Law and Regulation of Electronic Media

Second Edition

John R. Bittner

The University of North Carolina at Chapel Hill

PRENTICE HALL, *Englewood Cliffs, New Jersey 07632*

Library of Congress Cataloging-in-Publication Data
Bittner, John R.,

Law and regulation of electronic media / John R. Bittner. —2nd ed.
p. cm.
Rev. ed. of: Broadcast law and regulation. c1982.
Includes bibliographical references and index.
ISBN 0-13-085382-8
1. Broadcasting—Law and legislation—United States.
2. Telecommunication—Law and legislation—United States.
I. Bittner, John R., 1943- Broadcast law and regulation.
II. Title.
KF2805.B58 1994
343.7309'94—dc20
[347.303994] 93-41711
CIP

Acquisitions Editor: Steve Dalphin
Editorial/production supervision: Elizabeth Best
Copy Editor: Donna Mulden
Cover Design: Violet Lake Studio
Production Coordinator: Peter Havens

for

my family

Previously published as *Broadcast Law and Regulation*

A Paramount Communications Company
Englewood Cliffs, New Jersey 07632

Printed in the United States of America
10 9 8 7 6 5 4 3 2 1

ISBN 0-13-085382-8

Prentice-Hall International (UK) Limited, *London*
Prentice-Hall of Australia Pty. Limited, *Sydney*
Prentice-Hall Canada Inc., *Toronto*
Prentice-Hall Hispanoamericana, S.A., *Mexico*
Prentice-Hall of India Private Limited, *New Delhi*
Prentice Hall of Japan, Inc., *Tokyo*
Simon & Schuster Asia Pte. Ltd., *Singapore*
Editora Prentice-Hall do Brasil, Ltda., *Rio de Janeiro*

Contents

Preface

The world is undergoing a transformation in electronic communication as our society moves toward the frontiers of global information management. I can watch from my living room as CNN provides instantaneous coverage of events from almost any location on the globe, coverage which can have a profound effect on the politics of entire continents. Where once the telephone apparatus was contained in a large wooden box with a crank to summon an operator, today a portable phone fits in the palm of my hand and telephone companies are in the cable television business. Sitting at a personal computer it is possible to access interactive services with enough information to fill entire libraries. Framed against this backdrop is a 70-year-old local radio station which still airs swap-shop programs that can make you think time stands still. Within these contexts we begin our study of the control of electronic media. You will find the cultural and historical frameworks of our topic incorporated into many sections of this book; frameworks which influence the way media messages are shaped and transformed, creating a dynamic and evolving process we call law and regulation. In this book it has been my goal wherever possible to remove the law from the bonds of courts and regulatory agencies and place it in a pragmatic environment where people, not just media and messages, are affected by the process of policy making.

In addition to the topics and features of the previous edition, this completely revised edition of the book includes:

- An in-depth chapter on "Common Carrier" regulations providing a complete nontechnical overview of this increasingly important area of electronic media which is changing the way media messages are distributed and consumed.
- A separate chapter on "Cable" with an examination of cable regulation, including such topics as federal regulations, taxation of cable systems, rate setting, local franchising, analyses of cable television ordinances, franchise authorities, renewal, indecency, and due process.
- A chapter on the subject of "Satellites: Telecommunication in Space" introduces the reader to an area of regulation that is affecting every country that operates or uses satellite systems.
- Two separate chapters, "International Regulatory Frameworks" and "International Statutes and Codes," transport the reader into the international arena of law and regulation, including the regulatory environment for global information management and the web of legal issues that transcends national boundaries. Readers

are provided with an overview of the key international regulatory organizations which are setting the international policy agenda for controlling electronic media in the twenty-first century. In addition, these chapters provide specific examples of how laws and regulations originate and are integrated with the traditions and cultures of different countries. International organizations such as the International Telecommunication Union (ITU) and the European Community (EC) are discussed. Readers gain an awareness and understanding of international regulatory issues including such topics as regulated artistic and cultural integrity, language programming requirements, foreign libel law, financing and contract regulations, and other subjects. Readers gain a global awareness of electronic media law, the way culture and history impact on regulation, the way different countries approach policy making, and the statutes that evolve from different political and social systems.

• A chapter on "Ethics and Public Influence" including a discussion of public-interest pressure which details how the consumer can influence policy making, and why law and regulation do not evolve in a vacuum. The reader is sensitized to the fact that the messages we as consumers receive are influenced by a combination of ethical judgments, law and regulation, and public influence, and that the rich history of citizen involvement continues to help shape communication policy.

• Three separate chapters—"Political and Entertainment Programming," "The Broadcast Press," and "Commercial Programming"—examine how different regulations affect the programming we as consumers receive from the electronic media. The book helps the reader become a more responsible consumer of electronic media while being made aware of the underpinnings of control that affect practicing professionals.

• A chapter on "Broadcast Operations" exposes the reader to the world of administrative law applied to the daily realities of managing an electronic media enterprise. The reader is introduced to the day-to-day decision making in such areas as personnel matters, affirmative action, sexual harassment, hiring and firing, discrimination, tax law, risk and liability, and labor law. The chapter places the reader in the chair of the owners and managers who must juggle the profit-loss columns of commercial and noncommercial media while working in an environment of federal regulations, state statutes, and local ordinances.

• A chapter on "Wage and Hour Law in Station Operations" strips away the enigma of this specialized area of administrative law which directly affects every employee, intern, manager, and owner working in electronic media. The chapter provides an overview of wage and hour law, its developing interpretations applied to radio and television stations, and examples applied directly to station operations. Applied examples get behind the misperceptions of this specialized area of administrative law. The station's role in identifying exempt employees, special provisions for broadcasting, and how different employees such as assignment editors, producers, directors, and reporters are classified are all discussed. Removed are the myths behind what the law says and how it is applied, as well as the perceptions managers and employees have about each others' responsibilities in the workplace. The reader is alerted to what practicing professionals can expect on the job, in addition to recent developments in labor law and the interpretations of the Fair Labor Standards Act. Furthermore, a case dealing with collective bargaining in the television industry examines this related area of labor law.

• The chapter on the "Federal Communications Commission" details the organization and functioning of the primary agency in the United States responsible for the control of electronic media.

• A chapter on the "Federal Trade Commission" examines the agency that oversees truth in advertising which gained new importance during the era of deregulation in the Federal Communications Commission.

• A chapter on the subject of "Allied Regulatory Agencies" introduces the reader to agencies other than the FCC and the FTC which control or influence the regulation of electronic media in the United States, including the National Telecommunications and Information Administration, and others.

• A look back at the genesis of electronic media law and regulation is found in the chapter discussing regulation during "The Telegraph Era." The chapter places the reader at the roots from which many of today's regulatory concepts evolved. A companion chapter on "The Wireless Era" looks at the turbulent yet highly significant era of early radio.

• A chapter on "The Legal System and Legal Research" is the one contributed chapter to the book which is authored by a law librarian. It guides the reader through the multitude of sources where in-depth treatment of legal and regulatory issues can be found and where significant research can be launched.

In addition to the chapter material, the reader will also find pedagogical and learning aids in the book which are helpful in mastering more complex topics and issues. These aids include:

• More than 300 "Questions for Critical Analysis" which challenge readers to use critical-thinking skills in analyzing material from the perspective of how law, regulation, and policy affect both consumers and practicing professionals. The questions provide an incentive for readers to review material and provide instructors with a forum from which to launch class discussions.

• Cultural and historical perspectives are integrated throughout the book providing the reader with a broad, critically based approach to the study of law and regulation.

• Case examples are integrated into the book to bring the law alive and apply legal concepts to the actual day-to-day decision making in electronic media.

• "Material for Analysis" at the end of many chapters provides readers and instructors with the option to use additional analytical and critical-thinking skills through the use of cases and other material covering such varied topics as codes of ethics, truth in advertising, collective bargaining, FCC financial requirements, and other topics and issues.

• Summaries end each chapter with an overview of the material, giving readers a way to test their knowledge and to review key areas for a better understanding of important concepts.

• A glossary located at the end of the book is an accessible way of locating key terms.

In summary, this completely revised edition of the book is designed to introduce the reader to the full range of regulated telecommunication enterprises and their impact on society. The book is written with the goal of moving the reader beyond traditional broadcasting to the regulatory frontier of new technology, of global information management, while retaining the cultural and historical underpinnings of the field. Most important, the author has tried to make the journey into the law and regulation of electronic media an enjoyable journey, one which opens new horizons for the reader and broadens the reader's awareness of the impact law and regulation have on media in our society.

Finally, a word of caution. No book can be the ultimate source when it comes to legal matters concerning the field of electronic media. For readers who become involved in legal issues, be they on a personal or community level, *competent counsel with expertise in communication law should always be consulted.*

Acknowledgments

This book has been in revision since the first edition appeared more than ten years ago, but the past four years have been devoted exclusively to preparing this second edition. During this time many people have provided tremendous assistance in every facet of the book's development.

Many individuals and associations in international broadcasting and telecommunication provided material which found its way into this text. Their cooperation and assistance are gratefully acknowledged. Their titles reflect positions held at the time of their contact or correspondence with the author. Thanked especially are C. C. Chang, Chief of Public Relations at Taiwan Television Enterprise, Ltd. in Taiwan; Joan Chao, Deputy Chief of Listeners' Service Section at the Voice of Free China in Taiwan; and Yu Bu of the Foreign Affairs Bureau of the Ministry of Radio, Film and TV, in Beijing in the People's Republic of China.

In addition, thanks go to L. J. Heinsman of the International Affairs Department, Nederlandse Omroepprogramma Stichting, in Hilversum, the Netherlands; Drs. H. C. Homan of the Corporate Communications Office, Netherlands Broadcasting Services Corporation, Hilversum, the Netherlands; Travis Baxter, Station Manager with Radio Tara Limited, Radio Telefis Eireann, in Dublin, Ireland; Niels J. Langkilde, head of the Information Department of TV2/DANMARK; and the Press and Information Office of Radio Telefis Eireann, in Dublin, Ireland.

Also thanked are Geoff Carter, Membership Services Officer, Public Broadcasting Association of Australia, in Ultimo, New South Wales; P. Robertson, Media and Information Office of the Australian Broadcasting Corporation in Sydney; Jeff Rushton, Deputy Federal Director of the Federation of Australian Radio Broadcasters; Raimo Arhela of the International Relations Information Section of Oy. Yleisradio Ab. in Helsinki, Finland; K. Gross, head of the regulatory section of the Office of the General Directorate of Posts and Telegraphs for Denmark; Michael M. Jacobsen of the Board of Directors' Secretariat of Danmarks Radio; Niklaus Stuber, editor in chief, and Anton Brumann, both of Swiss Teletext, in Biel, Switzerland; the Secretariat of the Caribbean Broadcasting Union located in Barbados which provided information on the CBU and its membership; and N. Jasentuliyana, director of the Outer Space

Affairs Division at the United Nations is thanked for providing important information on the regulations of satellites.

Harold M. White, Jr., communications attorney, friend, scholar, and author in the area of space law, and former faculty member at the University of North Carolina at Chapel Hill, is thanked for his important work in this pioneering field of study and who, with his wife Rita Lauria White, authored important works which contributed to the chapter on satellite regulation. His insights on the field continue to be very valuable.

Additional people I am grateful to are James G. Mercer, Executive Director for Separations and Access, the United States Telephone Association, for assistance in general regulatory matters; Mary Steele of the North Carolina Public Utilities Commission for helping to direct me to the key areas of North Carolina Public Utilities Law; Dick MacKnight, Director of Corporate Information, U.S. West, for summarizing U.S. West's regulatory environment; Ron Fischmann of the Cable Advertising Bureau for information on cable contracts; Robert S. Sachs, Senior Vice President, Corporate and Legal Affairs, Continental Cablevision, Inc., for information on cable franchises; and Norman Black, Director of Public Affairs and Communications for the Cellular Telecommunications Industry Association, for his help in retrieving a number of important FCC publications in Washington, DC, and forwarding them to Chapel Hill.

Despite massive personnel and philosophical changes elsewhere in the company, Prentice-Hall/Simon & Schuster, which with this edition publishes my fifteenth book, has retained an excellent production organization.

Jolene A. Robinson, friend, an author's confidant on literature and life, executive assistant, copy editor, and stylistic consultant, is thanked for continued caring and diligence over the long history of this edition.

Ridley Kessler, Jr., Federal Documents Librarian at the Davis Library of the University of North Carolina at Chapel Hill, is thanked for his expertise and generosity in being available whenever I needed him by phone or in person. Having Ridley Kessler to assist an author is like having one's own campus branch of the Library of Congress. Obscure documents from the founding of the Republic to the latest decisions of federal agencies were never more than a phone call away. Also at the University of North Carolina at Chapel Hill, my friend and periodic personal secretary, Geraldine Taylor, deserves special thanks.

At the School of Journalism and Mass Communication at the University of North Carolina at Chapel Hill, Barbara Semonche, librarian at the school, was always willing to go the extra mile and access a database or locate just the book or periodical that was needed to round out a chapter. No one is better at meeting and understanding the research demands of faculty, especially under the pressure of deadlines. To have the services of a trained librarian and the resource of a specialized depository, were invaluable. Few authors are so fortunate.

Also at the School of Journalism and Mass Communication, Jo Bass helped with the industry liaison for the Radio Television News Directors Association of the Carolinas, and the campus chapter of the Radio-Television News Directors Association. In this area Linda Lumsden was also a valuable assistant. Mei-Ling Ying was a superb assistant during the final few months of research. The efficiency of Judy Meade and her staff kept the summer burdens off my shoulders, permitting me time to finish this manuscript. Robert Lauterborn deserves thanks for funneling to me the important legal materials in the field of advertising that continually cross his desk. More than once this material found its way into the book. Ranjeev Singh and Bill Carrington provided help and expertise in computer programming at one extremely critical juncture in the preparation of the manuscript. Without them this book would have been one chapter shorter. Agnès Ruhlmann is thanked for composing and translating permission requests for international documents.

Without exception, each one of my faculty colleagues in the School of Journalism and Mass Communication deserves my very deepest appreciation. At a time when some of public higher education has tragically become an impersonal bureaucracy for both faculty and students, one is truly fortunate when each day begins with a positive conflict over whether to spend the early morning hours working on one's book, or spending them with my faculty colleagues in Howell Hall at the University of North Carolina at Chapel Hill.

Within my own family, I owe a special indebtedness to Denise, and we both owe the blessing of companionship to Stormy. Although he may never achieve the literary fame of some of his peers, past and present, no animal has been there more when needed, or is more representative of what is right with the world. To my sons John and Donald, I express love and thanks for their understanding in hearing many times the answer, "Still working on my book," to their question, "What's happening, Dad?"

Beverly and Bill Long, and also Chuck and Louise Stone, remain special friends.

Introduction

While writing the introduction to this text, I am surrounded by electronic media. Many are subtle, taking on an unassuming, almost unnoticeable presence in my life. My first news of the day is the morning edition of *The Wall Street Journal*, delivered to my home long before dawn. Jogging in the predawn of a December morning, I am accompanied by a trusted companion of 14 years, a German shepherd named Stormy. We pass driveway after driveway where other papers have been dropped and in the next block are joined by Butterscotch, an Irish setter, and by Cinnamon, a golden retriever. Cinnamon's electronic fencing, an invisible electromagnetic pulse that triggers a small warning tone when Cinnamon nears the boundary of her yard, will keep Cinnamon from following us. Cinnamon looks dejected as Butterscotch and I continue on our route and drop out of sight at the next corner. Later Stormy and I bid farewell to Butterscotch and Cinnamon and go inside where I begin skimming the pages of the *Journal* and other papers.

The issue of the *Journal* I retrieved from the driveway is composed in another part of the United States where an electronic image of each page is beamed off a satellite 22,000 miles in space, then back to a satellite receiving dish at a printing plant in North Carolina. There, additional copy is added before the paper is printed and distributed. In the short time it took to finish my morning jog, millions of other papers were beamed and distributed to other parts of the world. The satellite signals carrying the pages of the *Journal* also beamed radio and television programs to area stations and to homes across the country. The technology that surrounds me this morning did not evolve in a legal or regulatory vacuum. For me to receive the morning paper, world conferences were convened and treaties were signed which now permit satellites to be launched, frequencies to be reserved, and international bodies to govern the operation of electronic media. Agencies such as the Federal Communications Commission, the Federal Trade Commission, the International Telecommunications Union all play a part in a dynamic framework of domestic and international laws and regulations which permit our society to function in this age of global information management. These laws and regulations touch the most sophisticated communication technologies, from the satellites that beam television pictures to millions of people, to the tiny receiver on Cinnamon's collar which had to pass FCC-approved specifications before it could be sold and marketed.

Along with the *Journal*, three other newspapers are delivered to my home. Each brings a different perspective on the news, and while these are not national newspapers like the *Journal*, they nevertheless are filled with information, much of which reached the city desks through electronic communication. Syndicated columns, wire service reports, even advertisements can be transmitted electronically. Common carrier-based communication such as the telephone provides links which can be used for voice communication as well as audio, data, and video. The local sportswriter covering a university basketball game can feed the story via telephone lines directly from a personal computer to the newspaper. The university sports information director can write another account of the game and like the sportswriter can transfer the text via telephone directly to the newspaper's data bank where an editor can call it up later and combine it with the sportswriter's own account of the game. If I want additional information about the game, I am able to select from a list of telephone numbers conveniently published on the back page of my local newspaper. By calling the number for sports, I will receive a voice recording recapping the game. The local telephone link is not regulated by national and international agencies. State public utility commissions play the major role in determining telecommunication policy affecting local telephone service.

Stormy walks into the kitchen reminding me it's time for his breakfast. After finishing a bowl of his favorite mixture, Stormy retires to the still warm hearth at the living room fireplace. Upstairs, Denise has already started her day by tuning in a local commercial radio station to hear local news, and then tuning in the public radio station and listening to "Morning Edition" from National Public Radio. Our local public broadcasting station is in the midst of a fund-raising campaign for a new building and tower. A few weeks earlier they completed an on-air telethon to raise money for operating expenses. The location of the new tower and an increase in power must be approved by the Federal Communications Commission. In addition, special permission from the FCC will be required when the radio station moves from its current facilities to its new building.

This morning the news from NPR carries stories from Africa and Europe. Correspondents in each of those areas telephone their reports back to NPR headquarters in the United States. The international telephone links are regulated by the same international agreements and government agencies that make it possible for the pages of *The Wall Street Journal* to reach me. During a network news break the station announces their telethon has been successful and they have exceeded their fund-raising goal. The fact that they engage in a telethon at all is the result of federal regulations which prohibit the station from airing commercials, and while they can embellish their donor announcements, they are prohibited from airing the extensive commercial copy heard on the local commercial radio station.

I am particularly fortunate because for me to own the radio receiver which tunes in the NPR station, I simply go to the store, purchase the device, and plug it in. In some other countries I would be required to pay an annual fee to own the receiver. A portion of these government-collected receiver fees would be returned to the state-controlled broadcasting system which in turn would produce programming. Later this morning I'll hear the public radio station again as background music at a local coffee shop I frequent. I'll also hear the morning news break from the British Broadcasting Corporation in London. The regulations that govern the BBC are much different than the ones that govern public radio in the United States.

On this particular morning I am leaving for Research Triangle Park, a high-technology region situated between three universities in central North Carolina. Here, a multitude of companies exist, most with international ties and engaged in the research and development of sophisticated products and services. A friend and Nobel Prize-winning scientist works in the Park at the American facility of a corporation headquartered in London. Throughout the day the corporate headquarters and the American facility will communicate electronically. International telecommunication links operate continuously and permit the exchange of data and faxes between the two facilities. To make it possible for the American facility to communicate with its British counterpart, regulatory agencies ranging from the state public utilities commission to the United Nations are involved.

My drive to Research Triangle Park is for the purpose of having breakfast with two close friends. At breakfast, Betty and George tell me the latest news they've retrieved from their interactive information service accessed via their personal computer. The news is from Europe where a *Times* of London story, capsuled and then accessed through their interactive information service, reports that a computer scanning process has uncovered new information about Leonardo da Vinci's famous painting of the Mona Lisa on display at the Louvre in Paris. In the future, more people like Betty and George will access information through interactive information services. These consumer-based services are opening up new regulatory challenges in such areas as libel law, which has traditionally been the domain of print and broadcast media. Cases have already reached the U.S. Supreme Court which have defined some of the limits of liability such services have when storing and permitting access to information.

Returning from breakfast, I tune in the local commercial radio station to listen to an update of the local news. Unlike the public station, news on the commercial station is interspaced with commercials which advertise such products as household goods, new cars, and an investment service. The ability of the local station to sell commercials is regulated by the same federal agency that permits the public broadcasting station to solicit donations and announce contributors to its telethon. The local news is free of government censorship, protected by the First Amendment to the U.S. Constitution. Some of my colleagues who work in other countries do not enjoy the freedom of speech and press we in the United States do. In some countries, government control of the media reaches all the way to spelling out requirements on dialects and the intonation of language. Although the news reports on the commercial station are free of government control, the commercials are not. Government control does exist over areas such as truth in advertising. The automobile dealership and the investment service, while generally free to advertise what they want to, can only do so as long as the advertising is truthful. To stretch the truth means running astray of the Federal Trade Commission. To lie means the risk of being shut down with the prospect of large fines.

By mid-morning back at my office at the university, Denise calls to inquire about a dinner meeting that evening. Her call is made from her car cellular phone using the latest technology that permits her to be in contact with any telephone anywhere in the world. The frequencies used by the telephone company, the telephone apparatus itself, and the privacy of the conversation are all regulated by the same state and federal agencies that oversee radio, television, satellite, and other types of electronic media. Soon after Denise calls, my colleague Chuck comes by my office door and tells me he has just received a call from an old friend who has been appointed by the President of the United States to a high-level government post. Chuck tells me the friend is flying to the news conference announcing his appointment and he telephoned Chuck from the airplane. Such common feats of personal communication were unheard of ten years ago. Denise's call, and Chuck's phone call from a friend, are the result of an increasingly frequent interlocking of high technology and international regulatory measures that permit new applications of personal communications in our lives.

In early afternoon a document arrives by fax from a professional organization outlining the highlights of federal cable television legislation. I have been asked to have lunch with a community group that wants to rewrite the local cable ordinance which comes up for renewal next year. When cable franchises come up for renewal, the emphasis shifts from the federal government to local municipalities which many times are the franchise authorities for cable television systems. The renewal process will begin a complex interaction of private enterprise and public administration, of cable companies and their competitors, and of federal and local government. In our town, some officials have already been visited by representatives from the regional telephone company suggesting it will be important not to put restrictions in the new cable ordinance which prohibit future telephone company entry into the local cable market.

Later, I stop by the administrative office in the academic unit where I teach. The dean is preparing to leave with a group of journalists and educators on a trip to Cuba. Because few international telecommunication agreements exist between my country and Cuba, much of the communication with Cuba which is necessary to arrange the trip, is being relayed through an office in Canada. In Cuba, the group will meet Carlos, an educator who teaches journalism there. For the professional broadcast journalists working in Cuba, the regulations governing their craft are much different than the regulations encountered by broadcast journalists in the United States.

By late afternoon a graduate student, a French woman who has returned to France for the holiday, calls to ask about her grades. Although Agnès is a continent away, her voice sounds as if she is in the next room. Connecting our conversation is fiber optic (*fibre optique*) cable, a key component on the frontier of the developing Integrated Services Digital Network which will eventually provide a web of global communication channels as well as new regulatory challenges in transborder information flow. At the cutting edge will be global information management, requiring new levels of cooperation between international organizations joining together to provide economic and social benefits through high technology to developing countries.

This evening Agnès is calling from a friend's apartment in Paris which overlooks the headquarters of Radio France. With international services broadcasting in French and other languages, Radio France's ability to serve an international audience without interference is made possible by agreements requiring the international registration of frequencies.

Paris is not the only stop on our journey through the field of electronic media. Before we finish this text we will spend part of our time in Washington, DC, the home of the Federal Communications Commission, and a host of other agencies which control electronic media in the United States. We will visit small towns such as Marble Head, Massachusetts, and large cities such as Los Angeles, California, and review the cable franchises of each. We will visit New York state where the public utilities commission influences both cable and common carrier law. Beyond the United States we will travel to such places as Switzerland, France, the Republic of China, Africa, Australia, Canada, and many places in between.

This is a book about law, but it is not a law book in the traditional sense. Integrated into the cases and the regulations are cultural and historical dimensions which add critical and important perspectives to the text. These cultural and historical dimensions are presented in the broader context of their impact on society and the way messages are transformed and altered. We will begin to see law and regulation as a dynamic and evolving process. We'll remove the law from the bonds of courts and agencies and place it in the context of the world at large where people are directly affected by communication policy.

We begin our journey through the text in a different place, at a different time. Our voyage begins as a cold, wet, piercing wind sweeps over England on the afternoon of October 5, 1832. The ship *Sully* is already four days late leaving port. An American professor of art named Samuel F.B. Morse is impatient with the delay and wants to return to America. Morse has been in Europe three years, perfecting his painting in France and Italy. Many of the friendships in America have been held together by long correspondence, and he yearns to see old colleagues and family. He takes the time to pen a short letter to a friend and writes about the upcoming voyage and about the "tremendous southwester" of a wind that is gnawing "in our teeth." We'll rejoin the voyage as we begin Chapter 1.

chapter one

The Telegraph Era

On board the *Sully,* a collection of dignitaries makes its acquaintance with Morse. Among them is Dr. Charles T. Jackson of Boston who one evening during a dinner-table conversation discusses the scientific theory of electromagnetism.[1] The topic fascinates Morse who conceives of the idea of making an electrical charge "visible" and using it for signaling purposes. On a sketchpad, Morse draws the first basic diagrams of what he later develops into the Recording Electric Magnetic Telegraph.[2] For Morse, however, the years in Europe have drained much of his finances and he returns home to devote his efforts to painting. The telegraph is relegated to his spare time.

Morse was not dealing with a new concept, but was instead adding the element of electromagnetism to the signaling process. Signaling telegraphs which used towers and semaphore systems with long mechanical arms and flags had been developed much earlier and were in common use. Frenchman Claude Chappe developed a series of semaphores in 1790. Other more "electronic" devices followed including the application of electricity to telegraphic communication by Samuel Thomas von Soemmerring in 1809 and Sir Francis Ronalds in 1816. The lack of reliable and sufficient power sources and the mechanical complexity of the systems were liabilities for both men.

THE FIRST PETITION TO CONGRESS FOR ELECTRICAL COMMUNICATION

In America, Morse was not alone in his interest in the telegraph. Captain Samuel C. Reid, a mariner, petitioned Congress on January 25, 1837 for funding to build a telegraph between New York and New Orleans via Washington, DC.[3] Although Reid's telegraph was a crude mechanical device, his original petition serves as an interesting example of one of the first pleas for technology funding in the beginnings of the electrical age.

Reid championed his cause by outlining his own credentials as both a native of Connecticut—of importance to the powerful New England congressional delegation—and his study of telegraph systems. He stated that for several years he had "applied himself to the study of the subject relating to the theory and practice of telegraphic communications."[4] Reid went on to point out that he had made himself practically acquainted with all the principal telegraphs that have been used in Europe for more than 40 years, and those of France and England in particular; and that he has "written a book and published the same upon the same subject."[5] Some of these early mechanical telegraphs had been employed in New York City as a means of communication between ships and the harbor.

In describing the mechanical telegraphs of Europe and New York, Reid outlined what he proposed to Congress to be a telegraphic link between New York and New Orleans and offered a cost estimate for the project:

> (I have) made an estimate of the probable cost and annual expense of a line of telegraphs from New York to the city of Washington, and thence to New Orleans, through the several inter-mediate cities, which will be exhibited when required. The distance between New York and Washington, being about 250 miles, would require 26 telegraphs, allowing 10 miles to each, and might be connected with the post offices of the several towns and cities through which the line should pass, and be under the control and government of the Post Office Department. Merchants and other citizens could be allowed the use of the telegraphs to carry on any commercial or other correspondence, by paying therefore a certain rate for any given number of words so transmitted. (I have) exhibited . . . plans and specifications to several of the Departments and other eminent personages in this city, who have expressed themselves warmly in favor of the project . . . (requests) that, after duly considering the subject, your honorable body will also be pleased to give it a favorable reception.[6]

It seems strange that if Reid was truly knowledgeable about the telegraphs of Europe, he would have alluded to the developing importance of electricity to the telegraph. Perhaps he felt that he needed to move quickly before electricity actually changed telegraphic communication forever. Congress, the wiser in this case, did not act favorably on his request. Less than a month later, however, Congress did move to inquire further about the technology of telegraphic communication and it is here that Samuel F. B. Morse advanced his system.

HOUSE RESOLUTION OF 1837

On February 3, 1837 the U.S. House of Representatives passed a resolution, "*Resolved*, That the Secretary of the Treasury be requested to report to the House of Representatives, at its next session, upon the propriety of establishing a system of telegraphs for the United States."[7] Levi Woodbury, then Secretary of the Treasury, prepared a circular dated March 10, 1837 for public distribution to knowledgeable and interested parties to respond to the Resolution. Titled *Circular to certain Collectors of the Customs, Commanders of Revenue Cutters, and other persons*, the circular read:

> With the view of obtaining information in regard to "the propriety of establishing a system of telegraphs for the United States," in compliance with the request contained in the annexed resolution of the House of Representatives, adopted at its last session, I will thank you to furnish the Department with your opinion upon the subject.
>
> If leisure permits, you would oblige me by pointing out the manner, and the various particulars, in which the system may be rendered most useful to the Government of the United States and the public generally. It would be desirable, if in your power, to present a detailed statement as to the proper points for the location, and distance of the stations from each other, with general rules for the regulation of the system, together with your sentiments as to the propriety of connecting it with any existing department of the Government, and some definite idea of the rapidity with which intelligence could ordinarily, and also in urgent cases, be communicated between distant places.
>
> I wish you to estimate the probable expense of establishing and supporting telegraphs, upon the most approved system, for any given distance, during any specified period. It would add to the interest of the subject if you would offer views as to the practicability of uniting with a system of telegraphs for communication in clear weather and in the day time, another for communication in fogs, by cannon or otherwise; and in the night, by the same mode, or by rockets, fires, etc. I should be gratified by receiving your reply by the first of October next.[8]

The U.S. House of Representatives, which 150 years later would be passing bills on the operation and development of communication systems for satellites in space, was taking its first step into the era of sophisticated technical communication. Years later the Federal Communications Commission would issue what is called a "Notice of Inquiry" to seek information about more complex telecommunication technologies and policies. The replies to this 1837 resolution passed by Congress included, among others, one from

Samuel Reid and two from Samuel F. B. Morse. Reid along with other respondents proposed a mechanical telegraph but Morse was the only one to propose a system using electricity.

RESPONSE TO THE 1837 HOUSE RESOLUTION

The letter which Morse sent to the secretary of the treasury in response to the House resolution is important for a number of reasons. It established for the first time an agenda of issues—issues which were important and which were necessary to establish the telegraph as "a public utility." Therein was laid the seed which later grew into a regulatory framework encompassing such technologies as telephones, microwave, satellite communication, cable television, and others. The following account is excerpted from Morse's letter to the secretary of the treasury dated September 27, 1837. Morse wrote:

Analogy to the Mail

The mail system, it seems to me, is founded on the universally admitted principle, that the greater the speed with which intelligence can be transmitted from point to point, the greater is the benefit derived to the whole community. The only question that remains, therefore, is, what system is best calculated, from its completeness and cheapness, to effect this desirable end?

Limitations of Other Systems

With regard to telegraphs constructed on the ordinary principles, however perfected within the limits in which they are necessarily confined, the most perfect of them are liable to one insurmountable objection—they are useless the greater part of the time. In foggy weather, and ordinarily during the night, no intelligence can be transmitted. Even when they can transmit, much time is consumed in communicating but little, and that little not always precise . . . As I have contracted to have a complete apparatus made to demonstrate at Washington by the 1st of January, 1838, the practicability and superiority of my mode of telegraphic communication by means of electro-magnetism, (an apparatus which I hope to have the pleasure of exhibiting to you,) I will confine myself in this communication to a statement of its peculiar advantages.

Instantaneous Transmission

First. The fullest and most precise information can be almost instantaneously transmitted between any two or more points, between which a wire conductor is laid: That is to say, no other time is consumed than is necessary to write the intelligence to be conveyed, and to convert the words into the telegraphic numbers. The numbers are then transmitted nearly instantaneously, (or, if I have been rightly informed in regard to some recent experiments in the velocity of electricity, two hundred thousand times more rapidly than light!) to any distance, where the numbers are immediately recognized, and reconverted into the words of the intelligence.

Weather Conditions

Second. The same full intelligence can be communicated at any moment, irrespective of the time of day or night, or state of the weather. This single point establishes its superiority to all other modes of telegraphic communication now known.

Size of Apparatus

Third. The whole apparatus will occupy but little space, (scarcely six cubic feet, probably not more than four;) and it may, therefore, be placed, without inconvenience, in any house.

Record of Message and Secrecy

Fourth. The record of intelligence is made in a permanent manner, and in such a form that it can be at once bound up in volumes convenient for reference, if desired. Fifth. Communications are secret to all but the persons for whom they are intended.

Post Office Control

As to "the propriety of connecting the system control of telegraphs with any existing department of Government," it would seem most natural to connect a telegraphic system with the Post Office Department; for, although it does not carry a mail, yet it is another mode of accomplishing the principal object for which the mail is established, to wit: the rapid and regular transmission of intelligence. If my system of telegraphs should be established, it is evident that the telegraph would have but little rest day or night.

Revenue From the System

The advantage of communicating intelligence instantaneously in hundreds of instances of daily occurrence, would warrant such a rate of postage, (if it may be so called,) as would amply defray all expenses of the first cost of establishing the system, and of guarding it, and keeping it in repair . . . In conclusion I would say, that if the perfecting of this new system of telegraphs (which may justly be called the American telegraph, since I can establish my claims to priority in the invention) shall be thought of public utility, and worthy the attention of Government, I shall be ready to make any sacrifice of personal service and of time to aid in its accomplishment.[9]

SECOND RESPONSE TO THE 1837 RESOLUTION

Morse sent a second letter to the secretary on November 28, 1837 which was also included in the report. He outlined the results of experiments conducted by himself and Professor Gale of the "University of the City of New York" and Alfred Vail of the Speedwell Iron Works in Morristown, New Jersey.[10] Morse's letter outlined successful communication over ten miles and his confidence in the operating system which he said could be used at any distance. Along with his letter he enclosed a report he had made to the *New York Journal of Commerce* on September 4, 1837, which showed the results of the experiments and included a diagram of the electrical impulses recorded when he sent two messages, one which read: "Successful experiment with telegraph," and a second which read: "Successful experiment with telegraph, September 4, 1937."[11]

REACTION AND REPORT OF THE COMMITTEE ON COMMERCE

The Committee on Commerce set about studying the replies made to the original House resolution and the circular distributed by the secretary of the treasury. In a report to the House of Representatives by Francis O. J. Smith, the chairman of the committee and Maine congressman, the Morse telegraph received enthusiastic support.[12] Typical of the tone of the report of the Committee on Commerce was the statement:

> It is obvious, however, that the influence of this invention over the political, commercial, and social relations of the people of this widely-extended country, looking to nothing beyond, will in the event of success, of itself amount to a revolution unsurpassed in normal grandeur by any discovery that has been made in arts and sciences, from the most distant period to which authentic history extends, to the present day.[13]

The chairman of the Committee on Commerce had not understated Morse's case, although history shows he was also trying to get some personal control of the telegraph and eventually owned a financial share in its success.[14]

Attached to the report was a statement from the Franklin Institute in Philadelphia which had tested the telegraph and was also positive. Again, addressing the issue of government control, the institute report stated, "The power of the invention, if successful, is so extensive for good and evil, that the Government alone should possess the right to control and regulate it."[15]

In addition, the committee was undoubtedly influenced by Morse's own correspondence.

CORRESPONDENCE TO THE COMMITTEE ON COMMERCE

On February 15, 1838 Morse wrote to Representative Francis O. J. Smith outlining a proposed experiment, and offering his own views on the control of the telegraph, stating:

> . . . If no insurmountable obstacles present themselves in a distance of one hundred miles, none may be expected in one thousand or in ten thousand miles; and then will be presented for the consideration of the Government the propriety of completely organizing this new telegraphic system as a part of the Government, attaching it to some Department already existing, or creating a new one, which may be called for by the accumulating duties of the present Departments.

Danger of Speculators

It is obvious, at the slightest glance, that this mode of instantaneous communication must inevitably become an instrument of immense power, to be wielded for good or for evil, as it shall be properly or improperly directed. In the hands of a company of speculators, who should monopolize it for themselves, it might be the means of enriching the corporation at the expense of the bankruptcy of thousands; and even in the hands of Government alone, it might become a means of working vast mischief to the republic. In considering these prospective evils, I would respectfully suggest a remedy which offers itself to my mind.

Appropriations for Expansion

Let the sole right of using the telegraph belong, in the first place, to the Government, who should grant, for a specified sum, or bonus, to any individual or company of individuals who may apply for it, and under such restrictions and regulations as the Government may think proper, the right to lay down a way of communication between any two points, for the purpose of transmitting intelligence; and thus would be promoted a general competition.

Separate Government Telegraph

The Government would have a telegraph of its own, and have its modes of communicating with its own officers and agents, independent of private permission, or interference with and interruption to the ordinary transmissions on the private telegraphs. Thus there would be a system of checks and preventives of abuse, operating to restrain the action of this otherwise dangerous power, within those bounds which will permit only the good and neutralize the evil.

Potential Revenue

Should the Government thus take the telegraph solely under its own control, the revenue derived from the bonuses alone, it must be plain, will be of vast amount. From the enterprising character of our countrymen, shown in the manner in which they carry forward any new project which promises private or public advantage, it is not visionary to suppose that it would not be long before the whole surface of this country (would be covered by telegraph).

First Refusal

If the Government is disposed to test this mode of telegraphic communication by enabling me to give it a fair trial for one hundred miles, I will engage to enter into no arrangements to dispose of my rights as the inventor and patentee for the United States, to any individual or company of individuals, previous to offering it to the Government for such a just and reasonable compensation as shall be mutually agreed upon. I remain, sir, respectfully, your most obedient servant, (Morse's signature).[16]

PROPOSED BUDGET

Morse also provided the Committee on Commerce with a proposed budget of $26,000 for his experimental telegraph. The committee recommended that Congress appropriate $30,000 to "meet any contingency not now anticipated, and to guard against any want of requisite funds in an enterprise of such moment to the Government, to the people, and to the scientific world . . ."[17]

With the report of the Committee on Commerce, the proposed budget of Morse, and the technology in place, the stage was set for the first government-sponsored and controlled test of the technology of the telegraph.

LOBBYING CONGRESS FOR THE TELEGRAPH

Although the time between the House resolution and the report of the Committee on Commerce was slightly more than 14 months, the wheels of Congress did not turn as speedily. A number of setbacks faced Morse, few of which he had much control over. He traveled to Europe seeking additional money for the development of the telegraph and engaged in numerous attempts, some more successful than others, to gain foreign patent rights.

LETTER TO THE SECRETARY OF THE TREASURY AND REPORT TO THE HOUSE

On October 27, 1838 Morse wrote the secretary of the treasury from Paris again requesting some indication of what Congress intended to do about the proposed appropriation and notifying the secretary that successful experiments had moved the telegraph beyond the experimental stage to the point where Congress could be funding an actual telegraph line instead of an experiment.[18] Morse's letter, excerpted as follows, was an exercise in persuasion, and although it did not show through in the letter, an exercise in desperation.[19] Along with indicating that an experiment was not necessary, he pushed for a firm decision as soon as possible and for the first time alerted the secretary of the treasury that the private sector and foreign investors were interested in the telegraph if the U.S. government was not.

Morse, perhaps feeling his best chance for future success still lay in the government appropriation, suggested the government might want its own telegraph line and offered a firm budget estimate of $520 per mile. He offered to accept any form of government accountability including the delay of his own compensation and concluded his letter by pointing out that the French government, after comparing telegraph systems from England, Germany, France, and the United States, was inclined to support the "American Telegraph" of Morse.

> . . . In case the Government should prefer to construct a line of the electro-magnetic telegraph . . . the aggregate expense of constructing (the telegraph) ready for use . . . will not exceed $520 per mile; and this includes two complete sets of wire, independent of each other, like a double railway, so that intelligence can be transmitted either way, at any moment . . .
>
> **Accountability for Expenditures**
>
> I can undertake to construct, by contract, any given length of telegraphic line at that rate, leaving the compensation for the use of the invention itself to the future decision of Congress, if such a course shall be preferred, or as an alternative that may better suit the views of Congress. I will construct for the Government any such line not less than 100 miles upon the most economical terms in my power, under any system of accountability which may be instituted, leaving, as before suggested, my own personal compensation (beyond current expenses) to the after decision of the Government. However, in either of the latter cases, I trust the Government will not desire me to preclude the invention from use in other parts of the Union, not selected by the Government for its own telegraphic line.
>
> **Rights-of-Way**
>
> The Government will also, in either case, obtain, at its own expense, the right of way requisite to lay and protect the telegraph, whithersoever it may lead. But as the highways are usually the most eligible in every respect for laying down the wires, no expense of any moment can arise from this source . . .[20]

CONGRESS APPROVES THE MORSE TELEGRAPH

Gradually Morse's finances were depleted and about the time it looked as though the telegraph would wither and be forgotten in Congress, just before adjournment on the night of March 3, 1843 the funding was approved for an experimental line between Washington to Baltimore.[21] The appropriation bill read:

> A BILL to test the practicability of establishing a system of electro-magnetic telegraphs by the United States.
>
> **Appropriation**
>
> Be it enacted by the Senate and House of Representatives of the United States in Congress assembled, That the sum of thirty thousand dollars be, and is hereby, appropriated, out of any moneys in the Treasury not otherwise appropriated, for testing the capacity and usefulness of the system of electro-magnetic telegraphs invented by Samuel F. B. Morse, of New York, for the use of the Government of the United States, by constructing a line of said electro-magnetic telegraphs, under the superintendence of Professor Samuel F. B. Morse, of such length and between such points as shall fully test its practicability and utility; and that the same shall be expended under the direction of the Secretary of the Treasury upon the application of said Morse.
>
> **Fund Disbursement**
>
> And be it further enacted, That the Secretary of the Treasury be, and he is hereby, authorized to pay, out of the aforesaid thirty thousand dollars, to the said Samuel F. B. Morse, and the persons employed under him, such

sums of money as he may deem to be a fair compensation for the services of the said Samuel F. B. Morse, and the persons employed under him, in constructing and in superintending the construction of the said line of telegraphs authorized by this bill.[22]

From many false starts, from disappointments, and at a time when its inventor was disillusioned and almost destitute, his dream was finally realized and the government took its first step toward supporting the "public utility." Work proceeded quickly with not unexpected setbacks and Morse produced a workable line between Baltimore and Washington, DC on May 24, 1844 at a cost of $27,500.[23] The now famous words "What hath God wrought" were transmitted successfully from Washington with his assistant Alfred Vail receiving the correct transmission and repeating it back to Washington.[24]

Morse made his report to Congress and offered to sell the rights to the telegraph to the government. In a letter to the Hon. George M. Bibb, then Secretary of the Treasury, Morse said, "Should the government be now disposed to possess the right of the proprietors, by giving them a fair consideration, I shall be ready to treat with them on the terms of the transfer."[25]

He went on to express his personal wishes by saying, "For myself, I should prefer that the government should possess the invention, although pecuniary interests of the proprietors induce them to lean towards arrangements with private companies."[26]

Morse's offer was not accepted. His asking price of $100,000 may have seemed high, since the original appropriation for the line between Baltimore and Washington was less than one third that much.[27] Even more important, the postmaster general was Cave Johnson who had been one of the telegraphs biggest foes in Congress.[28]

SMALL APPROPRIATION MEASURES FOR OPERATION

Two Congressional appropriations did, however, manage to elevate the line beyond experimental status for a short period of time.

Act of June 19, 1846

An act of June 19, 1846 appropriated funds:

For defraying the expenses of the magnetic telegraph from the city of Washington to Baltimore, four thousand dollars; this appropriation to be available, if need be, before the commencement of the next fiscal year; Provided, That the Postmaster-General be, and he is hereby, authorized to let, for a limited time, the aforesaid telegraph to any person who will keep it in operation for its earnings; or he may, under the direction of the President of the United States, sell the same.[29]

Act of August 10, 1846

An act of August 10, 1846 also appropriated money for miscellaneous items to the Post Office Department with a conditional clause reading: "Provided, That the proceeds of the telegraph between Washington city and Baltimore be . . . placed in the treasury of the United States for the benefit of the post-office department in the same manner as other revenues from postage."[30] The act of August 10, 1846 could be called the first experiment with electronic mail. Today, an electronic letter can be delivered to any one of thousands of post offices and other receiving stations worldwide. In 1846, however, neither this vision nor support for the government owning the rights to the telegraph were present.

GOVERNMENT SUPPORT FOR WESTWARD EXPANSION

The government's decision not to buy the rights to the telegraph did not appear to hinder its rapid development. News of Morse's successful experiment spread.

Right-of-Way from the Mississippi to San Francisco

Less than ten years later in 1855 Congress again found itself dealing with the telegraph and on February 17, 1855 it granted the right-of-way for construction of a line from the Missouri and Mississippi Rivers to the Pacific Ocean. The Pacific Telegraph Act stated that "Hiram O. Alden and James Eddy . . . are hereby authorized and empowered to construct, at their own expense, a line of telegraph from such point on the Mississippi or Missouri River as they may hereafter select through the public lands belonging to the United States, over which lands the right of way two hundred feet in width, for that purpose, is hereby granted to San Francisco, in California, in as a direct line as practicable." The act also established penalties for "voluntary or intentional injuries to said line or telegraph, or to any property thereto belonging, within the territories of the United States."[31]

Connecting Eastern Cities to the West

Further government support came in 1860 with the passage of the Electric Telegraph to the Pacific Act, which called for bids to construct a government telegraph which would connect with the cities of Washington, New Orleans, New York, Charleston, SC, Philadelphia, Boston, "and other cities in the Atlantic, Southern, and Western States," to the city of San Francisco. The act called for the line to "be open to the use of all citizens of the United States during the term of the said contract, on payment of the regular charges for transmission of dispatches."[32] Such charges were not to exceed $3.00 for a single dispatch of ten words.

RELATIONSHIP TO THE RAILROADS AND THE INTERSTATE COMMERCE COMMISSION (ICC)

Two years later in 1862 with legislation primarily designed to stretch the railroad into the West, the Pacific Railroad and Telegraph Act made provisions for a telegraph line to adjoin the railroad right of way to the Pacific Ocean.[33] An 1888 amendment to the 1862 legislation outlined the cooperative arrangements that were to exist between different telegraph companies and therefore assure that messages could be transmitted and received freely.[34] The 1888 Telegraph Lines Act affected railroads almost as much as telegraph companies and helped assure cooperation among government-subsidized companies. Railroads were closely tied to the developing telegraph industry since it was over railroad rights-of-way that many telegraph lines were placed, and much of the communication by telegraph concerned the schedules and cargo of the railroads. The 1888 legislation required both railroads operating telegraph lines and independent telegraph companies to cooperate. The Interstate Commerce Commission was responsible for enforcement. The law read in part:

Subsidized Companies

All railroad and telegraph companies to which the United States has granted any subsidy in lands or bonds or loan of credit for the construction of either railroad or telegraph lines. . . . (and which) shall extend its line to any station or office of a telegraph line belonging to any one of said railroad or telegraph companies, referred to in the first section of this act, said telegraph company so extending its line . . .

Equal Access Clause

. . . shall so operate without discrimination in favor of or against any person, company, or corporation whatever, and shall receive, deliver, and exchange business with connecting telegraph lines on equal terms, and affording equal facilities, and without discrimination for or against any one of such connecting lines; and such exchange of business shall be on terms just and equitable.[35]

Enforcement under the ICC

that if any such railroad or telegraph company referred to in the first section of this act, or company operating such railroad or telegraph line shall refuse or fail, in whole or in part, to maintain, and operate a telegraph line as provided in this act . . . then any person, company, corporation, or connecting telegraph company may apply for relief to the Interstate Commerce Commission, whose duty it shall thereupon be, under such rules and regulations as said Commission may prescribe, to ascertain the facts, and determine and order what arrangement is proper to be made in the particular case, and the railroad or telegraph company concerned shall abide by and perform such order; and it shall be the duty of the Interstate Commerce Commission, when such determination and order are made, to notify the parties concerned, and, if necessary, enforce the same by writ of mandamus in the courts of the United States, in the name of the United States, at the relation of either of said Interstate Commerce Commissioners:

Penalties and Inquiry Authority of the ICC

Provided, That the said Commissioners may institute any inquiry, upon their own motion, in the same manner and to the same effect as though complaint had been made . . . (a telegraph company who) shall refuse to abide by, or perform and carry out within a reasonable time the order or orders of the Interstate Commerce Commission, shall in every such case of refusal or failure be guilty of a misdemeanor, and, on conviction thereof, shall in every such case be fined in a sum not exceeding one thousand dollars, and may be imprisoned not less than six months;

Action for Damages

and in every such case of refusal of failure the party aggrieved may not only cause the officer or agent guilty thereof to be prosecuted under the provisions of this section, but may also bring an action for the damages sustained thereby against the company whose officer or agent may be guilty thereof, in the circuit or district court of the United States in any State or Territory in which any portion of the road or telegraph line of said company may be situated.[36]

Reporting requirements were also established by the act. Railroad and telegraph companies were required to file with the ICC copies of their contracts and agreements with other companies or persons including those using its rights-of-way. An inventory of lines and property and a report on the gross earnings and expenditures for the maintenance and operations involving connecting lines were to be filed annually with the ICC. It was in this era of expanding telegraph technology and application that the ICC firmly established itself in the business of regulating communication.

GRANTING THE RIGHT OF EMINENT DOMAIN

While the granting of individual rights-of-way was satisfactory, with the Post Roads Act of 1866 the government awarded all future construction projects the right of eminent domain—the right of the government to take land for the construction of the telegraph. The Post Roads Act, which would also later benefit the development of the telephone, read in part:

Right to Construct Lines

That any telegraph company now organized, or which may hereafter be organized under the laws of any State in this Union, shall have the right to construct, maintain, and operate lines of telegraph through and over any portion of the public domain of the United States, over and along any of the military or post roads of the United States which have been or may hereafter be declared such by act of Congress, and over, under, or across the navigable streams or waters of the United States.

Obstruction of Travel Prohibited

Provided, That such lines of telegraph shall be so constructed and maintained as not to obstruct the navigation of such streams and waters, or interfere with the ordinary travel on such military or post roads.

Power of Condemnation

And any of said companies shall have the right to take and use from such public lands the necessary stone, timber, and other materials for its posts, piers, stations, and other needful uses in the construction, maintenance, and operation of said lines of telegraph, and may pre-empt and use such portion of the unoccupied public lands subject to pre-emption through which its said lines of telegraph may be located as may be necessary for its stations, not exceeding forty acres for each station; but such stations shall not be within fifteen miles of each other.[37]

Establishing the Basis for Social Responsibility

The law did more than provide access to public lands. Even more important, the concept of eminent domain carries with it certain responsibilities for those who are granted the privilege. Among other things, the law ensures that everyone has an equal right to use the service and to guard against such things as discrimination and unreasonable fees. It also helped establish the basis for further control of the telegraph, eventually the telephone, and to some extent, the wireless and later the radio. After the 1866 legislation, most states enacted similar statutes.

INTERNATIONAL EXPANSION AND CONTROL

Along with subsidies and the granting of rights-of-way for domestic expansion of the telegraph, the government also encouraged international links.

Contractual Agreements with Great Britain to Link Newfoundland and Ireland

As early as 1857 Congress passed "An Act to expedite Telegraphic Communication for the Uses of Government in its Foreign Intercourse."[38] It charged the secretary of state, under the direction of the president, to contract for up to two ships to lay a "submarine cable" to connect existing telegraph lines between Newfoundland and the coast of Ireland. The legislation was contingent upon Great Britain also entering into the contract with the exact terms as those agreed upon by the United States.

Atlantic Cable Link via Bermuda and Azores

Ten years later in 1867 Congress passed a bill granting the American Atlantic Cable Telegraph Company in New York permission to construct and operate a "Submarine Telegraph Cable" on the Atlantic Coast of the United States, and established a telegraph link between the United States and Europe via the Bermudas and Azores Islands.[39] The American Atlantic Cable Telegraph Company obtained a 20-year approval with the stipulation that they had to commence "active operations" in two years from the passage of the act.

Additional Atlantic and Pacific Projects

Two additional acts of Congress, one in 1876 and another in 1877, continued the international expansion of the telegraph. A bill passed August 15, 1876 encouraged "telegraphic communication between America and Asia,"[40] authorized a group of investors and businessmen to "construct, lay, land, and maintain a line or lines of telegraph or submarine cable or cables on the Pacific coast of the United States of America, to connect American and Asiatic coasts by telegraph lines, wires or submarine cables. . . ."[41] The law established priority for messages with the government of the United States having first priority, telegraph companies having second priority, and private messages having third priority. Lines were to "be kept open to the public for the daily transmission of market and commercial reports and intelligence," and messages were to be forwarded "in the order in which they are received. . . ."[42]

The following year Congress supported connections with Europe by passing "An Act to encourage and promote telegraphic communication between America and Europe."[43] The provisions were in most ways similar to the 1876 legislation with some stipulations over rates and the provision that "no amalgamation, union, or sale of cable interests established under this act shall be made to any existing European or other cable-companies."[44] Each of the preceding acts were also important in the establishment of rate structures.

ESTABLISHING RATE STRUCTURES

As early as 1857 the government was establishing rates for the telegraph.

Secretary of the Treasury to Control Transatlantic Rates

The same law which authorized the submarine cable between Newfoundland and Ireland provided: "That the tariff of prices for the use of such submarine communication by the public shall be fixed by the Secretary of the Treasury of the United States and the government of Great Britain, or its authorized agent."[45]

Post Roads and Other "Postmaster-General" Authorizations

In 1866 the Post Roads Act gave the postmaster general authority to annually fix rates for telegraphic communication between departments of government.[46] One year later the 1867 legislation that provided for a submarine cable between the United States and Europe via the Azores stated, "That the government of the United States shall at all times have the preference in its use, upon terms that may be agreed upon between the Postmaster-General and the said company."[47] An 1876 law to encourage telegraphic communication between America and Asia stated that "Citizens of the United States shall enjoy the same privilege as to the payment of rates for the transmission of messages as are enjoyed by the citizens of the most favored nations."[48] One year later in 1877, the act to encourage telegraphic communication between America and Europe retained the same provision as the 1876 law along with a provision which said, "At-present tariff rates of messages shall be reduced to one-third or one shilling British currency, per word, over said new cable or cables."[49] For the remainder of the 1800s the role of the postmaster general as the regulator of rates was well established, except during wartime and for military purposes. The general appropriations bill of 1871 provided:

> That no part of this appropriation, nor of any appropriation for the several departments of the government, shall be expended for telegraphing between said departments and their officers or agents, except at rates first to be established by the Postmaster-General, under section two of chapter two hundred and thirty of the statutes of eighteen hundred and sixty-six (The Post Roads Act cited previously).[50]

A similar provision was included in another 1871 bill which appropriated money for deficiencies of previous fiscal years.[51] Samuel F. B. Morse, remember, had recommended in his 1837 response to the secretary of the treasury that the Post Office Department control the telegraph. With the settlement of the western regions of the United States, the role of the United States mail system and the telegraph was increasing in importance. In 1872 the government consolidated the statutes affecting the Post Office Department. Section 17 of the consolidation measure stated: "telegrams between the several departments of the government and their offices and agents, in the transmission over the lines of any company to which has been given the right of way, timber, or station lands from the public domain, shall have priority over all other business, at such rates as the Postmaster-General shall annually fix."[52]

GOVERNMENT CONTROL DURING CONFLICT

If a single event could be said to have propelled the telegraph and electrical communication into importance it was the War Between the States—the Civil War. Between 1861 and 1865 the Union and Confederate forces in the United States fought over much of the eastern United States and found the telegraph indispensable as an instrument of war.

The Civil War: Control and Revenue

Early in the Civil War Congress gave the president the authority to take control of "any and all telegraph lines in the United States" whenever "in his judgment the public safety" required it.[53] Army appropriation acts in both 1862[54] and 1863[55] awarded $500,000 for construction of the telegraph for military purposes. An 1862 revenue bill put a tax on telegraph messages which required that "no telegraph company or its agent or employee shall receive from any person, or transmit to any person, any dispatch or message without an adhesive stamp denoting the duty imposed by this act being affixed to a copy thereof, or having the same stamped thereupon and default thereof shall incur a penalty of ten dollars: Provided, That only one stamp shall be required, whether sent through one or more companies."[56]

Protection from Damage

Westward expansion of the United States into the territories west of the Mississippi River brought conflict with a number of Indian tribes and the construction of telegraph and railroad lines was often the catalyst. Protection from "savages" was part of an 1864 law encouraging expansion of the telegraph along the Pacific Coast mining areas. Section 3 of The Telegraph Communication Act of 1864 read in part:

> . . . in order to secure (the telegraph) from injury by savages or other evil-disposed persons, to the interruption of the public business, the Secretary of War is authorized to direct the commanders of the military districts or stations, and other officers, acting under authority of the United States in the territories traversed by said telegraph, to use any available force at their command to protect the same.[57]

Telegraph Provisions in Indian Treaties

Both President Abraham Lincoln and President Andrew Johnson signed Indian treaties which had provisions affecting the telegraph. A treaty approved in 1865 with the Shoshonee-Goship Bands of Indians in Utah Territory called for the telegraph lines constructed and operated under the authority of the United States "be continued without hindrance, molestation, or injury. . . ."[58] President Johnson secured the right to construct telegraph lines over lands occupied by the Sissiton and Warpeton Bands of the Dakota and Sioux in a treaty approved in 1867.[59] An 1871 Army appropriations measure gave the secretary of war authorization to negotiate with "a responsible party" for the construction of telegraph lines connecting the forts of the Dakota Territory.[60] Upon completion of each hundred miles of line he was authorized to pay the sum of $8,000, and an additional $80 per mile for any construction over an even hundred miles.[61] The bill carried a provision that "the money so paid shall be refunded to the United States in the use of said telegraph line at rates not higher than charged private individuals. . . ."[62] The contractor for the line received ownership when the money advanced for the line was refunded back to the United States in line charges. The government did, however, reserve the right to use the telegraph for "public purposes at such rates as may be just."[63]

TELEGRAPH PROTECTION ACT OF 1874

In 1874 protection was codified under the Telegraph Protection Act, which made it illegal to interfere with the construction or to damage telegraph lines:

> Be it enacted by the Senate and House of Representatives of the United States of America in Congress assembled, That any person or persons who shall willfully or maliciously injure or destroy any of the works or property or material of any telegraphic line constructed and owned, or in process of construction, by the United States, or that may be hereafter constructed and owned or occupied and controlled by the United States, or who shall willfully or maliciously interfere in any way with the working or use of any such telegraphic line, or who shall willfully or maliciously obstruct, hinder, or delay the transmission of any communication over any such telegraphic line, shall be deemed guilty of a misdemeanor, and, on conviction thereof in any district court of the United States having jurisdiction of the same, shall be punished by a fine of not less than one hundred nor more than one thousand dollars, or with imprisonment for a term not exceeding three years, or with both, in the discretion of the court.[64]

SPANISH-AMERICAN WAR TELEGRAPH TAX

In the spring and summer of 1898 the United States waged a brief war against Spain. The Spanish-American War was funded in part by a war-revenue measure passed on June 13, 1898, which included a tax on telegraph messages similar to the one passed in 1862 to provide revenue for the Civil War.[65] In the 1898 measure, officers and employees of telegraph or telephone companies were exempt when sending messages "concerning the affairs and service of the company." "Officers and employees of the Government on official business" were also exempt.[66]

THE TENTH CENSUS ACT: AN ACCOUNTING OF A TECHNOLOGY

By the last quarter of the nineteenth century, the telegraph had become not only an instrument of communication but an instrument of commerce that was of more than passing interest to the government. The government had already taxed the telegraph and as we have just read, it did so again in the Spanish-American War. When it became time to conduct the tenth census in 1889, the telegraph was included and the superintendent of the census was directed to:

> Require and obtain, from the owners, proprietors, or managers of every telegraph company, the following facts to wit: Name of corporation or company; terminal points connected; capital and capital paid up; length of lines in miles; miles of wire; number of officers; number of persons engaged in general administration; number of persons engaged as telegraph-operators; the number of messages transmitted by officers of the United States; the number of messages transmitted for the press; the number of messages transmitted for private parties; total number of messages transmitted; total receipts from messages; total expenditures of the company, exhibiting separately the amount expended for salaries, for repairs, and for general expenses.[67]

From the time Congress first appropriated money for Morse's experiments until the end of the century, it had become involved in the telegraph's development through subsidies to private enterprise, had taxed it for revenues including the support of war, had protected it from injury, and had included it in census data. A new technology, the telephone, was already in use and the government had accumulated 50 years of experience in regulating the first communication technology. The telegraph remained in use through 1991 when AT&T stopped offering telegraph service.[68] Even though the telephone surpassed the telegraph as the medium of choice for personal communication, the telegraph provided a written record of a transaction. Brokerage houses were some of the last customers for telegraphic communication.

SUMMARY

The roots of regulating electronic communication can be traced to the development of the telegraph. Samuel F. B. Morse's work eventually received government support which ultimately evolved into an international network of telegraph links. In the United States, early government support provided the thrust for the eventual international expansion of the telegraph. Secretary of the Treasury Levi Woodbury, in response to an 1837 House resolution, solicited proposals to establish a system of telegraphs "for any given distance, during any specified period."

The replies to the inquiry of the secretary of the treasury included two from Morse in which he proposed the only electrical system, clearly the most advanced for its day. After a series of discouraging setbacks, Morse received $30,000 in funding for an experimental line, completed in 1844 between Washington, DC and Baltimore at a cost of $27,500. Continued development of the telegraph took place but Morse's offer to sell the device to the government for $100,000 was rejected.

Two appropriation bills kept the Baltimore-Washington link operable and set up the first rate structure by providing that "the proceeds of the telegraph . . . be placed in the treasury of the United States for the benefit of the post-office department in the same manner as other revenues from postage."

Government support for westward expansion soon followed and eventually, the West and San Francisco were linked to major centers of the East. The Pacific Telegraph Act and the Electric Telegraph to the Pacific Act continued to aid development.

The Pacific Railroad and Telegraph Act assured cooperative arrangements between different telegraph companies. It also outlined the requirements for equal access to anyone who wanted to use the telegraph "with discrimination in favor of or against any person, company, or corporation whatever." Telegraph companies were held accountable to the Interstate Commerce Commission. Penalties were established and damage suits could be filed against the officers of telegraph companies who violated provisions of the act.

The right of eminent domain was conferred by the Post Roads Act of 1866 and further opened the door to government regulation, since eminent domain carries with it certain responsibilities for those who are granted the privilege.

International expansion and control occurred as early as 1857 with the passage of "An Act to expedite Telegraphic Communication for Uses of Government in its Foreign Intercourse." The law was enacted under the condition that Great Britain enact a law with the same "terms" as the United States. An 1867 act authorizing the Atlantic cable between the United States and Europe awarded a 20-year authorization to the American Atlantic Cable Telegraph Company. Laws passed in 1876 and 1877 continued international expansion and contained a provision that "no amalgamation, union, or sale of cable interests established under this act shall be made to any existing European or other cable-companies."

Congress dealt with rate structures in the 1857 legislation discussed earlier which gave the secretary of the treasury of the United States and "the Government of Great Britain, or its authorized agent" the authority to fix rates. The 1866, 1876, and 1877 legislation noted previously also dealt with rate structures.

The government made special provisions to control the telegraph during wartime, namely during the Civil War and again during the Spanish-American War. Both conflicts resulted in taxes on the telegraph for the purposes of raising war revenue. Legislation passed in 1864 helped protect the telegraph lines of the West from damage by Indians. The 1874 Telegraph Protection Act codified blanket protection to companies constructing and operating telegraph lines.

By the time of the tenth census in 1880, the telegraph was of such importance that the government called for an inventory of systems, income, messages, personnel, and expenditures. The telegraph remained in service through 1991, with brokerage houses being some of the last customers of the service.

MATERIAL FOR ANALYSIS

Only part of the fabric of the law and regulation of broadcasting and telecommunication is found in the acts of Congress or the statutes passed by the various states. Some of the most interesting and informative material comes from the courts. This was as true in the fascinating era of the telegraph as it is today. Moreover, much of the precedent for the way we approach the control of electronic media can be traced to an earlier generation of our technologies. In the short excerpts from the cases and other documents presented both here and in subsequent chapters, we will have the opportunity to expand our understanding of these approaches.

The telegraph, as did other technologies, went through some judicial growing pains. The courts had little experience to fall back on when it came to deciding cases which dealt with a technology that many judges and juries simply did not yet understand. Such issues as who held the rights to send telegraph messages over certain routes, whether Congress or the states could regulate the telegraph, and how much liability a telegraph company had for errors in transmission or delivery were all questions which the courts tried to answer.

First, read the account of the 1852 case of *Edward Shields* v. *Washington Telegraph Company*. The judge ruled in favor of the telegraph company noting that "influences from atmospheric causes are likely to change wires and pervert a telegraphic message." Here we see the comparisons made between the telegraph and common carriers (railroads, and so on). The comparisons with a common carrier as a basis for decisions about the telegraph were complex and difficult.

In the 1859 case of *Parks* v. *Alta*, we see a somewhat different interpretation than that of the Shields case. In *Parks* v. *Alta*, the court ruled against the telegraph company. Telegraph companies then began to protect themselves with agreements between the company and the senders of telegrams. Such agreements were upheld and to some extent the overall liability of telegraph companies lessened, as in the 1866 case of *Jonathan W. Ellis* v. *American Telegraph Company*.

EDWARD SHIELDS v. *WASHINGTON TELEGRAPH COMPANY*

In the Fifth District Court of New Orleans

Reported in C. Allen, *Telegraph Cases Decided in the Courts of America, Great Britain and Ireland.* New York: Hurd and Houghton, 1852, pp. 5–6.

. . . The plaintiff sued for $164 damages, arising from the incorrect transmission of a telegraphic dispatch, in which the word sixty-six was substituted in the price of oats, for *fifty*-six, the correct number. The company refunded the cost of the dispatch, but resisted any liability incurred by the mistake of the operator. As this is the first case of the kind tried, the principles laid down by the court are very interesting and important, as governing other cases. Judge Buchanan charged directly against any liability incurred by the company for mistakes of this kind; because uncontrollable influences from atmospheric causes are likely to change the wires and pervert a telegraphic message. It is unreasonable to apply the doctrine which applies to common carriers to a case like the present. The carrier is responsible for the merchandise intrusted to his care; but that merchandise has an appreciable value. The judge says:

> "What, on the contrary, is the test of appreciation of a message like that which the plaintiff received in this instance from his correspondent? The dispatch read or said, oats fifty-six, bran one-ten, corn seventy-three, hay twenty-five. The person who sent the dispatch made no explanation to the operator, and without explanation how could the operator know whether the numbers in question referred to dollars and cents or to bushels and bales? Again, how could the operator know whether the said dispatch conveyed an order to purchase or an account of sales? And if he were bound to infer the for-

mer, what information did the dispatch convey to his mind of the extent of the order? The meaning of the dispatch was a secret to all but the parties corresponding. Under these circumstances the value of the message transmitted was inappreciable, and this telegraph company had no means of knowing the extent of the responsibility which ought to be involved in its correct transmission, upon the principle contended for by the counsel for the plaintiff."

The judgement was for the plaintiff to the amount of three dollars and fifty cents—the cost of the message—which the company had offered to refund, and the costs of the court.

PARKS v. *ALTA CALIFORNIA TELEGRAPH COMPANY*

Supreme Court of California, 1859

13 California, 422

In this case, the plaintiff, a man named Parks, telegrammed an agent to collect a debt owed to Parks by a firm which was going out of business. An accident prevented the telegram from being sent. The other creditors got to the firm first, leaving no money to pay the debt owed to Parks. Parks sued the telegraph company for damages equal to the amount of the debt he was owed. A lower California court ruled "a telegraph company was not a common carrier; was not in any sense an insurer; (common carriers such as railroads were insurers of their goods) that a message had not any market value; and that the measure of damages was limited to the cost of the dispatch, which being two dollars and fifty cents, judgement therefor was rendered." Parks moved for a new trial and when that was denied he appealed to the California Supreme Court. The judge ruled in Parks' favor and wrote: The rules of law which govern the liability of telegraph companies are not new. They are old rules applied to new circumstances. Such companies hold themselves out to the public as engaged in a particular branch of business, in which the interests of the public are deeply concerned. They propose to do a certain service for a given price. There is no difference in the general nature of the legal obligation of the contract between carrying a message along a wire and carrying goods or a package along a route. The physical agency may be different, but the essential nature of the contract is the same. The breach of contract in one case or the other, is, or may be, attended with the same consequences; and the obligation to perform the stipulated duty is the same in both cases. The importance of the discharge of it in both respects is the same. In both cases the contract is binding, and the responsibility of the parties for the breach of duty is governed by the same general rules . . .

Suppose a man, on the eve of the expiration of a policy of insurance on his house, telegraphs to his agent to renew the policy immediately, the agent having the funds and the authority of the principal, and the telegraph company neglects to forward the message, and the house is burned a few days afterwards, could the company defend upon the ground that it could not be known whether the agent would have insured or not? . . . It seems to us that the loss of the debt would be the natural and proximate damages resulting from this breach of contract. And so in this case, the plaintiff had a debt for Gillingham & Co.; he wished to get out an attachment; he contracted with the defendant for the conveyance of a telegraphic message to his agent to take out an attachment; in the usual course of things, if the message had been delivered, the agent would have received it on the evening of the seventh; the papers could, with the most ordinary diligence, have been made out and the writ issued, early on the morning of the eighth; placed in the sheriff's hands shortly afterwards, the plaintiff's writ would have been entitled to precedence over most of these attachments; there was enough property, as seems to have been admitted, to secure the debt. If the facts warrant these conclusions, the plaintiff, we think, was entitled to judgement . . .

The opinion of the court below is not in accordance with these views, and the judgement is reversed and cause remanded for another trial.

JONATHAN W. ELLIS v. *AMERICAN TELEGRAPH COMPANY*

In the Supreme Judicial Court of Massachusetts

13 Allen, 266, 1866

A number of cases were decided against telegraph companies after the Parks case and many telegraph companies, in an effort to protect themselves, began using an agreement signed by the person sending the telegram. Agreements were designed to absolve the telegraph company of responsibility for errors in transmission and were permitted by state statutes. The agreements created a different kind of "contract" between the sender and the telegraph company than was emphasized in the Parks case. While such agreements did not always provide complete protection against suits and large damages—especially where negligence was proven—they did lessen the chance for damage rulings similar to the Parks case. In the Ellis case, a man named Ellis was the recipient of a telegram sent by H. T. Meserve from Boston which was supposed to read: "To J. W. Ellis, New Bedford. City Cambridge ten (10) men one hundred twenty-five dollars. H. T. Meserve." When the telegram was sent the figure "one-hundred twenty-five dollars" was changed to "one-hundred seventy-five dollars (175)." No additional fee had been paid by H. T. Meserve to have the telegram repeated and therefore help assure its accuracy. A superior court in Massachusetts ruled in favor of Ellis but the Supreme Judicial Court of Massachusetts disagreed and ordered a new trial. Presented next is the text of the agreement used by the American Telegraph Company followed by excerpts of the ruling by the Supreme Judicial Court of Massachusetts:

At the trial in the superior court, . . . it appeared that the message was offered to the defendants (American Telegraph Company) by H. T. Meserve upon a printed blank, and was in the following form:

> American Telegraph Company. Terms and conditions on which this and all messages are received by this company for transmission. In order to guard against and correct as much as possible some of thě errors arising from atmospheric and other causes appertaining to telegraphy, every important message should be repeated, by being sent back from the station at which it is to be received to the station from which it is originally sent. Half the usual price will be charged for repeating the message; and while this company in good faith will endeavor to send messages correctly and promptly, it will not be responsible for errors or delays in the transmission or delivery, nor for the non-delivery of repeated messages, beyond two hundred times the sum paid for sending the message, unless a special agreement for insurance be made in writing, and the amount of risk specified on this agreement, and paid for at the time of sending the message. Nor will the company be responsible for any error or delay in the transmission or delivery, or for the non-delivery of any unrepeated message, beyond the amount paid for sending the same, unless in like manner specially insured, and amount of risk stated hereon, and paid for at the time. No liability is assumed for errors in cipher or obscurely written messages; nor is any liability assumed by this company for any error or neglect by any other company over whose lines this message may be sent to reach its destination, and this company is hereby made the agent of the sender of this message to forward it over the lines extending beyond those of this company. No agent or employee is allowed to vary these terms, or make any other or verbal agreement, nor any promise as to the time of performance, and no one but a superintendent is authorized to make a special agreement for insurance. These terms apply through the whole course of this message on all lines by which it may be transmitted. Cambridge Livingston, Secretary. 145 Broadway, N. Y.

. . . It appears to have been taken for granted at the trial of the case, as it certainly was in the arguments of learned counsel at the bar of this court, that the rights of the parties were to be determined solely by having recourse to the rules and principles of the common law. This we think is an error. We entertain no doubt that these would have been found fully adequate to the satisfactory solution of the various questions to which the pursuit of this novel branch of human skill and industry will, in the course of time, necessarily give rise. But the legislature of this commonwealth have not deemed it wise or expedient to leave to the slow process of judicial determination the regulation of a business on which so many of the daily transactions of life, involving the most important rights and interests, are made to depend . . .

We are then to look into the provisions of the statute to ascertain how far they regulate and control the relative rights and liabilities of the parties to this suit. The only important clause bearing on the questions saved by the exceptions is found in the tenth section of the chapter of the General Statutes already cited. It is in these words: "Every company shall receive dispatches from and for other telegraph lines, companies, and associations, and from and for any person; and, on payment of the usual charges for transmitting dispatches according to the regulations of the company, shall transmit the same faithfully and impartially." . . .

Under this provision, an owner or manager of such a line becomes to a certain extent a public servant or agent. He is bound, under a heavy penalty, to the due and faithful execution of the service which he holds himself out as ready to perform. He cannot refuse to receive and forward dispatches; nor can he select the persons for whom he will act. He cannot transmit messages at such times or in such order as he may deem expedient. He is required to send them for every person who may apply, at a usual or uniform tariff or rate, without any undue preference, and according to established regulations applicable to all alike. There can be no doubt that, in view of the nature of the business, these requisitions are just and expedient. They certainly tend to prevent monopoly and exclusive privileges, and to secure to the public an equal enjoyment of the benefits arising from this new method of intercommunication between distant points. In some respects, they assimilate the duties and obligations incident to the employment to those which the law attaches to that of common carriers. But it is a mistake to say that the extent or degree of responsibility is the same. There is nothing in the statute which gives countenance to the suggestion, urged by the plaintiff's counsel, that owners or conductors of telegraphs are bound to warrant or insure the correct transmission of the messages which they undertake to send. Nor would it be just or reasonable to hold them to such a standard of diligence. The reasons of policy and expediency on which the rule of the common law is founded, which imposes on carriers of goods a liability for all losses not caused by the act of God or the public enemy, do not apply to the business of transmitting messages by means of the electric telegraph . . . The defendants were entitled to insist on a compliance with that part of their regulations which required that the message should be repeated, and the extent of the risk should be made known to them, if they were to be held to insure the safe and correct transmission of the message, or, in case of failure, to be responsible for all the damages consequent on delays or errors. Of this regulation the plaintiff had notice . . . *New Trial Granted*

The cases dealt with here provide a foundation for the understanding of more than just telegraph law. We shall see in other chapters that the issues which arose during the 1800s were also important to the development of law and regulation of the technologies which followed such as "wireless," modern radio and television, and modern common carriers such as the telephone. Even computers present some interesting legal challenges since the transfer of data can be compared to the transfer of goods and services over telephone systems which can be compared to common carriers.

QUESTIONS FOR CRITICAL ANALYSIS

- Why was the secretary of the treasury instead of some other department of government charged with issuing the first "notice of inquiry" on the telegraph?
- Why were "collectors of customs" and "commanders of revenue cutters" (somewhat equivalent to the modern U.S. Coast Guard) highlighted in the secretary's inquiry?
- If the system proposed to Congress by Morse was untried and untested, why didn't Congress move toward the more mechanical systems proposed by others?
- Morse's proposal referred to the telegraph as a "public utility." How did this concept compare to other public utilities of the 1830s and why would Morse use these words? Did it help persuade Congress in favor of the Morse system?
- Morse suggested that the telegraph should be under the control of the Post Office Department. Had he suggested another branch of government,

might it have influenced the way the telegraph was eventually regulated?

- The telegraph became an important instrument of military strategy, especially during the Civil War. Why didn't Morse suggest that this would be its primary use? Would such an argument have been more persuasive for Congress?
- The report of the Franklin Institute suggested the telegraph was such a powerful invention that the "government alone" should possess the right to control it. If you had been a member of Congress in the 1830s, would you have agreed with that assessment? If the invention was so powerful, could an argument be made against the government controlling it?
- How would the issue of freedom of the press as protected by the First Amendment to the Constitution impact on exclusive government control of the telegraph?
- In retrospect, had the government had exclusive control over the telegraph, would it have developed more or less rapidly than it did?
- Congress failed to act on Morse's original proposal, dragging out the matter almost to the point where Morse was without personal funds. When Congress did act, it appropriated $30,000, which was $4,000 more than he requested. Why would so much hesitation be followed by so much generosity?
- Why didn't the Post Office Department develop the telegraph as a "mail" service and use it as a means of earning revenue for the department?
- Why was the Interstate Commerce Commission chosen to enforce early telegraph laws?
- The 1876 legislation stated that "no amalgamation, union, or sale of cable interests established under this act shall be made to any existing European or other cable-companies." Why would such a provision be included?
- If the Interstate Commerce Commission was responsible for enforcement of telegraph law, why did the Post Office Department have authority to set rates?
- In the Shields case, the judge ruled in favor of the telegraph company. Why was this case any different than *Parks* v. *Alta*, which found in favor of the plaintiff and against the telegraph company?
- In the Shields case, the judge gave the opinion that the "telegraph company had no means of knowing the extent of the responsibility which ought to be involved in its correct transmission." Do you agree with this statement? Why shouldn't the telegraph company clearly understand its responsibility to accuracy, since it is crucial to its success?
- In the Ellis case, the statement is made that the "legislature of this commonwealth has not deemed it wise or expedient to leave the slow process of judicial determination . . ." to the regulation of the telegraph. Are courts a help or a hindrance to the regulation of fast-growing technologies?
- The Ellis case was heard in 1866. Would the same arguments hold up if the telegraph had achieved a degree of reliability equivalent to the modern telephone or to radio communication?

ADDITIONAL RESOURCES

Allen, C., ed., *Telegraph Cases Decided in the Courts of America, Great Britain, and Ireland*. New York: Hurd and Houghton, 1873.

Croswell, S. G., *A Treatise on the Law Relating to Electricity*. Boston: Little, Brown, 1895.

Gray, M. A., *Treatise on Communication by Telegraph*. Boston: Little, Brown, 1885.

Jones, S. W., *A Treatise on the Law of Telegraph and Telephone Companies*. Kansas City, MO: Vernon Law Book Co., 1906.

Scott, W. L., and M. P. Jarnagin, *A Treatise Upon the Law of Telegraphs; with an Appendix Containing the General Provisions of England, Canada, the United States, and the States of the Union, upon the Subject of Telegraphs*. Boston: Little, Brown, 1868.

chapter two

The Wireless Era

With a network of wires running across the United States, attention was focused on the prosperity of the industrial revolution. But all this would soon change. Guglielmo Marconi, flying an antenna kite in December 1901, heard the crackle of the letter "S" resounding in his earphones at Signal Hill, Newfoundland. As he received the signals from the English coast, magazines and newspapers heralded the feat, and Marconi's name flashed across the same telegraph wires that his own accomplishments would soon make obsolete. For Marconi, the experimental broadcast across the Atlantic was only the beginning. He was as much a businessman as an inventor, and as his empire began to stretch worldwide, it became a dominant force in the growing application of wireless to ship-to-shore communication.

INTERNATIONAL REQUESTS FOR REGULATION

In the United States and elsewhere, government attention turned to regulating wireless communication when the Marconi companies started to prohibit ships and shore stations from communicating with each other unless they were equipped with the Marconi equipment. Germany was especially affected by Marconi's strategy, since it housed a competing Slaby-Arco wireless system. Finally, the Germans took the initiative and in 1903 called a conference in Berlin, where a protocol agreement was reached for international cooperation in wireless communication. Three years later, Berlin hosted the first International Radiotelegraph Convention, out of which an agreement was signed by 27 nations. In the United States, the stage was now set for domestic legislation, which would embody the spirit of the Berlin agreement and foster safety and cooperation among American shipping interests.

ROOSEVELT'S MESSAGE TO CONGRESS

In a statement dated February 9, 1909, President Theodore Roosevelt sent a message to both the Senate and House discussing "Radio-Telegraphy on Passenger Steamers." Roosevelt pointed out the merits of the new "instrumentality for the preservation of life at sea" and praised American inventors for applying the technology which had developed in "another country." The president noted that the Navy Department had seen that the Atlantic, Gulf, and Pacific coasts were equipped with shore stations and that steps had been taken to prevent the establishment of a monopoly, at least in the United States. Roosevelt called on

Congress to enact a law which would require ocean-going steamships carrying "considerable numbers of passengers" on routes where wireless installations were operable to have adequate wireless equipment and competent operators.

THE WIRELESS SHIP ACT OF 1910

The year 1910 held few visions of commercial broadcasting stations as we know them today. Transatlantic experiments were less than a decade old, and Congress was only now thinking about safety applications of the new medium, especially for ships at sea. Some ships, but by no means all, had installed wireless apparatus. It was in this atmosphere that the Wireless Ship Act of 1910 was passed. Encompassing only four paragraphs, it set the stage for maritime communication:

Requirements for Shipboard Wireless

Be it enacted by the Senate and House of Representatives of the United States of America in Congress assembled, That from and after the first day of July, nineteen hundred and eleven, it shall be unlawful for any ocean-going steamer of the United States, or of any foreign country, carrying passengers and carrying fifty or more persons, including passengers and crew, to leave or attempt to leave any port of the United States unless such steamer shall be equipped with an efficient apparatus for radio-communication, in good working order, in charge of a person skilled in the use of such apparatus, which apparatus shall be capable of transmitting and receiving messages over a distance of at least one hundred miles, night or day: Provided, That the provisions of this act shall not apply to steamers plying only between ports less than two hundred miles apart.

Required Cooperation

Sec. 2. That for the purpose of this act apparatus for radio-communication shall not be deemed to be efficient unless the company installing it shall contract in writing to exchange, and shall, in fact, exchange, as far as may be physically practicable, to be determined by the master of the vessel, messages with shore or ship stations using other systems of radio-communication.

Penalties for Non-compliance

Sec. 3. That the master or other person being in charge of any vessel which leaves or attempts to leave any port of the United States in violation of any of the provisions of this act shall, upon conviction, be fined in a sum not more than five thousand dollars, and any such fine shall be a lien upon such vessel, and such vessel may be libeled therefor in any district court of the United States within the jurisdiction of which such vessel shall arrive or depart, and the leaving or attempting to leave each and every port of the United States shall constitute a separate offense.

Sec. 4. That the Secretary of Commerce and Labor shall make such regulations as may be necessary to secure the proper execution of this act by collectors of customs and other officers of the Government.[1]

For the United States, The Radio Act of 1910 was the first law covering wireless. The law did not mention radio stations as we know them today since the real age of radio had not yet arrived. Terms such as *licenses*, *wavelengths*, and other technical phrases associated with radio would come later.

THE RADIO ACT OF 1912

Wireless quickly achieved international recognition and many countries forged cooperative agreements. The United States, however, where wireless was not under complete government control as it was in some other nations, remained lax in these agreements. In April 1912, however, that all began to change when the ship Titanic sank in the North Atlantic after striking an iceberg. News of the sinking and contributions of wireless to the safety of the survivors were well chronicled. Four months before the Titanic sank the provisions of the 1906 Berlin treaty had been the subject of discussions in Congress. Those discussions, accompanied by the Titanic tragedy, resulted in passage of the Radio Act of 1912. It read in part:

Regulating "Commercial Intercourse" Among States and Nations

Be it enacted by the Senate and House of Representatives of the United States of America in Congress, That a person, company, or corporation within the jurisdiction of the United States shall not use or operate any apparatus for radio communication as a means of commercial intercourse among the several States, or with foreign nations, or upon any vessel of the United States engaged in interstate or foreign commerce, or for the transmission of radiograms or signals the effect of which extends beyond the jurisdiction of the State or Territory in which the same are made,

First Licensing Provision

or where interference would be caused thereby with the receipt of messages or signals from beyond the jurisdiction of the said State or Territory, except under and in accordance with a license, revocable for cause, in that behalf granted by the Secretary of Commerce and Labor upon application therefor; but nothing in this Act shall be construed to apply to the transmission and exchange of radiograms or signals between points situated in the same State: Provided, That the effect thereof shall not extend beyond the jurisdiction of the said State or interfere with the reception of radiograms or signals from beyond said jurisdiction; and a license shall not be required for the transmission or exchange of radiograms or signals by or on behalf of the Government of the United States,

Call Letters

but every Government station on land or sea shall have special call letters designated and published in the list of radio stations of the United States by the Department of Commerce and Labor. Any person, company, or corporation that shall use or operate any apparatus for radio communication in violation of this section, or knowingly aid or abet another person, company, or corporation in so doing, shall be deemed guilty of a misdemeanor,

Penalties for Non-Compliance

and on conviction thereof shall be punished by a fine not exceeding five hundred dollars, and the apparatus or device so unlawfully used and operated may be adjudged forfeited to the United States.

Sec. 2. That every such license shall be in such form as the Secretary of Commerce and Labor shall determine and shall contain the restriction, pursuant to this Act, on and subject to which the license is granted;

Citizenry Requirements

that every such license shall be issued only to citizens of the United States or Puerto Rico or to a company incorporated under the laws of some State or Territory or of the United States or Puerto Rico, and shall specify the ownership and location of the station in which said apparatus shall be used and other particulars for its identification and to enable its range to be estimated; shall state the purpose of the station, and, in case of a station in actual operation at the date of passage of this Act, shall contain the statement that satisfactory proof has been furnished that it was actually operating on the above-mentioned date;

Frequency ("Wave Lengths")

shall state the wave length or the wave lengths authorized for use by the station for the prevention of interference and the hours for which the station is licensed for work; and shall not be construed to authorize the use of any apparatus for radio communication in any other station than that specified. Every such license shall be subject to the regulations contained herein, and such regulations as may be established from time to time by authority of this act or subsequent acts and treaties of the United States.

Provisions in Times of Conflict

Every such license shall provide that the President of the United States in time of war or public peril or disaster may cause the closing of any station for radio communication and the removal therefrom of all radio apparatus, or may authorize the use or control of any such station or apparatus by any department of the Government, upon just compensation to the owners.

Personal Licensing

Sec. 3. That every such apparatus shall at all times while in use and operation as aforesaid be in charge or under the supervision of a person or persons licensed for that purpose by the Secretary of Commerce and Labor. Every person so licensed who in the operation of any radio apparatus shall fail to observe and obey regulations contained in or made pursuant to this act or subsequent acts or treaties of the United States, or any one of them, or who shall fail to enforce obedience thereto by an unlicensed person while serving under his supervision, in addition to the punishments and penalties herein prescribed, may suffer the suspension of the said license for a period to be fixed by the Secretary of Commerce and Labor not exceeding one year.

License for Employment and Supervisory Responsibilities

It shall be unlawful to employ any unlicensed person or for any unlicensed person to serve in charge or in supervision of the use and operation of such an apparatus, and any person violating this provision shall be guilty of a misdemeanor, and on conviction thereof shall be punished by a fine of not more than one hundred dollars or imprisonment for not more than two months; or both, in the discretion of the court, for each and every such offense: Provided, That in case of emergency the Secretary of Commerce and Labor may authorize a collector of customs to issue a temporary permit, in lieu of a license, to the operator of a vessel. . . .

Enforcement by Secretary of Commerce

These regulations shall be enforced by the Secretary of Commerce and Labor through the collectors of customs and other officers of the Government as other regulations herein provided for. The Secretary of Commerce and Labor may, in his discretion, waive the provisions of any or all of these regulations when no interference of the character above mentioned can ensue.

Temporary Licenses for Testing

The Secretary of Commerce and Labor may grant special temporary licenses to stations actually engaged in conducting experiments for the development of the science of radio communication, or the apparatus pertaining thereto, to carry on special tests, using any amount of power or any wave lengths, at such hours and under such conditions as will insure the least interference with the sending or receipt of commercial or Government radiograms, of distress signals and radiograms, or with the work of other stations. In these regulations the naval and military stations shall be understood to be stations on land.[2]

Much more encompassing than the 1910 legislation, the 1912 act provided for definitions of authority between federal and state governments and established call letters for government stations. Along with providing clauses for revoking a license and fines for violators, it also established the assignment of frequencies, stating that the license of the station would "state the wave length or the wave lengths authorized for use by the station for the prevention of interference and the hours for which the station is licensed to work: . . ." But in addition to these specified wavelengths, stations could still use "other sending wave lengths."

The 1912 act recognized the famous S-O-S distress signal, allowing it to be broadcast with a maximum of interference to override other stations. For the first time, the act defined *radio communication* as: "any system of electrical communication by telegraphy or telephony without the aid of any wire connecting the points from and at which the radiograms, signals, or other communications are sent or received." Other provisions of the act covered secrecy-of-messages restrictions to protect government stations' signals, rules for ship-to-shore communication, and a ban on stations refusing to receive messages from those which were not equipped with apparatus manufactured by a certain company. The act was a valiant effort to control wireless communication. But few legislators could foresee the exploding growth of the wireless and, even if they had, the legislative process could not begin to keep up with the new technology. It was not long before the regulatory framework began to crumble.

THE NATIONAL RADIO CONFERENCES: THE 1912 LAW IN TROUBLE

Before long, the United States and radio were involved in World War I. For the U.S. Navy, it meant hurriedly constructed wireless towers on warships. Taking over the country's radio stations, the government put a lid on radio's development for anything but wartime service. But when the war ended, it was like uncapping a bottle. All the pent-up enthusiasm was released, and new experimenters eagerly flocked to their equipment.

Although the Radio Act of 1912 had survived World War I, it was headed for trouble in an exploding radio industry. By the 1920s, the chaos on the spectrum had mushroomed out of proportion. In 1922 alone, receiving set sales climbed 1,200 percent. The airways were flooded with everything from marine military operations to thousands of amateur radio experimenters. Added to this flood was the advent of commercial radio and its powerful stations booming onto the air.

First National Radio Conference

In 1922, groups of government officials, amateur radio operators, and commercial radio representatives met in Washington, DC, for the First National Radio Conference.[3] The conference was addressed by representatives of opposing factions, all of whom had an interest in radio. Amateur radio operators were afraid that their privileges were going to be trimmed under the influence of such large commercial firms as General Electric and Westinghouse; whereas the large commercial firms were afraid that their privileges were going to be relegated to the military. After the rhetoric subsided, the conference split into three committees: amateur, technical, and legislative. Since interference was still the biggest problem, it was not surprising that the technical committee's recommendations received the most attention. Based on that report, legislation was introduced in Congress in 1923, but it never emerged from a Senate committee.

Second National Radio Conference

The Second National Radio Conference was held in 1923 and reaffirmed the problems of interference and recommended discretion in frequency allocations. Taking into account the commercial interests of the new medium, the conference suggested that allowing more stations on the air would only fragment an already shaky financial condition. Realizing that different geographical areas had different problems, the second conference suggested splitting up the country into zones, with each zone tackling its individual problems on a local basis. Legislation was introduced but it did not budge from congressional committees.

Third National Radio Conference

The interference continued and a Third National Radio Conference convened in 1924. Two major developments captured the attention of these delegates. First, "network" broadcasting had become a reality. AT&T's wired system and Westinghouse's short-wave system were proving that interstation connection was not only possible but also somewhat successful. Second, David Sarnoff, head of RCA, announced that RCA was going to experiment with the concept of superpower stations crisscrossing the country.

It is not surprising that the third conference recommended resolutions opposing monopoly and even encouraged government intervention. Nevertheless, the conference supported the development of network broadcasting, and although agreeing to let the superpower experiments proceed, warned that they "should only be permitted under strict government scrutiny."[4] On a request from Secretary of Commerce Herbert Hoover, legislation was not introduced and the decision was made to halt further legislative initiatives until still another national conference was convened.[5]

Fourth National Radio Conference

Convening in 1925, the Fourth National Radio Conference resulted in proposals which later became the foundation of the Radio Act of 1927. This conference suggested a system of station classifications and admonished Congress to pass some workable broadcast legislation. The delegates recommended preventing monopoly, installing five-year terms for licenses, requiring stations to operate in the public interest, providing for licenses to be revoked, and giving the secretary of commerce the power to enforce regulations. Its participants tried to guard against government censorship of programming, provide for due process of law, give the president control of stations in wartime, and see to it that broadcasting not be thought of as a public utility. But their good intentions were too late.

THE INTERCITY CASE

Despite the radio conference representatives' valiant efforts to make the 1912 law workable, law suits and legal opinions soon made it clear that the law was in serious trouble. Highlighting the problem in 1923 was *Hoover* v. *Intercity Radio Co., Inc.*[6]

Intercity had been engaged in telegraph communication between New York and other points under a license issued by the secretary of commerce and labor. Upon expiration, Intercity applied for and was denied a renewal because there was not enough space available on the spectrum for a frequency assignment that would not interfere with government and private stations. The issue went to court, where the judges ruled that the secretary had overstepped his bounds in refusing to renew Intercity's license. Cited as justification was a statement made by the chairman of the Committee on Commerce when the bill was passed to the effect that "it is compulsory with the Secretary of Commerce and Labor that upon application, these licenses shall be issued."

The interpretation meant the secretary of commerce and labor, although having the power to place restrictions on licenses and to prevent interference, could not refuse to issue a license as a means of curtailing that interference. The court stated: "In the present case, the duty of naming a wavelength is mandatory upon the Secretary. The only discretionary act is in selecting a wavelength within the limitations prescribed in the statute, which, in his judgement, will result in the least possible interference." The court went on to define the relationship between the restrictions and a radio license, stating: "The issuing of a license is not to be dependent upon the fixing of a wavelength. It is a restriction entering into the license. The wavelength named by the Secretary merely measures the extent of the privilege granted to the Licensee."

For the secretary of commerce and labor, the ruling was frustrating. Broadcasting had matured beyond the experimental and military stages. The secretary was faced with regulating a limited resource, and the court was telling the secretary that he had to give some of the available spectrum to everyone who wanted it. The act had charged the secretary with broad responsibilities, but the provisions of the act did not give the secretary the power to carry them out.

THE ZENITH RADIO CORPORATION CASE

Three years later came *United States* v. *Zenith Radio Corporation* et al.[7] Zenith had received a license which authorized it to operate on a wavelength of 332.4 meters on Thursday night from 10 to 12 p.m., "when the use of this period is not desired by the General Electric Company's Denver Station." Zenith clashed with the secretary when it operated at other times and on another unauthorized frequency. Yet the court ruled in favor of Zenith. The legal catch was a section of the 1912 law reading: "In addition to normal sending wave length, all stations . . . may use other sending wave lengths: . . ."

REQUEST OF THE CHICAGO FEDERATION OF LABOR

The crowning blow came when Acting Secretary of Commerce Stephen Davis answered a request from the Chicago Federation of Labor to construct a station.[8] The application itself had not even reached Washington before Davis wrote the federation telling them that all the wavelengths were in use, and that if the federation constructed a station, there would be no license forthcoming. Davis put the blame on the Fourth National Radio Conference, where it certainly did not belong, since the conference did not have the power to dictate policy. Some politicians began to be concerned, and as the situation grew worse and the stations continued to interfere with each other, the Office of the Secretary of Commerce sought an opinion from the attorney general.

REQUEST FOR AN OPINION FROM THE ATTORNEY GENERAL

In a letter of June 4, 1926, the secretary asked the attorney general for a definition of power. The questions posed in the letter, as interpreted by the attorney general were as stated:

1. Does the 1912 Act require broadcasting stations to obtain licenses, and is the operation of such a station without a license an offense under that Act?
2. Has the Secretary of Commerce authority under the 1912 Act to assign wave lengths and times of operation and limit the power of stations?
3. Has a station, whose license stipulates a wave length for its use, the right to use any other wave length, and if it does operate on a different wave length, is it in violation of the law and does it become subject to the penalties of the Act?

4. If a station, whose license stipulates a period during which only the station may operate and limits its power, transmits at different times, or with excessive power, is it in violation of the Act, and does it become subject to the penalties of the Act?
5. Has the Secretary of Commerce power to fix the duration of the licenses which he issues or should they be indeterminate, continuing in effect until revoked or until Congress otherwise provides?[9]

THE ATTORNEY GENERAL'S RESPONSE

The answer to the first question was affirmative. The act definitely provided for stations to be licensed, and stations operating without a license were clearly in violation.

As to the second question, the attorney general said that the secretary had the right to assign a wavelength to each station under one provision of the act, but that for the most part the stations could use whatever frequency they so desired, whenever they wanted. With the exception of two minor provisions, the attorney general also stated that the secretary had no power to designate hours of operation. Also lost was the argument over limiting power. The act stated that stations should use the "minimum amount of energy necessary to carry out any communications desired." The attorney general said: "It does not appear that the Secretary is given the power to determine in advance what this minimum amount should be for every case; and I therefore conclude that you have no authority to insert such a determination as a part of any license."

The third answer was obvious. Stations could use any other wavelength they desired. The act and courts had affirmed that point.

That also answered the fourth question. Since the secretary could not limit power or operating times beyond the actual license, stations were free to use other wavelengths with different power outputs and at different times than the license stated.

The attorney general said in answer to the fifth question that he could "find no authority in the Act for the issuance of licenses of limited duration."

COOLIDGE'S MESSAGE TO CONGRESS

Clearly, a law which only a decade earlier had seemed in firm control of the new medium was now almost worthless. Four months later, on December 7, 1926, President Coolidge sent a message to Congress. Much like Roosevelt had done in 1909, Coolidge had thrown the backing of the presidency behind legislation affecting radio. Coolidge, however, had a much more developed system of broadcasting with which to contend. He reminded Congress that for years the Department of Commerce had urgently requested the need for regulation which would help it carry out its regulatory functions and prevent interference between broadcasting stations. Coolidge noted that decisions of the courts had broken down the authority of the department and that if new legislation were not enacted the "great value" of broadcasting could be destroyed. He called for a separate "board" which could be brought together whenever action was necessary. Coolidge's message stated:

> The administration of the decision of the board and other features of regulation and promotion of radio in the public interest, together with scientific research, would remain in the Department of Commerce. Such an arrangement makes for more expert, more efficient, and more economical administration than an independent agency or board, whose duties, after initial stages, require but little attention, in which administrative functions are confused with semijudicial functions and from which of necessity there must be greatly increased personnel and expenditure.[10]

Congress stopped the further licensing of broadcasting stations until specific legislation could be passed.

THE RADIO ACT OF 1927: FORMING THE FEDERAL RADIO COMMISSION

Congress had been working on the Radio Act of 1927 before Coolidge's message. The 1927 law passed both houses of Congress and received the president's signature on February 23, 1927. The Radio Act of 1927 was administered by the secretary of commerce, and it provided for the formation of a Federal Radio Commission (FRC) to oversee broadcasting. The act was intended to remain in force for only a year, but it was subsequently extended until 1934. With court decisions as guides, Congress plugged the holes left by the 1912 law.

One provision of the 1927 act formed a Federal Radio Commission "composed of five commissioners appointed by the President, by and with the advice and consent of the Senate, and one of whom the President shall designate as chairman. . . ."[11] The law specified that each commissioner must be a citizen of the United States and that each would receive compensation of $10,000 for the first year of service. The commissioner system, as well as many other provisions of the 1927 legislation, later became part of the Communications Act of 1934. It was more than Coolidge had requested.

The Federal Radio Commission was organized into a series of divisions and sections. At the head of the Federal Radio Commission were the commissioners themselves, who presided directly over the three divisions.

PROVISIONS OF THE RADIO ACT OF 1927

Along with forming the FRC, other provisions in the 1927 act included dividing the United States into zones represented by the individual commissioners.

Zoning

No more than one commissioner could be appointed from any one zone. The first zone encompassed New England and the upper tip of the Middle Atlantic states, including the District of Columbia, Puerto Rico, and the Virgin Islands. The second zone included the upper Middle Atlantic states west to Michigan and Kentucky. The third zone encompassed the South, and the fourth and fifth zones the Great Plains and the West, respectively. The act provided for the licensing of stations, but only for a specified time, and gave the government considerable control over the electromagnetic spectrum.

States' Rights

The act also set out to define states' rights. Keep in mind that federal regulation over intrastate commerce, for which wireless was used, was not popular. So it was not surprising that the Radio Act of 1927 tried to avoid direct control of intrastate communication, while at the same time retaining control of communication across state borders. The act stated that the law's jurisdiction would extend "within any State when the effects of such use extend beyond the borders of said State. . . ."

Service

The most quoted provision came from Section 4, with its statement that stations should operate "as public convenience, interest, or necessity requires. . . ." In addition, Section 4 prescribed the "nature of the service to be rendered by each class of licensed station and each station within any class." Control over frequency, power, and times of operation was covered by the act, giving the FRC power to: "Assign bands or frequencies or wave lengths for each individual station and determine the power which each station shall use and the time during which it may operate." Coverage areas for stations were to be fixed by the FRC, and the commission was to have power over "chain" or network broadcasting. Stations were also required to keep operating logs.

Judicial Powers

In addition to regulating the industry, the 1927 act gave the commission quasi-judicial powers, with the "authority to hold hearings, summon witnesses, administer oaths, compel the production of books, documents, and papers and to make such investigations as may be necessary in the performance of its duties." The secretary of commerce was empowered to "prescribe the qualifications of stations operators, to classify them according to the duties to be performed, to fix the forms of such licenses, and to issue them to such persons as he finds qualified."

Operations

The secretary was also empowered to issue call letters to all stations and to "publish" the call letters. But before issuing a license, the government made certain that the prospective licensee gave up all rights to the frequency. The applicant had to sign a "waiver of any claim to the use of any particular frequency or wave length. . . ." Once granted, station licenses were limited to a three-year duration. Closing the wavelength loophole of the 1912 legislation, the 1927 law stated that: "The station license shall not vest in the licensee any right to operate the station nor any right in the use of the frequencies or wave length designated in the license beyond the term thereof nor in any other manner than authorized therein." The act also discouraged monopolies and prohibited the transfer of licenses without commission approval. It also gave the commission power to revoke licenses for "issuing false statements or failing to operate substantially as set forth in the license." The wording for Section 315 of the Communications Act of 1934 came from the 1927 legislation with: "If any licensee shall permit any person who is a legally qualified candidate for any public office to use a broadcasting station, he shall afford equal opportunities to all other such candidates for that office. . . ." Commercial broadcasting gained instant recognition and regulation by the requirement that paid commercials were to be announced as paid or furnished by the sponsor.

Construction Permits

Putting a station on the air was an important provision of the act. As we'll see later in this chapter, this issue also arose in the appeals process. Specifically, the act stated: "No license shall be issued under the authority of this Act for the operation of any station, the construction of which is begun or is continued after this Act takes effect, unless a permit for its construction has been granted by the licensing authority upon written application thereof." The law acknowledged that construction permits for stations would specify the "earliest and latest dates between which the actual operation of such station is expected to begin, and shall provide that said permit will be automatically forfeited if the station is not ready for operation within the time specified. . . ."

Anticensorship

The anticensorship provision, later to become incorporated into Section 326 of the Communications Act of 1934, was also included. That provision was followed with: "No person within the jurisdiction of the United States shall utter any obscene, indecent, or profane language by means of radio communication."

We can see the conflicts that could develop, not only between these two provisions but also in the "convenience, interest, and necessity" clause. It was not very long before the broadcasters and the government were arguing. Yet, the 1927 law became the foundation of contemporary broadcast regulation. It was simple and straightforward, and the courts gave it strong support.

COURT CHALLENGES TO THE RADIO ACT OF 1927

The Radio Act of 1927 was challenged with much the same ferocity, although not the same success, as the 1912 legislation. Researchers Don R. Le Duc and Thomas A. McCain examined the judicial processes that took place before the 1934 law went into effect. They concluded that the "federal judiciary, during the period in which it considered appeals from Federal Radio Commission decisions, generally supported the regulatory authority of the agency, and by providing such support, enhanced its ability to supervise the broadcasting industry."[12] Supervision of the industry was no small task. Because of the leniency of the 1912 legislation, it was necessary to control some of the stations already on the air in order to return stability to the industry.

The seriousness of each decision was embodied in the fact that federal judges had to distinguish between regulations on broadcasting stations serving the public and the traditional common carrier regulations that were more appropriate to public utilities. As Le Duc and McCain point out, unless a judge "could distinguish broadcast regulation from other types of government control, affirmance of the standard used by the FRC would allow all federal agencies much broader latitude in their regulatory functions."[13]

Affirming the FRC's Power

The authority of the FRC to refuse a license was first tested in the case of *Technical Radio Laboratory* v. *FRC*.[14] Technical Radio Laboratory operated station WTRL in Midland Park, New Jersey, but was denied a license renewal by the FRC, since there simply were not enough frequencies available for every station that wanted to be on the air. The court affirmed the FRC's decision. Further legal support for this power was affirmed in the case of *Carrell* v. *FRC*, when the FRC was upheld in its decision not to renew the licenses of stations WKBG, WIBJ, and WHBM, all operated by Carrell.[15]

Affirming the Public Interest Standard

The "public interest" standard of the 1927 law was to come under scrutiny by the courts in the case of *FRC* v. *Nelson Brothers Bond and Mortgage Co.*[16] The FRC had approved the application of station WJKS in Gary, Indiana, causing the termination of licenses for station WIBO, owned by Nelson Brothers, and station WPCC in Chicago. It is no surprise that the case went to court. The Circuit Court of Appeals overturned the FRC's decision, but the Supreme Court agreed to review the decision of the Appeals Court and ruled in favor of the FRC. The FRC gained more clout in the case of

Pote (Station WLOE) v. *FRC*, when the FRC denied the transfer of the license for station WLOE from Boston Broadcasting to William Pote.[17]

Federal Jurisdiction

One of the most sensitive areas of the Radio Act of 1927 was the concept of federal jurisdiction over intrastate commerce. The Radio Act of 1912 was weak in this regard, and although the Radio Act of 1927 tried to enact stronger measures, states' rights were nothing to tamper with. For this reason, the broadcasters found themselves confronted with licenses both at the federal and at the municipal levels. Brought to the court's attention in *Whitehurst* v. *Grimes, Chief of Police*, et al.,[18] the case arose when amateur radio station 9ALM was charged a local license tax by the city of Lexington, Kentucky. The tax came under a city ordinance, but a judge ruled that 9ALM's *federal* license preempted local control, due to the station's effect on interstate communication.

The law was further broadened in the case of *United States* v. *Gregg* et al.,[19] when the court said that "even an *unlicensed* party whose signal was admittedly only intrastate in range would come within the purview of federal control because . . . any signal on a channel within the spectrum of frequencies requiring federal licensing would have an 'effect' upon interstate communication."[20] The decision stopped an unlicensed Houston, Texas station, "The Voice of Labor," from operating without a license.

Due Process

Although the FRC did receive its share of support, unleashed federal power could and would not go unchecked. A series of decisions trimmed the ability of the FRC to act without regard to the rights and due process of the people involved. When the FRC limited the broadcasting rights of Westinghouse, the case went to court in *Westinghouse Electric and Manufacturing Co.* v. *FRC*.[21] The FRC was held in error for not permitting Westinghouse a hearing before taking action against it. Nevertheless, the FRC still had the "public convenience, interest, and necessity" clause as a basis for waiving a *public* hearing whenever it deemed appropriate.[22]

Broadcasters' Rights

Broadcasters gained support in cases affecting the construction of new stations. The FRC was taken to court by a Richmond, Virginia firm that had applied to construct a station in Roanoke. In the case of *Richmond Development* v. *FRC*, the court recognized the right of the construction permit holder to challenge the FRC when the commission refused to extend the time of the permit.[23] The court noted that the FRC knew that Richmond Development might not be able to complete construction when the permit was issued.

Additional support for the broadcaster came in the cases of *Reading Broadcasting* v. *FRC* and *Journal Co.* v. *FRC*.[24] Each of these cases protected the broadcaster against arbitrary action affecting a change of frequency, reduction in power, or limitations in hours of operation when the stations could show that, over an extended period of time, they had operated in the public interest.

THE BRINKLEY AND SCHULER CASES

Just as the FRC was restrained from arbitrarily imposing restrictions on stations that could show good performance records, it was supported in refusing renewals to licensees who did not meet the "public convenience, interest, and necessity." Such power was of concern, since, theoretically, to deny a license for material used on the station could be construed as an infringement on First Amendment rights of free speech.

Dr. Brinkley's KFKB Broadcasts

In the case of *KFKB Broadcasting* v. *FRC*, the FRC denied the renewal of station KFKB.[25] Among other items, the station had broadcast programs by Dr. John R. Brinkley, during which Dr. Brinkley prescribed medicine for patients who wrote him or the station about their problems. The prescriptions were listed by number, and the patients were advised to obtain the prescriptions from the Brinkley Pharmaceutical Association. Two such broadcasts the court found as typical were as follows:

> Here's one from Tillie. She says she had an operation, had some trouble 10 years ago. I think the operation was unnecessary, and it isn't very good sense to have an ovary removed with the expectation of motherhood resulting therefrom. My advice to you is to use Women's Tonic No. 50, 67, and 61. This combination will do for you what you desire if any combination will, after three months persistent use.

> Sunflower State, from Dresden, Kansas. Probably he has gall stones. No, I don't mean that, I mean kidney stones. My advice to you is to put him on Prescription No. 80 and 50 for men, also 64. I think that he will be a whole lot better. Also drink a lot of water.[26]

It is little wonder that Dr. Brinkley's prescriptions did not impress the court. Dr. Brinkley claimed that refusal to renew the license was a case of censorship. The court indicated that nothing had been prohibited from being aired prior to the broadcast, and that the FRC was assuming that the renewal of the license would encourage the same type of programming that was indicative of the station's past performance. The court stated: "In considering the question whether the public interest, convenience, or necessity will be served by a renewal of the appellant's license, the Commission has merely exercised its undoubted right to take note of appellant's past conduct, which is not censorship."[27]

Dr. Schuler and the Trinity Methodist Church, South

In a similar case, *Trinity Methodist Church, South* v. *FRC*, the right to refuse renewal of a license was further affirmed.[28] In this case, the Reverend Doctor Schuler was alleged to have used a radio station to attack the Roman Catholic Church. Trinity claimed that the refusal to renew the license violated the right of free speech, that it deprived Dr. Schuler "of his property without due process of law," and that the FRC decision violated the Radio Act of 1927 because there was not sufficient evidence to deny the renewal. It argued, therefore, that the FRC's decision was "arbitrary and capricious."[29] The evidence against Dr. Schuler included a contempt of court citation under appeal to the Supreme Court of California. The court criticized Schuler, stating:

> Appellant, not satisfied with attacking the judges of the courts in cases then pending before them, attacked the bar association for its activities in recommending judges, charging it with ulterior and sinister purposes. With no more justification, he charged particular judges with sundry immoral acts. He made defamatory statements against the board of health. He charged that the labor temple in Los Angeles was a bootlegging and gambling joint.[30]

In affirming the FRC's decision to deny Trinity's license renewal, the court seriously damaged arguments that such denials were in violation of either a licensee's right of free speech or of rights of due process. Keep in mind that the denial occurred after, not before, Dr. Schuler had aired his comments; thus it was not a form of prior restraint.

DEFINING THE 1927 LAW'S LIMITS OF AUTHORITY

When Congress passed the Radio Act of 1927, it provided in Section 16 that the Court of Appeals of the District of Columbia had the right to hear appeals to FRC decisions. So, if a broadcaster felt that an FRC decision was indeed "arbitrary and capricious," the broadcaster still had another forum in which to argue. But if the broadcaster was not satisfied with the appeals court's decision, could the case go all the way to the Supreme Court?

The General Electric Case

The first case to test the question was the *FRC* v. *General Electric Company*. In this case, as Le Duc and McCain point out, the court held that federal courts could now engage in fact finding with the authority of an administrative agency that could not have its decisions reviewed by the Supreme Court under the Judiciary Act of 1789.

Amending the Law's Section 16

Congress amended Section 16 on July 1, 1930. The 1930 legislation, which was also cited by the appeals court in the Brinkley case and used as a basis of appeal in the Schuler case, stated that the "review by the court shall be limited to questions of law and that findings of fact by the Commission, if supported by substantial evidence, shall be conclusive unless it shall clearly appear that the findings of the Commission are arbitrary or capricious."[31] In other words, if the FRC did its homework prior to delivering an opinion, the facts would stand as originally presented, and the appeals process would consist of arguments about the law.

From 1927 to 1934, the Radio Act of 1927 withstood challenges from all sides. It achieved the ability to regulate effectively the expanding medium of "wireless," which now encompassed the nation with entertainment and new programming envisioned by few of the 1910 pioneer regulators. It is hardly surprising that the 1927 law was liberally quoted in the Communications Act of 1934, the law governing contemporary broadcasting.

THE COMMUNICATIONS ACT OF 1934

It was becoming clear that broadcasting needed a new, more comprehensive regulatory agency. The FRC was still limited in its scope, having to share responsibilities with the U.S. Department of Commerce. And although the Commerce Department had at one time been an appropriate home, the predominant trend was toward the public consumption of radio, overshadowing its commercial uses. Although commercial stations would still far outnumber those directing their signals to the public, guarding the public's convenience, interest, and necessity was no small task.

Roosevelt Proposes the FCC

After a number of proposals to coordinate regulation had been examined, President Franklin D. Roosevelt sent to Congress on February 26, 1934, a proposal to create a separate agency, known as the Federal Communications Commission. Roosevelt's message said that the FCC should have the authority "now lying in the Federal Radio Commission and with such authority over communications as now lies with the Interstate Commerce Commission—the services affected to be all of those which rely on wires, cables, or radio as a medium of transmission."[32]

The change to a separate independent agency also resolved the dilemma that had plagued regulation under the FRC, in that an agency of "commerce" had been charged with administering issues which were inherently part of the free speech-free press clause of the First Amendment to the Constitution. It would be interesting to speculate what would have occurred in the future of legislation and the media of radio and television had the air waves continued to be viewed as instruments of "commerce."

Passage of the Communications Act

Congress responded to Roosevelt's proposal by passing the Communications Act of 1934. With it came the Federal Communications Commission, which in the next half century was to see its domain increase over everything from local radio to satellite communication, from intrastate to international communication. Although it took only five months for Roosevelt's message to become law, the scope of the FCC had already been hammered out in court challenges to the 1927 law.

Much of the 1927 law was left intact, including the guiding phrase, "public convenience, interest, or necessity," which was retained as a nebulous but very powerful component of the 1934 legislation.[33] A few minor changes dealt with the actual wording of the law. "Wave length" was changed to "frequency," and whereas the 1927 law was concerned with "wireless communication," the FCC was charged with governing both wire and wireless. As is the case with most laws, the 1934 legislation has been amended many times.

SUMMARY

This chapter traces the government's role in early broadcasting. The impetus for regulation took place as Marconi developed his international wireless empires and placed restrictions on communication between ships which were not using Marconi equipment. Germany, the home of the competing Slaby-Arco wireless system, was the first to call for control and hosted the Berlin meetings of 1903 and 1906. Following a statement from U.S. President Theodore Roosevelt, The United States placed its first controls on wireless with the Wireless Ship Act of 1910 which provided an early safeguard for ships at sea. It required them to be equipped with radio apparatus which could communicate with other ships and shore stations. Violations meant possible fines and court proceedings.

Two years later, spurred on partly by the sinking of the steamship *The Titanic*, the Radio Act of 1912 was passed and expanded on the 1910 legislation. The Radio Act of 1912, however, could not deal with radio's exploding growth during the 1920s. Some key areas of regulation included the regulation of commercial intercourse among states and nations, licensing provisions, call letters, penalties, citizen requirements, call letters, operating times, and enforcement.

Four national radio conferences convened and discussed how to bring the new medium under government control—control that was acceptable to the industry yet permitted the orderly use of the electromagnetic spectrum. Many parties, all with competing interests, used the national radio conferences to hammer out their differences.

Court cases also spelled trouble for the 1912 law. Intercity radio won a challenge to the 1912 law and was granted an operating license, even though no space was available on the spectrum for Intercity to operate its station. Zenith Radio Corporation also won a suit which gave it permission to operate at other times, frequencies, and power, beyond those which were stipulated in its original license. Opinions by the U.S. attorney general further complicated matters when the attorney general gave a detailed opinion more supportive of the ability of broadcasters to operate without restrictions under the 1912 law than the ability of the secretary of commerce to regulate broadcasting and stop the chaos caused by stations trying to outpower each other.

Finally, at the request of U.S. President Calvin Coolidge, Congress was called upon to pass legislation which would provide some form of new regulatory framework for radio broadcasting. Congress acted by passing the Radio Act of 1927 creating the Federal Radio Commission, the existence of which was renewed on a year-to-year basis while the FRC fought a series of court battles to affirm its control over radio. Seven years later, the Communications Act of 1934 passed Congress and established the Federal Communications Commission, a separate, independent, government agency.

MATERIAL FOR ANALYSIS

While a great deal of legal and technical information emerged from the national radio conferences, the reports in the trade publications of the era provided a layperson's view of the policy making which took place. One such report authored by Carl H. Butman appeared in a 1924 issue of the trade magazine *Radio News*.[34] Titled "Better Radio Service," the article is interesting because of its rich detail, highlighted on occasion by editorial-type prose.

A REPORT OF THE THIRD NATIONAL RADIO CONFERENCE

The first report of the Conference was made by Mr. W. D. Terrell, Chief Supervisor of Radio of the Department of Commerce, who is chairman of the sub-committee on general allocation of frequency or wavelength bands. The allocation for marine communication allows ship communication . . . radio compass stations . . . and radio beacons . . . with suitable protecting bands on either side. It was recommended that ships be no longer required to maintain the . . . adjustment as required by international regulations. The wave band reserved for marine telephone, colleges and Government use . . . was continued. The band for Government use . . . fixed by the previous Conference, was left unchanged. The band for broadcast purposes was extended . . . and cleared from all other types of service, thereby permitting its exclusive use for broadcasting.

The radio amateurs were allowed to retain the wave bands previously assigned, with slight changes.

Dr. George K. Burgess, Director of the Bureau of Standards, reported as chairman of the sub-committee on allocation of frequencies to broadcast stations. This allocation does not differ except in degree from the allocation now in force. The extension of the broadcasting service . . . allows a large number of simultaneous, non-interfering communication channels in this class. It was recommended that the present Class C licenses be discontinued, after November 15, 1924. This will make available several new channels for Class B broadcasting and will eliminate one of the most important causes for congestion in the broadcasting band. It is also recommended that the frequency assignments on the Atlantic coast be repeated on the Pacific coast. This has been shown to be practical in the experience of the Department. The zoning system of the United States was, therefore, changed in minor degrees to take care of this alteration and allow a large number of frequencies for the congested areas . . .

These changes in the allocation of frequencies to broadcast stations require that several alterations be made in existing assignments. Such changes are inevitable, but the reassignments should be made. It is recommended that a small continuing committee be designated by the

Conference to remain in Washington and collaborate with radio supervisors in a reassignment of the broadcast station frequencies in accordance with the recommendations of this Committee.

General George O. Squier, formerly Chief Signal Officer of the United States Army, reported that the work of Subcommittee No. 3 on general problems of radio broadcasting was practically completed after three extended sessions. This report states that due consideration has been given to the class of programs broadcast from various stations. After an extended discussion on the details of making recommendations to the Conference it has been deemed advisable for the Department to follow a "hands off" policy regarding material broadcast, as it is believed that each station desires to cover a certain field and to entertain or educate a certain class of people. To regulate the programs under these conditions would mean censorship, and official censorship is not recommended.

In regard to the changing of the requirements for operators' licenses, it has been recommended by this Committee that the present experiment and instruction grade of license be made more elastic if possible to permit the holders of such licenses to operate broadcast stations when such licenses are issued to professors of physics and fellows of the Institute of Radio Engineers, and men of equal qualifications. It has been deemed advisable that the operators employed at broadcast stations throughout the country should not be required to secure the same class of license as required for marine communication. The present so-called marine license insists that the holder have a thorough knowledge of all modern systems of radio communication, and as radio broadcasting and the apparatus pertaining thereto is a science within a science, this Committee recommends that a new class of operators' licenses be created, different from the license required of other types of service and the examination for it be based upon the needs of the broadcasting service.

The question of increased power for broadcast stations has been considered in detail, and the Committee has decided: "to determine the advisability of permitting the expansion of broadcasting by the employment of increased power beyond that prescribed in the regulations for Class B stations, and to permit the use of apparatus for this purpose to any individual and to remove certain limitations now prescribed for Class B stations, and for the purpose of observing what interference, if any, might result in public broadcast reception in the various localities, this Committee recommends that a new class of license be established and that licenses in this class shall be granted by the Secretary of Commerce, who shall have discretionary power to prescribe the type of apparatus, location, frequency, power requirements of operation of such stations, and that licenses for such stations shall be granted on an experimental basis only, and for such period or periods of time as the Secretary of Commerce may determine."

Although the Government refused to take off the lid in regard to power limitations, experimental licenses for high-power broadcasting are assured and it is up to the radio engineers to show the radio supervisors and the listening public the benefits of high-power broadcasting. The engineers of the Radio Corporation, who propose to erect a 40 to 50 k.w. station outside of New York in the near future, are going forward with their plans and will request the first superpower broadcasting license under a revised Class D or development permit. As soon as the technicians work out the details of minimum interference and set up the station, the public, within a range of a thousand miles of New York, at least, will have an opportunity of listening in on the R. C. A. super-broadcaster. No doubt, it will also carry to Europe and South America as well as all over the United States. If the inspectors or the public find that this station interferes seriously with the reception of other stations, the Department will cause it to close down, since this is a requirement of the special permit.

It is also probable that nine smaller broadcasters will also apply for permission to broadcast with 5 k.w. sets under the same conditions, and, as was pointed out, a broadcasting system of pure radio may soon be competing for radio popularity with the chain of the inter-connected stations served by the American Telephone and Telegraph Co., which has made possible nation-wide broadcasting.

Among the important decisions reached were: The addition of 30 wave channels for broadcast stations, bringing the total to 100 . . . A re-classification of broadcasters and the transfer of all Class E stations . . . improves the situation further, while the re-zoning of the country into six zones will further aid broadcast operation. This will provide a separate zone for the New England States, including New York City and part of New Jersey. Zone Two will comprise the remainder of the Atlantic states, Pennsylvania, West Virginia, and the western part of New York. Zone Three, Michigan, Ohio, Illinois, Kentucky, Tennessee,

West Georgia, Alabama and Mississippi; the Central States are divided horizontally, the southern states forming Zone Four, and the northern, Zone Five; all the Pacific States with Idaho, Utah and Arizona, constitute the Sixth zone. When assigning experimental stations high power licenses, the Department intends to use this system and in assigning new Class 1 stations.

Marine communications will be handled . . . giving the ships five channels instead of two, also removing coast-wide interference and congestion. Amateurs retain substantially the same wavelengths as heretofore, but benefit by low wavelengths assigned temporarily by the Department recently; all of which assures the amateurs an increase in channels over what they had a year ago, and permits greater latitude in 24-hour operation.

The conference voted not to interfere with broadcast programs, discouraging censorship definitely. The conferees found that simultaneous broadcasting of national events is practical over a large area and believes that nation-wide broadcasting by interconnecting stations deserves encouragement . . .

Hiram Percy Maxim, President of the American Radio Relay League, reported as chairman of the subcommittee on amateur problems. It was recommended by this committee that the use of receiving sets capable of radiating be discouraged for use on the short wave relay broadcast band.

In order to eliminate as far as possible the interference from amateur transmitting sets, it was recommended that, except in case of transmitters using coil antenna or loops, radiating system or a device producing an equivalent effect be required in all amateur transmitters. All of the amateur bands shall be open to telegraphic communication by tubes or devices producing similar effects . . .

QUESTIONS FOR CRITICAL ANALYSIS

- Although only two years separated the Wireless Ship Act of 1910 and the Radio Act of 1912, 15 years separated the 1912 law and the Radio Act of 1927. Why, as broadcasting began to develop in the late teens and early twenties, didn't Congress act to shore up the seemingly ineffective legislation?
- Experimental voice broadcasting arrived a full six years before the passage of the Radio Act of 1912. Why, then, didn't the law address the probable effects of this new development in wireless?
- Although the sinking of the *Titanic* rallied popular support for new regulations governing wireless, did it also create a certain "rush to judgment," resulting in a law inadequate for the years immediately following the passage of the Radio Act of 1912?
- What would have been the impact on future legislation and the broadcasting industry had the court ruled differently in *United States* v. *Zenith*?
- What would have happened if the court ruled differently in *Hoover* v. *Intercity Radio Co., Inc.*?
- Had the amateur radio operators' lobbying efforts been weaker when the national radio conferences were taking place, would the structure of American broadcasting have evolved differently?
- Were the national radio conferences effective, or did they just prolong the badly needed revisions in the Radio Act of 1912?
- If the legislative process in the early 1920s was too slow to patch up the Radio Act of 1912, how can today's political bureaucracy handle legislation governing such things as satellite communication?
- Why, with so much attention paid to radio's exploding popularity, did it take so long from the time the first major stations signed on the air, about 1920, to the time the Radio Act of 1927 materialized?
- Consider the five questions posed to the attorney general by the secretary of commerce in his letter of June 4, 1926. What might have happened to the structure of American broadcasting if the attorney general's answers had been different? Was any one of the secretary's questions more critical than the others?
- The Radio Act of 1927 proved a rather solid document when challenged in court between 1927 and 1934. What would have been the long-term effects on broadcasting if the document had proved weak and ineffectual?
- What cases challenging the Radio Act of 1927 were the most important in establishing the structure of broadcast regulation?

- The Communications Act of 1934 placed broadcasting under the Federal Communications Commission. How might our broadcasting system of today have evolved differently if broadcasting had remained in the Department of Commerce?
- In the report of the Third National Radio Conference found in the Material for Analysis section of this chapter, we learned that the frequency "band for broadcast purposes was extended . . . and cleared from all other types of service, thereby permitting its exclusive use for broadcasting." Why was broadcasting extended the privileged status of being protected from other services and its frequency band extended?
- In reading the report of the Third National Radio Conference, we learned that the Department of Commerce was advised to follow a "hands off" policy regarding the specific type of material radio stations would broadcast. Anything other than this "hands off" policy would be considered official censorship, which was not recommended. If broadcasting in the 1920s was faced with a more limited electromagnetic spectrum than is possible even today, why would the Department of Commerce not take a more controlling role over broadcast programming using the "public interest" and limited resource argument to regulate programming?
- In American colleges and universities, Departments of Journalism and Mass Communication, Speech Communication, Radio and Television, Communication, and similar departments exist. Why then did the participants of the Third National Radio Conference permit more leniency to the licensing of "Professors of Physics"?
- Why did the Third National Radio Conference decide that a different type of license should be issued to those operators employed by broadcasting services as opposed to people working in marine radio?
- The report of the Third National Radio Conference stated, "It is up to the radio engineers to show the . . . listening public the benefits of high-powered broadcasting." Why would radio engineers as opposed to programmers have the responsibility to show the listening public these benefits?
- The report of the Third National Radio Conference stated the public "within a range of a thousand miles of New York" would be able to listen to the RCA superstation. The report also indicated the station would carry to Europe and South America. The report of the conference went on to state: "If the inspectors or the public finds that this station interferes seriously with the reception of other stations, the Department will cause it to close down. . . ." If the superstation was going to reach within a thousand miles of New York and at times to Europe and South America, and if it was going to be closed down if it interfered with the reception of other stations, why would it be granted a special permit in the first place?
- With the ability of broadcasting to cover wide areas such as that of the superpower stations, why would the Department of Commerce use a zoning system as a means of assigning experimental stations high-powered licenses?
- Radio amateurs benefited from the national radio conferences. In the report of the third conference we learned that amateurs retained the same wavelengths as previous conferences but in addition were assigned frequency space at lower wavelengths, permitting greater latitude in their operations. Why were radio amateurs given preferential treatment when such serious issues as marine communication and radio broadcasting were of prime concern to the policy makers of that era? Why did the policy makers in the national radio conferences believe that "nation-wide broadcasting by interconnecting stations" deserved encouragement?

ADDITIONAL RESOURCES

Benjamin, L. M., "Broadcast Campaign Precedents from the 1924 Presidential Election," 31 *Journal of Broadcasting & Electronic Media* 449 (1987).

Bensman, M. R., "Regulation of Broadcasting by the Department of Commerce, 1921–1927," in *American Broadcasting: A Sourcebook on the History of Radio and Television*, eds. L. W. Lichty and M. C. Topping, New York: Hastings House, 60 (1975).

Burch, D., "Common Carrier Communications by Wire and Radio: A Retrospective." 37 *Federal Communications Law Journal* 85 (1985).

Geller, H., "Communications Law—A Half Century Later." 37 *Federal Communications Law Journal* 73 (1985).

Godfrey, D. G., "Senator Dill and the 1927 Radio Act," 23 *Journal of Broadcasting* 477 (1979).

Goldberg, H. "One Hundred and Twenty Years of International Communications." 37 *Federal Communications Law Journal* 131 (1985).

Hazlett, T. W., "The Rationality of U.S. Regulation of the Broadcast Spectrum." 33 *Journal of Law and Economics* 133 (1990).

Le Duc, D. R., and T. A. McCain, "The Federal Radio Commission in Federal Court: Origins of Broadcast Regulatory Doctrines," 14 *Journal of Broadcasting* 393 (1970).

Minasian, J. R., "Political Economy of Broadcasting in the 1920s," *Journal of Law and Economics* 391 (1969).

Sarno, E. F., "The National Radio Conferences," 13 *Journal of Broadcasting* 189 (1969).

chapter three

The Federal Communications Commission

The Federal Communications Commission was formed by Congress through the passage of the Communications Act of 1934, the major piece of legislation, often amended, which controls most of the electronic media in the United States. An independent agency of government with five commissioners, the FCC reports to Congress and governs everything from broadcasting to common carriers.[1] The radio station that wakes you up in the morning is regulated by the FCC, the rates you pay for long-distance telephone calls are regulated by the FCC, the type of circuitry in an automatic garage door opener is based on a standard established by the FCC. This chapter examines the organization of the FCC, its functions, and some of the ways it affects the day-to-day operations of telecommunication industries.

THE RELATIONSHIP OF THE FCC TO CONGRESS

Congress formed the Federal Communications Commission through the passage of the Communications Act of 1934, and Congress, as it does with other agencies of the federal government, monitors the FCC's activities.[2]

The Politics of Agency Regulation

Both the Senate, through the confirmation process for appointed FCC commissioners, and the House of Representatives through the power of the appropriations process, exert influence on the FCC. The executive branch of government, because the president has the power to appoint commissioners, also holds power over the FCC. Together, this triangle of influence makes communications policy a political process.

An example of how communications policy translates into Congressional politics can be seen during an attempt by the U.S. Senate to pass a cable regulatory measure. Senator Earnst Hollings was quoted as saying his vote in favor of regulation was "a chance to offset his vote against going to war in the Persian Gulf, which according to the polls did not sit well with his constituents," and "back home cable television is what his constituents want to talk about."[3]

Direct Involvement by Congress

Sometimes the influence of Congress over the FCC is direct and pointed, such as when FCC Chairman, Republican, and Bush administration appointee Alfred C. Sikes took office. Noted for both tough enforcement and a free-marketplace philosophy, Sikes quickly heard from Michigan Democratic Congressman Dingell who challenged the chairman's policies on radio deregulation. Dingell gave the FCC a deadline date to respond and his aide said "the Congressman would await FCC response before contemplating action—legislative or otherwise."[4] It wasn't the first time Dingell and Sikes had sparred. An earlier letter from Dingell questioned the commission's decision on syndication rules which was based on an "executive summary" instead of a final text. Sikes replied to Dingell saying administrative agency decision makers do not need final texts "as long as sufficient basis for reasoned decision making exists and the ruling when published adequately shows and explains the decision."[5]

Grass-Roots Influence

Issues can quickly emerge from grass-roots constituencies that communicate with Congress. For example, people take their television viewing seriously and cable television rates that strain the family budget can quickly become an issue members of Congress hear about from their local constituency. Moreover, a television station in a member's home district may also be a powerful editorial force that can influence voters and election outcomes. Like any other constituent, local radio and television managers and owners have their own local policy agendas and can lobby Congress just as any other constituents do.

Communication policy can also affect Congress through citizens groups which may be highly organized, have access to press publicity, and support a visible cause such as reducing sex and violence on television. Add the visible cause to such grass-roots influence as local churches and local parent-teachers organizations, and the ingredients exist to create a powerful lobbying force in Congress.

An example of how localized communication policy can become occurred in Chicago with the renewal challenge to a local television station which had been programming sexually-oriented pay-TV programming before changing its format to Spanish-language programming reaching Chicago's Hispanic community. A challenger used the sex-oriented programming as an issue and eventually won the right to the frequency. But what was already a controversial FCC decision turned even more complicated when New Mexico Democrat Congressman Bill Richardson got involved and called for hearings to review the decision before the Telecommunications Subcommittee of the House of Representatives. If that wasn't enough, no less than three other organizations or their representatives got involved including the Coalition in Defense of Access to Channel 44, the Latino Institute, and the United Neighborhood Organization. The dispute which continued for more than a decade even reached down to the level of a Chicago ward alderman who openly opposed the transfer of the license.[6]

Although the president makes the appointment and the allegiance of the FCC chairman is to the administration, the inability to work with Congress can have serious consequences. Evidence of this can be seen in the fact that prior to 1982 there were seven instead of the current five commissioners. Washington, DC communications attorneys, Erwin G. Krasnow and Michael Regan, who have written about and studied the FCC confirmation process, state, "Because a number of key legislators felt the seven FCC Commissioners had been unresponsive to Congress, Congress determined to send an even clearer parental message to its wayward children; in effect, casting two of them out of the family altogether."[7]

THE FCC CONFIRMATION PROCESS

The commissioners are appointed by the president, but it is the Senate which confirms the president's nomination.

The Political Process

While the president many times uses the appointment of FCC commissioners to advance the communications policy of the administration in power, Congress uses the confirmation process to try to control its own agenda. The give and take between the executive and legislative branches of government is sometimes harmonious, sometimes not. FCC chairmen in particular have traditionally been closely tied politically to the administration in power, and some have become noteworthy for making a major impact on telecommunication policy. That power to direct policy, and the relationship the commission has with Congress at any particular time, makes the confirmation process a serious matter.

As telecommunication policy becomes increasingly important in our society, more and more industry professional associations and lobbying groups are directly affected by the makeup of the FCC. These groups realize that individual senators many times make the difference in getting a person appointed to the commission who is sensitive to the economic goals of their regulated industry.

Powerful senators can influence the confirmation process. While the public side of the confirmation process tends to follow the expected advise and consent activities associated with other confirmations, a private side also accompanies the process. For example, a list of potential nominees may be circulated as "trial balloons" to see if certain people will incur the wrath of certain members of Congress, which could impede the confirmation process, or worse yet embarrass the president.

Knowing that Congress exercises appropriations control over the FCC and that the Senate must confirm the president's nominee, a president not wanting to face the embarrassment of having a nominee denied confirmation will sometimes turn to a congressional staff member or even a senator as potential nominees, knowing Congress will not likely reject one of its own.[8]

Members of Congress may have a key person they want to advance as a potential appointee, even though the nomination, if it is advanced, will not have much chance of success. Political contributors who are tied to the communications industry can become prospective nominees from the home state of an influential member of Congress. A particularly influential broadcaster with the proper political credentials can become a nominee. The nomination of an attorney with a communications law practice in a senator's home state can work to the advantage of both. The senator gets the visibility of identifying the prospective nominee while the attorney and the attorney's law firm get the advantage of prestigious local publicity.

Evaluating the Nominee

Once the nominee is selected and made public, a series of meetings with senators usually takes place before the candidate reaches the confirmation hearing. The opportunity to determine what the nominee's positions are on key issues is important for senators whose constituencies may be strongly affected by FCC policies or who serve on important committees in Congress which control communications policy. The Senate's Commerce Committee and its Communications Subcommittee are two areas where much of the major communication legislation originates.

At the actual confirmation hearing senators can extract promises from nominees about particularly sensitive communication policy matters. Any issue—from conflicts of interest, to deregulation, to affirmative action—can be discussed in confirmation hearings.[9] While not having the public impact of nominees to the Supreme Court, agency confirmation hearings are watched closely by the trade press, which reports to the industry about the qualifications and policy statements of the nominee.

THE ROLE OF THE AUTHORIZATION PROCESS

In addition to the confirmation process, two additional levels of control are exercised by Congress over the FCC. These are the authorization process and the appropriations process.[10]

Agencies of Congress are "authorized" by law, which in the case of the FCC is for a two-year period. Congressional authorization measures are the prelude to appropriations measures and Congress frequently takes its cues in appropriations from an agency's authorization measure. Like the confirmation process, Congress can cast a watchful eye over agencies during the authorization process, having the potential to manipulate an agency. The FCC is no exception. In the same era that whittled the number of commissioners from seven to five, the permanent authorization of the FCC was cut from a permanent authorization to a two-year authorization as part of a budget reconciliation measure. The House and Senate were the winners and gained systematic review and control over the FCC through the authorization process. Key communications policy matters and amendments to the Communications Act of 1934 can now become part of authorization and appropriation measures.

THE FCC AND THE APPROPRIATIONS PROCESS

Whatever power is lacking in the authorization process is regained in the appropriations process, which provides the FCC with its operating budget.

The Power of Appropriations

The appropriations process is one of the most powerful processes in Congress and those members of Congress who serve on appropriations committees control the purse strings and yield a great deal of power. Key policy matters can become the object of appropriations bills just as they can with authorization measures, but with money attached there is never any doubt about their importance. Many of the measures which do pass are the result of "riders" attached to budget appropriations frequently buried deep within legislation and rarely reported, even by the trade press.

Direct Control by Congress

Over the years a number of examples have emerged which show the interrelationship between politics, the commission, and appropriations. For example, when an influential Democrat chaired the Senate Commerce Committee, he stonewalled a $350,000 appropriation transfer requested by an outgoing Republican FCC chairman until a new Democrat FCC chairman could be named by the president. The FCC backed up the senator with a unanimous vote against the transfer. After the new Democrat FCC chairman was in place, the transfer was approved.[11]

In another example an appropriation measure was amended to include a prohibition against the FCC issuing waivers in its crossownership rules, which at the time were seen by some members of the Senate as favoring media baron Rupert Murdoch. In another case a senator was responsible for including a $750,000 appropriation in the FCC budget, which created a separate staff to develop a plan to make UHF television (operating above channel 13) compatible with VHF television (operating at channels 2–13 and below). The appropriations included directions stating: "This plan should address all the technical and regulatory aspects of achieving parity . . . (and) should also include indications of the probable need for any legislation necessary to fulfill the plan."[12]

THE EMERGING ROLE OF FEDERAL AGENCIES

The power to enforce and create regulations and to issue fines and review decisions is not new. The Interstate Commerce Commission was created in 1887 when the telegraph was well developed as the first medium of electrical communication. The telegraph had become a key link in not only interstate commerce, but with the construction of the Atlantic cable, international commerce. Various court decisions refined the technology of the telegraph by rulings which protected operators from crippling lawsuits and provided the telegraph and its successor, the telephone, with the ability to operate and expand unbridled.

FEDERAL AGENCY CONTROL OVER COMMUNICATION

Gradually the telegraph was replaced by the telephone and wireless was replaced by radio and voice broadcasting. Radio became a mass medium which resulted in the development of more and more stations, until the four national radio conferences attempted to bring the chaos of the airwaves under control. The end result of the conferences, although not a complete solution to the problem of interference, was the Federal Radio Commission as part of the Department of Commerce. But the Federal Radio Commission was still somewhat suspect and even though radio was in its infancy, the FRC did not have anywhere near the power of its successor, the Federal Communications Commission. Even then there was a sense of mistrust of the FRC and the power of the executive branch to influence communications policy. FRC commissioners were appointed for one-year terms only. Today a series of checks and balances, most prominent through the review of FCC decisions by the courts, results in an FCC that operates as an independent agency.

THE RELATIONSHIP OF THE FCC TO THE COURTS

To understand the relationship of the FCC to the courts, one must understand that the commission itself is an extension of the judicial process. The commission has enforcement power much like a police department, but within the FCC also exists judicial power much like a court, and the commission has the power to issue decisions on every regulatory matter that comes before it over such broad areas as license renewal, affirmative action, ownership of media properties, telephone rates, and a host of other communication matters. At the same time, the regulated industries affected by FCC policy have at their disposal an appellate process that can lead to the U.S. Supreme Court.

THE U.S. COURT OF APPEALS FOR THE DISTRICT OF COLUMBIA

Equally important to the early development of the Federal Radio Commission was the U.S. Court of Appeals for the District of Columbia, which was charged with hearing the appeals from the FRC.

Historical Perspective

Firmly anchored in our democratic system of checks and balances is the need for a court to oversee potential abuses of power, political influence gone awry, executive branch manipulation, special-interest influence, or just plain mistakes on the part of a government agency over the industry it is charged to regulate. Unlike today's Federal Communications Commission with an engineering office of skilled technical experts able to understand and interpret the technology the commission regulates, the FRC had no such extensive expertise.

While the appeals court was not in the engineering business, it did, however, perform a service by being a forum where those broadcasters who felt aggrieved by the new FRC could go for a hearing. The power of the appeals court was further enhanced by the fact that no specific provision for appeal to the Supreme Court was provided for. Congress had created a federal agency with a court to help. Together, in case after case, the power of the Federal Radio Commission was affirmed. The appeals court performed much like a partner with the FRC.[13] To a great extent, it was an extension of the FRC, an extension which could defer to the expertise of the commission, or participate more directly by molding communications policy through judicial decision. As familiarity can breed contempt, however, over the years the relationship has had its rough spots.

The Agency as Expert

At the heart of the relationship is the assumption that the agency is the "expert" in any proceeding. No longer is the Federal Communications Commission a throwback to the FRC. It is a seasoned federal agency which has been honed by playing hardball in litigation on a multitude of issues at all levels of the judicial process. As an agency of the federal government, more than one party has found the FCC also has persistence, which can be an expensive thorn in the sides of those who challenge it.

In administrative law, there is also a presumption that federal regulatory agencies should prevail in many cases because the agency is the expert when it comes to dealing with the industries they regulate. Also at issue is the fact that even though the FCC uses a long, arduous process of seeking comments and replies when developing regulations, the diversity among the tens of thousands of individuals and businesses which hold FCC licenses means there are always those who feel the U.S. Court of Appeals or the Supreme Court will have a more sympathetic ear than the federal agency that regulates them. Thus, if the funds are available, they will pursue litigation in the hope that they will win and to extend the life of their business if they lose.

Looking back over this relationship with the U.S. Court of Appeals for the District of Columbia, at least until the 1970s, the judicial review had been primarily centered on a narrow interpretation of the FCC rules and regulations, with an assumption that in many matters the expertise of the agency should prevail. "The consensus seems to be that the courts should restrict themselves to a determination of whether or not the agency has acted within its legislative mandate and whether or not it has reached its conclusions in a rational manner after exploring all material facts and issues."[14]

THE COURT OF APPEALS AS POLICY MAKER

By the 1960s, and especially in the 1970s, some key cases which came before the D.C. Circuit Court resulted in the court taking a more aggressive position as an interpreter of communications policy. The most celebrated case that opened a new era in broadcast regulation was *Office of Communication of United Church of Christ* v. *F.C.C.*[15] It changed the rules on who could take part in commission proceedings by permitting private citizens, the broadcast audience who makes up the listeners and viewers, to participate as parties in license renewal hearings. Prior to that time the FCC, with the court's approval, interpreted its own rules as limiting participation to: "1) licensees claiming a measure of economic injury that could adversely affect the public interest, and 2) parties claiming electrical interference from other stations."[16]

Other issues also came before the court, furthering its reputation as a formulator of communications policy. At some points the court went too far and was reprimanded by the U.S. Supreme Court. But between 1966 and the 1990s, the FCC and the D.C. Circuit Court have grappled over such major issues as forced divestiture of crossownership of broadcast and newspaper properties, equal employment opportunity, radio formats, obscenity, and others. For the FCC, those who study and research communications policy, and for the public which is affected by such policy, the role of the D.C. Circuit Court cannot be underestimated.

THE COMMISSIONERS

At the top of the commission hierarchy are five FCC commissioners, headed by a chairman. Appointed by the president of the United States and confirmed by the Senate, commissioners are prohibited from having a financial interest in any of the industries they regulate. No more than three commissioners can be from the same political party, and their terms are staggered. Appointees who fill the unexpired term of a commissioner may or may not be reappointed when that term expires.

Ability to Mold Policy

Commissioners, especially FCC chairmen, can have a significant influence over the commission's activities as well as communication policy. In recent years, chairmen Mark S. Fowler, Dennis Patrick, and Alfred Sikes have all left their mark on the FCC. Fowler served during the administration of President Ronald Reagan during the 1980s and oversaw major changes in such areas as the deregulation of broadcasting, a streamlining of FCC procedures, the growing importance of common carrier communication involving the telephone companies, and a scaling down of the size of the commission.[17] The philosophy of the Fowler chairmanship can be seen in the five objectives established during his tenure.

1. To create, to the maximum extent possible, an unregulated, competitive marketplace environment for the development of telecommunication.
2. To eliminate unnecessary regulations and policies.
3. To provide service to the public in the most efficient, expeditious manner possible.
4. To promote the coordination and planning of international communications which assures the vital interests of the American public in Commerce, Defense and Foreign Policy.
5. To eliminate government action that infringes the freedom of speech and the press.[18]

Postservice Industry Links

Commissioner Dennis Patrick followed Mark Fowler, was appointed by President Reagan, and continued much of the philosophy of the Fowler years at the FCC. As others have done in the past, Patrick left the FCC to go into private consulting and used the expertise gained at the commission to represent such clients as Time Warner, which later hired him full time to head a new Time Warner subsidiary, Time Warner Telecommunications. The relationship, called the "revolving door" by some critics, between FCC commissioners and staff and the industries they regulate can be seen in the makeup of the subsidiary. For example, joining Patrick in the early stages of Time Warner Telecommunications were three other former FCC employees. One was Patrick's legal assistant at the FCC, another a former attorney in the FCC's Mass Media Bureau, and a third a former head of the Mass Media Bureau. The subsidiary was described as focusing on "spectrum-based common carrier and private radio services."[19]

Regulating the Information Society

FCC chairman Alfred C. Sikes followed Patrick as an appointee of President George Bush. His term got off to a controversial start because of a split among commissioners on financial interest and syndication rules, but Sikes still gained some uniformity among commissioners to advance his own goals. In a *New York Times* News Service report on his early tenure at the FCC, which one newspaper headlined "Sparks fly as U.S. communications hot-wired: FCC boss has vigorous agenda," Sikes was characterized as having "a bold blueprint," and "in a hurry to put it in place."[20] The report said of Sikes:

> He wants to free up space on the crowded airwaves for advanced new services, from pocket-sized radio telephones to interactive television and satellite messaging, and reform the way people receive licenses. He is also bent on spurring competition by knocking down regulatory barriers that now segregate services into isolated fiefdoms for telephones, cellular service, cable television and broadcasting. He is pressing for legislation to lift key restrictions on the Bell telephone companies while forcing them to open their networks to new rivals.[21]

While ambitious, Sikes faced a tough job and the need to contend with significant economic and political forces impacting on FCC decision makers at a time when technology continued to push toward a global information society. Under President Bill Clinton, veteran and knowledgeable FCC commissioner James Quello served as acting chair of the commission until the confirmation of Reed Hundt. Under Hundt, observers feel that by the time the Clinton administration reaches the mid-1990s, Hundt's term will have seen a new emphasis on quality programming, more influence for public interest and citizens groups, and the support of the Clinton administration's telecommunication infrastructure.

CONDUCTING FCC BUSINESS

The commissioners hold regular meetings and executive sessions to oversee commission activities. Their meetings are open to the public, a procedure started under mandate by Congress. Closed meetings can be called by a majority vote of the entire commission. These meetings normally concern matters of national defense, manufacturers' trade secrets, criminal matters, or when the parties concerned with the FCC decision specifically request the meeting be closed.[22]

Along with the commissioners and members of the public, most meetings are attended by other FCC staff including the commission secretary. The meeting is organized through the secretary's office which is part of the Office of the Managing Director. The managing director, the general counsel, the chief of the Office of Plans and Policy are also frequently present. At commission meetings, commissioners customarily have a legal and engineering assistant present. If an agenda item originates in a specific FCC bureau then the chief of the bureau may be present to answer questions. The bureau chief may also have assistants present. Agenda items such as internal personnel matters, investigatory records, premature disclosure, and adjudicatory (judicial) matters can result in closing portions of a meeting. Meetings are announced no less than one week in advance along with a synopsis of what matters will be discussed. Based on the general counsel's recommendation, the commissioners then vote whether to close the meeting. A tape recording is made of all closed meetings.

FCC OFFICES

The FCC is organized around a group of offices and bureaus. Commission offices consist of the Office of Plans and Policy, Office of the Managing Director, Office of General Counsel, Office of Administrative Law Judges, Review Board, Office of Public Affairs, Office of Legislative Affairs, and Office of the Chief Engineer.[23]The organization of the FCC and offices and bureaus can change from time to time. A new FCC chairman, different commissioners, or changes in technologies or issues before the commission may produce an organizational change. The discussion of FCC organization which follows is very general. Think of the FCC in terms of its functions as well as being composed of various offices and bureaus.

The Office of Plans and Policy

The Office of Plans and Policy is responsible for developing the long-range policy decisions for industries which fall under FCC jurisdiction. It also is responsible for assessing the policy implications of FCC decisions, providing policy analyses and recommendations to the commission staff, and coordinating policy research. The chief of the Office of Plans and Policy recommends budgets and priorities for the commission policy research program and functions as the central account manager for all contractual research studies funded by the FCC.

Office of the Managing Director

While the FCC commissioners exercise power over many policy decisions, the real work of the FCC is under the direction of the FCC's managing director. The managing director serves under the FCC chairman as the chief operating and executive official of the FCC. The managing director supervises the various staff offices and administers the policy programs and FCC directives. Such administrative affairs as personnel, labor relations, budget and financial matters, data processing, procurement, office space, administrative services, records and security, are all under the managing director's guidance.

Office of the General Counsel

The general counsel is the commission's attorney, representing it before the courts. The general counsel also aids in the preparation of legislative programs fostered by the commission and works closely with the attorney general and the Justice Department in cases which involve prosecution or jurisdiction across agency boundaries. An example of this cooperation might be the prosecution of violations of the Criminal Code beyond those under the jurisdiction of the FCC. If a person steals radio equipment and then uses it to broadcast illegally, both the Justice Department and the FCC would become jointly involved in this matter.

Office of Administrative Law Judges

This office is the first rung of the ladder in the appeals process. The administrative law judges preside over hearings and render initial decisions, but it is not unusual for their decisions to be appealed. When two applicants for a broadcast license appear at a hearing, both have a major investment at stake, and a ruling in favor of one party will usually prompt the other to continue the appeals process.

Review Board

The Review Board is the second step in the FCC appellate process, between the administrative law judges and the commissioners. In some cases, the decisions of the administrative law judges are reversed by the Review Board, and then reversed again by the commissioners. This is not so much a reflection on the ability of the judges to adhere to judicial procedure as it is an indication of the desire of the offended to exhaust every administrative remedy.

In special cases, initial decisions can be reviewed directly by the commissioners. If, for example, a renewal decision goes against a licensee, the licensee can appeal to the Review Board, which consists of senior-level employees of the commission. Individual FCC bureaus can also appeal to the Review Board. If, for instance, a bureau rules against a licensee, and an administrative law judge rules in the licensee's favor, then the bureau can appeal to the Review Board. Either party can appeal that ruling to the commissioners, which, as a body, choose which cases to accept for review. The commissioners are the last appellate step before the matter goes into the federal courts.

Office of Public Affairs

This office is the public information arm of the commission. Informing the public of FCC regulatory requirements makes it possible for the public to participate in FCC decision making. Additional functions include keeping the public informed of the commission's decisions, encouraging and facilitating public participation in FCC decision making, and promoting minority participation. The office employs an assistant director for minority enterprise. Two separate subdivisions operate within the Office of Public Affairs: (1) the News Media Division, and (2) the Consumer Assistance and Small Business Division.

As the names of the two divisions imply, one deals with the press and radio and television news departments, the other concentrates on contact with the public and small businesses which may need the services of the FCC. For example, the operator of a local delivery service using a fleet of vehicles with two-way radios may need to contact the commission about a regulatory matter. The delivery service can contact the Consumer Assistance and Small Business Division for help in locating the office or bureau within the FCC which can assist the delivery service operator or answer questions.

Office of Legislative Affairs

Legislative programs of the FCC are instituted by the Office of Legislative Affairs.[24] Although an independent agency, the FCC must operate, as other agencies of government do, in a close working relationship with Congress. Congress can quickly become involved in FCC policies when pressure from the public impacts on the legislative branch of government as well as the FCC. For example, a public outcry over violence on television may result in constituents writing their congressman in addition to the FCC. Congress may decide to hold hearings on the issue and propose laws which the FCC might deem unenforceable. Close communication with the Office of Legislative Affairs during the hearing process may avoid difficulties later.

In addition to proposing legislation, the Office of Legislative Affairs assists in preparing formal testimony and briefing material for Congressional hearings. Informal briefing of Congressional staff members takes place on a regular basis. These informal briefings are especially valuable since much of the development of telecommunication policy takes place beyond the formal activities of Congress and many Congressional staffs change because of new members being elected to Congress. Answering written Congressional inquiries is also part of the responsibilities of the Office of Legislative Affairs.[25]

Office of Engineering and Technology

The Chief Engineer is the top technical office of the FCC. A large number of the staff are engineers and deal with such things as the number of stations in a given market, equipment testing and certification, frequency allocations, and modifications and requests for increases in power. At laboratory divisions of the office, new equipment is tested to see that it meets FCC specifications. Such authorization is necessary before it can be used for broadcasting purposes and sold commercially.[26]

FCC BUREAUS

Whereas much of the decision making takes place through the FCC offices, the regulatory and other functions performed by the commission take place through the bureaus. Four bureaus are responsible for the primary functioning of the commission: Mass Media, Common Carrier, Private Radio, and Field Operations.[27]

Mass Media Bureau

Broadcasting stations are regulated through the Mass Media Bureau. Cable matters including private microwave radio facilities used by cable systems fall under the Mass Media Bureau. If you decide to purchase a radio or television station, the Mass Media Bureau would be responsible for approving the sale. If you want to construct a new radio station, the Mass Media Bureau would be responsible for issuing the official FCC Construction Permit allowing you to begin construction of the station.[28]

Common Carrier Bureau

Telephone, telegraph, and satellite companies are regulated through the Common Carrier Bureau. For example, if you decided to establish a group of microwave relay stations across the United States and sell time on the relay stations to others who want to relay signals over long distances, you would be regulated by the FCC and fall under the Common Carrier Bureau. With the increased importance in common carrier communication, this bureau has taken on more importance in recent years, especially with more competition in the telephone industry.

Private Radio Bureau

The two-way radio which links a local police dispatcher with a fleet of patrol cars comes under the jurisdiction of the Private Radio Bureau. Radio services, private land mobile operations, private operational fixed microwave, aviation, marine, personal, amateur, and disaster radio services are under the Private Radio Bureau.[29] Our example of the delivery service using two-way radios fits here. Although initial contact may have been made through the Consumer Assistance and Small Business Division of the Office of Public Affairs, the issue would eventually reach the Public Radio Bureau.

Field Operations Bureau

The Field Operations Bureau to some degree spills over into the other three bureaus, since the bureau detects violations of radio regulations, monitors transmissions, inspects stations, and handles the investigations of complaints about interference.[30] The Field Operations Bureau maintains a network of field offices where people can obtain information about the FCC, which serve as public contact points for the commission, and where FCC license examinations are administered.

Field Operations Bureaus maintain sophisticated monitoring equipment which can detect illegal transmissions. Serious infractions of FCC rules or the operation of illegal radio stations can result in a "raid" where U.S. Marshals and FCC personnel join together to locate, seize, and take the station which is operating illegally off the air.

The bureau has limited powers of enforcement which can be exercised on site, with more serious matters being referred to a specific FCC bureau for action. For example, a technical violation at a radar or television station which results in a fine up to a certain amount can be handled by the Field Operations Bureau but a more serious infraction would be referred to the Mass Media Bureau's own Enforcement Division.

FUNCTIONS AND ACTIVITIES OF THE FCC

Now that we have an understanding of the organization of the FCC, we can use this understanding to examine more closely how the FCC operates and what issues impact on the commission's offices and bureaus.[31] Keep in mind that the sphere of influence over which the FCC has control is quite large and few agencies of government have such a direct effect on the public. Every time you talk on the telephone, every time you watch television or listen to radio, you are affected by FCC policy in some way. Few agencies are also more directly influenced by the public than the FCC. A number of public-interest and citizen groups concerned with the quality of television programming are in constant communication with the FCC, exerting pressure and pushing their agendas forward. Such groups also lobby Congress and the executive branch of government. In the paragraphs that follow, we will examine the legislative functions, policy development and support, working with advisory boards, working with interagency committees, working with other agencies of government, the public information functions, and enforcement.

LEGISLATIVE FUNCTIONS

Handled by the Office of Legislative Affairs, the FCC recommends to Congress new legislation, which amends the Communications Act. For example, a typical legislative package has included amendments which permit the license examination activities of the FCC to be subcontracted to private firms, allow the FCC to charge telephone companies for audits of their firms, prohibit malicious interference with radio communications, and increase the fines the FCC can levy against parties found guilty of violating FCC regulations.[32]

Some legislation may deal with the internal operations of the commission. For example, annual appropriations and authorization measures provide for such procedures as the extension of an FCC travel reimbursement program, modifying a collection schedule, and undertaking an experimental two-year program to hire older people to help with administrative and technical assistance at the FCC.[33]

LITIGATION ACTIVITIES

The FCC General Counsel is responsible for representing the FCC in court. At any given time, the commission is a party to numerous lawsuits, many on appeal from FCC decisions. Aggrieved parties can move beyond the FCC to the U.S. Court of Appeals if they want to challenge an FCC decision. It is not uncommon for stations and others to file an appeal, especially when large fines are involved or when the stakes are high, such as with the denial of a license.

The Scope of Litigation

A perusal of just a sampling of cases at the level of the appeals court illustrates the litigation functions of the FCC and the broad scope of the FCC's jurisdiction. In each of these cases the appeals court ruled in favor of the FCC. For example, in *Carlin Communications, Inc.* v. *FCC*, the court approved FCC regulations which required access codes or scrambled messages to be used when accessing sexually explicit telephone message services.[34] In *Rural Telephone Coalition* v. *FCC*, the court affirmed the FCC's authority to regulate certain telephone exchange costs in order to assure telephone rates in certain areas were affordable to the average subscriber.[35] In *National Association for Better Broadcasting* v. *FCC*, the court "upheld a Commission Report and Order concluding that subscription television and subscription direct broadcast satellite services" are not considered "broadcasting" under the Communications Act.[36]

Losing on Appeal

The agency does have some advantage in appeals, especially where highly technical matters are concerned, and in the cases just cited the FCC prevailed, at least at the level of the appeals court. However, there are many occasions when the appellate court does not rule in favor of the FCC, even when technical issues are at stake. When the FCC gave the go-ahead to a Florida applicant, Daytona Beach Community College, to use 12 channels of service devoted to instructional television, the U.S. Court of Appeals said the FCC had erred in not following its own rule limiting such grants to four channels in a single area of operation.[37] The appeal was filed by the Hispanic Information and Telecommunications Network Inc., which wanted to use four of the channels.

Occasionally, the FCC's own rules are cut down in an appeal. After enforcing a 24-hour ban on indecent programming, a group of media representatives including the National Association of Broadcasters and citizens groups took the FCC to the U.S. Court of Appeals and won a victory which struck down the ban as too restrictive and clashing with the First Amendment. Broadcasters wanted a "safe harbor" in which to deal with the programming more forthrightly and to have clearer guidelines to follow.[38]

POLICY DEVELOPMENT AND SUPPORT

Conducted through the Office of Plans and Policy, the FCC is engaged in the development of communications policy through research.

General Themes

General themes include ensuring increased competition in telecommunication industries and efficient and economic use of the electromagnetic spectrum. Such topics as the impact of advanced television systems, indecent broadcasts, telephone exchanges and rates, crossownership of broadcasting stations and newspapers by the same party, and children's television programming are some of the more general policy issues that confront the commission.

Preregulatory Research

When the commission passes rules and regulations or recommends major legislation to Congress, it is usually supported through studies which have examined the technical and economic impact of the regulation. For example, before passing rules governing the scrambling of satellite signals to the owners of home dish antennas, the FCC reviewed the public-interest implications of the rules. An FCC report on the matter also showed that not passing rules governing the piracy of satellite signals would erode the ability of satellite companies to obtain income for their programming, thus harming the consumer by limiting the availability of programming and the incentive to produce and acquire new programming. The report also determined that scrambling protects "programmers from commercial theft of their services and allows them to recover compensation from all who view their copyrighted works."[39] To pass laws and regulations, in addition to needing to enforce them, requires this type of analysis through policy research.

WORKING WITH ADVISORY BOARDS

With procedural safeguards in place to avoid conflicts of interest and political influence, the FCC and other government agencies can operate with the advice of advisory committees. One example is the 25-member Emergency Broadcast System Advisory Committee made up of senior-level representatives from the broadcasting, cable television, common carrier, and news service industries. Typical topics with which the committee deals are state and local emergency preparedness plans and training material for personnel who may be on duty when an emergency occurs.

WORKING WITH INTERAGENCY COMMITTEES

Different interagency committees, boards, and other groups work between agencies of government. Participating in the work of these interagency committees helps ensure that policies developed by the FCC do not conflict with those of other agencies. For example, emergency communications is the concern of such interagency groups as the National Telecommunications Committee and Information Systems Committee. These interagency committees can petition the FCC to create new rules and regulations and the commission can respond by invoking the required procedures to solicit comment and move the regulatory process forward. Interagency committees need not be involved in communication matters for the FCC to participate. For example, the FCC staff has helped to plan the communication needs for regional earthquake response by cooperating with the Subcommittee on Federal Earthquake Response.

WORKING WITH OTHER AGENCIES OF GOVERNMENT

Working directly with other agencies of government is also necessary. For example, considering new rules and regulations affecting that part of the electromagnetic spectrum used by the military necessitates coordinating policy with the Defense Department. Decisions affecting international communication may affect the State Department and even United Nations organizations. Deceptive station promotion practices fall under the control of the FCC but are also in the domain of the Federal Trade Commission. A broadcast station's affirmative action program is under the jurisdiction of the FCC but a station owner who discriminates in hiring can also become a party to actions by state agencies and the federal Equal Employment Opportunity Commission. The FCC's Field Operations Bureau may find itself providing assistance to such agencies as the Coast Guard, the Federal Aviation Administration, the FBI, the Secret Service, and other agencies which utilize radio communication. The FCC may also be called upon to work with state and municipal governments in policy planning.

PUBLIC INFORMATION FUNCTIONS

Public information, including public relations and news media relations, serves a number of functions within the commission. Handled through the Office of Public Affairs, the public information function entails making available to the public key FCC documents. For example, a researcher needing access to FCC documents can contact the Consumer Assistance area of the Office of Public Affairs.

Enforcement Support

Another function of the Office of Public Affairs is to give support to the enforcement activities of the FCC. Deterring crime is partially based on publicity. If in our society no one knew who was charged, found guilty, or what penalties they received, others would not learn from their mistakes. The same principle applies to the enforcement of communications law just as it does to a local newspaper publishing the names of speeding violators.

For the FCC, getting publicity out about the commission's enforcement activities aids in preventing other violations. The FCC-generated publicity of the surprise nationwide inspections of 1,000 radio and television towers to make sure they had the required painting and lighting caused many operators who were not inspected to pay attention and bring their own towers into compliance.[40] Pirate radio stations, long an FCC enforcement problem, were brought to the public's attention once again in the early 1990s by the Office of Public Affairs. While the number of pirate stations which were shut down was not unusual, the publicity paid to the enforcement activities was.[41] The connection between public affairs and enforcement was articulated by one chief of the Field Operations Bureau who was quoted as saying, "We would like to get compliance through education to the extent we can." The chief said, "We hand out literature and try to get press coverage. Generally, increasing the awareness in a given area is helpful toward getting compliance."[42]

Enhanced Visibility

Another advantage of the public-relations side of the commission is the fact that publicity for a federal agency keeps the agency visible in the eyes of Congress, which monitors the agency's activities and controls its funding through the appropriations process. If Congress does not feel an agency is active, then it can become an easy mark for budget cuts. The FCC's Field Operations Bureau, for example, was no stranger to budget cuts. During the era of federal deregulation during the 1980s, the bureau's staff went from 500 to well under 400.[43] Field offices were closed in such places as Cincinnati, Pittsburgh, and St. Louis. Monitoring equipment became old and less effective.

Staff Morale

Enhanced visibility can also improve staff morale. When an agency receives publicity for its work, it is one of the few external rewards the staff receives for what are many times routine jobs with little glamour. Writing about another federal agency, the Federal Trade Commission, a writer in *The Wall Street Journal* noted: "The Federal Trade Commission is enjoying a surge of largely admiring press coverage for its recently revived antitrust enforcement program. Staff morale has soared at an agency that had been reduced to glum irrelevancy during the Reagan years."[44]

ENFORCEMENT

One of the most publicized activities of the FCC is enforcement. Broadcasters are familiar with the Field Operations Bureau which conducts on-site investigations. If the FCC decides to vigorously pursue a case, the enforcement arm of the commission can extend beyond the Field Operations Bureau and the other bureaus into the courts. Other bureaus of the FCC will also become involved. For example, a delivery service's two-way radio system will fall under the Private Radio Bureau, where serious violations would be prosecuted, even though a Field Operations Bureau located in the delivery service's own region might be the first contact with the violator.

Regional Enforcement

Regional locations of the Field Operations Bureau provide a national network of monitoring services and enforcement support. For example, when the FCC wanted to concentrate on the pirating of satellite signals sent to home satellite dishes, the field offices of the Field Operations Bureau visited dealers suspected of selling the illegal equipment to descramble satellite signals. Illegal equipment was seized in four states.[45] Similar regional enforcement measures were necessary when a Cuban independence organization planned to start sending television signals to Cuba from a boat off the Florida coast. The Miami regional office spent 11 weeks involved in investigating and tracking activities because such broadcasts violated international law.[46]

Interagency Coordination

Enforcement activities are also coordinated with other agencies of government. For example, the sophisticated monitoring equipment of the Field Operations Bureau can be used to assist other agencies of government in sea and air rescue. Of major concern to all agencies are the many false alarms, accounting for 98 percent of all reports, generated by the emergency locater transmitters used in aircraft. The problem is serious enough that a False Alarm Working Group chaired by a Field Operations Bureau engineer has been formed to work with such agencies as the National Aeronautics and Space Administration to make workable a special monitoring device that will alert pilots when the emergency locater transmitter aboard an aircraft has been accidentally activated.

ENFORCEMENT AND CRITICISM

In all countries, and the United States is no exception, electronic communication is a regulated industry. The regulation now encompasses such diverse technologies as data transfer, broadcasting, telephones, satellites, and even the type of equipment consumers buy to receive or interact with these technologies. As we will read, the FCC has at its disposal a number of different measures to assure these regulated industries toe the line, operate in the spirit of competition but without interference to each other, all the while keeping in mind the needs of the consumer who is entitled to communication services which are in the public interest. Although much publicity surrounds the extent to which the commission has control over these regulated industries, there are areas over which the FCC does not have control and that is where our discussion begins.[47]

WHAT THE FCC DOES NOT REGULATE

Many people perceive the FCC as having broad powers of regulation. Consumers unhappy about something they have seen or heard on local radio or television may complain to the FCC. But the commission has very little control over the *content* of broadcast messages. With the exception of obscene and indecent programming—and even that area is somewhat nebulous—lotteries and deceptive advertising are about the only areas of programming the FCC can directly regulate without infringing on the First Amendment. Even when the FCC does act in these areas, court battles frequently arise.

Programming

The FCC cannot tell a station when to air a program. Nor can it tell a station when to run its commercials or public-service announcements. The FCC will not substitute its judgment for that of the local broadcaster in those areas. Although some network contracts prohibit editing of certain programs, that is solely an agreement between the network and the station, not the FCC. Despite the "no-editing" clauses, the licensee retains control over local programming, with the right to delete the network's entire program if it feels the program would not be in the public interest.

Although the FCC can act in the public interest to question heavy commercialization of radio and television, the direct authority to tell a station that it must air commercials does not exist. Similarly, the commission could consider the amount of public-service programming in a contested license renewal, but has no authority to tell a station what public-service programming to air. If the local licensee chooses to air public-service announcements for the Red Cross instead of the American Cancer Society, or no public-service announcement at all, that is the station's prerogative.

Lotteries and Prizes

Although lotteries are forbidden, the FCC has little jurisdiction over the conduct of legitimate contests, especially the awarding of prizes. If a station runs a contest, and you win a prize which does not satisfy you, the best recourse would be to deal directly with the station or the manufacturer of the prize. The FCC does not have the authority to tell the manufacturer to give you a different prize or help you obtain repairs for a defective item. Similarly, although stations broadcast a variety of sporting events, the FCC has no jurisdiction over the promoters or organizers of those sporting events. If your favorite boxer unexpectedly fails to appear on the local televised "Golden Gloves" championship, you are free to write the Boxing Commission, but the FCC won't be able to help you.

Foreign Stations

Similarly, the commission does not have any jurisdiction over countries whose radio or television signals cross into the United States. Although reciprocal international agreements oversee the use of the electromagnetic spectrum, the consumer in Michigan who complains to the FCC about a Canadian radio station would receive little satisfaction. A listener in southern California complaining to the FCC about a station in Mexico would experience similar frustration. An exception would be if the Canadian or Mexican station were operating off frequency and interfering with American stations, although even in these cases, the FCC would have to go through the U.S. State Department or the respective regulatory agencies in Canada and Mexico to solve the interference problem.

Allied Services

The FCC does not have jurisdiction over news-gathering organizations and press associations, either local or national.[48] Press associations, such as Associated Press and Reuters, are independent of the broadcast stations they serve and are not regulated by the FCC. Consumers who do not understand radio and television programming sometimes complain about news coverage. Not only does the FCC avoid control of programming, including news programming, but much of the information aired on radio and television reaches the station through such news services as Associated Press and other organizations. To the extent that such organizations use radio frequencies or satellites to transmit information, the FCC does have jurisdiction, but only in the technical sense.

Similarly, the commission does not directly regulate the radio and television networks, music rights organizations, or ratings services. The FCC does, however, regulate network owned and operated broadcasting stations, just as it does other stations. Music licensing firms such as ASCAP and BMI are independent organizations and are not involved in the activities that the commission regulates. These organizations, although directly involved in serving stations and collecting royalties from them for airing performers' works, are not under the jurisdiction of the FCC. In addition, audience measurement firms, such as Nielsen and Arbitron, are independent of the FCC, although a station's fraudulent use of audience ratings reflects on the licensee's commitment to serve the public interest and can trigger an FCC inquiry or investigation.

Libel and Slander

Libel and slander, making a defamatory untrue statement about someone during a radio and television broadcast, is another area over which the FCC has no jurisdiction. If you feel that you have been libeled or slandered (both terms sometimes apply to "broadcast" speech which is "published"), your best recourse would be to consult an attorney, not the FCC. Even in the case of license renewal, the FCC stays away from becoming involved in these matters. In fact, when defamation did become an issue in a license renewal, the FCC stated in part:

> It is the judgment of the Commission, as it has been the judgment of those who drafted our Constitution and of the overwhelming majority of our legislators and judges over the years, that the public interest is best served by permitting the expression of any views that do not involve, quoting from Supreme Court decisions, "a clear and present danger of serious substantive evil that rises far above public inconvenience, annoyance or unrest." . . . this principle insures that the most diverse and opposing opinions will be expressed, many of which may even be highly offensive to those officials who thus protect the rights of others to free speech. If there is to be free speech, it must be free for speech that we abhor and hate as well as for speech that we find tolerable or congenial.[49]

The First Amendment of the U.S. Constitution arises to protect free speech, even when that free speech is unpopular. In the same vein, program content which contains derogatory comments about sex, race, or religious beliefs also enjoys some protection under the First Amendment. Ethnic humor may offend some people, but any attempt to control this area of programming would, for the most part, be outside the FCC's jurisdiction.

FCC POWERS OF ENFORCEMENT

The Communications Act specifies that violators of its provisions will be penalized, and the commission has at its disposal a number of enforcement measures to keep the industries it regulates in tow. Depending on the type of violation, the commission can impose penalties ranging from a simple letter to revoking a station's license.[50]

Letters and Notices

Letters and notices are used for less serious matters without imposing a forfeiture. Missing exhibits from a license renewal or minor technical violations handled by the field office of the Field Operations Bureau are situations which might warrant an official letter or notice.

Forfeitures

The most common sanction placed upon a station is a forfeiture (fine), usually imposed because of a technical rule violation. More serious offenses result in higher fines. Typical of violations are the following: failure to calibrate a remote meter device; failure to maintain actual antenna input power as near as practical to authorized power; failure to maintain a receiver to monitor the Emergency Broadcast System.[51] More serious violations involve commercial operating practices. Typical violations are the following: fraudulent billing practices; failure to make time available to political candidates at the lowest unit charge; falsification of operating logs.[52] Violations in this category are considered serious enough that they can incur the maximum fine.

Short-term Renewals

Next to forfeitures, the most severe sanction placed upon a station is a short-term license renewal. The purpose of such a renewal is to give the commission an early opportunity to review what it sees as past deficiencies.[53] Typical of short-term license renewals are those issued for the following infractions:

1. Station's equal employment.
2. Utilization of broadcast facility to gain competitive advantage in nonbroadcast activities; fraudulent billing.
3. Inadvertent misrepresentations to the commission, falsification of logs; violation of logging rules; nonfulfillment of prior proposals concerning public-service announcements; lack of supervision and control over station operations.
4. Broadcast of false, misleading, or deceptive advertising in connection with the promotion of a contest.
5. Predetermining the outcome of a contest.
6. Fraudulent billing.
7. Conducting contests during audience survey periods ("hypoing").[54]

Alleged violations centering around commercial matters were responsible for most of these short-term renewals, indicating the seriousness that the FCC places upon such actions.[55] Fraudulent billing practices undermine the entire fabric of broadcasting and the FCC has little compassion for such violations.

Renewal Denials and Revocation

The most serious penalty the FCC can impose against a licensee is to deny it the right to operate, either through revoking its license or denying renewal of its license. The FCC has leveled such sanctions against noncommercial as well as commercial broadcasters. In a sweeping action, the FCC lifted the licenses of an entire state's educational television commission. It was a precedent-setting example, designed to show that the commission was not going to tolerate what it considered lack of service to an audience.

In addition to the example just stated, the reasons for lifting a license or denying a renewal vary considerably. The following three examples, all subject to appeal, show different reasons for denying a license. In one case the FCC denied the license renewal of a California noncommercial television station for alleged misrepresentation. The station claimed that equipment which wasn't delivered kept it off the air. The FCC said that was not the case and that a budget deficit, not equipment delivery, was the real reason the station was off the air.[56] In another decision the FCC voted unanimously to deny the renewal of a New York state radio station in a ruling which characterized the station owner as unfit to be a licensee after the manager allegedly made a racist remark to a job applicant and discriminated in a hiring decision. The commission said not awarding prizes in a contest also contributed to the decision.[57]

A Georgia AM-FM licensee found itself on the wrong side of the FCC Review Board, which went beyond the recommended $20,000 fine imposed by an administrative law judge and instead revoked the licenses for the AM-FM stations. The Review Board ruled that the licensee had transferred ownership of two stations bought at a distress sale without getting the transfer approved by the commission. One report of the proceeding detailed part of a particularly stinging rebuke by the Review Board which accused the licensee of "willful violation" of the statute, and went on to say the matter was "compounded by conduct fully as egregious as misrepresentation or lack of candor, and equally as telling as to its trustworthiness."[58]

An Arizona AM-FM operation had its license renewal denied by the FCC in an opinion which charged the owners with being unfit licensees in connection with what the FCC said were misrepresentations about management and ownership made some 15 years earlier. The case pointed out that time, even 15 years, does not heal all wounds and the license was awarded to the parties which challenged the license renewal.

Cease-and-Desist Orders

Over the years, cease-and-desist orders have been very rare, mostly because other sanctions such as fines are quite effective. In one case a minister asked the FCC to issue a cease-and-desist order prohibiting a station from dropping a religious program. The commission declined but reaffirmed it did have the authority to issue such an order.[60] A cease-and-desist order was also used to prevent a station from continuing to broadcast off-color remarks.[61]

FCC INSPECTIONS

Any broadcast station is subject to an FCC inspection. When an inspector arrives at the station or monitors the station from a remote location, such as a field truck, violation of a technical rule can result in an official communique from the commission.

Advisory Notice

For minor violations, the station may receive an Advisory Notice, which is somewhat analogous to a warning citation for a traffic violation. It is the least severe of the various official sanctions that can be placed upon an operator. The Advisory Notice tells the violator to correct any unsatisfactory condition. No written reply is required, but a copy is placed on file with the FCC.

Official Notice

More serious is the Official Notice of Violation, to which a written reply is required within ten days. The reply must be sent to the FCC office from which the violation notice originated. The written answer is critical and can determine what further action might be taken by the FCC. Stations are warned that one of the most, if not the most, serious rule violation is to lie or misrepresent something to the commission. In some cases, the commission may have accumulated considerably more evidence against a station than the notice itself details. Information from FCC remote monitoring may already be on file, and such information can quickly contradict an attempt by a licensee to gloss over a problem in a written reply.

The notice to which the broadcaster must reply originates from an individual inspector, monitoring station, or field truck. The reply, along with the FCC violation notice, is reviewed by the FCC and then forwarded to the Field Operations Bureau in Washington. It can stop there, or, if serious enough, it can go on to the Mass Media Bureau where a fine can be issued. In very serious circumstances, the matter may come before the full commission.

CONSUMER COMPLAINTS TO THE FCC

Although even the FCC recommends that an individual try first to iron out a complaint or difference with a local station, when this process becomes difficult or when communication breaks down, another avenue open to the individual is to communicate directly with the commission.

The Complaint Division

Complaints from the public are directed to the FCC's Complaint Division, which handles tens of thousands of letters a year about broadcast stations, approximately half of which are complaints. From these figures, it is clear a letter to a local broadcaster stands a much greater chance of receiving personal attention than a letter to the FCC. If, however, you are not satisfied with the local response and decide to pursue the matter at the level of the FCC, you are advised to follow guidelines similar to those which apply to writing to a local broadcaster.

Filing a Complaint

The most important point about your letter is to include only those items over which the FCC has jurisdiction. Many people are under the misconception that the FCC has total control over local broadcasters. Such is not the case. True, the FCC enforces many rules and regulations, but many of these concern the engineering practices of the station and have no relationship to programming and other operations. The FCC points out that it "cannot direct that a particular program be put on or taken off the air, nor are we arbiters of taste." The FCC's concern is with the total community,[62] "rather than with the personal preferences or grievances of the individuals."[63]

If you have complained first to the station involved, then include a copy of that correspondence with your letter to the commission. The exception to this procedure would be if, for some reason, you do not want your identity disclosed to the station and prefer to request the FCC to keep it confidential. Your complaint, however, may not be as effective if the letter is not included. As is the case when writing to a local broadcaster, complain promptly.

Content of the Complaint Letter

Include your full name and address, the call letters of the station, and a "statement of what the station has done or failed to do which causes you to file a complaint. Be as specific as possible. Furnish names, dates, places, and other details."[64] The organization of your letter is also important. Keep it simple and state the facts clearly. "If the facts are self-explanatory, avoid argument, let the facts speak for themselves. Avoid repetition or exaggeration. If you think a specific law or regulation has been violated, tell us what it is. If possible, use a typewriter, but if you do write by hand, take special pains to write legibly."[65] Assuming that you do write to the FCC, we'll examine what happens to your complaint.

Processing a Complaint

First, if you have not followed the guidelines specified in the preceding paragraphs, then you'll probably receive a form letter in the mail explaining the proper procedures and asking that you follow these. If, on the other hand, the information is complete and there appears to be a violation, your complaint will be investigated, most likely by a letter to the station or, in rare instances, by a personal visit from an FCC official. Such visits are called "field inquiries" and are infrequent because of the commission's limited investigatory staff. If the FCC staff feels that the station has violated one of the FCC rules, it can do one of three things. It may recommend sanctions be imposed on the station; it may direct remedial action or, where extenuating circumstances are present, it may note the violation but not recommend a sanction.

Although the inspection process is an integral part of the FCC enforcement process, it is only as effective as there are funds to staff FCC field offices and hire inspectors. Federal budget cuts have in the past hampered FCC enforcement efforts. For example, when the 1992 Cable Act was passed, sufficient appropriations did not exist at first to implement the measure. Changes in the funding of the FCC under the Clinton administration are designed to make the agency self supporting. The Clinton budget package passed in 1993 included provisions for regulatory fees to be paid by regulated telecommunication industries. The regulated industries were not happy with the measure. Not only did they feel they were being taxed unfairly, but with the fees in place, it would be easier to raise the fees in the future as the commission needed more funds. The full extent of a regulatory and funding policy, where the regulated pay the regulator, cannot be fully assessed.

INPUT TO FCC RULE MAKING

Keep in mind that FCC rules and regulations are designed to keep the broadcaster operating in the "public interest." But there are still practical limitations as to how far the commission can go. Some rules would simply be too costly to be practical. Others would not be feasible on a wide scale. Despite the fact that the FCC has the power to enact rules, the broadcaster must still be able to implement the commission's decisions. As a result, the commission is careful to take every opportunity to seek feedback on any proposed action from as many people as possible and from as many varying viewpoints as possible. A multistage process is used in formulating FCC regulations, and attention is given at every step to feedback from both broadcasters and the public.

PETITION FOR RULE MAKING

FCC decision making can begin in two ways. First, the commission can make a motion to consider a Petition for Rule Making. Second, any citizen or broadcaster can also contact the commission and submit a petition for rule making. The FCC staff will then examine the petition and determine whether it has merits.

As a highly abbreviated example, let's assume that a citizens' group you belong to has made a persuasive argument for rule making, that it is legally and technically sound, and that the FCC decides it wants to investigate the matter further. The commission now issues a file number, which opens the door for broadcasters and members of the public alike to comment on your proposal. As an example, we'll assume that you have petitioned the commission that all television stations should have public-access studios to permit the public to produce their own television programs.

Perhaps a senior-citizen consumer group feels that your proposal has merit and it also files comments with the FCC. They argue that the facilities would permit senior citizens to form their own television production companies and produce programs for national syndication. At the same time, television stations respond to your petition. They argue that the technical and administrative expense of a television studio for public use would be prohibitive. With all this information, the commission now takes the matter under advisement. We'll assume that the commission feels the petition still has some merit, but that they need more information.

The commission's next step is to issue a Notice of Proposed Rule Making and to give it a docket number. It then accepts both comments and reply comments to this notice. These are essentially written forms of discussion and debate. If, after evaluating the responses, the commission feels the proposal does not have merit, they can dispose of it by issuing a Memorandum Opinion and Order.

ISSUING THE FINAL DECISION

With all of these comments and reply comments available, the commission must now make a decision on the proposed rule making. It issues a Report and Order, in which it discusses all of the pro and con arguments for the proposed rule and states why it has arrived at its decision. The Report and Order is the commission's official notification of its final decision. If the proposal is complex, the commission may issue more than one Report and Order.

THE FCC'S NOTICE OF INQUIRY

At any point in the rule making process or while the commission is considering a rule making petition, it may issue a Notice of Inquiry, asking for more information on an issue.[66] This is the FCC's way of saying: "We want opinions before we proceed." Although broadcasters and the public can respond at any time, the Notice of Inquiry usually shifts the input process into high gear. Especially important to the FCC are comments from people who have had experience related to the proposed rule making or who would be directly affected by it. In our example, comments from the operator of a private television production company that understands the costs of running a studio would be more valuable than comments or reply comments from someone who has no experience and only a peripheral understanding of the issue. Notice of Inquiries have also been directed at the public and questionnaires used to solicit public opinion.

CRITICISM OF THE FCC

Because it is regulating a very "visible" industry, and because that industry directly affects all of us on a daily basis, the FCC has had its share of criticism from the public, the Congress, and even from the commissioners within its ranks. In the paragraphs that follow we will examine some of this criticism. The categories of issues discussed are by no means inclusive, but they also represent subjective opinions and do not necessarily apply to FCC operations at all times. Some are more general in nature, others are based on specific instances and involve specific practices and procedures.

Internal Document Distribution

The FCC's internal distribution process, in which comments from interested parties who write to the FCC to influence policy are distributed to staff members who read and categorize the comments, was criticized by professor Michael A. McGregor. McGregor studied the use of informal comments in rule-making proceedings (so called because commenters are not required to adhere to some of the strict guidelines placed upon those who participate formally in rule-making proceedings). McGregor contends:

> The distribution system within the Commission appears to be in disarray. Persons assigned to a particular rule-making proceeding may not be aware of a particular comment until that comment is referred to in reply comments. This is often the result of other commenting parties being served with copies of comments; these same comments, however, may never have been directed to staff persons assigned to the proceeding. In

other cases, employees may receive comments after all consideration of the proceeding is finished. Finally, the informal comments may not find their way to the public docket files. Evidence of this is found in the public files for the children's television proceeding. Over 1000 letters, by staff estimate, received by the Children's Television Task Force could not be located in the files. This may be the result of either misfiling (or nonfiling) by the public reference room employees, or misdelivery (or nondelivery) of the documents to the public reference room in the first place.[67]

The entire issue of informal comments raises the question of how much influence the average citizen, or for that matter citizen groups, have in the FCC decision-making process.

Relationship of the Commissioners to the Middle Staff

The relationship of the FCC's middle staff to the commissioners is another bone of contention among critics. Erwin Krasnow and Lawrence Longley point out that the middle staff exerts influence over the commissioners by controlling the channels of internal communication at the FCC.[68] Thus, when the commissioners need to choose among alternative policies, they must rely on the information that their staff feels is relevant and significant. Since hundreds of decisions are made every day, implementation of policy must be delegated to middle staff personnel.

Decision Making

Another criticism of the FCC is that it is sluggish in making important decisions. Krasnow and Longley point out that the FCC is "incapable of policy planning, of disposing within a reasonable period of time the business before it, of fashioning procedures that are effective to deal with its problems."[69] Still another case is that of the proceedings affecting the assignment of WHDH-TV in Boston. The case started in 1947, when WHDH filed an application for a license to operate Channel 5. The channel allocation was the subject of competing applications and FCC decrees for 25 years. It was one of the longest proceedings ever to transpire before the FCC. Professors Robert Smith and Paul Prince reviewed the chronology of the WHDH-TV case and concluded that there was no clear winner in the proceedings, but the public was a significant loser.[70] Sterling Quinlan, writing a book about the case, quotes a former commissioner as saying, "Let's face it. This was the Whorehouse Era of the Commission. When matters were arranged, not adjudicated."[71]

In another example, an attorney representing a group of petitioners to deny the renewal of a New York state AM radio station was quoted as expressing frustration over how long it took the FCC to act in the matter. Ten years elapsed between the time the original petition to deny was filed until the FCC's final decision. The attorney was quoted as saying, "I am frustrated that it has taken us this long and a threat to take them to court to get a decision that we ought to have gotten years ago."[72] The attorney went on to remark that the FCC "had to be dragged kicking and screaming into this thing and at every single stage . . . it was a consequence of us pushing to do it."[73]

Conflict of Interest

The commission has, on occasion, been called to task for potential conflicts of interest because its staff owned stocks of corporations regulated by the FCC. A staff report of the House Oversight and Investigations Subcommittee criticized members for transferring shares of stock in communication-related industries to immediate members of their own families, although the law did not prohibit that practice. Some of the stock ownership reported by the subcommittee included shares of General Electric owned by the spouse of a staff member, shares of AT&T owned by the spouse of a staff member in the Common Carrier Bureau, and shares of AT&T owned by the spouse of an engineer in charge of an FCC field office.[74]

Citizen Participation

McGregor's research cited earlier also applies here. Regulated industries are accustomed to hiring professional legal counsel to represent them before the commission on rule-making proceedings. Citizen groups and members of the general public often do not employ specialized counsel and can be at a disadvantage in having their comments considered.[75] Although submitting informal comments is somewhat easier because of fewer formal submission requirements, getting the informal comments of the public and citizen groups to be included in the decision process can be difficult, especially when the comments are misfiled or undelivered to the proper location in the FCC.

An earlier report prepared by the Rand Corporation suggested that the commission should do more to encourage citizen participation, one such effort being to support legislation that would provide financial assistance to citizen groups involved in Commission proceedings. High on the list of recommendations was the proposal to give citizen groups access to any evidence that might support their cause. Under current procedures a person or group can only gain access to information, called the *right of discovery*, after proceedings have begun in the courts or, in the case of the FCC, after a hearing has been designated.

Frequency Allocations

Not everyone feels that the way in which the FCC allocates frequencies on the electromagnetic spectrum is in the best interest of the public. For example, the designation of certain frequencies for marine use means that there are wide areas of the country where these frequencies go unused, simply because there is no demand for marine communication.[76] Moreover, this policy has perpetuated itself for years, and trying to change it now would involve major capital expenditures for the industries affected.

Local Station Concept

The commission's local station concept, allocating certain frequencies for lower-powered stations serving small communities, also has disadvantages in that it ties up a sizable portion of the spectrum for local station use. Critics point out that one means of lessening crowding on the spectrum would be to switch to regional allocations. The result of such a switch would be fewer higher-powered stations serving larger regions. Others counter that the idea, although technologically sound, becomes impractical when we think of the "local" service that would be lost.[77] A regional station in Chicago serving a small town in Illinois would be hard pressed to include the Illinois community's local news in its regional programming.[78]

EEO Compliance

Other criticism is based on the FCC's Equal Employment Opportunity (EEO) policies and on the role of citizens' groups in FCC decision making. A report by the Citizens' Communications Center claimed that the criteria for stations' compliance with the FCC's EEO requirements are vague and can be met by broadcasters who still discriminate.[79] The report also asserted that the commission requires an unrealistically high standard of proof of discrimination practices before designating a hearing in a renewal case. Another report critical of the commission's EEO policy was issued by the United States Commission on Civil Rights.[80] Yet, this report suggested that the FCC should improve the image of women and minorities in television programming, an area that many would argue is clearly outside the commission's jurisdiction.

SUMMARY

Formed by the Communications Act of 1934, the Federal Communications Commission operates as an independent agency of government. Despite its independent status, however, it maintains a close relationship with Congress, which is closely tied politically to the commission. Members of Congress frequently see the commission as an instrument of communication policy that directly affects their constituents.

Some of this policy originates at the grassroots level when the public complains to their local representative about television programming. While the First Amendment prohibits the FCC from directly controlling the content of programming, the commission can establish general guidelines on amounts of specific programming. Congress can hold hearings on the quality of programming and such hearings usually gain considerable publicity in local newspapers and on radio and television. Individual decisions of the FCC can gain the attention of Congress. Members of key committees engage in communication with FCC chairmen and the hearing process can always be used to elevate a policy issue and put pressure on the commission. Since radio and television stations are licensed to serve their local communities, even specific license renewals can gain the attention of members of Congress.

The confirmation process of FCC commissioners is a political process that involves the executive branch of government through the president's nomination of commissioners, and the Senate which confirms the nominations. FCC chairmen in particular are closely tied politically to the administration in power and can execute communication policy on behalf of the executive branch. Once the nomination is announced, a series of meetings takes place with key member of Congress. The confirmation hearings are another arena where nominees can be queried and where their prospective policy agendas are discussed.

The authorization and appropriations process are two additional ways Congress can influence the FCC. Authorization measures are blueprints for Congress to follow in appropriating money for an agency's activities. The authorization and the appropriations process can both be used to formulate communication policy through the use of riders which contain specific regulatory measures amending the Communications Act. Key policy initiatives can be rejected or approved using the authorization and appropriations process.

The role of federal agencies in communication policy dates back to the formation of the Interstate Commerce Commission which controlled the telegraph, wireless, and early radio. Gradually as radio developed, the airways became crowded and four national radio conferences provided the basis upon which the Federal Radio Commission was formed. Closely tied to the FRC was the U.S. Court of Appeals which affirmed many of the FRC's early decisions and today is part of the checks and balances affecting the operation of the Federal Communications Commission. Sometimes operating like a partner to the FCC, and other times an adversary, the U.S. Court of Appeals for the District of Columbia has played a significant role in the development of communications policy.

One of the more noteworthy decisions was in the case of *Office of Communication of United Church of Christ* v. *FCC*, which permitted private citizens, the listeners and viewers, to take an active role in FCC decisions. Previously, only those parties who were facing economic injury or interference could participate. The decision opened up the era of public-interest and citizen-group involvement in the formulation of communications policy.

The most direct influence over the FCC and communications policy is exercised by the commissioners. Commissioners are prohibited from having a financial interest in industries regulated by the FCC and no more than three commissioners can be from the same political party. Commission chairmen are sometimes noted for their own agendas and can exert influence over the commission's activities. In recent years the theme of a deregulated and competitive marketplace for communication technologies has been predominant at the FCC. Stricter enforcement of the rules and regulations which do exist has also been noted. Many former commissioners enter private industry or law practice and continue their ties to the commission.

The commission holds regular meetings and the agenda includes the issues which evolve from the various FCC offices and bureaus. Meetings are for the most part public, are announced in advance, and can only be closed for internal FCC personnel matters or classified material affecting the national defense. Commission meetings typically have representatives from the FCC offices and bureaus present as well as engineering personnel to answer questions about technical matters.

The FCC is organized into offices and bureaus. The Office of Plans and Policy is responsible for developing long-range policy decisions to industries which are regulated by the FCC. The managing director serves under the FCC chairman as the chief operating and executive official of the FCC. On the first rung of the ladder in the appeals process are the administrative law judges, while the Review Board is the second step in that process. The general counsel is the FCC attorney. The Office of Public Affairs is the public information arm of the FCC and the Office of Legislative Affairs coordinates the commission's legislative initiatives in addition to working with closely with Congress. Technical expertise is found in the personnel of the Office of Engineering and Technology.

FCC bureaus include the Mass Media Bureau which controls radio, television, and cable. Telephone regulation falls under the Common Carrier Bureau, while private radio communications fall under the Private Radio Bureau. The Field Operations Bureau is the enforcement arm of the commission.

The functions and activities of the FCC are tied to the various offices and bureaus. These include legislative functions which involve the FCC's own legislative agenda. Considerable effort is also expended on litigation. Decisions of the FCC are open to appeal and through the general counsel, the FCC operates as both plaintiff and defendant in the federal courts. Both regulatory and legislative initiatives are frequently preceded by policy and planning research and the FCC also finds itself working with advisory boards, interagency committees, and other agencies of federal, state, and municipal government. The public information functions include providing assistance and information to the public, working with the news media, and supporting the FCC's enforcement efforts. The enforcement efforts are coordinated through the regional Field Operations Bureaus.

In all countries electronic communications function under differing amounts of government control. In the United States the Federal Communications Commission has at its disposal rules and regulations which govern the industries it regulates.

Despite the enforcement powers invested in the commission, there are a number of areas the FCC does not control. For example, the FCC has very little control over radio and television programming. This lack of control is vested in the First Amendment guarantees of the U.S. Constitution and applies to everything except indecent and obscene material and the broadcasting of lotteries. Even these areas of programming have some limited First Amendment protection. In addition to not controlling the content of programming, the FCC avoids telling stations when to air programming.

The awarding of prizes, foreign broadcasting stations, and allied services are three additional areas the FCC does not control. If you don't like the prize your receive in a station contest, your recourse lies with the station or the manufacturer, not the FCC. Foreign stations come under the regulatory body controlling broadcasting in their respective countries. Music rights organizations serve the music industry and broadcasting through music licensing and royalty agreements, but the FCC does not control the music rights organizations.

Libel and slander, defaming someone on the air, are not matters the FCC handles. People who feel they have been defamed can consult an attorney skilled in media law, but the FCC will not help.

The FCC has at its disposal different enforcement measures ranging from the least severe, an official letter notifying the licensee of a minor technical violation, to the most severe, which is the revocation of a station's license. Between these two extremes, more serious notices can also be issued and forfeitures (fines) are available as deterrents. Short-term license renewals give the commission the opportunity to reevaluate a station's performance before issuing the standard renewal. On very rare occasions a cease-and-desist order has been issued.

Consumer complaints to the FCC are handled by the Complaint Division. Tens of thousands of letters are handled annually by the FCC, which is one reason a complaint is best sent first to the station involved. If you are dissatisfied with the outcome or the complaint is unresolved, you have the option of contacting the FCC. Some tips the FCC provides to those filing complaints include making sure the letter is typed, having complete documentation such as the station's call letters, frequency, time of the violation if a technical or programming complaint, and any other pertinent information that will permit the FCC to act on the matter. Without full documentation, it can be difficult for the commission to proceed with an inquiry or investigation.

Rules and regulations governing the operation of electronic communication are formulated through formal rule-making procedures. These procedures begin with a Petition for Rule Making and follow a process that permits comments and reply comments from affected parties.

The FCC has been criticized in a number of different areas. Some of this criticism occurs because so much of our society is affected by FCC decision making, and the commission regulates a very visible industry. This criticism takes many forms, from public comment to Congressional hearings, and has covered such areas as the internal document distribution, the relationship of the commissioners to the middle staff, decision making, conflict of interest, citizen participation, frequency allocation, the local station concept, and EEO compliance.

MATERIAL FOR ANALYSIS

GENERAL RULES OF PRACTICE AND PROCEDURE FOR THE FEDERAL COMMUNICATIONS COMMISSION

The following abridged excerpts from the rules of practice and procedure before the FCC deal with censure and suspension, employment of former commissioners, and other matters, all of which affect the daily operation of the commission. In excerpting the material which follows, part, section, and subsection designations have been deleted. Readers wanting the complete text of the rules should consult 47 CFR Part 1. Additional discussions of ethics are found in later chapters of the text, both in the main chapter and in the material for analysis.

Proceedings Before the Commission

The Commission may on its own motion or petition of any interested party hold such proceedings as it may deem necessary from time to time in connection with the investigation of any matter which it has the power to investigate under the law, or for the purpose of obtaining information necessary or helpful in the determination of its policies, the carrying out of its duties or the formulation or amendment of its rules and regulations. For such purposes it may subpoena witnesses and require the production of evidence. Procedures to be followed by the Commission shall, unless specifically prescribed in this part, be such as in the opinion of the Commission will best serve the purposes of such proceedings.

* * *

AUTHORITY FOR REPRESENTATION

Any person, in a representative capacity, transacting business with the Commission, may be required to show his authority to act in such capacity.

PERSONS WHO MAY BE ADMITTED TO PRACTICE

Any person who is a member in good standing of the bar of the Supreme Court of the United States or of the highest court of any state, territory, or of the District of Columbia, and is not under any order of any court suspending, enjoining, restraining, disbarring, or otherwise restricting him in the practice of law, may represent others before the Commission.

When such member of the bar acting in a representative capacity appears in person or signs a paper in practice before the commission, his personal appearance or signature shall constitute a representation to the Commission that, under the provisions of this chapter and the law, he is authorized and qualified to represent the particular party in whose behalf he acts. Further proof of authority to act in a representative capacity may be required.

CENSURE, SUSPENSION, OR DISBARMENT OF ATTORNEYS

The Commission may censure, suspend, or disbar any person who has practiced, is practicing or holding himself out as entitled to practice before it if it finds that such person:

Does not possess the qualifications . . . has failed to conform to standards of ethical conduct required of practitioners at the bar of any court of which he is a member; is lacking in character or professional integrity; and/or displays toward the Commission or any of its hearing officers conduct which, if displayed toward any court of the United States or any of its Territories or the District of Columbia, would be cause for censure, suspension, or disbarment.

Before any member of the bar of the commission shall be censured, suspended, or disbarred, charges shall be preferred by the commission against such practitioner and he shall be afforded an opportunity to be heard thereon.

FORMER COMMISSIONERS AND EMPLOYEES

No member, officer, or employee of the commission:

Whose active service with the Commission has terminated but who is receiving pay while on annual leave not taken prior to separation from such active service, or who is in any other leave status, shall appear as attorney or participate in the preparation or handling of any matter before, or to be submitted to, the Commission.

Restrictions on any former commission employee's acting as representative as to a particular matter in which the employee personally and substantially participated—

> No former Commissioner or Commission employee (including special Government employee) shall knowingly act as agent or attorney for, or otherwise represent, any other person (other than the United States) in any formal or informal appearance before, or, with the intent to influence, make any oral or written communication to the Commission on behalf of any other person in connection with any particular Commission matter involving a specific party in which the Commissioner or employee participated personally and substantially while so employed.

Two-year restriction on any former commission employee's acting as representative as to a particular matter for which the employee had official responsibility—

> No former Commissioner or Commission employee (including special Government employee), within two years after the

cessation of such employment, shall knowingly act as agent or attorney for, or otherwise represent, any other person (other than the United Sates) in any formal or informal appearance before, or, with the intent to influence, make any oral or written communication on behalf of any other person (other than the United States) to the Commission in connection with any particular Commission matter involving a specific party which was actually pending at the Commission and was under his or her official responsibility within one year prior to the termination of such responsibility.

Two-year restriction on a former senior employee's assisting in representation as to a matter in which the employee participated personally and substantially—

> No former Commissioner or senior employee . . . of the Commission (including special Government employee), within two years after the cessation of such employment, shall knowingly represent or aid, counsel, advise, consult, or assist in representing any other person (other than the United States) by personal presence at any formal or informal appearance before the Commission in connection with any particular commission matter involving a specific party in which he or she participated personally and substantially as an employee.

One-year restriction on a former senior employee's transactions with former agency on a particular matter, regardless of prior involvement—

> No former Commissioner or senior employee . . . of the Commission (other than a special government employee who serves for fewer than 60 days in a calendar year), within one year after such employment has ceased, shall knowingly act as agent or attorney for, or otherwise represent, any person (other than the United States) in any formal or informal appearance before, or, with the intent to influence, make any oral or written communication to the Commission on behalf of anyone (including himself or herself) other than the United States in connection with any particular Commission matter (whether or not involving a specific party) which is pending before the Commission or in which the Commission has a direct and substantial interest.

ETHICS LAWS GOVERNING THE FEDERAL COMMUNICATIONS COMMISSION

Ethical conduct expected of FCC employees has been made part of federal law and all FCC employees fall under one or more provisions of the law. The federal statutes deal with such actions as gifts and entertainment, financial interests, use of government property, misuse of information, indebtedness, gambling and betting, playing the lottery, and general conduct prejudicial to the government. In excerpting the material which follows, part, section, and subsection designations have been deleted. Readers wanting the complete text with section designations should consult 47 CFR Part 19.

Under "Ethical and Other Conduct and Responsibilities of Employees" federal regulations state:

SPECIFIC PROVISIONS

The regulations issued under this subpart contain provisions covering the standards of and governing the ethical and other conduct of FCC employees . . . They are not meant to restrict unduly a Commission employee's social activities. Each employee must judge for himself whether his social activities may or may not compromise or appear to compromise his position as a public servant.

Proscribed Actions

An employee shall avoid any action, whether or not specifically prohibited by this subpart, which might result in, or create the appearance of:

a. Using public office for private gain;
b. Giving preferential treatment to any person;
c. Impeding Government efficiency or economy;
d. Losing complete independence or impartiality;
e. Making a Government decision outside official channels; or
f. Affecting adversely the confidence of the public in the integrity of the Government.

Gifts, Entertainment, and Favors

. . . an employee shall not solicit or accept, directly or indirectly, any gift, gratuity, favor, entertainment, loan, or any other thing of monetary value, from a person who:

1. Has, or is seeking to obtain, contractual or other business or financial relations with the Commission ;
2. Conducts operations or activities that are regulated by the Commission; or
3. Has interests that may be substantially affected by the performance or nonperformance of his (the employee's) official duty; or
4. Is in any way attempting to affect the employee's official actions at the Commission.
5. Is offering anything of monetary value to an employee because of the employee's official position . . .

Family Associations, Loans, Other Gifts

1. Where obvious family (such as those between the parents, children, or spouse of the employee and the employee) or other personal relationships make it clear that it is those relationships rather than the business of the persons concerned which are the motivating factor;
2. Food and refreshments, not lavish in kind, may be accepted when: (i) offered free in the course of a meeting or other group function, not connected with an inspection or investigation, at which attendance is desirable because it will assist the Commission employee in performing his or her official duties; or (ii) provided to all panelists or speakers when a Commission employee is participating as a panelist or speaker in a program, seminar or educational conference. The Commission's Office of General Counsel shall make a prior written determination as to the propriety of accepting invitations from regulated entities or interested persons as described in (statutes) and shall keep a log of its decisions. Approval may be requested by any Commission employee or the organizer of the group function;
3. Loans may be obtained from banks or other financial institutions on customary terms to finance proper and usual activities of employees, such as home mortgage loans;
4. Unsolicited advertising or promotional material such as pens, pencils, note pads, calendars and other items of nominal intrinsic value may be accepted, as well as literature relating to the communications field.
5. Gifts given for participation in a program, seminar or educational conference may be accepted only when such gifts are:
   i. of nominal intrinsic value;
   ii. in the nature of a remembrance traditional to the particular sponsoring entity;
   iii. provided to all participants in the program . . .

An employee shall not solicit a contribution from another employee for a gift to an official superior, make a donation as a gift to an official superior, or accept a gift from an employee receiving less pay than himself. However, this paragraph does not prohibit a voluntary gift of nominal value or donation in a nominal amount made on a special occasion such as marriage, illness, or retirement.

An employee shall not accept a gift, present, decoration, or other thing from a foreign government unless authorized by Congress as provided by the Constitution . . .

(This section does not preclude) an employee from receipt of bona fide reimbursement, unless prohibited by law, for expenses of travel and such other necessary subsistence as is compatible with this part for which no Government payment or reimbursement is made. However, this paragraph does not allow an employee to be reimbursed, or payment to be made on his behalf, for excessive personal living expenses, gifts, entertainment, or other personal benefits, . . .

Outside Employment and Other Activity

The Commissioners are prohibited from engaging in any other business, vocation, profession, or employment. No Commissioner or employee of the Commission is permitted to be in the employ of or hold any official relation to any person subject to any of the provisions of the Communications Act. In addition, no Commissioner or employee of the Commission may engage in outside employment or other outside activity, with or without compensation, which is in conflict with or otherwise not compatible with the full and proper discharge of his duties and responsibilities as a Commission employee. Incompatible activities include but are not limited to:

1. Acceptance of a fee, compensation, gift, payment of expenses, or any other thing of monetary value in circumstances in which acceptance may result in, or create the ap-

pearance of a conflict of interest situation; or

2. Outside employment which tends to impair his mental or physical capacity to perform his Commission duties and responsibilities in an acceptable manner; or
3. Outside employment or activities (excluding the publication of articles) which reasonably might be regarded as official actions or bring discredit upon the Commission.

No professional employee of the Commission shall engage in the private practice of his profession unless specifically authorized by the Commission. Requests for such authorizations shall, in the case of employees generally, be submitted to the Head of the Office or Bureau to which the employee is assigned; in the case of Heads of Offices and Bureaus to the Chairman; and in the case of an employee in the immediate office of a Commissioner to the Commissioner. All pertinent facts regarding the proposed employment, such as the name of the employer, the nature of the work to be performed, and the amount of time involved shall be set forth.

Employees of the Commission are encouraged to engage in teaching, lecturing and writing that is not prohibited by law, the Executive Order, the Office of Personnel Management Regulations or the provisions of this chapter. However, an employee shall not, either with or without compensation, engage in teaching, lecturing or writing (including such as is involved in the preparation of a person or class of persons for a Office of Personnel Management or Foreign Service examination) that is dependent on information obtained as a result of his Government employment, except when that information has been made available to the general public or will be made available on request, or when the Chairman gives written authorization for the use of nonpublic information on the basis that its use is in the public interest. Except in the case of a Commissioner, articles which identify the author as a Commission employee shall include the following disclaimer.

The views expressed are those of the author and do not necessarily reflect the views of the Commission.

Documents prepared in the course of, and publications relating to, an employee's official duty shall not be used for his private gain. In addition, the Commissioners shall not receive compensation or anything of monetary value for any consultation, lecture, discussion, writing, or appearance the subject matter of which is devoted substantially to the responsibilities, programs, or operations of the Commission, or which draws substantially on official data or ideas which have not become part of the body of public information . . .

* * *

FINANCIAL INTERESTS

An employee of the Commission shall not have a direct or indirect financial interest that conflicts substantially, or appears to conflict substantially, with his Government duties and responsibilities.

An employee of the Commission shall not engage in, directly or indirectly, a financial transaction as a result of, or primarily relying on, information obtained through his Government employment.

No member of the Commission or person employed by the Commission shall: (i) Be financially interested in any company or other entity engaged in the manufacture or sale of telecommunications equipment which is subject to regulation by the Commission; (ii) Be financially interested in any company or other entity engaged in the business of communication by wire or radio or in the use of the electromagnetic spectrum; (iii) Be financially interested in any company or other entity which controls any company or other entity specified in clause (i) or clause (ii), or which derives a significant portion of its total income from ownership of stocks, bonds, or other securities of any such company or other entity; or (iv) Be employed by, hold any official relation to, or own any stocks, bonds, or other securities of, any person significantly regulated by the Commission under this act; . . .

except that the prohibitions established in this subparagraph shall apply only to financial interests in any company or other entity which has a significant interest in communications, manufacturing, or sales activities which are subject to regulation by the Commission.

To determine whether an entity has a significant interest in communications related activities that are subject to Commissions regulations, the Commission shall consider, without excluding other relevant factors . . . These criteria include: (i) The revenues and efforts directed toward the telecommunications aspect of the business; (ii) The extent of Commission regulation over the entity involved; (iii) The potential economic impact of any Commission action on that particular entity; and (iv) The public perception regarding the business activities of the company.

Financial Interests of Commission Employees

(In summary) . . . the main conflict of interest provisions applying to financial interests (of Commission employees) are:

(1) An employee may not, except in the discharge of his official duties, represent anyone else before a court or Government agency in a matter in which the United States is a party or has an interest. This prohibition applies both to paid and unpaid representation of another.

This prohibition does not extent to *(a)* representation of another person, without compensation, in a disciplinary, loyalty, or other personnel matter; or *(b)* the giving of testimony under oath or from making statements required to be made under penalty for perjury or contempt.

This prohibition may be waived under the express approval of the Government official responsible for his appointment in the case of an employee who represents, with or without compensation, his own parents, spouse or child or a person or estate he serves as a fiduciary, but only as to matters in which the employee has not participated personally and substantially as a Government employee and which are not the subject of his official responsibility.

An employee may not participate in his governmental capacity in any matter in which he, his spouse, minor child or outside business associate has a financial interest. This prohibition shall not apply if the employee advises the Government official responsible for his appointment of the nature of the matter, makes full disclosure of the financial interest, and receives in advance a written determination that the interest is not so substantial as to be deemed likely to affect the integrity of the employee's services.

An employee may not participate in his governmental capacity in any matter in which a person from whom he has accepted employment, or with whom he is negotiating for employment, has a financial interest. At the outset of negotiations with such a prospective employer, the employee shall notify his immediate supervisor. The supervisor shall review the employee's current assignments and responsibilities and discharge him from any assignments that could affect the interests of the prospective employer. The employee shall thereupon file a statement of disqualification and non-participation . . . The statement shall continue in effect until such time (if any) as the negotiations are unsuccessfully terminated.

An employee may not receive any salary, or supplementation of his Government salary, from a private source as compensation for his services to the Government. (i) This prohibition will not prevent an employee from continuing to participate in a bona fide pension plan or other employee welfare or benefit plan maintained by a former employer. (ii) This prohibition is not applicable to anyone serving the Government without compensation or to contributions, awards, or other expenses under the terms of the Government Employees Training Act . . .

Use of Government Property

An employee of the Commission shall not directly or indirectly use, or allow the use of, Government property of any kind, including property leased to the government, for other than officially approved activities. An employee has a positive duty to protect and conserve Government property, including equipment, supplies, and other property entrusted or issued to him.

Misuse of Information

Except as provided . . . or as authorized by the Commission, an employee shall not, directly, or indirectly, disclose to any person outside the Commission any information, or any portion of the contents of any document, which is part of the Commission's records or which is obtained through or in connection with his Government employment, and which is not routinely available to the public and, with the same exceptions, shall not use any such documents or information except in the conduct of his official duties. Conduct intended to be prohibited by this section includes, but is not limited to, the disclosure of information about the content of agenda items (except for compliance with the Government in the Sunshine Act), or other staff papers to persons outside the Commission and disclosure of actions or decisions made by the Commission at closed meetings or by circulation, prior to the public release of such information. This section does not prohibit the release of an official commission meeting agenda listing titles and summaries of items for discussion at an open Commission meeting. Also, this section does not prohibit the release of information about the scheduling of Commission agenda items.

Indebtedness

An employee shall pay each just financial obligation in a proper and timely manner, especially one imposed by law such as Federal, State, or local taxes. For the purpose of this section, a "just financial obligation" means one acknowledged by the employee or reduced to judgment by a court, and "in a proper and timely manner" means in a manner which the Commission determines does not, under the circumstances, reflect adversely on the Government as his employer. In the event of a dispute between an employee and an alleged creditor, this section does not require the Commission to determine the validity or amount of the disputed debt.

Gambling, Betting, and Lotteries

An employee of the Commission shall not participate, while on Government-owned or leased property or while on duty for the Commission, in any gambling activity including the operation of a gambling device, in conducting a lottery or pool, in a game for money or property, or in selling or purchasing a numbers slip or ticket . . . However, this section does not preclude activities: (a) Necessitated by an employee's law enforcement duties; . . .

GENERAL CONDUCT PREJUDICIAL TO THE GOVERNMENT

An employee of the Commission shall not engage in criminal, infamous, dishonest, immoral, or notoriously disgraceful conduct, or other conduct prejudicial to the Commission or to the Government.

QUESTIONS FOR CRITICAL ANALYSIS

- Although critics would be quick to point out any unnecessary growth in the federal bureaucracy, might there be justification for splitting off the common carrier services (telephone, telegraph) of the FCC into a separate regulatory agency and permit the FCC to concentrate its efforts more on radio and television broadcast stations?
- Should the Field Operations Bureau of the FCC have the authority to revoke a license?
- Is the communications field any more "crucial" and "dynamic" than other industries regulated by the government, such as the airlines or railroads?
- Is industry self-regulation a satisfactory alternative to government control of broadcast programming?
- The FCC issues some of its most severe penalties for violations of rules affecting commercial programming (fraudulent billing, and so on). Why are the penalties so strict in this area of programming?
- Why does the FCC consider one of the most serious violations to be willful misrepresentation?
- Should any fine, regardless of the amount, be brought before the FCC commissioners?
- The FCC has employed questionnaires as one method of soliciting reactions from the public. Do you feel that questionnaires to collect information are useful?
- If the criticism is justified that middle staff members exert influence over individual commissioners by controlling the channels of internal communication at the FCC, is there any solution to the problem?
- What are the advantages and disadvantages to the many layers of review, both within the FCC and the court system, that a broadcaster faces when challenging an FCC decision?
- Since the Review Board and administrative law judges are part of the FCC's own hearing process, how can operators charged with a violation and appearing before either the Review Board or the judges feel they have receive fair treatment?
- Does a truly fair and impartial hearing only occur at the level of the U.S. Court of Appeals or the U.S. Supreme Court, which is not part of the internal agency review process, or can a fair and impartial hearing take place at the different levels of review within the commission?
- Should the hearing and review process be revised so that any appeal beyond a regional Field Operations Bureau would be heard by a court separate and removed from agency control and influence?
- The FCC, as is the case with other federal agencies, has the power to investigate, subpoena witnesses, and produce evidence to determine compliance with its rules and regulations. Should the administrative agency whose rules and regulations are in question carry on its own investigation or should federal investigations be conducted solely by the Justice Department?
- Commissioners within two years after they cease employment with the FCC cannot represent anyone before the commission. Is this rule fair? Is the time after service appropriate?

ADDITIONAL RESOURCES

Albert, J. A., "The Federal Regulation of Broadcast Station Contests, or . . . What's the FCC Doing in the Cash Call Jackpot?" 15 *Loyola University of Chicago Law Journal* 261 (1984).

Campbell, E., "Television Violence: Social Science vs. the Law." 10 *Loyola Entertainment Law Journal* 413 (1990).

Dickey, J. W., Jr., "Broadcast-transmission of Pornography; A Serious Matter." 20 *Arkansas Lawyer* 21 (1986).

Dyk, T. B., "Full First Amendment Freedom for Broadcasters: The Industry as Eliza on the Ice and Congress on the Friendly Overseer." 5 *Yale Journal on Regulation* 299 (1988).

Ferris, C. D., and T. J. Leahy, "Red Lions, Tigers and Bears: Broadcast Content Regulation and the First Amendment. (Competing Public and Private Interests: Mass Media Regulation and the Constitution)." 38 *Catholic University Law Review* 299 (1989).

Fowler, M. S., and Daniel L. Brenner, "A Marketplace Approach to Broadcast Regulation." 60 *Texas Law Review* 207 (1982).

Frieden, R. M., "International Telecommunications and the Federal Communications Commission." 21 *Columbia Journal of Transnational Law* 423 (1983).

Gabel, D., "Divestiture, Spin-offs, and Technological Change in the Telecommunications Industry—A Property Rights Analysis." 3 *Harvard Journal of Law and Technology* 75 (1990).

Graham, B., "The State's Role in the New Age of Communications." 56 *Florida Bar Journal* 210 (1982).

Hagelin, T. M., and K. A. Wimmer, "Broadcast Deregulation and the Administrative Responsibility to Monitor Policy Change; An Empirical Study of the Elimination of Logging Requirements." 38 *Federal Communications Law Journal* 201 (1986).

McGregor, M. A., "Connections Among Deleted Underbrush Policies, FCC Character Standards, and State Criminal Law." 34 *Journal of Broadcasting & Electronic Media* 153 (1990).

Meisel, N. S., "The Equal Opportunity Doctrine: The Broadcast Executive Who Campaigns for Political Office Makes His Own Strange Bedfellow." 6 *Cardozo Arts & Entertainment Law Journal* 113 (1987).

Murchison, B. C., "Misrepresentation and the FCC." 37 *Federal Communications Law Journal* 403 (1985).

Naylor, Karen Sue, "Equal Time Equals Unequal Treatment to Newscaster Candidates." 9 *Loyola Entertainment Law Journal* 283 (1989).

Passler, R. G., "Carlin Revisited—What Does the Future Hold for the Seven 'Dirty' Words?" 65 *Tulane Law Review* 131 (1990).

Pfau, M., "A Channel Approach to Television Influence." 34 *Journal of Broadcasting & Electronic Media* 195 (1990).

Phillips, L. H., "Federal Preemption of Conflicting Telecommunications Regulations." 7 *Glendale Law Review* 141 (1987).

Pressler, L., and K. V. Schieffer, "A Proposal for Universal Telecommunications Service." 40 *Federal Communications Law Journal* 351 (1988).

Robinson, G. O., "The FCC in the Year 2000." 37 *Federal Communications Law Journal* 155 (1985).

Rubin, A. M., "Publication and the Flow of Information in Communication." 35 *Journal of Broadcasting & Electronic Media* 119 (1991).

Siff, A., "ISDNs: Shaping the New Networks That Might Reshape FCC Policies." 37 *Federal Communications Law Journal* 171 (1985).

Spaeth, S. M., "The Balance of Interests in Administrative Law and Telecommunications Regulation: Have We Broken the Scales?" 43 *Federal Communications Law Journal* 23 (1990).

chapter four

The Federal Trade Commission

While the Federal Communications Commission is the agency primarily responsible for regulating broadcasting and telecommunication, other federal agencies also play a role in the regulatory process. The Federal Trade Commission (FTC) has become increasingly concerned with the quality of broadcast advertising and in the early 1990s engaged in a renewed emphasis on enforcement and prosecution. The importance of the FTC in the study of broadcasting and telecommunication lies partially in the fact that the Federal Communications Commission during the deregulatory era of the Reagan presidency in the 1980s by default turned over to the FTC much of the enforcement responsibilities once shouldered by the FCC.[1] Former regulatory areas such as truth in advertising and the way stations promote and market themselves was left for the FTC and the various state statutes. Stations which knowingly participate in the creation of false and misleading advertising, and which fraudulently promote themselves through inflated ratings or extended coverage maps used in promotional brochures and advertising can fall under the enforcement arc of the FTC and state agencies. They may also open themselves up to civil litigation. Production companies which produce misleading program-length commercials can also come under FTC scrutiny.

SCOPE AND BACKGROUND OF THE FTC

The Federal Trade Commission is an agency charged with protecting the consumer, guarding against antitrust arrangements, and fostering competition in the marketplace. Its enforcement arm reaches into broadcast commercial programming because the FTC is charged with guarding against misleading commercials. When misleading commercials are aired, advertisers and advertising agencies come under FTC scrutiny. If the copy for a commercial is sold, written, and aired by a local television station, those who are engaged in selling, writing, and producing the commercial must understand the limits of responsible and truthful advertising, beyond which the Federal Trade Commission can become involved. Similarly, if that same station promotes itself through the use of inaccurate ratings data or artificially extends its coverage map in promotional literature, then an investigation by the FCC may also result in a notification to the Federal Trade Commission. When mergers of media companies are anticompetitive, then the FTC can step in and rule on antitrust grounds.

The Federal Trade Commission was formed in 1914 by enactment of the FTC Act. The act's purpose was succinctly stated in the phrase: "unfair methods of competition in commerce are hereby declared unlawful."[2] Closely related to the FTC Act was the Clayton Act, also passed in 1914, which guarded against corporate mergers that would lessen competition. Since 1914, the FTC Act has been amended many times. Some of the most familiar pieces of legislation are the 1966 Fair Packaging and Labeling Act and the 1969 Truth in Lending Act, which requires full disclosure of packaged contents and credit terms.

Like the Federal Communications Commission, the FTC has five commissioners, who are appointed by the president with the advice and consent of the Senate. No more than three commissioners can be from the same political party. The president designates a chairman. Of all the missions undertaken by the FTC, it is the consumer protection mission that impacts on the audience and users of broadcasting and telecommunication. From the marketing of cellular telephones to commercials for tanning salons, the FTC takes an enforceable interest in the way we do business.

THE CONSUMER PROTECTION MISSION OF THE FTC

The consumer protection mission of the FTC is directed by the agency's Bureau of Consumer Protection, which directs its efforts toward "eliminating unfair or deceptive acts or practices in or affecting commerce, with emphasis on those practices that may unreasonably restrict or inhibit the free exercise of consumer choice."[3]

Program Areas of Consumer Protection

The activities of the Consumer Protection Bureau of the FTC can be grouped into five "program" areas: (1) advertising practices, (2) marketing practices, (3) credit practices, (4) service industry practices, and (5) enforcement. Some overlap occurs between the different programs such as when an advertiser touts misleading credit terms and triggers attention from the advertising practices program, the marketing practices program, the credit practices program, and the enforcement arm. A basic understanding of FTC programs is necessary for consumers who respond to advertising and marketing and buy products and services. Such an understanding is also necessary for practicing professionals, some of whom are involved in broadcast sales. It is important to view the programs which follow as functions and practices, not the organizational-chart structure of the Federal Trade Commission.

Absolvement Clauses in Consent Agreements

The reader is alerted to the fact that coming under FTC scrutiny does *not* necessarily mean a company has engaged in any wrongdoing or violated any laws. Frequently an FTC public document will contain the names of companies which have engaged in trade practices the FTC has monitored, but the document may reflect activity at one stage of the monitoring or enforcement process only. Cases may also move on to other levels within the FTC, the U.S. Court of Appeals, or the U.S. Supreme Court, where a ruling may be overturned or modified.

Cases may also be withdrawn from adjudication by the commission at some point in a proceeding. Agreed-upon consent orders frequently contain the following language as part of an agreement between a respondent (company engaged in advertising, marketing, or selling a product or service) and the FTC:

> The respondent, its attorney, and counsel for the Commission having thereafter executed an agreement containing a consent order, an admission by the respondent of all the jurisdictional facts set forth in the complaint, a statement that the signing of said agreement is for settlement purposes only and does not constitute an admission by respondent that the law has been violated as alleged in such complaint . . . The Secretary of the Commission having thereafter withdrawn this matter from adjudication . . .[4]

Notice that the commission and the respondent accept jurisdictional facts in the case but the respondent does not admit to violating the law. The commission in turn withdraws the complaint from adjudication and settles the matter with a consent order between the respondent and the FTC. Notice also that the word *alleged* appears, which changes the meaning of the statement. The commission's order outlining the specific action to be taken by the respondent then follows.

Many companies which settle with the FTC through a consent order continue to do business and sell the same products or services, although the manner in which the product or service is advertised and marketed may have changed. Such orders do not necessarily mean anything is wrong with the product, but that scientific evidence did not exist to support the claims made in the advertisements and on that basis the FTC may have deemed the advertisements misleading. With this in mind, we'll begin our discussion with the advertising practices program of the Consumer Protection Bureau and in the next chapter will examine more closely specific FTC actions concerning advertising practices.

ADVERTISING PRACTICES

The advertising practices program is concerned with false and misleading advertising, both broadcast and print. It also monitors the claims made in advertising to assure that they are backed up by reputable tests and evidence. The FTC frequently enters into consent agreements with companies to cease and desist from making unsubstantiated claims in advertising. Alleged misrepresentation over such things as the range of cellular telephones, the ability of touch-tone phones to access allied services, diet supplements to enhance muscle growth, exaggerated savings on heating and cooling bills from heating and air-conditioning systems, and automobile fuel additives meeting established standards are just some of the advertising practices issues with which the FTC has dealt.

MARKETING PRACTICES

Marketing practices can involve advertising as well, but marketing practices also involve other functions in the movement of goods and services to consumers. The FTC describes its marketing practices mission with the statement: "to identify, halt, and redress injury caused by unfair and deceptive practices in the marketing and sale of a variety of products and services and to ensure that companies honor warranty and other contractual agreements."[5]

Cable Television Decoders and Cellular Telephones

Examples of marketing practices can be seen in a company selling cable television decoders and two companies selling telephone equipment.[6] The company selling cable decoders was required under FTC order to state in its sales catalogues that the unauthorized use of cable television equipment is against the law. A company selling cellular telephone equipment agreed not to "misrepresent the range of radiotelephone communication devices or their ability to transmit and receive messages simultaneously." The company was also prohibited from using such phrases as "up to" in range-related claims unless the range could be obtained "by an appreciable number of customers." A company selling telephone equipment agreed not to misrepresent its phones capabilities and disclose that its phones which looked like touch-tone phones only produced pulses like rotary phones. The agreement with the FTC prohibited the company "from misrepresenting the compatibility of its telephones with tone-accessed services, including alternative long-distance service and home-accessed computer services."

Cassette Tapes

Another example of marketing practices involved a marketer of cassette tapes which ended up agreeing to a federal court injunction as a settlement to a charge brought by the FTC that the company had falsely represented its plan where consumers paid from $1,260 to $1,700 to buy audio cassette tapes from a catalogue. "Under the injunction, the company agreed to pay refunds to certain customers and will not misrepresent any merchandise or services it offers."[7]

Broadcast Promotion and Sales

While a station's promotional advertisements fall under advertising, the practices engaged in by its sales staff are considered marketing. A promotional brochure containing misleading information about audience ratings or an extended coverage map which depicts the station as reaching an audience outside its true listening or viewing area would fall under marketing. Although a station manager may feel that the brochure goes to advertisers who are not sophisticated enough in their knowledge of coverage maps and audience ratings to cause a problem with the FTC, it is the competing station which gets a copy of the brochure and must compete in the marketplace against fraudulent promotional literature that can file the complaint and trigger the FTC inquiry. In theory, there is also nothing to stop a competing station from filing a complaint about a product commercial which they feel contains misleading statements of fact or claims which cannot be substantiated. Similarly, a competing product manufacturer, wholesaler, or retailer can file a complaint.

Salespersons and copy writers need to be alert to scientific claims which are not substantiated since these claims can fall under the FTC's marketing practices mission. A rug cleaner which claims in a commercial to remove blood when it won't and a diet supplement touted in a commercial to prevent cancer when it won't are commercials based on claims which are not substantiated and therefore constitute deceptive marketing as well as advertising.

Indirect Marketing Complaints

Indirect marketing problems can also arise. For example, if a broadcast commercial talks about a local club membership which permits the local member to have access to affiliate clubs in other locations and names the locations, then the local member should be able to gain access to those affiliate clubs. If they cannot because the affiliate club in another city will not honor the local membership, then the commercial copy needs to be changed, to say nothing of the sales practices which sold unsuspecting consumers on the affiliate membership privileges. Similarly, misrepresenting club membership fees as "dues" when in fact the prospective member ends up signing an undisclosed high-interest rate finance company contract which may be resold, go to a collection agency, or even small claims court and negatively affect the consumer's credit rating is a serious matter. If the misleading commercial copy is written by the station copy writer, the station may also find itself needing legal counsel.

State Consumer Protection Statutes

Many state consumer protection laws are quite strong and can provide for triple damages to consumers who are the victims of fraudulent marketing practices. In some states, even acting in good faith will not protect the business or its representatives from being held liable for misrepresentation. Broadcast sales personnel and copy writers should be knowledgeable in their state's consumer protection laws to protect themselves and their clients. Usually prompt restitution will help resolve a matter, but if a finance company has prepaid the cost of goods or services or the provider itself has engaged the unsuspecting consumer in a finance company contract, then the issue may become more difficult since the finance company may argue the binding language of the contract. Such dilemmas can put the station in the middle between their client and the consumer, especially if the consumer claims they heard about the product or service through the station's commercials.

Small-Claims Court Records

Sometimes it's a good idea to peruse the records of small claims court in a local community to see if certain types of businesses are using the court on a regular basis to collect debts from consumers who may have been unsuspecting victims of questionable sales practices. Such information, especially if a pattern exists, should alert the sales department that problems could develop with the account, either in the area of trade practices or possibly in getting paid for the commercials the station airs. Station news departments may also find interesting business-beat stories from small claims court as well as the public records of the state attorney general.[8]

CREDIT PRACTICES

Credit practices concern such areas as the full disclosure of credit terms required by law, the truthful representation of credit terms in sales, marketing, and advertising, and the collection of debts and the operation of credit systems. Broadcast salespeople need to be alert to state and federal credit disclosure laws which many times require such information as annual percentage rates and payout periods to be included in broadcast as well as print commercials. The federal Truth in Lending Act, the wording of which is copied in many state laws permitting the state attorney general to prosecute offenders, has important applications to the wording of broadcast as well as print commercials.

SERVICE INDUSTRY PRACTICES

The FTC's service industry practices program concentrates on furthering informed consumer choice and increasing the availability of "less expensive, safe and reliable services and products that consumers desire."[9] The program is also interested in facilitating "fair competitive opportunities for smaller manufacturers in the standards-setting process; and reduce consumer losses based on false or misleading information."[10]

Professional Trade Associations

A professional trade association's restrictions against advertising by its members is an example of a service industry practice that can incur FTC scrutiny. Broadcast advertising by professionals is not new and has been around since early radio, but over the years as more and more professionals began to advertise and as radio and television made more of an impact on our lives, some professional associations stepped in and became involved in restricting both the practice and content of advertising by professionals.

An example of restrictive advertising by professionals involved the Wyoming Board of Podiatry, the state association for certifying foot doctors. The FTC secured an agreement, the terms of which stopped the board from prohibiting its members from engaging in truthful advertising. An FTC report of the agreement stated that under the agreement the board could not "restrict or discourage podiatrists from truthfully advertising their goods and services by adopting rules or policies prohibiting such advertising, by suspending or revoking a podiatrist's license as a result of such advertising, or by declaring such advertising illegal or unethical."[11]

In another action the FTC stepped in when the Rhode Island Board of Accountancy was involved in the adoption of prohibitive measures restricting advertising by Certified Public Accounts.[12] In still another action the FTC ordered the American Academy of Optometry not to restrict its "members" and "prospective members" from engaging in truthful advertising. The academy was not restricted from adopting reasonable standards to guard against false or deceptive advertising.[13] Similar actions by the FTC have involved professional trade associations in other states.

Some professional associations and their members may feel that the advertising of certain professional services demeans a profession and its members, and some poorly produced broadcast commercials do, but that doesn't mean that truthful advertising of professional services can be prohibited. Today, it is not uncommon to see dentists, lawyers, chiropractors, and other professionals advertising their services on radio and television. While in the past most professionals were not the place broadcast salespeople would go to sell advertising, FTC actions have opened up the service industry to competition, and advertising is part of that competition. With the exception of businesses that are illegal, few restrictions exist on advertising if it is truthful.

Application Services for Cellular Telephone Systems

Other types of services also fall under the FTC's watch.[14] For example, application-preparation services for cellular telephone frequencies garnered FTC attention and the commission obtained a temporary restraining order against one company charged with misleading potential investors about the chance and profit potential of winning FCC lotteries for the right to build cellular telephone systems. The FTC also instituted criminal contempt proceedings against the company officers. In a similar case involving a group of related companies engaged in the same type business, the FTC obtained an order to require the defendants to establish a $400,000 fund to pay for the preparation of such applications and a company officer was fined $100,000.

ENFORCEMENT: THE INVESTIGATION PROCESS

The real power of the FTC lies in enforcement. In general terms the enforcement functions are designed to promote "a free and competitive market in which consumers can obtain and make use of truthful purchasing information and benefit from fair market practices."[15] At the root of the enforcement program is the investigatory process.[16] Here, the FTC can initiate an investigation on its own initiative or at the request of another party, which may issue an official complaint against an advertising claim or other trade practice. During the investigation, the commission can issue subpoenas or orders requiring persons to testify as well as produce documents. Anyone who is subpoenaed can file an opposition to the order or subpoena within ten days. The FTC can also hold investigative hearings and can order depositions to be taken.

ENFORCEMENT: AVAILABLE REMEDIES

The commission has at its disposal various remedies to correct what it may consider fraudulent trade practices. They include:

Assurance of Voluntary Compliance (Non-Adjudicative)

If the Commission believes the public interest will be fully safeguarded, it may dispose of a matter under investigation by accepting a promise that the questioned practice will be discontinued. A number of factors are considered by the Commission in the rare cases in which it accepts such a promise, including (1) the nature and gravity of the practice in question, and (2) the prior record and good faith of the party.[17]

Consent Order

Instead of litigating a complaint, a respondent may execute an appropriate agreement containing an order for consideration by the Commission. If the agreement is accepted by the Commission, the order is placed on the public record for sixty (60) days during which time comments or views concerning the order may be filed by any interested persons. Upon receipt of such comments or views, the Commission may withdraw its acceptance and set the matter down for a formal proceeding, issue the complaint and order in accordance with the agreement, or take such action as it may consider appropriate. Respondents in consent orders do not admit violations of the law, but such orders have the same force and effect as adjudicative orders.[18]

Adjudicative Order

An adjudicative order is based on evidence of record obtained during an adjudicative proceeding which starts when a complaint is issued. The proceeding is conducted before an Administrative Law Judge who serves as the initial trier of facts. After the hearings the judge within 90 days issues his initial decision, which is subject to review by the Commission on the motion of either party or on the Commission's own motion. Appeals from a final Commission decision and order may be made to any proper Court of Appeals and ultimately to the Supreme Court.[19]

Preliminary Injunctions

The Federal Trade Commission has statutory authority to seek preliminary injunctive relief in Federal district court against anyone who is violating or about to violate any provision of law enforced by the FTC.[20]

FILING AN FTC COMPLAINT

To better understand the FTC's enforcement process, let's imagine that you have received a complaint from the FTC, alleging that your company is falsely advertising through radio and television commercials a product it manufactures.[21]

The Letter

The first notice you would probably receive from the FTC would be a letter. You would then have the opportunity to reply to that letter and explain your position. The FTC at this point may decide that your arguments have merit and simply decide not to pursue. But if the FTC is not satisfied with your arguments, it may proceed to subpoena all pertinent files, such as the details of any product testing you may have undertaken.

Examining Files

If the files clearly show your claims not to be deceptive, then the FTC may consider your case closed. If, on the other hand, it is not content with your test results and still feels the advertising to be deceptive, the beginning of a negotiation process begins.

Negotiation

Two developments will normally take place during this phase. First, you may offer a consent order, stating that you will agree to remedy the problem, perhaps by taking your commercials off the air. The FTC then has an opportunity either to accept or to reject your consent agreement. If the commission accepts your agreement, it will be placed on the public record for 60 days. During that time, other parties can file pro or con comments on the agreement. If the evidence builds up against you, the FTC can withdraw from the consent agreement and begin formal proceedings.[22] If the consent order is signed, that usually ends the matter.

Issuing the Complaint

Let us assume that the evidence built up against you during the 60-day period was substantial, and that the FTC decides to proceed to issue a complaint. An administrative law judge rules on that complaint. The law judge issues a decision, which is then reviewed by the FTC commissioners.

Once again, you have two options. The FTC can decide either (1) to affirm or modify the decision of the law judge or (2) to dismiss the complaint. We'll assume that it was not your lucky day, and that the FTC decided to uphold the decision of the administrative law judge, which was to prohibit you from using the commercials in any future advertising. Once again, you have two choices.

The Option of Appeal

You can either accept the FTC decision and tell your ad agency to use new commercials, or you can tell your lawyers to appeal the FTC decision to the U.S. Court of Appeals. Regardless of which decision you make, one thing is certain: The road to the court has been both long and rough. You undoubtedly spent large sums of money fighting the case through the FTC, and you will now face additional expense in the appeals process. Keep in mind that although you may feel as though you have been overwhelmed by the power of a federal agency, the FTC would contend that such safeguards are for the benefit of the public. For the FTC, enforcement powers are a stern warning to advertisers to see that their advertising, marketing, and other practices meet the standards of truth and accuracy.

Maintaining Competition: Television Sports Contracts

In addition to its consumer protection efforts, the FTC is also the federal agency charged with assuring competition in the marketplace. The commission, through its Bureau of Competition, monitors a number of business practices including mergers and international antitrust, which is becoming more important as we move toward a global economy.

Television sports contracts fall under the umbrella of the FTC and in the early 1990s the FTC challenged college football television contracts. In its complaint the commission specifically zeroed in on Capital Cities/ABC and the College Football Association claiming the contract restricted competition and reduced the selection of games from consumers.[23] The contract worth a reported $215 million dollars involved more than 60 members of the CFA and football games contracted to be televised through 1995. It was not the first time television sports contracts had been involved in regulatory scrutiny. In 1984 the U.S. Supreme Court ruled that the National Collegiate Athletic Association violated antitrust laws by acting as "the sole, mandatory negotiating agent for all college teams in the bargaining for television rights."[24]

MERGERS

The FTC stepped into the recording industry and obtained a consent order from a group of record companies planning mergers to obtain prior FTC approval first, and to notify the FTC about any distribution agreements which were planned.[25] A better understanding of how the FTC approaches mergers can be seen by examining the actual text of the consent order.

A Proposed Merger and Trade of Commerce

The companies involved in the proposed merger were Warner Communications Inc., Warner Bros. Records, Inc., (collectively "Warner"), Chappell & Co., Inc., and PolyGram Records, Inc. (collectively "PolyGram").

> Warner and PolyGram have agreed to merge their prerecorded music business in the U.S. and in the rest of the world. In the United States, Warner will transfer its recorded music assets to the respondent Warner Bros. Records, Inc. PolyGram will transfer its prerecorded music business to respondent Chappell & Co. These two corporations will then merge, and the surviving corporation, Warner-PolyGram, Inc., will then issue new stock . . . The relevant product market in which to assess the competitive effects of the merger is the market for prerecorded music. The relevant geographic market in which to assess the competitive effects on the merger is the United States. The relevant market is moderately concentrated. Barriers to entry into the distribution of the relevant product are substantial. Both Warner and PolyGram are substantial competitors in the relevant product and geographic markets.[26]

The FTC contended that the effects of the proposed merger would have the potential to "substantially lessen competition or tend to create a monopoly" in the marketplace.

Effects of the Merger and Order

The possible effects of the merger as listed in the consent order would:

> Eliminate substantial actual competition between Warner and PolyGram in the relevant market;
>
> Eliminate substantial potential competition between Warner and PolyGram;
>
> Eliminate substantial actual and potential competition between the other companies engaged in the distribution of the relevant product; and
>
> Significantly increase the level of industry concentration in the relevant market.[27]

The order called for Warner to terminate all agreements related to the merger and to cease and desist from "acquiring, directly or indirectly, without prior approval of the Federal Trade Commission, any interest in, or any stock, share capital or assets of any major record company . . ."[28]

This particular example involved the merger of companies controlling the recording industry, but the FTC has the authority to enter into any proposed merger if there is reason to believe the merger would affect competition. That competition, accompanied by controls over the content of advertising, is designed to assure that consumers receive the most value for their dollar in a marketplace that remains competitive.

TRUTH IN ADVERTISING

Our attention now turns to cases that have been investigated by the FTC. It is in this arena of adjudication, of consent orders, of a company's doing business in the marketplace, that a much deeper understanding of FTC operations takes place. Of those areas with which the FTC deals, truth in advertising is the most visible, and to the consumer, one of the most important.

Agreed Limits of Admitted Liability

Keep in mind the point made earlier that while the companies involved in our discussions have engaged in practices which resulted in FTC actions, those companies may *not* have been guilty, or found guilty of violating the law. In addition, some have corrected practices which originally resulted in FTC actions and remain in business with revised advertising and marketing strategies, fully complying, ethically and legally, with the spirit of the Federal Trade Commission Act, under which the FTC operates.

In addition, remember that consent orders are frequently used by the FTC to engage an advertiser in an agreement which would require the advertiser to cease and desist from practices the FTC deems unacceptable. Such orders are powerful in themselves as a means of convincing an advertiser to change or stop a particular advertising or marketing strategy. The option of consent orders can also result in an issue being resolved very early in the negotiation process and eliminate the need for the Bureau of Consumer Protection to press the issue to a higher level in the commission or the courts. FTC consent orders typically contain a paragraph that reads:

> The respondent, its attorney, and counsel for the Commission having thereafter executed an agreement containing a consent order, an admission by the respondent of all the jurisdictional facts set forth in the complaint, a statement that *the signing of said agreement is for settlement purposes only and does not constitute an admission by respondent that the law has been violated as alleged in such complaint* . . . The Secretary of the Commission having thereafter withdrawn this matter from adjudication . . . (italics added)[29]

In reading the cases presented in this chapter, the preceding statement should be kept in mind. In the first example which follows, the FTC took action against a company advertising and selling ultrasonic pest control devices that claimed to use ultrasonic sound waves to eliminate pests. In addition to print material, television and radio commercials advertised the "Homefree" pest control device.

Product Television Commercial

The television commercial used to advertise the pest control device included a scene inside a home with a man and woman actor. The terms and abbreviations used in the story-boarded (artist's preliminary drawings with script arranged in a series of frames) script for the television commercial that follows refer to production elements used in producing the commercial: VIDEO is what appears on the television screen, SFX is the sound accompanying the video, ANNCR is the announcer's voice, "Pan" means to move the camera horizontally, SUPER is to superimpose words over the video, and TAG is the ending statement.

In the actual television commercial all of the production elements are merged into a cohesive artistic whole. The wording and capitalization of the following script is the way it appears in the Federal Trade Commission exhibit attached to the proceeding. Read the television and radio commercials as if you were a consumer considering the purchase of one of the pest control devices.

> VIDEO: CLOSE-UP of man, eyes rolling
>
> SFX: Loud buzzing . . . then SLAP!
>
> ANNCR: "Tired of being bugged by bugs? Fight back with the new electronic pest control that gets rid of fleas, flies, bugs, and . . ."
>
> VIDEO: Camera catches a dog scratching; man next to dog (also scratching)
>
> SFX: woman's scratching
>
> ANNCR: ". . . even rats and mice."
>
> VIDEO: Woman on chair
>
> ANNCR: "When you plug in HOMEFREE, the ultrasonic sound drives 'em right out of your house."
>
> VIDEO: Blank wall with AC outlet.
>
> ANNCR: "HOMEFREE keeps your home free from bugs, insects, rats, and mice . . ."
>
> VIDEO: Pan and Beauty shot in room.[30]
>
> ANNCR: ". . . and is safe for kids and pets. No harmful poisons or sprays to worry about."
>
> VIDEO: Family enjoying their peace in the room.
>
> SUPER: 100% non-toxic
>
> TAG: "HOMEFREE—The Ultrasonic Pest Control Available at . . ."
>
> VIDEO: Tight Beauty Shot, list of stores.[31]

In addition to the television commercial and print material, two radio commercials were also part of the marketing plan.

Product Radio Commercials

Two similar radio commercials were used as exhibits by the commission to illustrate advertising practices used by the manufacturer. With the tag line of 5 seconds, each has a running time of 60 seconds. The first commercial reads:

> LISTEN CAREFULLY. YOU ARE ABOUT TO HEAR THE SOUND OF A REVOLUTION IN HOME PEST CONTROL. THE SOUND OF ULTRASONIC WAVES UNLEASHED BY THE HOMEFREE ULTRASONIC PEST CONTROL SYSTEM. ARE YOU LISTENING? HERE WE GO: (THREE-FOUR SECONDS SILENCE) YOU DIDN'T HEAR IT, DID YOU? YOU WON'T. AND YOUR KIDS AND PETS WON'T. BUT FLEAS, FLIES, BUGS, EVEN RATS AND MICE WILL. AND THAT SOUND WE CAN'T HEAR, WILL DRIVE THEM CRAZY, AND OUT OF YOUR HOUSE FOR GOOD. THE HOMEFREE BLANKETS YOUR HOME WITH HIGH FREQUENCY SOUND ONLY PESTS, BUGS, AND RODENTS CAN HEAR. HOMEFREE COMBINED SCIENCE AND ELECTRONICS TO CREATE A PEST CONTROL SYSTEM THAT IS EFFECTIVE, AND EASY TO USE. ALL YOU DO IS PLUG IT IN. AND REMEMBER, YOU CAN'T HEAR IT WORK. YOU CAN ONLY SEE THE RESULTS! HOMEFREE ULTRASONIC.[32]

The second commercial is similar to the first. Read it as though you were considering buying the product.

> LISTEN VERY CAREFULLY. YOU ARE ABOUT TO HEAR THE SOUND OF THE HOMEFREE UNLTRASONIC PEST CONTROL SYSTEM HARD AT WORK, DRIVING BUGS AND RODENTS CRAZY, AND OUT OF YOUR HOUSE FOR GOOD. ARE YOU LISTENING? HERE IT IS: (THREE-FOUR SECONDS SILENCE) YOU DIDN'T HEAR IT, DID YOU? YOU WON'T. AND YOUR KIDS AND PETS WON'T. BUT FLEAS, FLIES, BUGS, EVEN RATS AND MICE WILL. AND THAT SOUND THAT WE CAN'T HEAR, IRRITATES THEM SO MUCH, THEY LEAVE YOUR HOME IN DROVES. THE HOMEFREE BLANKETS YOUR HOME WITH HIGH FREQUENCY ULTRASONIC WAVES THAT ONLY PESTS, BUGS AND RODENTS CAN HEAR. BY COMBINING SCIENCE AND ELECTRONICS, HOMEFREE HAS MADE PEST CONTROL EFFECTIVE, AND EASY TO USE. NO CHEMICALS, ODORS, OR SPILLS. ALL YOU DO IS PLUG IT IN. AND REMEMBER, YOU CAN'T HEAR IT WORK.

YOU CAN ONLY SEE THE RESULTS. HOMEFREE ULTRASONIC.[33]

Based on the three broadcast commercials and print material used to market the pest control device, the FTC obtained a consent order requiring the firm to stop marketing the device and prohibiting it from "making any performance or efficacy claims about any ultrasonic pest-control product unless it possesses and relies on competent and reliable evidence that substantiates its claims."[34] An understanding of how a federal agency prepares its argument in such a case is seen in a series of steps leading to the actual order issued by the commission.

The Complaint

The complaint stating the alleged violation includes the jurisdictional phrase giving the commission the power to act in the matter. In this case the company is identified as doing business under the laws of the State of California and that respondent (the company) "at all times mentioned herein, has maintained a substantial course of business, including the acts and practices as hereinafter set forth, which are in or affecting commerce, as [commerce] is defined in the Federal Trade Commission Act."[35] The complaint goes on to allege as stated in the FTC record (subheadings are added to, and paragraph references are deleted from the original document):

> In the course and conduct of its business, and for the purpose of inducing the purchase of the Homefree ultrasonic pest control product, respondent has disseminated, directly and through its marketers and distributors, various promotional materials, including suggested advertisements, sales brochures and promotional pamphlets, which contain statements respecting the performance of the Homefree ultrasonic pest control product. Examples of such promotional materials, which include the Homefree package, are attached hereto as Exhibits.
>
> **Advertised Claims**
>
> Through the use of statements referred to . . . and others not specifically set forth therein, respondent has represented, and is now representing, directly or by implication, that use of the Homefree:
>
> a. Eliminates rats, mice, cockroaches, and other pests from a purchaser's home or place of business.
> b. Eliminates rodents and insects from a purchaser's home or place of business within four to six weeks or sooner.
> c. Prevents rodents and insects from remaining in or entering an area in a purchaser's home or place of business where the Homefree device is in use.
>
> **Statement of Truth and Fact**
>
> In truth and in fact, use of the Homefree:
>
> a. Does not eliminate rats, mice, cockroaches, and other pests from a purchaser's home or place of business.
> b. Does not eliminate rodents and insects from a purchaser's home or place of business within four to six weeks or sooner.
> c. Does not prevent rodents or insects from remaining in or entering an area in a purchaser's home or place of business where the Homefree device is in use.
>
> Therefore, the representations set forth . . . were, and are, false and misleading.
>
> **Additional Claims**
>
> Alleging further violation of Section 5 of the Federal Trade Commission Act, the allegations . . . are incorporated by reference herein. Through the use of statements referred to . . . and others not expressly set out therein, respondent has represented, and is now representing, directly or by implication, that use of the Homefree:
>
> a. Effectively controls rats and mice in the home or place of business.
> b. Effectively controls insects, such as cockroaches, in the home or place of business.
> c. Eliminates the need to use, in the home or place of business, alternative rodent or insect control products such as traps, powders, sprays or other chemicals.
>
> **Statement of Truth and Fact**
>
> In truth and in fact, use of the Homefree:
>
> a. Does not effectively control rats and mice in the home or place of business. Any

reaction by rodents to the Home Free would, at best, only be of short duration. Rodents habituate to ultrasound and will return to their chosen nesting or feeding habitats even in the presence of such ultrasonic products.

b. Does not effectively control insects, such as cockroaches, in the home or place of business.

c. Does not eliminate the need to use, in the home or place of business, alternative rodent or insect control products such as traps, powders, sprays, or other chemicals.

Therefore, the representations set forth . . . were, and are, false and misleading.

Reasonable Basis—Substantiation

Alleging further violation of . . . the Federal Trade Commission Act, the allegations . . . are incorporated by reference herein.

Through the use of the statements referred to . . . and others not expressly set out therein, respondent has represented and is now representing, directly or by implication, that at the time of making the representations set forth . . . respondent possessed and relied upon a reasonable basis for those representations.

In truth and in fact, at such times, respondent did not possess and rely upon a reasonable basis for making those representations.

Therefore, the representation set forth . . . is, false and misleading.

The use by respondent of the aforesaid representations . . . and the placement, in the hands of distributors and retailers, of promotional materials through which others may have conveyed those representations, have had the tendency and capacity to mislead consumers and to induce the purchase of respondent's ultrasonic pest control products.

The acts and practices of respondent, as herein alleged, constituted, and now constitute unfair and deceptive acts or practices in or affecting commerce in violation of Section 5 of the Federal Trade Commission Act. The acts and practices of respondent, as herein alleged, are continuing and will continue in the absence of the relief herein requested.[36]

We can see from reading the FTC's case that the advertising copy played a key role in the commission's intervention. The claims of the manufacturer were based on the ability of the device to both eliminate and control pests by ultrasonic sound, and these claims were, by the FTC's contention, implied in the commercial copy. Based on the advertising copy, and the unsubstantiated claims made in the advertising, the FTC imposed a cease and desist order reading:

Cease-and-Desist Orders: Advertising

It is ordered, That respondent . . . do forthwith cease and desist from:

A. Representing, directly or by implication, that the Home Free or any other ultrasonic pest control product will:
   (1) eliminate cockroaches, rats, mice or other pests from a home or place of business;
   (2) eliminate rodents or insects from a home or place of business within four to six weeks, or within any other specified period of time;
   (3) protect an area where said product is in use in a home or place of business from rodents or insects, or will cause an area to be free of rodents or insects; or
   (4) serve as an effective alternative to the use of conventional products such as sprays, powders, traps or other chemicals in providing protection from insect and rodent infestation.

Cease and Desist Order: Unsubstantiated Claims

B. Representing, directly or by implication, any performance characteristic of any ultrasonic pest control product, unless at the time of making such representation respondent possesses and relies upon competent and reliable evidence which substantiates the representation. Evidence in the form of tests, experiments, analyses, research studies, or other evaluations shall be competent and reliable only if they are conducted in an objective manner by persons qualified to do so, using procedures generally accepted in the relevant professions or sciences to yield accurate, reliable, and reproducible results.

C. Representing, directly or by implication, that any ultrasonic pest control product is effective in providing protection from insect or rodent infestation in a home or place of business, unless at the time of making such representation respondent possesses and relies upon competent and reliable evidence which either directly relates to such home or place of business use conditions, or which can properly be applied to such conditions. Evidence in the form of tests, experiments, analyses, research studies, or other evaluations shall be competent and reliable only if they are conducted in an objective manner by persons qualified to do so, using procedure generally accepted in the relevant professions or sciences to yield accurate, reliable, and reproducible results.[37]

Notice that the cease and desist order covering advertising is based partially on alleged claims of the effectiveness of the pest-control device. Moreover, strict guidelines exist over what qualifies as a substantiated claim. Simply conducting an uncontrolled experiment, the unreliable results of which are then used to substantiate a claim, is not acceptable. As stated in the case of the pest-control device, evidence of a product's worth shall be based on competent and reliable tests "only if they are conducted in an objective manner by persons qualified to do so."[38] Such tests must also be conducted using generally accepted procedures.

Notification to Consumers

In addition to the cease and desist order the FTC also took exceptionally strong action in this case and required the company to issue a widely disseminated and prominently displayed notice to consumers stating that "THE FEDERAL TRADE COMMISSION HAS CHARGED THAT SUCH DEVICES ARE NOT EFFECTIVE FOR THE PURPOSES ADVERTISED."[39] The company was required to print the notice on tablets in sufficient quantities to meet expected consumer demand, and provide the tablets to each distributor and retail establishment that had been engaged in selling the devices.

The company was ordered to "take all steps necessary" to also place the notices in the public areas of the retail establishments where the notices would be most likely to be seen by customers. The commission even specified the notice was to be a wall poster at least 8-1/2 × 11 inches in size with 24-point type.

The consent decree required the notices to be placed in the Sunday edition of the newspapers in the local communities where the pest-control devices had been sold. In every community where the pest-control devices had been advertised in newspapers, magazines, radio, or television, the notice was to appear prominently in the newspaper of greatest general circulation.

Consumer Refunds and Reporting Requirements

The company was required under the consent decree to provide refunds to consumers who had purchased the pest-control devices directly, or to retailers who had sold the devices. The consent order also provided the FTC with a monitoring system to assure future compliance with the consent decree. The company was required to advise the commission in writing of the location and number of notices which had been placed in accordance with the order. In addition the company was required to provide a summary report of the consumer redress program which included a tabulation of the number of consumers who requested refunds and the dollar amount of the refunds. The company was also required to provide the FTC with the names and addresses of those who received reimbursements and to circulate a copy of the order to all of the present and future managerial employees of the company, its distributors, and independent sales agents.

What began as a business to sell technology to unsuspecting consumers ended with an FTC consent order. This particular case was more involved than most and the penalties for the company were time consuming, to say nothing of the implications for lost income.

ADVERTISING NONPRESCRIPTION DRUGS

Most of us have heard the term *ibuprofen* used in radio and television commercials. One such commercial for a drug store chain became an exhibit in a Federal Trade Commission case which charged Walgreen Co., the owners of Walgreen stores, with falsely advertising the over-the-counter drug Advil.

A Radio Commercial

Some of that advertising included the radio commercial for Advil reading (capitalizations and underlines are included in the original script as an exhibit in the proceeding):

> Here's good news for pain sufferers. One of the world's *most-prescribed* pain relievers—known to millions as Ibuprofen—is now available *without* a prescription, at Walgreens! Now you can buy it under the brand name *ADVIL*—spelled *A-D-V-I-L*—*ADVIL* for the temporary relief of minor arthritis pain . . . headaches and toothaches . . . muscle and backaches . . . and menstrual cramps. *ADVIL* . . . a highly effective, non-narcotic, anti-inflammatory pain reliever. *ADVIL* . . . now available *without* a prescription, at Walgreens![40]

The phrases of keenest interest to the FTC were the statements reading, "One of the world's *most-prescribed* pain relievers—known to millions as Ibuprofen—is now available *without* a prescription, at Walgreens! . . . ADVIL. . . . a highly effective, non-narcotic, anti-inflammatory pain reliever" (italics substituted for underlines in the actual text of the FTC proceeding).[41]

Material Representations

The FTC said, in singling out these and other phrases from other advertisements, that Walgreen's had "made the following material representations, directly or by implication:"[42]

a. Consumers can substitute "Advil, in over-the-counter dose levels, for prescription ibuprofen, because when so substituted, "Advil" provides all the same therapeutic benefits to consumers as prescription ibuprofen.

b. "Advil," in over-the-counter dose levels, provides anti-inflammatory benefit to consumers.[43]

The FTC considered the statements made in Walgreen's advertisements as false and misleading because, according to the FTC, Walgreen's did not have a basis to make the representations which were stated in their advertisements.[44]

Cease-and-Desist Order and Clinical Testing Requirements

The commission sought a consent decree containing a cease-and-desist order requiring Walgreen's to stop representing:

A. That any such product can be substituted by consumers, in over-the-counter dose levels, for a prescription form of the product, because when so substituted such product provides all of the same therapeutic benefits to consumers as the FDA-approved label indications for the prescription form of the product, unless at the time of making the representation respondent possesses and relies upon a reasonable basis substantiating such representation. Except as otherwise permitted by the provisions of paragraph IV hereinbelow, such reasonable basis shall consist of at least two adequate and well-controlled double-blinded clinical studies which conform to acceptable designs and protocols and are conducted by different persons independently of each other. Such persons shall be qualified by training and experience to conduct such studies.

B. That any such product provides anti-inflammatory benefits for arthritis or other conditions unless at the time of making the representation respondent possesses and relies upon a reasonable basis substantiating such representation. Except as otherwise permitted by the provisions of paragraph IV hereinbelow, such reasonable basis shall consist of at least two adequate and well-controlled double-blinded clinical studies which conform to acceptable designs and protocols and are conducted by different persons independently of each other. Such persons shall be qualified by training and experience to conduct such studies.[45]

Compare the order in the case of Walgreen's versus the order in the case of the pest-control device. Testing procedures for prescription and nonprescription drugs are much more standardized than for ultrasonic pest-control devices, and that is clearly articulated in the wording of the commercial for Advil. A copy writer preparing a commercial for a nonprescription drug can innocently make the mistake of claiming the drug is more effective than it is. Such terms as *nonprescription, doses, prescription strength,* and other phrases must be used with care when writing commercial copy for over-the-counter drugs.

ENFORCING WARNING LABELS

Numerous products in the marketplace require warning labels. We are probably most familiar with the warning label on a pack of cigarettes which warns against the dangers of smoking. Different federal agencies patrol the use of warning labels. The Food and Drug Administration is one such agency. Even where FDA warning labels are concerned, however, the advertising and marketing of a product comes under FTC jurisdiction when the advertising may circumvent the spirit of the warning labels. Two cases in point both concern the advertising of tanning devices.

Safety Claims

In separate cases two radio commercials, in addition to other advertising, were employed by two diffferent companies to market tanning devices which made safety claims. The first radio commercial, that could be adapted to different locations and operators, read (capitalizations and underlines are as they appeared in the original commercial as exhibited as evidence in the FTC proceeding):

> **Beautiful Tan!**
>
> (Theme established under)
>
> Getting a tan can be fun and easy! *(NAME)* is proud to announce that they are open and ready for business in *(Town)* at *(address).*
>
> *(Name)* features an exclusive European tanning process. There are no dangers of overexposure or burning that other tanning salon treatments bring! There are no boring stand-up sessions at *(name)*! You can be in luxury on our special SunBed while our SAFE built in lamps make you beautifully brown! You can look good all summer long! Let *(name)* help you keep your tan all year long! Call soon for your appointment.[46]

The second radio commercial for a tanning device marketed by a different company, which was a party to a separate FTC proceeding, also made safety claims. The radio commercial read (capitalizations and underlines are as they appeared in the original commercial as exhibited as evidence in the FTC proceeding):

> Here's something you really should know if you're searching for that perfect suntan! Doctors the world over warn constantly against over exposing your skin to sunlight! The sun sears, bakes, and burns the skin. It adds wrinkles and creases, and even the finest sunscreens can't protect you from that! So how do you avoid skin damage? Drop into *NAME. NAME* takes you out of the sun and tans you in minutes, *not* hours! *NAME,* using the Silver system, will tan you deeper and more safely than anything under the sun. The Silver tanning system filters out the UV-B rays the sun emits, the rays that scorch the skin, and intensifies the UV-A rays that tan the skin! Want the perfect tan? Introduce yourself to the Silver *tanning* system at *NAME*! Or call *NAME* at *PHONE NUMBER*! That's *NAME*! There's nothing like it under the sun![47]

The FTC objected to many of the claims made by the tanning systems, but singled out the phrase from the first commercial which read, "You can lie in luxury on our special SunBed while our SAFE built in lamps make you beautifully brown!"[48] In the second commercial the FTC singled out the phrase, "Silver system will tan you deeper and more safely than anything under the sun."[49]

Representations Versus Truth and Fact

For the two companies marketing tanning devices, the FTC challenged a number of claims made in both the radio commercials presented here as well as in other advertising engaged in by the two firms. Among the statements and depictions the FTC took issue with were claims that the tanning devices could not contribute to skin cancer, that the tanning devices could be used without protective eye wear (a claim made in one nonbroadcast advertisement), that the tanning device could not contribute to skin aging, and that the tanning devices could be used without the risk of any harmful side effects associated with the sun.[50]

The FTC countered with the statements that in truth and in fact the tanning devices could cause skin cancer, could not be used without protective eye wear, could contribute to skin aging, and were in fact associated with the harmful side effects of the sun.[51]

Required Warning Order

For both firms, the FTC issued an order requiring advertisements to contain reference to the mandatory FDA warning label found on tanning devices. The FTC order read in part:

> *It is further ordered,* That commencing one year after the date of service of this order respondent . . . a corporation, its successors and assigns, and its officers, agents, representatives, and employees, directly or through any corporation, subsidiary, division or other device, in connection with the advertising, offering for sale, sale or distribution of any tanning device, in or affecting commerce, as "commerce" is defined in the Federal Trade Commission Act, do forthwith cease and desist from making in any print advertisement, film, video tape or any other promotional material any representation, directly or by implication, that the tanning device is safe or safer than other devices or methods of tanning or that the device has health benefits unless the following statement is given:
>
> NOTICE—Read the mandatory FDA warning label found on every tanning machine for important information on potential eye injury, skin cancer, skin aging and photosensitive reactions.
>
> The above-required language shall be included in printed material printed in a typeface and color that are clear and conspicuous, and, in multipage documents, shall appear on the cover or first page; and in any film, video tape, or slide promotional material shall be included either orally or visually in a manner designed to ensure clarity and prominence; provided, further, that nothing contrary to, inconsistent with, or in mitigation of the above-required statement shall be used in any advertising or promotional materials.[52]

In addition to making reference to the mandatory Food and Drug Administration warning, the FTC order required the firms to distribute a copy of the order to such people and businesses as dealers, distributors, health clubs, beauty salons, and catalogue houses.

ENDORSEMENTS IN ADVERTISING

The "Rotation Diet" received a great deal of attention when it was announced as a weight reduction program that would permit you to diet only three days a week, for four days "be entirely free to eat whatever you want," and still lose weight.[53] If you think the idea sounds good, you aren't alone. According to one radio commercial, over 100,000 people were on the diet. The radio commercial read:

> PLEASE GET A PENCIL AND STAND BY.
>
> I'M GOING TO TELL YOU ABOUT AN EXCITING NEW DIET THAT IS SWEEPING THE COUNTRY. THERE ARE NOW OVER 100,000 PEOPLE ON THE ROTATION DIET—AND THESE PEOPLE ARE LOSING POUNDS WHILE EATING WHATEVER THEY WANT 4 DAYS EVERY WEEK.
>
> THAT'S RIGHT! ON THE ROTATION DIET EVERY TUESDAY, THURSDAY, SATURDAY AND SUNDAY ARE FREE DAYS WHEN YOU ARE ENTIRELY FREE TO EAT WHATEVER YOU WANT—AND AS MUCH AS YOU WANT. THE OTHER 3 DAYS YOU OPERATE ON A PERSONALIZED DIET THAT KEEPS YOUR ENERGY HIGH AND YOUR HUNGER LOW AND YOU'RE NEVER MORE THAN TOMORROW MORNING AWAY FROM BEING ABLE TO HAVE WHATEVER YOU WANT. FOR A FREE BROCHURE CALL NOW TOLL FREE.
>
> (800 telephone number)
>
> THAT'S
>
> (800 telephone number)
>
> ONCE AGAIN, FOR A FREE BROCHURE CALL
>
> (800 telephone number)
>
> SEE OUR AD IN THIS WEEK'S TV GUIDE[54]

Other advertisements emphasized the accomplishments of the diet in more direct terms, one such advertisement reading:

> Here's how the (diet) works: This amazing diet actually lets you eat and drink what and whenever you want on TUESDAYS, THURSDAYS, SATURDAYS AND SUNDAYS. You can have food like spaghetti, ravioli, fettuccine, and pizza. Bread and potatoes too. And desserts like chocolate

> layer cake, ice cream, banana splits, sundaes, pecan pie with whipped cream—whatever your favorites might be! You can even have double helpings of everything because that's the whole idea of the (diet). You're FREE to eat anything you want, as much as you want 4 days every week.[55]

There was more, however, than just the radio commercial in the advertising for the Rotation Diet. Endorsements by an expert and endorsements by those who used the diet were an important part of the marketing mix.

Expert Endorsement

The expert endorsement came from a clinical psychologist with a doctor of philosophy degree in psychology who had developed some of the "basic principles upon which the weight reduction and/or weight control programs" were based.[56] Appearing in the advertisements for the Rotation Diet, and using the title "doctor," the clinical psychologist was portrayed as possessing an expertise in psychology, as well as the physiological and psychological aspects of dieting. In one advertisement a question-and-answer interview with the psychologist contained the following exchange:

> Q. Does the Rotation Diet really work? Do people lose weight on it?
>
> A. It works extremely well. But as any doctor with years of experience in weight control knows, designing a way to lose weight is only a small part of the challenge. My years of observation of this diet convince me that its real breakthrough is the unique way it allows a person to find his or her right weight and stay there. . . .
>
> Q. How much weight can I lose?
>
> A. Women usually lose 8 to 20 pounds a month, men 12 to 25 pounds. The amount depends on many personal variables, including the total amount of weight you have to lose. . . .[57]

The FTC wasn't impressed and contended that the endorsement implied that: "Consumers can eat unlimited quantities of food four days a week and, regardless of how much they eat on those four days, still lose substantial amounts of weight on the Rotation Diet," when in truth and in fact "Consumers cannot eat unlimited quantities of food four days a week and regardless of how much they eat on those four days, still lose substantial amounts of weight. . . ."[58]

User Endorsements

In addition to the endorsements by the clinical psychologist, other user endorsements were part of the advertisement and marketing strategy:

> I really pig-out on my free days—pizza, cheesecake, beer, potato chips. I eat to my 'heart's content' and have still lost 57 pounds!' N.M., Princeton, NJ
>
> I save enough on my 3 diet days to more than pay for the whole week. The diet actually costs me nothing! J.A., Stowe, OH
>
> The all natural diet—no drugs or medicine! The Rotation Diet is really SANE and PROVEN SAFE!' C.D., Wilmington, DE
>
> I've lost over 70 pounds while eating all of the ice cream that I want 4 days every week. THIS IS THE MOST SUCCESSFUL DIET EVER!' P.A., Philadelphia, PA[59]

Some comments in the FTC's examples quoted so-called users who said they had been on the diet for six months and had only "ONE" diet day each week. Another user said Wednesday was the "free day" and it worked great.

Material Connections to the Advertiser

What the consumers reading and hearing about the diet did not know was that the clinical psychologist was linked to the advertiser, had a continuing role in the marketing of the diet, served as the director of the diet program's Professional Advisory Board, and provided advice on the products and diet program. Most important, and what the FTC objected to, was that he was compensated by the advertiser for his services. Moreover, some of the nonexpert people who endorsed the diet, some permitting their photographs to be used, were employees of the company. From the standpoint of the FTC, the failure of the company to inform the consumer of such material relationships was false and misleading.

The Commission's Order

On the subject of endorsements, the FTC consent order with the company marketing the diet called for the company to cease and desist from:

> Representing, directly or by implication, that any person has endorsed any such product, program or service, unless that person has committed that endorsement in writing and has authorized, in writing, its use in promotional or advertising materials, and unless respondents have good reason to believe that at the time of their representation that person continues to subscribe to the views presented.
>
> Failing to disclose any material connection, where one exists, between an endorser (except a celebrity endorser) of any such product, program or service and any respondent; provided, however, that a "*material connection*" shall mean, for purposes of this order, any relationship between an endorser of any such product, program or service, and any entity marketing such product, program or service which relationship would not reasonably be expected by consumers and, if known by consumers, might materially affect the weight or credibility given to the endorsement.[60]

The FTC order also called on the company to cease and desist from making the claim that a consumer could eat any quantity of food and still lose weight. The order called for the company to stop making any representation about weight loss, weight control, safety, and other claims in advertisements unless those representations were based on "reliable survey or other scientific evidence that substantiates the representation."[61]

PROGRAM-LENGTH COMMERCIALS

The FTC pays particular attention to program-length commercials.

Definition

Under the FTC's definition, program-length commercials, also called "program-length advertisements" or "infomercials," are defined as "any video advertisement that ends fifteen minutes or more after it begins."[62] Both the companies that used program-length commercials in their marketing strategies, and the production companies that produced the commercials, became the target of the FTC investigations.

Some program-length commercials are for legitimate products which have been tested and are marketed within the spirit of FTC guidelines. Others, however, are considered to be of little value and are marketed through false and misleading program-length advertisements which masquerade as normal programming, even to the point of taking commercial breaks to make the program appear objective and legitimate.[63]

Simulated Investigated Reports

Program-length commercials that are particularity troubling to the FTC are ones which purport to be investigative reports. Such was the case with a program-length commercial for BluBlocker sunglasses.[64] Marketed through a program-length commercial called "Consumer Challenge," the product appeared as the object of a so-called television "investigative report." But "Consumer Challenge" was not a "60-Minutes"-type program. According to the FTC, it was created by the company marketing BluBlockers for the sole purpose of selling BluBlockers.

FTC records identified three excerpts from the transcript of "Consumer Challenge" which showed how the program was presented as an investigative report which ostensibly examined the quality of BluBlocker sunglasses:

> Welcome to "Consumer Challenge," hosted by Jonathan Goldsmith, the show that examines the popular new products for you, the consumer, with investigative reporters Don Hale and Catherine Grant. Here's your host, Jonathan Goldsmith.
>
> On today's "Consumer Challenge" we investigate BluBlockers—a new product innovation or consumer rip-off?
>
> We interrupt this program for a special announcement. This program is unable to handle the number of calls requesting the sunglasses featured in this program. If you are interested in obtaining the BluBlocker sunglasses, you may call the manufacturer directly at the number shown here.
>
> Thanks for such a thorough job on your investigation on this topic. Remember, if you didn't get the ordering information, please stay tuned and it will be shown on the screen at the end of the show . . . Look for our next

> "Consumer Challenge," the show that challenges the products of our time to make you a better, more informed consumer in the future.[65]

In addition to disseminating the television program which claimed to be an investigative report examining BluBlocker sunglasses, the company tied in the content of its print advertisements and used the print advertisements to further publicize the report.

Print Advertising Tie-Ins

To further its complaint, the FTC singled out three excerpts from BluBlocker's print advertisements which read:

> "Consumer Challenge" TV show picks BluBlocker sunglasses as target for investigative report and ends up with surprise.
>
> We were upset. Our advertisement for BluBlocker high resolution sunglasses was selected to be exposed by the new commercial TV production, Consumer Challenge. "Is this advertisement about a major new product breakthrough or a real rip-off?" asked the show's host Jonathan Goldsmith. "We're going to find out." If you've ever watched 60 Minutes or 20/20 you could understand our fear. We were running the risk of Consumer Challenge taking a great product and ruining it on the air. Sales could plummet and our product could be destroyed by some clever editor or a jealous producer. But we were totally wrong.
>
> Obviously we are very proud of our achievement with the Consumer Challenge TV show. Whenever you can convey a very positive image of your product on a commercial TV production, it is very encouraging.[66]

Additional copy in the print advertising told of the benefits of the product, including other testimonials, one which stated that a famous wildlife photographer was sitting on the steps of his cabin and supposedly saw a mountain he hadn't seen before because of the high resolution of the sunglasses. Readers of the print ad were told, "If you have a chance, catch Consumer Challenge in your area. Check local time and listings."[67]

The FTC Complaint

The FTC complaint alleged that the advertisements and the program-length commercial were misleading in truth and in fact:

> "Consumer Challenge" is not an independent consumer program such as "60 Minutes" or "20/20," that conducts independent and objective investigations of consumer products like BluBlockers. It was created by . . . (marketer) . . . and produced at the request of . . . (marketer) . . . for the sole purpose of selling BluBlockers.
>
> The producers and investigative reporters of "Consumer Challenge" did not conduct an independent and objective investigation of BluBlockers without receiving any reimbursement or other financial benefit, directly or indirectly, from its marketers. . . . They were paid by . . . the production company on behalf of . . . (marketers) . . . for producing and acting in the advertisement.[68]

The FTC required the order to be distributed to each of the marketer's operating divisions and to notify the commission in writing, telling how they complied with the order.

Cease-and-Desist Order

The decision and order issued by the FTC called for the marketers of BluBlockers to cease and desist from:

> Misrepresenting, directly or indirectly, that such product has been independently investigated or evaluated.
>
> Misrepresenting, directly or indirectly, that an advertisement is an independent consumer or news program and not a paid advertisement.
>
> For a period of ten (10) years from the date of service of this order, failing to disclose clearly and prominently in any program length advertisement that the program is an advertisement or commercial. Such fact shall be disclosed at the beginning of the program. In addition, such fact shall be disclosed each time during the program that ordering instructions are given, provided however, that such additional disclosures need not appear more than twice during any half hour

period of the program. For the purposes of this order, *"program length advertisement"* shall mean any video advertisement that ends fifteen minutes or more after it begins.[69]

You may still find BluBlocker sunglasses marketed, but through a different message than the one which brought the FTC into the picture.

The Future of Program-Length Commercials

The FTC's crackdown on program-length commercials has brought Congress into the matter. It held hearings on the subject and heard testimony from the Association of National Advertisers, a trade group which called on the FTC to hold "producers and advertisers . . . to the same high standards for truthful, nondeceptive advertising as would be required for any other advertising format."[70] Marketers are paying attention to the FTC's watch over program-length commercials. One production company executive said he no longer accepts claims made by doctors trying to sell a product unless the production company conducted its own studies.[71] A marketer of bee pollen cures agreed to send a letter to the purchasers of the product telling them the program they saw was a commercial and the claims were unsubstantiated.[72]

The growth and development of cable television has opened up new opportunities for program-length commercials. Many cable channels have time to fill and program-length commercials are one way to fill it. Moreover, cable television is primarily controlled by municipalities. Controls over program content are sometimes not as restrictive as they are in over-the-air television, where stations must adhere to the public-interest spirit of the Communications Act. In over-the-air television the FCC is the primary governing agency, but where program-length commercials are employed, deceptive advertising, even on cable television, can result in a Federal Trade Commission investigation.

We can expect program-length commercials to continue, perhaps even increase, as new cable channels develop. At the same time, however, with the FTC looking over the shoulder of both advertisers and the production companies that produce program-length commercials, the content of those commercials will be less misleading and the products will need to be tested to substantiate the claims made by the advertiser.

IN-STORE TELEVISION

Cable television is not the only medium where advertising is growing. The growth of nonbroadcast video has also gained importance. The small videotape playback units and monitors that play continuous tape everywhere from automobile showrooms to clothing stores are becoming a common element in marketing strategies.

Advertising Advantages of In-Store Video

The advantages of in-store video are many. For example, the audience is usually captive and interested in the product. A person in a new car showroom is probably interested in cars. Any self-contained videotape presentation offers a chance for the dealer and automaker to present an advertising message highlighting the features of the new models without the competition and distractions of at-home television, where the set may be on but the viewer is at the refrigerator getting a snack. In-store video involves an active, not a passive, participant in the viewing process.

Production Advantages

Production advantages also arise with in-store video. For example, the commercial presented on an in-store video playback unit does not need to meet the production quality standards of over-the-air television, although many in-store presentations do. The playback unit is usually distinct from its surroundings and gains attention by its very presence. Consider how visible an in-store full-color video of ocean surfing with crashing waves and the latest beach fashions can be in the stationary surroundings of clothing racks in a department store. Longer commercials are also possible since the restrictions of over-the-air television, many times dominated by the time limits of network and syndicated programming, do not restrict the producer's creativity.

Regulatory Control Over the Content of In-Store Video

With all of these advantages, in addition to the lack of Federal Communications Commission control over in-store video, it would seem that most of what appears in these nonbroadcast presentations would be free of regulatory controls. Advertisers would have a much freer rein to present their products than would be possible in over-the-air television with its "public-interest" requirements. Don't be deceived, because that's not the case. The watchful eye of the FTC is monitoring these in-store commercial presentations just as much as the in-store detective is scouting for shoplifters.

As far as advertising is concerned, the Federal Trade Commission Act covers all media. An example of an in-store video advertisement that ended up in an FTC consent order was a commercial for bottled water. The commercial ran 1 minute and 50 seconds, much longer than the typical 10- to 60-second commercials on over-the-air television. Longer commercials give copy writers the opportunity to tell more, but sometimes what is said doesn't meet the FTC's requirements for truthful advertising.

In-Store Video Commercial

The product that brought FTC action was a device which attached to a standard water faucet and was suppose to produced quality water similar to the standards of bottled water. Part of the commercial, some of which the FTC took exception to, read as follows (video portion is in capital letters):

> Announcer: Now if you're buying and lugging lots of jugs of water to solve your drinking problem—
>
> VIDEO: MOTHER ENTER KITCHEN LUGGING GROCERY SACKS 7 JUGS OF DRINKING WATER—DAUGHTER GREETS HER & TAKES THE JUGS
>
> Forget it! Here's a better solution:
>
> SCENE FREEZERS—MATTE X OVER SCENE
>
> Make your own bottled water with this marvel of modern technology (product name).
>
> CUT TO HER HANDS SETTING DOWN BOTTLED WATER MAKER CARTON—SLOW ZOOM IN AS SHE OPENS TOP FLAP AND SLIDES OUT UNIT.
>
> As you know, many of America's drinking water sources are contaminated. Ordinary carbon-type filters cannot remove some of the nasty chemicals and minerals that may be lurking in your drinking water.
>
> DISSOLVE TO . . . POLLUTED STREAM . . . POLLUTION HEADLINES MOVING ACROSS SCREEN
>
> But the (product name) Reverse Osmosis membrane can separate these harmful molecules from water.
>
> DISSOLVE BACK TO SAME BOTTLED WATER MAKER BOX AS CAMERA CONTINUES TO ZOOM INTO "REVERSE OSMOSIS" TYPE PANEL
>
> (descriptions of contamination)
>
> . . . It also removes up to 99% of these pesticides and suspected cancer-causing chemicals.
>
> CHANGE TO CHEMICAL CHART & CLOSE GRAPHIC "REMOVES UP TO 99% OF THESE SUSPECTED CANCER-CAUSING CHEMICALS"
>
> . . . because inside, water flows slowly through this cellulose acetate membrane—separating harmful molecules from pure water.
>
> TITLE REMAINS AS BACKGROUND DISSOLVES TO CROSS SECTION ARTWORK OF UNIT[73]

Beginning with the paragraph reading "As you know . . . ," the FTC objected to the claims, and issued a consent order for the company selling the water filter to cease and desist from representing the product as treating or removing contaminants or reducing any health-related risks.

Graphics and Lessons for Producers

The FTC also singled out some of the graphics used in the advertisements for the water filter. The illustration of "tap water" consisted of "water molecules" which were represented by white circles, and the "contaminants" were represented by black dots. The graphic, however, showed all the "contaminants" being screened out by the membrane, something the FTC contended wouldn't happen.

The case of the water filter in the in-store video commercial highlights some lessons for producers. For example, just because the commercial is longer, there isn't any less responsibility to produce a commercial that isn't misleading and that must be based on substantiated claims. While the longer commercial may provide some creative flexibility, it also increases the chance of including information which will be misleading. Finally, spoken words are not the only indicator of a commercial's truthfulness. Graphics can also play a part and the FTC is just as apt to find fault with what is seen as with what is said.

THE REASONABLE BASIS FOR REPRESENTATIONS IN ADVERTISING

Throughout the examples of FTC involvement in this chapter, an overriding thesis emerges: Companies must be able to substantiate claims made in advertisements. The claims made in a commercial are not more important than being able to prove those claims. A commercial for a widget that cures baldness is fine if, in truth and in fact, the widget actually does cure baldness. If it doesn't or if you can't prove that it does, then airing the commercial is an open invitation for an inquiry from the Federal Trade Commission.

Evaluations of the Product or Service

Tests which substantiate and provide a "reasonable basis" for making claims are important to truthful advertising. The FTC looks unfavorably on inflated claims that cannot be proven. The language used in a consent order requiring a reasonable basis for substantiating a claim varies with the particular product, how inflated the claim is, and other mitigating factors. For the purposes of a consent order, "reasonable basis" consists of "competent and reliable" evidence:

> To the extent that the evidence of a reasonable basis consists of scientific or professional tests, experiments, analyses, research, studies or other evidence based on the expertise of professionals in the relevant area, such evidence shall be "competent and reliable" only if those tests, experiments, analyses, research, studies, or other evidence are conducted and evaluated in an objective manner by persons qualified to do so, using only procedures that are generally accepted in the profession as yielding accurate and reliable results.[74]

The FTC can also order an advertiser to maintain for copying and inspection by the FTC the records used to substantiate a claim and to provide to the FTC upon request all "test reports, studies, surveys, or other materials in its possession or control or of which it has knowledge that contradict, qualify, or call into question . . . the basis upon which respondent relied."[75] In other words the FTC wants companies to be alert to evidence that *does not* support their advertising claims as well as evidence that does.

Expert Endorsements

Of additional concern to the commission are claims made by so-called experts that endorse a product or service. Certain assumptions accompany an endorser who uses the title "doctor" as identified by an announcer or through the use of the designation "Dr." in a graphic. The consumer relies on such titles as a measure of integrity which reflects upon the product or service being sold. As such, the FTC expects these individuals to make endorsements only when the endorsement can be supported by the same reliable evidence that is required of other types of product testing. A company should not try to get around substantiating a claim by having an expert "doctor" endorse the product or service when no evidence exists to back up the endorsement.

The endorsement of a clinical psychologist was called into question by the FTC when the commission stated that the endorser did not have a reasonable basis for making the representations appearing in the ads. The commission suggested that an expectation would exist that such an expert would have "possessed and relied upon a reasonable basis for those representations."[76] The commission contended that the endorsement would be expected to consist of "an actual exercise of his expertise in evaluating (the product) with respect to which he is an expert, in the form of an examination or testing of the programs and products at least as extensive as someone with a similar degree of expertise would normally conduct in order to support the conclusions presented in the endorsement."[77]

THE USE OF "SURVEYS" IN ADVERTISING PRODUCTS AND SERVICES

In addition to exercising its control over claims and endorsements in advertising, the FTC also concerns itself with the use of so-called "surveys" in advertising.[78]

Reliability in Conducting Surveys

Conducting a reliable survey means obtaining a random sample of a representative group of people. A random sample involves giving everyone in the group an equal chance of being selected and the size of the sample must be large enough to accurately estimate the opinions or beliefs of the whole group based on the sample. In other words, if you are conducting a survey of doctors across the United States to solicit their opinions on the dangers of eating seafood versus beef, only sampling doctors in Boston would not be acceptable since doctors in Boston may have different opinions on the subject than doctors in Montana. Similarly, only asking five doctors what they thought would not be a large enough sample to estimate the opinion of all doctors. Using a sample of five doctors in Boston and then using the survey in advertising by claiming it is a national survey of doctors would be considered false and misleading, especially if the audience did not know you only sampled five doctors in Boston.

FTC Expectations for Using Surveys as Endorsements

The expectations of the FTC in the use of surveys to support advertising can be drawn from the wording of a cease-and-desist order issued to an advertising agency over the use of surveys to make representations about such products as stop-smoking aids, smoke alarms, water purifiers, baby food preparation kits, shower head attachments, and foot massagers. Although stated in the negative outlining what the agency could *not* do, the order offers an affirmative statement about the minimum expectations the agency has over survey use. The agency agreed to cease and desist from:

A. Employing, in any advertisement for any product, the word "survey" (or any comparable term), or basing any claim upon one or more surveys in whole or in part which states, either expressly or by implication, the beliefs, opinions, practices, recommendations, or endorsements of any professional group (or portion thereof) with expertise relative to the product, unless:

(1) a projectable sample was used and the sample size of and response rate to the survey were sufficiently large so as to allow meaningful projections to the population referred to in the advertisement with a reasonable degree of confidence unless there is a clear and conspicuous disclosure in the advertisement that the survey may not be representative of the population referred to in the advertisement;

(2) the survey was completed within three years prior to the date of the representation, unless there is other appropriate data which establishes a reasonable basis for concluding that the beliefs, opinions, practices, recommendations or endorsements of the members of the relevant professional population surveyed have not materially changed since the completion of the survey; and

(3) the survey was designed, executed and analyzed in a competent and reliable manner.

B. Representing, directly or by implication, that the beliefs, practices, recommendations or endorsements of members of any professional group with expertise relative to the advertised product have been surveyed or sampled unless the survey or sample directly solicits the beliefs, opinions, practices, recommendations, or endorsements of members of that group.[79]

Notice that the order stressed the need to sample the professional group whose opinions are being used as representations in the advertisements. Going back to our example of doctors, you could not sample doctors and then use the sample as a survey purporting to represent lawyers.

Although not discussed in the consent order, care must be taken not to break out a subgroup from a survey which is too small to make accurate statements about the subgroup's beliefs. For example, if you conduct a national survey of doctors, only five of which are pediatricians, then stating a "national survey of pediatricians" endorses a given product would be considered false and misleading. A statistical term called *sampling error,* which is determined by the size of the sample, would be much too large to justify any endorsement by the pediatricians.

SUMMARY

The Federal Trade Commission is placing renewed emphasis on enforcement and prosecution homing in on unscrupulous advertisers who use radio and television to mislead consumers. Stations, regardless of whether advertising is received from an agency or generated locally, need to understand the FTC and its enforcement process. In addition, stations need to be aware of state laws governing advertising.

The primary enforcement arm of the FTC is the Bureau of Consumer Protection. Five program areas fall under the bureau: advertising practices, marketing practices, credit practices, service industry practices, and enforcement. Many issues before the FTC are settled through consent agreements. Under a consent agreement the case is customarily withdrawn from adjudication at some point in the proceeding. The FTC and the advertiser agree on jurisdictional facts and the advertiser is not required to admit to violating the law. Companies can still operate after an FTC complaint is settled through a consent order and they frequently do, selling the same products but with revised advertising and marketing practices.

Advertising practices are concerned with false and misleading advertising, both broadcast and print. Marketing practices also involve advertising but encompass the movement of goods and services. Credit practices are concerned with the disclosure of credit terms and the truthful representation of credit terms in sales, marketing, and advertising. Credit practices also involve the collection of debts and the operation of credit systems. Service industry practices concentrate on creating informed consumers who use service industries.

Enforcement of FTC regulations begin with an investigation where the commission can issue subpoenas and other orders requiring testimony and the production of documents. One of the enforcement remedies available to the commission is the assurance of voluntary compliance which does not involve the adjudicatory proceedings. Consent orders permit a complaint to be negotiated with an agreement that the alleged practices will cease. More serious are adjudicative orders which involve a proceeding conducted by an administrative law judge who serves as the referee over the initial tier of facts. Preliminary injunctions are more serious still and seek injunctive relief in a federal district court.

The complaint process usually begins with a consumer or competitor complaining to the FTC about false advertising. The advertiser customarily receives a letter from the FTC with the opportunity to reply. At that point the issue can be dropped or the negotiation process begins. A consent order can evolve out of the negotiation process which if agreed to by the commission and the advertiser can end the matter. If, however, during the 60- day period for public comments during the negotiation phase considerable evidence builds up against the advertiser, then an administrative law judge may rule on the complaint. The advertiser has the option to appeal the decision or accept the decision of the administrative law judge.

While guarding against false advertising, the FTC has some responsibility to assure open competition in the marketplace, especially where advertising or marketing may restrict that competition. For example, the FTC has challenged football television contracts with some success, resulting in a U.S. Supreme Court decision that one type of contract between a conference and network violated antitrust laws. Mergers can also fall under FTC jurisdiction. A proposed merger of record companies resulted in an FTC-obtained consent order to review distribution agreements under the planned merger.

Truth in advertising applies to any product or service. Some examples discussed in this chapter include a television commercial used to advertise pest control through an ultrasonic sound device. The FTC reviewed advertising claims that the electronic sound device eliminated rats, mice, cockroaches, and other pests when in fact the device was not effective against those rodents and insects. The company under a consent agreement was ordered to provide refunds to consumers in addition to assuring the FTC of future compliance with the decree. A commercial for nonprescription drugs included a claim that an over-the-counter dose could be substituted for prescription levels. The commission has also used its power to enforce warning labels. When tanning salons were claimed safe, the FTC stepped in and enforced the mandatory FDA warning label on tanning devices.

Expert endorsements must also be treated carefully. Such endorsements must be from recognized experts and cannot be falsified or the subject of misleading language. Of particular concern are endorsements which cannot be proven, such as the claim that rotating a diet will result in weight loss without an accompanied reduction of caloric intake. The FTC has also stepped up its enforcement of program-length commercials which are defined as video advertisements that end 15 minutes or more after they begin. Both the companies who are marketing products and the producers of program-length commercials have been targeted for FTC investigations. Especially problematic to the commission are simulated investigative reports where the advertiser attempts to create in the minds of the public that they are watching an objective newscast reporting the results of product testing. Companies using program-length commercials have been advised not to make their products appear as though they have been independently investigated and evaluated when in truth and in fact they have not. In-store television, videotape playback units in retail establishments playing continuous tape which advertises a product or service, has also garnered the FTC's attention.

A special interest of the FTC is the basis upon which companies make claims about their products. Claims must be truthful and backed up by independent testing. Specifically, there must be a reasonable basis to assume product quality and it must be based on scientific and professional tests using the expertise of professionals in a relevant area.

Some advertisers use surveys to market their products. Conducting a reliable survey means obtaining a random sample which involves giving everyone in the group being sampled an equal chance of being selected. A projected sample must contain a sample size and response rate sufficiently large to allow for meaningful projections. In addition, the survey must be completed within three years of the date of the endorsement or representation and be executed and analyzed in a competent and reliable manner. Care must also be taken when breaking out subgroups in a survey since the sample size of the subgroup may be too small to make accurate and meaningful projections about the entire group.

MATERIAL FOR ANALYSIS

Companies which become the object of an FTC inquiry many times settle the matter through a consent order. The following consent order applies to a company engaged in the sale of a weight-reducing device.

IN THE MATTER OF *NUTRITONE, INC., ET AL.*

CONSENT ORDER, ETC., IN REGARD TO ALLEGED VIOLATION OF SEC. 5 AND 12 OF THE FEDERAL TRADE COMMISSION ACT

Docket C-3264. 1989

This consent order prohibits, among other things, a Massachusetts corporation from making any representations concerning the efficacy of electric muscle stimulation ("EMS") treatment programs and products, unless respondents possess reliable scientific evidence to substantiate the representations. Respondents are required to retain, for at least five years, records supporting any future advertising and also required to post a copy of the order on the premises.

* * *

COMPLAINT

The Federal Trade Commission, having reason to believe that Nutritone, Inc., a corporation, also trading and doing business as Body By Design, and . . . officers of said corporation ("respondents"), have violated Sections 5(a) and 12 of the Federal Trade Commission Act, and it appearing to the Commission that a proceeding by it in respect thereof would be in the public interest, alleges that:

PARAGRAPH 1. (a) Respondent Nutritone, Inc., is a Massachusetts corporation. Its principal office or place of business is (address).

(b) (respondents) are officers of the corporate respondent. They formulate, direct and control the acts and practices of the corporate respondent, including all the acts and practices alleged in this complaint below. Their principal office or place of business is the same as that of the corporation.

PAR. 2. Respondents have advertised, offered for sale, sold and distributed to the public an electric muscle stimulation program.

PAR. 3. Respondents have caused to be prepared and placed for publication and have caused the dissemination of advertising and promotional materials, including, but not limited to, the advertising and promotional materials attached hereto as Exhibits A through D to promote the sale of their electric muscle stimulation treatment program.

PAR. 4. The acts or practices of respondents alleged in this complaint have been in or affecting commerce, as "commerce" is defined in the Federal Trade Commission Act.

PAR. 5. In the course and conduct of their business, respondents have disseminated and caused the dissemination of advertisements and promotional materials for electric muscle stimulation, by various means in or affecting commerce and including *inter alia*, placing advertisements for broadcast by radio, in magazines and in newspapers distributed through the mail and across state lines, for the purpose of inducing, and which were likely to induce, directly or indirectly, the purchase of respondents' electric muscle stimulation program.

PAR. 6. Typical statements in such advertisements and promotional materials, disseminated as previously described, but not necessarily inclusive thereof, are found in advertisements and promotional materials attached hereto as (exhibits). Specifically, these advertisements and promotional materials contain the following statements:

1. Exercise 20 muscle groups simultaneously and achieve up to 1000 muscle contractions as in situps, pushups and leglifts.
2. Men develop the "V" shape.
3. Women tone stomachs, thighs and buttocks.
4. EMS can be the best workout of your life with significant strength gains.
5. Save time—in just 35 min. you can do the equivalent of 2 hours in the gym.
6. EMS is the *new* high technology way to tone or strengthen muscles for Men and Women.
7. No agonizing exercise—no pain.

PAR. 7. Through the use, *inter alia*, of the statements referred to in paragraph six and other statements contained in advertisements or promotional materials not specifically set forth herein, respondents have represented, and now represent, directly or by implication, that their electric muscle stimulation treatments:

1. Cause muscle contractions of comparable intensity to those produced when normal healthy people do conventional physical exercise such as situps, pushups and leglifts;
2. Change the girth of various parts of the body such as the stomach, buttocks, and thighs;
3. Provide all the health benefits to normal healthy people of rigorous physical exercise;
4. Provide greater health benefits and increases in strength for normal healthy people in a specified period of time than a program of rigorous physical exercise for the same time period;
5. Are the result of recent scientific and technological learning and experimentation; and

PAR. 8. In truth and in fact, respondents' electric muscle stimulation treatments consisting of low-frequency, low-current muscle stimulation:

1. Do not cause muscle contractions of comparable intensity to those produced when normal healthy people do conventional physical exercises such as situps, pushups and leglifts;
2. Do not change the girth of various parts of the body such as the stomach, buttocks, and thigh;
3. Do not provide all the health benefits to normal healthy people of rigorous physical exercise;
4. Do not provide greater health benefits and increases in strength for normal healthy people in a specific period of time than programs of regular gym exercises for the same time period;
5. Are not the result of recent scientific and technological learning and experimentation. Therefore, the representations set forth in paragraph seven are false and misleading.

PAR. 9. Through the use, *inter alia*, of the statements referred to in paragraph six, and other statements contained in advertisements and promotional materials not specifically set forth herein, respondents have represented and now represent, directly or by implication, that at the time of making the representations set forth in paragraph seven respondents possessed and relied upon a reasonable basis for these representations.

PAR. 10. In truth and in fact, at the time of those representations respondents did not possess and rely upon a reasonable basis for making such representations. Therefore, the representation set forth in paragraph nine was, and is, false and misleading.

PAR. 11. The acts and practices of respondents as alleged in this complaint, and the placement in the hands of others of the means and instrumentalities by and through which others may have used said acts and practices, constitute unfair and deceptive acts or practices in or affecting commerce and the dissemination of false advertisements in violation of Section 5(a) and 12 of the Federal Trade Commission Act.

DECISION AND ORDER

The Federal Trade Commission having initiated an investigation of certain acts and practices of the respondents named in the caption hereof, and the respondents having been furnished thereafter with a copy of a draft of complaint which the Boston Regional Office proposed to present to the Commission for its consideration and which, if issued by the Commission, would charge respondents with violation of the Federal Trade Commission Act; and

The respondents and counsel for the Commission having thereafter executed an agreement containing a consent order, an admission by the respondents of all the jurisdictional facts set forth in the aforesaid draft of complaint, a statement that the signing of said agreement is for settlement purposes only and does not constitute an admission by respondents that the law has been violated as alleged in such complaint, and waivers and other provisions as required by the Commission's Rules; and

The Commission having thereafter considered the matter and having determined that it had reason to believe that the respondents have violated the said Act, and that the complaint should issue stating its charges in that respect, and having thereupon accepted the executed consent agreement and placed such agreement on the public record for a period of sixty (60) days, now in further conformity with the procedure prescribed in Section 2.34 of its Rules, the Commission hereby issues its complaint, makes the following jurisdictional findings and enters the following order:

1. Respondent, Nutritone, Inc., is a corporation, d/b/a/ Body By Design, organized, existing and doing business under and by virtue of the laws of the Commonwealth of Massachusetts, with its office and principal place of business (address).

2. Respondents . . . are officers of the corporation.

3. The Federal Trade Commission has jurisdiction of the subject matter of this proceeding and of the respondents, and the proceeding is in the public interest.

ORDER

I.

It is ordered, That respondents Nutritone, Inc., a corporation, its officers, and (respondents), individually and as officers of the corporation, their successors and assigns, and respondents, agents, representatives, and employees, directly or through any corporation, subsidiary, division or other device, in connection with the advertising, offering for sale, selling or distribution of any electric muscle stimulation treatment program or product in or affecting commerce, as "commerce" is defined in the Federal Trade Commission Act, do forthwith cease and desist from representing, directly or by implication, contrary to fact, that any low-frequency (1000 Hz and below) electric muscle stimulation treatment or product:

A. Can cause muscle contractions of similar intensity to those produced by conventional exercise.

B. Will visibly change the girth of any part of the body without a reduction in caloric intake or participation in a weight loss program.

C. Provides similar or superior health benefits to those produced by rigorous conventional exercise for normal healthy people.

D. Provides, in the same or shorter time period, health benefits similar or superior to those produced by conventional exercise.

E. Are a result of any new or recent scientific and technological research and experimentation.

II.

It is furthered ordered, That respondents Nutritone, Inc., a corporation, its officers, and (respondents), individually and as officers of the corporation, their successors and assigns, and respondents' agents, representatives, and employees, directly or through any corporation, subsidiary, division or other device, in connection with the advertising, offering for sale, sale or distribution of any diet, strength development, or fitness program or product in or affecting commerce, as "commerce" is defined in the Federal Trade Commission Act, do forthwith cease and desist from making any representation, directly or by implication, concerning such program's or product's efficacy, or the comparability or superiority over other programs or products, or the results typically achieved by consumers of the program or product unless, at the time of making such representation respondents possess and rely upon competent and reliable scientific evidence that substantiates the representation; *provided, however*, that for purposes of this order for any test, analysis, research, study, or other evidence to be "competent and reliable" it must be conducted and evaluated in an objective manner by persons qualified to do so, using procedures generally accepted in the profession to yield accurate and reliable results.

III.

It is furthered ordered, That respondents shall for at least five years after the date of the last dissemination of the representation, maintain and upon request make available to the Federal Trade Commission for inspection and copying copies of:

1. All materials that were relied upon by respondents in disseminating any representation covered by this order.
2. All test reports, studies, surveys, or demonstrations in their possession or control that contradict any representation of respondents that is covered by this order.

IV.

It is furthered ordered, That respondents shall conspicuously post a copy of this order on their premises.

V.

It is furthered ordered, That the corporate respondent and the individual respondents shall notify the Commission at least thirty (30) days prior to any proposed change in the corporate respondent such as dissolution, assignment, or sale resulting in the emergence of a successor corporation, the creation or dissolution of subsidiaries or any other change in the corporation which may affect compliance obligations arising out of the order, or of any change in the position or responsibilities of (respondents) in regard to any corporation or subsidiary of which either is an officer and which corporation or subsidiary is, directly or indirectly, involved in the sale or distribution of any electric muscle stimulation treatment program or product.

VI.

It is further ordered, That respondents shall, within sixty (60) days after service of this order, file with the Commission a report, in writing, setting forth in detail the manner and form in which they have complied with this order.

QUESTIONS FOR CRITICAL ANALYSIS

- In what areas could regulatory conflicts develop between the Federal Communications Commission and the Federal Trade Commission?
- Should the Federal Communications Commission be charged with monitoring truthfulness in broadcast advertising while the Federal Trade Commission concentrates on the print media?
- Should local stations be required to monitor test results showing the reliability of products advertised on their stations?
- The five program areas covered by the Federal Trade Commission include advertising practices, marketing practices, credit practices, service industry practices, and enforcement. Should any additional areas be added, and if so what should they be?
- Would a sixth program area covering electronic media permit the FTC more latitude in enforcement, resulting in more truth and accuracy in radio and television commercials?
- Are FTC regulations really necessary or if we eliminated all regulations governing truth in advertising would consumers gradually develop the ability to make their own assessment of product worth and reliability?
- Many companies which settle an FTC consent order continue to do business and sell the same products, although advertised and marketed in a different way. Should consent orders go further and restrict the future sale and marketing of the product by the same company?
- Are small companies at a disadvantage in defending themselves against the FTC?
- The regulation of the telephone industry falls under the Common Carrier Bureau of the Federal Communications Commission. Should this bureau be responsible for enforcing marketing practices of cellular telephones?
- Cable television is also regulated by the Federal Communications Commission in addition to states and municipalities. Where cable television marketing practices are concerned, should the FTC relinquish its regulatory responsibility to the FCC or the appropriate state or local agency?
- Could local small-claims courts be used by consumers as a means of redress against companies advertising products which do not measure up to advertising claims?

- The Federal Trade Commission has exercised its authority over television football contracts between football conferences and networks. Should networks be required to deal exclusively with each individual college whose games it wants to televise and not negotiate with a football conference?
- Should individual radio and television stations be required to have commercial clearance departments where all copy is screened for truth in advertising?
- If a television commercial advertises a product or service which requires an FDA-approved warning label, should the content of the warning label be displayed in legible letters on the screen during the commercial? If not displayed for the entire commercial should the warning be displayed for a certain number of seconds during the commercial? If the warning label is not displayed as text would an audio warning label be an acceptable substitute?
- Should the federal government impose length limits on commercials therefore making program-length commercials illegal if they exceeded the length limit?
- The designation "Dr." is used with people who have different types of degrees. For example, an M.D. and a Ph.D. both use the prefix "Dr." When an endorser of a product uses the prefix "Dr.", should the type of degree designation be required following the person's name such as M.D. for medical doctors? Would some circumstances exist where the designation was not necessary such as a doctor cast against the backdrop of a hospital emergency room or a professor in a university library? Is the designation "Dr." abused in advertising and marketing and should a federal regulation be imposed whereby the designation cannot be used in the endorsement of products?

ADDITIONAL RESOURCES

Averitt, N. W., and T. Calvani, "The Role of the FTC in American Society." 39 *Oklahoma Law Review* 39 (Spring 1986).

Harris, J. D., "Legal Restrictions on Food, Drug, and Cosmetic Advertising." 43 *Food Drug Cosmetic Law Journal* 249 (March 1988).

Heald, P., "Money Damages and Corrective Advertising: An Economic Analysis." 55 *University of Chicago Law Review* 629 (Spring 1988).

Karns, J. E., "The Federal Trade Commission's Evolving Deception Policy." 22 *University of Richmond Law Review* 399 (Spring 1988).

Karns, J. E., "The Federal Unfair Trade Practice Standard after International Harvester: When is a Marketing Practice a Pure Omission?" 40 *Drake Law Review* 61 (Fall 1991).

Mathios, A., and M. Plummer, "The Regulation of Advertising by the Federal Trade Commission: Capital Market Effects." 12 *Research in Law and Economics Annual* 77 (1989).

Peeler, Lee C., and M. K. Rusk, "Commercial Speech and the FTC's Consumer Protection Program." 59 *Antitrust Law Journal* 985 (Fall 1990).

Schmidt, Richard M., Jr., and R. C. Burns, "Proof or Consequences: False Advertising and the Doctrine of Commercial Speech." 56 *University of Cincinnati Law Review* 1273 (Spring 1988).

chapter five

Allied Regulatory Agencies

In addition to the FTC, the executive branch of government has been actively involved in regulatory policy affecting radio and television. The National Telecommunications and Information Administration (NTIA) also plays a role, as does the U.S. Department of Justice. The Office of Technology Assessment (OTA) supports Congress by providing information for policy decisions on the effects of technology on our society. Elsewhere in this text is a discussion of the International Telecommunication Union (ITU) which works to coordinate the responsible use of the electromagnetic spectrum among countries. These allied agencies are important because telecommunication policy is not controlled by only one agency and policy planning must take into consideration the needs of all agencies of government which deal in some way with telecommunications. Neither the private sector nor government can regulate or plan without consulting each other. For example, while the Common Carrier Bureau of the Federal Communications Commission regulates the telephone industry, the White House Communications Agency, which is directed by the Defense Communications Agency, provides the telephone and telecommunications services to the White House and the Office of the President. In somewhat the same way, the FCC regulates commercial radio and television broadcasting in the United States, agreements executed through the ITU prevent interference between stations in the United States and those operating in other countries. When interference does occur, the Department of State becomes involved.

THE BEGINNING OF U.S. TELECOMMUNICATIONS REGULATION

Distinctions between different media and the carriers of communication are becoming increasingly blurred. Network programs travel over telephone company facilities or satellite systems linking domestic and international carriers of communication. Computers process all kinds of information—from election-night returns to cost-analysis figures to wire-service feeds. Trying to project cost analysis for a new cable system becomes more complex when we see the cable system being used for so much more than relaying television programs. When the electromagnetic spectrum is being shared by many different countries, all competing for their allotment of available frequencies, how does the United States determine international communications policy? Who looks out for the interests of government in its competition with private industry for use of the spectrum?

These questions force us to look beyond the term *broadcasting* to the term *telecommunications*, which incorporates all of the components of our new age of "information technology."[1] Telecommunications includes not only the evening network news but also electronic-funds transfers, where a computer does everything from depositing your paycheck to paying your electric bill. With this new growth of the telecommunications industry, much of which is already under the FCC's jurisdiction, it is not surprising that other agencies of government have taken an active interest.

THE NIXON ERA AND THE OFFICE OF TELECOMMUNICATIONS POLICY

The modern efforts to elevate telecommunications in importance took place in 1970 under President Richard Nixon, when he established the Office of Telecommunications Policy (OTP) in the executive office of the president. The OTP was formed by executive order, which was part of Nixon's reorganization plan. The executive order spelled out the charge to the OTP:

> (1) Serve as the President's principal advisor on telecommunications; (2) assure that the executive branch views are effectively presented to the Congress and the Federal Communications Commission on telecommunications policy matters; (3) review telecommunications research and development, system improvement and expansion programs, and programs for the testing, operation, and use of telecommunications system by Federal agencies, and (4) develop, in cooperation with the Federal Communications Commission, a comprehensive long-range plan for improved management of all electromagnetic spectrum resources.[2]

The director and the deputy director of the OTP were appointed by the president with the advice and consent of the Senate. Both were prohibited from holding any other jobs while serving in their respective capacities. With OTP taking control of the duties of the Office of Emergency Preparedness, that office was abolished.[3]

Pressure from the Executive Branch

The idea of the White House jumping feet first into communication regulation was not surprising to many political observers, but it was not to the liking of many people either. Vice-President Spiro Agnew had leveled strong criticism against the television networks in his famous Des Moines, Iowa speech of 1969. The OTP was sounding in theory like a "coordinating" and "advising" agency but the broadcasting industry was still wary. The executive order did state it would not "impair any existing authority or jurisdiction of the Federal Communications Commission,"[4] but with the president already able to appoint at least one FCC commissioner per year, the added influence of this White House directive seemed less than subtle.

The Whitehead Speech

Caution was replaced by outright concern in 1972, when OTP director Clay Whitehead used an Indianapolis, Indiana luncheon of the Society of Professional Journalists, Sigma Delta Chi, to level his own critique of the networks. The forum was appropriate for the Nixon administration. Indiana had been a big supporter of Nixon, and a luncheon of journalists is an optimum forum for publicity, even when the speaker is not always newsworthy. Whitehead's speech made national news.

Whitehead began by saying, "It's been easy for broadcasters to give lip service to the uniquely American principle of placing broadcasting power and responsibility at the local level." It's been too easy "for broadcasters to turn around and sell their responsibility along with their audience to a network at the going rate for affiliate compensation. . . . When affiliates consistently pass the buck to the networks, they're frustrating the fundamental purposes of the First Amendment free press provision." Then came the cake. Whitehead announced the administration's intention to sponsor legislation which would rescue local broadcasters from, what Whitehead called, the FCC's "trap door" by extending the time between license renewal.

Whitehead emphasized that *local* broadcasters would need to meet the needs of their local communities, regardless of where the programs originated. Second, broadcasters would need to show that they "afforded reasonable, realistic, and practical opportunities for the presentation and discussion of conflicting views on controversial issues." Neither idea was new, but Whitehead's statement did catapult them to the public's attention, and it gave the newspaper reporters something to write about.

Attempts to Control News Coverage

But there was more. The problem had been how to gain some control over news coverage, coverage with which the Nixon administration had long been dissatisfied. Dipping into a local or network news department was not something for which reporters or the First Amendment would stand still, but if anyone could control the broadcast journalists, it was their bosses, the people who signed the paychecks—*management*. Whitehead noted that when a disc jockey lined his pockets with payola money, management would take decisive action. Whitehead said "but men also stress or suppress information in accordance with their beliefs. Will station licenses or network executives also take action against this ideological plugola?" He said that "insulating station and network news departments from management oversight and supervision has never been responsible and never will be."

"Who else but management . . . can assure that the audience is being served by journalists dedicated to the highest professional standards? Who else but management can or should correct so-called professionals who confuse sensationalism with sense and who dispense elitist gossip in the guise of news analysis?"[5] The offer was now clear. If broadcast management would clean up local and network news bias, as perceived by the Nixon administration, the reward would be longer times between five-year license renewals.

The Cable Alliance

The OTP survived the early 1970s intact and continued to be involved in policy making. Finding an ally among cable operators, the OTP proposed deregulation of cable, so that it could prosper in a free, competitive atmosphere. Since the cable companies had not been making any great strides with the FCC and the Communications Act interpretations, the OTP was a breath of fresh air. The OTP stated that the "framework for the present regulation of cable communications is premised on a law that addresses only limited-signal technologies and that does not, therefore, recognize the potential for this new medium."[6] The OTP also encouraged commercial developments to replace the government-supported benefits of satellites, which were beaming educational television programming domestically and internationally.[7] The OTP also represented the United States in international treaty negotiations involving INTELSAT and the International Telecommunication Union (ITU), a United Nations organization involved in seeking cooperative international efforts in the development of telecommunication.

Opposition to the OTP

Yet whatever accomplishments the OTP did manage to achieve, it did so under a handicap. The Nixon administration's antinetwork views, as reflected in the Agnew and Whitehead speeches, placed a taint on the office from the very beginning. From a broadcaster's viewpoint, having another political appointee from the White House in addition to the FCC commissioners wasn't satisfactory.

THE FORMATION OF THE OFFICE OF TELECOMMUNICATIONS IN THE DEPARTMENT OF COMMERCE

Also in response to the executive order issued under President Nixon, the Department of Commerce formed the Office of Telecommunications (OT). The executive order stated that the OT would, among other things, "(1) conduct technical and economic research . . . ; and (2) conduct research and analysis on radio propagation, radio systems' characteristics, and operating techniques affecting the utilization of the radio spectrum . . ."[8] Fully 41 percent of the Office of Telecommunications budget came from jobs done for the OTP.[9]

Research and Policy Initiatives

The OT's applied research program analyses studied the effectiveness of transmission and receiver systems for the United States Information Agency's Voice of America.[10] The research program developed formulas which helped predict the "electronic" effectiveness of VOA transmissions months in advance, across a wide range of frequencies. Conducting research on the application of fiber optic technology, the OT formed the Task Force on Optical Communications, comprised of representatives from business, government, and education. The task force met to discuss new developments and applications of this technology. Research in public safety examined such areas as early warning systems for natural disasters, which could aid in predicting a potential disaster caused by natural phenomena and also beam radio and television warning signals directly to home receivers.[11]

International Telecommunications

In the area of international telecommunications, the OT worked closely with the United Nations' International Telecommunication Union (ITU) in planning international conferences and negotiations. Policy initiatives for World Administrative Radio Conferences (WARC) resulted from OT research and planning. The OT served in various capacities on two committees of the International Telecommunication Union. These committees, the International Radio Consultive Committee (CCIR), and the International Telephone and Telegraph Consultive Committee (CCITT) sponsor study groups that deal with technical problems of common interest to member nations and representing the interests of the United States and offering technical knowledge.[12]

In cooperation with the ITU, the OT conducted a series of fellowship programs to help educate specialists in ITU member countries. It also initiated a series of broadcast engineering consultancies for foreign countries.[13] OT also conducted seminars for other federal employees and maintained a public information program for non-government organizations.[14]

THE NATIONAL TELECOMMUNICATIONS AND INFORMATION ADMINISTRATION

When Jimmy Carter was elected president, the OTP became one of the targets of Carter's own reorganization efforts. Carter realized the OTP could very quickly turn into a political liability. Its pro-cable stance didn't thrill the commercial broadcasters. Research contracted by the office, regardless of how objective, was susceptible to charges of favoring administration policies. Unlike the FCC, where blame could be spread over all the commissioners, OTP critics could center theirs directly on the president and his administration. Carter appointed an "acting director" of the OTP and sent to Congress a proposal to move the OTP's functions out of the White House and into the Department of Commerce. The Office of Telecommunications was already in the Commerce Department, and it was already doing a large share of the OTP's work. Carter combined the OT and the OTP functions into a new Commerce Department agency called the National Telecommunications and Information Administration (NTIA).

Transition to the NTIA from the OT and the OTP

Specifically, the transition was provided for in President Carter's reorganization plan creating the NTIA through a five-step process. First, the reorganization plan first transferred all functions of the Office of Telecommunications Policy to the Department of Commerce. That moved it out of the White House control. Second, the reorganization plan then abolished the Office of Telecommunication Policy. Third, the reorganization plan then abolished the Office of Telecommunications in the Department of Commerce. Fourth, the reorganization plan then created an office of Assistant Secretary for Communication and Information in the Department of Commerce. Fifth, finally, the reorganization plan formed the National Telecommunications and Information Administration, with the Assistant Secretary for Communications and Information as agency head.

President Carter appointed Henry Geller as the first head of the agency. Geller had been a former deputy general counsel and general counsel of the FCC under two presidents and had served a stint with the Rand Corporation and later the Aspen Institute Program on Communications and Society. Although the NTIA's charge is still one of advising the president and is accountable to the executive branch, its removal from the Office of the President has at least presented the appearance of detachment and created the potential for better cooperation with other agencies of government.

Functions

Similar in many ways to the old Office of Telecommunications, the NTIA sees itself as having different primary functions.[15] These include: (1) Advise the president on telecommunication policy. (2) In coordination with the State Department develop programs and policies relating to international telecommunications including conferences and negotiations. (3) Coordinate telecommunications activities of the executive branch. (4) Assign frequencies to U.S. government radio stations. (5) Develop telecommunications policies pertaining to the nation's telecommunication economic and technological advancement. (6) Ensure that executive branch views on telecommunications matters are effectively presented to the Federal Communications Commission and Congress. (7) Study and make recommendations on the impact of the convergence of computer and communications technology.

The functions of the NTIA are organized under offices and a research institute.[16] These include: (1) the Office of Policy Analysis and Development, (2) the Office of International Affairs, (3) the Office of Spectrum Management, (3) the Office of Telecommunications Applications, and (4) the Institute for Telecommunication Sciences.

Office of Policy Analysis and Development

The NTIA's Office of Policy Analysis and Development (OPAD) examines policy issues operating in such areas as telecommunication industries, the telephone industry, broadcasting, and cable. During the 1980s under the executive branch, the office examined policies deregulating many of the telecommunications industries. A minority training and development program operates under the office and provides technical planning services for minority entrepreneurs. OPAD also participates and helps coordinate interagency policy making in the areas of domestic emergency preparedness.

Office of International Affairs

International telecommunication policy is formulated under the Office of International Affairs (OIA) in the NTIA. The movement toward integrated telecommunication systems across national boundaries, such as the technology of the Integrated Services Digital Network (ISDN) which standardizes international transmission standards, means that increased international cooperation is necessary for all countries to be able to communicate freely with each other. The increased importance in the role telephone systems play in delivering the information needs of tomorrow's consumers also means increased importance for the agencies which must coordinate international policies. OIA is actively involved in the assessment of other nation's telecommunication policies to determine how they will affect U.S. policy in the area of developing technology. Monitoring the legislative initiatives of other countries and working to lessen barriers to U.S. trade in telecommunications information services are two additional functions of the NTIA's Office of International Affairs.

Office of Spectrum Management

While the Federal Communications Commission is responsible for the nonfederal usage of the electromagnetic spectrum, the NTIA is responsible for the federal use of the spectrum and this federal use of the spectrum falls under the NTIA's Office of Spectrum Management. The FCC and the NTIA cooperate in the administration of federal and nonfederal use, since many times competing interests of federal and nonfederal uses necessitate dialogue in the policy planning process. Among the spectrum management functions of the Office of Spectrum Management (OSM) is the review of proposed federal communications systems to guard against interference with nonfederal uses of the spectrum, resolving operational problems on different frequencies, and performing technical analyses of the use on the electromagnetic spectrum.

The OSM is also a key player in the liaison with the ITU in planning U.S. participation in ITU world regulatory conferences. Working with the committees of the ITU, the OTM prepares the U.S. position and then participates, in cooperation with the Department of State, in the international frequency management arenas. The proposals formulated by the NTIA become the documents used by the Department of State in international negotiations over the use of the electromagnetic spectrum.

Office of Telecommunications Applications

The Office of Telecommunications Applications works with public television stations and administers planning and construction grants to such stations. Part of what is called the Public Telecommunications Facilities Program, the grants have helped establish more than hundreds of noncommercial television stations nationwide. In addition more than a thousand grants have been awarded to upgrade public radio and television programs since the grants were started in 1962.

Institute for Telecommunication Sciences

The NTIA's Institute for Telecommunication Sciences (ITS) is an agency which operated under the old Office of Telecommunications in the Department of Commerce and continued to operate under the NTIA after President Carter's reorganization plan took effect. To some extent the Institute is much like the Office of Engineering in the FCC in that the Institute is the technical expertise and support staff for all of the activities of the NTIA. It's also a centralized government laboratory for other government agencies which use ITS as a resource to help solve telecommunications problems. Its responsibilities include research and the development of performance criteria for telecommunications systems. The institute also studies wave characteristics in the electromagnetic spectrum to improve the efficiency of the spectrum.

U.S. GOVERNMENT USES AND COORDINATION OF TELECOMMUNICATION SERVICES

Between our discussion of the National Telecommunications and Information Administration, the agency responsible for policy and coordination of the federal government's use of telecommunications, and other federal government agencies involved in telecommunications administration and operations, it is necessary to grasp the enormous extent to which the federal government uses the electromagnetic spectrum and telecommunications services.[17] The tremendous increase in this use has been almost exponential. Not only have new services developed as the technology to provide them has become available, but the size and complexity of government has also increased. Our discussion which follows concerns only the federal government. Additional uses of the electromagnetic spectrum by state and local governments come under the control of the Federal Communications Commission and the federal government's use of the spectrum is coordinated through the National Telecommunications and Information Administration in an integrated regulatory framework that not only involves the FCC and the NTIA but the DCA and other agencies of government. Consider that the approach of one hurricane brings into use the agencies of the National Weather Service, the U.S. military spotter aircraft, emergency preparedness organizations, amateur radio, and commercial radio and television stations, all of which use radio frequencies and are regulated and managed by different government agencies.

In another example, a high-level military commander communicating with troops can involve telecommunications services regulated or coordinated by more than a dozen federal agencies. One set of regulations may apply in peacetime and completely different regulations in wartime, and the ability to switch between the two on short notice by a presidential directive is important. Although that much regulatory complexity may seem cumbersome and dangerously slow in the event that national security is threatened, keep in mind that the regulations, coordination, and contingency plans are in place long before they are needed so that operations proceed as smoothly as possible. Even then, however, international radio regulations may come into play when military operations are taking place in a foreign country where radio frequencies are allocated for local use without interference. When military operations begin, radio jamming can occur and it is necessary to use any frequency on a demand basis to complete the mission. Even in peacetime, the military's use of the electromagnetic spectrum is significant.

Military Uses of the Electromagnetic Spectrum

At the highest levels the military use of radio frequencies involves the National Command Authorities, the Joint Chiefs of Staff, and the commanders of the various military branches. One example of a military department's use of the spectrum is the U.S. Army, where radio is the primary medium of communication for Army tactical units.[18] Radio is used for the exchange of information and as liaison between units. It is also the only means of communication across enemy territory, large bodies of water, and over terrain where wires cannot be installed. These uses not only involve voice communication but the use of radio frequencies to relay computer data as well. In one form or another, the Army's use of the radio communications covers most of the spectrum's useable space. Instructional use of the spectrum for training purposes takes place at Army bases, causing higher concentrations of local radio-frequency use.[19] Army aviation operation uses the electromagnetic spectrum in air traffic control, in attack helicopters in tactical operations, and in other types of airborne personnel operations. In addition to all of these uses, the U.S. Army Corps of Engineers maintains more than 22,500 miles of navigable waterways, and at many points radio communication with passing vessels through locks and bridges takes place. In addition, the corps operates sensing devices at 66,000 dams which require more than 1,000 miles of microwave radio-relay systems.[20]

Other military operations, such as the Coast Guard, Navy, Marine Corp, Air Force, National

Guard, and military reserves, also use radio communications. For example, Navy fleet communication between ships and ashore commands uses radio frequencies, much of it mobile and over wide geographic areas including all oceans. Because of these mobile and geographic restrictions, radio waves are the only means of communications applicable to Navy operations. The Air Force and its various commands, such as the Tactical Air Command and the Strategic Air Command, use the entire breadth of the electromagnetic spectrum to achieve their missions. The Air Force, for example, operates about 10,000 aircraft, each using radio communication across multiple frequencies.

The Air Force Communications Command

An example of the different layers of military coordination in telecommunications is the Air Force Communications Command. Because of the number of Air Force aircraft in operation, there are special demands for air traffic control and navigational uses of radio communication. Managing these demands is the Air Force Communications Command which has the responsibility to install the air traffic control and navigation systems as well as provide the engineering support, the operations, and the maintenance of these services. For the Air Force, these services must be operational in both peacetime and wartime and their operation must be coordinated with the domestic, international, nongovernment, and nonmilitary air traffic control services.

The Naval Telecommunications System

Telecommunications services for the U.S. Navy and the U.S. Marine Corp are operated through the Naval Telecommunications System. The system operates worldwide and supports naval forces in oceans where the fleet operates. Along with the aboard telecommunications services, a network of onshore Area Master Stations provides links to the fleet.

Nonmilitary Government Uses of the Spectrum

In addition to military use of the spectrum, other government agencies also use radio frequencies, placing demands on the spectrum and necessitating coordination between regulatory agencies. For example, the U.S. Forest Service has 45,000 radios which are used in fire fighting, the management of recreational facilities, rescue operations, and the control of timber production and watersheds. In addition, thousands of other pieces of electronic equipment are used in research activities of the service. Just within the Agriculture Department alone, which is where the U.S. Forest Service falls, there are radio spectrum uses by such agencies as the Soil Conservation Service, the Federal Extension Service, Federal Grain Inspection Service, and the Plant Health Inspection Service.

The National Weather Service in the Department of Commerce uses radio communication at its field offices where weather radio transmitters broadcast regular weather radio reports to agriculture and maritime interests. There are more than 100 weather radar centers in operation, more than 100 weather balloon stations, and 300 weather radio stations all using radio frequencies. More than 4,000 data-collection platforms use data-collection radio-relay services of meteorological satellites. Some are coordinated between countries for weather forecasting, locating distress signals, and providing search and rescue services. The Department of Energy uses 6,000 radio frequencies from low-frequency to light-wave regions of the electromagnetic spectrum. The U.S. government's petroleum reserves program controlled from New Orleans uses five VHF-FM radio networks along the Gulf Coast. While the preceding list may seem extensive, it only scratches the surface of the demands placed on the spectrum for nonmilitary communication services. In the role of broadcasters, the United States Information Agency operates the Voice of America which consists of more than 100 medium-wave and shortwave transmitters in the United States and foreign countries. Microwave and satellite systems help relay the Voice of America broadcasts worldwide.

Telecommunication Services of the U.S. Government

To this point we have been discussing the federal government's use of services which require the use of the electromagnetic spectrum. Other federal government telecommunication needs are met by wired systems, with telephone and data communication being examples.[21] More detailed examples can be seen through such agencies as the Social Security Administration and the Internal Revenue Service. The Social Security Administration makes direct deposits available for people receiving social security checks. Customer inquiries, which at one time took weeks to answer, are now answered in a matter of minutes through data-based record accessing. The Internal Revenue Service is perfecting direct filing of tax returns to be used by paid tax preparers. It means if you file a tax return through your accountant, your accountant can use the same computer program used to prepare your tax return to file the return electronically with the Internal Revenue Service. Special telephone services for obtaining tax advice and special telephone services for the deaf and elderly are already available.

The Department of Health and Human Services uses telephone and data links for health care. A "Physician Data Query" service permits a personal computer to be used to access a medical library thousands of miles away. Government hospitals use telecommunication links for diagnosis. Telephone "hot lines" on everything from AIDS to cancer care are in operation and information can be obtained in different languages. A Medicare direct-charge credit service is under consideration which would permit patients to charge their prescriptions directly to the government.

MANAGING MILITARY TELECOMMUNICATIONS: THE DEFENSE COMMUNICATIONS AGENCY

As our worldwide communication systems become increasingly integrated, more agencies of government are becoming involved in using these channels of communication. Consequently, the roles that these agencies, services, and bureaus play are taking on new dimensions. Managing the military's telecommunications services is the Defense Communications Agency (DCA).

Coordinating the Needs of the Defense Department

Established in 1960 as a Department of Defense Management Organization, the DCA provides central management functions to certain communications-related activities of the Army, Navy, and Air Force.[22] The DCA's primary responsibility is the management and direction of the Defense Communications System (DCS), which includes all long-haul, point-to-point communications systems of the Army, Navy, and Air Force. Included under the DCS umbrella are supervision of circuitry by radio, wire, submarine cable, and satellites.

Global Organization

Along with the responsibilities for hardware and communication components of the DCS, the director of the agency oversees a vice director, deputy director for plans and programs, deputy director for operations, deputy director for command and control, deputy director for systems engineering, deputy director for military satellite communications, a comptroller, and about 1,500 military and 1,500 civilian support personnel.[23]

Operating as part of a worldwide communication network, the DCS has an operation control center located in Washington, DC. Area centers operate in such locations as the Pacific and Europe; and regional centers, which report to the area centers, are located in such areas as Japan and the Philippines. Both area and regional centers are in constant contact with each other. The DCS is also the "architect" of high-frequency and satellite communication related to defense. In this role, it plans the engineering requirements as well as the integration of the military departments' uses of satellite communication.

The telecommunication system, wired and unwired, operated by the DCS and administered by the DCA involves both private and government-owned and operated services. A voice network provides worldwide direct-distance telephone service and other voice-mode services through microwave links which are both ground and satellite based. In addition to telephone-type services, the DCA also manages the Defense Data Network which links Defense Department agencies.[24]

Along with the Defense Communications Agency's role as overseer of the DCS, the agency also oversees the National Communications System (NCS), discussed elsewhere in this chapter, which incorporates the major communication networks of the Department of State, Federal Aviation Administration, General Services Administration, National Aeronautics and Space Administration, Department of Energy, Central Intelligence Agency, Department of the Interior, Department of Commerce, and International Communications Agency.[25] Also falling under the DCA is the White House Communications Agency, also discussed elsewhere in this chapter.

NATIONAL SECURITY AND EMERGENCY PREPAREDNESS: THE NATIONAL COMMUNICATIONS SYSTEM

Following the Cuban missile crisis, President John F. Kennedy in an executive order of August 21, 1963 formed the National Communications System

(NCS) designed to integrate and link together those areas of the government most concerned with national security.

Executive Order Restructuring NCS Functions

Under an executive order issued by President Reagan on April 3, 1984, the NCS was restructured and charged with, "The coordination of the planning for and provision of national security and emergency preparedness communications for the Federal government under all circumstances, including crisis or emergency, attack, recovery and reconstruction."[26] The executive order called on the NCS to ensure the development of a national telecommunications infrastructure which:

> Is responsive to the national security and emergency preparedness needs of the President and the Federal departments, agencies and other entities, including telecommunications in support of national security leadership and continuity of government:
>
> Is capable of satisfying priority telecommunications requirements under all circumstances through use of commercial, government and privately owned telecommunications resources:
>
> Incorporates the necessary combination of hardness, redundancy, mobility, connectivity, interoperability, restorability and security to obtain, to the maximum extent practicable, the survivability of national security and emergency preparedness telecommunications in all circumstances, including conditions of crisis or emergency; and is consistent to the maximum extent practicable, with other national telecommunications policies.
>
> To assist in accomplishing its mission, the NCS shall:
>
> Serve as the focal point for joint industry-government national security and emergency preparedness telecommunications planning; and establish a joint industry-government National Coordinating Center which is capable of assisting in the initiation, coordination, restoration, and reconstruction of national security or emergency preparedness telecommunications services or facilities under all conditions of crisis or emergency.[27]

President Reagan's executive order also provided for the secretary of defense to appoint the manager of the NCS and the order charged the appointed manager with ensuring the NCS, "conducts unified planning and operations, in order to coordinate the development and maintenance of an effective and responsive capability for meeting the domestic and international national security and emergency preparedness needs of the Federal government."

Management of the National Communications System

The executive order charged the manager of NCS with integrating the NCS functions with other emergency management agencies of the government.[28] In addition the executive order called on the manager of NCS to develop:

> A recommended evolutionary telecommunications architecture designed to meet current and future Federal government national security and emergency preparedness telecommunications requirements.
>
> Plans and procedures for minimizing or removing technical impediments to the interoperability of government owned and/or commercially-approved telecommunications systems.
>
> Test and exercise programs and procedure for the evaluation of the capability of the Nation's telecommunications resources to meet national security or emergency preparedness telecommunications requirements . . .
>
> Implement and administer any approved plans or programs as assigned, including any system of priorities and preferences for the provision of communications services . . .[29]

The executive order under President Reagan spelled out responsibilities for the National Security Council under nonwartime conditions and those responsibilities included overseeing the activities of the NCS and advising and assisting the president in the development of telecommunications policy for emergency preparedness. Other agencies of government were also charged with developing plans for telecommunications services which would function under emergency conditions, and were given the authority to develop their own rules and regulations to implement those plans.

THE WHITE HOUSE COMMUNICATIONS AGENCY

The White House Communications Agency is under the direction of the Defense Communications Agency and is responsible for providing the communications services for the president as well as the president's family and staff. This includes the needs of the White House in the areas of telecommunications, computer systems, and audio-visual services.

OFFICE OF SCIENCE AND TECHNOLOGY POLICY

While the OTP was removed from the Executive Office of the President, it did not mean the end of the White House's involvement in telecommunication policy. The Office of Science and Technology Policy in the Executive Office of the President is a coordinating and advisory body to the president on a wide range of telecommunication matters.

Director's Responsibility

An example of this coordinating function is seen in the area of national security matters which are related to telecommunication. In an executive order (No.12472) which formed a system linking together government agencies operating or regulating communication systems involved in national security and emergency preparedness, the director of the Office of Science and Technology Policy was charged with providing:

> . . . information, advice, guidance and assistance, as appropriate, to the President and to those Federal departments and agencies with responsibilities for the provision, management, or allocation of telecommunication resources, during those crisis or emergencies in which the exercise of the President's war power functions is not required or permitted by law . . .[30]

The director of the Office of Science and Technology Policy was also charged with making:

> recommendations to the President with respect to the test, exercise and evaluation of the capability of existing and planned communications systems, networks or facilities to meet national security or emergency preparedness requirements and report the results of any such tests or evaluations and any recommended remedial actions to the President and to the National Security Council.[31]

In addition, the director or director's designate:

> shall advise and assist the President in the administration of a system of radio spectrum priorities for those spectrum dependent telecommunications resources of the Federal government which support national security or emergency preparedness functions. The Director also shall certify or approve priorities for radio spectrum use by the Federal Government, including the resolution of any conflicts in or among priorities, under all conditions of crisis or emergency. . . .[32]

Other federal agencies, including the Federal Communications Commission, coordinate their functions with the Office of Science and Technology Policy.

OFFICE OF TECHNOLOGY ASSESSMENT

Created in 1972, the Office of Technology Assessment (OTA) provides Congress with forecasts on the impact of technology in society. The issues tackled by the OTA range from technology on water supplies to solar-powered satellites.

Primary Functions

Specifically, the OTA is charged with bringing "a long-term global and comprehensive perspective to bear and to provide Congress with independent, authoritative, evenhanded assessments."[33] For Congress, the OTA is a ready source of digestible information on long-range goals, separate from the more narrow issues that confront the daily pattern of lawmaking. Projects for the OTA are initiated after the approval of a congressionally-appointed board composed of six senators and six congressmen. Initial requests for studies by the OTA can originate from the OTA director, the members of the Board, or from the chairpersons of congressional committees.[34] An Advisory Council comprising eminent professionals in the field of science and engineering also advises the OTA.

An example of an OTA technology assessment study is one that proposed to study education.[35] Communication satellites distributing television courses anywhere in the world open up new policy issues, associated not only with technology but with the future of education as well. The role of OTA in assessing this future perspective would include such areas as determining how technology is used as a means of improving the quality and availability of education in the formal and informal education systems; the implications of global educational technology for education and foreign policy; and the effect of new technologies of education on students' ability to acquire basic skills.[36]

OTA has conducted broad-based issue assessments of new technology in society. In one instance people responded to a request for priorities for the OTA to examine. From a list of items selected from individuals and publications, the OTA then focused its efforts on these high-priority items.

POLICY IMPLICATIONS OF GOVERNMENT TELECOMMUNICATION SERVICES

The complexity of the government's use of telecommunications, both spectrum-based and wired services, opens up important regulatory and policy considerations.[37] In the use of the electromagnetic spectrum, for example, pressure continues to mount from those who demand use of the spectrum for commercial services. Cellular telephone systems have grown dramatically and use frequencies once dedicated to other services. Technologies such as high-definition television (HDTV) use a greater portion of the electromagnetic spectrum than standard over-the-air broadcasting. Direct-broadcast satellite (DBS) systems are operating in other countries and promise to be in consumer demand in the United States by the mid-1990s. All of these services, and hundreds of others both domestically and internationally, compete for space on the spectrum. Policy makers must determine what services will be given priority. While the government has the internal mechanism to look out for its own interests, powerful political pressure can be applied by private business to meet their needs as well.

The federal government is also at the point where it must determine whether it can realize a savings from owning its own telephone system or leasing it through private business. Although private leasing arrangements have some advantages, it also means that suppliers are chosen through a bidding process, political pressure mounts to spread the government's business across many different suppliers, and the increased number of suppliers means a larger management role for the government. Because so much money has already been spent on communications equipment, there is a certain inertia to the system as it now exists. Increased government use of cellular telephone systems will continue to grow and sophisticated defense installations, both fixed and mobile, will use the spectrum for everything from radar to sophisticated communication networks between commanders at the highest levels to operational field units.

As the spectrum becomes more crowded, there is also the added cost of equipment which must be more sophisticated to operate in environments where interference and even the smallest frequency shifts are unacceptable. The sophisticated equipment is more expensive, which demands a greater share of federal budgets, some of which can themselves decline during recessionary times and the corresponding budget cuts. Finally, there is the need for people with the intelligence, both political and scientific, to plan and execute the next generation of services and to formulate the policy that must support those services in a global political environment.

U.S. DEPARTMENT OF JUSTICE

Sometimes called the largest law office in the world, the U.S. Department of Justice employees serve from the attorney general to the federal prison system.[38] Since 1968, the U.S. Department of Justice, through the Antitrust Division, has participated as a party in both adjudicatory and rulemaking proceedings at the FCC. The reason for its participation is that the United States is a statutory respondent in almost all appeals on FCC decisions. This means that a case would be titled, as a hypothetical example, *WAAA* v. *FCC and the United States*. The attorney general, who represents the United States, has delegated responsibility in these cases to the Antitrust Division, where it is discharged by the Appellate Section.

SECURITIES AND EXCHANGE COMMISSION

The legal ramifications of big corporate mergers and the financing of broadcasting properties have resulted in increased attention to the Securities and Exchange Commission (SEC).[39]

Securities Trading and the Crash of 1929

Following World War I, a surge of activity in securities trading took place, reaching a peak by 1929. Little public support occurred for requiring financial disclosure to prevent the fraudulent sale of stock. Credit was easy and people plunged into the stock market with a "rags to riches" enthusiasm. More than 20 million shareholders took part in securities trading. Brokers, many financed by big corporations, engaged in "margin" trading where small down payments could be used to pyramid paper profits. Then in 1929 it all collapsed in the Great Crash of the stock market, which brought the American economic system to the verge of disaster.

Abuses were uncovered in a government investigation which heard testimony from bankers, traders, and executives of the large brokerage houses. Public outcry resulted in the passage of law requiring full disclosure of securities offerings, to be enforced by the Federal Trade Commission. Another bill followed a year later that formed a separate government agency called the Securities and Exchange Commission.

Modern SEC Enforcement Areas

The Securities and Exchange Commission investigates and brings enforcement actions to stop violations in such areas as corporate reporting and accounting, insider trading, violations of regulated entities and associated persons, market manipulations, securities offerings, changes in corporate control, related party transactions, and others. For example, in the area of corporate reporting and accounting, financial disclosure is a high priority. Such actions as the improper valuation of assets and liabilities, improper reporting of revenue or income, and failure to have sufficient reserves to cover bad debts are all areas that can involve SEC enforcement actions. In the same area, not using generally accepted auditing standards can elicit SEC attention.

Regulated Entities

Regulated entities and associated persons account for the largest number of SEC actions. Broker-dealers, investment companies, and investment advisers are typical of regulated entities and associated persons. For example, the SEC has brought actions against a firm that wrongfully used a client's fully-paid securities in a stock loan deal. In another instance, action was brought against a brokerage firm that failed to properly supervise its sales staff, resulting in wrongfully conducted transactions. Some individuals and firms fail to register public offerings of stock or make misrepresentations in a stock offering. Not accurately reporting a change in the corporate control of a company based on who owns how much stock can result in SEC action. The SEC has brought action against defendants for manipulating the price of common stock through dominating the market and issuing false statements about future business prospects.

Nonpublic Information

People who buy or sell securities while in possession of nonpublic information can be guilty of insider trading. When successfully prosecuted, such individuals can incur loss of all profits made from insider trading, substantial penalties, and prison sentences. For example, in one action the office manager of a law firm received a sentence of three and one-half years plus five years probation after pleading guilty to an indictment which charged the individual with having tipped off defendants to prospective mergers which involved clients of the law firm.

The Broadcast Press

At first glance it may seem as though SEC regulations only affect stockbrokers or large publicly held companies. Not so. The SEC and the FCC can both become involved in such areas as local station operations, specifically, the station's news department. It is well established that a journalist who uses inside information from an unreleased news story to make a personal profit is in violation of securities law. For example, assume you obtain an advance copy of a press release telling about a new wonder drug from a pharmaceutical firm.

Knowing the price of the stock will go up after the announcement, you phone your stockbroker and buy a large quantity of the stock. You could be guilty of securities fraud and subject to federal prosecution. Moreover, the station may be liable as well and be subject to penalties from the FCC. Journalists have as much responsibility as stockbrokers when it comes to not making a profit on inside information. Some stations have policies which guard against this happening, for example, a disclosure policy for employees of the station, forbidding employees to buy stocks during the period immediately preceding the dissemination of information that might affect the price of the stock, prohibiting short-term trading by requiring an employee to hold a stock a certain length of time before selling it, or even requiring employees to publicly disclose information about stocks about which they might report.

SEC REPORTING REQUIREMENTS: THE 10K FORM

Companies trading in public securities and which fall under SEC regulations are required to file different public disclosure forms, the more common being the 10K which is frequently cited in corporate annual reports. The 10K form provides an important source of information about the operations of a company, ranging from the market value of its stock to the business characteristics of its subsidiaries. Anyone who is seriously considering investing in publicly held stock should understand and consult a company's 10K form before proceeding. The nonfinancial aspects of the 10K can also be informative. To understand some of the reporting requirements, we'll examine certain information contained in a 10K filed by Capital Cities/ABC, Inc.[40]

General Business Operations for a Television Network

Part of the 10K requires a description of business operations. In the case of Capital Cities/ABC, Inc., that includes stating that the company operates the ABC Television Network with its affiliated televisions, radio network, and radio stations. The company also provides programming for cable television. We can learn from the 10K that the company has more than 19,000 employees, of which more than 10,000 are in broadcasting, more than 9,000 are in its publishing enterprises, and more than 200 in corporate activities. The company earned the majority of its income from advertising sales in its broadcasting and publishing businesses. Other income came from book and record sales and from magazine circulation.

Broadcasting Operations

Broadcasting operations are described in the 10K reports as follows:

> Generally, the Company pays the cost of producing or purchasing the broadcast rights for its network programming and pays varying degrees of compensation to its affiliated stations for broadcasting the programs and commercial announcements included therein. Substantially all revenues from network operations are derived from the sale to advertisers of time in network programs for commercial announcements. The ability to sell time for commercial announcement and the rates received are substantially dependent on the quantitative and qualitative audience that the network can deliver to the advertiser.[41]

In addition to identifying the ABC Radio Networks, and the ABC Television Network, the 10K also contains a list of the radio and television stations with their call letters, city of operation, frequency, power, expiration date of the FCC license, and the ranking in the market. For example, WABC radio in New York City operates as 770 kilohertz with a power of 50,000 watts, and its license expired on June 1, 1991. In the 10K it is ranked number one in its market. The 10K also lists the companies "video enterprises," which include three cable television networks.

Competition: Other Networks

Analyzing the company's competition as required in the 10K shows the network competes with other networks, as do its owned-and-operated stations. The 10K requirement spelling out Capital Cities/ABC, Inc.'s competition reads in part:

> The ABC Television Network competes for viewers with the other television networks, independent stations and other media such as cable television, satellite television program services and video cassettes; in the sale of

> advertising time, it competes with the other television networks, independent television stations, suppliers of cable television programming, and other advertising media such as newspapers, magazines and billboards. Substantial competition also exists for exclusive broadcasting rights for television programming. The ABC Radio Networks likewise compete with other radio networks and radio programming services, independent radio stations, and other advertising media.[42]

Notice that competition goes beyond other networks to other media as well. The common thread among all media is the sale of advertising time.

Competition: Other Broadcasting Stations

In discussing the network's owned-and-operated stations, the 10K competition analysis for Capital Cities/ABC Inc. reads:

> The Company's television and radio stations are in competition with other television and radio stations and other advertising media such as newspapers, magazines and billboards. Such competition occurs primarily in individual market areas. Generally, a television broadcasting station in one market does not compete directly with other stations in other market areas. Nor does a group of stations, such as those owned by the Company, compete with any other group of stations as such. While the pattern of competition in the radio station industry is basically the same, it is not uncommon for radio stations outside of a market area to place a signal of sufficient strength within that area (particularly during nighttime hours) to gain a share of the audience.[43]

The "nighttime hours" refer to the fact that at night the radio-wave propagation in the electromagnetic spectrum causes signals to travel further and some other stations, depending on their license restrictions, may lower their power during nighttime. The competition section of the 10K also points out that management and experience, authorized power allowance, assigned frequency, network affiliation, local program acceptance, and the strength of the local competition all play a part in defining the competitive nature of the marketplace. The information in a 10K is important to those people who may be interested in investing in a company or researching the company for comparison purposes. The 10K form is a good place to get a better understanding of the financial health of a company as well as the market forces which are impacting on the industry within which the company operates.

Competition: Cable Television

In the case of Capital Cities/ABC, Inc., competition from cable television systems is discussed in the 10K. An excerpt from the analysis discusses how cable competes with conventional television:

> The most common sources of television service other than conventional television stations are cable television systems. Cable television can provide more competition for a station by making additional signals available to its audience. In addition, most cable television systems supply programming that is not available on conventional television stations. These include a wide range of advertiser-supported and subscription-supported video programming services. Subscription-supported video programming services are also provided by over-the-air television stations and multipoint distribution services which employ non-broadcast frequencies to transmit subscription television services to individual homes and businesses. Additional services are being provided or may be provided within the relatively near future by low power television stations and direct broadcast satellites.[44]

The Capital Cities/ABC, Inc. 10K also points out that the company's video services compete with other companies supplying program services through such media as video cassettes, videodiscs, television syndication, theatrical distribution, and conventional over-the-air broadcasting stations.

Regulatory Matters

In addition to describing the nature of the business, the financial picture, and the competition, the 10K also discusses regulatory matters which affect a company. For example, in the case of a broadcasting company the regulatory matters discussed in a 10K frequently concern the license renewals of owned-and-operated stations. General statements about pending legal matters may be referred to in a 10K, and then discussed in detail in another SEC form, the 10Q. In such areas as license renewal, the 10K will point out that broadcasting licenses are granted for a maximum period of seven years for radio and every five years for television.

The 10K will also inform the reader that there are periods when a renewal application is pending that competing applicants may file for the frequency. If a station's license renewal is tied up in the FCC or is encountering a challenge and litigation, then this information will typically appear in the 10K. Such sections can be quite lengthy and the company may provide background information on the FCC's rules and regulations so that the specific points of disclosure in the company's 10K form can be placed in the proper context and understood. For example, in discussing the joint holdings of broadcast and print properties in the same market, a brief description of the FCC's ownership rules might be included in the 10K form.

While a 10K form does not provide confidential information which would endanger the ability of a company to compete, it does provide a profile of the company which, when interpreted by knowledgeable people, is valuable in getting an understanding of how successful the company has been in the past, what the forces are which may impact on the marketplace, and what kinds of risks the company may face in the future.

THE COPYRIGHT OFFICE OF THE LIBRARY OF CONGRESS

Many radio programs and most major television and motion pictures are copyrighted, thus protecting the work from infringement and permitting the creator to receive just compensation for the use or copying of the work. The administrative structure of copyright in the United States is the Copyright Office of the Library of Congress. The Copyright Office was formed in 1870, more than 150 years after England enacted the Statute of Anne under which copyrights fell under statutory control instead of common law.[45] While most states enacted copyright laws following the American Revolution, the federal government did not become involved in copyrights until passage of the U.S. Constitution. Since 1897 the Copyright Office has been a separate division for the Library of Congress. Cataloguing more than one-half million pieces yearly, the Copyright Office has been called the keystone of the Library of Congress. It is the Copyright Office which officially records the copyrights of radio, television, and motion picture programs. Although registration is not required under copyright law, the Copyright Office will provide the forms and process the registration for those who want their works protected under the registration process. With computer software falling under copyright law, this expanding field is one more area over which the Copyright Office has jurisdiction.

DEPARTMENT OF LABOR

The Wage and Hour Division of the the U.S. Department of Labor enforces the Fair Labor Standards Act, which spells out the required compensation employees receive in such areas as minimum wage and overtime pay. Some precedent-setting lawsuits have come from employment practices involving compensation in the broadcasting industry and companies have found the courts take a conservative view when enforcing the statutes.

Enforcing Wage and Hour Laws

Federal and state laws determine the minimum wage employers are required to pay employees. But it is in the area of overtime pay that employers most frequently run afoul of the Labor Department. Federal regulations through the Fair Labor Standards Act (FLSA) require employers to pay at least minimum wage for the first 40 hours worked and then one and one-half time for any number of hours over 40. There are no restrictions at the federal level on how many hours someone can work, just that they are compensated for overtime. Various definitions are used to determine what constitutes a workweek and such things as fixed workweeks and fixed salaries come into play when applying the precise wording of the FLSA. Being on a salary does not necessarily exempt someone from overtime pay.

Exemptions from the Fair Labor Standards Act

Where the greatest ambiguity and awards for damages have occurred is in interpreting who is exempt from the overtime provisions of the FLSA. An executive exemption exists for people who are in management, who direct the work of two or more employees, who have the authority to fire and hire as well as promote people, and are engaged in exercising these duties for 80 percent of their time on the job.

Certain minimum compensation levels also exist to qualify for the exemption. An administrative exemption also exists for people at higher salaries and who perform nonmanual labor related to management. Size of the market also applies to radio and television stations with stations in populations of 100,000 or less or 25,000 population if they are 40 airline miles from the larger city.

In addition to the executive and administrative exemptions, a professional exemption also exists. The key for exemption in the professional category is for the person to work in an area which requires advanced knowledge in a field of science or learning obtained through prolonged specialized instruction. Work that is original and creative in nature in a recognized artistic field that demands such qualities as "invention," "imagination," and "talent" apply here. Doing work which is intellectual and varied also helps to qualify a person for the professional exemption for overtime pay.

SUMMARY

Where once communication policy meant the telegraph of Morse and the radio of Marconi, today international telecommunication links satellite, cable, and the airwaves to impact on the lives of millions of people daily. Modern telecommunication policy traces its roots in the United States to the presidency of Richard Nixon, who established the Office of Telecommunications Policy in the executive branch of government. The old OTP was the president's principal advisor on telecommunication, and developed telecommunications policy in cooperation with other agencies of government. In the 1970s the agency became politicized when its director Clay Whitehead used an Indianapolis luncheon of the Society of Professional Journalists to level a critique on the management of the broadcasting industry. Critics saw it as a veiled attempt to control news coverage and abridge the First Amendment through the abuse of power in the executive branch of government. In addition to the presence of the OTP, under an executive order of President Nixon, the Department of Commerce formed the Office of Telecommunications which was charged with conducting research on the economic and technical aspects of the telecommunications industry.

The OTP eventually became a target of President Jimmy Carter's reorganization effort, seeing it as a political liability with commercial broadcasters. OTP was transferred to the Department of Commerce and a reorganization abolished it along with the Commerce Department's Office of Telecommunications. Replacing the two agencies was the NTIA which continues to provide recommendations on telecommunication to the executive branch but in addition is responsible for setting policy and determining the telecommunications needs of the U.S. government. NTIA's functions include policy analysis and development, international telecommunication policy making, government use of the electromagnetic spectrum under the Office of Spectrum Management, and telecommunications technical support for public broadcasting. The U.S. government continues to be one of the major users of the electromagnetic spectrum. For example, military uses of the spectrum alone can be seen in such activities as the U.S. Army's technical units where information exchange between units on the field and command headquarters continents away takes place through radio communication. Aviation and air traffic control are two other users. Add to the U.S. Army's aircraft needs those of the U.S. Air Force with worldwide communications and air traffic control services. Other government uses include such agencies as the U.S. Forest Service with tens of thousands of radios used in fire fighting and recreational activities. The National Weather Service and the Department of Energy combined use tens of thousands of additional radio frequencies.

Of the agencies just mentioned, the military places the greatest demand on the spectrum. Managing the military's telecommunication services is the Defense Communications Agency. Formed in the Department of Defense in 1960, the DCA provides central management functions for long-haul and point-to-point communications for the armed forces. In addition the DCA oversees the National Communications System, which coordinates the networks of many other federal agencies. Formed after the Cuban missile crisis, which showed the Kennedy administration that the United States was vulnerable without an integrated government network for national security, the National Communications System was formed to be the focal point for joint industry-government telecommunications planning in such areas as national security and emergency preparedness. The White House Communications Agency under the

DCA is responsible for providing communication service to the president as well as his family and staff. The Office of Science and Technology and Policy in the Executive Office of the President coordinates a wide range of telecommunications matters. In addition to providing advice and guidance, the office coordinates its activities for specific emergency preparedness requirements with the National Security Council.

On the legislative side, the Office of Technology Assessment provides Congress with forecasts on the impact of technologies ranging from water supplies to solar-powered satellites. Since the United States is a statutory respondent in almost all appeals on FCC decisions, the U.S. Department of Justice plays a role in telecommunications policy and regulation. Of special interest is the Justice Department's Antitrust Division where the force of the Clayton Act can be used in broadcast matters such as proposed mergers and crossownership issues. Public-interest groups familiar with Justice Department procedures and personnel keep active in their attempts to influence telecommunications policy.

Where major corporations are involved in financing and mergers of telecommunications properties, the Securities and Exchange Commission may be involved. The SEC can investigate and bring enforcement actions in corporate reporting and accounting, insider trading, violations of regulated entities and associated persons, market manipulations, securities offerings, changes in corporate control, related property transactions, and others. Even broadcast news can come under SEC scrutiny if reporters use privileged information obtained during the journalistic process to profit from yet-to-be-announced stock market fluctuations. The most common public disclosure form the SEC requires is the 10K, frequently seen in corporate annual reports. Among other things, the 10K examines business operations, subsidiaries, and competition.

Two other agencies affecting electronic media industries are the Copyright Office of the Library of Congress and the U.S Department of Labor. The Copyright Office catalogues and protects millions of pieces of information including radio, television, and motion picture programs. It administers a copyright registration program and coordinates its activities to protect the copyrights of materials produced in the United States but distributed overseas. Enforcing the Fair Labor Standards Act under which wage and hour requirements fall is the U.S. Department of Labor. The Fair Labor Standards Act requires employers to pay at least minimum wage for the first 40 hours worked during a seven-day period, although some exceptions exist.

MATERIAL FOR ANALYSIS

In the 1988 National Telecommunications and Information Administration report *NTIA Telecom 2000*, policy makers examined international and domestic policy making in the year 2000. The following excerpts are from *NTIA Telecom 2000* and discuss some of the issues that will face international and domestic policy makers in the year 2000, especially the argument for a strong presence in the executive branch.[46]

INTERNATIONAL AND DOMESTIC POLICY MAKING IN THE YEAR 2000

Spurred by competition, less fettered by unnecessary regulatory burdens, and encouraged by Government, science and industry can create, develop, and distribute a wealth of telecommunications and information devices, processes, and networks that will dramatically enrich our society by the year 2000. The timing, extent, and cost of these enrichments will depend not only on creative and productive efforts, however, but also on the wisdom and forbearance of government policymakers and regulators, both in the United States and throughout the world. How key government decision makers treat—or permit others to treat—these technological advances, and whether they view the enormous changes that these developments portend as a welcome advance or a fundamental threat, can be expected to have a substantial impact upon the introduction of new services and technologies.

Regulators and policymakers in the United States have generally supported, or at least condoned, the technological and competitive advances driving our telecommunications and information policies, although at times with some hesitation and confusion. Some other countries are now also allowing some competition. Yet much of the rest of the world has not been nearly as supportive and has, in fact, constrained and even prohibited the introduction of new services and means of offering those services. In an era of global markets, a crucial challenge we face in international venues will be persuading other governments to liberalize access to their networks and markets, while maintaining a strong consensus in favor of marketplace solutions at home.

OVERVIEW OF CURRENT ARRANGEMENTS

. . . Since the dawn of modern telecommunications, when radio and wireline communications were first introduced, concern over issues such as ownership, access, universality, control, and spectrum interference have driven the organization and reorganization of U.S. regulatory and policy structures. Over the decades, as telecommunications has assumed an ever more prominent role in our economy and lives, the evolution of appropriate regulatory and policy structures has also become more essential, complicated, and perennially controversial.

Capitalizing on Opportunities and Protecting the Public

Although during the preceding half century, telecommunications and information technology, and associated businesses, have developed beyond the dreams of even the industry itself, the governmental regulatory mechanisms and means of developing telecommunications policy remain relatively unchanged from those adopted more than half a century ago. The chief focus of the Communications Act of 1934 was on the regulation of telecommunications, not necessarily its maximum development and promotion. The statute did direct the FCC to promote the larger and more effective use of radio, for example, and encouraged close oversight of telephone technology, to ensure that advances potentially beneficial to the country would be deployed. In general, however, the drafters of that legislation saw the talents and resources of industry presenting more of a challenge to the public interest than an opportunity for national progress.

One of the principal concerns . . . is how best to resolve the existing tension between our desire domestically to minimize Government's role while recognizing . . . that attenuation of Government involvement in an international context may have the practical effect, not of promoting market solutions, but rather aggrandizing the power of foreign, government-owned or controlled, communications monopolies.

Domestic and International Policy Paradigm

The trend domestically has plainly been toward a less interventionist, deregulatory role for Government, as previously discussed in this report. This approach, moreover, has clearly been justified and has yielded substantial public gains. But in the international arena, faced with foreign government-owned or controlled monopolies, restrictive practices, contentious battles over standards, and other controversies, an effective and active Federal Government role is required.

Too Short-Term and Reactive a Focus

By most estimation, the current organizational structure exhibits three fundamental defects: First, its outlook often tends to be reactive and skewed toward achieving short-term objectives rather than proactively establishing and working to reach long-range goals. The current policy making apparatus can often focus too much on maintaining the status quo, despite the influx of technological innovation and marketplace pressures. Rather than managing change to accomplish broad-based public interest goals, policymakers too often become preoccupied with arbitrating between narrow, turf-minded interests. A dynamic sector affected significantly by what government does or does not do needs a government that can act thoughtfully and at times relatively quickly.

In particular, there is a critical need for long-range policy planning, as opposed to the ad hoc response to a current crisis which has characterized many U.S. regulatory approaches. Examples of this ad hoc, reactive approach date back to the earliest days of telecommunications policy making. The first international radio conference was held in 1903 to overcome the refusal of the Marconi Company to receive messages over non-Marconi equipment. The first major Federal domestic telecommunications legislation, the Mann-Elkins Act, was passed in 1910, and placed interstate and foreign telephone and telegraph services under the regulatory jurisdiction of the Interstate Commerce Commission. It was largely a response to AT&T's acquisition of an interstate telephone service monopoly and the ensuing clamor for some kind of Federal regulation.

The need for quick responsive decision making will remain with us, but proactive, long-range policy making requires an ongoing creative approach to fundamental issues as well as immediate crises. Problems and issues necessarily overlap and interrelate. Yet policy has too often been formulated primarily as part of a discrete Government response to an existing crisis. This reflects the view that telecommunications has been a mission-support function, rather than a critical economic and social infrastructure item similar to post roads, navigable waterways, railroads, and interstate highways. While we may have been able to get away with this short-sighted approach in a simpler paper and voice communications-based past, we cannot afford this approach in the information age.

Dispersed Resources

Second, the allocation of financial and staff resources among a variety of particular agencies, most with only limited interests or responsibilities in communications and information policies, does not foster the development of effective communications policy or policymakers. As a result, experts in relatively narrow areas, or in broad areas with only a narrow communications interest, often fail to see the broader interplay of interdependent communications and information concerns. Not unexpectedly, this has produced a patchwork of roles and structures, rather than a coherent governmental framework for formulating and implementing national telecommunications policies and goals. And while the "cross-pollination" of expertise might fail to occur, forum shopping by interested parties does not.

Absence of Focused Responsibility

Finally, the current structure makes leadership—and effective Congressional oversight—difficult. So long as ultimate responsibility for most communications and information policy is fragmented among a multitude of agencies, and between domestic and international policy making, then short-term, makeshift solutions will too often emerge as a hastily-coordinated, lowest common denominator.

To some extent, some of this dispersion of real or perceived authority may be unavoidable. The structure of the Executive branch tends to mirror Congressional committee arrangements. As committee jurisdictions overlap, so too do those of Executive agencies, in telecommunications as in other areas. And, as telecommunications and information services become more important factors in other fields—trade and financial services, for instance—the number of potential participants in the telecommunications and information policy making will likely expand.

Circumstances in the U.S. Government are only slightly more confused and confusing than abroad. Squabbles among various . . . other governments over telecommunications and information issues are hardly uncommon. In the United States, however, our greater diversity, combined with the absence in too many instances of a final determiner of our telecommunication and information policies, has made effective international implementation difficult.

A Vulnerability Assessment

In the final analysis the problem is that for most issues there is, at times, no one in charge, and the buck does not stop anywhere. Our democratic republic embodies a variety of checks and balances, and separation of power concepts not typically present in parliamentary democracies. Disputes within the U.S. Government tend, therefore, to be harder to resolve. While not without advantages, the resulting diffusion of power tends to favor the status quo and inure to the benefit of incumbents. And, in a international context, this situation tends to benefit our trade rivals, some of whom demonstrably have mastered the ability to energize one part of the American Government against another.

WORKING TOWARD A SOLUTION

The problem thus is not merely the need for better coordination, but the need for coordinated decision making. Telecommunications has become a very high stakes sector with increasingly interdependent issues which require a highly integrated approach to adequately address policy issues. A lead policy agency must be proactive and not merely reactive. It must have a cross-disciplinary depth of skills encompassing economics, engineering, political science, and communications and intellectual property law, with both domestic and international dimensions. It must also be able to command sufficient acceptance within Government as well as the private sector in order to limit vulnerability to deliberate manipulation by foreign parties and interest groups.

A More Holistic Approach

By bringing these varied disciplines and perspectives together in a holistic approach, a lead telecommunications agency could achieve a synergy such that the whole will be greater that the sum of its parts. For example, if the issue is future directions for Direct Broadcast Satellite (DBS) services, a comprehensive policy—and hence the agency developing the policy—must consider such interrelated issues as the advent of high-definition television (HDTV), spectrum needs and orbital locations, the Space World Administrative Radio Conference, Regional Administrative Radio Conferences, demands by the developing world for a "New World Information Order," transporter data flows, commercial space policies, copyright protection, scrambling, broadcast policies premised on localism, antitrust, and even local zoning regulations. To ignore any of these issues may result in the development of flawed policy positions which undermine our goals in international forums.

CURRENT AGENCY RESPONSIBILITIES

More than two dozen agencies of the Federal Government, as well as many committees and subcommittees of the U.S. Congress, are involved in the development, implementation, and operation of U.S. telecommunications and information policy. For some agencies, telecommunications and information policy is a primary mission; for others an occasional sidelight. But each has different expertise, tools, and available forums in which to advance its goals. Each brings a different perspective, if not constituency, to an issue.

Within the Federal Government, power and oversight responsibility is shared by a host of agencies, some of which are concerned exclusively with domestic issues, some with international matters, and some with a combination of the two. There is a further split of authority and responsibility between those Federal Government agencies within the Executive branch (e.g., Departments of Commerce and State) and the Federal Communications Commission (FCC), an independent regulatory agency created by Congress. Additionally, the U.S Government has policy making agencies (e.g., FCC and Department of Commerce) and agencies predominantly involved as telecommunications users (e.g., Department of Defense).

In addition, in the domestic arena there is a split in authority between Federal and state policymakers and regulators. The latter are comprised primarily of state legislatures and public utility commissions whose area of responsibility is focused upon intrastate common carrier and private carrier issues. In order to avoid or reconcile conflicts between the Federal and state regimes in many instances, the Federal Communications Commission has established Joint Boards, made up of federal and state regulators, which make recommendations on such issues as the split of telephone revenues between the local and long distance portions of the network and the level of subscriber access fees.

Ensuing Problems

Rather than a panacea . . . (the) reorganization effort (forming the NTIA) failed to establish a dynamic policy making focal point with clear decision making authority. As earlier discussed, reorganization fragmented powers and dispersed responsibilities among many agencies. It also inserted several part-time telecommunications and information policymakers into the process, their lack of background and institutional expertise in either telecommunications or information policy notwithstanding. A consequence was a tendency for parties to weigh in on isolated issues and immediate dilemmas from a particular perspective, often unaware of the potentially profound ramifications of their recommendations on broader telecommunications concerns.

In the ensuing years, little has been done to reconcile the delegations of authority in the 1978 Executive Order with the potentially conflicting grants of authority found in other measures. This blurring of responsibilities may have affected overall Executive branch communications and information policy making even by those with the clearest powers and responsibilities. When a senior policymaker has a number of responsibilities, a natural inclination will be to devote greatest attention to those where his authority is clearest. That focus will have profound effects on planning, budgeting, and constancy. It will also sometimes result in staff frustration and in more decisions being made at the staff level.

CLARIFYING RESPONSIBILITIES

Despite almost universal agreement that problems remain in the structure of Government telecommunications policy making, a viable solution remains elusive . . .

Realizing that . . . fundamental organizational problems have existed and eluded solution for so long, however, should not diminish efforts now to deal with them. Telecommunications and information have become increasingly vital components of our economy and national life. As they grow in importance and affect more and more of our economy, these industries attract more intense and widespread interest. Yet we have clearly reached the point where the continued inability of our Government to get its own telecommunications policy "house" in order could seriously threaten to a significant degree the ongoing efficient developments of these key high-technology, "sunrise" industries and, therefore, the benefits which these technologies can deliver.

The Cost of Delay

This nation can no longer afford to have its Government as part of the communication policy making problem . . .

In an era of intense competition across global markets and rapidly developing technologies, we can ill-afford to hobble U.S. industry with the costs inherent in such delays. By perpetuating such institutional diversity, we will continue to afford interest groups, including foreign-based interests, an environment conducive to deliberate outside manipulation. The inability of Congress, through considered oversight, to ensure effective implementation of national policies and laws also is at risk under current arrangements.

Need for Action

Government reorganization is highly desirable if we are fully to exploit telecommunications technologies and capitalize on their economic and societal potential. The problems of coordination and policy leadership are particularly acute in international telecommunications.

As earlier discussed, this is due to the fact that U.S. firms typically cannot act unilaterally, but must act in concert with one or more foreign partners. In most other countries this means a government-owned or controlled entity. Competition is often frustrated by countervailing government intervention abroad. Dealing with this intervention becomes very difficult, if not impossible, when the U.S Government's policy process is disordered.

In view of the fragmented telecommunications policy making structure of the Executive branch, both between and occasionally even within agencies, it is not surprising that private industry is often confused as well. Private sector representatives in meetings during development of this report cited the fragmented, ambiguous grants of authority, and consequent problems. Many also called for an arbiter of U.S. telecommunications and information policy, short of raising each issue to the attention of the President.

EXECUTIVE BRANCH POLICY MAKING: A BLUEPRINT FOR THE INFORMATION AGE

To resolve these difficulties, any fully effective telecommunications and information policy entity must have sufficient expertise and authority. So equipped, it could then serve as a focal point for private sector interaction, government coordination, and foreign negotiations. In recognition of their vital importance to the nation, many in private industry maintain that telecommunications and information policy decisions also require high-level attention in the Executive branch. Because international telecommunications and information policies cannot be divorced from domestic issues in an era of global markets, moreover, any fully effective policy making entity should have expertise in both fields.

Clear Signals

Where a government places authority over a particular area of commerce signals, first, what it thinks are the most critical aspects of that area; and, second, dictates how other countries will react. If, for example, the lead agency for establishing U.S. communications and information policy were to be the State Department, it is likely foreign governments will think that the United States views these policies primarily as a means of projecting political power. In turn, these other nations will be inclined to respond by sending their own foreign ministry personnel to international negotiations and conferences.

We properly treat the telecommunications and information industries as essential parts of our commercial infrastrucure, both in and of themselves and as prime components of most other industries. U.S. policies that govern these industries are therefore developed primarily for sound economic reasons. We should avoid projecting the appearance that the United States views telecommunications and information policy primarily as an instrumentality of political power. The lead agency responsible for developing communications and information policies, and for presenting those views to foreign communications entities and ministries, should thus have broad commercial expertise.

Relationship Between the Executive Branch and the FCC

A clearly unified Executive branch, with a mandate for long-range policy planning, would go far toward meeting the challenges of technological advances and foreign developments. It would also minimize the confusion experienced by U.S. companies, foreign telecommunications authorities, and the FCC, which are currently confronted by diverse and conflicting views of individual Federal agencies. Perhaps equally important, the restructuring of Executive branch policy making would eliminate the incentive and ability for forum shopping in search of a more favorable policy decision.

A restructuring would provide a means for the Administration to balance the trade-offs between national security, trade policy, foreign relations, and economic policy and present a unified Executive branch position to the FCC and the world. Such balancing by a single Administration authority would accentuate the Executive branch's ability to formulate telecommunications and information policy from a holistic, cross-industry, and global perspective at a time when the FCC, ironically, has less and less influence, let alone control, over a wider segment of the telecommunications and information infrastructure.

CONCLUSIONS

1. International, and sometimes domestic, telecommunications and information policy under the current organizational structure is often reactive and skewed toward achieving short term objectives, focusing too much on maintaining the status quo, despite the influx of technological innovation and marketplace pressures.

2. The current structure invites forum shopping, and "divide and conquer" strategies by special interests, including foreign-based, and makes leadership and Congressional oversight difficult.

3. A lead telecommunications and information policy agency must have a cross-disciplinary depth of skill encompassing economics, engineering, political science, and communications and intellectual property law, with both domestic and international dimensions.

4. The FCC's direct supervisory powers over the overall telecommunications and information industries has steadily diminished due to deregulation of mass media and common carrier markets, increasing market shares of completely unregulated or less regulated industries, and FCC decisions to not regulate certain businesses.

5. Despite Congressional and Executive branch calls for improvements over many decades, the structure for telecommunications and information policy making remains part of the problem, not the solutions to the nation's telecommunications and information policy challenges.

6. It has been suggested at different times that a central telecommunications and information policy making agency be located in the Executive Office as a Special Advisor or Office of Telecommunication Policy, or even as a separate department, such as was created for transportation policy.

QUESTIONS FOR CRITICAL ANALYSIS

- What are the advantages or disadvantages of the NTIA as opposed to the existence in the early 1970s of the OT in the Department of Commerce and the OTP in the White House?
- What potential exists for the executive branch of government to influence broadcast policy through regulatory agencies?
- Why couldn't the work performed by the Office of Technology Assessment be performed by the Office of Plans and Policy of the Federal Communications Commission?
- If we consider the FCC as the "expert" agency involved in broadcast regulations, why is the U.S. Department of Justice so deeply involved in issues such as crossownership?
- What is the purpose of having the director of the Defense Communications Agency also manage the National Communications System?
- As a result of satellite technology, the flow of broadcast programming across national boundaries and the sharing of spectrum space with other nations is becoming increasingly important as a topic of policy making. What role will the U.S. Department of State play in the future of such policy, and how will that role be integrated with other domestic regulatory agencies?
- With so many distinctions between telecommunication services becoming more and more blurred, should a superagency be formed which combines all of the current regulatory efforts of the FCC, the NTIA, the FTC and other agencies?

- Are the terms *broadcasting* and *telecommunications* outdated terms and should they be replaced with such a term as *information technology*?
- Do you think the Office of Telecommunications Policy under the Nixon administration would have survived if it had not been politicized by agency staff?
- Clay Whitehead stated in his 1972 speech "insulating station and network news departments from management oversight and supervision has never been responsible and never will be." Do you agree with that assessment?
- What are the advantages and disadvantages of news departments over which management exercises close control?
- Should international telecommunications issues be the exclusive domain of the Department of State, since it is primarily responsible for diplomatic relations with other countries?
- Why do you think President Carter moved the OTP out of the executive branch and into the Department of Commerce before eliminating the agency and reorganizing the telecommunications regulatory infrastructure?
- Is there potential for interagency conflict between the FCC and the NTIA because both are concerned with allocating frequencies in the electromagnetic spectrum and administering telecommunications policy within the United States?
- Could jealousy exist toward the NTIA because of its closer association with the executive branch of government?
- Could the Institute for Telecommunications Sciences in the NTIA and the Office of Engineering in the FCC be combined under a federal agency concentrating on telecommunications technology?
- Could a White House communications agency be consolidated into some other regulatory structure?
- Should the executive branch of government be void of all telecommunications policy matters, delegating those responsibilities to agencies of government removed from the executive branch? Would such a move lessen the "politics" of regulation?
- Why does Congress need its own Office of Technology Assessment, when such agencies as the FCC and NTIA are also involved in making decisions about technology?
- Could the Federal Communications Commission better enforce the antitrust laws where broadcasting and telecommunications industries are concerned?
- The FCC works more closely with radio and television than does the Copyright Office of the Library of Congress. Should copyright registration of radio and television programs be under the Federal Communications Commission rather than the Copyright Office?
- Should the FCC also have the authority to enforce wage and hour laws in radio and television stations with the ability to levy fines against stations who are found in violation of wage and hour laws?
- Why do you think U.S. policy making has been more reactive than proactive, as suggested by the *NTIA Telecom 2000* report?
- How does one balance the need to support private free enterprise in the U.S. telecommunications industry with competition from foreign owned, government controlled, and sometimes subsidized telecommunications industries of other countries?
- The *NTIA Telecom 2000* report suggests that we have a patchwork of roles and structures rather than a coherent governmental framework for formulating and implementing telecommunication policies. Would a superagency governing telecommunication help to solve the patchwork problem? Would a superagency be less susceptible to the pressures of special-interest groups and private industry, which tend to influence policy making?

ADDITIONAL RESOURCES

Brotman, S. N., "Executive Branch Communications Policy Making: Reconciling Function and Form with the Council of Communications Advisors." 42 *Federal Communications Law Journal*, 51 (1989).

Wall, D., and J. Bradshaw, "The Television License: Prosecution and Poor Households." 26 *The Howard Journal of Criminal Justice* 47 (1987).

chapter six

Political and Entertainment Programming

Although the free press clause of the U.S. Constitution is used as a basis for prohibiting the government's intrusion into media content, and even though Section 326 of the Communications Act of 1934 prohibits censorship of radio and television programming, both the courts and the government have exercised the power to become involved in programming when the public interest warrants. In some areas, such as obscenity, the FCC has exercised this authority. In others, such as determining station formats, the commission has steered clear of involvement. It is the area of political programming, because of the fact such programming is at the core of the democratic process and can influence public opinion, regulations are specific and enforceable.

SECTION 315 OF THE COMMUNICATIONS ACT

Of all of the provisions of the Communications Act of 1934, few have received as much attention or notoriety as Section 315 which regulates political broadcasting. The provision instructs the broadcaster and the candidate on how the electronic media are to be used as part of our political system. It has an effect on how we, the consumers of broadcast communication, are informed about our electoral process. The "equal-time" provision of Section 315 states:

> If any licensee shall permit any person who is a legally qualified candidate for public office to use a broadcasting station, he shall afford equal opportunities to all other such candidates for that office in the use of such broadcasting station.

It is the equal-time provision that has received major criticism from both broadcasters and politicians. Archibald Cox remarked that "If we truly mean to restore openness and a sense of honor to our national life, we should acknowledge that equal time is dead and that broadcasters are as free as newspapers to determine what coverage to give candidates and their speeches."[1] Because of the equal-time provision, the press has backed away from coverage of candidate appearances precisely including White House requests for news coverage when a president is a legally declared candidate for public office.[2]

DEFINITIONS GUIDING EQUAL-TIME PROVISIONS

The Communications Act defines a legally qualified candidate as:

> any person who has publicly announced that he is a candidate for nomination by a convention of a political party or for nomination or election in a primary, special, or general election, municipal, county, state or national, and who meets the qualifications prescribed by the applicable laws to hold the office for which he is a candidate, so that he may be voted for by the electorate directly or by means of delegates or electors, and who:
>
> 1) has qualified for a place on the ballot or
>
> 2) is eligible under the applicable law to be voted for by sticker, by writing in his name on the ballot, or by other method, and
>
> i) has been duly nominated by a political party which is commonly known and regarded as such, or
>
> ii) makes a substantial showing that he is a bona fide candidate for nomination or office, as the case may be.[3]

In addition to this definition, there are hundreds of state and local statutes further clarifying political eligibility. Yet broadcasters are prohibited from exercising their own judgment as to who may be considered legally qualified. And it makes little difference if the candidate has a chance of winning. If the law says that the candidate is qualified, and if the candidate has publicly announced his or her candidacy, then the equal-time provisions apply. Those provisions also apply to cable television systems. Section 315 specifically defines a *broadcasting station* to include a "community antenna television system."

ANTICENSORSHIP PROVISIONS

As a further safeguard against unfair treatment to political candidates, Section 315 expressly prohibits the broadcaster from censoring the content of any political message. The law succinctly states that the licensee "shall have no power of censorship over the material broadcast under provisions of this section."

Up until 1959, broadcasters were in a quandary over the noncensorship rule, fearing it was only a matter of time until some candidate blatantly libeled an opponent, and the station would be sued for damages. The dreaded event happened that year in North Dakota, when U.S. senatorial candidate A. C. Townley charged on the air that the North Dakota Farmers' Union was communist controlled. The Farmers' Union sued the station and Townley for $100,000.[4] But the North Dakota Supreme Court ruled that the station was not liable and that the suit should have been brought against Townley alone. Undoubtedly, the Farmers' Union had thought about that, but knew that since Townley made only $98.50 a month, the prospect for recovering damages was not good.

The Farmers' Union appealed to the Supreme Court. Justice Black, in delivering the opinion of the Court, stated: "Quite possibly, if a station were held responsible for the broadcast of libelous material, all remarks even faintly objectionable would be excluded out of an excess of caution. . . . if any censorship were permissible, a station so inclined could intentionally inhibit a candidate's legitimate presentation under the guise of lawful censorship of libelous matter."[5]

An AM/FM station in Connecticut was fined $10,000 by the FCC for allegedly violating Section 315 after censoring the scripts of the Democratic and Fusion party candidates because they were supposedly in bad taste. The two candidates for mayor affected by the censorship action filed suit for damages. A circuit court judge ruled that because the stations were the only ones in Stamford, the government had delegated control over the airwaves to them, and therefore the censorship was actually federal action. This new twist in legal posture exemplifies the complex regulatory philosophy that can encompass Section 315. Although the decision was open to appeal, the legal interpretation of radio stations being instruments of the government opened up a whole new frontier of arguments dealing with the very basis of broadcast regulation. The RadioTelevision News Directors' Association joined with ABC, NBC, CBS, NAB, and PBS in filing an amicus curiae (friend of the court) brief on behalf of WSTC, arguing that broadcast licensees should not be considered instruments of government.

SECTION 315: OBSCENE AND INDECENT PROGRAMMING

In a memorandum from the chairman of the FCC to a U.S. congressman, broadcasters were alerted to their responsibility under Section 1464 of the

U.S. Criminal Code not to air obscene or indecent material and that Section 315 was not designed to supersede Section 1464. Thus, this one area of programming seems to be clearly within the broadcaster's or cablecaster's discretion.[6]

EXEMPTIONS TO THE EQUAL-TIME PROVISION

Exempt from the equal-time provisions are appearances by candidates on the following types of news programming:

(1) bona fide newscast,
(2) bona fide news interview,
(3) bona fide news documentary (if the appearance of the candidate is incidental to the presentation of the subject or subjects covered by the news documentary), or
(4) on-the-spot coverage of bona fide news events (including but not limited to political conventions and activities incidental thereto).

Political debates, including those sponsored by individual stations, are exempt when broadcast in their entirety and considered to constitute a bona fide newscast. At one time the FCC required the debate to be aired within 24 hours after it occurred but dropped that requirement in favor of the licensee's discretion to determine when in fact it remains a newsworthy event, regardless of how much delay is involved.

Traditional news programs are not the only programming designated as exempt. For example, *Donahue* has achieved exempt status under the "bona fide news interview" provision. Specifically, the commission found that the *Donahue* program "has been regularly scheduled for many years; the licensee has employed many techniques to retain absolute control over the program's production and broadcast; decisions on the format, content and participants are based on reasonable good faith journalistic judgement. . . ."[7] Tickets are distributed months in advance which prohibits, or at least safeguards against, someone using the program to espouse political views as a member of the audience. When one receives a ticket they have no way of knowing who the guests will be or the topic to be discussed.[8] Donahue himself was pointed to as being held responsible for adherence to many of the safeguards including cutting "off any questioner who fails to comply with these guidelines and restates questions in order to provide proper journalistic focus."[9]

As early as 1967 when the three commercial television networks carried the year-end interview with President Lyndon Johnson, Senator Eugene McCarthy requested equal time. McCarthy had just announced his candidacy for president and claimed that Johnson was also a legally qualified candidate. The interview series was not new. The networks had started it in 1962 with President John F. Kennedy.

The FCC denied Senator McCarthy's request. It based its decision on the grounds that the interview was exempt because Johnson was not an announced candidate for office. McCarthy appealed to the circuit court, and the court affirmed the commission's decision not to grant equal time. The court noted that since Congress had delegated the power to enforce Section 315 to the FCC, all the court could do was simply determine if the law was contrary to what Congress meant it to be, or was simply unreasonable. They found it to be neither and affirmed the FCC. The case did answer the question of when an incumbent president actually becomes a legally qualified candidate—whether it is when he or she announces his or her candidacy for reelection or at the time of the convention nomination.[10]

Although exemptions are rarely contested when part of a bona fide newscast, a station cannot simply log a program as a newscast and claim exemption. Allowing such an arbitrary application of Section 315 would make it easy for an unscrupulous broadcaster to bestow candidacy favoritism. To guard against this, the FCC looks at how long the program has been logged as news to determine whether it is bona fide. If a station has aired a 6:00 P.M. television newscast for five years and schedules in an appearance of a candidate, an opponent would have little grounds to demand equal time. On the other hand, if a candidate appears on an 8:00 P.M. program which is logged for the very first time as news, an opponent would have a legitimate request for equal time. Such requests must be made within seven days after the broadcast. The NAB's *Political Broadcast Catechism* lists seven elements in determining a bona fide program:

> The following considerations among others, may be pertinent: (l) the format, nature and content of the program; (2) whether the format, nature and content of the program has changed since its inception and, if so, in what respects; (3) who initiates the program;

(4) who produces and controls the program; (5) when was the program initiated; (6) is the program regularly scheduled; and (7) if the program is regularly scheduled, the time and day of the week when it is broadcast.[11]

SELLING TIME: THE LOWEST UNIT CHARGE

In addition to granting equal time to candidates, Section 315 also spells out how much they are to be charged for the use of broadcast facilities:

> (b) The charges made for the use of any broadcasting station by any person who is a legally qualified candidate for any public office in connection with his campaign for nomination for election, or election, to such office shall not exceed:
>
> (1) during the forty-five days preceding the date of a primary or primary runoff election and during the sixty days preceding the date of a general or special election in which such person is a candidate, the lowest unit charge of the station for the same class and amount of time for the same period, and
>
> (2) at any time, the charges made for comparable use of such station by other users thereof.

The preceding is known as the "lowest unit charge" rule. To understand it more clearly, assume that you are the sales manager for a television station. The station's rate card charges an advertiser $1,000 to buy a single one-minute commercial in prime time. An advertiser purchasing two commercials receives a discount and is charged only $850 per commercial. We'll assume that the rate card permits an advertiser purchasing 25 commercials to receive an even bigger discount, whereby each commercial costs $500. Along comes candidate John Doe, who is running for senator. Doe wants to buy just one commercial to remind his friends that he's running for office. He wants to run it in prime time. What will you charge him for the cost of his one commercial? You'll charge him $500. Even though he is buying only one commercial, the law states that you must charge him the "lowest unit charge." If he wanted to purchase a commercial in a fringe-time period, in which the rates are lower, then you would charge him the "lowest unit charge" for that time period.

It is easy to see why Section 315 is not the darling of many broadcasters. For example, station WGN in Chicago had a long-standing rule that candidates could purchase only a minimum block of five minutes of commercial time. In the Illinois presidential primary, a group wanted to buy 60-second and 30-second commercials promoting the candidate. These shorter commercials are often favored by candidates, since longer ones make some viewers change channels. When WGN said no, the committee petitioned the FCC, and the commission overruled WGN's five-minute policy, requiring it to sell the shorter commercials. To make matters more confusing, a year later, a Chicago mayoral candidate claimed that he could not buy program-length commercials on two Chicago stations.[12] The stations offered commercials of up to five minutes, and this time the FCC upheld the stations' right, not the candidate's. The decision clouded the decision issued a year earlier concerning WGN. The commission was quoted as saying that the "law giving a political candidate the same standing as commercial advertisers meant *only* that the candidate must be charged the lowest commercial rate for air time."[13] Some commissioners did not support the decision of the FCC giving the station control over the length of the commercial message. One commissioner was quoted as saying that the ruling would make it more difficult for candidates to gain access to broadcasting outlets.[14]

Many stations and account executives dealing with local politicians use an agreement form executed between the station and the candidate. One form offered by the NAB provides space to list the length of the broadcast, the hours, dates, times per week, total number of weeks, and rates for the commercial schedule used by the candidate. Total charges are included along with the dates of the first and last broadcast, as well as an explanation of the lowest unit charge, the fact that the information will be kept in the public file, and the agreement on the part of the candidate to hold the station harmless for any damages or liability that could occur as a result of the broadcast.

PERSONAL ATTACKS AND POLITICAL EDITORIALS

Although the FCC no longer enforces the Fairness Doctrine, certain provisions of the doctrine remain in place. Two of these are the personal attack rule and the rule governing political editorials.

Personal Attack Rule

The personal atack rule requires a station to notify an individual or group when an attack is made on their honesty, character, or integrity and to afford them the opportunity to use the station's facilities to reply. The provision governing personal attacks reads:

> (a) When, during the presentation of views on a controversial issue of public importance, an attack is made upon the honesty, character, integrity or like personal qualities of an indemnified person or group, the licensee shall, within a reasonable time and in no event later than one week after the attack, transmit to the persons or group attacked:
>
> (1) Notification of the date, time and identification of the broadcast;
>
> (2) A script or tape (or an accurate summary if a script or tape is not available) of the attack; and
>
> (3) An offer of a reasonable opportunity to respond over the licensee's facilities.
>
> (b) The provisions of paragraph (a) of this section shall not apply to broadcast material which falls within one or more of the following categories:
>
> (1) Personal attacks on foreign groups or foreign public figures;
>
> (2) Personal attacks occurring during uses by legally qualified candidates;
>
> (3) Personal attacks made during broadcasts not included in paragraph (b) (2) of this section and made by legally qualified candidates, their authorized spokespersons, or those associated with them in the campaign, on other such candidates, their authorized spokespersons or persons associated with the candidates in the campaign; and
>
> (4) Bona fide newscasts, bona fide news interviews, and on-the-spot coverage of bona fide news events, including commentary or analysis contained in the foregoing programs.[15]

Political Editorial Rule

The provisions of paragraph (a) also apply to editorials. In addition, when a licensee endorses or opposes a legally qualified candidate, within 24 hours the licensee must notify the other qualified candidate for the same office and afford that person same reasonable opportunity to reply. FCC rules governing political editorials read:

> (a) Where a licensee, in an editorial,
>
> (1) Endorses or,
>
> (2) Opposes a legally qualified candidate or candidates, the licensee shall, within 24 hours after the editorial, transmit to, respectively,
>
> (i) The other qualified candidate or candidates for the same office or,
>
> (ii) The candidate opposed in the editorial,
>
> (A) Notification of the date and the time of the editorial,
>
> (B) A script or tape of the editorial and
>
> (C) An offer of reasonable opportunity for the candidate or a spokesman of the candidate to respond over the licensee's facilities. Where such editorials are broadcast on the day of the election, the licensee shall comply with the provisions of this paragraph sufficiently far in advance of the broadcast to enable the candidate or candidates to have a reasonable opportunity to prepare a response and to present it in a timely fashion.[16]

STATE CONTROL OF POLITICAL ADVERTISING

Although broadcasting is an industry primarily under federal control, some states have not hesitated to include the electronic media when passing legislation controlling political advertising. For example, a state statute may require that "no media"—which includes radio and television—"shall charge a candidate, treasurer, political party or individual a rate for advertising in support of or opposition to a candidate, political party or political committee that is higher than the normal rate charged other customers for comparable advertising services."[17]

Some attempts at state control of political advertising have been rebuked by the courts. For example, a Texas law which required broadcasters to charge the lowest unit price at all times was found to violate the First Amendment and the Communications Act. The court said that such a law restricted the ability of the station to determine its programming and that in the case of federal elective offices the law might have conflicted with federal law.[18]

ACCESS: THE RELATIONSHIP OF SECTION 312 TO SECTION 315

Our discussion of Section 315 would not be complete without mention of another section of the Communications Act of 1934—Section 312—and how it relates to Section 315. Section 312 is actually a prerequisite to Section 315, since Section 312 clearly states that the station must not deny access to any candidate for federal office, regardless of what form that access takes. Section 312 cautions the broadcaster that a station license may be revoked: "for willful or repeated failure to allow reasonable access to or to permit purchase of reasonable amounts of time for the use of a broadcasting station by a legally qualified candidate for Federal elective office on behalf of his candidacy."

CANDIDATES FOR "FEDERAL" OFFICE

Notice that the law reads "Federal elective office." This clause has been a bone of some contention and confusion in interpretations of Section 315, especially when candidates at other than the federal level are involved. Some stations have used Section 312 as grounds for refusing to sell commercial time to candidates other than those running for federal offices. The advantage in such a policy is primarily economic. First of all, federal candidates number fewer than local candidates, translating into fewer political commercials. You may ask: "But isn't the station in business to sell commercials?" Yes, but remember that lowest unit charge. If a department store is paying a nondiscounted rate for commercials but cannot get on the air because of the plethora of political commercials sold at the lowest unit charge, then the station is losing money. Second, federal candidates often place their advertising through advertising agencies. Although the station must still give a discount to the agency, the number of commercials purchased is usually more than what candidates would purchase on their own. Thus, the overall dollar spent is closer to the actual profit made from typical business advertising. Third, the commercials from the agency are usually prerecorded, which eliminates the need for the local station to tie up its staff and facilities in helping a candidate to produce a commercial which may only run one time at the lowest unit charge.

By inserting the term *federal*, then, Section 312 left no definition of *reasonable access* for candidates running for state and local offices. Historically, the station has had some latitude for flexibility in such cases. In its *Guidelines* to political candidates, the commission says: "The licensee in its own good-faith judgment in serving the public interest may determine which political races are of greatest interest and significance to its service area, and therefore may refuse to sell time to candidates for less important offices, provided it treats all candidates for such offices equally."[19] A blanket refusal to sell any political advertising is, however, risky. Broadcasters have an obligation to their local communities, and information about candidates, even if purchased, is still an important part of that service.

STATE VERSUS FEDERAL ACCESS

A station refusing equal opportunities to purchase time is still on shaky ground if it refuses privileges to candidates running for nonfederal elective office while providing privileges to candidates for federal elective office. For example, one station refused to offer run-of-station commercials, which are the least expensive because they are purchased in bulk and aired at the station's discretion, to a candidate for state office. Instead, the station offered fixed-position commercials, which were more expensive. The FCC sided with the station. But in an appeal to the U.S. Court of Appeals in Washington, DC, the candidate won.[20]

Commercial networks have been found not to be exempt from the provisions of Section 312. The U.S. Supreme Court upheld an FCC ruling that ABC, NBC, and CBS had violated Section 312 by refusing to sell a presidential committee a half-hour of time to run a documentary kicking off a campaign for reelection.[21]

ACCESS TO NONCOMMERCIAL STATIONS

Noncommercial stations are not exempt from Section 312. That ruling came in 1976, when New York Senator James Buckley complained that he had not received reasonable access to five public broadcasting stations in upstate New York.[22]

Buckley claimed that the stations would not air a five-minute program that he had provided to them. But the stations felt that they had met the reasonable access requirement by carrying a debate between Buckley and his opponent, Daniel Moynihan. The FCC in a 6–0 decision agreed with Buckley, although indicating that each situation should be considered on an individual basis. They were not making policy for every noncommercial broadcasting station in the country.

Noncommercial educational stations which are not selling commercials but which operate on unreserved channels and whose charters or articles of incorporation permit them to charge for air time can also charge for political commercials.[23] They must, however, notify the FCC of the change in operating procedures. Since they probably do not have rate cards upon which to judge the lowest unit charge, these stations are usually safe in setting rates which are in line with other commercial stations in the same broadcast market.

PRINT VERSUS BROADCAST

Before concluding our discussion of political broadcasting, we should remind ourselves that the regulations we have been discussing apply only to the broadcast media and not to the print media. Under the rationale that the electromagnetic spectrum is a limited resource, the FCC has the authority under the Communications Act to institute such rules as it deems in the public interest. Section 315 and Section 312 are good examples. In print media enterprises, the editor or publisher has total discretion on who gains access to the paper and what is said about that person. With new technologies increasing the number of electronic communication channels, the future may see a relaxation of rules governing political broadcasting.

Even when the most precise language possible is used in court cases, FCC decisions, and amended rules and regulations, Section 315 is and will continue to be in a state of flux. With thousands of broadcasting stations and many more times that number of candidates, the law will continue to be challenged. As a responsible consumer of broadcast communication, you should try to remain alert to the individual issues in your own community which may arise from a dispute between a candidate and a station over the meaning of Section 315.

OBSCENE, INDECENT, AND PROFANE MATERIAL

One of the most complex areas of broadcast regulation is obscene, indecent, and profane material. The statutes governing obscene and indecent programming have evolved from both the Radio Act of 1927 and the Communications Act of 1934. The Radio Act of 1927 provided for penalties of up to $5,000 and imprisonment for five years for anyone convicted of violating the act, including its obscenity provisions. The Communications Act of 1934 changed this to $10,000 and two years in jail, stating that the violator's license could be suspended for up to two years. In 1937, the penal provisions covering obscenity were amended to include license suspension for those transmitting communications containing profane or obscene "words, language, or meaning. . . ." The license suspension was no longer limited to two years, and the word *meaning* became even more appropriate as television increased in popularity.[24]

In 1948, Congress lifted the obscenity provisions out of the Communications Act of 1934 and placed them into the United States Code. Thus, U.S. Criminal Code Section 1464 states: "Whoever utters any obscene, indecent, or profane language by means of radio communication shall be fined not more than $10,000 or imprisoned not more than two years or both."[25] "Radio communication" includes television. Both the Department of Justice and the FCC have the power to enforce Section 1464. Penalties include forfeiture of a license or construction permit and fines of $1,000 for each day the offense occurs, not to exceed a total of $10,000. The Justice Department can also prosecute under Section 1464 and send a licensee to jail.

Although paving the way for enforcing the code, the FCC still finds itself clashing not only with the First Amendment but also with the anticensorship provision of the Communications Act, which states in Section 326 that: "Nothing in this chapter shall be understood or construed to give the Commission the power of censorship over the radio communications or signals transmitted by any radio station, and no regulation or condition shall be promulgated or fixed by the Commission which shall interfere with the right of free speech by means of radio communication." The difficulty in enforcing the obscenity statute lies in a number of judicial conflicts that have developed since the 1948 codification. These have included not only the First Amendment dilemma stated previously but also different meanings for *indecency*, *profanity*, and *obscenity*; varied applications between print and broadcast media; and the application of different standards to different communities.

Definitions, Application, and Enforcement

Tracing the development of obscenity legislation takes us on a road leading back to English common law and libel law, starting in England in 1868 with the case of *Regina* v. *Hicklin*. In an appeal to the Court of Queens Bench, the court defined a test of obscenity as "whether the tendency of the matter charged as obscenity is to deprave and corrupt those whose minds are open to such immoral influences. . . ."[26] The definition cited in the Hicklin case was used as a basis for obscenity statutes in both the United States and England all the way into the twentieth century. Its primary thrust was that the publication had to be judged on its potential to reach the most susceptible of the audience. A series of cases upheld the Hicklin definition even into the 1930s.[27] Although the definition began to crumble, a Portland, Oregon, case brought broadcasting into the obscenity picture for the first time and found the Hicklin definition sufficient to warrant conviction.[28] In that case, Robert Gordon Duncan was charged with violating the obscenity statute of the Radio Act of 1927, and in 1931 was convicted in the case *Duncan* v. *United States*.[29] The main issue in the case was whether the language used by Duncan was obscene, indecent, or profane under the statute. The court based its decision on a definition similar to the one in the Hicklin case:

> In construing the word "obscene" as used therein, it has been uniformly held that, if the matter complained of were of such a nature as would tend to corrupt the morals of those whose minds are open to such influences by arousing or implanting in such minds lewd or lascivious thoughts or desires, it is within the prohibition of the statute. . . .[30]

Within the Duncan decision can also be found reference to both indecency and profanity. The court stated that indecent language, like obscenity, is language that has a "tendency to excite libidinous thoughts on the part of the hearers . . . and is calculated to arouse . . . sexual passions and desires." The court considered the words spoken by Duncan also to be profane in his references to an individual being damned and using the term "By God" irreverently.[31] Important to the Duncan decision as well as to decisions preceding it was the fact that the courts viewed a broadcast (or a publication) as obscene without examining the context of the remarks or the specific audience to whom it was directed. In 1936, the courts had enough of the Hicklin definition and in the case of *United States* v. *Levine*, although not dealing with broadcasting, established that a publication (a book in this case) should be considered in its entirety and by the effect it might have on the audience it would most likely reach.[32]

A landmark obscenity decision occurred in 1957 with the case of *Roth* v. *United States*.[33] In the Roth case, a legal test of obscenity was based on "whether to the average person, applying contemporary community standards, the dominant theme of the material taken as a whole appeals to prurient interests." The Court also believed that some obscenity statutes were unconstitutional when they punished "incitation to impure sexual thoughts, not shown to be related to an overt anti-social conduct. . . ." *Separating sex from obscenity*, the Court said: "sex and obscenity are not synonymous. Obscene material is material which deals with sex in a manner appealing to prurient interest."

Still another important obscenity ruling occurred in 1968, in the case of *Ginsberg* v. *State of New York*.[34] Sam Ginsberg operated a store on Long Island and was prosecuted under a New York law which made it a misdemeanor to sell a magazine to a minor under 17 years of age when the magazine showed female buttocks or breasts with less than "full opaque covering." After selling two "girlie" magazines to a 16-year-old, Ginsberg was found guilty under the statute. In its decision, the Supreme Court established what has become known as the "variable obscenity" concept. In other words, what may be obscene for children may not be for adults. We'll see shortly how both the Roth and the Ginsberg decisions became intertwined with subsequent broadcast rulings on obscenity.

As the print media continued to battle obscenity, broadcasting was developing some precedents of its own. In *United States* v. *Walker*, disc jockey Charlie Walker was found guilty by a jury of broadcasting offensive language on a radio station in Kingstree, South Carolina, from January to April 1960.[35] The statute used to convict Walker was the Criminal Code. As if that was not enough, when WDKD's license came up for renewal, the FCC denied it, and the case went to court in *Robinson* v. *Federal Communications Commission*.[36] Although the main issue in the license renewal was an alleged attempt to mislead the FCC with false evidence, the court also made reference to Charlie Walker's broadcasts as "vulgar," "indecent," and "filth." Left unclear in both cases was a true test of the obscenity issue, since the Walker case did not go beyond the district court, and the Robinson case was indirectly related to obscenity.

Although the Criminal Code prohibits "obscene, indecent, or profane language," the FCC attempted to stick with the actionable term of *indecent* and avoid *obscenity*, which had substantial precedent for defense in the First Amendment. In 1970, the commission fined noncommercial WUHY-FM $100 because an interview guest had supposedly expressed his view on current topics by "frequently interspersing" words which are slang for sexual intercourse and removal of bodily waste. Again, the fine was based on a charge of indecency, not obscenity. The commission went so far as to define indecency by stating "we believe that the statutory term, 'indecent' should be applicable, and that in the broadcast field, the standard for its applicability should be that the material broadcast is (a) patently offensive by contemporary community standards, and (b) utterly without social value."[37]

Topless Radio and George Carlin's Four-letter Words

Finally, in 1973, the FCC found itself squarely in the obscenity arena with a case involving a station in Oak Parks, Illinois. The topic for the call-in program was oral sex, and female listeners called the moderator with graphic descriptions of their experiences. The format, also employed at other stations, was known as "topless radio." Female listeners were not the only ones to contact the station. The FCC notified them of their apparent liability of $2,000 for violating *both* the indecency and obscenity clauses of the Criminal Code.[38] Sounding much like the court in *Roth* v. *United States*, the FCC quickly pointed out that it was not saying that sex was forbidden on the broadcast medium:

> We are emphatically *not* saying that *sex per se* is a forbidden subject on the broadcast medium. We are well aware that sex is a vital human relationship which has concerned humanity over the centuries, and that sex and obscenity are not the same thing. In this area as well as others, we recognize the licensee's right to present provocative or unpopular programming which may offend some listeners. . . .

Echoing the court in *Ginsberg* v. *State of New York*, the FCC noted that children were in the audience:

> There are significant numbers of children in the audience during these afternoon hours—and not all of a pre-school age. Thus, there is always a significant percentage of school age children out of school on any given day. Many listen to radio; indeed it is almost the constant companion of the teenager. In this very instance, the station received the following call complaining about the oral sex discussion. . . .
>
> *Female Listener*: Yes, hello, what I wanted to know about your show was how can you people be so frank about things like this out in the open—I was always taught to believe that what the husband and wife do is for their bedroom only and between themselves—now my daughter happens to be home and she's 13 and she accidently listened to this show, I mean, don't you think about children that are home from school?
>
> *Announcer*: Certainly, that's why we don't allow anyone on the air under the age of 18. There is evidence that this program is not intended solely for adults. On the February 16, 1973, program on "Do you always achieve orgasm?" the announcer moved from a discussion of orgasm to a comment aimed in large part at the 16–20 year-old audience. . . .

The FCC's action on the Oak Park station arose from still a third case of the annals of obscenity law, *Ginzburg* v. *United States*. In the Ginzburg case (spelled differently, and not to be confused with Ginsberg), a sharply divided Supreme Court upheld a fine and prison term for publisher Ralph Ginzburg on the charge that he was guilty of "commercial exploitation of erotica" in connection with alleged "pandering" of material which was supposedly "titillating" and appealed to "prurient interests." The dissenting justices were vehement in their disagreement with Justice Stewart, stating that although Ginzburg's conviction was upheld on the preceding grounds, he was not even charged with "commercial exploitation," "pandering," or "titillation"! Justice Stewart affirmed that he knew of no federal statute under which those three activities were a criminal offense. This, however, did not stop the FCC. In citing the station, the FCC stated: "There is here commercial exploitation, an effort at pandering. Formats like Femme

Forum, aptly called topless radio, are designed to garner larger audiences through titillating sexual discussions. The announcer actively solicits the titillating response. . . ."

Two groups, the Illinois Citizens' Committee for Broadcasting and the Illinois Division of the American Civil Liberties Union, asked the FCC to reconsider the ruling. When the commission declined, the Illinois Citizens' Committee for Broadcasting appealed in *Illinois Citizens' Committee for Broadcasting* v. *Federal Communications Commission*. The court upheld the FCC's action and in effect ruled that the commission was not acting unconstitutionally. Left untouched was an interpretation of *indecent*.

On the afternoon of October 30, 1973, WBAI-FM warned its listeners that the broadcast that would follow included sensitive language, which might be offensive to some. What followed was a recording by comedian George Carlin from his album *George Carlin: Occupation Foole*. Carlin's monologue was a satire on seven four-letter words which could not be used on radio or television because they depict sexual or excretory organs and activities. A month later, the FCC received a complaint from a man who said he was driving with his son and had heard the broadcast. It was the only complaint received about the broadcast, which had been aired as part of a discussion on contemporary societies' attitudes about language.

The FCC issued a ruling against WBAI-FM, and this time went back to *indecent* as the actionable term. Clarifying its definition of indecent language, the FCC stated that such language: ". . . describes, in terms patently offensive as measured by contemporary community standards for the broadcast medium, sexual or excretory activities and organs, at times of the day where there is a reasonable risk that children may be in the audience."[39]

In issuing its definition, the commission drew on both the Roth and the WUHY-FM decisions when referring to community standards and also applied the variable obscenity standard of the Ginsberg case. Yet this standard was not used to prohibit speech, but rather to "channel" it to a time when children weren't present. Still moving cautiously on obscenity, however, the FCC said that the language in the Carlin recording was not so much obscene as it was indecent. It defined indecent as distinguishable from obscene in that indecent language "(1) lacks the element of appeal to the prurient interest. . . . and (2) when children may be in the audience, it cannot be redeemed by a claim that it has literary, artistic, political, or scientific value." The commission did suggest that such material might be broadcast at night if it could be considered to have serious literary, artistic, political, or scientific value.

The commission also rationalized that broadcast media should be treated differently than print media for the purposes of regulating indecent material because broadcast media are intrusive, based on four considerations:

> (1) children have access to radio and in some cases are unsupervised by parents, (2) radio receivers are in the home, a place where people's privacy interest is entitled to extra deference; (3) unconsenting adults may tune in a station without any warning that offensive language is being or will be broadcast; and (4) there is a scarcity of spectrum space, the use of which the government must therefore license in the public interest.[40]

The commission reiterated that it was not in the business of censorship but that it did have a statutory obligation to enforce those provisions of the Criminal Code that regulated obscene, indecent, or profane language.

The United States Supreme Court upheld the FCC's decision after an appeals court rejected it.[41] The Supreme Court pointed out in *FCC* v. *Pacifica Foundation*:

> . . . . the broadcast media have established a uniquely pervasive presence in the lives of all Americans. Patently offensive, indecent material presented over the airwaves confronts the citizen, not only in public, but also in the privacy of the home, where the individual's right to be let alone plainly outweighs the First Amendment rights of an intruder. Because the broadcast audience is constantly tuning in and out, prior warnings cannot completely protect the listener or viewer from unexpected program content. To say that one may avoid further offense by turning off the radio when he hears indecent language is like saying that the remedy for an assault is to run away after the first blow. One may hang up on an indecent phone call, but that option does not give the caller a constitutional immunity or avoid a harm that has already taken place.[42]

The Howard Stern Case

The largest initial sanction imposed by the FCC for alleged indecency went against three stations for airing the "Howard Stern Show." A Los Angeles FM station was fined $105,000 for 12 broadcasts of the program that aired late in 1991.[43] Concern over the amount of the fines was expressed by the National Association of Broadcasters general counsel who said he was "troubled" by the fines which apparently had been issued without sufficient legal analysis in the letter admonishing the Los Angeles station.[44] Stern's controversial broadcasts dealt with sexual innuendo stronger than is heard on most radio stations and that some claimed went far beyond the seven dirty words case. Stations which aired the Stern show had mixed reactions to the fine. One affiliate said they were aware the show was controversial when they decided to carry the program. Another affiliate said they would review the show since fines drive up the cost of doing business.[45]

The Safe Harbor Regulatory Measure

Despite the FCC's determination to enforce a ban on indecency, challenges on First Amendment grounds resulted in a District of Columbia Court of Appeals ruling against the FCC 24-hour ban.[46] Under congressional mandate and the U.S. Supreme Court's decision to let the appeals court decision stand, the FCC adopted a safe harbor regulatory policy which forced such programming into a midnight to 6 A.M. time period when fewer children are in the broadcast audience.

An unusual application of the safe harbor regulatory policy, and also Section 315 and Sec. 312 of the Communications Act, occurred during the 1992 election. Section 315 requires reasonable access to legally qualified candidates for public office, and Sec. 312 prevents their political messages from being censored, the exception being obscene and indecent material. For willful or repeated failure to provide reasonable access a station can have its license revoked. To air indecent, obscene, or profane material can also result in the station running afoul of the law.

A Georgia television station found itself caught squarely between Sec. 315, Sec. 312, and the ban on indecent programming, when it was approached by a legally qualified congressional candidate who wanted to air a half-hour anti-abortion ad in a Sunday afternoon time period following a televised football game. The ad contained what the court said was indecent material stating:

> Specifically, beginning with the segment "Abortion in America: The Real Story," the videotape depicts the actual surgical procedure for abortion. During a short segment, approximately four minutes in length, the videotape contains graphic depictions and descriptions of female genitalia, the uterus, excreted uterine fluid, dismembered fetal body parts, and aborted fetuses. This portion of the videotape depicts these activities and materials in a manner which is patently offensive according to contemporary community standards. This is so in light of the context of the entire video. The Court further concludes that the evidence shows that the images, words, and depictions in the videotape would be readily understandable to children in the audience.[47]

In addition, the court pointed out that the "linchpin of indecency enforcement is the protection of children from inappropriate broadcast material."[48] The court granted the television station relief and permitted it to channel the paid political advertisement into the safe harbor time period, which the court said "best accommodates the two competing interests and rights: the interest in protecting children from indecent materials," and the candidate's right to broadcast the political advertisement.[49]

THE LICENSEE'S RIGHT TO CONTROL FORMATS

While the FCC has valiantly tried to regulate offensive language, it has not tried to dictate radio formats. In fact, the courts have tried to force regulatory power over this area on the commission—regulatory power it does not want, feels to be unconstitutional, and believes to be contrary to the intended purpose of the Communications Act.

Precedent for Format Control

Traditionally, the decision of what format a radio station provides for its audience has been the sole prerogative of the licensee. Over the years, stations have shifted formats to meet the pace of competition, not only from other radio stations but also from television. As television grew in popularity, radio decided to compete by incorporating specialized formats. The rock-and-roll of the 1950s thus became softrock, top-40 rock, progressive rock, oldie rock, and country rock. The diversity succeeded as radio stations were able to capture a specialized audience and attract advertisers wanting to reach that audience. But the marketplace dictated the diversity, not the FCC.

Then, 1970 placed government intervention on the doorsteps of the broadcasting industry.[50] It started in Georgia with the Citizens' Committee to Preserve the Voice of the Arts in Atlanta. In a U.S. Court of Appeals case, the group successfully preserved a classical music format of a local radio station. But the case that set the commission back on its heels involved station WEFM-FM in Chicago. Owned by the Zenith Radio Corporation and having programmed classical music since 1940, the station went up for sale. The prospective buyer, GCC Communications of Chicago, announced that it would change WEFM-FM's format to contemporary music. Citizen uproar abounded, but the FCC stood firm and approved the sale of the station. It rationalized that the Communications Act prohibited it from making decisions based on formats—in a sense from prohibiting the licensee from having the freedom to operate in the public interest. But the decision was appealed, and the Washington, DC District Court said the FCC erred and should have held a hearing prior to making a decision on the sale.

At this point, the FCC decided to take a closer look at its role in deciding station formats. It asked for opinions on the issue and broadcasters responded, aided by powerful lobbying from the National Association of Broadcasters. After considering the evidence, the FCC took an unprecedented stance in direct opposition to the court and said that it saw no reason to become involved in determining station formats.[51]

The Licensee's Right to Choose a Format: FCC Support

The FCC's first argument defending its stance was that it was unconstitutional for it to become involved in such decisions, and that opening up hearings every time a citizens' group complained about a change in format would create an administrative nightmare. Furthermore, the FCC felt that the marketplace was the arena in which formats should be decided. Audiences and advertisers could determine what best served the public interest. After all, broadcasting was still a business.

Another argument centered on the format itself. How could the FCC determine when format changes took place? The difference between classical and rock music was one thing, but differentiating between different types of rock music could be extremely difficult, let alone inappropriate, for a government agency. Furthermore, if the FCC were to rule on one format, to be equitable, it should examine every format of every station in every market. The commission would soon be telling each community what format was best and what radio station should program what format.

Nevertheless, to completely wash its hands of any further consideration of format selection did not seem appropriate. There was still the matter of making sure that stations served the public interest. FCC Commissioner Benjamin Hooks believed that the FCC should still ". . . take an extra hard look at the reasonableness of any proposal which would deprive a community of its only source of a particular type of programming."[52] Commissioner Hooks also felt that minorities should be serviced with programming, even if the marketplace did not inherently provide it. Those sentiments were echoed by citizens' groups. Among others, the Action Alliance of Senior Citizens of Greater Philadelphia protested that broadcasters direct their programming to groups who the advertisers pay the most to reach, thus discriminating against senior citizens. Spanish-American groups also felt that Spanish-culture formats might be eliminated without any recourse for the Spanish-American audience.

The arguments supporting the holding of hearings on formats during licensing proceedings again came to the forefront in the summer of 1979, when the U.S. Court of Appeals reaffirmed its position, criticizing the commission for being lax in its responsibility to "carry out its legal duties as interpreted by the court."

The U.S. Supreme Court agreed to hear the case and in 1981 ruled in favor of the FCC.[53] After a decade of wrestling with the issue of who could have final control over a format, the FCC's position that the licensee would determine the format gained the Court's approval. Specifically, the marketplace would become the regulator. Although the Supreme Court's decision would not stop a challenge to a format change, it did give the local broadcaster strong protection against such challenges.

RETAINING THE STATION'S RIGHTS IN SYNDICATION AGREEMENTS

The issue of format control is also important in syndicated programming. The FCC still feels, however, the licensee should be responsible for its format in order to serve public interest. Binding contracts can be offered to broadcasters by syndication companies. Consequently, stations should be alert to contracts with provisions which: (1) fix the number of broadcast hours; (2) prohibit AM-FM duplication; (3) prohibit subcarrier authorizations; (4) require the exclusive use of any musical format service or prohibit other sources of programming; (5) fix the amount of programming aired from a syndicator thereby giving up the station's right to control its programming; (6) prohibit certain announcements by the station; (7) fix the number of commercials broadcast; (8) limit the content or source of nonmusical programming; (9) fix the amount of air time for news, music, or other programming; (10) prohibit automatic gain control of company-supplied materials thereby permitting excessively loud programming to be aired which may result in interference with other stations and violate FCC technical rules.[54]

The key to the contracts is to retain flexibility. This is especially important in dealing with long-term contracts. The FCC does not want the licensee obligated to the degree that programming "in the public interest" might not air because of restrictions placed upon the station by the syndicator.

PRIME-TIME ACCESS

Concern over the dominance of network programming prompted the FCC in 1971 to take measures assuring that alternative programming would also be aired during the evening hours. Out of these measures came the prime-time access rules. The latest, the 1975 Prime Time Access Rule III (PTAR III), charges stations in the top 50 markets which are either network affiliated or network owned to clear an hour from network prime-time programming, which is 7:00 P.M. to 11:00 P.M. in Eastern and Pacific time zones and 6:00 P.M. to 10:00 P.M. in Central and Mountain time zones.[55] PTAR III was "refined" by order of the U.S. Second Circuit Court of Appeals in the case *National Association of Independent Television Producers and Distributors et al.* v. *FCC*.[56] The rule is designed to (l) give independent producers and syndicators a market for their programming and (2) encourage local stations to develop creative programming. By applying the rule to the top 50 markets, the FCC has successfully covered the nation. Yet the rule has been more successful in providing time for syndicated programming than in stimulating local creativity. The result has been a plethora of quiz and game shows in the 6:00 to 8:00 P.M. time periods across the country.

PTAR III stills allows a series of exemptions. Stations can broadcast network or off-network documentaries, public affairs, and children's programming. Public affairs programming is defined in the same terms as it is in the FCC logging rules, as "... talks, commentaries, discussions, speeches, editorials, political programs, documentaries, forums, panels, roundtables, and similar programs primarily concerning local, national, and international public affairs." Feature films can also be broadcast, as can network news programming of the fast-breaking variety of interest to the viewing audience. In other words, if a network provides its affiliates with coverage of a major news event, such as an assassination or a natural disaster, the local affiliates can carry the program and have it count as prime-time access. If a television station produces an hour of local news that immediately precedes the prime-time access hour—for example, local news from 6:00 to 7:00 P.M.—then the station can carry network news programming up to one-half hour into the access period, or until 7:30 P.M.

Sports programming is also exempt. If a sports event is scheduled to end at the beginning of prime-time access but lasts longer, stations are permitted to continue their sports coverage. Major sports events for which all of prime time is devoted to their coverage, such as New Year's Day football games or the Olympic games, receive the same exemption. Under continued scrutiny is the antiblackout law (Public Law 93-107), which permits the telecast of a home football game during prime time, but only if the game is sold out 72 hours before kickoff.

COPYRIGHT

Most of the content of broadcast programming can be copyrighted. A local commercial, for example, that was prepared by an ad agency or by someone at the station can fall under copyright.[57] A disc jockey's afternoon radio show can be copyrighted.[58] The original script of a television drama, the local or network evening news, and a sports documentary can all be copyrighted. Copyright law is designed to protect all of these from infringement by other parties who may want to use the material for personal gain.

We think most often of copyrighted material as being books, magazine articles, or pictures. But these examples only scratch the surface. Even an idea can be copyrighted if it can be recorded aurally or visually and retained as evidence of the idea's origin. Network news programs have been copyrighted for years as a protection against someone recording them and selling them as either entertainment or source material. Copyright gives musical recordings careful protection in an industry where pirated material is a constant concern.

Registration and Publication

Copyright exists from the time a work is "created" in "fixed" form. It immediately becomes the property of the author or entity which created it, regardless of whether it is registered as a copyrightable work or contains the legal mark of copyright.[59] But to protect a work from infringement, other measures are usually necessary. Copyright registration is one available means and involves completing the necessary forms, affixing a copyright notice to the work, and depositing a copy of the work with the Copyright Office of the Library of Congress.

Registration of a work for copyright purposes can occur when the work is published. The term *published* has different meanings depending on the type of work being copyrighted. For example, a published book appears in a different form than a phonograph record although both are considered published under copyright law. The Copyright Act defines publications as:

> . . . the distribution of copies or phonorecords of a work to the public by sale or other transfer or ownership, or by rental, lease, or lending. The offering to distribute copies or phonorecords to a group of persons for purposes of further distribution, public performance, or public display, constitutes publication. A public performance or display of a work does not of itself constitute publication.[60]

Important to an understanding of the definition is the sentence above which reads: "A public performance of a work does not of itself constitute publication." If you produce a television program and show it via television to a large audience, publication may not have taken place unless you offer the program for sale or lease. Publication is important in copyright law since when publication does take place all copies of the work should bear the notice of copyright. Such works bearing the notice of copyright must also by law be deposited with the Library of Congress. To improperly use the copyright notice but not then deposit the work can result in criminal penalties.

In most works a copyright notice consists of the letter "C" in a circle or the word "Copyright" or its abbreviation "Copr." followed by the year of first publication and the name of the copyright holder, such as: Copyright 1993, John Doe. For sound reproductions the copyright notice is somewhat different and consists of the letter "P" in a circle, followed by the year of the first date of publication. Broadly speaking, those works which can be copyrighted include: (1) literary works; (2) musical works, including any accompanying words; (3) dramatic works, including any accompanying music; (4) pantomimes and choreographic works; (5) pictorial, graphic, and sculpture works; (6) motion pictures and other audiovisual works; and (7) sound recordings. The length of a copyright is the length of the author's life plus 50 years.

Copyrighting Media Works

For the purposes of copyright, the medium of motion pictures, including television recordings, are considered "audiovisual works" and must consist of a series of related images that are "fixed" in some tangible medium of expression such as a film, tape, or disc and are intended to be shown by means of projection or other viewing equipment.[61] The images must impart the impression of motion. Other forms of audiovisual material, such as slides or filmstrips, can be copyrighted but are not considered "motion pictures." To "fix" in a tangible medium of expression means that the images must be sufficiently permanent or stable to permit it to be perceived, reproduced, or otherwise communicated for more than just "transitory duration." In most cases the copyright notice appears with or near the title, with the cast, credits, or similar information, or immediately following the beginning of the work, or immediately preceding the end of the work. In the case of a work which appears as a series, each part in the series should be copyrighted separately and distinguished from other parts in the series.

Phonorecords and the Compulsory License

The Copyright Act defines *phonorecords* as "material objects in which sounds other than those accompanying a motion picture or other audiovisual work are fixed." Records, tapes, and discs other than those that contain a soundtrack fall in the phonorecord category. When phonorecords have been distributed in the United States with the copyright owner's consent, under certain circumstances others may obtain a "compulsory license" to make and distribute the works. The compulsory license is most useful if the copyright owner does not want to negotiate with the intended distributor.

The compulsory license also permits the holder to make certain musical arrangements of the work as long as the basic melody and fundamental character of the work are not changed. The compulsory license does not entitle the person to make and distribute reproductions of the work for background music systems, jukeboxes, or broadcasting. The compulsory license only applies to distribution to the public for private use.

Foreign Copyrights

Copyrighting a work in one country does not necessarily mean copyright protection in other countries. If you produce and copyright a motion picture in the United States it may be public domain in Russia. No such thing as "international copyright" exists. In September 1955, the Universal Copyright Convention (UCC) came into force. Members of the UCC generally share copyright protection for member countries. Someone who is concerned about protecting copyright in another country should first research the laws of that country as they apply to foreign copyright protection. Even if a country is not a member of the UCC, national laws may exist which still offer copyright protection to holders of foreign copyrights.

"FAIR USE" STANDARDS: NONPROFIT EDUCATIONAL INSTITUTIONS

In coming to grips with a satisfactory interpretation of the "fair use" standard, a negotiating committee appointed by the chair of the House Subcommittee on Courts, Civil Liberties, and Administration of Justice established guidelines for educational institutions. While *not* having the power of law, the guidelines do offer some direction for administrators. The guidelines were developed to apply only to off-air recording by nonprofit educational institutions:

> A broadcast program may be recorded off-air simultaneously with broadcast transmission (including simultaneous cable re-transmission) and retained by a non-profit educational institution for a period not to exceed the first forty-five (45) consecutive calendar days after date of recording. Upon conclusion of such retention period, all off-air recordings must be erased or destroyed immediately. Off-air recordings may be used once by individual teachers in the course of relevant teaching activities, and repeated once only when instructional reinforcement is necessary, in classrooms and similar places devoted to instruction within a single building, cluster or campus, as well as in the homes of students receiving formalized home instruction, during the first ten (10) consecutive school days in the forty-five (45) day calendar day retention period. "School days" are school session days—not counting weekends, holidays, vacations, examination periods, or other scheduled interruptions—within the forty-five (45) calendar day retention period. Off-air recordings may be made only at the request of and used by individual teachers, and may not be regularly recorded in anticipation of requests. No broadcast program may be recorded off-air more than once at the request of the same teacher, regardless of the number of times the program may be broadcast. A limited number of copies may be reproduced from each off-air recording to meet the legitimate needs of teachers under these guidelines. Each additional copy shall be subject to all provisions governing the original recording. After the first ten (10) consecutive school days, off-air recordings may be used up to the end of the forty-five (45) calendar retention period only for teacher evaluation purposes, *i.e.*, to determine whether or not to include the broadcast program in the teaching curriculum, and may not be used in the recording institution for student exhibition or any other non-evaluation purpose without authorization. Off-air recordings need not be used in their entirety, but the recorded programs may not be altered from their original content. Off-air recordings may not be physically or electronically combined or merged to constitute teaching anthologies or compilations. All copies of off-air recordings must include the copyright notice on the broadcast program as recorded. Educational institutions are expected to establish appropriate control procedures to maintain the integrity of these guidelines.[62]

TELEVISION VIOLENCE AND CHILDREN'S PROGRAMMING: RE-EMERGING REGULATORY ISSUES

An issue that has surfaced periodically since television's infancy began to reemerge again in the mid-1990s as politicians hearing outcries from their constituencies moved to enter the debate on how much violence should be on television and what effect it has on society. The highly visible issue makes it a popular topic for political figures, many of whom gain local exposure from print media when they speak out on violence on television. But the issue is more than public relations. Serious scholars from many disciplines have researched the violence-behavior interface and found troubling links that point to more than a casual relationship between violence in the media and violence in society.

At the same time, the prospect of government censorship of the media flies in the face of the First Amendment. For First Amendment purists, any government control of television content is be seen as unacceptable and unconstitutional. For citizens groups opposing violence on television, the First Amendment is not the issue. They point out that over-the-air broadcasting, as one example, operates on a limited resource and is a pervasive force in our society. Control of the limited resource through such things as bans on cigarette advertising on radio and television has already established precedent. Moreover, networks and cable systems have long realized that violent programming attracts viewers. With many motion pictures already containing violence, television networks which own large film libraries containing violence, are in the position of having no alternative to reducing violence in their programming but to produce new entertainment products. Thus, the debate goes on.

Television Program Improvement Act

In an effort to get television networks to work jointly toward reducing violence, Congress passed the Television Improvement Act of 1990 which exempted, for an initial three-year period, the networks from antitrust law so they could consult with each other on the issue of television violence. The act stated:

> The antitrust laws shall not apply to any joint discussion, consideration, review, action, or agreement by or among persons in the television industry for the purpose of, and limited to, developing and disseminating voluntary guidelines designed to alleviate the negative impact of violence in telecast material.[63]

Included in the definition of "person in the television industry" was any entity producing programming for television. Major professional trade associations named in the law and coming under the definition were: the National Cable Television Association; the Association of Independent Television Stations, Incorporated; the National Association of Broadcasters; the Motion Picture Association of America and the Community Antenna Television Association. The exemption did not apply to "any joint discussion, consideration, review, action, or agreement which results in a boycott of any person."[64] Before the initial three-year period expired, industry representatives and policy makers were arguing the issues. Jack Valenti, spokesperson of the Motion Picture Association of America "advised critics of TV violence to look elsewhere for scapegoats."[65] Fifteen cable networks agreed to run warning labels, and ABC announced an 800 number people could call to determine which programs had a violence warning.[66] Most efforts were seen as attempts to ward off congressional threats of direct programming controls.

Children's Television Act

Taking action to limit the amount of commercial matter on children's television and putting teeth in the law by tying it to license renewal Congress passed the Children's Television Act of 1990, which took effect in 1991.[67] The act set commercial time limits in television programming directed to children—12 minutes per hour on weekdays and 10.5 minutes on weekends. Prohibited were program-length commercials in children's programming. Licensees must report at license renewal time if they have exceeded the limits.

Some criticism of broadcaster's compliance came from FCC audits which found broadcasters were using public service announcements and programs such as the *Flintstones* and *G.I. Joe* as examples of informational and educational programming.[68] For the most part, however, the commission said broadcasters were complying with the law and set the compliance figure at 90%.[69] The FCC did report, however, that fines totalling more than $90,000 had been assessed within two and one-half years after the law took effect. The commission did not give an accounting of how large the audience was for the stations which exceeded the limits.[70] Continued emphasis on the quality of children's television emerged from both the Senate and the White House. Because presidential First Lady Hillary Clinton entered the debate over the quality of television programming, and Senator Paul Simon, who sponsored the Television Program Improvement Act, has remained an outspoken critic of violence on television, both issues remain of interest to policy makers.

SUMMARY

Section 315 is the equal-time provision of the Communications Act and requires licensees to afford equal opportunities for legally qualified candidates for public office. The act sets out definitions for legally qualified candidates and as a safeguard against partisan programming, prohibits the broadcaster from censoring the content of any political message. Obscene and indecent programming is not permitted under Section 315 and licensees do have the discretion of not airing programming they feel may fall into the obscene or indecent category. Exemptions to the equal-time provision apply for such things as bona fide newscasts and interviews as well as political debates. In addition to the equal-time provision, stations are also required to adhere to the rules governing lowest unit charges. The lowest unit rule means that broadcasters must sell advertising to legally qualified candidates for public office at a rate equivalent to the lowest unit charge the station charges advertisers for the same class and amount of time.

Some states also enforce political advertising regulations and local broadcasters should be alert to state laws as well as federal regulations. Also closely related to Section 315 is Section 312 which requires stations to give access to any candidate for federal office. The station has the discretion to determine what type of access fulfills the requirement. Noncommercial stations are not exempt from Section 312. Noncommercial educational stations operating on certain unreserved channels and whose charters or articles of incorporation permit them to charge for air time can also charge for political commercials. If rate cards are not available, establishing the lowest unit charge based on rates in line with area commercial stations is acceptable.

The statutes governing obscene and indecent programming date back to the Radio Act of 1927, which provided penalties of up to $5,000 and imprisonment for five years for anyone who was convicted of violating the obscenity provisions of the act. In 1948 Congress lifted the obscenity provisions of the Communications Act of 1934 and placed them under the United States Code. Today penalties run as high as $10,000 for each offense. The Justice Department can prosecute under the United States Code and seek criminal penalties. Some difficulties exist in prosecuting obscenity cases, not the least of which is the difficulty in defining the terms *indecency, profanity, and obscenity*. Varied applications between print and broadcast media also exist.

One of the landmark obscenity cases occurred in 1957 in *Roth* v. *United States*, where a legal test of obscenity was based on whether the average person applying contemporary community standards found the material to appeal to prurient interest. In another case, *Ginsberg* v. *State of New York*, the obscenity law was applied to selling publications to a minor under 17 years of age when the magazine showed less than the full opaque covering of a woman's body. The FCC has enforced various obscenity cases, two of the more famous being the topless radio incident involving a station in Oak Park, Illinois. George Carlin's four-letter words also became an FCC enforcement issue when the commission ruled the law had been violated because the program had been aired during a time when children were likely to be in the audience. Controversial television personality and radio talk show host Howard Stern and his syndicator became the object of an indecency charge by the FCC for sexually explicit references made on his program.

Radio station formats became a court issue in the 1970s when a U.S. Court of Appeals decision successfully preserved a classical music format of a radio station in Atlanta. After other formats became an issue in the courts and at the commission, the FCC took a position that it was unconstitutional for the agency to become involved in format selection. In 1981 the U.S. Supreme Court ruled in the commission's favor. While a format can still be challenged, local broadcasters have strong protection against interference from outside groups pressuring the station to adhere to a particular type of programing.

In syndicated programming, the FCC has taken the position that stations must retain control. Although not having the force of official policy, the FCC guidelines which broadcasters follow can alert them to contracts which have restrictive clauses covering such areas as the number of broadcast hours or the number of commercials broadcast. Much of syndicated programming appears during the prime-time access hours.

Like printed material radio and television programs are copyrightable. Copyright exists for anything that is "created" or in "fixed" form. Copyright protection entails the registration of the copyrighted work, and either visually or aurally the copyright symbol or announcement must appear in the program. Educational institutions have a "fair use" standards for using copyrighted works. Under the fair use standards educational institutions are expected to establish appropriate control procedures to guard against copyright violations. For the most part a broadcast program can be recorded off the air simultaneously with a broadcast transmission. Off-air recordings can be made at the request of individual teachers but should not be regularly recorded in anticipation of requests. These guidelines do not have the force of law but are the result of a special negotiation committee appointed by the chair of the House subcommittee on courts, civil liberties, and administration of justice.

Concern over the quality of television programming resulted in Congress passing two laws in 1990 dealing with violence on television and the amount of commercial matter permitted in programming directed to children.

MATERIAL FOR ANALYSIS

Congress in 1990 passed the Children's Television Act limiting the amount of commercial matter which can occur in television programming directed toward children. In addition to requiring documentation of compliance at license renewal time, the act called for periodic audits to assure station compliance.

CHILDREN'S TELEVISION ACT OF 1990

Public Law 101-437, 101st Congress, H.R. 1677, 47 USC 303a, 104 Stat. 996.

An Act To require the Federal Communications Commission to reinstate restrictions on advertising during children's television, to enforce the obligation of broadcasters to meet the educational and informational needs of the child audience, and for other purposes. This Act may be cited as the "Children's Television Act of 1990."

TITLE I-REGULATION OF CHILDREN'S TELEVISION FINDINGS

Sec. 101. The Congress finds that-

(1) it has been clearly demonstrated that television can assist children to learn important information, skills, values, and behavior, while entertaining them and exciting their curiosity to learn about the world around them;

(2) as part of their obligation to serve the public interest, television station operators and licensees should provide programming that serves the special needs of children;

(3) the financial support of advertisers assists in the provision of programming to children;

(4) special safeguards are appropriate to protect children from over commercialization on television;

(5) television station operators and licensees should follow practices in connection with children's television programming and advertising that take into consideration the characteristics of this child audience; and

(6) it is therefore necessary that the Federal Communications Commission (hereinafter referred to as the "Commission") take the actions required by this title.

STANDARDS FOR CHILDREN'S TELEVISION PROGRAMMING

SEC. 102. (a) The Commission shall, within 30 days after the date of enactment of this Act, initiate a rulemaking proceeding to prescribe standards applicable to commercial television broadcast licensees with respect to the time devoted to commercial matter in conjunction with children's television programming. The Commission shall, within 180 days after the date of enactment of this Act, complete the rulemaking proceeding and prescribe final standards that meet the requirements of subsection (b).

(b) Except as provided in subsection (c), the standards prescribed under subsection (a) shall include the requirement that each commercial television broadcast licensee shall limit the duration of advertising in children's television programming to not more than 10.5 minutes per hour on weekends and not more than 12 minutes per hour on weekdays.

(c) After January 1, 1993, the Commission-

(1) may review and evaluate the advertising duration limitations required by subsection (b); and

(2) may, after notice and public comment and a demonstration of the need for modification of such limitations, modify such limitations in accordance with the public interest.

(d) As used in this section, the term "commercial television broadcast licensee" includes a cable operator, as defined in section 602 of the Communications Act of 1934 (47 U.S.C. 522).

CONSIDERATION OF CHILDREN'S TELEVISION SERVICE IN BROADCAST LICENSE RENEWAL

SEC. 103. (a) After the standards required by section 102 are in effect, the Commission shall, in its review of any application for renewal of a television broadcast license, consider the extent to which the licensee-

(1) has complied with such standards; and

(2) has served the educational and informational needs of children through the licensee's overall programming, including programming specifically designed to serve such needs.

(b) In addition to consideration of the licensee's programming as required under subsection (a), the Commission may consider-

(1) any special nonbroadcast efforts by the licensee which enhance the educational and informational value of such programming to children; and (2) any special efforts by the licensee to produce or support programming broadcast by another station in the licensee's marketplace which is specifically designed to serve the educational and informational needs of children.

PROGRAM LENGTH COMMERCIAL MATTER

SEC. 104. Within 180 days after the date of enactment of this Act, the Commission shall complete the proceeding known as "Revision of Programming and Commercialization Policies, Ascertainment Requirements and Program Log Requirements for Commercial Television Stations" . . .

QUESTIONS FOR CRITICAL ANALYSIS

- Some strong proponents of the First Amendment suggest that Section 315 should be abolished. Do you agree?
- Are the equal-time provisions of Section 315 fair and equitable? Do they conflict with the First Amendment?
- With so many different states having different laws governing candidate eligibility, should a federal law be enacted which standardizes state laws as they apply to candidate access and qualifications?
- A bona fide newscast is exempt from the equal-time provision. Could a station abuse this provision of the law?
- Could a station abuse the bona fide news documentary provision of the law?
- Is the lowest unit charge fair to small-market stations which may be on the border line of making a profit because of the size of their community, the number of viewers or listeners the station has, or the economic conditions?
- Since radio and television stations are federally licensed, should states be prohibited from having any control over political advertising aired on radio and television?
- Are the distinctions between obscenity, indecency and profanity realistic?

- Where would pornography fit into the definitions of obscenity, indecency and profanity?
- Is it possible to enforce fairly the provisions governing obscenity, indecency and profanity?
- Consider some of the explicit song lyrics which are common in today's popular music, and heard frequently on radio stations. In view of these explicit lyrics, were the sanctions against stations airing topless radio formats fair and equitable?
- If a community is served by only one radio station, should the government have the ability to control the format of the station, assuring that the station airs a sufficient amount of local news and information programming to serve the public interest? What would be considered a sufficient amount of news and information programming?
- Given the competitive nature of the broadcasting and cable industries, is a law exempting programming entities from antitrust laws a realistic way of contributing to the reduction in television violence?
- Are such measures as 800 numbers and violence warnings effective safeguards against television violence? Should there be any safeguards at all, or should the First Amendment prevail and no censorship of any type of programming be permitted?
- Even if the amount of violence on television is reduced, will violent-prone individuals seek out violent television programs, making government controls on violent programming moot?

ADDITIONAL RESOURCES

Donnerstein, E., B. Wilson, and D. Linz, "On the Regulation of Broadcasting Indecency to Protect Children," 36 *Journal of Broadcasting & Electronic Media* 111 (1992).

Hofbauer, D. L., " 'Cableporn' and the First Amendment: Perspectives on Content Regulation of Cable Television." 35 *Federal Communications Law Journal* 139 (1983).

Kleiman, H. M., "Indecent Programming on Cable Television: Legal and Social Dimensions." 30 *Journal of Broadcasting & Electronic Media* 275 (1986).

Kunkel, D., and B. Watkins, "Evolution of Children's Television Regulatory Policy." 31 *Journal of Broadcasting & Electronic Media* 367 (1987).

Meyerson, M. I., "The Right to Speak, the Right to Hear, and the Right not to Hear: The Technological Resolution to the Cable-Pornography Debate." 21 *University of Michigan Journal of Law Reform* 137 (1987).

Wardle, L. D., "Cable Comes of Age: A Constitutional Analysis of the Regulation of 'Indecent' Cable Television Programming." 63 *Denver University Law Review* 621 (1986).

chapter seven

The Broadcast Press

The broadcast press in America enjoys considerable freedom, but certain controls still exist with which the broadcast press must contend. Some of these are common to both print and broadcast journalism, such as reporters' shield laws and freedom of information laws. Depending on the particular state where they are in force, some laws are more restrictive than others. For example, some states fall back on the strength of the First Amendment and do not have reporters' shield laws. In states where shield laws do exist, some are highly restrictive.[1] In any case, these controls operate within the framework of the United States Constitution.

One of the strongest and most lasting statements in support of freedom of the press and against prior restraint came with the U.S. Supreme Court's decision in *Near* v. *Minnesota*.[2] The 1931 case was brought to court when a Minnesota statute prohibiting publication of certain "malicious, scandalous, and defamatory" material was used to stop publication of a newspaper called the *Saturday Press*. The *Press* had set out to clean up political corruption in Minneapolis and was found guilty of being a public nuisance by publishing defamatory remarks about the Jewish race, the *Minneapolis Tribune*, and the *Minneapolis Journal*. More specifically, the publication charged that a Jewish gangster was in control of gambling, bootlegging, and racketeering in Minneapolis, and that the law enforcement agencies were not performing their duties. The chief of police came under scrutiny and it was claimed the chief was having illicit relations with gangsters in addition to participating in graft. The mayor was singled out as derelict in his duty, and a member of the grand jury was accused of being in sympathy with the gangsters. The county attorney, who was also out of favor with the newspaper, was incensed by the articles and brought action against the publishers J. N. Near and H. Guilford to stop publication. The case went to the Minnesota Supreme Court, where the public nuisance statute was upheld. Near next took the case to the U.S. Supreme Court. Guilford, meanwhile, had been shot by gangsters. In issuing the majority opinion, Justice Hughes wrote in *Near* v. *Minnesota*:

> The fact that for approximately one hundred and fifty years there has been almost an entire absence of attempts to impose previous restrictions upon publications relating to the malfeasance of public officers is significant of the deep-seated conviction that such restraints would violate constitutional rights. Public officers whose character and conduct

remain open to debate and free discussion in the press, find their remedies for false accusations in actions under libel laws not proceedings to restrain the publication of newspapers and periodicals . . .[3]

THE ROLE OF THE U.S. CONSTITUTION

The relationship of the broadcast press to the Constitution is most closely aligned with the First Amendment's phrase: "Congress shall make no law . . . abridging the freedom of speech, or of the press . . ." To give some assurance that a state could not wholeheartedly negate the U.S. Constitution, the Fourteenth Amendment was passed, stating: "No State shall make or enforce any law which shall abridge the privileges or immunities of citizens of the United States; nor shall any state deprive any person of life, liberty, or property, without due process of law. . . ." The Fourteenth Amendment was not affirmed by the courts until 1925, when in the case of *Gitlow* v. *New York* the U.S. Supreme Court declared: "For present purposes, we may and do assume that freedom of speech and of the press—which are protected by the First Amendment from abridgement by Congress—are among the fundamental personal rights and liberties protected by the due process clause of the Fourteenth Amendment from impairment by the states."[4]

Affirmation or Delimitation?

The Constitution has not stopped the states from passing countless laws affecting the confidentiality of sources for both print and broadcast journalists; nor from passing laws affecting the right of access to public meetings or for cameras in the courtroom; nor from passing laws governing cable television. The twentieth-century concept of the electromagnetic spectrum as a limited resource has been used as a basis for more and more legislation and interpretation, although not without criticism. Former CBS commentator Eric Sevareid, addressing a meeting of the National Association of Broadcasters, remarked: "I could never understand why so basic a right as the First Amendment could be diluted or abridged simply because of technological change in the dissemination and reception of information and ideas."[5]

The broadcast press has continually had to fight for its rights as an equal partner with the print media under the First Amendment. This fight has included visible lobbying efforts by the NAB, such as its Declaration of Broadcast Freedoms, which was passed as a resolution by NAB's board. In the Declaration, the broadcasters stated that they: "will increase our vigilance in defending our rights to stand equal to the written press . . . and that we will use every proper means to defend, on behalf of those we serve, their inalienable rights to have a free electronic press." Spokespersons for the broadcasting industry have been equally vocal. CBS's William S. Paley once remarked that the First Amendment freedom, "presupposes, in us as broadcasters, a greater sense of responsibility. If we fail to see the dimensions of that responsibility and to measure up to them, we are in for constant threats of restrictions and policing."[6]

Broadcast Versus Print: Equal Status

Along with the rhetoric has come judicial support for the First Amendment's application to broadcasting. In the case of *CBS* v. *the Democratic National Committee*, Justice William O. Douglas wrote: "My conclusion is that the TV and radio stand in the same protected position under the First Amendment as do newspapers and magazines. The philosophy of the First Amendment requires that result, for the fear that Madison and Jefferson had of government intrusion is perhaps even more relevant to TV and radio than it is to newspapers and other like publications."[7] A panel of five justices of the New York State Supreme Court affirmed the right of WABC-TV to show a documentary about conditions in a children's home and the presiding justice wrote: "While the protection of freedom of the press is not absolute, the burden of demonstrating a condition which warrants a prior restraint is indeed a heavy one. Television broadcasting falls under the umbrella of protection afforded the press, for it too, in matters such as the subject under review, is engaged in the dissemination of information of public concern."[8] Ironically, while affirming the right to show the documentary, the court stopped the broadcast for five days to give the children's home time to appeal.

The spirit of the First Amendment is also inherent in the Communications Act of 1934 and in its amendments.[9] Section 315, dealing with political advertising, states that licensees ". . . shall have no power of censorship over material broadcast under the provisions of this section." Section 326 of the Communications Act of 1934, stated earlier in the Radio Act of 1927, states: "Nothing in this Act shall be understood or construed to give the Commission the power of censorship over the radio communications or . . . shall interfere with the right of free speech by means of radio communication."

FREE PRESS VERSUS FAIR TRIAL

A frequent battleground over the rights of the broadcast press is the First, Sixth, and Fourteenth Amendments to the U.S. Constitution. All three interact with issues surrounding the argument between a free press and a fair trial. Specifically, the First Amendment deals with a free press and states:

> Congress shall make no law . . . abridging the freedom of speech, or of the press . . .

The Sixth Amendment deals with fair trial and states:

> In all criminal prosecutions, the accused shall enjoy the right to a speedy and public trial, by an impartial jury . . .

The Fourteenth Amendment deals with due process and states:

> . . . nor shall any State deprive any person of life, liberty, or property, without due process of law; nor deny to any person within its jurisdiction the equal protection of the laws.

During an amendment clash, the press claims its rights of a free press under the First Amendment and the "public trial" guarantees of the Sixth Amendment as a basis for permitting cameras in court. Lawyers and judges opposed to such access fall in behind the "impartial jury" guarantees of the Sixth Amendment and the "due process" guarantees of the Fourteenth Amendment. At the center of this argument is the legal issue of both pretrial and trial publicity. It is especially visible where cameras in the courtroom are concerned.

CAMERAS IN COURT

The concern over cameras in courtrooms began before television was an accepted part of journalism. When Bruno Hauptmann was tried for kidnapping the son of the famed aviator Charles Lindbergh in 1935, the courtroom resembled more a county fair than a judicial proceeding. Reporters were falling over reporters, vendors were selling souvenirs, and when the judge barred cameras from the courtroom, an enterprising reporter managed to sneak a camera into the balcony and snap a picture of the courtroom that bannered in papers across the country. The scene did nothing to advance the cause of access for photojournalists.

The Rideau and Estes Cases

Such claims for constitutional priority were not founded merely in supposition or conjecture. The annals of case law are filled with overturned verdicts, appeals, and charges of biased juries because of the fact that the news media have been less than restrained in their coverage. The cases that stand out as being of particular interest include *Rideau* v. *Louisiana*.[10] In this case, the suspect was interviewed by a county sheriff, and the interview was filmed and played on local television. The suspect's confessions made during the interview and the subsequent televising of those confessions prompted the defense attorney to request a change of venue. A denial and subsequent guilty verdict caused the United States Supreme Court to reverse the conviction and state that the jury should have been drawn from a community whose residents had not seen the televised interview.

The case of Texas businessman Billie Sol Estes added fuel to the constitutional fire. Estes was tried and convicted of swindling. An appeals court affirmed the conviction, but when the case reached the United States Supreme Court in 1965, in *Estes* v. *State of Texas*, the conviction was reversed.[11] Massive national publicity surrounded the trial, and when it first went to court, the trial judge permitted television coverage of portions of the trial. In fact, the initial hearings were carried live. The scene was described in Estes by Justice Clark:

> Indeed, at least 12 cameramen were engaged in the courtroom throughout the hearing taking motion and still pictures and televising the proceedings. Cables and wires were snaked across the courtroom floor, three microphones were on the judges' bench, and others were beamed at the jury box and the counsel table. It is conceded that the activities of the television crews and news photographers led to considerable disruption of the hearings.

Justice Clark in Estes summarized four areas in which television could interfere with a trial: (l) Television can have an impact on the jury. The mere announcement of a televised trial can alert the community to "all the morbid details surrounding" the trial. "Every juror carries with him into the jury box, those solemn facts and thus increases the chance of prejudice that is present in every criminal case." (2) Television can impair the quality of testimony. "The impact upon a witness of the knowledge that he is being viewed by a vast audience is simply incalculable. Some may be demoralized and frightened, some cocky and given to overstatement; memories may falter. . . ." (3) Television places additional responsibilities on the trial judge. Along with other supervisory duties, the judge must also supervise television. The job of the judge "is to make certain that the accused receives a fair trial. This most difficult task requires his undivided attention." (4) On the defendant, television "is a form of mental if not physical harassment, resembling a police line-up or the third degree. The inevitable closeups of his gestures and expressions during the ordeal of his trial might well transgress his personal sensibilities, his dignity, and his ability to concentrate. . . ."

Experimenting with Cameras in Court

In 1972 the American Bar Association's House of Delegates approved a Code of Professional Responsibility, permitting the use of television in the courtroom for such activities as presenting evidence. Despite the Court's decision in *Estes*, broadcasters continued their fight to gain courtroom access for television cameras. Some progress was made during the 1970s. The 1970s also saw forward-looking measures from a small number of states including Alabama, Georgia, Florida, Indiana, Washington, and Nevada. For example, progress came in 1974 when the Washington State Supreme Court instructed a county superior court to select a trial and to experiment, for "educational" purposes, with televising it. The experiment was generally successful.[12] In Las Vegas, Nevada, during the fall of 1976, KLAS-TV televised a criminal court trial in color. Sixty hours of courtroom activity, including interviews with the defendant, jury, and attorneys, were videotaped and edited for a three-part, prime-time special. Florida's own experiments with cameras in court began in 1976 and were modified in 1977. A publicized trial took place in Florida in 1977 when a teenager was accused of murder. Segments of the trial appeared regularly on network television, calling national attention to the camera-courtroom issue. A few weeks later, when the verdict was read in an Indiana kidnapping case, cameras were again present, and the courtroom once again made national television.

Alabama is credited with establishing a substantial precedent. With the cooperation of the news media in Mobile, Alabama, Judge Robert H. Hodnette, Jr., of the Thirteenth Circuit Court of Alabama, drew up plans for the broadcast coverage of trials. The Alabama Supreme Court approved his plans, which became a model for other states to follow. The Alabama guidelines include among others the following provisions:

> No broadcasting, recording or photographing should detract from the dignity of the court proceedings.
>
> Persons desiring to broadcast, record or photograph official court proceedings must make a timely request to the Clerk of the Supreme Court prior to the hearing, trial or event, specifying the particular case, hearing or event for which coverage is desired.
>
> Written consent from attorneys and parties, if present, shall be obtained on a form, copies of which are available in the Clerk's office.
>
> Overhead lights, when provided, shall be switched on and off by the Marshal. No other lights, flashbulbs, flashes or sudden light changes, may be used except with the express authorization of the Marshal or the court.[13]

Under one of the provisions, reference is made to obtaining written consent from attorneys as well as the parties involved in the case. In Alabama, this involves a request form completed by the media representative desiring to cover the trial and a similar form completed by the attorney and parties involved. From that point on, the main responsibility of the court is to conduct a fair trial and the main responsibility of the media is to report the trial, not to disrupt it.

Georgia is another state that has approved broadcast equipment in court. Television stations in Atlanta broke the ice in 1977 by televising proceedings of the Georgia Supreme Court, while Atlanta radio stations patched into the court's public address system.[14] As in similar cases, this action necessitated a revision of the state's code of judicial conduct. Georgia's revised code now authorizes the "broadcasting, televising, recording, filming and taking of photographs in its courtroom, or the courtroom of any other state court of Georgia, during any judicial hearing."[15] The guidelines under which the code functions necessitate that both attorneys must give written approval before their oral arguments can be covered.[16]

The Chandler Ruling

In 1981 a breakthrough occurred when the U.S. Supreme Court again considered the issue of cameras in the courts. In the case of *Chandler* v. *Florida*, the U.S. Supreme Court ruled that Florida's own authorization of cameras (both television and still cameras), when subject to the control of the presiding judge and with guidelines which protected the criminal defendant's right to a fair trial, does not violate the U.S. Constitution. The ruling paved the way for states to adopt their own guidelines without fear of them being deemed unconstitutional. As we will now see, other states had proceeded to establish guidelines before the Chandler ruling. The American Bar Association ended its opposition to cameras in the courtroom by condoning "unobtrusive use of cameras" in an ABA resolution passed in 1982.

Canon of Judicial Ethics

Since the Lindbergh trial, everyone from Supreme Court justices to bar associations have grappled with the difficult issues of how much publicity is too much and *how* and *whether* television cameras and recording equipment interfere with a fair trial. The American Bar Association approved its famous Canon 35 two years after the Lindbergh trial. Amended in 1963 to include television, Canon 35 forbade either the taking of photographs or the broadcasting of court proceedings. Individual states were quick to affirm Canon 35's principles and place it in statutes affecting court proceedings. The Federal Rules of Criminal Procedures, specifically Rule 53, carry the prohibition of cameras in federal courts. And a special committee of the Judicial Conference of the United States reaffirmed Canon 35 in 1968, calling for prohibition of ". . . radio or television broadcasting from the courtroom or its environs, during the progress of or in connection with judicial proceedings. . . ."

The revised Canon 3A(7) reads:

> (7) A judge should prohibit broadcasting, televising, recording or photographing in courtrooms and areas immediately adjacent thereto during sessions of court, or recesses between sessions, except that under rules prescribed by a supervising appellate court or other appropriate authority, a judge may authorize broadcasting, televising recording and photographing of judicial proceedings in courtrooms and areas immediately adjacent thereto consistent with the right of the parties to a fair trial and subject to express conditions, limitations, and guidelines which allow such coverage in a manner that will be unobtrusive, will not distract the trial participants, and will not otherwise interfere with the administration of justice.

Clearly, the revised Canon 3A(7) still permits judges the latitude to close trials but also opens the opportunity for negotiation with the news media.

While acceptance of cameras in the courtroom is not universal, broadcast journalists can be optimistic about the future of cameras and recording equipment in judicial proceedings, especially in view of recent gains made in numerous states.[17] More than 75 percent of the states have some provision for admitting cameras to the courtroom, but the access standards vary considerably.[18]

Key Factors: Public Access, Responsible Constraint

The future status of cameras in court hinges on two key factors: (1) the willingness of the courts to recognize the public's right of access to trials by permitting in the courtroom the apparatus necessary to capture the actual sounds and sights of the court in session, and (2) the willingness of the broadcast press to use restraint and the highest degree of professional attitude and activity while covering a trial. Certainly, not all of the courts across the country are going to open their doors to broadcasting overnight. The process will continue to be slow and gradual, and many trials will remain closed at the request of the parties involved. Meanwhile, the talented courtroom artists who are employed by many of the networks and larger television stations will continue their craft of capturing on sketch pads the activity barred from the eyes of the television camera.

COVERING LEGISLATIVE PROCEEDINGS

Too many times, the sensational decisions of the judiciary and the ever-present charisma of the executive branch demand the media's attention at the expense of other issues which are being hashed out in the legislative branch. This holds true not only for the U.S. Congress but also for state legislatures as well. Just as the live television coverage of judicial proceedings has been of keen interest to broadcast journalists, so has television coverage of the legislative branches of government.

Early Issues in the Televising of Congress

Widespread attention to live coverage of the House of Representatives was attracted by the hearings conducted in 1974. But the issue itself is much older. As early as 1922, Representative Vincent Brennan introduced a joint resolution "providing for the installation and operation of radio-telephone transmitting apparatus for the purpose of transmitting the proceedings and debates of the Senate and the House of Representatives."[19] Between 1922 and 1974, the issue arose again many times. But in 1974, the previous proposals, which had been mostly stillborn, took on a new meaning when President Richard Nixon's involvement in a political scandal called Watergate brought impeachment discussions to the House Judiciary Committee, and television brought the live drama to the nation. The presence of television did not create all the liabilities critics said it would. On top of public opinion polls showing a new lack of confidence in Congress, the time was ripe for serious discussions. Hearings held in February and March of 1974 considered:

> First. How can the role of Congress be more fully and accurately covered in the news media? Second. How can spokesmen for Congress gain direct access more readily to the broadcast media to present congressional viewpoints on issues? Third. What additional facilities, staff and other supporting services, if any, are required to provide Congress with more adequate institutional capability in the area of mass communications?[20]

The summary of positions resulting from the 1974 hearings provides even today a succinct statement of a general philosophy inherent in the issues surrounding the live coverage of legislative proceedings:

> (1) Most Americans know less than they need to know about the workings of Congress and its constitutional role; (2) part of the blame for ineffective communication lies in Congress, in procedural constraints as well as in other aspects of its organization and operation which can—and should—be changed; and (3) declining public confidence in Congress—along with other democratic institutions—urgently demands corrective action, including provision for broadcast coverage . . .[21]

Equally important are points that have been made in opposition to live television coverage. Again, although applying primarily to the U.S. House of Representatives, they are echoed in state legislatures as well. Opponents claim that television in the legislative branch can:

> 1. Subject members to the pressures of performing before a mass audience, distracting them from concentration on complex issues, and inhibiting the necessary compromises that go into the making of legislative decisions.
> 2. Result in members having to spend more of their already too thinly divided time on the floor (to avoid being charged with 'absenteeism'), conflicting with committee work and other necessary duties elsewhere.
> 3. Limit or eliminate the use of revise-and-extend procedures, extending debate unnecessarily and requiring more floor time for consideration of legislation.
> 4. Place the less aggressive or articulate members at a disadvantage, providing at the same time a forum for a few to 'showboat' in an effort to appeal favorably to their constituents.
> 5. Require the installation of bright lights, bulky cameras, cumbersome cables, and the presence of technical personnel and commentators in the galleries, creating uncomfortable glare and other distractions in the chambers.
> 6. Present a distorted picture of the congressional process, focusing undue attention on the final stage of legislative activity, much of which is either too dull to be interesting or too complicated to be understandable to the average viewer or listener.[22]

After arguments on both sides were aired, in October 1977 the House voted 342-44 to open its chambers to television. The critics lined up with their final shots, as proponents called it an "electronic age" whose time has come.[23] Others heralded it as bringing full First Amendment freedom to the House for both print and electronic journalism. Still another called it a "historic moment." Opponents also chimed in, with one representative suggesting that a new "theme song" would surely appear as a lead-in to each opening session.[24] It hasn't. Still another claimed the House would change from a forum to a theater. It hasn't.

Amidst all of the rhetoric, there was a real concern over who would control the television feed's. The three commercial networks wanted unlimited control, and some representatives were in their corner. Others, like Representative James Cleveland, stated: "We are not going to turn this over to a monopoly of the big three TV networks."[25] One argument was that smaller radio and television stations would have to "pay through the nose" for feeds, while with House control, the feeds would be free.

In March 1979, the system went into full operation with the House in control and the news media shouting "Censorship!" House Speaker Tip O'Neill recognized the "chill" that existed between the House members and the broadcast press but predicted that someday, when the House became comfortable with the presence of cameras, the press would be able to bring their own equipment into the chambers to televise proceedings.[26] O'Neill denied any censorship, but the squabbles continue. The Cable Satellite Public Affairs Network (C-SPAN) now carries live coverage and the public television stations have been more supportive of the concept than the commercial stations.

Six months into the operation of the House system, the network news chiefs still had complaints. Sid Davis of NBC said: "It's like covering a football game with cameras that never focus on the coaches or the players on the sidelines,"[27] and Ed Fouhy (CBS) complained: "We'd like to go in there and do what we do everywhere else, with professionals taking pictures wherever there is news."[28] Another side of the legislature coverage issue, however, centers on the unknown results of unlimited television coverage in an atmosphere of competition. What would be the result if the networks had a free rein to cover and choose news on the "sidelines"? Would the demands of competitive journalism give the viewing audience television drama rather than the issues of government? Moreover, with so much of the real decision making going on in committees and hearings, witness the nationally televised hearings on Supreme Court Justice Clarence Thomas, is this where the real coverage issues of the future will be found, not on the House floor?

Coverage at the State Level

In legislatures where live television cameras are not permitted, the same two factors continually snarl access: (1) the necessity to garner enough votes to pass a full-coverage measure, and (2) the inability to muster a plan for the coverage. Sticky points include whether or not cameras should show all of the chamber. Can the gallery be seen? Do the cameras need to be in fixed positions? Who will determine what will and will not be televised? Will the charismatic representatives steal the show from their less "polished" counterparts? Will politicians play to the cameras, instead of doing their job?

Nevertheless, the broadcast press is making progress. With Congress paving the way, and with bodies such as the Illinois Commerce Commission opening proceedings to live broadcast coverage, more and more state bodies have followed suit. Moreover, legislatures do not wrestle as courts do with the classic constitutional dilemma of free press versus fair trial. Open coverage of state legislatures should continue to increase where responsible media behavior prevails and is accompanied by a unified attempt to gain access.

OPEN-MEETING LAWS

Closely aligned with televised coverage of legislative proceedings are open meeting laws which prohibit the press from being barred from official decision making by governmental bodies. Such laws may or may not permit the broadcast press to use cameras and recorders.

Accessibility

Generally, open-meeting laws can be judged on their degree of openness based on whether the laws have provisions which:

> (1) Include a statement of public policy in support of openness; (2) provide for an open legislature; (3) provide for open legislative committees; (4) provide for open meetings of state agencies or bodies; (5) provide for open meetings of agencies and bodies of the political subdivisions of the state; (6) provide for open County Boards; (7) provide for open City Councils (or their equivalent); (8) forbid closed executive sessions; (9) provide legal recourse to halt secrecy; (10) declare actions

taken in meetings which violate the law to be null and void; (11) provide for penalties for those who violate the law.[29]

The degree of openness varies from state to state with some states barring "electronic" meetings.[30] In other states there are laws that insure open meetings and guard against circumvention of the law by telephone, teleconferencing, or videoconferencing.[31] Personnel actions by government agencies are always an area of contention. In some states all personnel actions are open to the press and public and in others such actions are closed to protect the privacy of the people who are the subject of the personnel actions. Some state institutions form advisory committees to advise chief administrative officers, who in turn have final action on personnel matters. The advisory committees' recommendations many times are privileged and not considered open under the open meeting statute. In some cases the names of final candidates for government positions, such as the top three candidates for a college presidency at a state institution, are public record but the proceedings of the advisory search committees which discuss and eliminate less qualified candidates are closed to the press and public.

Provisions

Many state open-meeting laws have provisions which directly affect the radio and television media. Emergency notice of meetings, electronic meetings, and the actual recordings of meetings are three examples. For instance, one state's open-meeting law provides for notifying the news media when the media have made prior arrangements for such notification. The specific provision reads:

> For an emergency meeting, the public body shall cause notice of the meeting to be given to each local wire service, local radio station, and local television station that has filed a written request, which includes the newspaper's, wire service's, or station's telephone number, for emergency notice with the clerk or secretary of the public body or with some other person designated by the public body. This notice shall be given either by telephone or by the same method used to notify the members of the public body and shall be given immediately after notice has been given to those members. This notice shall be given at the expense of the party notified. An 'emergency meeting' is one called because of generally unexpected circumstances that require immediate consideration by the public body. Only business connected with the emergency may be considered at a meeting to which notice is given pursuant to this paragraph.[32]

A provision against circumventing the law by electronic means mentioned earlier reads:

> If a public body holds an official meeting by use of conference telephone or other electronic means, it shall provide a location and means whereby members of the public may listen to the meeting and the notice of the meeting required by this Article shall specify that location. A fee of up to twenty-five dollars ($25.00) may be charged each such listener to defray in part the cost of providing the necessary location and equipment.[33]

The obtrusiveness of electronic equipment, especially where lights are involved, has caused some states to regulate the placement of cameras and recording equipment in the meeting room. For example, one such provision reads:

> A public body may regulate that placement and use of equipment necessary for broadcasting, photographing, filming, or recording a meeting, so as to prevent undue interference with the meeting. However, the public body must allow such equipment to be placed within the meeting room in such a way as to permit its intended use, and the ordinary use of such equipment shall not be declared to constitute undue interference; provided, however, that if the public body, in good faith, should determine that the size of the meeting room is such that all the members of the public body, members of the public present, and the equipment and personnel necessary for broadcasting, photographing, filming, and tape-recording the meeting cannot be accommodated in the meeting room without unduly interfering with the meeting and an adequate alternative meeting room is not readily available, then the public body, acting in good faith and consistent with the purposes of this Article, may require the pooling of such equipment and the personnel operating it; and provided further, if the news media, in order to facilitate news cover-

age, request an alternative site for the meeting, and the public body grants the request, then the news media making such request shall pay any costs incurred by the public body in securing an alternative meeting site.[34]

ACCESS TO PUBLIC RECORDS

Closely related to open-meeting laws are freedom of information laws which permit access by the press and public to public records. A federal Freedom of Information Act permits access to records of the federal government, although it is filled with exceptions that block access to areas the government feels should remain confidential.

The Freedom of Information Act

Passed in 1976, the federal Freedom of Information Act helped the press gain access to all federal documents except in such areas as national security, internal personnel matters, trade secrets, personal or privileged financial matters, personnel and medical files, law enforcement investigatory records, certain reports of financial institutions, and certain geological and geophysical information concerning wells.[35]

A series of amendments to the law has expanded and clarified the exceptions just listed. Included, for example, are exemptions over the flow of information about hazardous waste products originating from the Consumer Product Safety Commission, audit selection procedures of the Internal Revenue Service, and information on the military and civilian use of nuclear material originating from the Department of Energy.[36]

The actual amount of "openness" which may exist in the federal government at any given time can be dependent on the administration in power. It is not possible to tell what the Clinton administration legacy will be, but a Reagan administration National Security Advisor ordered National Security Council staff members not to talk to reporters, and a CIA director halted a practice of occasional press briefings about unclassified material. Although later the ban was lifted, the Reagan staff ordered executive branch personnel not to talk to "any element of the news media."[37]

The same administration reversed a "presumption of classification" status in an executive order that made it easier to label informations as confidential. Whereas during the previous administration there had to be "identifiable damage" to national security, the Reagan order made even "speculative harm" sufficient for classification. Eliminated was a policy of systematically declassifying information after 20 years, and a new policy made it possible to classify a document indefinitely.[38] The publication of the book *The Puzzle Palace* resulted in the National Security Agency—the subject of the book—telling librarians at the Virginia Military Institute to withhold from the public the contents of a special collection the author had used to do his research.

Another Reagan era action which elicited more widespread publicity and criticism was a Justice Department order that Canadian documentary films about acid rain and nuclear arms be labeled "political propaganda." The U.S. Justice Department also told the Film Board of Canada that the Justice Department wanted the names of all individuals and groups who requested the films.[39]

News media access to information was further restricted by a presidential directive "requiring every federal employee with access to classified information to sign an agreement not to make unauthorized disclosures and to submit to lie detector tests in the event of an investigation into news leaks."[40] The FBI was given the authority to investigate news leaks even if no criminal activity was suspected.

Additional strains on the availability and credibility of information occurred when it was disclosed that the Reagan administration had engaged in the practice of deliberately manipulating news events to gain positive coverage for its policies. The National Security Council and the Central Intelligence Agency were reported by Knight-Ridder News Service to have jointly sponsored through the State Department's Office of Public Diplomacy a media campaign designed to influence press coverage of El Salvador.[41] The goal was to change the image of the country from war-torn to one of gradual stabilization. Knight-Ridder also reported a media campaign by the same Office of Public Diplomacy to influence media coverage of Central America by leaking to reporters stories that would be unfavorable to Nicaragua and favorable to El Salvador.[42]

Using the Federal Freedom of Information Act

Most federal records are open to the press and public with the exceptions discussed earlier. In most cases a step-by-step process can gain access to the sought-after information, albeit with some costs incurred for research and copy fees. The original request should be made to the executive director of the federal agency involved. Be as specific as possible in describing the exact information you are seeking and keep a copy of your request. State the Freedom of Information Act with the appropriate section. For example, after the greeting, such a letter of request might read:

> Pursuant to the Freedom of Information Act, 5 U.S.C. 552 and (you may need to cite the specific rule or regulation of the federal agency whose own rules make public documents of the agency eg. if writing the FCC you would add: and to Section 0.461 of the FCC's Rules and Regulations) I hereby request access to (identify records requested in as much detail as possible). If there is any charge for locating and copying this material, please let me know in advance if the cost will exceed $_____. I would appreciate a reply to this request by ___________ (date, giving the agency reasonable time to process the request, usually seven to ten working days). If the request is denied please indicate which section of the Freedom of Information Act is being relied on as legal basis for denial.[43]

Include your name, address, a telephone number, and date the letter. If you just want to examine the records and not make copies, then this should be made clear in your letter. When requests are denied, an application for review can be made to the agency within 30 days. Agencies are required to rule on an appeal within 20 business days. If unsuccessful on appeal to the agency, you may take the appeal to the U.S. district court in the district in which you reside, or where your principal place of business or the records are located.

In most cases, especially where unclassified information is held, requests are handled on a routine basis. In many instances an agency will operate a public information office where people can go to request information and where staff personnel are available to assist the public and the press. Other times, the route to gaining access to information can be incredibly difficult and frustrating. A journalistic investigation of CIA infiltration of more than 400 underground publications during the Vietnam War era of the 1960s and 1970s meant a three-year wait for information from CIA files. Along with the delays came a CIA estimate of fees totaling more than $60,000 and a demand for a deposit of $30,000. Eventually an agreement was reached between the journalist and the CIA that made information available on 38 papers.[44]

Access to Criminal Records

In most cases police records are open to the press and the public, although there are exceptions where ongoing investigations are involved. You will probably not receive a friendly welcome if you ask a police detective for an ongoing investigation file, and in many states you would not be entitled to such information. Police logs, which are kept daily by most police departments, are usually considered public record. The courts are, however, full of cases where attempts have been made to keep police logs and other noninvestigatory records secret. For example, in an Ohio rape case which resulted in death the local paper went to court and gained disclosure of the university police reports of the incident. The university argued that the information was private on grounds that it was trial preparation material and disclosure would interfere with law enforcement proceedings.[45] We might speculate whether the court-ordered disclosure would have taken place if the victim had lived.

In another case a Massachusetts private college argued that because it was not state supported its police logs were confidential in addition to the fact that student records were confidential under federal privacy law. A court ruled that the police logs of the private college were public record since a state law required all police logs to be open to the public.[46] A Florida court ruled that a sheriff department's police blotter, budget, and personnel records are open for personal inspection under the state's public records law.[47] These examples are only a sampling of the many different laws and interpretations.

SHIELD LAWS

While the concept of a free press is embedded in the Constitution, many states have dealt directly with the free flow of information through the passage of reporters' shield laws.

What Shield Laws Protect

Shield laws protect the anonymity of reporters' sources, notes, outtakes, and other materials used in the reporting process. For example, assume you are filming a documentary about drug use at a local high school. You conduct a series of interviews, carefully shielding the face of the interviewee from the cameras. The interviewee admits not only to using drugs but also to selling them illegally. You air the documentary on a local television station and later receive a summons to tell the county prosecutor whom you interviewed. The prosecutor wants to arrest your source for using and selling drugs. You refuse, are sentenced for contempt, and end up in jail. What recourse do you have, and what protection do you have against the prosecutor's inquiry?

The answer may lie in your state's shield law. Most comprehensive shield laws protect the confidentiality of reporters' sources as a natural outgrowth of freedom of the press, although some see them limiting the First Amendment, not protecting it. The emphasis on shield laws surfaced in earnest in the early 1970s, when reporters kept finding themselves behind bars for refusing to divulge their sources of information.

A State Shield Law

Considerable national publicity over the jailings of such reporters resulted, pressuring many legislatures either to enact new shield laws or to update old ones. Indiana, for example, updated its shield law to read:

> Any person connected with, or any person who has been so connected with or employed by a . . . newspaper or other periodical issued at regular intervals and having a general circulation or a recognized press association; a wire service as a bona fide owner, editorial or reportorial employee, who receives or has received his or her principal income from legitimate gathering, writing, editing and interpretation of news, and any person connected with a licensed radio or television station as owner official, or as an editorial or reportorial employee who received or has received . . . income from . . . announcing or broadcasting of news, shall not be compelled to disclose in any legal proceedings or elsewhere the source of any information procured or obtained in the course of his employment or representation of such newspaper, periodical, press association, radio station, or television station, or wire service, whether published or not published in the newspaper or periodical, or by the press association or wire service or broadcast or not broadcast by the radio station or television station by which he is employed.[48]

Some of the old laws passed years ago did not specifically protect the broadcast press, and broadcast reporters often found themselves spending time in jail until an appeals court freed them. Most, but not all, laws encompass all media. Some such as Oregon's also include cable television, wire services, and books. The specific statement in Oregon's statute determines a medium of communication as ". . . any newspaper, magazine or other periodical, book, pamphlet, news service, wire service, news or feature syndicate, broadcast station or network, or cable television system."

Regardless of how complete your own state's shield laws may be, there are certain areas in which courts still challenge a reporter's confidentiality. The weakest ground exists in the area of grand jury proceedings. Such proceedings are expected to be an arena for protection as well as prosecution. In *Branzburg* v. *Hayes*, the United States Supreme Court ruled that the press does not enjoy a separate privilege under the First Amendment any more than any other citizen.

While state shield laws do offer protection, the best route to avoiding conflict with a judge is to exercise care in the reporting process.[49] Many reporters, unfortunately, feel that a free press and the First Amendment entitle them to take liberties which common sense, and especially the courts, may dispute. When dealing with a confidential source, exercise care and ask yourself if the reason the source wants to remain confidential is because the information it is supplying is suspect in the first place. Ask yourself if you are being used and find out if the information can be verified from another source. Sometimes it may sound good on the air to use such phrases as: "A reliable source told us . . ."; "A source in the governor's office told us . . ."; "A government official said . . ."; and other forms of attribution which suggest that the reporter is "well connected" and doing a thorough job. But if the story cannot be verified from another source and the report damages a business or personal reputation, then the only alternative for someone seeking damages in a libel case is to subpoena the reporter. The judge, remember, is an attorney first and the law, not the press, is where her or his professional reputation rests. Many judges have little patience for reporters who have engaged in sloppy reporting practices when gathering information.

GAG ORDERS

Another regulatory issue facing the broadcast press is raised directly by the judges. Place yourself, for a moment, behind a judicial bench at a preliminary hearing, determining whether an accused murderer will stand trial. It is your responsibility as a judge to conduct a trial which seeks the truth before a fair and impartial jury. If anything less than that occurs, you can expect your decision to be appealed to a higher court and risk having the verdict overturned or a new trial ordered. How do you protect the defendant's rights to a fair trial? You may decide to issue a gag order, muzzling the press and prohibiting it from reporting certain details of the case.

Now return to being a reporter. You have an obligation as a reporter to inform the public. It is not your role to decide whether the community that watches the coverage of the crime may become so biased that a fair and impartial jury cannot be chosen. How do you handle the gag order? You can obey it. You can permit yourself to be muzzled and abide by the judge's decision. Many reporters would do just that. Others would be appalled at the thought. If you are, you could defy the court order and report the proceedings. That could also find you in the same cell with the reporter who refused to reveal a confidential source of information. You risk being found in contempt of court.

Judges, however, continue to issue gag orders, knowing that while the gag order is being appealed the business of the court can take place without the watchful eye of the press. In Bloomington, Illinois, the media sought, but was denied by the U.S. Supreme Court, a stay of two gag orders issued by two different judges in cases where juvenile defendants were involved. While the names of the defendants were well known in their communities, the judge would not permit the release of their names by the press.[50] Juveniles, however, represent a somewhat different legal matter than adults. Where adults are involved a gag order will usually be quashed, but many times too late to benefit the press, which is interested in accurate and timely reporting of a judicial proceeding.

ACCESS TO TRIAL AND PRETRIAL PROCEEDINGS

Closely related to the issue of gag orders is access to trial and pretrial proceedings. The vast majority of disputes are settled before trial.

Two cases determined the direction of pretrial access in recent years, each conflicting with the other's contitutional values. The cases, *Gannett Company, Inc.* v. *DePasquale* came down on the side of the Sixth Amendment and resulted in pretrial closures until *Press-Enterprises Co.* v. *Riverside County Superior Court* (P-E II) favored the First Amendment and opened pretrial proceedings.[51]

In the case of *Gannett* v. *DePasquale*, the Court held that the defendant, not the public or the press, is the key to the guarantee of a fair trial, and that judges have an affirmative duty to minimize the effects of pretrial publicity. When all litigants—the judge, the defendant, and the prosecutor—agree to a closed hearing, then it is legal and appropriate. The majority opinion, written by Justice Stewart, stated:

> Among the guarantees that the Sixth Amendment provides to a person charged with the commission of a criminal offense, and to him alone, is the "right to a speedy and public trial, by an impartial jury." The Constitution nowhere mentions any right of access to a criminal trial on the part of the public; its guarantee, like the others enumerated, is personal to the accused.[52]

Justice Rehnquist concurred in part:

> The Court's discussion of the need to preserve the defendant's right to a fair trial should not be interpreted to mean that under the Sixth Amendment a trial court can close a pretrial hearing or trial only when there is a danger that prejudicial publicity will harm the defendant.
>
> To the contrary, since the Court holds that the public does not have any Sixth Amendment right of access to such proceedings, it necessarily follows that if the parties agree on a closed proceeding, the trial court is not required by the Sixth Amendment to advance any reason whatsoever for declining to open a pretrial hearing or trial to the public.[53]

Jack Landau of the Reporters' Committee for a Free Press predicted that the decision would "encourage federal and state trial judges all over the nation to convert our open court system into secret judicial forums."[54] Echoing Landau's comments was Paul Davis, speaking as president of the Radio Television News Directors' Association. He said: "in its zeal to protect a defendant's right to a fair trial, the Supreme Court has seriously crippled the concept of public scrutiny without which the integrity of the American judicial system cannot survive."[55] While then Chief Justice Burger pointed out that the issue was *pre*trial and not trial, Landau pointed out that fully 89 percent of all criminal cases are settled during pretrial proceedings.[56] Glimmerings of hope for future decisions to swing the pendulum away from closed sessions came from Justice Blackmun, who wrote: "Publicity is essential to the preservation of public confidence in the rule of law and in the operation of courts. Only in rare circumstances does this principle clash with the rights of the criminal defendant to a fair trial so as to justify exclusion."[57]

Relief from *Gannett v. DePasquale* came with *Press Enterprise Co.* v. *Riverside Superior Court* (P-E II). The U.S. Supreme Court reversed the California Supreme Court and weighed in on the side of the First Amendment. A magistrate granted a defendant's motion to exclude the public from the preliminary hearing using a California statute that required such proceedings to be open unless "exclusion of the public is necessary in order to protect the defendant's right to a fair and impartial trial." The magistrate refused the *Press Enterprises's* request that the transcript of the proceeding, 4,239 pages of testimony gathered over eight weeks and filling 47 volumes, be released. The case was particularly newsworthy since the defendant, a nurse, was charged with killing 12 patients with massive does of the drug lidocaine used to treat heart conditions.

In a 7-2 decision, the U.S. Supreme Court ruled in favor of the newspaper's petition to open access to preliminary hearings. The Court pointed out that even the celebrated case of Aaron Burr for treason resulted in the probable-cause hearing being held in the Hall of the House of Delegates in Virginia because the courtroom was too small to hold everyone who wanted to witness the proceeding. In a decision written by Chief Justice Burger, the court cited previous cases and First Amendment principles in supporting openness. Fair trial, the Court said, is assured by the presence of neutral observers and many times the preliminary hearing is the only proceeding where the public has the opportunity to view the criminal justice system. Burger wrote that it is difficult for the people in a open society to accept what they can't observe. Openness assures fairness and the appearance of fairness. The Court emphasized that asserting that publicity might deprive a defendant of the defendant's right to a fair trial does not overcome that First Amendment right of access. The Court also criticized the magistrate for not seeking other solutions to complete closure. With *Press-Enterprise II*, the Court returned the weight of the First Amendment and access to pretrial proceedings to counterbalance the Sixth-Amendment effect of *Gannett* v. *DePasquale*.

ACCESS TO JURY SELECTION

The Gannett decision still needed clarification and some came when a California man was accused of raping and strangling a 15-year-old girl. When the prosecutor announced that he would seek the death penalty the Riverside, California *Press Enterprise*, the same company that would win the 1986 decision (P-E II), was prohibited by the trial judge from covering the jury selection process.[58] A request for a copy of the transcript of the proceeding was also denied. The California courts upheld the trial judge and supported arguments that jury selection entails asking very private questions of the prospective jurors. Individuals will be much more candid if they know their answers will not become part of press publicity. In this particular case it was reported that there was an "implied agreement between the court and prospective jurors that their right to privacy would be respected concerning their views on the death penalty."[59]

The U.S. Supreme Court in 1984 disagreed and ruled in the case of *Press Enterprise Co.* v. *Superior Court* that jury selection is presumed to be open and can only be closed in situations where the defendant's right to a fair trial is jeopardized or where very intimate information is being disclosed by a prospective juror.[60] Even in these situations a transcript with the prospective juror's name deleted can be released to the public and the press. Moreover, the judge must clearly state why no alternative to closure can be employed and such statements must be in enough detail that they can be reviewed by a higher court if the closure is appealed.

Access to Pretrial Discovery

To obtain facts assuring a fair and just trial, both parties can engage in "discovery" proceedings and obtain information about the other party. These pretrial discovery functions frequently uncover information that the press deems in the public interest. One perspective on how much information is public and therefore open to the press occurred in *Seattle Times Co.* v. *Rhinehart*.[61] When the *Seattle Times* and another paper covered a story about a spiritual leader and his foundation, the leader and the foundation sued for libel and invasion of privacy.

During discovery the newspaper sought the foundation's list of contributors to help defend themselves against the claim that the foundation had suffered damages because of the published articles. The foundation resisted compliance with the discovery request saying that the release of the information would adversely affect financial support to the foundation. The Washington State Supreme Court ordered the foundation to provide the newspaper with the information it requested. The foundation then sought and was granted a protective order that prohibited the newspaper from publishing the information. While such an order may appear to be a form of prior restraint violating the First Amendment, they are sometimes issued to guard trade secrets, and to protect parties from "annoyance, embarrassment, or oppression."[62] The court felt that it was necessary to avoid the "chilling effect" that disclosure would have on parties who may want to bring their cases to court.[63]

The U.S. Supreme Court in 1984 voted unanimously to uphold the Washington State Supreme Court. The decision affirmed the lack of any First Amendment right of public access to information obtained in pretrial discovery of civil cases. The decision did not affect criminal cases and did not prohibit the reporting of information which may be obtained from other sources even though the same information is uncovered during a discovery proceeding. For example, if the foundation's records had been public documents—such as a foundation operated by an agency of state government where a strong open records law exists—then the fact the information became part of a pretrial discovery would not prohibit it from being reported by the press.

The *Seattle Times* v. *Rhinehart* decision did not prohibit the release of all pretrial information in all cases. Judges still have considerable freedom to rule on the side of public disclosure when they feel it serves the public interest. For example, when claims were made that the oil companies had conspired to control the price of petroleum products, the documents were originally sealed.[64] Dow Jones, the parent company of *The Wall Street Journal*, moved to release the documents, many of which had been filed as pretrial briefs. A district judge agreed that the discovery information should be open to the public for a number of reasons, including the seriousness of the issue and the fact that taxpayer monies were used in bringing to trial and prosecuting the original suits. Among parties to the suits were the State of California and the City of Long Beach which argued certain petroleum companies had "conspired to drive down the price of domestic crude oil." An appeal to the 9th Circuit Court of Appeals in San Francisco affirmed the lower court decision to make public the pretrial discovery information. The U.S. Supreme Court refused to review the appellate court decision.

Access to Trials: Beyond DePasquale

Access to trials, as opposed to pretrial proceedings, has not been clearly interpreted by the courts. In 1980 the U.S. Supreme Court, hearing a case on appeal from the Supreme Court of Virginia, issued a 7-1 decision in support of First Amendment rights of journalists to attend criminal trials. In *Richmond Newspapers* v. *Commonwealth of Virginia*, the majority opinion of Justice Burger stated: "We hold that the right to attend criminal trials is implicit in the guarantees of the First Amendment; without the freedom to attend such trials, which people have exercised for centuries, important aspects of freedom of speech and of the press could be eviscerated."[66] In a concurring opinion, Justice Stevens said: "Until today the Court has accorded virtually absolute protection to the dissemination of information or ideas, but never before has it squarely held that the acquisition of newsworthy matter is entitled to any constitutional protection whatsoever."[67] Justice Brennan went on to concur, saying

> Secrecy is profoundly inimical to this demonstrative purpose of the trial process. Open trials assure the public that procedural rights are respected, and that justice is afforded equally. Closed trials breed suspicion of prejudice and arbitrariness, which in turn spawns disrespect for law. Public access is essential, therefore, if trial adjudication is to achieve the objective of maintaining public confidence in the administration of justice.
>
> But the trial is more a demonstrably just method of adjudicating disputes and protecting rights. It plays a pivotal role in the entire judicial process, and, by extension, in our form of government. Under our system, judges are not mere umpires, but, in their

> own sphere, lawmakers—a coordinate branch of government. While individual cases turn upon the controversies between parties, or involve particular prosecutions, court rulings impose official and practical consequences upon members of society at large. Moreover, judges bear responsibility for the vitally important task of construing and securing constitutional rights. Thus, so far as the trial is the mechanism for judicial factfinding, as well as the initial forum for legal decisionmaking, it is a genuine governmental proceeding.[68]

Access became more clouded, however, when the *Sacramento Bee* newspaper ran a story about a drug trafficking trial and one juror in the case was excused after reading the story. The judge, citing concern over news accounts reaching other jurors, closed the trial to the press and the public while hearing a motion to suppress evidence. The closures were upheld on appeal to the U.S. Court of Appeals for the 9th Circuit in San Francisco. The newspaper appealed to the U.S. Supreme Court in *Sacramento Bee* v. *U.S. District Court* but in an 8-1 vote the justices declined to hear the case.[69] It meant the judges still had some latitude to close trials when a fair trial, in their opinion, outweighed a free press.

Reasons for Court Closures

A report by The Reporters Committee for Freedom of the Press examined court closures and found a variety of reasons judges use to keep the press and sometimes the public from judicial proceedings.[70] The most frequently cited reason for closing a trial to the press is fear that publicity will prejudice a jury. Some states have closure laws, although overly encompassing closure statutes have been found to be unconstitutional. Potential embarrassment to trial participants can result in a closing, such as a community leader serving as a witness. Other closings have taken place when there was a fear for the safety of the trial participants. Proceedings involving juveniles are frequently closed to the press. National security is another reason closure can occur. These and other reasons point out that carrying a press card and having some Supreme Court decisions on your side will not necessarily get you in the courtroom door.

LIBEL

Libel is a false published statement about a person or institution that results in public hatred, contempt, or ridicule and one that can cause the person or institution harm. In libel law, the word *published* refers to both broadcast and print media. If something is *aired* on a radio or television station, it is considered *published*. Harm is not necessarily physical harm either. Being shunned by friends, losing business, or similar suffering can be construed as grounds for libel. In court, a libel suit brought against a reporter or station can cause substantial damages, running into the thousands or even millions of dollars. Irresponsible reporting is nothing to take lightly and can bring serious consequences. Even public figures, such as politicians or celebrities, can win libel suits if they can prove that a statement is false and malicious. While some well-known cases are the foundation of libel law, every reporter should be familiar with their individual state laws applied to libel since statutes differ from state to state. Knowing libel law at the state level is a prudent safeguard.

Foundations of Libel Law

In 1964, the case of *The New York Times Co.* v. *Sullivan* established the principle that only when deliberate knowledge of falsity or reckless disregard for the truth had been present could a public official collect damages for libel.[71] Proving deliberate knowledge of falsity and reckless disregard for the truth was exceptionally difficult, and time and time again the courts sided with the news media. In 1971, the case of *Curtis Publishing Co.* v. *Butts* expanded the rule used in *The New York Times* case to include public figures—in this instance, well-known college athletic officials.[72] The *Curtis* case dealt a severe blow to the old *Saturday Evening Post*, which saw itself liable for punitive and actual damages close to three-quarters of a million dollars.

Since the *Curtis* case, the courts have continued to define libel law—specifically what is and what is not a public figure, and what is required for damages. The 1974 case of *Gertz* v. *Robert Welch, Inc.* saw a prominent Chicago lawyer win a libel suit when he was falsely characterized by a right-wing magazine as being a communist and having a criminal record. Despite the fact that the lawyer was representing a client in a newsworthy proceeding, the court said that this action was not enough to place him in the category of a public figure.[73] A further refining of the definition of a public figure occurred in the 1976 case of *Time, Inc.* v. *Firestone*, when the well-known socialite, Mary Alice Firestone, was involved in a widely publicized divorce suit.[74] The court found that, because divorce is a private matter, she deserved some protection as a private person instead of being labeled a public figure in the traditional categories previously mentioned.

Other cases have helped to clarify the libel issue, although not necessarily in favor of the media. For example, jurisdiction became an issue in two cases where the U.S. Supreme Court ruled that a person can sue for libel where a publication circulates, not where it is published or originates. The same would probably apply to over-the-air radio or television signals. When a nationally circulated tabloid published in Florida was sued in California by California resident and actress Shirley Jones who claimed she had been libeled, the tabloid cried foul, saying it had no direct ties with California. But the U.S. Supreme Court affirmed in *Calder* v. *Jones* a lower court ruling which held that the editor of the tabloid and the reporter who wrote the story, both Florida residents, should be included as defendants in the suit. The First Amendment did not give any special protection to media defendants who were not residents of a state which, in this case, was where the plaintiff resided, and where the newspaper had substantial circulation.[75]

The ability to bring suit anywhere a publication is circulated was further affirmed when an associate publisher of *Penthouse* magazine sued *Hustler* magazine for libel after she had been portrayed in a *Hustler* cartoon and copy in a way she felt libeled her and invaded her privacy. After the statute of limitations ran out in other states, she filed suit in New Hampshire, where the court ducked the issue by saying that New Hampshire did not have jurisdiction. The U.S. Supreme Court in *Keeton* v. *Hustler* disagreed, saying *Hustler*'s circulation in New Hampshire was enough to give New Hampshire jurisdiction.[76] Both cases have implications for broadcast news and entertainment programming. The cases clearly permit a person to bring a libel suit virtually anywhere a signal reaches or a program is distributed, and such suits will not be restricted by state boundaries.

In another case the U.S. Supreme Court looked again at the way libel law was interpreted under the standards established in *The New York Times Co.* v. *Sullivan*. A publication described a company's stereo loudspeakers as creating sound which wandered about the room and made a piano sound as if it stretched from "wall to wall."[77] Bose Corp., manufacturer of the loudspeakers, sued the publication for libel. The judge found in favor of the plaintiff but the ruling was reversed on appeal after the appellate court considered separately the evidence used to support actual malice. The U.S. Supreme Court in *Bose* v. *Consumer Union* upheld the reversal and reaffirmed the principle of constitutional law that allows an appellate court to independently review factual evidence to determine if a trial judge has erred in interpreting the First Amendment rights of the press and the precedent of *The New York Times* v. *Sullivan* spirit of the actual malice test.[78]

Avoiding Libel

While knowledge of case law, the causes of libel, and defenses against it are important, even more important is avoiding libel.[79] Many libel suits originate through carelessness or haste. Other libel suits germinate when reporters are less than professional. For example, the pressure of deadlines always creates problems in getting accurate information. But no deadline is more important than accuracy. Unless the facts of a story are clear and verifiable, then the story should not air. Anything less can result in a plaintiff showing reckless disregard, the end result of which may be a guilty verdict and punitive as well as actual damages.

People are different than events. The sketchy details of hurricane damage is less serious than the sketchy details over an accused rapist. There is no margin for error in the latter story. Whenever a person's reputation is at stake, the story has the potential for igniting a fiery libel suit. Double check information and if it can't be independently verified by at least two sources, it should be held until further information is available. Even routine stories can cause problems since these may be the ones taken for granted. The seemingly uninteresting and unimportant details of a police blotter can injure the reputation of a private citizen. Even such public events as news conferences are filled with pitfalls when the person being quoted makes unproven accusations against another person, organization, business, or other group. Misquoting someone may come back to haunt a reporter in a court case where both the station and the reporter end up as codefendants. Where private citizens are involved, their privacy may be an issue. Invading it may trigger an invasion of privacy suit, even if the information reported in the story is true. Involuntarily being thrust into the news by a zealous news team can land the station and its personnel in court. Old pictures, file footage, or other "stock" video can misrepresent and damage someone's reputation.

Representing the Plaintiff

If you are an attorney representing a plaintiff in a libel action, you would be responsible for proving certain facts. First, the statement prompting the libel action would have to be *proved false*. That may not be difficult, however, since the simple lack of the defendant's ability to prove the statement true may be all that is necessary. Many reporters have ended up in court simply because they *thought* a statement was true but forgot that they needed to *prove* it to be true to successfully defend themselves against libel.

If you successfully prove that the statement is false, the second task is to prove that it was *published*. This is generally easy, since simply producing the news copy or a recording of the broadcast is all that is necessary. Examining the published copy, you would next need to prove that it was *defamatory*. Are the words used actually harmful? If a person is called an "embezzler" or an "adulterer," there is little question that the words are defamatory. Such words, which are defamatory on their face value, are called libel *per se*. If the words are not libelous on their face value, but only in the context of other words, they are called libel *per quod*. For example, if an on-air gossip column says that high school teachers John Doe and Jane Smith are going to make it legal and get married, it could imply that they have been living together or having an affair which, if causing them to be ridiculed in their local community could put the station in court.

More difficult elements to prove are *negligence* or *actual malice*, which are closely related. Was the reporter careless in handling the story? Were there other safeguards that could have been taken? If these safeguards were thrown to the wind, does that imply actual malice as defined by *New York Times*? Some negligence cases are easier to prove than others. If a program director testifies that the news director arrives drunk on the job and doesn't pay much attention to work, then the fact of negligence may seem to be cut and dried. But even less flagrant behavior can be construed as negligent. For example, if the reporter could have checked other news sources but didn't, it can be construed as negligence. What if the reporter had contacted one more person to verify the facts? What if the reporter had made an extra effort to get both sides of the story? Would the reporter then have aired the same story? Questions like these can weigh heavily on the minds of a judge or jury.

Finally, the plaintiff must be able to prove that he or she was *injured* by the publication of the defamatory material. Remember, libel damages have been awarded for nothing more than mental anguish. Being shunned by co-workers, even if a person keeps his or her job, can mean a decision in favor of the plaintiff.

You would have a great deal of latitude in questioning reporters about how the story developed, what took place during the preparation of the story, what was said between you and your news director or production crew, and any other question about the editorial process. Much of the liberty to do whatever is necessary to attempt to prove actual malice and a reckless disregard for the truth would be based in the U.S. Supreme Court decision of *Herbert* v. *Lando*.[80] Colonel Anthony Herbert was a retired Vietnam era Army officer who sued CBS over a broadcast that alleged a cover-up of wartime atrocities. CBS's Barry Lando produced the program. The case eventually was remanded by the U.S. Supreme Court back to the federal district court but the opinions expressed by the Supreme Court influenced procedures in trying libel cases. CBS claimed editorial privilege, specifically that the First Amendment prevented inquiry into the "state of mind" Lando and others possessed at the time the program was broadcast. "The District Court ruled the defendant's state of mind was central to the plaintiff's case and no constitutional privilege existed which would prevent, under the rules of Federal Civil Procedure, the discovery of any subject matter involved."[81] The case went to the court of appeals which ruled in favor of the First Amendment privilege but the Supreme Court in reversing the court of appeals upheld the reasoning of the district court. In a strongly worded opinion based on the foundation of individual rights the Supreme Court opinion read:

> We are thus being asked to modify firmly established constitutional doctrine by placing beyond the plaintiff's reach a range of direct evidence relevant to proving knowing or reckless falsehood by the publisher of an alleged libel, elements that are critical to plaintiffs such as Herbert. The case for making this modification is by no means clear and convincing and we decline to accept it.[82]

General Defenses Against Libel

While an attorney has a major task in proving libel, the defense can have an equally difficult time proving innocence. Three primary defenses are used in libel cases, although it is not always necessary to prove all three.

The first defense is *truth*. In some states, proving that a published statement is true is an absolute defense against libel. But remember, the key word is *proving*. Many a reporter has fallen victim to a rumor or unsubstantiated fact, only to find out after the story aired that it was fictitious. *Saying* that someone is taking money from the retirement fund is one thing. *Proving* it *conclusively* in court is something else. Even criminal charges can lead a reporter astray. The word *alleged* does not always stand up as a defense if the news media, by the extent and tone of their coverage, are less than objective in reporting the arrest and trial of an accused. If the person is found innocent, biased reporting can spell a libel suit.

A second defense is *qualified privilege*. Certain forums permit immunity from libel actions. For example, if a witness in a murder case testifies that she saw the accused enter the widow's house just after the crime occurred, and her testimony is reported on a newscast, there would be little grounds for the accused to sue the witness after the accused was found innocent. Remarks made at official proceedings, such as Congressional hearings or other legislative sessions, are also immune from libel. However, it is well to keep in mind that irresponsible reporting can still mean trouble if the privilege is abused.

Still another primary defense against libel is *fair comment*. This is a somewhat grey area of the law, and each situation is different. The press is permitted a certain amount of freedom to criticize such people as elected officials or government administrators. Here the defense must prove that it was in the public interest for the comments to be made and that the public interest was paramount. Again, this privilege can be abused. A politician's official functions can be criticized, but if that politician is living with another man's wife, without endangering his ability to carry out his duties as an elected official, to openly expose his living arrangement may be grounds for libel under an invasion of privacy statute.

Consent can also be a defense, but again, consent must be proven. Let us assume that a radio journalist records an interview with a doctor and asks the doctor's permission to air a story about the police chief's speculation that he is distributing illegal drugs. The doctor consents. The story airs. The doctor sues for libel. If the reporter does not have the doctor's consent on tape or in writing, proving that the doctor actually consented to the story being aired could be a sticky problem. In some states, reply and retraction can also be used as a defense against libel. Other states require that a personal apology be made by the media.

Libel law continues to evolve. In recent years, the courts, although still guaranteeing a free press, have looked more carefully at the press's responsibility in carrying out its functions. Moreover, when libel is proven, the damage awards can be staggering, even crippling. Television journalists are particularly vulnerable to libel, since libel can occur not only by word but by picture.

INVASION OF PRIVACY

Closely related to libel laws are invasion of privacy statutes.

Types of Statutes

These statutes are generally divided into four categories: appropriation, intrusion, private information, and false information. *Appropriation* refers to the unauthorized use of a person's picture or likeness for some commercial purpose. *Intrusion* can become an issue if an overzealous electronic wizard decides to bug someone's room or office to gather information for a story. Although intrusion is rarely an issue in cases involving the press, the recent emphasis on investigative reporting and the miniaturizations of electronic circuitry have increased the potential for abuse. Publishing *private information* about a person can result in an invasion of privacy suit. The difficulty lies in determining exactly what is private, and this difficulty is compounded when public officials are concerned. Publishing *false information* about a person's private life can be closely related to libel law; in fact, the two can overlap.

Privacy law is one of the more recent areas of developing judicial precedent. As we become more concerned about our privacy in an increasingly commercialized world, in which computers have the ability to store our most private secrets and investigative reporting continues to develop as a specialized field of journalism (albeit many times practiced by irresponsible and inexperienced reporters), more and more cases centering around invasion of privacy will find their way into the courts.

Avoiding Invasion of Privacy Suits

Like libel suits, avoiding invasion of privacy suits involves responsible reporting practices. Many times the desire to report a story, even the well-intentioned effort to get the facts, jeopardizes the privacy of another person. When a public official is involved, there is less chance of overstepping the bounds of responsible journalism. Not so with private individuals.

Some basic safeguards can help keep one from becoming a defendant.[83] For example, do not assume that simply because an individual is thrust into the public eye that he or she is fair game for a story. It is usually necessary to obtain consent before going onto someone's private property to record facts or pictures that are not in public view. When consent is required it must be given from someone in a position to grant it. A minor or retarded individual may not be a valid consenter. Even if consent is given to enter onto private property that does not entail consent to take photographs or make video or audio recordings. Moreover, a police or fire official does not necessarily have the authority to grant consent to enter or photograph private property. Even taking a picture or making a recording when neither is aired may be considered an invasion of privacy. Use of hidden cameras can result in even more serious repercussions for broadcast journalists.

Remember a person does not become a public figure when forced into the news against their will or through actions or events over which they have no control. Also remember that the First Amendment has not been used successfully against charges of trespassing.

SEARCH AND SEIZURE

Although few newsrooms have ever been faced with a search warrant, the experience can be a chilling reminder of what police-state tactics mean and how vulnerable the First Amendment is to challenge. Such was the *Stanford Daily* case where the U.S. Supreme Court upheld a surprise search on the offices of the student newspaper at Stanford University.

Zurcher v. *Stanford Daily*

The *Stanford Daily* case struck down most First Amendment protection that a news organization had against surprise searches of their premises. It gave police the right to search any premise upon showing that there was a reasonable chance that evidence of a crime could be found there, and the presence of a search warrant meant that the police could look anywhere for that evidence. Unlike a subpoena, which has a much better chance of being challenged in court, a search warrant is a much more immediate threat. Moreover, not every police officer will wait long enough for a local news outlet to call its attorney and wait until the warrant can be challenged or quashed. As an editorial in *Broadcasting* stated: "It will be a public-spirited cop indeed who chances upon evidence of a journalistic investigation of the local police and keeps the secret."[84]

KBCI-TV, Boise, Idaho

In July 1980, when inmates rioted at the Idaho State Prison in Boise, KBCI-TV, a CBS affiliate, entered the grounds of the prison and interviewed rioting prisoners on videotape. The Ada County prosecutor, who was not inside the prison with the television reporters, obtained a search warrant for the tapes. Police searched the newsroom of the station, going through files and desk drawers, and obtained two videotapes containing footage of the prison riot. While the station was being searched, two Ada County sheriff's deputies reportedly refused to allow one of the station's attorneys to leave his office in a nearby bank building. The Boise search-and-seizure incident was one of the first major searches of a newsroom to occur after the *Stanford* case. Idaho law did not provide for the issuance of a subpoena until a defendant had been named in a case and, in the prison riot incident, no defendant had been named when the warrant was secured and served.

Relief from Search and Seizure: Privacy Protection Act

The results of the *Stanford Daily* decision followed by the well-publicized Idaho incident (which included an interview with the prosecutor and the news director on ABC's *Nightline*) caused politicians to call for federal protection against newsroom searches. Many attorneys were in favor of protection since the newsroom searches caused them to realize that their offices were not immune from police intrusion.

Protection did arrive with the Privacy Protection Act. Taking effect in 1981, the act made it unlawful for a government officer or employee investigating or prosecuting a criminal offense to search for a work product possessed by someone reasonably believed to have a purpose to disseminate information to the public.[85] The key to the wording of the law is *work product*, and a distinction is made between *work product* and *documentary materials*. Specifically:

work product includes:

- reporter's, producer's and editor's notes and interviews, mental impressions, conclusions, opinions, theories,
- materials prepared, produced, authored or created in anticipation of their communication to the public, and
- materials possessed to be communicated to the public.[86]

documentary materials include:

- materials on which information is recorded, including but not limited to video and audio tapes, photographs, motion picture films, negatives, and other mechanically, magnetically or electronically recorded cards, tapes or discs, written or printed materials.[87]

Exceptions to the law do exist. If news personnel are believed to be in possession of material which directly relates to the commission of a crime or that seizing the material is necessary to prevent death or bodily injury, then police may still show up at the front door with a search warrant. As an example, if news personnel are in possession of stolen goods, then they would receive little protection under the law from being served with a search warrant.

Exceptions are also present when documentary material is considered as opposed to work product. For example, if law enforcement officials feel news personnel will destroy material when served by a subpoena, then they can argue for a search warrant. If a newsperson refuses to turn over material after being served by a subpoena (having failed to squash the subpoena) or if a delay typically caused by a subpoena should threaten the interests of justice, then law enforcement can argue for a search warrant. Despite the act, there are no guarantees search warrants will not be served in the future. If you are employed in a broadcast newsroom, it is a good idea to contact the station's attorney and familiarize yourself with the procedures to follow when served by a search warrant.

RIGHT OF PUBLICITY

In one of the more unusual cases to come before the Supreme Court, a circus performer sued an Ohio television station after the station broadcast his human cannonball act in its entirety on the evening news. Hugo Zacchini was shot from a cannon some 200 feet away, with each performance lasting about 15 seconds. On a directive from his superior, a reporter from a local station filmed the act against the wishes of Zacchini. After the film aired, Zacchini brought suit, claiming that his act had been "showed and commercialized without his consent."[88] The issue at hand is commonly termed the *right of publicity*. In the case of Zacchini, it was closely related to an invasion of privacy. In fact, the Ohio Supreme Court alluded to this fact when hearing the case, but nevertheless ruled in favor of the press, saying that the press must be given a wide latitude in determining how much of a story or incident it should include as part of the news.

The United States Supreme Court, in *Hugo Zacchini* v. *Scripps Howard Broadcasting Company*, however, took a much different view and reversed the lower court. The majority opinion, written by Justice White, stated:

> The broadcast of a film of petitioner's entire act poses a substantial threat to the economic value of that performance. As the Ohio court recognized, this act is the product of petitioner's own talents and energy, the end result of much time, effort and expense. Much of its economic value lies in the "right of exclusive control over the publicity given to his performance"; if the public can see the act for free on television, they will be less willing to pay to see it at the fair. The effect of a public broadcast of the performance is similar to preventing petitioner from charging an admission fee. "The rationale for [(protecting the right of publicity)] is the straight-forward one of preventing unjust enrichment by the theft of good will. No social purpose is served by having the defendant get for free some aspect of the plaintiff that would have market value and for which he would normally pay." . . .
>
> Moreover, the broadcast of petitioner's entire performance, unlike the unauthorized use of another's name for purposes of trade or the incidental use of a name or picture by the press, goes to the heart of petitioner's ability to earn a living as an entertainer. Thus in this

> case, Ohio has recognized what may be the strongest case for a "right of publicity"—involving not the appropriation of an entertainer's reputation to enhance the attractiveness of a commercial product, but the appropriation of the very activity by which the entertainer acquired his reputation in the first place. . . .
>
> There is no doubt that entertainment, as well as news, enjoys First Amendment protection. It is also true that entertainment itself can be important news. But it is important to note that neither the public nor respondent will be deprived of the benefit of petitioner's performance as long as his commercial stake in his act is appropriately recognized. Petitioner does not seek to enjoin the broadcast of his performance; he simply wants to be paid for it. . . .[89]

More supportive of the press's position was the dissenting opinion of Justice Powell, with which Justice Brennan and Justice Marshall concurred:

> Although the Court would draw no distinction, . . . I do not view respondent's action as comparable to unauthorized commercial broadcasts of sporting events, theatrical performances, and the like where the broadcaster keeps the profits. There is no suggestion here that respondent made any such use of the film. Instead, it simply reported on what petitioner concedes to be a newsworthy event, in a way hardly surprising for a television station—by means of film coverage. The report was part of an ordinary daily news program, consuming a total of 15 seconds. It is a routine example of the press fulfilling the informing function so vital to our system.
>
> The Court's holding that the station's ordinary news report may give rise to substantial liability has disturbing implications, for the decision could lead to a degree of media self-censorship. . . . Hereafter, whenever a television news editor is unsure whether certain film footage received from a camera crew might be held to portray an "entire act," he may decline coverage—even of clearly newsworthy events—or confine the broadcast to watered-down verbal reporting, perhaps with an occasional still picture. The public is then the loser. This is hardly the kind of news reportage that the First Amendment is meant to foster. . . .
>
> In my view, the First Amendment commands a different analytical starting point from the one selected by the Court. Rather than begin with a quantitative analysis of the performer's behavior—is this or is this not his entire act—we should direct initial attention to the actions of the news media: what use did the station make of the film footage? When a film is used, as here, for a routine portion of a regular news program, I would hold that the First Amendment protects the station from a "right of publicity" or "appropriation" suit, absent a strong showing by the plaintiff that the news broadcast was a subterfuge or cover for private or commercial exploitation.[90]

Although the case was a very narrow one, it did open up new issues, whereby news coverage of the performing arts will be approached with caution. A sword swallower, a juggler, or even the climactic scene from a local play could fall under the umbrella of the Zacchini ruling if a zealous performer decides to bring suit.

SUMMARY

Although the Constitution is designed to assure a free press, certain safeguards in the form of laws and regulations have also been designed to assure a more responsible press. Many of these laws and regulations concern broadcast journalism.

Ever since the Lindbergh kidnapping trial, judges have been less than enthusiastic about cameras in the courtroom. Television joined the ranks of equipment barred from the courts after the trial of Texas financier Billie Sol Estes. More recently, however, some states have begun to permit both television cameras in courtrooms and live coverage of judicial proceedings. Legislatures have also started opening up their proceedings to broadcast coverage, with both state and federal bodies experimenting with live coverage and videotaping of proceedings. Smaller television cameras and more compact recording equipment have aided the cause of the broadcast reporter.

Open-meeting laws are helping to assure access to legislative proceedings on the state level. Although statutes differ from state to state, most laws guard against the press being barred from government and court proceedings. Some laws are more complete than others, providing for open legislatures, county boards, city councils, and establishing penalties for infractions.

Shield laws protect the confidentiality of a reporter's sources. Although most of them provide adequate protection, they do not guarantee protection against contempt citations for refusing to reveal those sources.

Laws which assure access to public records are much the same as laws which assure open meetings. Both are designed to permit the free flow of information about governmental bodies conducting the public business. The 1976 Freedom of Information Act helped the press and public gain access to federal documents. Again, like open-meeting laws, the degree of "openness" varies and can be determined by the administration in office. Using the Freedom of Information Act entails knowing some basic procedures and requesting the precise documents you are seeking, although timely release of the information is by no means assured. In most states under most circumstances, criminal records are open. The exception is criminal records about juvenile offenders.

Judges trying to protect fair trials from being infringed upon by news media publicity will frequently issue gag orders, which prevent publication of court proceedings or facts surrounding a case. Although gag orders have not been upheld by the Supreme Court, they can have a stifling effect on the press, who must fight the legal battle to have such an order rescinded. Stronger precedent against pretrial publicity occurred in 1979, when the Supreme Court upheld the right to close such proceedings to the press when all parties involved agreed to the closing.

While access to trial and pretrial proceedings is affirmed by U.S. Supreme Court decisions, many judges still close proceedings. Access to jury selection and pretrial discovery have also been affirmed, although some exceptions still exist and judges fearing pretrial publicity of prejudicing a jury will be quick to deny access.

Two other controls faced by both the print and broadcast press are the libel and invasion of privacy laws. If a person is identified in a publication and defamed, that person may have grounds for a libel suit if he or she can prove that damages have occurred and that the reporter acted irresponsibly. Defending a libel suit can be difficult, and the defense must usually prove that the statement was true, that the person consented to having it published, or that it was privileged information, not subject to libel. An invasion of privacy suit can be brought if a person's likeness is used for commercial purposes without his or her permission, if a person's private life is intruded upon, or if false or defamatory information is published about an individual.

Search and seizure is another issue confronting the press. In the *Stanford Daily* ruling, police were given the authority to serve search warrants on premises occupied by news organizations and it was ruled that the organizations could not rely on First Amendment protection against such searches.

The ruling in the case of an Ohio performer who engaged in a "human cannonball" stunt has placed additional constraints on the press when it covers a live performance and the coverage decreases the potential for paid admission to the event.

MATERIAL FOR ANALYSIS

RTNDA CODE OF BROADCAST NEWS ETHICS

Founded in 1946 as the National Association of Radio News Directors, the Radio/Television News Directors' Association (RTNDA) today represents broadcast news directors and journalists in legislative and professional endeavors. It publishes a newsletter, the *RTNDA Communicator*. In addition to its code of ethics, the RTNDA lobbies for free press laws and against laws which it sees as restricting the free flow of information. When the FCC passed regulations governing children's programming, the RTNDA and other groups including the Reporters Committee for the Freedom of the Press, the Media Institute, a Washington-based research group, and the Society of Professional Journalists filed a joint brief with the FCC claiming the Children's Television Act violated the First Amendment. The groups said that while it was necessary for the FCC to enforce the laws "The Commission should minimize this infringement on the First Amendment rights of information media by interpreting and enforcing the act in the least restrictive manner."[91] The RTNDA keeps keenly aware of issues affecting the broadcast press and championing the causes of broadcast news. The RTNDA is primarily an organization for radio and television news directors, those who manage and make the decisions in the broadcast newsroom. The code reads:

> The responsibility of radio and television journalists is to gather and report information of importance and interest to the public accurately, honestly and impartially.
>
> *The members of the Radio-Television News Directors Association accept these standards and will:*
>
> 1. Strive to present the source or nature of broadcast news material in a way that is balanced, accurate and fair.
>   A. They will evaluate information solely on its merits as news, rejecting sensationalism or misleading emphasis in any form.
>   B. They will guard against using audio or video material in a way that deceives the audience.
>   C. They will not mislead the public by presenting as spontaneous news any material which is staged or rehearsed.
>   D. They will identify people by race, creed, nationality or prior status only when it is relevant.
>   E. They will clearly label opinion and commentary.
>   F. They will promptly acknowledge and correct errors.
> 2. Strive to conduct themselves in a manner that protects them from conflicts of interest, real or perceived. They will decline gifts or favors which would influence or appear to influence their judgements.
> 3. Respect the dignity, privacy and well-being of people with whom they deal.
> 4. Recognize the need to protect confidential sources. They will promise confidentiality only with the intention of keeping that promise.
> 5. Respect everyone's right to a fair trial.
> 6. Broadcast the private transmissions of other broadcasters only with permission.
> 7. Actively encourage observance of this Code by all journalists, whether members of the Radio-Television News Directors Association or not.

QUESTIONS FOR CRITICAL ANALYSIS

- Stop and consider the issue of a free press versus fair trial. Under what, if any, circumstances could one be justified in taking precedent over the other?
- How "open" is the open-meeting law in your state?
- How open is the shield law in your state?
- Justice William O. Douglas concluded: "TV and radio stand in the same protected position under the First Amendment as do newspapers and magazines." Although we read about a great many comparisons between newspapers and the broadcast press, how should we consider magazines in this framework?
- A newspaper went to court to compel disclosure of records of a rape incident where the victim died. The court granted disclosure. Do you agree with the court's decision? What if the victim had lived?
- What way should "magazine programs," such as CBS's *60 Minutes*, be afforded the same press freedoms as printed magazines?
- Are such programs news in the traditional sense of broadcast news, for example, the *CBS Evening News*? If not, what legal differences could be posed by such distinctions?
- If the press is guilty of unbalanced coverage favoring the executive branch of state governments, would permitting live radio and television coverage of legislative proceedings help correct this imbalance?
- Could the definition and application of the terms *work product* and *documentary materials* be applied differently to the print versus the broadcast media?
- Will cases involving one medium used as a precedent for another, such as deciding a newspaper case and applying it to radio, result in confusion about what can and cannot be classified *work product* and *documentary materials*?
- Can you see difficulties with newspersons, law enforcement officials, or courts distinguishing between the Privacy Protection Act's definitions of *work product* and *documentary materials*?
- In a typical newspaper office, information of an "editorial" nature is usually printed or written (stories, reporters' notes, pictures, negatives, and so on) and can be readily identified by the persons conducting the search. But what happens when the place to be searched is a broadcast newsroom?

- Video and audio tapes must be played to be "viewed." Could the police demand that tapes be played, so that they could determine what was applicable to the scope of the warrant?
- Would the use of station equipment and personnel to play the tapes disrupt the operation of the broadcast newsroom even more than in the case of a newspaper office? If so, do the arguments for First Amendment protection become stronger for the broadcast newsroom than for the newspaper office?
- Could difficulties exist in interpreting that section of the law which classifies a newsperson as someone "reasonably believed to have a purpose to disseminate information to the public"? How would the law treat a part-time student intern working intermittently in the newsroom of a local station?
- Do you agree with the majority opinion in *Herbert* v. *Lando* that there is no First Amendment constitutional privilege which would prohibit the plaintiff's ability to determine the "state of mind" of the defendant in a libel action?
- The Privacy Protection Act exempts material from protection from search warrants if there is reason to believe the materials would be concealed, altered, or destroyed by issuing a subpoena. Will this argument be used by some law enforcement officials to try and circumvent the law?
- Many radio and television journalists do not belong to the Radio-Television News Directors Association. What professional ethics govern their behavior?
- Codes of ethics are still only as strong as their enforcement sanctions. The RTNDA does not have an enforcement arm which monitors the actions of news directors or journalists the way the FCC monitors the operation of radio and television stations. Should professional associations have enforcement arms which could impose sanctions on members or would such actions be difficult to enforce, not appropriate for a professional association, and fly in the face of the First Amendment?
- If the codes of ethics are beneficial, why shouldn't they be made into FCC regulations and enforced by the commission?
- One provision of the RTNDA code of ethics calls upon members not to present as spontaneous news any material which is staged or rehearsed. Everyone from politicians to corporations "stages" press conferences, photo opportunities, and issues press releases to gain favorable publicity in the news media. Should reporters simply refuse to cover these types of events?
- How do reporters determine when a gift will influence their news judgment? Is a certain monetary value of a gift the cut-off point whereby it should be declined?
- The RTNDA code calls upon members to: Respect the dignity, privacy and well-being of people with whom they deal. What happens if a reporter is covering an event where a private citizen is injured and the individual asks that their name and picture not be used on the air?
- At conventions of professional associations, inexpensive briefcases with a corporate logo are sometimes presented to convention participants. Does accepting one of these briefcases violate the provision of the RTNDA code?

ADDITIONAL RESOURCES

Bator, P. M., "The First Amendment Applied to Broadcasting: A Few Misgivings." 10 *Harvard Journal of Law & Public Policy* 75 (1987).

Crain, W. Mark, and Brian L. Goff, "Televising Legislatures: An Economic Analysis." 29 *Journal of Law and Economics* 405 (October 1986).

Fein, B. E., "Regulating the Interception and Disclosure of Wire, Radio, and Oral Communications: A Case Study of Federal Statutory Antiquation." 22 *Harvard Journal on Legislation* 47 (1985).

Gartner, M. G., "Buncombe, Broadcasters and the First Amendment." 38 *Drake Law Review* 1 (1989).

Katsh, M. E., "Electronic Media and the First Amendment." 26 *Trial* 34 (1990).

Landever, A. R., "Electronic Surveillance, Computers, and the Fourth Amendment—The New Telecommunications Environment Calls for Reexamination of Doctrine." 15 *University of Toledo Law Review* 597 (1984).

Nadel, M. S., "A Unified Theory of the First Amendment: Divorcing the Medium from the Message." 11 *Fordham Urban Law Journal* 163 (1982–83).

O'Brien, S., "The Responsibility of the Electronic Press to Juvenile Audiences." 15 *Southwestern University Law Review* 653 (1985).

Rabel, T. R., "The Electronic Communications and Privacy Act: Discriminatory Treatment for Similar Technology, Cutting the Cord of Privacy." 23 *John Marshall Law Review* 661 (1990).

Wegner, J. M., "Home Interactive Media: An Analysis of Potential Abuses of Privacy." 29 *Journal of Broadcasting & Electronic Media* 51 (1985).

Wright, J., "The Protection of Corporate Privacy." 11 *International Business Lawyer* 119 (1983).

chapter eight

Regulating Commercial Programming

In the United States, broadcasting operates primarily as a commercial enterprise. Even public broadcasting stations secure income from government appropriations and donations to stay on the air. While commercial broadcasters must be concerned with the various regulations governing commercial programming, they must be equally aware of advertising's relationship to such issues as free speech and truthful presentations of commercials. Thus, to be fully versed in the field of commercial programming, we need to begin our discussion not in the station but in the courts, where we'll learn the framework for these "commercial" freedoms.

HISTORICAL PERSPECTIVES ON COMMERCIAL PROGRAMMING

Advertising as we know it today did not exist at the turn of the century. It was only when advertising "agents" began to move product information out of the classified sections of local newspapers and into larger type that the concept began. As magazines became popular, these agents could experiment with still larger ad formats and creative copy. The world of Madison Avenue had arrived.

The Beginnings of Broadcast Advertising: WEAF

For radio, advertising arrived in the early 1920s, when WEAF, the AT&T station in New York City, began selling blocks of commercial time for what then was known as toll broadcasting. In August 1922, New York City's Queensboro Corporation in order to sell real estate ushered in the era of commercial broadcasting with a set of five short programs to be aired over WEAF for a period of five days. For AT&T, the idea had considerable commercial merit and was a forward-thinking corporate strategy.

Criticism of Toll Broadcasting

The scheme of toll broadcasting, however, had its critics. One of the first to criticize the concept was the trade publication *American Radio Journal*. The *Journal* suggested as an alternative that (1) cities undertake and pay for programs on an entertainment basis; (2) the government charge the public and collect revenues from a large number of "radio subscribers"; or (3) the government tax the manufacturers of radio equipment, the people who distribute it, and the people who sell it.

Hitting even harder at the toll broadcasting concept was the well-known publication *Printers Ink*. This trade journal of early advertising concluded that "any attempt to make the radio an advertising medium, in the accepted sense of the term, would, we think, prove positively offensive to a great number of people." *Printer's Ink* was wrong. Radio was not totally offensive when commercial matter was supplemented with entertainment and news programming, and people did listen.

The Antitrust Issue

Since WEAF was the only outlet for firms wishing to advertise on radio, it began to attract a sizable number of sponsors. Meanwhile, AT&T continued to pour money into its "experimental" station and even tried to prohibit other stations from doing remote broadcasts using telephone company lines and equipment. In addition, the company started charging license fees for the use of AT&T's long lines for long-distance relay of radio.

AT&T's action was part of the competitive spirit found in broadcasting in the 1920s. Without any real federal regulation to control them, stations and their parent corporations were playing havoc with the airwaves. It was the issue of the long lines, however, that brought the Federal Trade Commission into the broadcasting arena. The FTC stated that AT&T's exclusivity over the use of long lines and toll broadcasting was anticompetitive and in violation of the Clayton Act, the government's major piece of antitrust legislation. Before the whole FTC matter could boil over, AT&T stopped, took stock of the role that public opinion might play in its profits, and decided it would be better not to push the issue. In a complicated arrangement of assets, AT&T exited from traditional over-the-air broadcasting and sold WEAF. The foundation for regulating broadcast advertising was thus firmly established.

REGULATION OF ADVERTISING: FIRST AMENDMENT ISSUES

In view of the billions of dollars spent on advertising, the thousands of stations in operation, and the fact that advertising is a powerful force in a democratic society, it is not surprising that the courts and the media have taken a keen interest in attempts to control advertising. What First Amendment protections are available to advertisers? How much can a sponsor brag about a product without being in violation of the law? We begin by examining the precedent for restricting advertising practices.

Valentine v. *Chrestensen*

One of the early cases that established precedent for quasi-government control over the distribution of advertising messages was brought to court in 1942.[1] The matter started in 1940, when a Florida resident named Chrestensen bought a Navy surplus submarine, moored it to the state pier in the East River in New York, and began charging admission for people to tour the sub. He advertised by distributing handbills, which the police said violated a New York Sanitary Code prohibiting distribution of commercial and business advertising matter on the streets. However, the police did tell him he could distribute handbills devoted to "information or a public protest." Chrestensen found a printer, and on one side of the handbill printed a protest about the City Dock Department refusing him permission to dock his sub at the city dock. On the other side of the handbill was the advertisement for tours of his sub, minus only a statement about the admission fee. The police again said "no." Chrestensen thought "yes" and proceeded to distribute the handbills anyway. The police again stepped in and stopped the distribution. Chrestensen sued, won in the district and circuit court of appeals, but lost at the United States Supreme Court. In *Valentine* v. *Chrestensen*, Justice Roberts wrote:

> The question is not whether the legislative body may interfere with the harmless pursuit of lawful business, but whether it must permit such pursuit, by what it deems an undesirable invasion of, or interference with, the full and free use of highways by the people in fulfillment of the public use to which streets are dedicated. . . .
>
> If that evasion were successful, every merchant who desires to (distribute) advertising leaflets in the streets need only append a civic appeal, or a moral platitude, to achieve immunity from the law's command.[2]

Although the Court did not rule on the *content* of the message, it did provide a municipality with the right to prohibit certain types of distribution. And while the *Chrestensen* decision might have dampened the history of free commercial speech if it had stood the test of time, other decisions gradually chipped away at it.

Pittsburgh Press v. *Pittsburgh Commission on Human Relations*

Another case was heard in Pittsburgh, Pennsylvania, when the Human Relations Commission sought to stop the *Pittsburgh Press* from using male and female categories in its help-wanted advertising.[3] The Human Relations Commission injected a city ordinance prohibiting discrimination in hiring and won the favor of the United States Supreme Court. The Court avoided a discussion of the specific *content* of the ads, however, and although the *Press* legitimately argued that advertising was its lifeblood, and that interference with it could damage the newspaper, the Court did not see the threat as significant enough to inject the First Amendment argument into its opinion. The Court pointed out that when a practice itself is illegal, the First Amendment principle is absent. The *Pittsburgh Press* case was too similar in nature to *Chrestensen* to clearly define First Amendment protection of commercial speech.

Bigelow v. *Virginia*

The Supreme Court came a bit closer to the First Amendment issue in 1975, when it ruled in *Bigelow* v. *Virginia* that a Virginia newspaper editor had First Amendment protection in publishing an advertisement encouraging women to go outside Virginia to obtain abortions, which were prohibited within the state.[4] Still considerable ambiguity existed. It was not a city ordinance that was being challenged, readers were not going to violate a law in Virginia by going out of state and the "distribution" of the advertisement was not at issue as it had been in *Chrestensen*. For more clarification it was necessary to wait until 1976 when the U.S. Supreme Court ruled in the case of *Virginia State Board of Pharmacy* v. *Virginia Citizens Consumer Council*.[5]

First Amendment Clarification: The Virginia Pharmacy Board Decision

Just how far the laws of the land could control the *content* of commercial speech was clarified in 1976, when a Virginia statute prohibiting licensed pharmacists to advertise the price of prescription drugs was found unconstitutional. The U.S. Supreme Court clarified many of the long-awaited issues regarding advertising and the First Amendment. In delivering the opinion of the Court, Justice Blackman wrote:

> It is clear, for example, that speech does not lose its First Amendment protection because money is spent to project it, as in a paid advertisement of one form or another. Speech likewise is protected even though it is carried in a form that is "sold" for profit, and even though it may involve a solicitation to purchase or otherwise pay or contribute money. If there is a kind of commercial speech that lacks all First Amendment protection, therefore, it must be distinguished by its content. Yet the speech whose content deprives it of protection cannot simply be speech on a commercial subject . . .
>
> Advertising, however tasteless and excessive it sometimes may seem, is nonetheless dissemination of information as to who is producing and selling what product for what reason, and at what price. So long as we preserve a predominantly free enterprise economy, the allocation of our resources in large measure will be made through numerous private economic decisions. It is a matter of public interest that those decisions, in the aggregate, be intelligent and well informed. To this end, the free flow of commercial information is indispensable. And if it is indispensable to the proper allocation of resources in a free enterprise system, it is also indispensable to the formation of intelligent opinions as to how that system ought to be regulated or altered. Therefore, even if the First Amendment were thought to be primarily an instrument to enlighten public decision making in a democracy, we could not say that the free flow of information does not serve that goal.[6]

In a concurring opinion, Justice Burger tempered the words of the majority opinion by noting, "I think it important to note also that the advertisement of professional services carries with it quite different risks from the advertisement of standard products." His opinion goes on to state:

> even with respect to expression at the core of the First Amendment, the Constitution does not provide absolute protection for false factual statements that cause private injury. In *Gertz* v. *Robert Welch*, 418 U.S. 323, 340, the

Court concluded that "there is no constitutional value in false statements of fact. . . ."

Since the factual claims contained in commercial price or product advertisements relate to tangible goods or services, they may be tested empirically and corrected to reflect the truth without in any manner jeopardizing the free dissemination of thought. Indeed, the elimination of false and deceptive claims serves to promote the one facet of commercial price and product advertising that warrants First Amendment protection—its contribution to the flow of accurate and reliable information relevant to public and private decision making.[7]

Regulatory Pressures

In the *Virginia Pharmacy Board* decision, the Court clarified the important questions about the First Amendment and commercial speech but did not unleash uninhibited commercial expression. Nevertheless, we are now at a place in the development of First Amendment law that gives great latitude to advertisers to say almost anything they want through commercial speech, as long as it is truthful. Moreover, a small station dealing with local merchants has no way of testing the legitimacy of every local product commercial that ends up on the air. The Federal Trade Commission can still put the bite on advertisers who do not heed the Supreme Court's opinion that "there is no constitutional protection in false statements of fact."

BROADCAST ADVERTISING: JURISDICTIONAL ISSUES

Advertising provides the revenue for commercial broadcasting. Regulations at both the state and federal level impact on this advertising and affect advertising's content as well as its dissemination.

Precedent for Jurisdiction

Although we tend to think of radio and television as being governed by federal law, as expressed in the Communications Act of 1934, state laws play an important part when advertising is involved. In the landmark case that applied state jurisdiction to broadcast advertising, a court upheld a New Mexico statute that prohibited a New Mexico radio station from accepting advertising from "across-the-border" Texas optometrists. The Texas advertising violated a New Mexico law regulating optometric advertising. In *Head* v. *New Mexico Board of Examiners in Optometry*, the U.S. Supreme Court upheld the New Mexico law and rejected the contention that the law interfered with interstate commerce and was thus preempted by federal law. In a concurring opinion, Justice Brennan said: "rather than mandate ouster of state regulations, several provisions of the Communications Act suggest a congressional design to leave standing various forms of state regulation, including the form embodied in the New Mexico statute."[8]

Robert Sadowski examined the subject of broadcasting and state statutes and found advertising to be second only to individual rights in the attention given it by state laws. Forty-three states have passed laws, which govern over 31 different areas of advertising affecting broadcasters.[9] The laws fall into two primary areas: (1) "general regulations, which govern fraudulent advertising, deceptive trade and consumer fraud practices," and (2) more specific regulations, covering "controls over foods, drugs, cosmetics, political advertising, and various other commodities such as insurance, loans, and real estate."[10] Eleven states have given protection to broadcasters who, in good faith, broadcast an advertisement that turns out to be deceptive. Although we do not hear much about prosecution, these state laws are more than just window dressing. In Mississippi, the Attorney General's office moved to stop an individual from advertising paintings which were supposedly painted by local "starving artists." The attorney general's office concluded that the paintings were mass-produced in Asia, and that all the profits went to the promoter.[11]

Federal Jurisdiction

At the federal level, the two principal agencies affecting broadcast advertising are the Federal Communications Commission and the Federal Trade Commission. The FCC can call upon its blanket "public-interest" clause to move in on an unscrupulous broadcaster involved in a deceptive advertising scheme.

More pervasive is the Federal Trade Commission, which keeps a watchful eye on advertising practices affecting both the broadcast and the print media. Only a tendency to deceive is sufficient to engage an FTC inquiry.[12] As was discussed previously in this text, the FTC has acted on many types of advertisements covering many different products.

Historically, one famous example of FTC action is the "Sandpaper Shave Case." A commercial for Rapid Shave shaving cream attempted to show the cream's merits by using it on a piece of heavy sandpaper.[13] An announcer spoke about the merits of the product, while Rapid Shave was being applied to what appeared to be sandpaper. The next thing you saw was a razor shaving the sandpaper. As it turned out, the razor did not immediately shave the sandpaper, and what was supposed to be sandpaper was really a type of plexiglass with sand affixed to it. After a series of decisions—including those of an FTC examiner, the FTC, and appeals to the Supreme Court—the Rapid Shave commercial was stopped. There were, however, convincing arguments that the public was not really harmed by the commercial and that Rapid Shave could in fact shave sandpaper after the sandpaper was soaked. Although the Rapid Shave commercial was amended, the FTC action did not prohibit all artificial props from television commercials.

The ITT Continental Baking Company, distributors of Profile Bread, ran corrective advertising to clarify earlier commercials which, the FTC alleged, misled people into thinking Profile Bread could help them lose weight. Firestone Tire and Rubber Co. agreed to pay $50,000 in penalties and $750,000 for a tire safety campaign to settle charges brought by an FTC order claiming that the company had aired misleading advertisements.[14] A substantial $550,000 of the settlement was appropriated for television commercials to air in major network news and sports programming. The FTC had pursued the company through the federal courts under provisions of the FTC act. In another case, the J. B. Williams Co. of New York agreed to an out-of-court settlement in a suit brought by the FTC concerning ads for Geritol.[15] The FTC claimed the commercials violated an FTC order prohibiting statements that the products "helped relieve tiredness, loss of strength, run-down feeling, nervousness or irritability without also saying that these symptoms usually result from iron deficiency and that Geritol could not help in these cases."[16]

SPONSOR IDENTIFICATION

Most commercials leave no doubt about who the sponsor is. Where there is doubt, however, the FCC can fall back on sponsor identification rules which read:

> When a broadcast station transmits any matter for which money, service, or other valuable consideration is either directly or indirectly paid or promised to, or charged or accepted by such station, the station at the time of the broadcast, shall announce (i) that such matter is sponsored, paid for, or furnished, either in whole or in part, and (ii) by whom or on whose behalf such consideration was supplied . . .[17]

Not acceptable under the rules are indirect references to the business. For example, a commercial which ends with the announcement that "this commercial is sponsored by your neighborhood hardware man" would not be acceptable, even if the "neighborhood hardware man" was a slogan frequently used by a local hardware store.[18] Notice that money does not have to be the "consideration." If a retail store gives a television station 25 compact discs under the implied agreement that a talk-show host will plug the retail store, then the "plug" must be announced as being "sponsored, paid for, or furnished" by the retail store.[19]

Special rules apply for political broadcasting and program content involving a controversial issue of public importance "for which any film, record, transcription, talent, script, or other material or service of any kind is furnished, either directly or indirectly to a station as an inducement for broadcasting such matter . . ."[20] When such matter is broadcast, FCC rules require "an announcement shall be made both at the beginning and conclusion of such broadcast on which such material or services" are used and "such film, record, transcription, talent, script, or material or service has been furnished to such station in connection with the transmission of such broadcast matter."[21] Only one announcement is necessary when the broadcast lasts five minutes or less.

An exception to the rules exist for "want ads" or classified advertisements which are sponsored by individuals, rather than companies. Sponsorship identification can be omitted under such circumstances but the station is required to maintain a list showing the name, address, and (where available) the telephone number of the individual placing the on-air advertisement. The list must be made available to members of the general public who have a "legitimate interest" in obtaining the information contained in the list, and the list must be retained for two years after the broadcast.[22]

GUARDING AGAINST FRAUDULENT BILLING

Fraudulent billing, although no longer regulated by the FCC, is still extremely serious and can occur in a variety of situations, the most common being co-op advertising. In co-op advertising, the manufacturer or major distributor of a product pays part of the cost of the advertising. To understand this concept, let's assume that the Ordinary Appliance Store sells a toaster manufactured by Tommy Toasters. Ordinary enters into an agreement with Tommy Toasters to split the cost of 100 commercials from station WAAA, but instead of mentioning Tommy Toasters, the Ordinary commercials talk about stoves and refrigerators. The cost of the commercials is $500. WAAA sends a bill for $250 to Ordinary and another $250 bill to Tommy Toasters for co-op advertising. The station is thus guilty of fraudulent billing.

Another variation of fraudulent billing would be for WAAA to send a bill to Tommy Toasters for more than the amount of the co- op advertising, such as $500 instead of $250, in the hope that Tommy would pay the bill without realizing the overcharge. If Tommy recognizes it, WAAA could claim it expected Tommy to pay only half the bill, since the remainder would be paid by Ordinary. A more direct form of fraudulent billing would be charging an advertiser for commercials that did not air, or overbilling an ad agency to recoup the 15 percent discount normally given agency orders. A subtle fraudulent billing practice would take the Ordinary portion of the bill in trade-out, such as having Ordinary furnish WAAA's lunchroom with a new stove at wholesale prices. Since the stove would cost Ordinary less than $250, Tommy Toasters would be paying more than half of the bill.

The federal government can still prosecute cases of fraudulent billing, as can the states. Private companies or individuals can also sue a station where fraudulent billing is involved and such actions can reflect on a station at license renewal time, especially if the renewal is contested.

NETWORK CLIPPING

Network clipping is the *practice of certifying to a network that a network commercial has been aired when in fact it has not. Network clipping* is also considered fraudulent billing. Not FCC enforced, network clipping is still open to action under local and state laws in such areas as racketeering and fair trade. Local affiliates provide networks with an accounting of all the network commercials that they air locally. Failing to air a commercial may cut the amount of compensation a station receives from the network. Nevertheless, when a station fails to air a commercial, either deliberately or inadvertently, the network is notified of that fact as part of the special certification report. Listing a network commercial as having been aired when it was not is considered fraudulent and may involve contract violations between the network and the station. The roster of commercial credits such as those shown at the end of a game show is considered commercial matter, and deleting it is also considered network clipping. Local stations are not prohibited from deleting network programming. What can be a violation of the law is a practice of deleting programming which contains advertising without notifying the network, thereby receiving compensation for services that were not rendered.

STATE REGULATION OF ALCOHOLIC BEVERAGE ADVERTISING

The FCC does not prohibit the advertising of hard liquor and other alcoholic beverages on radio and television. At one time the National Association of Broadcasters had a voluntary programming code in place which broadcasters could adhere to but the code is no longer in effect. Many broadcasters still voluntarily adhere to the provisions of the old code and many states have laws that restrict advertising of alcoholic beverages.

General Provisions

To understand how state statutes work, we can examine state laws in North Carolina. In that particular state, it is possible for restaurants to advertise the price of beer or wine but not brand names. Mixed drinks can also be advertised as long as the brand is not identified.[23] Grocery stores can advertise both the brand name and the price of beer and wine. Commercials for hard liquor are prohibited. Restaurants can also advertise special hours such as "happy hours," but the brand names of alcoholic beverages must not be mentioned.

Language, Co-op, and Restrictions to Minors

North Carolina law prohibits certain terms from being used, such as *high test, high proof, full strength,* and *extra strong*. Manufacturers, bottlers, importers, and wholesalers are treated a bit differently in that they can advertise the brand name but cannot list the price. Cooperative advertising between the retailer of beer and wine, such as a tavern or restaurant, and the wholesalers, distributors, bottlers, importers, producers, and manufacturers is prohibited. No program with content connected to a secondary or elementary school can contain commercials for alcoholic beverages. A commercial, for example, cannot contain "any statement, picture, or illustration inconsistent with the spirit of safety or safe driving programs," or "any subject matter or illustration inducing minors to drink."[24]

Claims and Test Results

In addition to the preceding provisions, the North Carolina regulation prohibits any statement that is false or misleading or which is an unfair comparison with a competitor's products. Test results, guarantees, and other representations that might mislead the consumer are prohibited. Stating that the beverage is "produced, blended, made, bottled, packed or sold under or in accordance with, any authorization, law, or regulation or any municipality, county or state, federal or foreign government," is prohibited unless it is specifically permitted by the laws of the governmental entity. Saying an alcoholic beverage originated from someplace it did not—such as calling a beverage "Kentucky whiskey" when it was made in Tennessee—is prohibited.

Tie-in Restrictions to the Flag and Armed Forces

A tie-in of the alcoholic beverage with a flag or the armed forces is prohibited.[25] The regulations state:

> Any statement, design, device or pictorial representation of or relating to, or capable of being construed as relating to the armed forces or the United States or the American flag, state flag, or any emblem, seal, insignia or decoration associated with any such flag of the armed forces of the United States; nor shall any advertisement contain any statement, device, design or pictorial representation of or concerning any flag, seal, coat of arms, crest or other insignia, likely to mislead the customer into believing that the product has been endorsed, made or used by, produced for or under the supervision of or in accordance with the specifications of the government, organizations, family or individual with whom such flag, seal, coat of arms, crest or insignia is associated.[26]

Tie-in to Athletes

Tie-ins to athletes are also prohibited. The regulations state:

> Any statement, picture or illustration implying that the consumption of alcoholic beverages enhances athletic prowess, or any statement, picture or illustration referring to any known athlete, if such statement, picture or illustration implies, or if the reader may reasonably infer, that the use of the product contributed to the athlete's athletic achievements.[27]

Our discussion has concerned regulation of commercials for alcoholic beverages in one state, North Carolina. In addition, the rules and regulations apply to all advertising, not just radio and television. Rules and regulations vary from state to state and an examination of your own state rules and regulations can provide additional insights into this area of the law.

STATION-CONDUCTED CONTESTS

The station-conducted contest has become a successful marketing tool for many licensees, especially in highly competitive markets. The various types of contests would fill a book, varying from spotting station bumper stickers on cars to big-money giveaways.

Areas for Possible Violations

FCC regulations governing contests read:

> A licensee that broadcasts or advertises information about a contest it conducts shall fully and accurately disclose the material terms of the contest, and shall conduct the contest substantially as announced or advertised. No contest description shall be false, misleading or deceptive with respect to any material term.[28]
>
> For the purposes of this rule:
>
> (a) A contest is a scheme in which a prize is offered or awarded, based upon chance, dili-

gence, knowledge or skill, to members of the public.

(b) Material terms include those factors which define the operation of the contest and which affect participation therein. Although the material terms may vary widely depending upon the exact nature of the contest, they will generally include: how to enter or participate; eligibility restrictions; entry deadline dates; whether prizes can be won; when prizes can be won; the extent, nature and value of prizes; basis for valuation of prizes; time and means of selection of winners; and/or tie-breaking procedures.

NOTE 2: In general, the time and manner of disclosure of the material terms of a contest are within the licensee's discretion. However, the obligation to disclose the material terms arises at the time the audience is first told how to enter or participate and continues thereafter. The material terms should be disclosed periodically by announcements broadcast on the station conducting the contest, but need not be enumerated each time an announcement promoting the contest is broadcast. Disclosure of material terms in a reasonable number of announcements is sufficient. In addition to the required broadcast announcements, disclosure of the material terms may be made in a non-broadcast manner.

NOTE 3: This rule is not applicable to licensee-conducted contests not broadcast or advertised to the general public or to a substantial segment thereof, to contests in which the general public is not requested or permitted to participate, to the commercial advertisement of non-licensee-conducted contests, or to a contest conducted by a non-broadcast division of the licensee or by a non-broadcast company related to the licensee.[29]

In general terms, the commission can be alerted when the following practices are involved:

1. Disseminating false or misleading information regarding the amount or nature of prizes;
2. Failing to control the contest to assure a fair opportunity for contestants to win the announced prize;
3. Urging participation in a contest, or urging persons to stay tuned to the station in order to win, at times when it is not possible to win prizes;
4. Failing to award prizes, or failing to award them within a reasonable time;
5. Failing to set forth fully and accurately the rules and conditions for contests;
6. Changing the rules or conditions of a contest without advising the public or doing so promptly;
7. Using arbitrary or inconsistently applied standards in judging entries;
8. Providing secret assistance to contestants or predetermination of winners;
9. Stating that winners are chosen solely by chance, when in fact chance played little or no part;
10. Broadcasting false clues in connection with a contest; and;
11. Conducting contests without adequate supervision.[30]

Applying FCC Contest Rules

The rule defines a contest as a "scheme in which a prize is offered or awarded, based upon chance, diligence, knowledge or skill, to members of the public." The *material terms* cited in the rule include how to enter or participate, the restrictions on eligibility, deadlines for entry, whether prizes can be won, when they can be won, "the extent, nature and value of the prizes," the basis for evaluating the prizes, the "time and means of selection of winners," and the method of breaking ties. The station is responsible for disclosing the material terms when the audience is told for the first time how to enter and "periodically" thereafter. The station can also disclose material terms through nonbroadcast media, such as newspapers or direct mail. Exemptions to the rule include "licensee-conducted contests not broadcast or advertised to the general public. . . ." The rule does not apply to commercials that mention a contest not sponsored by the licensee or conducted by some nonbroadcast division or company related to the licensee.

Management Responsibility

Responsibility in running contests is serious business, and lack of control over contest procedures can spell big trouble for broadcasters. Although alleged inappropriate considerations to political candidates were also an issue, the FCC denied renewal of the broadcast licenses of a group owner with stations in Indianapolis, Indiana; Omaha, Nebraska; and Vancouver, Washington primarily because of lack of such control.[31] In denying the renewals, the FCC said that although the political considerations were an issue, the "misconduct" in this area should "not be allowed to overshadow completely that fact that other misconduct has been proved which also has decisional significance. The FCC scheduled the renewal of the stations for a hearing as the result of "contest improprieties" and notified the station that "its manner of conducting contests would be investigated in the hearing."[32] It further contended that the "safeguards to protect the public from fraud in contests continue to be inadequate. . . ."[33] In its decision to deny renewal, the FCC stated that: "[the] stations conducted four contests in which their practices were not adequate to insure that no abuse would occur, and in at least two of those contests, [a] $1,000 Mystery Melody Contest and [b] Black Box Contest, actual misconduct did take place."[34]

Contests Directed to Children

Stations must be particularly careful when airing contests directed toward children. In Washington, DC, an adult viewer apparently became upset when, although he saw the children's program host dial his number, his phone did not ring. The program was prerecorded. A local newspaper publicized the incident, and the station, responding to an FCC inquiry about the matter, said that it had started to run an aural announcement to accompany an already-running video announcement that the program was prerecorded. The children's program had also promoted a "bike-a-day" for the winners, but had actually given away bags of toys for part of the contest period. The FCC thus felt that the contest was potentially misleading on a number of counts. For one thing, the video-only notice would be of little value to preschool children who could not read. Second, the bike-a-day promotion might mislead a child to believe that every child who answered the host's question would receive a bicycle, which was not the case. Third, the promise of bicycles as prizes when toys were actually awarded was clearly misleading.

The NAB also advises that information about the contest, including rules and eligibility requirements, should be kept on file as documentation should any problems arise after the contest ends.[35] Prizes of substantial value must be reported to the Internal Revenue Service. A certified account can provide specifics to a station when in doubt about reporting requirements.[36] Additional safeguards can also be developed including having releases signed by prize recipients.[37] Such releases state that the prize has been received, that the recipient will be responsible for paying any taxes which may come due, and that the recipient will turn to the manufacturer, not the station, if anything is wrong with the prize.

BROADCASTING LOTTERIES AND LOTTERY INFORMATION

To be considered a lottery, three things must be present: (l) prize, (2) chance, and (3) consideration. To better understand these three concepts, imagine that you are the general manager of a radio station and want to increase your ratings by conducting a contest. In the process, you also want to earn the station some money. You devise a scheme whereby listeners can purchase a gold star with a number on it. The gold stars cost $1.00 each and can be bought from local stores whose commercials run next to the promotional announcements for the contest. Each hour, you draw a number from a hat corresponding to a number on one of the gold stars. The person holding the winning number will receive a prize donated by the local stores. You are very careful to announce all of the material terms listed in our discussion of contests. Would you be in violation of the law? Yes. You would be broadcasting a lottery under the definition punishable by law.[38] The three lottery factors were all present in your contest. You awarded a prize to each person with a lucky number on his or her gold star. Second, the selection of the winning number was by *chance*, drawn from a hat. Chance is also present in spinning a wheel of fortune, in roulette, in selecting names of persons randomly generated by a computer, or in taking guesses on something in which knowledge is not necessary. The third element, *consideration*, was also present since you charged $1.00 for a gold star to enter the contest. Variations of the three elements can still classify a contest as a lottery. If it is necessary to purchase a product before receiving a gold star, then consideration is present. Keep in mind that a lottery must have *all three* conditions present—prize, chance, and consideration—to be defined as a lottery under law.

Lottery Statute

The statute under which violations are prosecuted is found in the United States Code, Title 18, the same law governing the broadcast of obscene, indecent, or profane language. Section 1304 governing lotteries states:

> Whoever broadcasts by means of any radio station for which a license is required by any law of the United States, or whoever, operating any such station, knowingly permits the broadcasting of, any advertisement of or information concerning any lottery, gift enterprise, or similar scheme, offering prizes dependent in whole or in part upon lot or chance, or any list of the prizes drawn or awarded by means of any such lottery, gift enterprise, or scheme, whether said list contains any part or all of such prizes, shall be fined no more than $1,000 or imprisoned not more than one year, or both. Each day's broadcasting shall constitute a separate offense.[39]

Section 1304 prohibits a person from broadcasting ". . . any advertisement of or information concerning any lottery. . . ." This means that broadcasters are prohibited from running announcements that tell about anyone else's lottery, as well as their own. If a local car dealer decides to devise a contest which meets the three elements of a lottery, airing commercials publicizing this contest could violate FCC regulations. Promotional contests involving banks and savings and loan institutions can be especially problematic.[40] When a person must first open a savings account in order to be eligible for a prize awarded in a free drawing, it is considered a lottery. Announcements do not have to be a commercial to violate the law. Simple community calendars or local bulletin boards announced as part of regular programming can trip up a broadcaster.

Enforcing Lottery Violations

In the case of *Ohio Quests, Inc.*, a licensee was found to have violated Section 1304 when an experienced operator made improper broadcasts.[41] In the case of *Laury Associates, Inc.*, the FCC determined that ignorance of the law was no excuse.[42] In the case of *University of Florida*, the FCC judged that even though a licensee may receive information in good faith for broadcast from an advertising agency, the licensee is still responsible for the content of the information being broadcast and accountable for violations.

The FCC also denied license renewal to a station for broadcasting information construed to be a lottery. The license of a Washington, DC station was revoked when, among other accumulated violations, it was found guilty of broadcasting a scheme whereby "ministers" enabled ". . . listeners to receive financial blessings, . . ." which turned out to be winning money in an illegal numbers game.[43] In the renewal hearing, a member of the Washington, DC police force testified that the illegal numbers game was prevalent in the station's listening area, and that people could place small bets on numbers determined by prices paid on horse races at a nearby track. The commission cited an "alleged testimonial," which had been read over the air:

> The first time I came to see you, I was blessed for $135 for a quarter, and the second time I came to see you I received $540 for a $1.00 investment. And the last time I was there I really hit the jackpot because I placed $10 where you told me to and the Lord blessed me with over $5,000.

The FCC noted that the ratio used for payoffs and referred to in the alleged testimonial "was the exact payoff for a winning number."

Many states conduct lotteries as a means of raising revenue. But there is a difference in broadcasting information about state lotteries. Stations in the state where the lottery is held or stations in a state where a state lottery is legal can broadcast information about state lotteries. Broadcasters in states where lotteries are not legal cannot. For example, North Carolina does not have a state lottery. Consequently, a radio station in North Carolina is prohibited from airing advertisements for the Virginia lottery, even though the station's signal contour is predominantly inside Virginia and Virginia has a lottery.

PROMOTIONS: THE PLUGOLA/PAYOLA ISSUE

In the 1950s the disclosure that disc jockeys were receiving cash and gifts from record promoters for plugging records on the air resulted in government investigations of the practice and subsequent rules to guard against such practices occurring in the future. Periodically the issue raises its head again, especially in radio, and stations must take the responsibility for establishing policies and insuring that payola—the practice of taking, and not disclosing payment in the form of money or other services of value for airing particular recordings and/or promoting recording artists, and plugola—

the practice of taking, and not disclosing payment in the form of money or other services of value for plugging goods or services on the air—does not occur.

The rules requiring the announcement on the air of payment for services is contained in the FCC rules governing commercial announcements already discussed. The disclosure requirement requires the following:

> **Employee Responsibility**
>
> (a) . . . any employee of a radio station who accepts or agrees to accept from any person (other than such station) who pays or agrees to pay such employee, any money, service or other valuable consideration for the broadcast of any matter over such station shall, in advance of such broadcast, disclose the fact of such acceptance or agreement to such station.
>
> **Producer Responsibility**
>
> (b) . . . any person who, in connection with the production or preparation of any program or program matter which is intended for broadcasting over any radio station, accepts or agrees to accept, or pays or agrees to pay, any money, service or other valuable consideration for the inclusion of any matter as part of such program or program matter, shall, in advance of such broadcast, disclose the fact of such acceptance or payment or agreement to the payee's employer, or to the person for whom such program or program matter is being produced, or to the licensee of such station over which such program is broadcast.
>
> **Supplier/Syndicator Responsibility**
>
> (c) . . . any person who supplies to any other person any program or program matter which is intended for broadcasting over any radio station shall, in advance of such broadcast, disclose to such other person any information of which he has knowledge, or which has been disclosed to him, as to any money, service or other valuable consideration which any person has paid or accepted, or has agreed to pay or accept, for the inclusion of any matter as a part of such program or program matter. . . .
>
> **Defining Limits**
>
> (f) The term "service or other valuable consideration" as used in this section shall not include any service or property furnished without charge or at a nominal charge for use on, or in connection with, a broadcast, or for use on a program which is intended for broadcasting over any radio station, unless it is so furnished in consideration for an identification in such broadcast or in such program of any person, product, service, trademark, or brand name beyond an identification which is reasonably related to the use of such service or property in such broadcast or such program.
>
> (g) Any person who violates any provision of this section shall, for each such violation, be fined not more than $10,000 or be imprisoned not more than one year, or both.[44]

To assure compliance with the rules some stations use sworn affidavits which contain language that states that the employee is familiar with the rules and follows them. Strongly worded memoranda to station personnel also help assure compliance.

CONSUMER CREDIT: PROTECTING A CLIENT

Broadcast salespersons frequently encounter advertisers who sell products permitting consumers to finance the purchase over time. While the Truth in Lending Act does not hold the media responsible for advertisements that do not fully disclose credit terms, broadcast salespersons can find themselves being asked by copy writers or sponsors the right way to disclose the terms of consumer credit. Giving the *wrong* advice to a sponsor could make the station liable. The problem is especially acute where small businesses are concerned or when a business ventures into consumer credit transactions with little experience.

Enforcement of Federal Regulations

Enforcement of the Truth in Lending Act is handled by a complex array of federal agencies.[45] For example, the Federal Trade Commission enforces the Truth in Lending Act where other federal agencies do not have jurisdiction. However, many other agencies do have specialized enforcement functions under the act.[46] Meat packers and stockyards, for instance, fall under the jurisdiction of the Department of Agriculture. Airlines come under the Civil Aeronautics Board and national banks come under the Comptroller of the Currency. Federal Land Banks as well as other agriculturally-oriented services come under the Farm Credit Administration. FDIC-insured banks which are not members of the Federal Reserve System come under the Federal Deposit Insurance Corporation. The Federal Home Loan Bank Board regulates advertising by savings institutions. The Federal Reserve Board enforces advertising regulations of state member banks that are part of the Federal Reserve System and federal credit unions fall under the National Credit Union Administration.

Spirit of the Truth in Lending Act

The spirit of the Truth in Lending Act is to protect the consumer against advertisements of any kind that might hide the true cost of merchandise or services.[47] The key to adhering to the letter and spirit of the law is "clear and conspicuous disclosure." For example, if a car dealership advertises a 10 percent financing on all new cars but does not tell the public that the rate is adjustable and gradually increases and the buyer pays off the car, then full disclosure did not take place. Practices such as this and a host of other "hidden" charges is what the Truth in Lending Act is designed to prohibit.

CATEGORIES OF CONSUMER CREDIT

Consumer credit, which is any credit primarily offered for "personal, family, or household purposes," can be categorized as open-end credit, closed-end credit, or consumer lease.

Open-End Credit

Examples of open-end credit are such things as "gas company credit cards, stores' revolving charge accounts, and cash-advance checking accounts."[48] In open-end credit: "(a) the creditor reasonably expects the customer to make repeated transactions; (b) the creditor may impose a finance charge from time to time on the unpaid balance; and (c) as the customer pays the outstanding balance, that amount of credit is, generally, once again made available to the customer."[49]

Closed-End Credit

Closed-end credit involves credit that is advanced for a specific amount of time. The amount financed, finance charge, and "schedule of payments are agreed upon by the lender and the customer."[50] For example, if you buy a chair and arrange credit directly with the furniture company to pay for the chair over a specified time period—such as six months—at a specific interest level resulting in a given monthly payment schedule you would be involved in a closed-end credit transaction.

Consumer Lease

Consumer lease occurs when personal property is leased to a private individual. The lease must be for more than four months. Even if the customer has the option of buying the merchandise at the end of the lease, it is still considered a lease under the Truth in Lending Act. The exception is when the customer's payments exceed the value of the personal property, such as making payments totaling $20,000 for an automobile that costs $18,000. In these cases, or when with only a nominal payment the person buys the property at the end of the payment period, it is a closed-end credit sale and not a consumer lease.

"TRIGGERING" TERMS AND DISCLOSURES IN CONSUMER CREDIT

What terms must be disclosed in a consumer credit or consumer lease transaction are determined by the actual phrasing of the commercial, which in turn may require specific disclosures on the part of the sponsor.

Statements for Open-End Credit

Six different statements or terms will trigger required disclosures for commercials that promote open-end credit. As outlined by the Federal Trade Commission, these "triggering" terms for open-end credit include:

1. a statement of when the finance charge begins to accrue, including the "free ride" period (if any).

   Examples:

   "Up to 30 days of free credit if you pay in full each month"

   "We charge interest from the date we receive notice of your purchase"

2. either the periodic rate used to compute the finance charge or the annual percentage rate.

   Examples:

   "Less than 2% per month"

   "Periodic rate—1-1/2% per month"

3. the method of determining the balance on which a finance charge may be imposed.

   Examples:

   "A small monthly service charge on your remaining balance each month"

   "Interest will be charged on your average daily balance each month"

4. the method of determining the finance charge, including a description of how any finance charge other than the periodic rate will be determined.

   Examples:

   "You only pay $1.00 each time you write an overdraft check"

   "Minimum finance charge: $.50 per month"

5. the amount of any charge, other than a finance charge, that may be imposed as part of the plan.

   Example:

   "There is a $35 annual membership fee to get your card"

6. the fact that the creditor will acquire a security interest.

   Examples:

   "A security interest will be taken on all goods purchased"

   "Secure your credit with a $1,000 certificate of deposit"[51]

If any triggering statements or terms are used, then three disclosures must take place. These include disclosing:

> (1) any minimum, fixed, transaction, activity, or similar charge that could be imposed; (2) any periodic rate that may be applied, expressed as an "annual percentage rate." The term "annual percentage rate" must be used. If the plan provides for a variable periodic rate, that fact must be disclosed; and (3) any membership or participation fee.[52]

An example of a disclosure statement that would meet the requirements of the Truth in Lending Act for open-end credit reads:

> Your ABC Credit Card monthly bill will include a $.50 transaction charge for each purchase you make during the month. In addition, a finance charge at the rate of 1% per month will be imposed on your unpaid balance. This is an annual percentage rate of 12%. The annual membership fee is $35.[53]

The FTC warns that general statements are not acceptable. For example, simply saying "a finance charge will be imposed" is not acceptable.

While triggering statements need to be watched, some latitude does still exist when preparing commercial copy. For example, statements such as "charge accounts available," "open a revolving budget account," "just say 'charge it'," "all major credit cards honored," "pay monthly," and "charge some cash," do not require disclosures.[54]

Statements for Closed-End Credit

Closed-end credit consists of a transaction, such as a loan, in which the schedule of payments, the amount of the loan, the specific payback period, and the finance charge are agreed upon by the lender and the consumer. Five triggering terms or statements can require disclosures in closed-end transactions. These terms and/or statements include:

1. the amount of the downpayment (expressed either as a percentage or as a dollar amount).

   Examples:

   "10% down"

   "$25 down"

   "90% financing"

2. amount of any payment (expressed either as a percentage or as a dollar amount).

   Examples:

   "Monthly payments less than $67"

   "Pay 5% each month"

   "$9 per month"

3. the number of payments

   Examples:

   "36 small payments are all you make"

   "48 monthly payments and you're all paid up"

4. the period of repayment (the total time required to repay).

   Examples:

   "Five years to pay"

   "36 months to pay"

   "4 year loans available"

5. the amount of any finance charge.

   Examples:

   "Financing costs less than $100"

   "Less than $100 interest"

   "$100 financing"[55]

When disclosure is required, the disclosure must include: "(1) the amount or percentage of the downpayment; (2) the terms of repayment; and (3) the 'annual percentage rate,' using that term spelled out in full. If the annual percentage rate may be increased after consummation of the credit transaction, that fact must be disclosed."[56]

A sample disclosure for closed-end credit that meets the requirements of the Truth in Lending Act could read: "No downpayment. Thirty-six monthly payments of $200 each. Annual percentage rate equals 24%." The word *downpayment* could be substituted with such terms as "15% cash required from buyer;" "a minimum $100 trade-in required," would meet the requirements. Remember the spirit of the law is full and conspicuous disclosure; thus; when in doubt and triggering terms or statements are made, it is best to err on the side of full disclosure.

Real estate firms frequently advertise on radio and television stations and, therefore, copy for such firms must also adhere to the Truth in Lending Act.[57] If only the annual percentage rate is stated, then disclosure statements are not required. Triggering terms for real estate transactions would include such statements as: "10% down," "payments of only $500 per month," "only 360 monthly payments," "you'll pay less than $500 per month," "30-year mortgages are available." In each of these cases the three disclosure statements must be made which include the annual percentage rate, the amount or terms of the repayment, and the amount of downpayment required.

As with open-end credit, a number of general statements can be made that will not trigger disclosures. For example, statements such as: "no downpayment," "18% annual percentage rate loans available here," "easy monthly payments," "loans available at 5% below our standard annual percentage rate," "low downpayment accepted," "pay weekly," "terms to fit your budget," and "financing available" are all acceptable and will not necessitate disclosure.[58]

Statements for Consumer Leases

As stated earlier, a consumer lease occurs when personal property is leased to private individuals. Three triggering terms or statements invoke disclosure in consumer lease commercials. They are:

1. the amount of any payment.

   Example:

   "Pay a mere $128 per month"

2. the number of required payments.

   Examples:

   "$133 per month . . . 36 month lease"
   "Low monthly payments on our four-year auto leases"

3. a statement that any or no downpayment, or other payment, is required at the beginning of the lease.

   Examples:

   "Lease now and make no payments for three months"
   "Only a small downpayment"
   "Leave your pocketbook behind and return home in your leased. . . ."[59]

When these triggering terms or statements are used, five areas of disclosure must be met. For consumer leases these include:

> (1) a statement that the transaction advertised is a lease;
>
> (2) the total amount of any payment (such as a security deposit or capitalized cost reduction) required at the beginning of the lease, or a statement that no such payment is required;
>
> (3) the number, amounts due dates, or periods of scheduled payments, and the total of such payments under the lease;
>
> (4) a statement of whether the customer has the option to purchase the leased property and at what time and price (the method of determining the price may be substituted for disclosure of the price); and
>
> (5) a statement of the amount (or a method of determining the amount) of any liabilities the lease imposes upon the customer at the end of the term; and, if the customer has such liability, a statement that the customer shall be liable for any difference between the estimated value of the leased property and its realized value at the end of the lease term.[60]

A sample disclosure statement that would meet the requirements of the Truth in Lending Act reads:

> Thirty-six month lease. No payments at the beginning of the lease, 36 monthly payments of $128 totaling $4,608.
>
> Customer has no option to purchase at the end of the lease.

> Customer will have no further liability unless auto has depreciated to less than 40% of its new car price. If so, customer is liable for that additional depreciation.[61]

Such phrases as "low monthly payments," "lease for less than it costs to buy," or "we lease to anyone" will not trigger disclosures.

In broadcasting, the triggering terms and statements for all types of credit transactions, be they open-end credit, closed-end credit, or consumer lease, can present problems in both the time available for most commercial copy and the ability of television to provide full and conspicuous disclosure. Clearly, the easiest solution to meeting the requirements of the Truth in Lending Act is not to use any triggering terms or statements. Unfortunately, not every selling situation will permit that flexibility. A competitor of an important sponsor may have developed a print advertising campaign based on statements that require disclosure. To meet your client's advertising needs you must develop commercials that also promote the same terms. Similarly, a station may enter into a cooperative promotional campaign where broadcast advertising must coincide with the sponsor's print campaign. When such situations develop, being aware of the truth-in-lending requirements can help to avoid placing your sponsor on the wrong side of the law.

DISCLOSURE OF WARRANTIES OR GUARANTEES

While the disclosure requirements for warranties and guarantees are not as complex as credit advertising, the FTC has issued guidelines, codified into law, which require certain statements when products are advertised with warranty or guarantee coverage.

Location for Customer Inspection

Specifically, the law states:

> If an advertisement mentions a warranty or guarantee that is offered on the advertised product, the advertisement should disclose, with such clarity and prominence as will be noticed and understood by prospective purchasers, that prior to sale, at the place where the product is sold, prospective purchasers can see the written warranty or guarantee for complete details of the warranty coverage.[62]

For example, a commercial might read: "Our Speedy bicycle is backed by a limited one-year warranty, a copy of which can be obtained at any one of our convenient locations." The fact that the bicycle is being advertised with a warranty required the disclosure statement telling the consumer where the warranty can be inspected. Similarly, a commercial with a guarantee might read: "We offer the best guarantee in the business. Read the details and compare wherever our fine products are sold."[63]

Commercials for Catalog Merchandise with a Warranty or Guarantee

Catalog merchandise presents a special case.[64] For example, since the catalog and not a retail store may be the only place to buy merchandise, then consumers must be given the address where they can write and secure a copy of the warranty or guarantee. A commercial for bicycle parts from a catalog outlet might read: "All of our parts are backed by our limited warranty. Write for a copy at P.O. Box. . . ." A warranty or guarantee may also be found in the catalog itself and identifying this fact is sufficient disclosure.

Satisfaction and Lifetime Guarantees

Sponsors must be careful not to use such terms as *satisfaction guarantee, money-back guarantee,* or *free trial offer,* unless they are willing to refund the "full advertised price of the product at the purchaser's request."[65] In addition, the commercial must list any limitations to the satisfaction guarantee or other similar representations. For example, if the satisfaction guarantee is conditional upon the consumer returning the unused portion of the merchandise, then this must be stated in the commercial. If the original packaging must be included, then this must also be made clear to the consumer.

If the word *lifetime* or *life* is used to promote the product warranty or guarantee, then the commercial must disclose exactly what is meant by such terms. For example, suppose lifetime warranty on a muffler means the life of the car. The commercial must state this clearly. Perhaps the lifetime warranty means the life of the car under the ownership of the person who originally purchased the muffler. The commercial must make this clear. Two examples encompassing the disclosure requirements are illustrated in the following statements. For a guarantee covering a muffler for the life of the car, the commercial might read:

> Our lifetime guarantee in the Whisper Muffler protects you for as long as your car runs—even if you sell it, trade it, or give it away![66]

A more restricted guarantee on a battery might read:

> Our battery is backed by our lifetime guarantee. Good for as long as you own your car![67]

Audio/Video Transmission Requirements

The manner in which disclosures are made is of concern to the Federal Trade Commission. Hiding the information about a warranty or guarantee in the corner of a television screen where no one can read it does not comply with FTC regulations.

Specifically, the audio/video transmission requirement reads:

> In television advertising, the Commission will regard any disclosure of the pre-sale availability or warranties as complying with (the requirements) if the advertisement makes the necessary disclosure simultaneously with or immediately following the warranty claim and the disclosure is made in the audio portion, or if in the video portion, it remains on the screen for at least five seconds.[68]

Since the video portion is not available in radio, the text of the commercial would need to make clear disclosures similar to those examples for the Whisper Muffler and battery discussed earlier.

SUMMARY

In many countries broadcasting operates as a commercial enterprise. Income from advertising fuels commercial stations in the same way that government appropriations and contributions support public broadcasting stations. Commercial broadcasting in the United States began in the 1920s when the AT&T station in New York sold blocks of time for a real estate corporation. Called "toll" broadcasting, the system had its critics who suggested alternative forms of funding were more appropriate, including having cities pay for programs and the government imposing a tax on "radio subscribers" as well as a tax on the manufacturers of radio equipment. A trade publication of the printing industry said advertising on radio was "totally offensive."

AT&T continued to experiment with its commercial station, at one point going so far as to prohibit competing stations from doing remote broadcasts using telephone company lines and equipment. The restrictive practice continued until the Federal Trade Commission intervened saying AT&T's exclusive control over the use of long lines and toll broadcasting violated the antitrust provisions of the Clayton Act. Rather than fight the issue in court, AT&T left the broadcasting business and sold its commercial station WEAF.

Local government control over advertising was affirmed in 1942 when a Florida resident bought a Navy surplus submarine and charged admission to tour the sub. After advertising the attraction by distributing handbills, the New York City Police Department intervened claiming the handbill distribution violated the New York sanitary code. When the entrepreneur was told he could only distribute handbills which were devoted to "information or a public protest," he printed a protest against the city dock department on one side of the handbill and publicized his submarine on the other. He was stopped again by police and sued, winning in district court but losing at the level of the United States Supreme Court. The justices ruled that simply appending the protest statement to the handbill was not enough to give him immunity from the law. Although the content of the message was not at issue, it did affirm the right to regulate the distribution of certain types of advertising messages.

When the Pittsburgh, Pennsylvania Human Relations Commission tried to stop the Pittsburgh press from using male and female categories in its help-wanted advertising, it relied on a city ordinance prohibiting discrimination in hiring. The Supreme Court ruled in favor of the city saying that when a practice is illegal, as was the use of separate male and female categories, the First Amendment principle was absent and would not apply in the case.

The Supreme Court did rule that a Virginia newspaper had First Amendment protection when it published an ad encouraging women to go outside the state for abortions. Although abortions were illegal in Virginia, going outside the state was not and First Amendment protection applied.

In still another clarification of the First Amendment's rule and the regulation of commercial speech, the U.S. Supreme Court ruled against a Virginia statute which prohibited licensed pharmacists from advertising the price of prescription drugs. While commercial speech today does not enjoy complete First Amendment protection, it does give great latitude to advertisers to say almost anything they want as long as it is truthful and can be proven using recognized testing procedures. The Federal Trade Commission and the courts continue to warn advertisers that there can be no constitutional protection for false statements.

Both state and federal law controls broadcast advertising even though stations themselves are licensed by the federal government. For example, a New Mexico law was upheld which prohibited New Mexico radio stations from accepting advertising from Texas optometrists. Texas advertising violated New Mexico law which regulated optometric advertising. Laws governing broadcast advertising at the state level can be categorized into those which govern fraudulent advertising, deceptive trade and consumer fraud practices, and regulations which control advertising of specific products.

Federal jurisdiction over advertising is primarily through the Federal Trade Commission, although the FCC can use its blanket public-interest clause to impose sanctions on an unscrupulous broadcaster, especially after an FTC complaint is upheld. Key elements which will trigger an FTC inquiry include the tendency to deceive, the advertiser's knowledge of falsity, the intent of the advertiser, the ability of the general public to understand the message, overall truthfulness, and lack of ambiguous content. Some of the landmark FTC decisions include challenges to a commercial showing a shaving cream's ability to soften sandpaper and a baking company advertisement touting low-calorie bread.

More specific regulations govern the day-to-day operations of commercial radio and television stations. For example, FCC rules require commercial sponsors to be identified on the air and although fraudulent billing is not regulated by the FCC, it is still extremely serious and can occur in a variety of situations, most commonly when co-op advertising is involved. The government at the state level can still prosecute cases of fraudulent billing and private parties can sue the station where fraudulent billing is an issue. Also not regulated by the FCC is network clipping, the practice of certifying to a network that a network commercial has been aired when in fact it is not. However, the practice is still considered fraud and fair trade and racketeering laws can be invoked.

Many state regulations apply to product advertising. For example, in one state restaurants can advertise the price of beer, wine, and mixed drinks but not brand names. Alcoholic beverages can be included in commercials as long as the brand is not mentioned. Grocery stores can advertise beer and wine but not hard liquor. State law prohibits certain terms from being used such as *high test* or *high proof*. Manufacturers, bottlers, and importers can advertise the brand name but not list the price and cooperative advertising between retailers and establishments is prohibited. Broad sections of the law deal with advertising to secondary and elementary schools. Talking about a competitor is permitted but false and misleading advertising is open to challenge.

Station-conducted contests are used as successful marketing tools for many licensees. In highly competitive markets contests play a major role in jockeying for rating positions and big money giveaways are common. In general terms, station-conducted contests are similar to advertising in that airing truthful information and not misleading the public are paramount. In addition, stations need to guard against using such practices as urging persons to stay tuned when it is not possible to win a prize, failing to award prizes, failing to set forth fully and accurately contest rules, changing the rules without notifying the public, using inconsistent judging standards, providing secret assistance, broadcasting false clues, and inadequate supervision of the contest. Particular concern exists when contests are directed toward children. Prizes of more than $600 must be reported to the Internal Revenue Service. Federal regulations govern the broadcast of a lottery. Three elements must be present for a lottery to exist: prize, chance, and consideration. Violations of lottery regulations are prosecuted under the United States Code.

Disclosures in the 1950s that disc jockeys were receiving cash and gifts for promoting records resulted in government investigations and new rules to guard against the practice which is called *plugola* or *payola*. The practice involves taking money or other services of value and not disclosing the payment. Most stations have safeguards against personnel taking gratuities in consideration for influencing the content of on-air programming. Employees, producers, syndicators, and suppliers are all part of the chain of decision making where payola practices can occur. In addition, employees can place themselves and the station at risk when accepting any service or item of value which influences programming. Some exemptions do exist. Service or property furnished without charge or at a nominal charge for use in connection with a broadcast is not included in the law.

Although the Truth in Lending Act does not hold the media responsible for advertisements that do not fully disclose credit terms, broadcast salespersons need to be alert to such regulations so as not to put the station's copy writers or the sponsors at odds with the law. The Federal Trade Commission is responsible for enforcement of the Truth in Lending Act. As an example, meat packers and stockyards fall under the jurisdiction of the Department of Agriculture, while airlines fall under the Civil Aeronautics Board. The spirit of the Truth in Lending Act is the protection of the consumer against advertisements which might hide the true cost of merchandise or services. The key element in adhering to the letter and spirit of the Truth in Lending Act is "clear and conspicuous disclosure."

Consumer credit can be classified as open-end credit, close-end credit, and consumer lease. Gas company credit cards and revolving charge accounts are open-end credit accounts. Close-end accounts result from financing a specific amount over a certain period of time. A consumer lease is when personal property is leased to a private individual. All three terms are used in broadcast advertising and certain disclosure terms are required under FTC regulations. Specific terms trigger consumer credit disclosure requirements. For example, triggering terms outlined under FTC regulations include such instances as when a finance charge begins a periodic interest rate or an annual percentage rate, the method for determining the balance and finance charge, and the amount of any charge. Whenever triggering statements take place, disclosures must occur.

Statements for close-end credit include the amount of downpayment when expressed as a percentage or a dollar amount, the amount of any specific payment, the number of payments, period of repayment, and the amount of any finance charge. Such terms require disclosure of the amount or percentage of the downpayment, terms of repayment, and the annual percentage rate. Statements which invoke disclosure requirements for consumer lease are the amount of any payment, number of required payments, and any or no downpayment.

Disclosure requirements also exist when warranties or guarantees are stated in a commercial or advertisement. For example, the location where potential customers can examine the details of the warranty coverage must be disclosed. Catalog companies are a special case since the audience cannot usually appear at the headquarters of the catalog company simply stating that the warranty or guarantee is located in the catalog is sufficient disclosure. Unless a sponsor is willing to refund the full advertised price of a product, care must be taken not to use such terms as *satisfaction guaranteed*, or *money-back guarantee*. In addition, the words *lifetime* or *life* when used to promote a product warranty or guarantee must have a full disclosure of what is meant by those terms. Because broadcast commercials have time constraints, *lifetime* and *life* warranties are sometimes avoided. The FTC can monitor the way a disclosure is made.

MATERIAL FOR ANALYSIS

Environmental claims in radio and television commercials have been common since the environmental movement began to sensitize consumers about the importance of everything from air pollution to recycling. Commonly referred to as *green marketing* or *environmental marketing*, many companies include environmental strategies in the advertising of their products and those which do not are at the least sensitive to how environmental concerns will affect the sale of their products. With a growing concern that advertisers were using misleading environmental marketing strategies and to help clear up confusion over exactly how far advertisers could go and what kind of copy would pass, the Federal Trade Commission in July 1992 issued its *Guides for the Use of Environmental Marketing Claims*, which are presented here. The guides point out that "some of the illustrative disclosures may be appropriate for use on labels but not in print or broadcast advertisements and vice versa." Important to keep in mind is the fact that even labels can become the source of commercial copy produced by creative copy writers who want to give the advertiser every advantage in the marketplace. Creative copy writers may inadvertently draw from labels or other advertising copy to develop the wording of a radio or television commercial. While liability may or may not be an issue, airing radio or television commercials for products which violate environmental marketing claims, even if only in labeling or print advertising, does not enhance the station's reputation with its audience and can result in annoying inquiries from a state or federal agency and strained relations with a client.

GUIDES FOR THE USE OF ENVIRONMENTAL MARKETING CLAIMS

THE APPLICATION OF SECTION 5 OF THE FEDERAL TRADE COMMISSION ACT TO ENVIRONMENTAL ADVERTISING AND MARKETING PRACTICES

A. STATEMENT OF PURPOSE:

These guides represent administrative interpretations of laws administered by the Federal Trade Commission for the guidance of the public in conducting its affairs in conformity with legal requirements. These guides specifically address the application of Section 5 of the FTC Act to environmental advertising and marketing practices. They provide the basis for voluntary compliance with such laws by members of industry. Conduct inconsistent with the positions articulated in these guides may result in corrective action by the Commission under Section 5 if, after investigation, the Commission has reason to believe that the behavior falls within the scope of conduct declared unlawful by the statute.

B. SCOPE OF THE GUIDES:

These guides apply to environmental claims included in labeling, advertising, promotional materials, and all other forms of marketing, whether asserted directly or by implication, through words, symbols, emblems, logos, depictions, product brand names, or through any other means. The guides apply to any claim about the environmental attributes of a product or package in connection with the sale, offering for sale, or marketing of such product or package for personal, family or household use, or for commercial, institutional, or industrial use.

Because the guides are not legislative rules under Section 18 of the FTC Act, they are not themselves enforceable regulations, nor do they have the force and effect of law. The guides themselves do not preempt regulation of other federal agencies or of state and local bodies governing the use of environmental marketing claims. Compliance with federal, state, or local law and regulations concerning such claims, however, will not necessarily preclude Commission law enforcement action under Section 5.

C. STRUCTURE OF THE GUIDES:

The guides are composed of general principles and specific guidance on the use of environmental claims. These general principles and specific guidance are followed by examples that generally address a single deception concern. A given claim may raise issues that are addressed under more than one example and in more than one section of the guides.

In many of the examples, one or more options are presented for qualifying a claim. These options are intended to provide a "safe harbor" for marketers who want certainty about how to make environmental claims. They do not represent the only permissible approaches to qualifying a claim. The examples do not illustrate all possible acceptable claims or disclosures that would be permissible under Section 5. In addition, some of the illustrative disclosures may be appropriate for use on labels but not in print or broadcast advertisements and vice versa. In some instances, the guides indicate within the example in what context or contexts a particular type of disclosure should be considered.

D. REVIEW PROCEDURE:

Three years after the date of adoption of these guides, the Commission will seek public comment on whether and how the guides need to be modified in light of ensuing developments.

Parties may petition the Commission to alter or amend these guides in light of substantial new evidence regarding consumer interpretation of a claim or regarding substantiation of a claim. Following review of such a petition, the Commission will take such action as it deems appropriate.

E. INTERPRETATION AND SUBSTANTIATION OF ENVIRONMENTAL MARKETING CLAIMS:

Section 5 of the FTC Act makes unlawful deceptive acts and practices in or affecting commerce. The Commission's criteria for determining whether an express or implied claim has been made are enunciated in the Commission's Policy Statement on Deception.[69] In addition, any party making an express or implied claim that presents an objective assertion about the environmental attribute of a product or package must, at the time the claim is made, possess and rely upon a reasonable basis substantiating the claim. A reasonable basis consists of competent and reliable evidence. In the context of environmental marketing claims, such substantiation will often require competent and reliable scientific evidence. For any test, analysis, research, study, or other evidence to be "competent and reliable" for purposes of these guides, it must be conducted and evaluated in an objective manner by persons qualified to do so, using procedures generally accepted in the profession to yield accurate and reliable results. Further guidance on the reasonable basis standard is set forth in the Commission's 1983 Policy Statement on the Advertising Substantiation Doctrine.[70] These guides, therefore, attempt to preview Commission policy in a relatively new context—that of environmental claims.

F. GENERAL PRINCIPLES:

The following general principles apply to all environmental marketing claims, including, but not limited to, those described in Part G below. In addition, Part G contains specific guidance applicable to certain environmental marketing claims. Claims should conform with all relevant provisions of these guides, not simply the provision that seems most directly applicable.

1. *Qualifications and Disclosures*: The Commission traditionally has held that in order to be effective, any qualifications or disclosures such as those described in these guides should be sufficiently clear and prominent to prevent deception. Clarity of language, relative type size and proximity to the claim being qualified, and an absence of contrary claims that could undercut effectiveness, will maximize the likelihood that the qualification and disclosures are appropriately clear and prominent.

2. *Distinction Between Benefits of Product and Package*: An environmental marketing claim should be presented in a way that makes clear whether the environmental attribute or benefit being asserted refers to the product, the product's packaging, or to a portion or component of the product or packaging. In general, if the environmental attribute of benefit applies to all but minor, incidental components of a product or package, the claim need not be qualified to identify that fact. There may be exceptions to this general principle. For example, if an unqualified "recyclable" claim is made and the presence of the incidental component significantly limits the ability to recycle the product, then the claim would be deceptive.

Example 1: A box of aluminum foil is labeled with the claim "recyclable," without further elaboration. Unless the type of product, surrounding language, or other context of the phrase establishes whether the claim refers to the foil or the box, the claim is deceptive if any part of either the box or the foil, other than minor, incidental components, cannot be recycled.

Example 2: A soft drink bottle is labeled "recycled." The bottle is made entirely from recycled materials, but the bottle cap is not. Because reasonable consumers are likely to consider the bottle cap to be a minor, incidental component of the package, the claim is not deceptive. Similarly, it would not be deceptive to label a shopping bag "recycled" where the bag is made entirely of recycled material but the easily detachable handle, an incidental component, is not.

3. *Overstatement of Environmental Attribute*: An environmental marketing claim should not be presented in a manner that overstates the environmental attribute or benefit, expressly or by implication. Marketers should avoid implications of significant environmental benefits if the benefit is in fact negligible.

Example 1: A package is labeled, "50% more recycled content than before." The manufacturer increased the recycled content of its package from 2 percent recycled material to 3 percent recycled material. Although the claim is technically true, it is likely to convey the false impression that the advertiser has increased significantly the use of recycled material.

Example 2: A trash bag is labeled "recyclable" without qualification. Because trash bags will ordinarily not be separated out from other trash at the landfill or incinerator for recycling, they are highly unlikely to be used again for any purpose. Even if the bag is technically capable of being recycled, the claim is deceptive since it asserts an environmental benefit where no significant or meaningful benefit exists.

Example 3: A paper grocery sack is labeled "reusable." The sack can be brought back to the store and reused for carrying groceries but will fall apart after two or three reuses, on average. Because reasonable consumers are unlikely to assume that a paper grocery sack is durable, the unqualified claim does not overstate the environmental benefit conveyed to the consumers. The claim is not deceptive and does not need to be qualified to indicate the limited reuse of the sack.

4. *Comparative Claims*: Environmental marketing claims that include a comparative statement should be presented in a manner that makes the basis of the comparison sufficiently clear to avoid consumer deception. In addition, the advertiser should be able to substantiate the comparison.

Example 1: An advertiser notes that its shampoo bottle contains "20% more recycled content." The claim in its context is ambiguous. Depending on contextual factors, it could be a comparison either to the advertiser's immediately preceding product or to a competitor's product. The advertiser should clarify the claim to make the basis for comparison clear, for example, by saying "20% more recycled content than our previous package." Otherwise, the advertiser should be prepared to substantiate whatever comparison is conveyed to reasonable consumers.

Example 2: An advertiser claims that "our plastic diaper liner has the most recycle content." The advertised diaper does have more recycled content, calculated as a percentage of weight, than any other on the market, although it is still well under 100% recycled. Provided the recycled content and the comparative difference between the product and those of competitors are significant and provided the specific comparison can be substantiated, the claim is not deceptive.

Example 3: An ad claims that the advertiser's packaging creates "less waste than the leading national brand." The advertiser's source reduction was implemented some time ago and is supported by a calculation comparing the relative solid waste contributions of the two packages. The advertiser should be able to substantiate that the comparison remains accurate.

G. ENVIRONMENTAL MARKETING CLAIMS:

Guidance about the use of environmental marketing claims is set forth below. Each guide is followed by several examples that illustrate, but do not provide an exhaustive list of, claims that do and do not comport with the guides. In each case, the general principles set forth in Part F above should also be followed.[71]

1. *General Environmental Benefit Claims*: It is deceptive to misrepresent, directly or by implication, that a product or package offers a general environmental benefit. Unqualified general claims of environmental benefit are difficult to interpret, and depending on their context, may convey a wide range of meanings to consumers. In many cases, such claims may convey that the product or package has specific and far-reaching environmental benefits. As explained in the Commission's Ad Substantiation Statement, every express and material, implied claim that the general assertion conveys to reasonable consumers about an objective quality, feature, or attribute of a product must be substantiated. Unless this substantiation duty can be met, broad environmental claims should either be avoided or qualified, as necessary, to prevent deception about the specific nature of the environmental benefit being asserted.

Example 1: A brand name like "Eco-Safe" would be deceptive if, in the context of the product so named, it leads consumers to believe that the product has environmental benefits which cannot be substantiated by the manufacturer. The claim would not be deceptive if "Eco-Safe" were followed by clear and prominent qualifying language limiting the safety representation to a particular product attribute for which it could be substantiated, and provided that no other deceptive implications were created by the context.

Example 2: A product wrapper is printed with the claim "Environmentally Friendly." Textual comments on the wrapper explain that the wrapper is "Environmentally Friendly because it was not chlorine bleached, a process that has been shown to create harmful substances." The wrapper was, in fact, not bleached with chlorine. However, the production of the wrapper now creates and releases to the environment significant quantities of other harmful substances. Since consumers are likely to interpret the "Environmentally Friendly" claim, in combination with the textual explanation, to mean that no significant harmful substances are currently released to the environment, the "Environmentally Friendly" claim would be deceptive.

Example 3: A pump spray product is labeled "environmentally safe." Most of the product's active ingredients consist of volatile organic compounds (VOCs) that may cause smog by contributing to gound-level ozone formation. The claim is deceptive because, absent further qualification, it is likely to convey to consumers that use of the product will not result in air pollution or other harm to the environment.

2. *Degradable/Biodegradable/Photodegradable*: It is deceptive to misrepresent, directly or by implication, that a product or package is degradable, biodegradable, or photodegradable. An unqualified claim that a product or package is degradable, biodegradable, or photodegradable should be substantiated by competent and reliable scientific evidence that the entire product or package will completely break down and return to nature, *i.e.*, decompose into elements found in nature within a reasonably short period of time after customary disposal.

Claims of degradability, biodegradability, or photodegradability should be qualified to the extent necessary to avoid consumer deception about: (a) the product or package's ability to degrade in the environment where it is customarily disposed; and (b) the rate and extent of degradation.

Example 1: A trash bag is marketed as "degradable," with no qualification or other disclosure. The marketer relies on soil burial tests to show that the product will decompose in the presence of water and oxygen. The trash bags are customarily disposed of in incineration facilities or at sanitary landfills that are managed in a way that inhibits degradation by minimizing moisture and oxygen. Degradation will be irrelevant for those trash bags that are incinerated and, for those disposed of in landfills, the marketer does not possess adequate substantiation that the bags will degrade in a reasonably short period of time in a landfill. The claim is therefore deceptive.

Example 2: A commercial agricultural plastic mulch film is advertised as "photodegradable" and qualified with the phrase "will break down into small pieces if left uncovered in sunlight." The claim is supported by competent and reliable scientific evidence that the product will break down in a reasonably short period of time after being exposed to sunlight and into sufficiently small pieces to become part of the soil. The qualified claim is not deceptive. Because the claim is qualified to indicate the limited extent of breakdown, the advertiser need not meet the elements for an unqualified photodegradable claim, i.e., that the product will not only break down, but will also decompose into elements found in nature.

Example 3: A soap or shampoo product is advertised as "biodegradable," with no qualification or other disclosure. The manufacturer has competent and reliable scientific evidence demonstrating that the product, which is customarily disposed of in sewage systems, will break down and decompose into elements found in nature in a short period of time. The claim is not deceptive.

3. *Compostable*: It is deceptive to misrepresent, directly or by implication, that a product or package is compostable. An unqualified claim that a product or package is compostable should be substantiated by competent and reliable scientific evidence that all the material in the product or package will break down into, or otherwise become part of, usable compost (*e.g.*, soil-conditioning material, mulch) in a safe and timely manner in an appropriate composting program or facility, or in a home compost pile or device.

Claims of compostability should be qualified to the extent necessary to avoid consumer deception. An unqualified claim may be deceptive: (1) if municipal composting facilities are not available to a substantial majority of consumers or communities where the package is sold; (2) if the claim misleads consumers about the environmental benefit provided when the product is disposed of in a landfill; or (3) if consumers misunderstood the claim to mean that the package can be safely composted in their home compost pile or device, when in fact it cannot.

Example 1: A manufacturer indicates that its unbleached coffee filter is compostable. The unqualified claim is not deceptive provided the manufacturer can substantiate that the filter can be converted safely to usable compost in a timely manner in a home compost pile or device, as well as in an appropriate composting program or facility.

Example 2: A lawn and leaf bag is labeled as "Compostable in California Municipal Yard Waste Composting Facilities." The bag contains toxic ingredients that are released into the compost material as the bag breaks down. The claim is deceptive if the presence of these toxic ingredients prevents the compost from being usable.

Example 3: A manufacturer indicates that its paper plate is suitable for home composting. If the manufacturer possesses substantiation for claiming that the paper plate can be converted safely to useable compost in a home compost pile or device, this claim is not deceptive even if no municipal composting facilities exist.

Example 4: A manufacturer makes an unqualified claim that its package is compostable. Although municipal composting facilities exist where the product is sold, the package will not break down into usable compost in a home compost pile or device. To avoid deception, the manufacturer should disclose that the package is not suitable for home composting.

Example 5: A nationally marketed lawn and leaf bag is labeled "compostable." Also printed on the bag is a disclosure that the bag is not designed for use in some compost piles. The bags are in fact composted in municipal yard waste composting programs in many communities around the country, but such programs are not available to a substantial majority of consumers where the bag is sold. The claim is deceptive since reasonable consumers living in areas not served by municipal yard waste programs may understand the reference to mean that composting facilities accepting the bags are available in their area. To avoid deception, the claim should be qualified to indicate the limited availability of such programs, for example, by stating, "Appropriate facilities may not exist in your area." Other examples of adequate qualification of the claim included providing the approximate percentage of communities or the population for which such programs are available.

Example 6: A manufacturer sells a disposable diaper that bears the legend, "This diaper can be composted where municipal solid waste composting facilities exist. There are currently [X number of] municipal solid waste composting facilities across the country." The claim is not deceptive, assuming that composting facilities are available as claimed and the manufacturer can substantiate that the diaper can be converted safely to usable compost in municipal solid waste composting facilities.

Example 7: A manufacturer markets yard waste bags only to consumers residing in particular geographic areas served by county yard waste composting programs. The bags meet specifications for these programs and are labeled, "Compostable Yard Waste Bag for County Composting Programs." The claim is not deceptive. Because the bags are compostable where they are sold, no qualification is required to indicate the limited ability of composting facilities.

4. *Recyclable*: It is deceptive to misrepresent, directly or by implication, that a product or package is recyclable. A product or package should not be marketed as recyclable unless it can be collected, separated, or otherwise recovered from the solid waste stream for use in the form of raw materials in the manufacture or assembly of a new package or product. Unqualified claims of recyclability for a product or package may be made if the entire product or package, excluding minor incidental components, is recyclable. For products or packages that are made of both recyclable and nonrecyclable components, the recyclable claim should be adequately qualified to avoid consumer deception about which portions or components of the product or package are recyclable.

Claims of recyclability should be qualified to the extent necessary to avoid consumer deception about any limited availability of recycling programs and collection sites. If an incidental component significantly limits the ability to recycle the product, the claim would be deceptive. A product or package that is made from recyclable material, but, because of its shape, size, or some other attribute, is not accepted in recycling programs for such material, should not be marketed as recyclable.

Example 1: A packaged product is labeled with an unqualified claim, "recyclable." It is unclear from the type of product and other context whether the claim refers to the product or its package. The unqualified claim is likely to convey to reasonable consumers that all of both the product and its packaging that remain after normal use of the product, except for minor, incidental components, can be recycled. Unless each such claim can be substantiated, the claim should be qualified to indicate what portions are recyclable.

Example 2: A plastic package is labeled on the bottom with the Society of the Plastics Industry (SPI) code, consisting of a design of arrows in a triangular shape containing a number and abbreviation identifying the component plastic resin. Without more, the use of the SPI symbol (or similar industry codes) on the bottom of the package, or in a similarly inconspicuous location, does not constitute a claim of recyclability.

Example 3: A container can be burned in incinerator facilities to produce heat and power. It cannot, however, be recycled into new products or packaging. Any claim that the container is recyclable would be deceptive.

Example 4: A nationally marketed bottle bears the unqualified statement that it is "recyclable." Collection sites for recycling the material in question are not available to a substantial majority of consumers or communities, although collection sites are established in a significant percentage of communities or available to a significant percentage of the population. The unqualified claim is deceptive since, unless evidence shows otherwise, reasonable consumers living in communities not served by programs may conclude that recycling programs for the material are available in their area. To avoid deception, the claim should be qualified to indicate the limited availability of programs, for example, by stating, "Check to see if recycling facilities exist in your area." Other examples of adequate qualifications of the claim include providing the approximate percentage of communities or the population to whom programs are available.

Example 5: A soda bottle is marketed nationally and labeled, "Recyclable where facilities exist." Recycling programs for material of this type and size are available in a significant percentage of communities or to a significant percentage of the population, but are not available to a substantial majority of consumers. The claim is deceptive since, unless evidence shows otherwise, reasonable consumers living in communities not served by programs may understand this phrase to mean that programs are available in their area. To avoid deception, the claim should be further qualified to indicate the limited availability of programs, for example, by using any of the approaches set forth in Example 4 above.

Example 6: A plastic detergent bottle is marketed as follows: "Recyclable in the few communities with facilities for colored HDPE bottles." Collection sites for recycling the container have been established in a half-dozen major metropolitan areas. This disclosure illustrates one approach to qualifying a claim adequately to prevent deception about the limited availability of recycling programs where collection facilities are not established in a significant percentage of communities or available to a significant percentage of the population. Other examples of adequate qualification of the claim include providing the number of communities with programs, or the percentage of communities or the population to which programs are available.

Example 7: A label claims that the package "includes some recyclable material." The package is composed of four layers of different materials, bonded together. One of the layers is made from the recyclable material, but others are not. While programs for recycling this type of material are available to a substantial majority of consumers, only a few of those programs have the capability to separate the recyclable layer. Even though it is technologically possible to separate the layers, the claim is not adequately qualified to avoid consumer deception. An appropriately qualified claim would be, "includes material recyclable in the few communities that collect multi-layer products." Other examples of adequate qualification of the claim include providing the number of communities with programs, or the percentage of communities or the population to which programs are available.

Example 8: A product is marketed as having a "recyclable" container. The product is distributed and advertised only in Missouri. Collection sites for recycling the container are available to a substantial majority of Missouri residents, but are not yet available nationally. Because the programs are generally available where the product is marketed, the unqualified claim does not deceive consumers about the limited availability of recycling programs.

5. *Recycled Content*: A recycled content claim may be made only for materials that have been recovered or otherwise diverted from the solid waste stream, either during the manufacturing process (pre-consumer), or after consumer use (post-consumer). To the extent the source of recycled content includes pre-consumer material, the manufacturer or advertiser must have substantiation for concluding that the pre-consumer material would otherwise have entered the solid waste stream. In asserting a recycled content claim, distinctions may be made between pre-consumer and post-consumer materials. Where such distinctions are asserted, any express or implied claim about the specific pre-consumer or post-consumer content of a product or package must be substantiated.

It is deceptive to misrepresent, directly or by implication, that a product or package is made of recycled material. Unqualified claims of recycled content may be made only if the entire product or package, excluding minor, incidental components, is made from recycled material. For products or packages that are only partially made of recycled material, a recycled claim should be adequately qualified to avoid consumer deception about the amount, by weight, or recycled content in the finished product or package.

Example 1: A manufacturer routinely collects spilled raw material and scraps from trimming finished products. After a minimal amount of reprocessing, the manufacturer combines the spills and scraps with virgin material for use in further production of the same product. A claim that the product contains recycled material is deceptive since the spills and scraps to which the claim refers are normally reused by industry within the original manufacturing process, and would not normally have entered the waste stream.

Example 2: A manufacturer purchases material from a firm that collects discarded material from other manufacturers and resells it. All of the material was diverted from the solid waste stream and is not normally reused by industry within the original manufacturing process. The manufacturer includes the weight of this material in its calculations of the recycled content of its products. A claim of recycled content based on this calculation is not deceptive because, absent the purchase and reuse of this material, it would have entered the waste stream.

Example 3: A greeting card is composed 30% by weight of paper collected from consumers after use of a paper product, and 20% by weight of paper that was generated after completion of the paper-making process, diverted from the solid waste stream, and otherwise would not normally have been reused in the original manufacturing process. The marketer or the card may claim either that the product "contains 50% recycled material," or may identify the specific pre-consumer and /or post-consumer content by stating, for example, that the product "contains 50% total recycled material, 30% of which is post-consumer material."

Example 4: A package with 20% recycled content by weight is labeled as containing "20% recycled paper." Some of the recycled content was composed of material collected from consumers after use of the original product. The rest was composed of overrun newspaper stock never sold to customers. The claim is not deceptive.

Example 5: A product in a multi-component package, such as a paperboard box in a shrink-wrapped plastic cover, indicates that it has recycled packaging. The paperboard box is made entirely of recycled material, but the plastic cover is not. The claim is deceptive since, without qualification, it suggests that both components are recycled. A claim limited to the paperboard box would not be deceptive.

Example 6: A package is made from layers of foil, plastic, and paper laminated together, although the layers are indistinguishable to consumers. The label claims that "one of the three layers of this package is made of recycled plastic." The plastic layer is made entirely of recycled plastic. The claim is not deceptive provided the recycled plastic layer constitutes a significant component of the entire package.

Example 7: A paper product is labeled as containing "100% recycled fiber." The claim is not deceptive if the advertiser can substantiate the conclusion that 100% by weight of the fiber in the finished product is recycled.

Example 8: A frozen dinner is marketed in a package composed of a cardboard box over a plastic tray. The package bears the legend, "package made from 30% recycled material." Each packaging component amounts to one-half the weight of the total package. The box is 20% recycled content by weight, while the plastic tray is 40% recycled content by weight. The claim is not deceptive, since the average amount of recycled material is 30%.

Example 9: A paper greeting card is labeled as containing 50% by weight recycled content. The seller purchases paper stock from several sources and the amount of recycled material in the stock provided by each source varies. Because the 50% figure is based on the annual weighted average of recycled material purchased from the sources after accounting for fiber loss during the production process, the claim is permissible.

6. *Source Reduction*: It is deceptive to misrepresent, directly or by implication, that a product or package has been reduced or is lower in weight, volume, or toxicity. Source reduction claims should be qualified to the extent necessary to avoid consumer deception about the amount of the source reduction and about the basis for any comparison asserted.

Example 1: An ad claims that solid waste created by disposal of the advertiser's packaging is "now 10% less than our previous package." The claim is not deceptive if the advertiser has substantiation that shows that disposal of the correct package contributes 10% less waste by weight or volume to the solid waste stream when compared with the immediately preceding version of the package.

Example 2: An advertiser notes that disposal of its product generates "10% less waste." The claim is ambiguous. Depending on contextual factors, it could be a comparison either to the immediately preceding product or to a competitor's product. The "10% less waste" reference is deceptive unless the seller clarifies which comparison is intended and substantiates that comparison, or substantiates both possible interpretations of the claim.

7. *Refillable*: It is deceptive to misrepresent, directly or by implication, that a package is refillable. An unqualified refillable claim should not be asserted unless a system is provided for: (1) the collection and return of the package for refill; or (2) the later refill of the package by consumers with product subsequently sold in another package. A package should not be marketed with an unqualified refillable claim, if it is up to the consumer to find new ways to refill the package.

Example 1: A container is labeled "refillable x times." The manufacturer has the capacity to refill returned containers and can show that the container will withstand being refilled at least X times. The manufacturer, however, has established no collection program. The unqualified claim is deceptive because there is no means for collection and return of the container to the manufacturer for refill.

Example 2: A bottle of fabric softener states it is in a "handy refillable container." The manufacturer also sells a large-sized container in the same market areas where it sells the small container. The claim is not deceptive because there is a means for consumers to refill the smaller container from larger containers of the same product.

8. *Ozone Safe and Ozone Friendly*: It is deceptive to misrepresent, directly or by implication, that a product is safe or "friendly" to the ozone layer. A claim that a product does not harm the ozone layer is deceptive if the product contains an ozone-depleting substance.

Example 1: A product is labeled "ozone friendly." The claim is deceptive if the product contains any ozone-depleting substance, including those substances listed as Class I or Class II chemicals in Title VI or the Clean Air Act Amendments of 1990, Pub. L No. 101-549, or others subsequently designated by EPA as ozone-depleting substances. Class I chemicals currently listed in Title VI are chlorofluorocarbons (CFCs), halons, carbon tetrachloride, and 1,1,1-trichloroethane. Class II chemicals currently listed in Title VI are hydrochlorofluorocarbons (HCFCs).

Example 2: The seller of an aerosol product makes an unqualified claim that its product "Contains no CFCs." Although the product does not contain CFCs, it does contain HCFC-22, another ozone-depleting ingredient. Because the claim "Contains no CFCs" may imply to reasonable consumers that the product does not harm the ozone layer, the claim is deceptive.

Example 3: A product is labeled "This product is 95% less damaging to the ozone layer than past formulations that contained CFCs." The manufacturer has substituted HCFCs for CFC-12, and can substantiate that this substitution will result in 95% less ozone depletion. The qualified comparative claim is not likely to be deceptive.

QUESTIONS FOR CRITICAL ANALYSIS

- What might have happened to the commercial broadcasting industry if AT&T had decided to keep WEAF and remain in the business of toll broadcasting?
- Critics of toll broadcasting claimed cities should undertake and pay for programs. Would such a plan have been practical?
- Could a tax be imposed on radio and television receivers and would it affect the broadcasting business?
- How might the regulation of broadcasting have been changed if the Supreme Court had ruled differently in *Virginia Pharmacy Board*? In *Valentine* v. *Chrestensen*?
- Do the regulations administered by the FTC and the fact that products can be "tested" provide adequate safeguards against false advertising? Would any additional safeguards withstand a test of constitutionality?
- While the FCC attempts to guard against unscrupulous contests run by broadcasters, the commission has no authority over or, for that matter, knowledge of contests constructed by other businesses that might buy commercial time to publicize such contests. Although a broadcaster is responsible for safeguarding against misleading advertising, many times management simply cannot police the contest of every company or organization buying commercials. In light of this situation, should more stringent FCC rules be enacted to prohibit broadcasters from publicizing on-the-air contests that the station does not conduct?
- Should complete First Amendment protection be given to advertising, thereby letting the consumer decide whether a commercial is an accurate representation of the product or service?
- Stations are prohibited from censoring the content of political ads even if the ads are decep-

tive. Would such a policy work for product advertising? Should the safeguards placed on products also apply to political advertising?

- Should stations be prohibited from accepting advertising which may be illegal in the state of a licensee, but permitted in states where the signal reaches?
- Is the FTC's "tendency to deceive" requirement too strong, or should actual deception be required before an advertisement is considered to run afoul of commission regulations?
- An advertiser may have a wholly innocent intent and still violate the law, according to federal guidelines. Is this requirement too strict, or should advertisers who inadvertently include misstatements of facts in their commercial copy be treated with leniency?
- By assuming that some consumers are ignorant, unthinking, and credulous, are government controls on truthful advertising too strict and should some level of intelligence be assumed when interpreting the rules more liberally?
- Should radio and television stations play a bigger role in monitoring the content of broadcast advertising even to the point of requiring stations to run corrective advertising free of charge if commercials are found to be misleading? Would such a rule be enforceable?
- Should the content of product advertising be restricted when it is directed at a child audience? For example, should commercials for cereal with a certain sugar content be kept off the air?
- Should the government restrict on radio and television advertisements which promote soft drinks with a high sugar or caffeine content? Should these restrictions be imposed only on commercials which are directed at children?
- Network programs frequently air over an entire country. Should the federal government enforce network clipping? Is any state sufficiently able to enforce network clipping or by removing the FCC from the enforcement process has the practice become unenforceable?
- What is the justification for state laws prohibiting the advertising of hard liquor when wine and beer are permitted to be advertised?
- In some states it is possible for restaurants to advertise the price of beer or wine but not brand names. Should restaurants be permitted to advertise price in addition to brand names?
- Calling a beverage Kentucky whiskey when it was made in Tennessee is prohibited. Why do prohibitions exist against generic state references to a product which may be produced in another state?
- If the brand name of potatoes is used in an advertisement, does it make any difference if the advertisement, says "Idaho" potatoes when the potatoes are grown in another state?
- Why in one state would the American flag, the Armed Forces, and athletes be prohibited from associating with alcoholic beverage advertising? One of the justifications for not having the American flag, state flags, or insignias tied to alcoholic beverage advertising is concern that the pictorial representation with a product will suggest endorsement. Is that concern legitimate or is too much protection being afforded the consumer?
- Should regulations exist which prohibit certain types of contests from airing during times when high concentrations of children are in the broadcast audience? What type of contests might be restricted?
- Would an alternative solution be to have the broadcaster investigate every contest publicized on the station to determine if it meets the criteria established by the FCC for contests conducted by broadcasters?
- Should there be regulations prohibiting broadcast publicity for businesses or events where the broadcaster knows a lottery takes place, even though the lottery itself is not publicized on the air? (Examples might be local fraternal lodges, race tracks, picnics, and so on.)
- A station is located in a state where gambling is illegal. Yet the station broadcasts commercials for a casino in a neighboring state, where gambling *is* legal. Since the station is licensed to serve the community where the station is located, should the station be prohibited from publicizing an activity which is illegal in the community it serves?
- With so many state lotteries developing around the United States are the rules prohibiting station-conducted lotteries outdated and should they be repealed?
- Stations have been reprimanded for broadcasting lottery information even when the information has been received in good faith from an advertising agency. Should some leniency be given broadcasters when agencies provide them with commercial copy which may inadvertently violate the FCC prohibitions against broadcasting a lottery?

- The determination of whether a good or service has "value" is a subjective one when enforcing laws concerning payola. Would a regulation be more effective if nothing could be received regardless of its value? Would a regulation be enforceable whereby a limit of say $100 dollars was placed on a gift and anything received of greater value would be considered payola?
- A frequent practice of credit card companies is to issue cards to college students who then run up charges and cannot afford to make payments on the balance. As a result, a student's credit ratings can be ruined for years into the future. Given that credit card companies engage in such practices, should their commercials require a warning to college students and others about the pitfalls of easy credit?
- Few individuals ever go to the trouble of reading the warranty or guarantee associated with most products. One California company advertised a videotape telling the consumer the tape could not be returned for a refund after the packaging seal was broken. What happens to a consumer when the videotape is defective but the purchaser has no way of knowing it is defective until after the seal is broken and the videotape is played? Should the consumer be permitted to return the tape for a complete refund? Is the requirement that the tape is not refundable after the seal is broken legal and enforceable?
- Some citizen groups and government agencies have argued for more controls over television advertising directed toward children. Some of these arguments center on a child's lack of ability to distinguish real from fictional televised situations and on the fact that children have not matured to the point where they are responsible consumers of persuasive campaigns.
- Contests, especially when tied into commercial campaigns, add yet another influence to a child's response to such campaigns. In view of these facts, should controls be placed on contests directed toward children—controls that go beyond current FCC guidelines?
- What issues surface when we attempt to apply theories of First Amendment free speech to "commercial" communication?
- Would it be wise to eliminate all controls on advertising and let the marketplace and the consumer be the ultimate judges of the validity of advertising claims?
- In businesses other than broadcasting, it is not unusual for the stronger of two businesses under the same owner to carry along a weaker business which needs financial help or is operating at a loss. In broadcasting, however, if combination rates are employed by two stations under the same owner, and the stations are not simulcasting, why should the FCC frown on the stronger station "carrying" along the weaker one? What effect would this have on a station's ability to operate in the public interest?
- Noncommercial public broadcasting stations, although not permitted to sell commercials, can obtain grants. When a specific program is made possible by a grant, the donor can be announced at the beginning and at the end of the program. The practice has elicited the ire of some commercial broadcasters, especially when public stations solicit funds from the same sources that commercial stations use to get advertising. The tension between commercial and public broadcasting gets even stronger when public stations heavily promote a program and include the name of the donor in such promotions. Should public broadcasting stations continue to be prohibited from selling advertising? Should such stations be even more restricted and be prohibited from announcing the names of donors at the beginning and end of programs? Are there other alternatives that would better serve both commercial and public broadcasting stations?
- Is the requirement that certification forms be signed by all employees an effective way of controlling special considerations that might be provided by companies who have a special interest in radio or television programming decisions? What additional safeguards could be taken against such abuses?
- Think of the products you use in your everyday life. Are some of these products considered environmentally safe and how might the commercial copy read which advertises the product on radio or television?
- In small markets, commercial copy may not go through the different checks which might occur if it were written at a large-market advertising agency. Should smaller-market radio and television stations be treated more leniently and permitted more flexibility in making environmental claims for their sponsors than stations in larger markets?
- The FTC will review the environmental marketing guidelines in 1995. Do you see any changes or additions in the guidelines which the FTC should take into consideration in amending them?

If a business, not a product, were named "Eco-Safe," would all of the products sold by the company need to be ecologically safe to meet FTC guidelines? Would the company run afoul of the FTC environmental marketing guidelines by airing commercials for their products if the products were not environmentally safe even if they made no environmentally safe claims?

ADDITIONAL RESOURCES

Brown, R., "Ad Hoc Access: The Regulation of Editorial Advertising on Television and Radio." 6 *Yale Law & Policy Review* 449 (1988).

Cherchiglia, D. K., "Changing Channels in Broadcast Regulation: Leaving Television Advertising to Containment by Market Forces." 34 *Case Western Reserve Law Review* 465 (1984).

Feldman, M. B., "Commercial Speech, Transborder Data Flows and the Right to Communicate under International Law." 17 *International Lawyer* 87 (1983).

Goldfarb, R., "Television Advertising: And Now a Word for Our Sponsors." 6 *Loyola Entertainment Law Journal* 256 (1986).

Griffin, R. C., "Broadcast Advertising: What Has It Done to the Audience?" 23 *Washburn Law Journal* 237 (1984).

Welkowitz, D. S., "Smoke in the Air: Commercial Speech and Broadcasting." 7 *Cardozo Law Review* 47 (1985).

Wildman, S. S., "Selecting Advanced Television Standards for the United States: Implications for Trade in Programs and Motion Pictures." 35 *Journal of Broadcasting & Electronic Media* 189 (1991).

Younger, S. "Alcoholic Beverage Advertising on the Airwaves: Alternatives to a Ban or Counteradvertising." 34 *UCLA Law Review* 1139 (1987).

chapter nine

Broadcast Operations

From the moment the idea for a new station is conceived, the managers and owners begin operating in a legal environment. At the core of that legal environment is the limited spectrum space available to operate radio and television stations. This legal environment is different than that which exists for newspapers. If the economy and population base can support them, any number of newspapers can be started in a local community without restriction. Not only will the newspapers enjoy immunity from most federal regulations, they will not be required to have a construction permit before beginning to publish, nor will there be restrictions on distributing the newspaper, such as being told where in town they may be published. Such areas as engineering data, their financial qualifications, and their commitment to minority hiring will not be under the watchful eye of the federal government. The newspapers can operate for as many years as they can remain profitable without being required to serve the public interest, face license renewals, or license challenges. It will not be necessary also for them to retain public inspection files which can be accessed by the public as well as federal inspectors who make unannounced visits.

For owners and managers of radio and television stations, the legal atmosphere in which they do business is complex and broad. Because the electromagnetic spectrum is a limited resource, they first face must apply for permission to use that limited resource. Whether or not they are granted permission to go on the air will be determined by such factors as the station's power, the contour or geographic area over which the station will broadcast, whether the station will be AM, FM, or television, and whether or not the station is commercial or noncommercial. Regulations differ between commercial and noncommercial stations. Approval of financial qualifications and commitment to affirmative action including the approval of a strategic plan to assure minority representation in employment is necessary before a station can operate. In any given day the broadcast manager will be confronted with all of the issues we have just discussed including ancillary issues such as employment, personnel, taxes, and other matters. From time to time managers may find themselves embroiled in issues which will demand specialized legal counsel. In this chapter we examine the legal and regulatory issues which impact on broadcast operations.

THE SPECTRUM AND FCC APPLICATION PROCEDURES

The law permits any qualified person, group, or company to apply to the FCC to construct an AM, FM, or TV station. The key is to find an available frequency and then be able to claim the frequency, sometimes in the face of opposition from competing applications. To better understand the process, for the uninitiated, a basic primer on frequencies and frequency assignments is necessary.[1] While at one time simply knowing about AM broadcasting frequencies was sufficient, today broadcasting is more complex. A broadcast manager may be responsible for an AM, FM, TV operation with satellite downlinks and uplinks all operating on different frequencies, with ndifferent legal requirements governing the construction and operation of such facilities.

A Spectrum Primer

All broadcasting stations operate at a given frequency on the electromagnetic spectrum. Historically, the spectrum has been an arena of contentious battling for space. Today, those early squabbles of the 1920s seem insignificant compared to the many stations and services that compete for space on the spectrum. In addition to domestic services of any one country, other countries compete for the same spectrum space. The spectrum itself can be compared to an electronic yardstick. At the low end of the yardstick is where radio waves are found, at the high end is light. In between we place communication services ranging from radio stations to fiber-optic communication. The FCC allocates space on the spectrum so that stations will not interfere with each other. When current is applied to a station transmitter it radiates electromagnetic energy into the atmosphere, much like ripples on a pond that emerge when a rock hits the water. The number of ripples on the surface of the pond could be counted. Using sophisticated equipment, we are able to theoretically count the number of electromagnetic waves that pass a given point every second. This theoretical counting process determines the frequency on which the station is broadcasting. The distance between waves is the wavelength, whether in the pond or in the atmosphere.

When one complete wave passes a given point it is called a *hertz* in honor of physics pioneer Henrich Hertz. One thousand hertz per second is called *hertz per second*, abbreviated as kHz. One million hertz per second is called a *megahertz* and abbreviated as MHz. By understanding hertz we can compute frequency. For example, 540,000 hertz per second is referred to as 540 kilohertz. On the lower end of your AM radio dial, this is the 540 position.

Waves are modulated in different ways. For example, AM broadcasting changes the range of the wave or its amplitude, thus the term *amplitude modulation* (AM). The frequency of the wave, not its amplitude, is changed in FM broadcasting, thus the term *frequency modulation* (FM). Television uses radio waves to transmit both the video and audio portion of the picture. The paths waves travel differ. Waves at the low end of the electromagnetic spectrum where AM broadcasting is found travel upward and bounce off the ionosphere. Other waves follow the contour of the ground and are called ground waves. Ground waves are found relatively close to the transmitting tower. At the higher frequencies, waves travel in a straight line or line-of-site. FM stations operate at a frequency where line-of-site broadcasting occurs.

The area in the 10,000 hertz range is the lowest frequency normally used for radio communication. From there upward that spectrum is sometime referred to as being divided into long waves, short waves, and microwaves. Other common divisions are referred to as VLF or the very low-frequency range consisting of that area below 30 kilohertz; LF or the low-frequency range between 30 to 300 kilohertz; MF or medium-frequency range from 300 kilohertz to 3 megahertz; HF or high-frequency from 3 to 30 megahertz; VHF or very-high frequency range between 30 to 300 megahertz; and UHF or ultrahigh-frequency between 300 to 3000 megahertz. A gigahertz is equivalent to 1,000 megahertz, and the range between 3 to 30 gigahertz is referred to as SHF or superhigh frequency. EHF or extremely high frequency ranges from 30 to 300 gigahertz. Gigahertz frequencies are where microwaves are found and such technologies as satellite communication operate in the gigahertz range.

Allocating Frequencies

The spectrum is divided into bands of frequencies. Within each band are primary and secondary applications. Secondary stations cannot interfere with primary service stations nor are secondary service stations protected from interference by primary service stations. Frequency allocations within a particular band are divided up among different types of users. For example, one band may belong to amateur radio, mobile service, and cellular telephone. Frequency assignments are the final subcategory of the different bands. The band historically used for AM radio has frequency assignments beginning at 540 kilohertz ranging up to

1600 kilohertz. Because an AM radio station needs only 10 kilohertz of operating space, 106 frequencies are available.[2] The FM band is divided into 100 assignments between 88.1 and 107.9 MHz. The frequency range of 88.1 to 91.9 MHz is reserved for noncommercial educational FM stations. To help understand how large the spectrum is, consider that the space occupied by AM broadcasting is 1/40,000 of the spectrum. Already there is fierce competition for every bit of useable spectrum space.

The Frequency Selection and Assignment Process

Any applicant for a broadcasting station would be well served to hire competent legal and engineering counsel unless the applicant possesses those skills and is certified accordingly. Even a simple unintentional technical or legal error can slow an application down for months or years and can open the applicant up to challenges. Once the decision to build a station is made, a consulting engineer must locate an available frequency or the applicant can select an available frequency from the FCC Table of Allotments.

Radio stations are designated on a "channel" basis. AM radio stations operate on clear, regional, and local channels. Clear channel stations are the high-powered stations serving wide areas of the country, and many have been operating since the early days of commercial radio. Local channels are assigned to lower-powered stations serving smaller communities. The Class I clear channel stations operate at a maximum power of 50,000 watts, secondary clear channel Class II stations operate between power levels of 250 and 50,000 watts. Many operate as daytime only stations, but applications for daytime only stations are no longer being accepted. Stations operating on regional channels operate at power levels between 250 and 5,000 watts except in Alaska, Hawaii, and Puerto Rico, where the maximum power permitted is 50,000 watts. Remaining frequencies exist for local channels operating with no more than 1,000 watts day and night.

An applicant for an FM station must locate an unused frequency in the area the applicant wants to serve. Remember that FM stations operate at frequencies where radio waves travel in a line-of-site. Tower height and terrain play a big part in determining how wide an area can be served. Here the FCC Table of Allotments is helpful. If no frequency is available on the Table of Allotments, an applicant can hire a consulting engineer to locate a frequency and petition the FCC to place it on the Table of Allotments. If the frequency is approved and added to the table, a filing period for the new frequency is established by the FCC, and any qualified applicant can apply. Six classes of commercial FM stations are available for frequency assignments ranging from a minimum power of 100 watts up to a maximum power of 100,000 watts. Because line-of-site is involved, and interference is less of a problem than it is on the AM frequencies, many FM stations operate at maximum power.

Like FM stations, TV applicants must locate an unused channel. Channels 2 through 13 are VHF channels and channels 14 through 69 are UHF channels. One can also apply to operate a television translator or a low-power television (LPTV) station. A translator station rebroadcasts signals from full-service stations. LPTV stations can also rebroadcast full-service stations, can originate their own programming, or operate as a subscription service. Any available channel can be assigned to translator or LPTV stations as long they do not interfere with other television stations.

General and Legal Requirements of the Application

The application for permission to construct a commercial broadcast station (construction must precede the application for a license to operate a station) is prepared on Form 301. (Other forms are used for licensing a station, license renewal, and the transfer of ownership). Form 301 requests information in seven areas: general information, legal qualifications, financial qualifications, program service statement, engineering data and antenna and site information, equal employment opportunity program, and certifications. Other requirements include a public notice requirement, wherein advertisements and announcements are made permitting others to comment on the application, and, if serious in their opposition, challenge the application.

The general information and legal qualifications sections request basic information, such as the name of the applicant, the type of station being applied for, the frequency being requested, and the location of the station. The FCC also wants to know if the applicant is an individual or some other entity such as a general partnership, limited partnership, or corporation. Partnerships and corporate applicants are required to provide more detailed information, and certain restrictions exist pertaining to who can own stock in the company. An alien, representative of an alien, or a foreign government or representative thereof cannot be licensed to operate a broadcasting station in the United States. Interest in other media properties is additional information that must be divulged in the application. An applicant must explain the citizenship of each shareholder. In the case of corporations, this can be reported as percentages determined by a sample survey using recognized statistical methods. In almost every case where husband and wife are applicants, both must meet the qualifications.

Preference to Minority Applicants

The courts have sent conflicting signals to applicants on whether women and minorities should have some preference in awarding licenses to competing applicants. In 1992 the U.S. Court of Appeals for the District of Columbia ruled in a 2-1 decision that an FCC decision to award a woman applicant ownership of a Maryland radio station in a contested proceeding with a male applicant was reverse discrimination and therefore unconstitutional.[3] The case drew publicity since the decision was written by Supreme Court Judge Clarence Thomas who had been serving on the appeals court when the case arose. The issue of sex discrimination and sexual harassment was a key issue during the Supreme Court confirmation hearings of Judge Thomas and the decision in the Maryland case drew fire from citizens' groups such as the Women's Legal Defense Fund which opposed Judge Thomas's confirmation to the Supreme Court. In addition, the court of appeals' 1992 ruling seemed to conflict in part with a Supreme Court decision in 1990 which supported preference to women and minorities in the awarding of station license, a point noted in the dissenting opinion of the appeals court judge. The issue remains unresolved, although there is some indication that the 1992 appeals court case focused on women only and the failure of the FCC to prove a link between women in positions of ownership and increased programming diversity.

Special Problems in Meeting Financial Qualifications

Financial qualifications demand that the applicant be financially able to operate the station, even during the early stages of operation when the station will suffer a loss due to a lack of advertising revenues. Financial qualifications of an applicant also come into play when a station is being purchased. In an application for a construction permit, the applicant must show sufficient liquid assets to construct the facility and operate it for three months without revenue. The commission cautions applicants that it is not the practice of the FCC to extend the time allotted for construction based on the inability of the applicant to meet financial obligations.

Potential pitfalls can also exist when financing a broadcast transaction.[4] Bank financing is sometimes difficult to obtain. In some communities, bankers may not know very much about the broadcasting industry and may shy away from taking a risk in a business of which they are skeptical. Even large national banks have moved their financing away from broadcasting, letting a few specialized banks with broadcasting expertise handle the risk. Bank examiners who must judge loans on the basis of collateral, cash flow, and stability sometimes have a difficult time interpreting the financial structure of a broadcast business. It is typically influenced by rating swings affected by such factors as the popularity of disc jockeys, news anchors, and fall lineups.

What many consider to be one of a station's most valuable assets, the station license, cannot be used as collateral for the repayment of a loan.[5] Stations must be responsive to their communities, not their creditors, reasons the FCC. In addition, bankers like collateral they can see such as land, trucks, buildings, and other assets that can be liquidated. Getting commitment for loans can also be difficult, since banks can have a problem time seeing the tangible result of a building and a tower. While they will issue a letter saying they are interested in financing the station, that's not good enough for the FCC. A definite legal agreement or assurance of liquid assets is necessary to meet the FCC's financial qualifications.

Because much of a station's overall worth is determined by billings, relations with the community, and relations with advertisers, and not just physical property, the financing package can be complex. Since a broadcast property cannot be transferred without FCC approval, selling the new station if it runs into financial problems can be difficult, especially if the station is involved in a bankruptcy action. In summary, applicants must have sufficient financial backing to be able to meet the FCC's expectations, and the bigger the property the bigger the financial pledge necessary to operate. While a three-month limit for a construction permit does not seem very long, any sensible applicant will have much more in liquid assets than what is necessary to operate for three months.

Required Engineering Data

A consulting engineer will determine what frequency is available or the Table of Allotments will be used to determine on what frequency the station will operate. The contour of the proposed signal will be included with the application, as will detailed information concerning geological surveys and environmental impact statements when necessary. An environmental impact study can be triggered when the station will be located in sensitive areas such as a wilderness area, a wildlife preserve, a flood plain, or when the station facilities will visually affect sites that are significant in American history.[6] High-intensity lights in residential neighborhoods can cause problems, as can exposure to low-level radiation emanating from the station transmitter.[7] Any involvement or requirements that must be met by local and state governments, such as zoning restrictions, must be detailed in the application under the engineering data section. For example, a radio station is a business, and as such can usually not be operated in an area zoned for residential-only dwellings unless an exception is granted by the government agency with authority over the zoned area.

Equal Employment and Certification Requirements

An equal employment model program must be filed with the application, although it is not as extensive as the program filed with license renewal. Any station proposing to employ more than five employees must file such a program and it must assure employment to women and minorities based on their representation in the community. The certification requirements concern the public notice which must be published and/or announced to the public. Certification that such dissemination takes place is made during the application process. Such items as contracts covering the purchase of a suitable transmitter site must accompany the application. While the site need not be purchased, assurance is necessary that the site will be obtainable if the application is approved.

In summary, completeness and honesty are prerequisites in completing an FCC application, whether to construct a new station, to transfer ownership of an existing station, or to change the site or facilities of an existing station.

CALL LETTER ASSIGNMENTS

Through international agreements, the FCC assigns call letters to domestic stations using the prefixes W, K, N, and A.[8] The United States has exclusive use of W, K, and N, but shares A with some other countries. Radio and television stations broadcasting to the general public get the K and W signs with the Ks going to stations west of the Mississippi River and Ws going to stations east of the Mississippi. A few exceptions exist, such as KYW in Philadelphia, Pennsylvania and KDKA in Pittsburgh, Pennsylvania. Other stations also get the W and K signs, such as those licensed to amateur radio operators. Both were operating before east and west designations went into force and they have kept their call letters. The Army and the Air Force, for example, are assigned the A prefix for their stations and the Navy and Coast Guard stations are assigned the N prefix. Call letters identify the nationality of a station, the type of station, and the specific station itself. Thus, KORN identifies the station as an American station broadcasting west of the Mississippi River. By checking a directory we can determine the frequency, power, and location of the station, which in the case of KORN is Mitchell, South Dakota.

To the stations that own them call letters are much more than just identifications. For amateur radio operators, for example, coveted call signs are those that contain a combination of letters making it easy to send Morse code. For commercial broadcasting stations, call letters can become important logos. History is rich with famous call letters and their slogans. For example, consider the following, some of which are no longer in use: WGN, Chicago, "World's Greatest Newspaper"; WCFL, Chicago, "Chicago Federation of Labor"; WGCD, Chester, South Carolina, "Wonderful Guernsey Center of Dixie"; and KABL in San Francisco representing San Francisco's "cable" cars.[9]

CALL LETTER DISPUTES

Stations can get federal service mark registrations for their call letters, helping to protect the call letters from infringement. The importance of the registered trademarks can be seen in disputes that must be resolved by the courts when stations come too close to infringing on each other's call letters. The FCC will assign a call letter to a station and let the state courts settle any infringement disputes. Two stations in Delaware litigated a dispute after the call letters on one station, even though it was assigned by the FCC, sounded too much like another station in the same market.[10] In the Delaware case, WBOT-TV and WBOC-TV were assigned to the same market. WBOC-TV had operated for more than 30 years in the market and spent large sums of money on advertising and promoting its call letters. WBOT-TV, on the other hand, wanted to use the call letters in conjunction with a slogan "We've got the best of times," to inform the public that it has reruns from the "best" era television movies. The case is interesting partly because of the testimony of a linguistics expert that showed how serious and important call letters are to a station, and partly because the judge identified the market as "call-letter" oriented because of the multitude of cable operators who determine what channel a station will appear on in any particular cable system.[11] Stations with call letters that are well promoted, well integrated into their marketing strategy, and to which large sums of money have been committed may want to consider registering the station call letters as a trademark.

LICENSE RENEWAL

Radio station licenses must be renewed every seven years, television station licenses every five years. The author of this text, when general manager of an FM radio station, took the station through three license renewal processes. Although all of the renewals were granted without any difficulty, some observations emerged which still remain vivid. The most important is planning. Waiting until license renewal time to find that operating practices and procedures have been neglected is serious and cannot be corrected. This is especially true where minority hiring is concerned. Equally important is the regular care and maintenance of facilities. Completing exhibits at the last minute is negligent and can be costly. Know the forms, know the process, know the obligations, and operate as though license renewal was an annual requirement. To some extent it is, since many annual reporting requirements must be certified as part of the renewal process.

License renewal requirements differ between radio stations and television stations. The FCC uses a postcard form for license renewal, but FCC inspectors periodically make unannounced visits to stations to determine if they are meeting their obligations in such areas as the completeness of the public inspection file. Regardless of the type of station involved, all stations must meet certain basic requirements such as equal employment guidelines. In addition, the station must certify that its annual employment reports, the ownership report, certification of interest in the station by foreign governments, and explanation of any adverse findings against the station by the courts or other administrative bodies are included in the file. As to adverse findings, the license renewal application must report

> judgements or decrees, including settlement, consent, and like agreements, where the misconduct occurred either in the operation of the station for which renewal is requested or in the conduct of the other broadcast and non-broadcast activities of the renewal applicant and parties to the application, such as all partners and all corporate officers, directors, and stockholders with a 10% or more ownership interest in the applicant.[12]

The station must certify that the public inspection file is up to date and that it contains the required documents. This encompasses such information as discussed earlier, including a copy of the last license renewal application, any change in the control of the station since the last renewal, the ownership and employment reports, annual lists of local problems, and the responsive programming which was broadcast to meet the problems.[13] Meeting the programming requirement is especially important, since any presumption of renewal is lost in a comparative hearing if the station has been negligent in meeting the needs of the community.

PETITIONS TO DENY IN APPLICATION PROCEEDINGS

Whether it is a license renewal, an application for a construction permit, or a transfer of station ownership, the right to petition the FCC to deny an application is afforded to anyone. When a petition to deny or a competing application is filed, the FCC schedules a hearing on the matter to be heard by an administrative law judge. A public notice of the hearing is made and applicants can amend the application with additional information but cannot use the process to strengthen an already filed application. After the hearing where the administrative law judge listens to evidence in the case, an initial decision is issued and is reviewed by the

FCC Review Board or the full Commission. The commission or the review board can hear arguments in the case and can modify or even reverse the decision of the administrative law judge. The final decision of the commission can also be appealed to the appeals court for the District of Columbia.

LEASING OTHER STATIONS' FACILITIES

Although stations are assigned call letters and a frequency by the FCC, certain circumstances permit stations to share each other's facilities. For example, when a Raleigh, North Carolina television station's tower collapsed in an ice storm, it arranged for its signal to be carried by a nearby television station licensed to Fayetteville, North Carolina. The Fayetteville station, not nearly as profitable as its Raleigh counterpart, and operating on a UHF frequency, saw the opportunity to gain some much needed income by leasing its channel to the Raleigh station.[14] The arrangement permitted the Raleigh station, operating at reduced power, to continue to operate on its normally assigned channel but also to have its programming carried on another channel in nearby Fayetteville. The relationship worked, except that the Raleigh station had double programming on some area cable systems that had carried both the Raleigh and Fayetteville stations. It was this dual exposure that caused a third competing station in Durham, North Carolina, to file a complaint against the Raleigh and Fayetteville stations after the Raleigh station began operating from its new tower. The Durham station complained that it wanted the stations on an equal playing field. The Raleigh station complained that the Durham action was motivated by competitive considerations since a ratings period was involved. Eventually the matter was resolved, but it demonstrates how stations must be keenly aware of the impact of their operating policies on their competition, and how a station must be prepared to respond to complaints from competing stations.

EQUAL EMPLOYMENT OPPORTUNITY PROGRAMS

The federal government's support for women and minorities to be well represented in the work force has been implemented by the Equal Employment Opportunity Commission and the requirement that affirmative-action measures be taken by business and industry throughout the United States. The FCC is one of the most aggressive agencies in enforcing affirmative action. The FCC has entered into a Memorandum of Understanding with the U.S. Equal Employment Opportunity Commission (EEOC) and shares information with the EEOC on equal employment matters. Specific charges against the station can be directed to either the FCC or a regional office of the EEOC. The FCC requires stations with more than five employees to file annual employment reports which must also be kept in the public inspection file. Simply having enough minorities on staff is not sufficient compliance. A station must apply affirmative action and equal employment opportunities to every job opening. Minimum standards that must be met include having a percentage of minorities in the top four job categories equal to half the percentage of minorities in the market. If, for example, 60 percent of a station's market consists of Native Americans, then the top four job categories (officials and managers, professionals, technicians, sales workers) in the station should have 30 percent Native Americans. Although stations with less than five employees are not required to have an affirmative action and equal employment opportunity program in writing, they are not exempt from complaints. Having a plan in place, regardless of the number of employees, is good protection. Having as few as 5 percent minorities in a market is enough to warrant meeting affirmative action hiring requirements.

As noted previously, the four top job categories are officials and managers, professionals, technicians, and people working in sales. The FCC's description of these top categories are as follows:

> *Officials and Managers*—Occupations requiring administrative personnel who set broad policies, exercise overall responsibility for execution of these policies, and direct individual departments or special phases of a firm's operations. Includes: Presidents and other corporate officers, general managers, station managers, controllers, chief accountants, general counsels, chief engineers, facilities managers, sales managers, business managers, promotion directors, research directors, personnel managers, news directors, operations managers, and production managers.
>
> *Professionals*—Occupations requiring either college graduation or experience of such a kind and amount as to provide a comparable

background. Includes: On-air personnel, correspondents, producers, writers, editors, researchers, designers, artists, musicians, dancers, accountants, attorneys, nurses, publicists, film buyers, rating and research analysts, systems analysts and programmers, financial analysts, state managers, cinema photographers, senior staff assistants, personnel interviewers, and continuity directors.

Technicians—Occupations requiring a combination of basic scientific knowledge and manual skill which can be obtained through about two years of post high school education, such as is offered in many technical institutes and junior colleges, or through equivalent on-the-job training. Includes: Engineers, technicians and engineering aides, transmitter, studio maintenance and master control engineers, and news camera, news sound, film lab and drafting technicians. Film editors, projectionists, and software specialists also fall into this category.

Sales—Occupations engaging wholly or primarily in direct selling. Includes: Sales account executives, sales analysts, account representatives, and sales trainees.[15]

Although the Federal Communications Commission delegates some enforcement of affirmative action to the EEOC, the FCC has taken steps to assure that broadcasting stations do not fall behind in their commitments to affirmative action.[16] By using the public-interest clause of the Communications Act, the FCC is able to put some teeth into its requirements. Its power is based on the rationale that, according to the FCC, a "broadcaster who refuses to hire minority and women employees will face a difficult, if not insurmountable obstacle to the presentation of programming to meet the problems, needs and interests of minorities and women." Although some reporting requirements for EEO compliance have been modified, many stations adhere to a model plan adopted by the FCC. It provides a good safeguard when affirmative action policies of a station are called into question by the EEOC or an employee.

THE AFFIRMATIVE ACTION PLAN

Stations can take a number of steps to help assure a successful affirmative action plan. Assume we are managing a television station in a medium-size market. Following are some safeguards that can help to assure compliance with affirmative action and equal employment opportunity programs. Requirements differ somewhat among different-size stations, and whether a station is on the air or a prospective owner is applying for permission to buy or operate a station. Some elements are part of the plan itself and other elements are necessary for the record keeping required by the FCC.

Statement of General Policy.
The first part of our program would consist of a statement committing the station to affirmative action in all areas of station business, which would include not only hiring employees but also promoting, compensating, and terminating them. Take note of the word *terminating*—if we aren't going to discriminate in hiring, then we can't discriminate in firing. Overall, the program must be a positive effort, assuring equal opportunity without regard to sex, race, national origin, color, or religion.

Responsibility for Implementation. Our next responsibility would be to implement our commitment. We would want to appoint someone at the station as our affirmative action administrator. If we have delegated the responsibility for firing and hiring to other administrators, then we will want to make sure that they also adhere to our commitment.

Policy Dissemination. But it is not enough merely to have an affirmative action program. We need to publicize it through such means as posters that tell applicants and employees where to write if they feel they have been discriminated against. The Department of Labor has posters available that contain such warnings. We could also put an affirmative action statement on the station's employment application.

Recruitment. Hiring is usually the easiest task in an affirmative action program. What takes work is obtaining a pool of applicants from which to choose. We will need to recruit people by advertising our job openings. In each ad, we will want to include a statement identifying our station as an equal opportunity employer. Potential women applicants can be reached via ads in newsletters; minorities can be reached through similar publications. Employment agencies and the placement services at local colleges are two additional avenues. Good referral sources are better than sources that rarely send the names of prospective applicants. Some broadcast managers recommend cutting off a service if it doesn't provide any applicant leads over a six-month period.[17]

Job Hires. We will want to keep track of women and minority employees hired in the past 12 months. If, in our opinion, not enough minority applicants are applying for positions, we will want to explain how we are going to improve our recruiting practices in the future.

Promotion. A responsible affirmative action program deals not only with hiring but with promotion. When openings develop within our organization, we should scan the current personnel to see who might be qualified for the jobs. If we find them, reward them. Visible opportunities for upward mobility of highly qualified people increase station morale. We would want to encourage women and minority employees to apply for advancement within the organization and keep a record of these promotions.

Training. If our station is small, developing a full-scale minority training program may be difficult. On the other hand, an internship program initiated with a local college can at least show a good-faith effort within our means.

Availability Survey. In order to compare the success of our program with the work force in our local area, we will need a recent availability survey. Such a survey discusses the percentages of women and minorities in the work force from which we can directly recruit—usually the metropolitan area in which the station is licensed or, in some cases, the county in which it is located.

Current Employment Survey. We would want to keep track of the number of women and members of minority groups employed by the station, and how many are in top management positions. We can supplement the information with a description of women and minority employees in all job classifications within the station.

The FCC requires the inclusion of statistical information in annual reports to the commission that detail the full-time and part-time employment statistics for the station. The FCC permits the station to tabulate data on annual reporting forms through the following minority identification measures. In this example, these measures are used to complete the minority identification section of FCC Form 395-B, the Broadcast Station Annual Employment Report.

> a. Minority group information necessary for this section may be obtained either by visual surveys of the work force, or from postemployment records. An employee may be included in the minority group to which she or he appears to belong or is regarded in the community as belonging.
>
> b. Since visual surveys are permitted, the fact that minority group identifications are not present on the company records is not an excuse for failure to provide the data called for.
>
> c. Conducting a visual survey and keeping postemployment records of the race or ethnic origin of employees is legal in all jurisdictions and under all federal and state laws. State laws prohibiting inquiries and record keeping as to race, etc., relate only to applicants for jobs, not to employees.
>
> d. FCC Form 395-B provides for reporting American Indians or Alaskan Natives; Asians or Pacific Islanders; Blacks, not of Hispanic Origin; Hispanics; and Whites, not of Hispanic origin, whenever such persons are employed. The category that most closely reflects the individual's recognition in his community should be used to report persons of mixed racial and/or ethnic origins.[18]

Effectiveness of the Affirmative Action Plan. Having an affirmative action plan is important but equally important is an evaluation of the plan's effectiveness. A periodic review every few months is necessary to ensure that the plan is meeting its goals. Meetings between management and the person responsible for administering the plan, or with supervisors charged with implementing it, are necessary to assure the plan's success.

Complaints and Special Problems. Stations need to keep a record of any complaints they have received about employment practices and an assessment of how effective the affirmative action plan is. For example, making an improvement in the plan and documenting the improvement is necessary to insure that the plan is effective and up to date. Periodic review of the program is mandatory good management practice.

AMENDMENTS TO EEO RULES UNDER THE 1992 CABLE ACT

Amendments to the equal employment opportunity requirements for both broadcasting and cable systems went into effect with the passage of the Cable Television Consumer Protection and Competition Act of 1992. As a preface to an inquiry into new EEO rules the law read: The Congress finds that

> (1) despite the existence of regulations governing equal employment opportunity, females and minorities are not employed in significant numbers in positions of management authority in the cable and broadcast television industries; (2) increase numbers of females and minorities in positions of management authority in the cable and broadcast television industries advances the Nation's policy favoring diversity and the expression of views in the electronic media; (3) rigorous enforcement of equal employment opportunity rules and regulations is required in order to effectively deter racial and gender discrimination."[19]

The act requires that the FCC prescribe revisions in the rules designed to promote equality of employment opportunities for females and minorities in a new set of job categories which includes both full-time and part-time employees. Stations and cable systems with more than five full-time employees are required to file with the commission, under the new annual statistical reports, statistical information by race sex and job title under the following:

- Corporate officers
- General manager
- Chief technician
- Comptroller
- General sales manager
- Production manager
- Managers
- Professionals
- Technicians
- Sales personnel
- Office and clerical personnel
- Skillcraft persons
- Semiskilled operatives
- Unskilled laborers
- Service workers[20]

In addition to the job categories, the 1992 legislation required the commission to revise regulations and require a midterm review of television broadcast station licensees' employment practices and at the midterm review notify the licensees of necessary improvements in recruitment practices that might be needed. In addition the 1992 legislation required the FCC within two years to conduct a review to consider:

> the effectiveness of its procedures, regulations, policies, standards, and guidelines in promoting equality of employment opportunity and promotion opportunity, and particularly the effectiveness of its procedures, regulations, policies, standards, and guidelines in promoting the congressional policy favoring increased employment opportunity for women and minorities in positions of management authority.[21]

AFFIRMATIVE ACTION CONSIDERATIONS IN HIRING PROCEDURES

To ensure a pool of applicants, advertisements are necessary. The wording of such advertisements would avoid statements that infer discrimination of any kind. The most obvious references are to age, sex, religion, race, or national origin. We will examine in our discussion of job interviewing how such references must also be avoided in questions asked of prospective employees. Statements that the station is an "affirmative action, equal opportunity employer" or similar phrasing can help make the commitment to affirmative action more conspicuous. Job applications should also be free of questions that could infer discrimination. Once the position is advertised, any procedure for selection of the candidate, such as contacting all applicants to be interviewed, or not considering tapes, must be adhered to rigorously to assure the integrity of the selection process. If selection procedures are spelled out in the advertisement and not followed, the station has little defense against a complaint.

Employment Interviews

Equally important to what appears in an advertisement or application is what is said during an employment interview. The National Association of Broadcasters in their *Broadcaster's Guide to Designing and Implementing an Effective*

EEO Program lists sensitive areas where interviewers can run afoul of EEO compliance.[22] The following paragraphs discuss some of these.

The most common pitfalls and the ones we hear the most about are interview questions dealing with age, sex, religion, and race. Any discrimination based on these factors is against the law. Questions that try to determine a person's age are not acceptable unless it can be shown that a person's age is a bona fide requirement for the job. That may be difficult to prove even if it is thought to be true. After individuals come to work, their personnel file can list their age but it cannot be a requirement for pre-employment inquiries. Making a person's sex an issue in hiring is illegal as well. The best advice is to not even allude to a question that might infer sex discrimination. Closely related topics can also cause problems. For example, the refusal to hire a woman solely because she is pregnant is sex discrimination. It is against the law to discriminate against a person because of their religion. If a person's religious beliefs prevent that individual from working on weekends, this cannot be used as a reason not to him or her. Any question about a person's race or color should be avoided.

Other questions may be more general but still should not be asked to avoid unintentional discrimination. For example, questions about a person's physical characteristics can cause problems. Questions should be avoided that suggest a weight or height requirement not affecting a person's ability to do the job. Remember, it would be difficult to prove a certain height or weight would be a requirement for employment. While an employer may ask if a person has a specific handicap that might affect a given job, broad questions such as "do you have any handicaps" should be avoided.

Other general questions about a person's background should be avoided. For example, a certain group of people, based on sex, race, national origin, or even family circumstances, may as a group have lower than average incomes. As a result, station management may be concerned that if they hire such an individual that person may leave bad debts all over town and embarrass the station. Consequently, station management asks questions about charge accounts, credit ratings, and other personal information. This suggests outright discrimination and prejudice, not because of the person's credit, but because of the socioeconomic group he or she belongs to—a group whose identity is primarily based on such things as sex, age, religion, race, or some other category. Having a prejudice against unwed mothers because you feel they will embarrass your station by not paying their bills may find you in court. Such a prejudice represents sex discrimination and may be easily proved by the testimony of the unwed mother who was asked the questions. Similarly, questions about an applicant's family status or relatives should be avoided with the exception of asking the names of relatives who may already work for the station. Some stations have policies against hiring relatives, although such policies can be unlawful if they prevent a station from meeting its affirmative action obligations.

Other areas of questioning beyond those discussed here can cause problems. Employers should be alert not only to the obvious questions to avoid but should also be sensitive to areas of questioning that might infer discrimination in employment interviews.

Special Problems in Administering Internship Programs

Internship programs can in some instances be viewed as an extension of the station's affirmative action plan, and problems can develop if the internship program is not handled properly. For example, by delegating responsibility for the selection of interns to a college or university, a station does not absolve itself of responsibility for affirmative action. If the college only recommends nonminorities to the internship program, and the internship program itself is void of minorities in a community where there is substantial minority representation in the population, then the program can become a liability to the station. Similarly, if a station has all minorities in its internship program but does not meet the minority hiring requirements in the station's full-time job categories, then the station can still become the target for review by the FCC or a possible target of a complaint. In addition, the station should remain alert to the possibility that interns may not be viewed as equivalent to full-time employees with significant responsibilities. An internship program may not therefore make up for deficient minority representation in other areas of the station.

If the station is involved in the selection of interns, care must be taken to ensure fairness and procedural integrity. For example, assume a station advertises a paid, 40-hour per week "internship" and asks local colleges to recommend two people as candidates. The station indicates in its job listing that the station will contact those people it wants to invite for personal interviews. By stating the station will contact the candidates it wants to interview, it assumes an affirmative responsibility to adhere to its own selection process. For example, if some of the students who are not recommended by their colleges don't wait to be contacted by the station and muscle their way in for interviews, the integrity of the selection procedures can be compromised. The people interviewed become part of the pool of candidates. The station would have a difficult time defending itself against charges of favoritism if one of the more aggressive candidates was selected for the internship when other students were not interviewed. A candidate who was not selected might feel the selection process unfair. Terms of employment can also raise issues. For example, if a station advertises a rotating internship program for a strict specific time period, say three months, and then extends the time an intern is employed, that may prevent other students from applying.

Management cannot afford to take internship programs lightly. If the program is not managed well, the college or university may sever its relationship with the station. In an economic climate where jobs are scarce the stakes are high, and tensions can run high as well. Unexpected problems can develop when people on the front line of the station's selection process have not been trained properly.

SEXUAL HARASSMENT

Broadcasters are becoming increasingly aware of the effects of sexual harassment both on individuals and on the operation of broadcasting stations. Sexual harassment can be viewed as a violation of civil rights law. What exactly constitutes sexual harassment is something which must be determined by the circumstances surrounding each incident. Moreover, because such incidents often occur in private, the testimony of the plaintiff and the defendant without the benefit of other witnesses makes the sexual harassment area of discrimination law particularly difficult to determine.

What Constitutes Sexual Harassment

The Equal Employment Opportunity Commission considers unlawful sexual harassment to occur:

> (1) When submission to such sexual conduct is "explicitly or implicitly" a condition of an individual's employment;
>
> (2) When submission to or rejection of such sexual conduct becomes the basis of employment decisions "affecting" an employee; or
>
> (3) When such sexual conduct has the purpose or effect of substantially interfering with an individual's job performance or creating an intimidating, hostile or offensive working atmosphere.[23]

Because charges of sexual harassment can result in a potential violation of a station's affirmative action policy, communications attorneys advise stations to make an affirmative effort to make employees aware of what constitutes sexual harassment, penalties for those engaging in sexual harassment, and procedures for filing complaints of sexual harassment which permit the person complaining to go above or around the person who is allegedly responsible for the offensive behavior. A mechanism for impartial investigations is also important. State laws come into play when sexual harassment become an issue, and charges of intentional infliction of emotional distress can appear as well.

Preventing Sexual Harassment

Most attorneys recommend a written policy against sexual harassment as a way of educating employees and of having a written record that the station will not tolerate sexually harassing behavior. The written statement can be an important defense in cases where a sexual harassment complaint is filed against a station, or the station finds itself a co-defendant with the person charged with the sexually harassing behavior. Written policies vary but good ones alert employees to the letter of the law and establish a nonthreatening complaint procedure. Also important is a practice of educating employees through workshops and training seminars. The station's attorney may be able to provide such training, or human resource professionals can be called upon, but the important thing is to conduct a responsible and serious seminar.

The workplace itself must be free of sexually harassing elements. Some of these are behavior based. For example, the three elements stated earlier and enforced by the EEOC involve contact between individuals—any individuals in any setting. If the station contracts with a delivery service and the delivery person engages in sexually harassing behavior with station employees, the station along with the delivery person and the delivery service can be the object of a sexual harassment complaint. Indirect harassment can also trigger complaints. Two people engaging in consenting affectionate behavior in the presence of other employees, when the other employees find the behavior creates an offensive, hostile, or intimidating work environment can be accused of sexually harassing behavior. If the two people are in a superior/subordinate role, the issue can be even more serious. Some employees may perceive the affectionate partner as receiving special favors, such as pay raises or promotions, based on his or her sex, not job performance.

Posters or cartoons in the workplace, if they are considered sexually offensive to other employees, can prove troublesome. Indirect actions by employers can also trigger complaints. A beer company ran television commercials showing a "bikini team" parachuting into a campsite carrying cases of beer for a group of men. Five female employees of the brewery filed a sexual harassment suit claiming the commercials contributed to sexual harassment at the brewery.[24]

The key to staying clear of sexual harassment in the workplace is to avoid verbal harassment, physical harassment, and visual harassment. Attorney Mary O'Melia, who conducts workshops on sexual harassment, lists some important "do nots."

- Do not allow sexually oriented jokes in the workplace.
- Do not allow habitual sexually oriented conversation.
- Do not make sexually oriented remarks or comments to co-workers or persons under one's supervision.
- Do not allow this conduct from others in the workplace.
- Do not make sexual demands, either implicit or explicit.
- Do not tie sexual favors in with job performance, appraisal, or promotions.
- Do not touch in a sexually oriented manner.
- Do not undress your employees with your eyes.[25]

Defending Against Sexual Harassment

Defending against a sexual harassment complaint can be complex. For one thing, many sexual harassment complaints originate from behavior which is only witnessed by the two people involved. The station or telecommunication company, especially when named as co-defendant, is forced into discrediting the credibility of the plaintiff. It can be an ugly proceeding, with very personal accusations on both sides. Verifying claims through impartial witnesses can help. In one complaint, a television station sales manager was accused of kissing an account executive and telling her "if you do everything right with this company, you will go a long way."[26] When the case went to district court two advertisers and a media buyer testified to the plaintiff's lack of service on their accounts. The testimony corroborated the testimony of the plaintiff's superiors. A written policy in the hands of every employee, posters alerting employees to the perils of sexual harassment, a complaint procedure that permits the employee to speak in confidence with management beyond their immediate supervisor, and workshops to sensitize employees to sexual harassment are helpful measures that can aid in a defense.

In conclusion, a productive workplace must be free of sexual harassment. The drain on the company in dealing with sexual harassment complaints can be enormous. People's lives, marriages, and incomes can be immediately affected by a single complaint, regardless of how legitimate it is. Frivolous complaints can, however, result in countersuits, and courts can find in favor of the defendants resulting in significant legal fees for the plaintiff who brought the complaint. Human nature being what it is, companies are not going to eliminate sexual attraction. Thus, they must work to avoid having sexual attraction result in harassment and interference with the productivity of the workplace. As society changes, as workshops are held, as a succession of cases and state and federal laws begin to curtail offensive behavior, sexual harassment in the workplace should diminish. Until then, workers must operate in an environment that is changing, and in some ways confusing and complex. Cynthia Crossen, writing in *The Wall Street Journal* about the issue of sex and power in the office said:

> Today those complex and thorny differences, once thrashed out around the kitchen table or on the front porch, are dramatized against the backdrop of filing cabinets, assembly lines and board rooms. That's where men and women flirt, compete, befriend, antagonize, irritate, love—nearly the entire spectrum of relationships between humans. And that's where the sexes have been trying to figure

out how two such different beasts can find some middle ground between sterile celibacy and sexual harassment.[27]

ISSUES IN DEALING WITH PERSONNEL

In addition to concern over discrimination and affirmative action, broadcasters must be alert to state and federal laws that govern the hiring and firing of station personnel. Personnel law, partly because of increased attention in the area of discrimination, is expanding to include other issues associated with hiring and firing station personnel.

The At-Will Doctrine

Some states continue to adhere to what is called the "employment at-will" doctrine, which gives employers considerable latitude in hiring and firing employees.[28] In general terms, managers operating stations in states where strong at-will statutes exist can terminate an employee for almost any reason short of illegal discrimination as defined by law. In other states the courts offer more protection to employees who may be treated unfairly or receive very harsh treatment by employers. In such states certain exceptions to the at-will doctrine exist. One is the "public policy" exception which protects whistle blowers or those employees who are asked to violate the law as a condition of employment. Thus, if a general assignment reporter is asked to drive an unsafe news vehicle that has failed state inspection and is fired for refusing, the reporter could sue and potentially receive punitive damages, job reinstatement, and back pay.

Implied Contracts

Contracts, both real and implied, have an impact on station management's ability to hire and fire employees. Stations that hire employees with open-end contracts generally have more latitude to dismiss an employee. The anchor person who is hired on a three-year written contract has more job security than the general assignment reporter who has no contract or an implied contract. Implied contracts can sometimes be upheld in court, however. If management verbally tells employees that they can work at the station as long as they want to, management may need to prove good cause before terminating such employees. Even then a legal fight may ensue. Advertisements for jobs can also spell trouble if such words as "career opportunity" are used, since such words can convey long-term employment. Disclaimers that state that no term of employment is promised can also protect station management and help preserve the at-will doctrine. Stations that publish and distribute employment handbooks may find such handbooks tantamount to employment contracts if specific conditions of employment and other employment practices are detailed in the handbook. Making such a handbook available at the time a person is hired and referring to the handbook as corporate policy can add to its credibility as a contractual instrument. Probationary periods can also cause problems if the employee is left with the impression that a job is assured after probation if he or she has shown satisfactory performance. Saying that during the probationary period a disc jockey can be terminated with or without cause may imply that after the probationary period the disc jockey will be fired only for good cause.

Other areas can also result in implied contracts. For example, performance reviews and appraisals can be troublesome if these periodic evaluations communicate to the employee that doing well on a performance review will guarantee employment. Such reviews should be used, and the employee should understand they are used for pay raises and promotion only, not as a guarantee of employment. Listing in station publications what conditions will justify termination of an employee (such as theft), may limit the ability to terminate an employee for other reasons. Care should be taken when using such lists in publications to indicate that they are examples, and other reasons may be grounds for dismissal. In summary, attorney L. Michael Zinser makes the following recommendations as preventive medicine when hiring:

> (1) Preserve the "at-will" doctrine by a statement in your employment application.
>
> (2) Preserve the "at-will" doctrine by a statement in your employee handbook.
>
> (3) Include in the employee handbook clear language stating that one named executive has the authority to make exceptions to the policies stated therein.
>
> (4) Carefully train all supervisors with hiring and firing authority to avoid creating situations which might become the basis for exceptions to the "at-will" doctrine.[29]

While it is possible to build safeguards against litigation, it is also possible to create an atmosphere that is inhuman and unproductive. The station where the manager feels uncomfortable complimenting an employee on good work because the manager is afraid it will imply a contract for continued employment will not be a productive or supportive workplace. Similarly, applications, handbooks, and ads that are so filled with legalese that they defeat the objective of good employee relations are of little use. In between the extremes of making promises that can't be kept, and safeguarding a station against lawsuits, there exist well-managed broadcast operations that have gained a reputation for being some of the best places to work in the industry.

Paying Personnel: Employees and Independent Contractors

Assume you are managing a radio station with a large front yard. You contract with a lawn service to mow the yard at the rate of $200 per month. When the lawn service company sends you a bill, you pay the bill. After one summer passes you are approached by a local gardener who offers to mow the lawn for $150 instead of the $200 you were paying the lawn-care service. You agree to the arrangement and simply issue a check to the gardener each time the lawn is mowed. Some days when it is raining you have the gardener do other things at the station, such as make repairs on the building. You buy the gardener some tools, set up a time schedule when she will not interfere with the regular activities of the station, and even decide to pay the travel expenses of the gardener to a flower and lawn exposition at the state capitol. Gradually the gardener's responsibilities increase until she works for your station only. At tax time you consider the gardener to have been what the Internal Revenue Service calls an independent contractor.

The Benefits of Independent Contractors

Independent contractors are not employees of the station but are hired independent of the station's regular employees. For many people, being an independent contractor has many advantages. For example, the independent contractor can usually deduct certain expenses such as automobile and long-distance travel. They can enroll in medical benefit plans that would be too expensive for an employer to provide. Tax depreciation benefits are afforded for real estate and other property directly connected with their business. The gardener, for example, could depreciate the truck she uses to haul the mower to the station. The construction or purchase price of part of the garage where the truck is parked could be depreciated by the gardener. A small room off the garage the gardener uses for an office could also be depreciated. If the gardener travels to a gardeners' convention, the cost of the travel may be deductible. For the station, hiring the gardener is much less expensive than hiring a full-time maintenance person for which the station would have to pay payroll and social security taxes as well as provide costly but necessary medical benefits.

The Tax Relationship with the Contractor

What seemed to be a nice arrangement, however, turns out to be a tax headache when the IRS challenges the independent-contractor status of the gardener, and instead claims the station should have treated the gardener as an employee and is liable for back taxes. The gardener meanwhile is also summoned to court and loses the tax deductions for the truck, the garage, the office, and the travel to the convention. What went wrong? The station developed too close a relationship with the gardener and committed some serious errors in defining the limits of this relationship. The IRS considers 20 different criteria when determining whether or not someone is an employee or an independent contractor.[30]

While we will not examine all of the criteria, some are noteworthy. For example, by setting the time the gardener came to work, the station manager broke one of the rules in dealing with independent contractors. While it may have been all right to hire the gardener to simply keep the lawn mowed as needed, setting a specific time to report to the work violated her independent-contractor status. Buying tools was another mistake. Independent contractors are assumed to work for many different people and the station would not buy tools for the gardener and expect her to use them at other places. By working solely for the station, the gardener further qualified herself as an employee and not an independent contractor. Paying travel expenses was another mistake. Not having a contract was still another error. It would not be necessary to have a contract with the lawn-care service since there would be no doubt about their status or services. The service has their own tools, they work on their own schedule, and they work for many different people.

This does not mean that stations should avoid hiring independent contractors. When the relationship meets the legal requirement of the law, such arrangements can be very satisfactory. A station might not be able to justify hiring a full-time news consultant, but hiring a news consultant as an independent contractor is beneficial. Hiring a writing coach for the news department is another example of an independent contractor. The independent contractor serves many different clients, pays all of the expenses, and works with many different stations.

LIMITING LIABILITY

Many radio and television stations engage in activities beyond programming and selling commercials. For example, promotional contests to gain listeners open up a number of legal and contractual questions that station management must be aware of. For example, most stations use promotional contests as a means of attracting an audience. Contests with prizes over a certain amount require the value of the prize to be reported to the Internal Revenue Service. Getting the winner of a valuable prize to sign a release limiting the station's liability may also prevent trouble down the road. Attorneys can draw up release forms, or sample forms are available from a number of different professional associations including the National Association of Broadcasters.

Awarding Prizes and Promoting Contests

A typical release form signed by the recipient of a prize of substantial value might contain the clause: "I understand and agree to be solely responsible for any and all taxes or duties which may be payable due to my receipt of the prize."[31] Other clauses of a good release form should spell out that the person receiving the prize releases the station from all claims that may arise from the contest or the prize. For example, if a station awards a prize toy that proves injurious to the winner's children, then the station wants to avoid being named a defendant in a lawsuit against the manufacturer of the toy. Protection can be afforded the station with such statements as: "With respect to any claims I may have as a result of the possession or use of the prize, I shall look solely to the prize's manufacturer or others in the chain of production and distribution of the prize excluding Station."[32] Specific wording of the release may use such terms as *officers and directors* and *employees*, so there is no mistake that everyone at the station who in any way may be connected with the prize or contest is covered under the release. While a release is no guarantee that the station would not be named in a lawsuit, it may help to mitigate damages.

Stations may also want to name contest winners or use their picture in promotional materials or advertising. When this takes place a release should also cover such use. A general clause might read: "so that Station (call letters) may promote the contest and the awarding of prizes, I hereby grant to Station (call letters) and its licensees the right to use my name, likeness, portrait, recorded voice and biographical material in connection with said promotions."[33]

When stations subcontract with another company to handle the promotion or contest, a contract with the subcontractor can help protect the station if the contract contains a clause placing the liability on the subcontractor and indemnifying the station. Such an indemnity agreement may contain a statement that calls on the subcontractor to "hold harmless" the station, any sponsors who may buy commercials as part of the contest promotion, and anyone who works at the station. Having the subcontractor be responsible for attorney's fees can also protect the station.

Guest Appearances

Guests who appear on programs pose special problems. Sometimes a guest will appear on a program, and later the recording of the program will be used for promotional purposes or as part of a news story. Without a release, the use of the recording for promotional purposes can result in a lawsuit because the original intent of the appearance was not for commercial purposes. Guests on a talk show who later find their picture used as a promotion for the talk show may decide to sue. If a guest who is a private person under the law does not want to be part of a news story, and can legitimately claim private-person status, having the person's picture appear as part of a news story can result in a claim against the station for invasion of privacy. A release protecting the station from such actions is prudent in many situations. Such a release will have the guests consent to having their picture or voice, or a reproduction of their voice or picture used for other purposes. Having the guests sign a statement indicating they acknowledge that the station or cable system is the sole owner of all rights to the program and the recordings of the program is important. Also having the guests agree to permit their names and likenesses to be used in advertising or promotional material is good protection. For guests under 18 years of age, the signature of a parent or legal guardian is necessary.

When a professional performer is involved, contracts and releases can become more complex. Unlike guests who appear without pay and whose livelihoods are not dependent on such appearances, performers must make a living by contracting for their time and artistic ability. Agents' commissions are involved, and the performer will usually take great pains to be compensated for each appearance, including future airings of any recordings of the program. Separate contract clauses may specify how many times and in what way the performer's likeness can be used in advertising or promotional materials. If guest appearances by the performer outside and beyond the appearance on the program are required, this will be spelled out in the contract. Some contracts become very specific trying to protect against any eventuality. For example, the wording in a release covering the appearance of a professional actor might give to the station the "irrevocable and unconditional power, right, privilege and permission to make, produce, reproduce, exhibit, distribute, publish and transmit by means of live broadcast or cablecast, film videotape, or any other similar mechanical or electronic method" the program on which the performer appears.[34] Getting what the stations pay for is covered with the clause: "Artist agrees to render services hereunder in a competent, painstaking, and artistic manner."[35] Gaining permission to copyright the program can guard against pirating, and copyright provides the station with the ability to earn income through further distribution of the program.

EMERGENCY BROADCAST SYSTEM REQUIREMENTS

The Emergency Broadcast System consists of AM, FM, and TV broadcast stations, including low-power TV stations, and nongovernment industry entities that volunteer to be part of EBS operations during a national, state, or local emergency.[36] Stations that are part of the local and state systems can be called upon to broadcast emergency messages, although participation at the local and state level is optional and at the discretion of local station management. Such events as hurricanes, tornados, and other weather warnings are typical of local emergencies where the EBS would be activated. At the national level, programming priorities are established for EBS programming. These include: Priority One—Presidential Messages; Priority Two—Operational (Local) Area Programming; Priority Three—State Programming; and Priority Four—National Programming and News. Stations that participate in the EBS remain on the air during a national emergency and are required to carry the messages from the president of the United States live at the time they are transmitted. Activation of the national EBS will preempt operation of the local-level and state-level EBS. During national emergencies, stations must reserve programming exclusively for the use of the president's messages and other information of importance to the nation.

Dissemination of Emergency Action Notifications

The national emergency information is disseminated through an Emergency Action Notification (EAN) issued by the White House.[37] The EAN message is then disseminated from the origination point on a dedicated network that reaches the radio and television networks, cable systems, common carriers, wire services, and other participating organizations. From there the EAN is disseminated to the networks' affiliates, the wire service subscribers, the off-the-air monitoring receivers of AM, FM, TV, and low-power TV stations, and other licensees. Participating cable systems send the messages to all subscribers. Any one of these arrangements receiving an EAN message will begin emergency actions at individual receiving points. State and local governments will disseminate information based on state-level and local-level EBS operational plans. FCC rules specify the receiving equipment stations must have to participate in the EBS:

> (a) Monitoring Requirement. To ensure effective off-the-air monitoring (FCC rule), as defined in FCC rules, all broadcast station licensees must install and operate, during their hours of operation, equipment capable of receiving the Attention Signal and emergency programming by other radio or television stations. This equipment must be maintained in operative condition, including arrangements for human listening watch or automatic alarm devices. It must be installed in the broadcast station, either at the trans-

mitter control location and/or studio location, in such a way that it enables the broadcast station staff, at normal duty locations, to be alerted instantaneously upon receipt of the attention signal and to immediately monitor the emergency programming. For situations where broadcast stations are co-owned and co-located (e.g., an AM and FM licensed to the same entity at the same location) with a combined studio facility, only one receiver is required if installed in the combined studio facility. The off-the-air signal monitoring assignment of each broadcast station is specified in the State EBS Operational Plan.

(b) Transmission Requirement. All broadcast licensees except noncommercial educational FM stations authorized to operate with transmitter output powers of 0.100 kW or less, and low-power TV stations, must install, operate, and maintain equipment capable of generating the Attention Signal (FCC rule) to modulate the transmitter so that the signal may be broadcast to other stations. The signal is used to alert other broadcast stations to the fact that the EBS is being activated at the national, state or local level. It is also used during the Weekly Tests involving the transmission and reception of the Attention Signal and Text Script in accordance with (FCC rule). This equipment must be installed in the broadcast station either at the transmitter control point and/or studio location in such a way that it enables the broadcast station staff at normal duty locations to initiate the two-tone transmission. For situations where broadcast stations are co-owned and co-located (e.g., an AM and FM licensed to the same entity at the same location) with a combined studio facility, only one generator is required if installed in the combined studio facility.[38]

On-Site Equipment Maintenance

In addition to installing equipment, stations are also charged with the responsibility of keeping the equipment maintained and in working order. FCC regulations governing this aspect of the EBS system are a continuation of the rules just cited, and state:

(c) The licensee has the responsibility to insure that the equipment used for off-the-air signal monitoring and generating the EBS Attention Signal is in functioning condition during all times the station is in operation, and to determine the cause of any failure to receive the Weekly Transmission Tests as described in (FCC rule). Appropriate entries must be made in the station log, indicating reasons why the Weekly Test Transmissions were not received.

(d) In the event that the equipment for receiving the Attention Signal and emergency programming transmitted by other stations, or the equipment for generating the Attention Signal, becomes defective, the station may operate without the defective equipment pending its repair or replacement for a period not in excess of 60 days without further authority of the Commission, provided that appropriate entries are made in the station log showing the date and the time the equipment was removed and restored to service. Weekly Test Transmissions of the Test Script, without the equipment for generating the Attention Signal, must still be conducted.

(e) If conditions beyond the control of the licensee prevent the restoration of the defective equipment to service within the above allowed period, informal request in accordance with (FCC rule) of this chapter may be filed with the Engineer in Charge of the radio district in which the station is operating for such additional time as may be required to complete repairs of the defective equipment.[39]

Operation During National-Level Emergency

Federal regulations spell out procedures stations follow in the event of a national emergency. Part of these regulations require an EBS Checklist, which summarizes procedures to be posted at normal duty positions where it is immediately available to employees responsible for EBS actions. When an EAN message is received, the station monitors the television networks and/or local cable systems for additional information. The authenticity of the EAN is verified by using a separate EBS Authenticator List. Certain stations are designated as primary transmitters of EAN messages. Other stations, including those who only monitor the EAN, have specific responsibilities in the event of the emergency. Once the EAN has been received and verified, a Standby Script contained in the EBS Checklist for Participating Stations is used until official program material from the White House or other national agency is received. Stations that provide foreign-language programming may transmit emergency announcements in English. In addition to these procedures, a significant number of other regulations exist that detail various operating requirements for local stations and the operation of the EBS system. While some stations may take EBS tests for granted, the FCC does not and care should be taken in making sure any station is in full compliance with EBS requirements.

MAINTAINING THE PUBLIC INSPECTION FILE

As the trustee of the public domain, broadcasting stations are required by law to keep certain documents and information open for public inspection.[40] Members of the general public are entitled to inspect documents from the file. What is contained in the public file varies somewhat among the different types of stations.

Technical Information

Typically, a public file contains technical information directly related to the construction and daily operation of the station. Construction permits, major changes in frequency, output power, or a change in the location of the station or the transmitters are typical inclusions. Minor technical information, such as specifications on the new antenna support wires, information about a new control board, or data about the new record racks, are not found or required in a public inspection file. If a new construction permit has been granted, and if the FCC grants an extension of the permit, the extension is in the public file. The file will also include correspondence related to these changes. A copy of the station's coverage area (contour maps) should be there, as should reports listing the ownership of the station, and any FCC decisions arising from a hearing on the station's license renewal.

Political Broadcasting and Citizen Agreements

Most of what a station does in the way of political programming is an open book to the public, including candidates and their opponents. Requests for political time by legally qualified candidates, a record of what was done with those requests, and the rate charged for that time are available. The spirit of the law behind the political file is to keep access to the airwaves open to legally qualified candidates. This prevents an unscrupulous broadcaster or politician from claiming that a candidate has not talked with the station or bought any advertising—thus discouraging the opponent from buying time—when in fact the candidate has purchased and aired a series of political commercials.

Citizen agreements are not common, but when written agreements do exist, they must be included in the public inspection file. FCC rules define a citizen agreement as: "a written agreement between a broadcast applicant, permittee, or licensee, and one or more citizens or citizen groups, entered for primarily noncommercial purposes." The definition:

> includes those agreements that deal with goals or proposed practices directly or indirectly affecting station operation in the public interest, in areas such as—but not limited to—community ascertainment, programming, and employment. It excludes common commercial agreements such as advertising contracts; union, employment, and personal services contracts; network affiliation, syndication, program supply contracts and so on. However, the mere inclusion of commercial terms in a primarily noncommercial agreement—such as provision for payment for fees for future services of the citizen-parties . . . (citing docket) would not cause the agreement to be considered commercial for the purposes of this section.[41]

To better understand the citizen agreement, assume WAAA radio's license renewal is challenged by a citizen group calling itself Better Wildlife Programming. WAAA enters into a written agreement with the group and agrees to program a certain number of hours each month dealing with wildlife management. The written agreement would therefore become part of the public inspection file. The FCC concerns itself with the overall record of a station serving its broadcast audience. Serious operational errors must occur before an individual challenge can be successful.

Claims Against the Station

A matter resulting in a claim against the station, such as a lawsuit that is unsettled, or any matter relating to an FCC investigation, must be in the public inspection file.[42] If the licensee has been advised of a complaint against it by the FCC, then this must be included. Only in cases where the claim is a private one and has been settled or barred by statute of limitations, or where the FCC has notified the station in writing that the material can be discarded, can the file be purged of the material.

Programs Meeting Community Issues

Every three months stations are required to place in their public inspection file the list of programs that provided the most significant treatment of issues facing the community served by the station. FCC rules require the list of programs to be filed on the tenth day of each calendar quarter (i.e., January 10, April 10, July 10, and October 10). The responsible broadcaster will include enough information about the program so that someone examining the file will be able to ascertain the name of the program, length of the program, the time and date it aired, the type of program (news, call-in, and so on), and a short narrative of the content of the program and how it dealt with the issue.[43] While there is no restriction on the maximum number of program issues to list, five to ten is an expected minimum. There is no need for the broadcaster to explain by what means an issue was deemed significant enough to warrant treatment by specific program(s). In addition to the materials already discussed, letters from the public are also kept in the public inspection file, as are descriptions of equal employment opportunity programs. Not included in the public inspection file is confidential personnel information of applicants and employees.

Location of Records

If the file is kept at the station, it is to be kept at the main studio or other accessible place.[44] It can also be kept at a public registry of documents, or at an attorney's office in the community served or to be served by the station. The public inspection file should be available for inspection any time during normal business hours. The station has a right to ask for personal identification but cannot interrogate someone about his or her motives for wanting to see the file. If you want certain documents copied, the station can charge you a reasonable fee to have the materials reproduced.

Retention of Letters

The public inspection file must contain letters from the public received by the licensee of commercial AM, FM, and TV broadcast stations. The exception is when the letter writer has requested the letter not be made public or when the licensee exercises the right not to include the letter because of its defamatory or obscene contents. Letters must be kept for three years after the date they are received and television stations are required to separate letters based on whether they apply to programming or nonprogramming. If comments in the letter cross both categories, the licensee files it in the category to which the letter writer has given the greatest attention.[45]

Children's Programming Records

For commercial TV stations the public inspection file must contain records which substantiate the station's compliance with the commercial limits on children's programming. Based on current regulations, this limit prohibits stations from broadcasting more than 10.5 minutes of commercial matter during hours when children's programming appears on weekends and not more than 12 minutes of commercial matter during children's programming on weekdays.[46]

On either an annual or quarterly basis, stations are required to include records in the file which demonstrate the extent to which the station has responded to the educational and informational needs of children in its overall programming. The records may also relate any special nonbroadcast efforts which enhance the educational and informational value of the programming. For example, distributing a study guide in local schools coordinated with a special program directed toward children would be the kind of information included in the file to meet this requirement. Of special interest to the commission is the identification of the "most significant programming" which meets these needs. Stations can make their children's programming records part of their issues/programs list or they can be kept as a separate list. At a very minimum the records should obtain the date, time, duration, and a brief description of the programming or nonbroadcast efforts the station feels best reflect its commitment to children's programming and informational needs.

Donor Liïst

Noncommercial stations have similar requirements concerning public inspection files as those of commercial stations. However, some exceptions do exist. For instance, noncommercial stations must include a list of the donors supporting specific programs. For example, if a public radio station sponsors a program and announces the names of donors or grants supporting the program, the names of these donors or the sponsors of the grants would be included on such a list. The list is required, however, regardless of whether or not the announcements are made on the air.[47]

PROMOTING THE STATION

Station promotions are as common to the broadcasting industry as commercials and sponsors. As is the case with other businesses, competing in the marketplace is fine, but such activities as misleading the public about coverage area or leadership in audience ratings, or artificially inflating rating surveys can bring down the wrath of the FTC, the FCC, and the rating services on a broadcaster.[48] Making a promotional announcement to the effect that "we're number one" when the station is actually third in the ratings, or calling itself the "leading news station" when a recognized rating service can dispute that claim opens the station to an FTC investigation. It could provoke a cease-and-desist order, a fine, or court proceedings.[49] The most common complaint about stations' promotional activities is hypoing. Hypoing is defined as "unusual advertising or other promotional efforts, designed to increase audiences only during the survey period."[50] The FTC, not the FCC, prosecutes hypoing violations. Although the FCC examines charges of hypoing at license renewal time and has issued short-term license renewals to stations involved in hypoing, it customarily forwards these complaints to the FTC.

Hypoing

The most common type of hypoing is a major station contest conducted when the rating services are taking their surveys. Stations have had listeners log the amount of quarter-hours they listen to the station during this time and award them money based on the amount of listening. These contests are closely aligned to the rating services' diary methods and problems arise when the contests are conducted only at survey time and not during other times of the year.

If a station calls the attention of the audience to a survey in progress, the rating company can note this on the cover of its published rating book. Abusing an audience rating can also mean trouble. The FCC cited a case in which a station employee received a diary and gave it to a station secretary, who promptly filled out the diary showing that her household had watched the station from sign-on until sign-off time. In another case, a licensee was accused of purchasing diaries from people who had received them from the rating companies.

The Federal Trade Commission guidelines covering station promotion and advertising go beyond hypoing.[51] They charge broadcasters with the responsibility for seeing that claims about the composition of their audiences are truthful, that survey data are interpreted accurately, and that surveys are cited as being only statistical estimates.

In a rule-making proceeding, the FCC examined possible regulations to govern the rating services.[52] The rules, which were not adopted, proposed a ban on "unusual advertising, contest or promotional activities" within four weeks of a rating period if the promotions were not conducted regularly throughout the year. Other provisions would have penalized stations for using old ratings data and banned for three months before a rating period any promotion that rewards people for "stating that they listen to the licensee's station." The rule was not adopted but did assure broadcasters that the commission was serious.

Arbitron clamped down on stations in Arizona and in Colorado that were conducting contests that could inflate diary responses.[53] Arbitron's sanctions could have included canceling the rating altogether, publishing a special supplement about the two stations, describing the inflationary contest in that supplement, and sending the supplement with an explanation to subscribing broadcasters, advertisers, and ad agencies as well as to the Advertising Research Foundation.[54]

Why are rating services so concerned about hypoing when they are paid by the station to conduct the survey? The rating services have learned that they can only be successful when the public and the industry have confidence in their products. Permitting stations to capriciously conduct hypoing and other questionable promotional activities can reflect poorly on both the rating services and their customers, the broadcasters.

Representing Coverage Maps

Another area related to station promotion is the accurate representation of station coverage areas. The geographic area covered by a station translates into audience size and, consequently, into advertising dollars. Abuse can abound in this area as readily as it can with audience ratings. In a station's promotional and advertising literature, a coverage map *must* be an accurate representation of the station's ability to reach its listeners. Some common inaccuracies associated with coverage maps are:

(1)Overstating the population in the station's coverage area.

(2)Labeling the map as "coverage survey" without additional explanation.

(3)Failing to identify the communities on the map.

(4)Using contours based on measurements not taken in accordance with Commission requirements.

(5)Failing to label contours or other map features legibly, and . . .

(6)Failing to include a mileage scale in the legend.[55]

Misrepresenting a coverage map can negatively reflect on the licensee, especially if the FTC rules against it.

Deceptive Programming

Deceptive programming employed as a means of station promotion can mean serious consequences. For example, one station faked a kidnapping of a station employee and broadcast the event in false news reports to add to the legitimacy.[56] Even though the station operated with an absentee owner, the FCC affirmed that the operating responsibility of an owner could not be delegated. Owners are still liable for the actions of their managers through which delegated authority passes. Moreover, it is necessary for a station to impress upon its employees the wrongfulness of deceptive practices. More than likely a penalty less serious than denial of a license will be imposed when policies against deceptive programming are in place and enforced by station management.

Another example of deceptive programming occurred when a station used letters prepared by the station staff and claimed they were letters from the broadcast audience.[57] Station employees were also used on the air but were identified as members of the broadcast audience. The FCC granted the station a short-term license renewal, among other sanctions, even though the station had instituted safeguards against such deceptive practices, had asked six employees to resign over the incident, and had strongly admonished in writing ten other employees.

We tend to think of news programming and editorializing as being the objective, factual part of broadcasting. Unfortunately, human nature can have its failings in these areas as well. Staged news events are rare but not unheard of. In one instance, the FCC investigated a network news crew's arranging for a person to walk up and challenge a National Guard line during a protest gathering.[58] When covering civil unrest, the author of this text encountered a news reporter from a competing station who actively sided with protesters, and identified plainclothes police officers to protesters. While not illegal in itself, it shows how one's involvement in a story can cloud news judgment and distort the objective representation of events.

Giving favorable news or editorial coverage to a business in which one has a financial interest, changing the facts of a story to protect a friend, deliberately engaging in trial or pretrial publicity to influence a case, failing to divulge to management or to the broadcast audience a personal or financial interest in an organization or individual that becomes the subject of a news story you write and air, or editorializing on an issue and supporting your position with knowingly false information are serious ethical matters that may turn into legal problems as well.

BROADCAST AND RECORDING OF TELEPHONE CONVERSATIONS

Calling parties are required to be notified that a telephone conversation is intended for broadcast. FCC rules governing the broadcast of telephone conversations read:

> Before recording a telephone conversation for broadcast, or broadcasting such a conversation simultaneously with its occurrence, a licensee shall inform any party to the call of the licensees' intention to broadcast the conversation, except for such parties aware, or maybe presumed to be aware from the circumstances of the conversation, that it is being or likely will be broadcast. Such awareness is presumed to exist only when the other party to the call is associated with the station (such as an employee or part-time reporter), or where the other party originates the call and it is obvious that it is in connection with a program in which the station customarily broadcasts telephone conversations.[59]

Applying the Rules to Everyday Regulations

A reporter who telephones a news source and wants to broadcast the comments of the party would notify the person that the telephone conversation is intended for broadcast. On the other hand, a caller originating a call to a radio talk show is assumed to be aware the call will be broadcast and therefore does not need to receive notification.

Broadcast of Taped, Filmed, or Recorded Material

If time is of significance, any taped, filmed, or recorded programming where an attempt is made to create an impression that the programming is occurring live must be announced as "taped, filmed, or recorded." FCC rules require the language of the announcement to be clear and using terms commonly understood by the public. Television stations have the prerogative of making the announcement visually or aurally.[60]

Rebroadcasts

Under certain circumstances broadcasting stations can rebroadcast transmissions from other broadcast or nonbroadcast stations.[61] Where another broadcast station is concerned, written permission must be obtained by the station wishing to repeat the signal and such written permission must be made available to the FCC upon request. Programs originated by the Voice of America (VOA) or the Armed Forces Radio and Television Services (AFRTS) cannot generally be rebroadcast domestically and only through special arrangements can any retransmission take place. Similarly, signals from foreign broadcast stations are also prohibited from being retransmitted without the consent of an originating station. Messages which originate by stations in the amateur and citizens band radio services can be broadcast at the discretion of broadcast licensees. In addition, time signals originating by the National Observatory and the National Bureau of Standards as well as the National Weather Service are permitted without specific authorization. Certain procedures require specific announcements to rebroadcast such services.

SUMMARY

Station operations involve the daily routine tasks of keeping the station operating and profitable. In most cases these tasks center around keeping abreast of FCC records and regulations, dealing with employees, working with attorneys, and other functions associated with the programming, engineering, and personnel sides of the station's operation.

Stations are able to operate because they occupy a reserved space on the electromagnetic spectrum. To apply for a permit to build and operate a broadcast station, an understanding of the spectrum is necessary. Historically, broadcasters have always battled for a place on the spectrum and in the early days of radio, crowding and interference were common. Today the spectrum is even more crowded, but some order has been brought to the frequency assignment process through international bodies and treaties. We speak of positions on the spectrum in terms of hertz, kilohertz, megahertz, and gigahertz for extremely high-frequency radio waves.

Larger portions of the spectrum are called bands and contain primary and secondary applications. Secondary stations cannot interfere with primary service stations nor are secondary service stations protected from interference from primary service stations. Applicants for a broadcast license normally hire competent legal and engineering counsel to process an FCC application. Even a simple, unintentional error can delay an application for months, and can open up the applicant to other charges if the application is contested. Stations are designated on a "channel" basis. AM stations operate on clear, regional, and local channels, and frequency allocations take these different service restrictions into consideration. FM and TV stations must locate an unused frequency, either through separate engineering studies or by using the FCC Table of Allotments. In addition to locating a frequency and meeting general and legal requirements, an applicant must also meet certain financial qualifications.

Special problems can arise in meeting the financial obligations to operate a station. For example, the applicant must prove that he or she is financially able to operate the station even if it suffers a loss. Bank financing is often difficult to obtain since banks like physical collateral, and the station's FCC license cannot legally be used as collateral. In addition, few banks have the expertise to understand the broadcasting industry, therefore shying away from making loans to radio and television stations. When the tower is to be located in a sensitive area, an environmental impact study is necessary. Other requirements include an equal employment opportunity plan and meeting basic certification requirements.

License renewal is less complex than applying to construct a new station. Radio station licenses must be renewed every seven years, television licenses every five years. Planning is important in any license renewal. Don't assume that it will be automatic, although many license renewals are. Be prepared at all times to handle objections, and have evidence available that the station has been operating in the public interest. The deregulatory era of the 1980s created false security among many general managers. Even if you win a license challenge, it can be time consuming, expensive, and result in damaging publicity. The FCC uses a postcard renewal form for license renewal but FCC inspectors can appear at any time and inspect the station. Among items required in license renewal are judgments, decrees, settlements, consents, certain engineering data, certification that the public inspection file is up to date, and that the station is meeting community issues with appropriate programming. A worst-case scenario is a petition to deny, filed against an applicant for a new station or a station seeking license renewal. Petitions to deny are argued before an administrative law judge and reviewed by the review board of the full commission.

Routine operating activities can sometimes result in legal problems. For example, one station leased the tower and frequency of a second station when the first station's tower collapsed in an ice storm. A third station filed a complaint against the first station claiming it had used the tower longer than was necessary, therefore extending its coverage area and gaining a favorable position on a local cable system. Call letter assignments and disputes can also cause problems. When a Delaware television station was assigned call letters that sounded like its competitor's, the competitor filed a complaint to protect its position in the marketplace.

Affirmative action and equal employment opportunity programs are closely monitored by the FCC. Needing careful scrutiny are the top job categories of officials and managers, professionals, technicians, and salespeople. Those categories must show a percentage of representation based on the population characteristics of the area served by the station. An effective affirmative action plan is also necessary for any station with five or more employees. Areas such as the responsibility for implementation, policy dissemination, recruitment, job hires, promotion, training, availability surveys, current employment surveys, the effectiveness of the affirmative action plan, and a record of complaints and special problems are important components. Station management must also be aware of affirmative action requirements in hiring procedures.

Guarding against sexual harassment is an extension of the station's affirmative action plan. The Equal Employment Opportunity Commission considers sexual harassment to occur when submission to sexual conduct is explicitly or implicitly a condition of an individual's employment, when submission to or rejection of sexual conduct becomes the basis for employment decisions affecting an employee, or when sexual conduct has the purpose or effect of substantially interfering with an individual's job performance. Some important "do nots" to avoid sexual harassment include not allowing sexually oriented jokes in the workplace, not allowing habitually sexually oriented conversation, not making sexually oriented remarks to other workers, and not making sexual demands that are either implicit or explicit.

Station managers must also be aware of basic personnel issues, especially when terminating employees. Some states adhere to a strict employment at-will doctrine, and such things as employee handbooks can form implicit contracts with employees. Employers can consider preserving the at-will doctrine in hiring and in employee handbooks and should carefully train supervisors in hiring decisions. Employees who are paid as independent contractors can offer savings to the station and tax benefits to the contractor. Care must be taken in having a relationship with the subcontractor that meets IRS requirements. For stations engaged in promotional contests, releases may be necessary to ensure that the recipient of the prize will pay all the taxes that may come due, and will not hold the station responsible for any defects or injury caused by defective merchandise. Contracts protecting the station and assuring quality service from guest artists are also common in larger stations that may hire performers for special promotions.

All stations are part of the Emergency Broadcast System, which can be activated in the case of a national emergency. Coordinated efforts with local agencies also provide early warning for severe weather conditions or other emergencies such as flooding. A monitoring requirement and a transmission requirement are part of FCC regulations. On-site maintenance is also required. A working knowledge of everything from FCC rules to administrative matters is necessary to operate in the legal environment of contemporary broadcasting.

In the area of FCC records, one of the more important items is the public inspection file. The file is open to public scrutiny at all times and can be examined by an FCC field inspector without warning. Since the general deregulatory trend of the FCC in the 1980s, the public inspection file is even more important as evidence of proper operating procedures and the licensee's commitment to the community served by the station. Although what is required in the public file differs slightly from station to station, some items are expected in every file. Basic engineering data in the file include such documents as construction permits, or recent major changes in the location of the studio, transmitter, or antenna. Political programming information is found in the file and includes requests for political advertising by legally qualified candidates. Although citizen agreements are rare, when one is in force it is found in the file. Citizen agreements are defined as written agreements "between a broadcast applicant, permittee, or licensee, and one or more citizens or citizen groups, entered for primarily noncommercial purposes." Any claims against the station, such as lawsuits, pending judgments, and other matters are found in the file. A list of programs that have addressed community issues are included although there is no requirement that the methodology used to determine the issues be present. The file must be kept at the station and available during regular business hours.

Most stations promote themselves through advertising, on-air promotions, and contests. As with any advertising, misrepresenting the station can have serious consequences. For example, inflating a broadcast rating through contests or manipulation of the data-gathering device, such as altering audience estimates by having station personnel fill out diaries, is an invitation for FCC or FTC action. Accurate representation of a station's coverage area in sales-promotion literature or external marketing is also necessary. If a station inflates and distorts the contour of its coverage map and sells advertising based on the inflated and inaccurate data, it can be considered fraud and endanger the license.

Deceptive programming used to promote the station can also result in serious consequences. One station allegedly faked a kidnapping of a station employee and broadcast the event as part of its newscast. Another station was charged with having its own staff write letters to the station and misrepresenting the letters as coming from the broadcast audience. Instigating or faking a newscast can be equally serious. Such actions as giving favorable news coverage to an advertiser, changing the facts of a story, or deliberately engaging in misleading pretrial publicity to influence a case are serious ethical problems that can become legal problems.

FCC rules govern the broadcast and recording of telephone conversations. Generally, the calling party must be informed or understand fully that the telephone call will be recorded or broadcast.

MATERIAL FOR ANALYSIS

Anyone wanting to construct a new AM, FM, or TV station, or make a change in existing facilities must complete FCC Form 301. The instructions for FCC Form 301, presented here in an abridged version, detail the different requirements that must be met before the FCC will grant permission to begin the construction process. After the station is complete, the applicant must apply for permission to test the transmitter and eventually must apply for a license to operate the station.

INSTRUCTIONS FOR FCC 301
APPLICATION FOR CONSTRUCTION PERMIT FOR COMMERCIAL BROADCAST STATION

GENERAL INSTRUCTIONS

I. GENERAL INFORMATION
II. LEGAL QUALIFICATIONS
III. FINANCIAL QUALIFICATIONS
IV-A. PROGRAM SERVICE STATEMENT
IV-B. INTEGRATION STATEMENT
V. ENGINEERING DATA AND ANTENNA AND SITE INFORMATION
VI. EQUAL EMPLOYMENT OPPORTUNITY PROGRAM
VII. CERTIFICATIONS

INSTRUCTIONS FOR SECTION I—
GENERAL INFORMATION

A. The name of the applicant stated in Section I shall be:

(1) if a corporation, the EXACT corporate name;

(2) if a partnership, the names of all general partners, and the name under which the partnership does business

(3) if an association, the name of the individual(s) authorized to act on behalf of the association, and the name of the association;

(4) if an individual applicant, the full legal name. In all other Sections of this form, the organization name alone will be sufficient for identification of the applicant . . .

INSTRUCTIONS FOR SECTION II—
LEGAL QUALIFICATIONS

A. . . . the words "party to this application" have the following meanings:

APPLICANT: the individual or entity seeking the proposed facilities.

INDIVIDUAL APPLICANT: the natural person applying for the facilities in his or her own right.

PARTNERSHIP APPLICANT: All partners, including limited partners. However, limited partners in a limited partnership are not considered parties to the application if the limited partners are not materially involved, directly or indirectly, in the management or operation of the media-related activities of the partnership and the applicant so certifies . . . Sufficient insulation of a limited partner for purposes of this certification would be assured if the limited partnership agreement:

(1) specifies that any exempt limited partner (if not a natural person, its directors, officers, partners, etc.) cannot act as an employee of the limited partnership if his or her functions, directly or indirectly, relate to the media enterprises of the company;

(2) bars any exempt limited partner from serving, in any material capacity, as an independent contractor or agent with respect to the partnerships media enterprises;

(3) restricts any exempt limited partner from communicating with the licensee or the general partner on matters pertaining to the day-to-day operations of its business;

(4) empowers the general partner to veto any admissions of additional general partners admitted by vote of the exempt limited partners;

(5) prohibits any exempt limited partner from voting on the removal of a general partner or limits this right to situations where the general partner is subject to bankruptcy proceedings, as described in . . . the Revised Uniform Limited Partnership Act, is adjudicated incompetent by a court of competent jurisdiction, or is removed for cause, as determined by an independent party;

(6) bars any exempt limited partner from performing any services to the limited partnership materially relating to its media activities, with the exception of making loans to, or acting as a surety for, the business; and

(7) states, in express terms, that any exempt limited partner is prohibited from becoming actively involved in the management or operation of the media businesses of the partnership.

Notwithstanding conformance of the partnership agreement to these criteria, however, the requisite certification cannot be made if the applicant has actual knowledge of a material involvement of the limited partner in the management or operation of the media-related business of the partnership. In the event that the applicant cannot certify as to the noninvolvement of the limited partners, the limited partners will be considered as parties to this application.

CORPORATE APPLICANT: All officers and directors and each owner of or subscriber to stock accounting for 5% or more of the outstanding votes in the corporation. However, where an individual or a single entity holds more than 50% of the applicant's voting stock, and a simple majority is all that is required to control corporate affairs, other stockholders are not considered parties to this application.

Where a corporation is a party to this application by virtue of its ownership or subscription to 5% or more of the voting stock of the applicant, each of the corporate stockholder's directors and "executive officers" (president, vice-president, secretary, treasurer, or their equivalents) is considered a party to this application UNLESS the applicant submits a statement establishing that an individual director or officer will not exercise authority or influence in areas that will affect the applicant or the proposed station. The applicant should identify the individual by name and title, describe the individual's duties and responsibilities, and explain why that person should not be attributed an interest in the corporate applicant or be considered a party to this application. In addition, a person or entity holding an ownership interest in the corporate stockholder of the applicant is considered a party to this application ONLY if that interest, when multiplied by the corporate stockholder's interest in the applicant, would account for 5% or more of the votes of the applicant. For example, where X owns or subscribes to stock accounting for 25% of the applicant's votes, only those stockholders of corporation X who hold stock accounting for 20% or more have a 5% indirect interest in the applicant (.25 × .20 = .05) and, therefore, are considered parties to this application. In applying the multiplier, any entity holding more than 50% of its subsidiary will be considered a 100% owner.

If any stockholder agreement exists pertaining to cooperative voting accounting for 5% or more of the votes, that block of stock is regarded as if held by a single entity, and any stockholder holding 5% or more of the stock in that block is considered a party to this application. An investment company, insurance company or trust department of a bank is not considered a party to this application if its aggregated holding accounts for less than 10% of the outstanding votes in the applicant AND IF the applicant certifies that:

(1) such entity exercises no influence or control over the corporation, directly or indirectly; and

(2) such entity has no representatives among the officers and directors of the corporation.

* * *

PARTNERSHIP APPLICANT: All holders of equity interests in the applicant that are not considered parties to the application, including all limited partners. In the event that there are more than fifty (50) owners of equity interests in the applicant, only those who own 5% or more of the total equity in the applicant are considered non-party equity owners . . .

CORPORATE APPLICANT: All holders of equity interests in the applicant that are not considered parties to the application, including all nonvoting stockholders, stockholders with less than 5% voting stock interest, and stockholders with less than a majority interest in voting stock where a single entity owns more than 50% of the voting stock. In the event that there are more than fifty (50) stockholders or owners of equity interests in the applicant, only those who own 5% or more of the total equity in the applicant are considered non-party equity owners for purposes of Section II.

ANY OTHER APPLICANT: All holders of equity interests in the applicant that are not considered parties to the application.

C. An attributable interest is an ownership interest in or relation to an applicant or licensee which will confer on its holder that degree of influence or control over the applicant or licensee as should subject it to limitation by the Commission's multiple ownership rules. Parties to the application are holders of attributable interests. Non-party holders of equity interests in the applicant are holders of nonattributable interests. While these holders of nonattributable interests are not considered parties to the application, Section II information must be provided for them. Moreover, they may have attributable interests in other media that are considered under the Commission's cross-interest policy which seeks to ensure the promotion and maintenance of arms' length competition between stations in the same area. For example, a limited partner in an applicant, who has made the above partnership certification, may have an attributable interest in a newspaper or broadcast station in the same area or in a station with contours that overlap the applicant's proposed station, or in a cable television (CATV) system that is located within the Grade B contour of a proposed television station . . . If so, the applicant is required:

(1) to identify the individuals or entities that have an attributable interest in another medium of mass communications in the area;

(2) to state the nature and extent of the interest in the applicant; and

(3) to identify the other medium and the nature and extent of the interest held.

In situations in which a marital relationship is involved, the interests held by one spouse are presumptively attributed to the other and both spouses may, unless this presumption is rebutted by an appropriate showing, be considered to be holders of attributable interests and parties to this application.

D. All applications must comply with Section 310 of the Communications Act as amended. Specifically, Section 310 proscribes issuance of a construction permit to an alien, the representative of an alien, a foreign government or the representative thereof, or a corporation organized under the laws of a foreign government. This proscription also applies with respect to any corporation of which any officer or director is an alien or of which more than 20% of the capital stock is owned or voted by aliens, their representatives, a foreign government or its representative, or by a corporation organized under the laws of a foreign country. This proscription could likewise apply to any corporation directly or indirectly controlled by another corporation of which (a) any officer is, (b) more than 25% of the directors are, or (c) more than 25% of the capital stock is owned or voted by aliens, their representatives, a foreign government or its representative. The Commission may also deny a construction permit to a corporation controlled by another corporation organized under the laws of a foreign country.

Section 310 of the Communications Act has been interpreted with respect to limited partnerships to prohibit equity contributions or voting interests of alien limited partners, which in the aggregate exceed 20% in a broadcast licensee or which in the aggregate exceed 25% in a partnership which holds a controlling interest in a broadcast licensee . . . The applicant must determine the citizenship of each officer and director. It must also determine the citizenship of each shareholder or else explain how it determined the relevant percentages. For large corporations, a sample survey using a recognized statistical method is acceptable for this purpose.

E. Commission policies and litigation reporting requirements for broadcast applicants have been revised with a view to focusing on misconduct which violates the Communications Act or a Commission rule or policy and on certain specified non-FCC misconduct which demonstrates the proclivity of an applicant to deal truthfully with the Commission and to comply with its rules and policies. The categories of relevant non-FCC misconduct include: (1) misrepresentations to any other governmental unit resulting in criminal or civil violations; (2) criminal convictions involving false statements or dishonesty; (3) certain felony convictions; and (4) adjudicated violations of anticompetitive or antitrust laws that are broadcast related.

INSTRUCTIONS FOR SECTION III— FINANCIAL QUALIFICATIONS

A. All applicants filing Form 301 must be financially qualified to effectuate their proposals. Certain applicants (i.e, for a new station, to reactivate a silent station, or if specifically requested by the Commission) must demonstrate their financial qualifications . . .

B. An applicant for a new station must attest it has sufficient net liquid assets on hand or committed sources of funds to construct the proposed facility and operate for three months without additional funds. In so certifying, the applicant is also attesting that it can and will meet all contractual requirements, if any, as to collateral, guarantees, donations, and capital investments . . .

C. Documentation supporting the certification of financial qualifications need not be submitted with this application but must be available to the Commission upon request. The Commission encourages that all financial statements used in the preparation of this application be prepared in accordance with generally accepted accounting principles.

D. (i)(a) the applicant must estimate the initial costs of constructing and operating the facility proposed in the application. The estimate for constructing the facility should include, but is not limited to, costs incurred for items listed below. In calculating costs for the items below, determine the costs for the items in place and ready for service, including amounts for labor, supervision, materials, supplies, and freight:

Antenna System (including antenna, antenna tower, transmission line, phasing equipment, ground system, controlling equipment and tower lighting);

RF Generating Equipment (including transmitter, tubes, filters, diplexer, remote control equipment, and automatic logger);

Monitoring and Test Equipment (including frequency monitor, modulation monitor, oscilloscope, dummy load, vectorscope, and video monitors);

Program Origination Equipment (including control consoles, film chains, cameras, audio tape equipment, video tape equipment, program and distribution amplifiers, limiters, and transcription equipment);

Acquiring Land;

Acquiring, Remodeling or Constructing Buildings;

Services (including legal, engineering, and installation costs); and

Other Miscellaneous items (including mobile and STL equipment, non-technical studio furnishings, etc.)

(b) the estimate must also include the costs of operating the proposed facility for the first three months, including the costs of proposed programming, without relying on advertising or other revenues to meet operating costs. To arrive at an estimate of the total costs to be met by the applicant, the total construction costs should be added to the estimated cost of operation for three months.

(2) The applicant must also identify, in the application, its sources of funding for the construc-

tion and operation of the proposed facility for the first three months. For each source of funding, the applicant must identify the source's name, address, telephone number, a contact person if the source is an entity, the relationship (if any) of the source to the applicant, and the amount of funds to be supplied by the source. The total amount of funds to be supplied by all the sources listed should equal or exceed the estimated cost of construction and operation . . .

The funding sources listed on the application should include, if applicable: existing capital, new capital, loans from banks (identified separately), loans from others (identified separately), profits for existing operations, donations, and net deferred credit from equipment suppliers (identified separately and determined by deducting from the deferred credit the down payment, payments to principal, and interest payments). (Note: if the first equipment payment is due upon shipment, the applicant must include five monthly payments; if due in 30 days, four monthly payments; if due in 60 days, three monthly payments; etc.)

. . . the applicant must also have on hand, at the time it files its application, BUT NEED NOT SUBMIT WITH THE APPLICATION, the following Documentation . . .:

A detailed balance sheet at the close of a month within 90 days of the date of the application showing the applicant's financial position.

A statement showing the yearly net income, after Federal income tax, for each of the past two years, received by the applicant from any source.

For each person identified in response to Question 3 . . . who has already furnished funds, purchased stock, extended credit, or guaranteed loans: A copy of the agreement obligating the party to furnish funds, showing the amount furnished, the rate of interest, the terms of repayment, and security, if any.

For each person identified in response to Question 3 . . . who has agreed to furnish funds, purchase stock, extend credit, or guarantee loans, a balance sheet or a financial statement showing: All liabilities and current and liquid assets sufficient to meet current liabilities; financial ability to comply with the terms of the agreement to furnish funds, purchase stock, extend credit, or guarantee loans; and net income after Federal income tax, received for the past two years.

Note: if the statement does not indicate current and liquid assets sufficient to meet the proposed commitments, the financial statement must be supplemented by a statement showing how non-liquid assets will be used to provide the funds, and the extent to which such assets have liens or prior obligations against them.

For financial institutions or equipment manufacturers, identified . . . who have agreed to make a loan or extend credit: The document by which the institution or manufacturer has agreed to provide the loan or credit, showing the amount of loan or credit, terms of payment or repayment of the loan, collateral or security required, rate of interest to be charged, and special requirements (e.g., moratorium on principal or interest, waiver of collateral, etc.); and a statement from any parties required to provide special endorsements showing their willingness to provide such endorsements.

E. It is Commission policy not to approve extensions of time for construction on the basis of financial inability or unwillingness to construct.

INSTRUCTIONS FOR SECTION IV-A— PROGRAM SERVICE STATEMENT

Applicant need only file a program service statement.

INSTRUCTIONS FOR SECTION IV-B— INTEGRATION STATEMENT

The applicant's integration statement must identify each principal who will participate in the management of the station, his or her position, duties and hours, and for each principal whether a qualitative credit will be claimed for minority status, past local residence, female status, broadcast experience or civic activity . . .

INSTRUCTIONS FOR SECTION V— ENGINEERING DATA AND ANTENNA AND SITE INFORMATION

A. An indication as to the specific transmitter make and model is not required on the application. Rather, any subsequent permit authorizing construction will require installation of a type accepted transmitter or one complying with the (FCC rule). Applicants for AM facilities are reminded of the maximum rated power limitations for transmitters . . .

* * *

C. (When applying for FM station construction permit a . . .) U.S. Geological Survey topographic quadrangle map upon which is marked the transmitter site (must be included). The Commission recommends that applicants submit at least one original copy of each appropriate full-scale USGS quadrangle map, if available, with the transmitter site properly marked and labeled.

In order to allow the Commission's processing staff to verify the correctness of the geographic coordinates provided in an FM application, it is necessary for this site map to show along the printed margin of both axes at least two coordinate markings, specifically labeled by the USGS, one on either side of the marked site.

Additionally, a scale of kilometers (if available) or miles and all of the identifying map information must be included. The site should be plotted on a full-scale map, and all of the contour lines must be clearly visible. Faded, smudged or otherwise illegible maps are unacceptable. Photocopies are acceptable in lieu of actual USGS maps, provided they are clear, dark and legible. It is not necessary to submit an entire map (although this is perfectly acceptable), but only as much as is necessary to fully comply with the requirements described above.

In certain cases it may be inconvenient to provide a full-scale photocopy which includes both the site and the margins. This can occur when the site lies toward the center of the map. In this case the following alternative is acceptable. Provide a full-scale copy of the Section of the map containing the site. This copy must include either four of the standard printed cross-marks or one margin and two cross-marks. Fine lines should be drawn between the marks in such a fashion as to enclose the site. Each of these lines should be labeled with the appropriate latitude or longitude. This full-scale map Section must include all the information specified in the previous paragraph. In addition, a reduced copy of the entire map must be included to allow the Commission's staff to verify that the lines have been correctly labeled . . .

E. The following guidance is provided for the questions regarding environmental impact . . .

(1) (Indicate) in the appropriate box to indicate whether a Commission grant of the proposed communication facility(ies) may have a significant environmental impact . . . Briefly, Commission grant of an application may have a significant environmental impact if any of the following are proposed:

(a) A facility is to be located in sensitive areas (e.g., an officially designated wilderness area, a wildlife preserve area, a flood plain) or will physically or visually affect sites significant in American history.

(b) A facility whose construction will involve significant change in surface features.

(c) The antenna tower and/or supporting structure(s) will be equipped with high intensity white lights and are to be located in residential neighborhoods.

(d) The facilities or the operation of which will cause exposure of workers or the general Public to levels of Radio frequency radiation in excess of the "Radio Frequency Protection Guides" recommended in "American National Standard Safety Levels with respect to Human Exposure to Radio Frequency Electromagnetic Fields, 800 kHz to 100 kHz," . . . by the Institute of Electrical and Electronics Engineers, Inc, 345 East 47th Street, New York, New York 10017.

(2) If you answer Yes, submit the required Environmental Assessment (EA). The EA includes for antenna towers and satellite earth stations:

(a) A description of the facilities as well as supporting structures and appurtenances, and a description of the site as well as the surrounding area and uses. If high intensity lighting is proposed or utilized within a residential area, the EA must also address the impact of this lighting upon the residents.

(b) A statement as to the zoning classification of the site, and communications with, or proceedings before and determinations (if any) made by zoning, planning, environmental or other local, state or federal authorities on matters relating to environmental effect.

(c) A statement as to whether construction of the facilities has been a source of controversy on environmental grounds in the local community.

(d) A discussion of environmental and other considerations which led to the selection of the particular site and, if relevant, the particular facility; the nature and extent of any unavoidable adverse environmental effects, and any alternative sites or facilities which have been or might reasonably be considered.

(3) The information submitted in the EA shall be factual (not argumentative or conclusory) and concise with sufficient detail to explain the environmental consequences and to enable the Commission, after an independent review of the EA, to reach a determination concerning the proposal's environmental impact, if any. The EA shall deal specifically with any feature of the site which has special environmental significance (e.g., wilderness area, wildlife preserves, natural migration paths for birds and other wildlife, and sites of historic, architectural, or archaeological value). In the case of historically significant sites, it shall

specify the effect of the facilities on any district, site, building, structure or object listed in the National Register of Historic Places, 39 Fed. Reg. 6402 (February 19, 1974). It shall also detail any substantial change in the character of the land utilized (e.g., deforestation, water diversion, wetland fill, or other extensive change of surface features). In the case of wilderness areas, wildlife preserves, or other like areas, the statement shall discuss the effect of any continuing pattern of human intrusion into the area (e.g., necessitated by the operation and maintenance of the facilities).

(4) The EA shall also be accompanied with evidence of site approval which has been obtained from local or federal land use authorities.

(5) To the extent that such information is submitted in another part of the application, it need not be duplicated in the EA, but adequate cross-reference to such information shall be supplied.

(6) An EA need not be submitted to the Commission if another agency of the Federal Government has assumed responsibility (a) for determining whether the facilities in question will have a significant effect on the quality of the human environment and, (b) if it will affect the environment, for invoking the environmental impact statement process.

INSTRUCTIONS FOR SECTION VI—EQUAL EMPLOYMENT OPPORTUNITY PROGRAM

A. Applicants seeking authority to construct a new commercial, noncommercial or international broadcast station, applicants seeking authority to obtain assignment of the construction permit or license of such a station, and applicants seeking authority to acquire control of an entity holding such construction permit or license are required to afford equal employment opportunity to all qualified persons and to refrain from discriminating in employment and related benefits on the basis of race. color, religion, national origin or sex . . . Pursuant to these requirements, an applicant who proposes to employ five or more full-time station employees must establish a program designed to assure equal employment opportunity for women and minority groups (that is, Blacks not of Hispanic origin, Asian or Pacific Islanders, American Indians or Alaskan Natives, and Hispanics) . . . If minority group representation in the available labor force is less than five percent (in the aggregate), a program for minority group members is not required. However, a program must be filed for women since they comprise a significant percentage of virtually all area labor forces. If an applicant proposes to employ less than five full-time employees, no EEO program for women or minorities need be filed.

B. Guidelines for developing an Equal Employment Opportunity program are . . . to be utilized only by applicants for new construction permits, assignees and transferees.

INSTRUCTIONS FOR SECTION VII—CERTIFICATIONS

A. Applicants for a new AM, FM or TV broadcast station or for a major modification of the authorized facilities of such stations . . . are required to give Public notice of the filing of their applications by publication in a local newspaper and/or by broadcast announcements . . .

B. An applicant need not have a binding agreement or absolute assurance of the availability of the transmitter site it proposes to utilize. However, the applicant must be able to show that it has obtained reasonable assurance that the proposed site is available to it. The Commission's requirements will be satisfied where an applicant has contacted the property owner or the owner's representative and has obtained reasonable assurance, in good faith, that the proposed site will be available for the intended purpose.

C. The original of this application form must be signed by the applicant . . .

QUESTIONS FOR CRITICAL ANALYSIS

- If the electromagnetic spectrum was not a limited resource, would it still be necessary for stations to be licensed?
- If the electromagnetic spectrum was not a limited resource, would small communities with one or two radio stations be able to support additional stations?
- If stations begin "transmitting" programs, not over the air but through fiber-optic cables, how would regulatory policy change in such areas as frequency assignments, financial qualifications, or other criteria used to award a construction permit or license?

- If the distribution of programming through fiber-optic cables becomes widespread, will federal, state, or local government take the lead in regulating "stations" using fiber-optic technology?
- If frequencies used for over-the-air broadcasting were vacated by radio and television stations, what pressures would be placed upon the FCC to reallocate these newly released frequencies for other services?
- What other services might dominate in demanding new space on the electromagnetic spectrum?
- Would a new policy for allocating frequencies be possible whereby the FCC would eliminate all primary stations and afford all other stations protection against interference?
- Frequency allocation is divided up among different users such as broadcasting, marine, amateur radio, and cellular telephone. Each service can claim a distinct benefit to their operations. For example, amateur radio operators argue that supporting amateur radio can result in new breakthroughs in applied communications. The cellular telephone industry argues it is an important source of consumer and business communication. Given the advantages of each type of service, how can the FCC justify cutting back one service to benefit another and what factors play a part in determining who gains frequencies and who loses them?
- With so many different sources of information available to consumers, is it really necessary for any radio or television station to be a high-powered station and broadcast beyond its immediate metropolitan area?
- Would a policy be feasible where some television stations would be asked to cut back their power, thereby permitting additional television frequencies to be assigned to smaller communities?
- Unlike a new broadcasting station, a new newspaper is not required to publish a public notice inviting other parties to comment before the newspaper starts publishing. Would the FCC be justified in eliminating the public notice requirement for a construction permit, thereby providing broadcasters with some of the rights newspapers enjoy?
- Would a local newspaper have any reason to challenge the application of a local radio station construction permit? Would such a challenge be taken seriously? If it would be taken seriously, on what grounds would it be considered?
- Why is it necessary for the FCC to concern itself with whether an applicant for a construction permit is a general partnership, limited partnership, or corporation?
- What is the rationale for giving preference to women and minorities in awarding a station license? Can women be at a political or economic disadvantage when applying for a construction permit?
- The FCC cautions applicants for a construction permit that it is not the practice of the commission to extend the time allocated for construction based on the inability of an applicant to meet its financial obligations. Is such a policy justified or does it keep individuals out of the industry who could make a significant contribution to programming and meeting the needs of an audience?
- Is the FCC unrealistic in showing a preference for material collateral such as land, trucks, buildings, and other assets which can be liquidated?
- Why is the station license not generally considered an asset for the purpose of meeting financial qualifications? Should it be?
- Broadcast financing is sometimes concentrated among a number of larger banks where particular expertise exists. Should the FCC, working with other government agencies, develop a system whereby smaller banks in local communities would be better prepared to offer financing to local radio and television stations? Would local lenders be skilled enough to make low-risk loans to local broadcasters?
- Would the risk be greater to small lending institutions than to larger banks which specialize in financing communications properties?
- Stations with less than five employees are exempt from filing an affirmative action plan. Is this policy justified?
- Could radio and television station call letters be assigned on the basis of states whereby each state would have a different prefix? What would be the advantage of such a system?
- With many radio stations using logo-type identification such as "Mix 98," "Kiss 100," and others, are call letters really necessary?
- Should the Federal Communications Commission stay out of call letter disputes and permit such disputes to be resolved through civil litigation only?
- Before allocating call letters, should the FCC examine other call letters awarded to the same

local area and determine if there is a potential for commercial infringement?

- Is the postcard renewal form used for radio stations an effective way of determining whether the station is meeting the needs of its local community?
- While the FCC requires a station to meet the needs of its local community, considerable latitude is given to stations in determining what those needs are. Should a more stringent review policy be imposed on stations requiring them to justify exactly how community needs are determined?
- Administrative law judges hear disputes over petitions to deny. These judges as part of the federal court system and tied to the agency in which they have jurisdiction are only one step in the federal court ladder. Could a policy be developed which puts the resolution of conflicts over petitions to deny under the jurisdiction of local district courts where a judge is more closely tied to the local community where the dispute originates?
- Under certain circumstances, one station can lease the facilities and the frequency of another station. Permission to engage in such leasing practices is many times based on temporary emergency conditions such as a natural disaster. Should a more lenient policy be developed by the FCC whereby two or more stations serving the same local community could share frequencies and programming back and forth at will? Assuming that such sharing practices were permitted and were adequately coordinated between the participating stations, would the audience benefit from such a policy?
- The FCC is an aggressive federal agency when it comes to monitoring affirmative action programs. Should the print media be required to administer the same affirmative action plans required by radio and television stations? Based on the First Amendment, could such a policy be enforced?
- The four top job categories enforced in FCC affirmative action plans are officials and managers, professionals, technicians, and people working in sales. Should any other categories be added to the FCC's affirmative action record keeping and enforcement policy? Examine the descriptions of these four categories found in the text and ask: Are the descriptions an accurate accounting of employees within each category? Is it possible to manipulate the categories through job titles or job descriptions, thereby usurping the spirit of affirmative action?
- Before being awarded a construction permit or a license renewal, should a station manager be required to certify skill in conducting employment interviews which avoid discrimination?
- Many stations conduct workshops to sensitize employees to the problems of sexual harassment in the workplace. Who is best qualified to conduct a sexual harassment sensitivity seminar which meets both the legal and personnel needs of a station?
- Read what constitutes sexual harassment. Can you think of any other incidents or conditions whereby sexual harassment would occur and should the definition of sexual harassment be expanded?
- Should both a man and a woman jointly conduct a sexual harassment seminar?
- Courts have determined that displaying sexually oriented posters in the workplace, including partially clad males or females, can be considered sexual harassment. Should other less obvious forms of sexual harassment also be eliminated in the workplace?
- Frequently, sexual harassment complaints, although private matters, become public knowledge. What legal issues can arise in an organization where an active sexual harassment complaint is unresolved?
- The at-will doctrine is primarily enforced at the state level. Should a federal employment at-will doctrine be imposed on radio and television stations since they operate with a federal license?
- Many employees work under "implied" contracts whereby a written document does not exist and the employee and employer operate over long periods of time in an atmosphere of mutual trust. Do written contracts prevent more or less opportunity for legal issues to emerge in an employee/employer relationship? Do written contracts lessen or increase the level of trust between employer and employee?
- Since periodic employment reviews and appraisals can result in implied contracts, should these appraisals be conducted by or in the presence of a skilled attorney? From a personnel and legal standpoint, would it be advisable to operate with as many contract employees as possible? What would be the benefits and liabilities of such a policy?

- Should stations use a blanket release policy for guest appearances regardless of whether the talent is an amateur or professional?
- Assess the federal regulations governing the Emergency Broadcast System. Do you feel the system can protect the public in a national emergency? Is the system open to sabotage?
- Most members of the public are not able to understand the complex technical information found in a public inspection file. Thus, should the requirement be eliminated?
- Coverage maps are used by stations in promotional materials distributed to advertising agencies and potential sponsors. Should stations be required to include a mileage scale showing the population within the coverage area? Should any additional information be included?
- Should foreigners be permitted to apply for a permit to construct a radio or television station?
- A requirement exists whereby a corporation is a party to a construction permit application if it subscribes to 5 percent or more of the voting stock and each of its executive officers is also considered a party to the application if they exercise authority or influence in the station. How would executive officers such as vice president, treasurer, or secretary working for a corporation with only 5 percent of the voting stock in a station be able to exercise control over it?
- If a corporation licensed to a foreign government operates in the United States and its executives are part of a local community's social, political, and economic structure, why should they be prohibited from applying for a construction permit or have significant investments in a local radio or television station?
- Why is an environmental assessment necessary when constructing a broadcast station? If the tower of a broadcasting station is located far away from the studio in a wilderness area, is an environmental assessment justified?
- High-intensity lights are used on the outside of many residential homes. Why is it necessary to have an environmental assessment if a broadcasting facility located in a residential neighborhood is equipped with high-intensity lights? In areas which are zoned for residential use, would a radio or television station construction permit run into public opposition if a building housing the facility was designed to look like a residential home?

ADDITIONAL RESOURCES

Bower, R., "Caution: FM Radio Broadcasting May Be Hazardous to What You Thought Was Your Service Mark." 5 *University of Bridgeport Law Review* 393 (1984).

Evans, A. B., "Are Minority Preferences Necessary? Another Look at the Radio Broadcasting Industry." 8 *Yale Law & Policy Review* 380 (1990).

Flick, S. R., "The Life, Death, and Rebirth of Section 319(a): The Prohibition of Premature Construction of Communications Facilities." 40 *Federal Communications Law Journal* 235 (1988).

Goriely, T., "Arbitrary Deductions from Pay and the Proposed Repeal of the Truck Acts." 12 *Industrial Law Journal* 236 (1983).

Holland, L. J., "Private International Broadcasting from the United States: Toward an Understanding of a Content Standard." 12 *North Carolina Journal of International Law and Commercial Regulation* 105 (1987).

Meeske, M. D. and J. Maunez-Cuadra, "Protecting Radio Call Letters and Slogans as Trademarks." 36 *Journal of Broadcasting & Electronic Media* 267 (1992).

Neal, A. C., "Recent Developments in Unfair Dismissal." 141 *New Law Journal* 1005 (July 19, 1991).

Rossini, M. J., "The Spectrum Scarcity Doctrine: A Constitutional Anachronism." 38 *Southwestern Law Journal* 827 (1985).

Stager, S. "Musical Performing Rights in the Television Industry: Has the Blanket License Finally Seen Its Demise?" 14 *Southwestern University Law Review* 569 (1984).

Stavitsky, A. G., "The Rise and Fall of the Distress Sale." 36 *Journal of Broadcasting & Electronic Media* 249 (1992).

Strauss, J. A., "The Performance Exemption under Section 110(5): Time for a Change." 22 *Duquesne Law Review* 669 (1984).

chapter ten

Wage and Hour Law in Station Operations

Growing out of the deplorable working conditions brought about by the Industrial Revolution of the late nineteenth and early twentieth centuries, the government began to take an active role in overseeing the treatment of workers in many different American industries. Today, various state laws apply to compensation, child labor, and overtime pay. At the federal level, employment practices in the United States are governed by the Fair Labor Standards Act (FLSA). Whether someone is an employee or operating a station which employs other people, understanding the basic principles of the FLSA is important to avoid unintentional mistakes which can be expensive if arbitrated in a disputed claim for compensation.

In broadcasting many different types of compensation exist, some exempt from the overtime pay and other provisions of the FLSA, others not. Moreover, the unusual nature of the broadcasting business makes it an unusual labor environment. For example, unlike other businesses a radio or television station cannot simply cut back and stay off the air when someone is sick or when a vacancy exists. A news department which suddenly finds itself covering a local crisis may need to have its personnel work longer hours. Having a basic understanding of wage and hour law can help avoid surprises when overtime pay is due employees, but for which money has not been budgeted. Even when unwritten agreements exist between employee "friends" who are "covering" for each other in a "trade out" of time due to one employee's illness, things can go wrong months later. Employees may become disgruntled and turn their wrath toward the station by claiming they were required to work overtime but not compensated. If an atmosphere exists where employees feel threatened if they complain, then that can compound the damages if a disputed claim goes against the station.

Understanding wage and hour law is important for both employees and employers. It can be an expensive and serious matter when a station manager operates over a long period of time and then finds employment practices have violated the Fair Labor Standards Act. Such violations can be costly as well as disruptive to the entire organization. Even past employees can sue under the FLSA, and they frequently do since they no longer work for the station and have nothing to lose. The lawsuits are often publicized by the local newspaper which covers the radio and television industry as an entertainment news beat.

Becoming well versed in labor law is not always the first priority of radio and television managers. After all, broadcasting is governed by the Federal Communications Commission and most managers have their hands full just dealing with FCC rules. Moreover, different managers have different strengths. Some managers come from legal backgrounds, others from programming, news, and engineering. Few are specialists in labor law. In this era of litigation, however, it is much better to understand the basics of labor law as a manager than as a defendant in a lawsuit when it is too late to change station policies. The reader is warned, however, that the discussions in this text are general in nature and that fine distinctions exist in the interpretations of wage and hour law. Competent counsel should be consulted before filing a complaint or becoming involved in a wage and hour dispute.

THE FAIR LABOR STANDARDS ACT: BACKGROUND

The Fair Labor Standards Act went into effect in October 1938. The act is administered and enforced by the Wage and Hour Division of the Department of Labor. While the wording of the law is the primary basis for court rulings in disputed wage and hour issues, the original act provided for "interpretations" of the law to be published by the Department of Labor and used as a basis for applying the FLSA to different employment situations. These interpretations, issued through the authority of the Wage and Hour Division, are used to clarify the meaning of the FLSA. Interpretations, while important, still do not carry the weight of the law itself when a disputed claim goes to court. Consequently, employers sometimes lose in court when they make the mistake of applying the interpretation instead of the actual wording of the FLSA to their particular dispute. (In the FLSA and the interpretations of the act, the term *he* and *his* is used. Such federal legal terminology, although outdated, is generic and applies to both male and female employees.)

The major provisions of the FLSA as they apply to broadcasting concern the exemptions to the overtime pay provisions. Broadcasting in particular is somewhat unusual because it has certain "artistic" and "professional" components which are treated differently in different parts of the industry. A radio station in a small market where the announcer reads the news will find that the announcer may be treated differently under the law than a news reporter at a radio station in a large market. Announcers and small-market stations are exempt from the overtime pay provisions, whereas a news reporter in a large market may not be exempt depending on that person's particular employment arrangement.

For anyone involved in a compensation dispute, competent counsel skilled in the understanding and practice of the FLSA should be retained, or a regional office of the Department of Labor should be consulted. Every employment situation is different, and it is difficult to apply working conditions in one station to those in another, even when the stations appear to be similar.

OVERTIME PAY PROVISIONS

In general terms, employees who are not exempt from the FLSA's overtime provisions must be paid one and one-half times their hourly rate of compensation for any hours worked over 40 hours in a given week.[1] This applies to employees of a station when a station is subject to the FLSA. While the 40-hour provision affects overtime pay, there is no limit under FLSA to the number of hours someone can work as long as they are paid overtime. Overtime is not usually required for working more than eight hours per day or for work on Saturdays, Sundays, or holidays, unless of course a separate contract has been agreed to by the station and employee to cover compensation during these times. In some cases the overtime provisions may apply if an employee works for two different stations but works more than 40 hours per week.[2]

The Workweek

A single workweek is the standard under which the FLSA is interpreted. You cannot average hours worked across two different weeks in applying the overtime standards of the act. For example, if a cameraperson in a station in a large metropolitan area works a total of 80 hours by working 50 hours the first week and 30 hours the second week, overtime provisions of the FLSA only apply to the first week when the cameraperson worked 50 hours, since the first week is the week that the cameraperson exceeded the 40-hour limit.

The overtime provisions apply regardless of whether the cameraperson is paid weekly, biweekly, monthly, or on another basis.[3] The workweek is considered fixed and consists of any consecutive 168 hours (seven consecutive 24-hour periods, or $7 \times 24 = 168$). A week can begin on any day and does not need to be the same day for all employees at the station.

Time of Overtime Payment

Overtime pay does not need to be paid on a weekly basis but must be paid no later than the time the usual pay period occurs. If overtime pay is irregular and must be computed, it can be paid at a reasonable time after the overtime pay is computed but no later than the next scheduled payday.[4] For example, if a satellite truck operator is paid on the fifteenth of each month and because of working a series of football games ends up working more than 40 hours per week, the overtime pay would appear in the paycheck at the next fifteenth after the overtime pay is computed.

The regular rate of pay upon which overtime is computed is not left to chance by the FLSA. Whatever the regular rate of pay is for the employee, that rate is used to compute overtime. Saying a person is paid a certain rate for 30 hours and another rate for 30 to 50 hours may not meet the criteria of the law if the effective rate of compensation for all 50 hours does not reflect compensation for overtime after the employee meets the 40-hour period. If for some reason an employee receives a retroactive pay increase, then overtime pay the employee is entitled to during the period covered by the retroactive pay increase must also be paid, and paid on the date the employee is compensated for the retroactive pay.

Figuring Hourly Rates of Pay

The FLSA makes it difficult for an employer to use creative compensation to get around the overtime requirement. As we have just read, the regular rate of pay under the FLSA is the rate per hour paid an employee. If an employee working a 40-hour week is paid a weekly salary and not exempt from the overtime requirements of the act, then the salary divided by 40 determines the hourly rate of pay.

If an employee works a 40-hour week and is paid monthly, then one way of computing the hourly rate is to multiply the pay-per-month by 12 (the number of months in a year), divide that amount by 52 (the number of weeks in a year), then divide that amount by 40 (the number of hours worked) to obtain the hourly wage upon which overtime is figured.

To better understand the preceding formula, consider, for example, that if a salaried employee makes $1,500 per month, the hourly wage is figured by multiplying $1,500 by 12 (the number of months in a year) which equals $18,000. The $18,000 is divided by 52 (the number of weeks in a year) which equals $346.15. The $346.15 is then divided by 40 (the workweek) which equals $8.65. The employee is compensated at the rate of $8.65 per hour and it is on this $8.65 per hour that overtime is figured at the rate of one and one-half times $8.65 for all hours worked in excess of 40 hours per week. If the employee works less than 40 hours, then that number of hours is divided into the salary.[5]

Salaried employees are not exempt from overtime pay simply because they are paid a salary. Other criteria to be exempt from overtime pay must be met, which will be discussed later in this chapter. Of course, to claim overtime pay an employee must be required to work *more* than 40 hours during a given week. Simply working additional hours voluntarily and then claiming the entitlement of overtime pay may not hold up with either your boss or the courts.

PRIZES AND AWARDS AS COMPENSATION

Stations offer prizes to listeners, viewers, and in large stations, prizes and awards may be awarded to employees. Sales contests and "suggestions" are two examples. These awards for activities not normally part of an employee's job still can amount to compensation. The FLSA interpretations state:

> (a) Where the prize is awarded for activities outside the customary working hours of the employee, beyond the scope of his customary duties or away from the employer's premises, the question of whether the compensation is remuneration for employment will depend on such factors as the amount of time, if any, spent by the employee in competing, the relationship between the contest activities and the usual work of the employee, whether the competition involves work usually performed by other employees for employers, whether an employee is specifically urged to participate or led to believe that he will not merit promotion or advancement unless he participates.
>
> (b) By way of example, a prize paid for work performed in obtaining new business for an employer would be regarded as remuneration for employment. Although the duties of the employees who participate in the contest may not normally encompass this type of work, it is the work of a kind normally performed by salesmen for their employers, and the time spent by the employees in competing for such a prize (whether successful or not) is working time and must be counted as such in determining

> overtime compensation due under the Act. On the other hand a prize or bonus paid to an employee when a sale is made by the company's sales representative to a person whom he recommended as a good sales prospect would not be regarded as compensation for services if in fact the prizewinner performed no work in securing the name of the sales prospect and spent no time on the matter for the company in any way.[6]

The FLSA provides for exemptions for people engaged in "outside" sales and these exemptions are discussed later in this chapter.

SUGGESTION SYSTEM AWARDS

A station manager decides to improve employee morale, engage employees in cost-savings ideas, try to instill more upward communication in the station, and generally let good ideas be recognized. The decision is made to put a "suggestion system," such as a suggestion box, in place and award prizes for the best suggestions. These prizes *can* fall under the FLSA as compensation.

> The question has been raised whether awards made to employees for suggestions submitted under a suggestion system plan are to be regarded as part of the regular rate. There is no hard and fast rule on this point as the term "suggestion system" has been used to describe a variety of widely differing plans. It may be generally stated, however, that prizes paid pursuant to a bona fide suggestion system plan may be excluded from the regular rate at least in situations where it is the fact that:
>
> (a) The amount of the prize has no relation to the earnings of the employee at his job but is rather geared to the value to the company of the suggestion which is submitted; and
>
> (b) The prize represents a bona fide award for a suggestion which is the result of additional effort or ingenuity unrelated to and outside the scope of the usual and customary duties of any employee of the class eligible to participate and the prize is not used as a substitute for wages; and
>
> (c) No employee is required or specifically urged to participate in the suggestion system plan or led to believe that he will not merit promotion or advancement (or retention of his existing job) unless he submits suggestions; and
>
> (d) The invitation to employees to submit suggestions is general in nature and no specific assignment is outlined to employees (either as individuals or as a group) to work on or develop; and
>
> (e) There is no time limit during which suggestions must be submitted; and
>
> (f) The employer has, prior to the submission of the suggestion by an employee, no notice or knowledge of the fact that an employee is working on the preparation of a suggestion under circumstances indicating that the company approved the task and the schedule of work undertaken by the employee.[7]

Particular care is necessary where subpart (f) of the rules is concerned. For example, an employee stops a manager in the hallway and makes a suggestion. The manager talks with the employee at length and then tells the employee to place the idea in the suggestion box so the manager can compensate the employee. That defeats the purpose of the exemption because the manager had knowledge and notice of the fact the employee was preparing the suggestion.

INDIVIDUAL CONTRACTS AND COLLECTIVE BARGAINING

Stations which have contracts with employees cannot be found guilty of violating the FLSA laws as long as the stations meet the minimum wage requirements and the overtime pay requirements for hours worked in excess of 40 hours. A collective bargaining agreement which meets overtime requirements and does not exceed a contract of 60 (sixty) hours per week, even for irregular hours, is usually considered to be within the standards set by the FLSA. The collective bargaining agreement must be made through negotiations with representatives of the employees. Stations operating under collective bargaining agreements operate within specialized areas of the Fair Labor Standards Act.

In summary, remember when applying the overtime provision of the FLSA that a typical workweek is any consecutive 168-hour period. Nonexempt employees who work more than 40 hours during that period may be entitled to overtime pay at the rate of one and one-half times their regular hourly rate. Salaried workers can also fall under the overtime provisions, depending on their duties and the hours worked, and some individual contracts or collective bargaining agreements determine the compensation levels beyond the specific interpretations of the FLSA.

FLSA EXEMPTIONS

Our attention now turns to those employees who are considered exempt from the overtime provisions of the FLSA. Keep in mind that the act itself took effect in 1938, before television stations proliferated the landscape and before cable television arrived.

Background

The FLSA was born in the industrialized, manufacturing economy of the late 1930s, not the high-technology service economy of today. Also, while such regulations as those enforced by the Federal Communications Commission have been kept mostly updated, there have been fewer revisions to the wage and hour laws. The Department of Labor instead uses the original interpretations of the act and subsequent court cases to determine enforcement policies. To some extent, this policy of judicial review, as opposed to frequent regulatory revision, is appropriate since virtually every employment situation has its own unique characteristics. Great diversity exists in the way radio and television stations are managed and operated. A small station may have the owner acting as a salesperson and news director. Even in larger stations employees sometimes wear more than one hat. Union stations operate with much more compartmentalized control and management than nonunion stations.

Terms

Terms as used in the FLSA and as they are interpreted in the broadcasting industry differ considerably. Someone involved in manufacturing and "production" as originally defined by the FLSA is a completely different person than someone involved in production at a television station. The former may be involved in the production of goods on a manufacturing company assembly line, while the latter sits inside a control room "producing" the evening news. Thus, as you read the interpretations of the exemptions to the overtime provisions, keep in mind that the frame of reference you have as a broadcaster or even as a station manager may be an entirely different one than a judge may have when hearing an appeal from a radio or television station caught in a messy compensation dispute. Nevertheless, the basis for the judge's decision will still rest with the letter of the FLSA as law, and also to a limited extent with the interpretations of the FLSA.

EXECUTIVE EXEMPTION TO OVERTIME PROVISIONS

Exemptions from the FLSA exist for an employee who is an "executive," "administrator," "professional," or "outside salesman." In other words, if you qualify as an executive, you may not be entitled to overtime pay. There is both a short test and a long test to determine if an employee is a bona fide executive with exempt status.

Criteria for Executive Exemption: Long Test

Using the long test, an employee in a bona fide executive capacity under the long test must meet all of the following criteria (emphases in italics added):

1. Their *primary duty* consists of the *management* of the station in which they are employed or in a customarily recognized *department or subdivision* of the station.
2. They customarily and regularly direct the work of *two or more employees.*
3. They have the authority to hire or fire other employees or whose suggestions and recommendations as to the hiring and firing and to the advancement and promotion or any other change of status will be given particular weight.
4. They *customarily and regularly exercise discretionary powers.*
5. They do not devote *more* than 20% of their time to work which is *not directly and closely related* to the work described in the points above. In other words, they must devote 80% of their time to executive activities and responsibilities as described in the points above.
6. They earn at least $155 per week.[8]

The FLSA states the preceding criteria do not "apply in the case of an employee who is in sole charge of an independent establishment or a physically separated branch establishment or who owns at least 20-percent interest in the enterprise in which he is employed."[9] For example, a television news reporter who is in sole charge of a regional bureau may come under this provision, depending on the reporter's other responsibilities. A bureau chief in sole charge of a regional news bureau would similarly come under this provision. Additional interpretations of the "sole charge" and the 20-percent rule are found later in this chapter.

Criteria for Executive Exemption: Short Test

In addition to the long test, a short test for executive exemption also exists. Specifically, persons are exempt as bona fide executives under the short test if they are compensated on a salary basis of not less than $250 per week and their primary duty consists of the management of the enterprise in which they are employed or of a customarily recognized department, and their work includes the customary and regular direction of the work of two or more employees.[10]

INTERPRETING THE EXECUTIVE EXEMPTION

As we read earlier in this chapter, the FLSA provided the administrator of the Wage and Hour Division of the U.S. Department of Labor the authority to develop interpretations of the FLSA as an aid to employers, employees, the courts, and the division in enforcing the provisions of the act. These interpretations are not the letter of the law, but they do provide us with an aid to more clearly understanding the law and eliminating some of its ambiguity. The interpretations are drawn upon frequently by the courts to justify decisions in compensation disputes.

Interpreting the Meaning of Management

Examples of what is meant by the term *management and primary duty* are provided in the act's interpretations. In most cases executives perform managerial duties which are easy to identify.

> For example, it is generally clear that work such as the following is exempt work when it is performed by an employee in the management of his department or the supervision of the employees under him: Interviewing, selecting, and training of employees; setting and adjusting their rates of pay and hours of work; directing their work; maintaining their production or sales records for use in supervision or control; appraising their productivity and efficiency for the purpose of recommending promotions or other changes in their status; handling their complaints and grievances and disciplining them when necessary; planning the work; determining the techniques to be used; apportioning the work among the workers . . .[11]

Interpreting When Management Is the Primary Duty

The determination of whether employees have management as their primary duty is determined by the specific employment conditions that exist in each enterprise. For example:

> The amount of time spent in the performance of the managerial duties is a useful guide in determining whether management is the primary duty of an employee. In the ordinary case it may be taken as a good rule of thumb that primary duty means the major part, or over 50 percent of his time, of the employee's time. Thus, an employee who spends over 50 percent of his time in management would have management as his primary duty. Time alone, however, is not the sole test, and in situations where the employee does not spend over 50 percent of his time in managerial duties, he might nevertheless have management as his primary duty if the other pertinent factors support such a conclusion. Some of these pertinent factors are the relative importance of the managerial duties as compared with other types of duties, the frequency with which the employee exercises discretionary powers, his relative freedom from supervision, and the relationship between his salary and the wages paid other employees for the kind of nonexempt work performed by the supervisor . . .[12]

The interpretations also spell out the application of the law to data processing, noting that "an employee who directs the day-to-day activities of a single group of programmers and who performs the more complex or responsible jobs in programming will be considered to have management as his primary duty."[13]

Defining a Department or Subdivision

Simply having the title of department head, director, supervisor, or other designation does not automatically qualify a person for the executive exemption.

> In order to properly classify an individual as an executive he must be more than merely a supervisor of two or more employees; nor is it sufficient that he merely participates in the management of the unit. He must be in charge of an have as his primary duty the management of a recognized unit which has a continuing function.[14]

Supervising Two or More Employees

To qualify as an executive supervising two or more employees, the employees must work in the department actually managed by the supervisor. For example, a radio station program director may not be considered exempt if the news staff of four employees is part of the news department and report to a news director, even if the news director reports to the program director. Programming may be considered a separate department from news and the program director's primary duty is supervising the announcers. Although supervision of the announcers may give the program director exempt status, it is the supervision of the announcers, not the news staff, that justifies the exemption.

The news director may be exempt but only if the news director and not the program director has the ability to fire and hire. Particular care must be taken when only two employees, or a very small number of employees, are under supervision since it is many times the case that with so few supervised employees, supervisors spend more than 20 percent of their time on other duties which are *not* exempt and therefore forfeit their exemption under the 20-percent rule.

Exercising Discretionary Powers

The criteria that an executive must "customarily and regularly" exercise discretionary powers can be confusing. For example, a television news reporter who daily goes into the field to cover stories may seem to customarily and regularly exercise discretionary powers. However, if the reporter's assignment is made by the news director or an assignment editor, the angle of the story is determined by the news director, and the video to be used on the air is ultimately selected by a producer, then the reporter is probably not exercising discretionary powers and may fail to meet the test for the executive exemption.

Defining Work Directly and Closely Related to Management

To qualify for an executive exemption, employees must not devote more than 20 percent of their time to work which is not directly and closely related to management of the enterprise. In interpreting the phrase "directly and closely related" to management, the Wage and Hour Division's interpretations state:

> (a) This phrase brings within the category of exempt work not only the actual management of the department and the supervision of the employees therein, but also activities which are closely associated with the performance of the duties involved in such managerial and supervisory functions or responsibilities. The supervision of employees and the management of a department include a great many directly and closely related tasks which are different from the work performed by subordinates and are commonly performed by supervisors because they are helpful in supervising the employees or contribute to the smooth functioning of the department for which they are responsible. Frequently such exempt work is of a kind which in establishments that are organized differently or which are larger and have greater specialization of function, may be performed by a nonexempt employee hired especially for that purpose.[15]

An example of how this provision applies can be seen in the work of accountants. If a person is hired exclusively to perform accounting work in a large organization, this work may not be exempt. On the other hand, in smaller organizations where accounting functions, such as budget preparation, are handled by supervisors, then this work could be interpreted as a management function and the time spent engaged in these accounting duties would be considered time spent on legitimate exempt management duties.

Being in Sole Charge of an Independent Establishment

You will remember there are two exceptions to the criteria for executive exemptions discussed earlier. The criteria do not "apply in the case of an employee who is in sole charge of an independent establishment or a physically separated branch establishment or who owns at least 20-percent interest in the enterprise in which he is employed."[16]

The sole-charge provision can, however, be confusing. To better understand the principle, consider that a regional news bureau is under the sole charge of a bureau chief who, through supervisory responsibilities, gains the executive exemption. The Wage and Hour Division's interpretations of these provisions help clarify the "sole-charge" rule.

To apply the interpretation to broadcasting, when you read the interpretation think of the "branch" as the regional news bureau separated from the station or network and under the direction of the bureau chief.

> Since the employee must be in "sole charge", only one person in any establishment can qualify as an executive under this exception, and then only if he is the top person in charge at that location . . . Thus, it would not be applicable to an employee who is in charge of a branch establishment but whose superior makes his offices on the premises. An example is a district manager who has overall supervisory functions in relation to a number of branch offices, but makes his office at one of the branches. The branch manager at the branch where the district manager's office is located is not in "sole charge" of the establishment and does not come within the exception. This does not mean that the "sole-charge" status of an employee will be considered lost because of an occasional visit to the branch office of the superior of the person in charge, or, in the case of an independent establishment by the visit for a short period on 1 or 2 days a week of the proprietor or principal corporate officer of the establishment . . .
>
> In order to qualify for the exception the employee must ordinarily be in charge of all the company activities at the location where he is employed. If he is in charge of only a portion of the company's activities at his location, then he cannot be said to be in sole charge of an independent establishment or a physically separated branch establishment . . .[17]

Nonintegrated Job Function

In some cases an employee may be in charge of a branch office or bureau but one function is not integrated into the bureau's activities. The interpretations of the FLSA point out that the executive exemption is not lost if:

> This one function is not important to the activities managed by the executive and constitutes only an insignificant portion of the employer's activities at that branch. Normally only one employee (at most two or three, but in any event an insignificant number when compared with the total number of persons employed at the branch) is engaged in the nonintegrated function for which the executive whose sole-charge status is in question is not responsible. Under such circumstances the employee does not lose his "sole-charge" status . . .[18]

An example of the nonintegrated function just described would be a regional news bureau where some desk space at the bureau is devoted to a salesperson selling time in the city where the regional bureau is located. The salesperson reports to the sales manager back at the station or network and not to the bureau chief.

As a general rule the responsibilities, duties, and salary of an employee determine whether the employee meets the criteria for exempt executive status. Titles are not sufficient to achieve the exemption.

ADMINISTRATIVE EXEMPTION TO OVERTIME PROVISIONS

In addition to executive exemptions, "administrative" exemptions to the overtime provisions of the FLSA also exist.

Criteria for Administrative Exemption: Long Test

The long test for administrative exemptions requires that the employee's primary duty meets all of the following criteria (emphases in italics added):

1. They perform office or *nonmanual* work *directly related to management policies or general*

business operations of his employers or his employer's customers.

2. They customarily and regularly exercise *discretion and independent judgement*.
3. They regularly and directly assist another person working in a bona fide executive or administrative capacity.
4. They perform under only general supervision work along specialized or technical lines requiring special training, experience, or knowledge.
5. They execute under only general supervision special assignments and tasks.
6. They do not devote more than 20% of their time to work which is not *directly and closely related* to the work described in the points above. In other words, they must devote 80% of their time to administrative activities and responsibilities as described in the points above.
7. They earn at least $155 per week.[19]

Criteria for Administrative Exemption: Short Test

A short test also exists for administrative exemptions. The short test requires the employees earn at least $250 a week, their primary duty must consist of performing office or nonmanual labor directly related to management or general business operations of the station, and they must perform work which requires them to customarily and regularly exercise discretion and independent judgment.[20]

INTERPRETING THE ADMINISTRATIVE EXEMPTION

In interpreting the administrative exemption, a fine line exists between what is exempt work and what is not exempt. Unlike the executive exemption which is somewhat more clearly defined because of the high-level responsibilities the employee assumes in the station, the administrative area can be more nebulous. For example, the specific tasks which require the exercise of discretion and independent judgment are clearly exempt from the overtime provisions.

This does not mean, however, that it is easy to determine when in fact discretion and independent judgment actually exist. Our example of the television newsroom applies here. A television reporter who is given complete freedom to cover whatever story the reporter wishes to cover, from whatever angle the reporter chooses, with whatever script and accompanying video the reporter chooses, is exercising discretion and independent judgment. On the other hand, when the reporter's tasks are highly directed, then the opportunity to exercise discretion and independent judgment may be absent.

Work Requiring Discretion and Independent Judgment

Some work may be performed by employees which may be routine and not require discretion and independent judgment, but "has a direct and close relationship to the performance of the more important duties."[21] This work, which is functionally related to the administrative duties, falls between work which is clearly exempt as discussed in the criteria and work which is clearly not exempt. This work, which falls between clearly exempt and clearly nonexempt work:

> . . . would appear to be routine, or on a fairly low level, and which does not itself require the exercise of discretion and independent judgement, but which has a direct and close relationship to the performance of the more important duties. The directness and closeness of the relationship may vary depending upon the nature of the job and the size and organization of the establishment in which the work is performed. This "directly and closely related" work includes routine work which necessarily arises out of the administrative duties, and the routine work without which the employee's more important work cannot be performed properly. It also includes a variety of routine tasks which may not be essential to the proper performance of the more important duties but which are functionally related to them directly and closely. In this latter category are activities which an administrative employee may reasonably be expected to perform in connection with carrying out his administrative functions including duties which either facilitate or arise incidentally from the performance of such functions and are commonly performed in connection with them.[22]

The key term in the preceding interpretation is *direct and close relationship*. When work, even though routine, has a direct and close relationship to administrative work, then performing this work may qualify as an exemption.

At the same time, the 20-percent rule must also be kept in mind. Too much routine or manual work may be interpreted as making the individual's job too routine to be considered administrative. This distinction is further clarified in the interpretation of the phrase "nonmanual work."

Interpreting Nonmanual Work

Although the FLSA specifically requires nonmanual work as a requirement for an administrative exemption, the interpretation of the law does not prohibit nonmanual work:

> The requirement that the work performed by an exempt administrative employee must be office work or nonmanual work restricts the exemption to "white-collar" employees who meet the tests. If the work performed is "office" work it is immaterial whether it is manual or nonmanual in nature. This is consistent with the intent to include within the term "administrative" only employees who are basically white-collar employees since the accepted usage of the term "white-collar" includes all office workers . . .
>
> (The interpretation of the law) does not completely prohibit the performance of manual work by an "administrative" employee. The performance by an otherwise exempt administrative employee of some manual work which is directly and closely related to the work requiring the exercise of discretion and independent judgement is not inconsistent with the principle that the exemption is limited to "white-collar" employees. However, if the employee performs so much manual work (other than office work) that he cannot be said to be basically a "white-collar" employee he does not qualify for exemption as a bona fide administrative employee, even if the manual work he performs is directly and closely related to the work requiring the exercise of discretion and independent judgement. Thus, it is obvious that employees who spend most of their time in using (instruments or equipment) or in performing repetitive operations with their hands, no matter how much skill is required, would not be bona fide administrative employees . . . An office employee, on the other hand, is a "white-collar" worker, and would not lose the exemption on the grounds that he is not primarily engaged in "nonmanual" work, although he would lose the exemption if he failed to meet any of the other requirements.[23]

In reading the preceding interpretation, the term *white-collar worker* appears. In practice, the term is *not* always interpreted in the literal sense but is used to refer to employees who perform administrative duties. Many radio stations, especially contemporary ones, have a corporate culture which results in few people wearing "white collars." The origin of the term *white collar* is from the era of manufacturing where the white-collar worker was clearly management and those who did not wear white collars worked in the production of goods. Nevertheless, in applying the FLSA, the term is still in use.

Work Directly Related to Management Policies: Basic Premise

The FLSA requires that an employee eligible for the administrative exemption of the FLSA must perform work directly related to management policies or general business operations. The station sales manager may therefore qualify for an administrative exemption and in some stations an executive exemption. In interpreting and enforcing the phrase "directly related to management policies or general business operation," the Wage and Hour Division provides some examples:

> The phrase "directly related to management policies or general business operations of his employer or his employer's customers" describes those types of activities relating to the administrative operations of a business as distinguished from "production" . . . In addition to describing the types of activities, the phrase limits the exemption to persons who perform work of substantial importance to the management or operation of the business of his employer or his employer's customers.
>
> The administrative operations of the business include the work performed by so-called white-collar employees engaged in "servicing" a business as, for example, advising the management, planning, negotiating, representing the company, purchasing, promoting sales, and business

> research and control. An employee performing such work is engaged in activities relating to the administrative operations of the business . . .
>
> As used to describe work of substantial importance to the management or operation of the business, the phrase "directly related to management policies or general business operation" is not limited to persons who participate in the formulation of management policies or in the operation of the business as a whole. Employees whose work is "directly related" to management policies or to general business operations include those whose work affects policy or whose responsibility it is to execute or carry it out. The phrase also includes a wide variety of persons who either carry out major assignments in conducting the operations of the business, or whose work affects business operations to a substantial degree, even though their assignments are tasks related to the operation of a particular segment of the business . . .[24]

Work Directly Related to Management Policies: Examples

The regulatory interpretations of the FLSA provide examples of what constitutes work directly related to management:

> Some firms employ persons whom they describe as "statisticians." If all such a person does, in effect, is to tabulate data, he is clearly not exempt. However, if such an employee makes analyses of data and draws conclusions which are important to the determination of, or which, in fact, determine financial, merchandising, or other policy, clearly he is doing work directly related to management policies or general business operations. Similarly, a personnel employee may be a clerk (or may determine) personnel policies affecting all the workers in the establishment. In the latter case, he is clearly doing work directly related to management policies or general business operations. These examples illustrate the two extremes. In each case, between these extreme types there are many employees whose work may be of substantial importance to the management or operation of the business, depending upon the particular facts . . .
>
> The test of "directly related to management policies or general business operations" is also met by many persons employed as advisory specialists and consultants of various kinds . . . account executives of advertising agencies . . . and many others.[25]

In examining the interpretations of the phrase "directly related to management policies or general business operations," some examples applied to broadcasting can be readily seen. For example, in a station or station group which employs an individual to manage personnel policies, that person would most likely be involved in administrative work. Those individuals who have group-wide personnel responsibilities most likely would fall under the executive exemptions. On the other hand, the person who works in the station's personnel department and collects and files résumés, even if engaged in interviewing applicants, may not qualify for either an administrative or executive exemption.

Many large stations have research departments which customarily examine ratings data and design promotional material to support the sales department. A statistician who works in the department and "crunches numbers" but plays a small role in determining how the numbers are used would not normally be exempt, while those who take the numbers and plan and design promotional strategies could be exempt. The key is whether the work is directly related to the management policies or business operations, and planning research and promotional strategies would be. Other criteria would, however, still have to be met, including the 20-percent rule.

PROFESSIONAL EXEMPTION TO OVERTIME PROVISIONS

People who work in bona fide professional capacities as defined by the FLSA are exempt from the overtime provisions of the law. The professional exemptions, especially in broadcasting provide some of the more difficult interpretations and each station is different.

Criteria for Professional Exemption: Long Test

The FLSA provides for professional exemption to the overtime provisions if the employee's primary duties meet all of the following criteria (emphases in italics added):

1. Their work requires knowledge of an advanced type in a field of science or learning

customarily acquired by a prolonged course of *specialized* intellectual instruction and study, as distinguished from a general academic education and from an apprenticeship, and from training in the performance of routine mental, manual, or physical processes.

2. Their work must be original and creative in character in a *recognized field of artistic endeavor* (as opposed to work which can be produced by a person endowed with general manual or intellectual ability and training), and the result of which depends primarily on *invention, imagination, or talent* of the employee.
3. Their work requires the consistent exercise of discretion and judgement in its performance.
4. Their work is predominantly *intellectual and varied* in character (as opposed to routine mental, manual, mechanical, or physical work) and is of such character that the output produced or the result accomplished cannot be standardized in relation to a given period of time.
5. They do not devote more than 20 percent of their hours worked in the workweek to activities which are not an *essential part of and necessarily incident to* the work described in the above points. In other words, they must devote 80% of their time to professional work as described in the points above.
6. They earn at least $170 per week.[26]

Notice the emphasis on the professional exemption is not as much the supervisory and administrative responsibilities as it is the specialized training and the creative and intellectual nature of the work performed.

Criteria for Professional Exemption: Short Test

The short test for professional exemption requires that the employee earn $250 per week and that the employee's primary duty includes work requiring knowledge of an advance type in a field of science and which requires the consistent exercise of discretion and judgment or work requiring invention, imagination, or talent in a recognized field of artistic endeavor.[27]

INTERPRETATIONS OF THE PROFESSIONAL EXEMPTION

Some general comments about the professional exemption are appropriate here. First, while certainly everyone who works in any position of semiresponsibility in a station may consider themselves a professional, this does not mean they meet the criteria under the FLSA. For example, a general assignment reporter with a degree in liberal studies may work under the highly structured direction of a news director and not be able to exercise enough discretion to qualify for the exemption. Similarly, the liberal arts training the reporter received in college may be considered general academic education as distinguished from "specialized intellectual instruction."

Quoted in a trade publication after a Louisiana television station lost a case in an FLSA dispute, Terry Etter, staff attorney for the National Association of Broadcasters said, "stations interested in maintaining overtime exemptions should take a number of precautions, such as requiring that news personnel have specialized degrees in broadcast journalism and giving news personnel more artistic freedom in choosing and developing stories and structuring newscasts."[28] This case and others clearly established that television news reporters are not automatically exempt from the FLSA's overtime provisions unless they meet strict tests as "professionals" as defined by the law.

Professional Work in a Recognized Field of Artistic Endeavor

Some television reporters may be surprised to learn they may not be considered professionals under the law even though they consider their work artistic in nature. After all, they shoot pictures and then mold those pictures through editing, using their own discretion, to create an artistic video product which appears on the air. Few would argue with the contention that a certain amount of artistic skill is necessary along with invention, imagination, and talent. Similarly, the person skilled in computer graphics who composes the scenes which appear on weather maps or as background in newscasts may very well consider themselves talented artists in the same way that a painter does or a syndicated cartoonist might.

The news writers who must compose news stories everyday may consider themselves artists in the same way that a nonfiction author does. Yet, these assumptions do not automatically make such people exempt professionals. Similarly, the "more responsible writing positions in advertising agencies" are clearly considered to be exempt professionals, but would a senior copy writer or assistant in the sales department of a radio station be entitled to the same exemption?[29] Perhaps. The tests for meeting the artistic professional criteria are very strict and narrow. The interpretations as defined by the Department of Labor read:

> (1) The work must be original and creative in character, as opposed to work which can be produced by a person endowed with general manual or intellectual ability and training. In the field of music there should be little difficulty ascertaining the application of the requirement. Musicians, composers, conductors, soloists, all are engaged in original and creative work within the sense of this definition . . . It is similarly met by cartoonists who are merely told the title or underlying concept of a cartoon and then must rely on their own creative powers to express the concept. It would not normally be met by a person who is employed as a copyist, or as an "animator" of motion-picture cartoons, or as a retoucher of photographs since it is not believed that such work is properly described as creative in character.
>
> (2) In the field of writing the distinction is perhaps more difficult to draw. Obviously the requirement is met by essayists or novelists or scenario writers who choose their own subjects and hand in a finished piece of work to their employers (the majority of such persons are, of course, not employees but self-employed). The requirement would also be met, generally speaking, by persons holding the more responsible writing positions in advertising agencies.[30]

Such fields as music, writing, and theater are interpreted by the Department of Labor as recognized fields of artistic endeavor.

Meeting the Invention, Imagination, and Talent Criteria

The interpretations of the FLSA applied to professional exemptions require "invention, imagination, and talent." According to the government's guidelines, "This requirement is easily met by a person employed as an actor, or a singer, or a violinist, or a short-story writer."[31]

Specific interpretations are made for employees of newspapers and these are sometimes referred to in rulings affecting broadcasters. Specifically, the interpretations state that in the case of employees of newspapers, the work must be "original and creative in character." In a statement with which some newspaper reporters might disagree, the interpretations state that, "obviously the majority of reporters do work which depends primarily on intelligence, diligence, and accuracy," but it is the minority whose work depends on invention, imagination, or talent.[32] Clearly, the interpretation of the FLSA applied to newspaper reporters does not automatically consider newspaper reporters exempt professionals, even though reporters may consider themselves writers.

Journalists as Professionals

As you read the interpretations which follow, make comparisons to the broadcast media and ask yourself if these same examples could apply to a radio or television newsroom. The interpretations state: "The field of journalism also employs many exempt as well as many nonexempt employees under the same or similar job titles."[33] The interpretations refer specifically to newspaper reporters and writers:

> (1) Newspaper writers, with possible exceptions in certain highly technical fields, do not meet the requirements . . . for exemption as professional employees of the "learned" type. Exemption for newspaper writers as professional employees is normally available under the provisions for professional employees of the "artistic" type. Newspaper writers of the exempt type must, therefore, be "predominantly original and creative in character." Only writing which is analytical, interpretative or highly individualized is considered to be creative in nature. (The writing of fiction to the extent that it may be found on a newspaper would also be considered as exempt work.) Newspaper writers commonly performing work which is original and creative within the meaning of (the professional exemption) are editorial writers, columnists, critics, and "top-flight" writers of analytical and interpretative articles.
>
> (2) The reporting of news, the rewriting of stories received from various sources, or the routine editorial work of a newspaper is not predominantly original and creative in character within the meaning of (professional exemption) and must be considered as nonexempt work. Thus, a reporter or news writer ordinarily collects facts about news

events by investigation, interview, or personal observation and writes stories reporting these events for publication, or submits the facts to a rewrite man or other editorial employee for story preparation. Such work is nonexempt work. The leg man, the reporter covering a police beat, the reporter sent out under specific instructions to cover a murder, fire, accident, ship arrival, convention, sport event, etc., are normally performing duties which are not professional in nature within the meaning of the act . . .

(3) Incidental interviewing or investigation, when it is performed as an essential part of and is necessarily incident to an employee's work, however, need not be counted as nonexempt work. Thus, if a dramatic critic interviews an actor and writes a story around the interview, the work of interviewing him and writing the story would not be considered as nonexempt work. However, a dramatic critic who is assigned to cover a routine news event such as a fire or a convention would be doing nonexempt work since covering the fire or the convention would not be necessary and incident to his work as a dramatic critic.[34]

Television reporters often do more than "write" the news. Frequently they cover the story, write the story, shoot their own video, and appear on camera. Many hold bachelor's degrees from accredited colleges and have majored in what some people would consider specialized areas such as radio-TV, journalism, speech, or communications. Would these people fit into the same definition as newspaper reporters and not be exempt from the overtime provisions because they do not qualify as "professionals" under the FLSA?

Radio and Television Announcers as Professionals

While Labor Department interpretations have not been developed for television reporters, people who work as announcers in radio and television are discussed in the department's interpretations which state:

> The determination of the exempt or nonexempt status of radio and television announcers as professional employees has been relatively difficult because of the merging of the artistic aspects of the job with the commercial. There is considerable variation in the type of work performed by various announcers, ranging from predominantly routine to predominantly exempt work. The wide variation in earnings as between individual announcers, from the highly paid "name" announcer on a national network who is greatly in demand by sponsors to the staff announcer paid a comparatively small salary in a small station, indicates not only great differences in personality, voice and manner, but also in some inherent special ability or talent which, while extremely difficult to define, is nevertheless real.[35]

Announcers as Professionals: Specific Duties

The regulatory interpretations spell out some of the duties announcers perform. You will notice that some of these examples appear outdated. The FLSA has relied on case law as opposed to amended regulations to enforce its provisions.

> The duties which many announcers are called upon to perform include: Functioning as a master of ceremonies; playing dramatic, comedy, or straight parts in a program; interviewing; conducting farm, fashion, and home economics programs; covering public events, such as sports programs, in which the announcer may be required to ad lib and describe current changing events; and acting as narrator and commentator. Such work is generally exempt. Work such as giving station identification and time signals, announcing the names of programs, and similar routine work is nonexempt work. In the field of radio entertainment as in other fields of artistic endeavor, the status of an employee as a bona fide professional . . . is in large part dependent upon whether his duties are original and creative in character, and whether they require invention, imagination, or talent. The determination of whether a particular announcer is exempt as a professional employee must be based upon his individual duties and the amount of exempt and nonexempt work performed, as well as his compensation.[36]

Notice the emphasis of the interpretation is on the artistic aspects of an announcer's duties and the department uses the artistic quality as a key factor to determine whether an announcer is professionally exempt. Questions exist over such matters as whether a news reporter covering a live event and needing to ad lib is engaging in exempt work.

The Professional Concept of Intellectual and Varied Work

The Wage and Hour Division does not make it easy to understand the concept of intellectual and varied work as described in the professional exemption. The key test applies to the "type of thinking which must be performed by the employee."[37] That test in itself is difficult to define. For example, an engineer in a radio station who plays the cartridge tapes for the announcer is not performing duties which would be considered intellectual and varied, despite the fact the engineer might be considered a professional. Depending on the engineer's background and other responsibilities, the work being performed would not qualify as professionally exempt. The "thinking" the engineer engages in is not varied.

What is sometimes frustrating for broadcasters, and other employers for that matter, is the need to define a professional's duties under the requirement that the work an employee engages in is intellectually varied. First, the employer is dealing with thought processes, not the easiest process to define. Second, in a dispute with the Department of Labor, the explanation is made even more difficult when dealing with officials and attorneys who may not have a background in broadcasting. Third, a judge who hears a case involving overtime pay may also lack any background or understanding of broadcasting. Decisions are based on a law which took effect in 1938 and has used the courts more than updated regulatory interpretations to determine the applicability of the law to employment practices in the broadcasting industry.

Defining Professional Work Considered Essential

A careful reading of the criteria for professional exemption sees that the 20-percent rule clearly identifies activities which are "an essential part of and necessarily incident to" the professional work.[38] This distinction is more clearly defined for the professional exemption than it is for the executive or administrative exemption which identifies work "directly and closely related to" administrative and executive duties.[39] The test of work being "essential and incident to" is a stronger test than the test of work which is "directly and closely related to." The test is especially applicable to routine work which when applied to the professional exemption must be "essential and incident to" the professional duties of the employee.

Professional Work in General

The Department of Labor is quick to point out that people working in a professional field are not necessarily professionally exempt under the FLSA. For example, the fact that a person works in engineering does not necessarily make that person a professional under the FLSA. The person's responsibilities as well as his or her training and background come into play. Similarly, having the title of engineer does not make a person an exempt professional. While the title of engineer is broad and covers many different types of work including work in broadcasting, people who have the title are not always professional engineers under the meaning of the FLSA.

OUTSIDE SALES EXEMPTION TO OVERTIME PROVISIONS

Employees classified as "outside salesmen" must meet the following criteria to be exempt under the FLSA.

1. They are employed for the purpose of, and are customarily and regularly engaged away from the station in making sales or obtaining orders or contracts for services or for the use of facilities for which a consideration will be paid by the client or customer.
2. They must not spend more than 20 percent of their working hours engaged in activities not listed above. Work performed incidental to and in conjunction with the employee's own outside sales or solicitations, including collections, shall not be regarded as nonexempt work.[40]

INTERPRETING THE OUTSIDE SALES EXEMPTION

The 20-percent rule is interpreted as meaning that if an employee engaged in sales traditionally works a 40-hour week, then the employee cannot spend more than eight hours (20 percent) in nonselling activities. The exemption is not available to those people who are being trained in sales. Specifically, "the exemption is applicable to an employee employed in the capacity of outside salesman and does not include employees training to become outside salesmen who are not actually performing the duties of an outside salesman."[41] No salary requirements are included in the outside sales exemptions. Keep in mind that many people who are involved in broadcast sales are paid on commission and their pay is irregular. Trying to apply such measures as the minimum wage or overtime to this type of compensation schedule can evolve into a mathematical nightmare that would tax the patience of attorneys as well as the courts.

COMBINATION EXEMPTIONS: TACKING

The FLSA provides for certain combinations of exemptions to qualify an employee as exempt from the overtime provisions. The combination exemptions are referred to as *tacking*, which means the tacking on of one exemption to another exemption. For example, when a person who does both professional and administrative work for 80 percent (no more than 20 percent of nonexempt work) of their workweek, the station may tack together the professional and the administrative work to obtain the exemption. Remember that the executive, administrative, and professional exemptions have salary requirements. When tacking occurs, the higher salary requirement of the combination must be met.

RADIO AND TELEVISION SMALL-MARKET EXEMPTION

Employees working in radio and television stations which operate in small markets or within a larger market but more than 40 airline miles from the principal city in the market, are exempt from the overtime pay requirements of the FLSA.[42]

Definition of the Small-Market Exemption

The FLSA identifies the station's studio as needing to be:

> (a) in a city or town of 100,000 population or less, according to the latest available decennial census figures as compiled by the Bureau of the Census except where such city or town is part of a standard metropolitan statistical area, as defined by the Bureau of the Budget, which has a total population in excess of 100,000; or
>
> (b) in a city or town of 25,000 population or less which is part of such an area but is at least 40 airline miles from the principal city of area.[43]

Interpreting the Census Terminology of the Exemption

In applying the law, census figures would be based on the 1990 census but the term *Standard Metropolitan Statistical Area* has been dropped from use in census terminology and new terminology substituted. The new terminology defines Metropolitan Statistical Areas (MSAs); Primary Metropolitan Statistical Areas (PMSAs); and Consolidated Metropolitan Statistical Areas (CMSAs), but the FLSA has not been amended to reflect the change, and stations operate under old terminology and census data pending the availability of the 1990 census figures and revision of the FLSA to reflect current census terminology.

Job Definitions of Announcers, News Editors, and Engineers

The FLSA exempts announcers, news editors, and engineers in small-market radio and television stations.[44] For the purpose of the small-market exemption, announcers are defined as "an employee who appears before the microphone or camera to introduce programs, read news announcements, present commercial messages, give station identification and time signals and present other similar routine on-the-air-material."[45] Announcers also "operate the studio control board, give cues to the control room for switching programs, make recordings, make the necessary preparations for the day's programming, play records, or write advertising, promotional or similar type copy."[46]

A news editor "gathers, edits, and rewrites the news. He may also select and prepare news items for broadcast and present the news on the air."[47] A chief engineer is defined in the FLSA as "an employee who primarily supervises the operation, maintenance, and repair of all electronic equipment in the studio and at the transmitter and is licensed by the FCC."[48] Because of the changing nature of the industry, varied employment conditions, and the outdated terminology, a competent communications attorney should be consulted to obtain the latest rulings where small-market exemptions are concerned.

APPLYING WAGE AND HOUR LAW TO STATION OPERATIONS

When the Fair Labor Standards Act was written, Congress gave the Department of Labor the authority to define key terms and to pass regulations and interpretations which could be used to enforce the provisions of the law. Later, specific measures were adopted which affected print journalism and the newspaper industry. Provisions within the law also apply to such people as announcers, engineers, and news editors, if these employees work in small markets as defined by the most recent census. Beyond those delineations, however, the act has been applied through individual court cases. Unlike the Federal Communications Commission which deals with technology and must come to grips on a regular basis with the future of the industry, the Department of Labor in its enforcement of the Fair Labor Standards Act is not quick to change the law and has permitted the courts to interpret the regulations governing such issues as minimum wage and overtime pay.

A disadvantage of such a policy is that with the exception of certain jobs in certain industries, the exemptions to the overtime pay provisions of the Fair Labor Standards Act remain purposefully general in nature to encompass as many different employment situations as possible. That theory of law and regulation is not new. The U.S. Constitution with its First Amendment guarantees of free press is one of the reasons some individual states have stayed away from passing laws governing the press. The states feel the general wording of the First Amendment is the best protection of a free press and by narrowly defining an issue through government regulation simply excludes other protections under the Constitution.

To some extent a similar philosophy exists in the enforcement of the Fair Labor Standards Act. Definitions and interpretations of the executive, administrative, professional, and outside sales exemptions are spelled out by the Department of Labor and left to the courts to mediate. Appellate courts representing different districts in the United States are many times more familiar with labor conditions and particular types of business in their respective regions.[49] Although decisions in a given appellate circuit apply only to that circuit, each decision nevertheless serves as a barometer of labor law enforcement and to similar businesses nationwide. To gain a deeper understanding of the FLSA, in this chapter we will examine the application of the Fair Labor Standards Act to the field of broadcasting, and specifically to television news.[50] In reading from case law quoted as examples in this chapter, it is not as important who won or lost as it is how the law was applied. Also, from your own knowledge of television newsroom operations, ask yourself if the decisions affirm your own impressions about the way television journalists are perceived as professionals, how television news is perceived as a profession, and what employment conditions exist in a television newsroom.

Before reading further, a review of the different categories of exemptions appearing earlier in this chapter is recommended.

EMPLOYER'S BURDEN OF PROOF

In applying the Fair Labor Standards Act, it is unequivocal who has the burden of proof in a compensation dispute. Clearly, it falls on the station's management to prove that a person is exempt from the overtime provisions. Thus, when a case goes to court, the station, *not* the employee, has the burden of proving that the employee is exempt because the employee's primary duties individually or combined, as when tacking applies, are classified as executive, administrative, or professional.[51] That burden of proof is not always easy, especially when it must be exercised as a defendant in a lawsuit. The station's failure to prove the employee *is* exempt virtually assures in the eyes of the court that the employee is *not* exempt. Even when the evidence seems balanced between the employee being exempt and not exempt, unless the proof is significant and persuasive to the contrary, the employee will often prevail because the station has simply not garnered overwhelming evidence to the contrary. In one instance the Department of Labor notified a station that the Department of Labor "approved of the station's compensation paid to its employees and said there was no violation" of the FLSA. Four years later the station found itself on the losing end of a lawsuit for overtime compensation.[52]

FINDINGS OF LAW AND FINDINGS OF FACT

As has been noted earlier, the enforcement of the FLSA has been left to a great degree to the courts. When cases do go to court the findings of "law" and the findings of "fact" are part of a court's basis upon which the decision is rendered.

Findings of Law

The findings of law are the application and the interpretation of the wording of the FLSA as it applies to the disputed claim, be it overtime, minimum wage, child labor, or whatever legal issue arises. In broadcasting, overtime is an issue of chief concern. However, as we have already seen, interpreting the FLSA is not an exact science. Well-intentioned managers have found themselves on the defendant side of lawsuits, faced with trying to prove in court that their employees are exempt and doing so under the nebulous interpretations of wage and hour law.

Findings of Fact

The findings of fact, or "historical facts" which set out to define the original terms of employment, go to the very heart of station operations. Such questions as exactly what an employee's duties are are sometimes difficult to prove, or defend against, especially when such things as job descriptions and contracts do not exist. Moreover, once a lawsuit is filed, it is too late to change station policy. Frequently, the employee's testimony can carry unusual weight since the employee is the one who may be perceived by the court as knowing best what his or her duties actually are. If more than one employee is a party to the suit, then collaborating testimony is possible and a many-against-one, employees-against-management scenario can result. Remember also it is the responsibility of the management of the station to prove the employee is exempt from being entitled to overtime pay.

Distinguishing Between Law and Fact

A court considering a compensation complaint under the FLSA must determine both law (the FLSA) and fact (including historical fact and the conditions of employment). Findings of fact can be difficult to overturn on appeal since they often involve somewhat mechanical tasks such as gathering testimony and cataloguing on-the-job activities, hours worked, and compensation. Exceptions, of course, do occur, such as determining the criteria for artistic duties. Distinguishing between law and fact can also be difficult and can affect the outcome of an appeal. As one court pointed out:

> First, there are findings of historical fact. These include such findings as whether the . . . employer controlled the number of hours the individual worked. These are subject to reversal only if clearly erroneous.[53] Second, there are findings as to . . . whether a particular job required "skill and initiative" and whether there was a "permanent" employer-employee relationship.[54] These, too, are fact findings, reviewed for clear error.[55] Finally, there is the district court's ultimate conclusion—that is, whether the individual is an "employee" under (the FLSA). "The ultimate finding . . . is not simply a factual inference drawn from historical facts, but more accurately is a legal conclusion based on factual inferences drawn from historical facts."[56] Such conclusions are subject to . . . review.[57]

Notice the phrase "is a legal conclusion based on factual inference drawn from historical facts." That phrase emphasizes the interrelationship between the law and the employment conditions, and more importantly shows how the FLSA is approached in more general terms, letting the facts as the employment conditions of each case guide the court's decision.

ESTABLISHING THE FACTUAL DUTIES OF THE EMPLOYEE

A key part of any lawsuit involving the FLSA is the description of the duties of each employee for which exemption is an issue. For example, read the job descriptions of the key employees of a television station involved in one compensation dispute which went to the appellate court. You may want to refer to these job descriptions as you read the application of the FLSA later in this chapter. The employees described next are general assignment reporters, producers, directors, and assignment editors (subheadings added):

> **General Assignment Reporters**
>
> General-assignment reporters usually receive a new coverage assignment each day. The assignment manager or an assignment editor tells the reporter the story to be covered, what she is expected to "shoot," and the intended angle or focus of the story. After the reporter interviews the persons that she or another . . . employee has arranged to interview, she obtains pertinent video footage, and then writes and records the text of the story, subject to review by the

producer. Some reporters help assemble the video and text narration; others rely on a video editor to put the final package together. General-assignment reporters are only infrequently assigned to do a series of reports focusing on a single topic or related topics. Successful reporters usually have a pleasant physical appearance and a strong and appealing voice, and are able to present themselves as credible and knowledgeable.

Producers

Producers are responsible for determining the content of the ten-to-twelve minute news portion of the station's thirty-minute newscast. They participate in meetings to decide which stories and story angles will be covered; they also decide the amount of time to be given a particular story, the sequence in which stories will be aired, and when to take commercial breaks. Producers have the authority to revise reporters' stories. All of the producers' actions are subject to approval by the executive producer.

Directors

Directors review the script for the newscast in order to prepare technical instructions for "calling" the show. The director decides which camera to use and on which machine to run videotaped segments or preproduction graphics. During the broadcast, the director cues the various technical personnel, telling them precisely when to perform their assigned tasks. The overall appearance of (the station's) newscasts, however, is prescribed by station management. The director therefore has no discretion concerning lighting, camera-shot blocking, closing-shot style, or the sequence of opening and closing graphics. KDFW's directors also direct some public affairs programming, which have no prescribed format but involve only simple camera work and a basic set. In addition, . . . directors screen commercials to be aired by the station to ensure that they meet the standards set by (the parent company).

Assignment Editors

Assignment editors are primarily responsible for pairing reporters with both photographers and videotape editors. They also monitor the wire services, police and fire department scanners, newspapers, and press releases for story ideas that conform to (station's) general guidelines. Assignment editors have no authority to decide the stories to be covered, but they may reassign reporters if they learn of a story requiring immediate action. Assignment editors operate under the supervision of the assignment manager.[58]

Based on what you have just read, based on your own knowledge, job experience, and understanding, consider your initial impressions of what these people would do on the job. Based on the key points of law reiterated earlier in executive, administrative, and professional exemptions of the FLSA, consider if these jobs would appear to be exempt as either an executive exemption, administrative exemption, or professional exemption, or a combination of any of the three. Remember also that the jobs performed by employees are a matter of fact as opposed to law. In court this type of information can be indisputable since the employees perform the duties on a daily basis and so much collaborative testimony exists over what type of job duties a person has that there may be little ambiguity in exactly what the person does on the job. Whether those duties qualify as exempt or whether those are the primary duties of the individual is another matter and comes closer to mixing fact and law.

APPLYING ARGUMENTS FOR AND AGAINST EXEMPTION

Based on what the jobs of the respective employees are, taken through documents and testimony, the station and employees argue for and against exemption. On the basis of these arguments, which tend to mix law and fact, the court must decide the case.

Station's Arguments: Employees as Artistic Professionals

For example, on the subject of reporters as artistic professionals under the regulations cited earlier, the station might argue the following:

> As to reporters, defendant argues that their writing is primarily original and creative and thus exempt . . . (station) also posits that TV reporters must have a "presence" on camera,

are hired not only for their journalistic skills but also because of intrinsic qualities with respect to their personality, voice, and manner, and are thus artistic professionals . . . As to producers and directors, defendant reasons that these employees are exempt because they use creativity in performing their job duties, particularly in using invention, imagination, and talent in preparing a format in such a manner as to make TV viewers stay tuned to (the station).[59]

Employees' Arguments: Not Exempt as Artistic Professionals

The employees, on the other hand, as plaintiffs who are bringing action for back overtime pay in the case, would contend they are not artistic professionals. In the case of reporters, their attorney might argue they are not artistic professionals:

> . . . because they do not perform original and creative writing. They are discouraged from including their own commentary or opinion in a story. There is a formula for putting together packages and in many respects a reporter is restricted and directed by management and the constraints of the story itself. The use of special effects and graphics by reporters does not change this result because there is a definite format and sameness to the special effects utilized. The station desires that there be uniformity in effects so that the viewer will be comfortable with the station. The manner in which graphics are used in packages is consistent and repetitive. Graphics are generally used in pieces where there are a number of statistics involved or when there are several points or statements which the viewer needs to keep in mind simultaneously. The reporters reject (the station's) reliance upon supposed inherent qualities of reporters, contending these are more germane to anchors. The reporters argue that their appearance on camera is brief, and that, while there is a minimum standard of presentability, there is not a particular look or voice quality required and there is, in fact, great variation among reporters.[60]

Producers may also contend that they are not artistic professionals under the definition of professional in the FLSA. A producer plaintiff might argue against the professional exemption:

> . . . because the selection of stories and formatting of a newscast is not creative. The selection and presentation of stories is generally dictated by the order of importance in which stories are played in other sources such as the newspaper, wire service, and network. Decisions to include or delete a story are not decisions of great consequence. The choices and selections available to producers fall only within a certain framework established by station management as to the type of stories that will be included within a particular newscast. Producers have substantial guidance from upper management as to the relative importance of stories. The executive producer reviews all formats.[61]

Directors could argue that they also are not artistic professionals:

> . . . because the directing they perform consists of no more than coordinating and does not allow for creative leeway that might be available to a director of documentary or dramatic films. Newscasts are specifically formatted by management and outside consultants. Decisions regarding the blocking of shots and lighting are made by the news director, a management position. The preproduction work that a director does is specifically formatted and repetitive with little room for director input. The calling of a show is a technical process that requires experience and skill but is in many respects simply mechanical. The aspects of a newscast or show that go awry are recurring in nature and directors do not use creativity and imagination in dealing with them.[62]

Based on the facts associated with the conditions of employment, the arguments of both the station and the employees, and the regulations as stated and interpreted in the FLSA, the court then makes a judgment applying the FLSA to the facts of the case. Keep in mind, however, that our example applies to just one station at a given point in time and to only the news department of that station. Stations involved in wage and hour disputes frequently change operating policies to the satisfaction of many of the parties involved and people working on other areas of a station have completely different job descriptions.

APPLYING FACT AND LAW TO THE CONDITIONS OF EMPLOYMENT

An example of a court applying the facts of a case to the law, the FLSA, can be seen in the following statement from a disputed overtime compensation claim concerning general assignment reporters as exempt professionals. Notice how the duties of the reporters (the facts) are linked to the criteria of the professional exemption (the law). Notice also the reference to the criteria for professionals listed earlier in the chapter.

> The court concludes . . . that general assignment reporters can be artistic professionals because significant technological advances in how broadcast news is gathered and presented to the viewer have required that reporters produce work that is original and creative in character, the result of which depends primarily on the invention, imagination, or talent of the employee. There is evidence that . . . reporters use originality, creativity, invention, imagination, and talent in their work. The proposition that they are artistic professionals is, in fact, not . . . far-fetched . . .[63]

Further weaving of the facts and the law occurs as the court engages in a commentary on the relationship between print and broadcast journalism, the former spelled out quite clearly in the FLSA, but spelled out more than three decades ago. Notice how the court makes specific reference to the distinctions between the two forms of journalism. Such distinctions are necessary on a case-by-case basis since it is print, not broadcast journalism, which is more clearly delineated in the FLSA. Further applying the facts to the law the court points out:

> These regulations were promulgated when television was in its relative infancy. The technological innovations brought about by color picture transmissions, satellite and electronic newsgathering, computer and electronic generated graphics, microwave transmissions, and videotape use, have all combined dramatically to transform television news as a visual medium. The regulations of 30 years ago appear to be influenced substantially by concepts more appropriately associated with print journalism. Newspaper writers produce work that depends primarily on intelligence, diligence, and accuracy. This is also an integral part of the work of a broadcast journalist. But TV reporters must also capture the viewer's attention, and enhance the viewer's understanding in a relatively short time frame by relating the news through the use of pictures, sound, and words—words that are understandable to the ear. These technological advances have rendered unpersuasive any generalized notion that broadcast journalists cannot be artistic professionals, and the court concludes that they can be found to be exempt, artistic professionals on the basis of *appropriate evidence* (emphasis added).[64]

A CRITICAL TEST: THE STATION'S BURDEN OF PROOF

On the surface it might seem that any broadcast journalist anywhere is an exempt professional. But note the important words *appropriate evidence*. Remember, under the Fair Labor Standards Act the burden of proof is on the station who is the employer. Despite the court's strong statements that broadcast journalists can be professionals, they must in the absence of specific regulations and interpretations under the FLSA, (1) perform the duties that qualify them as exempt professionals under the FLSA's current wording, (2) perform those duties at the particular station where the overtime compensation dispute originated, and (3) the station employer which has the burden of proof must be able to provide appropriate evidence sufficient enough to prove points 1 and 2. Despite the affirmative statements that general assignment reporters at some stations can be classified as exempt, this court ruled against the station stating:

> Nevertheless, the burden of proving the exemption, and in turn that the plaintiff-reporters are artistic professionals, rests with (the station). The exemptions are to be narrowly construed against (the station), and their application is limited to those plainly and unmistakably within their terms.

> Although the question is a close one, the court thus finds . . . that (the station) *did not prove by a preponderance of the evidence* that the work of its plaintiff-reporters is so "primarily" inventive or imaginative, or routinely original and creative, that the court can find they are artistic professionals (emphasis added).[65]

APPLYING A PROFESSIONAL EXEMPTION REGULATION

We can gain a deeper understanding as to how and why the court applied the particular employment conditions in this case and determined the television station's general assignment reporters were not exempt professionals and therefore were entitled to back overtime pay. Notice how the very specific duties of the reporters come into play when combining the facts of the case to the law.

Applying the Professional Exemption to Reporters

In applying the professional exemption regulation to general assignment television news reporters, the court determined that in this instance the reporters' work was not primarily "inventive," "imaginative," "original," and "creative." In the first paragraph the concept of burden of proof also raises its head again and, as the court states, "comes down to a burden of proof." The criteria of primary duty also appears. Even if a station can persuade the court that its employees do engage in duties which are original and creative and use invention, imagination, and talent, it must also shoulder the burden of proof that these duties are the primary duties of the employee. Notice also that despite the fact the courts may agree that the FLSA and its interpretations are out of date as far as television news is concerned, the fact that those criteria exist still causes the courts to rely on the letter of the law.

> . . . general assignment reporters do not do work that is so primarily inventive or imaginative, or routinely original and creative, that the court can hold that they are artistic professionals. The present case—like all wage and hour decisions—comes down to a question of proof. The exemptions are to be narrowly construed and applied only to those plainly and unmistakably within their terms. (The station) has not sustained its burden of proof by a preponderance of the evidence. (The station) did persuade the court that its reporters from time to time use creativity, invention, imagination, and talent in portions of their work. This is especially true in series packages and feature pieces and is also reflected in some of their daily work. (The station) failed to convince the court, however, that a reporter's artistic work represents the reporter's primary duties; that is, that a reporter's work is primarily inventive or imaginative or original and creative.[66]
>
> From a preponderance of the evidence, the court finds that the work of . . . reporters depends primarily on intelligence, diligence, and accuracy. Reporters are told which stories to cover and are informed of the focus or angle of the story before they cover it. They are often told whom or what type of person to interview. They use essentially a standard format of pictures and sound to cover most stories. They attempt to obtain both sides of a story and choose video and audio that informs the viewer and fairly sets out any competing viewpoints. There is a well-established format and sameness to the special effects that are utilized. Their work—day in and day out—is not predominantly original and creative because they do not produce analytical, interpretative, or highly individualized reporting. As with print journalists, the reporters ordinarily collect facts by investigation, interview, or personal observation and then write and report the events in a standard form, ranging from a VO to a package. Like print journalists, . . . reporters primarily use intelligence, diligence, and accuracy to report facts. They do not rely principally upon creativity, invention, or imagination. Local affiliate reporters are not, moreover, the modern-day version of the "name" announcer discussed in (the FLSA regulations).[67] At the local or regional market level the "name" announcers are the newscast anchors. The evidence at trial reflected that (the station) promotes its anchors but only rarely promotes reporters. While the evidence persuades the court that good reporting, in the aggregate, leads to a successful newscast, the evidence does not convince the court that individual reporters draw viewers in measurable numbers.

> Indeed, common sense dictates that if a profit-motivated operation . . . discovered that reporters—as individuals—measurably affected ratings, the station would tout the reporters to the viewing audience.[68]

Applying the Professional Exemption to Producers

In applying the professional exemption to producers, the court found that producers are not exempt professionals. Once again the key phrase from the FLSA, "invention, imagination, and talent" comes into play.

> The court finds next that producers are not exempt as artistic professionals. The court is not persuaded that their work is original and creative or that the result depends primarily upon the invention, imagination, or talent of the producer.
>
> The writing that a producer does is most closely akin to that of the "rewrite man" described in (the interpretations of the FLSA). Producers usually revise work prepared by reporters, wire services, or earlier broadcast news stories. Their work is not primarily original and creative. The court also rejects the contention that producers primarily use invention, imagination, and talent in formatting a newscast. There is some testimony that a talented producer can weave a newscast in a particularly pleasing manner and can add "bells and whistles" that differentiate one newscast from another. The preponderance of the evidence, however, supports the finding that producers follow accepted conventions in selecting lead stories, grouping related stories, pacing the broadcast, avoiding monotony in sequencing forms of stories, and incorporating stories that can be added or dropped. The court is persuaded from a preponderance of the evidence that producers do not depend primarily upon their invention, imagination, or talent in performing their jobs.[69]

In the court's decision we can again see the key phrase, "invention, imagination, or talent." This phrase, as nebulous as it might seem, is still the letter of the law and is applied as the letter of the law. Attorneys arguing a case must apply the terms in a persuasive manner that convinces the court to decide the case on one side or the other of a fine line which distinguishes a certain degree of creativity in the workplace.

Also, despite the fact that there is a world of difference between print and broadcast journalism, the fact that specific reference and criteria exist for print journalists causes many courts to still fall back on the interpretations for print journalists. In this instance, producers are compared to the "rewrite man" of print journalism. Some readers may even perceive a subtle demeaning tone to the court's text whereby even though the court rules in favor of the employees bringing action for back overtime pay, less stature is given to their work when it is defined by the court in the context of the legal terminology of the FLSA.

Applying the Professional Exemption to Directors

The court reached a similar conclusion in applying the professional exemption to directors and finding that directors, like producers, were not professionally exempt.

> The court finds that directors, like producers, are not exempt as artistic professionals. . . . directors are trained and experienced employees who have the resultant ability to cue other trained personnel to commence and complete a function in accordance with the director's cue. Directors do not primarily rely upon their invention, imagination, or talent in performing their work. Many of their decisions are obvious because station management has prescribed the "look" of the newscast in much detail. Directors have more leeway in public affairs programming but the court is persuaded by the evidence that, even here, . . . directors operate principally within accepted guidelines and do not function primarily upon the basis of invention, imagination, or talent.[70]

In denying the professional exemption to directors the court again falls back on the letter of the law through the phrase. In addition the burden of proof is reiterated by the court's statement that it is "persuaded by the evidence," that directors operate within accepted guidelines. Guidelines, when they do exist at a station, have the ability to create uniformity, uphold standards, and help assure quality. They can also help diminish the station's ability to classify employees as professionally exempt and enhance the employee's ability to successfully claim overtime pay.

APPLYING THE ADMINISTRATIVE EXEMPTION

The professional exemption in our example was applied to reporters. Stations may also consider newsroom employees to be administratively exempt. Although this exemption is more difficult for reporters since they traditionally work under one or more layers of supervision, it can sometimes apply to directors and producers. Nevertheless, the administrative exemption for these individuals is far from certain. The employee in an administrative function which qualifies as exempt from wage and hour law must "perform office or nonmanual work directly related to management policies or general business operations" and "must customarily and regularly exercise discretion and independent judgement."[71]

Care, however, must be made when generalizing about administrative duties. The courts use a strong interpretation for administrative exemptions and point out that frequently the terms *discretion and independent judgement* as used in labor law are misunderstood and misapplied. An employee who uses skill in applying techniques, procedures, or specific standards is not automatically performing administrative functions. Similarly, an employee who applies knowledge to prescribed procedures or in determining which procedure to follow is not necessarily performing an administrative function.[72]

Applying the Administrative Exemption to News Producers

Producers in some stations, depending on their responsibilities, would qualify for the administrative exemption. One court pointed out that determining whether news producers are administratively exempt is much like determining if television reporters are exempt as professionals. The determination is "a close issue which the court ultimately decides as a matter of proof."[73]

In other stations, however, and in particular large stations, producers may be far removed from the management functions of the station, may operate as part of a union, and may share a great many responsibilities with other middle-level staff, none of whom may be considered administratively exempt. The middle-level staff may collectively but not individually contribute to the management functions of the businesses to a degree that would warrant exemption.

In a case where producers were *not* considered to be administratively exempt, the primary duty of the producers, their actual responsibilities and job functions, and the station's burden of proof all reflected heavily on the court's decision (subheadings added):

> **The Primary Duty Test**
>
> The court finds first that . . . producers do not perform, as their primary duty, work that is directly related to management policies or general business operations. This is so because their work is not related to the "administrative" aspects of the business and is not of importance to the business as a whole to a "substantial degree." The work of . . . newscast producers . . . does not qualify as administrative work under the regulations. The regulations contemplate that administrative work includes advising management, planning, negotiating, representing, and promoting the company. The work of the . . . newscast producers, however, concerns the actual production aspect of (the station's) business.
>
> **Actual Responsibilities and Job Functions**
>
> . . . producers are responsible for the content of the news portion (10–12 minutes) of a particular newscast. They decide, based upon the relative importance and length of a story, the order in which news stories will air and prepare a format for the show. Producers time the newscast. If technical, logistical, or talent difficulties cause the newscast to run long or short, the producers are responsible for adding stories or deleting or altering the length of stories. The duties of the producer clearly relate to the production of . . . news department product and not to defendant's administrative operations . . . Producers thus fail to meet the first element necessary to be administratively exempt under the regulations. The producers also fail to meet the first element because their work does not consist of carrying out major assignments or work of substantial importance to (the station's) business as a whole, as those concepts are understood in FLSA jurisprudence.
>
> Newscast producers use techniques, procedures, repetitious experiences, and specific standards to carry out their work. The producer knows in advance how much

time is available for news (as opposed to weather, sports, and commercials). The standard length of the stories is dictated by station management and by the relative importance of the story. The standards for deciding how to lead a newscast, how to group and bridge related stories, and when and how to cut stories are known in the industry. Producers merely utilize their knowledge in following these prescribed procedures or in determining what procedures to follow. This process helps support station management's desire that one newscast appear similar to another, regardless who produced or directed it . . .

Burden of Proof

. . . the station has failed to meet its burden of proving that its producers perform work "directly related to management policies or general business operations" because of the substantial importance of their duties. The nature of the employee's work, and not the possible results or consequences, is the focal point of the regulations. As the court explains above, . . . producers use techniques, procedures, repetitious experience, and specific standards to perform their work. Many of the standards and procedures that they follow are dictated by station management or are otherwise known generally in the industry. The producers utilize their knowledge in applying these techniques or procedures as part of a skilled, integrated . . . production team. The producers thus do not perform work of such substantial importance that it is considered under the regulations to be "directly related to management policies or general business operations."[74]

We can see in reading the court's decision justification for the court's denial of the exemption. At the same time, however, we can see that if the producer is primarily responsible for the 10- to 12-minute portion of a newscast, then there may be ample time for the producer to engage in other duties which would make the person administratively exempt. If these other duties are closely related to the management functions of the business, then a station could argue for the exemption.

Applying Discretion and Independent Judgment to the Director

A key element in the administrative exemption is the necessity to prove the employee engages in "discretion and independent judgement." In this ruling we have a succinct example of the application of the FLSA's requirement of "discretion and independent judgement" applied to directors in a television newsroom. The court found that directors in this particular case did not meet the criteria, were therefore not administratively exempt, and as a result entitled to back overtime pay.

. . . directors are not exempt because their work does not require the exercise of discretion and independent judgment. The directors in question do perform some screening of commercials, direct public affairs programs, and direct preproduction work. These duties are analogous, however, to functions that the regulations consider to be non-exempt. The screening of commercials for technical acceptability and conformance with good broadcast standards is based on criteria established by station management. Directors, when screening commercials, are merely employing skill in the application of techniques and procedures, not discretion and independent judgment . . . The preproduction work is also principally technically oriented. Directors also direct one or more of the weekday and weekend newscasts. The "calling" of a newscast involves highly developed skills, executed under pressure and arduous time constraints, but does not involve discretion and independent judgment in the sense envisioned by the regulations. The director plans the sequence of the camera shots, the timing and sequence of special effects, and performs preproduction work. Station management and outside consultants, however, prescribe the "look" of the set and general policy concerning how the newscast is to be presented to the viewer. The flow of the show is actually dictated in large measure by station management's allocation of time to news, weather, and sports, and by how the news portion is stacked by the producer. Other decisions, such as the blocking of camera shots, are made by the news director . . . Directors do not supervise or assign the

> work that is performed by the various members of the technical crew. The director's duty is principally to coordinate the activities of various skilled people so that everyone is on the same time cue. A technical skill and expertise is involved, not an exercise of discretion and independent judgment concerning matters of significance or policy. [75]

The last sentence is particularly interesting. One might argue that to be able to use the sophisticated electronic equipment that is common in today's television newsroom, that the exercise of discretion and independent judgment is actually a prerequisite to technical skill and expertise. While technical skill and expertise are more readily identifiable and easily articulated in testimony because they are less abstract than discretion and independent judgment, the latter should nevertheless prevail and directors should be classified as administratively exempt at least on this one criteria.

Applying Discretion and Independent Judgment to Assignment Editors

Assignment editors at first glance might seem to be exempt administrators because the function of "assigning" direction to other employees involves supervision and administration. Moreover, making administrative decisions about what is or is not newsworthy involves independent judgment and discretion. However, this is not always the case and the lack of duties and responsibilities which involve discretion and independent judgment denies the exemption and entitles the employee to overtime pay.

> The assignment editor's duties consist of pairing reporters with photographers, monitoring police scanners for stories, and reviewing newspapers, press releases, and wire copy for possible stories. Assignment editors do make some decisions that involve the use of judgment . . . anything outside their narrowly circumscribed range of responsibility must be approved by station management. They do not exercise discretion and independent judgment in their work, especially not as to matters of significance.[76]

People who work in television news can testify to the fact that in many stations assignment editors have considerable administrative responsibility. But as is the case with other points of law, it is necessary to *prove* that an employee is exempt and in this case the conditions of employment did not generate enough proof to convince the court.

APPLYING THE CRITERIA OF THE EXECUTIVE EXEMPTION

One key element in applying the executive exemption is the necessity for the employee's primary duty to consist of the management of the station or a customarily recognized department or subdivision. In addition, the short test for the executive exemption requires the employee to customarily and regularly direct the work of two or more employees. Depending on the size of the station and its organization structure, management duties may be assigned to such individuals as directors and producers. In the absence of such clear management responsibilities, however, the executive exemption is difficult to prove.

The Primary Duty Criteria

For example, notice in the following decision how the issue of management as a primary duty is articulated by the court in denying the executive exemption to news producers and directors.

> The court holds that the duties of the producers and directors fall short of the necessary requirement of management as the primary duty. Factors useful in determining if management is an employee's primary duty include the amount of time spent in management activity, the importance of those management duties, the frequency of exercising discretion, and freedom from supervision. The directors and producers in the instant case spend almost no time in true management activity. The producers prepare and arrange the format of the show and do not manage other individuals who participate in the creation of the newscast. The other people with whom the producers come in contact (e.g., reporters, assignment editors, and associate producers) are all actually supervised or directed by management positions such as the assignment manager, executive producer, or assistant news director. The producers are not involved in the management activity contemplated by the

> regulations of training, supervising, disciplining, and directing and evaluating employees. The producers' primary duty is not management, but is to prepare the content and format of the newscast, and no major policy or management decisions are made by producers without obtaining permission from station management.
>
> The directors' primary duty likewise is not management. The directors take the format generated by the producer and set the manner of presentation of the newscast. In "calling" the show, the directors merely coordinate the activities of the various technical personnel so that everyone is on the same time cue. Directors do not manage the people involved in the technical production of the newscast, but merely coordinate the technical personnel who already know the production plan. The directors' primary duty does not constitute management activity as contemplated by the regulations. Directors do not participate in management policy and strategy decisions and make no decision of significance without permission by station management.[77]

The Supervisory Criteria

Another element in the executive exemption is the necessity under the short test for the exempt employee to engage in the customary and regular direction of the work of two or more employees. In denying the executive exemption to producers and directors the court determined:

> Each employee with whom the producers work is supervised and actually directed by station management, such as the assignment manager, executive producer, and assistant news director. Although producers may certainly impact other employees' jobs, these employees report directly to persons other than the producers.
>
> The evidence also persuades the court that directors do not in any sense supervise or assign the work performed by the various technical employees of the newscast. Each director has a supervisor who directs and assigns the director's work. The director simply coordinates technical employees, who have previously been assigned their tasks, when a particular function needs to be performed.
>
> The producers and directors are trained and skilled employees, working under narrowly prescribed guidelines of operation with little or no discretionary power as to matters of significance or management policy. They are part of an integrated production team where each skilled employee is responsible and accountable to someone in station management. They do not qualify as bona fide executives exempt from the FLSA.[78]

In the same case the court also found that assignment editors did not meet the criteria for executive exemption. The court pointed out that the duty of assignment editors at the station was to "... pair up reporters and photographers, monitor scanners, and review newspapers and wire copy for possible stories. Operating under well-settled guidelines, any unusual matter is immediately referred to management for decision."[79]

APPLYING COMBINATION EXEMPTIONS: TACKING

Combination exemptions called tacking can apply in a station, but the combinations must be the primary duty of the employee and result in at least 80 percent of the employee's time being spent on the exempt duties (no more than 20 percent of the employee's time being spent on nonexempt duties.) In a television newsroom, for example, if a news director is also functioning as a reporter, the combination of the professional exemption from the news director's reporting duties—assuming the news director would not be supervised and therefore have the freedom to use invention, imagination, and talent to a sufficient degree to qualify as being exempt—and the administrative or executive exemption from the news director's management and supervisory duties, could be combined to make the news director exempt. Of course the news director may also be exempt under the administrative or executive exemption without the need for tacking.

In our examples of the job descriptions and the applications of the FLSA to individual exemptions of reporters and others, tacking exemptions together can prove difficult. This is especially true if a court is convinced individual employees do not engage in any exempt work. The sum of nothing and nothing is still nothing, and arguing that tacking applies when individual exemptions are absent is many times futile.

INTERNSHIPS AND WAGE AND HOUR LAW

Internships can pose special problems for broadcasters. J. Laurent Scharff, RTNDA General Counsel writing in RTNDA Legal Notes advises stations that, "If *all* of the following criteria are complied with for a student internship, the student is not considered an 'employee' under FLSA and need not be paid accordingly":[80]

(1) the training, even though it includes actual operation of the facilities of the employer, is similar to that which would be given in a vocational school;
(2) the training is for the benefit of the trainees or students;
(3) the trainees or students do not displace regular employees, but work under their close observation;
(4) the employer that provides the training derives no immediate advantage from the activities of the trainees or students; and on occasion his operations may actually be impeded;
(5) the trainees or students are not necessarily entitled to a job at the conclusion of the training period; and
(6) the employer and the trainees or students understand that the trainees or students are not entitled to wages for the time spent in training.[81]

The six criteria are quoted from the Labor Department's WH Publication 1297, "Employment Relationship Under the Fair Labor Standards Act." Scharff goes on to state:

> While not made necessary by the first criterion, formal credit or other recognition by a college for an internship would be important support for a finding that the intern is not an employee subject to wage and hour requirements. The duties performed by the intern should be consistent with the second criterion, and, under that criterion and the third one, learning assignments must be well defined and closely supervised. Under the third and fourth criteria, the intern should not be given work that has the effect of displacing a regular employee from a substantial amount of work or which otherwise materially benefits the employer. Several young persons whom an insurance company was "teaching" in order to ascertain their interests in insurance careers were held to be employees because they prepared and mailed promotional materials for the company. The substance of the fifth and sixth criteria should be clearly communicated to interns before they are brought into the newsroom.[82]

COMPENSATION CLAIMS IN COURT

Compensation claims are always a disruption to station operations. If one employee is engaged in a compensation suit, then other employees may feel they are also entitled to overtime pay and therefore may join in the suit so as not to be left out if a decision goes against the station. Although all employees could file on behalf of themselves, expensive legal fees can be involved. Also, while employees may be covered by union contracts and have their jobs protected, any litigation which pits employees against management can take its emotional, financial, and organizational toll on everyone. Rumors repeated at other stations can make the situation even more frustrating in highly competitive markets.

A Compensation Audit

It is a good idea for every station which is not automatically exempt under the small-market rule to review the compensation levels of all employees. Competent counsel should be consulted and the station's attorneys should be made aware of the FLSA provisions. No one can be an expert in every facet of the law, which is why managers and stations retain competent communication counsel as well as local legal assistance to operate a broadcasting station. A healthy dose of legal prevention is usually money well spent. Disputes over compensation can drag on for years and drain the energy of many people who get involved.

The Realities of Labor Law

A legal action can be a frustrating experience for management because the law is well defined and enough cases have interpreted the FLSA that forging new ground can be difficult unless exceptional circumstances exist. Broadcasting has not been an industry exceptionally active in the labor law arena. As such, stations may find themselves in foreign territory with the need to educate their counsel on the intricacies of station operations while the counsel must then convince the court that the station is abiding by the letter of the FLSA. Meanwhile, an employee or group of employees without the burden of proof on their shoulders are the expert witnesses with considerable credibility when testifying about their own job duties.

MANAGEMENT AND STATION OPERATIONS

From management's perspective a compensation audit may help prevent disputes, but equally valuable is a review of station operations and a determination if employees who are considered exempt under the FLSA'S guidelines are engaged in on-the-job duties which will hold up in court. Cosmetic changes to try to circumvent the law won't work when it comes to proving an employee exempt. In some areas of station operations, however, changes in the administrative structure may help to move an employee toward exempt status. An employee may actually want to move to exempt status because of the stature, increased responsibilities, and opportunities for future career growth such a move to administrative or executive duties may provide.

The philosophy of management surrounding these decisions is best approached from the spirit of what is best for the employee as well as the station. For example, many employees are interested in improving their own job skills, their importance to the station, and also in becoming a productive part of an organization. That can only be accomplished by instilling in the employee a sense of self-worth which many times comes from giving the employee increased responsibilities. If those responsibilities are assigned by management with a genuine desire to improve the employee's value to the station and to themselves, the end result benefits everyone. Whether those responsibilities involve more artistic discretion common to the professional exemption, or more management responsibility associated with the administrative and executive exemptions is not as important as the value of professional growth for the employee and the organization.

A NOTE ON LABOR LAW AND THE IMPORTANCE OF TELEVISION NEWS

Two things need to be remembered in reviewing our examples applying the FLSA to a television news operation. The court cases quoted in the text as examples applying the FLSA affect only one station in one judicial district. Second, the examples apply only to the television news department of one station. Other stations may have different organizational structures and no one can refute the importance of television news to the overall operation, and the management of a television station.

While local news may only take up a small portion of the total broadcasting day, in competitive markets no programming is more important to the station's success in general and management's success in particular. It is not by accident that people with strong broadcast news backgrounds are managing some of the nation's most successful television stations in the nation's largest markets. Local news is also significant because a good audience rating in the local news, especially in the 6:00 P.M. block, can capture an audience and keep it tuned to the station for the prime-time programming which follows.

Good local news on affiliate stations is also important to the networks themselves. Local affiliates with strong local news programming help the network gain and hold the prime-time audience it needs to compete nationally. The sum total of the audience at network affiliate stations determines the ratings the networks achieve. Producing good local news can be the determining factor in keeping a station's network affiliation, especially in competitive markets.[83]

The decisions made in the news department play a big part in the operation of a station, from producing profits to affecting the morale of all employees. A first-place news rating in a competitive market can result in significant advertising revenues, the opportunity to publicize the station's position, and a bandwagon effect among audience members who will tune in the station because of its perceived image in the market. The importance of news programming is seen in the fact that many television station managers take an active role in the local news programming. The "news team" at many stations represents a management team as well as a journalistic team. In future FLSA cases, the importance of television news and its relationship to the management of the station may contribute to the station's ability to successfully exempt categories of employees which in the past were denied exemption.

SUMMARY

The Fair Labor Standards Act grew out of the industrialized society of the early twentieth century. The statute covers such areas as minimum wage, child labor, and overtime pay. For broadcasting and telecommunication, overtime pay is the primary concern. The FLSA is enforced by the Wage and Hour Division of the Department of Labor. With our society prone to litigation, it is important that we have a clear understanding of wage and hour law, from the perspective of both management and employees. In this text we deal with the FLSA in two different chapters. This chapter deals with the law itself, and a later chapter in the text deals with the application of the law to a television news operation.

In broadcasting many different compensation arrangements exist, from part-time employees, to employees who are considered artistic performers. In addition, the FLSA exempts some employees who work in stations operating in small markets. Because radio and television news content is unpredictable, some crises necessitate staff working overtime to cover breaking news events. Lacking a clear understanding of wage and hour law can result in unexpected challenges to a station's compensation package, the end result being a drain on emotional and financial resources, regardless of who wins a suit.

In studying the FLSA, both the letter of the law and the interpretations of the law come into play. The letter of the law is the original act as passed by Congress and amended. But when the law was passed Congress also gave the U.S. Department of Labor the authority to develop and incorporate into the regulations certain "interpretations" of the FLSA. These interpretations deal with specific examples of how the law can be applied. It is not possible, however, for every type of business or employment situation to be covered in the interpretations, and the Department of Labor has not attempted this task.

The Department of Labor has, on the other hand, permitted individual courts to mold the law on a case-by-case basis. Still, the interpretations as developed and published by the Department of Labor do carry weight, even though they are a guide for the courts and are not the letter of the law. Those who become involved in compensation disputes, and in some cases the attorneys that represent them, fail to understand the difference between the letter of the law as stated in the FLSA and the Department of Labor's interpretations of the law which accompany the FLSA.

Within the FLSA different provisions spell out the responsibilities of employers when it comes to overtime pay. For example, overtime pay is compensation paid for more than a 40-hour week. A week is defined as any consecutive 168 hours, which means a workweek can start at any time. Overtime pay is paid at the rate of one and one-half times the regular rate of pay and being paid a salary instead of an hourly wage does not necessarily mean an employer is exempt from paying compensation for overtime work. Formulas discussed in the chapter explain how rates of pay are determined.

Payment received through prizes and awards and suggestion systems may or may not count as traditional earnings. For prizes, the type of prize and the amount of time spent competing can impact on whether the prize is compensation. Awards for making suggestions are usually not related to an employee's earnings when the employee is not required to submit the suggestion.

The FLSA defines four exemptions to its overtime pay provisions. These exemptions are critical to an understanding of the wage and hour laws. The categories of employees who are exempt from the overtime pay provisions of the law are: executives, administrators, professionals, and people involved in outside sales. Long and short tests exist for executive, administrative, and professional exemptions.

An employee who qualifies for an executive exemption must work in management at the highest level of the enterprise. Executives must direct the work of at least two people, have the authority to hire and fire, exercise discretionary power, devote 80 percent of their time to these functions, and earn $155 per week under the long test and $250 per week under the short test. A key element of the executive and other exemptions is primary duty, which under the Department of Labor's interpretations generally means more than 50 percent of the employee's time.

An employee who qualifies for an administrative exemption performs office or nonmanual work directly related to management policies, regularly and directly assists another person working in a bona fide executive or administrative capacity, has only general supervision, spends at least 80 percent of their time in these duties, and earns $155 per week under the long test, and $250 per week under the short test.

An employee who qualifies for a professional exemption has advanced knowledge in a specialized course of study, completes work which is original and creative, consistently exercises discretion and judgment, completes work which is predominantly intellectual and varied, devotes 80 percent of their time to these tasks and earns $170 per week under the long test and $250 per week under the short test. A key element in the professional exemption is the ability to meet the test of work requiring invention, imagination, and talent.

The Department of Labor's interpretations make special provisions for radio and television announcers. Some work which announcers perform, such as announcing ad lib, is generally exempt under the professional exemption. People working in outside sales are generally exempt if they work mostly away from the station when making calls, and spend 80 percent of their time engaged in outside sales activity.

Announcers, news editors, and engineers in small-market stations are exempt under the FLSA. A small market generally is defined as a market having a population of 100,000 or below, based on census figures. The law has not been updated to include some of the new census terminology; thus, this portion of the FLSA is still somewhat difficult to interpret, and will continue to be until new terminology is incorporated into the regulations. The Fair Labor Standards Act was written with Congress giving the Wage and Hour Division of the Department of Labor enforcement powers and the responsibility for interpreting the law. The law covers such areas as minimum wage, overtime pay, and child labor. Overtime pay is the chief concern of broadcasters. Since it took effect in 1938, the FLSA has been interpreted by the courts which have developed case law as the primary means of applying the law to different employment situations.

The FLSA contains four exemptions: executive, administrative, professional, and outside sales. The first three were reviewed in this chapter. The executive exemption applies to high-level executives whose primary duty consists of the management of the station. Employees who are administratively exempt perform nonmanual work directly related to the management policies and general business operations. Professionally exempt employees have advanced knowledge in a specialized field or perform original and creative work in a recognized field of artistic endeavor.

Combination exemptions called tacking are possible such as combining work which is professionally exempt with work that is administratively exempt. To be exempt from the overtime pay provisions employees must have as their primary duty the responsibilities associated with each exemption.

In applying the FLSA it is the employer and not the employee that carries the burden of proof. Absent strong evidence to the contrary, the employee will normally prevail in a compensation dispute; thus, employers must be extra vigilant that their management and compensation policies are in line with the letter of the FLSA.

When applying the Fair Labor Standards Act to a compensation claim, the court will examine the findings of fact and the findings of law. Findings of fact are the specific details of the employment arrangement. Findings of law refer to the letter of the law as stated in the FLSA. What makes the FLSA somewhat difficult to defend against is the nature of the fact-finding process where the employees are the expert witnesses about their own job responsibilities and the FLSA is interpreted very narrowly by the courts.

As an example of findings of fact we examined the job descriptions of four categories of employees: general assignment reporters, producers, directors, and assignment editors. We then applied the FLSA and its interpretations to the job descriptions to determine whether or not any of the jobs would be exempt. Based on the jobs of the respective employees, in a compensation dispute the defendant employer and the plaintiff employee argue for and against exemption. For example, the station might argue that a reporter's writing is original and creative. The reporter seeking overtime pay might argue that his or her work is highly managed and therefore not original and creative.

Courts have recognized that broadcast journalism is distinct from print journalism and that it is possible for reporters to engage in creative and original work, which to qualify for exemption under the law must include work which involves "invention, imagination, and talent." Courts also point to the fact the FLSA interpretations of print journalism are more than 30 years old and therefore apply only in a limited way to broadcast journalism. If claiming a professional exemption for their employees, employers to win in court must still prove convincingly that the work their exempt employees perform results in work which meets the test of invention, imagination, and talent.

When applying the law to the administrative and executive exemptions, managerial duties, supervisory duties, and primary duties come into play. For example, executives must manage the business at the highest level. Administrators must assist in the management functions in a direct way and must supervise at least two or more employees. Tacking can be accomplished but the combination of the two duties which are tacked together must be the primary duty of the employee, must meet the higher salary test, and must involve at least 80 percent of the employee's time.

To avoid problems with compensation claims, station managers should conduct a compensation audit of their station and examine the compensation arrangement of every employee. Making sure the station is in line with the letter of the FLSA is important to avoiding compensation claims, potential litigation, and the disruption of station operations.

Station operations can sometimes be adjusted to give employees more responsibility and advance their professional growth while at the same time making them exempt. Such adjustments must be made in a spirit of a positive management philosophy which benefits both the station and the employee. Under no circumstances should adjustments be made simply to circumvent the law. Anyone contemplating a compensation claim should first seek counsel knowledgeable and experienced in the practice of wage and hour law.

MATERIAL FOR ANALYSIS

In addition to enforcing wage and hour law, the Department of Labor also enforces statutes as they apply to labor unions which represent workers in broadcasting, telecommunication, and other industries. This area of administrative law frequently deals with collective bargaining agreements, the right of workers to unionize, the rights of employers to recognize or not recognize unions, and numerous other areas of administrative law. When unions represent workers the labor contract becomes the document labor and management follow in the operation of the enterprise. While collective bargaining agreements cannot violate the law, such agreements can contain additional provisions designed to set the rules over which such matters as worker grievances, sick leave, seniority, and other issues can be aired. The case which follows is a National Labor Relations Board (NLRB) decision involving stations KOFY FM and KOFY TV in San Francisco, California. The dispute arose over whether management was required to recognize the American Federation of Television and Radio Artists (AFTRA). An administrative law judge originally heard the case and then the union filed a complaint with the NLRB, which delegated the matter to a three-member panel. Their ruling was in favor of the administrative law judge and the complaint was dismissed. Reading the short proceeding gives us an inside look at the operation of a unionized radio and television station, including brief testimony between station management and representatives of the union. The case has been edited to aid the reader in comprehending the primary argument, some citations and footnotes have been omitted. Names of corporate officers and respondents have been omitted without notation or the titles of individuals substituted for the individual's name, sometimes without notation. In the decision the plural term *Respondents* (KOFY FM and KOFY TV 20) is sometimes followed, albeit awkwardly for the reader, by the singular *has* or *was*, but should be read as synonymous with KOFY FM in the singular. KOFY FM was later combined for this hearing with KOFY TV 20. Readers wishing a complete text of the proceeding should consult the primary citation of the proceeding.

KOFY FM, KOFY TV 20 AND AMERICAN FEDERATION OF TELEVISION AND RADIO ARTISTS

Cases 20-CA-22544, 20-CA-22545

NATIONAL LABOR RELATIONS BOARD

137 L.R.R.M. 1219; 301 NLRB No. 93;1991 NLRB LEXIS 100 February 12, 1991

* * *

ORDER

The recommended Order of the administrative law judge is adopted and the complaint is dismissed.

* * *

The matter arose as follows:

The American Federation of Radio and Television Artists (the Union or the Charging Party) filed a charge with Region 20 of the National Labor Relations Board docketed as Case 20-CA-22544 against KOFY FM. On that same date the Union filed a second charge docketed as Case 20-CA-22545 against KOFY TV 20 (collectively with KOFY FM, Respondents). Following an investigation the Regional Director for Region 20 issued an Order Consolidating Cases, Consolidated Complaint and Notice of Hearing respecting the two cases . . .

The complaint alleges that the Union has been the recognized collective bargaining representative of appropriate bargaining units of Respondents' employees since September 1988 and that the parties reached full and complete agreement on a new contract with respect to each unit. The complaint further alleges that at all times since October 3, 1988 the Union has sought and at all times since March 1, 1989 Respondents has failed and refused to execute and/or be bound by the agreements reached. The General Counsel avers such conduct violates Section 8(a)(5) and (1) of the National Labor Relations Act (the Act). Respondents in their answer deny essentially all the allegations contending, inter alia, that the Union at no time represented a majority of employees in either unit, that Respondents neither recognized the Union as representative of their employees in the units at issue nor reached agreement with the Union and, finally, that even had they done so, such conduct is impermissible under the Act and cannot be the basis of an unfair labor practice in refusing to sign and/or abide by such agreements.

Findings of Fact

All parties were given full opportunity to participate at the hearing, to introduce relevant evidence, to call, examine and cross-examine witnesses, to argue orally and to file post-hearing briefs.

Upon the entire record herein, including helpful briefs from the General Counsel and Respondent, and from my observation of the witnesses and their demeanor, I make the following findings of fact.

I. Jurisdiction

At all times material, KOFY FM has maintained an office and place of business in San Francisco, California and has been engaged in the business of operating a radio broadcast station. At all material times KOFY FM in the course of its business operations has enjoyed annual revenues in excess of $100,000 of which at least $ 5,000 was received from customers located outside the State of California.

At all times material, KOFY TV 20 has maintained an office and place of business in San Francisco, California and has been engaged in the business of operating a television broadcast station. At all material times KOFY TV 20 has enjoyed annual revenues in excess of $ 100,000 of which at least $ 5,000 was received from customers located outside the State of California.

The parties agree and I find that Respondents, and each of them, are employers engaged in commerce and in a business affecting commerce within the meaning of Section 2(2), (6) and (7) of the Act.

II. Labor Organization

The Union is a labor organization within the meaning of Section 2(5) of the Act.

III. The Alleged Unfair Labor Practices

A. Background

Pacific FM is a corporation holding broadcast licenses for Respondents and a third station, KOFY-AM. Pacific FM acquired what became KOFY TV

20 in 1980, KOFY AM in 1986 and KOFY FM in May 1988. KOFY FM was acquired from Olympia Broadcasting which had operated the station under the call letters KKCY until late 1987 and KNIT thereafter.

KOFY TV and the Union entered into a collective bargaining agreement covering announcers in September 1986, which contract expired by its terms in August 1987. The contract was extended from time to time until it expired on May 31, 1988.

On September 7, 1988 Respondents' agent, KOFY 20's News Director and Pacific's FM Chief Financial Officer met with the Union's counsel and its Executive Director. The General Counsel and the Charging Party contend that on this date Respondents recognized the Union as representing the employees in the following units:

All full-time and regular part-time newspersons and announcers employed by Respondent at its FM radio station in San Francisco, California.

All full-time and regular part-time newspersons and announcers employed by Respondent at its television station in San Francisco, California.

Various communications and exchanges occurred through the period from this meeting into October 1988. The General Counsel and the Charging Party contend that as a result of these communications, Respondents entered into collective bargaining agreements respecting each unit. The Union sought Respondents' signature on contracts offered as reflecting agreements reached. Respondents ultimately refused to sign the contracts. The instant charges followed.

B. Issues and Arguments

A prima facie case that a valid agreement was reached between an employer and a union includes various factors. Thus, in a typical case it must be established, inter alia, that the Union represented a majority of employees in an appropriate unit, that the employer recognized the Union as the employees' representative and that complete agreement on a collective bargaining agreement covering terms and conditions of unit employees was reached.

In the instant case Respondents challenge the Union's majority in each unit, dispute the units' appropriateness, deny that recognition in either unit was granted and, furthers contest that agreement was reached with the Union with respect to either unit. The General Counsel and the Charging Party rely on certain legal arguments to establish critical aspects of their prima facie case.

The General Counsel contends that recognition and agreement accrued through the events of September and October 1988 as testified to by Union agents and supported by various documents introduced into evidence. The General Counsel further argues that Respondents did not challenge the validity of its recognition of the Union, i.e. the underlying majority employee support for the Union in either unit or the appropriateness of either unit for collective bargaining, until more than six months after recognition. The General Counsel argues . . .: "Therefore it is irrelevant whether the Union demonstrated its majority status at the time of Respondents' original recognition," and ". . . the appropriateness of the unit is not subject to attack beyond the Section 10(b) six-month period. Morse Shoe, Inc., 227 NLRB 391 (1976)."

C. The Threshold Time Bar Issue

The General Counsel's theory of the case requires findings of majority unit-employee support for the Union based on the time bar theory described above.[84] That theory, amply supported by a learned marshalling by Counsel for the General Counsel on brief of time bar precedent, depends in turn on the correctness of the factual assertion in her brief . . .:

"At no time prior to the filing of the charges [on March 17, 1989] did Respondents attempt to withdraw recognition of the Union based on objective considerations of a lack of majority status." It is appropriate to turn to the testimony relevant to this contention.

Respondent's agent testified that at the September 7, 1988 meeting he raised in various ways the fact that the employee complements in each unit had not yet been selected and that employee support for the Union could therefore not yet be tested. These contentions were disputed by Union agents.

Respondents' counsel testified that he was in telephone contact with the Union's Executive Director in January and February 1989 respecting Respondents' intentions regarding signing the contracts the Union had sent them. In two conversations Respondent's counsel told the union Executive Director he did not yet have a position on the question. In a third telephone conversation which the Respondents counsel placed as occurring "between the middle and two-thirds of the month" of February 1989, he testified: [Union's Executive Director] asked me what was going on, was the company going to sign the agreements which she had sent to me, and I told her that, no, the company wasn't going to sign them because I couldn't advise my clients to sign pre-hire agreements, and that even if we would get over that hurdle, that there were some substantial problems with the terms of the agreement.

* * *

She said that if that was the position the company was going to take, that AFTRA would have to file unfair labor practice charges against the company.

* * *

. . . I told her—I wasn't going to tell her not to, because I didn't see any change forthcoming in the company's position, although they were willing to meet to discuss it, and I wasn't going to close the door on that, but I wasn't going to ask her to refrain from filing unfair labor practice charges on the basis that something would definitely come out of those talks.

The Union's Executive director recalled only two telephone conversations with the Respondent's counsel, one in mid-January 1989 and a second in February 1989. Her memory of the second call is similar to Respondent's counsel's recitation of their second conversation save that, in Robert's memory, when Respondents counsel told her he did not have a position for her on whether or not Respondents were going to sign the proffered contracts, the Union's Executive Director testified:

And I expressed to (Respondent's counsel) that we were quite anxious about this . . . getting this resolved. That we could see no reason why the agreement should not be executed and implemented and that we were very concerned about getting the H&R matter resolved.

And that we were contemplating filing an unfair labor practice charge, if the company was not going to sign the agreements. And, (Respondent's counsel) said, "Well, you have to do what you have to do," essentially.

The Union's Executive director testified on rebuttal that in her second conversation with Respondent's counsel he made no mention of a pre-hire agreement or the Union's majority status.

I credit Respondent's counsel's recitation of the specifics of the third phone conversation with the Union's Executive Director and find that the Union's Executive Director had simply combined the latter two calls described by Respondent's counsel into a single call in her memory and failed to recall the specific refusal to sign made by Respondent's counsel or his supporting rationale concerning the prehire agreements. I so find because the demeanor of each witness convinced me each was speaking truthfully concerning the events. Given my view of the honesty of each witness, I find it much more likely that Union's Executive Director would fail to recall the specifics of this mid-February conversation than Respondent's counsel would grossly misrecall or fabricate the specifics of the third telephone conversation he related. Simply put, I find it more probable that Union's Executive Director misrecalled through failure of memory than Respondent's counsel misrecalled through fabrication of a third conversation with Union's Executive Director and the insertion of untrue statements made about prehire agreements. Accordingly, I find that Respondent's counsel told Union's Executive Director Respondents were not going to sign the agreements, inter alia, because they were "pre-hire agreements."

. . .I find the credited statement of Respondent's counsel in February to Union's Executive Director that Respondents would not sign the proffered contracts because they were "pre-hire" agreements is a sufficient communication of Respondents' theory that the Union did not possess valid majority support in the units so that this argument is not time barred because not raised within six months of the argued recognition. Thus, I find the words "pre-hire" as used by Respondents' labor counsel to the Executive Director of the Union may be held to encompass the technical circumstances presented by that term including the situation where recognition is granted and/or an agreement is reached at a time when an insufficient number of employees have been hired into the unit to make the action valid in law. Further, since all of February 1989 is within six months of September 7, 1988, Respondent's counsel's contentions were made within the six month period since the recognition.

Having found that Respondent's counsel timely asserted the majority issue as a defense, I find the General Counsel may not simply rely on the passage of time to avoid meeting the majority issue. Accordingly, I find the General Counsel bears the usual burden of proof on all issues including those of unit appropriateness and majority status herein. The General Counsel and the Charging Party having made no sustainable factual contentions respecting Union majority status at the relevant times in the units encompassed by the alleged collective bargaining agreements, I find the General Counsel has failed to establish such majority status. Accordingly, *I find Respondents was not obligated to recognize the Union as representative of employees in the units pled in the complaint nor obligated to sign or abide by the proffered contracts* (italics added). Accordingly, I further find Respondents have not acted in contravention of their obligations under the Act and have not violated the Act as alleged in the complaint. It follows further that I shall recommend that the complaint be dismissed in its entirety.

Conclusions of Law

On the basis of the above findings of fact and on the entire record herein, I make the following Conclusions of Law.

1. Respondents, and each of them, are employers engaged in commerce within the meaning of Section 2(2), (6) and (7) of the Act.

2. The Union is a labor organization within the meaning of Section 2(5) of the Act.

3. Respondent did not violate the Act as alleged in the complaint.

ORDER

Based on the foregoing findings of fact, conclusions of law, and the entire record herein, and pursuant to Section 10(c) of the Act, I hereby issue the following recommended Order.[85] The Complaint shall be and it hereby is dismissed.

Issued at San Francisco, California, this 4th day of June, 1990.

QUESTIONS FOR CRITICAL ANALYSIS

- Could a federal regulation be written whereby a station would be exempt from meeting the wage and hour standard during a breaking news event where employees must work more than a 40-hour week? Would such a regulation have merit? What would be its advantages and disadvantages?
- When the federal government officially declares an area a disaster area, why couldn't it also declare a moratorium on wage and hour laws letting reporters work more than 40 hours per week without receiving overtime pay? What might happen if such a law were to go into effect?
- Should the Federal Communications Commission and not the Department of Labor govern wage and hour laws when the laws apply to radio and television stations and the telecommunications industry?
- News department personnel know it is necessary to get the news out during emergencies and world crises. Could an argument be made that First Amendment issues are at stake where wage and hour law prohibits a station from covering an event because they do not have the budget to pay employees overtime?
- Would some type of First Amendment grounds exist for news department personnel to be exempt from wage and hour law?
- Should different regulations apply to radio and television news departments or other areas of station operation? For instance, it might be legal under new regulations to have overtime pay go into effect when a reporter works more than 50 hours in a given week.
- Do strict wage and hour laws make it difficult for employees to work additional hours on a volunteer basis so they can improve their skills and apply for better jobs at higher wages?
- Are wage and hour laws too strict when applied to prizes for sales contests or suggestion-box entries?
- A collective bargaining agreement which meets overtime requirements and does not exceed a contract of 60 hours per week is usually considered to be within FLSA standards. Is the 60-hour per week figure reasonable?
- Are the administrative and executive exemptions to wage and hour law so alike that they should be combined into a single category?
- Would a television news reporter in a nonunion station where reporters shoot their own video and prepare their own on-air packages be considered exempt professionals under the FLSA?
- A distinction is made in the FLSA interpretations between a print media cartoonist and a motion picture animator, the former being considered an exempt artistic professional, the latter not. Is this distinction justified? Is an animator of motion picture cartoons someone who relies on artistic talent just as much as a print media cartoonist?

- Do you feel the statement that "the majority of reporters do work which depends primarily on intelligence, diligence, and accuracy but not work which depends on invention, imagination or talent" is an accurate reflection of television journalism?
- Is the requirement that a professional exemption must involve "intellectually varied" tasks and responsibilities too vague to be applied fairly or interpreted with consistency?
- Read again the job descriptions for general assignment reporters, producers, directors, and assignment editors. Do you feel these descriptions apply to most television stations?
- Some broadcast professionals will argue that the future of broadcast journalism lies in stations using one person to write the story, report the story, shoot the video, position himself or herself and do his or her own standups, and package all of the elements into a story ready for airing. Using the reporter in this way, would the professional exemption to the FLSA apply?
- Courts still tend to fall back on FLSA interpretations from print journalism to decide broadcast wage and hour disputes. Why do judges sometimes fail to make the distinction between these two types of media?
- Should the Federal Communications Commission have jurisdiction over Department of Labor cases involving the recognition of unions as employee bargaining agents?
- Could issues surrounding a union contract ever impact on the ability of a station to serve the public interest, and if so should the content of union contracts be a matter which receives in-depth FCC review at the time of license renewal?
- Although union agreements may provide a set level of compensation for station employees, do such agreements tend to lessen the congenial atmosphere that might exist in a station where the union contract does not exist?
- From a management perspective which is more important, congeniality or compensation?

ADDITIONAL RESOURCES

Bachman, K. L., and A. H. Medansky, "The Wage-Hour Law: Highlights of the Fair Labor Standards Act of 1989." 21 *The Tax Adviser* 560 (September 1990).

Barnett, E., "FLSA Amendments Change More than Minimum Wage." 26 *Trial* 38 (September 1990).

Conaghan, J., "Statutory Maternity Pay under the Social Security Act 1986." 16 *Industrial Law Journal* 125 (June 1987).

Delikat, M., H. J. Levine, and B. G. Kempner, "The Explosive Growth of ERISA-Based Severance Pay Litigation." *Labor Law Journal* 404 (July 1987).

Murphy, A. J., and D. Nickles. "The Fair Labor Standards Act Amendments of 1985." 37 *Labor Law Journal* 67 (February 1986).

Prozzi, J. A., "Overtime Pay and the Managerial Employee: Still a 'Twilight Zone of Uncertainty'." 41 *Labor Law Journal* 178 (March 1990).

Prozzi, J. A., "Docking the Pay of Managerial Employees: The Wage and Hour Law's Potential Trap for the Employer." 42 *Labor Law Journal* 444 (July 1991).

Stieffel, R. A., "Qualified Separate Lines of Business Rules." 18 *Journal of Corporate Taxation* 275 (Autumn 1991).

chapter eleven

Cable

In the United States, Oregon and Pennsylvania hold claim to the beginning of cable television. Enterprising individuals in both states saw a way for communities far removed from television stations to get better reception by sharing an antenna located on top of an adjacent hilltop. From those small beginnings in 1948, cable systems have grown in size and number. Basic statistics are impressive.[1] More than 60 percent of television households receive cable, which reaches more than 55 million people. For those who have cable, viewing levels continue to increase and today average more than 18 hours of viewing per week. Annual expenditures for cable television are in excess of $20 billion.[2]

CABLE: THE BASIC CONCEPT

The components of the cable system consist of a headend, trunk cable, feeder cable (also called subtrunk), drop cables, and home terminal. The headend is the human and hardware combination responsible for originating, controlling, and processing signals over the cable system. A key part of the headend is the receiving antenna, also called the master antenna, which receives the incoming signals from distant television stations. The trunk cable is the main cable leaving the headend, and follows the main arteries of a community, such as the main thoroughfares. Off the trunk cable run the feeder cables to smaller areas, such as individual streets. From the feeder cable, a drop cable brings the signal along the final leg, into the subscriber's home television set. Spaced intermittently along the routes of the trunk and feeder cables are amplifiers, which boost the incoming signal.

Two-way cable systems operate in conjunction with a central computer and can function for public-opinion polling, remote reading of utility meters, at-home banking and shopping, monitoring of intensive-care patients, and other uses.

UNITED STATES v. SOUTHWESTERN CABLE CO.

The FCC began exercising its authority over cable in the early 1960s. By the mid-1960s the commission had established rules governing cable systems that received signals via microwave. In 1966, the test case came in *United States* v. *Southwestern Cable Co.*, where the Supreme Court upheld the FCC's right to regulate "interstate commerce by wire or radio". [3] The case developed when a cable company distributed the signals of Los Angeles television stations into the San Diego area. When the FCC limited the cable company's expansion of service, the issue reached the Ninth Circuit Court of

Appeals, which held that the commission lacked authority under the Communications Act to issue the order restricting the company's expansion. On appeal the U.S. Supreme Court affirmed the authority of the commission to issue the order restricting the cable company's expansion. The cable company argued that because cable was neither purely common carrier nor purely broadcasting, it did not fall under the Communications Act. The Supreme Court disagreed, stating in a majority opinion written by Justice Harlan: "Nothing in the language of (FCC rules), in the surrounding language, or the Act's history or purposes limits the Commission's authority to those activities and forms of communication that are specifically described by the Act's other provisions."[4] The Court reasoned that the FCC could act in advance of regulatory needs and that the commission had a statutory responsibility to plan ahead. Justice Harlan wrote: "The Commission has reasonably found that the successful performance of these duties demands prompt and efficacious regulation of community antenna television systems".[5]

1972 CABLE RULES AND CHANGES

By 1968, the FCC had started an official rule-making proceeding to develop comprehensive regulations for cable, which it issued in 1972.[6] After negotiations with Congress and the White House Office of Telecommunications Policy over program exclusivity and distant-signal importation, the new rules took effect. Broad categories of regulations consisted of "franchising standards, signal carriage, network program nonduplication and syndicated program exclusivity, nonbroadcast or cablecasting services, cross-ownership, equal employment opportunity, and technical standards."[7] Record-keeping requirements on finances and employment statistics were also required. Cable systems that originated programming came under the Fairness Doctrine and sponsor identification rules.

Modification of the rules began almost immediately as cable systems began to grow and new regulatory oversight began to strain the commission. By 1977 most of the franchising standards had been eliminated, a signal registration process replaced the certificate of compliance application process, and distant-signal carriage restrictions and syndicated program exclusivity rules were eliminated along with the requirement that cable systems file financial information with the FCC.[8]

REPEAL OF PAY CABLE RULES: THE HBO CASE

Pay cable programming rules were eliminated in 1977. In *Home Box Office, Inc.* v. *FCC*, the court ruled the FCC could not regulate pay cable to protect such programming as sports and motion pictures on conventional television.[9] FCC rules in force at the time required separate programming on pay television. Pay television operators, the FCC reasoned, were in a position to "siphon off" the best programming, thereby denying a large segment of the population programming that would be sold to pay services and denied to conventional broadcasters.

The court ruled that the real thrust of the FCC rules was to prevent competition and preventing competition was not a legitimate goal of the Communications Act. Also stressed in the decision was the court's opinion that cable was not a regulatory issue separate from broadcasting, and that even if the siphoning rules the FCC had imposed on pay cable were in the public good, the public good alone could not justify the commission's regulations.

> The commission has in no way justified its position that cable television must be a supplement to, rather than an equal of, broadcast television. Such an artificial narrowing of the scope of the regulatory problem is itself arbitrary and capricious and is ground for reversal. Moreover, by narrowing its discussion in this way the Commission has failed to crystallize what is in fact harmful about "siphoning."[10]

Cable television access rules also fell victim to the courts and other rules imposed by the commission began to create enforcement problems. By the early 1980s, a web of regulations had developed, and the list included such areas as local broadcast signal carriage, network program nonduplication protection, franchise fees, sports program blackouts, cross-ownership, equal employment opportunity, cable-originated programming, technical standards, cable television relay service, and record keeping and reporting.

THE CABLE ACT OF 1984

After patchwork legislation proved confusing and ineffective, Congress passed the Cable Communications Policy Act of 1984 bringing together under one law such issues as ownership, channel usage, provisions for issuing franchising and franchise renewals, rate structures and privacy, EEO policies, obscenity, lockboxes, and pole attachments.[11] The 1974 legislation established jurisdictional boundaries between federal, state, and local government. Rules were modified to incorporate provisions of the new law, which became effective on April 28, 1985.[12] The 1984 law was amended by the passage of the Cable Television Consumer Protection and Competition Act of 1992.[13]

THE CABLE ACT OF 1992

In the wake of complaints over rates and service, Congress again entered the cable regulation area in 1992 with a passage of a new law designed to give local franchising authorities additional regulation over cable systems, television stations the opportunity to enter into agreements with cable companies to carry local programming, and consumer protection measures associated with basic tier service. The arguments pro and con for the act resulted in a major lobbying effort by the cable industry and to some extent by the broadcasting industry on whether or not the cable act should be passed. A series of strongly worded commercials appeared on cable television systems and lobbying efforts organized by such trade associations as the National Association of Broadcasters brought the issue to the forefront of the political process. It became a campaign issue during the presidential election campaign which saw Bill Clinton and Albert Gore elected. Gore had been a supporter of the cable bill and had discussed cable regulation during some of his campaign appearances. President George Bush vetoed the Cable Television Consumer Protection and Competition Act of 1992 and it became the first veto overridden by Congress during the Bush administration.[14] Trade associations were quick to either hail the bill's passage or claim it was unconstitutional and move through the courts to block certain provisions of the law. Some of the provisions of the 1992 law included rate regulation, must carry, retransmission consent, program access, limitations on municipal liability franchise renewal, customer service, systems sales, ownership restrictions, and other provisions.

REGULATION OF RATES

Under the law, cable systems which are not subject to effective competition can be regulated by the FCC. Among other things, effective competition means that fewer than 30 percent of the households in the franchise area subscribe to the cable service of a cable system, and the franchise area is served by at least two unaffiliated multichannel video programming distributors. The term *multichannel video programming distributor* is defined as "a person, such as, but not limited to, a cable operator, a multichannel multipoint distribution service, a direct broadcast satellite service, or a television receive-only satellite program distributor, who makes available for purchase, by subscribers or customers, multiple channels of video programming."[15] That means most franchises do not have effective competition and therefore are eligible to have regulated rates. Authority to engage in such regulation requires the local franchising authority to petition the FCC and show that they have the personnel to administer such regulations. In addition, the local authority is required to certify with the FCC that the local authority has "procedural laws and regulations applicable to rate regulation" and that the authority has provided for "a reasonable opportunity for consideration of the views of interested parties."[16]

In determining whether or not local rates are reasonable a series of factors is taken into consideration, including the rates for similarly situated cable systems offering comparable cable programming services. Taken into account are facilities, costs of meeting regulations, the number of subscribers, the rates charged by the cable system, the relationship of rates to general consumer prices, capital and operating costs of the system, and the revenues from such income streams as advertising.[17] Specifically federal law states: "The Commission shall, by regulation, ensure that the rates for the basic service tier are reasonable."[18] The regulations are designed to achieve the goal of "protecting subscribers in any cable system that is not subject to effective competition from rates from the basic service tier that exceed the rates that would be charged for the basic service tier if such cable system were subject to effective competition."[19]

The commission has oversight authority if franchise authorities chose to engage in rate regulation. A cable operator or other interested person can petition the commission to review the regulation of the cable system by a franchising authority and if the commission finds that the franchising authority has acted inconsistently with federal statutes, the commission can order relief.[20] Relief can be granted through such means as the commission revoking a franchise authority's jurisdiction over a cable system until the authority complies with federal statutes.

The requirements for basic tier service require cable operators to include nonsuperstation commercial and noncommercial broadcast signals, the required public, educational and government access channels (PEG channels), in addition to any other services the cable operator wants to add to the basic tier at a reasonable rate. Purchasing the basic tier of service can be a legal requirement for access to premium channels but additional tiers cannot be added to the basic service as a condition for additional premium channels. The same regulations apply to access such services as pay-per-view. In addition, cable operators are prohibited from discriminating in the pricing of additional channels and services between those subscribers who only chose the basic service. The only exception permitted cable operators are for those systems which did not have the technology to facilitate access through only the basic tier of service. This exception, however, expires in the year 2002, ten years after the date of the 1992 enactment.[21]

Subscribers also have protection in the area of equipment leases including converter boxes. The FCC has the authority to develop standards and costs for "installation and lease of the equipment used by subscribers to receive the basic service tier, including a converter box and a remote control unit and, if requested by the subscriber, such addressable converter box or other equipment as is required to access programming . . ."[22]

CARRIAGE OF LOCAL COMMERCIAL TELEVISION SIGNALS

The most controversial part of the 1992 Cable Act was the must-carry rules. The rules were quickly challenged in court and their future remains somewhat unclear. Under the original legislation as passed in the 1992 Cable Act, cable operators are required to carry the "signals of local commercial television stations and qualified low power stations . . . Carriage of additional broadcast television signals . . . shall be at the discretion of such operator . . . "[23] The must-carry rules require cable systems "with 12 or fewer usable activated channels" to carry at least three local commercial television stations unless the system has 300 or fewer subscribers. In such case the system is exempt as long as the small system does not delete the signal of a broadcast television station.[24] Additional exemptions exist for cable operators without large-channel capacity and cable operators were required to carry the network affiliate closest to the headend of the cable system. The primary video and audio signal along with closed-captioning transmission of each local commercial television station on the system is required to be carried in its entirety.

A cable operator is not required to carry the signal of a local commercial television station that substantially duplicates the signal of another local commercial television station also carried on the system. In addition, the cable operator is not required to carry the signals of more than one local commercial television station affiliated with a particular broadcast network. In other words, if one ABC affiliate is carried and there are two ABC affiliates within the cable system's operating area, the cable operator is only required to carry one affiliate. The operator does have the discretion of carrying both affiliate stations, however, and both stations can count toward the required number of signals the operator is required to carry.

In addition, restrictions are imposed on the operator prohibiting the movement of channels on the cable system in the carriage of local commercial television stations. The operator is required to carry on the cable system the same channel number as the local commercial station or it can remain where it was already carried on the system, if the station so elects. For many stations it is advantageous not to tamper with the location of the channel since the audience in a given area may have become accustomed to a particular channel position. A different channel can also be used if mutually agreed upon by the station and the cable operator.

Every subscriber is afforded the opportunity of receiving the local commercial television stations. If the cable operator intends to delete or reposition a commercial station on the cable system, the operator must notify the station at least 30 days prior to their intended action and no deletion or repositioning can occur during a ratings period. The term *local commercial television station* does not include low-power television stations or television translator stations.

CARRIAGE OF NONCOMMERCIAL STATIONS

Similar to the requirements for commercial stations cable operators under the 1992 law must carry noncommercial stations as well. The law reads: "A cable operator of a cable system with 12 or fewer usable activated channels shall be required to carry the signal of one qualified local non-commercial educational television station . . . and may in its discretion, carry the signals of other qualified noncommercial educational television stations."[25] The rules are somewhat different for systems with 13 to 36 channels which are required to carry at least one qualified local noncommercial educational station but are not required to carry more than three stations. Where a noncommercial station is not available, the cable operator is required to import one to comply with the law. If the cable system had more than 36 channels as of March 29, 1990, it must carry the signal of each qualified local noncommercial educational television station which requests carriage. The exception is when noncommercial stations duplicate each other's programming.[26] Cable operators are prohibited from charging noncommercial stations for carriage, although the station can be required to bear the cost of delivering the signal to the cable system.

In addition to carriage requirements and retransmission consent provisions of the law, by October 1994 cable systems are barred from retransmitting the broadcast signals of a station without that station's consent and stations may elect between taking a must-carry position or a retransmission consent position.

RETRANSMISSION CONSENT

In addition to the must-carry rules, the retransmission consent provisions of the 1992 act were also controversial. Under the retransmission consent provision, cable systems must obtain consent to retransmit the signal of local stations. Remember, the act also requires cable systems to carry certain stations; thus, the new provision resulted in considerable high-powered negotiations between broadcasters and cable companies, both trying to comply with the law. Broadcasters were given a window in which they could exercise their right of carriage, or negotiate retransmission consent agreements. Overall, it became in the best interests of both cable operators and broadcasters to reach agreements. For those broadcasters choosing to simply exercise the must-carry provisions of the 1992 act, getting over the retransmission consent hurdle was easy, and the must-carry provisions of the act were given precedent over the retransmission provisions. For those broadcasters opting for retransmission consent over must-carry and deciding to negotiate, the road was a bit rougher, although some innovative deals were struck which may in the long run benefit both industries. When the first round of negotiations ended in 1993, no one could deny the fact that the cable operators and broadcasters were in a position to work more closely with each other in the future. Retransmission agreements are reviewed every three years.

Among the retransmission consent agreements were the straight compensation deal whereby the cable system compensates the television station to carry the station's signal. Other agreements, while still based on retransmission consent over must-carry, were struck without any money changing hands. Some agreements were negotiated on a group-wide basis whereby a group owner negotiated on behalf of all owned-and-operated television stations. Some networks, FOX in particular, provided, and charged, cable operators for a FOX cable programming channel. The cable systems in turn agreed to carry FOX television affiliates which in turn were compensated with some of the network's income from the cable deal. Still other agreements gave local television stations an additional cable channel to program separately from their broadcast station. Station managers were quick to point out they intended to use the newly acquired access channels for separate programming ventures, including 24-hour local news programming or local news programming during certain hours, with lease agreements with subcontractor programers during other time periods.

Local news is the one programming area which has not been able to move on a broad scale out of its traditional time periods of early morning, noon, drive-time, and late night. With cable audiences becoming conditioned to receiving CNN and *CNN Headline News* 24-hours a day, being forced to watch local news only when programmed continues to cause concern with many television news directors who feel they are losing audience to radio news and newspapers. For stations gaining an additional cable channel as a part of a retransmission consent agreement, the shackles were removed. All that was left was the time and investment to program the new cable channels with local news, sell ads, and hope the ventures into cable-distributed local news programming would be profitable. For television stations which are successful in launching successful local-news cable channels, the next round of negotiations on must-carry and retransmission consent may prove particularly interesting.

LEASED COMMERCIAL ACCESS

Cable operators required to designate channel capacity for commercial use may use excess channel capacity for programming from a qualified minority programming source or from any qualified educational programming source. The maximum amount of programming from the two sources may not exceed 33 percent of the channel capacity and the law prescribed new programming by prohibiting programming provided prior to July 1, 1990 as meeting the requirements of the minority and educational programming provision. *Qualified minority programming source* is defined as "a programming source which devotes substantially all of its programming to coverage of minority viewpoints, or to programming directed at members of minority groups, and which is over 50 percent minority owned . . ."[27] *Qualified educational programming source* is defined in the law as "a programming source which devotes substantially all of its programming to educational or instructional programming that promotes public understanding of mathematics, the sciences, the humanities, and the arts and has a documented annual expenditure on programming exceeding $15,000,000."[28]

CHILDREN'S PROTECTION FROM INDECENT PROGRAMMING

Children are given special protection under the law and cable operators are permitted to enforce a written and published policy which prohibits programming that the cable operator "reasonably believes describes or depicts sexual or excretory activities or organs in a patently offensive manner as measured by contemporary community standards."[29] Cable operators are required to place on a single channel all indecent programming as identified by program providers and the channel must be blocked unless the subscriber requests access to it in writing. Public, educational, or government access facilities cannot be used for the production of programming containing obscene material, promoting sexually explicit conduct, or soliciting or promoting unlawful conduct.

In addition the law also requires the cable operator to notify subscribers that a premium channel will be provided without charge and the subscriber has the right to request the channel be blocked. The term *premium channel* is defined as "any pay service offered on a per channel or per program basis, which offers movies rated by the Motion Picture Association of America as X, NC-17, or R."[30]

REGULATION OF CARRIAGE AGREEMENTS

Program Carriage Agreements between cable operators and multichannel video program distributors are regulated. Video programming vendors are people engaged in the production, creation, or wholesale distribution of video programming for sale. The law is designed to prevent a cable operator or other multichannel video programming distributor from requiring a financial interest in a program service as a condition for carriage on one or more of the cable operator systems. In addition, cable operators or other multichannel video programming distributors are prohibited from "coercing a video programming vendor to provide, and from retaliating against such a vendor for failing to provide exclusive rights against other multi-channel video programming distributors as a condition of carriage on a system."[31]

CONSUMER PROTECTION AND CUSTOMER SERVICE

Customer service was one of the main areas of complaint Congress used to justify passage of the 1992 legislation. The 1992 law established standards by which cable operators would fulfill customer service requirements which at a minimum required the FCC to establish requirements for office hours, telephone availability, installations, outages, service calls, and communications between the cable operator and the subscriber. Nothing in the new law prohibited cable operators and franchising authorities from agreeing to much stricter standards or the local authority to enforce those stricter standards.[32]

PROVISIONS FOR SPECIAL RELIEF

Exceptions to the rules are possible through provisions for special relief. The commission retains the right to waive any provision of the rules, impose additional or different rules, or issue rulings. Such relief can be requested through petition "by a cable television system operator, a franchising authority, an applicant, permittee, or licensee of a television broadcast, translator, or microwave relay station, or by any other interested person . . ."[33] The commission requires the parties involved in a dispute to have engaged in an attempt to solve the problem before it reaches the petition stage, and the petition must explain the steps taken to resolve the problem. When a petition for relief is filed, comments from interested parties can be filed in most cases within 30 days thereafter and the petitioner may also file replies to the comments.

In serious matters the commission can schedule hearings on the petition and the parties have the right to settle the issue without prejudice at any point prior to the commission taking final action on the matter. Much like broadcasting, the commission has at its disposal measures to enforce violations of the rules. City and state government may also have jurisdiction in a case. A forfeiture proceeding, which usually takes place without a hearing, can be initiated by the FCC, and the commission can issue an order requiring the cable operator to show cause why it should not cease and desist from activity resulting in the alleged violation. Parties who feel a cable operator has failed to provide commercial channel capacity where it is required, can bring an action in the district court in the judicial district where the cable system is located.[34]

REGISTRATION AND RECORDS REQUIREMENTS

Cable systems are required upon commencing operation to file a registration statement with the FCC. The registration statement contains the legal name of the operator and an identification number such as the social security number of the operator. Other basic information required on the registration statement includes the date the system began providing service, television broadcast signals to be carried, and the system's equal employment opportunity program when five or more full-time personnel are employed. After the registration statement is received, the FCC issues a public notice. The operator, if beginning operation before the registration statement is filed, is liable for any regulatory sanctions which may be imposed, such as cease and desist orders or forfeitures.

In addition to registration requirements a cable operator is required to be familiar with and have on hand the regulations governing cablecasting. Cable systems with more than 1000 subscribers are required to keep a public inspection file containing records on the system's EEO program, political cablecasting, and commercial records. The public inspection file must be maintained at the office where the operator collects subscriber fees or at another accessible place in the community, such as a public registry for documents or an attorney's office. A public inspection file must be available for inspection during regular business hours and photocopies of documents can be made upon request, with the inquirer being responsible for the costs of reproduction. Although the system operator can honor requests for documents from the public file by mail, no requirement is imposed for responding to mail requests. Commission representatives can gain access to the public inspection file "at any reasonable hour."

PUBLIC, EDUCATIONAL, AND GOVERNMENT ACCESS

Franchising authorities have the right under the Cable Act to require that cable systems provide access channels for public, educational, and government use (called PEG use). Prohibited is any editorial control over the content of programming on PEG channels. Federal law gives the franchising authority the ability to enforce any provision of the franchise covering PEG channels including "services, facilities, or equipment proposed by the cable operator which relate to public, educational, or governmental use of channel capacity . . ."[35] When PEG channel capacity is designated by the franchising authority the authority is required to prescribe: "(1) rules and procedures under which the cable operator is permitted to use such channel capacity for the provision of other services if such channel capacity is not being used for the purposes designated, and (2) rules and procedures under which such permitted use shall cease."[36]

CHANNELS FOR COMMERCIAL USE

When the 1984 Cable Act was passed, one of the intents of the legislation was to create a regulatory atmosphere whereby cable could develop as a medium of communication. Pursuant to this end, the act outlined conditions under which cable operators would provide channels designated for "commercial use," defined in the act as "the provision of video programming, whether or not for profit."[37]

Access Requirements

Only systems with 36 or more channels fall under the commercial-use regulations, unless the system was required to provide such channels prior to the enactment of the 1984 law. Systems with between 36- and 54-channel capacity must designate 10 percent of their channel capacity for leased commercial use, and systems with a capacity of more than 54 channels must designate 15 percent of their channels for such use. Local franchising authorities are prohibited from requiring channel capacity for commercial use in excess of the federally stated percentages and PEG channels do not count as commercial channel use. Editorial control by the cable operator over the content on commercial channels is prohibited.

Remedies for Denial of Access

The regulations provide for anyone aggrieved by the "failure or refusal of a cable operator to make channel capacity available for use pursuant to this section . . .

> to bring action against the cable system in the district court with jurisdiction over the system. Regulations state: "If the court finds that the channel capacity sought by such person has not been made available in accordance with this section, or finds that the price, terms, or conditions established by the cable operator are unreasonable, the court may order such system to make available to such person the channel capacity sought, and further determine the appropriate price, terms, or conditions for such use . . . and may award actual damages if it deems such relief appropriate.[38]

Evidence of prior violations by the cable system that establishes a pattern or practice of violations is sufficient for the commission to establish other rules requiring the operator to provide the "diversity of information sources" required in the law.

SUBSCRIBER PRIVACY PROTECTION

We may sit passively and watch television received on a local cable system and not give much thought to how much the cable company knows about us. What many system operators do know, however, is our telephone number, our address, what programs we are watching, and some idea of our household income because of medium income figures for our zip code. In addition, if we have subscribed to pay channels, this information is in the cable company records, as are the movies we watched through pay-per-view. What the cable company does with this information and the rights of the subscriber are spelled out in the cable regulations and are also contained in various statements found within local cable ordinances.[39] Specifically, the rules require that at the time of entering into an agreement to provide cable or other services, the cable company is required annually to provide the subscriber with a written statement that tells the subscriber the nature of information collected about the subscriber. The subscriber must be "clearly and conspicuously" informed of the nature of the information, the type of disclosure that will be made of the information, how long the information will be maintained, and how the subscriber can gain access to the information. An example of how one cable operator meets the requirements is seen in the following paragraphs from a cable company "Subscriber Privacy Notice":

1. So that we may continue to provide reliable, high quality service to you, we keep regular business records that contain your name, address, and other personally identifiable information. Such records include billing, payment, and deposit records, records indicating the number of your television sets connected to cable, and the service options you have chosen. We use this information to make sure that you are being properly billed for the services you receive. We also use this information for service calls, customer surveys, bill collection, and marketing needs, as well as for our own tax and accounting records.
2. We consider information we keep to be confidential. We may collect personally identifiable information from you and may disclose it to a third party if (a) you consent in advance in writing or electronically; (b) disclosure is necessary to render cable service and other services we provide to you and related business activities; or (c) disclosure is required under a court order, and you are notified of such order. Disclosure "necessary to render cable services" includes release of personally identifiable information to collection agencies, program guide suppliers, programming suppliers, billing and mailing houses and equipment suppliers. (For example, we may without your consent disclose your name and address to a collection service if required to collect past due bills.)
3. Unless you object, from time to time, we may disclose your name and address for mailing lists and other purposes, such as market research. Recipients of this information may use it for non-cable-related purposes, including

the sale of their products and services. We will not disclose the extent of your viewing or use of a particular service or the nature of any transaction you may make over the cable system, but we may disclose that you are among those who subscribe to a particular service. If you wish to remove your name from such lists or limit the use of your name at any time, please contact us at the system office.

4. We may also electronically test the system from time to time to determine whether you are being properly billed for the cable services you are receiving.

5. We will maintain the information about you for as long as we provide service to you, and for a longer time if necessary for related business activities. Ordinarily, for tax reasons, we would keep records for up to 5 years. When information is no longer necessary for our purposes, we will destroy the information unless there is a legitimate request or order to inspect the information still outstanding.

6. You have the right to inspect our records that contain information about you, correct any error in our information, and enforce your rights under federal law, including the right to recover statutory damages and costs. If you wish to inspect the records at our system office pertaining to you or to review your statutory rights, please contact us to set up an appointment during regular business hours.[40]

Not included in the subscriber notice or the rules are aggregate data where the individual subscriber is not identified. In addition, the cable operator cannot use the cable system to collect personal information without the subscriber's written "or electronic" consent. Damages, including punitive damages and reasonable attorney fees, are provided for violations of the subscriber privacy provisions of the cable rules. Under the privacy rules, states and local franchises can pass laws that are consistent with the federal regulations.

Provisions exist for government entities to gain access to personally identifiable information pursuant to a court order if the proceeding results in "clear and convincing evidence" that criminal behavior is involved and the information is material evidence in the case. Due process is still assured, however, to the subscriber who turns out to be the object of such a proceeding.

EEO AND POLITICAL BROADCASTING REQUIREMENTS

Equal employment opportunity (EEO) and political broadcasting requirements for cable systems are much the same as those for over-the-air broadcasting stations. Cable systems are responsible for an EEO program that includes defining the responsibility of each level of management to ensure "vigorous enforcement" of EEO policy, keeping employees informed of EEO rules, communicating the policy and employment needs to qualified applicants, conducting a continuing program to exclude prejudice, and conducting a "continuing review of job structure and employment practices . . . training, job design, and other measures needed to ensure genuine equality of opportunity to participate fully in all organizational units, occupations, and levels of responsibility."[41]

Political cablecasting rules also follow the rules governing conventional broadcast stations. For example, cable operators are not permitted to control the content of political cablecasts, and the lowest-unit charges that apply to broadcast stations also apply to cablecasting. Cable rules state that

> charges, if any, made for the use of any cable television system by any person who is a legally qualified candidate for any public office in connection with his campaign for nomination for election, or election, to such office shall not exceed . . . (dates where the rules apply) . . . the charges made for comparable use of such system by other users thereof.[42]

Specifically, the rules require that candidates

> shall be charged no more than the rate the cable television system would charge if the candidate were a commercial advertiser whose advertising was directed to promoting its business within the same areas as that encompassed by the particular office for which such person is a candidate. All discount privileges otherwise offered by a cable television system to commercial advertisers shall be available upon equal terms to candidates for public office.[43]

INDECENCY AND OBSCENITY ON CABLE TELEVISION

The U.S. Supreme Court has a long legacy of rulings centered on First Amendment issues.[44] Some decisions deal with limited spectrum space, which has an impact on the content of broadcasting.[45] Still others influence local municipalities and their limited ability to control locally distributed material.[46]

Because cable is inherently a locally regulated medium, and because communities take an active, sometimes emotional, interest in the content of cable programming, it is not surprising that local municipalities have attempted to regulate what the viewer can see. For example, over-the-air broadcasting has been used, albeit unsuccessfully, as a model to control cable television. In particular, *FCC* v. *Pacifica,* where comedian George Carlin's dirty words were an issue, has been cited as a rationale for local municipal control of indecency on cable.[47]

Obscenity is controlled at the federal level in the Cable Act, later amended to the Communications Act and part of the United States Code. The law reads: "Whoever transmits over any cable system any matter which is obscene or otherwise unprotected by the Constitution of the United States shall be fined not more than $10,000, or imprisoned not more than 2 years, or both."[48] At the local level, attempts to control indecency have failed, notably in two states, Utah and Florida.[49]

INDECENCY AND DUE PROCESS: *CRUZ* v. *FERRE*

A Miami, Florida cable television ordinance carried the wording: "No person shall by means of a cable television system knowingly distribute by wire or cable any obscene or indecent material."[50] Indecent was defined under the ordinance as "material which is a representation or description of a human sexual or excretory organ or function which the average person, applying community standards, would find to be patently offensive."

The ordinance provided for complaints to be submitted to the city manager, who could also initiate claims and was in charge of evaluating all claims against the system. An informal hearing was provided for, wherein the city manager governed the admissibility of evidence. Under the ordinance, the burden of proof was on the city, which was represented by the city attorney "or his designee." After a complaint and hearing, the manager would make a written finding. The only sanction provided for in the ordinance was the suspension of the license for up to nine days or the termination of the license.

A cable subscriber, Ruben Cruz, filed as a plaintiff a court action seeking to have the ordinance governing the control of indecent programming void on its face. HBO also intervened as a plaintiff and the district judge granted a motion voiding the indecent material portion of the ordinance and permanently enjoining the city from enforcing it. On appeal, the United States Court of Appeals for the 11th Circuit affirmed the findings of the lower court.

Over-the-Air Broadcasting versus Cable Television

A primary argument in *Cruz* v. *Ferre* was based on the George Carlin dirty words case, namely the intruding characteristic of broadcasting and its limited First Amendment protection. The court noted that broadcasting receives the most limited form of First Amendment protection and that the airwaves confront listeners in their home where an individual's right to be left alone outweighs the First Amendment rights of an intruder.[51]

In *Cruz* v. *Ferre,* the court carefully distinguished between cable and over-the-air broadcasting, noting:

> Unlike broadcast television, which sends over-the-air signals, cable television operates by transmitting programs to subscribers through coaxial cables or wires. These cables or wires are individually attached to ordinary television sets in subscribers' homes. Through the use of a converter, cable television can increase the channel capacity of a television set dramatically.[52]

The appeals court ruled:

> Although we recognize the complicated and uncertain area of constitutional interpretation which we are entering and the importance of the interests asserted by the city, we are persuaded that *Pacifica* cannot be extended to cover the particular facts of this case. . . . The Court's concern with the pervasiveness of the broadcast media can best be seen in its description of broadcasted material as an "intruder" into the privacy of the home. . . .

> (The cable subscriber) must affirmatively elect to have cable service come into his home. Additionally, the subscriber must make the additional affirmative decision whether to purchase any "extra" programming services, such as HBO. The subscriber must make a monthly decision whether to continue to subscribe to cable, and if dissatisfied with the cable service, he may cancel his subscription. . . . One of the keys to the very existence of cable television is the fact that cable programming is available only to those who have the cable attached to their television sets.[53]

"Because we determine that under the facts of the instant case the interests of the City of Miami are substantially less strong than those of the FCC in *Pacifica*, we believe that we must hold *Pacifica* to be inapplicable to this case."[54]

Breadth of the Ordinance and Due Process

In addition, the appeals court reasoned the Miami ordinance was too broad:

> Even if we were to find the rationale of Pacifica applicable to this case, we would still be compelled to strike the ordinance as facially overbroad. As the district judge noted, the ordinance "prohibits far too broadly the transmission of indecent materials through cable television. The ordinance's prohibition is wholesale, without regard to the time of day or other variables indispensable to the decision in Pacifica." *Cruz* v. *Ferre*, 571 F. Supp. at 131. The ordinance totally fails to account for the variables identified in *Pacifica*: the time of day; the context of the program in which the material appears; the composition of the viewing audience. In ignoring these variables, the ordinance goes far beyond . . . permissible regulation envisioned by the *Pacifica* Court.
>
> However noble may have been the city's intentions, we are constrained to recognize the limitations imposed by the Constitution and the opinions of the Supreme Court. The city's attempts through the challenged ordinance to regulate indecency on its cable television system exceeds these limitations.[55]

The issue of enforcement and the city manager's power to hear and rule on complaints was also addressed by the appeals court in *Cruz* v. *Ferre*.

Due Process and Lessons from the Case

Considering the issue of due process and the fundamental issue of fairness, the appeals court agreed with the district court, which found that concentrating the functions of "complainant, jury, judge and 'executioner' in one person ran a risk of arbitrary or capricious governmental action."[56] Under the Miami ordinance there existed an "intolerably high risk of unfairness," and . . . determinations in "an area of moral judgement that might well try the neutrality and impartiality of Solomon."[57]

From *Cruz* v. *Ferre* comes lessons for franchise authorities. First, while federal law may offer protection for the programming of obscene material, this is not necessarily the case for indecent material and the two are distinctly different as defined by law. Second, the use of court decisions based on over-the-air broadcasting are not necessarily suitable conditions upon which to make judgments about cable television, or write ordinances regulating cable television. Over-the-air television and cable television are different means of program distribution and are treated differently by the courts. Third, the First Amendment protection afforded cable is still unclear. First Amendment law has evolved for other media of communication and other types of speech distinct from cable television. Simply assuming that the First Amendment does not apply to subscriber-based wired communication in a particular instance is not wise. While not all programming is afforded First Amendment protection, that which is not evolves from very narrow definitions of disputable terms, such as *obscenity* and *indecency*. Fourth, due process must be considered when formulating the complaint procedure in any ordinance. An informal hearing process under the control of a city official may not meet the demands of due process when the complaint is forced into a court of law.

TAXATION OF CABLE TELEVISION

In the eighteenth century, a couple of hundred years before cable television, taxes were imposed on the press, primarily as a form of censorship intended to control the press and prevent it from criticizing government. A newspaper publisher too critical of government could find the paper subject to a tax, making it difficult to publish at a profit. To add to the control, government subsidies were often provided to publishers. Two hundred years later the United States Supreme Court in *Leathers* v. *Medlock* ruled that an Arkansas sales tax on cable television was constitutional and did not abridge the First Amendment rights of cable operators, even though other media were not subject to the sales tax.[58]

Rationale for Taxation: *Leathers* v. *Medlock*

Cable television distributed news is licensed by local government, operates under a franchise approved by local government, and can have its license to operate revoked by the government. It can, however, be taxed by government. *Leathers* v. *Medlock* generated controversy, not only because it singled out cable television for state taxation while exempting print media, radio, and television, but also because it was a powerful precedent for other states to follow during the recessionary years of the early 1990s. At that time revenue shortfalls were common, state governments were cutting back on services, Congress was trying to balance a federal budget by placing more burden on the states, and some states were openly considering taxes on advertising for all media.

In its rationale, the U.S. Supreme Court in *Leathers* v. *Medlock* said the Arkansas tax, levied on receipts from the sales of all tangible personal property and specified services, was not discriminatory. The same tax is also imposed on natural gas, electricity, water, ice, steam utility services, telephone, telecommunications, and telegraph services, among many others. The Court said the tax did not single out the press and therefore did not hinder the press as a watchdog of government activity. Moreover, the Court argued, the tax was not "content based" and nothing in the Arkansas law referred to the content of mass media. That last point was particularly significant because of all First Amendment protection, the protection of "ideas" is one of the strongest.[59]

Precedents for *Leathers* v. *Medlock*

Four cases stood out as precedent in *Leathers* v. *Medlock,* and all were used to show the clear distinction between why the Arkansas tax on cable television was constitutional and did not infringe on First Amendment rights, and why other cases did infringe on the First Amendment. The cases are significant because they form the basis for arguments clarifying when First Amendment principles can and cannot be applied to taxation measures. In *Groshean* v. *American Press Co.,* the U.S. Supreme Court considered a First Amendment challenge to a Louisiana law singling out weekly publications with circulations above 20,000 for a 2 percent tax on gross receipts.[60] Because the tax fell exclusively on 13 newspapers in the state, it was found discriminatory and unconstitutional. In *Minneapolis Star & Tribune Co.* v. *Minnesota Commissioner of Revenue*, a tax on the cost of ink and paper, exempted on the first $100,000 spent, was at issue. Eleven publishers accounting for only 14 of the state's 388 newspapers fell under the tax, and the Minneapolis Star and Tribune Company paid two thirds of all revenues.[61] The law was deemed unconstitutional because it singled out the press and targeted a small group of newspapers. Upon a similar rationale, the Court in *Arkansas Writers' Project, Inc.* v. *Ragland* found the selective taxation of the general interest magazine *Arkansas Times* was unconstitutional because it singled out a certain category of publication while exempting magazines devoted to sports and religion, as well as professional trade magazines.[62] The Court reasoned that the discrimination was based on content, and the tax operated in much the same way as that imposed on Minnesota's big newspapers. The support for content-specific publications as a criteria for determining constitutionality was further buttressed through the U.S. Supreme Court's opinion in *Regan* v. *Taxation with Representation of Washington*. Referring back to *Regan* v. *Taxation*, the Court in *Leathers* v. *Medlock stated*:

> In that case (*Regan* v. *Taxation*), we considered provisions of the Internal Revenue Code that discriminated between contributions to lobbying organizations. One section of the Code conferred tax-exempt status on certain nonprofit organizations that did not engage in lobbying activities. Contributions to those organizations were deductible. Another section of the Code conferred tax-exempt status on certain other nonprofit organizations that did lobby, but contributions to them were not deductible. . . . The tax distinction . . . did not trigger heightened scrutiny under the First Amendment.[63]

The vote in *Leathers* v. *Medlock* was seven to two with Justices Marshall and Blacknum dissenting. The dissent stressed that the "First Amendment prohibits singling out a particular information medium for heavier tax burdens that are borne by like-situated media," and noting also: "Although cable television transmits information by distinctive means, the information service provided by cable does not differ significantly from the information services provided by Arkansas' newspapers, magazines, television broadcasters, and radio stations."[64] In addition, the dissent argued: "This Court has recognized that cable operators exercise the same core press function of 'communication of ideas as do the traditional enterprises of newspaper and book publishers, public speakers, and pamphleteers.' "[65]

The taxing authority of *Leathers* v. *Medlock*, while giving a green light for states to tax cable television, did make it clear that such taxing authority was not tolerated when it is content-based, or stifles the free expression of ideas. Questions still arise as to why, if the state of Arkansas was looking for revenue, the legislature singled out cable television. One answer may lie in the fact that subscribers pay the tax as opposed to advertisers, and despite what Justices Marshall and Blacknum reasoned in their dissent, cable may not be seen as "press" in the eyes of many state legislators, Arkansas included.[66] A more serious issue, however, arises when one considers the interface between cable companies, their franchising authorities, and the ability to tax cable.

The Extent of Cable Taxation

The Arkansas sales tax is only one of many examples where the 5 percent franchise fee established under the federal Cable Act does not stop franchise authorities from tacking on other taxes, all of which are passed along to the consumer. How extensive these taxes are was detailed in testimony before a hearing of the U.S. House of Representatives by the Chairman and Chief Executive Officer of Continental Cablevision, Inc., Amos B. Hostetter, Jr. Showing the extent to which cable companies can be taxed, Hostetter testified:

> Municipal taxing of cable only begins with the 5% franchise fees. In Culver City, California, the City has imposed an 11% municipal utilities users tax on top of a 5% franchise fee. Together these two municipal taxes amount to two full months of each customers' yearly cable subscription fees. In addition, the L.A. county assessor has proposed a special cable television "possessory interest" property tax that amounts to an additional 1.5% of gross revenue per month over and above normal business property taxes. If this were not enough, (the governor) is seeking a 6% state telecommunications excise tax. With these proposed taxes, nearly one-fourth of our total revenues, or $9.40 dollars per subscriber per month would go to the city and state to pay franchise fees, utility users taxes, telecommunications taxes and special property taxes. By terms of the Culver City franchise, we are also required to provide channels for public, educational and government access; access facilities and equipment; and free basic service to municipal and school buildings. These are additional costs that must necessarily be absorbed by the consumers of cable services about whom the cities profess to be so concerned.
>
> In nearby Inglewood, California the tax story is much the same. As in Culver City, we pay 5% municipal franchise fees and face a county possessory interest tax equivalent to 1.5% of gross revenues and a state telecommunications excise tax of 6% of gross revenues. The only difference between the tax situation in Inglewood and Culver City is that Inglewood imposes a 10% instead of an 11% municipal utility users' tax. If the proposed possessory interest and telecommunications taxes pass, total fees and taxes will be "only" 22.5% instead of 23.5% of our gross revenues.
>
> The taxation trend we are seeing in Culver City and Inglewood is not confined to smaller cities. Just last month, (the mayor) proposed a 10% municipal utilities users tax on cable in Los Angeles . . .
>
> The trend in increased state and local cable taxes also goes well beyond California . . . (in Connecticut the Legislature) imposed gross receipts and sales taxes on cable that amount to 14% of gross revenues. In Richmond, Virginia, the City recently imposed a 5% utility users tax on cable on top of 3% franchise fees. Minnesota has just increase its sales tax on cable services to 6.5% of gross revenues. Mississippi, Texas, Vermont, and West Virginia have also imposed state sales taxes on cable services.[67]

Amos B. Hostetter, Jr.'s testimony also predicted that *Leathers* v. *Medlock* would "further accelerate legislative efforts to impose new cable television taxes." In testimony to the same House Subcommittee, Hostetter stated: "While cable operators can itemize these taxes on consumers' bills, in the end, consumers write one check to their cable company each month. And when they see the amount of that check going up without any related benefits, they blame their local cable operator, regardless of the cause."

A question emerges out of the tendency to tax cable television: Is the ability of local municipalities to tax cable beyond the 5 percent franchise fee, such as levying sales taxes or user excise taxes, a form of legislative blackmail or taxation without representation, whereby if the cable company complains about the tax measures it runs the risk of offending city officials who may retaliate at renewal time or rule against the cable company in a local dispute?

Property Tax Assessments

In addition to sales and other taxes on cable television, states have become more diligent in monitoring the value of cable systems for property tax purposes.[68] A cable television system is a business engaged in making a profit, owns land and equipment, and falls under property tax laws. Many cable systems have grown substantially in value over the years as systems have increased in size, popularity, and profitability. For example, in Idaho the State Tax Commission summoned records from 22 counties and asked them to explain why the assessment of their cable television systems did not reflect market value. The chief of the state's Real and Personal Property area of the State Tax Commission was the source of a newspaper report stating cable television systems in Idaho were valued as much as "10 to 15 times higher than the actual assessment" and cable companies not paying taxes on market value are "not paying their fair share."[69]

POLE ATTACHMENT RATE SETTING

Many cable companies attach their cables to poles owned by public utilities. After concern began to develop over the price utilities were charging cable companies, the FCC launched an inquiry on the matter, but determined it had little authority because pole attachment was not considered "communications by wire or radio" under the Communications Act.

Congress then became involved and enacted the federal Pole Attachments Act as a preventive measure against price gouging by public utilities who overcharged cable television operators for the use of utility poles. The Pole Attachments Act empowers the FCC to regulate pole attachment rates for cable television where no state regulation of pole attachment rates exists. Cable operators can seek relief through the FCC for alleged overcharging, and the FCC has the power to "regulate the rates, terms, and conditions for pole attachments to provide that such rates, terms, and conditions are just and reasonable. . . ."[70]

Rate Formula

The Pole Attachments Act permits the utility to receive compensation for permitting the cable company to attach its cable to a utility pole. Rates are determined on a per pole basis and provide that:

> a rate is just and reasonable if it assures a utility the recovery of not less than the additional costs of providing pole attachments, nor more than an amount determined by multiplying the percentage of the total usable space, or the percentage of the total duct or conduit capacity, which is occupied by the pole attachment by the sum of the operating expenses and actual capital costs of the utility attributable to the entire pole, duct, conduit, or right-of-way.[71]

In simplified terms, the utility can charge no more than what it costs to affix the cable attachment to the pole, and to maintain the cable attachment. The rate can also be figured on a percentage basis whereby if the cable attachment, for instance, takes up 2 percent of the useable space on the pole, and the operating expenses and capital costs for the entire pole are $100, then the cost to the cable operator would be $2.00.

Test of Authority

A test of the FCC's authority was settled in 1987 when the U.S. Supreme Court ruled in a case involving three cable companies seeking relief from alleged overcharging. In agreements with Florida Power Corporation, some dating back to 1963, the three cable companies using Florida

Power's poles were charged rates of $5.50, $6.24, and $7.15 per pole. After the FCC Common Carrier Bureau issued orders lowering the rates to $1.79 per pole, Florida Power sought FCC review of the bureau's actions. When the FCC review affirmed the bureau's rates, Florida Power appealed to the Eleventh Circuit Court of Appeals, which found in favor of Florida Power. On appeal to the U.S. Supreme Court in *FCC* v. *Florida Power* based on the Fifth Amendment's right to property guarantee, the Supreme Court ruled in favor of the FCC saying the action of the FCC in setting the rates did not result in a "taking" action under the Fifth Amendment's property standards. The unanimous nine-to-zero opinion written by Justice Marshall stated:

> Since the Act clearly contemplates voluntary commercial leases rather than forced governmental licensing, it merely regulates the economic regulations of utility company landlords and cable company tenants, which regulation is not a per se taking . . .
>
> The FCC order did not effect a taking under traditional Fifth Amendment standards, which permit governmental regulation of rates chargeable on the use of private property devoted to public purposes so long as the rates set are not confiscatory. Here, the rate imposed was calculated according to the Act's maximum rate formula, which is not confiscatory since it provided for the recovery of fully allocated costs, including the actual cost of capital.[72]

The Supreme Court pointed to the appeals court's incorrect reliance on *Loretto* v. *Teleprompter Manhatten CATV Corp.*, finding that it was improper for the government, which in Loretto was the State Commission on Cable Television, to require compulsory access to property.[73] Emphasized in *FCC* v. *Florida Power* was the *voluntary* arrangement between the power company and the cable company. The Supreme Court in *FCC* v. *Florida Power* made it clear it was not the amount charged but the actual renting that permits FCC jurisdiction. To rent or not to rent is a voluntary decision and public utilities are not required under FCC authority to give cable companies space on utility poles. Not decided in *FCC* v. *Florida Power* was whether *Loretta* v. *Teleprompter Manhatten CATV Corp.* would apply "if the FCC in a future case required utilities, over objection, to enter into, renew, or refrain from terminating pole attachment agreements."[74]

CABLE AND COPYRIGHT: THE COMPULSORY LICENSE

Under copyright law, cable systems are required to receive a compulsory license, permitting them to carry over-the-air signals pursuant to FCC rules. This license should not be confused with the contracts that govern the actual operation and fee schedule of the system. The copyright law views cable systems as commercial entities, involved in the "performance" of copyrighted works, and as such they must pay copyright fees under the compulsory licensing system. Fees collected by the Licensing Division of the Copyright Office are set and distributed by the Copyright Royalty Tribunal. Under the Copyright Office's compulsory license requirement, a cable company must adhere to four requirements. First, the cable system must register with the Copyright Office to obtain the compulsory license. Second, the cable system is required to list the stations it carries. Third, the cable system files a statement of account every six months. Fourth, a royalty payment accompanies the filing of the statement of account.

The cable system pays royalty fees for permission to retransmit broadcast signals, called *secondary transmission*, to subscribers. The amount varies and is determined by the size of the system. For example, small systems pay a semiannual fee which through the early 1990s remained a set fee under $28. Larger systems pay a percentage of their gross receipts. Such factors as the number of stations carried, the size of the market, and the gross receipts of the system all impact on the amount a cable system pays the Copyright Office under the compulsory license. A general analysis of the fee structure finds that the total amount of royalties collected is currently in excess of $200 million annually.[75] About two thirds of the cable systems in the United States are small systems serving small communities and fall into the category of cable systems that pay under $28 semiannually. The royalties collected from these systems account for less than 1 percent of the royalty payments. About 15 percent of the cable systems in the United States, roughly 2000, pay almost 98 percent of the total royalty fees.

Stations that want to collect their fair share of the money cable systems pay to the Copyright Royalty Tribunal must file a claim with the

Copyright Office. Stations cannot collect royalty fees simply because a cable system carries the signal. Requirements exist over whether the signal is a "distant" signal and whether its over-the-air signal is significantly viewed in the county where the cable system is located. Information on the station's claim form must include basic information such as the name of the licensee, call letters, period in which the claim is being executed, e.g., January 1, 1995 to December 31, 1995, and programming subject to royalties (such as station-produced programming or programs for which the station holds the rights or the copyright), and when the program(s) was aired.[76]

SYNDICATED EXCLUSIVITY AND SPORTS PROGRAMMING PROTECTION

Nonnetwork programs for which a television station has exclusive exhibition rights can receive protection from cable systems in the same market that might carry the programs through the importation of another station's distant signal.[77] Syndicated programs are programs "sold, licensed, distributed or offered to television station licensees in more than one market . . . other than as network programming."[78] The protection is afforded regardless of whether the local station holding the exclusive distribution rights is carried by the local cable system. When such programming is blacked out, the cable system can substitute other programming such as its own original programming, programming from another station, or other syndicated programming the cable system has purchased.

Sports events also receive cable retransmission protection. Referring to the definition of cable systems in FCC regulations, a "community unit"[79] is "a cable television system, or portion of a cable television system, that operates or will operate within a separate and distinct community or municipal entity. . . ."[80] Cable television community units that serve 1,000 or more subscribers cannot carry sports broadcasts transmitted by distant television stations if the sports events are blacked out on a local station. The holder of the right to the broadcast the sports event is the one responsible for notifying all affected cable systems. The cable system can substitute any other programming in place of the event that is subject to blackout. Notification must be received by the cable system no later than the Monday preceding the calendar week during which the blackout is requested.

NETWORK CABLE OWNERSHIP

Repealing a rule in effect for more than 20 years, the FCC in 1992 voted to permit networks to own cable systems.[81] Of special advantage to the networks are cable interests in major metropolitan areas where more than one cable system operates. Rules permitting network ownership of cable interests affect different companies in different ways. For example, for large conglomerates with many communication subsidiaries, getting into cable can be a logical step in diversification. General Electric, for example, which owns NBC, has the clout and financial base to experiment with new enterprising ventures. That may not be the case for all networks, especially at a time when network audience share is declining, affiliates suffer from an increase in cable advertising revenues, and economic uncertainty remains.[82]

LOCAL REGULATORY FRAMEWORKS

Much of the foundation of cable regulatory control is found at the local level. Unlike over-the-air broadcasting, which falls under federal control, cable also falls under state and local control. Many states have extensive cable regulations and some states administer the regulations under a separate commission. Local franchise authorities in hundreds of communities across the United States administer local municipal-based regulations. These state and local authorities establish service and operational requirements, have the power to levy franchise fees, and can make determinations about the availability of local access and commercially leased cable channels.

Types of local control vary considerably.[83] In smaller communities an administrative office may exist where local government establishes a regulatory presence much like the FCC. Some very small cable systems serving little more than housing developments may operate through the homeowners association with an agreement not amounting to more than a few pages. In a larger city the franchise, granted under the authority of a state cable commission, may consist of dozens of pages of complex legal matter. The office that administers the franchise may operate out of the state capital and consist of a well-staffed government unit or, at the local level, administration of the franchise can be one individual operating out of the mayor's office or the city planner's office. In some communities the city manager is the cable franchise authority with broad powers of enforcement.

LOCAL FRANCHISING

Franchising requirements were established under the 1984 Cable Act, which was amended by the Cable Television Consumer Protection and Competition Act of 1992.

Overall Provisions

Under the current law a franchising authority can award one or more franchises under its jurisdiction using public rights-of-way and easements, but taking into consideration the safety, functioning, and appearance of property and people. No area can be excluded from having cable service because of the income level of the residents in the local area. State commissions, where they exist, can require local cable systems to file tariffs listing the rates, terms, and conditions of service. Along with limiting the amount of franchise fees a franchising authority can collect, the original provisions of the act prohibited states from controlling rates for cable service.

Modification in the system and facilities is permitted as long as it does not result in lessening the "mix or quality of service." To modify the franchise the cable operator must demonstrate that it is commercially impracticable to comply with the requirements as specified in the original franchise. Provisions exist for the cable operator to drop a service if it is no longer available to the cable operator or the cost of the service is substantially in excess of what it was when the franchise was granted. Services can be arranged on different channels and moved among tiers, subject to certain restrictions affecting costs to subscribers. For the most part, not subject to modification are channels dedicated to public, education, or government access.

Renewal of the Franchise

Within a six-month period beginning three years before the franchise expires, provisions exist for the cable franchise authority to initiate on its own, or through the request of the cable operator, proceedings that afford the public in the franchise area "appropriate notice and participation" for the purpose of identifying cable-related community needs and reviewing the performance of the operator. After the proceeding, the cable operator can submit to the franchise authority a proposal for renewal of the franchise. Because of the increased sophistication of technology and available programming, the renewal proposal many times contains provisions for upgrading the system. Specifically the law reads:

> A franchising authority may, on its own initiative during the 6-month period which begins with the 36th month before the franchise expiration, commence a proceeding which affords the public in the franchise area appropriate notice and participation for the purpose of (A) identifying the future cable-related community needs and interests, and (B) reviewing the performance of the cable operator under the franchise during the then current franchise term. If the cable operator submits, during such 6-month period, a written renewal notice requesting the commencement of such proceeding, the franchising authority shall commence such a proceeding not later than 6 months after the date such notice is submitted.[84]

Additional proceedings, including opportunities for public input, can occur at the time of the renewal proposal and are required if the franchise is not to be renewed. The opportunity to introduce evidence exists in such proceedings, formal transcripts are made, and a written decision is required. Under certain circumstances, denying the renewal cannot be based on certain service failures unless the cable operator has been given the chance, through appropriate notice, to correct the deficiencies. When a franchise renewal is denied and the franchise authority takes control of the cable system, the franchise authority itself may decide to run the system or sell it to another operator. Such actions can result in court challenges and the process is not necessarily smooth, especially considering the capital investment originally made by the operator, or the value of the system to the operator or the operator's parent company. Nevertheless, when such a transfer does take place, the cable system must change hands at a fair market value.

Criticism and Loopholes

The existence of federal law does not necessarily create a favorable regulatory environment at the state or local level. The latitude afforded state and local franchise authorities can make operating a cable system difficult. The flexibility of local government to administer the franchise does not mean the process is always equitable. For example, cable companies that find themselves in a dispute with the franchise authority are sometimes frustrated by the franchise administrator's power to make broad sweeping judgments and rule in disputes without any check on its authority. These franchise-authorized administrators can end up sitting as complainant, jury, judge, and executioner, increasing the risk of capricious governmental action and making it difficult for a cable company to even admit evidence or call witnesses.[85] Such hearings are not generally part of the court system and therefore no one is under oath, evidence may not be able to be admitted properly, due process may be absent, and the entire proceeding is carried out by people unskilled at either negotiating disputes or the rules of judicial procedure. The end result is a procedural landfill which must be sorted out in the state or federal court system just to bring order and understanding to the process. The power that franchise authorities have through the wording of many franchises can be an invitation for the abuse of power, and that abuse can embroil the cable operator in a quagmire of bureaucracy while placing at risk the operator's investment, and subjecting both the investment and the cable system to the political whims of city officials.

THE CABLE TELEVISION ORDINANCE

At the core of the contractual relationship between the franchise authority and the cable system operator is the cable ordinance.[86] The discussion that follows lists just some of the provisions of a typical ordinance. Thousands of ordinances exist nationwide and each ordinance contains provisions that meet particular needs and conditions of a given community as well as its economic and political structure.

Definitions

As with any complex legal document, many ordinances contain definitions of terms. Terms such as *application*, to the proposal of the cable operator to obtain the franchise, *town*, which lists the name of the municipality, *commission*, such as the local or state regulatory commission having authority over the franchise, and *cable system*, which details the technical definitions. Some definitions are wordy. For example, consider just part of the first sentence of the definition of *cable system* from the Marblehead, Massachusetts cable license.

> Cable System: Community Antenna Television System, CATV System, or Cable Television Communications System—a facility which receives or originates video, audio, and data signals and distributes such signals through Subscriber and Institutional Networks to subscribing members or the public and institutions for a fixed or periodic fee, employing wires or cables passing along, over, under, across and upon streets, ways, lanes, alleys, parkways, bridges, highways, and other public places, including property over which the Town. . . .[87]

Length of Franchise

The ordinance will specify the length of the cable franchise. A cable system is a big capital investment for the cable operator. Because an area must be wired before cable service can be operational, that outlay necessitates long franchise periods to recapture the cost of constructing the system. For mature systems that have been in operation for many years and where the cost of the system has been recovered, a review of the franchise and the cable operator's performance at periodic intervals is not uncommon. A franchise might be awarded for ten years with the option to renew for five more years if satisfactory service is being rendered. Some older systems have franchises lasting 20 years. For the franchise authority, having as much control over the system as possible is beneficial, especially when the franchise will not be renewed for more than a decade. For the cable operator, as much protection as possible for the longest period of time is the ideal since investors want to know their capital investment is protected.

Franchise Transfer

A cable franchise that is in place for a 15-year term means there is a good likelihood that the cable system will change hands at some point within the 15-year period. Some ordinances contain a provision that the cable system will not change hands, or will change hands under certain approved circumstances, during a specified period of time after the franchise is renewed or the system is constructed. The franchise authority may elect to retain the right to choose the franchisee over the entire period of the franchise. When a cable system changes hands, the franchise authority must deal with new people and new management, and neither management nor the franchise authority have the benefit of a long-term relationship. Issues previously dealt with at a lunch between the city manager and cable manager may under new management end up in heated correspondence between the city attorney and the cable system's legal counsel.

Franchise Termination

Because the term of the franchise is long, franchise authorities typically protect themselves with provisions that specify under what circumstances the franchise can be terminated. Such provisions can be a bone of contention between the operator and the franchise authority at renewal time, with each trying to protect their own interests. Weak provisions can result in poor performance by the cable operator, excessively strict provisions can result in strained business relationships that sometimes end up in contentious court proceedings. Excessively strict provisions also can result in an atmosphere of day-to-day operational harassment whereby so many regulations exist and the threat of termination is always present that simple complaints gain the unjustified aura of major infractions and have the potential to get bogged down in a regulatory infrastructure that produces more bureaucracy than results. Excessive detail can also generate confusion and hair-splitting determinations by city officials charged with overseeing the franchise. Nevertheless, subscribers deserve protection, cable systems in many communities are a monopoly, and the franchise can tie the hands of both the operator and the franchise authority for long periods of time.

Some of the more obvious grounds for dismissal include an operator knowingly making false statements on a franchise or an operator failing to provide adequate service. Franchise termination typically requires a public hearing, although that does not mean the cable operator's rights or due process will be followed since such hearings are sometimes administered by city officials and not judges. When termination is an issue, the matter frequently goes into court, not only because of the seriousness of the issue but because the cable operator feels a judicial forum is necessary to be able to admit evidence and have the benefit of the rules of judicial procedure.

Some cities have extensive provisions granting a franchise authority the ability to revoke a franchise and terminate the operating agreement with the cable operator. Extremely detailed conditions for termination, although protecting the city and subscribers, can be difficult to administer and the source of frustration and strained relationships between the cable operator and the franchising authority. In abridged, paraphrased form, and quoting only partially from the franchise, the agreement between the cable operator and the City of Los Angeles states the franchise can be revoked for:

- Substantial failure to provide financial information.
- Substantial failure to meet technical performance standards.
- Substantial or repeated failure to provide any service to any person as required by the agreement.
- Substantial failure to comply with the standards, terms, or schedule of construction.
- Substantial failure to maintain the mix, level, and quality of service within the broad areas of video programming and other services.
- Abandonment of the system, in whole or in material part, without prior written consent of the city council.
- Substantial and repeated failure to comply with leased access requirements.
- Substantial failure to provide access channels and related facilities.
- Substantial failure to supply the government access channel and other support, equipment, and services.
- Substantial and repeated imposition for basic service of any nonstandard installation or other charges that are discriminatory.
- Substantial failure to comply with the interconnection requirements.
- Substantial and repeated failure to comply with the employment or purchasing provisions.
- Substantial and repeated failure to comply with the consumer service standards.
- Substantial failure to comply with the privacy rights of subscribers.
- Substantial failure to make any of the Franchise Fee compensation payments.
- Substantial failure to deposit in an escrow account any compensation arising from franchise disputes, contests, and other matters.

- Substantial failure to comply with many material rules, regulations, orders, or directives of the city issued pursuant to the police powers.
- The taking of any material action requiring approval or consent of the council without having first obtained consent.
- Substantial failure to furnish and maintain liability and indemnification insurance coverage.
- Persistent failure to furnish each plan required by the city.
- To engage in a course of conduct intentionally designed to practice any fraud or deceit.
- Failure to cooperate fully and faithfully with any lawful investigation, audit, or inquiry conducted by a city government agency.
- Any material written misrepresentation, intentionally made by or on behalf of the cable company in its proposal for the franchise.
- The conviction of the cable company, or affiliate person, director, executive, officer, (and other employees and affiliated persons) of any criminal offense.
- The conviction of any city officer, city employee, or city agent of the offense of bribery or fraud with respect to the cable agreement.
- Any material false entry made knowingly in the books or accounts or records of the cable company.
- Failure to comply with a duly constituted order or substantial ruling of any city regulatory body.

In addition to spelling out grounds to terminate the franchise, the agreement also lists procedures that are to be followed in the event there is an alleged failure by the cable company to comply with the material provisions of the agreement. The cable company has 45 days after being notified that an infraction has occurred to make a diligent effort to correct a problem and present facts and arguments refuting the alleged failure.

Renewal

Renewal provisions of a cable franchise are as important as conditions upon which a cable franchise can be terminated. When a clear understanding about intent and procedures is lacking, then an open invitation may exist for disagreements at renewal time to be decided in court. Some provisions of renewal may include the licensee notifying the franchise authority of its intention to renew and also providing the franchise authority with a written report on how the cable operator has complied with the provisions of the franchise. A clause stating that the issuing authority shall renew the license if the operator is in substantial compliance with the provisions of the franchise helps to a limited extent to protect the operator against arbitrary and capricious action on the part of city officials, most of whom will be a different group of people than when the franchise was first negotiated. A provision may also exist whereby the operator will be notified in writing well in advance if the franchise is not to be renewed. It permits the operator to plan for the possibility of going out of business, but also to appeal the decision. The time to have a firm understanding of renewal is at the time the franchise is approved, not later when questions arise and the only solution may be litigation.

Channel Capacity and Construction Standards

Some state commissions specify channel capacity, while in other areas the local authorities control channel capacity. The ordinance, however, will list that capacity and also contain provisions for public, educational, and government access channels. While franchise authorities do not control the equipment of the cable operator, equipment for provisions to operate access channels may be listed in the ordinance.

Construction and maintenance are continuing issues for the franchise authority and the cable operator. Some detail is important when issues such as tree trimming, access to easements and rights-of-way, and zoning requirements are involved. Local safety codes, building codes, and electrical codes at both the local and state level must be adhered to and provisions for such adherence can be listed in the cable ordinance. An ordinance may require an operator to use existing poles and conduits, and may refer to pole attachment agreements.

Bonds and Indemnity

Ordinances typically have cable operators carry liability insurance to assure that the municipality is held harmless in the event of injury to employees or anyone else associated with the cable system or who comes in contact with its equipment. If construction or extension of the system is an issue, then a construction bond is usually required, which helps ensure that the bills are paid if the cable company or its subcontractors run into financial difficulty before the system is finished and operational.

Interconnection and Access

Some ordinances provide for interconnection of the cable system with certain local institutions. For example, if the cable system has a two-way capability for security alarm purposes, then having the system connected to local emergency services such as fire and police might be provided. Other types of institutional connections with schools, museums, or local colleges can be included under the terms of the franchise. Access channels may be established and some cable systems are under contract to provide certain facilities for local access programming. Where a franchise fee is charged, such as 5 percent of gross revenues, the city may elect to have these funds contributed to a separate endowment whereby the funds, or a portion of them, are used to finance local productions. Viewing centers may be connected whereby large groups of people can view cable programs at a public auditorium.

Equal Opportunity Provisions

Although covered under federal and state laws, cable ordinances many times contain equal employment opportunity language assuring nondiscrimination in hiring and promotion and nondiscrimination in providing service to different areas of the city. Amendments to operator's EEO requirements were passed with the 1992 Cable Act and added additional job categories to the annual reporting requirements.

Standards for Safety

Safety codes can be written into a cable ordinance to help assure the safety of workers. For example, a cable ordinance for a Massachusetts town reads:

> The construction, maintenance and operation of the Cable System for which this License is granted shall be done in conformance with OSHA, the National Electrical Safety Code, the Massachusetts Electrical Code, the National Cable Television Standard Code, the Bell Telephone Systems Code of Pole Line Construction, the National Electrical Code, and the rules and regulations of the Commission and the FCC as the same exist or as same may be hereafter changed or amended and applicable to local codes.[88]

In addition to the provisions listed previously, other provisions may restate federal or state law governing cable television. The ordinance, after all, is the document of record between the franchise authority and the cable operator. Although it can be viewed as a contract, the ordinance is a contract honed through the legislative and political process. Issues may arise during a renewal hearing, through the recommendation of a city-hired consultant trying to get the best package for the franchise authority, through comparisons with other ordinances, or through peculiar community needs. For example, consider this provision in one local ordinance which states: "The Issuing Authority shall permit the Licensee to trim trees upon and overhanging all streets, alleys, sidewalks and public ways and places of the Town so as to prevent branches of such trees from coming in contact with the wires, cables and equipment of the Licensee, subject to the guidelines and regulations of the Tree Warden."[89]

STATE REGULATION OF CABLE

State government can play a major role in controlling cable.[90] State laws can be classified into three categories: pre-empt statutes, appellate statutes, and advisory statutes.

Types and Examples of State Cable Regulation

Pre-empt statutes are the strongest laws, and they take precedent over local regulations. With pre-empt statutes, cable falls under the jurisdiction of the Public Utility or Public Service Commission. Pre-empt statutes give considerable clout to a state commission, permitting it to issue and enforce a separate set of state cable regulations. These rules can govern everything from the day-to-day operation of the cable system, to collecting fees on gross revenue, to demanding financial collateral before allowing construction. A second type of control falls under the appellate statutes. Here, local municipalities retain some control over franchising, but the state has the power to review local agreements and be the final arbiter of disputes. Everything works fine until the state and a municipality disagree, then the municipality stands less than an even chance against the state. A less powerful state statute is the advisory statute. This is more popular with cable systems and municipalities, since it does not have either the clout or the enforcement power of a state commission. Some serve as "general guidelines," which serve as a reference for local government.

Examples of State Regulation

The extent of state regulatory authority can be seen in two states, New York and Connecticut. For example, New York law requires that a state Certificate of Confirmation be granted to a cable system before a franchise is valid.[91] Consumer protection is provided under the statute, which requires cable systems to notify the state cable commission 45 days before significant programming changes. Subscribers must be notified 30 days in advance of significant programming changes and can disconnect or downgrade the cable without charge within 45 days of receiving such notice. Extensive complaint procedures are in effect and require cable operators to keep on file their complaint procedures, and notify subscribers annually that such procedures are in effect. Billing practices must be disclosed at the time of installation, and bills must be itemized to show customers what they're paying for. Individual franchises must provide for bonds, insurance coverage, enforcement, EEO procedures, and 36-channel capacity. Technical standards are monitored and enforced, and for new cable systems or extended service the operator has 120 days to conduct a technical performance test and submit a report to the commission.

In Connecticut, cable systems must operate a business office and are prohibited from unreasonably discriminating against subscribers. Differential rates are permitted in justified situations.[92] Repair requirements are specified by law and at least one person must be on call 24 hours a day, seven days a week. Charges for downgrades and disconnections are prohibited and charges must cease when the customer notifies the cable company of the downgrade or disconnection. Cable operators are not permitted to repair television receiving equipment and each cable system must provide at cost the equipment that receives and decodes closed-captioned broadcasts for the hearing impaired. Sufficient phone lines must be operative to receive customer inquiries, complaints, and other requests. Outside the local exchange area a toll-free number must be available for subscribers. Larger systems with 30,000 or more customers are required to staff customer service phones at specific times and answering services must be available when phones are not staffed personally.

Advantages and Disadvantages of State Control

Proponents of state control argue the need for consistency among cable systems within a state. Such arguments gain support when two municipalities cannot resolve their jurisdictional differences over a cable system or when significantly differing fee structures provoke public outcry. Control of cable can also be a political plum for legislators, since it means control of a communication system, and communication influences public opinion. Since cable commissions can have a significant effect on cable growth within a state, appointment to the commission can be a sweet political reward for someone in the party in power.

Arguments against state control are equally vociferous, asserting that it presents an unnecessary duplication of law. States are sometimes caught in the middle between local and federal control, and meeting the requirements of one can violate those of the other. Opponents claim that state control throws local interests into a political arena with representatives who are looking out for their own interests, not for those of the local community. The "Big Brother" argument also pops up as people argue that when a state becomes too involved in cable, it can overstep into programming issues, which borders on censorship or propaganda.

SUMMARY

Cable television in the United States began in the states of Oregon and Pennsylvania. Enterprising individuals, in an attempt to improve reception from distant television stations, strung wires from an antenna located on a mountaintop and then sold connections to the antenna to the first cable subscribers. Today more than 60 percent of people receive cable, with annual expenditures predicted to reach $20 billion by the mid-1990s.

The basic concept of cable centers around the master antenna or headend. From the headend, trunk and feeder cables eventually connect with drop cables into the subscriber's home. Two-way cable systems offer interactive capabilities for two-way television, in-home banking and shopping, alarm systems, public-opinion polling, and other uses.

The exercise of FCC authority over cable began in the early 1960s when the commission started to enforce licenses for microwave systems used to carry cable signals from remote antennas to the master headend antenna. A 1966 test case over the commission's authority to regulate cable occurred with *United States* v. *Southwestern Cable Co.*, when a cable company in San Diego, California was prohibited from importing signals from Los Angeles. By 1968 the FCC had started formal rule making on cable regulation, covering such areas as syndicated program exclusivity, non-broadcast services, cross-ownership, and technical standards.

In 1977 the decision in *Home Box Office* v. *FCC* trimmed the FCC's authority to regulate pay cable, saying the Commission could not use its power to protect conventional broadcasters. Federal regulations became a patchwork effort until 1984 with the passage of the Cable Communications Policy Act of 1984, extensively revised in 1992. The Cable Act covered such areas as renewal requirements for local franchises, rate regulations, state and local authority, criminal and civil liability, obscene programming, technical specifications, and other provisions. Provisions enabling special relief were provided for, and registrations, records requirements, and rate structures are now part of federal regulations.

Cable systems which are not subject to effective competition can fall under local franchise authority rate regulation. Effective competition is defined so as to place most cable systems without effective competition and therefore subject to rate regulation. Factors taken into consideration in determining if local cable rates are reasonable include rates for similarly situated systems, cost of meeting regulations, capital and operating costs, and revenue.

Subscriber privacy rules are enforced at the federal level, and frequently at state and local levels. Rules require that at the time a subscriber enters into a service agreement, and annually thereafter, the cable operator is required to notify subscribers in a written statement of the nature of information collected about the subscriber.

Local franchise authorities have the power to require public, educational, and government (PEG) channels. Editorial control over the content of these channels is prohibited and franchise authorities, while able to set certain technical and equipment standards, cannot control the operation of the equipment. Cable operators may also designate channels for commercial use. EEO and political broadcasting requirements follow closely the requirements of conventional broadcasters. Cable systems must have an EEO policy that details the recruitment and hiring practices of the cable system. As with conventional broadcasters, cable operators must charge the lowest unit rate for political advertising, must treat all legally qualified candidates for the same public office fairly, and cannot censor the content of political advertising.

Communities take an active role in cable programming, especially at renewal time. Discussions of issues such as indecency and obscenity can be heated, and the regulation of programming falling into such categories can be controversial. At the federal level, being convicted of transmitting obscenity over a cable system carries a fine of not more than $10,000 or imprisonment of not more than two years, or both. One of the more important cases dealing with this issue was *Cruz* v. *Ferre*, which challenged a Miami, Florida cable ordinance on the grounds that it was too broad in its enforcement of "indecency." Although enforcement and hearings procedures were written into the local ordinance, sufficient due process was not provided the cable operator charged with violating the ordinance.

An emerging area of law concerns the taxation of cable television. While federal law requires a cap of 5 percent on franchise fees assessed to cable systems by the franchise authority, other taxes can be imposed on the system. In *Leathers* v. *Medlock*, an Arkansas tax on cable was upheld and found not to be discriminatory. Dissent in the case criticized singling out cable and distinguishing it from other media that were not taxed and were given more First Amendment protection. The extent of cable taxation is growing. In comments before a House subcommittee, one cable executive pointed to municipal utilities users' taxes, possessory interest taxes, state telecommunications excise taxes, gross receipts taxes, and sales taxes. Property taxes are also imposed on cable systems and some states monitor county assessments of cable systems to ensure adequate taxation is taking place. The federal Pole Attachments Act permits utilities to receive compensation for permitting cable companies to attach cable to utility poles. Rate structures for pole attachments are regulated to prevent price gouging.

Cable systems pay royalty fees under a compulsory license to retransmit distant signals of conventional broadcasters. The compulsory license is administered by the U.S. Copyright Office and royalties are paid to broadcasters through the Copyright Royalty Tribunal. Small systems pay a set fee and larger systems pay a percentage of their gross receipts.

Protection is afforded to broadcasters who own exclusive syndication rights to programming in a given market. A local cable system cannot import the distant signal of a television station carrying the same syndicated program to which a local television station owns exclusive distribution rights in the same market as the cable system. Sports blackouts must also be honored by cable systems. If television coverage of a local sports event is blacked out on a local television system, a cable system cannot import the television signal of a distant station carrying the event.

At the heart of cable regulation is the local cable ordinance. Ordinances vary considerably and can consist of a few operating regulations to large documents detailing every aspect of cable operation. More complete ordinances will contain definitions of cable terms, spell out the length of the franchise and what happens when the cable system is sold, the conditions under which franchises can be terminated, the specifics of franchise renewal, bonds and indemnity, interconnection and access, equal opportunity provisions, standards for safety, and other provisions.

In addition to local control, many states have regulatory structures governing cable television. For example, some states have pre-empt statutes, which take precedence over local regulations. Other states have appellate statutes whereby local ordinances have control over franchising but the actions of the local franchising authority are open to review by the state body. Other states have advisory statutes that serve as guidelines to local franchise authorities.

MATERIAL FOR ANALYSIS

The 1992 Cable Act is forthright in stating that nothing in the law prohibits "a local or municipal authority that is also . . . a franchising authority from operating as a multichannel video programming distributor in the franchise area . . ."[93] When the City Council of Morganton, North Carolina voted not to renew the cable franchise of Madison Cablevision, Inc., which had been in effect for 20 years, and decided to construct and operate its own municipally-owned cable system, Madison Cablevision, in an attempt to save its franchise, took the issue into the district court,[94] the North Carolina Supreme Court,[95] the U.S. Court of Appeals for the Fourth Circuit,[96] and eventually the U.S. Supreme Court where writ of certiorari was denied.[97] Madison, however, was at a major disadvantage from the beginning. The City of Morganton had begun renewal hearings 30 months prior to the effective date of the Cable Act of 1984, which would have given Madison some protection in the renewal process. Madison first sought relief in district court on the basis of claims covering such diverse issues as the First Amendment, free speech, constitutional conditions, equal protection, antitrust claims, breach of contract, tortious interference, due process, and civil rights.

The district court first granted partial summary judgment in favor of the City of Morganton, stayed further proceedings, and directed Madison to institute state court action with regard to certain state statutory and constitutional issues raised in Madison Cable's complaint. After the North Carolina Supreme Court resolved the state law issues in favor of the City of Morganton, the city then moved to have the district court reconsider the remaining claims.

Each level of review resulted in a judgment in favor of the city and the judgments were upheld on appeal. The district court's decision in *Madison Cablevision* v. *The City of Morganton* is an example of how complex the issues can become when franchise renewals are involved, how much authority municipalities as franchise authorities have in overseeing a cable system, how it is possible under one state's laws for a municipality to enter into a municipally-owned (and therefore government) cable business, and how state law adds another level of protection to the franchise authorities within a state.

Excerpts dealing with the constitutional aspects of the case follow Some citations are omitted for stylistic reasons, although appearing in the original text of the case. For a detailed reading of all issues in the case, the reader should consult the full texts of opinions in this matter.

MADISON CABLEVISION, INC. v. *THE CITY OF MORGANTON, NORTH CAROLINA, et. al.*

UNITED STATES DISTRICT COURT FOR THE WESTERN DISTRICT OF NORTH CAROLINA, SHELBY DIVISION

1990 U.S. Dist. LEXIS 18794

* * *

After considering the report of the various studies . . . the advice of attorneys, the testimony and comments made during the public hearing, the City Council voted not to renew Madison's franchise, and not to grant a franchise to (other companies expressing an interest). Instead the City Council voted to proceed with a plan to construct and operate a municipally owned and operated cable television system. The Council did not foreclose the possibility that at some future date it might reconsider the question as to whether more than one cable system for the City would be in the public interest. Sometime thereafter Madison was advised to submit to the Council within ninety days (90) a plan for an orderly removal of its equipment from the city-owned poles at the end of the franchise term as set forth in the franchise agreement.

Instead of submitting any plan for the removal of its equipment Madison brought this action seeking to prevent the City from requiring it to cease its cable operations in Morganton as provided under the franchise agreement. The complaint filed by Madison contains twelve claims for relief under both federal and state laws. The claims are as follows: (only claims 3, 4, 8, 10, and 12, which are based on constitutional grounds, are listed here for analysis.)

3. That the City violated Madison's rights guaranteed by the First and Fourteenth Amendments to the United States Constitution and Article I, Section 14 of the North Carolina Constitution.

4. That the City violated the equal protection clause of the Fourteenth Amendment to the United States Constitution.

8. That the Defendants deprived Madison of its constitutional rights in violation of 42 U.S.C.A. Section 1983.

10. That the Defendants breached the contract between Madison and the City.

12. That the City's option to purchase the franchisee's cable system at the expiration of the franchise is an unconstitutional and unenforceable provision of the franchise agreement.

* * *

FIRST AMENDMENT, FREE SPEECH, AND CONSTITUTIONAL CONDITIONS

The third and twelfth claims for relief allege that the ordinance in question violates freedom of speech provisions of the federal and state constitutions. Madison contends that the City violated its First Amendment rights by failing to renew its franchise when it expired and by deciding that the City would construct and operate a government owned and operated cable television system. The effect of this contention is that Madison is entitled under the First Amendment to continue to operate its cable television system in the City of Morganton even though its twenty-year franchise has expired and it is entitled to continue to use the city owned poles and rights of way on a permanent or indefinite basis. Madison also contends that cable operations must be equated to newspaper publishing. These contentions stretch the First Amendment far beyond which any court has gone thus far.

* * *

The complaint does not allege nor was there any evidence before the City Council to even suggest that the City sought to remove Madison because of the content or viewpoint of its cable television programming past, present or prospective. Accordingly, the City's legislative decisions not to franchise more than one cable operator and not to renew Madison's franchise should be resolved under the test in *United States* v. *O'Brien*, 391 U.S. 367, 88 S.Ct. 1673(1968):

> (A) government regulation is sufficiently justified if it is within the constitution power of Government; if it furthers an important or substantial governmental interest; if the governmental interest is unrelated to the suppression of free expression; and if the incidental restriction on alleged First Amendment freedoms is no greater than is essential to the furtherance of that interest. 391 U.S. at 377.

Both the decision not to renew Madison's franchise and the decision to grant a single franchise relate to the City's control over public property. Control over its property is within the constitutional powers of a local government. *Adderley* v. *Florida*, 385 U.S. 39, 47; 87 S.Ct. 242 (1966).

* * *

.. The decision by the Council not to renew Madison's franchise was supported by the record.

The record before the Court discloses that the Council's decision to grant a single franchise furthers the following substantial government interests: prevention of disruption in city streets and rights of way, see *Community Communications Co.* v. *City of Boulder*, 660 F.2d 1370, 1377–78 (10th Cir. 1981), cert. denied, 456 U.S. 1001 (1982); conservation of the space on city utility poles, *Clark* v. *Community for Creative Non-Violence*, 468 U.S. 288, 104 S.Ct. 3065 (1984); and ensuring that public rights-of-way are optimally used, in a manner that serves the public interest.

The Council's decision directly relates the evidence before it to these interests. The Council found that "overbuilding will require significant replacement of city property and may result in disruption of other city services." The Council stated that it wished to conserve relevant resources and protect against safety and other problems that might arise in the future. The Council further found that overbuilding, as an economic matter, would create long-term problems with little benefit to the City and its citizens.

Finally, the nonrenewal of Madison's franchise and the grant of only one franchise, by providing for access and similar channels of communications, while avoiding the harms of multiple systems and inadequate service, meet the final part of the O'Brien test. The Council's findings show that the City's interests would not be furthered by granting a franchise to Madison; they also show that the City would be more exposed to harm if there were multiple systems than with one system. This is enough. . . . The Council's decision not to franchise more than one cable operator clearly passes muster under O'Brien in light of the evidence before it, including the evidence offered by Madison.

* * *

The Court notes further that evidence showing that a substantial number of existing poles would have to be replaced is not contradicted by Madison's affidavits in opposition to the summary judgment motion.

Madison challenged these findings by submitting affidavits stating that, while there is not room for two systems on the utility poles now, the poles could easily be altered or replaced to accommodate additional systems. Because this Court has determined that the case should be decided on the basis of the record before the Council, the affidavits are irrelevant. Madison contends that it is proper to permit introduction of additional information because in its opinion the Council did not conduct a full investigation into overbuilding. The record shows the Council asked for detailed information concerning overbuilding, including the "extent and nature" of the work that would be required to permit overbuilding . . . The City is not required to endure the harms it foresees from multiple systems because of Madison's First Amendment claims. Therefore, the decisions challenged here not to renew Madison's franchise and not to grant multiple franchises satisfy the O'Brien standard as a matter of law.

Assuming arguendo that Madison's affidavits were relevant, they would fail to raise an issue of material fact requiring a trial. Accepting the allegations in the affidavits as true, the Court finds that it is evident that a substantial number of poles would have to be altered or replaced. The issue then would be whether Madison can demand that the City replace or renovate its utility poles so that a second cable operator can be accommodated in the future. This dispute is not a factual issue, but a legal question, and can be resolved on summary judgment, and must be resolved against Madison.

In any event, Madison has not challenged the evidence presented to the Council showing that the economic characteristics of cable in Morganton are such that granting two franchises would result in waste, deterioration of service and other harms; given cable's use of public property, the City's regulation of cable to avoid these harms is justified.

In view of the fact that North Carolina courts follow the O'Brien test, the Court's analysis above of O'Brien means that Madison's free speech claims under the North Carolina Constitution must be dismissed.

Madison relies upon *City of Los Angeles* v. *Preferred*, 476 U.S. 488, 106 S.Ct.2034, 90 L.Ed.2d 480 (1986), for support of its claims and for a denial of the motion for summary judgment. Madison also cites and relies upon *TCI of Key West* v. *United States*, 757 F.2d 1330 (D.C. Cir. 1985). In both *Preferred and Key West*, the First Amendment issues were considered. . . . This Court is not restricted in its inquiry to the allegations in the complaint, as were the courts in Key West and Preferred because the sufficiency of the claims are raised by summary judgment rather than on a motion to dismiss. The undisputed facts before the Court supply the information to this Court that was missing in these two cases.

In contrast to the situation in *Preferred,* here the City Council had a record before it from which it specifically found that economic and other harms will follow if there is more than one cable system in the City. And, again in contrast to Preferred, here the City Council found from the evidence, including the statement of Madison, that there is not enough room on utility poles for more than one system, and in contrast to Preferred and Key West, here the decision was supported by evidence that Madison's proposal did not meet the community needs.

Madison's federal and state freedom of speech claims must be dismissed. The considerations that make the decision not to renew Madison's franchise reasonable also justify repurchase and other limitations on Madison's expired franchise. Those limitations do not constitute unconstitutional conditions and the twelfth claim must also be dismissed. The ordinance on its face passes muster under the First Amendment. Madison offered affidavits in an attempt to show that City Council members acted with invidious motives, not appearing on the face of the ordinance on the record of the hearing before the Council. However, it has long been settled that it is not appropriate for courts to decide constitutional questions by engaging in a factual inquiry into legislative motives. Hence, the affidavits offered by Madison do not raise material issues of fact and the third and twelfth claims must be dismissed by way of summary judgment.

EQUAL PROTECTION

Madison raises in its fourth claim a series of equal protection issues. Because Morganton did not attempt to regulate the content of cable messages, and because the interests and concerns which make the City's action reasonable under the First Amendment also satisfy the standard of the Equal Protection Clause, the equal protection claims must also be dismissed.

* * *

DUE PROCESS

In its fifth and tenth claims for relief Madison alleges that the City's actions will deprive it of its property, either directly through failure to renew the franchise (fifth claim) or indirectly through the City's proposed action in providing cable services itself (tenth claim). It contends that the property right at issue in these claims is its franchise to operate a cable television system in the City of Morganton.

As a general matter, a franchisee's property rights are not violated when a company whose franchise has expired is replaced by a publicly owned system. Moreover, the holder of an expired franchise has no greater right than the holder of an unexpired franchise. The rule with regard to revocation or annulment of an existing franchise is simply that the franchise is a property right which may not be terminated without due process.

The Court has outlined above the procedure taken by the City Council to determine whether the franchise would be renewed and determined that its action was not arbitrary or capricious. Madison was afforded all the due process due it under federal and state law and the Constitutions.

* * *

Madison's contention that expenditures made to upgrade its cable system based on its unilateral expectation of extension of its franchise create property rights entitled to protection is without merit. Even if all the facts alleged by Madison were true it has alleged nothing which would make its investment of money reasonable in light of the impending expiration of its franchise. To the contrary the record before the Court indicates without question that it was unreasonable as a matter of law for Madison to upgrade its system on the basis of an unilateral expectation of renewal. Expenditures based on unilateral expectations do not create property rights. The Court concludes that Madison has lost no property interest protected by state law and therefore its constitutional claims alleging deprivation of property without due process are without merit. If the City elects to insist upon enforcing the provision of the franchise giving it the option to purchase Madison's equipment the parties would have to agree upon the value or a court of competent jurisdiction would determine such issue.

CIVIL RIGHTS

Madison set forth in its eighth claim that the Defendants have violated its civil rights under 42 U.S.C.A. Section 1983. The individual Defendants who are Council members and Mayor of the City of Morganton would be immune from suit for their legislative acts under Section 1983, but they are not sued in their individual capacity. The Court has determined that the Defendants are entitled to judgment in their favor on all the claims advanced by Madison. Therefore, the eighth claim states no claim for relief itself.

Madison's eleventh claim is that the City violated the public purpose requirements of the North Carolina Constitution by entering the public cable television business. As set forth above the North Carolina Supreme Court ruled against Madison on this issue and this Court adopts the ruling and will therefore dismiss the claim.

* * *

The Court finds and concludes that there is no genuine issue of any material fact and the Defendants are entitled to a judgment of dismissal of all the claims set forth in the complaint as a matter of law. A judgment of dismissal of all the claims will be entered simultaneously herewith. . . .

IT IS THEREFORE ORDERED, ADJUDGED, AND DECREED that the Defendants' motion for summary judgment be and the same is hereby allowed and the complaint is hereby dismissed with prejudice. The Plaintiff shall have and recover nothing of the Defendants and the Defendants shall recover their costs of the Plaintiff.

QUESTIONS FOR CRITICAL ANALYSIS

- Aside from the agreements with music rights organizations, standard broadcast stations do not face the paperwork and accountability to the Copyright Office that cable systems do. Why is there such concern over cable's copyright liability?
- The Copyright Act views cable systems as commercial enterprises engaged in the "performance of copyrighted works." Could the same definition be applied to over-the-air commercial broadcasters?
- One alternative to the compulsory licensing arrangement would be to have each cable system negotiate directly with the broadcast station or copyright owner fees for rebroadcasting their program. Would such an arrangement be workable, and would it be more or less satisfactory than the current compulsory license?
- Although the cable industry is regulated by the FCC, the industry also falls under the jurisdiction of various state and local authorities. On occasion, these different levels of jurisdiction conflict. Would it be wise for cable to be placed exclusively under the federal government, taking local and state authorities out of cable regulation altogether?
- Could these conflicts be resolved if a single level of government (local, state, or federal) had jurisdiction over cable? If so, which level would be appropriate?
- The public inspection file can be kept at "an attorney's office." Would this be intimidating to some members of the public or would it be more intimidating to have the file at the business office of the cable operator?
- In *Cruz* v. *Ferre*, if the city ordinance had not had such a serious penalty—suspension of the license for up to nine days, or suspension or termination of the license—would the wording of the ordinance prohibiting indecent material on the cable system have been as serious?
- In the Miami ordinance, did the city manager have too much power, such as the ability to rule on the admissibility of evidence?
- When the cable system can be represented by counsel and the city by the city attorney, is there any such thing as an "informal" hearing as provided for in the Miami ordinance?
- Similarly, when regulatory matters centering on sanctions and license termination can always go beyond municipal hearings and into the courts, as was the case in *Cruz* v. *Ferre*, are "informal" hearings ever really informal?
- If a city manager has the power to determine the admissibility of evidence in a cable hearing, can the refusal to admit evidence really encourage the proceeding to move beyond the informal hearing to the courts because an aggrieved party feels that only under the rules of judicial procedure will evidence be accepted into the proceeding, which will then result in a fair hearing?
- In a cable dispute, would a municipal judge overseeing an informal hearing and with the power to admit evidence, result in a hearing process that is more fair to the parties involved? Would the judge be less likely to be impartial if appointed rather than elected? If elected, what if a cable company PAC contributed to the judge's campaign?
- Could a sales tax on cable television services be construed to be a form of government censorship?
- What if a cable television company serving the

state capital vehemently criticized members of the legislature in a locally produced newscast? Could such criticism have political fallout through a state cable commission?

- Would legislators be more likely to vote in favor of a tax which placed an additional financial burden on the cable operator but raised new revenue for state government?
- Would legislators be less likely to impose such a tax out of fear of negative criticism?
- Would there be any type of safeguard to prevent such a tax and would it be held constitutional if challenged in court?
- What if the same cable television system was owned by the city and the political party in power in city government was different than the political party in power in state government? Could such circumstances perpetuate ill feelings and further increase the likelihood of the state imposing additional taxes on the cable system?
- Would it be necessary to impose the same tax on all cable systems, not just the one operating in the state capital?
- Would a U.S. Supreme Court composed of justices more supportive of First Amendment rights than those expressed by the majority opinion in *Leathers* v. *Medlock* result in a fundamental change in the government's approach to mass media, and specifically the taxation of mass media?
- Newspapers have traditionally been viewed as *the press* or *news media*, while cable television sometimes is labeled an *entertainment medium*. Does this distinction between the press and entertainment media result in different legislative action that singles out cable television for one type of government action and newspapers for a different type of government action?
- In many states, the core of cable regulation rests not with state government, but with local municipalities. Is it possible that in states where cable television is controlled primarily by local municipalities that can tax cable, jealousy could result between state and local government whereby state government feels slighted if it does not receive its fair share of revenue from cable services?
- Would a state sales tax be constitutional if it only taxed premium services, such as HBO and Showtime, and not basic cable service?
- What are the advantages and disadvantages of different cable regulatory frameworks, such as an elected board versus a city manager?
- Many cable systems now possess two-way and data-processing capabilities. What new policy issues will arise as this technology becomes more widespread?
- Since local municipalities have the power to determine many of the conditions of a cable franchise, as well as to determine who gets the franchise, do cable systems that originate their own news programming run a risk of repercussions if they criticize local government?
- What safeguards and recourse are available to cable companies that feel they have been wronged by local officials because of criticism occurring on cable news programming?
- It is becoming commonplace for cable systems to be linked together via satellite, and for cable systems to originate as well as distribute programming. The technology is available, and it could soon be practical for cable systems to be linked across continents. New regulatory issues will arise that integrate the policies affecting cable with those of satellite communication. Ask yourself: What are some of these issues and what role would international law play in the future development of a worldwide cable system?
- Many nations, including the United States, are major producers and suppliers of international television programming. Many programs seen in the United States are seen in foreign countries. In some cases, programs from the major production centers of the United States are produced for direct export. In a world where multiple cable channels will increase the demand for diversified programming, what role will heavy producers and suppliers of programming play in influencing world opinion, as well as in international communication policy?
- Will countries with high technology, regardless of their position in world affairs, be in a stronger position to influence international communication policy?
- The Cable Act of 1992 defines programming from a qualified educational source to be educational or instructional in nature in promoting the public understanding of mathematics, the sciences, the humanities and the arts. Should any additional categories have been added to the 1992 legislation?

- The Cable Act also requires the source to have annual expenditures on programming exceeding $15 million. Why would this arbitrary figure be placed in the statute and do you feel it may restrict quality educational programming from smaller production companies that may not have annual expenditures this great? Do you feel this provision of the law could withstand a court challenge? Are there any constitutional grounds for repealing this requirement?
- In the 1992 Cable Act, cable operators can enforce a written and published policy prohibiting indecent programming. Should cable operators be the ones to determine whether or not programming is indecent and could this section of the law be used to censor programs which the cable operator feels are offensive but which under a court test might not be found to be indecent as measured by a local community standards?

ADDITIONAL RESOURCES

Brenner, D. L., "Cable Franchising and the First Amendment: Preferred Problems, Undesirable Solutions." 10 *Comment* 999 (1988).

Clarkson, R. L., "The Invalidation of Mandatory Cable Access Regulations." 7 *Pepperdine Law Review* 469 (1980).

Fowler, D. L., "Diverse Programming vs. Community Standards: The Constitutionality of Municipal Censorship of Leased Access Cable." 27 *San Diego Law Review* 493 (1990).

Kowal, K., "Local Access Bypass." 37 *Federal Communications Law Journal* 325 (1985).

Lloyd, F. W., "Cable Television's Emerging Two Way Services: A Dilemma for Federal and State Regulators." 36 *Vanderbilt Law Review* 1045 (1983).

Mueller, W., "Controversial Programming on Cable Television's Public Access Channels: The Limits of Governmental Response." 38 *De Paul Law Review* 1051 (1989).

Saylor, D. J., "Municipal Ripoff: The Unconstitutionality of Cable Franchise Fees and Access Support Payments." 35 *Catholic University Law Review*, 671 (1986).

chapter twelve

Common Carrier Regulations

The term *common carrier* dates back to the early days of transportation and the people and companies engaged in "carrying" goods from one location to another. One of the legal characteristics of a common carrier is the requirement that no one can be refused service if they are able to pay the required rate or fare. Private carriers or contract carriers, as distinguished from common carriers, are not obligated to make their services available to everyone.

Gradually, telegraph and telephone companies fell under the definition of common carrier. In the courts, some of the legal precedents arising from transportation, such as liability for undelivered goods and the requirement of public access, were applied to these same companies. In addition to telegraph and telephone companies, railroads, pipelines, and companies owning telephone lines and telegraph cables were encompassed by laws governing common carriers.

COMMUNICATION GAINS COMMON CARRIER STATUS

Telegraph and telephone communication gained common carrier status with a 1910 federal law passed to amend earlier common carrier legislation. The 1910 law read:

> That the provisions of this Act shall apply to any corporation or any person or persons engaged in the transportation of oil or other commodity, except water and except natural or artificial gas, by means of pipelines, or partly by pipelines and partly by railroad, or partly by pipelines and partly by water, and to telegraph, telephone, and cable companies (whether wire or wireless) engaged in sending messages from one State, Territory, or District of the United States, to any other State, Territory, or District of the United States, or to any foreign country, who shall be considered and held to be common carriers within the meaning and purpose of this Act.[1]

In addition the act established categories of service and a requirement of reasonable charges stating:

> All charges made for any service rendered or to be rendered in the transportation of passengers or property and for the transmission of messages by telegraph, telephone, or cable, as aforesaid, or in connection therewith, shall be just and reasonable; and every unjust and unreasonable charge for such service or any part thereof is prohibited and declared to be unlawful: *Provided*, That messages by

> telegraph, telephone, or cable, subject to the provisions of this Act, may be classified into day, night, repeated, unrepeated, letter, commercial, press, Government, and such other classes as are just and reasonable, and different rates may be charged for the different classes of messages: *And provided further*, That nothing in this Act shall be construed to prevent telephone, telegraph, and cable companies from entering into contracts with common carriers, for the exchange of service.[2]

The 1910 law added to legislation passed in 1866 that gave telegraph companies and eventually telephone companies the right to construct, operate, and maintain lines over lands in the public domain and gave special rate privileges to the federal government.[3]

THE ORIGINS OF A REGULATED TELEPHONE INDUSTRY

To understand the structure of the telephone industry, one must go back to the beginnings of the telephone itself.[4]

The Invention of Alexander Graham Bell

Invented by Alexander Graham Bell, the telephone grew out of experimental work on what was called in 1875 a "harmonic telegraph."[5] Bell and two partners, Gardiner Green Hubbard and Thomas Sanders, entered into an agreement in 1875 to invent the new device with Sanders's money, Hubbard's legal advice, and Bell's skill as an inventor of sorts. Bell, with an assistant named Thomas Watson, fashioned a device to emulate the human voice with a vibrating metal reed stretched over a membrane.

The first patent on the device was filed on April 6, 1875, and granted on March 7, 1876, a few days prior to the first successful experiment of the telephone and the famous words, "Mr. Watson, come here, I want you," spoken to Watson by Bell. Four additional patents followed, all under an agreement by the three men called the Bell Patent Association. The word *telephone* did not appear in the early patents. The inventors originally saw themselves as improving the telegraph. When the word *telephone* did appear, it was in the new company formed by the three original partners called the "Bell Telephone Company, Gardiner G. Hubbard Trustee," later to become the Bell Telephone Company.[6] The company leased rather than sold telephones, which in the long run was a good idea, but in the short run resulted in a shortage of capital. Sanders, however, had ties with New England financial circles and interested a group of business leaders in investing in the telephone's development in New England. From this arrangement the New England Telephone Company was formed in 1878. The two companies eventually merged into the National Bell Telephone Company.[7]

Western Union, Exchanges, and AT&T

Western Union had also managed to get into the telephone business with equipment designed by Thomas Edison and Elisha Gray.[8] Western Union's telephone system flourished, as did Bell's. Western Union and Bell fought patent battles until the two settled out of court, with Western Union agreeing to pay royalties on new Bell patents and giving Bell exclusive rights to their already developed patents. Eventually, Western Union agreed to stay out of the telephone business, and Bell agreed to stay out of the telegraph business.[9] The settlement, requiring a special session of the Massachusetts legislature, resulted in the telephone company retaining the right of: "manufacturing, owning, selling, using and licensing others to use electrical speaking telephones and other apparatus and appliances pertaining to the transmission of intelligence by electricity . . ."[10] The settlement also resulted in the formation of a new company called the American Bell Telephone Company, which purchased the stock of the National Bell Telephone Company.

The National Bell Telephone Company had meanwhile been developing a system of telephone exchanges.[11] The new company would connect the various exchanges with one another so that long-distance calling could take place. This was accomplished by forming a Long Lines division within the new American Bell Telephone Company. The Long Lines division became a full-fledged subsidiary called the American Telephone and Telegraph Company (AT&T). Gradually AT&T constructed a network of lines throughout the United States and internationally. Eventually, the child swallowed the parent and AT&T became the parent company.

THE EARLY REGULATORY ENVIRONMENT

Of importance to our study of telecommunication is the regulatory environment within which the early telephone industry developed. Telephones developed through a different technology than broadcasting. Radio, for example, uses the electromagnetic spectrum, which is a limited resource, and which formerly the Interstate Commerce Commission, and today the Federal Communications Commission, regulates through a "limited resource" and "public-interest" philosophy. In addition, the federal government, as opposed to state government, regulates radio. Telephone companies, on the other hand, developed as a series of locally run companies in different states. Because many telephone companies were local exchanges covering just the communities they served through wired connections, they did not fall under federal jurisdiction.

Because it was engaged in connecting different local exchanges, AT&T developed under a somewhat different regulatory structure. Differences also existed between radio and telephone in the way the federal government gained the necessary information to execute a fair and equitable regulatory policy. Radio stations, for example, were not financially interconnected. Individual stations, with the exception of those used for radio telegraph messages, were not common carriers. Prior to commercial radio, the real regulatory challenge was in controlling interference between stations, a problem not encountered in the regulation of telephone companies since wired systems did not pose electromagnetic interference difficulties. For regulatory purposes, the economic status of the industry as a whole could be determined rather easily through an accounting of income through advertising.

Rate Structure and Patents

The challenge facing the regulation of telephone companies was one of rate structure—how the interface between long-distance carriers such as AT&T and local exchanges would be handled, meshing the federal regulations of the FCC with the regulations of the state public utility commissions. If someone at one local exchange called someone at another local exchange, and the call was transferred through a long-distance carrier, all three played a part in the interconnection and all three were theoretically compensated. Gradually, regulatory policy at both the state and federal levels developed a uniform system of accounts which, although not perfect or foolproof, did manage to satisfy Congress, the ICC, and after 1934, the FCC.

The early patent battles also compounded the problem. The 1876 awarding of the Bell patent didn't stop entrepreneurs from getting into the telephone business. Hundreds of companies sprang up, and hundreds of patent infringement suits, many successful, were filed by Bell, forcing the competitor out of business. When the patent issue did reach the U.S. Supreme Court, the Bell patents were upheld.[12] The original Bell patents expired in 1893, opening the way for the real growth of independent telephone companies, many of which served small rural communities. A large number of these small independent companies were eventually swallowed up by AT&T, which also acquired a large stock interest in its competitor, Western Union.

AT&T's Presence

Larger companies competing with AT&T began to feel that they were unfairly being kept out of the long-distance market by Bell's stranglehold on local independents with contracts for restrictive access. The administration of U.S. President Woodrow Wilson brought a favorable atmosphere for antitrust action against AT&T and other companies in an era favoring competition. The end result of this antitrust atmosphere was AT&T Vice-President N.C. Kingsbury forging a compromise with the federal government. In the 1913 compromise, AT&T committed itself to disposing of its entire holdings in Western Union stock, valued at $30 million, with certain exceptions, discontinuing the acquisition of other telephone companies that operated in competition with the Bell system, and agreeing to arrange interconnections with independent telephone companies for toll long-distance calling. In addition to independent companies being bought by AT&T, other independents began to merge with one another for increased profitability, and the larger independents gained some economic and political clout. In 1921 the federal government added to AT&T's acquisition possibilities with the passage of the Willis-Graham Act allowing for telephone company mergers free of antitrust actions. The law was not popular with independents but was tempered by a statement from AT&T Vice-President E. K. Hall, who told independent companies that except in special cases purchase of independents or consolidation would not be AT&T's general policy.[13]

The Willis-Graham Act came after World War I and affected the regulation of radio broadcasting as well as telephones. The war had seen the growth and development of radio-telegraph communication. Thousands of radio amateurs emerged who had served as radio-telegraph operators during the war and who had some lobbying clout. As part of the war policy, between August 1, 1918 and August 1, 1919, AT&T was under the control of the U.S. Post Office. Two federal regulatory policies emerged from this brief direct control. In the first place revenues from long-distance service became a subsidy for local calling. Second, the government developed a nationwide standard for long-distance rates based on annual costs. Since that time, independent telephone companies, AT&T, and other long-distance carriers have emerged.

Today there are more than 1,000 independent telephone companies in the United States. Some are large, such as GTE. Beginning in 1935 as General Telephone Corporation, GTE followed an expansion and acquisition plan somewhat parallel to the strategy of AT&T. It acquired equipment suppliers through the acquisition of Sylvania Electronics Company and others, and moved into satellite, international, and long-distance communication through mergers, resulting in US Sprint.

AT&T meanwhile had acquired and developed part of the Western Electric Manufacturing Company in 1881. The company later became Western Electric, wholly owned by AT&T. Western Electric was the manufacturing and supply arm of AT&T, in an arrangement whereby Western Electric would manufacture and buy for resale to AT&T equipment and other supplies needed by AT&T to run its business. While AT&T was not obligated to buy from Western Electric, economies of scale made it difficult not to do so. AT&T had also developed a significant research arm in Bell Labs, another wholly-owned company started in 1924.

THE 1949 ANTITRUST ACTION AND SETTLEMENT

In 1949 the government stepped in and filed antitrust proceedings against AT&T and Western Electric, charging them with conspiracy and violation of the Sherman Antitrust Act. The government wanted the AT&T-Western Electric alliance split up, for Western Electric to divest 50 percent of its stock in Bell Labs, for the three companies to license their patents to others on a nondiscriminatory basis, and for the Bell operating companies under AT&T to buy all equipment and supplies through competitive bidding.[14] The defendants argued forcibly against divestiture saying that the status quo made available equipment

> of advanced design and high quality at prices substantially lower than would be obtainable in the absence of such unification. It facilitated the standardization of equipment which is essential to efficient operation of interconnected telephone systems. . . . The ultimate beneficiaries of this unification are the users of telephone service, who thereby obtain better service at lower cost.[15]

In the same year the independent telephone companies received a boost when Congress permitted the Rural Electrification Administration to loan money to telephone companies enabling them to connect rural areas and expand into new locations. On January 24, 1956, the 1949 antitrust suit was settled under a consent decree. Concentrating on patents and royalties, the consent decree did not address the monopoly issue.[16]

> The settlement placed most of its emphasis on patents, owing largely to AT&T's hold on the patent of the newly discovered transistor. The settlement formalized an already existing policy to allow any applicant the use of some 8,600 existing AT&T patents, without having to pay royalties to AT&T. The rationale for this was based in part on the recognition that AT&T research and development were publicly subsidized. In a bow to AT&T, however, companies which applied to use AT&T patents had to share their own patents with AT&T. . . . The Consent Decree constituted a combination of minimal AT&T concessions and the construction of new regulatory barriers. It called for Western Electric to institute uniform cost accounting procedures and enjoined Western Electric from paying any patent royalties to AT&T (which could inflate the rate base). Most significant for the future, AT&T agreed not to engage in any activities external to those of a regulated communications carrier (except importantly, for military work). In exchange, the Consent Decree legally sanctified AT&T as a vertically integrated monopoly.[17]

The consent decree immediately came under fire from the government for having been agreed to under pressure from the U.S. Department of

Defense and the U.S. Atomic Energy Commission. Among other documents, a letter from Secretary of Defense C. E. Wilson to the attorney general spoke to the issue of AT&T's role in national defense work and claimed the antitrust case would threaten the continuation of the work.[18] The letter stated: "This is the reason that the severance of Western Electric from the system would effectively disintegrate the coordinated organization which is fundamental to the successful carrying forward of these critical defense projects, and it appears it could virtually destroy its usefulness for the future."[19] The Department of Justice's change of position and settlement prompted Congress to get involved.

The consent decree is credited with playing a part in the enactment of the *Antitrust Procedures and Penalties Act* that now requires court approval before a consent decree can be accepted in government-initiated antitrust actions. Congress felt that the Department of Justice was subject to economic and political pressures and that the public interest could be abridged without some type of review.[20] Despite the criticism that followed the consent decree, AT&T remained a vertically integrated company. It had escaped divestiture, and since consent decrees cannot be used as *prima facie* evidence in private antitrust suits, AT&T escaped litigation from companies that might have used a decision against AT&T and Western Electric to advance their own cases against the two and seek damages for the loss of business allegedly suffered because of the monopoly.

THE HUSH-A-PHONE CASE

Gradually, challenges to AT&T's hold on the marketplace began to emerge. When the Hush-a-Phone Corporation wanted to market a mechanical device that would attach to the telephone and permit enhanced conversations to occur in noisy conditions, AT&T objected and the FCC supported the restriction. The court of appeals reversed the FCC on the basis that Hush-a-Phone's device was mechanical and not electrical and did not cause harm to the telephone apparatus.[21] AT&T was, however, able to retain at that point its restrictions against electrical devices attached to the telephone. But the issue of antitrust was raised in the case, especially as it applied to AT&T, a regulated company which had controlled the entry of a nonregulated business, Hush-a-Phone, into the marketplace.

The FCC also ordered AT&T to file new "tariff" schedules, tariff being a public document that sets forth the services of a common carrier, including the rates charged for such services, governing rules, regulations, and practices related to those services.[22] Specifically, the FCC directed AT&T to rescind and cancel any tariff regulations to the extent that they prohibited a customer from using a device that did not injure people and did not harm the telephone system. The FCC went on to state, "As we construe the court's opinion, a tariff regulation which amounts to a blanket prohibition upon the customer's use of any and all devices without discriminating between the harmful and harmless encroaches upon the right of the user to make reasonable use of the facilities . . ."[23]

THE CARTERFONE DECISION

Hush-a-Phone also dislodged the first chip in the AT&T stone and paved the way for the 1968 Carterfone decision.[24] The Carterfone device was substantially different than the Hush-a-Phone device. Invented by Thomas F. Carter and produced and marketed by Carter Electronics Corp., the Carterfone was designed to be connected to a two-way radio at the base station serving a mobile radio system. When callers on the radio and the telephone are both in contact with the base station, the operator at the base station placed the handset of the operator's telephone in a cradle in the Carterfone device. A voice control circuit in the Carterfone device then automatically switched on the radio transmitter when the telephone caller was speaking. When the caller stopped speaking, the radio returned to the receive mode. The operator could monitor the conversation and control the voice volume.[25]

AT&T's Complaint

The AT&T complaint against Carterfone was based on the tariff regulation that stated:

> No equipment, apparatus, circuit or device not furnished by the telephone company shall be attached to or connected with the facilities furnished by the telephone company, whether physically, by induction or otherwise except as provided. . . . In case any such unauthorized attachment or connection is made, the telephone company shall have the right to remove or disconnect the same; or to suspend the service during the continuance of said attachment or connection; or to terminate the service.[26]

When AT&T and other companies advised subscribers that the Carterfone device would potentially subject them to penalties under the FCC tariff, Carterfone brought an antitrust action in the district court. The court reserved the right to rule on the issue of antitrust, but because of the technical issues involved, passed the matter on to the FCC under the doctrine of primary jurisdiction that vested in the FCC the right to determine the "justness, reasonableness, validity, application, and effect of the tariff and practices here involved."[27] Several parties intervened after the FCC scheduled a public hearing on the matter. Carter then filed a formal complaint under the Communications Act. Hearings were held and the examiner in the case determined there was a need for the Carterfone, the device did not have an adverse effect on the telephone system, and that applying the tariff against Carterfone was unjust and unreasonable.

FCC Adopts the Examiner's Findings

The FCC adopted the examiner's findings but also found the restrictive tariff to be "unreasonable, discriminatory, and unlawful," and that such provisions should be stricken. Drawing from the reasoning in the *Hush-a-Phone* decision, the FCC said restrictions against "foreign attachments" were an "unwarranted interference with the telephone subscriber's right reasonably to use his telephone in ways which are privately beneficial without being publicly detrimental."[28] The FCC went on to state:

> There has been no adequate showing that nonharmful interconnection must be prohibited in order to permit the telephone company to carry out its system responsibilities. The risk feared by the examiner has not been demonstrated to be substantial, and no reason presents itself why it should be. No one entity need provide all interconnection equipment for our telephone system any more than a single source is needed to supply the parts for the space probe . . .
>
> Nor can we assume that the telephone companies would be hindered in improving telephone service by any tendency of the manufacturers and users of interconnection devices to resist change. The telephone companies would remain free to make improvements to the telephone system and could reflect any such improvements in reasonable revised standards for nontelephone company provided devices used in connection with the system. Manufacturers and sellers of such devices would then have the responsibility of offering for sale or use only such equipment as would be in compliance with such revised standards. An owner or user of a device which failed to meet reasonable revised standards for such devices, would either have to have the device rebuilt to comply with the revised standards or discontinue its use. Such is the risk inherent in the private ownership of any equipment to be used in connection with the telephone system.
>
> The present unlawfulness of the tariff also permeates its past. It has been unreasonable and unreasonably discriminatory since its inception, for the reasons given above. That the telephone companies may not have known prior to the proceedings herein that the Carterfone was in fact harmless is irrelevant, since they barred its use without regard to its effect upon the telephone system. Furthermore the tariff was the carrier's own. It was not prescribed by the Commission. It has remained subject to complaint and to a finding that it has been unlawful since its inception . . .
>
> In view of the unlawfulness of the tariff there would be no point in merely declaring it invalid as applied to the Carterfone and permitting it to continue in operation as to other interconnection devices. This would also put a clearly improper burden upon the manufacturers and users of other devices. The appropriate remedy is to strike the tariff and permit the carriers, if they so desire, to propose new tariff provisions in accordance with this opinion.[29]

In *Carterfone*, telephone systems were opened to new equipment by nontelephone manufacturers which would enhance, but not be harmful to, telephone technologies. Although the antitrust issue was not a major part of the proceeding, the fact that Carter had filed on antitrust grounds meant the issue was not mute. Moreover, since *Hush-a-Phone* was the precedent for *Carterfone*, two cases now existed that struck at AT&T's hold in the marketplace and eliminated its restrictive tariff on external equipment attachments.

THE ABOVE 890 PROCEEDING

Three years after *Hush-a-Phone*, the *Above 890* proceeding resulted in the FCC authorizing the use of frequencies above 890 megacycles for private companies to offer new services to consumers. The *Above 890* proceeding was significant because it dealt with the allocation of space on the electromagnetic spectrum. Also, the *Above 890* hearing provided a micro case study on a variety of early telecommunication policy issues. *Above 890* examined a list of specific issues, some of which are applicable to our discussion.

The Interconnection Question

One question posed by the FCC in the *Above 890* proceeding was: "What effect would the authorization of private point-to-point systems where common carrier facilities are available have on the ability of the common carriers to serve the general public and, if such effect is detrimental, the specific nature, extent and magnitude of such detriment?"[30] As could be expected, the common carriers argued that permitting private microwave systems to compete with common carriers would hamper the improvement of an efficient nationwide communications system, and that regulatory bodies such as the FCC would be reluctant to require telephone companies to install facilities if it would impact negatively on the telephone company's well-being. Common carriers also argued that to license the private operators would increase the demand on the electromagnetic spectrum, which would not be in the public interest. Another argument by common carriers was that the entry of private operators would cause added cost burdens on individuals and small businesses who would continue to use common carriers.

The private sector, on the other hand, argued that telephone common carriers should devote their time to filling the back orders for telephone service that were building up, and new revenue from such increased service would offset some of the revenue loss telephone companies claimed they would suffer with the entry of the private operators. Private operators also argued that private users would lease more wire line connections to tie in smaller terminals to the principal microwave systems, therefore contributing to the income of the common carriers.

The Question of Economic Protection

The commission also asked:

> Is there any obligation on the part of the Commission under the provisions of the Communications Act to protect the users of common carrier service from any adverse economic effects that the carriers might suffer from the operation of private point-to-point systems? If there is no statutory obligation, is it desirable in the public interest for the Commission to establish this as a matter of policy?[31]

Arguments followed expected lines with the common carriers arguing the FCC did have a statutory obligation to protect them from a loss of business. The private operators argued the opposite position and added that it should be a policy position of the FCC to support a freedom of choice for consumers as to which type of communication they would employ. They also pointed to the area of mobile communications where private mobile communication systems already operated in competition with similar services provided by common carriers. The common carriers argued that rates for the general public would increase, that a duplication of facilities would be wasteful, that there was no national policy in favor of competition, and that a splintered national communications system would be detrimental to the national defense. They also argued that because the electromagnetic spectrum was a limited resource that "chaos" would prevail if eligibility to operate microwave services were offered to other users.[32] Western Union joined the common carriers and argued that because they already competed with the telephone companies, private lines, and airmail, that adding still more competition was actually "a perversion" of the concept of competition.[33]

The Question of Competition and Monopoly

The commission asked:

> Would a policy of restricting or denying a private point-to-point system because common carrier facilities are available be inconsistent with any of the provisions of the Communications Act? Would such restrictions result in a lessening of competition or a fostering of monopoly in the manufacture,

> sale, use, or provisions of communications facilities contrary to the public interest?[34]

Again the common carriers argued that the restriction or denial of licenses would violate the act. Private operators said it would not. The private operators also said it would lessen competition and foster monopoly. They weren't alone. The Justice Department, which had just three years earlier emerged with a consent decree instead of a clear victory in their antitrust suit against AT&T and Western Electric, stepped in on the side of the private operators saying they believed the wording of the Communications Act indicated:

> . . . a congressional intent to rely upon competition to regulate and develop the communications field to the greatest possible extent. Those provisions of the act regulating common carrier activities proceed upon the principle that direct regulation must be substituted for competition. This principle is inconsistent with the principle of competition, and is applicable in those areas where the common carriers already had monopolies when the Communications Act of 1934 was enacted. There is nothing in the Communications Act to indicate that any particular portion of the radio spectrum, such as the microwave region, should be turned over to the common carriers. We believe that reconciliation of the two methods of regulation requires that the common carrier concept be given as limited application as the terms of the Communications Act will permit.[35]

In addition to the Justice Department, the Office of Civil and Defense Mobilization filed comments that appeared to appease both parties, saying on one hand that private systems would contribute to a limited extent to the national defense, but from a defense planning standpoint such systems would help mostly at the local level. An opposing argument, however, pointed out that in a wartime crisis there would be an increased demand for communication services and the private systems could help meet the demand.

The Commission's Decision

After hearing responses to 19 different issue questions, the commission issued its decision in broad terms, saying the FCC had no "express obligation" to protect users of common carriers from adverse economic effects. The commission also observed that the common carriers had not made a conclusive showing that unrestricted licensing would have an impact on their ability to serve the general public. Although the commission admitted that it could not make decisions on speculation, the issue of economic effects did warrant continued surveillance. The commission rejected the argument of limited spectrum-space, saying there were ample frequencies available at that time and orderly, systematic, authorizations based on technical criteria could be applied to the allocation of spectrum space to private users. It also pointed out that the common carriers had declined to provide service to some areas that were remote and isolated, and that private systems had been constructed to meet the needs of users. Private systems were also seen as being able to meet the needs of flexibility in their hour-to-hour operational and administrative needs. The FCC reasoned that equipment manufacturing and development would also be enhanced by the entry of private operators. With the issuance of *Above 890*, the gates were opened for the entry of private point-to-point suppliers of services. An early major player to take advantage of the policy that started with *Above 890* was Microwave Communications, Inc., today known as MCI, a billion-dollar player in telecommunications.

THE MCI FILING AND DECISION: A PIVOTAL POINT

Taking advantage of the developing FCC policy toward more liberal entry into the marketplace and undoubtedly sensing the trend toward less protection for common carriers, MCI in 1963 filed for a permit to construct a point-to-point microwave link between Chicago, Illinois, and St. Louis, Missouri.[36] Like the *Above 890* proceeding, the MCI decision by the FCC is rich in information about how the fledgling private carriers developed, the heated policy differences within the commission itself over how to interpret "competition" and the "public interest," the use of the electromagnetic spectrum, the way in which parties to the proceeding entered evidence, their persuasive strategies, and the risks taken by a federal agency in the new and developing telecommunications market.

MCI's permit was granted in a four-to-three vote. Dissenting opinions abounded. In retrospect, when one considers the way the telecommunication industry has developed after the divestiture of AT&T and the role of the early players such as MCI, the MCI decision had broad implications for the future of the telecommunications landscape. The proceeding is also an excellent case study of what transpires when a new entrant wants to compete against long-established players, which in this case were the telephone companies. When one considers the fact that if companies such as MCI had not achieved a foothold in the marketplace, by the time the AT&T divestiture occurred, there would have been little economic or technical base for the development of a free-enterprise type of telecommunication infrastructure in the United States.

MCI's Technical Specifications

The MCI proposed system was a limited common carrier microwave radio service for "interplant" and "interoffice" communication needs of small businesses. Keep in mind that microwaves are at the upper end of the electromagnetic spectrum where line-of-site transmission propagation patterns exist, where hops of about 30 land miles are necessary, and where frequencies are discussed in terms of millions of cycles (hertz in today's terminology), as opposed to thousands of cycles per second for AM broadcast radio frequencies. At these frequencies, considerable amounts of information can travel over frequencies with these billions of cycles of bandwidth. It was for this reason the *Above 890* proceeding was so important. MCI proposed channels with bandwidths of 2 kilocycles for either the entire length of the system or for specific segments. Customers could also lease broadband frequencies of 48, 250, or 1,000 kilocycles for data transmission. Not only would MCI be offering lower rates but customers who had less than full-time communication needs could purchase half-time use provisions. A party-line arrangement was proposed with up to five subscribers per channel with prorated rate reductions. MCI also proposed combining channels into the larger bandwidths for data transmission along with fewer restrictions than other common carriers, therefore providing greater flexibility for customers as well as reduced costs.

Challenges to MCI's Application

Filing against the application were such well-known names in the communications industry as Western Union, General Telephone Co. of Illinois, the Associated Bell System Companies, AT&T, Illinois Bell, and Southwestern Bell. The FCC scheduled a hearing on the challenge to determine among other things:

> (a) whether the established common carriers offer services meeting the needs which MCI proposes to meet in the area which MCI proposes to serve; (b) whether the grant of MCI's application would result in wasteful duplication of facilities; (c) whether MCI is financially qualified to construct and operate its proposed facilities; (d) whether there is a need for MCI's proposal; and (e) whether operation of MCI's proposed system would result in interference to existing common carriers.[37]

The examiner assigned to the case found after considering the evidence and pleadings in the hearing that although there was duplication of services over this route there were services MCI could offer that others did not, that the system would work, and that MCI was financially qualified. The FCC decision grouped the issues into: (1) MCI's financial qualifications, (2) the need for MCI's proposals, (3) the reliability of service, (4) the efficient utilization of the frequency spectrum, and (5) the feasibility of loop service, which was the ability of MCI's customers to connect with existing switching systems.

MCI's Financial Qualifications

MCI estimated construction costs for the system at $564,000, a figure the examiner found reasonable. Opposing carriers argued that MCI had underestimated the costs of the system, omitted essential equipment items from the estimates, and would be unable to market enough channels to raise revenues. MCI's estimates were based on a quote from Collins Radio Co. to which MCI appended their own estimate for installation costs from an electrical manufacturing firm. Collins had agreed to sell MCI the equipment at 10 percent down financed over 60 equal monthly payments. MCI estimated its actual operating expenses for the first year at just under $230,000. Along with loans and escrow, it projected operating revenues based on being able to market 75 channels in the first year.

How close the projections for profits were can be seen in figures emerging from the proceeding. For example, $8,000 in surplus cash was projected after the sale of stock.[38] FCC commissioner Robert E. Lee in his dissenting opinion said, "suffice it to say that the examiner found MCI financially qualified based on rough estimates with $8000 in assets over liabilities and characterized it as a shoestring operation. I believe that the MCI cost estimates do not include certain essential equipment which would wipe out the $8000 cushion many times over."[39] Nevertheless, the majority felt that adequate service could be provided and the lack of funds, even for equipment, did not constitute a deficiency in MCI's financial qualifications.

The Need for MCI's Proposals

The examiner determined that there existed a need for services at lower rates than was being provided by other carriers and that MCI could meet that need. Opposing carriers argued otherwise. Rate structures have always been a bone of contention among carriers and regulatory agencies. The FCC did not enter the debate, instead concluding that the primary issue in the proceeding was whether the public interest would be served and that the majority of the commissioners said it would. About the ability to provide service, the FCC again pointed to channel spacing, especially the availability of 2-kilocycle channels as opposed to other carriers who offered only 4-kilocycle service, the less than full-time needs of subscribers, and a reduced rate for party-line connections. Flexibility was another strong point in favor of MCI. As evidence the FCC cited testimony from an Ann Arbor, Michigan company that leased computer time and said they were forced to buy more bandwidth than necessary under current tariffs. Other features stressed by the FCC were the interoffice and interplant arrangements. The issue of cost averaging also emerged, the process whereby customers in remote areas are charged the same as those in more densely populated areas, even though construction and operation of equipment to reach remote subscribers cost more. Because MCI would secure business over the lucrative route of Chicago to St. Louis they were accused of "cream skimming" the most profitable business without the need to service other less profitable remote areas. The issue had appeared before, but in the MCI proceeding the commission made a strong policy statement on the subject:

> Moreover, if we were to follow the carriers' reasoning and specify as a prerequisite to the establishment of a new common carrier service that it be so widespread as to permit cost averaging, we would in effect restrict the entry of new licensees into the common carrier field to a few large companies which are capable of serving the entire Nation. Such an approach is both unrealistic and inconsistent with the public interest. Innovations in the types and character of communications services offered or economies in operation which could not at once be instituted on a nationwide basis would be precluded from ever being introduced. In the circumstances of this case, we find the cream skimming argument to be without merit.[40]

AT&T meanwhile was caught in an inconsistency when it argued that "no public need exists for the sharing provisions of the MCI proposal." MCI pointed to AT&T's tariff filing in December of 1968 where AT&T proposed a "joint user arrangement under certain private lines furnished to a customer."[41] The disclosure of the letter, especially by MCI and in an FCC proceeding, undermined AT&T's argument. The FCC noted that it could not "ignore statements made by a party in filings with the Commission which contradict or are inconsistent with the position taken by that party in an adjudicatory proceeding."[42]

Reliability of Service

The common carriers argued that MCI would not be able to provide reliable service on the basis of its physical plant and facilities, its system maintenance, and clarity of its signal. A key piece of evidence presented by the common carriers centered on the estimated percentage system reliability. While MCI presented a reliability estimate of 99.9 percent, which some might argue was too high, the common carriers estimated reliability at 85 percent, which the FCC said was too low. The rationale in giving MCI the benefit of the doubt was its proposal not to offer the kind of high-density communication system offered by the telephone companies and Western Union. At the time of the decision, the FCC was considering setting reliability standards for microwave systems, but felt it was inconsistent with the public interest to defer action on the MCI request until such standards were adopted.

In addition to system reliability, the proceeding got down to such basics as to what type of housing would shelter MCI's equipment. One cannot help but stop and consider the scenario of industry giants such as the Bell companies in a federal wrestling match with a small, then relatively unknown, rival on subjects such as metal tool sheds. In what today almost seems like a patronizing issue, the carriers said the unheated tool sheds and a backup eight-hour battery power supply would not suffice in the event of a power failure. Again, the FCC was unconvinced and pointed out that the quality of the equipment or even its cost was not an issue. The only issue was if it would work. The sheds, the FCC said, were waterproof, and that while "working conditions in the sheds in case of a breakdown would not be of the best, there is nothing in the record to justify a finding that they are not usable."[43] By dealing with such issues the FCC also sent a signal to other potential entrants that it wasn't necessary to have designer-label facilities in order to succeed in obtaining construction permits for systems that would compete with the well-established companies.

Efficient Utilization of the Frequency Spectrum

An argument against MCI was that MCI would not make the fullest use of the spectrum, using one backup channel for each working channel. While the FCC recognized this was a problem they were lenient and said that the application should not be rejected for that reason. In making their determination the commission stated:

> Furthermore, in determining whether there is a frequency wastage we must take into account the benefits to be derived by the public from the proposed common carrier facilities, and to weigh these benefits against the disadvantages alleged by the opposing carriers. . . . When frequencies are used to meet a significant unfulfilled communications need, we do not believe that such use may be considered as "inefficient."[44]

Today, the same issues still present themselves, but technology has produced ways to use frequencies more efficiently, and new areas of the electromagnetic spectrum that were once unusable have been opened up to new communication services.

The Feasibility of Loop Service

For MCI's proposal to work there needed to be some way to connect the MCI microwave system to the local telephone exchanges (a *loop*). Common carriers opposing MCI's entry argued the loop service was not technically feasible and there was no provision in their tariff to provide such service. Moreover, the common carriers said they would not voluntarily provide loop service. Again ruling in favor of MCI, the commission said since carriers would not voluntarily provide loop service, they would retain jurisdiction over the proceeding and that MCI could return to the commission with a request to order interconnection. Absent a showing that interconnection was not technically feasible, the order to provide loop service would be in the public interest.

Issue by issue, the FCC ruled in favor of MCI. In sometimes almost defiant language the FCC came down on the side of a company that wanted to compete with a huge national telephone system. As if they could not control the giants within the framework of regulation and antitrust, they moved in an area where they did have jurisdiction—the opening up of new competition. The issue was significant enough that the three commissioners who voted against MCI's application, including the chairman of the FCC, issued or joined in dissenting opinions.

Dissenting and Separate Opinions

The dissenting opinions are worthy of note, not only for their policy implications but their language. FCC Chairman Rosel H. Hyde called the decision "diametrically opposed to sound economic and regulatory principles." He asked why the FCC condoned this "obviously grossly inefficient use" of the electromagnetic spectrum.

> Because, they say, of low cost and flexibility. . . . For no other reason than that it is proposing a typical "cream-skimming" operation. . . . The effect of the majority decision is to destroy the principle of nationwide average ratemaking. . . . This entire case is a classic example of an inefficient, uneconomic misallocation of resources.[45]

Another dissent came from Commissioner Robert E. Lee in which Commissioner James J. Wadsworth joined. Lee stated: "A common carrier must be held to a very high standard of public service which is even greater than that required of a broadcaster." Arguing the interconnection issue, Lee wrote: "It is inconceivable that the Commission is now going to permit (a microwave system) to be built which is of no use to the public without interconnection. I think we have put the cart before the horse."

Of the opinions issued with the decision, none was more colorful than that of Nicholas Johnson, who voted with the majority in support of MCI, and who during his term on the FCC was an outspoken critic of the commission, a consumer advocate, and noteworthy for his colorful prose. When he left the commission a *Broadcasting* magazine editorial said "Good Riddance."[46] On this occasion, he probably garnered the same feelings from the common carriers. Commissioner Johnson wrote:

> What do the proponents of regulation fear about this radical experiment with competition? "Cream skimming." Once an honorable enough agricultural undertaking, the expression is now used as an economic pejorative. . . .
>
> The telephone rate system is riddled with subsidies. In the first place, the telephone company itself deals in cream skimming. The really high-cost low-revenue subscribers—those who live in rural America—would never have had telephone service had they waited for Bell to ring. They had to get government assistance through the Rural Electrification Administration, their own cooperative telephone services, and non-Bell microwave carriers. In the second place, Bell has notoriously undercharged for those services in which it is engaged in competition—making up the difference by soaking those subscribers over whom it has a monopoly. . . .
>
> We can never know that a new product or service offered in the marketplace will become economically viable. Henry Ford couldn't know for sure. We cannot know for sure about MCI. . . .
>
> But I am not satisfied with the job the FCC has been doing. And I am still looking, at this juncture, for ways to add a little salt and pepper of competition to the rather tasteless stew of regulatory protection that this Commission and Bell have cooked up.[47]

And so, ten years after *Above 890*, the nation and its telecommunication industries and regulators had stepped into a new arena of services. Within 12 months after its decision in the MCI application, 37 additional applicants filed for permission to construct facilities and to operate as specialized common carriers. Ten of those applications came from companies associated with MCI, and one was for a nationwide system estimated at $350,000,000 in direct competition with the Bell system.[48] Although inviting litigation, in 1971 the FCC announced a policy formally opening the gates to entry by specialized common carriers stating,

> there are grounds for a reasonable expectation that new entry will have some beneficial effects, and there is no reason to anticipate that new entry would have any adverse impact. . . . We further find that a general policy in favor of the entry of new carriers in the specialized communications field would serve the public interest, convenience and necessity.[49]

MCI AND EXECUNET: COMPETITION IN LONG-DISTANCE SERVICES

MCI moved ahead aggressively in providing services as a specialized common carrier. The industry, the FCC, and the courts realized that microwaves, not just copper wires, were an alternative transport system for communication. The latter had been a major premise upon which the Bell system was able to argue, especially with its manufacturing arm, Western Electric, that Bell alone could best handle the nation's telephone needs. Through affiliated companies MCI was operating a long-distance point-to-point service nationwide by the mid-1970s with a service called "Execunet," an early direct-dial long-distance service. A customer would contact the local exchange service with one number, then punch in a customer number, then the area code and calling number of the telephone in the distant city. By using the local exchange service, MCI had its own long-distance network, even though it took the dialing of more numbers to access the system.

The First Phase of Litigation

The ability to introduce and keep Execunet in the market occurred by way of the *Execunet* decision giving MCI and others the go-ahead in the private long-distance market, even in the face of early FCC opposition.[50] The *Execunet* decision, issued by the court of appeals for the District of Columbia, overturned an earlier FCC decision that required MCI to cease and desist from offering and operating the Execunet service.[51] The decision of the appeals court showed the uncertainty and contradiction that gripped the FCC in this early era of regulation, and spoke briefly to the prospect of an

AT&T monopoly. When MCI began offering Execunet, AT&T took the unusual initiative of subscribing to the service and then apparently having AT&T representatives approach individual FCC commissioners and FCC staff through ex parte contacts. AT&T then filed a complaint outlining its allegations.[52] The FCC forwarded the AT&T complaint letter to MCI saying comments would be appreciated. MCI responded saying Execunet was a "private-line" service it was permitted to offer and that AT&T's complaint was untimely and should be rejected. It complained of the ex parte lobbying by AT&T, pointed out that MCI's licenses were not limited by FCC rules, and pointed to AT&T's comments in a previous proceeding (Docket 19117) in which AT&T took the position that the FCC "had no statutory authority to require prior approval of new services that were to be offered over existing facilities of a domestic carrier, but instead could regulate such services, if at all, only under the tariff provisions of the Communications Act."[53] MCI also contended that the report in Docket 19117 said new services could be offered by merely filing a tariff.

The FCC responded without holding a hearing or disclosing the details of AT&T's argument by sending MCI a letter telling the specialized carrier that its "tariff F.C.C. No. 1 is hereby rejected insofar as it purports to offer Execunet service . . ."[54] The FCC said it could only offer private-line services under existing facilities, stating: "In encouraging multiple entry and the development of competition in the supply of domestic communications, we have maintained a distinction between the so-called monopoly switched telephone services now being furnished by AT&T and all other classes of existing and potential specialized services."[55] MCI, the FCC said, sought authorization to offer only private-line services, and that it was granted authority to offer only such services. MCI immediately sought relief, finding it in the District of Columbia Circuit Court, which ruled that the FCC had failed to comply with the Administrative Procedures Act. FCC hearings were held, but under the watchful eye of the District of Columbia Circuit Court, which had obtained jurisdiction in the matter. When the hearings concluded another FCC opinion emerged and again MCI was not authorized to offer the Execunet service.

Final Opinion on Appeal

When the District of Columbia Appeals Court issued its opinion, the FCC was again overturned. The appeals court pointed to the FCC's "novel" interpretations of the rules and approach to the issue. In a commentary of the FCC's procedures, the justices wrote:

> The fact that an administrative practice is novel does not, of course, mean that it is wrong. However, novelty is a warning signal that all may not be well, especially in the instant case in which the Commission has itself failed to discuss the statutory warrant for the new course it has adopted. When the Communications Act is considered in detail, it becomes apparent that novelty has led to error in this case.[56]

The cream-skimming issue arose again, whereby the specialized common carriers would only set up business in the most lucrative areas, thereby "cream-skimming" income, while more established carriers would be left to service less profitable routes. The appeals court reasoned that as the cream-skimming issue was not relevant to the original MCI decision, it for most purposes did not apply here either. Referring to the FCC's earlier rulings covering specialized common carriers, the appeals court reiterated the thrust of the specialized common carrier ruling, stating:

> In granting the facilities authorizations on the basis that public interest finding, the Commission did not perhaps intend to open the field of common carrier communications generally, but its constant stress on the fact that specialized carriers would provide news, innovative, and hitherto unheard-of communications services clearly indicates that it had no very clear idea of precisely how far or to what services the field should be opened . . .
>
> Because the Commission has not so far determined that the public interest would be served by creating an AT&T monopoly . . . , it may not properly draw any inferences about the public interest from the bare fact that another carrier's proposed services would compete in that field.[57]

An Emerging Issue of AT&T Monopoly

In its concluding statement the appeals court backed itself into the issue of an AT&T monopoly stating:

> The Commission has no general authority to insist that carriers receive its approval before

> filing tariffs proposing new services or rates. Only if the Commission has determined that the public convenience and necessity may require that new services receive advance approval can it then reject a tariff as unauthorized. In so holding we have not had to consider, and have not considered, whether competition like that posed by Execunet is in the public interest. That will be the question for the Commission to decide should it elect to continue these proceedings. In that eventuality the Commission must be ever mindful that, just as it is not free to create competition for competition's sake, it is not free to propagate monopoly for monopoly's sake. The ultimate test of industry structure in the communications common carrier field must be the public interest, not the private financial interests of those who have until now enjoyed the fruits of de facto monopoly.[58]

Even after the appeals court decision telling MCI that it could continue its Execunet service, the FCC the following year ruled that AT&T did not need to offer connecting service to a specialized common carrier offering similar services to AT&T's long-distance services. Again the appeals court reversed the commission. Finally, after AT&T agreed to offer interconnection service at negotiated rates, the FCC ruled that the long-distance services that had been in contention in the MCI cases could now be offered on a competitive basis. Moreover, the issue of a monopoly was not something confined to the appeals court or the FCC.

THE PREDIVESTITURE ANTITRUST ACTION

Three years earlier in 1974 another antitrust suit had been brought against AT&T, Western Electric, and Bell Labs. The mood of the Department of Justice, the position of the courts, and of competitors was articulated years later:

> . . . for thirty years . . . , the Congress, the courts, the Federal Communications Commission, and state regulators wrestled with the problem of what to do about the Bell System monopoly, its arrogance in dealing with competitors and consumers, and its power to shut out competition. One Department of Justice lawsuit was filed and aborted; regulators issued edicts that were largely ignored; Congress investigated but could not come to a decision; and a second federal lawsuit and several private actions were filed in the courts where they remained pending for a number of years. In the meantime, competitors languished and the American ideal of free and fair competition remained absent from the telecommunications industry. When ultimately the decree that governs this case was negotiated between the parties and approved by the Court, it resolved the problem of claimed monopolistic conduct in telecommunications by going to its root.
>
> That root was the control by the Bell System in the local telephone switches—in which it had a monopoly—and its simultaneous presence in several other markets (long-distance, telecommunications manufacturing, and information services)—in which it had competitors. The competitors in each of these markets were suffering from an insuperable disadvantage: they could reach their ultimate customers only by connecting their circuits and products to the Bell System's local switches, the only technologically available avenue to the homes, offices, and factories of America where the individual telephone instruments are located. It followed that these competitors were at the mercy of the Bell System's managers, who could with ease discriminate against them by charging exorbitant prices, or refusing to attach competitors' products altogether. The Bell System was also able to subsidize its competitive products with funds syphoned off from the monies paid in by the ratepayers, thus to undercut the prices charged by independent firms and drive them out of business.
>
> The quite predictable result was that no independent long-distance manufacturing, or information company really got off the ground: for practical purposes, the Bell monopoly remained just that.[59]

In January 1982, after an eight-year battle, a settlement was announced that changed the face of the American telephone industry.

ISSUING THE MODIFIED FINAL JUDGMENT

In the settlement, the Justice Department called for separating local exchange carriers from the long-distance network, AT&T. Later that same year a

"Modification of Final Judgement," commonly called the MFJ, was approved by U.S. District Court Judge Harold Greene. As part of the MFJ, AT&T was permitted to keep Western Electric as its equipment supplier, its long lines, Bell Labs as its research arm, and the terminal equipment used for long-distance interconnections. AT&T divested itself of its local operations. The Bell companies were separated from AT&T, and long-distance communication was opened up to more competition. The 22 Bell operating companies (BOCs) were regrouped into seven regional holding companies (RHCs), which consist of: Pacific Telesis Group covering California and the lower western states; US West, which includes the northwestern states as well as much of the upper Midwest and some of the lower Southwest; Southwestern Bell Corporation, which covers Texas and the lower Midwest; BellSouth, which covers the Southeast; Bell Atlantic, which includes the Middle Atlantic states; and NYNEX, which includes New England.[60] The RHCs could provide, but not manufacture, new equipment for use in the home. The RHCs also inherited the assets, powers, and the obligations under the MFJ of the 22 Bell operating companies.

Equipment already installed at the time of the MFJ remained with AT&T and AT&T could provide new equipment. AT&T shareholders retained stock in the parent company and were assigned a proportionate interest in the local companies. With the consent decree, the competitors of AT&T were given access to the local exchanges. AT&T in turn was free to offer consumers equipment that could be rented or purchased and used in connection with local or long-distance telephone systems.[61]

REVISING THE MFJ

Gradually, through triannual reviews, various provisions of the MFJ began to be rescinded by Judge Greene. Of particular interest to broadcasters and the newspaper publishers was the information provider provision of the MFJ that kept the RHCs from becoming involved in developing the content of electronic data bases, such as electronic newspapers. In addition, the development of fiber-optic cable, which permitted large amounts of information to be carried over tiny glass fibers, meant that given the go-ahead and the technology, the telephone companies could eventually engage in the delivery of video information. Although still mandated by the Communications Act to provide universal telephone service, broadcasters and newspaper publishers saw the telephone companies as a threat. Major lobbying efforts by the American Newspaper Publishers Association (ANPA) were complimented by concerns expressed by the National Association of Broadcasters. The RHCs meanwhile engaged in their own lobbying and education program to get some of the restrictions of the original MFJ lifted.

Permitting Entry into Nontelecommunications Services

The 1987 triannual review of the MFJ resulted in the removal of the restriction over RHCs operating nontelecommunication businesses without the approval of Judge Greene's court. The original MFJ restricted entry into nontelecommunications enterprises unless a waiver was granted, which virtually all were upon petitioning of the court. The onslaught of waiver requests, however, took the court by surprise. Dozens of far-reaching requests were filed.

Judge Greene's court had imposed four conditions upon the granting of waivers: new businesses of the RHCs had to be operated through separate subsidiaries; the RHC's subsidiary had to obtain its own debt financing on its own credit; the total net revenue pursuant to the enterprise granted under the waiver could not be more than 10 percent of the RHC's total net revenues; and the subsidiary could be monitored by the court. The restrictions were designed to protect against cross-subsidization, whereby telephone company revenues could be used to subsidize the new enterprise. Also necessary was the assurance that the telephone company would not neglect its commitment to universal telephone service in favor of more glamorous enterprises.

Lifting of the restrictions on entry into nontelecommunications businesses was based on a number of rationales. For one, the court found itself granting the waivers anyway, so having a hurdle of court approval became unnecessary. In addition, the waiver process placed a burden on the planning and decision making of the RHCs. The new businesses did not appear to be resulting in questions of antitrust law, which was the primary thrust of the original restrictions. Of continuing concern to the court was the possibility that the RHCs in their desire to diversify would concentrate their efforts on the "more glamorous, albeit more speculative" businesses to the neglect of the traditional telephone operations. If that became the case, then the court suggested that either Congress or the FCC would see its way clear to address the problem.

The rationale for the removal of the non-telecommunication business restrictions seemed almost as significant as the restrictions themselves. For one, the FCC had been cited in other decisions, including the 1987 review, for its lack of effectiveness in policing the abuses that had plagued the telephone industry. One official, who headed the Common Carrier Bureau of the FCC between 1974 and 1978, who worked for the section of the FCC in charge of regulating the Bell System, testified: "I didn't feel that . . . we were at all effective in . . . controlling competitive practices or creating an environment for really full and fair competition," and "that, for a variety of reasons, there was a special regulatory void with respect to the Operating Companies."[63] Second, it was doubtful that after fighting the Department of Justice, decades of antitrust litigation, the MFJ, and the complexities of common carrier regulation and deregulation, Congress wanted to get too deeply involved in this regulatory arena. Even after the restrictions on electronic publishing were lifted, the cries of foul by the ANPA did not produce legislation. Judge Greene himself had been the target of lobbying campaigns, unusual in their intensity and in the fact they were directed at him by name. It was clear during this era that the outcome of his triannual reviews was so uncertain that lobbyists felt they had a significant chance of influencing him through the press as much as they did through the filing of briefs.

Removing Restrictions on the Entry of Information Providers

Another significant restriction lifted in the 1987 triannual review was the ability of RHCs to offer "gateway" entry to information providers. Judge Greene pointed to the potential public interest served by the development of a national videotex system, a concept then already operational in such countries as France and Japan. Judge Greene's review pointed to the arguments that the success of foreign systems was linked to the basic government ownership of the telephone network and the subsidies provided for allied services. In the United States, unlike France, there did not exist easy access by consumers. The typical consumer in America who wanted to link up to a remote data base needed a home computer, a modem, subscription to the remote data service, an account number, an access code, and knowledge of how to negotiate the menu to gain access to the desired information. Government subsidy was not seen as a viable solution to the development of easy access or system development. Moreover, the French government's subsidies were seen as difficult to replicate in the United States and would amount to basic telephone company subsidies. Although the possibility of such subsidies was not ruled out, it was not considered a feasible solution to the current problem. What did appear necessary, however, was the need to jump start the use of an infrastructure for a national videotex service. After all, one could argue from a global perspective that if information has value, then to compete internationally the United States needed to develop its own information system and be able to integrate this system with other parts of the world. Judge Greene stated:

> After considering the subject in some detail and with great care, the Court has become convinced, first, that, if the authority of the Regional Companies is carefully limited, the risk of anticompetitive action by these companies, while not insignificant, is, on balance, outweighed by other considerations; second, that the broad scale and the reasonable cost criteria necessary for a successful system can be met only by permitting the Regional Companies to provide the necessary infrastructure components for efficient videotex services on an integrated basis; and third, that it is probable that a well-run, adequately publicized system could perform a useful service, and that it might attract a sufficient number of subscribers so that it could operate on an economically sound basis.[64]

Gateway entry for information providers was provided, but for the time being, the restriction remained on the RHCs originating their own information. For anyone understanding the technology, the ability of the court to decide cases on the basis of antitrust issues *and* the public interest, some phrases in Judge Greene's decision stood out: "Accordingly, the Court will, in the present context, once again take into account values, in addition to . . . an environment free of anticompetitive (activity) . . . " He stated that divestiture was not an exercise in "abstract reasoning." It had as its "fundamental purpose the promotion of competition in the telecommunications market, to the end that the (public) might benefit from today's and tomorrow's telecommunications technology in this information age."[65]

Lifting Restrictions on Electronic Publishing

Judge Greene later lifted the restriction and allowed the RHCs to offer information services that would compete with traditional print media.[66] Under his own court-ordered stay, later criticized by the federal appeals court that lifted the stay in a 3-0 ruling, he opened the door to new electronic publishing ventures.[67] The group caught most off guard was the American Newspaper Publishers Association. Through their spokesperson and president-CEO Cathleen Black, the ANPA had tried to lobby Congress to pass legislation blocking the RHCs from getting into the information services business, sensing that a lifting of the restrictions was inevitable. When the restrictions were removed, Black was quoted as saying the phone companies "will be able to take advantage of [their] monopoly position to hamper other information services," and that the decision might "drive newspapers out of business."[68] The ANPA had earlier argued against the RHCs' involvement by claiming, among other things, that letting RHCs become information providers meant "ruling against fair competition and the rights of consumers."[69] The ANPA said they would still seek relief from the FCC, the courts, and state public utility commissions.

STATE REGULATIONS: PUBLIC UTILITY COMMISSIONS

Common carriers fall in a regulatory scheme shared by both federal and state government. Regulation generally falls under the authority of state public utility commissions.[70] State commissions are concerned with overseeing universal telephone service and an equitable rate base that is fair to the consumer and provides the common carrier with sufficient operating income and profit.

State public utility commissions—which go under different names such as *public service commission, department of public utilities, public service board,* and others—are mostly made up of three or five members, although some have seven. These state commissions are supported by staffs which handle the day-to-day activities of different departments such as rates, engineering, accounting, financial, and legal. Qualifications vary and run from age requirements, specific types of college degrees, and literacy, to more general requirements such as in South Carolina where appointment requires "the best qualified people." The backgrounds of commissioners vary greatly. Some are political appointees with no knowledge of public utilities or common carriers. Commissioners serve from four to ten years, depending on the state. Studies report that one in four does not have a college degree.[71] Legal training predominates with engineering second. Commissioners are bound together professionally by the National Association of Regulatory Commissioners, the membership of which extends to those working on federal commissions.

A continuing issue in common carrier regulation by state commissions is the issue of the commissions' independence.[72] For example, other branches of state government influence the work of state public utility commissions. In states where the governor appoints commissioners, the natural tendency may be to appoint commissioners who will fulfill the governor's own agenda, itself under the lobbying arm of the carriers themselves. Governors may also have the power to appoint the commission's chair, a key individual in setting the public and private agenda of a commission. Courts also play a role, since some commission decisions can be appealed. Courts, however, are confined to the review of matters of law, not findings of fact since the latter is within the administrative charge of the commission. State legislatures can control commission activity and jurisdiction through the passage of legislation and budget appropriations. Moreover, commissions can only enforce what they have been given the power to enforce. Some state legislatures have the power to review proposed rules and regulations and many legislatures have the power to confirm appointees.

STATE REGULATION OF RADIO COMMON CARRIERS

State regulatory commissions are involved in many different industries classified as public utilities and common carriers. Federal and state jurisdictions overlap in many of these areas. An example of state regulation of a common carrier affecting radio and telecommunications is a radio common carrier. The term *radio common carriers* under such a provision is defined by one state as:

> every corporation, company, association, partnership and person and lessees, trustees, or receivers, appointed by any court whatsoever owning, operating or managing a busi-

> ness of providing or offering a service for hire to the public of one-way or two-way radio or radio telephone communication whether interconnected with the land line telephone system or not and licensed by the Federal Communications Commission . . .[73]

While the FCC may issue a license to anyone using a two-way radio transmitter and receiver, and the design and manufacture of the transmitter and receiver must meet FCC specifications, a state can also regulate common carrier radio communication when it is deemed in the public interest and part of a service offering two-way radio communication for hire. An example of such a service would be a medical doctor whose communication service consists of two-way radios (beeper radios) and base station(s) used to communicate among members of a county medical society.[74] In addition, the state can regulate the rates charged by such a service, require that it issue a certificate of public convenience and necessity, and prescribe "appropriate and reasonable rules and regulations" governing the issuance of such certificates. The state may also protect other radio common carriers, who were in business first and serving the same area as a new applicant, by requiring a showing that the service already in operation is inadequate.

STATE REGULATION OF TELEPHONE CARRIERS

Although historically the FCC was concerned with regulating interstate telephone and states with regulating intrastate telephone, the distinctions have become blurred as some local exchange carriers are offering interconnection services that make them long-distance carriers. Some also offer cellular service. States have adopted for their own regulatory structure the rules and regulations used by the FCC for interstate carriers.[75] In some cases the wording of the state utility commission's regulations is similar, or exactly the same, as those of the FCC.

Uniform System of Accounts, Construction Plans, and Tariffs

Most notable among state regulations is the Uniform System of Accounts as prescribed by the Federal Communications Commission. Excerpted from the unabridged provisions are the following requirements, which offer a perspective on the way states attempt to regulate local exchange carriers:

> Each local exchange carrier with nonregulated operations shall provide to the Public Staff two copies of its cost allocation plan or cost allocation practices relating to the allocation of joint costs between regulated and nonregulated operations. Subsequent updates and revisions shall be provided within 30 days of implementation.
>
> Each local exchange carrier shall provide the Public Staff with two copies of its list of accounts and subsidiary record codes by name and number together with a brief description of each. Subsequent updates and revisions shall be provided within 30 days of implementation.
>
> Accounting records shall be maintained in a manner such that a reasonable audit trail exists with respect to all affiliated company transactions . . .[76]

Telephone companies can also be required to file construction plans, objectives, and capital expenditures. Such information is designed to give the state public commission

> . . . an overall understanding of the company's primary service objectives, its plans for major service improvements or extensions, an outline of its plans for introducing new services, new exchanges, or new service areas, its anticipated plant and customer growth, and its anticipated technological changes in rendering or extending service. The statement shall represent the company's best estimate and most current view of those construction activities required for the immediate future. The statement may be conditioned to reflect revisions based on changed conditions and demands, altered priorities, and progress on projects underway but not completed. A narrative discussion of such plans, objectives, and contingencies may be included. To the extent practicable, projects for service improvements shall be listed by exchanges for location purposes. Internal construction budgets which contain the same, or substantially the same, information required to be filed by this rule may be submitted in substitution, in whole or in part . . .[77]

Tariffs are filed by a common carrier to register the rates it will charge consumers. Every consumer must then be charged the same rate. For example, the toll charge to call between two cities for a given amount of time is the same no matter who uses the telephone. Each regulated telephone company is required to have on file with the state commission a copy of its tariffs. It addition to the tariff, a map showing the service area covered by the telephone company can be used to show areas where a flat rate applies and outer areas where toll charges apply. Changes in rate structures must be filed and approved by the state commission with jurisdiction over the service area. Although not a tariff per se, state commissions require 911 emergency numbers to be available in service areas where they are technologically feasible.

Connection Subsidy Programs

Some areas have programs where low-income households are eligible for reduced rates and therefore are able to obtain telephone service. These assistance programs provide important communication links for the elderly, the infirm, mothers with dependent children, and other people under social welfare programs. Such programs provide a reduction in the charges for installation and a deferred payment schedule. Verification of eligibility can be achieved through income tax statements or by social welfare agencies.

Extended Area Service

Extended area service (EAS) connects two or more telephone exchanges together; thus, flat rate calling is permitted between the exchanges. For example, local exchange telephone companies A, B, and C provide exclusive service to three different adjoining communities. The Chambers of Commerce of the three communities get together and petition the state public utility commission to offer EAS. If granted, the residents of any community can call the other two communities for the same flat rate. Support for EAS service can consist of surveys, resolutions, letters from civic groups, elected officials, and other affected subscribers. Public hearings may add further evidence to the request. Polling of affected subscribers can also be used and a simple majority of valid ballots will result in the approval of EAS service. Commissions usually disregard geographic area as a precondition and stress instead the public-interest dimensions of the case.

Service Objectives and Financial Data

Each regulated local exchange service falls under prescribed objectives for service. Examples of typical service objectives are:

Description	Objective
Direct distance dialing completion	95 percent
Operator "0" answer time	90 percent within 10 seconds
Directory assistance answer time	85 percent within 10 seconds
Public paystations out-of-order	10 percent maximum

To make intelligent decisions about rate structures, service, and other matters, state commissions also require basic financial data on local exchange operations. A company balance sheet, income statements for the current and prior year, depreciation reserves, analysis of salaries and wages, long-term debt interest charges, preferred stock issuances and dividends, and miscellaneous information on access lines, number of employees, and stock dividends are required.

Resale of Telephone Services

The next time you see a notice in a store window for a public FAX machine, you may see the cost of using the FAX in bold letters near the machine. Those bold letters may fulfill a requirement of a state regulation for people offering FAX services to the public, which is the resale of a telephone service.

Other locations of resale of telephone services are also available, such as hotels, restaurants, nursing homes, rest homes, licensed retirement homes, private clubs or student living quarters furnished by educational institutions, temporarily subleased residential premises, and some other types of businesses. Wherever a resale arrangement is available, it is governed by tariffs and the state utility commission. Certain contract requirements also exist between the provider and the end user. Typical provisions in such a contract include:

(a) A statement of the terms and conditions of service including current rates and termination charges, if any;

(b) A statement that the user may obtain service directly from the local telephone company;

(c) The name and telephone number of a representative of the provider to whom complaints should be addressed;

(d) A statement that the user may submit unresolved complaints about quality of service to the Utilities Commission;

(e) A statement that at least thirty days written notice will be given prior to any rate increase;

(f) A statement that the contract shall be voidable at the option of the end-user and without further liability to the end-user if the contract is breached by the reseller or sharer;

(g) A statement specifying when rates may be changed and the amount of increase that may be imposed during the contract period;

(h) A statement that rates, charges, payment arrangements, rules on disconnection and deposit requirements are not regulated by the . . . Utilities Commission . . .[78]

Advertising and Bill Inserts

With the increased flexibility of business operations, nontelecommunications enterprises, political campaigns, competing exchange and long-distance services, the opportunity to use the monthly telephone statement as an advertising and marketing device increases substantially. State commissions have established rules for such inserts to try to prevent abuse. Statements saying "This Message Is Not Paid for by the Customers" are required. Capital letters are legally required for nonutility advertisements used as bill inserts. Telephone companies are required to keep expense records associated with such advertising for three years from the date the bill insert was last disseminated. In attempts to prevent cross-subsidization, telephone companies are prohibited from recovering from rate payers any direct expenditure for the printing, distribution, handling, or mailing of the nonutility advertisements.

SEPARATIONS AND ACCESS

The complexity of regulation surrounding common carriers engaged in telecommunication has centered around the issue of separations and access. Separations mean the way costs are "separated" between the long-distance carriers and the local telephone exchanges. Access is concerned with who has access to the system. The issue of separations and access can be understood more clearly with the following example.

The Difficulty of Determining Separations

Assume two cities in different states are connected by only one highway and access to the highway is gained by a series of interchanges at different cities along the route. The interchanges and access ramps were built inside the city limits and the cities operate the toll booths at each interchange. When travelers want to use the highway, they get on at the nearest local interchange and get off when they reach their destination. Sometimes their route is short and the travel is all within one state. The toll is also less than that charged for using the highway for longer trips. Now ask yourself, of all the money which is collected at the various interchanges, who gets what amount?

We could argue that if all the travel is within one state, then that state should get all of the toll. But what if travel took us through both states, how should the toll be allocated? Perhaps it could be proportioned among the interchanges along the route, but only two of the interchanges were used, the one where we entered and the one where we exited. Also, how should the toll be allocated among the cities that built the interchanges? Should the exit and entry interchanges divide the toll? Should the busiest interchanges get the most money or should more money be allocated to the state(s) whose road links the two busiest interchanges?

Even though the states did not build the interchanges, the cities that operate those busy interchanges are feeding more traffic onto the highway and causing more wear. Shouldn't the state with the busiest section of road get a higher percentage of tolls? If more wear is occurring, should the states, which must repair the highway, get more, and the cities get less? We must also ask who will make the final determination on the allocation of tolls. Will it be the states? The cities that control the interchanges? The federal government, which also contributes funds for the construction and maintenance of the highways?

Distributing Costs and Revenues

The complexity of these issues is analogous to the way telephone systems determine how costs between local exchanges and long-distance carriers are allocated, in addition to determining who will gain access to the system. As an historical example, the Bell System offered telephone service on both an interstate and intrastate basis.[79] Interstate calls were regulated by the FCC, and intrastate calls were regulated by state public utility commissions. AT&T's Long Lines Department provided interstate and overseas telephone services. Local telephone companies and Bell operating companies, because they provided access to AT&T lines, were engaged in both types of service. A local long-distance call needed both the services of the local telephone company to connect the customer and AT&T to complete the long-distance call. Such elements as initial costs of the system, depreciation, income, and access were not easily determined, let alone regulated. Gradually the states and federal government developed a way of allocating costs, called separations procedures. Sampling the number and types of calls during a specific time period and estimating total usage was one way of allocating tolls and costs. As Phillips details:

> For settlements within the Bell System, all revenue collected from interstate operations were pooled each month, and expenses and taxes allocated to interstate operations for each company were repaid to them out of those revenue. The remaining net revenues, which represented the amount for return, were distributed to the Long Lines Department and the operating companies on the basis of the net investment each contributed to the total net investment of interstate services. If the Long Lines Department, for example, provided 35 percent of the total net investment, it would receive 35 percent of the remaining net revenues.[80]

After divestiture and with the advent of new competition in the industry, the separations procedures remain controversial. With many carriers competing for long-distance business, with many local telephone companies still needing to offer customer access to their exchanges, costs have been transferred to end users. To some degree such costs, while remaining controversial, provide stability to the system, accounting efficiency, cost allocations, and regulatory oversight.

FEDERAL REGULATION OF TELEPHONE COMMON CARRIERS

With the exception of the judiciary's oversight role, and antitrust issues that fall under the Department of Justice, the federal government's regulation of telephone is through the Common Carrier Bureau of the FCC. Federal control of common carriers is approached from a different regulatory perspective than other communication technologies such as broadcasting or cable. Control of broadcasting is based on the assumption that there is a limited amount of space on the electromagnetic spectrum and licenses are awarded to those individuals who promise to operate in the public interest.

While we may all listen to radio or watch television, few of us ever buy advertising on these media and fewer still own a station. Common carriers such as telephones, however, are used by everyone. Unlike broadcasting, they developed as a regulated monopoly. Today, telephone companies are corporations in transition. They are moving away from their traditional roles as providers of telephone service only to multifaceted conglomerates involved in both telecommunications and nontelecommunications businesses. Despite this diversity, however, the FCC retains control over their common carrier functions. That control ranges over such areas as filing tariffs, governing interlocking directorates, extension of lines and service, dealing with foreign governments, and requiring standardized accounting procedures called the Uniform System of Accounts.

Tariff Filings

Tariffs are filed by telephone companies before any business can be conducted for which the public can be charged a fee. The FCC must approve the tariff before a new service can be offered or rates can be imposed. FCC rules require that all tariffs, along with meeting clerical standards such as the size of paper, must include in a letter of transmittal the name and address of the carrier, the date and transmittal number, and the date upon which the tariff will take effect if approved by the commission. Tariffs must also include a cost analysis with projected expenses and revenue over the next 12-month period. The FCC may designate the tariff filing for an investigation before it is approved; thus, the tariff filing is also the carrier's best case and must be complete with enough supporting documents to withstand the investigation.

For private-line rate structures, the commission uses a variety of criteria to approve private-line tariffs. Private-line rate structures have the best chance of being approved when they comply with the following five guidelines:

(1) Rate structures for the same or comparable services should be integrated;

(2) Rate structures for the same or comparable services should be consistent with one another.
(3) Rate elements should be selected to reflect market demand, pricing convenience for the carrier and customers, and cost characteristics; a rate element which appears separately in one rate structure should appear separately in all other rate structures;
(4) Rate elements should be consistently defined with respect to underlying service functions and should be consistently employed through all rate structures; and
(5) Rate structures should be simple and easy to understand.[81]

Carriers are justified in departing from the guidelines, but must still show that its tariff is "just, reasonable, and nondiscriminatory." A list of connecting or other participating carriers must also be included. Carriers which are concurring in the tariff filing of another carrier must file a statement of concurrence reflecting the rates and regulations governing "through service."

Interlocking Directorates

The commission defines officers and directors, interlocking directors, and commonly owned carriers as follows:

> (a) "Officer or director" shall include the duties, or any of the duties, ordinarily performed by a director, president, vice president, secretary, treasurer, or other officer of a carrier such as general counsel, general solicitor, general attorney, comptroller, general auditor, general manager, general commercial manager, chief engineer, general superintendent, general land and tax agent, or chief purchasing agent;
>
> (b) "Interlocking director" shall mean a person who performs the duties of "officer or director" in more than one carrier . . .
>
> (c) "Commonly owned carriers" shall mean two or more carriers, one of which directly or indirectly owns more than 50 percent of the stock of the other carrier or carriers, or 50 percent of more of whose stick is owned directly or indirectly by the same person.[82]

FCC rules prohibit a person holding the position of officer or director in more than one carrier unless special permission is obtained from the commission. Affected carriers are those which have been found by the commission to have market power and are defined as *dominant carriers*, or where a designation has not been made but where a carrier has *not* been found to be nondominant. Some exceptions to this requirement do exist for cellular phone licensees. Special provisions also exist when two or more carriers are commonly owned.

Extension of Lines and Discontinuance of Service

Federal regulations require the monitoring of a carrier's expansion or discontinuance of service.[83] A carrier proposing to construct a new line or extend an existing line must show how the proposed construction or extension will service the "public interest, convenience, and necessity." In addition, information contained in the filing must include the points between which the proposed facilities are to be located and a description of the applicant's existing facilities between these points. Other information required by the commission includes the number of circuits proposed and the estimated load demand on those circuits. Basic topographical information must show terrain, cities and towns, populations, state boundaries, important operating centers, repeaters, and relay points. Where lease facilities are being used, details of the lease agreement must be included in the filing. Economic justification for the expansion must be made and a cost analysis including estimated revenues are required. If the construction will have a significant impact on the environment, then an environmental statement must accompany the filing.

Discontinuance, reduction, or impairment of service also requires a filing with the FCC.[84] Approval must be obtained before such action can be taken by the carrier. Exceptions exist for emergencies where less formal requests can be made. Emergency requests must include the nature and estimated duration of interrupted service, the effect upon rates, the nature of substituted service, and how original service will be restored as "expeditiously as possible." Similar requests to those used in emergencies apply to the discontinuance of service at military installations because of deactivation.

THE UNIFORM SYSTEM OF ACCOUNTS

Telephone companies developed as regulated monopolies. Even with their ability to engage in nonregulated telecommunications enterprises, their common carrier operations remain under federal control. For the government to be able to approve tariffs and assure universal service, telephone companies must provide extensive and detailed financial information about their operations. Called the Uniform System of Accounts, this financial picture contains a breakdown of items that permit the FCC to conduct an ongoing audit of the carrier's fiscal health. Hundreds of categories exist in the total account breakdown the FCC requires of the telephone industry. Categories include those directly relating to telecommunications, that is, from "repairs of pole lines," to such categories as "rest and lunch rooms expenses," "door checks and door stops," and "fences and hedges." The following partial breakdown of primary account categories shows just some of the information required by the FCC.[85]

Depreciation	Retained Earnings
Operating Income	Fixed Charges
Local and Toll Revenues	Operating Revenues
Operating Expenses	Office Salaries
Investments	Current Assets
Stock	Long-Term Debt
Current Liabilities	Accrued Liabilities
Telephone Plant Accounts	Deferred Credits

A further breakdown of just two of the preceding categories, Operating Revenue Accounts and Operating Expense Accounts, shows some of the subcategories of information required.

- OPERATING REVENUE ACCOUNTS
  - Local Service Revenues
    - Subscribers' station revenues.
    - Public telephone revenues.
    - Service stations.
    - Local private-line services.
    - Other local service revenues.
    - Interstate access revenues.
    - End-user revenues.
    - Carrier's carrier facilities revenues.
    - Special access revenues.
    - Intrastate access revenue.
  - Toll Service Revenues
    - Message tolls
    - Wide-area toll services.
    - Toll private-line services.
    - Other toll service revenues.
  - Miscellaneous Revenues
    - Telegraph commissions.
    - Directory advertising and sales.
    - Rent revenues.
    - Revenues from general services and licenses.
    - Other operating revenues.
    - Uncollectible Revenues
- OPERATING EXPENSE ACCOUNTS
  - Maintenance Expenses
    - Repairs of pole lines.
    - Repairs of aerial cable.
    - Repairs of underground cable.
    - Repairs of buried cable.
    - Repairs of submarine cable.
    - Repairs of aerial wire.
    - Repairs of underground conduit.
    - Shop repairs and salvage adjustments.
    - Test desk work.
    - Repairs of central office equipment.
    - Installations and repairs of station equipment.
    - Repairs of buildings and grounds.
    - Repairs of public telephone equipment.
    - Depreciation.
    - Maintaining transmission power.
    - Employment stabilization.
    - Other maintenance expenses.
  - Depreciation and Amortization Expenses
    - Depreciation.
    - Extraordinary retirements.
    - Amortization of intangible property.
    - Amortization of telephone plant acquisition adjustment.
  - Traffic Expenses
    - General traffic supervision.
    - Service inspection and customer instruction.
    - Operators' wages.
    - Rest and lunch rooms.
    - Operators' employment and training.
    - Central office house services.
    - Miscellaneous central office expenses.
    - Public telephone expenses.
    - Other traffic expenses.
    - Joint traffic expenses.
  - Commercial Expenses
    - General commercial administration.
    - Advertising.

Sales expense.
Connecting company relations.
Local commercial operations.
Interstate billing and collection expenses.
Intrastate billing and collection expenses.
Public telephone commissions.
Directory expenses.
Other commercial expenses.
Interstate carrier's carrier expenses.
Intrastate carrier's carrier expenses.

General Office Salaries and Expenses
Executive department.
Accounting department.
Treasury department.
Law department.
Other general office salaries and expenses.

Other Operating Expenses
Insurance.
Accidents and damages.
Operating rents.
Relief and pensions.
Telephone franchise requirements.
Expenses charged to construction.

Interpretations of the accounting procedures, some dating back to 1936, remain as part of FCC regulations and can be used as a reference when questions arise. Interpretations, however, are not substitutes for the actual accounting system or the FCC rules that govern them. Typical of an interpretation is a case dated March 13, 1939 which reads:

> Question: What account shall be credited with amounts of interest which have accrued on advances from affiliated companies when such advances are classified as long-term debt?
>
> Answer: Amounts of such interest are includible in account 2400. "Accrued liabilities," until the interest becomes payable, at which time such amounts are includible in account 2320. "Accounts payable," first subdivision prescribed by paragraph (b), except that the amount of such interest payable as is not subject to current settlement shall be included in account 2250, "Advances from affiliated companies."[86]

Carriers are given some flexibility to develop temporary or experimental accounts. The experimental accounts cannot impair the integrity of the Uniform System of Accounts, and carriers earning in excess of $1 million must notify the FCC of the purpose and nature of the experimental or temporary accounts within 30 days after the accounts are activated. Carriers may subdivide accounts when required by a state public utility commission.

EXTENSION OF CREDIT FOR CANDIDATES FOR FEDERAL OFFICE

Section 401 of the Federal Election Campaign Act of 1971, Public Law 92-225, is incorporated into FCC rules and regulations governing common carriers.[87] The rules state the general conditions under which extension of unsecured credit by a common carrier can be granted to a candidate for federal office. The issue arises when campaign headquarters is being equipped, when cellular phones are being activated, and similar circumstances.[88]

Definitions

Similar to definitions governing political broadcasting, a *candidate* is defined as:

> . . . an individual who seeks nomination for election, or election, to Federal office, whether or not such individual is elected, and an individual shall be deemed to seek nomination for election, or election, if he has (1) taken the action necessary under the law of a State to qualify himself for nomination for election, or election, to Federal office, or (2) received contributions or made expenditures, or has given his consent for any other person to receive contributions or make expenditures, with a view to bringing about his nomination for election, or election, to such office.[89]

The terms *election, federal office, person,* and *unsecured credit* are defined as follows:

> (b) "Election" means (1) a general, special, primary, or runoff election, (2) a convention or caucus of a political party held to nominate a candidate, (3) a primary election held for the selection of delegates to a national nominating convention of a political party, and (4) a primary election held for the expression of a preference for the nomination of persons for election to the office of President.

> (c) "federal office" means the office of President or Vice President of the United States: or of Senator or Representative in, or Delegate or Resident Commissioner to, the Congress of the United States.
>
> (d) "Person" means an individual, partnership, committee, association, corporation, labor organization, and any other organization or group of persons.
>
> (e) "Unsecured credit" means the furnishing of service without maintaining on a continuing basis advance payment, deposit, or other security, that is designed to assure payment of the estimated amount of service for each future 2 months period, with revised estimates to be made on at least a monthly basis.[90]

Notice the definitions and rules are written to apply to candidates for *federal office*, and do not apply to candidates for any other office.

Rules Governing the Extension of Unsecured Credit

A carrier is not obligated to extend unsecured credit, but it can if it meets certain requirements. These requirements call for all candidates for the same federal office to also be extended unsecured credit. In other words, if a candidate running for Congress, a federal office, is afforded unsecured credit, that candidate's opponent(s) must also be afforded unsecured credit. Before the carrier can extend unsecured credit, FCC regulations require it must secure an application for service that identifies "the applicant and the candidate" and "must specify if the candidate assumes responsibility for the charges . . ." Regardless of whether the candidate accepts responsibility, the applicant must be liable for payment upon demand or the carrier can discontinue service.

Upon issuing a bill, if the carrier has not received payment at the end of a 15-day period, then the applicant must be notified within seven days of such notice that payment must be received within seven days or service will be discontinued. The carrier is further required to take appropriate action within the law to collect what is due. Reports to the FCC are also required listing the name of the candidate, name and address of the applicant, the balance due the carrier, the reason for nonpayment, payment arrangements, and the date the service was discontinued. In addition the carrier is responsible for reporting to the commission the date, nature, and status of any action under the law the carrier has undertaken to collect.

STATE AND FEDERAL REGULATORY PROBLEMS

Conflict can develop between state and federal control, and at issue is the ability of both to engage in meaningful regulatory oversight. For example, while a company such as Western Electric continues to play a role in telephone communications, the FCC has no control over it. RHCs are free to venture, almost without accountability, into nontelecommunications businesses. There is ample opportunity for cross-subsidization of these enterprises by using the income from common carrier regulated operations to subsidize nonregulated businesses. While the FCC has some control over the common carrier operations, they do not exercise control over all nontelecommunications businesses. Added to these complex issues is the fact that some aspects of the telephone industry come under federal jurisdiction and some under state commissions. Regional companies operate across state boundaries making oversight difficult. No one state is capable of being sufficiently apprised of the financial picture of an RHC operating in many different states.

Simply getting access to information upon which to make regulatory decisions can be difficult. For example, when the National Association of Regulatory Commissioners tried to conduct an audit of five RHCs (Bell Atlantic, BellSouth, US West, Ameritech, and Pacific Telesis), they met with limited success and faced attempts to block access to accounting and cost-allocation records. The information they received was of poor quality; the audit revealed customers of several RHCs had been forced to subsidize competitive subsidiaries of the RHCs, lines of service such as Yellow Pages had been transferred from the telephone companies to unregulated subsidiaries; and telephone income was transferred to parent RHCs.[91] The uncomfortable relationship between the telephone companies and state government is seen in comments from the 1987 triannual review of the MFJ:

> According to the Ohio Consumer's Counsel, Bell of Pennsylvania offered $100 million for state economic development in exchange for deregulation legislation . . . A recent comprehensive report of the operations of NYNEX complains about the inability of regulators

> over the opposition of NYNEX to secure financial data, to halt diversion of economies achieved by the regulated segment to the benefit of non-regulated operations, and similar problems . . . And the trade press reported recently that US West informed state regulators in its area that the location of its planned research laboratory would depend upon the fate of deregulation legislation or upon requested rate increases, a charge US West has denied.[92]

With further deregulation of common carrier telephone operations, the movement of the RHCs into new nontelecommunications enterprises, the lobbying effectiveness of telephone companies, joint ventures between telephone companies, and complex wired and unwired technologies offering new subscriber services, the ability to regulate these carriers may prove even more difficult and frustrating for federal and state governments in the future.

REGULATING ON-LINE INFORMATION SERVICES

On-line information services are an emerging area of law. Common carriers represent one aspect of this emerging area, but other dimensions exist as well. For example, a common carrier such as a telephone company can carry information between an on-line data base and a subscriber's home. All sorts of information can be carried over the phone lines, such as verbal communication between two people, facsimiles, photographs sent via picture phone or through facsimile, video and audio, and other forms of electronic communication. Much of that information is potentially libelous, in that the information disparages someone's good name and is arguably "published." On-line information services operate in a number of different ways and have different contractual relationships with both subscribers to their services, as well as suppliers of information. Unless there is a contractual relationship with the service that gives the company operating the on-line data base significant control over the information, then these on-line services are shielded from liability. One case arose when the on-line data base company, CompuServe, found itself a defendant in "a diversity action for libel, business disparagement, and unfair competition, all resulting from allegedly defamatory statements made in a publication carried on a computerized database."[93] The court ruled in favor of CompuServe's motion for summary judgment involving all claims asserted against it and in effect removed CompuServe as a defendant in the case.

The plaintiffs who brought libel and other actions claimed that on separate occasions Rumorville USA had allegedly published through its electronic newsletter allegedly false and defamatory statements about them and that CompuServe carried the statements. There was no "employment, contractual, or other direct relationship" with the codefendants. CompuServe had no opportunity to review the contents of the electronic newsletter before it was uploaded into CompuServe's computer banks. Also, CompuServe did not receive part of any fees that the codefendants charged its subscribers; instead receiving the standard on-line time usage fees from those people accessing the electronic newsletter. CompuServe also maintained that before this action was filed, it had no notice of any complaints about the contents of the electronic publication.

In finding in CompuServe's favor and removing it as a codefendant in the case, the court found:

> The requirement that a distributor must have knowledge of the contents of a publication before liability can be imposed for distributing that publication is deeply rooted in the First Amendment, made applicable to the states through the Fourteenth Amendment. "The constitutional guarantees of the freedom of speech and of the press stand in the way of imposing" strict liability on distributors for the contents of the reading materials they carry. *Smith v. California*, 361 U.S. 147, 152-53 (1959). In *Smith*, the Court struck down an ordinance that imposed liability on a bookseller for possession of an obscene book, regardless of whether the bookseller had knowledge of the book's contents. The Court reasoned that "Every bookseller would be placed under an obligation to make himself aware of the contents of every book in his shop. It would be altogether unreasonable to demand so near an approach to omniscience." And the bookseller's burden would become the public's burden, for by restricting him the public's access to reading matter would be restricted. If the contents of bookshops and periodical stands were restricted to material of which their proprietors had made an inspection, they might be depleted indeed. Although Smith involved criminal li-

ability, the First Amendment's guarantees are no less relevant to the instant action: "What a State may not constitutionally bring about by means of a criminal statute is likewise beyond the reach of its civil law of libel. The fear of damage awards . . . may be markedly more inhibiting than the fear of prosecution under a criminal statute."[94]

CompuServe's . . . product is in essence an electronic, for-profit library that carries a vast number of publications and collects usage and membership fees from its subscribers in return for access to the publications. CompuServe and companies like it are at the forefront of the information industry revolution. High technology has markedly increased the speed with which information is gathered and processed; it is now possible for an individual with a personal computer, modem, and telephone line to have instantaneous access to thousands of news publications from across the United States and around the world. While CompuServe may decline to carry a given publication altogether, in reality, once it does decide to carry a publication, it will have little or no editorial control over that publication's contents. This is especially so when CompuServe carries the publication as part of a forum that is managed by a company unrelated to CompuServe.

With respect to the Rumorville publication . . . CompuServe has no more editorial control over such a publication than does a public library, book store, or newsstand, and it would be no more feasible for CompuServe to examine every publication it carries for potentially defamatory statements than it would be for any other distributor to do so. "First Amendment guarantees have long been recognized as protecting distributors of publications. . . . Obviously, the national distributor of hundreds of periodicals has no duty to monitor each issue of every periodical it distributes. Such a rule would be an impermissible burden on the First Amendment."[95] (computerized database service "is one of the modern, technologically interesting, alternative ways the public may obtain up-to-the-minute news" and "is entitled to the same protection as more established means of news distribution").[96]

On other points of law, the court also rejected the claim of unfair competition and vicarious liability. The CompuServe case was one of the early actions to set a precedent for shielding an on-line data base from liability for the actions of companies who subcontracted with the data base to store information and then sell that information to subscribers.

The court did not decide on the issue of libel in this proceeding. That issue remained unresolved for the other defendants. The contractual relationship that existed did not give CompuServe control over the contents of the electronic newsletter, and that lack of control helped shield it from potential liability. In addition, the district court, in citing First Amendment law, made it clear that the issue of free press applied to this case, insofar as the distributor of the information was concerned.

SUMMARY

Regulation of common carriers dates back to the earliest days of the transportation industry when carriers were first obligated to make their services available to anyone who could pay the rate or fare. Gradually, telegraphs and telephones were added to the definition of common carrier, and regulation of these two technologies evolved from the Interstate Commerce Commission to the Federal Communications Commission. By 1910, federal law required just and reasonable rates be charged for services. Individual telephone and telegraph companies could enter into contracts for the exchange of services.

Telephones were originally leased, not sold, and from the invention of Alexander Graham Bell evolved a number of early corporations, the most prominent of which was the National Bell Telephone Company. Western Union also entered the telephone business, which resulted in years of patent battles between the two companies. Eventually, through an act of the Massachusetts legislature the dispute was settled. Western Union agreed to stay out of the telephone business and Bell agreed to stay out of the telegraph business. Long-distance telephone communication grew. Gradually, the Bell system was consolidated into the American Telephone and Telegraph Company (AT&T).

Because telephone companies were engaged in both intrastate and interstate communication, a dual regulatory framework developed with regulatory power shared between states and the federal government. First attempts to protect the Bell patents failed and hundreds of telephone companies grew up in the late 1800s and early 1900s. Finally, with a U.S. Supreme Court decision, the patents were upheld and many of the smaller local telephone companies became part of AT&T. Despite the Supreme Court ruling, peace did not ensue and many independents felt constrained by the larger AT&T.

In 1913 AT&T Vice President N.C. Kingsbury forged a compromise with the federal government averting antitrust complications for the company. Under the agreement, AT&T disposed of Western Union stock, agreed to stop buying up independent telephone companies, and agreed to arrange interconnections with independents so they could provide long-distance service. In 1921 the Willis-Graham Act permitted telephone company mergers free of antitrust action. AT&T made a public statement that acquisition was not their general policy. They did, however, continue to develop the company and acquired Western Electric manufacturing, which produced and resold to AT&T the equipment it needed to develop its long-distance lines and expand the Bell system.

By 1949 AT&T again found itself the object of antitrust action. The government wanted the AT&T-Western Electric alliance split up, and for Western Electric to divest half its stock in Bell Labs, the research arm of AT&T. Again averting litigation, the antitrust action was settled as a consent decree, albeit a controversial one.

It wasn't long before challenges to AT&T's hold on the marketplace began to emerge. A company called Hush-a-Phone wanted to market a mechanical device that attached to a telephone and enhanced conversations conducted under noisy conditions. Supporting the telephone company, the FCC prohibited connecting the device but the court of appeals disagreed and reversed the finding, forcing open the grip AT&T had on the marketplace. Ruling that the device was mechanical and not electrical, the court agreed the device could not harm the telephone equipment. AT&T was ordered to file new tariffs with the FCC rescinding any tariff regulations that prohibited a customer from using a device that did not injure people and did not harm the telephone system.

The next case that had an impact on competition in the telephone industry was *Carterfone*. With Carterfone, a voice-control circuit automatically switched on a radio transmitter when the telephone caller spoke into the mouthpiece. When the caller stopped speaking, the voice circuit returned to the receive mode. When activated, Carterfone permitted two-way communication without the inconvenience of a manual on-off switch. When AT&T told subscribers that using the Carterfone would subject them to potential liabilities, Carterfone sued and eventually won on antitrust grounds. Using the precedent of *Hush-a-Phone*, *Carterfone* was able to show the device would not harm the telephone apparatus to which it was attached.

The third case in the string of rulings supporting open competition was *Above 890*. In *Above 890* the FCC ruled that ample frequencies existed and the area of the electromagnetic spectrum above 890 kHz could be used for point-to-point communication by private carriers.

The first company to successfully take advantage of the FCC's more liberalized entry into telecommunications was MCI, which applied to operate a private microwave service between Chicago and St. Louis. The timing was right for MCI. By a four-to-three vote, MCI won approval for the system, but the decision also offered insights into how the FCC would approach the issue of private carriers. The commission made it clear that if arguments entered by the established carriers to keep MCI out of the marketplace were accepted, then little competition would exist in the industry. Overruled were challenges and objections to MCI's financial qualifications, the technical feasibility of the system, MCI's proposed rate structure, cream skimming, the reliability of the proposed service, the efficient utilization of the spectrum, and loop service interconnects. Dissenting opinions of FCC commissioners were also filled with strong arguments against the proposal, but the four-to-three vote meant MCI was in the communications business and the face of telecommunications had changed. MCI then applied to offer direct-dial long-distance service through a network of affiliate companies it had developed. The FCC disapproved, but MCI won on appeal saying the FCC had incorrectly interpreted the rules and argued successfully that while MCI service may have been different, it did not warrant being rejected. Still undaunted, the FCC ruled the following year that AT&T did not need to offer connections to MCI, but that position was reversed by the court of appeals also and AT&T agreed to offer interconnection service at negotiated rates.

What waited in the wings, however, was more serious. A Justice Department antitrust action filed in 1974 against AT&T, Western Electric, and Bell Labs was eventually settled in 1982. The settlement, executed under a Modification of Final Judgment (MFJ) overseen by U.S. District Court Judge Harold Greene, resulted in AT&T keeping its long lines and long-distance services, Bell Labs, and its equipment supplier, Western Electric. The 22 Bell operating companies (BOCs) were regrouped into seven regional holding companies (RHCs): Pacific Telesis Group covering California and the lower western states; US West, which includes the northwestern states as well as much of the upper Midwest and some of the lower Southwest; Southwestern Bell Corporation, which covers Texas and the lower Midwest; BellSouth, which covers the Southeast; Bell Atlantic, which includes the Middle Atlantic States; and NYNEX, which includes New England. The RHCs could provide, but not manufacture, new equipment for use in the home. The RHCs also inherited the assets, powers, and the obligations under the MFJ of the 22 Bell operating companies. Gradually the MFJ was revised during triannual reviews by Judge Greene. RHCs were permitted to enter nontelecommunication markets with few restrictions. Restrictions on RHCs being information providers were lifted, as were restrictions on such enterprising businesses as electronic publishing.

In addition to the federal government's involvement in the regulation of common carriers, state public utility commissions also control much of the telephone industry. Much like federal government control through the FCC, state commissions oversee the provision of universal service and equitable rate structures. Most public utility commissions have three or five commissioners with varying qualifications stipulated by state law. Commissioner backgrounds vary. The National Association of Regulatory Commissioners is the professional organization which binds together both state and federal commissioners. The independence of state commissions is an issue in the state regulation of common carriers. For example, in states where the governor appoints commission members, politics can play a disproportionate role in selecting commissioners. In some states the legislature retains the power to review regulations passed by the state commission.

Although the federal government is most closely associated with the regulation of radio broadcasting to the public, states have the power to regulate radio common carriers, which offer two-way or one-way communication services such as beepers. Radio transmitters used in such services are licensed by the FCC, but states have a public-interest right to regulate the offering of services to the user.

States also have extensive control over telephone common carriers. An examination of one state provides examples. For instance, administering the Uniform System of Accounts, approving construction plans, and approving tariffs are all within state jurisdiction, although there is some overlap with the federal government. Some states have connection subsidy programs where those needing special assistance can receive a subsidy for connection and service. States can also rule on extended service areas where interconnection between different carriers permits flat-rate calling over a wide geographic area. Resale of telephone services can also fall under state jurisdiction. States can impose restrictions over how advertisements and bill inserts are used.

At the heart of the regulatory process are separations and access. Separations refer to the split between telephone operations devoted to intrastate services and interstate services. Access refers to access to the system.

Federal regulation of communication common carriers rests primarily with the FCC's Common Carrier Bureau. Federal regulations govern such things as tariff filings, interlocking directorates, extension and discontinuance of service, and administering the Uniform System of Accounts. Also under the bureau are rules governing the extension of credit to candidates for federal office. Basically, while unsecured credit can be offered to candidates, restrictions apply to billing and collection procedures. All candidates for the same office must be treated equally. If, for example, unsecured credit is offered to a candidate for one federal office, then all candidates for the same office must be offered service with unsecured credit.

With the changing nature of the telephone industry, problems can develop in the ability of both the state and federal government to effectively regulate the industry. For example, while Western Electric continues to be a big player in telecommunications, it is not regulated by the FCC. Most nontelecommunications enterprises are unregulated and potential problems of cross-subsidization have emerged whereby the profits from regulated areas of the industry are used to subsidize nonregulated, high-risk enterprises. RHCs operate across state boundaries making it difficult for any one state to effectively oversee their operations.

An emerging area of law is the regulation of on-line information services. An early case exploring this area involved CompuServe, which was named as a codefendant in a libel suit over the content of information on one of its on-line bulletin board services. Since CompuServe did not have an opportunity to preview the material that appeared on its bulletin boards, it argued successfully that it should not be a codefendant in the case. The court stated, "CompuServe has no more editorial control over such a publication than does a public library, book store, or newsstand."

MATERIAL FOR ANALYSIS

The National Telecommunications and Information Administration inquiry into the policy issues and the structure of the telecommunications industry in the year 2000 (also excerpted elsewhere in this text) brought together leaders from government, academia, and industry to participate in NTIA TELECOM 2000 meetings. These meetings permitted a sharing of the vision of telecommunications and information goals for the next century. The following material for analysis is also from the report NTIA TELECOM 2000 published by NTIA. It deals with regulatory issues that will have an impact on privacy, information flow, and intellectual property in our information age and the role that federal legislation will play in dealing with these issues.[97]

TELECOMMUNICATIONS AND THE INFORMATION AGE: ISSUES IN PRIVACY, INFORMATION FLOW, AND THE PROTECTION OF INTELLECTUAL PROPERTY

By the turn of the century, what technology will enable us to do with information will have profoundly changed our lives. Individual, business, and national prosperity will hinge, to a significant degree, upon the ability to use and control information. It is becoming a hackneyed phrase, but nevertheless it is tomorrow's reality: the advent of the information age stands to revolutionize our way of living as much as the industrial revolution altered the agrarian society that preceded it.

Computers and telecommunications technology will permit more individuals and businesses to operate from their homes or from a number of remote locations. New telecommunications network capabilities and innovative services will also provide individuals the ability to select, edit, and print verbal, audio, and video information—to become "electronic publishers." These and other developments will likely have consequences that could significantly affect traditional concepts of privacy, and ownership and control of intellectual property. Conceivably, they could substantially alter the relative roles of creators, distributors and users of arts, entertainment, information, and data.

In earlier times, written information and oral communications could be controlled by the speaker or publisher more easily. Unauthorized copies of books and maps could be made and secrets could be violated, of course, but access to information was generally limited to the circle of users selected by the speaker or publisher.

Electronic transmission, however, has vastly increased the potential for unintended use of information. This has caused concern, particularly where prior experience had caused people to develop an expectation of either privacy or unrestricted use with respect to the information in question. Many owners of home satellite receivers, for example, both in the United States and abroad, view unencrypted television network "feeds" relayed via satellite that are not intended for public reception, but rather for processing and subsequent distribution through network studios. More ominous is the demonstrated ability of computer hobbyists and others to gain unauthorized and potentially destructive access to corporate databases and networks, and even the public-switched telephone network. The vast amount of information handled by telecommunications and computer networks, coupled with the ease of access and speed with which volumes of data can be copied, altered or erased, heighten the importance of information policy issues as we approach the 21st Century. Thus, issues such as privacy, security, international control of information flows, and definition and enforcement of intellectual property rights (e.g., copyrights, patents, and trade secrets) have become more important to individuals, businesses, and government—and promise to be even more important in years to come.

INFORMATION POLICY MUST BALANCE THE RIGHTS OF THE INDIVIDUAL AND THE WELFARE OF SOCIETY

Information policy issues often arise out of a tension between individual or corporate property rights, and conflicting needs or desires of society. In the late 1970s and early 1980s, for example, individuals who purchased home satellite receivers at a cost of $2,000 to $15,000 were initially able to freely view satellite-transmitted video programs, by intercepting over-the-air satellite signals intended for cable systems and broadcast stations. When the affected industries asserted that such viewing infringed upon ownership rights of programmers, many who had installed satellite receivers claimed a right to view any programming they could pick up. Congress was enlisted to balance these conflicting claims, and ultimately allowed dish owners to receive and view such unencrypted signals. On the other hand, courts have held that government may limit the accessibility of information considered obscene, or which would jeopardize national security. Thus, information policy addresses, in general, issues surrounding both the flow of information and the controls which are sometimes thought necessary to direct that flow.

Fundamental National Policies

Our democratic tradition rests on longstanding and familiar assumptions that the American public and, ultimately, the national interest, will be best furthered by encouraging the maximum range of information options—the ability of everyone to choose freely among diverse and antagonistic sources of news and information.

The challenge for communications policymakers in the past was twofold. On the one hand, the impact of electronic information services, broadcasting especially, was plainly growing. On the other, regulatory and other factors were limiting the number of information suppliers, and thus limiting the proportion of the people who could express their opinions and ideas through electronic media. Concern with respect to control of information and information flows was growing, as was the importance of information to the country.

Government faced a fundamental choice between embarking on more intensive regulation of information suppliers versus taking steps to increase their number. It chose the latter, a course facilitated by changes in technology and costs that made competition among existing and new suppliers of information feasible.

As policymakers seek, in the coming decades, to maintain an appropriate balance between individual freedoms and societal interests, they should continue to encourage even more diversity, both in the sources and nature of information available. Policies promoting competition are highly desirable in this regard, as First Amendment and competitive values are closely related. Both seek to allow the maximum number of participants, and in so doing, to minimize the control which any one participant, including the government, may command.

The "free market of ideas" that Mr. Justice Holmes wrote about some 70 years ago is undeniably essential to the effective functioning of our democracy. It is most likely to be ensured by fostering diverse sources of information.

Information Issues for the Twenty-first Century

As electronic transmission of information becomes more efficient and ubiquitous, new opportunities and challenges will arise. Two trends in the transmission of information in particular will need to be assessed in terms of their possible effect on information policies: (1) even as the costs associated with transmission decline, the *value* of the information transmitted is increasing; and (2) as technologies proliferate and become more versatile, information becomes more accessible.

These trends generally increase conflicting pressures: on the one hand, proprietors of increasingly valuable information seek to restrict or control access to it and, perhaps, to raise the price of such access. On the other hand, users and others desiring access to information have greater incentives to find a way to overcome such restrictions as the value of information increases. Additionally, public policies may affect accessibility of information because of First Amendment concerns or international relations, apart from marketplace forces.

The range of issues grouped under the term *information policy* has changed over time and undoubtedly will continue to evolve as we approach the twenty-first century. As we look toward the year 2000, some of the most important issues in information policy can be broadly categorized as follows:

* protection of personal privacy in light of data collection, manipulation, and dissemination

by government and private firms, and the sometimes related need to ensure security of some information;

* "free flow" of information across national boundaries; and

* intellectual property rights and limitations, both domestic and international.

The balance of this chapter takes up each of these areas, briefly describing how they might evolve in the twenty-first century. It may not be possible or advisable for government to attempt to manage each of these areas of information policy. It is important, however, for government to remain knowledgeable and ready to respond where appropriate.

INFORMATION ACCESS AND DISSEMINATION

As technologies create new means to access, manipulate, and disseminate information, economic opportunities will increasingly arise for individuals, firms, and government to profit. In some instances, however, other individuals or companies would rather not have this information collected, used or disseminated. Whether there should be legal means available to prevent (or prevent interference with) such collection, use or dissemination will be one of the key questions posed to citizens, Congress, and other governmental bodies.

Establishing Reasonable Standards

What may be the most formidable challenge for information policy will be the necessity of drawing lines between permissible and impermissible information access and dissemination. Judgments ultimately will rest with citizens, who will make their views known through their purchasing decisions, through their elected officials, and through their lawyers.

Consumers today have opportunities to limit the use of their names and addresses when credit card companies or mail order houses sell their mailing lists. If enough consumers express privacy concerns, it is conceivable these and other firms will offer confidentiality of subscription and billing information as a marketing tool.

Alternately, where market forces appear insufficient to strike an appropriate balance between user needs and societal goals, elected officials at the local, state, and federal levels will be called upon to legislate such a balance. For example, when copyright owners in the recording industry objected to stores that rented records and tapes and, in some cases, sold blank tapes and made recording equipment available on the premises, Congress passed legislation that virtually eliminated the commercial audio taping industry. Although some considered this to be anticonsumer legislation, it was evident that the rental of audio recordings had harmed the recording industry by reducing the number of releases during the years audio rental existed, thus ultimately risking greater harm to the public.

SAFEGUARDING PRIVACY

Privacy issues have arisen since well before the founding of this nation. Indeed, the Fourth and Fifth Amendments to the Constitution are intended to protect individuals against certain physical intrusions affecting them or their property. Legal scholars long ago articulated the individual's "right to be left alone," and that concept has since been recognized by the Supreme Court as an important national value.

Communications and Information Focus

Although the concept of privacy has been central to debates over issues ranging from search and seizure to personal practices and reproductive rights, privacy issues in the context of telecommunications and information policy are considerably more focused. The focus here has been, first, on the interception of private electronic communications, or what in the context of traditional voice telephone calls was referred to as "wiretapping." This concern has expanded with the advent of new technologies and the growth of services such as cellular telephones, electronic mail, facsimile transmissions, and the networking of computers.

The second focus has been on the collection, use, and dissemination of information in the home, the workplace, or by government or quasi-government agencies. This second group of issues is sometimes called "records privacy." An individual's concern about the collection and distribution of sensitive or revealing personal information such as financial or medical records may be twofold: the loss of control over information once it has been disclosed, and the accuracy of that information as it is distributed and redistributed.

Interception

Interception of private communications has long been the object of federal and state protection. The Fourth Amendment to the Constitution, supplemented by wiretapping, postal, and other statutes, placed strict limits on wiretapping, electronic eavesdropping, and the opening of mail by government agencies, as well as protecting against many such acts by private individuals. As technology changed, there was a perceived need to update applicable statutes to provide similar protections for these newer means of communication. The industries involved recognized that such protections could be "good business," and could avoid a possible consumer backlash against use of such new systems if they felt unprotected. These developments led to the Electronic Communications Privacy Act of 1986, which updated the wiretap laws to cover these new technologies. As communications technology continues to evolve in the twenty-first century, we can expect similar evolution in these types of protection.

Government Recordkeeping

With respect to records privacy issues, twenty-first century policymakers should continue to distinguish between two areas: first, the collection and use of information about individuals by government, and second, the collection and use of information by private firms for commercial purposes. The federal government's collection and use of information about individuals is addressed primarily by the Privacy Act of 1974. At the heart of the Privacy Act lie general information principles including: (1) there should be no secret record systems; (2) individuals should be able to see and correct records about themselves; and (3) information collected for one purpose should not be used for another.

The procedures by which individuals may gain access to certain records kept by the government (with some important exceptions such as records pertaining to national security, trade secrets, or privileged or confidential information) are described by the Freedom of Information Act. For example, individuals may seek to block others' access to "personnel and medical files and similar files kept by Government the disclosure of which would constitute a clearly unwarranted invasion of personal privacy." The practice of "computer matching," or comparisons between databases, is the subject of pending legislation that would establish procedures and safeguards. The government's collection and use of information has spawned court cases and will, in all likelihood, continue to be an important area of information policy.

Recordkeeping by Private Industry

Privacy concerns with respect to recordkeeping and the use of information by private industry began attracting political attention in the early 1970s. Congress thus far has addressed such privacy issues on a sectorial basis.

Some information policy experts argue that the United States should follow a different model and attempt to craft omnibus recordkeeping legislation that would apply across the board to many industries and types of records. This is a model employed in other countries. On the other hand, the U.S. experience has demonstrated that it is generally better to tailor safeguards for use in affected industries.

Congress and the public have proven capable of recognizing, and in an effective, targeted way, solving problems as new industries or services have developed. For example, important pieces of privacy legislation have been passed affecting several sectors including: credit reporting, financial services, cable television, and certain electronic transmissions. Such a targeted approach, which responds to specific problems and the unique characteristics of an industry, is less likely than omnibus, "least common denominator" legislation, to retard the development of new and socially useful industries and services. Brief descriptions of some of these laws will illustrate the kinds of specific protections devised by the Congress:

First, credit investigation and reporting agencies must: (1) make their records available to the subject (although they do not have a duty to tell an individual when he or she has become the subject of a credit check); (2) establish procedures for correcting information; and (3) disclose information only to authorized customers. One large credit reporting company is affirmatively contacting individuals about whom it has records, and for a modest charge providing them with a copy of the records and notification when inquiries about those records are made. Such an action would appear to be in anticipation of public privacy concerns, in addition to any pecuniary or other benefit to the firm.

Second, individuals are protected from unwarranted government access to personal financial records under the Right to Financial Privacy Act of 1978. Additionally, financial institutions providing electronic funds transfer services are required to notify any customers of any third-party access to customer account information.

Third, privacy provisions of the 1984 Cable Act require a cable television system operator to inform subscribers of the nature of personally identifiable information collected by the system operator, and other details of how and when that information will be used. The law also restricts the kinds of information a cable operator may collect or disclose, and requires the cable operator to destroy data after its use.

Fourth, electronic communications such as cellular radio, private satellite transmissions, paging devices, digital communications, and other computer-to-computer data transfers are protected from unauthorized private and governmental interceptions. Service providers making unauthorized intentional disclosures of confidential communications may be subject to civil lawsuits and criminal sanctions may be imposed for intentional interception, impermissible access to stored data, or disclosure.

As these examples illustrate, when specific activities are widely perceived as transgressing personal privacy bounds, it is likely the public and their elected officials will respond. For example, when a federal judge was under consideration for appointment to the Supreme Court in 1987, a Washington, DC newspaper carried a story revealing the record of the nominee's videotape rentals at a home video store. Within weeks, bills had been introduced in Congress to prohibit video stores from divulging customer records.

SECURITY OF INFORMATION

A separate, though related, issue arises when information required to be held securely is disclosed more widely than the holder and subject wish, because the storage or transmission of the information, or both, is not secure. One way to maintain security is to destroy information that is no longer needed. To date, the Cable Act is the only legislation that requires that personal data be destroyed after its use.

Maintaining security of computer databases is often a necessity for private firms because of their proprietary nature. Companies increasingly take steps to limit the number and identity of people with authorized access, employ the use of passwords and "locks" on databases, and develop other security plans. Where the information collected is not directly related to the financial condition of a firm, but may still contain sensitive material (e.g., individual records), security measures may also be essential. In the areas of electronic funds transfer, securities and commodities trading, and other electronic transactions which may be targeted for financial gain by interceptors, security is of critical concern. The Congressional Office of Technology Assessment has noted that:

> [t]here is a blend of optimism and pessimism in the computer technology community about the future of computer security problems. On the one side, experts correctly point out that the technology of securing computer systems is improving steadily . . . [and that] computerized systems, even if not perfectly secure, are often far more secure than the manual systems they replaced.
>
> On the other side . . . since security has not been historically a high-priority goal in the design of information systems . . . security hardware and software are often added as an afterthought rather than integrated into the system from the beginning . . . [Further,] advances in the technology of protection may not be adequate to deal with the complex systems now being built.

Through a combination of improvements in security technology and specific legislation where needed, adequate safeguards should be established to protect against unauthorized access and misuse of information. Congress, for example, passed legislation to address liability where unauthorized electronic funds transfers occur. This may be a model for measures in other areas.

The problem of the security of information goes beyond unauthorized access and use. Unauthorized access and alteration or deletion of data or records has also become a significant concern. Our increasing dependence on electronic records systems for crucial purposes, such as financial transactions or payroll records, increases the damage that can be done, purposefully or through modern forms of vandalism. There have been discussions, for example, of hospitals concerned that they might administer the wrong drugs to patients, or even be forced to shut down, if someone were to access and alter their electronic records.

We may be aware today of only a fraction of the potential risks involved in global, instantaneous, high-capacity networks combining voice and data transmission with computer access and control. The telecommunications industry has long been affected by fraudulent use of networks by computer hackers, "blue boxes," and the like. Nor is this necessarily an exclusively American problem. Government agencies in Japan and West Germany, for example, currently are exploring means of cost effectively minimizing such abuses. This is an area where more effort, including intergovernmental discussions, may be needed.

FUTURE PRIVACY PRIORITIES

Citizens, businesses, and public agencies are embracing the technologies of the information age. They welcome the improved speed, quality, and new capabilities these electronic communications technologies and services can provide. People are increasingly aware, however, that as access, manipulation, and dissemination of information becomes both easier and more profitable, the opportunities for abuse of information also are enhanced.

Reaching a Sound Balance

It is not yet clear what activities citizens will perceive to constitute an unwarranted abuse of privacy, nor whether they will assume that reduced privacy is one of the unavoidable trade-offs to enjoy the fruits of the information age. It is essential, however, that individuals become sufficiently informed about the capabilities of telecommunications and data processing systems to make informed choices, and where necessary, to guide elected officials in legislating necessary privacy protections.

In pursuing the goal of adequate security and privacy safeguards in the twenty-first century, there likely will arise both technical and marketplace solutions to the problems of unwanted use and misuse of information. Additionally, the trend toward assuring individual protection evident on the part of Congress (as well as state legislatures and other government bodies) should continue.

Technological Remedies

Markets, and particularly unregulated markets, can be tremendously resilient and creative, and provide solutions to difficult problems. In the area of new technological solutions, for example, film and home video producers are hopeful that a new technology called "macrovision" will permit prerecorded video cassettes to be encoded so as to prevent unauthorized copying. Whether further legislation will be passed, given these market developments, is thus uncertain.

A second example illustrates that markets can also respond to public concerns, in this case, increasing demand for construction of "Sensitive Compartmentalized Information Facilities" (SCIFs). These ultra-secured rooms in office buildings are needed, for example, by firms intent on maintaining security of information. As one report noted

> Regardless of the high construction costs . . . builders, architects and commercial real estate specialists said there will be a need for SCIF space as long as there is the need for companies to perform classified research.

These examples serve to illustrate an important point. The "electronic tools" made possible by technology can also make possible new ways to enhance privacy and information security.

Finally, we have no reason to believe that government will be any less willing or able to address privacy and security concerns with legislation where appropriate than has been the case in the 1970s and 1980s. Not every legislative proposal becomes law, of course, but the track record of successful Congressional actions targeted to problems in this area has been impressive thus far and argues against attempts to find an all-encompassing omnibus approach. As noted earlier, an omnibus approach risks stifling the development of technologies with enormous potential for constructive use.

ENSURING FREE FLOW OF INFORMATION

The globalization of markets has been expedited by advances in technology that permits firms to communicate more quickly, completely and efficiently throughout the world. In turn, advances in technology have been spurred by increased demand in world markets. Without doubt, the amount of information transmitted across national borders has grown enormously.

U.S. Commitment

Since the end of World War II, the United States has advocated a policy of "free flow" of information, goods, capital, and labor throughout the world. The policy of free flow has been variously defined, often meaning:

> An extension of the First Amendment prohibition against laws "abridging the freedom of speech, or of the press," and in the sense expressed by Article 19 of the Universal Declaration of Human Rights;
> The absence of impediments imposed *inadvertently* as a consequence of regulations not directed at information flows per se;
> The absence of laws or regulations that *intentionally* impose restrictive conditions on the location of data-processing facilities, or on the transmission beyond borders of certain kinds of information (the motivations may be purely economic and not political, content may be of no particular concern to the regulators);
> The absence of governmental attempts to re-

quire disclosure—for economic, social, or political reasons—of the content of information being processed or transmitted.

As other countries, the United States has acknowledged limited exceptions to the general principle of free flow with respect to privacy, intellectual property rights, and national security requirements. The United States should, however, continue to advocate the basic principle of free flow of information in its international telecommunications and information policies.

This longstanding policy yields important economic and noneconomic benefits. First, U.S. firms have been able to operate in other countries because essential communications activities can be carried on across borders. As world markets become more competitive, U.S. firms will require even better worldwide communications capabilities. Advanced technology will not suffice if countries limit the ability of firms to transmit data and other information into and out of their territory. Second, free flow of information maintains a robust marketplace of ideas, contributing to the ability of citizens of the United States and other countries to communicate and resolve issues effectively.

In recent years, although the free flow concept has been defined variously by different governments, a consensus has been evolving that the global benefits of unrestricted flows of information warrant maximum flows of information among countries. One important breakthrough was the 1985 Declaration on Transborder Data Flows, adopted by the Organization for Economic Cooperation and Development (OECD). As noted by the OECD, this "Data Declaration" was the:

"first international effort to address economic issues raised by the information revolution. It addresse[d] the policy issues arising from transborder data flows such as intracorporate flows, computerized information services and scientific and technological exchanges. . . ."

In the data declaration, the OECD members stated, among other things, that:

. . . National policies which affect transborder data flows reflect a range of social and economic goals, and that governments may adopt different means to achieve their policy goals;

[Members are] aware of the social and economic benefits resulting from access to a variety of sources of information and of efficient and effective information services;

[and] . . . that Member countries have a common interest in facilitating transborder data flows, and in reconciling different policy objectives in this field.

Therefore, "the governments of OECD Member countries expressed their intention to promote access to data and information, to develop common approaches for dealing with the transborder data flow issues. They agreed to undertake further work on the main issues emerging from transborder data flows."

INFORMATION FLOW POLICIES FOR THE FUTURE

While the OECD data declaration is a step in the right direction, not all countries share the spirit of cooperation evidenced there. In addition, each country's implementation of laws addressing information flows may subtly (or not so subtly) affect the degree of "free" flow. Quotas or other limitations on the number or value of film and video products used by many countries would appear not to conform to the spirit of a free flow policy.

Effects on Investment and Trade

Global trade can be adversely affected when trading partners have asymmetrical information policies. Imbalances in information flows across national borders may directly or indirectly offer firms from one country a competitive advantage over firms from another. The achievement and maintenance of unrestricted information flows is especially important as world markets become increasingly global. Manipulation of information flows must not be used as a weapon in world trade; rather, countries should recognize that they have a common interest in facilitating transborder data flows, and in reconciling different policy objectives regarding information flows.

INTELLECTUAL PROPERTY RIGHTS

The creation and commercial use of intellectual property—the subject of copyright, patent, trademark, service mark, and trade secrets law—is playing an increasing role in the U.S. and world economies. This report focuses on copyright issues since they are the most related to the telecommunication and information industries, although most of the statements made here might apply to other areas of intellectual property.

Ensuring Adequate Protections

As previously noted, as technologies proliferate and advance, the information transmitted often becomes more valuable. Adequate intellectual property laws and enforcement of those laws are two necessary ingredients to ensure that creators have sufficient incentives to write, paint, sculpt, film, and record new works. If adequate protection and enforcement is not maintained, creativity will be discouraged, and incentives to produce will be reduced. In contrast, through strong intellectual property protections, there will be an expanding pool of creators and new works.

Striking a Sound Balance

In order to balance the rights of creators with the needs of users, the Congress through the copyright law has established important exceptions to practices that would otherwise constitute infringement. Perhaps the most important of these copyright exemptions is the "fair use" concept, which permits private and noncommercial entities to use copyrighted works in a limited way without liability. One of the most well-known "fair use" exemptions has become the right of an individual to videotape copyrighted television programs for personal use—a practice which, if strictly construed, would be a copyright violation. By the turn of the century, tensions between users and owners of intellectual property will, if anything, heighten and new conflicts such as the home videotaping controversy will have arisen.

MEETING PUBLIC AND NATIONAL NEEDS

Strengthening intellectual property protection must be high on the national list of priorities for the twenty-first century. As the amount of video transmission capacity increases, it will become important to ensure adequate incentives to produce additional programming, in order to afford the public more choice. Additionally, the U.S. economy has become increasingly dependent on information-based industries.

Protecting strong U.S. trade positions in industries based on intellectual property has become as important as reducing the trade deficit in goods, particularly in the telecommunications and information services sector. Indeed, the United States strongly supported the inclusion of intellectual property in the General Agreement of Tariffs and Trade Uruguay round of negotiations.

Both domestically and abroad, however, public understanding of the principles underlying intellectual property rights is losing ground to a widespread view that individuals have a right to reproduce works as they wish, particularly if it is easy and cheap to do so. A recent public opinion survey concluded, among other things, that the vast majority of the public finds acceptable—such that they would be willing to do it—some forms of unauthorized copying of copyrighted material. Copyright industries have sought to influence public attitudes about intellectual property. For example, the data processing industry distributed a brochure which read:

> *People who would never walk into a store and shoplift a software product think nothing of making several copies of the same software. The results are the same. The act is just as wrong.*

Within the United States, public attitudes and the heavy demand for entertainment products (e.g., video tapes, audio recordings) and computer software may pose the greatest obstacles to adequate intellectual property protection. Beyond our borders, however, additional complications arise due to the uneven and even nonexistent legal protection of intellectual property. The laws in many countries are either poorly enforced or have not been amended to reflect technological developments.

In addition, other governments employ various means to limit U.S. access to their markets. Five of the most common and serious tactics include:

1. Quota limitations on U.S. products—laws may limit the number of titles imported or distributed or the number of prints or cassettes imported or distributed; laws may require an amount of "screen time" be devoted to national products; similarly, many countries require that a certain amount of broadcast programming originate domestically.
2. Inadequate intellectual property protection—copyright laws may be unenforced, out of date, inadequate, or nonexistent, thereby permitting widespread piracy and counterfeiting.
3. Service barriers—discriminatory laws may require that products to be exhibited in a given country must be printed or reproduced in that country or may prohibit U.S. firms from opening local offices for distribution.
4. Import duties and tariffs—excessive and/or discriminatory tariffs are often levied on U.S. information products.
5. Subsidies—governments create incentives by tax laws, loans, trade promotion agencies, and other means which favor domestic information products, to the disadvantage of U.S. firms.

One of the ways in which the United States has worked with other countries to support and strengthen intellectual property laws worldwide is through bilateral and multilateral agreements. Important bilateral agreements were made in the 1980s with Taiwan, Hong Kong, Singapore, and South Korea, and agreements were expected to be reached with Indonesia, Malaysia, and Thailand that would substantially reduce the amount of pirated and counterfeited goods produced in Southeast Asia.

Policies for the Future

Both domestically and abroad, the United States must continue to maintain and advocate strong intellectual property protections. Large scale piracy and counterfeiting must be curbed through vigorous government prosecution and punishment, as well as through actions taken by private firms to detect and stop such actions.

Perhaps more importantly, however, it is necessary for the public to appreciate that the unauthorized use of intellectual property is just as wrong as the unauthorized use of tangible property. The copyright law has carved out important exceptions to liability for certain, largely noncommercial, private uses of copyrighted works, and so strikes a good balance between the wants and needs of copyright holders and the good of society. It is fundamentally important that the link between intellectual property rights and the creation of more and different art, entertainment, information, and data be made clearer in the minds of all citizens. If individuals, particularly young people, do not respect intellectual property rights because they do not understand the vital function they serve as an incentive for creators and producers, government cannot force such respect on society. A workable copyright system is never enacted by law alone, experts have noted, but rather it evolves as a social system, which may be bolstered by law. (Conclusions and recommendations follow. Numbers are for this text only and do not appear in the NTIA version.)

CONCLUSIONS

1. By the year 2000, new telecommunications and information technologies and services will likely have consequences that could significantly affect traditional concepts of privacy, information flows and the ownership and control of intellectual property.

2. The vast amount of information handled by telecommunications and computer networks, coupled with the ease of access and speed with which volumes of data can be copied, altered, or erased, heighten the importance of information policy issues as we face the twenty-first century.

3. Today, we may be aware of only a small part of the potential risks involved in global, instantaneous, high-capacity networks combining voice and data transmissions with computer access and control.

4. In pursuing the goal of adequate privacy and security safeguards in the twenty-first century, there likely will arise both technical and marketplace solutions to problems of unwanted use and misuse of information.

5. Congress and the public have proven capable of recognizing and solving privacy problems in a targeted way as new industries and services have developed.

6. With respect to international flows of information, other countries have policies different from the United States and resulting global trade can be adversely affected by asymmetrical information policies.

7. If intellectual property is not vigorously protected, creative works will be discouraged and the incentives to make more will be reduced. In contrast, through strong intellectual property protections, there will be an expanding pool of creators and new works.

8. Over the past thirty years, copyrighted intellectual property has contributed an increasing percentage of the Gross National Product.

9. Both domestically and abroad, public understanding of the principles underlying intellectual property rights is losing ground to a widespread view that individuals have a right to reproduce works, particularly if it is easy and cheap to do so.

10. Beyond our borders, additional complications arise due to the uneven and even nonexistent legal recognition of intellectual property, and laws are often unenforced or have not been amended to reflect technological changes.

RECOMMENDATIONS

1. Individuals need to become sufficiently informed about the capabilities of telecommunications to make choices that reflect their level of concern about privacy.

2. Government must remain prepared, if necessary, to act quickly and effectively to protect personal privacy and ensure information security. Specific legislative and judicial remedies should continue to be devised as warranted, rather than developing omnibus legislation.

3. The United States should in all bilateral and multilateral relationships continue to promote the unrestricted flow of information (with internationally agreed upon exceptions) across national borders.

4. Individuals and governments must recognize, and act in accordance with, the recognition that adequate intellectual property laws and enforcement of those laws is necessary to ensure an expanding pool of creators and new works.

5. The U.S. government must adopt and enforce intellectual property laws domestically and must continue to work for stronger protection and enforcement by other countries to maintain a strong U.S. trade position and to promote the creation and dissemination of literary, artistic, musical, and other information-based works worldwide.

QUESTIONS FOR CRITICAL ANALYSIS

- In the MCI application to construct point-to-point microwave facilities, the common carriers argued the system was only going to be 85 percent reliable. The FCC said that estimate was too low, even though MCI claimed 99.9 percent reliability, which some would argue was too high. If the common carriers had been less pessimistic, would they possibly have won the favor of the FCC, injected more credibility into other testimony and evidence, and perhaps persuaded one of the commissioners to vote for the common carriers?
- The vote in the MCI application decision was four to three. What would have happened to the American telecommunication infrastructure if the vote had been four to three against MCI?
- In the MCI application for construction permits to construct its first point-to-point microwave service, a dissenting opinion in the FCC's decision to grant the permits came from Commissioner Robert E. Lee, of which Commissioner James J. Wadsworth joined: "A common carrier must be held to a very high standard of public service which is even greater than that required of a broadcaster." Do you agree with that statement? On what basis would Commissioner Lee make such a remark and how would he justify it?
- If common carriers, especially telephone systems, used mostly wired communication systems to which everyone had access, and broadcasters used over-the-air systems to which only a few have access, why would broadcasters be held to lower standards to be considered to be operating in the "public interest"?
- Couldn't one argue that because far fewer people are granted broadcast licenses than can use the telephone, broadcasters should adhere to a much higher standard of operating in the "public interest" than common carriers?

ADDITIONAL RESOURCES

Beall, R., "Developing a Coherent Approach to the Regulation of Computer Bulletin Boards." 7 *Computer-Law Journal* 499 (1987).

Burnside, R. S., "The Electronic Communications Privacy Act of 1986: The Challenge of Applying Ambiguous Statutory Language to Intricate Telecommunication Technologies." 13 *Rutger Computer & Technology Law Journal* 451 (1987).

Katsh, M. E., "The First Amendment and Technological Change: The New Media Have a Message." 57 *George Washington Law Review* 1459 (1989).

Larson, A. C., and W. E. Kovacic, "Predatory Pricing Safeguards in Telecommunications Regulation: Removing Impediments to Competition." 35 *Saint Louis University Law Journal* 1 (1990).

O'Kief, W. G., The Laissez-faire Approach to Telecommunications Rate Regulation." 24 *Creighton Law Review* 649 (1991).

Stanley, W. B., "High Basic Service Rates and Connection Charges: Wrong for the Telephone Industry." 114 *Public Utilities Fortnightly* 23 (1984).

Weisman, D. L., "Default Capacity Tariffs: Smoothing the Transitional Regulatories Asymmetries in the Telecommunications Market." 5 *Yale Journal on Regulations* 149 (1988).

Whitten, M., "The Passing of POTS: Transition in Telecommunications." 53 *Oklahoma Bar Journal* 2215 (1982).

chapter thirteen

Satellites: Telecommunication in Space

When government officials, radio amateurs, and radio broadcasters met in the 1920s to work out a solution to crowding on the electromagnetic spectrum, their primary concern was the equitable apportionment of frequencies so that everyone with a special interest in radio could share this valuable resource. Prior to the national radio conferences, stations would simply raise their power or move their frequencies to bump competing stations off the airwaves. Beyond ship-to-shore communication, little concern existed over international regulation. Less advanced countries had not developed radio, and international agreements were primarily over the use of "wireless" for maritime communication.

Today, 70 years after the national radio conferences of the 1920s, the regulation of satellite communication encompasses many of the same concerns over frequency crowding, as well as a host of other issues. For example, the technology used to send signals from a remote news crew back to a local station uses satellites as the communication link between the crew and the home studio. In the United States, the process is relatively simple. Crews are able to phone a satellite carrier, reserve time and a frequency, and complete the transmission. Many news operations have dedicated satellite time guaranteeing them a satellite link to meet their needs. In European countries, however, even in the early 1990s such guarantees are not possible. For example, different countries have different rules governing satellite news transmission.[1] Many news operations pay fees to the government to ship their equipment to international events and to transmit feeds back to their stations. Some countries have multiple layers of regulations. Forward measures through the European Community are being proposed that could create an EC-type FCC operating across international boundaries and permitting satellite news gathering in Europe to be under one regulatory framework, but many obstacles still exist.

EARLY MILESTONES

To understand how and why satellites are regulated we must first gain a basic understanding of how satellite communication developed. The first satellite launched into orbit was the Russian satellite Sputnik I in October 1957. Sputnik, about the size of a basketball, operated on a frequency near today's FM radio band and was monitored by radio amateurs. In the heat of the Cold War, little cooperation between the then Soviet Block nations and the United States existed in space travel or space communication. Responding to the surprise launch of Sputnik, and stressing science education in schools, the United States announced an ambitious space exploration program that eventually put astronauts on the moon in July 1969.

Telstar

In satellite communication, the first significant link occurred on July 10, 1962 with the launch of AT&T's Telstar satellite, which relayed television pictures between Europe and the United States. Weighing 170 pounds, light in comparison to today's satellites, Telstar was a cooperative effort between AT&T and the National Aeronautics and Space Administration (NASA). Powered by solar energy, Telstar passed in view for about 45 minutes every time it passed over the earth. It orbited with an apogee of 3,052 miles, its highest point, and a perigee of 593 miles, its lowest point. Programming was limited to a seven-minute taped program with Jacques M. Marette, the French minister of Postal Services and Telecommunications, and musical arrangements by French performers. The British signal followed the French program with a test pattern and then a live broadcast by Britain's Deputy Chief Engineer, Captain Charles Booth.

The press coverage of the Telstar launch called attention to the rivalry in television technology between Britain and France, since the French were able to monitor signals much better than the British, but the British were able to offer a live program as opposed to the French taped program. The press coverage in the United States also centered on the role of NASA, which had received money from AT&T to launch Telstar. The agreement between the two also called for the free availability of any inventions to any company that requested them. Immediately following the successful launch, AT&T's stock briefly became one of the most active on the stock exchange. David Sarnoff, the chairman of RCA, proposed a single company to deal with international communication matters, following closely a similar proposal by U.S. President John F. Kennedy.[2] Western Union, also feeling the heat of the AT&T accomplishment, supported the Sarnoff idea. Because the program used in the United States broadcast was produced by AT&T, CBS broke away from the network pool coverage of the event and did not carry the remarks of AT&T board chairman Frederick R. Kappel. Jack Gould, the television critic of *The New York Times*, criticized the sight of government dignitaries serving as a "passive gallery" for private corporations and predicted that the lasting value of international television would be determined not in "laboratories in the sky but in offices on the ground."[3]

Synchronous Orbit

The primary disadvantage of Telstar and its generation of satellites was its limited ability to remain over a given point of the earth for more than about 45 minutes. This meant that when the satellite passed out of view the television relay was interrupted until the satellite returned into view again. What was necessary for uninterrupted satellite communication was to place the satellite in a position where it would remain stationary above the earth's surface. The solution was to position a satellite above the equator at a height that would keep it in orbit and synchronize the satellite's rotation with earth's rotation, thus making the satellite appear stationary and create a permanent link—a fixed, stationary antenna in space—for television communication and other applications. The achievement came a year after Telstar with the successful positioning of the Syncom II satellite, following the unsuccessful attempt to place Syncom I in a *synchronous orbit*—also called a *geostationary orbit*—six months earlier.

COMMUNICATIONS SATELLITE ACT OF 1962

Prior to the launch of Telstar, Congress passed the Communications Satellite Act of 1962. Among its provisions was the formation of a private communications satellite corporation to manage the participation of the United States in global international satellite communication.

Forming COMSAT

The act called for the corporation to be a profit-making company and not an agency of government. The president of the United States appointed the first 13 incorporators, who served as a temporary board of directors until successors were elected at the first stockholders' meeting. Board members were required to be citizens of the United States with one board member serving as chair. Financing of the corporation was through an initial stock offering as stipulated by the act, which stated:

> The corporation is authorized to issue and have outstanding, in such amounts as it shall determine, shares of capital stock, without

> par value, which shall carry voting rights and be eligible for dividends. The shares of such stock initially offered shall be sold at a price not in excess of $100 for each share and in a manner to encourage the widest distribution to the American public.[4]

Broad powers were awarded the corporation. In order to achieve its objectives and carry out the purposes of the act, it was given authorization to:

> (1) plan, initiate, construct, own, manage, and operate itself in conjunction with foreign governments or business entities a commercial communications satellite system;
> (2) furnish, for hire, channels of communication to United States communications carriers and to other authorized entities, foreign and domestic; and
> (3) own and operate satellite terminal stations when licensed by the Commission. . . .[5]

Also included in the activities of the corporation was authorization:

> (1) to conduct or contract for research and development related to its mission;
> (2) to acquire the physical facilities, equipment and devices necessary to its operations, including communications satellites and associated equipment and facilities, whether by construction, purchase, or gift;
> (3) to purchase satellite launching and related services from the United States Government;
> (4) to contract with authorized users, including the United States Government, for services of the communications satellite system.[6]

The Communications Satellite Corporation, today referred to as COMSAT, was conceived.

International Policy Provisions and Interagency Responsibilities

Among other provisions, the Communications Satellite Act of 1962 articulated the policy of the United States in developing an international satellite system, specifically stating: "It is the policy of the United States to establish, in conjunction with other countries, as expeditiously as practicable a commercial communications satellite system . . . which will serve the communications needs of the United States and other countries, and which will contribute to world peace."[7] The act went on to outline the private corporation and private enterprise approach to meeting the mandate of a global system:

> The new and expanded telecommunication services are to be made available as promptly as possible and are to be extended to provide global coverage at the earliest practicable date. In effectuating this program, care and attention will be directed toward providing such services to economically less developed countries and areas, as well as those more highly developed, toward efficient and economical use of the electromagnetic frequency spectrum, and toward the reflection of the benefits of this new technology in both quality of services and charges for such services.
>
> In order to facilitate this development and to provide for the widest possible participation by private enterprise, United States participation in the global system shall be in the form of a private corporation, subject to appropriate governmental regulation. It is the intent of Congress that all authorized users shall have nondiscriminatory access to the system; that maximum competition be maintained in the provision of equipment and services utilized by the system; that the corporation created under this Act be so organized and operated as to maintain and strengthen competition in the provision of communication services to the public; and that the activities of the corporation created under this Act and of the persons or companies participating in the ownership of the corporation shall be consistent with the Federal Antitrust Laws.[8]

Areas of authority were assigned to the president of the United States, NASA, and the FCC. Seven areas of responsibility were assigned to the executive branch. The president was to: (1) aid in planning and development of the system; (2) provide continuous review for all phases of the program; (3) coordinate the activities of governmental agencies dealing with telecommunication; (4) supervise the relationships with foreign governments; (5) insure arrangements for foreign participation in the use of the communications satellite system; (6) assure the availability of the satellite system for general governmental purposes; and (7) use the authority of the president to coordinate efficient use of the electromagnetic spectrum and technical compatibility in the United States and abroad.

NASA was charged with advising the FCC on technical characteristics of communication satellites and consulting with the new private corporation on technical characteristics of satellite systems. Cooperating with the corporation in research and development and furnishing the corporation a reimbursable basis for launch support, service, maintenance and other services were also part of its charge.

Broad areas were covered under the FCC's responsibilities including: (1) ensuring competition in the procurement of apparatus, services, and equipment for the developing satellite system; (2) ensuring nondiscriminatory access and use of the satellite system; (3) requiring the construction of the system to provide services to foreign countries when advised to do so by the State Department; (4) ensuring compatibility for interconnection with other systems; (5) establishing accounting regulations which ensure fair rate structures; (6) approving technical aspects of the system to meet regulatory mandates; (7) granting construction permits; (8) authorizing the issuance of COMSAT stock; (9) insuring additions by COMSAT to the system which were in the public interest; (10) requiring additions to the system by carriers to meet the public interest; and (11) passing rules and regulations to carry out the provisions of the act.

The initial meeting of 13 incorporators of the new Communications Satellite Corporation took place in Washington, DC on October 22, 1962.[9] The new company lacked money, employees, even offices, and had little more to guide it but the act that had created the company. The group of people putting it all together, however, had some impressive credentials. Sidney Weinberg was senior partner of the investment company Goldman Sachs & Co., Phil Graham headed the *Washington Post* and chaired the incorporators, David Kennedy was chair of Continental Bank of Chicago; Leo Welch was the recently retired chair of Standard Oil, and Bruce G. Sundlun had a wide range of business experience in areas ranging from broadcasting to executive aviation. Continental Bank became the company's first financial agent, partly because David Kennedy raised overnight the first $5 million in operating capital for the new company. Graham's recommendation that an executive committee be formed was quickly rebuffed on grounds that everyone had been appointed with equal authority and an executive committee would delegate the other members to second-class status.[10]

THE FORMATION AND OPERATION OF INTELSAT

The phrases in the Communications Satellite Act of 1962 calling for the development of a global satellite system were more than just words. They represented a commitment of the United States to build the global system and to put the political and economic muscle behind the commitment. In the same year the act was passed the General Assembly of the United Nations passed a resolution supporting the belief that satellite communication would facilitate contact with peoples of the world.[11] Another statement of support came in the *Treaty of Principles Governing the Activities of States in the Exploration and Use of Outer Space, Including the Moon and Other Celestial Bodies*, which stated "Outer Space . . . shall be free for exploration and use by all states without discrimination of any kind, on a basis of equality . . . and there shall be free access."[12] The international satellite network evolving from the efforts of COMSAT and other countries was originally called the International Satellite Consortium, which became the International Telecommunications Satellite Organization (INTELSAT). Today a network of INTELSAT satellites rings the earth providing not only video but data and voice relay for the communication needs of different countries.

The Road to International Agreements

COMSAT's statutory mission to develop a global satellite system meant the immediate commencing of international negotiations, which were not without obstacles. The United States operated its telecommunications industries as mostly private enterprises, while most European nations placed telecommunication under government control through their postal, telegraph, and telecommunications administrations.[13] In addition, the international telecommunication infrastructure was built on cables—undersea and terrestrial—with a history dating back to the late 1800s. Joining European government interests with American private enterprise was not simple for a new technology such as satellite, which could be much more invasive and had much wider cultural and political implications than cable. Space exploration and technology were at the frontier of the balance of power, especially after the then Soviet Union launched its first Sputnik satellite in 1957.

Tensions existed in Europe since many countries did not want to be second in the space race, could not effectively negotiate with Cold War Russia, and did not have the technology to move quickly enough to pre-empt the position of the United States in rocketry and satellite research and development.

Precedent for private-government relationships did exist between the United States and other countries, primarily through the AT&T, ITT, RCA, and Western Union international agreements. The firms were well known in Europe and AT&T had made a strong commitment to support COMSAT from the very start of COMSAT's operations. In a crucial meeting of the European Conference of Post and Telecommunications held in December 1963 in Karlsruhe, Germany, representatives of COMSAT and AT&T, the American representatives, faced a Europe cautious and negative toward U.S. efforts to move rapidly ahead with a global satellite system.

The entire concept of an international satellite network could have been delayed had it not been for the "forthright and unequivocal statement by the AT&T representative at the meeting, James E. Dingman" who stated AT&T's intention to use satellite communication.[14] The statement of Dingman, who was AT&T's vice chair at the time, conveyed a "sense of seriousness and urgency to all the PTT administrations of Europe."[15] Additional European planning meetings followed. A second critical meeting took place in Tokyo in 1964 at the invitation of the Japanese and the Australians, both of whom had big investments in cable and had not been represented in the European meetings. After commitments from the United States to work with Japan and Australia, the Europeans invited both countries and Canada to enter future conferences. After attempts to negotiate with the Soviet Union failed, they were left out of the INTELSAT planning and the program moved forward without them. The interim agreement creating INTELSAT was signed on August 20, 1964. A few weeks later Israel signed and after the State Department heralded the fact in a press release, the League of Arab states joined. Close ties between the United States and Latin America, and a commitment from Brazil, brought countries from that region into INTELSAT. On April 6, 1985, the Early Bird satellite built by Hughes Aircraft Company was successfully launched and became the first satellite in the INTELSAT series.

The Financial Base for INTELSAT

Internal accounting and billing procedures needed to be developed before INTELSAT could function.[16] Each new country joining INTELSAT and acceding to the interim agreement meant adjusting ownership shares. Since international funds transfer varied between countries, a policy was established that the date of accession occurred when the money reached the bank. Accounting and contract negotiations had to be worked out between COMSAT and NASA, the launch contractor. COMSAT was the manager of INTELSAT and a management fee, originally agreed upon as $150,000, had to be worked out. Tariffs for using the Early Bird satellite were negotiated and were based on such factors as "future program assumptions, projections of circuit leases, provisions for launch failures, depreciation periods, treatment of spare satellites, rate of return, and the period over which costs would be averaged. . . ."[17]

INTELSAT Membership and Structure

INTELSAT membership was originally opened to any country that was part of the initial interim agreement. The interim agreement was superseded by both the definitive agreements and the operating agreement. Membership is afforded when a country accedes to the agreements. Each signatory, more than one hundred, has an investment share in INTELSAT that is equal to its percentage of the total use of the system. Revenue for INTELSAT comes from charges to use the system. COMSAT represents the United States in INTELSAT.

The structure of INTELSAT consists of an Assembly of Parties, which meets every two years to consider long-term and constitutional issues; a Meeting of Signatories composed of designated telecommunications entities such as COMSAT, which meets each year to consider operational, technical, and financial issues; a Board of Governors, which is an executive committee meeting more frequently; and an Executive Organ, which is a permanent secretariat headed by a Director General.[18]

The Assembly of Parties is comprised of representatives of all parties to the definitive agreements. The Meeting of Signatories is composed of all signatories to the operating agreement. Representation to the Board of Governors is available to any signatory to the operating agreement, or to any group of signatories. Five or more signatories from the same ITU region may join together to obtain representation on the Board of Governors. No more than two such groups may represent a single region and no more than five groups may achieve representation. The Board of Governors is responsible for all decisions concerning the design, development, construction, establishment, operation, and maintenance of the INTELSAT space segment.

EMERGING POLICY IMPLICATIONS OF INTELSAT

Since its inception, INTELSAT has remained a dominant figure in international satellite communication. Its genesis was through the efforts of the United States when the Communication Satellite Act created COMSAT, and when the United States negotiated and helped form the INTELSAT system. While positioning the United States as an early entrant in international satellite communication, the Communication Satellite Act also positioned the United States in a high-profile, controlling role in INTELSAT. At one time the United States owned as much as 60 percent of the international satellite network. Today because other countries have joined INTELSAT and because of the way ownership shares are allocated, the U.S. ownership is in the 20 percent range. More than a hundred other countries that also are signatories to the INTELSAT agreements share in the ownership of INTELSAT.

Different Regulatory Approaches

What separates the United States from some other countries is the way in which regulatory policies are developed. For example, a basically democratic and capitalistic form of government operates with a strong private impetus to the development of broadcasting and telecommunications. Private enterprise has in the past, and continues today, to play a dominant role in the U.S. telecommunications infrastructure. From the early entries of the fledging broadcasting networks such as CBS, NBC, and Mutual to the modern-day telecommunication giants such as AT&T and the regional Bell operating companies, private enterprise has forged the framework for developments in communications technology.

In many European countries and elsewhere, telecommunication development has been under strong government control. For years the PTTs owned, operated, and controlled the access of foreign nations to their internal telecommunications infrastructures. Although efforts to deregulate some of the state monopolies under agreements forged through the European Community may open up competition, many PTT-type controls still exist. Thus, INTELSAT has had to deal with political and economic structures ranging from the free enterprise system to almost total government control.

Competition with Other Satellite Networks

INTELSAT also competes with other satellite networks. Russia and East European countries are connected largely through INTERSPUTNIK, a regional satellite network. The countries that previously formed the Soviet Union rejected the opportunity to participate in INTELSAT, and consequently INTERSPUTNIK evolved. Although closer ties to the West have materialized since the breakup of the Soviet Union, INTERSPUTNIK remains a connecting force in Eastern Europe.

One of INTELSAT's primary profit routes is across the Atlantic where large amounts of voice and video communications take place. It is on these high-profit channels that INTELSAT's concern was most notably focused in the 1980s with the introduction of private carriers attempting to compete with the INTELSAT network. The opportunity for that competition developed under the Reagan administration with the enactment of the Foreign Relations Authorization Act of 1985, which permitted limited competition with INTELSAT. The most visible competitor has been Pan American Satellite (PANAMSAT). Pan American Satellite, the first to enter the marketplace after the passage of the Foreign Relations Authorization Act and the FCC's decision in 1985 to permit separate international satellite systems to exist, applied to the FCC for permission to operate a satellite system linking much of North and South America with Western Europe as far east as Austria. Although eventually Pan Am was able to get its satellite in orbit, INTELSAT met the Pan Am application with strong opposition, buttressed by formidable arguments against the entry of a private satellite operator into what had been an international satellite monopoly.[19]

Opposition to Pan American Satellite

COMSAT, as the United States signatory to INTELSAT, was quick to point out the origin of the INTELSAT agreements. These require that other nations consult and coordinate with INTELSAT whenever satellite systems are developed in an effort to assure technical compatibility and to avoid significant economic harm to INTELSAT. Because the United States is a party to that agreement, COMSAT argued that the United States was undermining its own position in the international network by supporting the entry of private international satellite networks. Coordination and consultation with INTELSAT, COMSAT executives pointed out, was not the only issue since many other private systems had developed, but were primarily domestic and regional. As such, they did not pose any significant economic harm to INTELSAT. Pan American, however, was seeking to compete in that lucrative North America-Europe route, which was the heaviest traffic route for INTELSAT and one of its most lucrative. Here the argument that the entry of PANAMSAT would cause economic harm began to emerge. COMSAT had enjoyed the benefits of a corporation under the protection of the INTELSAT agreements.

COMSAT opposition was backed up by a unanimously adopted resolution passed at a meeting of the INTELSAT signatories in 1983, emphasizing the underlying purposes for which INTELSAT was created. Basically the spirit of the resolution claimed that permitting access to private carriers would cause financial problems, that is, higher rates, for INTELSAT users.[20] Approval of the entry of a private carrier would also, COMSAT argued, hurt U.S. foreign policy interests since the United States was in a somewhat enviable position of having INTELSAT's director general be an American. For an American to head the INTELSAT organization at a time when the United States was permitting private entry into the marketplace and undermining the INTELSAT agreements was particularly embarrassing, COMSAT claimed.

The interest of Third World nations was another argument used to oppose the entry of Pan American Satellite. Although not having the technical capability to be major players in international satellite development, over three fourths of INTELSAT members came from the Third World. Relationships with this segment of the membership would be strained by competition. Economic benefits to the United States through its relationship with INTELSAT were also not overlooked. At the time, NASA was a major benefactor of INTELSAT launch services, which totaled more than $700 million by 1984, in addition to more than $900 million in satellite construction contracts that had gone to United States industry.[21]

Another argument against Pan American Satellite's entry was that U.S. foreign policy would be seen as unpredictable, and based on the short term. To institute a policy that would disrupt the INTELSAT agreements could reinforce the perception that U.S. foreign policy was erratic. As one COMSAT executive stated:

> There has also been a widespread view that, at least in some respects, U.S. foreign policy proceeds in fits and starts, that it is all too frequently an on-again, off-again proposition. The U.S. commitment to INTELSAT provides significant confirmation that the United States can in fact be a reliable partner in a major international undertaking. The value of this demonstration of reliability reaches well beyond INTELSAT itself.[22]

Economic concerns also emerged. A Department of Commerce spokesperson was quoted as saying some nations feared that private carriers would "skim the cream off the most lucrative routes across the Atlantic."[23] The argument was not new and had been most prominently used by AT&T in early attempts to block the entry of MCI into domestic wired service between Chicago and St. Louis in the United States. The Commerce Department position was reinforced by INTELSAT, which said if projected revenues went down the only alternative the carrier would have would be to raise rates.

The crash of NASA's *Challenger* space shuttle in January 1986 did not help things. Insurance premiums soared for spacecraft launches. Added to the risk of its entry into the marketplace being blocked by policy and regulatory hurdles, Pan American Satellite found itself short of cash. Part of the network was sold off and a financial restructuring package occurred.

The delay of Pan American Satellite's entry, as well as that of other carriers also applying to enter the marketplace, permitted INTELSAT to shore up its political and economic defenses. INTELSAT has now been able to position itself to serve and market to specific regions. One satellite, for example, is designed to primarily serve broadcasters who have found limited availability over heavily used channels, especially between America and Europe. Additional orbital slots have been claimed by INTELSAT over the Pacific, and INTELSAT, while facing more competition, is itself in a much stronger position to compete.

Meanwhile, PANAMSAT called upon the FCC to reopen a proceeding and consider the structure of COMSAT. At issue is whether COMSAT's private-line services, which include video, should now be separated for accounting purposes as a subsidiary, so that the regulated dominant carrier protection afforded the International Satellite Network could not be used to unfairly compete against private carriers such as PANAMSAT. Joining PANAMSAT in calling for a reopening of the proceeding are such well-known American firms as CapCities/ABC, CBS, NBC, and Turner Broadcasting System.[24]

UNITED NATIONS COMMITTEE ON THE PEACEFUL USES OF OUTER SPACE (COPUOS)

After the 1957 launch of Sputnik, it became clear that outer space was the new frontier in the development of technology for defense and communication. Heightened by Cold War tensions between the United States and the Soviet Union, the United Nations through a General Assembly Resolution in 1958 created the United Nations ad hoc committee on the Peaceful Uses of Outer Space.[25] By forming the committee, the United Nations recognized that the earth's surface could no longer define the parameters of our attempts for international cooperation. One year later the ad hoc committee became the permanent Committee for the Peaceful Uses of Outer Space (COPUOS) with the passage of a second United Nations Resolution embodying the principles that space would serve mankind and support the "well-being of peoples."[26] Within COPUOS two permanent subcommittees operate, the Legal Subcommittee and the Scientific and Technical Subcommittee. Tension between the two space superpowers of the 1950s and 1960s, the Soviet Union and the United States, resulted in a compromise over how the body would function. Somewhat nontraditional by United Nations standards, COPUOS operates by consensus and without a veto mechanism.

One example of the Legal Subcommittee's work can be seen in a statement concerning the principles governing the responsibility, liability, and compensation for damages caused by objects launched into space. The Legal Subcommittee reached consensus on a draft of the principles, which state in part:

> . . . each State which launches or procures the launching of a space object and each State from whose territory or facility a space object is launched shall be internationally liable for damage caused by such objects or their component parts. This fully applies to the case of such a space object carrying a nuclear power source on board. Whenever two or more States jointly launch such a space object, they shall be jointly and severally liable for any damage caused . . .
>
> . . . damage shall be determined in accordance with international law and the principles of justice and equity in order to provide such reparation in respect of the damage as will restore the person, natural or judicial, State or international organization on whose behalf a claim is presented to the condition which would have existed if the damage had not occurred.
>
> For the purposes of this principle, compensation shall include reimbursement of the duly substantiated expenses for search, recovery and clean-up operations, including expenses for assistance received from third parties.[27]

Typical of deliberative bodies everywhere, detail in wording and phraseology can pose significant problems. For example, in reporting the consensus of the draft principles, the Legal Subcommittee went on to state that once agreement had been reached on all principles, "the Subcommittee would address outstanding issues such as the use of the terms 'should' and 'shall' and would consider whether any adjustments would be necessary to ensure that the principles are properly interrelated and balanced and would have their intended effect."[28] Some agenda items of the Legal Subcommittee remain in place over many years. Issues of earth sensing by satellite and nuclear power are two of these issues. Another consistent agenda item is stated as:

> Matters relating to the definition and delimitation of outer space and to the character and utilization of the geostationary orbit, including consideration of ways and means to ensure the rational and equitable use of the geostationary orbit without prejudice to the role of the International Telecommunication Union.[29]

ADOPTING THE COPUOS RECOMMENDATION FOR A TREATY ON OUTER SPACE

It became clear during the early years of COPUOS that an instrument of international law would need to exist to assure that the mission of COPUOS and other bodies concerned with space could be achieved. COPUOS recommended a treaty and the U.N. General Assembly adopted the recommendation for a "Treaty on Principles Governing the Activities of States in the Exploration and Use of Outer Space, Including the Moon and Other Celestial Bodies."[30] The treaty took effect a year later and has since been known as the U.N. Outer Space Treaty, or Space Charter, which some have characterized as the Magna Charta for space.[31] The preamble of the treaty reads in part:

> The States Parties to this Treaty,
>
> - Inspired by the great prospects opening up before mankind as a result of man's entry into outer space, Recognizing the common interest of all mankind in the progress of the exploration and use of outer space for peaceful purposes,
> - Believing that the exploration and use of outer space should be carried on for the benefit of all peoples irrespective of the degree of their economic or scientific development,
> - Desiring to contribute to broad international co-operation in the scientific as well as the legal aspects of the exploration and use of outer space for peaceful purposes,
> - Believing that such co-operation will contribute to the development of mutual understanding and to the strengthening of friendly relations between States and peoples . . .,
> - Convinced that a Treaty on Principles Governing the Activities of States in the Exploration and Use of Outer Space, including the Moon and Other Celestial Bodies, will further the Purposes and Principles of the Charter of the United Nations,
> - Have agreed . . . :[32]

Keep in mind that the treaty was drafted through the consensus process operating in COPUOS, a more difficult process than voting because the consensus infers unanimous agreement and support. Legal principles embodied in the treaty are summarized by White and White:

- International law and the Charter of the United Nations shall apply to space activities.
- Outer space shall be free for exploration, use, and scientific investigation.
- There can be no claims of sovereignty or territory by nations on Earth over locations in space, other than over objects launched from Earth.
- Outer space and celestial bodies are the province of all mankind and should be used only for peaceful purposes.
- Nuclear weapons, weapons of mass destruction, military bases and maneuvers are banned from space.
- The launching state retains jurisdiction over space objects launched from Earth.
- Governments are liable for damage caused on Earth by their space objects.
- Private interests are recognized as having freedom of action in space as long as a government or group of governments on Earth authorize, assume responsibility for, and continually supervise their activities. Signatory nations, therefore, have a duty to oversee the activities of their citizens and commercial space ventures.
- As "Envoys of Mankind," astronauts are due noninterference and all necessary assistance in distress.
- Steps must be taken to ensure that the natural environments of celestial bodies not be contaminated by earth organisms and that the Earth not be contaminated by extraterrestrial organisms.[33]

Although working papers, treaties, resolutions, and other instruments of international collaboration and diplomacy continue to appear, it was the Outer Space Treaty that laid the groundwork for the application of international law in outer space as well as satellite communication.

ISSUES CONFRONTING COPUOS AND THE LEGAL SUBCOMMITTEE

When a problem on communication policy or law confronts a single country there is a common legal framework in which to resolve issues and settle disputes. That is not always the case where international law is concerned and many different countries vie for a common solution to a problem, basing their input on indigenous statutes. As the development of satellite communication and the increased use of outer space as a resource began to confront different United Nations organizations, the Legal Subcommittee found itself playing an increasingly important role in ironing out the differences between countries.

The work of the Legal Subcommittee spans a breadth of issues ranging from the use of the geostationary orbit to the use of nuclear power in space. In any given year a multitude of issues will be placed before the Legal Subcommittee and different countries may file working papers with different opinions on how to deal with those issues. Each meeting of the Legal Subcommittee works with an agenda usually established through previous meetings. Some agendas remain in place for long periods of time, others are rather fleeting.

Definition and Delimitation of Outer Space

Examining just one issue, the "definition and delimitation" of outer space, shows the way in which the Legal Subcommittee comes to grips with different approaches to telecommunication policy. For example, using 1988–1992 as a reference point, the working group dealing with this topic began to determine if a separate legal regime should be established for the control of the geostationary orbit.[34] At issue was a demarcation line between air space and outer space and whether or not that demarcation line was a legal or technical issue. Some delegations to the Legal Subcommittee suggested that the issue should be resolved with a binding international instrument to which countries would agree. The framework for the exploration of outer space would therefore go beyond the original 1967 Outer Space Treaty. Specific scientific issues evolved from the meetings such as the determination of exactly where air space and outer space should be divided. One working paper suggested that 110 kilometers above sea level would be a boundary line upon which a legally binding international instrument could be developed. The suggestion was made that an international agreement could establish air space and the right of "innocent passage" through which any state could pass in the launching of a space vehicle.

Some delegations objected to the demarcation line suggesting that no such definition or delimitation of outer space was necessary. They suggested that such a demarcation line would create practical problems in the peaceful exploration of outer space and that utmost freedom should be given to all countries for that peaceful exploration. Some delegations did point out that if substantial practical problems arose in the future, the issue of the demarcation line could be considered. Other delegations suggested that creating a demarcation line would subject flying objects to various legal regimes as it crossed between the arbitrary boundary of one regime and another. In other words, a legal framework for air space might be different than a legal framework for outer space. Still other delegations objected, saying that a demarcation line was already widely recognized.

Access to Orbit

Another issue discussed frequently in the Legal Subcommittee during this period was equitable access to the geostationary orbit. Some delegations felt that a separate legal regime was necessary to deal exclusively with the geostationary orbit and that legal principles should develop out of existing space law to regulate equitable access to the orbit. Under such proposals, the Committee on the Peaceful Uses of Outer Space as well as the ITU would be the bodies responsible for both the political and legal questions relating to access. Other delegations took the position that the geostationary orbit was subject to the 1967 Outer Space Treaty and therefore was not subject to any claim of sovereignty. Given that the Outer Space Treaty encompassed the geostationary orbit, they argued that there was no need for a separate legal regime. Some members felt that equitable access should take into consideration the role of developing countries who had not yet developed sophisticated space technology. Out of the various discussions that took place general agreement evolved in two areas: (1) that the geostationary orbit was a limited natural resource, and (2) a claim of national sovereignty could not be made for any position in the orbit.

The Geostationary Orbit and Issues of National Sovereignty

A working paper submitted by Kenya took the position that the geostationary orbit was linked to national sovereignty. Kenya's working paper stated:

> The geostationary satellite orbit is a physical fact linked to the reality of our planet because its existence depends exclusively on its relation to gravitational phenomenon generated by the Earth and therefore should not be considered in the concept of outer space;
>
> By implication of the foregoing the geostationary satellite orbit is part of the territory

over which equatorial countries should exercise their national sovereignty.[35]

Kenya's position referred to previous world administrative radio conferences where some representatives contended that the segments of the geostationary orbit that were located above the equatorial countries and their respective territories were intended to bring "genuine benefits" to the inhabitants of those countries. Kenya stressed that the geostationary orbit should not serve the interests of a few advantaged countries which would be the sole beneficiaries of the natural resource, to the detriment of the developing countries. Similar draft working papers were submitted by Columbia, Ecuador, and Indonesia. An opposite view to countries proposing territorial jurisdiction over the orbit was presented by West Germany prior to unification. The report of the Legal Subcommittee included an extensive comparison between the German position and those of the equatorial countries.

Contrasting Policy Positions

Examining the preceding comparison illustrates these divergent views. For example, the position of the equatorial countries differed from the German position, which was that the geostationary orbit as well as outer space was not subject to claims of sovereignty by means of use, occupation, or any other means.[36]

The equatorial countries also took the position that those countries with advanced space technology should facilitate and accelerate the transfer of information to developing countries so that the developing countries could achieve the capability to use the orbit as a means of serving their national development objectives. The German working paper left the issue unstated. The German working paper also did not deal with the removal of nonoperational space objects, whereas the position of the equatorial countries was that those states or international organizations which have placed space objects in geostationary orbit should take all necessary steps to remove nonoperational or unutilized objects from the orbit. The German working paper also took the position that the geostationary orbit was an integral part of outer space and subject to the 1967 Outer Space Treaty, whereas the working papers of the equatorial countries left that issue unstated.[37]

ITU RADIO REGULATIONS GOVERNING SATELLITES

Beyond the regulations of individual countries, control over satellite communication occurs through the International Telecommunication Union and its Radio Regulations. Periodically amended through treaties and world administrative radio conferences, the ITU's Radio Regulations cover such things as the use of the geostationary orbit, frequency assignments, frequency registration, nuclear power in space, protection of astronauts, and search and recovery of launch vehicles and space orbiters.[38]

Definitions

Key definitions set the framework for applying the Radio Regulations to satellite communication and reflect common terminology used in international telecommunication law. Examples of some of these terms important to the understanding of satellite law include:

- Deep Space: Space at distances from the Earth approximately equal to, or greater than, the distance between the Earth and the Moon.
- Spacecraft: A vehicle which is intended to go beyond the major portion of the Earth's atmosphere.
- Satellite: A body which revolves around another body of preponderant mass and which has a motion primarily and permanently determined by the force of attraction of that other body.
- Active Satellite: A satellite carrying a station intended to transmit or retransmit radio communication signals.
- Reflecting Satellite: A satellite intended to reflect radio communication signals.
- Orbit: The path, relative to a specified frame of reference, described by the center of mass of a satellite or other object in space subjected primarily to natural forces, mainly the force of gravity.
- Inclination of an Orbit (of an earth satellite): The angle determined by the plane containing the orbit and the plane of the Earth's equator.
- Period (of a satellite): The time elapsing between two consecutive passages of a satellite through a characteristic point on its orbit.

- Altitude of the Apogee or of the Perigee: The altitude of the apogee or perigee above a specified reference surface serving to represent the surface of the Earth.
- Geosynchronous Satellite: An earth satellite whose period of revolution is equal to the period of rotation of the Earth about its axis.
- Geostationary Satellite: A geosynchronous satellite whose circular and direct orbit lies in the plane of the Earth's equator and which thus remains fixed relative to the Earth; by extension, a satellite which remains approximately fixed relative to the Earth.
- Geostationary-Satellite Orbit: The orbit in which a satellite must be placed to be a geostationary satellite.[39]

Other definitions relating to broadcasting space communication and telecommunication also appear in the Radio Regulations. For example, *telecommunication* is defined as "Any transmission, emission or reception of signs, signals, writing, images and sounds or intelligence of any nature by wire, radio, optical or other electro magnetics systems."[40] The definition of *space radio communication* is "Any radio communication involving the use of one or more space stations or the use of one or more reflecting satellites or other objects in space."[41] Additional terms defined in the Radio Regulations include *inter-satellite service, space operations service, aeronautical mobile-satellite service, radionavigation-satellite service,* and others.

Definition-based Regulatory Issues

Although definitions used in the Radio Regulations are rather straightforward, Rumphorst points out that concern has developed over the way they are applied to satellite communication.[42] For example, under the Radio Regulations the definition of *broadcasting service* reads: "A radio communication service in which the transmissions are intended for direct reception by the general public."[43] The regulations define the term *radio communication service* as: "A service as defined in this section involving the transmission, emission and/or reception of radio waves for specific telecommunications purposes."[44] Individual statutes within different countries may define a broadcasting service as a medium carrying sound and video images over such technologies as cable or fiber optics. The clash occurs when moving into other areas of international law such as copyright. Where the Berne Convention applies the word *broadcasting* to only over-the-air transmissions, the transmission of information through other means such as cable or wired systems is defined separately. Two other definitions also show the difficulty in strict application to contemporary satellite communication. For example, ITU Radio Regulations define *broadcasting-satellite service* as: "A radio communication service in which signals transmitted or retransmitted by space stations are intended for direct reception by the general public."[45] Closely related to broadcast satellite service is the *fixed-satellite service,* which the Radio Regulations define as: "A radio communication service between Earth stations at specified fixed points when one or more satellites are used; in some cases this service includes satellite to satellite links. . . ."[46]

The difference in the two definitions lies in the conditions for reception of the satellite signal. Radio Regulations permit the administration of a given country to assign a frequency to the allocated fixed service as long as the frequency is not intended for the signal to be received by the general public. Stated succinctly, private reception of signals transmitted from fixed-service satellite is prohibited. Penalties also exist. Individual countries are bound to take the necessary measures to prohibit the unauthorized interception of radio communications not intended for the general use of the public and to impose penalties for divulging the contents of the private radio communications used in the fixed-satellite services.[47]

Stop and consider the typical cable television system. The headend antennae more than likely contains a series of satellite dishes, all of which receive programming that is then distributed through cable to the general public. Rumphorst emphasizes that this rather universal means of transporting signals and distributing them to the public in strict application violates the Radio Regulations since the signals are relayed through a fixed-satellite service. The issue becomes even more complex when such a factor as the administration of individual telecommunication systems is taken into consideration. For example, some countries have privately owned systems, others are publicly owned systems. Rumphorst notes that other administrative agencies such as the Counsel of Europe with its Transfrontier Television Convention and the European Community Television Without

Frontiers directives all add to the complexities of international law over the growing field of satellite communication.[48]

Frequency Assignments

ITU Radio Regulations also govern the coordination of frequency assignments for satellite communication. For example, a country planning a satellite network follows specific procedures that include notification of the frequency assignments and the orbital position of the satellite to the International Frequency Registration Board of the ITU.[49] Radio Regulations require that a country intending to establish a satellite network notify the IFRB "not earlier than 5 years and preferably not later than 2 years before the date of service the frequency and orbital position of the satellites intended to be used in the network."[50] In turn the IFRB will publish in its weekly circular all of the information provided, and comments on the published information are then solicited. Countries that feel the frequency or orbital location or intended use of the network may interfere with their own satellite systems can then respond. Disagreements are resolved through the ITU. Radio Regulations require that:

> the administration responsible for the planned system shall first explore all possible means of meeting its requirements, taking into account the characteristics of the geostationary-satellite networks of other systems, and without considering the possibility of adjustment to systems of other administrations. If no such means can be found, the administration concerned is then free to apply to other administrations concerned to solve these difficulties. . . .[51]

Countries receiving the request are asked to explore all possible means of meeting the needs of the country requesting a resolution of the disagreement, including the possibility of relocating geostationary space stations or changing frequencies. The IFRB offers its assistance to countries involved in the resolution of disputes. Other regulations govern such matters as the accuracy of the antennas used in geostationary satellites, and making sure that the pointing direction and the frequency separation necessary to avoid interference with other satellite systems are correct.

WARC RESOLUTIONS

In addition to the Radio Regulations of the ITU, World Administrative Radio Conferences (WARC) pass resolutions that can influence telecommunication policy and set the stage for revision of the Radio Regulations. Resolutions range everywhere from Relating to Information on the Propagation of Radio Waves Used in the Determination of the Coordination Area to resolutions that deal with agreements for space-station links, global maritime distress and safety systems, and improvements in the design and use of radio equipment.[52] An early resolution dealing with equal rights of the geostationary satellite orbit and frequency bands was passed by the World Administrative Radio Conference held in Geneva, Switzerland in 1979. In general terms, the resolution establishes policy for eliminating any priority of an individual country or groups of countries when using geostationary orbit positions:

> *considering*
>
> that all countries have equal rights in the use of both the radio frequencies allocated to various space radio communication services and the geostationary-satellite orbit for these services;
>
> *taking into account*
>
> that the radio frequency spectrum and the geostationary-satellite orbit are limited natural resources and should be most effectively and economically used;
>
> *having in mind*
>
> that the use of the allocated frequency bands and fixed positions in the geostationary-satellite orbit by individual countries or groups of countries can start at various dates depending on the requirements and readiness of technical facilities of countries;
>
> *resolves*
>
> 1. that the registration with the IFRB of frequency assignments for space radio communication services and their use should not provide any permanent priority for any individual country or groups of countries and should not create an obstacle to the establishment of space systems by other countries;
>
> 2. that, accordingly, a country or a group of countries having registered with the IFRB frequencies for their space radio communication

services should take all practicable measures to realize the possibility of the use of new space systems by other countries or groups of countries so desiring;

3. that the provisions contained in paragraphs 1 and 2 of this Resolution should be taken into account by the administrations and the permanent organs of the Union.[53]

The same WARC passed a resolution on the use of geostationary-satellite orbits for the planning of space services. It articulated that the geostationary-satellite orbit and the radio-frequency spectrum are limited natural resources and as a result there is a need for equitable access to those resources and their efficient and economical use. The resolution went on to state that different countries can take advantage of those resources at different times and that there are growing requirements for countries to pay particularly close attention to the relevant technical aspects when using the orbit based on the geographical location of the particular country.[54]

THE EUROPEAN SPACE AGENCY

Concurrent with the development of rocketry and satellites in the United States, other parts of the world were moving forward in space technology. In Europe the effort was cooperative through a succession of international organizations leading up to the formation of the European Space Agency (ESA). The forerunners of the ESA conducted space research, developed rocketry for the launch of heavy satellites, and played a part in the negotiations with INTELSAT. These functions were carried out by the European Space Research Organization (ESRO), the European Organization for the Development and Construction of Space Vehicle Launchers (ELDO), and the European Conference on Satellite Communications (CETS). Each was a forerunner to, and played a part in, the formation of the European Space Agency.

Today the European Space Agency works cooperatively with the United States and NASA participating in a number of joint projects, one of the most notable being the Spacelab experiments, bringing together the first non-American astronaut to fly in the *Space Shuttle*, Dr. Ulf Merbold, with a NASA crew in the flight of the *Space Shuttle Columbia* on November 28, 1983. Another cooperative effort was the launching of the Hubble Space Telescope from the *Space Shuttle Discovery*. The cooperative relationship that now exists was preceded by some rough going during the early INTELSAT negotiations between the United States and European delegations on INTELSAT. John A. Johnson, one of COMSAT's chief negotiators, recalls:

> The Europeans had decided to caucus among themselves on every issue and to negotiate on the basis of a single position, at least so far as their formal statements were concerned. That was difficult for us to contend with. . . . Fortunately, because of certain natural interests in common and also because of the groundwork that had been prudently established ahead of time, we were able to reach wide areas of agreement at the very outset with the Japanese, the Australians, and the Canadians: Hence, while we were outnumbered by the Europeans, we were not without allies, and very important allies.[55]

A better understanding of the genesis of the ESA, the role of different organizations, and the formative years of European satellite technology can be gained by tracing the history of the three organizations which preceded the ESA—ESRO, ELDO, and CETS.

The European Space Research Organization (ESRO)

The development of the technology, organization, and regulation of European space research and satellite applications centered around two areas: (1) basic research, and (2) launch and rocketry.[56] The contemporary development of the research component can be traced back to a succession of organizations.

- International Council of Scientific Unions (ICSU)
- Committee on Space Research (COSPAR)
- European Organization for Nuclear Research (CERN)
- European Study Group on Space Research (ESGSR)
- European Preparatory Commission on Space Research (COPERS)
- European Space Research Organization (ESRO)

In 1954 the International Council of Scientific Unions (ICSU), a nongovernment organization designed to facilitate scientific understanding, formed a Committee on Space Research (COSPAR). After COSPAR was formed, a group of scientists took the initiative to use the model of the European Organization for Nuclear Research (CERN) to form under the auspices of CERN a more formal organization, the European Study Group on Space Research (ESGSR). The ESGSR was formed with strong backing by the French. Under the auspices of that organization there developed the European Preparatory Commission on Space Research (COPERS), which was charged with setting up a more permanent body. The charge, which was drawn up after a series of meetings during 1960 and 1961, was to study the possibilities of establishing a European organization designed to foster cooperation in space research. The convention establishing the European Space Research Organization (ERSO) entered into force on March 20, 1964.

The first director general of ESRO was Professor Pierre Auger of France who had served as the executive secretary of COPERS. After COPERS met for the last time on March 23, 1964, ESRO held its first meeting immediately thereafter. Already prepared for the new ESRO were scientific and technical programs and experimental projects involving sounding rockets and two small satellites.[57] The convention under which ESRO operated required collaboration among European countries engaged in space research and technology for peaceful purposes. Members of the ESRO convention were Belgium, Denmark, France, the Federal Republic of Germany, Italy, the Netherlands, Spain, Sweden, Switzerland, and the United Kingdom. Austria, Norway, and Ireland were granted observer status.

The European Organization for the Development and Construction of Space Vehicles (ELDO)

While ESRO was in its formative stages, the United Kingdom made the decision to abandon its nuclear-deterrent project based on a ground-to-ground ballistic system.[58] The research and development of rocketry conducted as part of the deterrent program provided the foundation for a cooperative effort in the launch of heavy-payload satellites. France had been conducting research on a rocket capable of launching light satellites, but by placing the French rocket on top of the British rocket it became the second stage of a heavy-payload launch system. In addition, by combining the research and development of other European nations, an even larger three-stage rocket was possible.

At a diplomatic conference in 1961 there evolved a document for the establishment of a European Organization for the Development and Construction of Space Vehicle Launchers (ELDO). By 1962 six European countries, Belgium, France, the Federal Republic of Germany, Italy, the Netherlands, and the United Kingdom, had agreed to the new organization's convention. Australia also signed because of a contract with the United Kingdom permitting the British to use the Woomera, Australia testing range.[59]

Based on the terms of the convention governing ELDO, the organization's purpose was the development and construction of space vehicles, in particular rockets that could carry heavy payloads. Paris was selected as the headquarters of the organization and the Woomera firing range in Australia was made available to member states. Specific countries had responsibility for different phases of the program. The Federal Republic of Germany had responsibility for the third stage of the launcher; Italy for the initial series of satellite test vehicles; Belgium for the ground guidance stations; and the Netherlands for long-range telemetry links and associated ground equipment.[60] The convention also required that the test firings of the first-stage rocket would occur at Woomera while the site of the second- and third-stage firings would be determined at a later date. ELDO later constructed its own launching base in Guiana.

The European Conference on Satellite Communications (CETS)

The United States was moving forward with COMSAT's international satellite network under INTELSAT when Europe decided to enter the INTELSAT program with a unified voice. Under the initiative of the French, there convened in Paris in 1963 a European Conference on Satellite Communications (CETS), the main purpose of which was to develop a policy through which Europe would participate in the INTELSAT negotiations. A series of CETS meetings took place in Paris, London, and Rome prior to the signing of the INTELSAT interim agreement in August 1964.[61]

Problems in the Functioning and Relationships of ESRO, ELDO, and CETS

A series of problems began to plague the three organizations, both in terms of their own internal functioning and their relationships with each other. ESRO abandoned two of its early projects, an astronomical observatory and a mission to study comets. Some countries began to withdraw their financial support for certain projects and Spain asked that its contributions to ESRO be reduced because of its own economic problems. A lack of agreement on budget priorities further strained the organization. Calls for the restructuring of the ESRO resulted in various reforms being introduced. They weren't enough, however, to cushion ESRO against the disagreements between members when some countries proposed that ESRO move out of purely research satellite deployment to application satellites. Aware of the progress made in the United States in both metrological and communications satellites, the pressure to compete fully and be part of the economic benefits of the new generation of satellites was substantial.

ELDO was also facing financial problems. The early budget projections were inadequate for ELDO to carry out its missions, and disagreements developed over how much money ELDO would need and who would pay the increased costs. Programs dropped behind schedule, further complicating matters and straining relations within the organization. Supplementary funds were granted but even these proved insufficient when technical difficulties occurred in test firings. A particularly costly failed launch in 1971 caused a rethinking of the ELDO concept of building launchers exclusively for European use.

CETS continued to work within the framework of the INTELSAT negotiations and gradually became involved as the overseer of a contentious European communication satellite program designed to help create European solidarity. The satellite program, however, ran into political trouble, was eventually taken out of CETS, and with the conclusion of the INTELSAT negotiations CETS lost its raison d'être. It ceased its activities in 1970.

Solving Organizational Problems: The European Space Agency Takes Shape

At a conference of the heads of ELDO in 1966 it was decided a new area for closer cooperation in space research was necessary and a proposal was made for the formation of a European Space Conference.[62] The conference took place in Paris the same year and resulted in a resolution recognizing the need for coordination of scientific and technological space research facilities. "On a practical level the Conference decided to set up subordinate bodies appropriate for its objectives, namely: a committee of alternatives; a program working group to draw up an inventory of European space programs, resources and facilities; and a committee responsible for looking into the legal conditions under which the Conference could take on institutional form."[63] International pressure to move forward in space research resulted in short deadlines for the subordinate bodies to complete their work. A second European Space Conference was held in Rome one year later. Other meetings followed. Proposals were hindered on some occasions by political disagreements and helped in others by joint projects. Finally, a convention creating the European Space Agency was agreed to in 1975. Under the terms of the convention, which took effect in 1980, ELDO ceased to exist and ESRO became the European Space Agency.

Legal and Organizational Structure of the ESA

The convention establishing the ESA and agreed upon by the member countries created a council with representatives from each member country, and a director general. The council is the ESA's political and legislative organ. Both the council and the director general are supported by an international staff. The council, under the terms of the convention, is a sovereign political organ and is entitled to hold meetings at the ministerial level.[64] ESA also has the privilege of immunity afforded other international organizations. The ESA Convention differs from the old ESRO operating document in that ESA has much broader areas of activity, emphasizes application as opposed to just research, and stresses joint undertakings. While the council has the option to set up subordinate boards to review specific projects, this is not a requirement.

ESA Regulations Governing Contracts

The contract regulations of the ESA regulate the procurement policy of the organization.[65] Under the ESA's contract regulations, certain requirements must be met.[66] For example:

> Contracts must be placed on the basis of the optimum combination of economy of cost and technical excellence. . . . Technical quality and cost effectiveness depend, in the first instance, on the quality and realism of the re-

> quirements imposed by the Agency and the conditions under which industry is asked to bid. An assessment of tenders as to quality and cost is made, in as objective a manner as possible, by an exhaustive evaluation procedure that involves a wide range of expertise, of which more than half is drawn from staff not directly concerned with the management of the ensuing contract. The result of this evaluation is the recommendation of the best offer. (The Industrial Policy Committee) approves the proposed procurement approach, and in particular whether the contract should be placed by open competition or by direct negotiation.[67]

Although the ESA's contract regulations require open competition where possible, some firms have achieved such dominance in space technology that other firms cannot bid on highly sophisticated projects. In addition, certain projects may be restricted to certain member countries, which means the primary contract must be placed with that country. Some prime contractors have merged, further limiting the ability of more than one firm to bid.[68] Final decisions on who gets the contract is made by the ESA's Industrial Policy Committee, which takes into account the excellence of the project and the cost. One feature of the contract-awarding process is designed to ensure that the work is distributed among participating countries in proportion to their contributions. The "geographical distribution of fair return" is known before bids are solicited and it becomes a management responsibility to assure the spirit of the contract regulations is met.[69]

Quality is built into programs through a performance incentive scheme. The potential profit a contractor receives can be controlled by the ESA and increased or reduced depending on the contractor's performance as measured against predetermined criteria. For example, a project completed ahead of time with improved performance results could result in a bonus. One that does not measure up could cost the contractor money. Predetermined criteria include "delivery against required dates, technical performance as evidenced in ground tests, and performance in orbit, including operational life."[70]

OTHER INTERNATIONAL SATELLITE GOVERNING ORGANIZATIONS

Both INTELSAT and the ESA have dominated much of the industrialized world's entry into satellite communication. Other organizations, however, have gained in stature as satellites play increasingly important roles in linking nations through space. Of particular interest are the International Organization of Space Communications (INTERSPUTNIK), the International Maritime Satellite Organization (INMARSAT), the Arab Satellite Communication Organization (ARABSAT), and the European Telecommunications Satellite Organization (EUTELSAT).[71]

International Organization of Space Communications

INTERSPUTNIK, named after the first communication satellite launched into space by the Soviet Union, was created in 1971 by the INTERSPUTNIK Foundation Agreement, which came into force upon ratification in July 1972.[72] INTERSPUTNIK is governed by a board that consists of the representatives of numerous countries, each country having one vote. Heading the board is a director-general, working in coordination with a supervised Auditing Committee consisting of three members elected by the board. Members of INTERSPUTNIK are primarily countries associated with the former Soviet Union and now the countries of Eastern Europe.

Some of the signatories to the INTERSPUTNIK Foundation Agreement include Bulgaria, Cuba, Hungary, Korea, Poland, Romania, Vietnam, Russia, Germany, and others. Since 1983 the system has operated as a commercial international satellite network. Telephone communication and broadcasting are the two primary uses of the INTERSPUTNIK system. News items are exchanged regularly among member stations over the network. Individual agreements also exist between INTERSPUTNIK and other international space communications organizations such as the Council for Mutual Economic Assistance (CMEA), the Council on International Cooperation and the Study and Utilization of Space (INTERCOSMOS), the International Radio and Television Organization (OIRT), INMARSAT, and ITU.

The International Maritime Satellite Organization

During Operation Desert Storm in 1991, a radio journalist in a Middle East desert needing to communicate with a local radio station or network in another country could open a suitcase-size portable satellite antennae system complete with portable transmitter and power unit and have it operational within five minutes. From the middle of the desert the satellite transmitter was able to connect with INMARSAT. Primarily designed for international shipping, INMARSAT evolved out of an initiative of the International Maritime Organization, which convened during 1975 and 1976.

INMARSAT was formed through an operating agreement permitting nations to become signatories of a convention stating the organizational and administrative structure of INMARSAT. INMARSAT's space segment is designed to be used by ships of all nations without discrimination. Established with its headquarters in London by an agreement with the government of the United Kingdom, INMARSAT has legal status in the United Kingdom and has within the United Kingdom the same legal privileges as a corporation.

Somewhat like INTELSAT, INMARSAT has limited protection from competitive regional and national satellite systems. Any member state of INMARSAT is required to notify the organization when it plans a separate space facility to meet any of the services offered by INMARSAT. INMARSAT is then empowered to make nonbinding recommendations helping to assure technical compatibility and avoid "significant economic harm."[73] Somewhat unusual in its private-public structure, INMARSAT is managed through interrelated private and public entities with an international obligation to provide public telecommunications while at the same time operating as an economically viable organization. A permanent working relationship exists between governments, especially in the area of technical cooperation. Any state can be a signatory to the INMARSAT Convention.

The technical aspects of the INMARSAT system include satellites and support facilities that are either leased or purchased by INMARSAT. Of these a space segment includes operational and spare satellites in geostationary orbit covering the three main ocean regions. Coast-earth stations connect the space segment of INMARSAT with individual countries' telecommunication networks, which are owned domestically by private companies or operated by PTTs. INMARSAT network coordinating stations in each region assign space-segment capacity to the satellites and earth stations while the ship-earth stations are purchased or leased by the individual maritime owners and operators. An operations control center at INMARSAT headquarters monitors and coordinates the operational activities of the network.

The administrative structure of INMARSAT consists of an assembly, a council, and a directorate:

> The *Assembly* is composed of representatives of all parties and meets once every two years. Its functions include the review of INMARSAT activities, purposes, general policy and long term objectives, and the making of recommendations thereon to the Council. Each party has one vote.
>
> The *Council* normally consists of twenty-two representatives of signatories or groups of signatories: eighteen with the largest investment shares and four elected by the *Assembly* on the principle of just geographical representation and with due regard to the interest of the developing countries. Policy making in INMARSAT is primarily the responsibility of the Council. Having due regard to the views and recommendations of the Assembly, the Council is required to provide for the space segment necessary for carrying out the purposes of INMARSAT in the most economic, effective, and efficient manner. The Council is therefore responsible for all main financial and operational decisions. The Council meets at least three times a year. Signatories on the Council have a voting power equivalent to their investment shares, except that most signatories may cast more than 25% of the total voting participation.
>
> The *Directorate* is headed by the Director-General, who is the chief executive and legal representative of the organization and is responsible to, and under the direction of, the Council. The Director-General is appointed by the Council for six years, subject to confirmation by the parties. The Directorate carries out the day-to-day activities of the organization.[74]

INMARSAT has the responsibility for determining the performance standards that coastal stations and ships use to interact with the INMARSAT satellites. A second-generation space segment went into operation in the 1990s and INMARSAT's growth has moved the satellite network to over 10,000 users.[75] INMARSAT is also attempting to secure international agreements between countries, some of which prohibit using communications equipment in coastal areas. An active research program operates within the organization and has applied satellite technology through INMARSAT to such areas as aeronautical communication.

The Arab Satellite Communication Organization

Signed in 1976, the Arab Satellite Communication Organization (ARABSAT) coordinates the telecommunications activities of the PTTs in the Arab countries. Headquartered in Riyadh, Saudi Arabia, the objective of ARABSAT is the establishment and maintenance of a regional telecommunication system for the Arab region. It provides the television program exchange for the Arab areas, in addition to telephone and data transmission. Three main organs comprise ARABSAT:

> The General Assembly is composed of all ARABSAT Ministers of Post, Telephone and Telegraph, and Telecommunications, and meets once a year. Its functions include the review of ARABSAT activities, purposes, general policy, and long term objectives in the making of recommendations thereon to the Board of Directors.
>
> The Board of Directors, composed of representatives of nine member States, of which five, the highest shareholders are permanent, and four are elected by the General Assembly every two years.
>
> The Executive Organ headed by the Director-General, . . . is the chief executive and legal representative of the organization, and is responsible to, and under the direction of, the Board. The Executive Organ is composed of a number of administrative units or sections which are defined in the ARABSAT internal regulations. The Executive Organ carries out the day-to-day activities of the organization.[76]

ARABSAT satellites are designed for launch on the *Space Shuttle* or the Ariane system. A control network operates out of Dirab, near Riyadh, with a secondary station located near Tunis.

European Telecommunications Satellite Organization

The space segment of European telecommunications is under the auspices of the European Telecommunications Satellite Organization (EUTELSAT). Seventeen European telecommunications administrations created EUTELSAT in 1977. It operated with provisional status until 1985 when 26 European countries signed an intragovernmental convention and operating agreement. Headquartered in Paris, EUTELSAT's organization consists of an Assembly of Parties, made up of representatives of the member countries; a Board of Signatories composed of the representatives of the different telecommunications entities who belong to EUTELSAT; and an Executive Organ headed by a director general.[77] The primary uses of the system are for telephone and television communication as well as data and service to the European Broadcasting Union's Eurovision system. Close cooperation exists with other organizations including the ITU, INTELSAT, and the ESA.

THE U.S. COMMERCIAL SPACE LAUNCH ACT

In the United States the ability of the private sector to enter the satellite business was enhanced in 1984 by the passage of the Commercial Space Launch Act.[78] The rationale for the act is stated in Sec. 2, which declares that:

(1) the peaceful uses of outer space continue to be of great value and to offer benefits to all mankind;
(2) private applications of space technology have achieved a significant level of commercial and economic activity, and offer the potential for growth in the future, particularly in the United States;
(3) new and innovative equipment and services are being sought, created, and offered by entrepreneurs in telecommunications, information services, and remote sensing technology;
(4) the private sector in the United States has the capability of developing and providing private satellite launching and associated services that would complement the launching and associated services now available from the United States Government;
(5) the development of commercial launch vehicles and associated services would enable the United States to retain its competitive position internationally, thereby contributing to the national interest and economic well-being of the United States;
(6) provision of launch services by the private sector is consistent with the national security interests and foreign policy interests of the United States and would be facilitated by stable, minimal, and appropriate regulatory guidelines that are fairly and expeditiously applied; and
(7) the United States should encourage private sector launches and associated services and, only to the extent necessary, regulate such

> launches and services in order to ensure compliance with international obligations of the United States and to protect the public health and safety, safety of property, and national security interests and foreign policy interests of the United States.[79]

The U.S Commercial Space Launch Act goes on to state its purpose is to promote economic growth and entrepreneurial activities through the private sector by simplifying and expediting commercial launch licenses to facilitate and encourage the utilization of government-developed space technology. The act provides for the secretary of transportation to issue licenses permitting private firms to operate launch sites in the United States and foreign nations. Payloads must comply with all requirements of federal law and the secretary has the power to terminate or suspend a launch if it is determined that the launch will be detrimental to public safety, national security, or foreign policy interest of the United States. The secretary of transportation retains the right to place federal officers or employees or any other individual as an observer at any launch site and to monitor the licensee or private contractor at any time.

Private companies also have the ability to purchase launch sites at fair market value. Private operators are required to carry liability insurance, hold-harmless agreements, proof of financial responsibility, and any other insurances that may be necessary to protect the United States from liability, loss, or injury involving government facilities or personnel. Sufficient insurance must be in effect to cover any international obligations the United States may incur as a result of the launch.[80] Consultation is required with the secretary of defense on matters affecting national security and the secretary of state where any launch affects foreign policy. While prohibiting states to pass laws inconsistent with any provision of the act, nothing precludes a state from passing regulations with additional or more stringent requirements than those contained in the act. The act encourages consultation between the secretary of transportation and states to "simplify and expedite the approval of space launch activities."[81]

FCC REGULATIONS GOVERNING DIRECT- BROADCAST SATELLITES

Federal Communications Commission Regulations define *direct-broadcast satellite service* as: "a radio communication service in which signals transmitted or retransmitted by space stations are intended for direct reception by the general public. In the Direct Broadcast Satellite Service the term *direct reception* shall encompass both individual reception and community reception."[82]

Development and Rationale

In an effort to permit entrepreneurs to enter the DBS service, the FCC has operated with a liberal policy of entry into the satellite industry. Still operating under an experimental phase, the rules have been codified with minimal restrictions for entrants to meet the FCC's application procedures. The formulation of FCC policy began with a Notice of Inquiry released in 1980 requesting comments on two FCC reports, one dealing with the technical characteristics of DBS and another with regulatory policies.[83] Two months after the original Notice of Inquiry the FCC received an application from Satellite Television Corporation, a subsidiary of COMSAT, to begin construction of a satellite-to-home broadcasting system. In 1981, the FCC approved the COMSAT application and concurrently issued a Notice of Proposed Policy Statement and Rule Making.[84] Additional applications soon followed. Seven were accepted by the FCC. One was partially accepted and were five rejected as incomplete and unacceptable.[85] In developing its rules the FCC determined that DBS could serve the public interest by providing service to remote areas, making additional channels of television programming available, tailoring programs to small audiences with specialized tastes, provide innovative services such as high-definition television and educational programming, including the transmission of medical data.[86]

Authorization

Authorization to operate a direct-broadcast satellite service cannot be granted to any alien or the representative of any alien, a foreign government or its representative, a corporation organized under the laws of a foreign government, or any corporation in which any officer or director is a alien. If more than one fifth of the capital stock in a company is owned or voted by aliens or the representatives of a foreign government, then that corporation cannot operate a direct-broadcast satellite system. Also, if one fourth of the board of directors are aliens or if the commission finds that granting the license is not in the public interest, it will also deny awarding the license. The same rules apply to parent companies, so a subsidiary company cannot apply independently of a parent to operate a DBS service.

Requests for Orbits and Frequencies

Applicants can request specific orbital positions and frequencies and must show the type of service intended to be provided along with all pertinent technical information. In addition, the application is placed on public notice for 45 days, during which other parties may file comments and partitions. The original application can be amended within a 45-day period and given the same consideration as the original application. However, if original applications have included requests for particular frequencies or orbital positions, the original application will take priority.

License terms for interim direct-broadcast satellite systems are for five years and the conditions include necessitating the holder of the construction permit to begin construction or at least contract for construction within one year of the grant of the construction permit. The satellite station also is required to be operational within a six-year period of the date of the construction permit unless an exception is made by the FCC. Transfer of the construction permit is not a justification for extending any of the deadlines. Technical requirements are based on the WARC regulations and of prime consideration is whether or not the system will interfere with other operational or planned systems. FCC regulations also require an equal employment opportunity policy to be enforced.

DBS Service Obligations

Under a provision passed with the Cable Television Consumer Protection and Competition Act of 1992, DBS operators have certain obligations to carry noncommercial educational and informational programming. Providers of DBS video programming services are required to reserve a portion of their channel capacity equal to not less than 4 percent, that's no more than 7 percent exclusively for noncommercial programming of an educational or informational nature.[87] The provider must meet the requirements of the law "by making channel capacity available to national educational programming suppliers, upon reasonable prices, terms, and conditions, as determined by the Commission . . ."[88] A determination of the reasonable prices can take into account the nonprofit character of the programming service and any federal funds that are used to support the programming.

Developing Policy

More permanent regulations over satellite communications will depend on a number of factors as the industry develops. One is the classification of the service as broadcasting or common carrier. For some satellite operators, leasing space makes them a common carrier. DBS, if contracted with those suppliers, would be considered under common carrier regulations. In other areas where the DBS operators originate programming they would fall under the broadcasting statues. Larson and other critics of the FCC policy toward DBS have identified potential disadvantages to the current policy framework.[89] For example, one possible adverse effect is on local broadcasting. DBS operators serve a national audience, and if they significantly siphon off the audience for local television and radio services it would run afoul of the FCC's emphasis on supporting local broadcasting. Such siphoning could trigger lobbying efforts by such groups as the National Association of Broadcasters, which represents the local radio and television industry. Although the Communications Act of 1934 provides the FCC with the authority to award licenses based on a public-interest standard much broader than local service, nevertheless the issue of local service remains visible.[90] Also under consideration is the economic impact that DBS might have. If DBS is supported by commercial advertising, significant audience drain could affect the revenues of local television and radio stations. At a time when the FCC is developing policy toward high-definition television (HDTV), policy that supports the economic structure of local television broadcasting, DBS could pose problems in the long run. Some spectrum-crowding issues could also emerge. Fixed-satellite services operate in the same frequency as DBS and at some point these services, along with private microwave links, may need to change frequencies.

POLICY IMPLICATIONS OF DIRECT-BROADCAST SATELLITES

As is the case with conventional broadcasting frequency assignments, the use of outer space has been on a first-come, first-served basis. This, however, has presented problems that are not easily solved within the framework of international law where sovereign states approach regulation from different perspectives. Although the United Nations and ITU governance has been effective, primarily because the issue has been frequency interference rather than programming, that effectiveness could be reduced with the widespread development of direct-broadcast satellites. For example, DBS systems are designed with powerful transmitters "broadcasting" over wide expanses of the earth's surface and crossing national boundaries. The very design of DBS is to reach small earth antennas at the level of the individual consumer, "grass-roots" in American political terminology, not institutions. Such broadcasts can have a much more direct and invasive impact than satellites used for point-to-point communication or navigation.

Program Control

The issue of industrialized nations having access to more than their fair share of orbital slots is an old one. Add to this equation the concern that nations obtaining orbital slots will use them for DBS. Should international regulations control the programing of DBS satellites since they influence so many people? Under United States law the answer is grounded in the First Amendment and is an unequivocal "no." But what happens when DBS satellites provide entertainment programming to entertainment starved regions? Psychologists suggest that television addiction among illiterate impoverished nationals is likely to result.[91] Political programming, even though couched unintentionally in entertainment programs, is much more invasive and threatening than nonpolitical programs. To make the issue even more complex, one must ask who, if anyone other than the sovereign state that produces and distributes the programming, should regulate it. Satellites, while sophisticated instruments of mass communication, cannot follow the precise boundaries of a country, especially small countries, and therefore keeping such signals in check may not be realistic. Proliferation of small receiving antennas further aggravates the problem. Because of the value, importance, and eventual popularity of DBS, international treaty negotiation will examine whether orbital slots for DBS warrant more regulation than satellites used for other purposes.

Common Carrier DBS

Consider the power of a foreign leader who can rent a DBS channel and talk directly to politicians and the public in democratic societies where the balance of power in the electoral process flows continuously between voters and elected officials. Theoretically, a well-established DBS leasing system could provide any leader with the means to reach any audience anywhere in the world where receiving antennas exist. In addition, treaties themselves are not always effective instruments of control. For example, Bailey points: "If these treaties are not customary international law, then States which are not parties to the treaties may serve as bases for which other States could vicariously circumvent the treaties to which they are bound without actually breaching those treaties or violating customary international law."[92] Bailey goes on to note that some countries that are not parties to a treaty could sell satellite time to other countries who want to target, and through communication, disrupt another country. The ability of countries to withdraw from treaties could pose additional burdens on the regulatory process.

TARIFF SCHEDULES

Rates for using satellites are spelled out in the tariff schedule, which lists the rates charged for leasing time and frequencies on the satellite. Different factors determine how much the user will be charged. For example, a user who leases a satellite for a year is charged less per hour than a user who only wants the satellite for a one-time transmission. Generally, rate structures are determined by hours of daily use, short- or long-term lease, time of day of service (prime- or nonprime-time use), and protection status (protected, nonprotected, or preemptible service).[93]

Other factors can affect the rates charged users. For example, occasional users will be charged more than regular users. Video users may be charged one rate for the space segment of the satellite link and additional charges for terrestrial links. The amount of spectrum space can also affect rates. Video signals use more bandwidth than audio-only signals, and two-way transmission can cost more than one-way transmission. The number of earth stations reached by the satellite footprint may also affect the rate the user is charged.

CONTINUING FACTORS AFFECTING THE REGULATION OF SATELLITE COMMUNICATION

Such issues as common carriers, electronic and satellite news gathering, the coordination of domestic and regulatory frameworks, and the assignment of frequencies and orbital positions only touch the core of satellite regulation. Satellites today are used for such telecommunication applications as data and telephone communication, video, navigation, and weather monitoring. Consider that there are aeronautical mobile satellites, amateur radio satellites, maritime mobile satellites, broadcast satellites, direct-broadcast satellites, and metrological satellites, to name just a few examples.

Economic and Political Structure

As we have seen with the European Space Agency's Contract Regulations, the economic and political structure of a region will determine its regulatory structure. For example, built into the ESA Contract Regulations are performance guidelines that are more complex and sophisticated, and some would argue more effective and efficient, than the simple lowest-bidder approach. In addition, the ESA must deal with different internal political structures among member countries whereas the United States and NASA do not. Although competition has been injected into the process through the initiatives of the European Community, much of European telecommunication is still controlled by individual PTTs. Economic conditions peculiar to one country can affect the entire organization. Currency-exchange rates can result in budget shortfalls. Political turmoil can further complicate matters, all of which have an impact on regulatory frameworks.

The Use of the Spectrum

Consider the different issues that arise every time a communication satellite is launched.[94] Most basic is frequency assignment. Great advances have been made in the use of the electromagnetic spectrum since the radio conferences of the 1920s. Today the useful area of the spectrum has stretched into the billions of hertz (cycles) per second. Satellites can operate in an area of the spectrum spanning approximately 30 billion hertz, but even so much negotiating exists at world administrative radio conferences over how the spectrum shall be allocated. Many different uses for satellites exist, not all of which are employed in such areas as broadcast communication or satellite news gathering. Add to this the fact that more than just a specific frequency is at issue when a satellite is launched. How long the frequency will be in use, and how much of the spectrum will be used also play a part in regulating satellites. Highly populated industrialized regions of the earth have more uses for satellite technology and therefore need more frequencies. In addition, the laws of physics transcend laws of nations, are not flexible, and create parameters upon the use of the spectrum. Satellites used for strictly domestic purposes can still spill over into other countries, making the use of the spectrum a constant international issue.

Orbital Positions

The geostationary orbit around the earth is not infinite. It is, like the frequency spectrum, a limited resource with currently about 1,800 parking spaces for satellites available. Consequently, the parking spaces must be regulated to avoid interference and, to a limited extent, outright collision between satellites. Although the probability of a physical collision is not high, the chance of a political collision is. Many of the industrialized nations with technology and sophisticated rocket propulsion systems moved ahead early in the space race. They also captured prime parking spaces in the geostationary orbit. While ample parking spaces exist in the geostationary orbit, not everyone can park where they want to. It is of little value to Australia to park a satellite on the other side of the globe where the footprint can't reach Australia. When frequency allocation is added to the issue of orbital position, the political landscape can become a contentious battleground. Just as highly populated regions of the earth have greater demands on frequency, they also have greater demands on the geostationary orbit. Of particular interest in the future will be the more populous regions placing demands on the geostationary orbit arc serving North America, the area over the Atlantic Ocean serving Western Europe, and the area over the Indian Ocean serving Eastern Europe and the USSR.[95]

Collision probabilities are based on such factors as the position of the satellite in relation to other satellites, the life of the satellite, whether the satellite is active or inactive, the size of the satellite, and the stability of the satellite. A problem at launch that causes a satellite to tumble uncontrollably in outer space will result in a greater probability of collision than a launch that results in an accurate stable positioning.

If a stable satellite were able to be placed permanently in a stable position, risks of collision would be minimal. Satellites, however, do not always remain stable. When a satellite drifts out of orbit, about ten years after positioning, the probability of collisions increases. Large satellites with extended solar panels inflate the risk even further. While all of these issues present problems, solutions to lessen the regulatory burden and increase the efficiency of the geostationary orbit are emerging rapidly. Advancements in antenna design, the ability to compress multiple signals into the same frequency permitting more efficient uplink and downlink capabilities, satellite-to-satellite relays in space, and other advanced systems provide more efficient use of the orbit.

Debris Collision in Space

In recent years the attention of COPUOS has focused on the growing problem of space debris and the potential hazards of unusable material in orbit. This emphasis and awareness was highlighted by the chair of COPUOS, Peter Jankowitsch of Austria, in opening remarks to the delegates at the beginning of COPUOS's thirty-third session.[96] Citing impressive statistics, he told the delegates that more than 7,000 known and trackable space objects circle the earth, and many more are there but undetectable. About 350 of these are active satellites, the rest are considered space debris and do not serve a useful function. Among the nonuseable objects are satellites that have outlived their usefulness but remain in space, disposable parts of missions and launches, and fragments resulting from the breakup of satellites and boosters. Jankowitsch stated that concern is increasing over such matters as

> the safety of manned space flight; accidental re-entry of space hardware; contamination of nuclear material in space and on the ground; damage to or loss of active satellites through collisions; debris proliferation through secondary collisions; crowding in the geostationary ring; interference with astronomical observations on the ground and in space; and interference with experiments in space.[97]

Jankowitsch pointed to the fact that space debris constitutes an "unacceptable" risk to people and materials, both in space and on the ground. Currently, little can be done about what is already in orbit, and cleaning operations are beyond the present technical capabilities of space technology. While atmospheric drag eventually pulls objects to earth, drag cannot be controlled. New emphasis in the planning stages of space flight must take place, and this involves improved spacecraft designs. COPUOS will continue to face the legal and technical ramifications of this problem in the future.

The Satellite Footprint

The footprint of a satellite is that area on the earth's surface covered by the satellite's signal. The total area visible to a satellite is more than 9,000 kilometers of the earth's surface but satellites are designed to target specific geographic regions. Although this area can be seen from the satellite, it is not the total useful area. Useful area is determined by such factors as the angle necessary for the ground antenna to communicate with the satellite and how the terrain and location of the antenna can impact on the communication link. A satellite uplink antenna on a mountaintop can be more efficient than one located in a valley where the mountain interrupts the line-of-sight signal. A satellite designed to communicate with a small fixed location on the earth's surface is more easily managed, from the perspective of both technology and regulation, than one positioned to communicate with large parts of a continent.

Channel Depth, Distribution, and Directionality

The tension existing between PANAMSAT and COMSAT's international satellite network shows the keen competition that can exist between companies wanting to gain a share of the satellite market. The decision by COMSAT to locate satellites in the Pacific region is a pre-emptive business strategy as well as a stake of claim on orbital slots and frequencies. As more countries expand their use of satellite communication and as developing countries want to gain a share and benefit in the technology of satellites, more demand for orbits and frequencies will exist. Basic international legal principles underlie three factors paramount to the effective utilization of the orbit and the application of technology. As Rothblatt explains, these three factors include channel depth, channel distribution, and channel directionality.[98] Policies governing satellite communication all support these three concepts.

The first factor, channel depth, is concerned with the capacity of the channel to handle messages. A small amount of channel depth means that only a small number of messages can be transmitted at any one time, whereas a large amount of channel depth means that the communication channel can handle a large number of messages.[99] Increased channel depth can occur by the application of technology that will do one of two things: (1) expand the electromagnetic spectrum into higher frequencies where there is less crowding and where more information can be included beyond the gigahertz range, and (2) expand the capacity of the channel by splitting it into different beams or piggybacking signals through compression techniques. In a regulatory framework where a country or satellite system is awarded a given frequency that includes a specific amount of bandwidth, the fully applied technologies can significantly enhance the value of the frequency.

Channel distribution refers to the footprint of the satellite. Satellites used for international transcontinental purposes apply a larger footprint than domestic or regional satellites. A policy interpretation of channel distribution exists within the ITU that encourages the entrance of developing countries into satellite communication, thereby fostering a policy that the largest number of satellites benefit society. Some scholars contend that channel distribution was one of the underlying reasons for the development of INTELSAT.[100]

The difference between channel directionality and channel distribution lies in the fact that the former is concerned with making the satellite available to as many people as possible who want to uplink and transmit information, whereas the latter is concerned with making it available to as many people as possible who want to receive information, i.e., the satellite footprint. Both, however, benefit from more efficient use of the spectrum. Some attempt has been made in the ITU's Radio Regulations to distinguish between those using satellites for point-to-point communication and the broader-based broadcasting services such as DBS. However, the legal definition between the two is becoming increasingly blurred.[101]

Merging Technology and Policy

Overall, international satellite policy has favored users of new frequencies by placing them in a legal position that forces later entrants to alter their planning of new satellite systems, protecting those who had been granted first-come, first-served status. Thus, if a country is able to develop technology that can utilize new areas of the electromagnetic spectrum, the ability to gain access to that spectrum for experimental and planning purposes provides a legal basis for future claims on that portion of the spectrum. Registering the frequency with the ITU's International Frequency Registration Bureau adds to the legal clout of the early entrant. Inherently, there is some disadvantage for late entrants since it is necessary for them to alter their own plans so as not to interfere with the system already in place. The country or system occupying the frequency is not required to give up part of the spectrum so that a new entrant can enter the marketplace. Although international law and policy evolving out of world administrative radio conferences support a negotiated settlement, even if one side must accommodate the other, the fact remains that early entrants do have a negotiating and legal advantage.[102]

As international satellite policy emphasizes more and more access to the orbit and frequencies, countries have moved aggressively to take advantage of domestic satellite systems. This means increasing the number of users within a given country, and increasing the size and capacity of domestic systems, making them available for different types of users such as private telephone, data, and television broadcasting. In the United States, for example, in the two-year period between 1992 and 1994, three American companies' launch schedules project the use of nine domestic satellites, including two of AT&T's Telstar series, three of GE Americom's SATCOM series, and four of Hughes Communication's GALAXY series.[103]

Although the three factors—channel depth, channel distribution, and channel directionality—have long played a part in the development of satellite policy, whether one will be prioritized over the other in future policy making remains uncertain. Developments in technology favor countries that have been able to venture into new areas of the electromagnetic spectrum and have developed techniques for increased channel capacity. Industrialized nations are at an advantage. The issues spill over into launch capacity since spacecraft such as the *Space Shuttle* are capable of both launching and providing maintenance of satellite systems.

The future may see a solution to equitable access through a merger of engineering and policy making.[104] For example, one policy approach is to consider that at any given time a certain number of orbital slots and a given amount of spectrum space exist. Hypothetically a certain amount of bandwidth might be allocated to every country. Once allocated, a country could sell, lease, or barter the bandwidth. Countries would be able to lease their allocated channels to other countries and other uses. The downside of such a measure would still be an inherent advantage for industrialized countries with more sophisticated technology capable of more efficient use of spectrum space.

A future scenario might also stipulate that the authorization to operate a satellite system be contingent upon the system operator using part of the allocated bandwidth for other international users who may need a particular orbital slot and frequency to meet their own communication needs. Access to the satellite would be legislated through international agreements and rate structures determined by a type of technology currency exchange. Proponents of the system could argue that it creates the maximum and most efficient use of both the orbital slot and available frequencies. A particular value of such a system would be increased access by developing countries that may not have launch capability but who would gain access and benefits through an international common carrier-type policy framework.

Social Benefits

Opponents to such a system might argue that "socialized" allocation of frequencies and resources would stifle an entrepreneurial surge in technology. When we stop and consider that satellites can be an important part of the Third World's development process, the advantage of access for any nation and the equitable allocation of resources become increasingly important. Telecommunications can be viewed as a complement to other national investments such as transportation, water, and natural resources that can raise the productivity levels in such industries as agricultural commerce, international trade, tourism, and even social services, all enhancing the quality of life.[105] The same portable satellite system that a radio reporter uses in the middle of the desert to phone back stories on an international conflict is used in areas hit by natural disasters, providing quick and efficient emergency communication that would save lives. In underdeveloped nations estimates range as high as 5 percent of telephone calls being for emergency and medical purposes. Experimental satellite networks have been used to aid doctors who must deal with outbreaks of cholera after typhoons and earthquakes. In South Pacific regions satellites have been used to telex information between suppliers resulting in lower product prices. Howell points to Sri Lanka where farmers use telephone communication relayed by satellite to learn the prices of coconuts and other produce. With this information they are able to bargain up prices. Downtime of equipment can be cut significantly when spare parts can be ordered through a telephone call as opposed to experiencing long delays through other types of communication.

The Case for Pan-African Satellites

In portions of Africa one of the major obstructions to profitable free trade is geographical isolation and the lack of communication systems.[106] Howell argues that access to satellite communication through arrangements with other nations can continue to enhance the productivity and development of Third World nations. How the policy implications of those needs are dealt with remains to be seen. One proposal to ensure access for developing nations is for any individual or entity to be able to acquire a type of common stock in a satellite system.[107] Such stock would be traded on a type of international stock exchange, thus permitting many Third World countries to develop venture capital, in addition to private-sector confidence through goodwill. Reasonable dividends could be controlled through such international organs as the ITU and a form of international price supports could enhance stockholder and investor confidence in such systems.[108] The advantage of expanding telecommunications systems to developing nations and instituting policy decisions to assure such expansion is seen by many as a major benefit to enhancing world trade and commerce. As Howell points out in arguing for a Pan-African satellite system:

> Decisions by telecommunications operators and developing countries to improve and expand their networks will create a major market for the owners of telecommunications technology and expertise, and the manufacturers of equipment. A more comprehensive world system will mean an increase in international traffic from which all operators will benefit. Where information flows so does commerce. A growth in world trade and other contacts will increase understanding among peoples. Effective and expanded telecommunications both within and between countries will make the world a better and safer place.[109]

Important in such considerations is the way the electromagnetic spectrum is allocated. Where international allocation of satellite resources is concerned, more attention is paid to the availability of orbital slots and frequencies than the benefit of the satellite to the population. Perhaps the future of international space law will evolve to the point where the social benefits and international public interest are taken into consideration when granting permission to operate a satellite system. Such a policy could result in some protection against unethical practices through coordinated international regulation, not through a patchwork of public-interest laws, government control, and restricted ownership.

Benefits in Economic Growth

The stimulation of the commercial broadcasting industry and common carrier sectors through satellite communication could stimulate economic growth in the private sector, enhancing the marketability of goods and services and urban trade.[110] In addition, isolated African communities would be connected with one another building both communication bridges and trade bridges benefitting Africa and other parts of the world. Because some underdeveloped nations do not have an efficient terrestrial infrastructure available to them, satellite communication could provide a means whereby all parts of the nation can be linked through space. Howell points to India where the telecommunications infrastructure that had been developed by the British in the 1880s was generally in disrepair when India launched its INSAT satellite system. The system now provides satellite communication, including broadcasting, to hundreds of thousands of villages throughout the region.[111] Although the system has come under criticism because of its broadcast in predominantly English and Hindi languages, which rural Indians do not speak, and its control by the educated elite, it nevertheless has provided a basis for India to move into the telecommunications age.

The examples of Africa and India point to current and potential benefits of satellite communication beyond the industrialized nations. Somewhere between the outlying villages where basic survival is the primary concern, the policy-making bodies of the ITU, and telecommunications administrations of industrialized nations, there may lie a merger of needs, politics, and economies permitting the full potential of satellite communication as a productive international social force.

Emerging Policies and Enforcement

Significant changes in the planning and allocation of satellite orbits and frequencies took place in the late 1980s with the world administrative radio conferences held in 1985 and 1988. Specifically, after considerable haggling and a deadlocked meeting, representatives to the 1985 conference put a new allocation process in place whereby all countries would be awarded specific orbital positions and frequencies. This permitted developing countries to have the same access rights as industrialized nations. Industrialized nations are still able to acquire additional orbital slots to meet their communication needs. In addition, multilateral planning meetings are being initiated.[112] The new policy has not been met with unanimous enthusiasm. Countries such as the United Kingdom, the United States, and Germany claim that congestion in the geostationary orbit is speculative, and, in particular, the British argue that because of this speculative approach there is no reason to develop satellite policy for fixed allocation frequencies or orbital positions prior to a country's satellite program being underway.[113]

The British buttressed their arguments by pointing out that only a few countries have had difficulties in coordinating any new satellite systems with existing satellite operators. Other countries such as Columbia do not agree with this assessment. Underdeveloped nations also perceive themselves at a disadvantage because of the ITU's limited enforcement. With the exception of the International Frequency Registration Board, which has been successful in coordinating the assignment of frequencies for satellite communication, the ITU has no visible enforcement arm to be able to control actions by any of its member nations who violate the spirit of international agreements.

Industrialized nations have not been innocent in failing to coordinate their activities with the ITU and the IFRB. For example, the United States embarrassingly had to admit that it had failed to coordinate with the ITU when it placed an RCA satellite in operation. Only when Cuba asked permission to put a satellite at the same orbital slot did the United States admit the omission and then correct it.[114] Given that failed coordination has taken place in the past, the increasing pressure to put satellites in orbit can make other countries uncomfortable when a large industrialized nation is singled out as not complying with ITU regulations. Such actions can quickly make other nations, especially developing countries, feel that they are at an even greater disadvantage because of the technological edge of the industrialized countries.

A future satellite policy allocating orbital slots and frequencies to countries based on an equitable guarantee of access for every country will elevate the position of smaller nations and require coordination—including diplomacy—between the Third World and the developed nations. The United States in particular is seen as a big player in this arena since its satellites occupy a large portion of the geostationary arc ranging from Hawaii to Bermuda.[115]

SUMMARY

Issues surrounding the regulation of satellite communication are more complex than the issues that faced policy makers in the 1920s trying to work out a solution to the crowding of radio stations. In a world of satellites, the International Telecommunications Union and other agencies work together to form an equitable regulatory framework. That framework not only concerns itself with allocating frequencies but also the positioning of satellites in orbit, collision risk factors, and disputes between countries, some with entirely different regulatory philosophies.

The satellite era can be traced back to the launching of the Russian satellite Sputnik I in October 1957. About the size of a basketball, it opened up the space race, which eventually saw the launch of AT&T's Telstar satellite in July 1962. Powered by solar energy, Telstar passed in view about every 45 minutes and sent television programs between the United States and Europe. Although heralded as the future of communication and a political event in itself, it suffered from the fact that it could not position itself at one point over the earth for continuous communication. That problem was solved one year later with the successful launch of SYNCOM II, the first satellite placed in geostationary orbit positioning itself over the equator where signals could be bounced without interruption.

In 1962 the United States Congress passed the Communications Satellite Act of 1962, which formed the Communications Satellite Corporation (COMSAT) and propelled the United States toward the development of satellites for communication purposes. Broad powers were awarded the corporation, which included the planning, initiating, construction, ownership, management, and operation of satellite systems in cooperation with foreign governments. A particularly important provision called on the United States to enter into cooperative agreements with foreign countries to create new and expanded telecommunications services as promptly as possible, and "to provide global coverage at the earliest practicable date." Different agencies of the government had different responsibilities. To the executive branch went such responsibilities as aiding in the planning and development of the system. NASA was charged with advising the FCC on technical matters and providing launch services. The FCC was charged with, among other things, ensuring competition, granting construction permits, and passing rules to carry out the provisions of the act.

The portion of the Communications Satellite Act of 1962 that called for the development of the global satellite system resulted in the formation of the International Telecommunications Satellite Organization (INTELSAT). COMSAT's statutory mission for the development of global systems resulted in a series of international negotiations, many of which contained significant obstacles. Gradually, however, INTELSAT grew to more than 100 participating companies. It has managed to grow and function successfully even though its members represent many different regulatory structures.

One of INTELSAT's primary profit routes has been across the Atlantic where large amounts of video and voice communications take place. It was not without concern when the United States passed the Foreign Relations Authorization Act of 1985 permitting limited competition with INTELSAT. INTELSAT in turn launched a major effort to prevent the entry of upstart Pan American Satellite. INTELSAT argued against the authorization of the PANAMSAT application saying that it violated the original agreements that formed INTELSAT, agreements requiring other nations to consult and coordinate with it not only to assure technical compatibility but to protect INTELSAT from significant economic harm. The unanimously passed resolution claimed access to private carriers would cause serious financial problems for INTELSAT users. Other arguments against PANAMSAT's entry included suggestions that Third World nations lacking technical capabilities would be at a disadvantage if private carriers were permitted to enter the market. INTELSAT also claimed United States foreign policy would appear erratic if INTELSAT agreements were disrupted, and a Department of Commerce spokesperson went so far as to suggest that private carriers would "skim the cream" off the most lucrative routes between the United States and Europe. PANAMSAT was eventually able to enter the private satellite sector, while concurrently calling on the FCC to reopen the proceeding and consider the structure of COMSAT, the U.S. signatory to INTELSAT.

The 1957 launch of Sputnik also resulted in an international effort by the United Nations to form the Committee for the Peaceful Uses of Outer Space. Two permanent subcommittees operate within COPUOS. The most significant from a regulatory standpoint is the Legal Subcommittee. Various issues are handled by the subcommittee, some of which include the definition and delimitation of outer space, access to orbit, issues of national sovereignty, and contrasting policy positions. For example, some countries have suggested that a demarcation line should separate air space and outer space, while other countries argue that no boundary exists. Some countries have argued access to orbit should be restricted over equatorial countries while COPUOS and the subcommittee have been successful in upholding the position that the geostationary orbit is a limited natural resource and a claim of national sovereignty cannot be made for any orbital position.

International regulations are primarily through the ITU's Radio Regulations, which govern satellite communication. The Radio Regulations define key terms associated with space and international law, although the definitions themselves are not without controversy. Such terms as *broadcasting service* and *radio communication* raise the issue of which best defines the medium carrying sound or video images over such technologies as cable and fiber optics that are linked to satellite systems. Primary among ITU's efforts is the registration of frequency assignments through the International Frequency Registration Board and resolutions adopted by world administrative radio conferences. Although not as strong as the radio regulations, the WARC resolutions do communicate international policy.

Other agencies also play a part in the coordination and regulation of satellite communication. These include the European Space Agency, one of the earliest, which has a rich history of international development emerging from a series of predecessor organizations that dealt with such areas as satellite technology, satellite policy, and launch services. The ESA operates under a convention agreed upon by member countries and consisting of a council with representatives from each member nation operating under a director general. The council is the ESA's political and legislative organ and both the council and director general are supported by an international staff. Important to the ESA are the Contract Regulations, which regulate the procurement policy of the organization. The final decision on who is awarded a contract is made by the ESA's Industrial Policy Committee, which takes into account both the cost and general excellence of the project. Contracts are awarded on a geographical distribution and fair-return basis.

Other international organizations also coordinate satellite policy. The International Organization of Space Communications began in 1972, primarily among communist countries. Some of the signatories to the original INTERSPUTNIK agreement included Cuba, Hungary, Korea, Poland, Romania, Vietnam, Russia, and others. The International Maritime Satellite Organization began in 1979 and operates a worldwide network primarily devoted to serving the international maritime interest of member nations. Limited protection exists for INMARSAT requiring notification to the organization when outside facilities are planned that will interface with the INMARSAT network. The Arab Satellite Communications Organization coordinates telecommunications activities for Arab countries. Headquartered in Riyadh, Saudi Arabia, ARABSAT maintains a regional telecommunication system for the Arab nations. The space segment of European telecommunications is coordinated by the European Telecommunications Satellite Organization. Created by 17 European administrations in 1977 and headquartered in Paris, EUTELSAT's organization consists of an Assembly of Parties, a Board of Signatories, and an Executive Organ headed by a director general.

Private interest in satellite communication in the United States was enhanced in 1984 with the passage of the Commercial Space Launch Act. The act's primary purpose is to promote economic growth and entrepreneurial activities by expediting ways for private companies to launch and operate satellite systems. Licenses are issued by the secretary of transportation and payloads must comply with all requirements of federal law. Under the act's provisions, private companies can purchase launch sites at fair market value. Private operators are required to carry liability insurance and proof of financial responsibility. If a private launch affects foreign policy, consultation with the secretary of defense is required.

In an effort to promote satellite development, the FCC in the United States has imposed minimal regulatory measures on companies wanting to enter the satellite industry. FCC regulations are primarily concerned with coordinating frequency assignments with international organizations. Regulations covering direct-broadcast satellites center around an applicant's request for specific orbital positions and frequencies and the necessity of showing the type of service that the contractor intends to provide along with all pertinent technical information. License terms for interim DBS systems are for five years and the applicant must begin construction within one year of receiving a construction permit. Completion of the system is required within a six-year period from the date of the construction permit, unless a specific exemption is made by the FCC.

Rates for using satellites are spelled out in tariff schedules. For example, a user who leases a satellite over long periods of time traditionally pays less per hour than a user who only wants to use a satellite for one-time transmission purposes. Rate structures are determined by hours of daily use, short- or long-term lease, time of day, and protection status. The amount of spectrum space requested by the user can also affect rates. Audio signals take up less spectrum space than video signals.

A number of policy implications are emerging as the DBS industry develops, including such matters as orbital positioning. DBS is potentially a very powerful communications tool and underdeveloped nations remain concerned that industrialized countries will receive more than their fair share of orbital slots. Common carrier use of DBS is another issue since being able to lease and program a DBS system would permit anyone with the financial and programming means to direct television programming anywhere in the world.

Many factors will continue to influence the regulation of satellite communication. The world's economic and political structures will both play a part. A healthy world economy permits the opportunity for more entrepreneurs to enter the satellite industry, especially DBS. While more efficient use of the electromagnetic spectrum is taking place, it remains a limited resource and demands on the most valuable frequencies remain. The geostationary orbit is another limited resource and only a limited number of spaces exist for satellites to rotate the earth above the equator. These "parking spaces" are regulated to avoid interference and the potential for collision between satellites. Different parts of the world have more demand for satellite communication, and therefore the most populated areas and most profitable routes are the most crowded.

In addition, policy issues in the regulation of satellite communication will center around three areas: channel depth, channel distribution, and channel directionality. Channel depth refers to the capacity of a channel to handle messages. Channel distribution is the footprint of the satellite and the geographic area that is covered by the satellite signal. Directionality refers to the number of people who are capable of uplinking and therefore transmitting signals via satellite. The future may see the merging of technology, policy, and social benefits, where the awarding of frequencies and orbital positions is based not only on the ability of a country to develop a satellite system but its ability to show on an international scale the social benefits of its satellite service.

MATERIAL FOR ANALYSIS

PRINCIPLES GOVERNING THE USE BY STATES OF ARTIFICIAL EARTH SATELLITES FOR INTERNATIONAL DIRECT TELEVISION BROADCASTING

Adopted by the United Nations General Assembly at its 100th plenary meeting, on 10 December 1982 (resolution 37/92, annex).

A. Purposes and objectives

1. Activities in the field of international direct television broadcasting by satellites should be carried out in a manner compatible with the sovereign rights of States, including the principle of non-intervention, as well as with the right of everyone to seek, receive and impart information and ideas as enshrined in the relevant United Nations instruments.

2. Such activities should promote the free dissemination and mutual exchange of information and knowledge in cultural and scientific fields, assist in educational, social and economic development, particularly in the developing coun-

tries, enhance the qualities of life of all peoples and provide recreation with due respect to the political and cultural integrity of States.

3. These activities should accordingly be carried out in a manner compatible with the development of mutual understanding and the strengthening of friendly relations and co-operation among all States and peoples in the interest of maintaining international peace and security.

B. Applicability of international law

4. Activities in the field of international direct television broadcasting by satellite should be conducted in accordance with international law, including the Charter of the United Nations, the Treaty on Principles Governing the Activities of States in the Exploration and Use of Outer Space, including the Moon and other Celestial Bodies, 27 January 1967, the relevant provisions of the International Telecommunication Convention and its Radio Regulations and of international instruments relating to friendly relations and co-operation among States and human rights.

C. Rights and benefits

5. Every State has an equal right to conduct satellite activities in the field of international direct television broadcasting by satellite and to authorize such activities by persons and entities under its jurisdiction. All States and peoples are entitled to and should enjoy the benefits from such activities. Access to the technology in this field should be available to all States without discrimination on terms mutually agreed upon by all concerned.

D. International co-operation

6. Activities in the field of international direct television broadcasting by satellite should be based upon and encourage international co-operation. Such co-operation should be the subject of appropriate arrangements. Special consideration should be given to the needs of the developing countries in the use of international direct television broadcasting by satellite for the purpose of accelerating their national development.

E. Peaceful settlement of disputes

7. Any international dispute that may arise from activities covered by these principles should be settled through established procedures for the peaceful settlement of disputes agreed upon by the parties to the dispute in accordance with the provisions of the Charter of the United Nations.

F. State responsibility

8. States should bear international responsibility for activities in the field of international direct television broadcasting by satellite carried out by them or under their jurisdiction and for the conformity of any such activities with the principles set forth in this document.

9. When international direct television broadcasting by satellite is carried out by an international intergovernmental organization, the responsibility referred to in paragraph 8 above should be borne both by that organization and by the States participating in it.

G. Duty and right to consult

10. Any broadcasting or receiving State within an international direct television broadcasting satellite service established between them requested to do so by any other broadcasting or receiving State within the same service should promptly enter into consultations with the requesting State regarding its activities in the field of international direct television broadcasting by satellite, without prejudice to other consultations which these States may undertake with any other State on that subject.

H. Copyright and neighboring rights

11. Without prejudice to the relevant provisions of international law, States should co-operate on a bilateral and multilateral basis for protection of copyright and neighboring rights by means of appropriate agreements between the interested States or the competent legal entities acting under their jurisdiction. In such co-operation they should give special consideration to the interests of developing countries in the use of direct television broadcasting for the purpose of accelerating their national development.

I. Notification to the United Nations

12. In order to promote international co-operation in the peaceful exploration and use of outer space, States conducting or authorizing activities in the field of international direct television broadcasting by satellite should inform the Secretary-General of the United Nations, to the greatest extent possible, of the nature of such activities. On receiving this information, the Secretary-General should disseminate it immediately and effectively to the relevant specialized agencies, as well as to the public and the international scientific community.

J. Consultations and agreements between States

13. A State which intends to establish or authorize the establishment of an international direct television broadcasting satellite service shall without delay notify the proposed receiving State or States of such intention and shall promptly enter into consultation with any of those States which so request.

14. An international direct television broadcasting satellite service shall only be established

after the conditions set forth in paragraph 13 above have been met and on the basis of the International Telecommunication Union and in accordance with these principles.

15. With respect to the unavoidable overspill of the radiation of the satellite signal, the relevant instruments of the International Telecommunication Union shall be exclusively applicable.

QUESTIONS FOR CRITICAL ANALYSIS

- In the 1920s when radio broadcasters met to work out a solution to crowded frequencies, the national radio conferences resulted in the formation of the Federal Radio Commission under the Radio Act of 1927. Think back to the organization of the FRC and ask Would such an agency be able to function as a regulator of satellite communication?
- Since the ITU has little enforcement power, what would stop a country from simply raising the power of its satellite to bump competition off the air the way radio stations did prior to the enactment of the Radio Act of 1927?
- How would the international community react and what could they do to stop a country from using a high-powered satellite to jam other nations' satellite systems?
- When Telstar was launched, *The New York Times* critic Jack Gould criticized government dignitaries for serving as a "passive gallery" for private corporations. Was this criticism justified?
- Jack Gould also predicted that the lasting value of international television would be determined not in "laboratories in the sky but in offices on the ground." What did he mean and do his predictions run true today?
- When the Communications Satellite Act of 1962 was passed, Congress created a private corporation to develop a new communications technology. Would the current political climate permit such a corporation to be formed today or would the lobbying efforts of private enterprise stifle such legislative intent?
- Can you think of any communications technology on the horizon that might necessitate congressional legislation to spur private enterprise into developing the technology? What about HDTV?
- Considering that the president of the United States appointed the first 13 incorporators of COMSAT, was the company ever really free of political influence in the years of its formative development?
- The Communications Satellite Act of 1962 required coordinated interagency functions to bring about a commercial communications satellite system. With so many different responsibilities split between the executive branch of government, NASA, and the FCC, how did COMSAT manage to succeed and not succumb to regulatory bureaucracy?
- What would have happened to COMSAT if the early interpersonal conflicts between some of the founding board members had not been resolved?
- Since the Communications Satellite Act of 1962 was the impetus for international negotiations to develop INTELSAT, is it possible the international community still perceives the United States as the primary player in satellite communication, with the ability to dominate the economic, technical, and political arenas controlling the development of satellite technology?
- What would have happened if international negotiations between INTELSAT's early signatories had broken down and the interim agreement creating INTELSAT had not been signed and approved?
- Under its current framework heavy users of INTELSAT have larger investment shares in the network. Does this structure favor wealthy industrialized nations with considerable technology and financial resources?
- When INTELSAT was originally formed, do you think the organization could foresee the entry of major private players in satellite communication competing for INTELSAT's business and resources? Would the interim agreement have guarded against such entry? If the interim agreement did guard against such entry, would it have been successful and could it have been enforced?
- Given the U.S. free enterprise system and democratic principles, how could it justify joining in the unanimously adopted resolution passed at a meeting of the INTELSAT's signatories in 1983, which claimed that access of private carriers would cause financial problems for INTELSAT users?
- Is the foreign policy value of a consistent approach to international telecommunications

policy important enough to warrant a protection of the original INTELSAT agreements and the prohibition against the entry of outside private companies into the international satellite market?

- Is the argument that private carriers might skim the cream off the most lucrative satellite routes justifiable in preventing private carriers from entering the international satellite business?
- Could COPUOS operate if its legislative mechanisms consisted of majority rule and a veto instead of the consensus process without a veto mechanism that now governs it?
- One part of the 1967 Outer Space Treaty is the provision that no claims of sovereignty or territory by any nation on earth can be made over any location in outer space. Does this statement effectively prohibit signatories to the treaty from making any territorial claim to orbital spaces above their territories?
- How can some equatorial countries have legitimate claim on territorial rights to orbital space above their respective geographical areas? Why then were some countries able to advance the argument that less developed nations under the geostationary orbit had special rights to orbital space?
- Speculate what type of international incident might be created if a country did not honor the spirit of the Outer Space Treaty and provide assistance to an astronaut in distress.
- Is there a sound argument for separating air space and outer space? Can such a delimitation be articulated effectively through international law? Can a demarcation line between air space and outer space be enforced in international law? Would such a demarcation line stifle the peaceful exploration of outer space? Is there a sound argument in the suggestion that such a demarcation line would subject flying objects to various legal regimes as an object crossed over the arbitrary boundaries from one regime to another?
- Should a separate legal regime be established to deal exclusively with access to the geostationary orbit?
- Should less developed nations that do not have sophisticated space technology be guaranteed access to the geostationary orbit in the future, regardless of how crowded it might become?
- Consider the statement in the working papers submitted by Kenya, which states "the geostationary orbit is a physical fact linked to the reality of our planet because its existence depends exclusively on its relation to gravitational phenomenon generated by the Earth and therefore should not be considered in the concept of outer space." Can such a claim be defended on the principles of physics? Can the claim be defended from the standpoint of international law?
- When two opposing policy positions are advanced by two countries, one of which has the capacity to operate a satellite network and the other a less developed nation with little technical expertise and resources, does the developed nation have a stronger political position within international governing bodies?
- Examine the definitions of *satellite* and *active satellite* as found in the ITU Radio Regulations and stated in this chapter. Is is possible that the two definitions could cause policy disagreement or confusion when applied to the regulation of satellite communication?
- Two provisions of the 1979 WARC resolution passed in Geneva concerning the registration of frequencies with the IFRB suggest that registration does not provide any permanent priority to a country or group and should not create an obstacle to the establishment of space systems by other countries. Another provision of the resolution states that countries registering with the IFRB should take every measure to realize the possibility of the use of new space systems by other countries or groups. Do these provisions provide a legal means by which less developed countries can argue access to frequencies and orbital positions in the future?
- With organizations such as INTELSAT, are other coordinating space agencies such as the European Space Agency, INTERSPUTNIK, INMARSAT, and others really necessary?
- INMARSAT's primary purpose is for maritime communication. Considering the use of portable satellite transceivers such as those used for remote broadcasting during crises, should INMARSAT's role in the international community be enhanced?
- Some international satellite organizations such as INTERSPUTNIK developed because of the desire of communist countries not to participate in an international satellite organization such as INTELSAT. With many communist countries becoming more democratic, should the barriers between the two organizations be eliminated and merged into a single international network?

- Whenever security interests are involved, private satellite companies launching payloads must, under the U.S. Commercial Space Launch Act, consult with the Defense Department and the secretary of defense. Is this requirement an effective measure against the launch of satellites for illegal or subversive purposes?
- FCC regulations permit the development of direct-broadcast satellite services by creating as few regulatory obstacles as possible. Is this lenient regulatory policy justified? Does the lenient policy provide a significant advantage to the early entrants into the DBS market?
- In political broadcasting, the lowest unit rule applies whereby political advertisers must be charged the lowest unit rate when purchasing advertising time on radio and television stations. Should similar rules be enforced for DBS systems, and is there anything preventing, under the guarantees of the First Amendment, foreign leaders from attempting to influence American political processes, either directly or indirectly?
- Because of the potential power to reach millions of people from outer space, should content controls be placed on the programming of DBS systems?
- Would such content controls be justified under the Communications Act whereby frequencies are limited resources? Would such content controls be justified under the First Amendment?
- Should an international policy be put in place whereby orbital positions and frequencies are only awarded after the applicant is required to show the social benefits of the proposed satellite service? Should a similar provision apply to economic benefits?

ADDITIONAL RESOURCES

Borrelli, D. J., "Telecommunications—Satellite and Earth Station Use—Further Developments in Satellite Telecommunications." 11 *Suffolk Transnational Law Journal* 551 (1988).

Frieden, R., "Getting Closer to the Source: New Policies for International Satellite Access." 37 *Federal Communications Law Journal* 293 (1985).

Gorove, K. M., "Thirteenth Annual Conference on the Global Telecommunications Revolution, Columbia University School of Law, March 29, 1985." *Journal of Space Law* 36 (1985).

Leive, D. M., "INTELSAT in a Changing Telecommunications Environment." 25 *Jurimetrics Journal* 82 (1984).

Maule, R. W., and D. S. Brust, "Satellite Marketing Under Scrutiny." 10 *Communications and the Law* 17 (1988).

Rothblatt, Martin A., "Legal Symposium Panel of Space Telecommunications Issues, International Telecommunication Union Forum 83, Geneva, Oct. 18, 1983." 12 *Journal of Space Law* 74 (1984).

Solana, Alan M., "The International Telecommunication Union and the Third World's Quest for Equitable Access to the Orbit-Spectrum Resource." 4 *Boston College Third World Law Journal* 183 (1984).

Speck, P. K., "Competition in International Satellite Telecommunications: Alternative Avenues." 20 *Texas International Law Journal* 517 (1985).

chapter fourteen

International Regulatory Systems

During the early 1900s, the global monopoly of Marconi and his radio companies affected the safety of international shipping interests. Through various regulatory measures the monopoly was constrained, and the government stepped in to regulate electronic media. From the government-owned and controlled broadcasting systems of Europe to the private enterprise of the United States, broadcasting flourished.

Gradually, the international organizations that were once charged with regulating the telegraph increased their sphere of influence to include broadcasting, the telephone, and the new communication technologies of the twentieth century. Increasingly, satellite communication which can beam voice, video, and data communication anywhere in the world has made us acutely aware that no one country can successfully regulate media that are capable of instant global impact. In addition, such intrinsic factors as competition, cultural norms, political diversity, and technology make it difficult for the electronic media to operate in complete freedom without any controls.

Working in cooperation with the regulatory agencies and administrations of individual countries, international regulatory agencies and organizations play an important role in coordinating regulatory policy. In some cases the influence of the organization is worldwide, such as the International Telecommunications Union of the United Nations. In others it is more regional such as the European Community, which is foremost an economic and political body, but in recent years has engaged in the regulation of the electronic media.

Organizations established to coordinate the activities of broadcasting and telecommunication across national boundaries also play a part in the regulatory sphere. By belonging to these organizations and subscribing to their by-laws, broadcasters place themselves in semicontractual terms within the control of the organizations where the member must adhere to the goals of the body. Organizations such as the European Broadcasting Union and the Union of National Radio and Television Organizations of Africa have benefited members by developing program exchanges, technical standards, legal services available to members, and even training programs. Quasi-legislative bodies such as general assemblies, not unlike those found in government, operate within the organizations; they pass by-laws and in some cases rely on larger organizations such as the United Nations to help ensure compliance. Because of their effect on international broadcasting, these organizations remain important. Many operate as regulatory bodies set up within individual countries to control broadcasting and telecommunication inside national boundaries. Many are specialized agencies of the United Nations and as such are public international organizations with a great deal of autonomy, are treaty based, are affiliated with the United Nations through an instrument of agreement with the United Nations Economic and Social Council, and operate within the sphere of international law. The first part of this chapter will deal with the regulatory agencies and organizations that affect control of the electronic media and the second part of the chapter concentrates on examples of specific laws and regulations.

THE INTERNATIONAL TELECOMMUNICATION UNION

The International Telecommunication Union is a United Nations organization responsible for coordinating the use of telecommunications among nations.[1] It does not have the enforcement powers of the Federal Communications Commission. Rather, it is a collective body of sovereign states and is only as strong as the willingness of the sovereign states to abide by its treaties. In other words, if a country violates an ITU agreement, no "field office" will revoke licenses or impose forfeitures. ITU's sovereign states view it not so much as an independent agency but as an arena in which to negotiate the use of telecommunication.

Early Telegraph: The International Telegraph Union

The history of the International Telecommunication Union dates back to 1849, when the impact of the telegraph was dawning on Europe. In that year, Austria and Prussia signed a treaty to join their telegraph lines. By 1865, the treaties that had been signed and the new technology prompted 20 European states to meet in Paris to approve the International Telegraph Convention with its set of Telegraph Regulations. In international telecommunication, the term *convention* is a multilateral treaty agreed upon by the signers. Out of the Paris Convention came a series of telegraph conferences. At the Vienna conference in 1868, the International Bureau of Telegraph Administrations was formed. Located in Berne, Switzerland, it became known as the Berne Bureau, and it was charged with a variety of administrative functions. It was staffed and funded mostly by the Swiss. The periodic conferences and the Berne Bureau collectively became known in 1875 as the International Telegraph Union, with the International Telegraph Convention as its charter. By 1885, the International Telegraph Union was involved with telephone as well as with telegraph.

Emerging Wireless: The Radio-Telegraph Union

At this same time, Marconi was tinkering with the new technology that would soon revolutionize the world's concepts of communication. The rapid corporate development of the British Marconi Wireless Company created a worldwide monopoly. This irritated the German government to the point that it convened a conference in 1903 to resolve some of the problems resulting from the monopoly, specifically the failure of ships equipped with Marconi apparatus to communicate with ships equipped with apparatus manufactured by other companies. Six of the eight sovereign states in attendance signed an agreement which, although mostly protocol, became the foundation for international radio regulations. The agreement called for wireless stations to "operate, as far as possible, in such a manner as not to interfere with the working of other stations."[2]

Further international cooperation emerged from the first International Radio-Telegraph Conference in 1906. There, 27 nations adopted the Radio-Telegraph Convention and specific Radio-Telegraph Regulations. Realizing that radio was a rapidly changing technology, the nations also made provisions to meet at periodic administrative conferences. The Berne Bureau, already serving the telegraph and telephone interests, was designated to handle the administrative duties of the radio organization. Gradually the Radio-Telegraph Convention (agreements) and the periodic conferences together came to be called the Radio-Telegraph Union.

The Complex Task of Merging Organizations and Conventions

Except for the fact that they shared the Berne Bureau, the two organizations—the International Telegraph Union and the Radio-Telegraph Union—operated independently in 1932. It was in that year that the two were combined. First, their respective conventions, the International Telegraph Convention and the Radio-Telegraph Convention, were combined into a single unified convention called the International Telecommunication Convention. Second, both organizations were then combined. The International Telegraph

Union and the Radio-Telegraph Union became the International Telecommunication Union, with the new combined convention as its official charter called the International Telecommunication Convention. The respective radio, telegraph, and telephone regulations of the previous organizations were welded into three sets of international regulations—radio, telegraph, and telephone—and called the International Telecommunication Convention.

FUNCTION AND ORGANIZATION OF THE ITU

The primary functions of the International Telecommunication Union include, among others: (1) effective allocations of the radio frequency spectrum and registration of radio frequency assignments; (2) coordinating efforts to eliminate harmful interference between radio stations of different countries and to improve the use made of the radio frequency spectrum; (3) fostering the creation, development, and improvement of telecommunication equipment and networks in new or developing countries by every means at its disposal, especially its participation in the appropriate programs of the United Nations; (4) promoting the adoption of measures for ensuring the safety of life through the cooperation of telecommunication services; (5) undertaking studies, making regulations, adopting resolutions, and benefiting all members and associate members.[3]

At any given time, the ITU may send cooperative teams of experts to help developing nations establish modern communications systems. On an annual basis, upwards of 300 experts are out on field missions, and 400 people are undergoing training in telecommunication services. ITU's technical cooperation activity continues to center on promoting and developing regional telecommunication networks, strengthening the telecommunication technical and administrative services in developing countries, and developing the human resources required for telecommunications.[4] The ITU also sponsors numerous feasibility studies for new systems of communication. In addition, it is directly involved in negotiations to secure funding sources for new telecommunication systems. Some of these sources include the International Bank for Reconstruction and Development, the African Development Bank, the Asian Development Bank, and regional banks.

The machinery to carry out the functions of ITU is housed in six areas, which have evolved out of various conferences and mergers over the years.[5]

Plenipotentiary Conference

The Plenipotentiary Conference is the supreme body of the ITU. It is composed of all of the ITU member nations, and it meets approximately every seven years to revise the International Telecommunication Convention. It differs somewhat from other U.N. conferences in that it tackles a complete, not a partial, revision of the convention and, compared to other conferences, it meets rather infrequently. The interrelationship of the members of the ITU and the political process was evidenced at one conference where members debated whether the ITU should go beyond its traditional role as a monitor of frequency standards to more general responsibilities including the use of foreign aid to help developing nations expand their telecommunications capabilities. The body voted to accept the expanded role and committed $360 million to the effort, in addition to establishing a new body within the ITU called the Telecommunications Development Bureau. Budget commitments for the new bureau were made through the 1990s. Historically, the United States opposed the increased role of the ITU into development support but has gradually changed its policy position and made significant diplomatic inroads into international telecommunication policy.[6]

Administrative Council

The Administrative Council is composed of members elected on a regional basis. The council meets each year to conduct business between the Plenipotentiary Conferences.

Administrative Conferences

Administrative conferences are called periodically to revise the regulations annexed to the convention. The radio conferences, called World Administrative Radio Conferences (WARC), examine such issues as international allocation of the electromagnetic spectrum.

International Consultative Committees

We learned earlier that the two international consultative committees are the International Radio Consultative Committee (CCIR) and the International Telephone and Telegraph Consultative Committee (CCIT). Both the CCIR and CCIT consist of plenary assemblies that meet every three to five years, periodically convened study groups, and full-time specialized secretariats. The committees makes recommendations in such areas as technical specifications for equipment. The origin of the CCIT dates back to a 1955 merger of two separate committees: the CCIF, which dealt with telephone, and the CCIT, representing telegraph interests. The CCIT and CCIF were originally formed at the 1926 Paris Conference of the International Telegraph Union. The CCIR traces its founding to the 1927 Washington Radio-Telegraph Conference.

International Frequency Registration Board (IFRB). The IFRB is composed of five elected members—reduced from nine in 1965 as a compromise with those who wanted the IFRB abolished altogether. The board is responsible for adopting international telecommunication technical standards, and it maintains a master register of international frequency use. When a country desires to use a certain frequency, it notifies the IFRB, which then determines if the use will meet the regulations of the ITU and not interfere with other registrants.

General Secretariat. The General Secretariat carries out the administrative duties of the ITU. It consists of an elected secretary general and deputy secretary general. The General Secretariat does not have the authority to establish policy.

CRITICISM OF THE ITU

As with any organization of international magnitude, the ITU has many critics, and continuing measures are undertaken to reorganize it and change or redistribute its policy and administrative functions. Sovereign states are very much concerned with autonomy where their communication systems are concerned. This attitude has caused resistance to any increase in power for the ITU beyond its current registry and coordinating functions. The relationship with the United Nations still remains somewhat of a stumbling block, since nations that are not U.N. members cannot be members of the ITU. In fact, one recommendation for changing the ITU is to open its membership to all countries of the world.[7]

It has been recommended that the ITU should have the ability to arbitrate conflicts between its members and also have some enforcement powers over its conventions, since a convention or regulation once ratified and accepted by the member countries becomes international law. Both of these courses would require the establishment of full-scale judicial machinery, although this would bring with it the problem of enforcement. Other suggestions for improving the ITU include establishing an international communication research center to supplement the work now being done at the domestic level, and expanding technical assistance.

ITU WORLD ADMINISTRATIVE RADIO CONFERENCES

The World Administrative Radio Conferences (WARC) that are called by the ITU are most important in affecting telecommunication policy worldwide.

Scope of the Conferences

These conferences meet periodically to consider limited and general topics of importance to member nations and the world use of communications. An example of a limited WARC would be one that deals with satellite communication. Another limited WARC topic is cellular phones services because with our movement toward a global society the use of satellites for more personal telephone communication is becoming a technical reality. Such issues also have particular interest to developing countries which have been isolated and through new technologies have new opportunities to communicate and participate in the world order. The complexities of such issues can be seen in the fact that in the United States telephone companies are private entities. In many countries the telephone companies are operated through state-owned or state-sanctioned monopolies which comprise the postal, telephone, and telegraph companies. It takes an international organization to sort through these ownership and regulatory differences and hammer out agreements that benefit all countries in their mutual use of the limited resource of the electromagnetic spectrum.[8]

More general conferences might review the entire international use of the electromagnetic spectrum and establish policy for that use well into the next century. Since each country has one vote, the superpowers do not necessarily control policy the way they do in other international negotiations. The conference examines frequency use based on different regions of the world, with a common goal of permitting the greatest latitude of spectrum use without interference.

The Planning Process

The planning for a WARC begins long before the meeting date, for policy first must be formulated on a national basis and then presented to the international conference. A number of government agencies are involved in this policy formation in the United States, including the FCC. The FCC may issue notices of inquiry, seeking responses from broadcasters on various topics of importance to the WARC. Special FCC publications may call the WARC meeting to the attention of the public and citizens' groups. At the same time, the commission may establish a series of FCC working groups to deal with specific types of communication needs. These groups develop recommendations for such topics as aeronautical mobile, amateur radio, aural AM broadcasting, aural FM broadcasting, auxiliary broadcast services, broadcasting satellite, domestic land mobile radio, fixed satellite, international broadcasting, land mobile radio, maritime mobile, private microwave, radio astronomy, radio relay, and television broadcasting.

Armed with this feedback, the FCC then develops in cooperation with the other agencies policies reflecting the needs of each of those areas represented. The U.S. Department of State takes over at that point, officially representing America at the international conference. Whenever a treaty is agreed upon at a conference such as a WARC, the State Department presents the treaty for ratification by the president with the advice and consent of the Senate. Once signed, the treaty becomes international law.

European Broadcasting Union

The European Broadcasting Union (EBU), governed by Swiss law, is a nongovernmental and noncommercial (nonprofit) organization cooperating with other broadcasting organizations in Western Europe.[9] The EBU also operates Eurovision, a European television-exchange network of member nations and organizations. Major American television networks are associate members of the EBU.

Founding of the EBU

EBU's history dates back to 1925 and the International Broadcasting Union (IBU) founded in Geneva, Switzerland. The IBU was formed for the purpose of seeking cooperation among nations, to exchange radio programs, and to plan policy for frequency assignments. The organization was little more than a letterhead during the turmoil of World War II. After the war a second organization, the International Radio Organization (OIR), was formed and the two organizations existed simultaneously.[10] The concept of two united organizations eventually failed and the OIR moved to Prague. At the prodding of the BBC, members of the IBU and other interested individuals and organizations met in Torguay, United Kingdom in 1950 and formed a new organization, the EBU. Assets of the IBU were transferred to the EBU and the IBU was dissolved. The new organization placed its headquarters in Geneva and formed a Technical Center in Brussels. A Legal Committee, Radio Program Committee, Television Program Committee, and Technical Committee were formed with a Technical Center located in Brussels, Belgium. Stated aims of the EBU are in part: (1) to support the interests of broadcasting organizations and to establish relations with other broadcasting organizations or groups; (2) to promote and coordinate studies and ensure the exchange of information on all matters of general interest to broadcasters; (3) to promote the development of broadcasting; (4) to seek the solution, by means of international cooperation, of any differences that may arise; and (5) to ensure its members respect the provisions of international agreements.[11] The power of the EBU rests with the cooperation of its individual members through the general assembly.

The Legal Committee: Representation and Contract Work

Of the different permanent committees operating as part of EBU, the Legal Committee is of greatest interest to the field of broadcast and telecommunication regulation. The Legal Committee is frequently the EBU's representative to other broadcasting and legislative organizations worldwide. For example, the EBU attends meetings convened by the World Intellectual Property Organization, participates as an observer in the meetings of the Council of Europe's Mass Media Bureau, and maintains relations with the European Space Agency. Of special interest to the Legal Committee is contract law involved in programming exchanges and retransmission through cable television and satellite systems.

In the area of contracts, the Legal Committee has constructed model agreements for program exchanges among different European broadcasting organizations, many state controlled. Model contracts exist in such areas as mechanical reproduction rights, the use of commercial records and music, and the distributions of cable television programming. In addition to contracts, the Legal Committee assists groups that want to express their views through the passage of declarations or resolutions which state policy but may not function as a multilateral treaty or contract. Negotiation of radio and television sports contracts can also be handled through the Legal Committee. Radio and television sports programming is increasing throughout the world and Europe is no exception. Such events as the Olympic Games and the World Football Cups present the need for an organization such as the EBU to handle the complexities of international negotiations and contracts, many between different countries as well as different private and government entities.

Research and Publication Function

Research and publication is another function of the Legal Committee. The committee is frequently asked to provide information on payments for programing or the rights to authors for script adaptations. Periodic questionnaires are circulated to EBU members asking what type of legal information is needed and most useful and then the EBU will arrange for research to obtain and collate this information. Results of the questionnaires are then disseminated to members through various publications and newsletters. These publications are intended as working tools for other organizations' legal departments or government bodies planning legislation affecting broadcasting.

INTERNATIONAL RADIO AND TELEVISION ORGANIZATION

The International Radio Organization which split off from the EBU, moved to Prague, Czechoslovakia in 1950.

Background and Operation

Seventeen countries were originally with the OIR. At the 1959 conference in Helsinki, Finland, television was added to the organization as it became the International Radio and Television Organization (OIRT). A program exchange began a year later, giving birth to the Intervision system which exchanges programs among OIRT members and others who want to participate. Since its beginnings, membership in OIRT has included broadcasting organizations in Eastern Europe, Asia, the Middle East, and elsewhere.[12]

The OIRT cooperates with other broadcasting organizations throughout the world, and as a consultative body to UNESCO, the OIRT adheres to various U.N. articles.[13] In addition, the OIRT also collaborates with PTT authorities in various countries and carries on an active program of research to upgrade the sound and video technology of member organizations. The budget of the OIRT is based on membership fees, and the working languages of the organization are Russian and German.

Membership in the OIRT is open to any broadcasting organization directly responsible for radio and television services or any national organization that constitutes a legal entity having control of a radio and television service. Members can either obtain active or associate status, the latter not permitting the right to vote in the organization. Some of the organizations with which the OIRT has cooperative ties include the EBU, the Asia-Pacific Broadcasting Union, the Arab States Broadcasting Union, the Caribbean Broadcasting Union, and the International Olympic Committee.

The Intervision System

As is the case with many international broadcasting organizations, program exchanges are a major benefit of membership. For the OIRT, this has also been the case. For example, prior to the declarations of independence of many Eastern European countries in the late 1980's and early 1990s, this was also the case for the OIRT. Intervision developed as a program exchange whereby countries could exchange information, much of it news, educational, and cultural affairs programming, produced by government-owned and controlled television systems. The activities of Intervision are governed by the Intervision Council which consists of representatives of all member broadcasting organizations.

In annual meetings, the Intervision Council considers problems associated with program development and exchange, and determines ways to implement the decisions and resolutions of the OIRT governing bodies. Working groups reporting to the Intervision Council are responsible for dealing with issues concerning different program exchanges. For example, at any given time a working group may exist on such matters as news exchange, educational programs, children and youth programs, sports programs, literary and dramatic programs, and others. Participation in a working group is voluntary and member broadcasting organizations can delegate one representative to each group for a two-year term.

The daily exchange of television news programs among OIRT members is the responsibility of two centers, the Intervision Program Co-ordination Center and the Intervision Technical Co-ordination Center. Satellites, land lines, and air mail are all used to implement the program exchanges. Exchanges are also conducted between associate members of Intervision such as CNN in the United States and NHK in Japan. Intervision claims to be the first organization to regularly use satellite relay for news exchanges, primarily to serve the broadcasting systems of Cuba and Vietnam. More extensive satellite installations now provide worldwide exchange capabilities.

Technical and Legal Support

Technical assistance for OIRT and the news exchange is provided through the OIRT Technical Commission which sets technical standards and is responsible for all technical requirements implemented through executive decisions of the OIRT General Assembly and Administrative Council. Study groups exist within the Technical Commission and include such areas as international sound transmission, television, wave propagation, and network planning. The Technical Commission maintains contact with other organizations and helps coordinate the technical requirements for program exchanges.

An Economic and Legal Commission consisting of representatives from each OIRT member organization meets once each year to analyze the financial, administrative, organizational, and legal projects submitted by the Administrative Council and the General Assembly. Under the direction of a commission chairperson, the budgets, planning, and legal questions about the OIRT's international activities fall under the Economic and Legal Commission.

What will be interesting to see in the future is to determine if changes in the political structure of Eastern Europe will result in major changes in the organization, membership, or operation of OIRT. The position of many democratic countries is the unrestricted free flow of information, void of any government interference. The independence movement in Eastern Europe, while not yet producing major changes in the ownership of television systems, has nonetheless made people aware of news programming produced without government control or political constraints. Thus, whereas television programming in the past contained the state-controlled messages produced by state-owned television systems, the future may see less government control. While that may seem ideal from the perspective of a democratic society, it can be a threatening thought to those in power in more authoritarian regimes. The new politics of Eastern Europe will mean new opportunities, but also new challenges to organizations such as OIRT.

CARIBBEAN BROADCASTING UNION

Formed in 1970, the Caribbean Broadcasting Union (CBU) operates to facilitate the flow of broadcast programming between the Caribbean nations.[14] It represents both private and public broadcasting systems in English-speaking and Dutch-speaking Caribbean areas. In addition, associate membership is granted to broadcasting systems outside the Caribbean. Such organizations as the BBC in the United Kingdom, and CNN and NBC in the United States are associate members. The CBU's permanent secretariat is located in Barbados and assists in the movement of program material among members. In addition to member support, funding for the CBU's activities is received from such organizations as the United Nations and the Canadian International Development Agency. Significant legal activity is found in the CBU's negotiation of rates with outside program suppliers. For example, broadcast rights are negotiated for the Olympic Games, World Cup Football, and international cricket matches from such places as Australia, England, India, and Pakistan. Stations receiving the broadcasts share the costs of programming. The CBU also arranges for the satellite interconnects and rate structures for news coverage such as elections and national disasters.

UNION OF NATIONAL RADIO AND TELEVISION ORGANIZATIONS

When the telegraph was in it infancy, Africa was a continent already in transition. For centuries a rich source of cultural and language diversity, the late 1800s and colonialization brought Africa under the control of European powers. Already diverse cultures were further fragmented by other cultures and other languages such as English, Portuguese, French, and Arabic. Gradually, however, over a 60-year period, Africa began to assert its independence.

The Formation of the URTNA

By the 1960s the era of postindependence had arrived and the first Pan-African organization created during this era was the Union of National Radio and Television Organizations of Africa (URTNA).[15] URTNA's original purpose was to help provide a link between African broadcasting organizations during the postindependence era and to establish a common professional institution. Initial meetings took place in 1960 and 1962 resulting in the URTNA's by-laws being adopted by the organization's General Assembly. Today, the URTNA remains essentially the same as when it was founded. Financial support for the union comes from membership fees, grants, income from publications, donations, and other activities.

From a group of broadcasting organizations of less than 24 independent African countries the URTNA grew to more than 40 active members by the mid-1980s.[16] The objectives of the URTNA include settling disagreements among members, assuring members adhere to the provisions of international and inter-African agreements relating to radio and television, assisting members in negotiating agreements with other organizations, and negotiating on behalf of URTNA members. Membership is afforded to any broadcasting organization within Africa willing to adhere to the statutes of the URTNA. Membership is conditional upon approval of the general assembly.

Organization

The URTNA functions are performed through the general assembly, the administrative council, and the bureau which is supported by a secretary general who presides over a general secretariat, a board of directors, and a legal adviser. Other boards and commissions also function within URTNA.

The general assembly is the supreme body of the organization and is presided over by a president. Having final authority in all matters related to URTNA, it is comprised of the membership and convenes once each year. Extraordinary sessions can be called by the president or by a two-thirds vote of the membership. Legislative issues are forwarded to the general assembly by the administrative council which is the policy-making part of URTNA and analogous to the president's cabinet in the United States. The administrative council, like the general assembly, meets once each year. Along with initiating policy, the council recommends new members to the general assembly, delegates authority to the secretary general, and appoints special commissions and study groups.

The bureau is much like an executive committee and consists of the president and two vice presidents. It operates like an expediting mechanism to implement decisions and take initiatives without convening the general assembly or the administrative council. The secretary general is the chief executive officer of the organization. As the head of the General Secretariat, the secretary general oversees a division of URTNA that implements the recommendations of the Administrative Council, administers the union's budget, and between meetings of the council and General Assembly is empowered to "take any relevant action to ensure the coordination of the activities of the Union's various permanent organs."[17] Among the commissions operating within URTNA is one dealing with program exchange and cultural affairs, one dealing with administrative and legal matters, and a technical commission. Study groups, less formal than commissions, are appointed to deal with issues as the need arises.[18]

The legal adviser is appointed by the General Assembly and handles legal matters such as copyright. For example, not all countries have the same copyright laws. The legal adviser must determine provisions that protect the use of visuals, completed programs, and the rights of developing countries where no copyright exists. Providing counsel to member countries on the advisability of signing treaties and how becoming signatories may affect a nation's ability to do business within the URTNA are other roles fulfilled by the legal adviser. To keep abreast of changes in international telecommunication law, the legal adviser participates in various international meetings such as those of the World Intellectual Property Organization.

The Program Exchange and Centers

When the union was founded one of its major objectives was to develop a program exchange among members. That objective remains today and program exchange has become one of the union's focal points. Originally members contributed programs to a radio program pool where programs were reproduced and air freighted to members. Television programs, on rare occasions, were also contributed. In 1976 a permanent Program Exchange Center was created, partially based on a concern that television programming that was the available for exchange contained little information of relevance to Africa. Keep in mind that the union was established in an era of postindependence and the lack of African-oriented programming reflected the opposite goal of the union's founders. Today the permanent Program Exchange Center works toward developing television production facilities and standards with an eye to providing African programming for Africa, not western programming for Africa, although the latter's influence remains.

Control over technical matters within the union is the responsibility of the Technical Center and a subsidiary unit, the Monitoring and Measuring Center. All authority over technical matters is delegated to the Technical Center. This authority includes centralized monitoring of all broadcasting signals of radio and television stations in member countries. Somewhat like the Federal Communications Commission's Office of Plans and Policy in the United States, the Technical Center of the union engages in study of regulatory-technical issues confronting member countries. For example, one study examined the effects that sand and dust storms have on satellite broadcasting.[19]

Training opportunities also exist for union members through the Inter-African Rural Radio Studies Center (CIERRO). A Management Board governs the CIERRO and meets at the end of each academic year. Chaired by the union's president, the management board defines the educational programs of the center adapting them to the needs of member countries.

Telecommunications and the URTNA

Telecommunications, like broadcasting, has impacted on Africa. URTNA is involved in the development of telecommunications through relations with other organizations such as the Pan-African Telecommunications Network. The network operates as a common carrier that has the potential to be a conduit for the relay and exchange of programs. Special working groups periodically deal with such issues as satellite fees, rural telecommunications, and other matters.

THE FEDERATION OF AUSTRALIAN RADIO BROADCASTERS

Internal professional associations exist in many countries and their activities range from providing members with industry news through a professionally oriented publication to negotiating rights for programs. One example of an association that gets involved in legal and regulatory matters is Australia's Federation of Australian Radio Broadcasters (FARB). Like professional associations in many countries, the FARB lobbies for its members in the various legislative and regulatory bodies of Australia. It also engages in other professional activities such as providing training seminars for managers and working with educational institutions in Australia that train broadcast professionals.

In addition to these more traditional activities, however, the FARB also accredits advertising agencies who work with the commercial broadcasters; thus, helping to assure its members that the agencies are professionally competent and have a satisfactory credit rating.[20] In addition, the FARB negotiates on behalf of its members with labor unions such as the Actors and Announcers' Equity of Australia, the Australian Journalists' Association, and the Professional Radio and Electronics Institute of Australia. In Australia, the FARB works in conjunction with the Australian Broadcasting Tribunal. The FARB also clears commercials in specific product categories for its members.[21] The FARB provides its members with advice on a range of copyright matters and can negotiate rights on behalf of its members. Negotiations are also conducted for member stations to use the overseas news material of the Australian Associated Press.

COUNCIL OF EUROPE

The Council of Europe was formed following World War II to promote European unity.[22] Each member state must recognize the rule of law and guarantee its citizens human rights. In the legal arena the council works toward coordinating legislation among its member states. More than 100 different multilateral treaties have been drawn up for ratification among the member states. Many treaties are open to nonmember states and these treaties help promote international cooperation beyond Europe. An umbrella committee called the European Committee on Legal Cooperation handles matters of commercial, administrative, and international law.

For example, a 1965 agreement on pirate radio stations helps prevent interference from pirate radio stations operating in international waters.[23] Each party to the treaty is responsible for enforcing violations in its own territorial waters. In the area of telecommunication, guaranteeing an individual's right of privacy when personal information is stored in data banks continues to be a concern of the council. Countries that sign a multilateral treaty on data protection undertake to assure that their internal laws comply with these same principles of protection. If these safeguards assuring privacy do not exist, then the signers of the treaty agree to prohibit the storing of sensitive personal information on individuals. Although enforcement remains a problem, the council through its treaties tries to eliminate "data havens" where individuals have information stored about them in a different country than where they live and without the individual's ability to know about such storage, correct inaccuracies, access the information, or purge it.

EUROPEAN COMMUNITY

The European Community (EC) is becoming increasingly influential in world affairs. Beginning in the 1980s the EC began to take an active interest in the regulation of broadcasting and telecommunication. The EC is an outgrowth of three different organizations that evolved after World War II, the European Coal and Steel Community, the European Economic Community, and the European Atomic Energy Community.

Background and Organization

First to be formed was the European Coal and Steel Community, which in 1952 was established through international treaty and became the organization through which workers were allowed to work in any of six European countries without restrictions, and through which trade barriers on coal and steel were also removed between the member countries.[24] The European Coal and Steel Community set the stage for more formal cooperation in other trade areas and eventually the formation of the European Economic Community and the European Atomic Energy Community formed through the Treaty of Rome, later amended, which went into effect on January 1, 1958.[25]

The European Community, encompassing its member countries, is the umbrella term given to all three organizations and is organized around five principal units: The Council of Ministers, the Commission, the European Parliament, the European Court of Justice, and the European Council. The first three are much like the legislative branches of government. For example, the Council of Ministers is made up of representatives appointed by the member governments.[26] The Council then appoints the Commission. The European Parliament is made up of elected representatives. As part of a system of checks and balances, the Parliament and the Commission can overrule the Council of Ministers. A two-thirds majority vote of censure by the Parliament can discharge the Commission.

Although not a formal legislative unit of the EC, regular meetings are also held by the European Council which consists of the heads of government of the EC member countries. Because of the participants, the meetings of the European Council receive considerable publicity but the real work of the European Community is done by the three legislative areas.

European Court of Justice

The European Court of Justice is the supreme judicial body of the European Community, but unlike the U.S. Supreme Court, it does not accept criminal cases.[27] Those are handled exclusively by the EC member states. Unlike the U.S. Supreme Court which must let a case come up through the lower courts, sometimes for decades before it reaches the U.S. Supreme Court, the European Court of Justice can issue advisory opinions on any case involving EC law and can accept at any time cases from the lower-level trial courts of the member states when EC law is concerned. If the lower trial court, however, decided to issue its own decision, the European Court of Justice cannot act as an appellate court. Under the Treaty of Rome the highest court of each member country is suppose to refer all cases involving EC law to the European Court of Justice. This does mean that all countries do, however, and if they do not there is little the European Court of Justice can do to enforce the judicial review provisions of the treaty.[28]

Legislative Branches' Involvement in Regulatory Matters

In addition to the European Court of Justice, the legislative branches of the EC have been active in regulations affecting broadcasting and telecommunication in the European Community. For example, a decision involving British Telecom found that the EC's competition rules don't apply to telecommunications. That ruling has resulted in the Commission Member States shall also ensure that broadcasts do the standpoint of "directives." Directives can be issued by the Commission without going through the normal legislative procedures involving the European Parliament and the Council of Ministers. For example, in the area of telecommunications, the Commission issued a directive calling on individual countries to end their state-held monopolies over telecommunications. Such monopolies are frequently under the country's postal, telephone, and telegraph administrations, the PTTs.

Under the Commission directive the PTTs in EC member countries are called upon to split into different legal entities, separating their regulatory and their commercial operations.[29] Such a system is similar to the United States where, for example, private commercial telephone companies exist but the companies are regulated by the government. In many European countries, both the regulation and the ownership of the company are under the government's PTT. The Commission's directive calling for the splitting up of the regulatory and commercial activities of PTT's has not resulted in automatic compliance. Countries such as France, Belgium, Italy, and Germany appealed the directive to the European Court of Justice. Only the Netherlands supported the measure.[30]

The Commission is also attempting to open up the bidding process through state PTT monopolies. Under a proposed directive PTTs could keep on hand a list of potential suppliers or announce each bid independently considering all of the bids submitted for that particular project. Impacting on these and other procedures is the General Agreement on Tariffs and Trade (GATT). The GATT is frequently brought up when concern arises about opening national boundaries in the EC to free trade and protecting countries that may be hurt by trade restrictions. Some ambiguity exists over whether telecommunications comes under the GATT provisions, however, and these issues remain unresolved. In the meantime, telecommunications hardware and services continue to grow. The Commission has proposed open bidding regardless of nationality, but where bids are equal, favoring bids which have at least a 50 percent EC-member involvement. Perceptions of fair treatment for non-EC members, including the United States, are particularly troublesome with the 50 percent provision.

Advertising Directives

In recognition of the power and influence of the electronic media, and the role of advertising in supporting those media, the EC Council of Ministers issued a directive to prohibit misleading advertising and to provide for penalties for those who engage in disseminating deceptive advertising messages. An EC press release announcing the first advertising directive stated,

> The messages capable of being received on TV screens in European homes will include not only conventional television programs but the pages of daily newspapers or other print media published in other parts of the world, and an extensive repertoire of sport and cultural entertainment material prerecorded and available via computer-controlled request codes accessible to individual subscribers.[31]

The release went on to note that it is already technically possible to engage in "armchair shopping," saying "The trader of the future can use the TV screen as a shop window for the merchandise of his department store, take orders by telephone code which will be automatically recorded for direct delivery to individual customers . . . ," while the shopper's bank account is automatically debited. The announcement stressed that these new systems are costly as well as convenient, and that: "The time has come for international regulation of advertising messages in all the main print and electronic media. This directive of the Council on misleading advertising is a timely first response to the needs of the new advertising age."[32]

Among other parts of the directive are provisions whereby persons who feel advertisements are misleading can bring action through the courts or designated administrative authorities to stop misleading advertising. Even prior restraint is possible whereby an advertisement which is considered misleading can be stopped before it is disseminated. Such measures are understandably controversial. The council directive attempted to remain sensitive to the need for quick resolution of contested matters since advertising can be diffused rapidly, and those with goods and products to sell must be able to advertise to generate demand for the goods and services. Much like the Federal Trade Commission's substantiation requirements for advertising claims, the directive gave authorities the power to require proof of advertised claims. Additional advertising directives have been issued, such as the "Television Without Frontiers" directive, as the EC continues to grapple with both the content and the power of the advertising media in post-1992 Europe.

The EC's Television Without Frontiers Directive

One of the more publicized directives issued by the European Community is the "Television Without Frontiers" directive which sets guidelines for the free flow of television broadcasting within the EC.[33] The directive attempts to come to grips with estimates in the EC that the total number of television hours broadcast within the European Community will reach 400,000 in the 1990s, up from 250,000 hours in the 1980s.

Some of the more controversial provisions of the directive are restrictions on the amount of television programming which can be produced by non-EC member countries. The directive calls for a majority of programs to be produced by EC nations, and even that amount was down from the 60 percent figure initially proposed by France. In a verbal exchange between spokespersons of the American motion picture industry, U.S. trade officials, and EC officials, strong opinions about the directive were unleashed. Jack Valenti, the president of the Motion Picture Association of America, said the directive "hurls a lance right at the heart of the U.S. industry's future."[34] Valenti went on to say: "Has culture botulism yet appeared anywhere in Europe? Is the culture in any of these European countries so flimsily anchored that European consumers must be caged and blinded else their links with their past, like an exploding star, vanish? Or is the real game not culture, but commerce?"[35] U.S. trade officials cited the directive as protectionism and tried to put a First Amendment-type spin on the directive saying it restricted the content of programming. Their concern was understandable, not only because of the special interests they represent but because the U.S. program sales to the EC represent half of the U.S. television industry's worldwide income.[36]

EC officials responded to the American criticism calling it unjustified. EC Commission Vice President Martin Bangemann said the criticism was "all the more unjustified because in the bilateral free trade agreement between the United States and Canada, the United States has explicitly recognized that cultural products are not to be placed on the same footing as other merchandise. They have formally accepted to respect very strict quotas concerning U.S. audiovisual products on Canadian soil."[37] EC Commission President Jacques Delors stated in the same release: "I must say to the United States, we have the right to exist and to maintain our traditions. There is no European culture, but several. Each country should be able to defend its own. At least, we should be given the time to do it. There will be no protection of the European market, . . . but no laissez-faire either."[38]

What is interesting about the exchange between the countries is that the United States took the position that television was commerce and the European Community took the position that it is culture.[39] Commerce can be regulated by trade tariffs and other measures, and the European Community itself is primarily an economic and political body. Culture, on the other hand, is a much more nebulous entity and is much more difficult to classify as a regulated commercial property. If television is commerce, then such measures as the General Agreement on Tariffs and Trade (GATT) which regulates international trade could apply to the directive. Moreover, the United States and other non-EC member countries could seek relief through another legislative body of the EC or the European Court of Justice. The "cultural" definition, however, makes that relief much more illusive.

Not everyone saw the directive in the way Valenti or other U.S. trade officials did, feeling that there were opportunities for joint productions with EC-member countries and the increase in the number of television hours would provide more income and more profits for U.S. producers engaged in these productions. The Trans-Atlantic Dialogue on European Broadcasting, a working group of senior communications industry officials, said the directive would provide "new opportunities for growth and cooperation within Europe and with other countries."[40]

EUROPEAN CONFERENCE OF POSTAL AND TELECOMMUNICATIONS ADMINISTRATIONS

Many European countries combine the functions of the post office and telecommunications, which includes telephone systems, in an internal postal, telegraph, and telecommunication administrative structure under PTTs. In some cases these PTTs are involved with broadcasters. For example, in Switzerland the Swiss Broadcasting Corporation is a private company organized as an association and nonprofit. Its primary role, however, is programming. The technical aspects of broadcasting are delegated to the PTT. The PTT is responsible for all matters relating to the construction, operation, and the upkeep of broadcast transmitters and relay equipment. Sound and video links between studios and transmitters are also the responsibility of the PTT. In Denmark the cable systems fall under the telephone company which are under the PTTs. The broadcasting law in Denmark states, "A telephone company, or, in State telephone areas, the Corporation of Posts and Telecommunications, may . . . devise a plan for connection of communal aerials and other cable systems to the networks of the telephone company . . . "[41] In the Netherlands the PTT is responsible for collecting fees for the use and ownership of radio and television receivers.

The organization that coordinates the activities of PTTs is the European Conference of Postal and Telecommunications Administrations. The organization's abbreviation is CEPT after the French translation. Formed in Montreaux, Switzerland in 1959, the CEPT lists as its primary functions:

> The implementation of work and services of common interest. The simplification and improvement of postal and telecommunication services. The examination of questions concerning the organizational, technical and operational aspects of services. The joint consideration of proposals submitted to congresses and conferences of the international Postal and Telecommunications bodies. The exchange of information and officials.[42]

Two levels of administration are found within the CEPT, the Plenary Assembly which deals with issues jointly affecting the various PTTs and also the administration of the organization, and the Postal Commission and Telecommunications Commission which report to the Plenary Assembly and handle matters of concern to either postal or telecommunications operations. For example, the Plenary Assembly is responsible for incorporating administrative offices into the organization to assist it in managing its operations. It has negotiated through the International Monetary Fund a standardized financial structure permitting the equitable transfer of funds and the settling of accounts between member PTTs. The Telecommunications Commission, on the other hand, has concentrated on developing such areas as satellite communications, transatlantic links, data transmission, and standardization of equipment among member PTTs.

THE TELECOMMUNICATIONS COMMISSION

The growth of telecommunication services throughout Europe has increased the importance and activity of the Telecommunications Commission of the CEPT. For example, the CEPT has worked cooperatively to develop a European satellite system and arrange the necessary agreements with the European Space Agency. Through the work of the Telecommunications Commission, CEPT has helped to define the technical standards and strategic planning for the data transmission systems in Europe. Working in cooperation with the United States and Canada, CEPT has helped to develop fiber-optic transatlantic links between Europe and North America. The future development of Integrated Services Digital Networks (ISDN) promises more involvement by the CEPT and its Telecommunications Commission as internal ISDN systems link together.

Within these developments a rich legal and regulatory arena exists which must be dealt with before any real cooperative venture can succeed. For example, although similarities exist among PTTs, differences exist in their structure, depending on the type of government within which they operate. Those PTTs embracing the spirit of the European Community's charge of separate legal entities for operational and regulatory matters present one structure which must mesh with countries resisting such separation. In satellite communication, agreements negotiated through the International Telecommunications Union, the ITU, and such organizations as the European Space Agency necessitate working through different international agencies, treaties, and international frequency allocations as well as internal regulatory structures. Tariffs, the schedule of prices and fees, must be negotiated through international agreements. Agreements must also be negotiated between organizations cooperating with the CEPT, such as the European Broadcasting Union and others. Technical matters alone impact on international law as the CEPT and the Telecommunications Commission work to encourage among PTTs the development of such services as teleconferencing, fiber optic networks, mobile communications, and telephone systems. For the CEPT, these jurisdictions present a challenge to maintain unity and credibility in its own sphere while working toward international contacts on a broad scale.

WORLD INTELLECTUAL PROPERTY ORGANIZATION

Without international agreements, copyright would only apply to artistic works in the country in which those works were registered and there would be no inherent protection for those works in other countries. So that those who create copyrighted works have some degree of international protection for the works they create, individual countries, referred to as states in international law, have entered into multilateral treaties. These various conventions protect copyright across international boundaries. At the heart of these conventions is the organization based in Geneva, Switzerland, called the World Intellectual Property Organization (WIPO).[43]

The Origin of the WIPO

The roots of the WIPO date back to 1883 when in Paris a treaty for the protection of industrial property was adopted. That treaty, called the Paris Convention for the Protection of Industrial Property, then joined together with the Berne Convention for the Protection of Literary and Artistic Works into a central administrative structure known as the United International Bureau for the Protection of Intellectual Property. This organization operating under various names became the WIPO, one of a group of designated specialized agencies affiliated with the United Nations.

Objectives of the WIPO

The objectives of the WIPO are to promote the protection of intellectual property throughout the world and to help ensure administrative cooperation among nations in the area of copyright protection. Especially important to WIPO is the encouragement of international treaties for copyright protection and the modernization of legislation to keep copyright protection current and applicable to different media across international boundaries. These treaties are centralized and to some degree administered through WIPO's International Bureau in Geneva.

Of direct interest to broadcasting is the The International Union for the Protection of Literary and Artistic Works, which is administered by the WIPO's International Bureau. The International Union, also called the Berne Union for Berne, Switzerland where it was formulated, states that each member state must accord the same protection to the copyright of the nationals of the other member states as it accords to that of its own nationals. Agreed upon minimum standards for protection are included with special provisions for developing countries. The WIPO's International Bureau, along with administering the International Union for the Protection of Literary and Artistic Works, initiates new projects and carries out existing projects for the promotion of copyright protection. It centralizes information and keeps members informed of new development in copyright law through its publication *Copyright* (*Le Driot d'auteur* in French). The International Bureau, which is the depository for most of the treaties administered by the WIPO, is funded by the member states as well as fees it collects through copyright registration.

THE UNIVERSAL POSTAL UNION

In countries with PTTs, telecommunication falls under an administrative framework that includes postal services as well as telephone and telegraph services. International cooperation of postal services is the responsibility of the Universal Postal Union (UPU) modeled after the agreements that forged cooperation among telegraph systems in the late 1800s.[44] The International Telegraph Union was founded in 1865 and in 1874 the first International Postal Congress opened in Berne, Switzerland. From that conference came the General Postal Union.[45] The 1874 meeting also established within the General Postal Union an International Bureau which has been permanently located at Berne ever since. Because so many countries subscribed to the regulatory measures established at Berne in 1874, three years later the name of the organization was changed to the Universal Postal Union.

Historical Context

The history of postal regulation, however, goes back much earlier to the origins of the Roman Empire and early civilizations of China, Egypt, Africa, wherever traces of communication systems exist. Within these early civilizations the ruling class used a system of human relays to move information throughout their own geographical spheres of influence and from one country to another. Later, monasteries developed a similar courier system for religious purposes. Gradually private citizens were permitted to use these systems to communicate with one another.

The first postal agreements occurred through the efforts of Franz von Taxis in the sixteenth century and resulted in France, Austria, Germany, the Netherlands, Italy, and Spain joining together to assure unhindered flow of information through different currencies and different countries. But postal systems for the most part were still large and disorganized. At the beginning of the 1800s in Germany alone there were 30 different postal systems in operation. Rates were in local currencies, weights were calculated differently; thus, long-distance postal carriage was expensive and complex. When steam power and railways arrived, postal officials realized they needed an efficient system to compete. From Great Britain through the efforts of Roland Hill came the postage stamp and standardized rates. From Germany came models for the consolidation of the postal system, namely through the work of Henrich Von Stephan whose efforts help create a unified system in his own country by the 1870s.

Von Stephan felt that simplifying and standardizing the postal system of different countries would result in substantial benefits and prepared a 14-point draft for the 1874 meeting in Berne. For the most part it was adopted. Other international conferences have also been noteworthy. The Vienna Conference in 1891 established a means whereby newspapers from different countries could be distributed through the mails. The Hague Conference in 1927 established regulations to govern international airmail service and subsequent conferences brought in aeronautical authorities from different countries to improve the airmail provisions. The London Congress in 1929 introduced the concept of the "small packet" to the postal service.

Contemporary Operations

Since the Berne meeting of 1874, countries throughout the world have become members of the UPU and today international postal systems are still one of the world's most reliable and efficient means of communication. World War II and the founding of the United Nations changed somewhat the process by which countries can join the UPU, and to some extent imposed political dimensions to an organization that had been exclusively economic and technical. Nevertheless, postal systems, which in some ways both compete with and complement telephone and telegraph communications have managed a remarkable amount of cooperation among different countries.

Today the UPU is a coordinating agency serving postal systems throughout the world that have a combined total of more than 650,000 post offices, many with allied telecommunication services. The UPU, a specialized agency of the United Nations, is organized around a Congress, Executive Council, a Consultive Council for Postal Studies, and an International Bureau.

Each of the areas has a specific function within the UPU. The Congress is composed of representatives from each of the member countries and is the supreme body of the UPU. Convened every five years, the Congress studies and revises the acts of the UPU and can accept legislative proposals from the members, the Executive Council, or the Consultative Council for Postal Studies. Congress elects the Executive Council made up of 40 members with due care for geographical distribution. Meeting every year, the Executive Council assures the continuity of the UPU's work including providing legal counsel. Congress also elects the Consultative Council for Postal Studies made up of 35 people who are responsible for studying the problems of individual postal administrations. The Consultative Council's reports are published as the "Collection of Postal Studies."

Operating since the beginning of the union is the International Bureau. The International Bureau is the permanent administrative component of the UPU and provides services to member countries, settles disputes, and considers requests for amendments to the act of the UPU. The International Bureau also acts as a settlement agent for debts relating to transit charges, terminal dues, and international reply coupons.[46] Close cooperation exists between the UPU and the International Telecommunications Union, both of which are United Nations organizations and both of which are involved in communications.

The future role of the UPU will be molded to some degree by new telecommunication services, which like the advent of steam power and railroads almost a century ago, will compete with the postal service as a means of personal communication. The technologies of FAX, lower and more competitive international telephone rates, will impact on postal systems. Yet even with the growth of new telecommunication technologies that transcend national boundaries, nothing is more resilient to political strife than the postal service. In addition, in countries where sophisticated communication technologies reach only the affluent, the postal service is available to every class of person. For these reasons, a complete understanding of telecommunication as a means of personal communication also requires an understanding of the postal service.

SUMMARY

From the Federal Communications Commission in the United States to tribunals and unions found in Europe, Africa, and elsewhere, broadcasting is regulated by many different government and quasi-government organizations. Much of the regulatory framework for broadcasting began in the twentieth century when Marconi's expanding empire necessitated systematic control over the communication links that protected worldwide shipping interests. Laws and regulations governing the telegraph gradually expanded to encompass radio and television. International organizations such as the International Telecommunication Union molded cooperative agreements across national boundaries.

The ITU is a United Nations organization responsible for coordinating the use of telecommunications among nations. Although not having the enforcement powers of the FCC, it is an arena for negotiated treaties concerning the use of the electromagnetic spectrum. The ITU's history dates back to 1849 when Austria and Prussia signed a telegraph agreement. From succeeding conferences grew new organizations and new treaties. The International Bureau of Telegraph Administration was formed in Vienna in 1868 and later became the International Telegraph Union. The increased importance of wireless resulted in the formation of the Radio-Telegraph Union which merged with the International Telegraph Union, forming the International Telecommunication Union. Today the ITU's functions include allocating space on the spectrum, supporting telecommunication systems in developing nations, and promoting the adoption of measures for ensuring safety through cooperative telecommunication services. Today the ITU is organized around the Plenipotentiary Conference which is the supreme body of the ITU. An Administrative Council is composed of members elected on a regional basis. Administrative conferences are called periodically to revise the regulations of the ITU and international consultative committees operate with full-time secretariats.

World Administrative Radio Conferences meet periodically to evaluate different telecommunication topics of policy such as satellite communications. Planning begins long before the meeting date. In the United States, different agencies of government coordinate negotiation strategies. The FCC forms working groups to study specific issues and other departments such as Defense and State begin preparations to represent all agencies of government as the chief representative of the United States.

The European Broadcasting Union is made up of associate and active members that operate the Eurovision system, a European television-exchange network. EBU grew out of the International Broadcasting Union founded in Geneva, Switzerland in 1925. Some of the goals of the EBU are to establish relations with other broadcasting organizations, ensure the exchange of information related to broadcasting, promote the development of broadcasting, seek solutions to problems through international cooperation, and ensure members respect international agreements. Of special interest to members is the legal and contract work performed by the Legal Committee of the EBU. The committee is often the representative of the EBU and its members at international meetings and the committee has constructed model agreements to assist members in negotiating programming rights. Negotiation of international sports broadcasting contracts and helping members pass declarations and resolutions are two additional functions performed by the EBU's Legal Committee.

After World War II, a second organization called the International Radio Organization operated simultaneously with the EBU. The International Radio Organization eventually broke off and became the International Radio and Television Organization located in Prague. Much like the EBU, the International Radio Television Organization operates a program-exchange service called Intervision and assists members in negotiating programming rights. Associate and active membership categories exist with the organization and like the EBU, cooperative ties exist with other international broadcasting organizations. An

Economic and Legal Commission meets each year to consider policy matters submitted to it by the administrative bodies of the organization, the Administrative Council and the General Assembly.

Facilitating programming between Caribbean nations is the Caribbean Broadcasting Union. Representing both English-speaking and Dutch-speaking Caribbean areas, the CBU legal activities include the negotiation of rates with outside suppliers. Sports broadcasting rights are negotiated for the Olympic Games, World Cup Football, and international cricket matches from such places as Australia, England, India, and Pakistan. Stations receiving the broadcasts share the costs of programming. The CBU also negotiates satellite interconnects and rates for news coverage such as elections and national disasters.

Operating in Africa is the Union of National Radio and Television Organizations. Emerging out of the postindependence era of the 1960s, the union's original purpose was to help join together African broadcasting organizations and provide a common professional association. Initial meetings in Nigeria in 1960 and 1962 resulted in by-laws being approved. Among URTNA's functions are helping to settle disputes between members, assuring compliance with inter-African agreements, and assisting members in negotiating new agreements on behalf of URTNA members. A General Assembly, an Administrative Council, a Bureau, and a General Secretariat under a secretary general are the administrative parts of the URTNA. A legal adviser appointed by the General Assembly is responsible for legal matters including advising members on international copyright law and how becoming signatories to treaties will affect the members relationship with the URTNA. Control over technical matters within and among the union's members is the responsibility of a Technical Center operating as a subsidiary unit of the Monitoring and Measuring Center.

Concerned with legal and regulatory matters in Australia is the Federation of Australian Radio Broadcasters. FARB has a lobby arm working with different national and provincial legislatures and agencies. It also serves as an accrediting organization for advertising agencies that want to place media buys with local broadcasters. In addition, FARB provides members with negotiating services for union contracts and advises members on copyright matters. FARB negotiates contracts with the Australian Associated Press for the use of overseas news material.

Following World War II the Council of Europe was formed to coordinate legislation among member states. In the area of broadcasting and telecommunication the council's European Committee on Legal Cooperation plays the most important role. A 1965 agreement on pirate radio stations tries to prevent interference from stations operating without any authorization in international waters. Guaranteeing an individual's right of privacy when personal information is stored in data banks is another concern of the council. Through treaties, the council tries to prevent data havens from cropping up where individuals can have data stored about them in a different country with little opportunity to access or purge the information.

Becoming increasingly important in world affairs is the European Community. In the 1980s the EC began to take an active interest in regulating broadcasting among member nations. The lifting of trade barriers and a common currency in Europe will continue to elevate the role of the EC in the realm of broadcasting and telecommunication. The supreme judicial body of the EC is the European Court of Justice which can review under certain circumstances the decisions of courts within EC member countries. In addition to the Court, the EC Commission, the European Parliament, and the EC's Council of Ministers can become involved in legislative and judicial matters. By issuing directives that in theory apply to all EC member countries, the EC is able to influence economic and regulatory policy. One of the more controversial directives is the Television Without Frontiers Directive, which calls for the majority of programming aired on stations in EC countries to be produced by EC member states.

Although organizations such as the European Broadcasting Union, Intervision, the EC, and others influence and regulate broadcasting, telecommunication services such as telephone systems fall under individual PTTs in different countries. The organization that coordinates these PTTs is the European Conference of Postal and Telecommunications Administrations. Formed in Montreaux, Switzerland in 1959, the goals of the administration include simplifying postal and telecommunication services among different countries, examining technical and operational aspects of these services. Two levels of administration within the organization are the Plenary Assembly at the first level which deals with issues affecting the PTTs, and a Postal Commission and Telecommunication Commission at the second level which deal with operations.

International copyright protection is provided by the World Intellectual Property Organization. While many countries have their own copyright laws, the WIPO coordinates these statutes within the context of international law. WIPO's beginnings date to Paris in 1883 when the protection of international property was adopted through a treaty called the Paris Convention. A central administrative structure growing out of the Paris Convention was the Bureau for the Protection of International Property, which eventually became the WIPO. The WIPO's International Bureau administers another organization called the Union for the Protection of Literary and Artistic Works, which affords each member state the same copyright protection as other member states.

In countries where sophisticated communication technologies reach only the affluent, the postal service is available to every class of citizen. Worldwide, postal services are entering into news telecommunication services. Coordinating this involvement on a global scale is the Universal Postal Union. Historically the UPU dates back to the telegraph era and is an outgrowth of the treaties that grew out of the telegraph becoming an international medium in the 1800s. In some countries the postal service finds itself in competition with new telecommunication services that use telephone, data, and satellite systems to send and receive messages. In other countries the postal service is more a partner to such services which are regulated by government-operated PTTs.

MATERIAL FOR ANALYSIS

The European Community is becoming more involved in the regulation of broadcasting. Through council directives, it is able to influence regulations among EC member nations and also impact on the radio and television industries of other countries, as was the case when the Television Without Frontiers Directive was passed. That directive, excerpted here in part, (some subheadings and reference to specific provisions have also been deleted) was preceded by directives that restrict advertising in the EC, including tobacco products that the European Parliament banned in 1992.[47] EC directives are not legally binding on member countries but do send a strong message. In many cases EC member countries fall into line with the directives and change their own laws to meet the wishes of the EC.

TELEVISION WITHOUT FRONTIERS DIRECTIVE OF THE EUROPEAN COMMUNITY

Addressed to the Member States and Done at Luxembourg 3 October 1989

* * *

Whereas the objectives of the Community as laid down in the Treaty include establishing an even closer union among the peoples of Europe, fostering closer relations between the States belonging to the Community, ensuring the economic and social progress of its countries by common action to eliminate the barriers which divided Europe, encouraging the constant improvement of the living conditions of its peoples as well as ensuring the preservation and strengthening of peace and liberty;

Whereas the Treaty provides for the establishment of a common market, including the abolition, as between Member States, of obstacles to freedom of movement for services and the institution of a system ensuring that competition in the common market is not distorted;

Whereas broadcasts transmitted across frontiers by means of various technologies are one of the ways of pursuing the objectives of the Community; whereas measures should be adopted to permit and ensure the transition from national markets to a common programme production and distribution market and to establish conditions of fair competition without prejudice to the public interest role to be discharged by the television services;

Whereas the Council of Europe has adopted the European Convention on Transfrontier Television;

Whereas the Treaty provides for the issuing of directives for the coordination of provisions to facilitate the taking up of activities as self-employed persons;

Whereas television broadcasting constitutes, in normal circumstances, a service within the meaning of the Treaty;

Whereas the Treaty provides for free movement of all services normally provided against payment, without exclusion on grounds of their cultural or other content and without restriction of nationals of Member States established in a Community country other than that of the person for whom the services are intended;

Whereas this right as applied to the broadcasting and distribution of television services is also a specific manifestation in Community law of a more general principle, namely the freedom of expression as enshrined in Article 10 (1) of the Convention for the Protection of Human Rights and Fundamental Freedoms ratified by all Member States; whereas for this reason the issuing of directives on the broadcasting and distribution of television programmes must ensure their free movement in the light of said Article and subject only to the limits set by paragraph 2 of that Article and by Article 56 (1) of the Treaty;

Whereas the laws, regulations and administrative measures in Member States concerning the pursuit of activities as television broadcasters and cable operators contain disparities, some of which may impede the free movement of broadcasts within the Community and may distort competition within the common market;

Whereas all such restrictions on freedom to provide broadcasting services within the Community must be abolished under the Treaty;

Whereas such abolition must go hand in hand with coordination of the applicable laws; whereas this coordination must be aimed at facilitating the pursuit of the professional activities concerned and, more generally, the free movement of information and ideas within the Community;

Whereas it is consequently necessary and sufficient that all broadcasts comply with the law of Member State from which they emanate;

Whereas this Directive lays down the minimum rules needed to guarantee freedom of transmission in broadcasting; whereas, therefore, it does not affect the responsibility of the Member States and their authorities with regard to the organization—including the systems of licensing, administrative authorization or taxation—financing and the content of programmes; whereas the independence of cultural developments in the Member States and the preservation of cultural diversity in the Community therefore remain unaffected;

Whereas it is necessary, in the common market, that all broadcasts emanating from and intended for reception within the Community and in particular those intended for reception in another Member State applicable to broadcasts intended for reception by the public in that Member State and the Provisions of this Directive;

Whereas the requirement that the originating Member State should verify that broadcasts comply with national law as coordinated by this Directive is sufficient under Community law to ensure free movement of broadcasts without secondary control on the same grounds in the receiving Member States; whereas, however, the receiving Member State may, exceptionally and under specific conditions provisionally suspend the retransmission of televised broadcasts;

Whereas it is essential for the Member States to ensure the prevention of any acts which may prove detrimental to freedom of movement and trade in television programmes or which may promote the creation of dominant positions which would lead to restrictions on pluralism and freedom of televised information and of the information sector as a whole;

Whereas this Directive, being confined specifically to television broadcasting rules, is without prejudice to existing or future Community acts of harmonization, in particular to satisfy mandatory requirements concerning the protection of consumers and the fairness of commercial transactions and competition;

Whereas co-ordination is nevertheless needed to make it easier for persons and industries producing programmes having a cultural objective to take up and pursue their activities;

Whereas minimum requirements in respect of all public or private Community television programmes for European audio-visual productions have been a means of promoting production, independent production and distribution in the abovementioned industries and are complementary to other instruments which are already or will be proposed to favor the same objective;

Whereas it is therefore necessary to promote markets of sufficient size for television productions in the Member Sates to recover necessary investments not only by establishing common rules opening up national markets but also by envisaging for European productions where practicable and by appropriate means a majority proportion in television programmes of all Member States; whereas, in order to allow the monitoring of the application of these rules and the pursuit of the objectives, Member States will provide the Commission with a report on the application of the proportions reserved for European works and independent productions in this Directive; whereas for the calculation of such proportions account should be taken of the specific situation of the Hellenic Republic and the Portuguese Republic; whereas the Commission must inform the other Member States of these reports accompanied, where appropriate by an opinion taking account of, in particular, progress achieved in relation to previous years, the share of first broadcasts in the programming, the particular circumstances of new television broadcasters and the specific situation of countries with a low audio-visual production capacity or restricted language area;

Whereas for these purposes "European works" should be defined with prejudice to the possibility of Member States laying down a more detailed definition as regards television broadcasters under their jurisdiction in accordance with Article 3 (1) in compliance with Community law and account being taken of the objectives of this Directive;

Whereas it is important to seek appropriate instruments and procedures in accordance with Community law in order to promote the implementation of these objectives with a view to adopting suitable measures to encourage the activity and development of European audio-visual production and distribution, particularly in countries with a low production capacity or restricted language area;

Whereas national support schemes for the development of European production may be applied in so far as they comply with Community law;

Whereas a commitment, where practicable, to a certain proportion of broadcasts for independent productions, created by producers who are independent of broadcasters will stimulate new sources of television production, especially the creation of small and medium-sized enterprises; whereas it will offer new opportunities and outlets to the marketing of creative talents of employment of cultural professions and employees in the cultural field; whereas the definition of the concept of independent producer by the Member Sates should take account of that objective by giving due consideration to small and medium-sized producers and making it possible to authorize financial participation by the coproduction subsidiaries of television organizations;

Whereas measures are necessary for Member States to ensure that a certain period elapses between the first cinema showing of a work and the first television showing;

Whereas in order to allow for an active policy in favour of a specific language, Member States remain free to lay down more detailed or stricter rules in particular on the basis of language criteria, as long as these rules are in conformity with Community law, and in particular are not applicable to the retransmission of broadcasts originating in other Member States;

Whereas in order to ensure that the interests of consumers as television viewers are fully and properly protected, it is essential for television advertising to be subject to a certain number of minimum rules and standards and that Member States must maintain the right to set more detailed or stricter rules and in certain circumstances to lay down different conditions for television broadcasters under their jurisdiction;

Whereas Member States, with due regard to Community law and in relation to broadcasts intended solely for the national territory which may not be received, directly or indirectly, in one or more Member States, must be able to lay down different conditions for the insertion of advertising and different limits for the volume of advertising in order to facilitate these particular broadcasts;

Whereas it is necessary to prohibit all television advertising promoting cigarettes and other tobacco products including indirect forms of advertising which, whilst not directly mentioning the tobacco product, seek to circumvent the ban on advertising by using brand names, symbols or other distinctive features of tobacco products or of undertakings whose known or main activities include the production or sale of such products;

Whereas it is equally necessary to prohibit all television advertising for medicinal products and medical treatment available only on prescription in the Member State within whose jurisdiction the broadcaster falls and to introduce strict criteria relating to the television advertising of alcoholic products;

Whereas in view of the growing importance of sponsorship in the financing of programmes, appropriate rules should be laid down;

Whereas it is, furthermore, necessary to introduce rules to protect the physical, mental and moral development of minors in programmes and in television advertising;

Whereas although television broadcasters are normally bound to ensure that programmes present facts and events fairly, it is nevertheless important that they should be subject to specific obligations with respect to the right of reply or equivalent remedies so that any person whose legitimate interests have been damaged by an assertion made in the course of a broadcast television programme may effectively exercise such right or remedy. (Has therefore adopted this directive):

(Article 1) Definitions

(a) "television broadcasting" means the initial transmission by wire or over the air, including that by satellite, in unencoded or encoded form, of television programmes intended for reception by the public. It includes the communication of programmes between undertakings with a view to their being relayed to the public. It does not include communication services providing items of information or other messages on individual demand such as telecopying, electronic data banks and other similar services;

(b) "television advertising" means any form of announcement broadcast in return for payment or for similar consideration by a public or private undertaking in connection with a trade, business, craft or profession in order to promote the supply of goods or services, including immovable property, or rights and obligations, in return for payment. Except for the purposes for Article 18, this does not include direct offers to the public for the sale, purchase or rental of products or for the provision of services in return for payment;

(c) "surreptitious advertising" means the representation in words or pictures of goods, services, the name, the trademark or the activities of a producer of goods or a provider of services in programmes when such representation is intended by the broadcaster to serve advertising and might mislead the public as to its nature. Such representation is considered to be intentional in particular if it is done in return for payment or for similar consideration;

(d) "sponsorship" means any contribution made by a public or private undertaking not engaged in television broadcasting activities or in the production of audio-visual works, to the financing of television programmes with a view to promoting its name, its trade mark, its image, its activities or its products.

* * *

(Article 4) Promotion, Distribution, and Production

Member States shall ensure where practicable and by appropriate means, that broadcasters reserve for European works, within the meaning of Article 6, a majority proportion of their transmission time, excluding the time appointed to news, sports events, games, advertising and teletext services. This proportion, having regard to the broadcaster's informational, educational, cultural and entertainment responsibilities to its viewing public, should be achieved progressively, on the basis of suitable criteria.

* * *

(Article 5) Member States shall ensure, where practicable and by appropriate means, that broadcasters reserve at least 10% of their transmission time, excluding the time appointed to news, sports events, games, advertising and teletext services, or alternately, at the discretion of the Member States, at least 10% of their programming budget, for European works created by producers who are independent of broadcasters. This proportion, having regard to broadcasters" informational, educational, cultural and entertainment responsibilities to its viewing public, should be achieved progressively, on the basis of suitable criteria; it must be achieved by earmarking an adequate proportion for recent works, that is to say works transmitted within five years of their production.

* * *

(Article 6) . . . the contribution of co-producers of those States to the total co-production costs is preponderant and the co-production is not controlled by one or more producers established outside those States.

The works referred to in (the above paragraph) are works made exclusively or in co-production with producers established in one or more Member States by producers established in one or more European third countries with which the Community will conclude agreements in accordance with the procedures of the Treaty, if those works are mainly made with authors and workers residing in one or more European States.

* * *

(Article 7) Member States shall ensure that the television broadcasters under their jurisdiction do not broadcast any cinematographic work, unless otherwise agreed between its rights holders and the broadcaster, until two years have elapsed since the work was first shown in cinemas in one of the Member States of the Community; in the case of cinematographic works co-produced by the broadcaster, this period shall be one year.

(Article 8) Where they consider it necessary for purposes of language policy, the Member

States, whilst observing Community law, may as regards some or all programmes of television broadcasters under their jurisdiction, lay down more detailed or stricter rules in particular on the basis of language criteria.

This chapter shall not apply to local television broadcasts not forming part of a national network.

Television Advertising and Sponsorship (Article 10)

1. Television advertising shall be readily recognizable as such and kept quite separate from other parts of the programme service by optical and/or acoustic means.
2. Isolated advertising spots shall remain the exception.
3. Advertising shall not use subliminal techniques.
4. Surreptitious advertising shall be prohibited.

(Article 11) Advertising Insertions

1. Advertisements shall be inserted between programmes. Provided the conditions contained in paragraphs 2 to 5 of this Article are fulfilled, advertisements may also be inserted during programmes in such a way that the integrity and value of the programme, taking into account natural breaks in and the duration and nature of the programme, and the rights of the rights holders are not prejudiced.
2. In programmes consisting of autonomous parts, or in sports programmes and similarly structured events and performances comprising intervals, advertisements shall only be inserted between the parts or in the intervals.
3. The transmission of audiovisual works such as feature films and films made for television (excluding series, serial, light entertainment programmes and documentaries), provided their programmed duration is more than 45 minutes, may be interrupted once for each complete period of 45 minutes. A further interruption is allowed if their programmed duration is at least 20 minutes longer than two or more complete periods of 45 minutes.
4. Where programmes, other than those covered by paragraph 2, are interrupted by advertisements, a period of at least 20 minutes should elapse between each successive advertising break within the programme.
5. Advertisements shall not be inserted in any broadcast of a religious service. News and current affairs programmes, documentaries, religious programmes, and children's programmes, when their programmed duration is less than 30 minutes shall not be interrupted by advertisements. If their programmed duration is of 30 minutes or longer, the provisions of the previous paragraphs shall apply.

(Article 12) Television advertising shall not:

(a) prejudice respect for human dignity;

(b) include any discrimination on grounds of race, sex or nationality;

(c) be offensive to religious or political beliefs;

(d) encourage behavior prejudicial to health or to safety;

(e) encourage behavior prejudicial to the protection of the environment.

(Article 13) All forms of television advertising for cigarettes and other tobacco products shall be prohibited.

(Article 14) Television advertising for medicinal products and medical treatment available only on prescription in the Member State within whose jurisdiction the broadcaster falls shall be prohibited.

(Article 15) Television advertising for alcoholic beverages shall comply with the following criteria:

(a) it may not be aimed specifically at minors or, in particular, depict minors consuming these beverages;

(b) it shall not link the consumption of alcohol to enhanced physical performance or to driving;

(c) it shall not create the impression that the consumption of alcohol contributes towards social or sexual success;

(d) it shall not claim that alcohol has therapeutic qualities or that it is a stimulant, a sedative or a means of resolving personal conflicts;

(e) it shall not encourage immoderate consumption of alcohol or present abstinence or moderation in a negative light;

(f) it shall not place emphasis on high alcoholic content as being a positive quality of the beverages.

(Article 16) Television advertising shall not cause moral or physical detriment to minors, and shall therefore comply with the following criteria for their protection:

(a) it shall not directly exhort minors to buy a product or a service by exploiting their inexperience or credulity;

(b) it shall not directly encourage minors to persuade their parents or others to purchase the goods or services being advertised;

(c) it shall not exploit the special trust minors place in parents, teachers or other persons;

(d) it shall not unreasonably show minors in dangerous situations.

(Article 17) Sponsored television programmes shall meet the following requirements:

(a) the content and scheduling of sponsored programmes may in no circumstances be influenced by the sponsor in such a way as to affect the responsibility and editorial independence of the broadcaster in respect of programmes;

(b) they must be clearly identified as such by the name and/or logo of the sponsor at the beginning and/or the end of the programmes;

(c) they must not encourage the purchase or rental of the products or services of the sponsor or a third party, in particular by making special promotional references to those products or services.

2. Television programmes may not be sponsored by natural or legal persons whose principal activity is the manufacture or sale of products, or the provision of services, the advertising of which is prohibited by Article 13 or 14.

3. News and current affairs programmes may not be sponsored.

(Article 18) Amount of Advertising

1. The amount of advertising shall not exceed 15% of the daily transmission time. However, this percentage may be increased to 20% to include forms of advertisements such as direct offers to the public for the sale, purchase or rental of products or for the provision of services, provided the amount of spot advertising does not exceed 15%.

2. The amount of spot advertising within a given one-hour period shall not exceed 20%.

3. Without prejudice to the provisions of paragraph 1, forms of advertisements such as direct offers to the public for the sale, purchase or rental of products or for the provision of services shall not exceed one hour per day.

* * *

(Article 22) Protection of Minors

Member States shall take appropriate measures to ensure that television broadcasts by broadcasters under their jurisdiction do not include programmes which might seriously impair the physical, mental or moral development of minors, in particular those that involve pornography or gratuitous violence. This provision shall extend to other programmes which are likely to impair the physical, mental or moral development of minors, except where it is ensured, by selecting the time of the broadcast or by any technical measure, that minors in the area of transmission will not normally hear or see such broadcasts.

Member States shall also ensure that broadcasts do not contain any incitement to hatred on grounds of race, sex, religion or nationality.

(Article 23) Right of Reply

1. Without prejudice to other provisions adopted by the Member States under civil, administrative or criminal law, any natural or legal person, regardless of nationality, whose legitimate interests, in particular reputation and good name, have been damaged by an assertion of incorrect facts in a television programme must have a right of reply or equivalent remedies.

2. A right of reply or equivalent remedies shall exist in relation to all broadcasters under the jurisdiction of a Member State.

3. Member States shall adopt the measures needed to establish the right of reply or the equivalent remedies and shall determine the procedure to be followed for the exercise thereof. In particular, they shall ensure that a sufficient time span is allowed and that the procedures are such that the right or equivalent remedies can be exercised appropriately by natural or legal persons resident or established in other Member States.

4. An application for exercise of the right of reply of the equivalent remedies may be rejected if such a reply is not justified according to the conditions laid down in paragraph 1, would involve a punishable act, would render the broadcaster liable to civil law proceedings or would transgress standards of public decency.

5. Provision shall be made for procedures whereby disputes as to the exercise of the right of reply or the equivalent remedies can be subject to judicial review.

(Article 26) Not later than the end of the fifth year after the date of adoption of this Directive and every two years thereafter, the Commission shall submit to the European Parliament, the Council, and the Economic and Social Committee a report on the application of this Directive and, if necessary, make further proposals to adapt it to developments in the field of television broadcasting.

QUESTIONS FOR CRITICAL ANALYSIS

- Is there any way the International Telecommunications Union could succeed if it had international enforcement powers similar to the Federal Communications Commission in the United States?
- What would happen in the ITU if one of the sovereign states decided to completely disregard the ITU conventions?
- Can you think of any instance where an issue would become so controversial and important to a sovereign state that it would find it necessary to disregard the ITU's conventions and develop telecommunication policy without regard to its international consequences?
- How is it possible for the ITU to emerge as a successful international organization when so many different technologies and political frameworks needed to be brought together in a cohesive agency?
- Is an ITU really necessary or could individual countries simply develop agreements with other nations to provide a cooperative relationship in which telecommunication could operate across national boundaries?
- Are developing nations at a disadvantage in the ITU and the United Nations?
- Is the ITU only as strong as the United Nations and the willingness of its member nations to cooperate in international telecommunication regulation?
- What kind of political pressure can individual nations impose on the policy-making of the ITU?
- In the planning process for WARC, policy must be formulated on a national basis and then presented to the international conference. What are some of the pitfalls that could develop during the internal planning process within one country prior to a WARC, and what would you consider the possible cause of these pitfalls?
- In view of the changes that have taken place this decade in Eastern Europe is there justification for considering the unification of such agencies as the OIR and the EBU?
- The negotiation of international contracts for such events as the Olympic Games and the World Football Cups are handled through the European Broadcasting Union. Should or could the ITU be responsible for negotiating such agreements?
- One of the organizations which has cooperative ties with the International Radio and Television Organization is the International Olympic Committee. Why would the IOC have cooperative agreements with International Radio and Television Organizations?
- Technical assistance for OIRT is provided through the technical commission which also sets technical standards and is responsible for all technical requirements implemented through the OIRT's General Assembly and Administrative Council. Would the coordination of technical assistance through an international organization ever stifle the development of technology instead of enhancing it?
- The Caribbean Broadcasting Union arranges for satellite interconnects and rate structures for news coverage during such events as elections and national disasters. Is there a danger in an international organization arranging for these interconnects and rate structures or would it be more effective for each country to negotiate separately with interested news organizations?
- How effective can an organization such as the Union of National Radio and Television Organizations of Africa be in protecting the rights of developing countries where no copyright law exists?
- Can an organization whose primary responsibility is coordinating Pan-African Broadcasting assume successfully the joint responsibilities of other areas of enforcement such as copyright?
- The URTNA monitors broadcasting signals of radio and television stations that are in member countries. The Technical Center conducts the monitoring to help study regulatory-technical issues confronting member countries much the way a Federal Communications Commission joint office of Plans and Policy in a Field Operations Bureau might operate. Using the URTNA's Technical Center as a model, could one develop an argument for combining the Plans and Policy Office with the Field Operations Bureau of the Federal Communications Commission in the United States?
- The Federation of Australian Radio Broadcasters has developed an accreditation program for advertising agencies. Would such an accrediting program work in the United States if it was administered by the Federal Communications

Commission? Could it work if it was administered by a nongovernment agency such as the National Association of Broadcasters?

- The Council of Europe administers a 1985 agreement on pirate radio stations to help prevent interference from pirate stations operating in international waters. If a country can only enforce interference in its own territorial waters, what is the advantage of signing an agreement with an organization such as the Council of Europe?
- The Council of Europe safeguards on privacy require signers of the treaty insuring rights of privacy to agree to prohibit the storing of sensitive personal information on individuals. How can one determine what is or is not sensitive personal information and who should make that determination? What are the dangers of "data havens" where individuals have information stored about them in a different country than where they live and how can such "data havens" be controlled in an era of high technology and international telecommunications?
- Would there be some advantage to the European Court of Justice of the European Community accepting criminal cases which it currently does not?
- The European Court of Justice can issue advisory opinions on any case involving EC law and can accept at any time cases from lower level trial courts located in EC member states. What is the advantage of the European Court of Justice issuing advisory opinions on cases involving EC law?
- Individual sovereignty is protected by each country's right to issue its own decisions. What advantages or disadvantages would there be to the European Court of Justice operating in much the same way as the United States Supreme Court in that it would be the final appellate court for any EC member country?
- What are some of the advantages of opening up the bidding process through state PTT monopolies and is there a danger of accepting low bids at the expense of quality which may interfere with not only the country where the bid is accepted but other countries that may participate in integrated telecommunication systems?
- One of the strongest critiques of the EC's Television Without Frontiers directive came from Jack Valenti of the Motion Picture Association of America. He said the directive "hurls a lance right at the heart of the United States industry's future." Do you think Valenti's criticism is warranted?
- How do you feel about Jack Valenti's strongly worded statement: "Has culture botulism yet appeared anywhere in Europe? Is the culture in any of these European countries so flimsily anchored that European consumers must be caged and blinded else their links with the past, like an exploding star, vanish?"
- Valenti went on to state that the real gain in the Television Without Frontiers directives is commerce not culture. Do you feel this is an accurate assessement?
- In Switzerland the Swiss Broadcasting Company is a private corporation whose primary responsibility is programming. The technical aspects of Swiss broadcasting are delegated to the PTT. Are there advantages or disadvantages to this separation of programming and technical matters? Are there advantages or disadvantages to the PTT having responsibility over the cable system as it does in Denmark?
- Some countries still do not have copyright laws protecting intellectual property including radio and television programs. How could the World Intellectual Property Organization be more effective in bringing these countries into its fold?
- An international organization which has been less effected by political strife and turmoil is the Universal Postal Union. Giving its ability to be isolated from many of the economic and political problems that plague other international organizations, would the UPU be a good organization to oversee some of the world's telecommunications entities?

ADDITIONAL RESOURCES

Asher, D. A., "International Telecommunications: Radio Marti—Radio Broadcasting to Cuba Act." 25 *Harvard International Law Journal* 483 (1984).

Chiron, S. Z., and L. A. Rehberg, "Fostering Competition in International Telecommunications." 38 *Federal Communications Law Journal* 1 (1986).

Cleveland, H., "The Twilight of Hierarchy: Speculations on the Global Information Society." 45 *Public Administration Review* 185 (January–February 1985).

Huntley, J. A. K., "Recent Developments in European Telecommunications Law." 3 *Computer Law & Practice* 49 (November–December 1990).

Kageyama, S., "International Cooperation and National Sovereignty—Unchanged Role of National Sovereignty in the Provision of International Telecommunication Services." 16 *Case Western Reserve Journal of International Law* 265 (Spring 1984).

Kinn, R. A., "United States Participation in the International Telecommunication Union: A Series of Interviews." 9 *Fletcher Forum* 37 (1985).

Levin, H. J., "Regulating the Global Commons: A Case Study." 12 *Research in Law and Economics* 247 (1989).

Potts, W. J., Jr., and J. E. Dunstan. "Creeping CANCOM: Canadian Distribution of American Television Programming to Alaskan Cable Systems." 7 *Pace Law Review* 127 (1986).

Ramsey, T. J., "The Role of Telecommunication in the Conduct of Foreign Affairs." 4 *New York Law School Journal of International and Comparative Law* 51 (1982).

Wall, S. A., "The British Telecommunications Decision: Toward a New Telecommunications Policy in the Common Market." 25 *Harvard International Law Journal* 184 (1984).

Zolf, S., "International Trade in Telecommunications: Liberalization or Beggar Thy Neighbor?" 2 *Review of International Business Law* 331 (1988).

chapter fifteen

International Statutes and Codes

To this point our discussion has concentrated on the regulatory agencies and organizations which exercise control over the electronic media. Our attention now turns to specific laws and regulations. We will begin by discussing cultural restrictions and requirements and then move to other areas of regulatory control. While many different types of regulatory structures exist, depending on the political and legal traditions of a country, our examples are drawn from a small group of countries for the purposes of comparison and analysis. With such comparisons, which include in some instances brief mentions of the United States, one must not generalize to other countries or regions solely based on the examples which appear here. Examples drawn from the regulations governing the Canadian Broadcasting Corporation do not apply to all electronic media in Canada. Some of the countries used as examples in this chapter are Australia, Canada, Denmark, Egypt, Finland, Iceland, Japan, the Netherlands, the Republic of China, Sweden, Switzerland, and Wales.

CULTURAL RESTRICTIONS AND REQUIREMENTS

When the European Community issued its "Television Without Frontiers Directive" requiring a majority of television programming in EC countries to be of European origin, the Motion Picture Association of America and U.S. trade officials said the directive was damaging to America's interests and may even have been a restraint on trade. The EC saw it differently and pointed out the right of European countries to protect their own culture. EC president Jacques Delors responded with words quoted elsewhere in this text by saying, "I must say to the United States, we have the right to exist and to maintain our traditions. There is no one European culture, but several."[1] Not only was Delors correct, something U.S. policy makers sometimes ignore, but many countries legislate cultural integrity into their broadcasting regulations. That legislated integrity has gained significance as satellites now make it possible for a broadcaster thousands of miles away to transmit signals which can blanket entire continents. The availability of satellite receiving dishes, becoming smaller and less expensive, permit more and more people to pick up signals from distant transmitters.[2]

Cultural Emphasis in External Services

This emphasis on culture can be seen in a number of countries. For example, a "Programme Policy Document" of Radio Nederland, the external shortwave broadcasting service, states, "Radio

Nederland being a Dutch organization is closely tied to Dutch society and Dutch culture."[3] The policies of Radio Nederland go on to stress the importance of Dutch culture as well as the obligation of the service to communicate with Dutch citizens whether living in the Netherlands or elsewhere.

Canada's external service, Radio Canada International, is mandated by the Canadian Broadcasting Corporation "to provide a program service designed to attract an international audience with the purpose of further developing international awareness of Canada and the Canadian identity by distributing, through shortwave and other means, programs which reflect the realities and quality of Canadian life and culture . . . "[4] CBC's own mandate charges it with safeguarding, enriching, and strengthening the cultural, political, and social fabric of Canada and providing programming which is "predominantly Canadian in content and character."[5]

Japan's Broadcast Law, which established Nippon Hoso Kyokai (NHK), Japan's public broadcasting service financed by license fees, requires NHK to follow such guiding principles as satisfying "the wishes of the people as well as to contribute to the elevation of the level of culture." It goes on to require NHK "to strive to assist in the nurturing and popularization of new culture as well as in the preservation of outstanding culture . . . "[6]

Cultural Emphasis in Domestic Services

In the Netherlands the Dutch Cultural Broadcasting Productions Promotion Fund awards grants for the development and production of programs which stress Dutch culture. Members of the Board of Directors of the Dutch Cultural Broadcasting Fund come not only from broadcasting but also film and the performing arts.[7]

In Sweden the agreement in force between the government and the Swedish Television Company states that the Swedish Television Company has an obligation "to convey news, and to comment upon or otherwise illustrate events and processes, providing all-round information that the population needs to orient itself, and to form an opinion on social and cultural issues."[8] The agreement goes on to require the Swedish Television Company

> to promote artistic and cultural innovation, and make creative use of the medium in artistic forms of expression; to monitor and scrutinize events and developments in the arts, and, in an interplay with Sweden's cultural life at large, make known and stimulate various cultural activities; to cater to a reasonable extent to a variety of interests in such areas as religion, culture and science.[9]

The Swiss Broadcasting Corporation, which operates a broadcasting system covering four different regions of Switzerland, each with its own language, is required by law to produce programs which take into account the cultural diversity of the nation and act as a binding force which will strengthen national unity and solidarity.[10] Specifically, the license granted to the SBC by the Swiss federal government and enforced by the Swiss Federal Department of Transport, Communications and Energy says,

> The programmes transmitted by the SBC must maintain and further cultural values of the nation and should contribute to spiritual, moral, religious, civic and artistic development . . . Programmes must be conceived so as to serve the interests of the nation, strengthen national unity and solidarity, and contribute to international understanding. The shortwave transmissions should serve to strengthen the bonds linking Swiss residing abroad with their homeland and should help to promote Switzerland's image abroad.[11]

Controls Over the Amount and Quality of Cultural Programming

Some countries have restrictions on the amount of programming which must be of local origin, thereby attempting to maintain cultural identity and support local production companies. The Program Foundation of the Netherlands Broadcasting Corporation is responsible for coordinating the programs of different groups which are granted programming time domestically. The Netherlands Media Act requires that 20 percent of the programs provided by the foundation must be of a "cultural nature."[12] On the broad scale is the "Television Without Frontiers Directive" of the European Community. Internal restrictions are found in such countries as Denmark where the statutes governing the national television service TV2 require it to strive toward having half of the service's programming devoted to Danish/Nordic productions.[13] In Iceland broadcasters are required by law to "promote the Icelandic history and cultural heritage. A significant rule is the obligation to translate all foreign television programs distributed to the public."[14] In addition, broadcast regulations require programming to show the diversity of Icelandic life. Support for these requirements comes from the "Cultural Fund" supported by a 10 percent tax on advertising revenue aired on Iceland's broadcasting stations.

Australian broadcasters are overseen by the Australian Broadcasting Tribunal which carries a mandate to "determine the standards to be observed by licensees in respect of the broadcasting . . . of programs."[15] Australian artists and performers receive encouragement from a provision requiring licensees to ensure "that not less than 20 percent of the time occupied in the broadcasting of music each day by a licensee shall consist of performances by Australians."[16] In addition, local religious services are assured of air time by a provision directing "every holder of a commercial broadcasting station license, commercial radio license, public broadcasting license or public radio license to transmit, free of charge, Divine Worship or other matter of a religious nature for a period totalling not less than one hour each week."[17]

Some of the strictest controls on cultural programming are found in the Orient. The Republic of China, although not entirely successful in enforcing its broadcast regulations, strives to require no less than 20 percent of broadcasting time on radio and television stations be devoted to educational and cultural programs which augment traditional culture and provide inspiration to the national spirit and consciousness.[18] In addition, the law reads: "Educational and cultural programs should coordinate with the nation's goals of advocating ethics, democracy, and scientific knowledge, to enable all citizens of this country to achieve a balanced development of body and mind."[19] Cartoons, especially foreign cartoons, are of concern to programmers and TV production standards require that "50% of each foreign cartoon aired should exemplify values such as the following: empathy, ethical behavior, respect for knowledge, and social consciousness."[20] Entertainment programs shall be devoted to promoting Chinese culture. Foreign language programs must be presented with Chinese subtitles or with Mandarin narration. Even the appearance of foreign performers is controlled with a regulation reading: "If a foreign performer is invited to take part in a domestic television program, the station shall act in accordance with the regulations concerned, report in detail on the contents of the performance, and submit a biographical sketch and a photo of the performer to the Government Information Office for approval."[21] An awards program administered by the Government Information Office recognizes "great achievements" in the promotion of Chinese culture and "significant contributions to cultural interflow in handling international relay of programs."[22]

Cultural-Political Provisions

Cultural-political standards also spill over into advertising in the Republic of China. Evidence of this can be seen in a paragraph from the statute regulating television advertising production dealing with political figures and national shrines stating:

> Television advertisements that refer to or include the national flag, other national emblems, Dr. Sun Yat-sen the late president Chiang Kai-shek, or portraits of present national leaders shall do so with due respect. Historical and religious figures in general, and such sites as the Presidential Offices, Sun Yat-sen Memorial Hall, the Chiang Kai-shek Memorial Hall, Martyrs' Shrine, etc. shall also be treated accordingly.[23]

History shows that other countries at times represent the opposite end of the free-market spectrum. Egypt under President Gamal Abdul Nasser is another example of the impact of regulated cultural-political programming as discussed in a *Journalism Monograph* authored by Munir K. Nasser.[24] When president of Egypt, Gamal Abdul Nasser became interested in radio and television as an instrument of political power. At the same time, Egypt was exerting a significant cultural influence over much of the Arab world. Muir Nasser points out in the *Monograph* that, "Egypt became the vanguard in Arab film, music, songs, live theater, journalism, literature, and the arts. Egypt's film industry dominated Arab markets for decades and built a favorable image for Egypt among Arab audiences. Egyptian music and songs were also very popular among Arab listeners."[25] For these listeners, radio was the ideal medium to advance the cultural and political goals of Nasser.

The Egyptians' appreciation for music is part of the country's heritage and Gamal Abdul Nasser exploited it on radio. Egyptian singers were commissioned to record songs touting Egyptian unity and each singer was expected to contribute a certain number of songs each year toward the Nasser regime. Hundreds of songs were written in support of Egypt's Aswan High Dam built by Nasser.

Hundreds of other songs stressed Arab unity. A song by Egyptian singer Um Kulsoum became so popular through radio that it became both Egypt and Iraq's national anthem.[26] The fact that a popular song could achieve such status speaks to both power of music as part of the culture and the power of radio to perpetuate that culture. When television arrived in Egypt in 1960 it became an important medium to disseminate the visual arts which already reflected the Nasser-directed cultural-political atmosphere in the country.

As we study international broadcasting systems, we must remain aware that the power of radio and television are important to any ruling party, regardless of whether they come to power through force or free elections. As was the case with Egypt, politics and culture can be indistinguishable from each other.

REGULATIONS AFFECTING LANGUAGE

Where the political and cultural needs of a nation are strongly tied to its language, broadcast law may contain provisions which require certain amounts of time be devoted to a given language, provisions affecting the pronunciation of a given language or dialect, or may restrict the use of certain types of language in categories of programming such as advertisements. For example, we have already read how Switzerland's broadcasting system is organized to serve different geographical regions of the country speaking different languages. Agreements between the national government and the Swedish local broadcasting companies state: "An all-round supply of programmes in the Swedish language shall be provided . . . "[27] In Canada the law requires programming provided by the Canadian Broadcasting Corporation be in English and French . . . "[28] Also in Canada the advertising standards of the Canadian Broadcasting Corporation state: "The correct use of language is, other than to depict typical characters or situations, an important element of CBC commercial presentation standards. Advertising messages should also avoid the impression of excessive loudness and be presented at a pace that can be comfortably followed."[29] In Wales the Welsh Fourth Channel is charged with providing programs in the Welsh language for Welsh speakers.

Maintaining Language Integrity

The Republic of China is one example of a very specific language policy incorporated into its broadcast regulations. As part of a policy of political and cultural unity, the speaking of pure Mandarin is emphasized. The language, even though it has many written commonalties, is difficult to understand when different Mandarin dialects are spoken. Consequently, the broadcast law contains a specific section devoted to language. The official government standards for television program production call on all personnel working in broadcasting: "To promote policies concerning the use of Mandarin to unify the nation in language and speech."[30] News is to be broadcast in Mandarin except "in the case of important government actions or momentous news, it may be broadcast in other languages once an information form has been properly filed."[31] In addition, any foreign names or technical terms used in a newscast "should be translated into standard Mandarin for pronunciation purposes." The primary statement of policy concerning language use on broadcast stations in the Republic of China is much more encompassing:

1) Avoid mispronunciations.
2) Avoid deliberately speaking Mandarin with a regional accent.
3) Avoid indecent or rude expression.
4) Avoid mimicking stuttering.
5) Do not deliberately use language that attacks or ridicules others.
6) In any situation unrelated to the Chinese Communists, terms associated with Chinese communism should be avoided.
7) Any language used in a program should be used according to the principles of Chinese language and culture.
8) Any vulgar or deprecating terms should not be used in reference to a people, a character-type, or a profession.
9) Avoid using vulgar or gangster expressions such as "Ma-tzu," "T'iao-tzu," "Liutzu," or "Chao-tzu."
10) Names of characters should also be free of vulgarity. Such reproachful terms as Shih yao-ch'ien, Greedy for Money even when Dead, T'ao Ta-feng, Porter of Nightsoil, Lang Hsin, Wolf-hearted, Kou-fei, Dog Lungs, are not acceptable.
11) Double-entendres that are lewd or vulgar should be avoided.
12) When interviewing a guest on a program, the host or hostess should address him politely and refrain from indiscriminate mocking.

13) In any dubbed foreign program, the place names should be rendered so as not to create any geographic misunderstandings; characters' names should be rendered as close in sound to the original as possible so as to avoid unfavorable allusions to other people.[32]

Broadcast commercials in the Republic of China also fall under regulations governing television advertising production.[33]

Language Requirements in Commercials

Regulations call for all TV commercials to be in Mandarin and provincial dialects may appear in commercials only in programs produced in those dialects. With the exception of identifying foreign-made products, foreign languages are not permitted in commercials. When foreign language identifications are used, Mandarin is still required as the main focus of the commercial. In commercials where foreign names are used, they must conform "to the requirements of Foreign Language Trademark Registration as maintained by the Central Standards Bureau, Ministry of Economics."[34] Finland also governs language use in commercials. Under the language section of the terms and conditions of the national broadcasting service, the general guidelines as interpreted by the The Finnish Language Division of the Finnish Research Center for Domestic Languages state that the broadcast regulations require:

> Good standard language is grammatically correct and only makes use of generally recognized vocabulary. Standard language is an effective idiom when the message is meant to be understood throughout the language community, which consists of individuals of different ages who have different backgrounds in terms of education and experiences and who speak different local and social dialects. In commercials, however, the idiom must be chosen according to the target group.
>
> The speech and text used in a commercial should generally be consistent so that one can easily ascertain from the overall style whether the intention is to use normal standard language, informal colloquial language, young people's language, some special jargon such as sporting slang or some local dialect. Language and picture should be connected in such a way that the selected idiom seems natural and according to anticipations in the situation and environment portrayed. If the aim is to create a deliberate contrast between picture and language for a humorous effect, the presentation should make it easy for the viewer to realize the exceptional nature of the situation. Intentional language mistakes or expressions which are of questionable correctness must not be used. When the intention is to use colloquial language, it should be remembered that the slang colored everyday language used in the capital is not the standard form of spoken Finnish. If a local dialect is chosen as the idiom, special attention should be given to the authenticity of its language.[35]

The guidelines used by Finland also state that commercials should be in "domestic languages" and that commercials made for international use should include a Finnish translation.

PROGRAMMING TO CHILDREN

In many countries, statutes or codes exist over the content of children's programming. The Netherlands, Australia, Canada, Finland, and the Republic of China provide examples. For instance, in the Netherlands film censorship regulations have categories of films for people under 12 or 16 years of age. When these films are shown on television the "provider of the program must make an announcement to this effect in the course of the program, immediately before the beginning of the program component in question."[36] In Australia the Advertising Code of the Media Council states commercials cannot contain any reference to dangerous practices which would result in the "physical, mental, or moral harm" to children, and advertisements are forbidden which urge children to pressure their parents to purchase a product or service.[37]

Restrictions on Advertised Products Directed Toward Children

The Canadian Broadcasting Corporation's (CBC) advertising standards are in accordance with the Canadian Radio-television and Telecommunications Commission. The CBC does not accept advertising of any kind when a program itself is directed toward children 12 years of age and under. A message considered "child-directed" for children 12 years of age and under is defined as messages "on behalf of a product or service for which children under 12 years of age are the only users or form a substantial part of the market as users and the message presented in a manner that appeals primarily to children."[38] Children's advertising which is accepted for other types of programs must be limited to not more than four minutes per hour or two minutes for any half-hour period. When a commercial is directed toward children 12 years of age and under and broadcast over CBC facilities the message is regulated by the following provisions:

> Truthfulness in fact and intent: Commercials must be complete in pertinent information, in fact as well as in intent. The advertised product should perform in real life as it appears to perform in the commercial, otherwise the reason it won't must be reasonably attainable by an average child.
>
> Acknowledgement of missing parts: The advertised product must be sold in as complete a form as it is shown in the commercial, otherwise the missing parts must be acknowledged in video and audio.
>
> Establishment of relative size: The relative size of each product should be clearly established. With the ability of television to alter true dimensions and especially with unsophisticated viewers, something must appear with the advertised product that is common to most children's everyday environment, e.g., a telephone, coins, a child, etc.
>
> Scheduling frequency: No single product, premium or service advertised to children may be promoted more than once during any half-hour period. This limitation does not apply to a program that is fully sponsored by a single advertiser.
>
> Product availability: Advertising for any product or service that is not generally available through outlets in a given station's coverage area is subject to immediate withdrawal.[39]

The CBC standards also restrict certain products from appearing in child-directed commercials. These include, among other products: drugs, vitamins in any form, make-up items such as perfumes and nail polish that would normally be marketed to adults, products not intended for use by children such as gasoline, products which are dangerous such as sharp objects.[40] In addition, products are prohibited in children's commercials which encourage a range of values that is inconsistent with moral, ethical, or legal standards of current Canadian society, e.g., products that require the use and eventual destruction of edible foods as playthings.[41] Other regulations apply to social status and fantasy personalities.

Restrictions on Persuasive Appeals to Children

Persuasive appeals are also regulated. For example, appeals to children are prohibited where children are portrayed as being under the influence of alcohol, playing inside a refrigerator, ignoring traffic regulations, accepting gifts from strangers, playing with matches, or depictions that show children engaged in socially unacceptable behavior such as questionable table manners and rudeness toward adults.[42] Price-minimizing words such as "only," "just," "a bargain," and "costs so little" are restricted. Asking Mommy or Daddy to buy something is not permitted and demeaning children by inferring they will be socially unaccepted if they do not own a particular product is not permitted. Not acceptable is toy advertising that makes direct comparisons with previous-year models when the claims are not valid. Real-life or fantasy personalities are restricted such as endorsements by puppets, persons, and characters costumed to look like well-known cartoon or other characters.[43]

Identifying Child-Centered Messages

To distinguish child-centered messages from messages which may involve products consumed by children but are found in commercials directed toward adults, the CBC advertising standards point to such factors as how the product is used in the commercial and by whom. For example, soft drinks may be consumed by children but when the commercial clearly contains actors who are older people (alone or with children), or when the commercials have adult vocabulary, then they are considered adult-directed commercials and do not fall under the children's advertising restrictions. The final assessment of whether the commercial is child-centered or adult-directed depends on the primary appeal of the message, how the video and audio combine to create the message. In addition to the advertising standards themselves, regulations require prior approval of all commercial messages before they appear on CBC facilities.

If the Canadian advertising standards were introduced as legislation in the Congress of the United States, arguments for and against the restrictions would quickly emerge. For example, some public-interest groups might find the standards appealing. After all, to the average citizen, the standards could be interpreted as basic common sense. However, accustomed to operating in a free marketplace, many advertising agencies, civil libertarians, and even government agencies could oppose the restrictions as too broad and unenforceable. For example, take any commercial on television which is directed toward young children and ask is the commercial directed to children 12 years of age and under or is the message 13 years of age and under? That distinction would be one which many people might disagree on, yet it becomes a matter of law when stated in a content regulation affecting television commercials.

Additional concerns would arise over the makeup of the board which oversees the approval of commercials since some groups would argue it would be impossible to bring together a group of people who agree and reflect the tastes of a large population. How such a board is appointed would be another consideration. Would the appointments be political, industry-based, or consumer-oriented? Social scientists might argue that to censor certain content would only make the same message more appealing when seen in other contexts, such as comic books, or home videos. All of these issues point to the controversy that can surround content regulations which are very specific and directed toward a specific segment of the population.

To get an additional insight on international regulations affecting children we can turn to Finland. As is the case in Canada, the advertising regulations affecting television commercials seen on the national television service also encompass the child audience.

Children as Viewers and Performers

Finland examines children as viewers but also as performers in television commercials. For example, regulations affecting children as viewers point out that "children comprise a considerable portion of the viewing audience," and commercials on Finland's commercial television company require that "the content of commercials intended for children must be carefully considered since they appeal to children as users of the product or influence them by their example."[44] The regulations go on to state that particular care must be taken with regard to the following:

> Commercials must not present situations which if imitated by children might cause injury to themselves or others.
>
> Commercials for products intended for children may not include expressions regarding price such as "for mere pocket money" or direct appeals to children such as "but, try, you will get or you will experience" etc.
>
> Commercials advertising toys and hobby items may not use presentations or special effects which might give children a misleading impression of the product or its use. In principle the product must be present in the form in which it is available commercially. If the product must be assembled, painted, moulded etc. the result shown in the commercial must be what a child can achieve with reasonable effort. The commercial must not give an exaggerated impression of the ease of the work involved.[45]

Anyone who has ever assembled a toy or bought a disassembled piece of merchandise where the directions read "easy instruction enclosed," or "assembled with easy instructions," might look upon the Finnish regulation on "exaggerated impression" as ideal in any country. In Finland, however, the directive takes on new meaning and is enforceable. Children as performers also fall under the Finnish regulations which state:

> The unnecessary use of children in commercials should be avoided. There are nevertheless situations in which the use of children serves a purpose in the advertising of products. In such cases care must nevertheless be taken not to create the impression that children are being exploited in order to sell the product. In considering the use of children as performers attention must always be given to the product and its nature and whether the presence of children may create possible detrimental effects. Children may not advertise a product in words or speak about the product in a commercial. Nor may children appear in sweets commercials. In deciding whether to use children in commercials, the script must always be submitted to MTV for approval.[46]

In comparison to the commercials seen on television in the United States, the Finnish regulations might require adjustment in the content of many American commercials, especially in the case of sugared cereals, and some soft drink and candy products. The Finnish regulation preventing children from advertising a product in "words or speak about the product" would add additional restrictions. Children are frequently seen in commercials in the United States, many with speaking roles.

The Child's Development in a Television Environment

For additional examples of regulations governing the content of programming directed toward children we can turn back to the Republic of China. In the standards which govern TV program production, children are singled out as an audience to which those who work in the Chinese television industry have a special responsibility. Chinese regulations require those working in the industry:

> To work hard to understand children's interests and needs, and then to provide them with appropriate entertainment that will enhance their willingness to study and, also, promote their balanced development, both physical and mental.
>
> To help our children cultivate positive attitudes toward life in modern society as law-abiding, responsible citizens.
>
> To cultivate children's ability to tell right from wrong and to identify themselves on the basis of social norms, to prepare them towards their future social life.
>
> To provide children with role models towards emulation of positive behavior, to assure a tendency toward good habits.
>
> To support, and coordinate with, school education and attempt to supply what is deficient in formal school education programs in order to promote the creativity and ability for independent thinking of all children.[47]

Keep in mind that the regulations enforced by the Republic of China apply to all programming, not just advertising. As viewed from an American perspective, the last two paragraphs of the "responsibilities" section would perhaps create the greatest controversy if introduced as legislation in the United States. For example, children appear in programming in many different roles, some of which would not bee seen as providing children with "role models towards emulation of positive behavior." Also, to require programming which attempts to correct the deficiencies of local schools makes the statement that the local schools are deficient, something which would cause local school officials and national education groups to rise up in protest. The "responsibilities" section of the program regulations are stated in more general terms than the "Principles of Program Production" which require specific content in children's programming. The program production standards for the Republic of China require the following:

> All Children's programs should have educational content and pay due attention to the physical and mental health of children, as well as to the development of healthy personalities. For this reason, the distinctions between right and wrong, good and evil, success and failure, should be obvious and illustrate cause and effect.
>
> Children's programs should stress such qualities as the development of the intellect, cultivation of a sense of community and the communal good, obeying laws, physical exercise, and acting to improve life, in order to guide children to a correct, mature philosophy of life.
>
> Children's shows should avoid exposing the ugly, weird, mean, shocking and abnormal aspects of society.
>
> No commercials or program announcements unfit for viewing by children may be broadcast during children's programs.
>
> All content that may affect the safety of children is to be avoided.
>
> Mondays through Fridays, all TV networks should schedule daily half-hour children's programs between 18:00 and 19:00 hours. On Saturdays and Sundays, an hour-long program should be scheduled. Two of these programs must be self-produced. If a network wishes to increase its airing time for children's programs, only self-produced programs will be allowed.
>
> At least 50% of each foreign cartoon aired should exemplify values such as the following: empathy, ethical behavior, respect for knowledge, and social consciousness.
>
> When dubbing cartoons, attention should be paid to naturalness and harmony; weird piercing sounds should be avoided.
>
> The broadcasting of imported cartoons should avoid those containing a violent or militaristic ideology.
>
> The amount of children's programming should be increased on children's holidays.[48]

Although not directed specifically at children's programming, program standards also call for dramatic programs to pay special attention to the

> integrity of the structure, the wholesomeness of the themes, the reasonableness of the plot development, and the coherency of interpersonal relations . . . Only one network may air a kung-fu drama in (the 8 to 9 p.m. time slot) Monday to Friday. This serial may not exceed thirty episodes. At any time, except during this time slot, each station may broadcast a kung-fu drama which may not exceed two hours in length. However, all three networks may not simultaneously broadcast kung-fu dramas.[49]

Pre-emptive Regulations on Advertising's Effect on Children

The Republic of China incorporates concern for children into its advertising regulations as well. Although some sections of the advertising law do not specifically use the Chinese equivalent of *child* or *children* in the language of the law, the conditions nevertheless can apply to children. Statements such as: "Advertising should not depict the actual swallowing or drinking of medicines."[50] More specific controls on advertising directed toward children are found in the regulations governing television production of commercials. The advertising which is directed at children and youths in the Republic of China should not, according to regulations, impair their morals, incite or encourage children to participate in dangerous activities, be poor role models for others, employ methods that specifically induce children to press their parents to purchase products, induce children into negative views of their parents or their parents' judgments and thus damage family relationships, or imply that those who do not come in possession of the promoted product will be negatively perceived.[51]

The strict codes governing children's programming is one of the reasons some foreign countries have been apprehensive about the importation of American television programming, even though such programming has proved popular. The development of satellites has increased the amount of programming which can be received from outside a country's boundaries and cultural intrusion remains an important issue. The "Television Without Frontiers Directive" of the European Community speaks in some ways to this issue. Ad agencies which use American marketing strategies are not always welcome guests in countries where the culture has rejected, somewhat because of internal regulations, the flamboyant style of some commercials and programs produced in the United States.[52]

GENERAL PROVISIONS FOR THE REGULATION OF ADVERTISING

In addition to the regulations governing children's advertising already discussed, countries have rules and regulations governing the content and placement of commercials. In some countries products such as alcohol or tobacco are prohibited, while in others such products are able to be advertised on radio and television but with certain guidelines. The basic premise of advertising codes is found in their preambles, prefaces, and basic principles which are usually phrased in general terms. For example, a sampling of some these broad directives include Finland where commercials must not "awaken negative attitudes" toward television advertising. In the Republic of China nude or overly romantic scenes which might influence the mental health of youth are prohibited. In the Republic of China television advertising (including films or tapes and picture slides) should report factual information and services concerning the products offered, which in turn through their sales strengthen the economy and improve living standards. In addition Republic of China guidelines state:

> TV advertising must stick to the truth, provide attractive, quality pictures, and tender accompanying sound and dialogues in moderate tones to elevate advertising practices. Advertising subject matter should be suitable for open family discussion. TV advertising content may not deceive or mislead viewers in any way . . . Deceptive or misleading presentation techniques are prohibited. Advertising content and effects should not contravene public peace or social morals. Low humor and immoral implications shall not be employed to attract viewer's attention. Advertising content should not contravene established and basic views of life, but should respect public mores and the wholesome community atmosphere . . . In order to assure the equality and freedom of competition, TV advertising may not directly or indirectly malign or spread slander concerning the products of others . . .[53]

Comparing the advertising regulations of the Republic of China to the relatively free atmosphere that commercial speech enjoys in the United States, some clear distinctions emerge. For example, numerous products advertised on television in the United States would not be suitable for family discussion on the Republic of China's television system. Some 900 number services, certain health and hygiene products, and other products would run afoul of the regulations. Similarly, some American beer commercials would call into force the "low humor and immoral implications" phrase, and although advertisers in the United States cannot slander another product without running the risk of a lawsuit, the rigor with which product comparisons are made would be risky business in the Republic of China.

Similar themes to those of the Republic of China are found the "basic principles" statement of MTV Finland which states

> Advertising messages must be presented with refinement and in good taste. Commercials must not be of such a nature as to awaken negative attitudes towards TV advertising. Commercials may not use words or pictures which are aimed at or may defame competitors, competing products or other fields of business, occupations or organizations. The content of commercials intended for children must be carefully considered since they appeal to children as users of the product or influence them by their example.[54]

In addition, Finland's regulations require commercials to be shown before and after programs, unless the programs are of a certain length. Programs lasting at least 20 minutes in length can have one commercial break, and programs of 35, 50, or 70 minutes in length can have two, three, or four commercial breaks, respectively. In addition to general statements, specific guidelines exist as well. The code of advertising of the Media Council of Australia states:

> Advertisements shall not encourage dangerous behavior and shall not encourage illegal or unsafe road usage practices. Advertisements shall not engage in unlawful discrimination and shall not demean the dignity of men, women, or children. Advertisements shall not contain anything which in the light of generally prevailing community standards is likely to cause serious offence to the community or a significant section of the community.[55]

In addition to being truthful and not misleading, advertisements must be clearly distinguished as advertisements and controversial advertisements must disclose the source of the advertisement. Unduly exploiting superstitions and playing on fear is not permitted and advertisements must "not disparage identifiable products, services or competitors in an unfair or misleading way."[56] Scientific, statistical or other research data quoted in advertisements must not be misleading nor irrelevant, and testimonials used in advertisements must honestly reflect the sentiments of the individuals represented.[57] Claims in testimonials are subject to the same rules as other advertising.

The advertising standards of the Canadian Broadcasting Corporation are similar to those of the countries just discussed. For example, the Canadian regulations for the CBC are unacceptable if they omit relevant information or arrange accurate information in such a way that the audience is mislead. A separate Competition Act in Canada prohibits false and misleading advertising. Other standards under the CBC rules require advertising to be evaluated in relation to its acceptability in the home, in mixed company, and in family or social groups. Canadian regulations governing advertising on the CBC state that:

> The various characteristics of racial and ethnic backgrounds and religious convictions should be treated with dignity and decency, as must such things as physical, mental or speech imperfections. They must not be held up as subjects of ridicule. Also, individuals or groups should not because of age, occupation, creed or sex be disparaged, exploited or unfairly represented. The Corporation is particularly sensitive to sex-role stereotyping and encourages advertisers to present both sexes fairly in all types of occupations roles.
>
> Commercial approaches should not encourage or depict as being desirable any activity that is contrary to widely held standards of behavior. Messages may not demand audience attention through use of the shock value of double entendre or undue exploitation of sex, nudity or violence.[58]

The Canadian regulations governing the CBC also prohibit advertisements which raise controversial issues, regulations which would run afoul of the First Amendment if they were applied to the United States. The rationale for the Canadian regulations is that the airwaves "must not come under the control of any individual or group who because of wealth, special position, etc. might be better able to influence listener or viewer attitudes on a contentious issue."[59] CBC advertising regulations state that

> commercial messages scheduled on CBC stations may not constitute or contain statements or opinions of a controversial nature, or attempt to persuade the audience to adopt a particular attitude or course of action on a subject that is controversial. Social, economic or political comment or opinion that is contentious may not be used in commercials regardless of the advertiser submitting the material.[60]

Such issues can be seen and discussed in other types of programming but not in advertising. Paid political commercials are possible but fall under the Canada Elections Act.

SPECIFIC PRODUCT PROVISIONS IN ADVERTISING REGULATION

In addition to the more general statements contained in the preambles and introductory paragraphs of advertising codes, specific products are singled out for regulatory control.

Examining the advertising regulations of four countries, we find first that in Denmark commercials on the national TV 2 service are prohibited for drugs, beer, wine, spirits, and tobacco. In addition, commercials for "financial pressure groups and religious and political views shall not be allowed."[61] Other regulations governing advertising in Denmark are established by the Minister for Transport and Communications. In Canada commercials are not prohibited for beer, wine, cider, and alcoholic beverages that do not have more than a 7 percent alcohol content, and only then when provincial law allows. Scripts for these products must still be approved by the Alcoholic Beverage Broadcast Advertising Advisory Committee of Canada.[62] In Finland alcohol and tobacco products are banned and drug advertising is only permitted when it serves "to enlighten the consumer." In addition to alcohol, tobacco, and drugs, Finland prohibits advertising "morally questionable publications and audio and video recordings." Political organizations and causes cannot advertise on radio and television in Finland.[63] The Republic of China prohibits even submitting advertising to the government for review if the advertising contravenes public morals, promotes superstition and other scientific-contradicting facts such as fortune telling and astrology, gambling, products that do not conform to import procedures, and funeral services and mortuaries.[64]

Generally Prohibited Product Categories

The amount of control differs among countries. Some countries have general controls over certain products while others are highly specific. For example, the Republic of China has strict controls over personal hygiene products, while in other countries a common sense rule of good taste applies. In the United States false advertising claims are handled primarily by the Federal Trade Commission, while in other countries the agencies which control radio and television also patrol the content of radio and television commercials to see if they meet government standards. Some countries have rules requiring prescreening of radio and television commercials while other countries, the United States being one, mostly deal with false advertising after the commercials air.

Medicines

Medicine is an area that many countries deal with at the level of the broadcaster airing the commercial or the company producing the commercial. For example, specific regulations over what are called *therapeutic goods* exist in Australia. Therapeutic goods are products which are used in "the preventing, diagnosing, curing or alleviating of a disease, ailment, defect or injury in persons (and) the influencing, inhibiting or modifying of a psychological process in persons . . . ," including such things as testing for pregnancy and matters of contraception.[65] An advertisement for therapeutic goods cannot contain any statements which claim the product is effective for the prevention, relief, or cure of a disorder which should be under the care of a physician. Certain diseases and disorders, such as arthritis, alcoholism, anemia, fertility, hernia, psoriasis, sinus infections, venereal disease, and others either are restricted from being discussed in advertisements or have restrictions on what can and cannot be said about drugs which claim to provide relief. For example, diseases transmitted through sexual intercourse must only be discussed in the context of contraception and reducing the risk of transmission of disease. A product taken by arthritis sufferers can only be advertised as providing temporary relief of pain. Other laws govern advertising in Australia including the Trade Practices Act which states "A Corporation shall not, in trade or commerce, engage in conduct that is misleading or deceptive."[66] The Trade Practices Act encompasses all media. The Broadcasting Act of Australia and relevant acts in the individual states also can govern the content of radio and television commercials.

In the Republic of China drug and therapeutic advertising must be within parameters approved by the health department. In addition, commercials for medicines should not show "weird or obscene or exaggerated gestures or postures or expressions," commercials must not "disillusion viewers via before-and-after pictures showing the claimed results of use of the product," and advertising should not imply sexual or obscene material or include language which is not in public use. In addition, doctors, nurses, medical or pharmaceutical associations, or famous persons cannot be associated with advertising for therapeutic medicines. Restrictions prohibit showing anytime between 7:30 and 9:30 p.m. someone swallowing or drinking medicines, medicines for colds, liver malfunctions, gastric problems, hemorrhoids, fractures, bruises, of medicines affecting the brain. Those producing and airing commercials for drugs are warned that the commercials should not "induce people to think they have already contracted a serious disease."[67] Medical products may not be offered as free gifts in advertising, regardless of what product or service is being advertised.

Medical Warnings

In Australia, warnings must appear or be heard in television and radio commercials. In radio commercials up to and including 20 seconds in length the phrase "use only as directed" must appear in the script. If the radio commercial is over 20 seconds then one of the following warnings, or words to that effect, must appear: (1) Use only as directed for minor and temporary ailments. (2) Prolonged use may be harmful. Use only as directed. (3) Use only as directed and consult your doctor if pain persists. If the radio commercials runs over 45 seconds then two of the three warnings must be in the script. Similar rules apply for television commercials but the warnings must be clearly visible when supered on the screen.

Weight-Loss Programs

As is the case in the United States and elsewhere, diets and weight-loss programs receive considerable exposure on radio and television. Australia's Advertising Code treats such programs in a separate section titled "slimming." Anyone advertising a diet plan or products aiding in weight loss must submit a certificate from a registered dietitian stating the plan will produce adequate amounts of "protein, vitamins and minerals," and that the diet plan is safe and capable of achieving the results which it claims. Food regulations of the various Australian states and territories can also govern advertising for weight-reduction plans and any plan that calls for less than 800 calories per day cannot be advertised. Some detailed aspects of the restrictions prohibit combining the loss of measurements from different parts of the body. For instance, it is acceptable to claim a weight-reduction plan can eliminate three inches off your waist and three inches from your hips, but it is not acceptable to say the weight-loss plan will eliminate six inches from your body. In addition, advertisers of weight-loss plans in Australia can't include such products as vibrators, inflatable garments, Turkish baths, soaps or essences, laxatives, hypnosis, body wraps, and similar products in their weight-loss commercials. Acupuncture and products claiming to increase the metabolic rate of the body are also prohibited. Ads must also refrain from claiming a specific amount of weight will be lost in a specified amount of time.

Contests and Investments

The CBC's Advertising Standards in Canada deal with contests and investing. Rules for all contests broadcast on CBC facilities must be approved by the CBC legal department. Rules must also be submitted to the CBC Advertising Standards office. When a contest falls within the lottery section of the Criminal Code, then the contest must be licensed and the advertiser must submit proof of licensing as well as the script and contest rules. Advertising the investment of nongovernment bonds, shares, and securities is regulated in Canada. Any advertising for a financial institution "including credit unions, banks, trust companies, stock brokers etc., that promote investment in plans such as registered retirement savings, investment certificates, shares, income securities, etc." is subject to legal review as are advertisements for investment shares in cooperatives.[68]

Motion Pictures

Motion pictures in many countries are seen as a powerful social and political tool and safeguards exist to regulate both the content and marketing of motion pictures which are seen on television. For example, while cigarettes can be advertised in Australia, cigarettes cannot be advertised in theaters in conjunction with films which are rated "G" or "PG," nor can cigarette advertising appear in cinemas during school holiday periods.[69] In the Republic of China regulations govern the advertising of motion pictures on television. For example, excessive "uncouth, absurd, violent or bloody, or obscene images" are prohibited and all commercials must identify the motion picture's restricted rating. Those with restricted ratings cannot be advertised during children's programs and all motion picture advertising, regardless of the rating, must be approved by the Government Information Office in addition to meeting the requirements of other statutes such as the Motion Picture Law, and the Radio and Television Law.[70]

ADVERTISING PRODUCTION STANDARDS

Some set regulatory standards governing the production quality of broadcast commercials.

General Requirements

Finland is one country where broadcasters are told that special effects, both video and sound, must not be disruptive and commercials cannot give the impression that any attempt is being made to influence the viewer's subconscious.[71] Flashing a picture rapidly on the screen would be an example of using special effects in an attempt to persuade the viewer through appeals to the subconscious. Similarly, special effects cannot be used to mislead the viewer into believing something is wrong with the sound or visual quality of their television set. Subliminal advertising is regulated in the Republic of China where television announcements lasting a few seconds, called "flash-card" ads, must appear for at least five seconds and two sequential flash-card ads cannot overlap. Flash-card ads are limited to 30 units with each digit in a phone number and each syllable of a foreign word counted as a unit (Coca-Cola is thus four units).[72] Other commercials must be at least ten seconds long and "hawking methods, light or sound contrasts, or other techniques that invoke emotional unrest in audiences should be avoided."

Technical Requirements

In Finland, specific technical requirements are spelled out for advertising on MTV, Finland's commercial television company. Frame sizes for 16mm and 35mm are listed with the safe-action area listed for both. The safe-action area is that portion of the television screen which will always be in plain view, regardless of what make or model of television receiver is in use or how old the receiver is. The terms and conditions advertisers must adhere to placing the text and other essential information in the commercial within this safe area, while background information such as scenery not critical to the persuasive message can extend beyond the safe area.

In addition to correct use of the safe-action area, commercials must be filmed so that at least six picture frames without sound appear at the beginning of the commercial and 30 picture frames without sound at the end. The requirement helps assure proper threading and projection of the commercial. Technical requirements also apply to film quality. For example, the terms and conditions point out that the photochemical processing of television films is different than theater films. Film intended for television broadcast must be processed differently under different requirements than film which would be processed for theater viewing. Because not everyone owns a color television set, advertisers are told that colors which show up well on black-and-white television screens should be selected when chosing the colors to use in the commercial.

Video tape commercials also have specific technical requirements at Finland's MTV. Commercials are only accepted on a specific size tape, sound mixing must meet specific levels, and any mixed sound must be adjusted to all other program sound. In other words, loud commercials are not permitted. Producers are limited to third-generation copies to preserve the technical quality of the commercial. Much like film, video tape also has a safe-action area within which essential information must appear. A certain amount of empty tape must precede and follow the commercial. Terms and conditions for advertisers go so far as to state what size reel the commercial must be recorded and stored on and in what type box it must be delivered. Technical requirements also exist for 35mm slides with the safe-action area specified. Specifications for the audio tape accompanying the slide are listed as are tape speed and glass framing requirements. The name of the client and the producer must be submitted with all commercials.

NEWS PROGRAMMING

In the United States news programming is to some extent driven by the First Amendment. Only limited control exists in the amount and content of news programming seen and heard on American radio and television. The public-interest clause of the Communications Act creates a broad-based responsibility for broadcasters, but requirements that certain amounts of news and public-affairs programming be aired for the most part have been eliminated from FCC regulations. License challenges can still include a lack of news and public-affairs programming as a basis for claiming a station does not satisfactorily serve its community, but even then the First Amendment makes it difficult to win on such grounds alone. Obscenity and pornography rules apply to all programming but test cases which apply obscenity or pornography to news programming are rare. Certain political broadcasting statutes, such as Section 315, can affect news programming. Libel in the United States is a remedy after a broadcast has been aired, but not necessarily as prior restraint. Unlike the United States, other countries have specific rules and regulations which, if not directly controlling the content of news programming, infer certain responsibilities. For example, regulations governing the operation of Danmarks Radio, while supporting free speech with the clause "importance shall be attached to considerations for the freedom of information and speech," the law also reads in news "importance shall be attached to objectivity and impartiality."[73] In Denmark's granting of licenses to local radio and television authorities permit local "daily newspapers and district newspapers" to have a "controlling influence in a company, association, or similar body" awarded a local radio or television license and where "daily newspapers or district papers have the controlling influence" the presupposition exists "that the local radio or television station fulfills a function as forum for a broad local debate."[74]

Election Coverage

Political broadcasting statutes differ depending on how authoritarian a government is and what type of political process operates in a given country. Some regulations mirror those of more democratic institutions. Finland's Administrative Council of the Finnish Broadcasting Company (YLE) requires that candidates for political office be given "equal status."[75] This applies to candidates for presidential elections as well as candidates for lesser offices. At this point, however, regulations become more strict. For example, at the time a candidate is nominated for a national election and the name of the candidate has been forwarded to the central election committee, YLE must seek to avoid mentioning the names of the candidates except in connection with special election programs. Reference to the candidate is permitted when it is necessary "in the context of reporting news" but regulations call for broadcasters not to give "special advantage" to one candidate over another. In most cases the restrictions apply one month prior to an election. If a politician appears in programs which are not "election" programs, such as news and current affairs programs, broadcasters are charged with making sure no politician acquires a "special advantage" for either the candidate or the party represented. The restriction on candidates does not apply to the president of Finland.

Objectivity

Although journalism ethics in the United States purport objectivity in reporting, that objectivity is mostly found in journalism textbooks and professional association's codes of ethics. That is not the case elsewhere. The Republic of China regulations governing broadcast news contain two clauses which would make most American news directors wince.[76] In one section of the Republic's regulations governing news coverage is the statement: "News reports should be objective, accurate, and complete." In another section of the same regulations appears the statement: "A news report should emphasize the bright side of society." Other provisions include the following statements:

> . . . News commentaries should be fair and just. Should there be any mistake, the TV network should make the necessary corrections on it own initiative in order to ensure its credibility.
>
> The use of materials related to the Chinese Communist regime should be timely; reports should avoid any undesirable consequences.
>
> News gathering should be conducted in a proper manner and by proper means. Especially in those cases involving major crimes, it is not appropriate for a reporter to hinder the legal process of investigation or enforcement.

> News programs may not broadcast as photo, picture, or the name of any criminal suspect who is a minor. Proper attention should be paid to the rights of his or her kin.
>
> Any news of social crimes should not be aired in the first half of the news broadcast; the volume of coverage should also be limited. However, cases of momentous import may be mentioned in a summary manner during the news outline.
>
> . . . It is not allowable to depict the way a crime was committed when reporting or commenting on a crime or an undesirable societal phenomenon. Reports should avoid exaggerating sex and violence.
>
> No deliberate comment should be made on legal cases in progress.[77]

The practice of promoting a program during a newscast by making the program part of a news story is common on American television. Prime-time investigative reports, for example, may have teasers which appear in the newscast preceding the report. Not so in the Republic of China. There a provision exists which tells stations that their news reports should "avoid reporting on other programs from the same station." In other words newscasts should not contain stories which may be promoting or hyping programs appearing on the station at different times.

Libel and Privacy

Libel law in the United States balances the power of the First Amendment which gives broadcast and print journalists the right to publish or broadcast almost anything they wish. But if the reporter is careless in selecting what parts of a story to include and what parts to omit, in collecting facts, in editing or writing a story, the reporter is careless and that carelessness damages the name of an individual or unfairly invades the person's privacy, then the person can sue for libel and/or invasion of privacy. If the person is a public figure or a public official then that person must prove malice. What damages the person libeled may be entitled to depends of the state libel law. There's nothing in FCC regulations to punish a station's news department for libeling someone. If the person lives in Norway, however, and the state broadcasting system, NRK, broadcasts a program exposing someone to "unwarranted prejudice" or invades someone's privacy, then he or she can turn to the Complaints Tribunal which can determine if NRK, when asked to rectify the alleged misinformation acted properly. In both countries, however, there is a tug and pull between the rights of the press on the one hand and the rights of the individual on the other to protect one's reputation.

In Japan, where some of the American legal system has been incorporated into Japanese law, libel takes on a somewhat different perspective. Kyu Ho Youm writing in *Journalism Quarterly* cites a 1907 Penal Code in Japan, still in effect, which calls for punishment by imprisonment in a forced labor camp for not more than three years or a fine of not more than 1,000 yen if one person defames another person by publicly alleging facts *regardless of whether such facts are true or false* (italics added). No distinction is made between libel and slander under the Penal Code.[78] The Penal Code was revised after World War II by incorporating the concept of "public interest" into the statute which, as Youm points out, provides "limited justification for defamatory crimes."[79] Under the revised code, the truth is recognized as a defense but only when the public interest is involved. The dead cannot be libeled in Japan unless the statements made are untrue.

A Civil Code in Japan provides for monetary damages to be awarded to the defamed in addition to other suitable measures of which an apology in the mass media is one alternative.[80] In Japan prior restraint is possible under unusual circumstances through a judicial injunction "to balance freedom of expression and the right of an individual to his reputation," as well as protecting the individual from future defamation.[81] At the same time, however, Japanese courts have also recognized the deterrent effect of prior restraint and said it should be used only in exceptional circumstances. Despite these exceptions, Youm cites legal scholars who point out that overall the Japanese press is free of government restrictions and has been listed as one of twelve countries with the "lowest inclination to control."[82] Youm concludes by stating: "Japan strives both constitutionally and statutorily to strike a balance between press freedom and the reputational interests of individuals. The Constitution explicitly guarantees freedom of the press, while the freedom may be qualified on grounds of the public welfare interest."[83]

FINANCING

Wide disparity exists in the way broadcasting systems are financed. In the United States, for example, advertising is the primary means of income for commercial radio and television stations. Public broadcasting stations in the United States are financed through a multitier system of contributions from individuals, corporations, foundations, and government grants. Combined, the contributions and grants permit the public stations to operate without the direct support of advertisers. Although companies who support public broadcasting are permitted a commercial-type announcement publicizing their support in association with a product or service, public stations do not as a rule air full-length commercials.[84] Commercial stations, however, have few restrictions and can air commercials of any length as long as the public is aware that they are watching a paid advertisement. The government provides little financial support for commercial radio and television stations with the exception of government agencies which may occasionally buy advertising.[85]

Pros and Cons of Regulated Financing

In some countries, however, "financing" means something entirely different than it does in the United States. Combination arrangements exist whereby stations receive both government funding and advertising. Other stations are supported wholly by tax revenues. Still other countries use "receiver fees" whereby the consumer pays the government a fee for the privilege of owning a radio or television receiver and the privilege of being able to watch television and listen to radio. In some countries the financing arrangement has developed through tradition and laws that have been in force for half a century. In others a change in the political structure has signaled a new approach to financing radio and television enterprises. Eastern Europe is one example where developing capitalism means experimenting with more traditional broadcast advertising as opposed to government announcements listing the names of products available in the local government warehouse. In some countries government financing of broadcasting has meant a way of assuring the ruling party or dictator retains control of the communication channels and therefore control of the power structure. It is for this reason that many parts of the world have very few radio and television stations, even though there is ample spectrum space available.

Scholars are able to argue the merits and demerits of almost any financing structure. For example, in the United States the commercial nature of radio and television keeps the broadcasting system relatively free from government control, even though the system is regulated by the Federal Communications Commission.[86] One can argue the merits of such a system in a democracy. We might argue that the public broadcasting system in the United States whereby grants and contributions fund the system is advantageous because local stations are not beholding to local advertisers and are more closely tied to the audience of local contributors. Critics, however, would argue that because a relatively few number of corporations fund public broadcasting, as opposed to the hundreds of thousands of different businesses that buy commercials on nonpublic stations, public broadcasting is unduly influenced by some of America's biggest corporations. Still others would argue that both systems of financing are worthy of high praise because the American public receives "free" TV, as opposed to being charged for the privilege of owning a radio or television receiver. Those who work and live in a country where receiver fees, sometimes referred to as "license fees," are used as a basis of financing would argue that their system is far superior because the public pays for the service and there is even less influence by government and private business. While every system of financing has its supporters and detractors the important thing to remember is that there is wide diversity among nations in the way broadcasting is financed.

Regulating Receiver Fees

To get a better understanding of how the receiver fee system operates and how it is regulated we can examine some countries where receiver fees are in place. One of the largest fee systems exists in Japan where approximately 33 million people pay receiver fees to support Nippon Hoso Kyokai, Japan's internationally recognized broadcasting system.[87] The license fee system has permitted the financial base for Japan to become one of the most technologically advanced broadcasting systems. Other advancements in receiver and transmitter technology as well as high-definition television are evidence of its prosperity. To some extent, the dominance of NHK, which has been part of Japanese society since NHK grew out of the Tokyo Broadcasting Station in 1925, is reflected in the growing economic influence that Japan has enjoyed in the last quarter of the twentieth century.

The fee system in Japan operates in a complex regulatory structure, which in theory at least is designed to shield it from government influence. The organization starts with NHK's Board of

Governors which is the highest decision-making organ of NRK. The 12-member board is appointed by the prime minister with consent of both houses of Japanese government, collectively called the National Diet. The board has considerable power and can appoint as well as dismiss the chairman, the chief executive officer, and the NHK auditors who oversee the activities of the chairman and the chairman's executive vice chairman. From NHK's standpoint, this gives the Board of Governors the power to decide on important matters relating to NHK's operations and "aims at ensuring freedom of expression in broadcasting, and independence from any outside influence, such as political forces."[88]

Although receiver fees are collected by the people the income does not automatically go to NHK, nor does NHK have the power to set fees. That process is part of the budget review directed by the National Diet. NHK presents a budget and operational plan each year to the National Diet and submits a financial report, inventory, and balance sheet to the minister of posts and telecommunications. The prime minister can comment on the documents, as can the minister of posts and telecommunications. Comments can be added by both, and the plan submitted to the National Diet through the Cabinet by way of the Board of Audit. Within each of the National Diet's two houses are Standing Committees on Communications, much like telecommunications committees exist in both the House and Senate in the United States. These committees deliberate and decide whether to approve NHK's budget.

The monthly receiver fee is also decided and becomes part of a budget package approved by the National Diet. The Broadcast Law is designed to shield NHK from political pressure over its content by providing that: "Broadcast programs shall never be interfered with or regulated by any person, except in the case where he does so under the powers provided by law."[89] According to NHK, its domestic service does not receive other income such as investment or financial assistance from business or organizations linked to business.

Administering a Receiver Fee System

In Sweden a receiver fee is also used to finance the national television service. High fees are paid for color television receivers. With language that is indicative of a utility structure with typical quarterly billing procedures, the law reads:

> Any person in possession of a receiver for the reception of visual transmissions with or without sound (television receivers) shall pay a general receiver charge . . . per part of a calendar quarter. If the receiver is designed for the color reception of visual transmissions with or without sound, the possessor shall further pay an additional charge . . . per calendar quarter. If the charge first becomes due during the current period of charge, the charge shall be reduced to the amount corresponding to the number of days that remain of the period. The charge shall be paid to such authority as the Government may appoint.[90]

The language used in Sweden is not that much different than that found in other countries.

For a family owning more than one television, Sweden charges only a single fee per household when the other television receivers are used by the family "or full-time border." A single fee structure also exists for nursing homes, hotels, hospitals, schools, and boarding houses. If the television receiver is used in a motor vehicle such as a recreational vehicle, the fee paid for the home receiver also covers its use in the motor vehicle. Diplomats are exempt from paying receiver fees and having a video tape recorder attached to the receiver does not increase the fee.

Norway requires that anyone selling a radio or television receiver to another person report the transaction to the Norwegian Broadcasting Association. Regulations also apply to the importing and selling of receivers. Anyone who imports receivers, parts for receivers, or antennas must report the transaction to the NRK. The NRK is also charged with assuring certain quality standards and specifications for the equipment.[91] NRK inspectors have access to the accounts of importers and can examine contracts and other relevant documents. Inspectors also have access to the premises where receivers are "manufactured, stored, or distributed." Special duties on imported receivers can be assessed by the Norwegian Parliament. The Parliament also sets fines for anyone who violates any of the regulations governing fees and imports.

If you are delinquent in not paying your receiver fee in Norway your television set can be seized without legal action and sold to cover the amount of the unpaid fees. The Netherlands Media Act spells out the following provisions for the collection of fees:

> At least one month before the beginning of the period in which the license fee is to be

> paid, a written notice stating the amount of the license fee payable for that period shall be sent to the registered holder by or on behalf of the Director-General.
>
> If the license fee is not paid punctually, the holder shall receive a warning notice in writing sent by or on behalf of the Director-General, requesting him/her to fulfil his/her obligations. The holder shall be charged the cost of sending this notice.
>
> The Director-General or a person acting on his behalf may order the sealing of reception devices and appoint the holder or another person as the keeper of the sealed reception devices, if the holder fails to pay his/her license fee arrears and the cost of sending the warning notices. The holder shall be charged the cost of sealing the reception devices . . .
>
> The devices shall not be unsealed until the license fee and the costs of sending warning notices and performing the sealing procedure have been paid.[92]

The Netherlands defines family living in a household as "spouses or other persons living together on a permanent basis and forming a joint household (and) parents and those of their children, stepchildren or adoptive children who live with them."[93] Two levels of license fees exist in the Netherlands and regulations governing who pays what can be a bit confusing. For instance, if you own a television receiver you pay an "A" fee and if you own a radio you pay a "B" fee, unless you own a radio which is located in the same room as the television and then the "A" fee can cover both. No fees are paid for receiving devices located in vehicles or vessels. If you are in the business of selling, repairing, transporting, or storing television receivers, then fees are not charged for receivers in your possession which are part of your business. Fees are waived for certain categories of handicapped people. In addition to receiver fees, advertising is found on Dutch television in time slots allocated to the Radio and Television Advertising Association.

LIABILITY FOR PROGRAM CONTENT

Different levels and degrees of liability exist in broadcasting. For example, in the United States the owner and manager of a radio and television station hold the most responsibility for what takes place at the station and the content of programming. That responsibility is enforced through the use of terms such as *licensee* more than individual titles such as *owner* or *manager*. In news departments, programming will usually violate state laws governing privacy and libel before running afoul of the FCC, which by legal tradition steeped in the First Amendment, has been kept from exercising excessive control over radio and television news programming. Individuals who feel they have been libeled will find it easier to turn to the courts than the FCC.

Broadcasting Liability Acts

In many foreign countries the responsibility for programming and the liability for program content is spelled out in detailed terms. For example, in Finland the Broadcasting Responsibility Act is the force of law covering the content of broadcast programming. Anyone who commits "an offense" under the Broadcasting Responsibility Act is liable under criminal law. An accessory to the offense is also held liable with the greatest responsibility falling on the shoulders of what Finnish law calls the program "editor." The state broadcasting service is required to designate a responsible program editor for each program aired on its system. Even if other people are responsible for producing the content of the program, the program editor can still be fined for the violations. The sentence can run up to 12 months' imprisonment and a fine unless the program editor is able to prove that all due caution was taken in preventing the offense.

Specifically prohibited are programs with criminal content and if those programs result in damage of any kind the program editor is responsible. The most serious offenses under the act are the following:

> defamation such as slander, insult, and dishonoring the memory of the deceased; religious offenses such as blasphemy and violation of freedom of worship; offenses directed at the state, for example violating the honor of the head of state or a friendly nation, dishonoring the coat of arms or other insignia of such a state, defamation of a foreign state and violating the honor of a diplomatic representative of a foreign state.[94]

Copyright violations also fall under Finland's Broadcasting Responsibility Act.

Sweden's Broadcasting Liability Act is similar in some ways to Finland's but different in others.[95] A program supervisor is responsible for offenses under Sweden's law but Sweden makes a point of legislating into its broadcasting statutes the spirit of its Freedom of Press Act which governs the print media. Under the Broadcasting Liability Act each program is assigned a program supervisor who is charged with preventing "offenses." Nothing can be put over the air unless it first receives the approval of the program supervisor. The program supervisor's name is kept in an official register which is open to the public. Once assigned to a program the program supervisor is liable for any offense against "freedom of expression." Where live broadcasts are concerned the person who appoints the program supervisor can declare that everyone who participates in the program is liable for its content.

Due Process

Due process for those charged with offenses under Sweden's Broadcasting Liability Act are tried in the Stockholm District Court. Some other Swedish courts also have jurisdiction over issues involving freedom of the press and these courts may also hear cases originating under the Broadcasting Liability Act. The justice chancellor, much like a prosecutor, can initiate proceedings against those who are liable under the act. With a six-month statute of limitations from the date of broadcast, the justice chancellor has jurisdiction to prosecute either freedom of expression issues or other matters which fall under the act. Strong confidentiality measures also exist in such proceedings and the program supervisor can avoid disclosing the script writer or "creator" of the program. The court hearing a case can order such disclosure in the interests of a fair trial, however. Fines, similar to those which would be levied for contempt of court proceedings in the United States, can be levied by Swedish courts if parties to an action refuse to divulge who provided information for broadcast. Swedish law also provides for the publishing of rules for program production companies to take measures to preserve evidence and for private individuals to inspect that evidence.

QUALIFICATIONS OF BROADCASTING PERSONNEL

In the United States persons wanting to own a broadcasting station are expected to have certain qualifications which permit them to operate and own a broadcasting property. For example, personal qualifications are necessary and are spelled out in FCC regulations and in the forms necessary to apply for permission to construct a broadcasting station and to put it on the air. Individuals who have an attributable interest in another medium of mass communication in the same geographic area where the station will operate must be listed on the FCC form and the nature and extent of the interest must be divulged.

Rationale for Regulating Qualifications for Ownership

The regulation exists to prevent undue concentrations of media power in a given market and the ability of one individual to control the channels of communication. Controlling the channels of communication can also mean controlling public opinion. FCC regulations prohibit issuing a construction permit to an alien, a representative of an alien, a foreign government, or a representative thereof.[96] Citizenship requirements also exist and marital relationships when both husband and wife have an interest in a broadcast property will come to bear on an application for construct a station. FCC regulations in the United States state, "in situations in which a marital relationship is involved, the interests held by one spouse are presumptively attributed to the other and both spouses may, unless this presumption is rebutted by an appropriate showing, be considered to be holders of attributable interests and parties to this application regarding whom full information is called for."[97] The control exerted over who can and cannot own a broadcasting property is not unusual. Some would argue the channels of communication are too important and powerful not to be regulated in some way, if for no other reason then political and social stability. In examining some of the regulations imposed in countries other than the United States, we turn to the Republic of China.

Regulated Qualifications for Middle-Management Personnel

People who are disqualified in the Republic of China from serving in important positions as staff members or officers of a radio and television station are those who have committed or instigated others to commit such acts as sedition, treason, or espionage. The mentally ill, people who don't reside in the country, or have illegally deprived others of their civil rights are also prohibited from serving in these capacities. Those who are qualified to hold positions of responsibility must meet one of the following qualifications:

> Previously have been a responsible officer of radio or television enterprises or served as a newspaper or magazine publisher.
>
> Previously have served as chief officer of a department or radio or television enterprises, or of a newspaper or magazine.
>
> Previously have served in a recommended appointment job in the government service or its equivalent, or in a higher position for over five years.
>
> Have had one's qualifications as a professor and related teaching experience duly recognized by the Ministry of Education.
>
> Have graduated from either local or overseas colleges and universities in related majors or departments and served more than eight years with a radio or television enterprise duly recognized by the Ministry of Education.
>
> Have graduated from either local or overseas colleges and universities in related majors or departments and served more than eight years with a radio or television enterprise duly recognized by the Ministry of Education.[98]

Qualifications for news, programming, and business departments also exist and at least one qualification from a list of qualifications must be met. For example, radio and television news directors must have served in that capacity at some other location and have graduated from a journalism-related course in a local or overseas department of a college or university. Having served as an associate professor teaching courses related to journalism or having worked for more than seven years in broadcasting, television, or journalism will also qualify for the position of news director. Programming department heads must have similar qualifications, including working in a similar capacity somewhere else, working three years in radio or television journalism or a related field, or working in the radio, television or film industry for more than seven years. Heads of business management departments fulfill the same qualifications related to their own areas of expertise. All three positions can be held by people who have previously served in a "recommended appointment job in the government service or its equivalent, or a higher position, of a relevant nature."[99]

Staff personnel must also meet certain qualifications. For example, program producers or hosts, announcers, editors, and directors must be college graduates and have more than three years of working experience in similar capacities. Reporters and "news compilers" must be college graduates or pass "high-level" government examinations. Continuing education programs are offered and employees are expected to participate in special training programs and attend lectures.[100]

COMPLAINT PROCEDURES

In the United States viewers or listeners who have been the subjects of a radio or television program have a number of options available if they feel they have been treated unfairly on the air. Not all options are effective or inexpensive.

Feedback: The Legal Construct

Libel law as it is applied in the United States, for example, requires the individual to seek legal counsel who must then interpret state statutes and case law to determine if the individual has in fact been libeled. If sufficient grounds exist to pursue a case, the individual can file a libel suit against the station. The individual also has the option of asking the station to correct any factual errors in a subsequent broadcast or even to give the individual the opportunity to reply. What form that reply takes, however, is at the discretion of the station. The station may decide the story stands on its own merits and will choose not to make any correction or provide the opportunity for a response. The individual, of course, has the option of pursuing the lawsuit. The court, if it rules against the station in a libel case, can in some states assess the station for actual and punitive damages. Other complaint mechanisms are available by writing the Federal Communications Commission where the letter of complaint will become part of the station's file. In most cases the station will be notified of the complaint by the FCC. Simply writing the FCC, however, does not guarantee any action on the part of the commission or the station. If the program where the questionable reference occurred is a news program, then the First Amendment offers a station operating in the United States certain protections not available in many other countries. If the person is a public figure or public official then the station may be entitled to even more protection against complaints or libel actions.

In the United States, only on rare occasions, and then primarily when the Fairness Doctrine was enforced, does the FCC place itself in a position of dictating to a station that it should broadcast a reply based on a complaint. Although corrective advertising can be ordered by the United States Federal Trade Commission, the order is issued to the advertiser and not a particular radio or television station or network.[101]

The Right to Reply

Other countries have more formal complaint procedures in place and offer the individual more immediate recourse, including some rights to reply. For example, Swedish law states that the Swedish Television Company "shall correct false information as necessary."[102] The same law goes on to state: "Anyone with a justified claim to refute a broadcast statement shall be given the opportunity to reply. Requests for the correction of misinformation or a right of reply shall be considered promptly. If the request has been made in writing, the company shall inform the Broadcasting Commission . . . " The Broadcast Commission can the approve or disapprove of the complaint. If a request for the correction of misinformation is approved, "such correction shall be broadcast without undue delay in a context that the viewing public will find appropriate. If a request for a right to reply is approved, a reply shall be transmitted as soon as possible in, or in connection with, a programme of the same or similar character as that to which the complaint relates."[103]

In Norway complaints must be submitted to the Norwegian Broadcasting Corporation (NRK) within 30 days of the date of the broadcast but the time limit is flexible in special cases. Complaints are evaluated at the level of the NRK which can act on the matter or pass it on to a Complaints Tribunal which has the authority to decide if a program broadcast by the NRK "has exposed anyone to unwarranted prejudice or invaded his privacy."[104] The Complaints Tribunal determines if NRK has acted properly in handling the complaint. NRK is required to keep programs against which complaints have been lodged available until after the tribunal has acted on the complaints.

The Norwegian Complaints Tribunal is composed of a chairperson with two other members and their personal deputies. All three members must be present for the tribunal to take action and each member is required to have "the competence of a judge." Cases of the tribunal are discussed in writing except when the tribunal chooses to hear oral arguments in a case. Each party in a complaints case is provided the opportunity to respond but when a plaintiff brings a complaint the tribunal finds has little merit, it can dismiss the complaint without factual consideration. Dissenting votes are possible when the tribunal rules, and final decisions with dissenting opinions are made public. The tribunal can decide if its rulings and dissenting opinions should be broadcast by the NRK.

Denmark also has a Broadcasting Complaints Commission similar to that of Norway. For example, complaints against programs on Danmarks Radio must be filed within four weeks of the broadcast, but the decision on the complaint made to Danmarks Radio can be appealed to the Broadcasting Complaints Commission.[105] The commission consists of three members appointed for four years. The chairperson of the Broadcasting Complaints Commission is appointed by the minister for transport and communications and "must meet the general requirements for appointment to the office of High Court Justice."[106] In addition the broadcast law states: "The Broadcasting Complaints Commission may direct Danmarks Radio to correct misrepresentations of facts in broadcasts by Danmarks Radio and may determine the contents, form and place of such corrections. Such adjudications of the Commission cannot be appealed against any other administrative authority."[107] The same procedure exists for complaints made against Denmark's TV 2 television networks.

SUMMARY

International statutes and codes range from very broad directives such as those issued by the European Community affecting broadcasting in EC-member countries, to very specific statutes which control the use of language dialects in a single country. These more specific statutes and codes are becoming increasingly important as satellites make it possible for any station with the right technology to broadcast globally. In addition traditional economic and political barriers are being torn down, such as the development of new alliances in Eastern Europe and movements toward a single currency and common trade agreements in Western Europe. In this chapter we examined specific statutes and codes governing such areas as culture, language, programming to children, advertising regulations, advertising production standards, news programming, financing, liability for program content, qualifications of broadcasting personnel, and complaint procedures.

Many external services have regulations which govern both the content and the amount of cultural programming. Radio Nederland airs programming centering around the Dutch culture. Canada's external service, Radio Canada, is mandated to air programs which further develop an international awareness of Canada and which reflect the realities of Canadian life and culture. Domestically, the Program Foundation of the Netherlands Broadcasting Corporation coordinates air time awarded to different political and social groups and the law requires that 20 percent of the programs provided by the foundation itself must deal with Dutch culture. Swedish Television Company's agreement with the Swedish government requires the company to promote artistic and cultural innovation. Similar requirements exist for Switzerland. The amount of cultural programming is also regulated in some countries. In Australia support for Australian artists is enhanced by regulations requiring not less than 20 percent of music programming be performed by Australians. The Republic of China has a similar statute. Cultural requirements are also found in advertising in such countries as the Republic of China, and history teaches us that in Egypt during the reign of Gamal Abdul Nasser music on radio was a major force promoting Arab nationalism.

Whereas in the United States the presence of English on radio and television is taken for granted and domestically regulations do not exist governing language use, that is not the case in some other countries. Restrictions apply in such countries as the Republic of China where Mandarin is the legislated official language of some parts of the broadcasting system. Both French and English language requirements exist in Canada, and in Finland language heard in commercials must be grammatically correct and make use of only a generally recognized vocabulary.

One of the most heavily regulated areas is programming directed toward children. The Canadian Broadcasting Corporation has strict guidelines over what type of commercial appeals can be directed toward children. Finland also regulates commercials directed toward children. Among other things, commercials in Finland must not present situations which may cause children injury to themselves or others. Regulations in Finland also cover children as performers where the unnecessary use of children in commercials is prohibited. In the Republic of China people working in the radio and television industry are charged with the responsibility for governing the overall content of children's programming which includes working hard to understand children's interests and providing them with appropriate entertainment which will enhance their willingness to study. Pre-emptive regulations over the content of commercials directed toward children are also found in the Republic of China and include a provision that advertising must not entice children to pressure their parents to buy products.

Advertising is regulated and both general and specific provisions exist. General provisions are usually stated in the preambles and prefaces of advertising codes and regulations. In Finland advertising cannot awaken negative opinions toward advertising. In the Republic of China advertising cannot use nude or overly romantic scenes. Also in China, advertising cannot contravene established views of life and should respect public mores. Similar themes to those of China are found in Finland where advertising messages must be presented with refinement and good taste. The placement of ads is also regulated in Finland where programs lasting at least 20 minutes can have only one commercial break. In many countries regulations control the advertising of specific products. Medicines, medical warnings, weight-loss programs, contests, investments, and motion pictures are examples. Advertising production standards are also upheld through regulations. In Finland, requirements govern what parts of the television screen must contain the key elements of a commercial message.

While the First Amendment in the United States restricts the government's involvement in news programming, other countries have stricter requirements. Political broadcasting in Finland requires candidates for political office be given "equal status." Other countries have regulations which attempt to assure accuracy and objectivity. In the Republic of China stations are prohibited from promoting other programming at the station in their news reports. Libel and privacy law guard the rights of the individual in the United States and such laws also exist in other countries. Japan has libel and privacy law in place that is modeled to some extent after libel and privacy law in the United States.

Financing of broadcasting systems is determined by the type of regulated financial structure that exists. Commercials provide income for stations in the United States and public stations receive funding from the government and private contributions. In some other countries receiver license fees are used as income. Japan is one example. Receiver fees in Japan are determined by the government in a complex arrangement whereby the National Diet confirms a 12-member NHK board appointed by the prime minister. The fees go to the government and are factored into a budget review which helps determine NHK's operating budget. Other fee systems exist in Sweden and Norway. In Norway, anyone selling a receiver must report the transaction to the Norwegian Broadcasting Association.

Liability for the content of programs is part of the regulations of many countries. In Finland the Broadcasting Responsibility Act is in force. Anyone violating the law is open to criminal prosecution. Copyright violations also fall under the act. Sweden has a Broadcasting Liability Act much like Finland's. Each program in Sweden is assigned a program supervisor who is charged with the overall responsibility for the program. Due process is legislated into Sweden's Broadcasting Liability Act.

In the Republic of China the qualifications of broadcasting personnel are spelled out in broadcast law. The mentally ill, people who have been disqualified from serving in important provisions of government, and those who have committed acts of sedition, treason, or espionage are all prohibited from holding staff positions in radio and television stations. Those who can serve in positions of responsibility can have such qualifications as previously serving as a responsible officer in a print or broadcast facility. Staff personnel holding positions as program producers or hosts, editors, and other jobs must be college graduates and have more than three years of work experience in similar capacities.

People who feel they have been treated unfairly in the United States can turn to the courts for redress. In other countries this option is also available but other avenue also exist. For example, in Sweden a right to reply is in force for anyone who is the subject of a report by the Swedish Television Company, provided the Broadcasting Commission rules in their favor. Similar provisions exist in Norway for programs aired by the Norwegian Broadcasting Corporation. In Norway a Complaints Tribunal oversees the reply provisions of the law. A Broadcasting Complaints Commission operates in Denmark.

MATERIAL FOR ANALYSIS

An overview of the broadcasting system of the Nordic countries finds many diverse regulatory frameworks. For example, in Iceland broadcasting is controlled by the Icelandic State Broadcasting Service which derives its income from license fees. Norway's radio and television are under the control of the Norwegian Broadcasting Corporation which is also financed by receiver fees. In Finland, broadcasting is controlled by the Finnish Broadcasting Company which operates local radio stations carrying commercial programming. In Sweden a community radio service permits any nonprofit organization not involved in broadcasting to obtain a low-power radio transmitter license from the Swedish Telecommunications Administration. In Denmark, broadcasting is controlled by Danmarks Radio. The following sections which are excerpted from the The Radio and Television Broadcasting Act of Denmark permit a closer look at one country and how it regulates its radio and television services.[108] The reader is reminded that what follows are excerpts and that paragraphs, part, and section numbers have been deleted without notation.

DENMARK'S RADIO AND TELEVISION BROADCASTING ACT

With Latest Amendments and Translation by Danmarks Radio

GENERAL PROVISIONS RELATING TO THE BROADCASTING AND DISTRIBUTION OF SOUND RADIO AND TELEVISION PROGRAMMES

Danmarks Radio shall have the right to broadcast, through transmitting networks, sound radio and television programmes intended for reception by the general public.

TV2 shall have the right to broadcast, through transmitting networks, sound radio and television programmes intended for reception by the general public.

Companies, associations and similar bodies and local authorities, who have been granted a licence . . . may broadcast through transmitting networks, programmes intended for reception by the general public pursuant to the provisions laid down in the licence so granted.

Communal aerials and other cable systems for distribution of sound radio and television programmes to private households may be used for distribution of: (i) Programmes of Danmark Radio and other Danish programmes which are broadcast by means of transmitting networks . . . (ii) Foreign sound radio and television programmes which can be received direct on frequencies reserved for radio broadcasting or which are transmitted to the system by the Directorate General of Posts and Telecommunications or a telephone company, also comprising programmes transmitted via communication satellites with a view to redistribution to communal aerial and other cable systems. (iii) Foreign sound radio and television programmes broadcast via communication satellites and received through a communal aerial system according to licence pursuant to . . . the Radio Communication Act.

Sound radio and television programmes may also be transmitted by means of communal aerials and other cable systems to private households in the following cases: (i) Danmarks Radio has the right to let programmes be distributed. (ii) TV 2 has the right to let programmes be distributed. (iii) Companies, associations and similar bodies and local authorities, which have been granted a licence . . . may distribute programmes pursuant to the provisions laid down in the licence so granted. (iv) The Commission . . . may in special circumstances grant a licence for the distribution, within certain local areas and for short periods of time, of programmes relating to individual events of a local nature . . . (v) Distribution of programmes may take place without a licence by means of systems which do not comprise more than 25 cable connections in a building or a group of neighboring buildings.

Owners of communal aerials and other cable systems for premises used for private dwelling shall be obliged to ensure that a distribution will take place, within the system, of television programmes of Danmarks Radio or other nationwide programmes or regional television programmes designated for reception in a certain area which are transmitted pursuant to current legislation.

If the systems comprise more than eight channels, a channel shall be made available to local television programmes broadcast or distributed in the area concerned . . .

* * *

The Minister for Transport and Communications shall lay down rules for installation and operation of communal aerials and other cable systems for distribution of sound radio and television programmes to private households. In the rules may be included regulations concerning the following circumstances: (i) Authorization for the establishment, extension, lay-out and use of communal aerials and other cable systems, including user influence on choice of programmes in systems not owned by the users. (ii) Installation and operation of a network to and between communal aerials and other cable systems and also concerning ownership of such a network. (iii) Transmission of foreign sound radio and television programmes for distribution . . . (iv) Overall Rules governing the charging of fees for communal aerials for connection to and reception from networks of the telephone companies and the Corporation of Posts and Telecommunications and monitoring to ensure observance of such rules. (v) That communal aerials and other cable systems may operate outside of the borders of a municipality only under certain local conditions. (vi) The technical manufacture of communal aerials and other cable systems and typological approval of the installation equipment used . . .

The Minister for Transport and Communications may authorize the Directorate General of Posts and Telecommunications or a telephone company to install and operate communal aerials and may lay down consequent rules.

Authority to install and operate communal aerials and any network to and between communal aerials may be granted on the condition that the telephone company concerned or, in State telephone areas, the Corporation of Posts and Telecommunications, may later, against reimbursement, acquire such parts of the systems concerned as are necessary for extension of the public telecommunications networks. Conditions for any such take-over shall be vested in the authority.

Authority to install and extend communal aerials and other cable systems for distribution of sound radio or television programmes to private households shall be granted after due application to the local authority administration.

Authority to install and extend communal aerials and other cable systems shall be granted based on an assessment as to whether an appropriate utilization is made of the possibilities for connection as contained in an approved plan . . . or a current planning scheme about which agreement exists between the local authority administration and the telephone company, or, in State telephone areas, the Corporation of Posts and Telecommunications.

A telephone company, or, in State telephone areas, the Corporation of Posts and Telecommunications, may, in consultation with the local authority administration, devise a plan for supply to the municipality or parts thereof indicating points for connection of communal aerials and other cable systems to the networks of the telephone company, or, in State telephone areas, of the Corporation of Posts and Telecommunications. The plan shall also be approved by the Minister for Transport and Communications who may make alterations to the plan before approval.

* * *

DANMARKS RADIO

Danmarks Radio shall be an independent public institution whose obligation to the general public is to broadcast sound radio and television programmes covering dissemination of news, information, entertainment, and arts. In the planning of programmes decisive importance shall be attached to considerations for the freedom of information and speech, and it shall be endeavored to provide quality, diversity and variety. In the dissemination of news, importance shall be attached to objectivity and impartiality.

Danmarks Radio may provide other programmes including broadcasting to other countries and produce programmes for distribution in some other manner than through broadcasts.

Danmarks Radio may provide other services in connection with programmes or with a view to utilizing the technical equipment, special expert knowledge etc.

In pursuance of rules laid down by the Minister for Transport and Communications, Danmarks Radio is obliged to broadcast information to the general public of importance with respect to preparedness.

The services of Danmarks Radio shall be financed from fees charged for the use of radio and television receiving sets, and from income from sale of services etc.

Danmarks Radio shall be governed by a Board composed of eleven members to be officially appointed by the Minister for Transport and Communications. One member (the Chairman) shall be appointed by the Minister for Transport and Communications and nine members shall be appointed by the Danish Parliament (the "Folketing"). One member shall be appointed by the permanent staff of Danmarks Radio. The Minister for Transport and Communications shall appoint the Vice Chairman from among the members appointed by Parliament.

* * *

The General Programme Advisory Committee is an advisory body which shall discuss Danmarks Radio's programme services and which may give opinions to that effect to the Board and Management.

Rules on composition and activities of the Committee shall be laid down in the statute of Danmarks Radio.

A County Programme Advisory Committee shall be set up for each county and the City of Copenhagen and District of Frederiksberg jointly according to rules laid down by the County Council. The County Programme Advisory Committee is an advisory body whose task is to follow Danmarks Radio's regional programme activity and who may give opinions to that effect and about the programme activity otherwise to the General Programme Advisory Committee . . . Members shall be appointed for a term of four years.

* * *

LOCAL RADIO AND TELEVISION BROADCASTING

The Commission . . . may grant licenses to companies, associations and similar bodies to carry on radio and television broadcasting by means of transmitting networks or cable systems within a local area.

A licence will be granted only subject to fulfillment of the following conditions: (i) Where a licence is granted to a company, association or similar body, the majority of the members of the Commission must be residents of the local area. (ii) The sole object of the company, association or similar body shall be radio and television broadcasting. (iii) Commercial enterprises with the exception of daily newspapers and district papers shall not be allowed to have the controlling influence in any such company, association, or similar body. Licence to companies, etc., in which daily newspapers or district papers have the controlling influence presupposes that the local radio or television station fulfills a function as forum for a broad local debate.

Local authorities have a right to be granted a licence as . . . if the objects of the programme activity of the local authority will be solely to provide production and transmission facilities for the benefit of interested citizens, and to transmit information relating to the local authority.

The holder of a licence shall carry on the programme activity independently. The programme activity shall not comprise programmes broadcast simultaneously by another holder of a licence unless this is warranted by special local affairs in each individual case. In addition, the Minister for Traffic and Communication may permit simultaneous broadcasting of a programme in cases of very special circumstances.

* * *

A licence shall be granted for a fixed period not to exceed three years for radio and five years for television. Renewal of a licence may be granted at the expiration of the period.

An application for licence to broadcast shall describe the programme activity so that the Commission . . . can ensure that it has connection with the local area. When considering applications, the Commission shall endeavor to ensure that the individual local area will have an overall programme activity of a comprehensive nature.

In connection with granting of a licence the Commission may include a condition that the programme activity be exercised in conformity with the application.

The holder of a licence shall record and for three months store all transmissions on tape in accordance with the rules laid down by the Minister for Transport and Communications. In connection with the hearing of a case concerning programme activity the holder may be called upon to hand over recordings of the transmissions. If it is deemed necessary in connection with the hearing of cases concerning programme activity, the holder may be called upon to store tapes for a period exceeding three months.

The holder of a licence shall take care that every transmission has an executive producer. The producer shall, to the widest possible extent, know about the persons who have taken part in or in any other way contributed towards the transmission.

The holder of a licence shall take care that at the end of every programme the producer is named.

* * *

TV 2

TV 2 is an independent institution, the objects of which are, through independent programme activity, to provide and transmit nationwide and regional television programmes. When drawing up programmes, decisive importance shall be attached to quality, versatility and variety. When drawing up programmes in the regional TV 2 enterprises . . . importance shall also be attached to the connection with the region.

TV 2 shall produce news transmissions and programmes of topical interest. Other programmes shall be acquired mainly through purchases from other producers.

The daily transmission time for commercials shall not exceed ten minutes on the nationwide programme and five minutes on the regional programme. Commercials shall be transmitted only in blocks between programmes . . .

TV 2 shall be governed by a Board of five members (the Central Board), to be officially appointed by the Minister for Transport and Communications. The Members shall be appointed by the Minister for Transport and Communications, and between them they shall represent insight into matters of media, culture and management. The regional Boards . . . jointly shall appoint one representative each with no voting rights on the Central Board.

* * *

The Minister for Transport and Communications shall set up a General Programme Advisory Committee. The members shall be appointed for a term of four years.

The General Programme Advisory Committee is an advisory body which shall discuss the programme activity of TV 2, and which may give its opinion to the Central Board and the Management.

* * *

The Regional Committee of Representatives shall act as the General Programme Advisory Committee for the regional enterprise. The General Programme Advisory Committee is an advisory body, which shall discuss the regional enterprise, and which may give its opinion about this to the Management and to the Manager.

* * *

THE BROADCASTING COMPLAINTS COMMISSION

Any complaints of certain programmes or programme series broadcast by Danmarks Radio shall be lodged with Danmarks Radio within four weeks after the programme or programme series was transmitted.

Decisions of Danmarks Radio regarding a complaint . . . may be appealed against by the person with respect to whom the decision was made . . .

The Broadcasting Complaints Commission may deal only with cases referred to it within four weeks after the person concerned was apprised of the decision of Danmarks Radio.

The Broadcasting Complaints Commission shall be composed of three members to be appointed by the Minister for Transport and Communications for a term of four years at a time. One of the members must meet the general requirements for appointment to the office of High Court justice.

* * *

The Broadcasting Complaints Commission may direct Danmarks Radio to correct misrepresentations of facts in broadcasts by Danmarks Radio and may determine the contents, form and place of such corrections. Such adjudications of the Commission cannot be appealed against to any other administrative authority. The Broadcast Complaints Commission shall not otherwise be empowered to make decisions having binding effect on Danmarks Radio but may only give opinions on matters before it.

Opinions given by the Broadcast Complaints Commission shall be published. The Commission may, in each case, direct Danmarks Radio to broadcast an announcement of the opinion given by the Board and determine the manner and form of such an announcement.

* * *

TV ADVERTISING ADVISORY COMMITTEE

The Minister for Transport and Communications shall appoint a TV Advertising Advisory Committee.

The TV Advertising Advisory Committee: (i) shall offer advice to the Minister for Transport and Communications concerning the contents of TV commercials, (ii) shall call attention to violations of rules concerning contents of TV commercials and may direct the Company . . . to publish, during the transmission time set aside for commercials, the decision without delay and without any additional comments, and (iii) may direct the Company . . . to rectify false information about actual facts which have been transmitted in a commercial . . .

The TV Advertising Advisory committee shall consist of three members to be appointed by the Minister for Transport and Communications for a term of four years.

The Minister for Transport and Communications shall lay down detailed rules concerning the composition and activity of the TV Advertising Advisory Committee.

QUESTIONS FOR CRITICAL ANALYSIS

- Can cultural integrity effectively be regulated into broadcast and telecommunication policy?
- Is it more important to regulate cultural integrity in broadcasting services beamed outside national borders or is the rationale stronger for imposing cultural integrity regulations on internal broadcasts?
- How is it possible for a broadcasting system to "contribute to the elevation of the level of culture," as stated in the Japanese broadcasting law?
- What are the advantages of assuring cultural integrity in the regulation of a broadcasting system? If the United States passed a regulation requiring broadcasting stations to place emphasis on the "culture" of the United States, could the law be enforced?
- Is it more important to control the quality or to control the amount of cultural programming?
- Is it better for a country to have broadcast regulations which promote national culture but are difficult to enforce than to have regulations which can be enforced but are not as strict in protecting cultural integrity?
- If one is attempting to promote cultural integrity, are some types of programs more important to control than others?
- What are the political advantages, if any, of regulations which require a certain percentage of programming in a certain language?
- Are there any political advantages to encouraging the correct use of language? Are strict language requirements more important in commercials than in news or entertainment programming?
- In the Netherlands categories of films for people under 12 or 16 years of age are a part of the film censorship regulation. How does one determine

if a film or for that matter a radio or television program meets a specific age category?

- Canadian broadcasting corporations standards distinguish between commercials which have adult vocabulary. How does one determine if the vocabulary in a commercial is "adult"?
- Would the requirement in the Republic of China that programs should "avoid exposing the ugly, weird, mean, shocking and abnormal aspects of society" be permitted in American television?
- Should the United States pass more restrictive legislation which would place controls on advertising such as those found in some other countries?
- Under CBC guidelines commercials should not encourage or depict as being desirable any activity that is contrary to widely held standards of behavior. How is it possible in any society to determine what are widely held standards of behavior?
- Is it possible to determine what "undue exploitation of sex, nudity or violence" consists of?
- If the United Nations proposed a resolution banning all advertising for beer on radio and television among member nations, would the United States support such a resolution?
- Under Australia's advertising regulations radio commercials up to and including 20 seconds in length must have the phrase "use only as directed" when medicines are advertised. If the commercial is over 20 seconds, then longer warnings must appear. Is the length of the commercial a satisfactory way to regulate the content of medical warnings?
- Under Japanese law prior restraint is possible under unusual circumstances to balance freedom of expression and the right of individuals to their reputation. Do you feel that such prior restraint is warranted? Would it be legal in the United States?
- What would happen in the United States if the Federal Communications Commission passed a Broadcast Financing Act which imposed a license fee on the owners of radio and television receivers and then distributed the fee to networks with a specific number of people in the listening or viewing audience?
- Should the United States pass laws requiring certain qualifications for people who work in the radio and television industry?
- Examine the qualifications required in the Republic of China for staff members or officers working in a radio or television station. Could such laws be imposed on the broadcasting industry in the United States and are the qualifications reasonable?
- In Denmark the Broadcasting Complaints Commission may direct Danmarks Radio to correct misrepresentations of facts and can determine the content form and place of such corrections. Moreover, the commission cannot be appealed to any other administrative authority. Do you consider such a process equitable and fair?
- Under Denmark law a TV Advertising Advisory Committee offers advice on the contents of television commercials. Would such a committee, if formed by the government, be able to operate effectively in the United States? Would such advisory committees at the regional and local level be an effective way to influence positively the content of television programming?

ADDITIONAL RESOURCES

Coutts, J. A., "Maintaining Broadcasts from Pirate Radio Stations." 55 *Journal of Criminal Law* 179 (1991).

"International Chamber of Commerce Draft Uniform Rules of Conduct for Interchange of Trade Data by Teletransmission (UNCIDO); Special Joint Committee on Uniform Rules for Communication Agreements." 3 *Computer Law & Practice* 105 (January–February 1987).

Kilb, B. D., "International Telecommunications: Competition in Overseas Service." 22 *Harvard International Law Journal* 207 (1981).

Kolossov, Y. M., "Prospects for an International Treaty on Telecommunications." 27 *California Western Law Review* 173 (1990).

Nugter, A. C. M., and J. M. Smit, "The Regulation of International Telecommunication Services: A New Approach." 14 *North Carolina Journal of International Law and Commercial Regulation* 191 (1989).

Rankin, T. M., "Business Secrets Across International Borders: One Aspect of the Transborder Data Flow Debate." 2 *Computer Law & Practice* 106 (1986).

Zimmerman, J. A., "Transborder Data Flow: Problems with the Council of Europe Convention, or Protecting States from Protectionism." 4 *Northwestern Journal of International Law & Business* 601 (1982).

chapter sixteen

Ethics and Public Influence

While regulations guide many decisions in broadcasting and telecommunication, codes of ethics also play a part. Codes are designed to help assure professional conduct in such areas as news, advertising, and other business practices. Unlike law and regulations, a code of ethics is not exact and many times lacks the enforcement provisions contained in a law or regulation. Some exceptions, however, do exist. For example the National Advertising Division and the National Advertising Review Board operate without legal parameters, but the wide acceptance of both organizations make them effective watchdogs of deceptive advertising. Codes also have a preventive effect by keeping regulators out of the business of controlling information. Where a code or a professional organization is able to police their profession and with the law encourage members to responsible behavior, then there is little incentive for government to become involved since the problems are seen as not existing or at least being under control.

Ethics rules are in place in government agencies where the regulators themselves are found. The federal government has enacted laws governing the ethical conduct of employees. State statutes can contain ethics codes for such people as judges. Listed as Canons of Judicial Ethics, these codes many times parallel national canons and can be found in some statutes wherever rules of judicial procedure to practice before courts or commissions are described. On the international level, codes of ethics such as the Advertising Code of the National Chamber of Commerce have become the model for laws and regulations governing advertising in many countries.

ETHICS LAWS GOVERNING THE FEDERAL COMMUNICATIONS COMMISSION

Ethical conduct expected of FCC employees has been made part of federal law and all FCC employees fall under one or more provisions of the law. The federal statutes deal with such actions as gifts and entertainment, financial interests, use of government property, misuse of information, indebtedness, gambling and betting, playing the lottery, and general conduct prejudicial to the government.[1] Under "Ethical and Other Conduct and Responsibilities of Employees," federal regulations prescribe that FCC employees will not: use their office for private gain, give preferential preference to any individual, impede government efficiency, remain impartial, make government decisions outside official channels, or affect the confidence of the public in the integrity of government. Each employee must determine if their social activities infringe on ethics rules. Detailed information is spelled out in the rules governing gifts and entertainment. Employees are instructed to be alert to anyone offering anything of monetary value which might affect decisions in their official positions as FCC employees. Food and refreshments may be accepted when offered free in the course of a meeting. The FCC's Office of General Counsel can make a determination as to the propriety of accepting invitations in which a question of conflict of interest arises.

Documents prepared in the course of an employee's official duty cannot be used for private gain and commissioners cannot receive anything of value for any consultation, lecture, or writings. Regulations do not prevent an employee from receiving an award for meritorious service if it is given by a charitable, religious, professional, or social organization as well as similar groups which do not appear to create a conflict of interest or give an award which would appear to influence the employee's official position.

Financial interest rules are specific and prevent an employee from having a direct or indirect interest in any company which is subject to commission control. That includes companies which are engaged in any use of the electromagnetic spectrum. Family members are also subject to FCC regulations. For example, an employee may not participate in any official capacity in any activity in which a member of the employee's family (spouse or minor child) has a financial interest. Similarly, employees cannot receive any outside compensation for which they also receive government compensation. Paying debts are also covered and employees are required to pay all debts in a timely manner.

AMERICAN BAR ASSOCIATION CODE OF JUDICIAL CONDUCT

The American Bar Association developed an official position governing the conduct of the judiciary almost 50 years before it formally adopted its Code of Judicial Conduct in 1972. Originally called the Canons of Judicial Ethics, the current Code remained in force with periodic amendments until a comprehensive review was completed in 1990.[2] The language of the Code has been incorporated into many other documents, including government regulations which makes it enforceable as a matter of law in some states.[3] Within the code are canons which detail the behavior expected of judges in the exercise of their official duties. The five canons' primary statements read:

1. A judge shall uphold the integrity and independence of the judiciary.
2. A judge shall avoid impropriety and the appearance of impropriety in all of the judge's activities.
3. A judge shall perform the duties of judicial office impartially and diligently.
4. A judge shall so conduct the judge's extra-judicial activities as to minimize the risk of conflict with judicial obligations.
5. A judge or judicial candidate shall refrain from inappropriate political activity.[4]

The code applies to anyone, whether or not a lawyer, who is an officer of a judicial system and performs judicial functions. Administrative law judges are "generally affiliated with the executive branch of government rather than the judicial branch and each adopting jurisdiction should consider the unique characteristics of particular administrative law judge positions in adopting and adapting the Code for administrative law judges."[5] Retired judges also fall under the code as long as they are subject to recall to perform judicial functions.

THE BUSINESS AND PROFESSIONAL ADVERTISING ASSOCIATION (B/PAA)

A number of professional advertising associations take part in self-regulatory efforts. The Business and Professional Advertising Association's (B/PAA) Code of Ethics focuses on guarding against misleading statements in advertising. Provisions of the B/PAA Code of Ethics include such statements as: "claims made must be capable of substantiation." It furthermore stresses that: "no form of advertising should be prepared or knowingly accepted that contains or suggests false, exaggerated, or misleading statements, claims, or implications." The B/PAA code also discourages advertising that unfairly disparages products or any that "plays on superstitions and fears of others for the purpose of exploitation. . . ." Other provisions ban vulgar and offensive advertising, advertising that would harm users, or advertising that distorts the meanings of quotations or other statements attributable to speakers or authors.

AMERICAN ADVERTISING FEDERATION (AAF)

Similar to the B/PAA Code of Ethics is the advertising code subscribed to by the American Advertising Federation. This nine-point, succinctly worded code of ethics, which has been in effect since 1965, states:

1. *Truth*—Advertising shall tell the truth, and shall reveal significant facts, the concealment of which would mislead the public.
2. *Responsibility*—Advertising agencies and advertisers shall be willing to provide substantiation of claims made.
3. *Taste and Decency*—Advertising shall be free of statements, illustrations, or implications which are offensive to good taste or public decency.
4. *Disparagement*—Advertising shall offer merchandise or service on its merits, and refrain from attacking competitors unfairly or disparaging their products, services or methods of doing business.
5. *Bait Advertising*—Advertising shall offer only merchandise or services which are readily available for purchase at the advertised price.
6. *Guarantees and Warranties*—Advertising of guarantees and warranties shall be explicit. Advertising of any guarantee or warranty shall clearly and conspicuously disclose its nature and extent, the manner in which the guarantor or warrantor will perform and the identity of the guarantor or warrantor.
7. *Price Claims*—Advertising shall avoid price or savings claims which are false or misleading, or which do not offer provable bargains or savings.
8. *Unprovable Claims*—Advertising shall avoid the use of exaggerated or unprovable claims.
9. *Testimonials*—Advertising containing testimonials shall be limited to those of competent witnesses who are reflecting a real and honest choice.[6]

The federation's code parallels in some ways that of the Business and Professional Advertising Association. Especially important to both codes is the method of dealing with competitors' products. Comparative advertising became the object of a Federal Trade Commission investigation into advertising self-regulation in 1976. Concluding its investigation in 1979, the FTC said it would challenge industry advertising codes that in any way restrained comparative advertising.[7] The FTC pointed out that language in many of the codes of ethics could be interpreted as discouraging comparative advertising, and it warned that "restrictive use of anti-disparagement rules" would be subject to FTC attack.[8] The government investigated 23 different organizations, including the American Advertising Federation, the American Association of Advertising Agencies, the NAB, the three major commercial networks, the Counsel for Better Business Bureaus, and such specific product organizations as the Cosmetic Toiletries and Fragrances Association, the American Petroleum Institute, the Wine Conference of America, the Soap and Detergent Association, and the Pharmaceutical Manufacturers' Association. Many trade organizations, such as those just listed, had or continue to have their own codes of ethics or guidelines for advertising but such codes are voluntary, and at the point that a code begins to restrict lawful advertising by prohibiting certain categories of goods or services from being advertised, then the FTC may very likely step in.[9]

ADVERTISING CODE OF THE INTERNATIONAL CHAMBER OF COMMERCE

Many regulations governing advertising, whether self-regulatory or part of international statutes, are an outgrowth of the Advertising Code of the International Chamber of Commerce. In some statutes the code is referred to in the preamble of regulations governing the content of advertising, in others, specific provisions of the code are repeated almost verbatim. Along with a statement of basic principles, the code treats such issues as decency, honesty, truth, product comparisons, the use of testimonials, product denigration, privacy, unfair attribution of goodwill, imitations, labeling and identifications, safety, ads to children, and general responsibilities for the advertisers.

ECONOMIC PRESSURE FOR ADVERTISING SELF-REGULATION

Companies can limit their sponsorship of programs showing gratuitous sex and violence because it does not fit their corporate image or they are under pressure from public-interest groups. Such actions are a form of economic pressure for self-regulation and are common in the broadcasting industry. Religious groups and consumer organizations have been especially active in applying such pressure to advertisers.

The issue of economic pressure for advertising self-regulation occurs with the advent of broadcasting itself, but one of the more visible cases in the modern era of television occurred in

1977 when ABC television aired its comedy series, *SOAP*. A soap-opera spoof with a sexually-oriented theme which today would seem tame, *SOAP* was launched amidst criticism from the Christian Life Commission of the Southern Baptist Convention; dissatisfaction from smaller religious groups, such as the Roman Catholic Bishops Office in Providence, RI; and industry criticism, echoed by such people as the Chairman and President of Westinghouse Broadcasting Co.[10] While the show did managed to remain profitable and on the air, its early start was clouded by an uproar over sexual inferences. Vlasic Foods and Jovan, Inc. were among those who publicly dropped their sponsorship. The president of Vlasic Foods declared that his company had decided to drop the series because the program was not consistent with Vlasic's media strategy and family-oriented commercials and that the company had received numerous negative letters from religious groups.[11] Some stations were consequently shy about carrying the series.

Advertiser boycotts, while sometimes controversial, have been used as a press strategy to influencing programming. Trade publications have reported boycotts of sponsors organized by such groups as the Moral Majority and the Coalition for Better Television as having a significant effect.[12] One marketing executive at a meeting of the Association of National Advertisers was quoted as saying "I hate to give these groups something to crow about, but . . . their influence is strong and they've gotten the attention of our management, we have to factor it into every decision we present."[13] A Toyota marketing manager was quoted as saying his company felt "threatened and vulnerable" because such pressure was a violation of freedom of speech and Toyota had no choice but to advertise on TV.

Phil Donahue's program *Donahue* was the object of a boycott by a Chicago-area group called the National Federation for Decency and the national-based Coalition for Better Broadcasting. The groups charged the program with being too sex oriented. The National Federation for Decency issued a statement saying the group did not question the right of the program or Donahue to have whatever guests he wants on the air, or the right of the stations to run the show but the group wanted to "pass the information on to friends and the general public" what companies support the show. A spokesperson for the decency group said they had no problems with programs on breast-feeding and rape but objected to programs on sex therapy and family planning and contraception.[14]

Advertisers associated with violent programming have been the object of boycotts. The National Coalition on Television Violence launched a boycott campaign against General Mills, McDonald's, Kellogg's, General Foods, and Mattell because, as the coalition claimed, the groups sponsored half of all violent Saturday morning TV cartoons. The group defined violence as "an intentional and hostile use of force by one person against another."[15] Minor weight was given to acts such as pushing, grabbing, or restraint. The Knights of Columbus and the Joelton Church of Christ in Tennessee took independent action by calling on the public to "withhold patronage" and "clean up TV," respectively. While the FCC prods many broadcasters into self-restraint, state government has also had a history of becoming involved in self-regulation. The New York State Assembly reacted to a report on the food commercials carried on children's television.[16] Although the report was criticized for its methodology, the Assembly nevertheless focused on its main conclusion: The commercials needed to be counteracted. The report charged that "long-range effects of eating patterns encouraged by advertising include obesity, diabetes, heart disease, numerous other conditions, and possibly cancer."[17] Based on these and other recommendations of the report, the assembly called for broadcasters in New York state to "pledge in their license renewal applications to carry educational and informative food and nutritional and public service announcements during time periods when children make up a significant part of the audience and when food commercials are being carried."[18] The report also called for the state to develop a means of intervention in FCC proceedings and called on the state's Consumer Protection Board to represent the public before the FCC.

POLITICAL PRESSURE FOR ADVERTISING SELF-REGULATION

Through citizen group pressure, state legislatures and local communities have become involved in regulating video distributed through local rental stores. In some states minors work in video rental stores and rent tapes with Motion Picture Association of America restricted "R" ratings to minors. The Junior League of Bronxville, New York joined with other Junior Leagues in the United States to increase public awareness of the problem.[19] Requirements against distribution to minors have been passed in such states as Maryland, Tennessee, and Georgia. The constitutionality of such laws beyond the local communities where the stores are located remains unclear.

Past cases have struck down the MPAA ratings as a way of regulating whether a film is obscene. Such determinations must be made by local authorities, not a national trade association. Moreover, the MPAA code has no legal teeth. It is voluntary and penalties do not exist for theater owners who fail to adhere to the rating's labels. Beyond video stores, the pressure on over-the-air broadcasters from state government has been minimal. The precedent for exclusive jurisdiction of the FCC in these areas restrains state governments from becoming overly involved. Nevertheless, with the growth of cable some programming pressure has been shifted to the state and local level.

THE NATIONAL ADVERTISING DIVISION AND THE NATIONAL ADVERTISING REVIEW BOARD

The emphasis on self-regulation of broadcast advertising first manifested itself in 1971, when the industry set up a mechanism to curtail deceptive advertising. The two-part system functions as (1) the National Advertising Division (NAD) of the Council of Better Business Bureaus (CBBB) and (2) the National Advertising Review Board (NARB).

The system can trace its roots back to 1930, when review committees of advertising professionals were created to monitor deceptive advertising. Even more concern arose during the Great Depression, when stronger amendments to the Federal Trade Commission Act were passed in 1938. The prosperity of the 1950s seemed to lull self-regulation proponents, however, and uptrends in the economy lessened both public criticism and government intervention. The consumer era of the 1960s saw government once again stepping in with truth-in-packaging legislation and with public safety acts centered around motor vehicles and cigarette smoking. Renewed efforts at self-regulation materialized in the early 1970s, after a 1969 report by the American Bar Association criticized the Federal Trade Commission for being acquiescent to broadcasting practices. Enter the NAD and the NARB.

How does the NAD operate? First, the division evaluates the complaint or question that has been filed. It can either dismiss the complaint or contact the advertiser for additional documents to substantiate or refute the complaint. If the NAD is not satisfied with the advertiser's substantiation, it can ask the advertiser to change or discontinue the advertising message. If the advertiser agrees, then the NAD dismisses the complaint. But if the advertiser disagrees, the complaint can be appealed to the NARB.

At the NARB, the chairperson appoints a review panel, which evaluates the complaint and either dismisses it or again asks the advertiser to change or discontinue the message. If the advertiser agrees, as with the NAD, the panel can dismiss the complaint. If the advertiser refuses, the matter is then referred to a government agency for further action.

Cases reaching the final review stage of the NARB have dealt with everything from oil companies to electric razors. One panel dismissed a complaint against an oil company when it found the company had substantially documented its survey data, ruling that country singer Johnny Cash did not deliver a deceptive testimonial. Another complaint was dismissed against a vitamin manufacturer when the panel ruled that the value of iron supplements for women of child-bearing age had been established. Yet the NARB ruled that an electric shaver manufacturer's advertising claims were false, especially in comparison with competing shavers.

It is also not unusual for either the NAD or the NARB to become involved in legal disputes, not necessarily as a major litigant, but as a result of a civil suit being filed against an advertiser during the sometimes lengthy review process. When this happens, the final opinion of the NARB can clearly have an impact on the outcome of the case. While not having any legal or formal authority, the NARB's policy of turning unresolved disputes over to federal agencies has given it enough clout to be taken very seriously by many members of the advertising industry.

RTNDA CODE OF BROADCAST NEWS ETHICS

The Radio-Television News Directors Association (RTNDA) was founded in 1946 as the National Association of Radio News Directors. The organization today represents primarily news directors, the people who manage newsrooms, not reporters, although associate membership is open to these individuals, educators, and others. The official publication of RTNDA is the magazine *RTNDA Communicator*. RTNDA is also active in

Washington lobbying circles where First Amendment issues are stake. Campus chapters of the organization are found in some of the larger, well-known journalism and broadcasting programs in colleges and universities. The RTNDA is also active in filing friend of the court briefs on First Amendment issues. Among other provisions the RTNDA Code of Ethics calls on members to "strive to present the source or nature of broadcast news material in a way that is balanced, accurate and fair," and to "evaluate information solely on its merits as news, rejecting sensationalism or misleading emphasis in any form."[20] The text of the RTNDA Code can be found in the Materials for Analysis section at the end of Chapter 7.

CODE OF THE SOCIETY OF PROFESSIONAL JOURNALISTS

In 1909, a group of student reporters on a small university campus in the Midwest formed a journalism organization called Sigma Delta Chi, later to be called the Society of Professional Journalists–Sigma Delta Chi. The accounts of that first meeting indicate that the real purpose was to form a group more resembling a typical college fraternity than an organization with professional direction.[21] The constitution of the new "secret fraternity" read: In Order to associate college journalists of TALENT, TRUTH and ENERGY into a more intimately organized unity of good fellowship, with the element of mysticism as a binding force in order to assist the members in acquiring the noblest principles of journalism . . .[22] The code of ethics was adopted at the national convention of the Society in 1973. Among other provisions, the code calls on journalists to protect the freedom of the press "as an inalienable right of people in a free society."[23]

ALLIED PROFESSIONAL AND EDUCATIONAL ASSOCIATIONS

In addition to the groups already mentioned, other professional societies exist to improve standards and promote specific interests of their memberships. For example, the American Women in Radio and Television (AWRT) was formed in 1951 to improve the quality of broadcasting and support the advancement of qualified women in the radio and television industry. Women in Communications, Inc. (WICI) was founded in 1909 by seven female journalism students at the University of Washington, who christened it Theta Sigma Phi. The name of the organization was changed in 1972, and its objective was described then as being to "unite women engaged in news, advertising, public relations and other fields of communication and to recognize distinguished achievements of such women."[24] Other activities of the organization include job and salary surveys of its members, lobbying for First Amendment legislation, and opposition to court decisions unfavorable to journalists.[25]

Wire services such as the Associated Press have organizations which serve broadcasters. The Associated Press Broadcasters (APB) began in 1951 as a committee to assist AP executives with the radio news report. Today, the organization holds an annual convention, and regional and state organizations meet regularly with award programs and publications.[26] Other broadcast organizations operate in the field of education. The Broadcast Education Association (BEA), for example, is an arm of the NAB, founded in 1955 to improve broadcast education. It offers both individual and institutional memberships. The BEA publishes the *Journal of Broadcasting and Electronic Media*.[27] The Association for Education in Journalism and Mass Communication (AEJMC) was founded in 1912 as the American Association of Teachers of Journalism. AEJMC has become a national organization of college and secondary journalism teachers, administrators, and practitioners. Along with publishing the *Journalism Quarterly*, the organization holds an annual convention, handles a placement service, and sponsors scholarships.[28] The organization receives partial support for its operations from foundations.[29]

PRESS COUNCILS

Press councils are organizations that are designed to perform a watchdog function over both the print and broadcast press.

National News Council

Envision the following scenario: Professional organizations are wrestling with codes of ethics; Congress and the state governments are wrestling with the issue of protecting the confidentiality of reporter sources and whether to write such protections into law; the networks are recoiling under criticism that they are too powerful and monopolistic. The date is 1973. The Twentieth Century

Fund commissions a 15-month study into such wrestlings and criticisms. The result is the formation of the National News Council (NNC).

The 15-member NNC is designed to promote accurate and fair reporting while defending the free press. A year after its inception, the council began accepting complaints from any citizen in the United States who wanted to file a charge of unfair news reporting. Although the council received considerable publicity in academic journalism circles, some larger organizations initially refused to support its activities. Such major institutions as *The New York Times*, the Associated Press, NBC, and ABC refused cooperation.[30] Despite this resistance, however, the council has continued to function and to process complaints from a wide variety of organizations. Its activities are published in a yearly summary titled *In the Public Interest*, and in 1977, the *Columbia Journalism Review* started to carry reports of its activities.[31] The NNC also sponsors fellowships for first-year law students and graduate journalism students at the council's headquarters in New York. Private organizations and other institutions have funded the NNC; the organization does not accept any government assistance. Even though the NNC continues to function, the data are scant on how effective it is in fostering a more responsible press. The NNC has no formal power over any medium and relies on publicity for its clout.

State Press Councils

What many consider to be the role model for the NNC is the Minnesota Press Council (MPC), organized in 1971 as the only statewide press council in the United States. Like the NNC, the MPC has no formal power, and it too relies on publicity for its impact. Original support for the council came from the Minnesota Newspaper Association, but the association severed its relationship when the council's first official act was to declare itself independent from the newspaper trade organization.[32] The early years of the council saw a small budget, no staff or office, and meetings conducted on volunteered time by its members. Although beginning as a newspaper organization, the council brought the broadcast press under its fold in 1977 by adding three broadcast members to its 24-member group. Membership is divided equally between the journalistic community and the public, with the chairman of the council being a jurist from the Minnesota Supreme Court. Some attribute the success of the council to the fact that numerous complaints are settled among the parties involved before the council itself has to act.

Although primarily print oriented, similar press councils have sprung up all over the country. Foundation support from the Mellett Fund financed experimental press councils in Bend, Oregon and Redwood City, California.[33] Other Mellett Fund grants established councils in Cairo and Sparta, Illinois; Littleton, Colorado; and Honolulu, Hawaii. The Cairo council dealt primarily with the issue of media coverage of race relations. Similar race-relation–oriented councils were developed with Mellet Fund support in Seattle and St. Louis. Because of a lack of support, the St. Louis council lasted for only five meetings, and the Cairo group survived just ten months of operation. With varying amounts of success, Peoria, Illinois; Hilo, Hawaii; and Eagle Valley, Colorado have also operated municipal press councils.[34] As with the Minnesota and the National News Councils, these municipal councils have been primarily void of power to force change on any medium.

Although press councils are a commendable idea, their widespread effect has been at best unassessed and at worst minimal. As noted earlier, data do not exist on the influence they exert on either the local or the national press, and the indifference of many media or the lack of proper emphasis has hindered these evaluative efforts.[35]

CITIZEN AND PUBLIC-INTEREST GROUPS: THE EARLY MOVEMENT

While operating in the public interest has traditionally meant serving the mass audience, broadcasters must also deal with special interests. More and more public-interest—or *citizen* groups, as they are called—have gained a voice in both network and local station policy, operations, and programming.

United Church of Christ Decision

The citizen movement gained significant ground in the 1966 case of *United Church of Christ v. Federal Communications Commission*, which gave citizen groups the authority to intervene and take an active part in proceedings involving broadcasters and the FCC.[36] For too long, many felt, had there been a closed association between the FCC and the industry it regulated. For too long had the FCC simply adhered to the status quo. The court pointed out that the traditional issues—electrical interference and economic injury—were no longer the only basis for citizen intervention. Circuit Judge Warren Burger, who served as Chief Justice of the U.S. Supreme Court during a series of decisions on the rights of the press, said in the *United Church of Christ* decision: "After nearly five decades of operation, the broadcast industry does not seem to have grasped the simple fact that a broadcast licensee is a public trust subject to termination for breach of duty."[37] Assessing the relationship of a regulatory agency such as the FCC, Burger wrote: "Taking advantage of this 'active interest' in the . . . quality of broadcasting rather than depending on governmental initiative is also desirable, in that it tends to cast governmental power, at least in the first instance, in the more detached role of arbiter rather than accuser."[38] Defending public participation, Burger wrote: "We cannot believe that the congressional mandate of public participation, which the Commission says it seeks to fulfill, was meant to be limited to writing letters to the Commission, to inspection of records, to the Commission's grace in considering listener claims, or to mere non-participating appearance at hearings."[39]

Early Encouragement for Citizen Pressure

The encouragement that citizen groups gained from the *United Church of Christ* case opened the participatory floodgate. Added to this encouragement was the mood of the times. It was the late 1960s, a time of antiestablishment protest over the United States' frustrating commitment to the Vietnam war. The civil rights movement was pushing ahead, calling for equality for blacks and other minorities. The resulting atmosphere confronted broadcasters with demands from a variety of individuals and organizations. Some took direct action, putting to use the statement of support from the *United Church of Christ (UCC)* decision. By 1971, there were some 50 petitions to deny license renewals.[40] Other groups wanted access to station programming and were granted it, even being allowed to produce on-air programming. Not every group was concerned about minorities, or license renewals, or even access. Some organizations, such as the Action for Children's Television (ACT), wanted to improve television programming for children and to make people more aware of the medium's potential and of how to responsibly consume television.

Encounters between broadcasters and citizen groups have had varied results. Broadcasters gained a new sensitivity to groups which had previously been virtually and, consequently, unserved. Alerted to these elements in the community, some stations broadened their newsbeats to include issues facing these people. One example was in California, where Chicanos received more coverage consideration. Another station in Texas provided coverage of and for blacks.

Some experiences brought confrontations, and broadcasters were quick to point out that certain groups, while labeling themselves with broad descriptive titles, represented only a handful of people. Many of these groups were temporary, lasting only as long as their enthusiasm or their money held out. But others with good organization and leadership became a major force in broadcast reform.

CHARACTERISTICS OF A CITIZEN GROUP: THE LEGACY OF ACTION FOR CHILDREN'S TELEVISION

In 1992 regulators, broadcasters, and many who over the years had followed the public-interest movement in broadcasting were surprised when Peggy Charren, the founder of the advocacy group Action for Children's Television (ACT), announced she was shutting down ACT at the end of 1992.[41] With the aid of a grant from the Lilly Endowment, Charren did some soul searching about the future of the organization and determined it was time to pass on its legacy to other groups who could carry on ACT's charge of improving the quality of children's television. Also contributing to her decision was the passage in 1990 of the Children's Television Act which limited the number of commercials on children's television programming and requires television stations to show how they provide educational programming for children. The effectiveness of the group was affirmed by the chief sponsor of the bill who gave ACT credit for bringing the problems of children's television to the attention of policy makers.

Historical Notes

A brief look back at ACT's history profiles one of the most effective public-interest groups in the history of television, decidedly one of the largest, most active, and best-organized citizen groups participating in broadcast reform. Started informally among parents and other interested professionals, ACT was conceived in 1968 and incorporated as a nonprofit public organization in

1970.[42] The main direction of its early discussions and organizational meetings was to determine how to make children's television a constructive force by educating parents in the responsible use of the medium. It also set out to influence legislators and sponsors on the potential benefits of television and on the regulatory and economic climate best suited to recognize and encourage those benefits. The respect for ACT among government agencies and in the industry remained solid throughout its history. One ACT publication listed ACT's aims as:

> To encourage and persuade broadcasters and advertisers to provide programming of the highest possible quality designed for children of different ages; to encourage the development and enforcement of appropriate guidelines relating to children and the media; to encourage research, experimentation and evaluation in the field of children's television.[43]

The power of the organization was reflected by the fact that when ACT first approached the FCC with its well-publicized petition to eliminate commercials on children's television, the FCC received 100,000 comments on the proposal. Leonard Gross, writing about citizen groups for *TV Guide*, said that the petition and the national response put ACT on the political map.[44]

The organization produced numerous publications, including a professional newsletter and library guide. Additional information was disseminated through press releases and, when major issues arose, news conferences. Excerpts from the following ACT press release describing the results of a pre-Christmas television monitoring study was typical of ACT's punch:

> Toy commercials accounted for 84 percent of all children's advertising in the afterschool hours on a New York City independent TV station during the holiday season, and for 47.5 percent of all network children's ads, according to a study of "Pre-Christmas Advertising to Children" released today by Action for Children's Television (ACT). . . . (shows) product descriptions seldom give more than very minimal product information. Although products are visually represented, it is often difficult for the child (or adult) to determine the materials, physical dimensions, operational procedures, or other necessary consumer information. . . . Warnings or cautions about the use of products are seldom given, even though the product itself may sometimes include such information." . . . (there is) frequent use of visual distortion and other special effects, which may be perceived literally by the child viewer and lead to unrealistic expectations of product performance . . . According to Peggy Charren, President of ACT . . . , "the Pre-Christmas study proves that children's advertising is still misleading and unfair to young viewers." She emphasized the "necessity for regulatory action to compel the broadcasting and advertising industries to desist from practices that manipulate and confuse the members of the child audiences."[45]

The Issues and ACT's Closing

The 1990 Children's Television Act was just one of a long line of issues the organization became involved in during its history. In 1976 ACT sought an injunction against television advertisements for Spiderman vitamins. Part of ACT's criticism of the vitamin ads was the use of the comic-book character Spiderman as the spokesman, and the promotion of the vitamins as chewable and candy-like; which, according to ACT, created a "completely distorted notion of the medicinal contents of the bottle."[46]

Not all of ACT's positions opposed the broadcasting industry. When the FCC's Family Viewing guidelines attempted to control fringe prime-time programming, ACT joined with the National Citizens' Committee for Broadcasting, another public-interest group, and filed a "friend of the court" brief on the side of the Writers' Guild of American West. The brief claimed that Family Viewing violated "the public's paramount First Amendment right to maximum program diversity."[47]

Government hearings provided another forum. Chief spokesperson at the hearings was ACT founder, Peggy Charren. Failure of the Federal Trade Commission to respond to ACT's petitions for restriction of advertising for foods, vitamins, and toys on children's programs became a familiar topic.[48] Appearing at a hearing on FTC oversight, Charren testified: "We seek only to secure and protect the rights of our children to be safe and healthy, and their freedom to learn how to make responsible choices and decisions that are based on an unclouded presentation of information."[49] ACT also called on the FTC to restrict television advertising for phone services directed at children. The use of advertisements to entice children to call 900-prefix telephone numbers which charge high rates for calls brought an ACT petition against sports score 900 numbers, Dial-Santa, scoop lines, and dial-a-Muppet. ACT cited one six-year-old who called Santa enough times to run up a telephone bill in the hundreds of dollars. ACT pointed out that a special problem existed with 900 numbers because of "latchkey" children who are home without adult supervision before parents return from work.[50]

Hard-hitting confrontations were not unusual for ACT and trade associations were not immune from ACT's scrutiny. When the National Association of Broadcasters published a "Guide to Innovative Programming," ACT said in a Washington press conference that the booklet "murders the truth, deceives the public and cheats children."[51] Peggy Charren accused NAB of "premeditated deception," and the issuing of "false data" which hindered the ability of Congress to advance the public interest.[52] The NAB defended the guide, stood by its statements, and maintained the booklet had been published to stimulate new ideas.

ACT also joined with other citizen and public-interest groups to support issues and causes. Jointly with the United Church of Christ, ACT called for an FCC investigation into promotions on television which the groups charged were in violation of sponsor identification regulations. The groups criticized broadcasters for airing programs which contained "commercial matter" in the form of promotions but not sufficiently labeling the programming as promotions. The groups pointed to an article in a Washington, DC newspaper where CBS marketing had arranged for a Coke machine to be placed in the corridor of a school television feature in exchange for Coca-Cola's promise to advertise heavily on the show.[53] The CBS vice president for program services defended the CBS deal saying the contribution Coca-Cola made to the program justified the credits which read "Sponsored, in part, by Coca-Cola."

One of the reasons Charren listed for closing ACT was so other organizations would pick up the fight for better children's television. She saw herself and ACT as always being there and consequently some other grass-roots and national organizations stayed out of the children's programming arena. Six months before ACT closed, Charren was quoted as saying, "I think it was a little jolting to the PTA and others to realize that ACT's not here any longer. It's like we pushed the little birds out of the nest and said 'Fly'."[54]

OFFICE OF COMMUNICATION OF THE UNITED CHURCH OF CHRIST

Another pioneer organization in the public-interest field is the Office of Communication of the Church of Christ. Constantly educating broadcast consumers about their rights, the office has also become deeply involved in the broader issues of programming and regulatory reform. An early victory occurred in 1964 when it petitioned the FCC to deny the license renewal of a Jackson, Mississippi television station, charging the station with discrimination and censorship of programming. In the 1966 *United Church of Christ* case discussed earlier, the appeals court ordered the FCC to conduct a hearing in the case. After the hearing, the FCC again renewed the license, but the office persisted with a second appeal. Three years later the court ruled the license must be vacated and called for the FCC to invite other applications. That case opened the door for the citizens' movement.

Typical of strong charges issued by the office came in 1977 when the General Synod of the United Church of Christ passed its Pronouncement on Exploitative Broadcast Practices. Coming down hard on excessive sex and violence in broadcasting, the pronouncement called for Congress to impose FCC-enforced oversight on stations, requiring them to air programs which reflected the tastes and desires of the community.

During its history, the Office of Communication has not been known for empty rhetoric. It backs up its stands with a staff of full-time personnel and a ready bank of consultants and lawyers. Its "Check Your Local Stations" program of community workshops trains local community leaders to work toward improving broadcast service and employment of minorities. The church's membership, well in excess of a million, can mount a sizable crusade toward an established goal, and the office is generally respected among regulators and industry people. Typical of the church's systematic evaluation projects was the EEO Project in Broadcasting and Cable asking 3,000 volunteers to visit local radio stations and catalogue hiring data. Among the specific objectives of the project were the bringing about of a "substantial increase in the number of women and minorities in broadcasting and cable television jobs," the monitoring of FCC employment practice guidelines, and "to alert the FCC to stations and cable systems making little or no effort to hire, train or promote minorities and women, and to press the Commission to take action against such operators."[55]

The UCC said in its letter to the volunteers:

> With the enclosed EEO *Action Guide* we hope to study hiring, job classification and promotion of minorities and women at every radio and television station and every cable system across the country . . . Our ultimate goal is to bring about a substantial increase in the number of minorities and women who are in jobs in broadcasting and cable where policy decisions are made.[56]

The project questionnaire included extensive reporting requirements and directions to participants with instructions which told volunteers about stations' public inspection files:

> These files contain copies of license renewal applications and other official documents describing the station's ownership, programming and employment practices. They are kept at the station's main studio or other locations in the community, and must be available for examination at all times during regular business hours. Any member of the public may use the station's public inspection files.[57]

Within the 16-page questionnaire were extensive data-gathering strategies including an interview with the station's general manager with such questions as: "What job titles are included by this station under each of the top five job categories?" And: "What are the sex and minority group identifications for the persons holding each job title?"[58] Adding endorsed support for the UCC project were the Black Citizens for Fair Media, an attorney advising Hispanic community groups, and the Media Project of the Legal Defense and Education Fund of the National Organization for Women.[59] In another study presented to the House of Representatives Subcommittee on Telecommunications, the UCC presented evidence it said showed the FCC's deregulatory policies were not working and that the goal of localism and local origination programming had not developed as the FCC planned.[60]

LOCAL CITIZEN GROUPS

While large, formal organizations work toward broadcast reform at the national level, many smaller, less visible groups work at the local level to accomplish similar goals. Local groups of parents or community leaders in small communities are gathering financial support from foundations to conduct television awareness seminars, program monitoring, and negotiations with local stations. The size of these groups can range anywhere from a few concerned parents to hundreds of supporters. In some cases, the local groups align themselves with national groups. Others remain independent.

Cable television, because it is regulated at the local level, is often the genesis for local citizen action. In Denver, Colorado, a local group called Citizens for Open Cable was formed during hearings on who would be awarded the Denver cable franchise. The group joined with the Mountain States Legal Foundation in filing a suit challenging the awarding of the cable franchise in what was termed a *de facto permit* to provide cable service to a half-million residents.[61] In Raleigh, North Carolina a citizen group called Citizens for Competitive Bidding launched a petition drive to force the city to stop negotiations with the current cable franchise holder and seek bids from other companies.[62] In Raleigh, as in other cities, a sufficient number of petitions can force local government to hold a referendum on an issue and submit the matter to the voters.

SCOPE OF CITIZEN GROUP ACTIVITIES

While focusing national attention on broadcasting issues is one function of citizen and public-interest groups, they may also become more directly involved in the operation of stations and cable systems.

Petitions to Deny

Except for attempting to block the sale of a station or set standards for who should buy one, filing a Petition to Deny at license renewal time is among the most complicated and expensive ventures in which citizen groups take part. Although any individual has the right to respond to a proposed license renewal, filing a Petition to Deny a renewal is a serious undertaking. Citizen groups which do file such petitions have the advice of an attorney and the ability to pay for that advice, not only at the local level, but also in Washington, DC. Despite the complexity and expense, many citizen groups are actively involved in license proceedings.

The types of issues involved in Petitions to Deny are varied. One of the most frequent is discrimination in employment. It is relatively easy by using employment reports to determine the percentage of minority employees in a particular station and to determine whether or not it meets its quota, based on the percentage of minority group members in the population served by the station. Somewhat harder to prove are discrimination charges concerning particular individuals.

In one instance, citizen groups presented 25 stations in Tennessee and Indiana with eight separate Petitions to Deny, charging that the stations had discriminated against blacks in both employment and programming services.[63] One of the petitions charged concentration of ownership of broadcasting and newspaper interests, while others zeroed in on employment and service to the black community.[64] The Indiana challenges charged a station with firing a black announcer and then changing the format of a jazz and black literature program that the announcer had created.[65] The FCC, however, has mostly remained out of format issues and gives the local station wide latitude to program whatever it wants to.

Discrimination in employment was charged by the National Organization of Women (NOW) in petitions filed against two network-owned stations.[66] When the FCC failed to act with sufficient speed on the petitions, the U.S. Court of Appeals stated that the lack of action amounted to rejection of the petition and commanded the FCC to act. Other groups have used the courts to pressure the FCC into action. When the Feminists for Media Rights of Lancaster, Pennsylvania, had waited 14 months for the FCC to act on a petition against a Lancaster TV station, they took the matter to the U.S. Court of Appeals. Charges in their petition included undue concentration of ownership in broadcasting and newspapers, as well as interests involving cable television.[67]

In many cases, the money to fight a license challenge as well as the enthusiasm of the group's organizers runs out, and stations win by default. In still other cases, the petitions contain errors, which detract from the overall credibility of the challenges. Courts have criticized petitions for generalities, and even for such basic mistakes as listing the wrong owner or even the wrong city served by a station. Nevertheless, petitions are something with which broadcasters must contend. The amateur efforts of the past are being replaced by experienced groups, who are willing and able to challenge broadcasters.

Influencing Program Decision Makers

Other citizen groups work toward changing broadcast programming through such means as access to program producers, influencing FCC policy and decision making, or having access to the airwaves in order to produce their own programming.

Morality in Media launched a direct-mail campaign against obscene and indecent material on cable TV. A pretested letter sent to a list of 44,000 known donors to causes and subscribers to religious publications paid for itself in return contributions. The group sent another mailing to approximately 200,000 people using former Dallas Cowboy's quarterback Roger Staubach as a spokesperson. Staubach asked readers to return an enclosed postcard to their mayors (local government awards cable franchises). The letter also asked for contributions to support the group's battle against what it called pornography on cable television. Staubach's letter suggested that "local controls are necessary since the Federal Communications Commission, the courts, many states and communities, keep passing the buck on the pornography issue, particularly on cable's public access channels and on the pay networks."[68] Examples of unfit programming cited in the letter were a young man offering "services" of other men and boys, women being tied and beaten and raped, demonstrations of deviant sexual acts, and sexual bondage. R-rated movies were also criticized in a published interview with the Rev. Morton Hill, president of Morality in Media, who was quoted as saying many of the R-rated films "include sex scenes showing everything except actual penetration. Neither these sequences nor scenes of simulated intercourse or sodomy should be allowed on the home screen . . ."[69]

Network programming's portrayal of women has been criticized by the National Commission on Working Women, saying that one season's shows portrayed a world of "male buddies where women are invisible, irrelevant or victimized."[70] Administering a program of "Alice Awards" to promote and reward programs which do portray women in a way seen as positive by the commission, the organization uses a strategy of publicly recognizing what it considers good programs while speaking out against objectionable ones. Comments about one group of Alice Award winners included statements that stations have reached a new level of maturity where it isn't necessary to have a billboard flashing "women's issue" because such issues are in the mainstream. "When a reporter announces that the evening news feature highlights an employment issue—whether it's pension problems, sexual harassment or the effects of layoffs on last-hired workers—today that reporter is more likely to say that the issue just happens to affect women disproportionately."[71] Although groups such as Morality in Media and the National Commission on Working Women do not have regulatory control over programming, their influence nevertheless can be felt in the programming marketplace. Producers and directors, while needing to be conscious of profits, are also sensitive to bad publicity and the good publicity and prestige that come from winning awards. At the same time, television can be a high-visibility issue which can aid in raising money for the organization.

In addition to direct-mail campaigns and awards programs, public-interest groups at both the local and national level can put pressure on broadcasters. For example, during the brief Gulf War of 1991, CNN reporter Peter Arnett remained in Baghdad, Iraq and reported the war for CNN. Because Arnett's reports were considered by some to come from "enemy territory" they were criticized as being anti-American. A coalition of groups described as "pro-American" tried to force Arnett out of Baghdad through, among other tactics, newspaper ads asking "Are You Outraged?" and calling Arnett "The U.S. Voice of Baghdad." Accuracy in Media Chairman Reed Irvine called for a boycott of CNN, urged the public to contact CNN parent company head Ted Turner, and was quoted as saying that Arnett's broadcasts were helping to spread Iraq's propaganda in America. The intensity of Accuracy in Media's rhetoric heated up with Irvine claiming that during wartime the rules change and the press cannot remain neutral. Besides Accuracy in Media, such groups as The Victory Committee, the American Conservative Union, American Defense Foundation, Americans for High Frontier, Blinded American Veterans Foundation, Vietnam Veterans Institute, Conservative Congressional Committee, and Concerned Women of America were all reported as participating in the effort.[72]

Stations in Miami and Chicago made programming and management decisions after groups of black citizens became involved in a movement to change programming and management. A Miami, Florida television station dropped the program *Crime Check* after it was criticized by a coalition of black leaders for portraying blacks unfairly.[73] The president of the Miami-Dade branch of the NAACP and a coalition of black groups called Summit 2000 claimed the stations programming was insensitive to blacks. The station replaced the program with another show which it said had broader coverage. In Chicago, civil rights spokesman, the Rev. Jesse Jackson, joined a local Operation PUSH-organized boycott against a network-owned Chicago station after the station demoted a black anchor because of ratings. The network appointed a black general manager for the station and Jackson claimed credit.

Monitoring Broadcast Programming

An alternative action for citizen groups has been to monitor broadcast programming, especially sex and violence on television. In one early effort in the late 1970s the National Parent Teacher Association (PTA) launched a national awareness effort to alert its members and the public to both the effects of violence on television and to the advertisers who supported violence with their ads.[74] The PTA first held a series of hearings around the United States, at which experts and the public discussed the effects of television violence. Then came the list of programs and sponsors. Sterling Drug Co. was named the "most offensive" advertiser because it placed its ads in programs the PTA raters considered to be low in quality and high on violence. Shows which showed up on the PTA's most-violent list included the police series *Starsky and Hutch*, the detective program *Charlie's Angels*, and the adventure show *Wonder Woman*. Some programs were also criticized for their "sexploitation." Programs praised as "most commendable" included the family-oriented *Little House on the Prairie*.[75]

The PTA also criticized commercials. Addressing advertisers sponsoring prime-time programming, the PTA said,

> The type of commercial most offensive was the feminine hygiene product, frequently advertised during prime-time. Teenagers watching television with dates, in either a family setting or amid peers, were most disturbed and embarrassed. Even mature women found the ads distressing and felt

> that the market was not so competitive nor the purchasers so sparse that companies would suffer from limiting their advertising to appropriate print media.[76]

The PTA also recognized advertisers which sponsored three or more of the "exemplary" shows and avoided low-quality shows.

On the issue of sex on radio, the Reverend Jesse Jackson came out against what was reported as "flagrant abuses of responsibility in the record industry where sex and violence is concerned."[77] Jackson saw a relationship between suggestive sexy lyrics and rhythms and responsibility among youths. A threatened boycott was used to attempt to change such lyrics and to alert the radio stations that might play such songs.

Television producers have also been the object of citizen group criticism. When Norman Lear decided to drop John Amos, who played the father figure in the comedy series *Good Times*, the National Black Media Coalition based in Washington, DC said it would look into the possibility of boycotting products advertised on the show. A press release from the coalition said black children need positive black male images, and that taking the father out of the show would eliminate TV's only positive black adult male character.[78] Lear claimed that the father figure in *The Jeffersons* and Fred Sanford in *Sanford and Sons* were positive black male images, but the coalition disagreed. The issue became somewhat moot when John Amos left the show to star in the highly acclaimed *Roots*, a series about the emergence of a black family from their African heritage into the twentieth century.

Encouraging Responsible Consumers

Part of the PTA's involvement in the citizen movement has included teaching interested members how to react to television at the local level, how to identify programming which contains excessive sex or violence, and how to communicate with government, the broadcasters, and advertisers. Other organizations have used similar measures to pressure for change by educating the public on what to watch for and how to react. A similar strategy of placing the responsibility on the consumer is promoted by a San Francisco citizen group, the Committee on Children's Television. Some of the questions as part of their "Guidelines for Selecting Television for Children" ask:[79] Does the program appeal to the audience for whom it is intended? Does the program present racial groups positively and does it show them in situations that enhance the Third World child's self-image? Does the program present gender roles and adult roles positively? Does the program present conflict that a child can understand and does it demonstrate positive techniques for resolving conflict?

The Christian Life Commission of the Southern Baptist Convention sponsors a campaign to help people be critical consumers of television programs. Some of the recommendations for responsible television viewing include: (l) study personal television viewing patterns and keep a record of programs watched to determine the amount of time spent with television; (2) plan television viewing and use the time responsibly by turning television on only for specific programs, thus controlling it instead of its controlling you; (3) parents should discuss commercials with children, guiding them against materialism; (4) families should watch television together and then discuss issues encountered in life.

The Center for Population Options based in Studio City, California issued a "Guide for Responsible Content in Television," designed to sensitize the industry to the importance of positive portrayals of sex for the purpose of helping to control teenage pregnancy. The center's suggestions include, among others:

> Sex should be recognized as a healthy and natural part of life. Parent and child conversations about sex are important and healthy and should be encouraged. It should be shown that not only the young, unmarried and beautiful have sexual relationships. Not all affection and touching must culminate in sex. Couples having sexual relationships should be portrayed with feelings of affection, love and respect for each other. Consequences of unprotected sex should be discussed or shown.[80]

The sexual aids suggestions appeared in trade publications and were published by the Caucus for Producers, Directors and Writers.

The examples of these and other citizen groups' efforts provide a wide latitude for action. The groups are not directly involved in changing or even lobbying for broadcast regulation. Rather, they encourage the public to take the responsibility and consume with care. While many people feel that the bureaucracy of government and the networks prevent any opportunity for change, they can see the value of the individual and parental approach to controlling how television affects their daily lives.

PERSPECTIVES ON THE FUTURE OF THE CITIZEN MOVEMENT

The future of the citizen movement and its effect on broadcast regulation and policy are tied to a number of important questions. Among them: Do citizen groups really represent broad constituencies? Does even a very popular citizen group with several thousand members speak on issues representative of an entire national population? Even if such groups do represent issues salient to larger populations, is the larger population that much concerned, and does it feel deeply enough about those issues to warrant changes in programming or policy? These questions become even more important when citizen groups become involved in challenging broadcasters at license renewal time. Here, small groups can get down to very specific measures, designed to change the operation and programming of a station. A frequent criticism of citizen groups is that do not represent large groups of individuals and therefore should not be given the weight they receive in policy making. Another criticism is whether the citizen group is concerned primarily with raising money rather than improving the quality broadcasting.

SETBACKS FROM DEREGULATION

One of the more powerful weapons citizen groups had at their disposal was the Fairness Doctrine. In general terms the Fairness Doctrine required broadcasters to provide equal time to the coverage of local issues which had a significant impact on the community they serve. The FCC has since stopped enforcing the Fairness Doctrine, yet there remain vestiges of political support in Congress to make the doctrine law. The time between license renewals has been lengthened, which forces citizen groups to intervene in a station's operating procedures at much longer intervals than in the past. Ownership requirements have been changed dramatically, especially in radio where the FCC has increased the number of stations any one owner can hold. Where once the major commercial networks such as CBS, NBC, and ABC commanded a large share of the viewing audience, citizen groups could exert widespread change by putting pressure at the network level. Since the 1970s, network viewing has decreased from the 90 percent range to the 60 percent range, resulting in more fragmented audiences. New technologies, smaller and smaller subgroups within the mass audience, changes in regulatory posture, and broadcaster skill in dealing with citizen group challenges will all play significant roles in the future life of citizen groups and professional associations who influence through nonregulatory ways the content of radio and television programming.

SUMMARY

Codes of ethics exist at national and international levels and provide a means whereby professional societies and organizations can influence the content of broadcast programming as well as set practitioner standards for their membership. The ethics laws that govern the activities of FCC employees deal with such areas as gifts and entertainment, financial interests, use of government property, misuse of information, indebtedness, gambling and betting, playing the lottery, and other measures. The American Bar Association Code of Judicial Conduct contains canons which govern the conduct of judges in such areas as integrity, impartiality, quasi-judicial activities, extra-judicial activities, reporting compensation, and political activity.

Two business and professional codes are those of the Business and Professional Advertising Association and the American Advertising Federation. Among other provisions the BPAA code stresses that no form of advertising should appear that contains false, exaggerated, or misleading statements. The BPAA code also discourages advertising that unfairly disparages products or any advertising that plays on superstitions. The AAF code is more detailed and deals with such subjects as truth, responsibility, taste and decency, disparagement, bait advertising, guarantees and warranties, price claims, unprovable claims, and testimonials.

The Advertising Code of the International Chamber of Commerce is a model that many countries have incorporated into their own statutes governing the content of advertising, both broadcast and print. Some of the provisions of the code include the requirement that advertising should be legal, decent, honest, and truthful. In addition the code calls for advertisements not to abuse the trust of the consumer or exploit a consumer's lack of experience and knowledge, not to take unfair advantage of the goodwill attached to the trade name or logo of another firm, and not to exploit the natural credulity of children or the lack of experience of young people.

Economic and political pressure impacts on self-regulation in advertising. For example, companies can limit their sponsorship of programs which contain what the company feels is too much violence or sexual content. Vlasic Foods and Jovan, Inc. were some of the first companies to register their dissatisfaction with this type of programming. The New York State Assembly became involved in broadcast issues when it challenged broadcasters in New York state to pledge in their license renewals that they would carry public-service advertisements promoting nutrition.

The National Advertising Division and the National Advertising Review Board emphasize self-regulation by hearing deceptive advertising claims much in the same way the Federal Trade Commission does. The difference, however, is in the fact that a federal agency is not involved. A finding against an advertiser by the Federal Trade Commission can bring substantial fines, to say nothing of the loss experienced through high legal bills and sometimes being required to cease advertising the product altogether.

As press organizations, the Radio-Television News Directors Association and the Society of Professional Journalists both have codes of ethics. The RTNDA represents broadcast journalists in both legislative and professional endeavors. The RTNDA code calls on broadcast journalists to gather and report the news accurately, honestly, and impartially. More specific to the RTNDA code are subparts which call on members to evaluate information solely on its merits as news, guard against using audio or video material in a way that deceives the audience, label opinion and commentary, and acknowledge and correct errors. The ethics code of the Society of Professional Journalists deals with such areas as responsibility, freedom of the press, ethics, accuracy and objectivity, fair play, and mutual trust. The society, like the RTNDA is actively involved in lobbying efforts on First Amendment issues and the two organizations frequently join together in filing friend of the court briefs on issues of interest to journalists. Other professional organizations have standards which apply to their members. American Women in Radio and Television and Women in Communication, Inc. are two examples. Wire service associations such as the Associated Press Broadcasters also sensitize members to issues affecting broadcast journalism.

Press councils perform watchdog functions over both broadcast and print journalism. The National News Council came into existence in 1973 during a time when states were dealing with reporters' shield laws, the networks were being criticized for monopolistic practices, and journalists were being jailed for refusing to divulge their sources. The NNC receives no government support and relies on publicity and professional support to perform its functions of overseeing the press. State press councils also exist, one of the earlier ones being in Minnesota. Over the years state and local press councils have appeared in such places as Bend, Oregon and Redwood City, California.

Another important arena in self-regulation are citizen and public-interest groups. These organizations can be broad in scope and deal with all broadcast programming, or be more narrowly focused and deal with a specific aspect of programming, such as children's programming. The citizen and public-interest movement gained significant ground in the 1966 case brought by the United Church of Christ which gave citizen groups the authority to intervene and take an active part in FCC proceedings. Citizen and public-interest groups participate in a wide range of activities including becoming involved in station license renewals. When a station fails to meet its programming commitments or affirmative action requirements, it can find its license being challenged at renewal time. Even if the station wins, the publicity can be damaging in the marketplace. Direct attempts to influence program decision makers, monitor broadcast programming, boycott advertisers, and engage in campaigns to encourage responsible consumers are all within the scope of citizen groups. Citizen groups have achieved a number of reforms in broadcast programming, station operations, and policy making.

MATERIAL FOR ANALYSIS

ETHICS LAWS GOVERNING THE FEDERAL COMMUNICATIONS COMMISSION

Ethical conduct expected of FCC employees has been made part of federal law and all FCC employees fall under one or more provisions of the law. The federal statutes deal with such actions as gifts and entertainment, financial interests, use of government property, misuse of information, indebtedness, gambling and betting, playing the lottery, and general conduct prejudicial to the government. In excerpting the material which follows, part, section, and subsection designations have been deleted. Readers wanting the complete text with section designations should consult 47 CFR Part 19.

Under "Ethical and Other Conduct and Responsibilities of Employees" federal regulations state:

SPECIFIC PROVISIONS

The regulations issued under this subpart contain provisions covering the standards of and governing the ethical and other conduct of FCC employees . . . They are not meant to restrict unduly a Commission employee's social activities. Each employee must judge for himself whether his social activities may or may not compromise or appear to compromise his position as a public servant.

PROSCRIBED ACTIONS

An employee shall avoid any action, whether or not specifically prohibited by this subpart, which might result in, or create the appearance of:

(a) Using public office for private gain;

(b) Giving preferential treatment to any person;

(c) Impeding government efficiency or economy;

(d) Losing complete independence or impartiality;

(e) Making a government decision outside official channels; or

(f) Affecting adversely the confidence of the public in the integrity of the government.

GIFTS, ENTERTAINMENT, AND FAVORS

. . . an employee shall not solicit or accept, directly or indirectly, any gift, gratuity, favor, entertainment, loan, or any other thing of monetary value, from a person who:

(1) Has, or is seeking to obtain, contractual or other business or financial relations with the Commission;

(2) Conduct operations or activities that are regulated by the Commission; or

(3) Has interests that may be substantially affected by the performance or nonperformance of his (the employee's) official duty; or

(4) Is in any way attempting to affect the employee's official actions at the Commission; or

(5) Is offering anything of monetary value to an employee because of the employee's official position . . . .

FAMILY ASSOCIATIONS, LOANS, OTHER GIFTS

(1) Where obvious family (such as those between the parents, children, or spouse of the employee and the employee) or other personal relationships make it clear that it is those relationships rather than the business of the persons concerned which are the motivating factors;

(2) Food and refreshments, not lavish in kind, may be accepted when: (i) offered free in the course of a meeting or other group function, not connected with an inspection of investigation, at which attendance is desirable because it will assist the Commission employee in performing his or her official duties; or (ii) provided to all panelists or speakers when a Commission employee is participating as a panelist or speaker in a program, seminar or educational conference. The Commission's Office of General Counsel shall make a prior written determination as to the propriety of accepting invitations from regulated entities or interested persons as described in (statutes) and shall keep a log of its decisions. Approval may be requested by any Commission employee or the organizer of the group function;

(3) Loans may be obtained from banks or other financial institutions on customary terms to finance proper and usual activities of employees, such as home mortgage loans;

(4) Unsolicited advertising or promotional material such as pens, pencils, note pads, calendars and other items of nominal intrinsic value may be accepted, as well as literature relating to the communications field.

(5) Gifts given for participation in a program, seminar or educational conference may be accepted only when such gifts are: remembrance traditional to the particular sponsoring entity; (iii) provided to all participants in the program . . .

An employee shall not solicit a contribution from another employee for a gift to an official superior, make a donation as a gift to an official superior, or accept a gift from an employee receiving less pay than himself. However, this paragraph does not prohibit a voluntary gift of nominal value or donation in a nominal amount made on a special occasion such as marriage, illness, or retirement.

An employee shall not accept a gift, present, decoration, or other thing from a foreign government unless authorized by Congress as provided by the Constitution . . .

(This section does not preclude) an employee from receipt of bona fide reimbursement, unless prohibited by law, for expenses of travel and such other necessary subsistence as is compatible with this part for which no Government payment or reimbursement is made. However, this paragraph does not allow an employee to be reimbursed, or payment to be made on his behalf, for excessive personal living expenses, gift, entertainment, or other personal benefits, . . .

OUTSIDE EMPLOYMENT AND OTHER ACTIVITY

The Commissioners are prohibited from engaging in any other business, vocation, profession, or employment. No Commissioner or employee of the Commission is permitted to be in the employ of or hold any official relation to any person subject to any of the provisions of the Communications Act. In addition, no commissioner or employee of the Commission may engage in outside employment or other outside activity, with or without compensation, which is in conflict with or otherwise not compatible with the full and proper discharge of his duties and responsibilities as a Commission employee. Incompatible activities include but are not limited to:

(1) Acceptance of a fee, compensation, gift, payment of expenses, or any other thing of monetary value in circumstances in which acceptance may result in, or create the appearance of a conflicts of interest situation; or

(2) Outside employment which tends to impair his mental or physical capacity to perform his Commission duties and responsibilities in an acceptable manner; or

(3) Outside employment or activities (excluding the publication of articles) which reasonably might be regarded as official actions or bring discredit upon the Commission.

No professional employee of the Commission shall engage in the private practice of his profession unless specifically authorized by the Commission. Requests for such authorizations shall, in the case of employees generally, be submitted to the Head of the Office or Bureau to which the employee is assigned; in the case of an employee in the immediate office of a Commissioner to the Commissioner. All pertinent facts regarding the proposed employment, such as the name of the employer, the nature of the work to be performed, and the amount of time involved shall be set forth.

Employees of the Commission are encouraged to engage in teaching, lecturing and writing that is not prohibited by law, the Executive Order, the Office of Personnel Management Regulations or the provisions of this chapter. However, an employee shall not, either with or without compensation, engage in teaching lecturing or writing (including such as is involved in the preparation of a person or class of persons for a Office of Personnel Management or Foreign Service examination) that is dependent on information obtained as a result of his Government employment, except when that information has been made available to the general public or will be made available on request, or when the Chairman gives written authorization for the use of nonpublic information on the basis that its use is in the public interest. Except in the case of a Commissioner, articles which identify the author as a Commission employee shall include the following disclaimer:

The views expressed are those of the author and do not necessarily reflect the view of the Commission.

Documents prepared in the course of, and publications relating to, an employee's official duty shall not be used for his private gain. In addition, the Commissioners shall not receive compensation or anything of monetary value for any consultation, lecture, discussion, writing, or appearance the subject matter of which is devoted substantially to the responsibilities, programs, or operations of the Commission, or which draws substantially on official data or ideas which have not become part of the body of public information . . .

FINANCIAL INTERESTS

An employee of the Commission shall not have a direct or indirect financial interest that conflicts substantially, or appears to conflict substantially, with his Government duties and responsibilities.

An employee of the Commission shall not engage in, directly or indirectly, a financial transaction as a result of, or primarily relying on, information obtained through his Government employment.

No member of the Commission or person employed by the Commission shall: (i) Be financially interested in any company or other entity engaged in the manufacture or sale of telecommunications equipment which is subject to regulation by the Commission; (ii) Be financially interested in any company or other entity engaged in the business of communication by wire or radio or in the use of the electromagnetic spectrum; (iii) Be financially interested in any company or other entity which controls any company or other entity specified in clause (i) or clause (ii), or which derives a significant portion of its total income from ownership of stocks, bonds, or other securities of any such company or other entity; or (iv) Be employed by, hold any official relation to, or own any stocks, bonds, or other securities of, any person significantly regulated by the Commission under this act; . . .

Except that the prohibitions established in this subparagraph shall apply only to financial interests in any company or other entity which has a significant interest in communications, manufacturing, or sales activities which are subject to regulation by the Commission.

To determine whether an entity has a significant interest in communications related activities that are subject to Commissions regulations, the Commission shall consider, without excluding other relevant factors . . . These criteria include: (i) The revenues and efforts directed toward the telecommunications aspect of the business; (ii) The extent of Commission regulation over the entity involved; (iii) The potential economic impact of any Commission action on that particular entity; and (iv) The public perception regarding the business activities of the company.

FINANCIAL INTEREST OF COMMISSION EMPLOYEES

(In summary) . . . the main conflict of interest provisions applying to financial interests (of Commission employees) are:

(1) An employee may not, except in the discharge of his official duties, represent anyone else before a court or Government agency in a matter in which the United States is a party or has an interest. This prohibition applies both to paid and unpaid representation of another.

This prohibition does not extend to a (a) representation of another person, without compensation, in a disciplinary, loyalty, or other personnel matter; or (b) the giving of testimony under oath or from making statements required to be made under penalty for perjury or contempt.

This prohibition may be waived under the express approval of the Government official responsible for his appointment in the case of an employee who represents, with or without compensation, his own parents, spouse or child or a person or estate he serves as a fiduciary, but only as to matters in which the employee has not participated personally and substantially as a Government employee and which are not the subject of his official responsibility.

An employee may not participate in his governmental capacity in any matter in which he, his spouse, minor child or outside business associate has a financial interest. This prohibition shall not apply if the employee advises the Government official responsible for his appointment of the nature of the matter, makes full disclosure of the financial interest, and receives advance a written determination that the interest is not so substantial as to be deemed likely to affect the integrity of the employee's services.

An employee may not participate in his governmental capacity in any matter in which a person from whom he has accepted employment, or with whom he is negotiating for employment, has a financial interest. At the outset of negotiations with such a prospective employer, the employee shall notify his immediate supervisor. The supervisor shall review the employee's current assignments and responsibilities and discharge him from any assignments that could affect the interests of the prospective employer. The employee shall thereupon file a statement of disqualification and non-participation . . . The statement shall continue in effect until such time (if any) as the negotiations are unsuccessfully terminated.

An employee may not receive any salary, or supplementation of his Government salary, from a private source as compensation for his services to the Government. (i) This prohibition will not prevent an employee from continuing to participate in a bona fide pension plan or other employee welfare or benefit plan maintained by a former employer. (ii) This prohibition is not applicable to anyone serving the Government without compensation or to contributions, awards, or other expenses under the term of the Government Employees Training Act . . .

USE OF GOVERNMENT PROPERTY

An employee of the Commission shall not directly or indirectly use, or allow the use of, Government property of any kind, including property leased to the government, for other than officially approved activities. An employee has a positive duty to protect and conserve Government property, including equipment, supplies, and other property entrusted or issued to him.

MISUSE OF INFORMATION

Except as provided . . . or as authorized by the Commission, an employee shall not, directly or indirectly, disclose to any person outside the Commission any information, or any portion of the contents of any document, which is part of the Commission's records or which is obtained through or in connection with his Government employment, and which is not routinely available to the public and, with the same exceptions, shall not use any such documents or information except in the conduct of his official duties. Conduct intended to be prohibited by this section includes, but is not limited to, the disclosure of information about the content of agendas items (except for compliance with the Government in the Sunshine Act), or other staff papers to persons outside the Commission and disclosure of actions or decisions made by the Commission at closed meetings or by circulation, prior to the public release of such information. This section does not prohibit the release of an official commission meeting agenda listing titles and summaries of items for discussion at an open Commission meeting. Also, this section does not prohibit the release of information about the scheduling of Commission agenda items.

INDEBTEDNESS

An employee shall pay each just financial obligation in a proper and timely manner, especially one imposed by law such as Federal, State, or local taxes. For the purpose of this section, a "just financial obligation" means one acknowledged by the employee or reduced to judgement by a court, and "in a proper and timely manner" means in a manner which the Commission determines does not, under the circumstances, reflect adversely on the Government as his employer. In the event of a dispute between an employee and an alleged creditor, this section does not require the Commission to determine the validity or amount of the disputed debt.

GAMBLING, BETTING, AND LOTTERIES

An employee of the Commission shall not participate, while on Government-owned or leased property or while on duty for the Commission, in any gambling activity including the operation of a gambling device, in conducting a lottery or pool, in a game for money or property, or in selling or purchasing a numbers slip or ticket . . . However, this section does not preclude activities: (a) Necessitated by an employee's law enforcement duties; . . .

GENERAL CONDUCT PREJUDICIAL TO THE GOVERNMENT

An employee of the Commission shall not engage in criminal, infamous, dishonest, immoral, or notoriously disgraceful conduct, or other conduct prejudicial to the Commission or to the Government.

QUESTIONS FOR CRITICAL ANALYSIS

- Although critics would be quick to point out any unnecessary growth in the federal bureaucracy, might there be justification for splitting off the common carrier services (telephone, telegraph) of the FCC into a separate regulatory agency and permit the FCC to concentrate its efforts more on radio and television broadcast stations?
- Should the Field Operations Bureau of the FCC have the authority to revoke a license?
- Is the communications field any more "crucial" and "dynamic" than other industries regulated by the government, such as the airlines or railroads?
- With the U.S. Constitution guaranteeing freedom of the press, is a code of ethics such as that subscribed to by RTNDA really necessary? If it is, what purpose does it serve?
- As new technologies, such as fiber optics and satellite communication, open up many more

channels of communication to the average consumer, will industry self-regulation be less or more important?

- If enough new channels of communication become operable through the technological advances of cable and satellite communication, could the government completely deregulate radio and television, letting self-regulation guide the future of the industry?
- If it develops that less government regulation *is* possible, what areas of broadcast operations or programming would self-regulation *not* be able to control effectively?
- A reported arrangement between CBS marketing and Coca-Cola resulted in a Coke machine being placed in the corridor of a school used in a program appealing to young adults. Two citizen groups criticized the use of the Coke machine as a commercial production that violated FCC regulations. CBS defended the arrangement, which was based on an agreement that Coke would also advertise heavily on the program, saying the marketing arrangement was listed in the credits. Should advertisers be permitted to place promotional products in a television program or should the FCC prohibit such placement on the grounds that it violates the rules requiring the identification of sponsors?
- The code of ethics of the Business and Professional Advertising Association bans vulgar and offensive advertising. How is it possible to determine if advertising is offensive?
- One provision of the American Advertising Federation Code requires testimonials to be "limited to those of competent witnesses who are reflecting a real and honest choice." What do you feel is meant by "a real and honest choice"?
- Comparative advertising, although to some extent controlled by the Federal Trade Commission, is an effective form of persuasive communication. Should comparative ads be regulated more closely than other types of advertising?
- Are boycotts of an advertiser's products an effective way to influence television programming on the local level?
- Can an organization sponsoring a boycott of an advertiser's products contribute to or hinder the effectiveness of the boycott, depending on the public's perception of the organization and its goals?
- Given that the First Amendment to the Constitution protects journalists in almost every phase of their profession, is it really necessary for any code of ethics to exist which in any way applies to the reporting process?
- Many educators belong to professional and educational associations. Should such associations have codes of ethics that apply to professors of journalism, communication, or media law? If so, what might those codes entail?
- Now that Action for Children's Television no longer exists, will other organizations be more or less effective in applying public influence on policy issues affecting children's television?
- What are the advantages of a church, such as the United Church of Christ, becoming involved in broadcast policy making?
- Are local public-interest and citizen groups, which are closely tied to the community a station serves, more effective in influencing the programming of that station than would be a national public-interest group?
- One of the 12 questions as part of its guidelines for selecting television for children of the National PTA asks if the program appeals to the audience for whom it is intended. (A program for 12-year-olds should be different from a program for 6-year-olds.) How could one determine into what age category a program falls?
- Some citizen and public-interest groups stress consumer awareness and the responsible consumption of television programming. Is this a better approach than trying to influence the programming of television stations?

ADDITIONAL RESOURCES

Chamberlain, B. F., "Lessons in Regulating Information Flow: The FCC's Weak Track Record in Interpreting the Public Interest Standard." 60 *North Carolina Law Review* 1057 (June 1982).

Charren, P., "Children's Advertising: Whose Hand Rocks the Cradle?" 56 *University of Cincinnati Law Review* 1251 (Spring 1988).

Farrington, D. G., "Private Plaintiffs and the Public Interest." 33 *Hastings Law Journal* 985 (March 1982).

Haring, J. R., and K. B. Levitz, "The Law and Economics of Federalism in Telecommunications." 41 *Federal Communications Law Journal* 261 (July 1989).

Lee, D. E., "Public Interest, Public Figures, and the Corporate Defamation Plaintiff." 81 *Northwestern University Law Review* 318 (Winter 1987).

Michalik, A. P., "The Public Interest Standard in the Communications Act and the Hearing Impaired." 25 *Boston College Law Review* 893 (July 1984).

Nader, R., and W. B. Schultz, "Public Interest Law with Bread on the Table." 71 *Denver University Law Review* 74 (February 1985).

chapter seventeen

The Lingering Fairness Debate

Closely related to Section 315, which we discussed earlier in this text, is the *Fairness Doctrine*. First issued in 1949, the Fairness Doctrine concerns itself with assuring the fair treatment of controversial issues of public importance.[1] Its current status is an outgrowth of both court cases and FCC inquiries dating back to 1941 with the famous *Mayflower* decision. The FCC re-examined the doctrine in 1964, 1974, and 1976 and then stopped enforcing the doctrine, reasoning that it was an undue burden and an abridgement of the First Amendment. Under the Clinton administration renewed efforts may take place to formally enact the doctrine into federal law. Currently the doctrine is repeated and not enforced. This chapter presents a history of the doctrine as well as the issues which are debated over its viability in an era of new technologies, more media outlets including cable and additional radio and television stations, and the ever-present First Amendment.

EARLY POLICIES ON FAIRNESS

The Federal Radio Commission, in discussing the limited spectrum space, noted that if issues "are of sufficient importance to the listening public, the microphone will undoubtedly be available. If not, a well-founded complaint will receive the careful consideration of the commission."[2] Concern over this fairness issue crystallized in 1941 with the *Mayflower* decision, involving station WAAB in Boston.[3] The Mayflower Broadcasting Corporation petitioned the FCC to give Mayflower the facilities of WAAB. Although the FCC ruled in favor of WAAB, the station was strongly criticized by the commission for its practice of "editorializing." The FCC stated that it is " . . . clear that with the limitations in frequencies inherent in the nature of radio, the public interest can never be served by a dedication of any broadcast facility to the support of his own partisan ends."[4] The FCC offered the opinion that: "A truly free radio cannot be used to advocate the causes of the licensee. . . . In brief, the broadcaster cannot be an advocate."[5] It is difficult to determine how many stations were editorializing in 1941, but the *Mayflower* decision successfully discouraged others from jumping on the editorial bandwagon.

While the *Mayflower* decision was stifling editorials, the Code of the National Association of Broadcasters was stifling discussion of controversial issues by prohibiting the purchase of commercials to air those issues. It wasn't long before one station was caught in a triangular conflict among the FCC, the NAB Code, and the First Amendment. Station WHKC in Columbus, Ohio, believing that it was operating in the public interest, adhered to the NAB Code and promptly found itself in a dispute with a labor union. The union claimed that the station had refused to sell it time and had censored the scripts it had submitted.

The union filed a petition against WHKC's license renewal. The FCC held a hearing on the matter in August 1944 and heard the argument about the NAB Code. By October, the union and the station had agreed to a compromise. The agreement broke with the code and prohibited any further censorship of scripts, dropping the station's policy that banned selling time for controversial issues. The agreement stated: "With respect to public issues of a controversial nature, the station's policy will be one of open-mindedness and impartiality."[6] It went on to state that the station would "make time available . . . on a commercial basis, for the full and free discussion of issues of public importance, including controversial issues. . . ." The FCC, in accepting the agreement, recognized that the radio spectrum was limited and not available to everyone who desired access. But it added that stations still had to make time available without censorship and without discrimination for a full discusssion of issues.

Further support for airing controversial issues occurred in 1946, when Robert Harold Scott of Palo Alto, California, filed a petition asking the FCC to revoke the licenses of radio stations KQW, KPO, and KFRC. Scott claimed that he wanted time to expound his views about atheism, providing a balance for the station's "direct statements and arguments against atheism as well as for indirect arguments, such as church services, prayers, Bible reading, and other kinds of religious programs."[7] Scott's petition did not result in the stations' license revocations, but the FCC did reaffirm in its decision its views on access and fairness and affirmed the freedom of speech clause of the First Amendment. The commission also stated that the mere fact of an issue being unpopular did not alleviate the broadcaster's responsibility to make time available for opposing views on "current controversial issues of public importance."

With the Scott and the WHKC decisions, the FCC made it clear that it expected stations to be responsive to issues that were controversial and of public importance and not to avoid them simply because they were unpopular. Still left unclear, however, was the whole subject of the *Mayflower* decision discouraging editorializing. The issue had its moot points since commentators had appeared for years and delivered statements on the air which could easily have been considered equivalent to editorializing.

ISSUING THE FAIRNESS DOCTRINE

The commission began to tackle the editorializing issue in March and April of 1948 when it held eight days of hearings on the subject. Other persons filed written motions. Out of these hearings came a statement issued by the FCC on June 1, 1949, under the heading: *In the Matter of Editorializing by Broadcast Licensees*. It was to become known as the *Fairness Doctrine*. In the doctrine, the commission reasserted its commitment to free expression of controversial issues of public importance, as stated in the WHKC and Scott decisions. It also *reversed* the *Mayflower* decision by supporting broadcast editorials. The commission came "to the conclusion that overt licensee editorialization, within reasonable limits and subject to the general requirements of fairness . . . , is not contrary to the public interest."[8] In the matter of Editoralizing by Broadcast Licensees, at the same time, it cautioned broadcasters against abuse of the editorial:

> It should also be clearly indicated that the question of the relationship of broadcast editorialization, . . . to operation in the public interest, is not identical with the broader problem of assuring "fairness" in the presentation of news, comment or opinion, but is rather one specific facet of this larger problem. . . . In the absence of a duty to present all sides of controversial issues, overt editorialization by station licensees could conceivably result in serious abuse. But where, as we believe to be the case under the Communications Act, such a responsibility for a fair and balanced presentation of controversial public issues exists, we cannot see how the open espousal of one point of view by the licensee should necessarily prevent him from affording a fair opportunity for the presentation of contrary positions or make more difficult the enforcement of the statutory standard of fairness upon any licensee.

What had been only one decade earlier the ultimate discouragement was now unqualified support for broadcasters to air their subjective views.

ADDITIONAL SUPPORT FOR FAIRNESS

As expected, complaints were soon filed with the FCC alleging abuse of the Fairness Doctrine. In 1950, the FCC inquired about the practice of a station broadcasting a series of programs supporting the National Fair Employment Practices Commission (NFEPC). The station replied that it had not presented the views of those opposing the NFEPC. The FCC informed the station that it had not acted properly. The NFEPC issue was of public importance simply because the station had broadcast so many programs on the subject. In short, it was a controversial issue of public importance, and the station had not been fair in presenting both sides.[9]

In another case, a station broadcast a series of programs about pay TV, with much of the content opposing pay TV. In an FCC hearing, the question arose of whether or not the station had complied with the requirements of the Fairness Doctrine with these programs. The station argued that although the pay TV issue was a controversial issue nationally, it did not feel that it was controversial to the local area served by the station. Again, the station was advised that it had not acted properly. And the FCC again noted that because the station had broadcast considerable programming about pay TV, it had elevated the issue to local importance. Moreover, after presenting a network program with balanced views on the subject, the station pre-empted local programming to present the views of a senator who was opposed to the issue "with the apparent design of neutralizing any possible public sympathy for pay TV which might have arisen from the preceding network forum."[10]

THE FAIRNESS PRIMER

In 1964, the FCC published its first set of guidelines since the Fairness Doctrine's inception in 1949. The 1964 document, commonly called the *Fairness Primer*, brought together the representative FCC rulings that had transpired over those years.[11] It gave people an opportunity to study the FCC's decisions, as well as shedding light on other stations' practices and policies, showing where complaints might be warranted, and guiding stations on how to meet Fairness Doctrine requirements.

Still waiting, however, was a major legal test of the constitutionality of the Fairness Doctrine. This came in an appeals court case in 1967, which reached the Supreme Court in 1969. Called the *Red Lion* decision, it affirmed the constitutionality of the Fairness Doctrine.[12]

THE *RED LION* DECISION

The *Red Lion* decision involved the Red Lion Broadcasting Company of Red Lion, Pennsylvania. In November 1964, the Reverend Billy James Hargis lashed out on Red Lion's radio station against the author of a book about Barry Goldwater. The author, Fred J. Cook, was held in low esteem by Hargis, who detailed what he felt to be the less favorable aspects of Cook's career as a writer. Cook contacted the station for a chance to reply to Hargis. But the station claimed that it did not have to offer free time to Cook unless he could prove that there was no commercial sponsorship available to present his views. Cook went to the FCC, which ruled in his favor, citing the Fairness Doctrine. In the case of *Red Lion Broadcasting Co.* v. *Federal Communications Commission*, the appeals court upheld the FCC's decision.

At that point, the Radio-Television News Directors Association entered the picture and appealed the case once more, this time to the United States Court of Appeals for the Seventh Circuit in Chicago. In the case of *Radio-Television News Directors Association* v. *United States*, the court ruled that the Fairness Doctrine's personal attack and editorial rules would "contravene the First Amendment."[13] But RTNDA's victory was short-lived. The FCC then took the case to the Supreme Court, which reviewed both the circuit and the appeals court decisions. The Supreme Court ruled:

> In view of the prevalence of scarcity of broadcast frequencies, the Government's role in allocating those frequencies, and the legitimate claims of those unable without governmental assistance to gain access to those frequencies for expression of their views, we hold the regulations and ruling at issue here are both authorized by statute and constitutional.[14]

With this, the Supreme Court upheld the FCC and reversed the decision in the RTNDA case. The Fairness Doctrine was now not only a broadcast regulation issued by the FCC but one that had been reaffirmed by judicial precedent by the highest court in the land.

PERSONAL ATTACK AND POLITICAL EDITORIALIZING

One area of the Fairness Doctrine that remained somewhat nebulous concerned the broadcast of direct personal attacks against individuals or organizations. In an attempt to clarify the responsibilities of broadcasters in this area, the FCC issued an advisee in July 1963 on how to handle personal attacks.[15] The advisee called upon broadcasters to transmit the text of the attack to the person or group attacked and to offer time for a reply. The same applied to editorials, and broadcasters were again reminded of their responsibilities for overall fairness.

But the advisee was just that—advice. The FCC felt that it needed to strengthen this advice into a requirement. So when the *Red Lion* issue came to the attention of the FCC, it decided that this was the time for a ruling. On August 14, 1967, the FCC's rules regarding personal attack went into effect and required a broadcaster to offer a responsible opportunity to respond to an attack on one's honesty, character, or integrity. A complete discussion of the personal attack rules appear in the chapter dealing with political and entertainment programming. The rules exempt foreign groups or foreign public figures, certain types of attacks made by political candidates during campaigns, and, with the same provisions as Section 315, various bona fide news events.

The FCC has extended the personal attack rule to cover comments made "in relation to" a given broadcast as well as on the broadcast itself. This extension occurred after a politician was called a "coward" by a talk show host two hours after a program on meat boycotts had been aired. The "coward" remark was in relation to the politician's participation in the boycott program. The FCC said that the station should have notified the politician about the charge, but the U.S. Court of Appeals overruled the FCC; saying that the commission had just extended the personal attack rule, and that the station could not have predicted the new interpretation. The court also said, however, that the rule *could* be extended in future incidents, and the FCC made it clear that this would become policy.[16] At the same time that it spelled out the new personal attack policy, the FCC also spelled out new rules covering editorials which require reasonable access for a qualified candidate to respond to an endorsement of his or her opponent. The political editorial rules are also found in the chapter dealing with political and entertainment programming.

With these 1967 rules, broadcasters know exactly what is expected of them when such incidents occur on their stations. They do, however, have the discretion to determine what constitutes a personal attack. Here, the FCC has permitted broadcast management to remain in charge of its local programming—if not carte blanche, at least somewhat uninhibited by a federal agency.

THE FAIRNESS DOCTRINE AND BROADCAST ADVERTISING

The FCC's position on the fairness issue is that the *overall* programming of a station should reflect its commitment to fairness, not just a single program. Advertising's role in this programming became a contested issue when WCBSTV was approached by New York lawyer, John W. Banzhaf, who requested equal time to reply to cigarette commercials. WCBS-TV refused to grant him time, but the FCC agreed with Banzhaf. The FCC's decision was upheld by the appeals court, which tried to confine the decision to cigarette advertising. But that was too much to hope for, and over the years, the Fairness Doctrine has been applied to many factions of advertising. Cigarette advertising was meanwhile banned on radio and television after 1971 by the Public Health Cigarette Smoking Act of 1969.

In another case, the Media Access Project, Inc. (MAP) contended that Georgia Power Company had sponsored ten commercials which lobbied for a rate increase pending before the Georgia Public Service Commission. MAP complained that two stations in Augusta, Georgia, had not met their obligations under the Fairness Doctrine by avoiding an effort to redress what MAP considered an imbalance of programming. The stations contended that the issue was not controversial, since the hearings on the rate increase were being held in Atlanta, not Augusta, which was the area served by the stations. They also suggested that the advertisements were "institutional" and thus not even covered under the Fairness Doctrine. Moreover, one of the stations had broadcast contrasting viewpoints on nine different occasions. The FCC, however, said that these programs were not enough to balance what it felt was a controversial issue. The commission directed the stations to inform it of what programming they had broadcast or intended to broadcast to present contrasting viewpoints on the issue.[17]

In a sweeping FCC order, eight California stations were caught in a Fairness Doctrine controversy over programming about nuclear power plants. At a time when people in California were being asked to sign a petition for a referendum on nuclear power plants, the stations aired commercials sponsored by the Pacific Gas and Electric Company. The commercials promoted nuclear power and power plants. Citizen action groups brought the matter to the FCC's attention and in 1974 filed an action against 13 stations. The commission found that five stations had presented the issue fairly, with programming advancing the antinuclear stand. Eight others were required to show the FCC how they intended to comply with the Fairness Doctrine. The commission felt that the issue was controversial and of public importance and it investigated "to the minute" the amount of time the stations had devoted to different sides of the issue.[18]

When Texaco sponsored commercials showing pieces of a puzzle being fitted together, and representing different phases of the oil industry, the FCC said that it was a controversial issue and aired at a time when legislation was pending in Congress to break up the oil companies. The complaint was filed by the Media Access Project against NBC, ABC, and Washington, DC stations WRC-TV and WTOP-TV. The FCC ruled in favor of the two networks and WRC, but said that WTOP-TV had to present viewpoints of those who favored the breakup of the oil companies.

But not all of the complaints against broadcasters have ended up in favor of the complainants. For example, a resident of Poland Springs, Maine, asked a local television station for equal time to present arguments against the use of snowmobiles. Snowmobiles had been advertised on the station as making winter "just one big fun-filled season."[19] The resident claimed that because the Maine legislature was considering a bill to regulate snowmobiles, and because the resident felt the machines to be dangerous to wildlife and vegetation, he should be able to present his views under the Fairness Doctrine. The FCC ruled that the commercials were standard product commercials, and that the resident was not entitled to air time. The appeals court upheld the FCC and said that the commercials were not directed toward the snowmobile controversy.

In another case, the Polish-American Congress, Inc. complained that the broadcasting of Polish jokes on ABC's *Dick Cavett Show* were actually attacks disguised as ethnic humor. The Broadcast Bureau of the FCC ruled that the jokes were not attacks on Polish-Americans, "since it had not been shown that there was any controversy in this country concerning the intelligence or other qualities of Polish-Americans."[20] The Polish-American Congress requested that the entire Commission review the ruling of its Broadcast Bureau. The request was denied, and the case went to the court of appeals. The court ruled that the jokes did not constitute a controversial issue and did not require the network to offer free time for a response. The Supreme Court refused to review the lower court's decision.

Three stations in San Francisco and two in Los Angeles became involved in a Fairness Doctrine complaint after broadcasting commercials for Chevron F-310 gasoline. Alan F. Neckritz and Lawrence B. Ordower of Berkeley, California, contended that the commercials presented only one side of a controversial issue: whether or not Chevron F-310 helped to solve air pollution. The FCC ruled that the commercials did not deal with a controversial issue of public importance, but instead were statements of a claim of product efficiency. Neckritz appealed to the Washington, DC circuit court. In a decision on June 28, 1974, the appeals court ruled in favor of the FCC.[21]

The FCC's decisions are not always upheld. When NBC broadcast its documentary, "Pensions: The Broken Promise," the FCC requested the network to indicate how it would meet its obligations under the Fairness Doctrine. NBC felt that it had been fair in presenting the documentary and should not be required to offer additional time on the matter. The network took the matter to court, and the court ruled in its favor. The appeals court "disagreed with the FCC's judgment that the documentary was unbalanced on the *broad issue* of overall pension plan performance for workers, and the network was reasonable in asserting that the documentary was on the *less controversial issue* of 'problems' with pensions."[22]

PENALTIES FOR ABUSE: THE WXUR DECISION

Although the FCC has a variety of sanctions to impose upon broadcasters who violate its rules, the most stringent is to deny renewal of a broadcast license. This maximum penalty was imposed on station WXUR in Media, Pennsylvania, after the FCC determined that the station had violated the Fairness Doctrine by openly criticizing groups and individuals, yet not informing them of their right to reply. The station had been operated by Brandywine Main Line Radio, Inc., which was wholly owned by the Faith Theological Seminary under the direction of fundamentalist preacher Carl McIntire. McIntire's group applied for ownership of the station in 1965, but the FCC approved the application only on the basis that the group would "provide the opportunity for the expression of opposing viewpoints on controversial public issues."[23] When renewal time arrived, citizens protested. The FCC revoked the station's license, finding that "Brandywine failed to establish any regular procedure for previewing, monitoring or reviewing its broadcasts, and thus did not regularly know what views were being presented on controversial issues of public importance."[24]

The FCC decision was appealed in *Brandywine-Main Line Radio, Inc.* v. *Federal Communications Commission*. The court upheld the FCC, pointing out that almost immediately after the new owners took over, the station started airing a series of programs characterized as "The Hate Clubs of the Air." The commission found the other evidence substantial and the public outcry considerable. One complaint was filed with the Media, Pennsylvania Borough Council, and the Pennsylvania legislature even passed a resolution condemning the programming practices of Carl McIntire.[25]

Despite the fact that the case represented a precedent for Fairness Doctrine penalties, one of the more widely quoted aspects of the case came in a dissenting opinion from Chief Judge Bazelon of the Washington, DC appeals court, which heard the *Brandywine* litigation. Bazelon believed that the decision to revoke the license was a prima facie affront to free speech and press. He suggested that the time had come for "the Commission to draw back and consider whether time and technology have so eroded the necessity for governmental imposition of Fairness obligations that the Doctrine has come to defeat its purpose in a variety of circumstances. . . ."[26] Two years later, the FCC issued a "re-evaluation" of the Fairness Doctrine.

One of the most celebrated cases occurred in West Virginia in 1976, when station WHAR was hit by a Fairness Doctrine complaint from, among others, Representative Patsy Mink, who was supporting anti-strip-mining legislation in Congress. In the *Patsy Mink* case, the FCC ruled in favor of the complainants in one of the best examples of how the commission could assert its authority and affirm a station's duty not only to air but to seek out issues of importance to a local community. In the *Patsy Mink* case, the FCC itself determined what was and was not an important issue in Clarksburg, West Virginia. It found that strip mining was important, and determined that the issue came under the Fairness Doctrine.

THE FAIRNESS REPORT: 1974

Undoubtedly sensing the consternation of broadcasters, the public, and the courts over the Fairness Doctrine, the FCC filed a Notice of Inquiry in 1971, seeking opinions on the applicability and usefulness of the doctrine as well as its interpretations.[27] Out of the inquiry came a statement by the FCC in 1974, commonly known as the *Fairness Report*.[28] Broadcasters who thought the report might provide some relief from the Fairness Doctrine were disappointed. The commission did, however, attempt to clarify some of the issues that had raised problems. As it stands, the report is the document currently guiding broadcasters in meeting their obligations under the Fairness Doctrine.

Determining Adequate Time for Opposing Viewpoints

The report reiterated that the licensee had an "affirmative responsibility" to provide a "reasonable" amount of time for the presentation of important issues. Although it was still up to the licensee to determine how much time to devote to presentations, the report made it clear that the commission believes that the "medium can make a great contribution to an informed public opinion." But it was "not prepared to allow this purpose to be frustrated by broadcasters who consistently ignore their public interest responsibilities." The report regarded strict adherence to the Fairness Doctrine as the single most important requirement in the operation of a station and an essential element for license renewal.

The report also cautioned broadcasters against falling back on their network to meet fairness requirements. The responsibility could not be delegated to any other "person or group" or be "unduly fettered by contractual agreements. . . ." The FCC felt that "stations, in carrying out this responsibility, should be alert to the opportunity to complement network offerings with local programming on these issues, or with syndicated programming."

But how will these quasi-hands-off policies contribute to an informed public opinion? The commission felt that even though it was not requiring that equal time be made available, the requirement that contrasting viewpoints be provided would "greatly increase the likelihood that individual members of the public will be exposed to varying points of view."

Defining a Controversial Issue

One of the most difficult issues confronting the commission and broadcasters alike is just what constitutes a controversial issue. If you were a broadcaster, how would you determine this? First you would check the 1974 *Fairness Report* guidelines. For example, the mere fact that an issue is newsworthy and receives attention in the press does not necessarily mean that the Fairness Doctrine is applicable to it.[29] However, the amount of media coverage *is* something to consider. So is the amount of attention the issue receives from government officials and "other community leaders." But even with these factors, the broadcaster is still faced with a "subjective evaluation of the impact that the issue is likely to have on the community at large." The report specifies: "The licensee should be able to tell with a reasonable degree of objectivity, whether an issue is the subject of vigorous debate with substantial elements of the community in opposition to one another." Yet broadcasters and the public are cautioned that the "Fairness Doctrine was not designed for the purpose of providing a forum for private disputes of no consequence to the general public."

Identifying the Issue

Closely related to defining an issue is *identifying* it. That may seem quite simple, but often an issue is camouflaged by unrelated discussions. In recognizing this fact, the 1974 *Fairness Report* used the example of a community debate on a school bond issue:

> The broadcast presents a spokesman who forcefully asserts that new school construction is urgently needed and that there is also a need for substantial increases in teachers' salaries, both principal arguments advanced by proponents of the bond issue. The spokesman, however, does not explicitly mention or advocate passage of the bond issue. In this case, the licensee would be faced with a need to determine whether the spokesman had raised the issue of whether the school bonds should be authorized (which is controversial), or whether he had merely raised the question of whether present school facilities and teacher salaries are adequate (which might not be at all controversial).

How would you rule if you were managing a broadcasting station? According to the report: "The licensee's inquiry should focus not on whether the statement bears some tangential relevance to the school bond question, but rather on whether the statement in the context of the ongoing community debate, is so obviously and substantially related to the School bond issue as to amount to advocacy of a position on that question."

If, for example, the program was logged as a discussion of the school-bond issue, then there would be little question that the Fairness Doctrine would apply. If the spokesman was the chairperson of a committee actively supporting the bond issue, then this would be an instance to provide time to people opposing the issue. Regardless of the examples, the broadcaster has the final say, notwithstanding an FCC review, and every community and local issue presents its own set of problems.

Providing Opportunities for Contrasting Viewpoints

One of the hazy areas of the report deals with the way broadcasters provide time for opposing viewpoints. Perhaps here more than in any other area, the FCC has adopted a hands-off policy, staying away from strict reprisal unless the licensee has acted in an "arbitrary and unreasonable fashion." For the commission to interfere too heavily with this process would mean a head-on collision with the First Amendment, especially where news programming is concerned. Consequently, the report indicates that although "the Licensee has a duty to play a conscious and positive role in encouraging the presentation of opposing viewpoints," the FCC does not believe that it is necessary to establish a "formula" in locating spokespersons. If, on the other hand, the licensee does not present opposing viewpoints, then the FCC expects the broadcaster to be "prepared to demonstrate that he has made a diligent, good-faith effort. . . ."

The report also acknowledges that an issue may have more than two sides, and that the licensee has an obligation to present different opinions or "shades" of opinion. But the FCC reaffirms that "equal" time is not necessary: "we have long felt that the basic goal of creating an informed citizenry would be frustrated if for every controversial item or presentation on a newscast or other broadcast the licensee had to offer equal time to the other side." The report does specify certain actions which clearly are abuses of the Fairness Doctrine. For example, if one side of an issue is presented in prime time and the other side after midnight, then a complaint might be justified. Or an imbalance "might be a reflection of the total amount of time afforded to each side, or the frequency with which each side is presented, . . . or of a combination of factors."

The commission reiterates that it will not issue an equal-time "formula" per se, but that in examining a fairness complaint, it may examine the ratio of time made available to opposing viewpoints. This, too, can be difficult. Transcripts of programs may not be available, and relying on listener or management recollections can be shaky. Yet in dealing with commercials, the formula concept becomes easier to interpret, as in the case of the eight California stations caught in the nuclear power issue. The mere discussion of the commission's time concepts in this case gave broadcasters their first "formula" to follow as a Fairness Doctrine guideline.

Rethinking the Decision on Cigarette Advertising

The 1974 report also reconsidered advertising. The FCC admitted that its original decision, upheld in *Banzhaf* v. *Federal Communications Commission*, should not be viewed as current policy and that, in retrospect, "we believe that this mechanical approach to the Fairness Doctrine represented a serious departure from the Doctrine's central purpose. . . ." The report reflected the commission's opinion that "standard product commercials, such as the old cigarette ads, make no meaningful contribution toward informing the public on any side of any issue." Reflecting on all this, had the Public Health Cigarette Smoking Act not been passed in 1969, there might have been strong arguments to return "product" cigarette advertising to radio and television after the issuance of the 1974 *Fairness Report*.

RECONSIDERATION OF THE FAIRNESS DOCTRINE: 1976

In 1976, the FCC again examined the Fairness Doctrine.[30] Coming on the heels of the 1974 report, the commission's action was prompted by petitions filed by citizen groups wanting more access. Overall, the FCC found the 1974 document to be in good health. It reaffirmed its decision to apply the Fairness Doctrine to advertisements that deal with public issues, not just the advertising that lauds the merits of a given product. It also agreed that editorials should come under the doctrine's regulatory umbrella. The commission ruled that a "tenuous" relationship to an issue would not trigger the doctrine. In its 1976 *Memorandum Opinion and Order*, it reiterated that it would still let the broadcaster decide what was necessary to meet the doctrine's requirement, and that if a broadcaster was found in error, the commission would probably just direct the station to offer time to the opposing issue.

RELATING THE FAIRNESS DOCTRINE TO SECTION 315

Confusion frequently arises over the interpretations of the Fairness Doctrine and Section 315. Part of this confusion results from the imprecise use of the two concepts in everything from popular literature to the reports of uninformed broadcasters. Both documents are designed to afford "equal opportunities" if not "equal time" to opposing points of view. But remember, Section 315 deals with *political* broadcasting and candidates for public office, regardless of what they say.

Let us assume that an incumbent candidate for Congress talks about the construction of a flood-control dam during a local radio program. The dam has been hotly contested in the station's community, and could easily be classified as a controversial issue of public importance. After the candidate's broadcast, his opponent requests and is granted the opportunity to appear on the program. But the opponent, instead of discussing the flood-control dam on the program, talks about urban renewal. Has the broadcaster met the requirements of Section 315 and the Fairness Doctrine?

We could assume that with the appearance of both candidates, the requirements of Section 315 have been satisfied. But that is *not* necessarily the case as far as the Fairness Doctrine is concerned. Since the incumbent discussed a controversial issue of public importance, he triggered the

Fairness Doctrine machinery. So the broadcaster, under the Fairness Doctrine, must still present an opposing view to the flood-control project. If the opponent had discussed his opposition to the dam, then perhaps that would have fulfilled the requirement. But he didn't. Now along comes a spokesperson for the group opposing the dam. That person is also given the opportunity to appear on the station, this time to speak in opposition to the dam. But keep in mind that the broadcaster might not be *required* (although it is advisable) to give "equal time" for the spokesperson's viewpoints.

It is also important to remember that although Section 315 exempts most news programming, the Fairness Doctrine does not. The FCC is not going to dictate news content, but if controversial issues of public importance are heard on news programs, then in some way the broadcaster has the obligation to present opposing sides of those issues. And even Section 315 states that the news programming exemptions do not excuse broadcasters from "the obligation imposed upon them under this Act to operate in the public interest and to afford reasonable opportunity for the discussion of conflicting views on issues of public importance."

THE FAIRNESS DOCTRINE UNDER ATTACK: ISSUES AND CRITICISM

In addition to being one of the most important pieces of broadcast regulation that exists, the Fairness Doctrine is also one of the most highly criticized. Those who cry out against its alleged injustices do so loudly; those who support it are equally intense. Supporters base their arguments on concepts we have already discussed in detail, for example, limited spectrum space, the need to assure responsible use of the spectrum by providing all sides of opposing viewpoints, assuring open and unchecked views in a marketplace of ideas, fostering unbiased news reporting, and guaranteeing the presentation of programming devoted to issues of public importance. Critics feel that the doctrine is at best an unnecessary restraint, at worst a blatant case of government intrusion, colliding head on with the First Amendment. Between these two extremes are a multitude of opinions from an abundance of spokespersons.

General criticism has come from such industry sources as NBC's Julian Goodman, who remarked:

> The Fairness Doctrine has discouraged the very type of discussion it purports to foster. It has done this by giving Government the right to intervene as a frequently partisan editor in the process of broadcast journalism. . . . The Fairness Doctrine has been a muzzle on broadcast journalism's pursuit of stories and issues the public should know about and it has enabled the Government to stand at the broadcaster's shoulder and ask him to justify or amend his journalistic effort.[31]

At the heart of the criticism is the limited resource of the electromagnetic spectrum. The right of government to establish regulations for broadcasting has traditionally been based on the fact that the spectrum has only so much room, and thus not everyone can operate a broadcasting station. Therefore, the rules that guide broadcasters in their "privilege" not "right" to operate a station are both legal and appropriate. It is under this limited-resource concept that the Fairness Doctrine operates. Is this a legitimate justification for the doctrine?

Back in 1964, Joseph L. Brechner, President and General Manager of an Orlando, Florida television station, spoke to the National Broadcast Editorial Conference. In his address, later published in the *Journal of Broadcasting*, he said:

> In almost no area in this great country, with its vastly developed broadcasting system, is there a likelihood of a single viewpoint or political position, an area which could be said to be dominated or tyrannized by a broadcaster. On the contrary, broadcasting and broadcasters represent or offer the protection against single-newspaper editorial tyranny.[32]

Echoing Brechner's sentiment, FCC Chairman Richard Wiley suggested, when the FCC was reconsidering the Fairness Doctrine in 1976, that the commission suspend the doctrine in some larger markets on an experimental basis. His suggestion remained just that—a suggestion.

Another analysis of the limited-resource argument was posted by Herbert W. Hobler, President of the Nassau Broadcasting Company of Princeton, New Jersey. Addressing the 1975 New Jersey Broadcasters Association, he said:

> There are today, only 1,774 daily newspapers in this country—many of which are actually only six-day newspapers. There are some

7,640 weeklies, of all sizes and shapes. That's a total of 9,400 newspapers—and a total of 500 *less* papers than existed ten years ago. In 1973 alone, 169 went out of business and 78 merged. Another way to look at this is that there are close to 500 *less* editorial opinions available to the public. . . . There are some 7,737 commercial radio and TV stations in this country—and all of them are on seven days a week. And that's an INCREASE of 2,072 stations in the past ten years.[33]

Notwithstanding the merits of the Fairness Doctrine, other critics disagree with the print-broadcast analysis. The Communications Law Committee of the American Bar Association contends:

> Critics of the Fairness Doctrine thus miss the point when they argue that there are thousands more radio broadcast licensees than daily newspapers. The matter is not a question of the scarcity of broadcast facilities as compared to daily newspapers. Whatever the economics of the daily newspaper field, it is technologically open to all. Radio is inherently not so open. The government must license or there will be a pattern of frequency interference. It chooses one licensee for a frequency and forecloses all others—a crucial difference from the print media.[34]

However, the Law Committee has some persuasive legal arguments against the Fairness Doctrine. It cites the case of the *Miami Herald Publishing Co.* v. *Tornillo*, which struck down a Florida statute requiring the right of reply to people attacked in newspaper editorials.[35] The U.S. Supreme Court concluded:

> The choice of material to go into a newspaper, and the decisions made as to limitations on the size and content of the paper, and treatment of public issues and public officials—whether fair or unfair—constitute the exercise of editorial control and judgment. It has yet to be demonstrated how governmental regulation of this crucial process can be exercised consistent with First Amendment guarantees of a free press. . . .

The committee suggests that the right of reply statute "has the same commendable purpose as the Commission's Fairness Doctrine . . ." but asks: "Why is the FCC's rule as to broadcast journalism consistent with the First Amendment and Florida's print statute inconsistent?"[36] The answer again lies in the limited-resource concept that gives the government the power to regulate broadcasting.

The Law Committee suggested the possibility of substituting access programming for what it termed "governmentally-regulated fairness."[37] How would access programming work? Instead of being concerned primarily with the *content* of programming, the broadcaster would provide ample opportunity for opposing viewpoints and the presentation of issues of public importance. Note that the emphasis is on providing the *opportunity*, as opposed to the current emphasis not only on opportunity but on the actual content of programming. At the same time, the Committee recommends that if the "regulated" approach is to remain, then there should still be "wide discretion in the licensee to make Fairness judgments," and the Fairness Doctrine scrutiny should come primarily at license renewal time, as opposed to the "ad-hoc" consideration of complaints whenever they occur.

THE ERA OF DEREGULATION: FCC SUPPORT FOR REASSESSMENT/REPEAL

Consistent with the deregulatory atmosphere of the Fowler era at the FCC, the Commission conducted an inquiry into broadcasters' obligations under the Fairness Doctrine and issued a *Report* in 1985 strongly critical of the Doctrine.[38] In many ways it was opposite the stance taken in the past when the Doctrine was generally supported by the FCC. The FCC advanced seven major arguments in its *Report*. These were: (1) the Fairness Doctrine lessens the amount of diverse views available to the public; (2) the Fairness Doctrine inhibits expression of unorthodox opinions; (3) the Doctrine places the government into the intrusive and constitutionally disfavored role of scrutinizing program content; (4) the Doctrine creates an opportunity for intimidation of broadcasters by government officials; (5) the Doctrine imposes unnecessary economic costs upon broadcasters and the Commission; (6) more information sources in the marketplace decrease the need for the Fairness Doctrine; and (7) the Fairness Doctrine cannot be justified on the basis that it protects either broadcasters or the public from undue influence.

An examination of the FCC's position better explains the commission's opinion as stated in the *Report*. Many arguments echoed the comments of others quoted in the preceding paragraphs and elsewhere.

Lessens Diversity of Views

The FCC called the Fairness Doctrine a two-pronged instrument, the first being an affirmative obligation to air controversial issues of public importance, the second being the licensee's obligation to respond with balanced programming.[39] The FCC stated that the overwhelming majority of complaints it received related to the second prong, the failure of the licensee to respond with balanced programming. Any broadcasters faced with such a scenario, the FCC contends, will shy away from as much controversy as possible to avoid being caught in the second prong. The FCC buttressed its position with examples of stations shying away from political advertising, establishing actual policies against airing controversial issues, the chilling effect of possible legal burdens, elimination of issue-oriented advertising, and others.

The Expression of Unorthodox Opinions

Over the years, the FCC has supported stations that stayed away from certain issues because the issues were not considered "significant" public issues. Issues that were not significant did not fall under the obligations required by the Fairness Doctrine. Therein was the problem. Many unorthodox opinions, by the very fact that they are unorthodox, do not fall into the category of "significant." The result is that many unorthodox opinions are not aired.[40]

Government Intrusion

To enforce the Fairness Doctrine, the FCC contends that it must arbitrarily involve itself in program content, even to the point of counting minutes and seconds aired on one side or the other of the issues in contention.[41] Such government intrusion is the antithesis of a free marketplace of ideas. Even such assessments as the frequency of the broadcast and the degree of audience exposure can be tallied. This includes news programming.

Government Intimidation

As government officials, the FCC contended, the enforcement arms can intimidate broadcasters who air opinions with which they disagree.[42] Some politicians can use the Fairness Doctrine to intimidate broadcasters who do not air viewpoints consistent with the politician's position on an issue.

Cost Burdens on Broadcasters and the FCC

As with any regulation, costs are involved. Financially, a station and the FCC incur costs through negotiating Fairness Doctrine complaints, hiring legal counsel to help defend and resolve disputes, and to process the required paperwork associated with enforcement.[43]

Increased Information Sources in the Marketplace

The Fairness Doctrine was established at a time when there were fewer radio and television stations than there are today and even fewer cable channels. In addition, other technologies, such as low-power television, multipoint distribution systems, and other technologies increase the number of information channels available, therefore making the Fairness Doctrine unnecessary. More channels permit more opportunities for divergent viewpoints.[44]

Undue Influence

The commission contended in its *Report* that the argument that broadcasters would be pressured and influenced by special-interest groups was fallacious.[45] They felt that broadcasters had the ability to retain control over their programming and that the First Amendment forbids government intrusion in editorial decisions of the print media. Broadcast journalism should enjoy the same protection.

The well-publicized and widely disseminated *Report* brought forth a flurry of action by those trying to get the Fairness Doctrine repealed. The Radio-Television News Directors Association, long an opponent of the Doctrine, filed briefs as part of other proceedings in the U.S. Court of Appeals and cited the FCC *Report* as evidence.

ISSUES IN SUPPORT OF THE FAIRNESS DOCTRINE

At first glance, especially with all of the visible rhetoric and support for appeal, it may appear that the Fairness Doctrine is a cousin to a bygone era of broadcast regulation, no longer appropriate in a contemporary society where many media abound. But filed as comments to the FCC *Report* were arguments in support of retaining the Doctrine (although these were many times relegated to footnotes and dismissed by the Commission).[46] Others have echoed similar arguments in other forums, speeches, and writings.

Limited Resource as Legal Precedent

As we have already read, central to opposition to the doctrine is the First Amendment to the U.S. Constitution which assures a free press. This has been the central core of arguments against the Doctrine. While the First Amendment makes a good argument, it is still the concept of the electromagnetic spectrum as a limited resource which has kept the Fairness Doctrine in place and which much of legal precedent is based upon.

Fallacy of the Multiple-Channel Argument

Moreover, the arguments of a multitude of channels in the marketplace has some flaws. First, while cable has experienced substantial growth, it is viewed by many as primarily an entertainment medium. Even with millions of subscribers, cable still serves a very small percentage of the public. Much of the public still tends to have loyalties to traditional news sources that serve the local community. Other technologies such as low-power television have never scratched the surface of their potential and still reach a minute segment of the population.

Single-Service Communities

Hundreds of communities in the United States are served by a single radio station, and where newspapers do exist, many are published once weekly, thus giving the local radio station a monopoly six days a week over information. The management of such stations is many times tied to the financial infrastructure of the community. Unpopular issues or those that can cost advertising dollars can be avoided much more easily when a Fairness Doctrine is not present to assure diversity of opinions. The fact that the public in such communities may be served by other nearby stations does not mean that those stations spend much, if any, time dealing with the local communities' controversial issues of public importance.

Journalistic versus Management Decision

The First Amendment argument also homes in on the "journalistic" function of the media but it is many times in the offices of the general manager, not the newsroom, where decisions are made about what political advertising to run or on what issue to do an editorial. Without a Fairness Doctrine in place, a general manager supporting a local political cause can turn the editorial power of the station for or against a cause without any need to offer balanced programming.

Big Money: Local Issues

One of the by-products of our media age has been the proliferation of political action committees and other groups, some of which have enormous fund-raising power and the ability to channel funds to candidates who support their political causes. In the past, these groups have concentrated their support on federal candidates. With the Fairness Doctrine gone, national political organizations can funnel funds to local grass-roots candidates and causes, and provide money for radio and television commercials with messages that can be vicious and dramatic in their attacks. Local candidates who could not afford to buy time would have little recourse to counter with opposing views. Local politicians, less experienced in big-time politics and sometimes more susceptible to being bought or influenced by outside money would accept outside influence money and sophisticated political advertising insensitive to the best interest of the local community and be free from the fear of programming to balance viewpoints.

The Lobbyist and the Public

While many broadcasters have opposed the Fairness Doctrine, there is no indication that those who have spoken the loudest represent the majority, much less the general public. For example, the National Association of Broadcasters has been a powerful foe of the Fairness Doctrine, but the NAB understandably must oppose measures that place burdens—regulatory, philosophical, or financial—upon the commercial broadcasting industry. The NAB can be one of the loudest voices and most effective lobbying forces in Washington representing commercial broadcasters, but the NAB's constituency is the broadcasting industry, not necessarily the general public.

The Public's Position: Unknown Quantity

In all of the arguments for and against the Fairness Doctrine, little is known about how the public feels. Ostensibly the FCC should represent the public interest but on the issue of the Fairness Doctrine there is little known about how the public feels except through the comments of some citizen groups. Even these, however, like the NAB, do not necessarily represent the public at large. Some public-opinion surveys have asked "mother-and-apple pie" questions eliciting percentages that support one view or another but without a clear indication of whether the public really understands such complex subjects as freedom of marketplace ideas or the limited resource of an electromagnetic spectrum. Moreover, since a typical public-opinion survey is not equipped to educate and ask questions at the same time, it must rely on the latter. In such matters the public may be superficially polled and then purported to be represented in Washington. Hypothetically, one could argue that questions such as "Do you favor equal freedoms for both broadcast and print media?" can elicit a high percentage of "yes" responses, but when such data are used to support a major regulatory change as complex as the Fairness Doctrine the argument is weak.

Deregulation Now: Pay Later

Some commercial broadcasters are themselves skeptical of the entire deregulatory era, pointing out that when no one has any rules to play by, the ability to plan and manage a station can be even more difficult. For example, even if the Fairness Doctrine remains repealed, it would not change the station's mandate under the Communications Act to operate in the public interest. The station manager who has little to be held accountable for in the day-to-day operation of a station may find himself or herself caught in an inescapable trap at license renewal time when a competing applicant comes forth with evidence of denied access to the airwaves, unbalanced programming, personal attacks in editorials, and other actions which result in either losing the station license or defending it at a much greater financial loss than would have been necessary in resolving a Fairness Doctrine complaint. One could argue that the elimination of the Fairness Doctrine will show in the long run to be a cruel hoax on the commercial broadcasters who later find themselves in more and deeper hot water when the stakes are higher and it's too late to change a pattern of irresponsible broadcasting not in the public interest. The Fairness Doctrine as a safety net and guide will no longer exist.

The Fairness Doctrine and Partisan Programming

The Fairness Doctrine was established as a response to broadcasters who engaged in partisan programming and refused access to opposing viewpoints. While it may be argued (although not necessarily substantiated) that the Fairness Doctrine inhibits free expression of divergent viewpoints, we know nothing about how broadcasters would over the long-term respond to no doctrine. Will it result in increased partisan politics in other types of programming? For example, we might argue that the Fairness Doctrine already applies to religious programming. Politics in the pulpit is nothing new but without the Fairness Doctrine in place, partisan politics in the electronic pulpit of the airwaves may reach new heights. Partisan issues disguised in other types of programming, such as docudramas, documentaries, and so on, would become more frequent. Stations would engage in much more partisan politics, and assuming the argument of multiple channels of communication offering divergent views is fallacious, the public would be ill-served and uninformed.

Fairness and Government Licensed Stations

Many stations are licensed by government agencies. We fail to realize that the public broadcasting station at a local college may be licensed to the college, which in turn is supported by tax dollars. Regardless of how "independent" the station is, it still would be considered a voice of government. Without a Fairness Doctrine, the ability of governors, state legislators, even college presidents, to become directly involved in partisan programming would increase. The college president who is a personal friend of the governor and whose college receives state appropriations might find herself or himself in an awkward position if the college station editorialized in favor of the governor's opponent or supported one side of a local municipal issue that separated the "town and gown."

Political Pressure on the FCC

While the FCC may argue that the Fairness Doctrine can result in government intimidation and intrusion, the FCC itself is susceptible to the same political intrusion and intimidation.

Finally, one cannot overlook the outside political influence that can play a part in FCC decisions. For example, an administration in power (keep in mind that the president appoints FCC commissioners) that relies heavily on the broadcast media to carry partisan views through weekly radio addresses or other forums tempered its remarks so as not to invoke the Fairness Doctrine on broadcast affiliates which carry such programs. In the absence of a Fairness Doctrine, the freedom to carry out personal attacks and much more partisan messages is greater. Thus, for a party or politician in power, which has at its disposal an outlet (broadcast affiliates) and the money to fund the production and distribution of partisan messages, the Fairness Doctrine is not a friend. Without the Fairness Doctrine we could argue that the FCC would no longer be a filter protecting the public from direct and partisan involvement from other agencies of government as well as from high-ranking government officials.

ELIMINATING THE BALLOT-ISSUE COROLLARY

The FCC further scaled back the Fairness Doctrine by eliminating the ballot-issue provision of the doctrine.[47] In a 3-to-2 vote the FCC used a case involving the Arkansas AFL-CIO and the Committee Against Amendment 2 which filed a joint complaint against station KARK-TV, charging the station with failing to give sufficient coverage to a ballot proposition to be voted on in the general election. Despite theses issues the Fairness Doctrine remains a political issue closely hinging on the party in power in the White House. The Fairness Doctrine appears a long way from being enforced. During the Clinton presidency a change in policy may take place.[48]

SUMMARY

The Fairness Doctrine is closely related to and often confused with Section 315 of the Communications Act. Section 315 is primarily concerned with political advertising and access, whereas the Fairness Doctrine is concerned with overall balanced programming when dealing with controversial issues of public importance.

From the passage of the Radio Act of 1927, a fairness-type requirement has been an issue in broadcast regulation. In 1941 the matter came to the forefront with the *Mayflower* decision, which stifled editorializing. The courts wrestled with the issue of fairness until 1949 when the FCC enacted the Fairness Doctrine, requiring broadcasters to present balanced programming of controversial issues of public importance. Since its passage in 1949 the FCC has reviewed the Fairness Doctrine five times on a formal basis and more frequently on a case-by-case basis. The *Red Lion* decision upheld the constitutionality of the Fairness Doctrine and has withstood other challenges through the years.

Most recently, the FCC examined the doctrine in 1985 as part of the deregulatory push by Mark Fowler, FCC chairman, and Ronald Reagan appointee to the FCC. In the 1985 *Report* the Commission outlined seven issues, which the commission contended would be the basis for repealing the Doctrine. These included: (1) the Fairness Doctrine lessens the amount of diverse views even though in theory it was designed to do just the opposite; (2) the administration of the Fairness Doctrine inhibits the expression of unorthodox opinions; (3) the operation of the Fairness Doctrine places the government into an intrusive and constitutionally disfavored role of scrutinizing programming; (4) the Fairness Doctrine creates the opportunity for intimidation of broadcasters by governmental officials; (5) the Fairness Doctrine imposes unnecessary economic costs upon broadcasters and the commission; (6) the need for the Fairness Doctrine is diminished in the light of the increased number of media outlets—"channels" of communication—in the marketplace; and (7) the Fairness Doctrine cannot be justified on the basis that it protects either broadcasters or the public from undue influence.

Others, some of whom responded to the FCC's original inquiry resulting in the 1985 report, argued that the Fairness Doctrine should not be repealed. Issues supporting the retention of the Fairness Doctrine include: (1) The limited-resource concept is still a basis for legal precedent and also the basis for the *Red Lion* and other decisions upholding the Fairness Doctrine. (2) Media outlets have not increased to the point where the Fairness Doctrine is unnecessary. Cable reaches only a small segment of the population and other technologies such as low-power television, multipoint distribution, and others reach even smaller audiences, some being almost experimental in nature. (3) Many communities are still served by a single radio station which has a six-day-a-week monopoly over news and information. (4) Arguments for repeal are based on First Amendment issues, yet many decisions about such things as political programming and advertising are made at the level of management and not in the newsroom. (5) Political action committees and other organizations supporting various causes will have the ability to support through paid political advertising local issues heretofore avoided because of the risk of invoking the Fairness Doctrine. (6) Much opposition to the Fairness Doctrine comes from lobbying groups whose constituency is the commercial broadcasting industry. Even then, there is no indication that such lobbying represents the majority of broadcasters. (7) Little is known about how the public views the Fairness Doctrine, such views being important to gauge a true understanding of what would be in the "public interest." (8) Some feel that deregulation may turn out to be a cruel hoax leading broadcasters astray to make mistakes that later will cost them their license. A Fairness Doctrine complaint is much easier to deal with than a license challenge. (9) Elimination of the doctrine will permit new amounts of partisan programming. While we know that some broadcasters are hindered by the doctrine, we have no way of determining what type of programming will be unleashed if the Fairness Doctrine is repealed. (10) Stations which are licensed by the government may see new pressures to conform to the political party in power. (11) More political pressure is really behind moves to repeal the Fairness Doctrine, mostly encouraged by the Mark Fowler/Ronald Reagan orientation to deregulation.

Regardless of the future of the Fairness Doctrine, it remains one of the most important, albeit controversial, pieces of broadcast regulation.

ADDITIONAL RESOURCES

Brennan, T. A., "The Fairness Doctrine as Public Policy." 33 *Journal of Broadcasting & Electronic Media* 419 (1989).

Ecabert, G. S., "The Demise of the Fairness Doctrine: A Constitutional Reevaluation of Content-based Broadcasting Regulations." 56 *University of Cincinnati Law Review* 999 (1988).

Gray, K. B., "Fairness Doctrine Termination: Extinction of an Unenforceable Theory." *Suffolk University Law Review* 22 (Winter 1988).

Hedblom, M. K., "Returning Fairness to the Broadcast Media." 7 *Law & Inequality: A Journal of Theory and Practice* 29 (1988).

Hyde, R. H., "FCC Action Repealing the Fairness Doctrine: A Revolution in Broadcast Regulation." 38 *Syracuse Law Review* 1175 (1987).

Perry, G., "The First Amendment versus the Right to Be Heard: Bickering and Political Mayhem Resulting from the Repeal of the Fairness Doctrine by the FCC." 20 *Texas Tech Law Review* (1989).

Richards, R. D. "Resurrecting the Fairness Doctrine: The Quandary of Enforcement Continues." 37 *Cleveland State Law Review* 559 (1989).

chapter eighteen

Understanding the Legal System and Legal Research*

Every facet of our society is affected by the increasing influence of the law. In communications this is strikingly apparent with the growing body of statutes, regulations, and administrative and judicial decisions that direct the actions of every radio and television station, every newspaper and magazine, every cable company, every reporter, every editor and news director. To be properly informed and to stay abreast of changes are part of the responsibilities of the members of the field. As students, you have the opportunity to begin to develop the necessary skills.

Legal research is different than most other types of research and consequently students attempting it for the first time are often intimidated by the enormity of the task. It is time consuming, but it should not be feared and can be mastered with some patience and enthusiasm. Understanding the legal system and the materials it generates will help dispel the mystique.

You may find it useful to read through these pages the first time without trying to master the material. This will give you the range of sources available. Every source may not be necessary for your research. The issues you cover and the strategy you choose will dictate the appropriate material.

There are some sources discussed here that may not be available in a general academic library. Law school libraries will offer the most complete set of materials. If you are not near a law school and your college library does not contain the needed material, try the court library at your county seat. If you are near the state capitol, there is usually a large legal collection available at the state library or the appellate court library. Depository libraries for U.S. government publications are likely to have much of the material, and there are at least two such libraries in each Congressional district. As a last resort, try to obtain the material through interlibrary loan, although a clear idea of what you need is necessary for this method. When in doubt, check with a reference librarian for assistance.

THE LEGAL SYSTEM

To research any aspect of the law effectively, it is important to understand the structure of the legal system. There are three branches of the government: the legislative, the executive, and the judicial, and each branch plays a part in the develop-

*This chapter was written by Colleen Kristl Pauwels, Associate Professor and Law Library Director, Indiana University School of Law, Bloomington, Indiana.

ment of the law. The legislature enacts the law, the executive agencies administer the law, and the courts rule on the interpretation, applicability, and constitutionality of the law as well as provide rulings in other special areas.

Under our federal constitution, each state is sovereign and each has jurisdiction over all legal matters governed by its own constitution and statutes. Federal courts have jurisdiction over matters involving the U.S. Constitution and laws enacted by Congress; treaties and disputes involving ambassadors, public ministers, and consuls; laws relating to navigable waters; and controversies between the United States and individuals, between two states, or between individuals from different states.

The federal court system has a three-tiered structure. Its trial-level courts are called district courts and there is at least one district court in each state. The intermediate appellate-level courts are called the courts of appeals. These courts are divided into 13 circuits. The first 11 circuits are regional and include three or more states. These regional circuits are referred to by number; for example, New York is in the second circuit, California, the ninth circuit, and Indiana is in the seventh circuit. The District of Columbia has its own circuit and hears most of the appeals involving federal agencies. The federal circuit, created in 1982, hears appeals from throughout the country regarding patents, public contracts, and customs. The final level or court of last resort within the federal courts is the U.S. Supreme Court.

Most states have the same three-tiered court structure: trial level, intermediate appellate level, and court of last resort. The names of the courts may vary somewhat from state to state, but they function in the same way.

The American court system operates in accord with the doctrine of stare decisis, a principle of law that means as courts interpret the law, cases hold as precedents for similar cases in that jurisdiction in the future. It is not only essential, then, to know the statute or regulation that is to be followed, but also to locate prior cases that have interpreted the law and therefore have set the precedent for future rulings. For this reason, various forms of legal materials must be consulted for effective research.

A LEGAL RESEARCH STRATEGY

Legal research materials can be divided into three large categories. Primary sources include the actual forms of the law, such as constitutions, statutes, regulations, and administrative agency and court decisions. The second category includes the various finding aids and indexes used to locate the primary sources. The third group includes all secondary materials, such as books and journal articles, that discuss the laws and the related issues.

Choosing the proper strategy at the outset will save valuable time and will make more effective use of the materials available. The first step is to get a clear idea of what it is you want to know. This can be done by consulting a variety of secondary sources. This material can provide good background to help define your issue. The use of these materials alone, however, does not constitute legal research. When you have redefined the question and pinpointed the issue or issues involved, you must identify and retrieve all the primary material. It is important here to be both comprehensive and up to date in your search. One decision can change a whole body of previous law and so careful attention must be paid to all the material.

SECONDARY MATERIAL

Annotated Law Reports

There are several types of secondary material that can be consulted. *American Law Reports* or *ALR* selects state and federal cases and includes with the opinion an analytical essay on the subject of the decision. These annotations analyze the issues of the case and discuss its impact. One of the assets of each annotation is that it brings into perspective the current standing of case law in other jurisdictions. This is a valuable source to use at the outset of your research to develop your background information or narrow your topic.

Journals and Periodicals

Reviewing the periodical literature is another excellent way to develop background knowledge. There are many specialized journals and periodicals that discuss legal issues in communications and media law. Some of these specialized journals include:

- Access Reports
- Advertising Age
- Broadcasting
- Bulletin of the Copyright Society of the U.S.A.
- Cardoza Arts & Entertainment Law Journal

- Communications and the Law
- Communications Lawyer
- Copyright Bulletin
- Federal Communications Law Journal
- Hastings Communications and Entertainment Law Journal: Comm/Ent
- Hofstra Entertainment & Copyright Law Digest
- Journal of Art & Entertainment Law
- Journalism Quarterly
- News Media and the Law
- Student Press Law Center Report
- University of Miami Entertainment & Sports Law Review

In addition, law journals that are not solely concerned with media law often contain important articles discussing the developments in the field. Law journals are of particular importance because some of the finest legal scholars contribute to them. These journals can also provide analyses of court decisions more rapidly than books can. Journals are published by law schools, legal associations, and commercial houses.

Periodical Indexes

Articles in general periodicals, as well as those in the law journals, can be found through periodical indexes. *Readers' Guide to Periodical Literature* indexes general and media journals. *Public Affairs Information Service Bulletin*, or *P.A.I.S.*, indexes a selection of law and media journals and other magazines concerned with public affairs issues. These indexes can be found in most academic libraries. There are several legal periodical indexes. *Index to Legal Periodicals* and *Current Law Index* are two of the most comprehensive. Both indexes are available as paper indexes or in CD-ROM format. The CD-ROM equivalents are *WilsonDisc—Index to Legal Periodicals* and *LegalTrac*. Although some academic libraries may subscribe to one of these law periodical indexes, they are more often found in law school libraries.

Books

A great number of books have been written on media law topics. Some will be available in your library and can be found through a subject search of its holdings. To make sure the material is as current as possible, it is still best to consult the primary sources whenever possible.

Law Dictionaries

While reading, you may come across words or phrases that you do not understand. There are several legal dictionaries that will define the terms for you. *Black's Law Dictionary* is the most common and is often found in academic libraries.

PRIMARY MATERIALS

After defining your topic, your search should focus on primary material. Primary sources include: constitutions and statutes, regulations, the rulings of administrative agencies, and the decisions of the courts.

A constitution, whether for a state or the federal government, is the framework for that government. It delegates power and responsibilities to the government and defines the rights and liberties of its citizens. It is the supreme law of the jurisdiction and supersedes all other forms of law.

Statutes are the form of law enacted by the legislative body. The Congress and most state legislatures are bicameral or two house systems. The legislation must proceed through both houses and be signed by the chief executive before it is enacted into law.

Regulations are the product of agencies. Under authority delegated by the legislature, agencies, such as the Federal Communications Commission and the Federal Trade Commission, may adopt rules which set policy or establish procedures to be followed for compliance with a statute. Regulations have the force of law and are enforced by the executive agency.

Administrative rulings are the quasi-judicial decisions of the executive agencies. As part of their enforcement responsibilities, agencies hold hearings and may hand down opinions, orders or decisions clarifying issues or mandating action. The FCC and FTC are the two primary agencies concerned with communications issues.

Court decisions are the rulings of the various units of the court system. The decision or judgment of the court is generally accompanied by an opinion at the appellate level, but an opinion is only occasionally included with trial-level decisions. At the appellate level, where there is more than one judge, the opinion, if it has the support of the majority of the court, is called the opinion of the court and is offered to clarify the reasoning behind the decision. These opinions provide the courts with the precedents used in subsequent cases. If there is a disagreement in the court regarding the reasons offered to justify the judgment, or even regarding the judgment itself, concurring and/or dissenting opinions are written and signed by the judges who wrote them.

Legal Citations

To use legal material effectively, it is important to understand legal citation form. Legal citations to statutes, regulations, decisions, and most other law materials follow a uniform method of citation that is much different from the citations you ordinarily see in books and periodicals in other areas. The standard method for legal materials consists of giving the volume of the work, an abbreviation of the title of the work, and the first page of the case decision or periodical noted. Therefore, you might see cited 88 Colum.L.R. 156. This is the citation for an article in volume 88 of the *Columbia Law Review* that begins on page 156.

For citations to court decisions from the U.S. Supreme Court, you will often see the following:

> *The New York Times* v. *United States*, 403 U.S. 713, 91 S.Ct. 2140, 29 L.Ed.2d 822 (1971).

What has been given here is the name of the case (*The New York Times* v. *United States*) and three citations for different reporters or sets of volumes where you can find the same case. These are called parallel citations—three places to find the same case. The date in parenthesis indicates the year the case was decided.

There are two major exceptions to the basic legal citation form. Some looseleaf services cite to paragraph numbers as well as, or instead of, page numbers. For example, Pike and Fischer *Radio Regulation*, a looseleaf service that pulls together statutes, cases, and administrative agency materials, uses page numbers for cases (e.g., 37 RR 2d 744) but paragraph numbers for the other materials (e.g., RR ¶ 69.58). In the U.S. Code or other statute volumes, the proper citation is to section numbers (e.g., 5 U.S.C. § 315). A sign is usually, but not always, used for paragraph (¶) and section (§).

Here are some abbreviations of the legal materials that you are most likely to encounter. For a more detailed list of abbreviations, look in the back of *Black's Law Dictionary*.

A.B.A.J.—American Bar Association Journal
A.L.R.—American Law Reports
A.L.R. 2d—American Law Reports (2nd series)
A.L.R. 3d—American Law Reports (3rd series)
A.L.R. 4th—American Law Reports (4th series)
A.L.R. 5th—American Law Reports (5th series)
A.L.R. Fed—American Law Reports, Federal cases
Am.Jur.2d—American Jurisprudence Second (edition)
A., A.2d—Atlantic Reporter, Atlantic Reporter, 2nd series
Cal. Rptr.—California Reporter
C.F.R.—Code of Federal Regulations
C.J.S.—Corpus Juris Secundum
Colum.L.R.—Columbia Law Review
F., F.2d—Federal Reporter, Federal Reporter, 2d series
F.C.C.—Federal Communication Commission Reports
F.C.C.2d—Federal Communication Commission Reports 2d series
F.C.C. Rec.—F.C.C. Record
F.R.—Federal Register
F.Supp.—Federal Supplement
F.T.C.—Federal Trade Commission Reports
F.T.C.2d—Federal Trade Commission Reports, 2d series
Harv.L.R.—Harvard Law Review
L.Ed.—U.S. Supreme Court Reports, Lawyers' Edition
L.Ed.2d—U.S. Supreme Court Reports, Lawyers' Edition 2d
series LW U.S.—Law Week
Med.L.Rptr.—Media Law Reporter
N.E., N.E.2d—Northeastern Reporter, Northeastern Reporter, 2d series
N.W., N.W.2d—Northwestern Reporter, Northwestern Reporter, 2d series
N.Y.Supp., N.Y.Supp.2d—New York Supplement, New York Supplement, 2d series
P., P.2d—Pacific Reporter, Pacific Reporter, 2d series
R.R.—Pike and Fischer Radio Regulation (unofficial cite)
R.R.2d—Pike and Fischer Radio Regulation, 2d series (unofficial cite)
Rad. Regs. (P & F)—Pike and Fischer Radio Regulation (official cite)
Rad. Regs.2d (P & F)—Pike and Fischer Radio

Regulation 2d series (official cite)

S.Ct.—Supreme Court Reporter

S.E., S.E.2d—Southeastern Reporter, Southeastern Reporter, 2d series

So., So.2d—Southern Reporter, Southern Reporter, 2d series

Stan.L.R.—Stanford Law Review

S.W., S.W.2d—Southwestern Reporter, Southwestern Reporter, 2d series

U.Chi.L.R.—University of Chicago Law Review

U.S.—U.S. Reports

U.S.C.—U.S. Code

U.S.C.A.—U.S. Code Annotated

U.S.C.S.—U.S. Code Service

Yale L.J.—Yale Law Journal

Some case citations will provide—in addition to the volume, reporter system, and first page of the case—the year the decision was released and, in some instances, the jurisdiction of the court. For example:

> *United States* v. *Hunter*, 459 F.2d 205 (4th Cir. 1972).

This citation tells you that the U.S. Court of Appeals for the Fourth Circuit handed down this decision in 1972.

Finding Constitutions and Statutes

Constitutions and statutes are available in several sources. As statutes or public laws are passed, they are compiled in chronological order. Federal laws can be found in *Statutes at Large*. State laws are called session laws and are issued under a variety of titles such as *Acts of Indiana* or *Laws of Minnesota*.

More workable forms of statutes are codes. Codes, available for both federal and state statutes, are subject arrangements of the laws in force. The authorized or official code for federal statutes is called the *U.S. Code*. Some states also have official codes with varying titles. These official codes contain only the text of the statutes and the constitution. There are, however, annotated codes, published commercially, that include the legislative background along with each section of the law, as well as a summary of each court case that has interpreted the law. The two annotated codes for federal laws are the *United States Code Annotated* and *United States Code Service*. There is also an annotated code for each state. All codes are updated, to include current amendments and cases, by pamphlet supplements usually inserted in the back of each volume and called pocket-parts.

Indexes provide access by subject, popular name, or law number. A version of the code and session laws for the United States and your home state are available in most academic libraries. A collection of all state codes is usually available only in law school libraries.

Other sources of the federal statutes in the communications area are two looseleaf services, Pike and Fischer *Radio Regulation* and Commerce Clearing House *Trade Regulation Reporter*. These services compile the statutes and other primary materials relevant to many communications issues involving broadcasting and advertising. They are updated regularly, but these sources cannot be relied on for their comprehensiveness and the codes should be consulted for verification as well as for citing purposes. These services are ordinarily available only in large academic or law school libraries.

Legislative history is the term used for the publications generated during the passage of each bill. These materials often shed light on the legislative intent of a particular statute and are sometimes used by the courts for clarification. Legislative history is rarely available for state laws but it can readily be found for federal legislation. Material published in the *Congressional Record*, House and Senate Reports, and Congressional hearings are all parts of the legislative history. This material can be found through a variety of indexes available in many academic libraries. Your reference librarian can help you locate the material you need.

Finding Regulations

Federal regulations are published as they are issued in a daily publication called the *Federal Register*. They are then compiled annually in the *Code of Federal Regulations*. Its index provides access through subject or agency, or by authorizing statute. It is not particularly thorough, however, and assistance from a librarian might save time. Because of the somewhat complex updating system, finding the most current material is more difficult in this source. Currency is essential and care must be taken to find all the material. Both sources can be found in many academic libraries.

The two looseleaf services in communications, Pike and Fischer *Radio Regulation* and Commerce Clearing House *Trade Regulation*

Reporter, include regulations specific to the issues they cover. Like any looseleaf service, however, they cannot be relied upon for comprehensive coverage and you should verify your research in the official source. These looseleaf services are not routinely found in academic libraries but are available in many law school libraries.

State agency regulations are becoming available in a growing number of states but still often can only be obtained through the issuing agency. A reference librarian can assist you in finding these regulations.

Finding Administrative Agency Decisions

Federal administrative decisions are published by the individual agencies. Older decisions and notices related to communication law can be found in the *Federal Communications Commission Reports*. Since 1986 the *FCC Record* has been published, which includes a comprehensive compilation of decisions, reports, public notices, and other FCC documents. The decisions regarding advertising and other trade issues are published in the *Federal Trade Commission Reports*, which contain the full text of all opinions as well as orders and decrees of the agency.

These official sets are delayed several months before publication, and for this reason, commercially published looseleaf services are used for the most current agency decisions. Those that include communications law issues are Pike and Fischer *Radio Regulation* and Commerce Clearing House *Trade Regulation Reporter*. Although they are not comprehensive sources, most of the important decisions are included. These services are not generally found in academic libraries, but are available in many law school libraries. The official version of the decision reports may be found in academic libraries and particularly those that are depositories for U.S. government publications.

Most states do not routinely distribute the decisions of their administrative agencies. Although some are available for the largest states, most must be obtained directly from the agency.

Availability of Court Decisions

Because of the principle of stare decisis, court decisions form the largest body of legal research materials. Publications called *reporters* contain the decisions and opinions of the judges for cases in various jurisdictions. There are thousands of cases reported in these sets each year. Many cases, although decided, are not reported, however. The overwhelming majority of cases at the trial level have little consequence beyond the parties involved; therefore, there is no value or justification for the expense of publishing them. It is important to remember that although some cases are discussed by the news media at the trial level, since they pertain to a new or budding point of law, it is the rare trial-level case that is available through the standard reporters. Ordinarily transcripts of these cases can only be obtained from the clerk of the local court where the case was tried.

The court decisions may be published by the state or federal government or by a commercial publishing company. The reporters authorized by the government for publication are called *official* reporters. These reporters, although often preferred for citing purposes, are not different in any substantive way from the commercial or unofficial reporters. In actuality, the commercial reporters are often more easily obtained and therefore more commonly held by libraries.

It is important to reiterate here that a court decision is only valid as precedent within the jurisdiction of that court. That is, an Indiana case cannot be used as precedent for a subsequent New Jersey case; what is ruled in the Second Federal Circuit is not precedent in the Fifth Federal Circuit. Cases in other jurisdictions can be used by the courts as a persuasive authority but they do not control the ruling of courts in other jurisdictions. Finding the appropriate case in the correct jurisdiction is essential to your research.

A Shortcut to Finding Decisions

The field of communications has several looseleaf services that bring together court cases from all jurisdictions. The service most commonly found in academic libraries is the Bureau of National Affairs *Media Law Reporter*. It includes the full text of opinions from all U.S. Supreme Court cases dealing with these issues and most important cases from other jurisdictions. It has an easy-to-use index as well as a summary or digest of each case included. Its frequent updates include a news section discussing new cases in the field and it also mentions periodical articles on related issues. It is not a comprehensive source, but it does include the most important cases in media law. Many academic libraries that cannot afford the great expense of the individual reporters may subscribe to this service.

There are other services that also include statutes, regulations, and some administrative agency decisions. Pike and Fischer *Radio Regulation* and Commerce Clearing House *Trade Regulation Reporter* are the sets concerned with issues related to communications. These provide the same access to decisions but they often are only available in law school libraries.

Court Reporters—The Supreme Court

U.S. Supreme Court decisions are published officially in a series called *U.S. Reports*. In addition, two commercial versions are published. The *Supreme Court Reporter*, a publication of West Publishing Company, and the *U.S. Supreme Court Reports, Lawyers' Edition* (commonly called *Lawyers' Edition*) is published by Lawyers' Cooperative Publishing Company. All of these reporters include every U.S. Supreme Court decision. The commercial versions vary only in the kind of supplementary material they include in addition to the opinions.

Prior to the publication of the bound volumes, each of the Supreme Court reporters publishes paperback pamphlets called advance sheets. These advance sheets are issued regularly to provide quick access to recent decisions. The advance sheets have the same pagination that will appear in the final bound volume and can be used and cited in the same way.

Looseleaf services, such as Bureau of National Affairs *U.S. Law Week* and Commerce Clearing House *Supreme Court Bulletin* also contain the full text of these opinions, sometimes within two weeks of the decision. Academic libraries often subscribe to one of these sources if the reporters are not available.

Court Reporters—Lower Federal Courts

Printed decisions of the federal courts of appeals and district courts are only available through commercial reporters. The most comprehensive of these reporters are published by West. The courts of appeals decisions are available in *West's Federal Reporter*. As part of their jurisdiction, these courts hear appeals from the administrative agencies. These appeals are usually, but not always, heard in the District of Columbia circuit.

District court or trial-level cases can be found in West's *Federal Supplement*, but it reports only a fraction of the total number of district court cases. Other sources such as looseleaf services or computer systems may contain some cases not available in the West reporters, but there are many that go unreported in any source.

Court Reporters—The State Courts

Most states publish official reporters for the court of appeals and Supreme Court. Advance sheets are not ordinarily published, and there is often a considerable delay before the bound volumes are available. For these reasons, the commercial reporters provide the primary access to state court decisions.

The National Reporter System, published by West, is the most inclusive of the reporters. The series includes a group of regional reporters incorporating all the reported cases in the state courts. There are seven regional reporters: Atlantic, Pacific, Southern, Southwestern, Southeastern, Northwestern, and Northeastern. The *New York Supplement* and the *California Reporter* have been added to supplement the reporters for the two states with the most active courts. Remember that although the National Reporter System includes all reported cases, this does not mean it includes every state case. There are no trial court cases included and only a selection of appellate cases. Advance sheets are available for each segment of the National Reporter System, providing current reporting of state cases.

FINDING LEGAL MATERIAL BY COMPUTER

There are a number of computer systems currently available that provide access to legal materials. Two of the most common are LEXIS and WESTLAW. Both of these systems provide full text searching of court opinions from all jurisdictions, state and federal statutes, regulations, and federal agency decisions. In addition, they each contain a growing collection of secondary sources, such as law journals, available through these services. LEXIS has a companion service called NEXIS which is a full text database that includes a wide range of periodicals and newspapers. WESTLAW includes the DIALOG system to provide similar coverage of research available in periodical literature. These systems are in virtually all law school libraries; however, there may be some restrictions on use. Because of the value of these computer databases to the general academic community, academic libraries are beginning to subscribe to the services. If LEXIS/NEXIS or WESTLAW is available, ask a librarian if your research would be facilitated by this approach.

FINDING AIDS

The digest is the most comprehensive subject approach to court decisions. By identifying each of the legal issues discussed in the opinion, the case is summarized or digested together with others concerned with the same issue. There are a number of digests ranging from those including all reported cases to those concerned with an individual state. The most important thing to remember when using any digest is to select the digest most appropriate for your needs. Do not use the most comprehensive one when a selective digest will do. A librarian can help you determine the right digest for your research.

Legal encyclopedias are another basic legal research source. They combine a summary of the current case law on an issue with a case-finding element. There are two general legal encyclopedias and one for each state.

Because there are so many cases decided each month, it is difficult to be sure that a particular case is still valid today. It may have been overruled or modified by a later decision. There may also have been cases with similar issues that may have altered the interpretation in some way. *Shepard's Citations* provides the judicial history and further court interpretation for all published decisions. There is a series of volumes for each reporter, both official and unofficial, which enables you to (1) locate further appeals or parallel citation of your case; (2) verify the current status of your case by finding if it has been overruled or upheld by subsequent cases; and (3) locate other cases on the same or similar point of law. There are also *Shepard's* volumes to update statutes, regulations, and administrative decisions, as well as for some secondary material. Ask a librarian how to use the series. This source can be found in all law school libraries, but rarely in academic libraries.

SUMMARY

The growing influence of the law has made legal research an essential skill for members of the communications field. Understanding the legal system is the first step toward mastery of this skill.

The legislative, executive, and judicial branches all play a part in the development of the law. The various forms of law—the constitution, statutes, regulations, and administrative and judicial decisions—make up the primary sources to be consulted when determining the law on a specific issue.

The proper strategy is essential for effective legal research, however. By first consulting background material to gain insight on the issues involved, you will get a clearer idea of the way to approach your research. Periodical articles and books provide valuable assistance in this task.

The primary sources must then be consulted. Locating the appropriate statutes, the implementing regulations, and the judicial or administrative interpretation are all steps toward a comprehensive search of the law. Many different sources can be consulted along the way and there are various indexes and finding aids to assist you. Looseleaf services such as the BNA *Media Law Reporter* or Pike and Fischer *Radio Regulation* provide shortcuts in your research by compiling primary material such as statutes, regulations, and decisions on communication law issues.

ADDITIONAL RESOURCES

Books: The Legal System

Baum, L., *American Courts: Process and Policy*, 2nd ed. Boston: Houghton Mifflin, 1989.

Cataldo, B. F., *Introduction to Law and the Legal Process*, 3rd. ed. Malibar, FL: R.E. Krieger Publishing Co., 1987.

Grilliot, H. J., and F. A. Schubert, *Introduction to Law and the Legal System*, 5th ed. Boston: Houghton Mifflin, 1992.

Jewell, M. E., and S. C. Patterson, *The Legislative Process in the United States*, 4th ed. New York: Random House, 1986.

Keefe, W. J., and M. S. Ogul, *The American Legislative Process: Congress and the States*, 8th ed. Englewood Cliffs, NJ: Prentice Hall, 1993.

Neubauer, D. W., *Judicial Process: Law, Courts, and Politics in the United States*. Pacific Grove, CA: Brooks/Cole Publishing Co., 1991.

Reynolds, W. L., *Judicial Process in a Nutshell*, 2nd ed. St. Paul, MN: West Publishing Co., 1991.

Van Geel, T., *Understanding Supreme Court Opinions*. New York: Longman Publishing Group, 1991.

Books: Legal Research

Cohen, M. L., R. C. Berring, and K. C. Olson, *How to Find the Law*, 9th ed. St. Paul, MN: West Publishing Co., 1989.

Cohen, M. L., R. C. Berring, and K. C. Olson, *Finding the Law; An Abridged Edition of "How to Find the Law, 9th."* St. Paul, MN: West Publishing Co., 1989.

Jacobstein, J. M., and R. M. Mersky, *Fundamentals of Legal Research*, 5th ed. Westbury, NY: Foundation Press, 1990.

Jacobstein, J. M., and R. M. Mersky, *Legal Research Illustrated*, 5th ed. Westbury, NY: Foundation Press, 1990.

Kunz, C. L., D. A. Schmedemann, A. L. Bateson, M. P. Downs, and C. P. Erlinder, *The Process of Legal Research; Successful Strategies*, 3rd ed. Boston: Little, Brown and Co., 1992.

Olson, K. C., and R. C. Berring, *Practical Approaches to Legal Research*. New York: Haworth Press, 1988.

Teply, L. L., *Legal Research and Citation*, 4th ed. St. Paul, MN: West Publishing Co., 1992.

Appendix

After months of debate and lobbying efforts by both the broadcasting and cable industries, Congress passed the Cable Television Consumer Protection and Competition Act of 1992. The first major overhaul of federal cable legislation since the 1984 legislation, the 1992 act returned to the FCC the power to regulate cable rates where effective competition was lacking at the local level, and rates were determined to be too high. After a delay in enforcement caused by a lack of appropriations, the specific provisions of the 1992 act began to develop as FCC regulations, albeit in the midst of court challenges and negotiations between broadcasters and cable companies over carriage of local network affiliate stations and retransmission consent. Excerpted below are sections of the act dealing with rate regulations, carriage requirements and retransmission consent.

CABLE TELEVISION CONSUMER PROTECTION AND COMPETITION ACT OF 1992

Public Law 102–385, 106 U.S. Stat. 1460, October 5, 1992, Citing Sec. 623

SEC. 2. FINDINGS; POLICY; DEFINITIONS.

(A) FINDINGS.

The Congress finds and declares the following:

(1) Pursuant to the cable Communications Policy Act of 1984, rates for cable television services have been deregulated in approximately 97 percent of all franchises since December 29, 1986. Since rate deregulation, monthly rates for the lowest priced basic cable service have increased by 40 percent or more for 28 percent of cable television subscribers. Although the average number of basic channels has increased from about 24 to 30, average monthly rates have increased by 29 percent during the same period. The average monthly cable rate has increased almost 3 times as much as the Consumer Price Index since rate deregulation.

(2) For a variety of reasons, including local franchising requirements and the extraordinary expense of constructing more than one cable television system to serve a particular geographic

area, most cable television subscribers have no opportunity to select between competing cable systems. Without the presence of another multichannel video programming distributor, a cable system faces no local competition. The result is undue market power for the cable operator as compared to that of consumers and video programmers.

(3) There has been a substantial increase in the penetration of cable television systems over the past decade. Nearly 56,000,000 households, over 60 percent of the households with televisions, subscribe to cable television, and this percentage is almost certain to increase. As a result of this growth, the cable television industry has become a dominant nationwide video medium.

(4) The cable industry has become highly concentrated. The potential effects of such concentration are barriers to entry for new programmers and a reduction in the number of media voices available to consumers.

(5) The cable industry has become vertically integrated; cable operators and cable programmers often have common ownership. As a result, cable operators have the incentive and ability to favor their affiliated programmers. This could make it more difficult for noncable-affiliated programmers to secure carriage on cable systems. Vertically integrated program suppliers also have the incentive and ability to favor their affiliated cable operators over no affiliated cable operators and programming distributors using other technologies.

(6) There is a substantial governmental and First Amendment interest in promoting a diversity of views provided through multiple technology media.

(7) There is a substantial governmental and First Amendment interest in ensuring that cable subscribers have access to local noncommercial educational stations which Congress has authorized, as expressed in section 396(a) (5) of the Communications Act of 1934. The distribution of unique noncommercial, educational programming services advances that interest.

(8) The Federal Government has a substantial interest in making all no duplicative local public television services available on cable systems because—

(A) public television provides educational and informational programming to the Nation's citizens, thereby advancing the Government's compelling interest in educating its citizens;

(B) public television is a local community institution, supported through local tax dollars and voluntary citizen contributions in excess of $10,800,000,000 since 1972, that provides public service programming that is responsive to the needs and interests of the local community;

(C) the Federal Government, in recognition of public television's integral role in serving the educational and informational needs of local communities, has invested more than $3,000,000,000 in public broadcasting since 1969; and

(D) absent carriage requirements there is a substantial likelihood that citizens, who have supported local public television services, will be deprived of those services,

(9) The Federal Government has a substantial interest in having cable systems carry the signals of local commercial television stations because the carriage of such signals is necessary to serve the goals contained in section 307(b) of the Communications Act of 1934 of providing a fair, efficient, and equitable distribution of broadcast services.

(10) A primary objective and benefit of our Nation's system of regulation of television broadcasting is the local origination of programming. There is a substantial governmental interest in ensuring its continuation.

(11) Broadcast television stations continue to be an important source of local news and public affairs programming and other local broadcast services critical to an informed electorate.

(12) Broadcast television programming is supported by revenues generated from advertising broadcast over stations. Such programming is otherwise free to those who own television sets and do not require cable transmission to receive broadcast signals. There is a substantial governmental interest in promoting the continued availability of such free television programming, especially for viewers who are unable to afford other means of receiving programming.

(13) As a result of the growth of cable television, there has been a marked shift in market share from broadcast television to cable television services.

(14) Cable television systems and broadcast television stations increasingly compete for television advertising revenues. As the proportion of households subscribing to cable television increases, proportionately more advertising revenues will be reallocated from broadcast to cable television systems.

(15) A cable television system which carries the signal of a local television broadcaster is assisting the broadcaster to increase its viewership, and thereby attract additional advertising revenues that otherwise might be earned by the cable system

operator. As a result, there is an economic incentive for cable systems to terminate the retransmission of the broadcast signal, refuse to carry new signals, or reposition a broadcast signal to a disadvantageous channel position. There is a substantial likelihood that absent the reimposition of such a requirement, additional local broadcast signals will be deleted, repositioned, or not carried.

(16) As a result of the economic incentive that cable systems have to delete, reposition, or not carry local broadcast signals, coupled with the absence of a requirement that such systems carry local broadcast signals, the economic viability of free local broadcast television and its ability to originate quality local programming will be seriously jeopardized.

(17) Consumers who subscribe to cable television often do so to obtain local broadcast signals which they otherwise would not be able to receive, or to obtain improved signals. Most subscribers to cable television systems do not or cannot maintain antennas to receive broadcast television services, do not have input selector switches to convert from a cable to antenna reception system, or cannot otherwise receive broadcast television services. The regulatory system created by the Cable Communications Policy Act of 1984 was premised upon the continued existence of mandatory carriage obligations for cable systems, ensuring that local stations would be protected from anticompetitive conduct by cable systems.

(18) Cable television systems often are the single most efficient distribution system for television programming. A Government mandate for a substantial societal investment in alternative distribution systems for cable subscribers, such as the "A/B" input selector antenna system, is not an enduring or feasible method of distribution and is not in the public interest.

(19) At the same time, broadcast programming that is carried remains the most popular programming on cable systems, and a substantial portion of the benefits for which consumers pay cable systems is derived from carriage of the signals of network affiliates, independent television stations, and public television stations. Also cable programming placed on channels adjacent to popular off-the-air signals obtains a larger audience than on other channel stations. Cable systems, therefore, obtain great benefits from local broadcast signals which, until now, they have been able to obtain without the consent of the broadcaster or any copyright liability. This has resulted in an effective subsidy of the development of cable systems by local broadcasters. While at one time, when cable systems did not attempt to compete with local broadcasters for programming, audience, and advertising, this subsidy may have been appropriate, it is no longer and results in a competitive imbalance between the two industries.

(20) The Cable Communications Policy Act of 1984, in its amendments to the Communications Act of 1934, limited the regulatory authority of franchising authorities over cable operators. Franchising authorities are finding it difficult under the current regulatory scheme to deny renewals to cable systems that are not adequately serving cable subscribers.

(21) Cable systems should be encouraged to carry low-power television stations licensed to the communities served by those systems where the low-power station creates and broadcasts, as a substantial part of its programming day, local programming.

(B) STATEMENT OF POLICY.

It is the policy of the Congress in this Act to—

(1) promote the availability to the public of a diversity of views and information through cable television and other video distribution media;

(2) rely on the marketplace, to the maximum extent feasible, to achieve that availability;

(3) ensure that cable operators continue to expand, where economically justified, their capacity and the programs offered over their cable systems;

(4) where cable television systems are not subject to effective competition, ensure that consumer interests are protected in receipt of cable service; and

(5) ensure that cable television operators do not have undue market power vis-a-vis video programmers and consumers.

* * *

(A) COMPETITION PREFERENCE; LOCAL AND FEDERAL REGULATION

(1) IN GENERAL.—No Federal agency or State may regulate the rates for the provision of cable service except to the extent provided under this section and section 612. Any franchising authority may regulate the rates for the provision of cable service, or any other communications service provided over a cable system to cable subscribers, but only to the extent provided under this section. No Federal agency, State, or franchising authority

may regulate the rates for cable service of a cable system that is owned or operated by a local government or franchising authority within whose jurisdiction that cable system is located and that is the only cable system located in such jurisdiction.

(2) PREFERENCE FOR COMPETITION.—If the Commission finds that a cable system is subject to effective competition, the rates for the provision of cable service by such system shall not be subject to regulation by the Commission or by a State or franchising authority under this section. If the Commission finds that a cable system is not subject to effective competition—

(A) the rates for the provision of the basic cable service shall be subject to regulation by a franchising authority, or by the Commission if the Commission exercises jurisdiction pursuant to paragraph (6), in accordance with the regulations prescribed by the Commission under subsection (b); and

(B) the rates for cable programming services shall be subject to regulation by the Commission under subsection (c).

(3) QUALIFICATION OF FRANCHISING AUTHORITY.—A franchising authority that seeks to exercise the regulatory jurisdiction permitted under paragraph (2)(A) shall file with the Commission a written certification that—

(A) the franchising authority will adopt and administer regulations with respect to the rates subject to regulation under this section that are consistent with the regulations prescribed by the Commission under subjection (b);

(B) the franchising authority has the legal authority to adopt, and the personnel to administer, such regulations; and

(C) procedural laws and regulations applicable to rate regulation proceedings by such authority provide a reasonable opportunity for consideration of the views of interested parties.

(4) APPROVAL BY COMMISSION.—A certification filed by a franchising authority under paragraph (3) shall be effective 30 days after the date on which it is filed unless the Commission finds, after notice to the authority and a reasonable opportunity for the authority to comment, that—

(A) the franchising authority has adopted or is administering regulations with respect to the rates subject to regulation under this section that are not consistent with the regulations prescribed by the Commission under subsection (b);

(B) the franchising authority does not have the legal authority to adopt, or the personnel to administer, such regulations; or

(C) procedural laws and regulations applicable to rate regulation proceedings by such authority do not provide a reasonable opportunity for consideration of the views of interested parties.

If the Commission disapproves a franchising authority's certification, the Commission shall notify the franchising authority of any revisions or modifications necessary to obtain approval.

(5) REVOCATION OF JURISDICTION.—Upon petition by a cable operator or other interested party, the Commission shall review the regulation of cable system rates by a franchising authority under this subsection. A copy of the petition shall be provided to the franchising authority by the person filing the petition. If the Commission finds that the franchising authority has acted inconsistently with the requirements of this subsection, the Commission shall grant appropriate relief. If the Commission, after the franchising authority has had a reasonable opportunity to comment, determines that the State and local laws and regulations are not in conformance with the regulations prescribed by the Commission under subsection (b), the Commission shall revoke the jurisdiction of such authority.

(6) EXERCISE OF JURISDICTION BY COMMISSION.—If the Commission disapproves a franchising authority's certification under paragraph (4), or revokes such authority's jurisdiction under paragraph (5), the Commission shall exercise the franchising authority's regulatory jurisdiction under paragraph (2) (A) until the franchising authority has qualified to exercise that jurisdiction by filing a new certification that meets the requirements of paragraph (3). Such new certification shall be effective upon approval by the Commission. The Commission shall act to approve or disapprove any such new certification within 90 days after the date it is filed.

(B) ESTABLISHMENT OF BASIC SERVICE TIER RATE REGULATIONS.

(1) COMMISSION OBLIGATION TO SUBSCRIBERS.—The Commission shall, by regulation, ensure that the rates for the basic service tier are reasonable. Such regulations shall be designed to achieve the goal of protecting subscribers of any cable system that is not subject to effective competition from rates for the basic service tier that exceed the rates that would be charged for the basic service tier if such cable system were subject to effective competition.

(2) COMMISSION REGULATIONS.—Within 180 days after date of enactment of the Cable Television Consumer Protection and Competition Act of 1992, the Commission shall prescribe, and periodically thereafter revise, regulations to carry out its obligations under paragraph (1). In prescribing such regulations, the Commission—

(A) shall seek to reduce the administrative burdens on subscribers, cable operators, franchising authorities, and the Commission;

(B) may adopt formulas or other mechanisms and procedures in complying with the requirements of subparagraph (A); and

(C) shall take into account the following factors:

(i) the rates for cable systems, if any, that are subject to effective competition;

(ii) the direct costs (if any) of obtaining, transmitting, and otherwise providing signals carried on the basic service tier, including signals and services carried on the basic service tier pursuant to paragraph (7) (B), and changes in such costs;

(iii) only such portion of the joint and common costs (if any) of obtaining, transmitting, and otherwise providing such signals as is determined, in accordance with regulations prescribed by the Commission, to be reasonably and properly allocable to the basic service tier, and changes in such costs;

(iv) the revenues (if any) received by a cable operator from advertising from programming that is carried as part of the basic service tier or from other consideration obtained in connection with the basic service tier;

(v) the reasonably and properly allocable portion of any amount assessed as a franchise fee, tax, or charge of any kind imposed by any State or local authority on the transactions between cable operators and cable subscribers or any other fee, tax, or assessment of general applicability imposed by a governmental entity applied against cable operators or cable subscribers;

(vi) any amount required, in accordance with paragraph (4), to satisfy franchise requirements to support public, educational, or governmental channels or the use of such channels or any other services required under the franchise; and

(vii) a reasonable profit, as defined by the Commission consistent with the Commission's obligations to subscribers under paragraph (1).

(3) EQUIPMENT.—The regulations prescribed by the Commission under this subsection shall include standards to establish, on the basis of actual cost, the price or rate for—

(A) installation and lease of the equipment used by subscribers to receive the basic service tier, including a converter box and a remote control unit and, if requested by the subscriber, such addressable converter box or other equipment as is required to access programming described in paragraph (8); and

(B) installation and monthly use of connections for additional television receivers.

(4) COSTS OF FRANCHISE REQUIREMENTS.—The regulations prescribed by the Commission under this subsection shall include standards to identify costs attributable to satisfying franchise requirements to support public, educational, and governmental channels or the use of such channels or any other services required under the franchise.

(5) IMPLEMENTATION AND ENFORCEMENT.—The regulations prescribed by the Commission under this subsection shall include additional standards, guidelines, and procedures concerning the implementation and enforcement of such regulations, which shall include—

(A) procedures by which cable operators may implement and franchising authorities may enforce the regulations prescribed by the Commission under this subsection;

(B) procedures for the expeditious resolution of disputes between cable operators and franchising authorities concerning the administration of such regulations;

(C) standards and procedures to prevent unreasonable charges for changes in the subscriber's selection of services or equipment subject to regulation under this section, which standards shall require that charges for changing the service tier selected shall be based on the cost of such change and shall not exceed nominal amounts when the system's configuration permits changes in service tier selection to be effected solely by coded entry on a computer terminal or by other similarly simple method; and

(D) standards and procedures to assure that subscribers receive notice of the availability of the basic service tier required under this section.

(6) NOTICE.—The procedures prescribed by the Commission pursuant to paragraph (5) (A) shall require a cable operator to provide 30 days' advance notice to a franchising authority of any increase proposed in the price to be charged for the basic service tier.

(7) COMPONENTS OF BASIC TIER SUBJECT TO RATE REGULATION.—

(A) MINIMUM CONTENTS.—Each cable operator of a cable system shall provide its subscribers a separately available basic service tier to which subscription is required for access to any other tier of service. Such basic service tier shall, at a minimum, consist of the following:

(i) All signals carried in fulfillment of the requirements of sections 614 and 615.

(ii) Any public, educational, and governmental access programming required by the franchise of the cable system to be provided to subscribers.

(iii) Any signal of any television broadcast station that is provided by the cable operator to any subscriber, except a signal which is secondarily transmitted by a satellite carrier beyond the local service area of such station.

(B) PERMITTED ADDITIONS TO BASIC TIER.—A cable operator may add additional video programming signals or services to the basic service tier. Any such additional signals or services provided on the basic service tier shall be provided to subscribers at rates determined under the regulations prescribed by the Commission under this subsection.

(8) BUY-THROUGH OF OTHER TIERS PROHIBITED.—

(A) PROHIBITION.—A cable operator may not require the subscription to any tier other than the basic service tier required by paragraph (7) as a condition of access to video programming offered on a per channel or per program basis. A cable operator may not discriminate between subscribers to the basic service tier and other subscribers with regard to the rates charged for video programming offered on a per channel or per program basis.

(B) EXCEPTION; LIMITATION.—The prohibition in subparagraph (A) shall not apply to a cable system that, by reason of the lack of addressable converter boxes or other technological limitations, does not permit the operator to offer programming on a per channel or per program basis in the same manner required by subparagraph (A). This subparagraph shall not be available to any cable operator after—

(i) the technology utilized by the cable system is modified or improved in a way that eliminates such technological limitation; or

(ii) 10 years after the date of enactment of the Cable Television Consumer Protection and Competition Act of 1992, subject to subparagraph (C).

(C) WAIVER.—If, in any proceeding initiated at the request of any cable operator, the Commission determines that compliance with the requirements of subparagraph (A) would require the cable operator to increase its rates, the Commission may, to the extent consistent with the public interest, grant such cable operator a waiver from such requirements for such specified period as the Commission determines reasonable and appropriate.

(C) REGULATION OF UNREASONABLE RATES.

(1) COMMISSION REGULATIONS.—Within 180 days after the date of enactment of the Cable Television Consumer Protection and Competition Act of 1992, the Commission shall, by regulation, establish the following:

(A) criteria prescribed in accordance with paragraph (2) for identifying, in individual cases, rates for cable programming services that are unreasonable;

(B) fair and expeditious procedures for the receipt, consideration, and resolution of complaints from any subscriber, franchising authority, or other relevant State or local government entity alleging that a rate for cable programming services charged by a cable operator violates the criteria prescribed under subparagraph (A), which procedures shall include the minimum showing that shall be required for a complaint to obtain Commission consideration and resolution of whether the rate in question is unreasonable; and

(C) the procedures to be used to reduce rates for cable programming services that are determined by the Commission to be unreasonable and to refund such portion of the rates or charges that were paid by subscribers after the filing of such complaint and that are determined to be unreasonable.

(2) FACTORS TO BE CONSIDERED.—In establishing the criteria for determining in individual cases whether rates for cable programming services are unreasonable under paragraph (1)(A), the Commission shall consider, among other factors—

(A) the rates for similarly situated cable systems offering comparable cable programming services, taking into account similarities in facilities, regulatory and governmental costs, the number of subscribers, and other relevant factors;

(B) the rates for cable systems, if any, that are subject to effective competition;

(C) the history of the rates for cable programming services of the system, including the relationship of such rates to changes in general consumer prices;

(D) the rates, as a whole, for all the cable programming, cable equipment, and cable services provided by the system, other than programming provided on a per channel or per program basis;

(E) capital and operating costs of the cable system, including the quality and costs of the customer service provided by the cable system; and

(F) the revenues (if any) received by a cable operator from advertising from programming that is carried as part of the service for which a rate is being established, and changes in such revenues, or from other consideration obtained in connection with the cable programming services concerned.

(3) LIMITATION ON COMPLAINTS CONCERNING EXISTING RATES.—Except during the 180-day period following the effective date of the regulations prescribed by the Commission under paragraph (1), the procedures established under subparagraph (B) of such paragraph shall be available only with respect to complaints filed within a reasonable period of time following a change in rates that is initiated after that effective date, including a change in rates that results from a change in that system's service tiers.

(D) UNIFORM RATE STRUCTURE REQUIRED.

A cable operator shall have a rate structure, for the provision of cable service, that is uniform throughout the geographic area in which cable service is provided over its cable system.

(E) DISCRIMINATION; SERVICES FOR THE HEARING IMPAIRED.

Nothing in this title shall be construed as prohibiting any Federal agency, State, or a franchising authority from— (1) prohibiting discrimination among subscribers and potential subscribers to cable service, except that no Federal agency, State, or franchising authority may prohibit a cable operator from offering reasonable discounts to senior citizens or other economically disadvantaged group discounts; or (2) requiring and regulating the installation or rental of equipment which facilitates the reception of cable service by hearing impaired individuals.

(F) NEGATIVE OPTION BILLING PROHIBITED.

A cable operator shall not charge a subscriber for any service or equipment that the subscriber has not affirmatively requested by name. For purposes of this subsection, a subscriber's failure to refuse a cable operator's proposal to provide such service or equipment shall not be deemed to be an affirmative request for such service or equipment.

(G) COLLECTION OF INFORMATION.

The Commission shall, by regulation, require cable operators to file with the Commission or a franchising authority, as appropriate, within one year after the date of enactment of the Cable Television Consumer Protection and Competition Act of 1992 and annually thereafter, such financial information as may be needed for purposes of administering and enforcing this section.

(H) PREVENTION OF EVASIONS.

Within 180 days after the date of enactment of the Cable Television Consumer Protection and Competition Act of 1992, the Commission shall, by regulation, establish standards, guidelines, and procedures to prevent evasions, including evasions that result from retiering, of the requirements of this section and shall, thereafter, periodically review and revise such standards, guidelines, and procedures.

(I) SMALL SYSTEMS BURDENS.

In developing and prescribing regulations pursuant to this section, the Commission shall design such regulations to reduce the administrative burdens and cost of compliance for cable systems that have 1,000 or fewer subscribers.

(J) RATE REGULATION AGREEMENTS.

During the term of an agreement made before July 1, 1990, by a franchising authority and a cable operator providing for the regulation of basic cable service rates, where there was not effective competition under Commission rules in effect on that date, nothing in this section (or the regulations thereunder) shall abridge the ability of such franchising authority to regulate rates in accordance with such an agreement.

(K) REPORTS ON AVERAGE PRICES.

The Commission shall annually publish statistical reports on the average rates for basic cable service and other cable programming, and for converter boxes, remote control units, and other equipment, of—(1) cable systems that the Commission has found are subject to effective competition under subsection (a) (2), compared with (2) cable systems that the Commission has found are not subject to such effective competition.

(L) DEFINITIONS.

As used in this section—

(1) The term "effective competition" means that—

(A) fewer than 30 percent of the households in the franchise area subscribe to the cable service of a cable system;

(B) the franchise area is—

(i) served by at least two unaffiliated multichannel video programming distributors each of which offers comparable video programming to at least 50 percent of the households in the franchise area; and

(ii) the number of households subscribing to programming services offered by multichannel video programming distributors other than the largest multichannel video programming distributor exceeds 15 percent of the households in the franchise area; or

(C) a multichannel video programming distributor operated by the franchising authority for that franchise area offers video programming to at least 50 percent of the households in that franchise area.

(2) The term "cable programming service" means any video programming provided over a cable system, regardless of service tier, including installation or rental of equipment used for the receipt of such video programming, other than (A) video programming carried on the basic service tier, and (B) video programming offered on a per channel or per program basis.

* * *

SEC. 4. CARRIAGE OF LOCAL COMMERCIAL TELEVISION SIGNALS.

Part II of title VI of the Communications Act of 1934 is amended by inserting after 613 (47 U.S.C. 533) the following new section:

SEC. 614. CARRIAGE OF LOCAL COMMERCIAL TELEVISION SIGNALS.

(A) CARRIAGE OBLIGATIONS.

Each cable operator shall carry, on the cable system of that operator, the signals of local commercial television stations and qualified low power stations as provided by this section. Carriage of additional broadcast television signals on such system shall be at the discretion of such operator, subject to section 325(b).

(B) SIGNALS REQUIRED.

(1) IN GENERAL.—(A) A cable operator of a cable system with 12 or fewer usable activated channels shall carry the signals of at least three local commercial television stations, except that is such a system has 300 or fewer subscribers, it shall not be subject to any requirements under this section so long as such system does not delete from carriage by that system any signal of a broadcast television station.

(B) A cable operator of a cable system with more than 12 usable activated channels shall carry the signals of local commercial television stations, up to one-third of the aggregate number of usable activated channels of such system.

(2) SELECTION OF SIGNALS.—Whenever the number of local commercial television stations exceeds the maximum number of signals a cable system is required to carry under paragraph (1), the cable operator shall have discretion in selecting which such stations shall be carried on its cable system, except that—

(A) under no circumstances shall a cable operator carry a qualified low power station in lieu of a local commercial television station; and

(B) if the cable operator elects to carry an affiliate of a broadcast network (as such term is defined by the Commission by regulation), such cable operator shall carry the affiliate of such broadcast network whose city of license reference point, as defined in section 76.53 of title 47, Code of Federal Regulations (in effect on January 1, 1991), or any successor regulation thereto, is closest to the principal headend of the cable system.

(3) CONTENT TO BE CARRIED.—

(A) A cable operator shall carry in its entirety, on the cable system of that operator, the primary video, accompanying audio, and line 21 closed caption transmission of each of the local commercial television stations carried on the cable system and, to the extent technically feasible, program-related material carried in the vertical blanking interval or on subcarriers. Retransmission of other material in the vertical blanking internal or other nonprogram-related material (including teletext and other subscription and advertiser-supported information services) shall be at the discretion of the cable operator. Where appropriate and feasible, operators may delete signal enhancements, such as ghost-canceling, from the broadcast signal and employ such enhancements at the system headend or headends.

(B) The cable operator shall carry the entirety of the program schedule of any television station carried on the cable system unless carriage of specific programming is prohibited, and other programming authorized to be substituted, under section 76.67 or subpart F of part 76 of title 47, Code of Federal Regulations (as in effect on January 1, 1991), or any successor regulations thereto.

(4) SIGNAL QUALITY.

(A) NONDEGRADATION; TECHNICAL SPECIFICATIONS.—The signals of local commercial television stations that a cable operator carries shall be carried without material degradation. The Commission shall adopt carriage standards to ensure that, to the extent technically feasible, the quality of signal processing and carriage provided by a cable system for the carriage of local commercial television stations will be no less than that provided by the system for carriage of any other type of signal.

(B) ADVANCED TELEVISION.—At such time as the Commission prescribes modifications of the standards for television broadcast signals, the Commission shall initiate a proceeding to establish any changes in the signal carriage requirements of cable television systems necessary to ensure cable carriage of such broadcast signals of local commercial television stations which have been changed to conform with such modified standards.

(5) DUPLICATION NOT REQUIRED.—Notwithstanding paragraph (1), a cable operator shall not be required to carry the signal of any local commercial television station that substantially duplicates the signal of another local commercial television station which is carried on its cable system, or to carry the signals of more than one local commercial television station affiliated with a particular broadcast network (as such term is defined by regulation). If a cable operator elects to carry on its cable system a signal which substantially duplicates the signal of another local commercial television station carried on the cable system, or to carry on its system the signals of more than one local commercial television station affiliated with a particular broadcast network, all such signals shall be counted toward the number of signals the operator is required to carry under paragraph (1).

(6) CHANNEL POSITIONING.—Each signal carried in fulfillment of the carriage obligations of a cable operator under this section shall be carried on the cable system channel number on which the local commercial television station is broadcast over the air, or on the channel on which it was carried on July 19, 1985, or on the channel on which it was carried on January 1, 1992, at the election of the station, or on such other channel number as is mutually agreed upon by the station and the cable operator. Any dispute regarding the positioning of a local commercial television station shall be resolved by the Commission.

(7) SIGNAL AVAILABILITY.—Signals carried in fulfillment of the requirements of this section shall be provided to every subscriber of a cable system. Such signals shall be viewable via cable on all television receivers of a subscriber which are connected to a cable system by a cable operator or for which a cable operator provides a connection. If a cable operator authorizes subscribers to install additional receiver connections, but does not provide the subscriber with such connections, or with the equipment and materials for such connections, the operator shall notify such subscribers of all broadcast stations carried on the cable system which cannot be viewed via cable without a converter box and shall offer to sell or lease such a converter box to such subscribers at rates in accordance with section 623(b)(3).

(8) IDENTIFICATION OF SIGNALS CARRIED.—A cable operator shall identify, upon request by any person, the signals carried on its system in fulfillment of the requirements of this section.

(9) NOTIFICATION.—A cable operator shall provide written notice to a local commercial television station at least 30 days prior to either deleting from carriage or repositioning that station. No deletion or repositioning of a local commercial television station shall occur during a period in which major television ratings services measure the size of audiences of local television stations. The notification provisions of this paragraph shall not be used to undermine or evade the channel positioning or carriage requirements imposed upon cable operators under this section.

(10) COMPENSATION FOR CARRIAGE.—A cable operator shall not accept or request monetary payment or other valuable consideration in exchange either for carriage of local commercial television stations in fulfillment of the requirements of this section or for the channel positioning rights provided to such stations under this section, except that—

(A) any such station may be required to bear the costs associated with delivering a good quality signal or a baseband video signal to the principal headend of the cable system;

(B) a cable operator may accept payments from stations which would be considered distant signals under section 111 of title 17, United States Code, as indemnification for any increased copyright liability resulting from carriage of such signal; and

(C) a cable operator may continue to accept monetary payment or other valuable consideration in exchange for carriage or channel positioning of the signal of any local commercial television station carried in fulfillment of the requirements of this section, through, but not beyond, the date of expiration of an agreement thereon between a cable operator and a local commercial television station entered into prior to June 26, 1990.

(C) LOW POWER STATION CARRIAGE OBLIGATION.—

(1) REQUIREMENT.—If there are not sufficient signals of full power local commercial television stations to fill the channels set aside under subsection (b)—

(A) a cable operator of a cable system with a capacity of 35 or fewer usable activated channels shall be required to carry one qualified low power station; and

(B) a cable operator of a cable system with a capacity of more than 35 usable activated channels shall be required to carry two qualified low power stations.

(2) USE OF PUBLIC, EDUCATIONAL, OR GOVERNMENTAL CHANNELS.—A cable operator required to carry more than one signal of a qualified low power station under this subsection may do so, subject to approval by the franchising authority pursuant to section 611, by placing such additional station on public, educational, or governmental channels not in use for their designated purposes.

(D) REMEDIES.—

(1) COMPLAINTS BY BROADCAST STATIONS.—Whenever a local commercial television station believes that a cable operator has failed to meet its obligations under this section, such station shall notify the operator, in writing, of the alleged failure and identify its reasons for believing that the cable operator is obligated to carry the signal of such station or has otherwise failed to comply with the channel positioning or repositioning or other requirements of this section. The cable operator shall, within 30 days of such written notification, respond in writing to such notification and either commence to carry the signal of such station in accordance with the terms requested or state its reasons for believing that it is not obligated to carry such signal or is in compliance with the channel positioning and repositioning and other requirements of this section. A local commercial television station that is denied carriage or channel positioning or repositioning in accordance with this section by a cable operator may obtain review of such denial by filing a complaint with the Commission. Such complaint shall allege the manner in which such cable operator has failed to meet its obligations and the basis for such allegations.

(2) OPPORTUNITY TO RESPOND.—The Commission shall afford such cable operator an opportunity to present data and arguments to establish that there has been no failure to meet its obligations under this section.

(3) REMEDIAL ACTIONS; DISMISSAL.—Within 120 days after the date a complaint is filed, the Commission shall determine whether the cable operator has met is obligations under this section. If the Commission determines that the cable operator has failed to meet such obligations, the Commission shall order the cable operator to reposition the complaining station or, in the case of an obligation to carry a station, to commence carriage of the station and to continue such carriage for at least 12 months. If the Commission determines that the cable operator has fully met the requirements of this section, it shall dismiss the complaint.

* * *

SEC. 6. RETRANSMISSION CONSENT FOR CABLE SYSTEMS.

Section 325 of the Communications act of 1934 (47 U.S.C. 325) is amended—

(1) by redesignating subsections (b) and (c) as subsections (c) and (d), respectively; and

(2) by inserting immediately after subsection (a) the following new subsection: (b)(1) Following

the date that is one year after the date of enactment of the Cable Television Consumer Protection and Competition Act of 1992, no cable system or other multichannel video programming distributor shall retransmit the signal of a broadcasting station, or any part thereof, except—

(A) with the express authority of the originating station; or

(B) pursuant to section 614, in the case of a station electing, in accordance with this subsection, to assert the right to carriage under such section.

(2) The provisions of this subsection shall not apply to—

(A) retransmission of the signal of a noncommercial broadcasting station;

(B) retransmission directly to a home satellite antenna of the signal of a broadcasting station that is not owned or operated by, or affiliated with, a broadcasting network, if such signal was retransmitted by a satellite carrier on May 1, 1991;

(C) retransmission of the signal of a broadcasting station that is owned or operated by, or affiliated with, a broadcasting network directly to a home satellite antenna, if the household receiving the signal is an unserved household; or

(D) retransmission by a cable operator or other multichannel video programming distributor of the signal of a superstation if such signal was obtained from a satellite carrier and the originating station was a superstation on May 1, 1991. For purposes of this paragraph, the terms 'satellite carrier,' 'superstation,' and 'unserved household' have the meanings given those terms, respectively in section 119(d) of title 17, United States Code, as in effect on the date of enactment of the Cable Television Consumer Protection and Competition Act of 1992.

(3)(A) Within 45 days after the date of enactment of the Cable Television Consumer Protection and Competition Act of 1992, the Commission shall commence a rulemaking proceeding to establish regulations to govern the exercise by television broadcast stations of the right to grant retransmission consent under this subsection and of the right to signal carriage under section 614, and such other regulations as are necessary to administer the limitations carried in paragraph (2). The Commission shall consider in such proceeding the impact that the grant of retransmission consent by television stations may have on the rates for the basic service tier and shall ensure that the regulations prescribed under this subsection do not conflict with the Commission's obligation under section 623(b)(1) to ensure that the rates for the basic service tier are reasonable. Such rulemaking proceeding shall be completed within 180 days after the date of enactment of the Cable Television Consumer Protection and Competition Act of 1992.

(B) The regulations required by subparagraph (A) shall require that television stations, within one year after the date of enactment of the Cable Television Consumer Protection and Competition Act of 1992 and every three years thereafter, make an election between the right to grant retransmission consent under this subsection and the right to signal carriage under section 614. If there is more than one cable system which services the same geographic area, a station's election shall apply to all such cable systems.

(4) If an originating television station elects under paragraph (3)(B) to exercise its right to grant retransmission consent under this subsection with respect to a cable system, the provisions of section 614 shall not apply to the carriage of the signal of such station by such cable system.

(5) The exercise by a television broadcast station of the right to grant retransmission consent under this subsection shall not interfere with or supersede the rights under section 614 or 615 of any station electing to assert the right to signal carriage under that section.

(6) Nothing in this section shall be construed as modifying the compulsory copyright license established in section lll of title 17, United States Code, or as affecting existing or future video programming licensing agreements between broadcasting stations and video programmers.

Notes

Chapter 1

[1] Source for the quotations in the last sentence of the Introduction and also of this chapter's early history of the telegraph is from: E. L. Morse, ed., *Samuel F. B. Morse: His Letters and Journals* (New York: Boston, Houghton Mifflin, 1914), pp. 5–7.

[2] Ibid., p. 7. Important to later patent suits (somewhat common for inventors, especially during the early history of electronic communication as witnessed not only by Morse but later Marconi and de Forest) were the sketches he made on the return to America on the vessel *Sully*. A certified copy of the original sketch was eventually placed in the National Museum in Washington, DC (1914). The original drawing included a magnet, the source of electricity being based on the theories of electromagnetism. Some Congressional indexes of the era referred to such work under the heading "animal magnetism." Dr. Charles T. Jackson claimed later to have given Morse all of his ideas but J. Francis Fisher, a Philadelphia attorney, provided the following testimony:

> In the fall of the year 1832 I returned from Europe as a passenger with Mr. Morse in the ship *Sully*, Captain Pell master. During the voyage the subject on an electric telegraph was one of frequent conversation. Mr. Morse was most constant in pursuing it, and *alone* the one who seems disposed to reduce it to practical test, and I recollect that, for this purpose, he devised *a system of signs* for letters to be indicated and marked by quick succession of strokes or shocks of the galvanic current, and I am sure of the fact that it was deem by Mr. Morse perfectly competent to effect the result stated. I did not suppose that any other person on board the ship claimed any merit in the invention, or was, in fact interested to pursue it to maturity as Mr. Morse then seemed to be, nor have I been able since that time to recall any fact or circumstance to justify the claim of any person other than Mr. Morse to the invention. (Source: E. L. Morse, p. 11)

[3] Petition of Samuel C. Reid, "Praying for the Establishment of a Line of Telegraphs from New York to New Orleans," 24th Congress, Sess. 11, January 26, 1837, *U.S. Serial*, Vol. 298, pp. 107–108. To aid the reader in grasping the material, when quoting documents throughout this text, especially in the case of more complex material, the author has on occasion added paragraph breaks where none may have appeared in the original document. (Author's note: In most of the quoted material, the seventeenth-century spelling has been changed to contemporary usage.)

[4] Ibid.

[5] Ibid.

[6] Ibid.

[7] As referenced and quoted in the letter from the Secretary of the Treasury, Levi Woodbury, "Transmitting a Report upon the Subject of a System of Telegraphs for the United States," 25th Congress, 2d Session, December 11, 1837, *U.S. Serial*, Vol. 322, House Doc. No. 15.

[8] Ibid.

[9] Ibid.

[10] Ibid.

[11] Ibid.

[12] Report of Committee on Commerce, "Electro-Magnetic Telegraphs," 25th Congress, 2d Session, April 6, 1838, *U.S. Serial*, Vol. 335, House Doc. No. 753.

[13] Ibid.

[14] Ibid.

[15] Ibid.

[16] Ibid.

[17] Ibid.

[18] The letter was presented by Secretary of the Treasury, Levi Woodbury, to Samuel Cushman who had become chairman of the Committee on Commerce. Cushman presented the letter in a report to the House of Representatives on January 4, 1839.

[19] An additional letter dated August 10, 1842 to Congressman Boardman of Connecticut contained an offer from

Morse to conduct a demonstration between the "President's house, or one of the Departments, and the Capitol and the Navy Yard, so that instantaneous communication can be held between these three points at pleasure, at any time of day or night, at any season, in clear of rainy weather, and ready to their examination during the next session of Congress, so that the whole subject may be fairly understood." Boardman's reply was not encouraging. He wrote: "The Treasury and the Government are both bankrupt, and that foolish Tyler (President John Tyler) has vetoed the tariff bill; the House is in bad humor and nothing of the kind you propose could be done." Source: E. L. Morse, ed., *Samuel F. B. Morse: His Letters and Journals*, pp. 175–177.

[20] Letter from the Secretary of the Treasury, Samuel Cushman, transmitting to Congress, "A letter from Professor Morse, on the subject of his electro-magnetic telegraph," 25th Congress, 3d Session, January 4, 1839, *U.S. Serial*, Vol. 346, House Doc. No. 58.

[21] After an 89-to-83 vote in the House and a long delay in the Senate.

[22] The original wording of the bill appeared in an earlier report from the Hon. Charles G. Ferris of New York in a Commerce Committee Report dated December 30, 1842 ("Electro-magnetic Telegraphs," Report No. 17, 27th Congress, 3d Session, House of Representatives) in which the postmaster general was to administer the funds. The words *postmaster general* were replaced by the words *secretary of the treasury*.

[23] *Congressional Globe*, Vol. XIII, June 5, 1844, p. 643. "I beg leave to state that the perfect practicability of the system has been fully and satisfactorily established by the work already completed. The subject is respectfully submitted to the consideration of Congress, for such further directions in the matter as may be deemed expedient."

The report details the operations and states that "although the estimates were that the cost of the conducting wires in pipes would be $583 per mile, and on posts $350, the actual cost was considerably less; and that, of the $30,000 appropriated by Congress, $3500 remains unexpended, and will probably suffice for current expenses till Congress sees fit to extend the experiment."

[24] Although Morse himself was a religious man, the words themselves were chosen by Annie Ellsworth, the daughter of the commissioner of patents and Morse's friend H. L. Ellsworth, from the Bible, the twenty-third verse of the twenty-third chapter of Numbers. It was Annie Ellsworth who had first notified Morse of the passage of the bill, at which time he told her she could pick the first message when the line was completed. (*Samuel F. B. Morse: Letters and Journals*, pp. 199 and 222.)

[25] "Magnetic Telegraph. Letter from the Secretary of the Treasury, transmitting a letter from Professor Morse, relative to the magnetic telegraph." 28th Congress, 2d Session, December 23, 1844, *U.S. Serial*, Vol. 464, House Doc. No. 24. (The letter was in support of extending the telegraph to New York.)

[26] Ibid.

[27] E. L. Morse, ed., *Samuel F. B. Morse: His Letters and Journals*, p. 232.

[28] Ibid.

[29] "An Act making Appropriations for the Service of the Post-Office Department for the Year ending thirtieth June, eighteen hundred and forty-seven," 39th Congress, Sess. I, Ch. 31, June 19, 1846. *U.S. Stat.*, Vol. 9, p. 19.

[30] "An Act making Appropriations for the civil and diplomatic Expenses of Government, for the Year ending the thirtieth Day of June, eighteen hundred and forty-seven, and for other Purposes," 39th Congress, Sess. I, Ch. 175, August 10, 1846, *U.S. Stat.*, Vol. 9, p. 85.

[31] "An Act authorizing the Construction of a Line of Telegraph from the Mississippi or Missouri Rivers to the Pacific Ocean," 33rd Congress, Sess. I, Ch. 112, February 17, 1855, *U.S. Stat.*, Vol. 10, p. 610.

[32] "An Act to facilitate Communication between the Atlantic and Pacific States by Electric Telegraph," 36th Congress, Sess. I, Ch. 137, June 16, 1860, *U.S. Stat.*, Vol. 12, p. 41.

[33] "An Act to aid in the Construction of a Railroad and Telegraph Line from the Missouri River to the Pacific Ocean, and to secure to the Government the Use of the same for Postal, Military, and Other Purposes," 37th Congress, Sess. II, Ch. 120, July 1, 1862, *U.S. Stat.*, Vol. 12, p. 489.

[34] "An act supplementary to the act of July first, eighteen hundred and sixty-two, entitled 'An act to aid in the construction of a railroad and telegraph line from the Missouri River to the Pacific Ocean, and to secure to the Government the use of sale for postal, military, and other purposes,' and also of the act of July second, eighteen hundred and sixty-four, and other acts amendatory or said first-named act," 50th Congress, Sess. I, Ch. 772, August 7, 1888, *U.S. Stat.* Vol. 25, p. 382.

[35] The clause should not be confused with discrimination on the basis of contemporary definitions of sex, age, race, religion, or national origin.

[36] Ibid., pp 383–384.

[37] "An Act to aid in the Construction of Telegraph Lines, and to secure to the Government the Use of same for postal, military, and other Purposes," 39th Congress, Sess. I, Ch. 230, July 24, 1866, *U.S. Stat.*, Vol. 14, pp. 221–222.

[38] "An Act to expedite Telegraphic Communication for the Uses of the Government in its Foreign Intercourse," 34th Congress, Session III, Ch. 95, March 3, 1857, *U.S. Stat.*, Vol. 11, p. 187.

[39] "An Act to grant to the American Atlantic Cable Telegraph Company, of New York, the Right of Way and Privilege to lay, land, and operate a Submarine Telegraph Cable on the Atlantic Coast of the United States, and establish Telegraph Communication between the United States and Europe, via the Bermudas and Azores Islands," Sess. I., Ch. 15, March 29, 1867, *U.S. Stat.*, Vol. 11, p. 10.

[40] "An Act to encourage and promote telegraphic communication between America and Asia," 44th Congress, Sess. I., Ch. 293, August 15, 1876, *U.S. Stat.*, Vol. 19, p. 201.

[41] Ibid.

[42] Ibid.

[43] "An Act to encourage and promote telegraphic communication between America and Europe," 44th Congress, Sess. II, Ch. 63, February 20, 1877, *U.S. Stat.*, Vol. 19, p. 232.

[44] Ibid. Cable refers to telegraph; cable television did not appear until the 1940s.

[45] "An Act to expedite Telegraphic Communication for the Uses of the Government in its Foreign Intercourse," 34th Congress, Session III, Ch. 95, March 3, 1857, *U.S. Stat.*, Vol. 11, p. 188.

[46] "An Act to aid in Construction of Telegraph Lines, and to secure to the Government the Use of the same for postal, military, and other Purposes," 39th Congress, Sess. I, Ch. 230, July 24, 1866, *U.S. Stat.*, Vol. 14, p. 221.

Note: The Post Roads Act is sometimes cited as the beginning of the regulation of electronic communication but the reader encountering such referrals should keep in mind the early stipulations placed upon Morse in his earliest telegraph experiments, namely the expenditure of appropriations and also the 1857 law cited in the previous footnote.

[47] "An Act to grant to the American Atlantic Cable Telegraph Company, of New York, the Right of Way and Privilege to lay, land, and operate a Submarine Telegraph Cable on the Atlantic Coast of the United States, and establish Telegraph Communication between the United States and Europe, via the Bermuda and Azores Islands," 40th Cong., Sess. I., Ch. 15, March 29, 1867, *U.S. Stat.*, Vol. 15, p. 10.

48 "An Act to encourage and promote telegraphic communication between America and Asia," 44th Congress, Session. I., Ch. 293, August 15, 1876, *U.S. Stat.*, Vol. 19, p. 201.

49 "An Act to encourage and promote telegraphic communication between America and Europe," 44th Congress, Sess. II, Ch. 63, February 20, 1877, *U.S. Stat.*, Vol. 19, p. 232.

50 "An Act making Appropriations for sundry civil Expenses of the Government for the fiscal Year ending June thirty, eighteen hundred and seventy-two, and for other Purposes," 41st Congress, Sess. III., Ch. 114, March 3, 1871, *U.S. Stat.*, Vol. 16, p. 495.

51 "An Act making Appropriations to supply Deficiencies in the Appropriations for the Service of the Government for the fiscal Years ending June thirty, eighteen hundred and seventy, and June thirty, eighteen hundred and seventy-one and for former Years, and for other Purposes," 41st Congress, Sess. III., Ch. 115, March 3, 1871, *U.S. Stat.*, Vol 16, p. 520.

52 "An Act to revise, consolidate, and amend the Statutes relating to the Post-Office Department," 42nd Congress, Sess. II., Ch. 335, June 8, 1872, *U.S. Stat.*, Vol. 17, p. 287.

53 "An Act to authorize the President of the United States in certain Cases to take Possession of Railroad and Telegraph Lines, and for other Purposes," 37th Congress, Sess. II., January 31, 1862, *U.S. Stat.*, Vol. 12, p. 334.

54 "An Act making Appropriations for the Support of the Army for the Year ending the thirtieth of June, eighteen hundred and sixty-three, and additional Appropriations for the Year ending thirtieth of June, eighteen hundred and sixty-two, and for other purposes," 37th Congress, Sess. II., Ch. 133, July 5, 1862, *U.S. Stat.*, Vol. 12, p. 505.

55 "An Act making Appropriations for the Support of the Army for the Year ending the thirtieth of June, eighteen hundred and sixty-four, and for a Deficiency for the Signal Service for the Year ending June thirty, eighteen hundred and sixty-three," 37th Congress, Sess. III., Ch. 25, February 9, *U.S. Stat.*, Vol. 12, p. 642.

56 "An Act to provide Internal Revenue to support the Government and to pay Interest of the Public Dept.," 37th Congress, Sess. II., Ch. 119, July 1, 1862, *U.S. Stat.*, Vol. 12, p. 432.

57 "An Act to encourage and facilitate Telegraphic Communication between the Eastern and Western Continents," 38th Congress, Sess. I., Ch. 199, July 1, 1864, *U.S. Stat.*, Vol. 13, p. 340.

58 "Treaty between the United States of America and the Shoshonee-Gosip Bands of Indians, concluded at Tuilla Valley, October 12, 1863; Ratification advised, with Amendment, by the Senate, March 7, 1864; Amendment assented to, November 24, 1864; Proclaimed by the President of the United States, January 17, 1865," *U.S. Stat.*, Vol. 13, p. 681.

59 "Treaty between the United States of America and the Sissiton and Warpeton Bands of Dakota or Sioux Indians; Concluded February 19, 1867; Ratification advised, with Amendments, April 15, 1867; Amendments accepted April 22, 1867; Proclaimed May 2, 1867," *U.S. Stat.*, Vol. 15, p. 505.

60 "An Act making Appropriations for the Support of the Army for the Year ending June thirty, eighteen hundred and seventy-two, and for other Purposes." 41st Congress, Sess. III., Ch. 116, March 3, 1871, *U.S. Stat.*, Vol. 16, p. 522.

61 Ibid.

62 Ibid.

63 Ibid.

64 "An act to protect lines of telegraph constructed by the United States from malicious injury and obstruction." 43th Congress, Sess. I., Ch. 461, June 23, 1874, *U.S. Stat.*, Vol. 18, p. 250.

65 "An Act To provide ways and means to meet war expenditures, and for other purposes," 55th Congress, Sess. II., Ch. 448, June 13, 1898, *U.S. Stat.*, Vol. 30, p. 448.

66 Ibid.

67 "An act to provide for taking the tenth and subsequent censuses," 45th Congress, Sess. III., Ch. 195, March 3, 1879, *U.S. Stat.*, Vol. 20, p. 478.

68 "AT&T Cuts Off Telegraph Service," *News and Observer*, Raleigh, NC, December 18, 1991, p. 10C.

Chapter 2

1 The Wireless Ship Act of 1910, Public Law 262, 61st Congress, June 24, 1910.

2 The Radio Act of 1912, Public Law 264, 62d Congress, August 13, 1912. Sec. 1.

3 See Edward F. Sarno, Jr., "The National Radio Conferences," *Journal of Broadcasting* 13 (Spring 1969), 189–202.

4 Ibid. For a summary of the role of the Department of Commerce during this period, see Marvin R. Bensman, "Regulation of Broadcasting by the Department of Commerce, 1921–1927," in Lawrence W. Lichty and Malachi C. Toppings, eds., *American Broadcasting: A Source Book on the History of Radio and Television* (New York: Hastings House, 1975), pp. 544–555; see also Carl H. Butman, "Better Radio Service," *Radio News* 6 (December 1924).

5 A third legislative defeat, coming on the heels of two previous unsuccessful attempts, would have been politically humiliating. The entire issue could have become bogged down in a legislative quagmire while the turmoil in the radio industry continued unabated.

6 *Hoover* v. *Intercity Radio C., Inc.*, 286 F. 1003 (D.C. Cir), February 25, 1923.

7 *United States* v. *Zenith Radio Corporation* et al., 12 F. 2d 614 (N.D. Ill.), April 16, 1926.

8 Eric Barnouw, *A Tower in Babel: A History of Broadcasting in the United States* (New York: Oxford University Press, 1966), p. 175.

9 Attorney General's Opinion, 35 Ops. Att'y Gen. 126, July 8, 1926.

10 H. Doc. 483, 69th Congress, 2d Session, December 7, 1926.

11 The Radio Act of 1927, Public Law 632, 69th Congress, February 23, 1927, sec. 3.

12 Don R. Le Duc and Thomas A. McCain, "The Federal Radio Commission in Federal Court: Origins of Broadcast Regulatory Doctrines," *Journal of Broadcasting* 14 (Fall 1970), 393–410.

13 Ibid., p. 395.

14 *Technical Radio Laboratory* v. *FRC*, 36 F. 2d 111 (1929). Although not all of the cases challenging the FRC are found in the main body of this text, Le Duc and McCain cite 41 key cases setting legal precedents for FRC authority. The student or teacher who wishes to engage in detailed research centering on these cases should see the Le Duc and McCain article cited in footnote 11, specifically pages 407–410, or the cases listed in the "Additional Resources" section of Chapter 1.

15 *Carrell* v. *FRC*, 36 F. 2d 117 (1929), as cited in Le Duc and McCain, "The FRC in Federal Court," pp. 396 and 407.

16 *FRC* v. *Nelson Brothers Bond and Mortgage Co.* (*Station WIBO*), 289 U.S. 266 (1933), as cited in Le Duc and McCain, pp. 396–397 and 409.

17 *Pote (Station WLOE)* v. *FRC*, 67 F. 2d 509 (1933), as cited in Le Duc and McCain, pp. 397 and 410.

18 *Whitehurst* v. *Grimes, Chief of Police*, et al., 21 F. 2d 787 (1927), as cited in Le Duc and McCain, pp. 389 and 407.

19 *United States* v. *Gregg* et al., 5 F. Supp. 848 (1933), as cited in Le Duc and McCain, pp. 398 and 410.

20 Le Duc and McCain, p. 398.

[21] *Westinghouse Electric and Manufacturing Co.* v. *FRC*, 47 F. 2d 415 (1931), as cited in Le Duc and McCain, pp. 399 and 408.

[22] Le Duc and McCain, p. 399.

[23] *Richmond Development* v. *FRC*, 35 F. 2d 883 (1930), as cited in Le Duc and McCain, pp. 400 and 407.

[24] *Reading Broadcasting* v. *FRC*, 48 F. 2d 458 (1931), and *Journal Co.* v. *FRC*, 48 F. 2d 461 (1931), as cited in Le Duc and McCain, pp. 401 and 408.

[25] *KFKB Broadcasting* v. *Federal Radio Commission*, 47 F. 2d 670 (1931).

[26] Ibid.

[27] Ibid.

[28] *Trinity Methodist Church, South* v. *Federal Radio Commission*, 62 F. 2d 850 (1932).

[29] Ibid.

[30] Le Duc and McCain, "The FRC in Federal Court," p. 402.

[31] Act of July 1, 1930 (4658 at 844).

[32] S. Doc. 144, 73d Congress, 2d Session, February 26, 1934, President Franklin D. Roosevelt's message to Congress, suggesting the formation of the Federal Communications Commission.

[33] Section 326.

[34] C. H. Butman, "Better Radio Service," *Radio News*, 6 (1924), 901, 1106–1109.

Chapter 3

[1] Government uses and operations of broadcasting and telecommunications fall under the National Telecommunications and Information Administration (NTIA).

[2] Three articles in particular are useful in studying this relationship. All three were co-authored by Washington, DC communications attorneys Erwin G. Krasnow and Michael Regan. The author gratefully acknowledges the importance of the articles in preparing this section on the relationship of the FCC to Congress. See E. G. Krasnow and M. Regan, "Legislating Conduct at the FCC: Congress and the FCC Authorization Process," *Broadcast Financial Journal* (March–April 1989), pp. 4–6; E.G. Krasnow and M. Regan, "Advice, Consent, and Politics: Congress and the FCC Confirmation Process," *Broadcast Financial Journal* (September–October 1989), pp. 10–12; E. G. Krasnow and M. Regan, "Congress, the FCC, and the Appropriations Process: the Power of Purse Strings," *Broadcast Financial Journal* (March–April 1990), pp. 8–10.

[3] "Broadcasters Win Retains Consent in S.12," *Broadcasting*, May 20, 1991, p. 30.

[4] "Dingell Challenges Policies in Letter to Sikes," *Broadcasting*, April 29, 1991, p. 20. The legislative tug and pull was not new for Dingell, who at the time of the exchange was serving as Chairman of the House Energy and Commerce Committee. Dingell was also one of the strong proponents of the Fairness Doctrine, which the FCC stopped enforcing after an FCC inquiry and an opinion paper heavily weighted against the doctrine was issued by the commission.

[5] "Dingell Challenges Policies in Letter to Sikes," *Broadcasting*, April 29, 1991, p. 20.

[6] An account of the issue is found in "Chicago TV Case Draws Hill Interest," *Broadcasting*, February 11, 1991, p. 33.

[7] E. G. Krasnow and M. Regan, "Legislating Conduct at the FCC: Congress and the FCC Authorization Process," *Broadcast Financial Journal* (March–April 1989), pp. 4–6, citing p. 6.

[8] As was the case with Rep. Charlotte Reid of Illinois in 1971 under President Richard Nixon when Nixon's original choice ran into an Internal Revenue Service audit. Source: E. G. Krasnow and M. Regan, "Advice, Consent, and Politics: Congress and the FCC Confirmation Process," *Broadcast Financial Journal* (September–October 1989), pp. 10–12; citing p. 12.

[9] E. G. Krasnow and M. Regan, "Advice, Consent, and Politics: Congress and the FCC Confirmation Process," *Broadcast Financial Journal* (September–October 1989), pp. 10–12. Promises can also be extracted in meetings with senators prior to the confirmation hearings.

[10] See E. G. Krasnow and M. Regan, "Legislating Conduct at the FCC: Congress and the FCC Authorization Process," *Broadcast Financial Journal* (March–April 1989), pp. 4–6.

[11] The matter involved Senator Ernest "Fritz" Hollings, a Democrat from South Carolina and Republican FCC Chairman Richard Wiley. Source: E. G. Krasnow and M. Regan, "Congress, the FCC, and the Appropriations Process: the Power of Purse Strings," *Broadcast Financial Journal* (March–April 1990), pp. 8–10; citing p. 9.

[12] Senator Lowell Weicker, Republican of Connecticut, as cited in: E. G. Krasnow and M. Regan, "Congress, the FCC, and the Appropriations Process: the Power of Purse Strings," *Broadcast Financial Journal* (March–April 1990), pp. 8–10; citing p. 9.

[13] The partnership concept and the history of the relationship of the FRC, the FCC, and the D.C. Circuit Court is chronicled in a monograph published by the Association for Education in Journalism and Mass Communication and authored by professor John H. Pennybacker. See J. H. Pennybacker, "The Limits of Judicial Review: The FCC, the U.S. Court of Appeals for the District of Columbia, and the Supreme Court," *Journalism Monograph No. 116* (September 1989), 30 pp. The partnership concept has been articulated in a number of cases, for example in *Greater Boston Television Corp.* v. *F.C.C.*, 444 F.2d, 841, 851–52(1969).

[14] J. H. Pennybacker, "The Limits of Judicial Review: The FCC, the U.S. Court of Appeals for the District of Columbia, and the Supreme Court," *Journalism Monograph* No. *116*, (September 1989), 30 pp.; citing Paper, "Judicial Scrutiny of the FCC: The Illusion of Usurpation," *B.U.L. Review*, (1972), p. 664.

[15] *Office of Communication of United Church of Christ* v. *F.C.C.*, 359 F.2d 994 (1966)

[16] J. H. Pennybacker, "The Limits of Judicial Review: The FCC, the U.S. Court of Appeals for the District of Columbia, and the Supreme Court," *Journalism Monograph No. 116*, (September 1989), p. 7.

[17] By 14 percent. Source: *Managing Director's Report to the Chairman on Sixth Year Accomplishments*, April 1987. Chairman's transmittal letter listed a reduction in the size of the commission staff between 2,153 on FY 1980 to 1,855 projected for FY 1987.

[18] *Managing Director's Report to the Chairman on Sixth Year Accomplishments*, April 1987.

[19] "Patrick to Head Time Warner Subsidiary," *Broadcasting*, May 27, 1991, p. 52.

[20] *Raleigh News and Observer*, Raleigh, NC, June 2, 1991, pp. 1F, 6F. Reprint of *The New York Times* News Service article by Edmund L. Andrews.

[21] The article also noted the strong industry pressure and "brutal" lobbying at the FCC by the movie interest over the passage of the financial interest and syndication rules. *Raleigh News and Observer*; Raleigh, NC, June 2, 1991, p. 1F. Reprint of *The New York Times* News Service article by Edmund L. Andrews.

[22] A report of the commission's first open meeting is chronicled in "Like a Day with the Sunshine at the FCC," *Broadcasting*, 46 (March 28, 1977), 29. Procedural policy was announced in "FCC in the Sunshine," *NAB Highlights*, 3 (March 7, 1977), 2. Material for this section was also drawn from material provided by the FCC's Consumer Assistance and Small Business Division.

[23] As discussed in FCC publications, *FCC Annual Reports*, *Broadcasting Yearbook*, and "How the FCC Is Organized into

Offices and Bureaus," *Communication News* 14 (January 1977), 46–48. "FCC Makes Over Broadcast Bureau," *Broadcasting* 45 (April 5, 1976), 53, and the *FCC Annual Report*, 1984.

[24] The Office of Legislative Affairs was established at the end of fiscal year 1987 and the beginning of fiscal year 1988.

[25] In any one fiscal year, thousands of inquiries are answered.

[26] *FCC Annual Report*, 1984, pp. 3–5.

[27] Ibid.

[28] It may also be necessary to receive approval from local authorities. For example, the office building which is being constructed to house the transmitter, offices, and studios of the station would need a local building permit. Other permits would be required before you could start broadcasting to test the transmitter and other facilities. At some point an FCC license would be necessary to operate full time.

[29] Ibid.

[30] *FCC Annual Report*, 1984 and *NAB Counsel Memorandum* L-421, August 1984. The FCC policy statement listing sample violations and forfeitures included the following partial list:

Safety: All tower lights are out and the FCC has not been notified within the required 30 minutes ($2000), Majority of the tower lights are out and/or the loss of the top flashing beacon ($1000). Tower lights are not observed at least once each 24 hours ($500). Temporary warning lights not present during construction ($1000). Tower not properly painted ($750). *Interference-Harm Actual Potential*: Overpower operation, frequency tolerance, modulation limits, spurious and harmonic emission ($1000–2000). Failure to cease operation by remote control when a malfunction occurs in the remote control section ($300). Station operating under post-sunset authorization such as operating 50 percent overpower or operating one-half hour or longer after the station was required to sign off ($1000). *Administrative and Nontechnical*: Failure to maintain and have a complete public inspection file ($300). Failure to have a licensed operator on duty ($200). Willfully or repeatedly incorrect log entries ($1000).

[31] Drawn from the 1988 and 1989 fiscal year annual reports.

[32] Federal Communications Commission Authorization Act of 1987. Reported in the FCC's 1988 fiscal year report.

[33] Federal Communications Commission Authorization Act of 1987. Reported in the FCC's 1988 fiscal year report, p. 9.

[34] *Carlin Communications, Inc.* v. *FCC*, 837 F.2d 546 (2d Cir. 1988).

[35] *Rural Telephone Coalition* v. *FCC*, 838 F.2d 1307 (D.C. Cir. 1988).

[36] *National Association for Better Broadcasting* v. *FCC*, 849 F.2d 665 (D.C. Cir. 1988).

[37] "Appeals Court Says FCC Incorrectly Read Rule," *Broadcasting*, January 30, 1989, p. 61.

[38] "Court Throws Out the FCC's 24-Hour Indecency Ban," *Broadcasting*, May 20, 1991, p. 33.

[39] As capsuled in the *FCC Annual Report* for fiscal year 1988, p. 16.

[40] "FCC Rules: The Force Is With Them," *Broadcasting*, June 7, 1991, pp. 100–101.

[41] Ibid.

[42] Ibid.

[43] Ibid.

[44] P. M. Barrett, "Business Complains FTC Goes Too Far, Pressing Its Cases After Losing in Courts," *The Wall Street Journal*, April 16, 1991, p. B10A.

[45] 1988 *FCC Annual Report*, p. 55.

[46] Specifically, the 1982 International Telecommunications Convention.

[47] Based on: "The FCC and Broadcasting," *FCC Broadcast Bureau Publication #8310-100.*

[48] "Staged" news events are not considered to be operating in the public interest, however.

[49] "The FCC and Broadcasting."

[50] More specifically, the Field Operations Bureau can issue a Notice of Apparent Liability (NAL) and a Notice of Forfeiture (NOF). It also has the power to mitigate or cancel forfeitures (fines) and can refer collection of forfeitures to the United States Attorney's Office.

The Field Operations Bureau can issue a Notice of Radio Station Conditions for minor rule violations or when it spots problems which are not yet rule violations but could be if left uncorrected. No response is required for the Notice of Radio Station Conditions but the Field Operations Bureau keeps track of such notices for future visits and reference. For more serious violations the Field Operations Bureau can issue an Official Notice of Violation which requires a station to respond. The Field Operations Bureau will not normally hesitate to issue a notice just because a station operator or manager is cooperative and the station must substantiate any claim that it cannot afford to pay a forfeiture imposed by the bureau.

[51] Technical violations usually fall under subordinate personnel such as engineering staff.

[52] Violations such as fraudulent billing can usually be traced directly to management and are much more serious. Moreover, a "victim" (the advertiser or sponsor) also exists outside the station.

[53] Authority granted by the same statute that permits forfeitures.

[54] *FCC Annual Report*, 1974, p. 37.

[55] One study, by Maurice E. Shelby, investigated 156 short-term license renewals granted by the commission in the decade immediately following the passage of the statute. It showed that 113 stations (72 percent) received one-year renewals, 29 stations (19 percent) received renewals for more than one year (but less than three), and 14 (9 percent) were licensed for less than a year. Three main reasons accounted for the majority of short-term renewals: (1) improper control over station operation, which generally meant the owner was not adequately supervising employees; (2) repeated rule violations, both technical and programming; and (3) performance versus promise, or, in other words, that the licensee was not living up to the promises made in the previous license renewal. Source: Maurice E. Shelby, Jr., "Short-term License Renewals: 1960–1972," *Journal of Broadcasting*, 18 (Summer 1974), 277–88.

[56] "FCC Yanks license. . . . ," *Broadcasting*, May 9, 1988, pp. 61–62.

[57] "Commission to take away AM license," *Broadcasting*, February 27, 1989, p. 42.

[58] "FCC revokes licenses of Georgia AM-FM," *Broadcasting*, November 7, 1988, p. 53.

[59] "FCC Upholds Denial of Arizona Radio Renewals," *Broadcasting*, May 20, 1991, p. 61.

[60] *FCC Annual Report*, 1974, p. 78.

[61] See, for example; Donald M. Gillmor and Jerome A. Barron, *Mass Communication Law* (St. Paul, MN: West Publishing Company, 1974), p. 889. Citing: Richard Sneed, *15 P. & F. Radio Reg.* 158 (1967). The FCC fluctuates in its enforcement of obscenity matters, as evidenced by a 24-hour ban against such broadcasts, which was not upheld in a 1991 appeals court decision.

[62] FCC *Procedural Manual*, n.d.

[63] FCC *Procedural Manual*, n.d.

[64] FCC *Procedural Manual*, n.d.

[65] FCC *Procedural Manual*, n.d.

[66] One of the first "notices" as a process affecting communication technology was when the federal government issued a call for proposals to build a telegraph.

[67] M. A. McGregor, "The FCC's Use of Informal Comments in Rule-Making Proceedings," *Journal of Broadcasting and Electronic Media,* 30 (Fall 1986), pp. 413–425, citing p. 422. "Reply comments" are comments made in reply to earlier comments and come at a different point in the rule-making proceeding.

[68] Erwin G. Krasnow and Lawrence D. Longley, *The Politics of Broadcast Regulation,* p. 24.

[69] Ibid.

[70] Robert R. Smith and Paul T. Prince, "WHDH: The Unconscionable Delay," *Journal of Broadcasting* 18 (Winter 1973–74), 85–86.

[71] See also Sterling Quinlan, *The Hundred Million Dollar Lunch* (Chicago: J. Philip O'Hara, 1974), p. 4.

[72] "Commission to take away AM License," *Broadcasting,* February 27, 1989, p. 42.

[73] Ibid.

[74] "FCC Berated for Policy on Stockholdings of the Employees," *Broadcasting* 46 (May 30, 1977), 8, 30. In addition, an earlier summary report on the commission was completed by researchers Johnson and Dystel who summarized and divided their own critique of the FCC into seven areas. They contended that: (1) The FCC delves into areas beyond its expertise and issues beyond its ken. (2) It takes years to resolve important cases. (3) The FCC is manipulated by its own staff and the industries it is supposed to regulate, and that such manipulations result in precedents that return to "haunt" the commission. (4) Principled decision making does not exist, because the FCC no longer approves of its own rules and precedents, but ignores them instead—either by waiving them or evading them. (5) The commission ignores its own administrative principles and those established by the judiciary. (6) The commissioners decide cases they don't understand. (7) The FCC has yet to develop "rational" policies for governing its day-to-day decisions. Source: N. Johnson and J. Dystel, "A Day in the Life of The Federal Communications Commission," *Yale Law Journal,* 82 (July 1973), 1575–1634. Although the report is now almost 20 years old, the significance of it rests with the fact that some of the criticisms are still being heard.

[75] McGregor, p. 413.

[76] Marc C. Franklin, *The First Amendment and the Fourth Estate* (Mineola, NY: Foundation Press, 1977), pp. 465–466.

[77] Ibid., p. 466. It is interesting to note that, although not adhering to "regional" assignments of frequencies on a domestic scale, international agreements on frequency management are regional. This points out the peculiar nature of the electromagnetic spectrum as a resource. When the overall territory (the world) is big enough, regional allocations are practical. Moreover, the political realities of trying to localize spectrum management on a world scale make the task almost prohibitive.

[78] This argument also applies to the Fairness Doctrine which the FCC stopped enforcing in the 1980s. Some argue that one of the reasons the Fairness Doctrine is not needed is because there are so many stations serving many different audiences and providing a diversity of viewpoints. But this argument fails to consider that the local station concept is alive and well and based on local service. Because of this policy, many smaller communities have only one radio station serving the community and covering local issues. Where a weekly newspaper exists or no newspaper at all, that one radio station has a monopoly on viewpoints. Regional allocations may not improve diversity, but the policy of local service also results in the trade-off of creating the "viewpoint monopoly" for the local station.

[79] *Window Dressing on the Set: Women and Minorities in Television* (Washington, DC: United States Commission on Civil Rights, 1977).

[80] Ibid.

Chapter 4

[1] *Policy Statement and Order,* MM Docket No. 83-842, 57 R.R. 2d 913 (1985), *aff'd sub nom, Telecommunications Research and Action Center* v. *FCC,* 800 F.2d 1181 (D.C. Cir. 1986).

[2] *Your FTC: What It Is and What It Does* (Washington, DC: Federal Trade Commission, 1977).

[3] Federal Trade Commission, 1986 *Annual Report,* p. 11.

[4] 102 F.T.C. 1734, Docket 9113, *In the Matter of Ford Motor Company,* (1983). Such statements also include the following language:

> The Commission having considered the matter and having thereupon accepted the executed consent agreement and placed such agreement on the public record for a period of sixty (60) days, and having duly considered the comments filed thereafter by interested persons pursuant to Section 3.25 of its Rules, now in further conformity with the procedure prescribed in Section 3.25(f) of its Rules, the Commission hereby makes the following jurisdictional findings and enters the following order.

[5] Federal Trade Commission, 1986 *Annual Report,* p. 14.

[6] Source for the examples of the company selling cable television decoders and the two companies selling telephone equipment, including the material in quotation marks, is: Federal Trade Commission, 1986 *Annual Report,* pp. 29–30.

[7] Federal Trade Commission, 1986 *Annual Report,* p. 14.

[8] Federal Trade Commission reports, especially if they are timely and accessed when released, can provide stories for business-beat reporters about the trade practices of national chains which may have franchises in the local area. Government documents are frequently public record, much like court cases, although the wording of news reports should keep in mind issues in libel law which necessitate truthful and factual reporting.

[9] Federal Trade Commission, 1986 *Annual Report,* p. 18.

[10] Ibid., p. 18.

[11] Ibid., p. 37.

[12] Ibid., p. 8.

[13] Ibid., p. 31.

[14] Cellular telephone application-preparation services as cited as the first and subsequent cases against such companies and cited in: Federal Trade Commission, 1986 *Annual Report,* p. 19.

[15] Federal Trade Commission, 1986 *Annual Report,* p. 20.

[16] *Your FTC: What It Is and What It Does* (Washington, DC: Federal Trade Commission, 1977), p. 25.

[17] Ibid., p. 26.

[18] Ibid.

[19] Ibid.

[20] Ibid.

[21] "The FTC Advertising Review Process," *Advertising Age,* 48 (July 11, 1977), 142.

[22] *Your FTC,* p. 26.

[23] P. M. Barret and D. Kneale, "FTC to Charge ABC Sports, College Group in TV Pact," *The Wall Street Journal,* September 6, 1990, p. B1.

[24] Ibid.

[25] 108 F.T.C. 105, Docket 9174, (1986).

[26] Ibid.

[27] Ibid.

[28] Ibid.

[29] For example, as found in: 108 F.T.C. Reports 62, Docket C-3196, (1986).

[30] This particular frame shows an attractive (interior "Beauty" shot) shelf display with books, plants, and dishes.

[31] 108 F.T.C. Reports 62, Docket C-3196, (1986). Exhibit G in the proceeding.

[32] 108 F.T.C. Reports 62, Docket C-3196, (1986). Exhibit H in the proceeding.

[33] 108 F.T.C. Reports 62, Docket C-3196, (1986). Exhibit I in the proceeding.

[34] 108 F.T.C. Reports 62, Docket C-3196, (1986).

[35] Ibid.

[36] Ibid.

[37] Ibid.

[38] Ibid.

[39] 108 F.T.C. Reports 62, Docket C-3196, (1986), Attachment A in the proceeding.

[40] 109 F.T.C. Reports 165, Docket C-3214, (1987), Exhibit E in the proceeding.

[41] 109 F.T.C. Reports 165, Docket C-3214, (1987), as cited in the text of the proceeding at 157.

[42] 109 F.T.C. Reports 165, Docket C-3214, (1987).

[43] Ibid.

[44] Although the then FTC chairman voted in the negative.

[45] 109 F.T.C. Reports 165, Docket C-3214, (1987). Consent order contains the statement: " . . . the signing of said agreement is for settlement purposes only and does not constitute an admission by respondent that the law has been violated as alleged in such complaint."

[46] 110 F.T.C. Reports 511, Docket C-3230, (1988), Exhibit E in the proceeding.

[47] 110 F.T.C. Reports 380, Docket C-3225, (1988), Exhibit B in the proceeding.

[48] 110 F.T.C. Reports 511, Docket C-3230, (1988), Exhibit E in the proceeding.

[49] 110 F.T.C. Reports 380, Docket C-3225, (1988), Exhibit B in the proceeding.

[50] 110 F.T.C. Reports 511, Docket C-3230, (1988); and 110 F.T.C. 380, Docket C-3225, (1988).

[51] Ibid.

[52] As stated in both proceedings: 110 F.T.C. Reports 511, Docket C-3230, (1988); and 110 F.T.C. Reports 380, Docket C-3225, (1988).

[53] 110 F.T.C. Reports 37, Docket 9194, (1987), Exhibit F in the proceeding. The diet was also identified in FTC documents as the "Freedom Diet" and the "Rotation-Freedom Diet."

[54] 110 F.T.C. Reports 37, Docket 9194, (1987), Exhibit F in the proceeding. The commercial contained the actual 800 number.

[55] 110 F.T.C. Reports 37.

[56] Ibid.

[57] Ibid.

[58] Ibid.

[59] Ibid.

[60] Ibid.

[61] Ibid.

[62] 111 F.T.C. Reports, 522, Docket C-3248, (1989).

[63] J. Lipman, "FTC Zaps Misleading Infomercials," *The Wall Street Journal*, June 6, 1991, p. B1.

[64] 111 F.T.C. Reports, 522, (1989).

[65] Ibid.

[66] Ibid., Exhibit A in the proceeding.

[67] Ibid.

[68] Ibid.

[69] Ibid.

[70] J. Lipman, "FTC Zaps Misleading Infomercials," *The Wall Street Journal*, June 6, 1991, p. B1.

[71] Ibid. However, it is unlikely that the FTC would accept a production company's tests for many of the products doctors advertise.

[72] Ibid.

[73] 111 F.T.C. Reports 623, Docket C-3249, (1989). Exhibit B in the proceeding.

[74] 111 F.T.C. Reports 623, (1989).

[75] 110 F.T.C. Reports 380, (1988).

[76] 110 F.T.C. Reports 37, (1987).

[77] Ibid.

[78] For example, a major advertising agency became involved in an FTC action after it used *surveys* in advertising products. The FTC said the word *survey* could not be used in advertising unless the survey was current and conducted using acceptable methods. As discussed in: 97 F.T.C. Reports 333, (1981).

[79] 97 F.T.C. Reports 333, (1981).

Chapter 5

[1] *Telecommunication*, without the "s," commonly refers to the "process" of information transfer. The term *telecommunications* refers not only to the process but also to the industries and to the components of those industries that are in some way related to the process.

[2] Executive Order No. 11556, Reorganization Plan No. 1 of 1970, September 4, 1970, Richard M. Nixon, President of the United States (section 2).

[3] Ibid., (section 13).

[4] Ibid., (section 14).

[5] Remarks of Clay T. Whitehead, Director, Office of Telecommunications Policy, Executive Office of the President, Meeting of the Indianapolis Chapter of the Society of Professional Journalists-Sigma Delta Chi, December 18, 1972 (copy of the address provided by the OTP).

[6] Office of Telecommunications Policy, *Activities and Programs 1975–1976*, p. 5.

[7] For example, NASA's ATS-6 satellite network.

[8] Office of Telecommunications: U.S. Department of Commerce, *Progress Report 1976*, p. 22. The early organization of the OT encompassed four major units, the activities of which have been incorporated into the National Telecommunications and Information Administration. The four units as organized under the OT were: The Institute for Telecommunication Sciences, the Policy Research Division, the Analytical Support Division, and the Spectrum Management Support Division. They continue to operate to some degree in similar fashion in the NTIA.

[9] Ibid., p. 5.

[10] Ibid., p. 9.

[11] Ibid., pp. 11–12.

[12] The initials correspond to the French identification of the organizations.

[13] *Progress Report 1976*, pp. 13–14.

[14] Ibid., pp. 20–28.

[15] "International and Domestic Policy Making in the Year 2000," in *NTIA Telecom 2000*, (Washington, DC: National Telecommunications and Information Administration), 1988, p. 169.

[16] From NTIA public information materials.

[17] Helpful in completing this section, as well as other discussions of the U.S. government's role in telecommunication was: W. R. Slye, "Federal Government Use of Telecommunications," in *NTIA Telecom 2000*, (Washington, DC: National Telecommunications and Information Administration), 1988.

[18] Source for the section on military uses of the electromagnetic spectrum: W. R. Slye, "Federal Government Use of Telecommunications," pp. 360–364.

[19] Fort Hood, Texas; Fort Bragg, North Carolina; Fort Bliss, Texas; Fort Still, Oklahoma; Fort Lewis, Washington (Yakima Training Facility).

[20] W. R. Slye, "Federal Government Use of Telecommunications," p. 362.

[21] Ibid., pp. 352–353.

[22] Source materials for the discussion of the Defense Communications Agency include: *NTIA Telecom 2000*, (Washington, DC: National Telecommunications and Information Administration), 1988; "DCA is the Key Link in Military Communications Systems," *Communications News* 15 (July 1978), 52–55.

[23] Ibid., p. 52.

[24] W. R. Slye, "Federal Government Use of Telecommunications," pp. 357–358.

[25] Ibid., p. 54.

[26] "Assignment of National Security and Emergency Preparedness Telecommunications Functions," Executive Order 12473, *Federal Register*, 49, April 3, 1984, 13471.

[27] Ibid. Section and paragraph designations have been omitted.

[28] Different emergency preparedness functions operate in addition to the NCS, one being the Federal Emergency Management Agency.

[29] "Assignment of National Security and Emergency Preparedness Telecommunications Functions," Executive Order 12473, *Federal Register*, 49, April 3, 1984, 13471. Section and paragraph designations have been omitted.

[30] "Assignment of National Security and Emergency Preparedness Telecommunications Functions," The White House, Executive Order 12472, April 3, 1984, *Federal Register*, 49, No. 87, April 5, 1984, Presidential Documents, 13474.

[31] Ibid.

[32] Ibid.

[33] *OTA Priorities 1979*, Washington, DC: *Office of Technology Assessment*, p. i. Additional background information is drawn from the OTA publication "What OTA Is, What OTA Does, How OTA Works," (February 1985).

[34] Ibid., p. 15.

[35] Ibid., p. 19.

[36] Ibid.

[37] W. R. Slye, "Federal Government Use of Telecommunications," pp. 378–381.

[38] Most helpful in the preparation of material on the U.S. Department of Justice was attorney Kenneth Robinson of the department. His efforts on the author's behalf in providing information are gratefully acknowledged. Most helpful also was Linda Cobb-Reiley's paper, "The Department of Justice and the Federal Communications Commission: Interactions and Conflicts in the Formulation of a Newspaper-Television Station Cross-Ownership Policy," presented at the 1978 annual meeting of the Association for Education in Journalism. (Note: Notes 25–40 are from Cobb-Reiley's paper, "The Department. . . .")

[39] Information about the Securities and Exchange Commission discussed in this chapter came from: ". . . *good people, important problems and workable laws,*" *50 Years of the U.S. Securities and Exchange Commission*, Washington, DC: Securities and Exchange Commission, 1984, 76 pp.; Securities and Exchange Commission, Annual Report, 1985, 145 pp.; discussions of specific enforcement actions are found in the Annual Report, pp. 2–6. The impact of big business and broadcasting can be grasped by reading D. A. Odell, "The Metromedia Leveraged Buy Out," *Duke Law Magazine*, 3, No. 2 (1985), 21–25. Information on "The Broadcast Press" and financial reporting is from NAB Counsel memorandum No. L-504 (February 1985), "SEC Shows an Interest in the Financial Conflicts of News Personnel: FCC Policies also Apply," prepared by R. Bortnick, and NAB Legal Intern.

[40] The material described under this section is not quoted verbatim from the 10K, except where noted by indentation. The 10K used here for illustrative purposes was filed by Capital Cities/ABC, Inc., pursuant to Section 13 or 15d of the Securities Exchange Act of 1934. The 10K is for the fiscal year ended December 28, 1986.

[41] Capital Cities/ABC, Inc. 10K for the fiscal year ending December 28, 1986.

[42] Ibid.

[43] Ibid.

[44] Ibid.

[45] Two cases in England affirmed the statutory effect of the Statute of Anne (1710) covering copyrights: *Miller* v. *Taylor* (1769) assured authors the rights to their works and *Donaldson* v. *Becket* (1774) affirmed the Statue of Anne as taking precedent over common law and eliminating any future common law claims to copyright in England.

[46] "International and Domestic Policymaking in the Year 2000," *NTIA Telecom 2000*, (Washington, DC: National Telecommunications and Information Administration), 1988, pp. 163–184.

Chapter 6

[1] Archibald Cox, in a speech delivered to the Anti-Defamation League of B'nai B'rith, New York, December 7, 1976.

[2] As in the case of Gerald Ford on a tax-cut issue: Source: Associated Press, October 7, 1975.

[3] Section 73.120 of the Communications Act of 1934. Two publications have updated rules and regulations and have provided guidelines to broadcasters in interpreting Section 315. These are: "Uses of Broadcast and Cablecast Facilities by Candidates for Public Office," Fed. Reg. 5796; and "Licensee Responsibility under Amendments to the Communications Act of 1971," FCC *Public Notice*, June 5, 1974, 47 FCC 516 (1974).

[4] *Farmers' Educational and Cooperative Union of America, North Dakota Division*, v. *WDAY*, 89 N. W.2d 102, 109 (N.D. 1958).

[5] *Farmers' Educational and Cooperative Union of America* v. *WDAY, Inc.*, 360 U.S. 525, 79 S.Ct. 1302, 3 L.Ed. 2d 1407 (1959).

[6] NAB Counsel Memorandum, "Political Broadcasting Update," April 1985 No. L-509 prepared by C. J. Blakekey, Esq., p. 3. The issue arose when *Hustler* magazine publisher Larry Flynnt planned to broadcast obscene commercials supporting his anticipated presidential candidacy.

[7] NAB Counsel Memorandum, "Political Broadcasting Update," pp. 2–3.

[8] Ibid.

[9] Ibid.

[10] "NAB Supports Your Right to Delay Political Broadcasts," *NAB Highlights*, 3 (March 28, 1977), 1.

[11] "RTNDA Says Coverage of Political Debates Should Not Be Limited," *RTNDA Communicator*, 21 (April 1977), 6. The brief was in the case of *United Church of Christ* v. *F.C.C.*

[12] *McCarthy* v. *Federal Communications Commission*, 390 F. 2d 471 (D.C. Cir. 1968).

[13] *Political Broadcast Catechism*, 8th ed. (Washington, DC: National Association of Broadcasters, 1976), p. 7.

[14] "Hook Wants FCC off the Fence on Section 315," *Broadcasting*, 31 (May 16, 1977), 36–38.

[15] 47 CFR Ch.I(10-1-91 Edition) 73.1920.

[16] 47 CFR Ch.I(10-1-91 Edition) 73.1930.

[17] North Carolina Association of Broadcasters, *Nuts n' Bolts of Political Broadcasting*, Raleigh, NC: NCAB, n.d., p. 11.

[18] "Political Ad Law Void," *The News Media & the Law*, (November/December 1984), p. 35.

[19] "Use of Broadcast and Cablecast Facilities by Candidates for Public Office," FCC *Public Notice*, March 16, 1972; 37 *Fed. Reg*. 5804 (March 21, 1972).

[20] "FCC Overturned on Lowest Units for Politicians," *Broadcasting*, 49 (October 27, 1980), 46.

[21] "Double Jeopardy for Networks in C-M Decision," *Broadcasting*, 49 (March 17, 1980), 29–30.

[22] "FCC says Public Stations Must Give 'Reasonable' Amount of Access to Candidates," *Broadcasting*, 45 (November 1, 1976), 53–54.

[23] "Use of Broadcast and Cablecast Facilities by Candidates for Public Office," FCC *Public Notice*, March 16, 1972; 37 *Fed. Reg*. 5805 (March 21, 1972).

[24] For the early development of legal precedent in the area of regulating obscene, indecent, and profane programming, see James Walter Wesolowski, "Obscene, Indecent, or Profane Broadcast Language as Construed by the Federal Courts," *Journal of Broadcasting*, 13 (Spring 1969), 203–219.

[25] Title 18, United States Code (Codified June 25, 1948, Ch. 645, 62 Stat. 769).

[26] *Regina* v. *Hicklin*, L. R. 3 QB. 360 (1868). For a discussion of the Hicklin case, see Donald M. Gillmor and Jerome A. Barron, *Mass Communication Law* (St. Paul, MN: West Publishing Co., 1974), pp. 329–330.

[27] In particular: Ex parte *Jackson*, 96 U.S. 727 (1878): *United States* v. *Bennett*, 24 Fed. Cas. 1093 (N.Y.S.D. 1879); *United States* v. *Harmon*, 45 F. 414 (D.C. Kan, 1891) rev'd 50 F. 921 (C.C.); *People* v. *Friede*, 133 Misc. 611, 233 N.Y.S. 565 (1929).

[28] Weakening of the Hicklin decision is seen in *United States* v. *Kennerley*, 209 F. 119 (S.D.N.Y. 1913); *Halsey* v. *New York Society for the Suppression of Vice*, 191 App. Div. 245, 180 N.Y.S. 836 (1920); *United States* v. *Dennett* 39 F. 2d 128 (1931).

[29] *Duncan* v. *United States*, 48 F. 2d 128 (1931).

[30] 48 F. 2d 128, 132, as cited in Wesolowski, "Obscene, Indecent, or Profane Broadcast Language."

[31] Ibid.

[32] *United States* v. *Levine*, 83 F. 2d 156 (2d Cir. 1936), as cited in Gillmor and Barron, *Mass Communication Law*, p. 330.

[33] *Roth* v. *United States*, 354 U.S. 476, 77 S.Ct. 1304, 1 L.Ed. 2d 1498 (1957). Decided at the same time as *Alberts* v. *State of California*.

[34] *Ginsberg* v. *State of New York*, 390 U.S. 629, 88 S.Ct. 1274, 1277 (1968).

[35] In re *Palmetto Broadcasting Company (WDKD)*.

[36] *Robinson* v. *F.C.C.*, 334 F. 2d 584 (1964).

[37] In re *WHUY-FM Eastern Educational Radio*, 24 F.C.C. 2d 408 (1970).

[38] Sounderling Broadcasting Corporation, WGLD-FM, 27 Radio Reg. 2d 285 (F.C.C., 1973). The appeals case affirming the FCC ruling is *Illinois Citizens' Committee for Broadcasting* v. *Federal Communications Commission*, 515 F. 2d 397 (D.C. Cir. 1975). The *Ginzburg* ruling cited in the text is *Ginzburg* v. *United States*, 383 U.S. 463, 86 S.Ct. 942, 16 L.Ed. 2d 31 (1966). See also Charles Feldman and Stanley Tickton, "Obscene/Indecent Programming: Regulation of Ambiguity," *Journal of Broadcasting*, 20 (Spring 1976), 273–282.

[39] *Pacifica Foundation*, 56 F.C.C. 2d 94 (1975).

[40] Ibid.

[41] *Pacifica Foundation* v. *Federal Communications Commission*, U.S. Court of Appeals, District of Columbia, CA, No. 75-1391, March 16, 1977. Also see footnote 7 of the decision and the Amicus Brief, quoting statement of John A. Schneider before the House Subcommittee of Communications, July 15, 1975, p. 9.

[42] Ibid., footnote 19 of the *Pacifica* decision.

[43] Joe Flint, "FCC's Stern Fined: Record $105,000," *Broadcasting* (November 2, 1992) pp. 55–56.

[44] Joe Flint, "FCC's Stern Fined: Record $105,000," *Broadcasting* (November 2, 1992) p. 55 quoting NAB Associate General Counsel Steven Bookshester.

[45] Joe Flint, "FCC's Stern Fined: Record $105,000," *Broadcasting* (November 2, 1992) p. 56.

[46] *Action for Children's Television v. F.C.C.* 290 U.S. App. D.C. 4, 932 F.2d 1504 (D.C. 1991)

[47] *Gillett Communications of Atlanta, Inc. d/b/a WAGA-TV5*, v. *Daniel Becker, Daniel Becker for Congress Committee, and the Federal Communications Commission*, United States District Court for the Northern District of Georgia, Atlanta Division, 807 F. Supp. 757; 1992 U.S. Dist. LEXIS 17366; 20 Media L. Rep. 1947 (1992).

[48] In the Matter of Liability of Sagittarius Broadcasting Corporation, 1992 FCC LEXIS 6042, (October 23, 1992), citing *Action for Children's Television* v. *F.C.C.*, 271 U.S. App. D.C. 365, 852 F.2d 1332, 1340 (D.C. 1988).

[49] *Gillett Communications of Atlanta, Inc. d/b/a WAGA-TV5*, v. *Daniel Becker, Daniel Becker for Congress Committee, and the Federal Communications Commission*, United States District Court for the Northern District of Georgia, Atlanta Division, 807 F. Supp. 757; 1992 U.S. Dist. LEXIS 17366; 20 Media L. Rep. 1947 (1992).

[50] "Origins of the Format Change Controversy," *Broadcasting*, 45 (August 2, 1976), 21. *Citizens' Committee to save WEFM* v. *FCC*, 506 F. 2d 246 (D.C. Cir. 1974); *Citizens' Committee to Preserve the Voice of the Arts in Atlanta* v. *F.C.C.*, 436 F. 2d 263 (D.C. Cir. 1970).

[51] "FCC Defends Licensee Right to Choose Radio Formats," *Broadcasting*, 45 (August 2, 1976), 21.

[52] "FCC Urged to Take Another Look at Its Format Ruling," *Broadcasting*, 45 (September 6, 1976), 42.

[53] *Federal Communications Commission et al.* v. *WNCN Listeners Guild et al.*, 450 U.S. 582, 101 S. Ct. 1266, 1981 U.S. LEXIS 10, 67 L. Ed. 2d 521, 49 U.S.L.W 4306.

[54] The list is adapted from FCC, Docket No. 19743, Inquiry into Subscription Agreements between Radio Broadcast Stations and Musical Format Service Companies. Adopted: November 4, 1975; released November 7, 1975, p. 8.

[55] *Third Report and Order* in Docket No. 19622, FCC 75-542, May 13, 1975. The different times result from different network feed times to affiliates in the various time zones. For two perspectives on the sports antiblackout issue, see Ira Horowitz, "Sports Telecasts: Rights and Regulations," *Journal of Communication*, 27 (Summer 1977), 160–168; and John J. Siegfried and C. Elton Hinshaw, "Professional Football and the Anti-Blackout Law," *Journal of Communication*, 27 (Summer 1977), 169–174.

[56] *National Association of Independent Television Producers and Distributors* et al. v. *F.C.C.*, CA No. 75-4021, April 21, 1975.

[57] A commercial should be registered as a copyrighted work, however.

[58] Except for cable radio retransmission, the disc jockey's program would typically be copyrighted if it were placed in syndication.

[59] The Copyright Act (title 17, U.S. Code) is summarized in publications of the Copyright Office, Library of Congress, Washington, DC. Copyright basics are discussed in Circular R1; U.S. Government Printing Office, 1985, No. 491–561. Material cited in this section is noted by Circular No. Actual wording of the law should be used in making interpretations for purpose of counsel.

[60] Circular R1, p. 5. "Before 1978, statutory copyright was generally secured by the act of publication with notice of copy-

right, assuming compliance with all other relevant statutory conditions. Works in the public domain on January 1, 1978 (for example, works published without satisfying all conditions for securing statutory copyright under Copyright Act of 1909) remain in the public domain under the current Act.

Statutory copyright could also be secured before 1978 by the act of registration in the case of certain unpublished works and works eligible for ad interim copyright. The current Act automatically extends to full term copyright (section 304 sets the term) for all works in which ad interim copyright was subsisting or was capable of being secured on December 31, 1977." Citing Circular R1, p. 5.

[61] As discussed in Circular R45, "Copyright Registration for Motion Pictures Including Video Recordings," p. 3. "Before 1912, motion pictures were not probably protected as 'photographs' in many cases. In 1912, two new classes of motion pictures were added to the list of works eligible for copyright registration: Class L for 'photoplays' and class M for 'motion pictures other than photoplays.' " The Copyright Act of 1976 (effective January 1, 1978) dropped the distinction between Class L and Class M, and lumped all motion pictures together as part of the larger category of audiovisual works. (citing Circular R45, p. 3.)

[62] "Guidelines for 'Fair Use' of Videotapes for Educational Purposes," *Chronicle of Higher Education*, December 16, 1981, p.12.

[63] Television Improvement Act of 1990, 47 USC 303c, 104 Stat. 5127.

[64] Ibid.

[65] "Violence Debate Heats Up, Shifts from D.C. to L.A.," *Broadcasting & Cable* (August 2, 1993), pp. 12–13, citing p. 12.

[66] Ibid.

[67] Children's Television Act of 1990, 47 USC 303a, 104 Stat. 996.

[68] Kim McAvoy, "FCC Gets Into the Children's Act," Broadcasting & Cable (July 26, 1993), pp. 42–43.

[69] Ibid., p. 43.

[70] Ibid.

Chapter 7

[1] A shield law passed in 1992 in South Carolina is one example.

[2] *Near* v. *Minnesota*, 238 U.S. 697, 707, 1 Media L. Rep. 1001, 1003 (1931).

[3] *Near* v. *Minnesota*, 238 U.S. 697, 707, 1 Media L. Rep. 1001, 1003 (1931).

[4] *Gitlow* v. *New York*, 268 U.S. 652, 666 (1925).

[5] Eric Sevareid, in a speech delivered at the "First Amendment Confrontation," during the 55th Annual Convention of the National Association of Broadcasters, March 28, 1977.

[6] Paley's remark was quoted by Archibald Cox during a speech by Cox to the Anti-Defamation League of B'nai B'rith, on the occasion of Paley's receiving the First Amendment Freedoms Award, December 7, 1976, in New York City.

[7] *CBS* v. *The Democratic National Committee*, 412 U.S. 94 (1973); William Small, "The First Amendment/Radio and Television: Treated Like Distant Cousins," *The Quill* (September 1976), p. 32.

[8] "State Court Holds Free-Press Rights Are Applicable to Broadcasting," *Broadcasting*, 45 (April 12, 1976), 59.

[9] The Communications Act of 1934, Public Law 416, 73rd Congress, June 19, 1934, amended. Additional perspectives on the First Amendment's relationship to the Communications Act are found in: "Electronic Journalism and First Amendment Problems: Recommendations of Communications Law Committee, Section of Science and Technology, American Bar Association," *Federal Communications Bar Journal*, 29 (1976), 1–62.

[10] *Rideau* v. *Louisiana*, 373 U.S. 723, 10 L.Ed. 2d 663, 83 S.Ct. 1417 (1963).

[11] *Estes* v. *State of Texas*, 381 U.S. 532, 85 S.Ct. 1628, 14 L.Ed. 2d 543 (1965). The reader wishing a good current discussion of issues surrounding cameras in court can consult the Florida Guidelines: *In re Petition of Post-Newsweek Stations*, 5 Med. L. Rptr. 1047.

[12] "Cameras in the Courtroom," *The Quill*, 63 (April 1975), 25.

[13] Alabama Supreme Court as approved with the cooperation of the news media in Mobile, Alabama, and Judge Robert H. Hodnette, Jr., of the Thirteenth Circuit.

[14] "Georgia Supreme Court Lets Cameras In," *Broadcasting*, 46 (September 26, 1977), 51.

[15] Ibid.

[16] Ibid.

[17] Depending on a particular state's "degree of openness."

[18] "Law Poll: Lawyers Aren't Convinced that TV Belongs in Courtroom," *American Bar Association Journal*, 65 (September 1979), 1306, 1308.

[19] *Congressional Record*, 62 (1922) 3130. As Cited in Ronald Garay, "Implementing Televised Coverage of Sessions of the U.S. Congress," *Journalism Quarterly*, 55 (Autumn 1978), 527. Garay's article is an excellent historical review of the development of live radio and television coverage of the U.S. House of Representatives.

[20] *Congressional Record*, 119 (1974) 42724, as cited in Garay, "Implementing Televised Coverage," p. 529.

[21] U.S. Congress, *Broadcasting House and Senate Proceedings*. Interim report of the Joint Committee of Congressional Operations on Congress and Mass Communications, 93rd Congress, 2d Session, 1974 (Sen. Rept. No. 93-1275), p. 20, as cited in Garay, "Implementing Televised Coverage," p. 530.

[22] Ibid., p. 19. Garay, "Implementing Televised Coverage," p. 530.

[23] "The House Will Let Cameras In," *Broadcasting*, 46 (October 21, 1977), 25.

[24] Ibid.

[25] Ibid.

[26] "House Blacks Out Votes as Coverage by Cameras Begins," *Broadcasting*, 45 (March 26, 1976), 100–102. Of particular objection to the news media was the practice of blacking out everything but the tally board during voting. Some felt that seeing the representatives actually voting was as important as seeing the vote totals. The RTNDA sent a letter of protest to Speaker O'Neill.

[27] "In-House Television," *Broadcasting*, 48 (September 24, 1979), 61.

[28] Ibid.

[29] John B. Adams, *State Open Meeting Laws: An Overview* (Columbia, MO: Freedom of Information Foundation), 1974.

[30] Ibid., pp. 24–29.

[31] See discussions in "University Secrecy Challenged," *The News Media and the Law* (March/April 1983), pp. 27–28; "Law Bars Phone Meetings," *The News Media and the Law* (November/December 1984), pp. 29–30.

[32] North Carolina Statutes, Article 33C, 1979.

[33] Ibid.

[34] Ibid.

[35] Adapted from S. Nevas and T. Etter, "Law On Your Side—Getting News From Local Police and Government," *RadioActive* (February 1981), pp. 6–7.

[36] "Reagan Shuts Off Public Information," *The News Media and the Law* (September/October 1983), pp. 33–34.

[37] Ibid.

[38] Ibid.

[39] Ibid.

[40] Ibid.

[41] A. Chardy, "Reagan OK'd as many as 50 covert operations," Knight-Ridder News Service, *The Raleigh News and Observer*, November 23, 1986, p. 19A.

[42] Ibid.

[43] Adapted from FCC guidelines on using the Freedom of Information Act.

[44] "FOI Suit Opens CIA Files On Underground Papers," *The News Media and the Law* (March/April 1983), p. 29.

[45] The case involved the Beacon Journal Publishing Co. and the University of Akron (Ohio). See "Police Records Opened to Press in Four States," *The News Media and the Law* (June/July 1982), 25. *Beacon Journal* v. *Univ. of Akron*, 6 Med.L.Rptr. 2390 (Ohio Sup Ct. Dec. 30, 1980).

[46] The case involved Boston College and the student newspaper *The Heights. The Heights* filed suit against the Trustees of Boston College to win access to the information. Citing: Ibid. "Police Records . . ." *The Heights* v. *Boston College*, Civ. No. 81-5229 (Mass. Sup. Ct. Middlesex Dec. 31, 1981).

[47] "Police Records . . ." *Times Publishing Co.* v. *Pinellas County Sheriff's Dept.*, No. 80-5416-17 (Fla. Cir. Ct., Pinellas County Feb. 2, 1981). The Times Publishing Company brought suit against the sheriff's department. In ruling in favor of the publishing company, the court noted that the Florida public records law had been liberally interpreted to include everything except specifically exempted information and that included rejecting exemptions for work product and personnel information. Citing: Ibid. "Police Records . . ."

[48] Section 1. IC 1971, 34-3-5-1, 1973. See also: John R. Bittner, "Politics and Information Flow: The Oregon Shield Law," *Western Speech*, 39 (Winter 1975), 51–59; *Shield Laws: A Report on Freedom of the Press, Protection of News Sources and the Obligation To Testify*, Lexington Council of State Governments, Kentucky, 1973; D. Eshelman and A. Barbour, "Legal References on Newsmen and Compulsory Disclosure," *Journal of Broadcasting*, 17 (Winter 1972-73), 37–50; V. Blasi, "The Newspersons Privilege: An Empirical Study," *Michigan Law Review*, 70 (December 1971), 229–235, 28-. Recent cases which dealt with confidentiality include *State v. Bachanan*, 250 Oregon 244, 436 p. 2d 729, cert. denied, 392 U.S. 905, 88 S.Ct. 2055, 20 L.Ed. 2d 1363 (1968), which involved the editor of a student newspaper; and *Branzburg* v. *Hayes in the Matter of Pappas* and *United States* v. *Caldwell*, 408 U.S. 665, 92 S.Ct. 2646, 33 L.Ed. 2d 626 (1972), concerning a reporter who authored a story about a chemical process changing marijuana into hashish.

[49] With the assistance of *NAB Counsel*, L-419, "The Qualified Privilege to Protect Confidential and Unnamed Sources," (July 1981), p. 6.

[50] "Secret Courts," *The News Media and the Law*, (Spring 1985), p. 13. *The Daily Pantagraph, et al.* v. *Judge Baner*, No. 84-J-S, slip op. (Ill. 11th Cir. Oct 14, 1984). *Decatur Newspapers, et al.* v. *Judge Bigler*, No. 84-J-24 (Union Co. Ill. Jan. 28, 1985), supervisory order denied, No. 61502 (Ill. March 28, 1985). See also Roger M. Grace, "The Courts v. the News Media: Is the Conflict Necessary?" *Case and Comment*, 79 (March-April 1974), 3–10; Tom Petersen, "Gag Orders in Iowa Reversed through Media Pressure," *RTNDA Communicator*, 30 (July 1976), 6; Stan Crock, "A Flurry of Gag Rules," *The Quill*, 62 (March 1974), 21–23; Lyle Denniston, "What Next for Burger's Nebraska Loophole?" *The Quill*, 65 (May 1977), 24–25.

[51] *Gannett Company, Inc.* v. *DePasquale*, 443 U.S. 368 (1979). *Press-Enterprise Co.* v. *Superior Court of California for the County of Riverside* (P-E II), No. 84-1560; 478 U.S. 1; 106 S. Ct. 2735; 1986 U.S. LEXIS 120; 92 L. Ed. 2d. 1; 54 U.S.L.W. 4869; 13 Media L. Rep. 1001; (1986). State courts were quick to jump on the bandwagon of DePasquale, citing the case as a precedent.

[52] *Gannett Company, Inc.* v. *DePasquale*, 443 U.S. 368 (1979).

[53] Ibid.

[54] "High Court Rules Defendant Rights Supersede Those of Press, Public," *Broadcasting*, 48 (July 9, 1979), 46.

[55] Ibid.

[56] Ibid.

[57] Ibid.

[58] As reported in: "Jury Selection Must Be In Public," *The News Media and the Law*, (January/February 1984), p. 21.

[59] Ibid.

[60] *Press Enterprise Co.* v. *Superior Court*, 52 U.S.L.W. 4113 (U.S., Jan. 18, 1984) (No. 82-556); 464 U.S. 501, 10 Med. L. Rep. 1161 (1984) See also: Jacqueline S. Chamberlaine, "A Prize-Winning News Librarian!," News Library News, 7 (Spring 1985), pp. 20–21; with an editor's note by Barbara P. Semonche.

[61] Accounts of the *Seattle Times Co.* v. *Rhinehart* are from "Secret Courts," *The News Media and the Law*, (Spring 1985), p. 13; "The Press and Courtroom Rights," NAB Counsel, L-419 (August 1984), 4–5; Citation: *Seattle Times* v. *Rhinehart*, 98 Wash. 2d 226, 654 P. 2d 673 (1982), petition for cert. filed, 51 U.S.L.W. 3791 (U.S. April 22, 1983) (No 82-1721).

[62] *NAB Counsel*, L-419 (August 1984), 4.

[63] Ibid., p. 5.

[64] "Dow Jones Wins Document Fight," *The News Media and the Law*, (Spring 1985), pp. 13–14.

[65] Ibid., p. 14. Citation: *In Re Coordinated Petroleum Proceedings*, 101 F.R.D. 34 (C.D. Cal. 1984), mandamus denied, 53 U.S.L.W. 3325 (U.S. Oct. 29, 1984) (No. 84-479).

[66] *Richmond Newspapers Inc.* v. *Commonwealth of Virginia*, 448 U.S. 555 (1980).

[67] Ibid.

[68] Ibid.

[69] "Sacramento Bee Stung," *The News Media and the Law*, (June/July 1982), p. 1. Citing: *Sacramento Bee* v. *U.S. District Court*, 7 Med. L.Rptr. 1929 (9th Cir. Sept. 14, 1981), cert. denied 50 U.S.L.W. 3911 (May 17, 1982).

[70] "Courts Closed for Wide Variety of Reasons Other Than Publicity," *The News Media and the Law*, (June/July 1981), pp. 52–53.

[71] *New York Times* v. *Sullivan*, 376 U.S. 254, 84 S.Ct. 710 (1964).

[72] *Curtis Publishing Co.* v. *Butts*, 388 U.S. 130, 87 S.Ct. 1975, 18 L.Ed. 2d 1094.

[73] *Gertz* v. *Robert Welch*, 418 U.S. 323, 94 S.Ct. 2997, 41 L.Ed. 2d 789 (1974).

[74] *Times, Inc.* v. *Firestone*, 424 U.S. 448 (1976).

[75] *Calder* v. *Jones*, 52 U.S.L.W. 4349 (U.S. Mar. 20, 1984).

[76] *Keaton* v. *Hustler Magazine, Inc.*, 52 U.S.L.W. 4346 (U.S. Mar. 20, 1984).

[77] *Bose* v. *Consumers Union*, 7 Med. L. Rptr. 2481 (D. Mass. Dec. 20, 1981).

[78] *Bose* v. *Consumers Union*, 104 S.Ct. 1949 (1984).

[79] One of the best sources of information on avoiding libel is Bruce W. Sanford's *Synopsis of the Law of Libel*. First published in 1977, subsequent editions have been updated and made applicable to the latest legal interpretations. The original edition was distributed by Scripps-Howard and copyrighted by Baker Hostetler and Patterson, Cleveland, Ohio.

[80] *Herbert* v. *Lando* 99 S.Ct. 296, 441 U. S. 153, 4 Media L. Rep. 2575 (1979).

[81] Fed. Rule Civ. Proc. 26 (b) as cited in *Herbert* v. *Lando* 99 S.Ct. 296, 441 U. S. 153, 4 Media L. Rep. 2575 (1979).

[82] *Herbert* v. *Lando* 99 S.Ct. 296, 441 U. S. 153, 4 Media L. Rep. 2575 (1979).

[83] Adapted from "How to Avoid Privacy Suits," *The News Media and the Law*, (Summer 1986), p. 7.

[84] "Nothing Sacred," *Broadcasting*, 47 (June 12, 1978), 82.

[85] Privacy Protection Act, 1980. Especially helpful in the preparation of the section on search and seizure was NAB Counsel, L-029 available to the author in the final stages of this manuscript's preparation.

[86] Ibid.

[87] Ibid.

[88] *Hugo Zacchini* v. *Scripps-Howard Broadcasting Company*, United States Supreme Court, 1977, 2 Med. L. Rptr. 2089.

[89] Ibid.

[90] Ibid.

[91] Robert Naylor, Jr., "Media groups say TV act too strict," Associated Press, reported in the *News and Observer*, Raleigh, NC, (February 3, 1991), p. 3E.

Chapter 8

[1] 316 U.S. 52 (1942).

[2] Ibid.

[3] 413 U.S. 376, 389, 1 Media L.Rep. 1908, 1915 (1973).

[4] 421 U.S. 809, 1 Media L. Rep. 1919 (1975).

[5] 425 U.S. 748, 1 Media L. Rep. 1930 (1976).

[6] Ibid.

[7] Ibid.

[8] *Head* v. *New Mexico Board of Examiners in Optometry*, 374 U.S. 424 (1963). As cited in Robert P. Sadowski, "Broadcasting and State Statutory Laws," *Journal of Broadcasting*, 18 (Fall 1974), 435.

[9] Ibid.

[10] Ibid.

[11] *NAB Highlights*, 3 (May 9, 1977), 4. Station liability for deceptive advertising is discussed in Leon C. Smith, "Local Station Liability for Deceptive Advertising," *Journal of Broadcasting*, 25 (Winter 1970–71), 107–112.

[12] See: Earl W. Kinter, *Michigan Law Review*, 64 (May 1960), 1280–1281.

[13] *Federal Trade Commission* v. *Colgate-Palmolive Co.*, 380 U.S. 374, 85 S.Ct. 1035 (1965). See also Harold L. Nelson and Dwight L. Teeter, Jr., *Law of Mass Communications* (Mineola, NY: Foundation Press, 1973), pp. 537–540.

[14] "Firestone Agrees to Pay for Remedial Ads," *Broadcasting*, 45 (February 23, 1976), 73.

[15] "Williams Settles with FTC over Geritol Ads," *Broadcasting* 45 (January 19, 1976), 45.

[16] Ibid.

[17] 47 CFR Ch.1 (10-1-91), Sec. 73.1212.

[18] Although monitoring and enforcement can be dificult.

[19] 47 CFR Ch.1 (10-1-91), Sec. 73.1212.

[20] 47 CFR Ch. 1 (10-1-91 Edition), 73.1211(D).

[21] Ibid.

[22] Want-ads exceptions are found at 47CFR Ch. 1 (10-1-91 Edition), 73.1211(G).

[23] Information on state regulation of alcoholic beverage commercials is from the April 13, 1984 issue of the "Legal and Government Affairs Review" memorandum of the North Carolina Association of Broadcasters. It cites and describes the rules and regulations affecting the advertising of alcoholic beverages which took effect on May 1, 1984, and were distributed to ABC Permittees by Marvin L. Speight, Jr., chairperson of the Alcoholic Beverage Control Commission.

[24] Ibid.

[25] North Carolina has a large military population.

[26] Ibid.

[27] Ibid.

[28] Section 73:1216.

[29] Section 73:1216. [41 FR 43152, Sept 30, 1976].

[30] FCC Public Notice, March 1974, as cited in NAB Legal Memorandum, "Licensee-Conducted Contests," October (L-612).

[31] FCC 75-127, 29849. (Docket No. 19122); (Docket No. 19123); (Docket No. 19124); (Docket No. 191265).

[32] Ibid.

[33] Ibid.

[34] Ibid.

[35] Ibid.

[36] Specifically the filing of IRS Form 1099.

[37] "Limiting Station Liability Through Releases," NAB Legal Memorandum, August 1983 (L-336), pp. 4–6.

[38] 47 CFR (10-1-91) 73:1211.

[39] Title 18, United States Code, Section 1304.

[40] "Promotions for Savings Accounts May Be Illegal," *Broadcasting*, 46 (March 28, 1977), 75.

[41] *Ohio Quests, Inc.*, 8 F.C.C. 2d 859 (1967).

[42] *Laury Associates, Inc.*, 27 F.C.C. 2d 870 (1971).

[43] F.C.C. 75-1018 (36929). In re Applications of United Television Company, Inc. (WFAN-TV) Washington, DC, for Renewal of License (Docket No. 18559), United Television Company, Inc. (WFAN-TV) Washington, DC (Docket No. 18561), for Construction Permit (Docket No. 18561); United Broadcasting Company, Inc. (WOOK) Washington, DC, for renewal of License (Docket No. 18562); Washington Community Broadcasting Co., Washington, DC, for Construction Permit for New Standard Broadcast Station (Docket No. 18563). Adopted September 9, 1975; Released September 12, 1975.

[44] Sec. 507 (U.S.C. Sec. 508—).

[45] Federal Trade Commission, "How to Advertise Consumer Credit," Washington, DC: Superintendent of Documents, (1986), p. 2, note 1.

[46] Ibid, p. 5.

[47] Ibid, p. 4.

[48] Ibid.

[49] Ibid.

[50] Ibid., p. 6.

[51] Ibid., pp. 6–7.

[52] Ibid., p. 8.

[53] Ibid., p. 6.

[54] Ibid., p. 9.

[55] Ibid., p. 9.

[56] Ibid., pp. 11–15.

[57] Ibid., p. 9.

[58] Ibid., p. 18.

[59] Ibid., p. 18.

[60] Ibid., pp. 18–19.

[61] Ibid.

[62] Regulations concerning the advertising and disclosure of warranties and guarantees are found in Section 239.2, of the Code of Federal Regulations, Ctation: 16 C.F.R. Sec. 239.2 (1986).

[63] Ibid. (Used as an example in the codified regulations.)

[64] Ibid.

[65] 16 C.F.R. Sec. 239.3 (1986).

[66] Example from 16 C.F.R. Sec. 239.4 (1986).

[67] Ibid.

[68] Note 1 in 16 C.F.R. 239.2 (1986).

[69] *Cliffdale Associates, Inc.*, 103 F.T.C. 110, at 176, 176 n.7, n.8,

Appendix, *reprinting* letter dated Oct. 14, 1983, from the Commission to The Honorable John D. Dingell, Chairman, Committee on Energy and Commerce, U.S. House of Repesentatives (1984) (Deception Statement).

[70] 49 Fed. Reg. 30,999 (1984); *appended to Thompson Medical Co.*, 104 F.T.C. 648 (1984).

[71] These guides do not address the claims based on a "lifecycle" theory of environmental benefit. Such analyses are still in their infancy and thus the commission lacks sufficient information on which to base guidance at this time.

Chapter 9

[1] In addition to FCC regulations in Title 47 of the Code of Federal Regulations (CFR) the source for the preparation of this section of the text is FCC Information Bulletin, "Frequency Allocation," April 1988, 7 pp.

[2] In addition to FCC regulations in Title 47 of the Code of Federal Regulations (CFR), the source for this section of the text is FCC Information Bulletin, "How to Apply for a Broadcast Station," periodically updated.

[3] First reported in the press. See M. L. Carnevale and P. M. Barrett, "Court Strikes Down FCC Policy Favoring Women in Granting Broadcast Licenses," *The Wall Street Journal*, February 20, 1992, p. B6.

[4] See M. S. Senter, Jr., and L. M. Crakes, "Financing Broadcast Transactions: Avoiding the FCC Pitfalls," *Broadcast Financial Journal* (May-June 1990), pp. 4–8. Although dealing with the transfer of station ownership, many of the principles apply to obtaining financing for a new station.

[5] The rationale, upheld by the courts, is based on the policy that a broadcaster must first and foremost be responsible to the community served by the station and giving up that responsibility to the demands of creditors would abridge that responsibility. See M. S. Senter, Jr., and L. M. Crakes, "Financing Broadcast Transactions: Avoiding the FCC Pitfalls," *Broadcast Financial Journal* (May-June 1990), p. 5.

[6] FCC Form 301, Section V(D)(a.).

[7] See "Radio Frequency Protection Guides," recommended in "American Historical Standard Safety Levels with respect to Human Exposure to Radio Frequency Electromagnetic Fields, 300 kHz to 100 GHz," (ANSI C95. 1-1982), by the Institute of Electrical and Electronics Engineers, Inc. 345 East 47th Street, New York, New York 10017.

[8] Certain stations, such as radar and diathermy (heat-measuring devices) operations are exempt. General information on call letters can be found in the FCC publication, "Station Identification and Call Signs," Federal Communications Commission, April 1988, 4 pp.

[9] "Station Identification and Call Signs," Federal Communications Commission, April 1988, p. 2.

[10] W. M. Borchard, "Call Letter Case Illustrates 'Trap'," *Advertising Age*, September 15, 1986, p. 58. William M. Borchard, who wrote the *Advertising Age* article, is identified in the article as a New York copyright and trademark attorney and a special media correspondent for the U.S. Trademark Assn. The linguistics expert was reported to have testified that no call letters were more similar than WBOC and WBOT.

[11] Case law has not always supported the frequency designation number as infringement, however. Borchard cites an earlier Georgia case in which two stations with "99 FM" were not infringing on each other because the 99 described an approximate location on the dial. Source: W. M. Borchard, "Call Letter Case Illustrates "Trap"," *Advertising Age*, September 15, 1986, p. 58.

[12] FCC Form 303-S, Guidelines.

[13] As listed in 73.3526 and 73.3527 of the FCC Rules.

[14] The complaint is chronicled in B. Langford, "WTVD files complaint against WRAL, WKFT," *The News and Observer*, Raleigh, NC, November 21, 1990, p. 5D.

[15] Top four job categories are defined in FCC Form 395-B.

[16] While reporting requirements have been modified over the years, the original basis for model affirmative action plans originated with Docket No. 20550, FCC 76-426, released July 26, 1976.

[17] P. G. Escobar, "EEO Deregulation Brings Tougher Standards," *Broadcast Financial Journal* (September-October 1989), pp. 18, 19.

[18] Minority group identification records are found in FCC Form 395-B Instructions.

[19] Public Law 102-385, 106 stat. 1460, October 5, 1992. Sec. 22(a)(1)-(3).

[20] Public Law 102-385, 106 stat. 1460, October 5, 1992. Sec. 22 amending section 634(d)(3) of the Communications Act of 1934.

[21] Public Law 102-385, 106 stat. 1460, October 5, 1992. Sec. 334(g).

[22] E. G. Aird, *A Broadcaster's Guide to Designing and Implementing an Effective EEO Program* (Washington, DC: National Association of Broadcasters, 1980), pp. 29–34. The author gratefully acknowledges the importance of this document in the preparation of the material in the text concerning affirmative action considerations in hiring.

[23] EEOC Sexual Harassment Guidelines. Additional perspectives on sexual harassment in the workplace can be found in K. A. Thurston, "Sexual Harassment: An Organizational Perspective," *Personnel Administrator* (December 1980), pp. 59–64; C. R. Klasoon, D. E. Thompson, and G. L. Luben, "How Defensible is Your Performance Appraisal System?" *Personnel Administrator* (December 1980), pp. 77–83. A summary advisory and procedural statement is NAB Counsel L-026 authored by communications attorney Wade H. Hargrove of the firm of Tharrington, Smith & Hargrove, Raleigh, NC.

[24] "Bikini Team Lawsuit," *The Wall Street Journal*, November 11, 1991, p. B4.

[25] Attorney Mary O'Melia conducts sexual harassment workshops for faculty and students at the University of North Carolina at Chapel Hill and serves as assistant director of affirmative action at the same university.

[26] "Sexual Harassment in Broadcasting," NAB Legal Counsel Memorandum prepared by Frank H. Stewart and Mark J. Stepaniak, April 1987. The article summarizes the case of *Neville* v. *Taft Broadcasting Co. and WGR-TV*, CIV-82-622C, (W.D.N.Y. January 16, 1987).

[27] C. Crossen, "Sex and Power in the Office. Are You From Another Planet, Or What? . . . " *The Wall Street Journal*, October 18, 1991, p. B1.

[28] The author acknowledges the following sources in the preparation of this section of the text: L. M. Zinser, "The Employment-At-Will Doctrine: Developments and Some Preventive Medicine, NAB Counsel Memorandum, February 1985, 6 pp.; S. D. Goland, "Implied Employment Contracts: Avoiding the Pitfalls," NAB Counsel Memorandum, January 1986, 8 pp.

[29] L. Michael Zinser, "The Employment-At-Will Doctrine: Developments and Some Preventive Medicine," NAB Counsel Memorandum, February 1985, p. 6.

[30] See also T. J. O'Rourke, "Independent Contractor or Employee," *Broadcast Cable Financial Journal* (May-June 1991), pp. 40–46; J. R. Urquhart III, Esq., "The IRS, Independent Contractors, and You," *Broadcast Cable Financial Journal* (May-June 1991), pp. 47–52.

[31] See Steven Muchnick, "Limiting Station Liability Through Releases," NAB Counsel Memorandum, August 1983.

[32] Adapted from "Limiting Station Liability Through Releases."

[33] Ibid.

[34] Quoted material from: "Limiting Station Liability Through Releases," p. 10.

[35] "Limiting Station Liability Through Releases," p. 10.

[36] EBS regulations are found in Code of Federal Regulations, Title 47, Part 73, Subpart G.

[37] As the procedures are defined in 73.931.

[38] 73.932.

[39] Ibid.

[40] 47 C.F.R. Sec. 73.3516 and subparts.

[41] 47 C.F.R. Sec. 73.3516 (a) (1), (1985).

[42] 47 C.F.R. Sec. 73.3516 (e) (2), (ii), (1985).

[43] 47 C.F.R. Sec. 73.3516 (a) (8), (9), (1985).

[44] 47 C.F.R. Sec. 73.3516 (d), (1985). A general discussion of the public inspection file issue can be seen in C. Tyrie and C. Clift III, "Broadcast Public Files: FCC Requirements, Station Performance and Public Use," *Journal of Broadcasting*, 28 (Summer 1984), 305–313.

[45] 47 C.F.R. Ch. 1 (10-1-91 Edition), sec 73.1202.

[46] 47 C.F.R. Ch. 1 (10-1-91 Edition), sec 73.670.

[47] 47 C.F.R. Ch. 1 (10-1-91 Edition), sec 73.3527.

[48] The Federal Trade Commission's statement on the matter of deceptive claims over coverage maps dates back to 1965. "FTC Issues Statement Regarding Deceptive Claims of Broadcast Audience Coverage," FTC Public Information Office, News Release of Thursday, July 8, 1965.

[49] A Cedar Rapids, Iowa, station came under criticism from two competitors for calling itself "Eastern Iowa's Leading News Station." The station claimed that one rating service had verified its claim, while the competitors claimed that two other surveys refuted it. A complaint against the station was filed with the FCC by the competitors. (Source: Correspondence to the FCC from Edgar F. Czarra, of the law firm of Covington and Burling, Washington, DC, representing the station, September 9, 1976).

[50] Based on FTC's 1965 guidelines, cited in *Report and Order*, in Docket No. 20501, FCC 76-226, March 10, 1976.

[51] Ibid.

[52] Notice of Proposed Rulemaking in Docket No. 20501, FCC-643, adopted May 29, 1975.

[53] J. P. Fordan, "Arbitron Blows Whistle on Station Games," *Advertising Age*, 48 (May 2, 1977), 12.

[54] Ibid.

[55] Jim Popham, "Charting a Straight Course at the FCC," *Radioactive*, 2 (November 1976), 6.

[56] The author acknowledges the NAB Counsel memorandum, "Deceptive Programming: Some Preventive Guidelines," (November 1983), 7 pp. in the preparation of this section on deceptive programming. Citing: *Walton Broadcasting, Inc.*, 47 R.R. 2d (P&F) 1233, 1240 (1980).

[57] Ibid., "Deceptive Programming . . ."

[58] Ibid.

[59] 47 C.F.R. Ch. 1 (10-1-91 Edition), sec 73.1206.

[60] 47 C.F.R. Ch. 1 (10-1-91 Edition), sec 73.1208.

Chapter 10

[1] FLSA, Section 7(a). Interpretation at Part 778.100, 29 CFR Ch. V, (7-1-90 Edition), 463–464. All references to the act or the interpretations are from the 1990 CFR. Page numbers differ depending on where the part cited appears in the CFR. Note: Hereafter, citations appear in the abbreviated form only, and cite the part of the CFR under which the interpretation is published. To keep as closely as possible to the literal interpretation of the law, portions of this chapter may quote verbatim from the law or its interpretations, yet may not always be cited in every case because of stylistic requirements. Persons wanting to read the exact text or the expanded regulations and interpretations should consult the most recent edition of the CFR under the appropriate section number. Anyone involved in disputed claims for compensation should consult competent counsel or the Wage and Hour Division of the Department of Labor. This text is for the purpose of providing a forum for discussion and a basic understanding of the concepts related to the FLSA and should not be considered the source upon which any claim is negotiated. Only the law itself, cases which interpret the law, and to a limited extent the interpretations of the Wage and Hour Division are suitable as a basis for resolving disputed claims.

[2] Issues concerning dual employment are discussed in Part 785 and should be consulted by counsel when a disputed claim arises.

[3] 778.104.

[4] 778.106.

[5] See 778.109 and 778.113.

[6] 778.332.

[7] 778.333.

[8] Based on, but quoted only in part from 541.1, interpreting Section 13(a)(1) of the FLSA. In applying the list to a specific compensation issue the reader should consult the actual wording of the FLSA and its interpretations to determine applicability.

[9] 541.1 (e).

[10] 541.1 (f).

[11] 541.102.

[12] 541.103.

[13] 541.103.

[14] 541.104.

[15] 541.108. The regulatory interpretation (541.108) uses the illustration of a timekeeper which adds additional insight to the interpretation:

(b) Keeping basic records of working time, for example, is frequently performed by a timekeeper employed for that purpose. In such cases the work is clearly not exempt in nature. In other establishments which are not large enough to employ a timekeeper, or in which the timekeeping function has been decentralized, the supervisor of each department keeps the basic time records of his own subordinates. In these instances, as indicated above, the timekeeping function is directly related to the function of managing the particular department and supervising its employees. However, the preparation of a payroll by a supervisor, even the payroll of the employees under his supervision, cannot be considered to be exempt work, since the preparation of a payroll does not aid in the supervision of the employees or the management of the department. Similarly, the keeping by a supervisor of production or sales records of his own subordinates for use in supervision or control would be exempt work, while the maintenance of production records of employees not under his direction would not be exempt work.

[16] 541.1 (e).

[17] 541.113.

[18] 541.113.

[19] Based on, but quoted only in part from 541.2, interpreting Section 13(a)(1) of the FLSA. In applying the list to a specific compensation issue, the reader should consult the actual wording of the FLSA and its interpretations to determine applicability.

[20] 541.2.

[21] 541.202.

[22] 542.202.

[23] 541.203(a)(b).

[24] 541.205.

[25] 541.205.

[26] 541.3.

[27] 541.3.

[28] "Louisiana TV Station Settles Overtime Suit," *Broadcasting*, May 20, 1991, p. 58.

[29] 541.303 specifically identifies "the more responsible writing positions in advertising agencies."

[30] 541.303.

[31] Ibid.

[32] Ibid.

[33] 541.303(f).

[34] 541.303(f)(1)(2)(3). The () appearing in the text of the interpretations are inserted by the author of the text and refer to Part 541.3 and subparts thereof.

[35] 541.303(e)(1)(2).

[36] Ibid.

[37] 541.306(a).

[38] 541.3 (a) through (c).

[39] 541.1(e) for administrative work, and 541.2(d) for executive work.

[40] Based on, but quoted only in part from 541.5, interpreting Section 13(a)(1) of the FLSA. In applying the list to a specific compensation issue, the reader should consult the actual wording of the FLSA and its interpretations to determine applicability.

[41] Based on, but quoted only in part from 541.5, interpreting Section 13(a)(1) of the FLSA. In applying the list to a specific compensation issue, the reader should consult the actual wording of the FLSA and its interpretations to determine applicability.

[42] Definitions of job descriptions and small-market exemptions are quoted from: 29 CFR Ch. V (7-1-92) Part 793, Sections 793.7-793.18, pp. 897–900.

[43] Ibid.

[44] Ibid.

[45] Ibid.

[46] Ibid.

[47] Ibid.

[48] Ibid.

[49] Agricultural industries of the Southeast or Midwest, industrialized companies in the Northeast, and marine industries of the Northwest are some examples.

[50] *Dalheim* v. *KDFW-TV*, 706 F. Supp. 493, LEXIS 16073, (N.D.Tex. 1988). FLSA is at 29 U.S.C. 201–209 (1988). On appeal: *Edward W. Dalheim, et al.*, Plaintiffs-Appellees, v. *KDFW-TV*, Defendant-Appellant, U.S. Court of Appeals for the Fifth Circuit, 918 F.2d 1220; 1990 U.S. App. LEXIS 21479; 18 Media L. Rep. 1657. In quoting from the circuit court's decisions, some citations and legal terminology have been omitted (where noted . . .) and footnotes which do appear refer to the citations as they appear in the district court and circuit court decisions in both KDFW-TV actions. Statements and commentary in this text associated with the application of the law as it occurred in KDFW-TV are not designed to reflect on the merits of the case or the arguments presented by KDFW-TV or its employees. The excerpts from the district court and the circuit court cases are for illustrative purposes only and designed as an aid in explaining the process by which the FLSA is applied in an actual employment situation.

[51] *Arnold* v. *Ben Kanowsky, Inc.*, 361 U.S. 388, 392, 80 S. Ct. 453, 456, 4 L.Ed.2d 393 (1960). Also, *Idaho Sheet Metal Works, Inc.* v. *Wirtz*, 383 U.S. 190, 206, 86 S. Ct. 737, 747, 15 L.Ed.2d 694 (1966).

[52] *Dalheim* v. *KDFW-TV*, 706 F. Supp. 493 (N.D.Tex. 1988).

[53] *Brock* v. *Mr. W Fireworks, Inc.*, 814 F.2d 1042 (5th Cir.), cert. denied, 484 U.S. 924, 108 S. Ct. 286, 98 L.Ed.2d 246 (1987); and Id. at 1044.

[54] *United States* v. *Silk*, 331 U.S. 704, 715, 67 S. Ct. 1463, 1469, 91 L.Ed. 1757 (1947).

[55] Brock, 814 F.2d at 1044.

[56] Id. at 1045.

[57] Id. Excerpt is from: On appeal: *Edward W. Dalheim, et al.* v. *KDFW-TV*, Defendant-Appellant, U.S. Court of Appeals for the Fifth Circuit, 918 F.2d 1220; 1990 U.S. App. LEXIS 21479; 18 Media L. Rep. 1657. Some citations have been eliminated when citing the KDFW-TV. Parenthetical () references to FLSA are to Section 3(e).

[58] *Edward W. Dalheim, et al.* v. *KDFW-TV*, U.S. Court of Appeals for the Fifth Circuit, 918 F.2d 1220; 1990 U.S. App. LEXIS 21479; 18 Media L. Rep. 1657. Job descriptions were much more extensive in the district court case leading to the appeal *Dalheim* v. *KDFW-TV*, 706 F. Supp. 493, LEXIS 16073, (N.D.Tex. 1988). FLSA is at 29 U.S.C. 201–209 (1988).

[59] *Dalheim* v. *KDFW-TV*, 706 F. Supp. 493, LEXIS 16073, (N.D.Tex. 1988). FLSA is at 29 U.S.C. 201–209 (1988).

[60] Plaintiffs, producers, and directors argued the same: *Dalheim* v. *KDFW-TV*, 706 F. Supp. 493, LEXIS 16073, (N.D.Tex. 1988). FLSA is at 29 U.S.C. 201–209 (1988).

[61] *Dalheim* v. *KDFW-TV*, 706 F. Supp. 493, LEXIS 16073, (N.D.Tex. 1988). FLSA is at 29 U.S.C. 201–209 (1988).

[62] Ibid.

[63] Ibid.

[64] Ibid.

[65] Ibid.

[66] For a case determining that plaintiffs had talent and training for original artistic production and that the work required this capability, but that the employees were nonexempt because their work was not predominantly of that character, see *Stranger* v. *Vocafilm Corp.*, 151 F.2d 894 (2d Cir. 1945).

[67] 541.303(e)(1).

[68] *Dalheim* v. *KDFW-TV*, 706 F. Supp. 493, LEXIS 16073, (N.D.Tex. 1988). FLSA is at 29 U.S.C. 201–209 (1988).

[69] Ibid.

[70] Ibid.

[71] Based on, but quoted only in part from 541.2, interpreting Section 13(a)(1) of the FLSA. In applying the list to a specific compensation issue, the reader should consult the actual wording of the FLSA and its interpretations to determine applicability.

[72] 541.2.

[73] Note 16 in: *Dalheim* v. *KDFW-TV*, 706 F. Supp. 493, LEXIS 16073, (N.D.Tex. 1988).

[74] *Dalheim* v. *KDFW-TV*, 706 F. Supp. 493, LEXIS 16073, (N.D.Tex. 1988). Note also:

> Although the court need not consider the second element—independent judgment and discretion—the court observes that a more lenient test applies when the short test is applicable. Under the Sec. 541.2(b) long test, an employee must "customarily and regularly" exercise independent judgment and discretion; under the Sec. 214(a) short test applicable in this case, the employee's primary duty must simply "include work requiring the exercise of discretion and independent judgment." See *Dymond* v. *U.S. Postal Service*, 670 F.2d 93, 95 (8th Cir. 1982). (Note 17 in Dalheim.)

[75] *Dalheim* v. *KDFW-TV*, 706 F. Supp. 493, LEXIS 16073, (N.D.Tex. 1988). Note also:

> Other cases have held that highly trained technicians who exercise no discretion, control, or administrative functions, but rather must always consult a superior on any major policy change, are not exempt under the FLSA. See, e.g., *Martin* v.

Penn Line Services Inc., 416 F.Supp. 1387 (W.D. Pa. 1976); *Reeves* v. *International Telephone & Telephone Corp.*, 357 F.Supp. 295, 301 (W.D. La. 1973). See also *Pezzilo* v. *GTE Information Systems*, 414 F. Supp. 1257 (M.D. Tenn. 1976), aff'd, 572 F.2d 1189 (6th Cir. 1978) (computer programmers not exercising discretion and judgment but exercising job skill). Source: Dalheim at note 18.

[76] *Dalheim* v. *KDFW-TV*, 706 F. Supp. 493, LEXIS 16073, (N.D.Tex. 1988).

[77] Ibid.

[78] Ibid.

[79] Ibid.

[80] J. Laurent Scharff, "Structuring Student Internships to Avoid Problems," RTNDA *Legal Notes* (October 1992), 2 pp.

[81] Ibid.

[82] Ibid.

[83] Network owned and operated stations affiliated with the parent company network.

[84] From KOFY FM, KOFY TV 20 and AMERICAN FEDERATION OF TELEVISION AND RADIO ARTISTS; Cases 20-CA-22544, 20-CA-22545 NATIONAL LABOR RELATIONS BOARD; 137 L.R.R.M. 1219; 301 NLRB No. 93;1991 NLRB LEXIS 100; February 12, 1991; Note 2 in the original decision:

Neither the Union nor the General Counsel attempted to show that the Union had the support of a majority of employees in either unit at the time of recognition or any other time. Respondent adduced unchallenged evidence that on September 7, 1988 neither unit was significantly staffed. The presumption of majority status the Union enjoyed in the unit covered by the extended 1986 contract, see Barrington Plaza and Tragniew, Inc., 185 NLRB 962 (1970), does not automatically extend to the far larger unit covered by the purported KOFY TV 20 contract. On this record I find neither actual evidence nor any benefit of presumption which may sustain the General Counsel's burden of proof on this issue, should the General Counsel's time bar argument not preclude direct consideration of the units' expressed sentiments regarding representation.

[85] From KOFY FM, KOFY TV 20 and AMERICAN FEDERATION OF TELEVISION AND RADIO ARTISTS; Cases 20-CA-22544, 20-CA-22545 NATIONAL LABOR RELATIONS BOARD; 137 L.R.R.M. 1219; 301 NLRB No. 93; 1991 NLRB LEXIS 100; February 12, 1991; note 5 in the original decision: "If no exceptions are filed as provided by Section 102.46 of the Board's Rules and Regulations, the findings, conclusions, and recommended Order shall, as provided in Section 102.48 of the Rules, be adopted by the Board and all objections to them shall be waived for all purposes."

Chapter 11

[1] *1992 Cable TV Facts* (New York: Cabletelevision Advertising Bureau, Inc.), 57 pp.

[2] Based on a projected expenditure of almost $20 billion in 1992. Source: *1992 Cable TV Facts* (New York: Cabletelevision Advertising Bureau, Inc.), p. 4.

[3] *United States v. Southwestern Cable Co.*, 392 U.S. 157, 88 S.Ct. 1994, 20 L.Ed.2d 1001 (1968).

[4] Ibid.

[5] Ibid.

[6] The proceeding to revise the rules occurred under Docket 18397. A discussion of the compromise made in the 1972 rules and an example of the issues that can confront a local change of service can be found, respectively, in Harvey Jassem, "The Selling of the Cable TV Compromise," *Journal of Broadcasting*, 17 (Fall 1973), 427–436; and Norman Felsenthal, "Cherry-Picking, Cable, and the FCC," *Journal of Broadcasting* 19 (Winter 1975), 43–53. The full citation of the Southwestern case is *United States* v. *Southwestern Cable Co.*, 392 U.S. 157 (1968). The 1972 rules were issued in *Regulatory Developments in Cable Television* (Washington, DC: Federal Communications Commission, May 1977), definitions cited on pp. 7–8; see also the most recent editions of the *Cable Sourcebook*, and *FCC Information Bulletin* #13632.

[7] *FCC Information Bulletin*, (January 1990), p. 3.

[8] Ibid.

[9] *Home Box Office, Inc.* v. *FCC*, 567 F.2d 9 (D.C. Cir. 1977); cert. den. 434 U.S. 829 (1977).

[10] Ibid.

[11] Public Law 98-549. See also Michael O. Wirth and Linda Cobb-Reiley, "A First Amendment Critique of the 1984 Cable Act," *Journal of Broadcasting & Electronic Media*, 31 (Fall 1987), 391–407.

[12] Report and Order in MM Docket No. 84-1296, 50 FR 18637 (1984), modified, 104 FCC 2d 386 (1986), 60 RR 2d 514 (1986).

[13] Public Law 102-385, 106 Stat. 1460, October 5, 1992. As with all federal communications law, both acts amend the Communications Act of 1934.

[14] Public Law 102-385, 106 stat. 1460, October 5, 1992. Section numbers as cited both in the 1992 act and in the notes of this text refer to the amended section numbers of the Communications Act of 1934 (47 U.S.C. 531 et seq.) as amended by the 1992 legislation. Subheadings appearing in this text are the same as subheadings appearing in the Public Law 102-385. Much of the 1992 Cable Act amends specific sections of the Communications Act of 1934, which in turn is published in the United States Code and from which regulations evolve and are published in the Code of Federal Regulations. For additional information on such citations refer to the chapter on "The Legal System and Legal Research" which concludes this text.

[15] Public Law 102-385, 106 stat. 1460, October 5, 1992. Sec. 2. Amending Section 602 of the Communications Act of 1934.

[16] Public Law 102-385, 106 stat. 1460, October 5, 1992. Sec. 623.

[17] Ibid.

[18] Ibid.

[19] Ibid.

[20] Ibid.

[21] Ibid.

[22] Public Law 102-385, 106 stat. 1460, October 5, 1992.

[23] Ibid., Sec. 614.

[24] Ibid.

[25] Ibid., Sec. 615.

[26] Ibid.

[27] Ibid., Sec. 9.

[28] Ibid.

[29] Ibid., Sec. 10.

[30] Ibid., Sec. 15.

[31] Ibid., Sec. 616.

[32] Ibid., Sec. 632.

In addition the law prevents cable operators from selling and transferring the ownership—called trafficking in cable systems—of the cable system within a 36-month period following the acquisition or initial construction of the system.

[33] 47 CFR Ch.I (10-1-91 Edition), 76.7(a). The discussion of the rules applying to special relief is drawn from 47 CFR Ch.I (10-1-91 Edition), 76.7(a)–(g).

[34] 47 CFR Ch.I (10-1-91 Edition), 76.10(a)–(c).

[35] Cable Communications Policy Act of 1984, Public Law 98-549, II, Sec. 611(a)–(f).

[36] Ibid., Sec. 611(d).

[37] Ibid., Sec. 612.

[38] Ibid.

39 Cable Communications Policy Act of 1984, Pubic Law 98-549, at section 631. The discussion of cable rules either paraphrases or quotes directly (which may or may not appear in quotation marks in the text) from this section of the law.

40 Subscriber Privacy Notice of Carolina Cable, Chapel Hill, North Carolina.

41 47 CFR Ch.I (10-1-91 Edition), 76.73. Also as amended in Public Law 102-385, 106 stat. 1460, October 5, 1992. Sec. 22.

42 47 CFR Ch.I (10-1-91 Edition), 76.205.

43 Ibid.

44 *Gitlow* v. *New York*, 268 U.S. 652, 45 S. Ct. 625, 69 L. Ed. 1138 (1925); *Chaplinsky* v. *New Hampshire*, 315 U.S. 568, 62 S. Ct. 766, 86 L. Ed. 1031 (1942); *New York Times* v. *Sullivan*, 376 U.S. 254, 84 S. Ct. 710, 11 L. Ed. 2d 686 (1964); *Brandenburg* v. *Ohio*, 395 U.S. 444, 89 CS. Ct. 1927, 23 L. Ed. 2d 430 (1969); *Roth* v. *United States*, 354 U.S. 476, 77 S. Ct. 1304, 1 L. Ed. 2d 419 (1973); *Miller* v. *California*, 413 U. S. 15, 93 S. Ct. 2607, 37 L. Ed. 2d 419 (1973). See also Howard M. Kleiman, "Indecent Programming on Cable Television: Legal and Social Dimensions," *Journal of Broadcasting and Electronic Media*, 30 (Summer 1986), 275–294.

45 *FCC* v. *Pacifica Foundation*, 438 U.S. 726, 98 S. Ct. 3026, 57 L. Ed. 2d 1073 (1978).

46 *Miller* v. *California*, 413 U. S. 15, 93 S. Ct. 2607, 37 L. Ed. 2d 419 (1973).

47 *FCC* v. *Pacifica Foundation*, 438 U.S. 726, 98 S. Ct. 3026, 57 L. Ed. 2d 1073 (1978). Unsuccessfully argued to uphold the indecency prohibition of the Miami, Florida cable franchise in *Cruz* v. *Ferre*, 571 F. Supp. 125 (S.D.Fla. 1983), upheld in *Cruz* v. *Ferre*, 755 F.2d 1415 (11th Cir. 1985).

48 Cable Communications Policy Act of 1984, Public Law 98-549, at section 639.

49 *Community Television of Utah, Inc. v. Roy City*, 555 F.Supp. 1164 (D.C. Utah 1982); *Community Television* v. *Wilkerson*, 611 F. Supp. 1099 (D.C. Utah 1985; Jones v. Wilkerson, 800 F.2d 989 (10th Cir. 1986), affirmed without opinion, 107 S.Ct. 1559 (1987); *Cruz* v. *Ferre*, 571 F. Supp. 125 (S.D.Fla. 1983), upheld in *Cruz* v. *Ferre*, 755 F.2d 1415, 57 Rad. Reg. 2d (P & F) 1452 (11th Cir. 1985).

50 City of Miami Ordinance No. 9223, adopted on October 19, 1981, established the regulation of cable television in the City of Miami. Ordinance No. 9332, enacted on November 19, 1981, granted Miami Cablevision, a joint venture of Americable of Greater Miami, Inc., and Miami Telecommunications, Inc. a nonexclusive, revocable license to operate a cable system in Miami. A third ordinance, No. 9538, regulated indecent and obscene material and became the object of a lawsuit. Obscene was defined under the same ordinance as "(i) whether the average person, applying contemporary community standards, would find that the work, taken as a whole, appeals to the prurient interest; (ii) whether the work depicts or describes, in a patently offensive way, sexual conduct specifically defined by the applicable state law; and (iii) whether the work, taken as a whole, lacks serious literary, artistic, political or scientific value." The discussion of the Miami ordinance and *Cruz* v. *Ferre* is from *Cruz* v. *Ferre*, 755 F.2d 1415 (11th Cir. 1985).

51 *FCC* v. *Pacifica Foundation*, 438 U.S. at 748–49, 98 S.Ct. at 3039–40.

52 *Cruz* v. *Ferre*, 755 F.2d 1415 57 Rad. Reg. 2d (P & F) 1452 (11th Cir. 1985).

53 Ibid. Notes and citations omitted. Exercising a bit of colorful prose, the court in footnoting the statement that "cable programming is available only to those who have cable attached to their television sets," pointed to a Brief of Appellants in the *Cruz* case arguing on behalf of the validity of the city ordinance. In n6 the appeals court in the Cruz case said: "appellants seem to want to extend Justice Stevens's 'pig in the parlor' analogy. See Brief of Appellants at 16 ('it makes no difference whether the pig enters the parlor through the door of broadcast, cable, or amplified speech: government is entitled to keep the pig out of the parlor'). It seems to us, however, that if an individual voluntarily opens his door and allows a pig into his parlor, he is in less of a position to squeal."

54 *Cruz* v. *Ferre*, 755 F.2d 1415 57 Rad. Reg. 2d (P & F) 1452 (11th Cir. 1985). Notes and citations omitted.

55 Ibid.

56 Citing the district court in *Cruz* v. *Ferre*, 571 F. Supp. at 133.

57 *Cruz* v. *Ferre*, 571 F. Supp. at 133.

58 *Leathers* v. *Medlock*, 111 S. Ct. 1438; 113 L. Ed. 2d 494; 59 U.S.L.W. 4281; Media L. Rep. 1953; 1991 U.S. LEXIS 2220.

59 The "ideas" concept was anchored in *Regan* v. *Taxation with Representation of Washington*, 461 U.S. 540 (1983).

60 *Grosjean* v. *American Press Co.*, 297 U.S. 233 (1936).

61 *Minneapolis Star & Tribune Co.* v. *Minnesota Commissioner of Revenue*, 460 U.S. 575 (1983).

62 *Arkansas Writers' Project, Inc.* v. *Ragland*, 481 U.S. 221 (1987).

63 *Regan* v. *Taxation with Representation of Washington*, 461 U.S. 540 (1983). Citations omitted. Citation for *Cammarano* v. *United States* is as follows: *Cammarano* v. *United States*, 358 U.S. 498 (1959).

64 *Leathers* v. *Medlock*, 111 S. Ct. 1438; 113 L. Ed. 2d 494; 59 U.S.L.W. 4281; Media L. Rep. 1953; 1991 U.S. LEXIS 2220.

65 Citing: *Los Angeles* v. *Preferred Communications, Inc.* 476 U.S. 488, 494 (1986).

66 Although cable as a news medium is well documented throughout the United States through local access programming and cooperative arrangements with local broadcasters.

67 Testimony of Amos B. Hostetter, Jr., Chairman and Chief Executive Officer, Continental Cablevision, Inc., Before the Subcommittee on Telecommunications and Finance of the U.S. House of Representatives, June 27, 1991.

68 See for example: Harvey T. Boyd and Richard Keenan, "Property Taxes: What You Should Know and Can Do," *Broadcast Cable Financial Journal* (July–August 1990), pp. 10–13.

69 "Assessments of Cable Television Questioned," *The Record*, Council, Idaho, January 4, 1989, p. 1.

70 47 U. S. C. @ 224(b)(1).

71 Ibid.

72 *Federal Communications Commission*, et al. v. *Florida Power Corp.* et al. 480 U.S. 245; 107 S. Ct. 1107; 1987 U.S. LEXIS 937; 94 L. Ed. 2d 282; 55 U.S.L.W. 4236; 62 Rad Reg. 2d (P & F) 287; 14 Media L. Rep. 1455.

73 *Loretto* v. *Teleprompter Manhattan CATV Corp.* 458 U.S. 419.

74 *Federal Communications Commission*, et al. v. *Florida Power Corp.*, et al., at n6.

75 From Robert G. Picard, "Copyright Royalty Payments Top $200 Million as Payments by Cable Triple," *Broadcast Cable Financial Journal* (July–August 1991), pp. 8–9, 11. Picard's analysis is based on records of the U.S. Copyright Office, based on 1989 figures. The payment schedule at that time required from the smallest systems a payment of $28 semiannually.

76 Detailed in NAB Counsel Memo L-8809, May–June 1988.

77 Rules covering syndicated exclusivity are found at 47 CFR I (10-1-91 Edition) 76.151.

78 Syndicated programs as defined at 76.5(o).

79 47 CFR Ch I (10-1-91 Edition) 76.5(dd).

80 47 CFR Ch I (10-1-91 Edition) 76.67.

81 First press reports of the rule change were carried in "FCC Votes to Allow Networks to Buy Cable Systems; Limits are Established," *The Wall Street Journal*, June 19, 1992, p. B8.

82 Reaction to the announcement was mixed. CBS main-

tained it did not want to enter the cable business and was committed to over-the-air broadcasting. Independent TV operators said they were worried about program diversity and competition. Capital Cities/ABC said they would wait and see while weighing individual situations. Source: "FCC Votes to Allow Networks to Buy Cable Systems; Limits are Established," *The Wall Street Journal*, June 19, 1992, p. B8. Some of the networks' statements could be seen as public relations efforts.

[83] An early examination of this issue is contained in V. Sparkes, "Local Regulatory Agencies for Cable Television," *Journal of Broadcasting*, 19 (Spring 1975), 228–229.

[84] Cable Television Consumer Protection and Competition Act of 1992, Public Law 102-385, October 5, 1992. Sec. 18. Amending Section 626(a) of the Communications Act of 1934.

[85] See for example *Cruz* v. *Ferre*, 755 F.2d 1415 57 Rad. Reg. 2d (P & F) 1452 (11th Cir. 1985). Also: Testimony of Amos B. Hostetter, Jr., Chairman and Chief Executive Officer, Continental Cablevision, Inc., Before the Subcommittee on Telecommunications and Finance of the U.S. House of Representatives, June 27, 1991.

[86] Sources for the discussion of provisions of a cable ordinance primarily consist of Grainger R. Barrett, "Franchising Cable TV Today," *Popular Government* (Winter 1980), pp. 1–5, 18; the cable franchises of Marblehead and Springfield, Massachusetts and the Hollywood-Wilshire area of the City of Los Angeles; and where cited, the testimony of Amos B. Hostetter, Jr., Chairman and Chief Executive Officer, Continental Cablevision, Inc., Before the Subcommittee on Telecommunications and Finance of the U.S. House of Representatives, June 27, 1991, hereafter cited in the notes as "Hostetter testimony, p." No assumption should be made that a specific provision applies to a specific franchise without consulting the original franchise document. As stated in the main text of the chapter, thousands of franchise documents exist nationwide with great variation in terms and conditions. The provisions discussed here are for the purposes of example only and should not be seen as constituting the typical or ideal franchise, since a franchise authority many times has provisions that apply to the peculiarities of a particular franchise area. Such things as the number of cable companies, the social climate of the community, the economic and political conditions, the party in power at the time the franchise was awarded, and regulations can all have an impact on the provisions of the ordinance in effect.

[87] Final Cable Television License for the Town of Marblehead, Massachusetts, Section 1, Definitions. Hereafter referred to as "Marblehead Cable License."

[88] Marblehead Cable License, Section 19(b).

[89] Marblehead Cable License, Section 18(b).

[90] An early assessment of the issue is found in Frederick W. Ford and Lee G. Lovett, "State Regulation of Cable Television, Part I: Current Statutes," *Broadcast Management/Engineering*, 10 (June 1974), 18, 21, 50, Frederick W. Ford and Lee G. Lovett, "State Regulation of Cable TV, Part II: States with No CATV Statutes: Short-Term and Long-Term Trends," *Broadcast Management/Engineering*, 30 (June 1974) 20, 21, 22.

[91] Examples are from Article 28 of the New York State Executive Law. All examples are subject to revision and are presented here as summarized as Appendix D and Appendix E in Hostetter testimony.

[92] Examples from C.G.S. 16-333 and R.S.C.A. 16-333.

Chapter 12

[1] An act to create a commerce court, and to amend the act entitled "An Act to Regulate Commerce," approved February 4, 1887, as heretofore amended, and for other purposes. H.R. 17536. 61st. Congress, Sess. II. Ch. 309, June 18, 1910, U.S. Stat. Vol. 36, p. 539.

[2] Ibid., p. 546.

[3] "An Act to aid in the Construction of Telegraph Lines, and to secure to the Government the Use of same for postal, military, and other Purposes," 39th Congress, Sess. I, Ch. 230, July 24, 1866, *U.S. Stat.*, Vol. 14, pp. 221–222.

[4] Many sources detail the corporate history of the telephone industry. Among those consulted for this section of the text are Charles F. Phillips, Jr., *The Regulation of Public Utilities: Theory and Practice* (Arlington, VA: Public Utilities Reports, Inc., 1988); *The History of the Telephone Industry* (Washington, DC: United States Telephone Association, n.d.); Robert Britt Horwitz, "For Whom the Bell Tolls: Causes and Consequences of the AT&T Divestiture," *Critical Studies in Mass Communication*, 3 (June 1986), 119–154; Chancy, *Bell Telephone Quarterly*, (July 1923) (reprinted 1979).

[5] Of interest is the account that Bell had been carrying on studies with a laboratory device called the phonautograph, which made mechanical tracings of sound vibrations. He made an improved phonautograph, using the bones and drum of a human ear procured for him by a friend, Dr. Clarence Blake. Bell explained how his experiments with this improved instrument led him to his conception of the telephone as follows: "I was much struck by the disproportion in weight between the membrane and the bones that were moved by it; and it occurred to me that if such a thin and delicate membrane could move bones that were, relatively to it, very massive indeed, why should not a larger and stouter membrane be able to move a piece of steel in the manner I desired? At once the conception of the membrane speaking telephone became complete in my mind. . . . The arrangement thus conceived in the summer of 1874 was substantially similar to that shown . . . in my patent of March 7, 1876." Bell described to his father, while on a visit to the family home at Brantford, Ontario, on this date (1874) his conception of his electric speaking telephone using his undulating current principle. (*Events in Telecommunications History*, pp. 2–3.). date (1874) added.

[6] Prior to the formation of the company, on August 10, 1876, the world's first long-distance telephone call (one-way) was received at Paris, Ontario, by Bell from his father and uncle at Brantford, Ontario, over telegraph lines 8 miles and 68 miles long. Referring to this call, Bell said: "This Brantford experiment is of historical interest . . . because it led to the discovery of the proper combination of parts in a telephone to enable it to become operative upon a long line; and because upon this occasion occurred the first transmission of the human voice over a telegraph line in which the transmitting and receiving telephone was miles apart."

Permission to use this telegraph line was granted by Lewis B. McFarlane, a telegraph manager, who entered the telephone business in 1879, was president of the Bell Telephone Company of Canada from 1915 to 1925 and chairman of the board from 1925 to 1930. (*Events in Telecommunications History*, p. 3.)

[7] Hubbard offered to sell the telephone invention to Western Union for $100,000, but the offer was refused (*Events in Telecommunications History*, p. 3.)

[8] Elisha Gray worked his way through Oberlin College as a carpenter. His work in physics at Oberlin quickly narrowed to electrical applications. He invented a self-adjusting telegraph relay, a telegraphic switch and a repeater. He continued in the firm of Gray and Barton only two years, after which he devoted himself entirely to electrical research. Gray was working on a harmonic telegraph at the same time as Bell, and perfected what he called a telephone to transmit musical sounds. The idea of transmitting vocal sounds occurred to him, and on February 14, 1876, he filed a caveat (a confidential report of an invention which is not fully perfected) in the U.S. Patent Office. His caveat indicated that he was on the same track as Bell, but had not worked out his transmitter as fully. And on that same day, but a few hours earlier, Alexander Graham Bell had filed a patent application for his telephone, thus anticipating Gray. Gray's

most important invention thereafter probably was the telautograph which transmits facsimile handwriting and drawings. At the time of his sudden death in 1901, he was experimenting on underwater signaling to vessels at sea. (*Events in Telecommunications History*, p. 2.)

[9] Competition in the telephone business developed from the Western Union Telegraph Company through its newly established subsidiaries, the American Speaking Telephone Company and the Gold & Stock Telephone Company. These companies used Thomas A. Edison transmitters and Elisha Gray receivers.

The Handset Telephone—Robert G. Brown, who became chief operator at the Western Union (Gold & Stock) exchange in New York City, devised in 1878 (possibly in April but more probably in May) the first handset, mounting an Edison transmitter and a Gray receiver on a bar of metal. Brown was sent to France in 1879 to open an exchange at Paris. There his handset was lightened to make it more easily handled by operators. It became popular in France and Europe despite limitations that made it unacceptable in the United States, and for years was known as the French or Continental telephone. Brown died at St. Petersburg, Florida, October 2, 1947, at the age of 93. (*Events in Telecommunications History*, p. 5.)

[10] William Chauncy Langdon, *Bell Telephone Quarterly* (July 1923). Reprinted in 1979 by the Bell System, p. 5.

[11] The District Telephone Company of New Haven, organized by licensee George W. Coy along with Walter Lewis and H. P. Frost, had 21 subscribers. (*Events in Telecommunications History*, p. 5.) "First" exchanges the following year (1879) included:

February	Louisville, KY
February 15	Minneapolis, MN
February 24	Denver, CO
March	Indianapolis, IN
March 15	New Orleans, LA
April 1	Richmond, VA
April 2	Providence, RI
April 26	Toronto, Canada
May 1	Montreal, Canada
June	Omaha, NE
June 1	Burlington, VT
June 4	Topeka, KS
June 11	Dubuque, IA
August 1	Augusta, GA
August 15	Camden, NJ
August 21	Galveston, TX
August 26	Charleston, SC
September 1	Portland, ME
September 1	Brantford, Canada
September 20	Raleigh, NC
September 22	London, Canada
November 1	Little Rock, AR
November 15	Mobile, AL
December	Nashville, TN

(*Events in Telecommunications History*, p. 7.)

[12] 126 U.S. 1 (1988).

[13] *The History of the Telephone Industry* (Washington, DC: United States Telephone Association), n.d., p. 7. This publication, as well as works by Phillips and Horwitz, cited later, were helpful in providing background information about this era and this section of the text.

[14] Charles F. Phillips, Jr., *The Regulation of Public Utilities: Theory and Practice* (Arlington, VA: Public Utilities Reports, Inc., 1988), p. 688.

[15] *United States* v. *Western Electric Co., Inc.* and *American Telephone & Telegraph Co., Inc.* Civil Action No. 17-49 (D.N.J. 1956); Answer printed at page 1807 of Consent Decree Program of the Department of Justice (Hearings before the Antitrust Subcommittee of the Committee on the Judiciary, House, 85th Cong., 2d sess.), U.S. Government Printing Office, 1958, Part II, Vol. I, pp. 1723–1795, and cited by Charles F. Phillips, Jr., *The Regulation of Public Utilities: Theory and Practice* (Arlington, VA: Public Utilities Reports, Inc., 1988), p. 688.

[16] Robert Britt Horwitz, "For Whom the Bell Tolls: Causes and Consequences of the AT&T Divestiture," *Critical Studies in Mass Communication*, 3 (June 1986), 128–129.

[17] Robert Britt Horwitz, "For Whom the Bell Tolls: Causes and Consequences of the AT&T Divestiture," *Critical Studies in Mass Communication*, 3 (June 1986), 128. Citing: *United States* v. *Western Electric Co., Inc.* and *American Telephone & Telegraph Co., Inc.* Civil Action No. 17-49 (D.N.J. 1956); A. Lewis, "AT&T Settles Antitrust Case; Shares Patents," *The New York Times*, January 25, 1956, pp. 1, 16; G. F. George, "The Federal Communications Commission and the Bell System: Abdication of Regulatory Responsibility," *Indiana Law Journal*, 44 (1969), 459–477.

[18] U.S. House of Representatives. 85th Congress, 2nd Session. Interstate and Foreign Commerce. Network Broadcasting (Report No. 1297). Washington, DC: U.S. Government Printing Office; as cited by Horwitz, p. 129.

[19] U.S. House of Representatives. 85th Congress, 2nd Session. Interstate and Foreign Commerce. Network Broadcasting (Report No. 1297). Washington, DC: U.S. Government Printing Office; as cited by Horwitz, p. 129.

[20] Pub. L. 93-528, Dec. 21, 1974, 88 Stat. 1706.

[21] *Hush-a-Phone Corp.* v. *United States*, 238 F.2d 266 (D.S. Cir. 1956).

[22] As noted in *Black's Law Dictionary*, 6th ed., (1990), pp. 1456–1457.

[23] Cited from note 2 in Carterfone.

[24] In the Matter of Use of the Carterfone Device in Message Toll Telephone Service, 13 FCC 2d 420 (1968), recon. denied, 14 FCC 2d 571 (Adopted June 26, 1968).

[25] The description of the workings of the device are paraphrased from the FCC ruling: In the Matter of Use of the Carterfone Device in Message Toll Telephone Service, 13 FCC 2d 420 (1968), recon. denied, 14 FCC 2d 571 (Adopted June 26, 1968).

[26] 2.6.1 General Provisions, of tariff FCC No. 263, issued January 2, 1968, Effective February 1, 1968, superseding tariff FCC No. 132 which was the tariff under which the action was originally instituted. As cited in Appendix A of the Carterfone decision.

[27] *Carter* v. *AT&T*, 250 F. Supp. 188, 192 (N.D. Texas, 1966). The United States Court of Appeals for the Fifth Circuit affirmed the district court's decision on August 17, 1966 in *Carter* v. *American Telephone and Telegraph Co.* 365 F. 2d 486 (5th Cir., 1966).

[28] *Hush-a-Phone Corp.* v. *United States*, 238 F.2d 266 (D.C. Cir. 1956).

[29] In the Matter of Use of the Carterfone Device in Message Toll Telephone Service, 13 FCC 2d 420 (1968), recon. denied, 14 FCC 2d 571 (Adopted June 26, 1968), pp. 423–425.

[30] In the Matter of Allocation of Frequencies in the Band Above 890 Mc., 27 FCC 359 (Adopted July 29, 1959), Docket No. 11866.

[31] Specifically, citing *FCC* v. *RCA Communications, Inc.*, 346 U.S. 86, 91 (1953). In the Matter of Allocation of Frequencies in the Band Above 890 Mc., 27 FCC 359 (Adopted July 29, 1959), Docket No. 11866.

[32] The argument seems particularly artificial in view of the fact that squatters rights as a matter of policy had already developed in the broadcasting industry.

[33] Dealing with antitrust and issues of competition is also the domain of the Justice Department.

[34] As in the previous issue question, parties responded by briefs.

[35] Keep in mind that the *Hush-a-Phone* decision had already occurred and the consent decree had been entered into three years earlier in 1956.

[36] The FCC scheduled a hearing on the matter which was held between February 13, 1967 and April 19, 1967 under Hearing Examiner Herbert Sharfman. The final decision was issued on August 13, 1969. In Re Applications of Microwave Communications, Inc. For Construction Permits to Establish New Facilities in the Domestic Public Point-to-Point Microwave Radio Service at Chicago, Ill., St. Louis, Mo., and Intermediate Points., 18 FCC 2d 953 (1969), recon. denies, 21 FCC 2d 825 (1970).

[37] In Re Applications of Microwave Communications, Inc., 18 FCC 2d 953 (August 13, 1969), p. 954.

[38] In addition MCI proposed to have $151,500 in an escrow account, $50,000 from a loan from Louis-Joliet Bank, and operating income of $272,000. The FCC accepted a figure of $129,920 income to be likely and indicated it would be sufficient. (p. 956)

[39] Commissioner James J. Wadsworth joined in the dissent. The equipment said lacking was customer drop equipment, which is used to connect the system to the subscriber. Other pleadings pointed to the lack of ratio-squared circuitry said to cost $108,000. The FCC concluded such equipment could be added later, could purchase it on the installment basis. (p. 957)

[40] In Re Applications of Microwave Communications, Inc., 18 FCC 2d 953 (August 13, 1969), p. 961.

[41] Ibid., p. 960.

[42] Ibid., p. 962.

[43] Ibid., p. 963.

[44] Ibid., p. 965.

[45] All dissenting opinions are part of the text of the decision and found on pp. 971–976 in In Re Applications of Microwave Communications, Inc., 18 FCC 2d 953 (August 13, 1969).

[46] *Broadcasting* (December 17, 1973) and discussed in Sydney W. Head and Christopher H. Sterling, *Broadcasting in America: A Survey of Television, Radio, and New Technologies*, 4th ed. (Boston: Houghton Mifflin, 1982), p. 456.

[47] In Re Applications of Microwave Communications, Inc., 18 FCC 2d 953 (August 13, 1969), pp. 976–978.

[48] As quoted in Charles F. Phillips, Jr., *The Regulation of Public Utilities: Theory and Practice* (Arlington, VA: Public Utilities Reports, Inc., 1988), p. 698, and citing, among others, David E. Evans (ed.), *Breaking up Bell* (New York: Elsevier Science Publishing Co., 1983).

[49] Re Specialized Common Carrier Services, Docket No. 18920, Notice of Inquiry, 24 FCC 2d 318 (1970), First Report and Order, 29 FCC 2d 870, 920 (1971), recon. denied, 31 FCC 2d 1106 (1971), aff'd sub nom. Washington Utils. & Transp. Comm. v. Federal Communications Commission., 513 F. 2d 1142 (9th Cir. 1974), cert. denied, 423 U.S. 836 (1975), as cited in Charles F. Phillips, Jr., *The Regulation of Public Utilities: Theory and Practice* (Arlington, VA: Public Utilities Reports, Inc., 1988), p. 698.

[50] MCI Telecommunications Corporation, Microwave Communications, Inc., and *N-Triple-C Inc., Petitioners* v. *Federal Communications Commission and United States of America.* 561 F.2d 365; 41 Rad. Reg. 2d (P & F) 191; 182 App. D.C. 367, Argued April 28, 1977, July 28, 1977. Hereinafter cited as *MCI Telecommunications Corp.* v. *FCC*, 561 F.2d 365 (D.C. Cir. 1977). Also referred to in the text and elsewhere in these notes as Execunet.

[51] As cited in note 1 of *MCI Telecommunications Corp.* v. *FCC*, 561 F.2d 365 (D.C. Cir. 1977): The orders are a letter order of July 2, 1975 (FCC 75-799) and the Decision in MCI Telecommunications Corp., 60 FCC 2d 25 (July 13, 1976). The letter order is set out at Appendix B of the second order, 60 FCC 2d at 62–64.

[52] Discussion of the ex parte contacts and office demonstrations of Execunet are detailed in the decision of the D.C. Circuit court.

[53] In the Matter of Establishment of Rules Pertaining to the Authorization of New or Revised Classifications of Communications on Interstate or Foreign Common Carrier Facilities, and Amendment of Part 63.60-63.90 of the Rules, Notice of Proposed Rule Making, 27 FCC 2d 36 (1971); Report and Order, 39 FCC 2d 131 (1973).

[54] Cited at note 12 in *Execunet* as MCI Telecommunications Corp., supra note 1, Appendix B, 60 FCC 2d at 64.

[55] MCI Telecommunications Corp. v. FCC, 561 F.2d 365 (D.C. Cir. 1977).

[56] Ibid.

[57] Citing in *Execunet* at note 68: See Specialized Common Carrier Services, supra note 26, 29 FCC 2d at 905-914 (69070).

[58] MCI Telecommunications Corp. v. FCC, 561 F.2d 365 (D.C. Cir. 1977). Also citing as notes 70 and 71: n70 See *FCC* v. *RCA Communications, Inc.*, 346 U.S. 86, 96-97 (1953); *Hawaiian Telephone Co.* v. *FCC*, 498 F.2d 771, 776-777 (D.C. Cir. 1974); n71 Cf., e.g., *Carroll Broadcasting Co.* v. *FCC*, 258 F.2d 440 (D.C. Cir. 1958).

[59] Notes and citations omitted. *United States of America, Plaintiff*, v. *Western Electric Company, Inc.*, et al., Defendants; Civil Action No. 82-0192; United States District Court for the District of Columbia, 673 F. Supp. 525; 1987 U.S. Dist. LEXIS 10003; 1987-2 Trade Cas. (CCH) P67, 815 (September 10, 1987, Decided and Filed).

[60] Two of the companies, Southern New England Telephone and Cincinnati Bell were unaffected by the divestiture since AT&T owned a minority interest in them.

[61] Formerly called American Bell, in 1983 it was renamed as a result of further negotiations in which AT&T agreed to cease using the name Bell except for Bell Labs.

[62] Notes and citations omitted. *United States of America, Plaintiff*, v. *Western Electric Company, Inc.*, et al., Defendants; Civil Action No. 82-0192; United States District Court for the District of Columbia, 673 F. Supp. 525; 1987 U.S. Dist. LEXIS 10003; 1987-2 Trade Cas. (CCH) P67, 815 (September 10, 1987, Decided and Filed), at p. 98.

[63] For example: *United States of America*, Plaintiff, v. *Western Electric Company, Inc.*, et al., Defendants; Civil Action No. 82-0192; United States District Court for the District of Columbia, 673 F. Supp. 525; 1987 U.S. Dist. LEXIS 10003; 1987-2 Trade Cas. (CCH) P67, 815 (September 10, 1987, Decided and Filed), at page 7 and citing the transcript at pages 10469-70, 10475. Also pages 29 and 31 address the issue of FCC oversight.

[64] Notes and citations omitted. *United States of America*, Plaintiff, v. *Western Electric Company, Inc.*, et al., Defendants; Civil Action No. 82-0192; United States District Court for the District of Columbia, 673 F. Supp. 525; 1987 U.S. Dist. LEXIS 10003; 1987-2 Trade Cas. (CCH) P67, 815 (September 10, 1987, Decided and Filed), at p. 89.

[65] Notes and citations omitted. *United States of America*, Plaintiff, v. *Western Electric Company, Inc.*, et al., Defendants; Civil Action No. 82-0192; United States District Court for the District of Columbia, 673 F. Supp. 525; 1987 U.S. Dist. LEXIS 10003; 1987-2 Trade Cas. (CCH) P67, 815 (September 10, 1987, Decided and Filed), at p. 89.

[66] *United States of America* v. *Western Electric Company, Inc.*, et al., 767 F. Supp. 308; 1991 U.S. Dist. LEXIS 9706; 1991–92 Trade Cas. (CCH) P69, 503; 69 Rad Reg. 2d (P & F) 793; 123 P.U.R. 4th 521 (1991).

[67] *United States of America* v. *Western Electric Company* et al., National Association of Broadcasters, Appellant, and consolidated cases. 1991 U.S. App. LEXIS 33098 (1991).

[68] Bob Davis, "Regional 'Bells' Cleared to Offer News and Data," *The Wall Street Journal*, October 8, 1991, pp. B1, B10.

[69] Christy Fisher, "Bell Ruling Rings Alarm: ANPA Gets Ready to Fight Against New Phone Services," *Advertising Age*, July 29, 1991, p. 1.

[70] The section dealing with state public utility commissions, is drawn from Charles F. Phillips, Jr., *The Regulation of Public Utilities: Theory and Practice* (Arlington, VA: Public Utilities Reports, Inc., 1988), pp. 123–129.

[71] William T. Gormley, Jr., *The Politics of Public Utility Regulation* (Pittsburgh: University of Pittsburgh Press, 1983), p. 189; as cited in Phillips, *The Regulation of Public Utilities: Theory and Practice*, p. 130.

[72] Also from Charles F. Phillips, Jr., *The Regulation of Public Utilities: Theory and Practice* (Arlington, VA: Public Utilities Reports, Inc., 1988), pp. 123–129.

[73] Example taken from Article 6A, *Radio Common Carriers*, Part 62-119(3), from *North Carolina Public Utilities Laws and Regulations*, (1989-90 Edition), p. 88. See also 62-120, through 62-122.

[74] *Utilities Commission* v. *Simpson*, 32 N.C. App. 543, 232 S.E.2d 871 (1977), aff'd, 295 N.C. 519, 246 S.E.2d 753 (1978).

[75] Examples of state regulation of telephone common carriers found in this section of the text are from *North Carolina Public Utilities Laws and Regulations*, (1989–90 Edition).

[76] The discussion of the Uniform System of Accounts is drawn from the state of North Carolina's *North Carolina Public Utilities Laws and Regulations*, (1989–90 Edition), pp. 471–472, and citing Rule R9-2.

[77] Ibid., p. 472, citing Rule R9-3.

[78] Ibid., pp. 506–507, citing Rule R14-5.

[79] The historical perspective for separations and access is drawn from Charles F. Phillips, Jr., *The Regulation of Public Utilities: Theory and Practice* (Arlington, VA: Public Utilities Reports, Inc., 1988), pp. 215–218.

[80] Footnote omitted. Charles F. Phillips, Jr., *The Regulation of Public Utilities: Theory and Practice* (Arlington, VA: Public Utilities Reports, Inc., 1988), p. 216.

[81] 47 CFR Ch.1 (10-1-85 Edition), Part 61.40.

[82] Ibid., Part 62.2.

[83] Ibid., Part 63.01.

[84] Ibid., Part 63.62.

[85] Ibid. The list is for illustrative purposes and is not in the order the items appear in FCC regulations.

[86] Ibid., Part 33, App. A.

[87] Ibid., Part 64.801.

[88] The issue of misuse of cellular phones has arisen in election campaigns where a candidate's cellular telephone calls can be monitored illegally by others who frequently work for the opponent's campaign.

[89] 47 CFR Ch.1 (10-1-85 Edition), Part 64.803.

[90] Ibid.

[91] *United States of America*, Plaintiff, v. *Western Electric Company, Inc.*, et al., Defendants; Civil Action No. 82-0192; United States District Court for the District of Columbia, 673 F. Supp. 525; 1987 U.S. Dist. LEXIS 10003; 1987-2 Trade Cas. (CCH) P67, 815 (September 10, 1987, Decided and Filed), at p. 75, footnotes and citations omitted. Audit description based on comments quoted in the action as follows: Comments of Washington Utilities and Transportation Commission at 3-5 citing "Summary Report on the Regional Holding Company Investigations," National Association of Regulatory Commissioners, Washington, DC, September 18, 1986. Similar findings were reported by the staff of the California Public Utilities Commission with respect to Pacific Telesis, as cited: California Public Utilities Commission, A Report on Pacific Bell's Affiliated/Subsidiary Companies, Proceeding No. A.85-01-034, Exec. Summary at 2-3 (June 3, 1986). Citation at note 254.

[92] First . . . : Reply at 13. Second. . . : New York State Department of Public Service, Report on NYNEX Corporation and Affiliates (March 1987). Citation for US West: *Communications Week*, August 3, 1987, at 1.

[93] *Chubby, Inc., a Corporation d/b/a/ Skuttlebut, and Robert G. Blanchard*, Plaintiffs, v. *ConpuServe Inc., d/b/a Rumorville, and Don Fitzpatrick*, individually, Defendants. United States District Court for the Southern District of New York. 776 F. Supp. 135, 19 Media L. Rep. 1525, 1991 U.S. Dist. LEXIS 15545, October 29, 1991. Footnotes are added in the quotation for stylistic reasons and do not necessarily appear in the original decision.

[94] *Chubby, Inc., a Corporation d/b/a/ Skuttlebut, and Robert G. Blanchard*, Plaintiffs, v. *ConpuServe Inc., d/b/a Rumorville, and Don Fitzpatrick*, individually, Defendants. Citing *The New York Times Co.* v. *Sullivan*, 376 U.S. 254, 277 (5y4) (citation omitted).

[95] *Chubby, Inc., a Corporation d/b/a/ Skuttlebut, and Robert G. Blanchard*, Plaintiffs, v. *ConpuServe Inc., d/b/a Rumorville, and Don Fitzpatrick*, individually, Defendants. Citing *Lerman* v. *Flynt Distributing Co.*, 745 F.2d 123, 139 (2d Cir. 1984), cert. denied, 471 U.S. 1054 (1985); see also *Daniel* v. *Dow Jones & Co.*, 137 Misc.2d 94, 102, 520 N.Y.S.2d 334, 340 (N.Y. Civ. Ct. 1987).

[96] *Chubby, Inc., a Corporation d/b/a/ Skuttlebut, and Robert G. Blanchard*, Plaintiffs v. *ConpuServe Inc., d/b/a Rumorville, and Don Fitzpatrick*, individually, Defendants. Some citations and footnotes are omitted from the text of the quote from the district court's decision.

[97] Chapter 7 in the report is titled: "Privacy, Information Flows, and Protection of Intellectual Property in the Information Age," *NTIA Telecom 2000*, (Washington, DC: National Telecommunications and Information Administration), 1988, excerpts are from pp. 131–147.

Chapter 13

[1] Gerald Oberst Jr., "Monday Memo: 'Each country in Europe has a different regulatory system for SNG service'," *Broadcasting*, August 10, 1992, p. 14.

[2] Anthony Lewis, "Sarnoff Suggests Industry Merger," *The New York Times*, August 8, 1962, pp. 1, 14.

[3] Jack Gould, "TV: Telstar and World Broadcasting," *The New York Times*, July 11, 1962, p. 71.

[4] Communication Satellite Act of 1962, Public Law 87-624, Sec. 304(a.).

[5] Ibid., Sec. 305 (a.).

[6] Ibid., Sec. 305 (b.).

[7] Ibid., Sec. 102(a.).

[8] Ibid., Sec. 102(c.).

[9] The first 20 years of COMSAT are chronicled in issue Number 12 of the company magazine *COMSAT: Communications Satellite Corporation Magazine* (1983). Authors cited in references to articles published in the special anniversary edition of the magazine are "remembrances" of the authors and edited by the magazine's editors.

[10] In addition to having the executive committee idea quashed, Graham had arranged for a stenotypist to record the meeting, only to have Sidney Weinberg threaten to walk out if the stenotypist stayed because Weinberg felt the stenotypist would cause people to "posture for the record." The stenotypist left. Source: Bruce G. Sundlun, " 'Fireworks' At First Incorporators Meeting," *COMSAT: Communications Satellite Corporation Magazine*, no. 12 (1983), pp. 13–14.

[11] Cited from Benno Signitzer, *Regulation of Direct Broadcasting from Satellites: The U.N. Involvement* (New York: Praeger Publishers, Inc., 1976), p. 21.

[12] Ibid., p. 22. The term *states* refers to sovereign countries, not states of the United States.

[13] The early formation of COMSAT in the international arena is from John A. Johnson, "Starting Intelsat, The First

Negotiations," *COMSAT: Communications Satellite Corporation Magazine*, no. 12 (1983), pp. 15–19. Johnson served in various roles with the company including chairman and chief executive officer of Comsat General Corporation. During the 1960s he was at different times chairman or vice chairman of the Interim Communications Satellite Committee (ICSC), the temporary governing body of INTELSAT which ceased operations when the INTELSAT definitive arrangements were signed in 1971.

[14] John A. Johnson, "Starting Intelsat, The First Negotiations," *COMSAT: Communications Satellite Corporation Magazine*, no. 12 (1983), p. 16.

[15] Ibid.

[16] The financial start up is chronicled in Carl J. Reber, "Starting Intelsat, The Financial Perspective," *COMSAT: Communications Satellite Corporation Magazine*, no. 12 (1983), pp. 20–22.

[17] Ibid., p. 21.

[18] Rita Lauria White and Harold M. White, Jr., *The Law and Regulation of International Space Communication* (Boston: Artech House, 1988), p. 217.

[19] A number of publications chronicle the early tension between INTELSAT and Pan American Satellite. See for example: Joel R. Alper, "The Case Where INTELSAT: Applications for Competitive Systems Raise many Concerns," *COMSAT: Communication Satellite Corporation Magazine*, no. 13 (1984), pp. 5–7; Wreatham E. Gathright, "U.S. Foreign Policy and INTELSAT," *COMSAT: Communication Satellite Corporation Magazine*, no. 13 (1984), pp. 7–11; Edward J. Martin, "INTELSAT: The Future Course," *COMSAT: Communication Satellite Corporation Magazine*, no. 13 (1984) pp. 11–12; "U.S., INTELSAT Wrestle with PANAMSAT Application," *Broadcasting*, October 13, 1986, pp. 62–63; "Trying to Break Satellite Monopoly," *Insight*, June 6, 1988, pp. 43–45.

[20] Joel R. Alper, "The Case for INTELSAT: Applications for Competitive Systems Raise many Concerns," *COMSAT: Communication Satellite Corporation Magazine*, no. 13 (1984), p. 6.

[21] Joel R. Alper, "The Case Where INTELSAT: Applications for Competitive Systems Raise many Concerns," *COMSAT: Communication Satellite Corporation Magazine*, no. 13 (1984), p. 6.

[22] Wreatham E. Gathright, "U.S. Foreign Policy and INTELSAT," *COMSAT: Communication Satellite Corporation Magazine*, no. 13 (1984) p. 11.

[23] "Trying to Break Satellite Monopoly," *Insight*, June 6, 1988, p. 44.

[24] Peter Lambert, "The Competitors Fear Even More Effective INTELSAT," *Broadcasting*, July 27, 1972, p. 54.

[25] United Nations General Assembly Resolution 1348 (XIII), December 13, 1958.

[26] United Nations General Assembly Resolution 1472 (XIV), December 12, 1959.

[27] Principles 8 and 9 of the draft principles relevant to the use of nuclear power sources in outer space, in accordance with General Assembly resolution 45/72, and quoted from the "Report of the Committee on the Peaceful Uses of Outer Space," General Assembly, forty-sixth session, Supplement no. 20 (A/46/20), 1991, pp. 17–18.

[28] "Report of the Committee on the Peaceful Uses of Outer Space," General Assembly, forty-sixth session, Supplement no. 20 (A/46/20), 1991, p. 19.

[29] As seen in annual reports of COPUOS, and citing the 1991 annual report, p. 21.

[30] Treaty on Principles Governing the Activities of States in the Exploration and Use of Outer Space, Including the Moon and Other Celestial Bodies; 18 UST 2410, TIAS No. 6347, 610 UNTS 205 No. 8843, opened for signature at Moscow, London, and Washington, on 27 January 1967. At note 1: "Coming into force on 10 October 1967, the date of deposit of the instruments of ratification by five Governments, including the Governments designated as Depository Governments under the Treaty, i.e., the Governments of the Union of Soviet Socialist Republics, the United Kingdom of Great Britain and Northern Ireland and the United States of America, in accordance with paragraph 3 of article XIV." Hereinafter cited as "Outer Space Treaty."

[31] Rita Lauria White and Harold M. White, Jr., *The Law and Regulation of International Space Communication* (Boston: Artech House, 1988), p. 242.

[32] Outer Space Treaty.

[33] Summarized in Rita Lauria White and Harold M. White, Jr., *The Law and Regulation of International Space Communication* (Boston: Artech House, 1988), pp. 242–243.

[34] "Report of the Legal Subcommittee on the work of its twenty-seventh session (14–31 March 1988)," A/AC.105/411, 8 April 1988.

[35] Kenya Cola? working paper (A/AC.105/C.2/L.155 of 2 April 1986).

[36] The German working paper is cataloged as (A/AC.105/C.2/L.153 of 24 March 1986).

[37] A comparative discussion of the equatorial nations working papers and the German working paper is from "Report of the Legal Sub-committee on the work of its twenty-sixth session (16 March–3 April 1987)," A/AC.105/385, 16 April 1987, pp. 51–52.

[38] International Telecommunication Union, Radio Regulations. The Regulations are periodically updated and can be located in most major international depositories. (ISBN 92-61-01221-3).

[39] International Telecommunications Union, Radio Regulations, section VIII, technical terms relating to space. Chapter 1, article 1, RR1-22—RR1-23. Definitions cited in this text are from the 1982 edition of Radio Regulations, revised in 1985, 1986, and 1988.

[40] International Telecommunications Union, Radio Regulations, Article 1, No. 4, 1.2, RR1-1.

[41] International Telecommunications Union, Radio Regulations No. 9, 1.7, RR1-2.

[42] W. Rumphorst, "Convergent Technology and New Services: Legal Problems in Using Satellites for Transmission of Programmes to the General Public," *Telecommunication Journal*, 57 (March 1990), 183–188.

[43] International Telecommunications Union, Radio Regulations, Article 1, No. 36, 3.17, RR1-5.

[44] International Telecommunications Union, Radio Regulations, Article 1, No. 20-3.1-RR1-3.

[45] International Telecommunication Union, Radio Regulations, no. 37, 3.18, RR1-5.

[46] International Telecommunication Union, Radio Regulations, Article 1, No. 22, 3.3, RR1-3.

[47] International Telecommunications Union, Radio Regulations, Article 23, No. 1993 (a) 1994 (b).

[48] W. Rumphorst, "Convergent Technology and New Services: Legal Problems in Using Satellites for Transmission of Programmes to the General Public," *Telecommunication Journal*, 57 (March 1990), p. 186.

[49] As defined in ITV Radio Regulations.

[50] International Telecommunication Union, Radio Regulations, Article 11, No. 1042, RR11-1.

[51] International Telecommunication Union, Radio Regulations, Article 11, No. 1051, RR11-2.

[52] Resolutions cited are RES 60-1/3, RES 101-1/3, RES 203-1/2, RES 67-1.

[53] Resolution No. 2, "Relating to the Equitable Use by All Countries, with Equal Rights, of the Geostationary-Satellite Orbit and of Frequency Bands for Space Radio Communication Services," RES 2-1.

[54] Resolution No. 3, "Relating to the Use of the Geostationary-Satellite Orbit and to the Planning of Space Services Utilizing it," RES 3-1.

[55] John A. Johnson, "Starting Intelsat, The First Negotiations," *COMSAT: Communications Satellite Corporation Magazine*, no. 12, (1983), pp. 17–18.

[56] Source for the history and development of the European Space Agency is *Twenty Years of European Cooperation in Space* (Paris: European Space Agency, 1984), 259 pp.

[57] Under the work of COPERS.

[58] *Twenty Years of European Cooperation in Space* (Paris: European Space Agency, 1984), p. 16. The background for ELSO is chronicled in *Twenty Years* . . . , pp. 16–17, 23–25.

[59] Denmark, which had taken part in the negotiations, was granted observer status but did not sign the convention.

[60] The policy was for all member countries of the European Conference of Postal and Telecommunications Administrations (ECPT).

[61] *Twenty Years of European Cooperation in Space* (Paris: European Space Agency, 1984), p. 17.

[62] The seven founding members of ELDO participated, Denmark and Spain also took part, Austria, Greece, Ireland, Sweden, and Switzerland attended as observers. *Twenty Years of European Cooperation in Space* (Paris: European Space Agency, 1984), p. 27.

[63] *Twenty Years of European Cooperation in Space* (Paris: European Space Agency, 1984), pp. 27–28.

[64] Ibid., p. 30.

[65] Ibid., pp. 221–222.

[66] Article 5 of the ESA Contract Regulations.

[67] *Twenty Years of European Cooperation in Space* (Paris: European Space Agency, 1984) p. 221.

[68] Ibid., p. 221.

[69] Ibid., p. 221.

[70] Ibid., p. 224.

[71] *Space Activities of the United Nations and International Organizations* (New York: United Nations, 1986), 271 pp.; A/AC.105/358.

[72] Ibid., pp. 148–149.

[73] Ibid., p. 153.

[74] Ibid., p. 154.

[75] Ibid., p. 157.

[76] Ibid., p. 159.

[77] Ibid., p. 161.

[78] Public Law 98-575, 98 Stat. 3055.

[79] Ibid.

[80] Ibid., Sec. 15 (a), Sec 16.

[81] Ibid., Sec. 21.

[82] Rules governing direct-broadcast satellites are found in part 100, 47 CFR Ch.1 (10-1-91 Edition).

[83] Notice of Inquiry, 45 Fed. Reg. 72,719 (1980). The early development of DBS broadcasting and the FCC's development of policies is reviewed in Paul B. Larsen, et al., "DBS Under FCC and International Regulations," *Vanderbilt Law Review*, 37 (January 1984), 67.

[84] 86 FCC 2d 719 (1981).

[85] Interim Direct Broadcast Satellite Applications, 46 Fed. Reg. 32,497 (1981). As discussed in Larsen, et al.

[86] Report and Order, 90 FCC 2d 676, 680–682 (1982).

[87] Public Law 102-385, 106 stat. 1460, October 5, 1992. Sec. 335(b)(1).

[88] Ibid., Sec. 335(b)(3).

[89] Notice of Inquiry, 45 Fed. Reg. 72,719 (1980). See also Paul B. Larsen, et al., "DBS Under FCC and International Regulations," *Vanderbilt Law Review*, 37 (January 1984), 67.

[89] 86 FCC 2d 719 (1981), pp. 83–85.

[90] Communications Act of 1934, Sec. 307(b), 47 U.S.C. Sec. 307(b) (1976).

[91] See "Comment: Direct Broadcast Satellites: Implications for Less-Developed Countries and for World Order," *Virginia Journal of International Law*, 66 (1971), 75; as cited at note 7 in James Edwin Bailey, III, "Comment: Current and Future Legal Uses of Direct Broadcast Satellites in International Law," *Louisiana Law Review*, (January 1985), p. 701.

[92] James Edwin Bailey, III, "Comment: Current and Future Legal Uses of Direct Broadcast Satellites in International Law," *Louisiana Law Review*, (January 1985), pp. 701–702.

[93] Abraham Schnapf, *Communication Satellites: Overview and Options for Broadcasters* (Washington, DC: National Association of Broadcasters, 1982), p. 26.

[94] The author gratefully acknowledges the work of Rita Lauria White and Harold M. White, Jr. in developing this section of the text. Mr. White's courses on space communication law and ethics taught at the University of North Carolina at Chapel Hill, the Whites' other writings, and specifically their book, *The Law and Regulation of International Space Communication* (Boston: Artech House 1988), all contributed important insights.

[95] Rita Lauria White and Harold M. White, Jr., *The Law and Regulation of International Space Communication*, (Boston: Artech House, 1988), p. 14.

[96] Chairman's Opening Remarks, "Report of the Committee on the Peaceful Uses of Outer Space," General Assembly, forty-fifth session, Supplement No. 20 (A/45/20), 1990, pp. 30–31.

[97] Statistics are based on a NASA Satellite Situation Report. Also cited was the *RAE Table of Earth Satellites 1957–1986* (London: Macmillan, 1987), which listed more than 17,000 space objects over that period, including fragments. "Report of the Committee on the Peaceful Uses of Outer Space," General Assembly, forty-fifth session, Supplement No. 20 (A/45/20), 1990, pp. 30–31.

[98] A discussion of this issue can be found in Martin A. Rothblatt, "Satellite Communication and Spectrum Allocation," *The American Journal of International Law*, 76 (January 1982), 56–77. How many messages can be handled at one time by a satellite channel is determined by measuring bits per second (bps). According to Rothblatt, 56,000 bps are required to convey the human voice. Citing Rothblatt at n10.

[99] Martin A. Rothblatt, "Satellite Communication and Spectrum Allocation," *The American Journal of International Law*, 76 (January 1982), 59. A quantitative definition of channel depth is "message volume per unit of time."

[100] Martin A. Rothblatt, "Satellite Communication and Spectrum Allocation," *The American Journal of International Law*, 76 (January 1982), 63.

[101] See, for example, W. Rumphorst, "Convergent Technology and New Services: Legal Problems in Using Satellites for Transmission of Programmes to the General Public," *Telecommunication Journal*, 57 (March 1990), 183–88.

[102] Martin A. Rothblatt, "Satellite Communication and Spectrum Allocation," *The American Journal of International Law*, 76 (January 1982), 59.

[103] "Satellites: Next Generation," *Broadcasting*, (July 27, 1992), p. 55.

[104] Martin A. Rothblatt, "Satellite Communication and Spectrum Allocation," *The American Journal of International Law*, 76 (January 1982), 63–77. Specifically, Rothblatt has suggested a jurimetic approach whereby quantitative measures are applied to the three factors of depth, distribution, and directionality.

[105] See, for example, Roy Carleton Howell, "International Telecommunications and the Law: The Creation of Pan African Satellites," *Howard Law Journal*, 31, (1988), 575–641. The article

provides a lengthy discussion of the economic viability of a Pan-African satellite network.

[106] Roy Carleton Howell, "International Telecommunications and the Law: The Creation of Pan African Satellites," *Howard Law Journal*, 31, (1988), 575 at notes 2 and 5.

[107] Ibid., p. 598.

[108] Ibid.

[109] Ibid., p. 599 at n58.

[110] Ibid., p. 607.

[111] Ibid., p. 628.

[112] Gregory C. Staple, "The New World Satellite Order: A Report from Geneva," *The American Journal International Law*, 80 (July 1986), 703.

[113] Ibid., p. 706.

[114] Ibid., p. 709.

[115] Ibid., p. 706.

Chapter 14

[1] Discussion of the history, organization, function, and issues facing ITU can be found in: David M. Leive, *International Telecommunications and International Law: The Regulation of the Radio Spectrum* (Dobbs Ferry, N.Y.: A. W. Sijthoff, Leyden, and Oceana Publications, 1971); John and Mary R. Markle Foundation and the Twentieth Century Fund, eds., Global Communications in the Space Age: Toward a New ITU (New York: John and Mary R. Markle Foundation and the Twentieth Century Fund, 1972).

[2] Harold K. Jacobson, "The International Telecommunication Union: ITU's Structures and Function," in John and Mary R. Markle Foundation and Twentieth Century Funds, eds., *Global Communications in the Space Age: Toward a New ITU* (New York: John and Mary R. Markle Foundation and the Twentieth Century Fund, 1972), p. 40

[3] International Telecommunication Convention (Montreux, 1965). See also: Jacobson, "The ITU," pp. 40–41.

[4] *United Nations Yearbook* 27 (1973), 955.

[5] As discussed in Leive, *International Communications*, pp. 32–40; and *Global Communications*, pp. 6–7.

[6] "U.S. Representatives to ITU Pleased with Nice Conference," *Broadcasting* (July 24, 1989), p. 84.

[7] *Global Communications*, pp. 8–9.

[8] An interesting perspective on these issues is seen in "An Open World Policy for Telecommunications," *Broadcasting*, (October 19, 1987), pp. 33–40. An interview with U.S. State Department's ambassador Diana Lady Dougan. See also: "U.S. Pleased with WARC Results," *Broadcasting* (October 10, 1988), p. 41.

[9] Source material for the section on the European Broadcasting Union includes, but is not limited to: European Broadcasting Union, (Geneva: EBU), 1985, 35 pp.; Kalbermatten, R. de, "The European Broadcasting Union," *INTERMEDIA* (December, 1977), pp. 25–30; Press releases on the Eurovision News Exchanges, July 5, 1984; Eurovision's 30th Anniversary, June 6, 1984.

[10] The juxtaposition of the initials results from translation.

[11] Adapted from Kalbermatten, R. de, "The European Broadcasting Union," *INTERMEDIA* (December, 1977), p. 25.

[12] At one time or another members have included broadcasting organizations in such countries as Bulgaria, Cuba, Estonia, Hungary, Korea, Laos, Lithuania, Moldavia, Poland, Romania, Vietnam, Afghanistan, and Yemen.

[13] Information about the OIRT is from material provided the author by the OIRT Publications Office in Prague. A special acknowledgement is made to Zygmunt Trzebiatowski of the OIRT Secretary General's Office for making this information available (updated through 1985).

[14] Information on the Caribbean Broadcasting Union was provided the author by the secretariat located in Barbados.

[15] Material for this section of the text was provided the author by the Office of the Secretary General of the URTNA. "Background Information On URTNA," unpublished document, URTNA, 1982. A brief profile of the URTNA is also contained in any recent edition of the *World Radio TV Handbook*, A. G. Sennitt, ed. (New York: Billboard Publications).

[16] Associate memberships are also possible and are afforded to organizations outside Arica.

[17] "Background Information On URTNA," unpublished document, URTNA, 1982, p. 9.

[18] URTNA commissions are made up of seven members and elected to serve two-year terms. Commissions are answerable to the Administrative Council.

[19] "Background Information On URTNA," unpublished document, URTNA, 1982, p. 14.

[20] "The Australian Commercial Radio Industry," Monograph published by the Federation of Australian Radio Broadcasters, September 1988.

[21] An appeals process for such clearance is in place in Australia.

[22] Information on the Council of Europe is from The Council of Europe: A Concise Guide, (Strasbourg: The Council of Europe), 1982, 85 pp.

[23] "European Agreement for the Prevention of Broadcasts Transmitted From Stations Outside National Territories," European Treaty Series No. 53, January 22, 1965.

[24] Belgium, West Germany, Italy, the Netherlands, Luxembourg, and France.

[25] The Treaty of Rome was signed on March 25, 1957, taking effect on January 1, 1958. It has since been amended by other treaties.

[26] The EC as of 1991 consisted of Belgium, Denmark, France, Greece, Ireland, Italy, Luxembourg, the Netherlands, Portugal, Spain, the United Kingdom, and Germany. As the economic power of the EC continues to increase, other countries will undoubtedly be brought into the EC. The Soviet Union requested membership in the EC but was denied full member status. Shortly after the request in 1991, the independence movement among the Russian Republics transformed the Soviet Union into a group of more independent and loosely structured countries, which for the EC, will mean increased trade opportunities with individual countries in Eastern Europe. Shortly after declaring their independence from the Soviet Union in 1991, the Baltic States requested membership in the EC, at first denied on the grounds that their economic system was not yet developed to the point where it would be strong enough to compete on an equal footing with other EC member nations.

[27] Of particular value to this section is L.C. White, "The Court of Justice: The E.C.'s Lawmaker," *Europe* (June 1989), 41–42.

[28] "According to Professor Roger Goebel of the Fordham University School of Law, the French *Conseil d'Etat* has, in several instances, refused to refer cases. . . . " Citing L.C. White, "The Court of Justice: The E.C.'s Lawmaker," *Europe* (June 1989), 42.

[29] As discussed in E. De Bony, "E.C. is Prying Open its Telecommunications Markets," *Europe*, (April 1989), pp. 18–19.

[30] Bids of more than $200,000 are affected. Source: E. De Bony, "E.C. is Prying Open its Telecommunications Markets," *Europe*, (April 1989) p. 18.

[31] "EEC Consumers Protected Against Misleading Advertising in Electronic Age," Press Release from the Commission of the European Communities, No IP(84)234, Brussels, 1984.

[32] "EEC Consumers Protected Against Misleading Advertising in Electronic Age," Press Release from the Commission of the European Communities, No IP(84)234, Brussels, 1984.

[33] Belgium and Denmark voted against the directive.

[34] J. Valenti, *The European Community Makes Ominous Sounds About Broadcast Quotas*, remarks to the U.S. State Dept. Advisory Comm. on Int'l Com. and Info. Pol'y, Washington, DC, at 3 (July 17, 1989), as cited in F. H. Cate, "The European Broadcasting Directive," American Bar Association Section of International Law and Practice, Communications Committee Monograph Series 1990/1. Citation is as cited in Cates.

[35] Valenti as cited in Cates.

[36] J. Johnson, "In Search of . . . The European T.V. Show," *Europe*, (November 1989), pp. 46–47, citing p. 46.

[37] "European Community Adopts TV Without Frontiers Directive," EC press release, No. 33/89 (October 4, 1989), quoting Vice President Martin Bangeman.

[38] "European Community Adopts TV Without Frontiers Directive," EC press release, No. 33/89 (October 4, 1989), quoting Vice President Martin Bangeman.

[39] The concept of "culture" in arguing the issue of the directive is seen in C. G. Artwick, "Culture or Commerce: The European Community and 'Television Without Frontiers'," paper presented at the annual meeting of the Association for Education in Journalism and Mass Communication, Minneapolis, MN, 1990; and L. J. Bjork, "Cultural Domination and Sovereignty: The Development of European TV Quotas, 1981–89," paper presented at the annual meeting of the Association for Education for Journalism and Mass Communication, Minneapolis, MN, 1990.

[40] Citing Cates at note 54: *European Ministers' Broadcast Directive Seen as Positive, Cooperative Step for European TV Program Production Industry* (Oct. 3, 1989) (news release) (available from the Annenberg Washington Program, 1445 Pennsylvania Ave., N.W., Suite 200, Washington, DC 20004).

[41] Denmark's Act No. 421 of 15 June 1973, with amendments published through December 1988.

[42] *CEPT Twenty Fifth Anniversary*, Montreaux, 1984, p. 6.

[43] Material for the discussion of WIPO is from *WIPO*, a general information booklet published by the WIPO, (Geneva: WIPO), 1985, 72 pp. Some material is verbatim from WIPO, with lengthy quotations noted with appropriate attribution.

[44] H. Daniel, "One Hundred Years of International Postal Co-Operation," *Union Postale*, (November–December 1974), pp. 165–174. Sources for this section of the text are the previously cited publication in addition to the following publications from the Universal Postal Union: *The Universal Postal Union: Its Creation and Development* (Berne, Switzerland: International Bureau of the Universal Postal Union, 1983), booklet, 20 pp.; *Constitution of the Universal Postal Union* (Berne, Switzerland: Universal Postal Union, 1985), 47 pp.; *List of Member Countries of the Universal Postal Union* (Berne, Switzerland: Universal Postal Union, 1985), 11 pp.; *The Universal Postal Union: Specialized Agency of the United Nations* (Berne, Switzerland: Universal Postal Union, 1985), booklet, 11 pp.

[45] An earlier conference in Paris in 1863 and the adoption of a document titled *Result of the Deliberations of the International Postal Conference at Paris* helped set the stage for the 1874 Berne meeting. The Paris document, while not binding on any country, did result in many countries simplifying their postal systems and regulations. Source: H. Daniel, "One Hundred Years of International Postal Co-Operation," *Union Postale* (November–December 1974), p. 166.

[46] *The Universal Postal Union: Specialized Agency of the United Nations* (Berne, Switzerland: Universal Postal Union, 1985), p. 5.

[47] The 150–123 vote also banned tobacco company sponsorship in sporting events. Germany, Britain, the Netherlands, and Greece opposed the ban while France, Spain, Portugal, Ireland, Belgium, Luxembourg, Italy, and Denmark favored it. Source: First press reports of the Parliament's vote appeared in February 1992, citing the *News and Observer*, Raleigh, NC, February 2, 1992, p. 10c.

Chapter 15

[1] "European Community Adopts TV Without Frontiers Directive," EC Office of Press and Public Affairs, October 4, 1989.

[2] Ironically, one of the factors contributing to the growth of satellite receivers has been the restrictive programming policies of some governments. See R. G. Harris, "Telecommunications Policy in Japan: Lessons for the U.S.," paper presented to the Conference on Public Utility Economics & Regulation, Monterey, CA, July 6, 1988.

[3] "40th Anniversary of Radio Nederland, The International Service," publication of Radio Nederland (booklet), 1987, p. 14.

[4] "RCI Overview," Radio Canada International public information statement, August 1, 1986.

[5] Canadian Broadcasting Act of 1968 as cited in the CBC's corporate operating plan for 1988 thru 1993, published October 1, 1987.

[6] Article 44 of Japan's Broadcast Law, enacted in 1950. NHK is an outgrowth of the Tokyo Broadcasting Station dating back to 1925.

[7] The Netherlands Media Act, Sec. 170, par. 1–5.

[8] "Agreement Between the State and the Swedish Television Company," in accordance with Sections 5 and 6 of the Radio Act (1966:755).

[9] "Agreement Between the State and the Swedish Television Company," concluded between the State and the Swedish Television Company (SVT) in accordance with Sections 5 and 6 of the Radio Act (1966:755).

[10] Government License, Article 13, Para. 1, as cited in SBC's overview booklet on the SBC service.

[11] "The Swiss Broadcasting Corporation," public information document of the SBC, (October 1986).

[12] The Netherlands Media Act, Sec. 51, par. 5.

[13] "Nordic Television in Transition," Nordic Council of Ministers publication, Copenhagen, n.d., p. 5.

[14] As required by the Icelandic State Broadcasting Service and cited in "Nordic Television in Transition," Nordic Council of Ministers publication, Copenhagen, n.d., p. 10.

[15] Australia: Section 16 (1) (d) of the 1942 Broadcasting and Television Act in force.

[16] Australia: Section 16 (1) (d) of the 1942 Broadcasting and Television Act in force.

[17] Section 103 of the Broadcasting and Television Act of 1942.

[18] The Enforcement Rules of the Broadcasting & Television Law in the Republic of China, Chapter 3, Article 18. Approved on December 24, 1976 by the Executive Yuan. Third emendation passed on April 30, 1988.

[19] Republic of China Standards for TV Program Production, Section 3 (II)(B)(1). Passed by Executive Yuan on April 30, 1983, Second emendation passed October 15, 1987.

[20] Republic of China Standards for TV Program Production, Section 3 (II)(E)(7). Passed by Executive Yuan on April 30, 1983, Second emendation passed October 15, 1987.

[21] The Enforcement Rules of the Broadcasting & Television Law in the Republic of China, Chapter 3, Article 27, Approved on December 24, 1976 by the Executive Yuan. Third emendation passed on April 30, 1988.

[22] Republic of China Broadcasting and Television Law, citing Chapter I, Article 3; Chapter III, Article 19; Chapter V, Article 36. Promulgated by the President on January 8, 1976.

[23] Republic of China Regulations for Television Advertising Production, (II) (18). Approved by Letter, (85) Gin Kuang, 3 Tze No. 06039, April 21, 1985.

[24] M. K. Nasser, "Egyptian Mass Media Under Nasser and Sadat," *Journalism Monograph* No. 124, published by the Association for Education in Journalism and Mass Communication, (December 1990), 26 pp. Munir K. Nasser authored the monograph when serving as assistant executive director of the United Palestinian Appeal in Washington, DC. All references to Egyptian mass media during the Gamal Abdul Nasser era are from the Monograph.

[25] M. K. Nasser, "Egyptian Mass Media Under Nasser and Sadat," *Journalism Monograph* No. 124, (December 1990), p. 7.

[26] Munir Nasser cites an observer who counted 300 songs for the Aswan Dam and more than 220 for Arab unity. Nasser, p. 7.

[27] Agreement Between the State and the Swedish Local Radio Company, in accordance with Sections 5 and 6 of the Radio Act (1966:755), general provisions, part 7.

[28] Section 3(1)(n)(iii). Recommendations for minor changes were made as part of a CBC Brief to the Legislative Committee considering Bill C-136 in August 1988.

[29] *Advertising Standards of the Canadian Broadcasting Corporation (French: Code Publicitaire)*, 1987, p. A1.

[30] Republic of China Standards for TV Program Production, Section 2 (A)(7). Passed by Executive Yuan on April 30, 1983, Second emendation passed October 15, 1987.

[31] Republic of China Standards for TV Program Production, Section (3)(2)(A)(1). Passed by Executive Yuan on April 30, 1983, Second emendation passed October 15, 1987.

[32] Republic of China Standards for TV Program Production, Section (3)(I)(D)(1–13). Passed by Executive Yuan on April 30, 1983, Second emendation passed October 15, 1987.

[33] Republic of China Regulations for Television Advertising Production. Approved by Letter, (85) Gin Kuang 3 tze No. 06039, April 21, 1985.

[34] Republic of China Regulations for Television Advertising Production, (II)(19)(c.). Approved by Letter, (85) Gin Kuang 3 tze No. 06039, April 21, 1985.

[35] MTV Finland, *The Television Advertising Terms and Conditions* (Helsinki: MTV Finland), n.d., p. 4. The policy is articulated by The Finnish Language Division of the Finnish Research Center for Domestic Languages.

[36] The Netherlands Media Act, Sec. 71, par. 3.

[37] Advertising Code of the Media Council of Australia, Part 12, effective June 1989.

[38] *Advertising Standards of the Canadian Broadcasting Corporation* (French: *Code Publicitaire*), 1987, p. B4.

[39] *Advertising Standards of the Canadian Broadcasting Corporation* (French: *Code Publicitaire*), 1987, pp. B1–B2 and citing paragraphs (a) through (e) in the first part of Section B.

[40] *Advertising Standards of the Canadian Broadcasting Corporation* (French: *Code Publicitaire*), 1987, p. B2 and citing paragraphs (a) through (e) under the Unacceptable Products subsection of Section B.

[41] *Advertising Standards of the Canadian Broadcasting Corporation* (French: *Code Publicitaire*), 1987, p. B2 and citing paragraphs (a) through (e) under the Unacceptable Products subsection of Section B.

[42] *Advertising Standards of the Canadian Broadcasting Corporation* (French: *Code Publicitaire*), 1987, pp. B2–B3 and citing paragraphs (a) through (h) under the Unacceptable Content subsection of Section B.

[43] *Advertising Standards of the Canadian Broadcasting Corporation* (French: *Code Publicitaire*), 1987, pp. B2–B3 and citing paragraphs (a) through (h) under the Unacceptable Content subsection of Section B. Prohibitions do not apply to the following: (i) to such personalities, characters, and so on as they appear on the package; (ii) to characters created by an advertiser for promotional purposes; (iii) to professional actors or announcers not featured on children's programs; (iv) when such personalities, characters, and so on make factual statements about nutritional or educational benefits. (When premiums are used in commercials . . .) The product or service of the advertiser must receive at least equal emphasis. Promotion of the premium may not exceed one half of the commercial time or 20 seconds, whichever is less. Premium: A premium is defined as anything offered with or without additional cost that is likely to induce purchase of the advertiser's regular product or service. Commercials to preschoolers: Messages for products or services intended primarily for use by children of preschool age that directly address the preschooler, e.g., "Hey kids, wait till Mom and Dad hear you play a tune."

[44] MTV Finland, *The Television Advertising Terms and Conditions* (Helsinki: MTV Finland), n.d., p. 5, citing Part V: Children and advertising; subpart 14: Children as viewers. Second quotation citing the same regulations, Part I(C), Basic principles.

[45] MTV Finland, *The Television Advertising Terms and Conditions* (Helsinki: MTV Finland), n.d., p. 6, citing Part V: Children and advertising; subpart 14 (a) through (c): Children as viewers.

[46] MTV Finland, *The Television Advertising Terms and Conditions* (Helsinki: MTV Finland), n.d., p. 6, citing Part V: Children and advertising; subpart 15: Children as performers.

[47] Republic of China Standards for TV Program Production, Section 2 (B)(1) through (6). Passed by Executive Yuan on April 30, 1983, Second emendation passed October 15, 1987.

[48] Republic of China Standards for TV Program Production, Section 3(II)(E)(1) through (10). Passed by Executive Yuan on April 30, 1983, Second emendation passed October 15, 1987.

[49] Republic of China Standards for TV Program Production, Section 3(II)(F)(2). Passed by Executive Yuan on April 30, 1983, Second emendation passed October 15, 1987.

[50] Republic of China Regulations for Television Advertising Production, (II)(23)(f). Approved by Letter, (85) Gin Kuang 3 tze No. 06039, April 21, 1985.

[51] Republic of China Regulations for Television Advertising Production, (II)(26). Approved by Letter, (85) Gin Kuang 3 tze No. 06039, April 21, 1985.

[52] Eastern Europe is one example where advertising has been rather staid and where products have been chosen for their utilitarian value, not the gadgets and gimmicks.

[53] Citing Republic of China Regulations for Television Advertising Production, (II)(1–3, 6–8, 11–14). Approved by Letter, (85) Gin Kuang 3 tze No. 06039, April 21, 1985.

[54] MTV Finland, *The Television Advertising Terms and Conditions* (Helsinki: MTV Finland), n.d., p. 6, citing Part I: Basic principles, subparts (a–d).

[55] Advertising Code of the Media Council of Australia, introductory points 4–11 and 13–14, effective June 1, 1989.

[56] Ibid.

[57] Ibid.

[58] *Advertising Standards of the Canadian Broadcasting Corporation (French: Code Publicitaire)*, 1987, p. A1.

[59] Ibid., p. A2. To some extent the regulation can be compared to measures which at one time were enforced through the Fairness Doctrine in the United States. The Fairness Doctrine encouraged vigorous discussion of controversial issues but wanted them balanced. Public broadcasting stations at one time were not permitted to editorialize but that rule was eventually

struck down by the courts. Many public stations still do not editorialize because of a fear of offending donors.

[60] Ibid.

[61] Denmark Act No. 421 of June 15, 1973 on Radio and Television Broadcasting with amendments., Par II(B), Section 15y(2).

[62] *Advertising Standards of the Canadian Broadcasting Corporation (French: Code Publicitaire)*, 1987, p. C2.

[63] The Basic Agreement Between YLE and MTV, summary document published by YLE, n.d.

[64] Other prohibitions include products which are not preregistered for review, graveyards, exploiting death, notices of missing persons, standard classified advertising, product names that have the potential in themselves to induce harmful effects. Republic of China Regulations for Television Advertising Production, (II)(21)(a. through g). Approved by Letter, (85) Gin Kuang 3 tze No. 06039, April 21, 1985.

[65] Advertising Code of the Media Council of Australia, Therapeutic Goods, definition (2)(1)(i–iii), effective June 1, 1989.

[66] The Australian Trade Practices Act of 1974, (Section 52 Part V Consumer Requirements).

[67] Republic of China Regulations for Television Advertising Production, (II)(23)(a through n). Approved by Letter, (85) Gin Kuang 3 tze No. 06039, April 21, 1985.

[68] *Advertising Standards of the Canadian Broadcasting Corporation (French: Code Publicitaire)*, 1987, p. A6.

[69] Advertising Code of the Media Council of Australia, Cigarette Advertising, (6)(1–2), effective June 1, 1989.

[70] Republic of China Regulations for Television Advertising Production, (II)(29)(a through d). Approved by Letter, (85) Gin Kuang 3 tze No. 06039, April 21, 1985.

[71] MTV Finland, *The Television Advertising Terms and Conditions* (Helsinki: MTV Finland), n.d., p. 5, citing Part IV(5): Use of Special Effects.

[72] Republic of China Regulations for Television Advertising Production, (II)(31). Approved by Letter, (85) Gin Kuang 3 tze No. 06039, April 21, 1985.

[73] Radio and Television Broadcasting Act of Denmark, citing Section 6.(1).

[74] Ibid., citing Section 15a.(1))(iii).

[75] "Special Provisions Concerning Political Programs," Approved November 26, 1982. Public information document of YLE.

[76] Regulations governing news coverage in the Republic of China are found in Republic of China Standards for TV Program Production, Section 3 (II)(A)(2 through 8). Passed by Executive Yuan on April 30, 1983, Second emendation passed October 15, 1987.

[77] Omitted sections (. . .) are those quoted in the previous paragraph. Republic of China Standards for TV Program Production, Section 3 (II)(A)(2 through 8). Passed by Executive Yuan on April 30, 1983, Second emendation passed October 15, 1987.

[78] Information on libel law in Japan is from K. H. Youm, "Libel Law and the Press in Japan," *Journalism Quarterly*, 67 (Winter 1990), 1103–1112.

[79] Ibid., p. 1105.

[80] Ibid., p. 1106.

[81] Ibid., p. 1107.

[82] Ibid., p. 1109. Citing: J. C. Merrill, "Inclination of Nations to Control Press and Attitudes on Professionalization," *Journalism Quarterly*, 65 (Winter 1988).

[83] Youm, p. 1111.

[84] Occasional exceptions exist during experimental funding arrangements.

[85] The Defense Department being one example.

[86] This does not mean that a broadcast lobby does not exist or that there aren't trade-offs to achieve a favorable regulatory climate.

[87] Information about the financing and structure of Japanese broadcasting is from materials provided the author by NHK's Audience and Public Relations Bureau, January 1991.

[88] "The Structure of NHK," *NHK Factsheet*, (January 1991).

[89] Ibid.

[90] Act Concerning Charges for the Possession of Television Receivers, 24 May 1978 (SFS 1978:478) last amended 1987 (SFS 1987:233).

[91] Such safeguards are also in place in the United States and regulated by the Federal Communications Commission.

[92] The Netherlands Media Act, Sec. 120, 121, par. 1, 2, 4.

[93] Ibid., Sec. 114, par. 4 (a–b).

[94] Interpretation of Finland's Broadcasting Responsibility Act by Oy. Yleisradio Ab. The Broadcasting Responsibility Act of March 12, 1971 came into effect on September 1, 1971. Enforcement of the act has been incorporated into the Statute on Broadcasting Responsibility issued on August 6, 1971.

[95] The Broadcasting Liability Act, December 30, 1966 (SFS 1966:756), last amended 1986 (SFS 1986:1211).

[96] Instructions for Section II (B), Legal Qualifications, FCC Form 301.

[97] Ibid.

[98] Republic of China Regulations for the Administration of the Responsible Officers and Staff Members of Radio and Television Enterprises, Part V (1–5). Issued by the Government Information Office of the Executive Yuan, June 24, 1983.

[99] News, programming, and management positions are outlined in: Republic of China Regulations for the Administration of the Responsible Officers and Staff Members of Radio and Television Enterprises, Part VI–VII (1–5, respectively). Issued by the Government Information Office of the Executive Yuan, June 24, 1983.

[100] Due process is afforded employees. The law states "Both commendations and chastisements of responsible officers and staff members of radio and television enterprises shall proceed in conformity with the stipulations of the Radio and Television Law." Citing Republic of China Regulations for the Administration of the Responsible Officers and Staff Members of Radio and Television Enterprises, Part IX–XVI. Issued by the Government Information Office of the Executive Yuan, June 24, 1983.

[101] The exception would be if the station itself is the advertiser, such as a promotion campaign for a station in a competitive market. If the station oversteps its bounds such as claiming their power is 100,000 watts when it is only 50,000, then a complaint by a competing station to the FTC would usually trigger an inquiry.

[102] Agreement Between the State and the Swedish Television Company, in accordance with Sections 5 and 6 of the Radio Act (1966:755), General provisions, part 12.

[103] Ibid., General provisions, parts 12, 13, and 14. Similar provisions are found in agreements with the Swedish radio companies.

[104] Norwegian Broadcasting Act, June 13, 1980, Chapter 4 (15)(1).

[105] Act No. 421 of 15 June 1973 on Radio and Television Broadcasting with Latest Amendments, published by Danmarks Radio, December 1988, Part III, Section 16.

[106] Act No. 421 of 15 June 1973 on Radio and Television Broadcasting with Latest Amendments, published by Danmarks Radio, December 1988, Part III, Section 17 (2). By royal decree of June 3, 1988 the Directorate General of Posts and Communications transferred enforcement of broadcast regulation from the Ministry of Cultural Affairs to the Ministry of

Transport and the name of the Ministry of Transport was changed to the Ministry of Transport and Communications.

[107] Act No. 421 of 15 June 1973 on Radio and Television Broadcasting with Latest Amendments, published by Danmarks Radio, December 1988, Part III, Section 18 (1)(2).

[108] The act has been subsequently amended.

Chapter 16

[1] Citing Subpart B-Ethical and Other Conduct and Responsibilities of Employees. All are from 47 CFR Ch1 (10-1-91 Edition).

[2] "Preface," ABA Code of Judicial Conduct, current revisions adopted by the House of Delegates of the American Bar Association on August 7, 1990.

[3] Similar language is found in the regulations governing the Public Utilities Commission which controls telecommunication services in North Carolina. Code of Judicial Conduct, Adopted September 26, 1973, As amended, North Carolina Public Utilities Laws and Regulations, 1989–1990 Edition.

[4] ABA Code of Judicial Conduct, current revisions adopted by the House of Delegates of the American Bar Association on August 7, 1990.

[5] "Application of the Code of Judicial Conduct," ABA Code of Judicial Conduct, current revisions adopted by the House of Delegates of the American Bar Association on August 7, 1990.

[6] Code of Ethics of the American Advertising Federation, from "Professional Paper No. 6," Women in Communications, Inc., July 1976.

[7] "FTC Ends Self-Regulation Probe," *Advertising Age*, 50 (July 9, 1979), 8.

[8] Ibid.

[9] One example at the time of the inquiry was the Financial Advertising Committee on Ethics (FACE), a group formed in 1975 to assist self-regulatory efforts in bank advertising. Its guidelines dealt with those areas most susceptible to misrepresentation, such as free banking services, free checking accounts, savings claims, package services, premiums and giveaways, deposit insurance, and information related to interest rate computations. FACE stated that: "free service (other than free checking) may be advertised only if the service is an unconditional gift and does not require another tie-in service; free checking accounts may be advertised, provided there is no charge for other parts of the service such as monthly statements, checks, or other instruments." See "Banks Adopt Ethics Code and Guidelines for Advertising," *Broadcasting*, 45 (September 13, 1976), 35.

[10] "Advertisers Feel Pressure on 'SOAP'," *Broadcasting*, 46 (August 29, 1977), 22.

[11] "ABC Strong in Net Survival Test; Stragglers Face Early Extinction," *Advertising Age*, 48 (September 26, 1977), 2.

[12] "Advertisers Confirm TV 'Morality' Impact," *Advertising Age*, November 16, 1981, pp. 3–4.

[13] Ibid.

[14] " 'Donahue Named As a Target of Boycott'," *Broadcasting*, August 10, 1981, p. 68.

[15] Diane Mermigas, "TV Violence Group Plans to Boycott 5 Advertisers," *Advertising Age*, February 3, 1983, p. 9.

[16] "N.Y. State Report Urges Reforms in Ads Aimed at Children," *Broadcasting*, 46 (May 9, 1977), 80–81.

[17] Ibid., p. 81.

[18] Ibid.

[19] Jon Nordheimer, "Groups Target Monitors' Access to Violent Videos," N.Y. Times News Service, reported in the *Durham Morning Herald*, Durham, NC, June 17, 1987, p. B1.

[20] As published in *RTNDA Communicator*, (January 1990), p. 10.

[21] William M. Glenn, *The Sigma Delta Chi Story* (Coral Gables, FL: Glade House, 1979).

[22] Ibid.

[23] The Society of Professional Journalists Code of Ethics was first adopted in 1926 and revised in 1973, 1984, and 1987.

[24] Ibid., p. 25.

[25] Ibid., p. 25.

[26] Ibid., p. 24.

[27] Ibid., p. 28.

[28] Ibid., p. 27.

[29] Ibid., p. 27.

[30] W. Robert Nowell, *Press Councils in the United States and Abroad* (Bloomington, IN: Center for New Communications, School of Journalism, Indiana University, 1979), pp. 8–9.

[31] Ibid.

[32] Fred Johnson, "The Minnesota Press Council: A Study of Its Effectiveness," *Mass Communication Review*, (Winter 1976/77), pp. 13–18.

[33] Nowell, *Press Councils*, p. 8.

[34] Ibid.

[35] J. Edward Gerald of the University of Minnesota critiqued the press council concept saying: "A press council is only one of the remedies indicated by modern times by which newspapers and the broadcasting stations can proceed to improve community understanding and media credibility. The press council remedy is quite narrow in terms of the whole problem." Source: Johnson, "The Minnesota Press Council," p. 19.

[36] *Office of Communication of the United Church of Christ* v. *Federal Communications Commission*, 359 F. 2d 944 (D.C. Cir.), 1966.

[37] Ibid.

[38] Ibid.

[39] Ibid.

[40] "The Struggle over Broadcast Access," *Broadcasting*, 40 (September 27, 1971), 24.

[41] Press reports of the decision to shut down ACT included Jennifer Moore, "Peggy Charren's Closing ACT," *The Chronicle of Philanthropy*, July 28, 1992, pp. 24–26.

[42] The information of the history and operation of ACT is taken from *Actfacts* (Newtonville, MA: Action for Children's Television, n.d.).

[43] *Actfacts*, p. 4.

[44] Leonard Gross, "Television Under Pressure," *TV Guide*, 23 (February 22, 1975), 4–7.

[45] "ACT Survey of Pre-Xmas Children's TV Finds Ad Time Up, Toy Prices High," press release from ACT, September 7, 1976.

[46] "ACT Seeks Injunction against Hudson TV Ads for Spiderman Vitamins," *Action for Children's Television News*, 5 (Winter 1976), 1, 13.

[47] "ACT Joins with NCCB vs. the Family Hour," *Action for Children's Television News*, 5 (Summer 1976), 8.

[48] "House Subcommittee Hears ACT Testimony and FTC's Silences," *Action for Children's Television News*, 5 (Spring 1976), 8.

[49] "ACT Prods the FTC for Response to 'Buried' Petitions," *Action for Children's Television News*, 4 (Spring/Summer 1974), 8.

[50] "ACT Calls on FTC to Restrict TV Ads for Phone Services Aims at Children," *Broadcasting*, August 12, 1985, p. 36.

[51] "ACT Blasts NAB's Children's Programming Survey," *Broadcasting*, April 16, 1984, p. 42.

[52] Ibid.

[53] "Citizens Groups Say They've Spotted Unidentified Paying Object," *Broadcasting*, January 30, 1989, pp. 59–60.

[54] Jennifer Moore, "Peggy Charren's Closing ACT," *The Chronicle of Philanthropy*, July 28, 1992, p. 26.

[55] Action Guide of the United Church of Christ Office of Communication EEO Project in Broadcasting and Cable, (1981), p. 3.

[56] July 1981 letter from Janice M. Engsberg to volunteers participating in the EEO project of the United Church of Christ Office of Communication.

[57] United Church of Christ Office of Communication Questionnaire for the EEO Project in Broadcasting, (1981), p. 1. The statement said: "*No appointment is necessary.*" (Italics in the original statement.)

[58] United Church of Christ Office of Communication Questionnaire for the EEO Project in Broadcasting, italics in original, (1981), p. 8.

[59] Action Guide of the United Church of Christ Office of Communication EEO Project in Broadcasting and Cable, (1981), p. 3.

[60] "UCC Study Says Broadcasters are not Giving Viewers Enough Local Programming," *Broadcasting*, May 13, 1991, p. 45.

[61] "Denver Lawsuit Challenges Cable Franchise Exclusivity," *Advertising Age*, October 25, 1982, p. 58.

[62] Todd Cohen, "Cable Bidding Draws Support, Opposition," *News and Observer*, Raleigh, NC, October 31, 1982, pp. 1A, 18A.

[63] "Blacks Continue Renewal Pressures in Tenn., and Ind.," *Broadcasting*, July 12, 1976, p. 28.

[64] Ibid.

[65] Ibid.

[66] "Yardsticks Discriminate Too?" *WICI National Newsletter*, (April 1975), p. 3.

[67] "Too Much Time?" *Broadcasting*, 45 (October 4, 1976), 48.

[68] Maurine Christopher, "Morality in Media Tackles Cable," *Advertising Age*, August 24, 1981, p. 12.

[69] Ibid.

[70] "Network TV's Treatment of Women Criticized," *Broadcasting*, November 11, 1985, pp. 54–56.

[71] Ibid. The comment applied to the 1985 television season.

[72] "Group Launches Campaign to 'Pull Plug' on CNN's Arnett," *Broadcasting*, February 18, 1991, p. 61.

[73] "WSVN-TV Pulls Show After Complaints," *Broadcasting*, September 24, 1990, p. 50.

[74] Nancy F. Millman, "PTA Raps Advertisers Linked to Low Quality Shows," *Advertising Age*, 50 (February 19, 1979), 10.

[75] Ibid.

[76] Ibid.

[77] "Sex and Violence in Rock Meets Resistance," *Broadcast Management/Engineering*, 13 (January 1977), 6.

[78] "Boycott Threatened against Lear Show," *Broadcasting*, 45 (June 14, 1976), 50.

[79] "Guidelines for Selecting Television Programs for Children," Committee on Children's Television, 1976.

[80] The Center for Population Options sexual content suggestions are found in "Sexual Aids," *Broadcasting*, October 13, 1986, p. 72.

Chapter 17

[1] *In the Matter of Editorializing by Broadcast Licensees*, 13 F.C.C. 1246, June 1, 1949.

[2] *Great Lakes Broadcasting Co.*, 3 F.R.C. Ann. Rep. 32 (1929), modified on other grounds, 37, F.2d 993 (D.C. Cir.) certiorari dismissed, 281 U.S. 706 (1930); as cited in: Marc A. Franklin in collaboration with Ruth Korzenik Franklin, The First Amendment and the Fourth Estate. (Mineola, NY: Foundation Press, 1977), p. 601.

[3] *In the Matter of the Mayflower Broadcasting Corporation and the Yankee Network, Inc. (WAAB)*, 8 F.C.C. 333, 338, January 16, 1941.

[4] Ibid.

[5] Ibid.

[6] In re *United Broadcasting Co. (WHKC)*, 10 F.C.C. 515 June 26, 1945.

[7] In re *Petition of Robert Harold Scott for Revocation of Licenses of Radio Stations KOW, KPO and KFRC*, 11 F.C.C. 372, July 19, 1946.

[8] *In the Matter of Editorializing by Broadcast Licensees*, 13 F.C.C. 1246, June 1, 1949.

[9] "Applicability of the Fairness Doctrine in the Handling of Controversial Issues of Public Importance," 29 *Fed. Reg.* 10416 (July 25, 1964).

[10] Ibid.

[11] Ibid.

[12] *Red Lion Broadcasting Co.* v. *Federal Communications Commission*, 127 U.S. App. D.C. 129, 381 F.2d 908 (9167). *Red Lion Broadcasting Co., Inc.* v. *Federal Communications Commission; United States* v. *Radio-Television News Directors Association*, 395 U.S. 367, 89 S.Ct. 1794, 23 L.Ed. 2d 371 (1969). The cases are well documented in numerous legal texts. (Further citations of the case in this book are listed as *Red Lion*.)

[13] *Radio-Television News Directors Association* v. *United States*, 400 F.2d 1002 (7th Cir. 1968).

[14] *Red Lion*.

[15] "Broadcast Licensees Advised concerning Stations' Responsibilities under the Fairness Doctrine as to Controversial Issue Programming," F.C.C. 63-734, July 25, 1963.

[16] "FCC Extends Rule on Personal Attacks," *Broadcasting*, 45 (August 9, 1976), 39.

[17] *FCC Annual Report*, 1974, p. 18.

[18] "Fairness Case Goes against Eight California Radio Stations," *Broadcasting*, 45 (May 24, 1976), 40, 42. A discussion of the legal aspects of editorial advertising is found in Milan D. Meeske, "Editorial Advertising and the First Amendment," *Journal of Broadcasting*, 17 (Fall 1973), 417–426.

[19] Associated Press, March 22, 1976.

[20] *FCC Annual Report*, 1974, p. 19.

[21] Ibid.

[22] Frederick W. Ford and Lee G. Lovett, "Fairness Doctrine: 1974 Part II," *Broadcast Management/Engineering*, 10 (November 1974), 20, footnote 2. Also, *FCC Annual Report*, 1974, p. 19.

[23] Gillmor and Barron, *Mass Communication Law*, p. 834.

[24] *Brandywine-Mainline Radio, Inc.* v. *Federal Communications Commission*, 473 F.2d 16 (D.C. Cir. 1972). The case is also studied as an example of group defamation under the Fairness Doctrine (Donald M. Gillmor and Jerome A. Barron, *Mass Communication Law*, St. Paul: West, 1979, pp. 795–868.)

[25] Gillmor and Barron, *Mass Communication Law*, p. 846.

[26] *Brandywine-Mainline Radio, Inc.* v. *Federal Communications Commission*. Also cited in the FCC's 1974 *Fairness Report*.

[27] *In the Matter of the Handling of Public Issues Under the Fairness Doctrine and the Public Interest Standards of the Communications Act*, 30 F.C.C. 2d 26 (1971).

[28] *In the Matter of the Handling of Public Issues under the Fairness Doctrine and the Public Interest Standards of the Communications Act*, 48 F.C.C. 2d 1 30 RR 2d 1261; "Fairness Doctrine and the Public."

[29] *Healey* v. *F.C.C.*, 148 vs. App. D.C. 409 (1972).

[30] *Memorandum Opinion and Order on Reconsideration of Fairness Doctrine*, 36 RR 2d 1021 (1976).

[31] Julian Goodman, "Freedom the First Priority," speech delivered to the Anti-Defamation League Dinner in Atlanta, Georgia, December 6, 1975.

[32] Joseph L. Brechner, "A Statement on the 'Fairness Doctrine'," *Journal of Broadcasting*, 9 (Spring 1965), 109. In the *Journal* article, Brechner's quotation is in italics.

[33] Herbert W. Hobler, "The Fair Less Doctrine," speech delivered to the New Jersey Broadcasters Association's annual convention, Wildwood Crest, New Jersey, June 25, 1975.

[34] Recommendations of the Communications Law Committee, Section of Science and Technology, American Bar Association, "Electronic Journalism and First Amendment Problems," *Federal Communications Bar Journal*, 29 (November 1, 1976), 10.

[35] Ibid., p. 9. *Miami Herald Publishing Co.* v. *Tornilla*, 418 U.S. 241, 258 (1974).

[36] Recommendations of the Communications Law Committee.

[37] Ibid., p. 15.

[38] The Commission released the *1985 Fairness Report* on August 23, 1985. Citation for the inquiry: The proceedings are Inquiry into Section 73.1910 of the Commission's Rules and Regulations Concerning Alternatives to the General Fairness Doctrine Obligations of Broadcast Licensees in Gen. Docket No 84-282, 102 FCC 2d 145 (1985), petition to review docketed sub nom. *Radio-Television News Directors Association* v. *FCC*, No 85-1691 (D.C. Cir. filed October 22, 1985) (*1985 Fairness Report*).

[39] Ibid. Also: *Syracuse Peace Council* v. *FCC*, 867 F.2d 654 (D.C. Cir. 1989). *cert. denied*, 110 S.Ct. 717 (1990).

[40] Ibid.

[41] Ibid.

[42] Ibid.

[43] Ibid.

[44] Ibid.

[45] Ibid.

[46] Ibid.

[47] As reported in H. A. Jessell, "Fairness Doctrine Whittled Further," *Broadcasting*, January 6, 1992, p. 16.

[48] Postelection remarks during the week of November 6, 1992.

Glossary

Active satellite A satellite carrying a station intended for transmitting or retransmitting radio communication signals.

Adjudicative order Decision issued by an administrative law judge. Can be appealed to any proper court of appeals.

Amendment A revision, change, or modification to a document. An amendment to a constitution adds to the scope of the constitution. Pleadings and other proceedings of law may be amended.

Amicus curiae A friend of the court. Although not a party to the proceeding, amicus curiae briefs may be filed by interested parties to add to appeals. For example, RTNDA and the Society of Professional Journalists frequently file amicus curiae briefs concerning First Amendment matters.

Apogee The point farthest from the earth during a satellite's orbit.

Appropriation A certain amount of money devoted to a specific purpose. Agencies and projects are funded by appropriation measures.

Avail Available time for commercial sponsorship.

Bona fide In good faith.

Bond A promise to pay the debt of the bondholder, usually in a specific amount of time with a specified amount of interest. Construction bonds are common in the cable industry and are frequently required by franchising authorities to assure the bills are paid during the construction of a new cable system.

Call letter The call sign of a station. In the United States, stations west of the Mississippi begin with the letter K and those east of the Mississippi with the letter W. A few exceptions exist such as KYW in Philadelphia and KDKA in Pittsburgh. Stations in other countries begin with other prefixes.

Cease-and-desist order Order issued by an administrative agency requiring a specific practice to stop. For example, the FTC will issue a cease-and-desist order stopping the advertising of a product because of misleading claims.

Certiorari A writ issued by a higher court to a lower court. For example, the U.S. Supreme Court employs a writ of certiorari to choose cases it will hear on appeal. Many writs of certiorari are denied and may be designated by the abbreviated citation "cert. den.".

Channel depth The capacity of a satellite channel to handle messages.

Citizen agreement An agreement between a citizen or public-interest group and a radio or television station.

Consent order Agreement between a federal agency and a potential defendant which settles the dispute without it going to trial.

Contour The geographic area covered by a station's signal.

Copyright Registered protection for a print or nonprint work. International copyright protection exists through cooperative agreements between countries.

Coverage map A map showing the geographic area covered by the station's signal.

Cream skimming Term frequently used in debate over common carrier issues. The term describes a business practice where only the most lucrative customers and their service areas are served by the carrier, resulting in a charge of cream skimming.

Deep space Space at distances from the earth approximately equal to, or greater than, the distance between the earth and the moon.

Direct-broadcast satellite A powerful satellite used to broadcast television signals direct to small home satellite receiving antennas.

Downlink Communication channel between a transmitting antenna on a satellite and a receiving antenna on earth.

Effective competition A term used in cable television which is generally considered to exist when a franchise area receives at least three unduplicated off-the-air broadcast signals.

Electromagnetic Magnetic field caused by electrical impulses constantly present in the atmosphere. Used as the source of physical energy carrying radio waves.

Electromagnetic spectrum Reference measure for electromagnetic energy. Different frequencies are at different positions on the electromagnetic spectrum, which is a limited resource affecting telecommunication policy.

Emergency Action Notification National emergency alert issued by the White House and distributed through the Emergency Broadcast System.

Emergency Broadcast System A programming network used in emergencies. The system can be activated through the White House issuing an Emergency Action Notification.

Eminent domain In the right of eminent domain, land is reserved for the public good which can be taken through government action to use the land for public purposes. For example, the government can exercise the right of eminent domain to take private property for the construction of roads, telegraph lines, and railroads.

Fair rate of return In cable systems, a rate of return on investment takes into account appropriate costs, including but not necessarily limited to capital costs, basic cable programming, customer service labor, and ancillary costs attributable to obtaining and transmitting signals carried on the basic tier of a cable system.

Finding of fact A ruling or determination based on factual evidence in a case as opposed to a finding based on the law. On appeal, findings of fact are usually not an issue unless clearly erroneous evidence is uncovered.

Finding of law Findings of law are the basis for appeals and refer to court decisions based on findings of fact which apply to the evidence in a case.

Footprint Geographic area on earth covered by a communication satellite signal.

Franchise fee A fee the cable operator pays the franchise authority.

Franchising authority Government unit responsible for issuing a franchise to a cable television system. In most cases local government is the franchising authority for a local cable system.

Gateway entry The ability of information providers to gain access to common carrier facilities.

Geostationary orbit *See* Synchronous orbit.

Headend Control center of a cable television system.

Hertz A unit of electromagnetic energy. The term is synonymous with cycle, such as cycle per second or hertz per second. Frequencies are determined by the number of radio waves passing a certain point in one second. Each wave is referred to as a cycle or hertz.

High-definition television A high-resolution television system permitting large-screen display with enhanced picture quality.

Indemnity One party agrees to assume responsibility for a loss. For example, if a cable system defaults on a construction contract the loss may be shifted to the bondholder who agrees to indemnify the franchise authority.

Independent contractor An individual who contracts with a station, cable system, and so on for a specific amount of work, who is not an employee of the station, and who does not receive station benefits. For example, hiring a consulting engineer to evaluate the site for a new tower would be engaging the services of an independent contractor, since the consultant is independent of the station and not one of the station's employees.

Integrated Services Digital Network (ISDN) Standardized digital transmission system used in telecommunications.

Job hire A record of who was hired in a station during a given period of time. Used to determine compliance with affirmative action regulations.

Loop service Telephone connection where a local carrier connected to individual subscribers is interconnected with a long-distance common carrier, thereby providing a complete communication loop.

Lottery A contest by chance. In broadcast regulations, to be considered a lottery three elements must be present: prize, chance, and consideration.

Lower-power television A television station operating with low power and covering a small geographic area. The FCC has allocated a number of low-power television frequencies which operate in smaller communities.

Lowest unit charge Federal regulation requiring stations to charge political candidates the lowest rate for a specific time period.

Multipoint distribution service Television programming which is distributed through microwave transmission systems to subscribers owning microwave receiving antennas.

National radio conferences Four national conferences held in the 1920s in the United States to develop a regulatory framework for the growing radio industry. Out of the conferences emerged the Radio Act of 1927 which formed the Federal Radio Commission.

Notice of inquiry Published notice of the FCC requesting information on an issued designated for potential policy making.

Payola The practice of taking and not disclosing payment in the form of money or other services of value, for airing particular recordings and/or promoting recording artists. Closely related to and sometimes defined synonymously with *plugola*.

Perigee The point closest to the earth during a satellite's orbit.

Period (of a satellite) The time elapsing between two consecutive passages of a satellite through a characteristic point on its orbit.

Plenipotentiary The term means something invested with full power and is used frequently in international regulation such as the Plenipotentiary Conference which is the supreme body of the International Telecommunications Union.

Plugola The practice of taking and not disclosing payment in the form of money or other services of value, for plugging goods or services on the air. Closely related to and sometimes defined synonymously with *payola*.

Preliminary injunction Issued by a court or agency to bring to a stop a specific practice pending the resolution of a dispute.

Private utility A utility where access is restricted and not available to everyone.

Program-length commercial Television advertisement that ends 15 minutes or more after it begins.

Public domain A document, radio or television program, film, or other work which is not subject to copyright protection. The term is also used in association with the electromagnetic spectrum whereby broadcasting stations are trustees of this limited resource considered to be in the public domain.

Public notice Issued by a regulatory agency to bring an issue to the attention of the public and inform the public of the agency's position on a given issue.

Public utility A utility where everyone has equal access, such as a public telephone system. A private utility restricts access.

Reasonable access A good faith judgment permitting political candidates access to radio or television advertising.

Reflecting satellite A satellite intended to reflect radio communication signals.

Release A signed contract releasing a station from liabilities used for talent and prize recipients.

Resolution Technical term describing the clarity of a television picture. High-definition television pictures have a higher resolution than standard television pictures. European television pictures have a higher resolution than American television pictures. In legal terminology a statement of policy by a legislative body such as: "Resolved, that the secretary of the treasury be requested to report to the House of Representatives . . ."

Satellite A body which revolves around another body of preponderant mass and which has a motion primarily and permanently determined by the force of attraction of that other body. For example, a communications satellite revolves around the earth. The motion of the satellite is determined by the attraction of the earth.

Satellite master antenna television A satellite dish is used to receive television signals which are then distributed through cable to individual dwellings in the same complex. The system is frequently used in office buildings and apartments.

Separations A common carrier term used to describe the way costs are separated between long-distance carriers and the local telephone exchanges.

Spacecraft A vehicle which is intended to go beyond the major portion of the earth's atmosphere.

Specifications Standards which must be met. For example, specifications will be written into a government proposal advertising for bids for a new satellite system. A local school system might write specifications into a proposal for a closed-circuit television system. Contractors may then bid on the system which must meet the specifications outlined in the proposal.

Subscribers People who subscribe to a programming service such as cable television.

Supra Refers to an earlier part of a book such as an earlier note or footnote. More common in legal texts than other works where op. cit. or the last name of the author will be used in succeeding references.

Synchronous orbit Orbit of a satellite that is synchronous with the rotation of the earth, therefore permitting the satellite to be "fixed" above a given geographic area for communication purposes. Also called *geostationary orbit*.

Tacking A term used in wage and hour law where exemptions are "tacked" together, such as tacking together professional and administrative work to obtain an exemption from wage and hour requirements.

Tariff A listing of the rates charged for access to a public utility.

Testimonial A statement about the value of a product or service, usually by a well-known personality.

Tie-in One advertisement related through copy or visual identity with another advertisement for the same, or a different product. For example, a car dealer may join with a soft drink company to promote one another in their commercials.

Toll broadcasting A term used in early radio for stations that aired commercials. It was first applied to WEAF radio.

Transponder A device which sends and receives signals of specific wavelengths. For example, communication satellites have a certain number of transponders and each transponder occupies a portion of the electromagnetic spectrum used for satellite communication.

Uplink Communication channel between a transmitting antenna on earth and the receiving antenna on a satellite.

Workweek Defined in wage and hour law as seven consecutive 24-hour periods. A workweek can begin on any day and does not need to be the same day for all employees.

Zones Geographical areas defined by legislation. For example, early broadcast policy was based on dividing the United States into different zones.

INDEX TO CASES AND LEGAL CITATIONS

INDEX TO NAMES AND SUBJECTS